Rand McNally

WORLD ATLAS

Rand McNally

WORLD ATLAS

Grolier Incorporated
Danbury, Connecticut

RAND McNALLY WORLD ATLAS

ISBN 0-7172-5324-4

Printed and manufactured in the United States of America.

CONTENTS

USING THE ATLAS . . . . **I•7 - I•8**

FLAGS OF THE WORLD . . . . **I•9 - I•15**

WORLD TIME ZONES . . . . **I•16**

REFERENCE MAPS . . . . **1 - 128**
Map Symbols and Index Map 1
World . . . . 2 - 3

Europe . . . . **4 - 5**
Scandinavia 6
British Isles 7
Central Europe . . . . 8 - 9
France and the Alps . . . . 10 - 11
Spain and Portugal . . . . 12 - 13
Italy . . . . 14 - 15
Southeastern Europe . . . . 16 - 17
Baltic and Moscow Regions . . . . 18 - 19

Asia . . . . **20 - 21**
Northwest Asia . . . . 22 - 23
Northeast Asia . . . . 24 - 25
China, Japan, and Korea . . . . 26 - 27
Eastern and
Southeastern China . . . . 28 - 29
Japan . . . . 30 - 31
Southeastern Asia . . . . 32 - 33
Burma, Thailand, and
Indochina . . . . 34 - 35
India and Pakistan 36
Southern India and Sri Lanka 37
Northern India and Pakistan . . . . 38 - 39
Eastern Mediterranean Lands 40

Africa **41**
Northern Africa . . . . 42 - 43
Southern Africa . . . . 44 - 45
Eastern Africa and Middle East 46

Antarctica **47**

Pacific Ocean . . . . **48 - 49**

Australia . . . . **50 - 51**
New Zealand 52

South America **53**
Northern South America . . . . 54 - 55
Southern South America 56
Southeastern Brazil 57
Colombia, Ecuador, Venezuela,
and Guyana . . . . 58 - 59

Atlantic Ocean **60**

North America **61**
Mexico . . . . 62 - 63
Central America
and the Caribbean . . . . 64 - 65

Canada . . . . ***66 - 67***
Alberta 68
British Columbia 69
Manitoba 70
New Brunswick, Nova Scotia,
and Prince Edward Island 71
Newfoundland 72
Ontario 73
Quebec 74
Saskatchewan 75

United States of America . . . . ***76 - 77***
Alabama 78
Alaska 79
Arizona 80
Arkansas 81
California 82
Colorado 83
Connecticut 84
Delaware 85
Florida 86
Georgia 87
Hawaii 88
Idaho 89
Illinois 90
Indiana 91
Iowa 92
Kansas 93
Kentucky 94
Louisiana 95
Maine 96
Maryland 97
Massachusetts 98
Michigan 99
Minnesota 100
Mississippi 101
Missouri 102
Montana 103
Nebraska 104
Nevada 105
New Hampshire 106
New Jersey 107
New Mexico 108
New York 109
North Carolina 110

USING THE ATLAS

Maps and Atlases

Satellite images of the world (figure 1) constantly give us views of the shape and size of the earth. It is hard, therefore, to imagine how difficult it once was to ascertain the look of our planet. Yet from early history we have evidence of humans trying to work out what the world actually looked like.

Twenty-five hundred years ago, on a tiny clay tablet the size of a hand, the Babylonians inscribed the earth as a flat disk (figure 2) with Babylon at the center. The section of the Cantino map of 1502 (figure 3) is an example of a *portolan* chart used by mariners to chart the newly discovered Americas. The maps in this atlas, show the detail and accuracy that cartographers are now able to achieve.

In 1589 Gerardus Mercator used the word *atlas* to describe a collection of maps. Atlases now bring together not only a variety of maps, but an assortment of tables and other reference material as well. They have become a unique and indispensable reference for graphically defining the world and answering the question *where*. With them routes between places can be traced, trips planned, distances measured, places imagined, and our earth visualized.

FIGURE 1

FIGURE 2

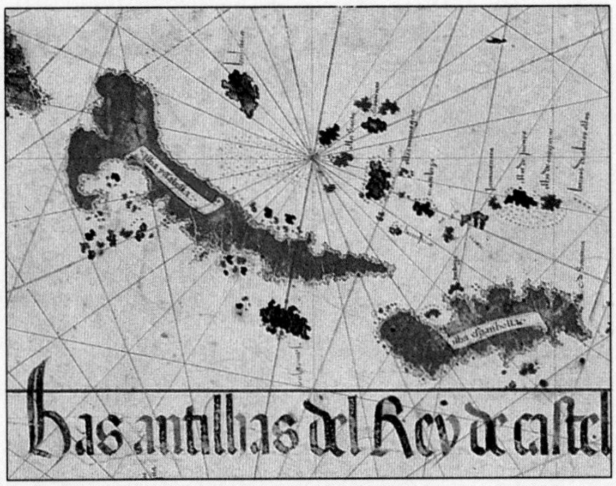

FIGURE 3

Sequence of the Maps

The world is made up of seven major landmasses: the continents of Europe, Asia, Africa, Antarctica, Australia, South America, and North America. The maps in this atlas follow this continental sequence. To allow for the inclusion of detail, each continent is broken down into a series of maps, and this grouping is arranged so that as consecutive pages are turned, a continuous successive part of the continent is shown. Larger-scale maps are used for regions of greater detail or for areas of global significance.

Getting the Information

To realize the potential of an atlas the user must be able to:

1. Find places on the maps
2. Measure distances
3. Determine directions
4. Understand map symbols

Finding Places

One of the most common and important tasks facilitated by an atlas is finding the location of a place in the world. A river's name in a book, a city mentioned in the news, or a vacation spot may prompt your need to know where the place is located. The illustrations and text below explain how to find Yangon (Rangoon), Burma.

Yancheng, China	**B9**	28
Yandoon, Burma	**F3**	34
Yangjiang, China	**G9**	26
Yangon (Rangoon), Burma	**B2**	32
Yangquan, China	**D9**	26
Yangtze see Chang, stm., China . .	**E10**	26
Yangzhou, China	**C8**	28

FIGURE 4

1. Look up the place-name in the index at the back of the atlas. Yangon, Burma can be found on the map on page 32, and it can be located on the map by the letter-number key *B2* (figure 4). If you know the general area in which a place is found, you may turn directly to the appropriate map and use the special marginal index.

2. Turn to the map of Southeastern Asia found on page 32. Note that the letters *A* through *H* and the numbers *1* through *11* appear in the margins of the map.

3. To find Yangon, on the map, place your left index finger on *B* and your right index finger on *2*. Move your left finger across the map and your right finger down the map. Your fingers will meet in the area in which Yangon is located (figure 5).

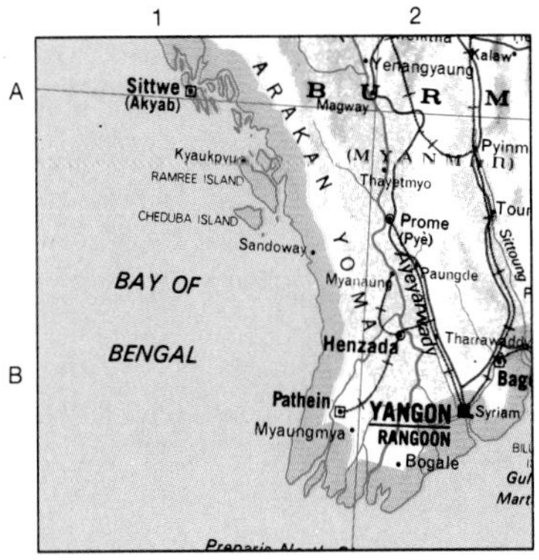

FIGURE 5

Measuring Distances

In planning trips, determining the distance between two places is essential, and an atlas can help in travel preparation. For instance, to determine the approximate distance between Paris and Rouen, France, follow these three steps:

1. Lay a slip of paper on the map on page 10 so that its edge touches the two cities. Adjust the paper so one corner touches Rouen. Mark the paper directly at the spot where Paris is located (figure 6).

FIGURE 6

2. Place the paper along the scale of miles beneath the map. Position the corner at 0 and line up the edge of the paper along the scale. The pencil mark on the paper indicates Rouen is between 50 and 100 miles from Paris (figure 7).

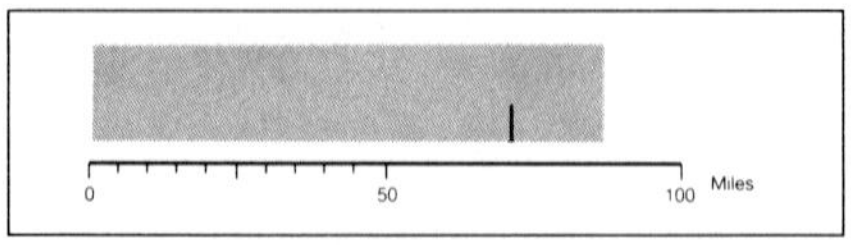

FIGURE 7

3. To find the exact distance, move the paper to the left so that the pencil mark is at 100 on the scale. The corner of the paper stands on the fourth 5-mile unit on the scale. This means that the two towns are 50 plus 20, or 70 miles apart (figure 8).

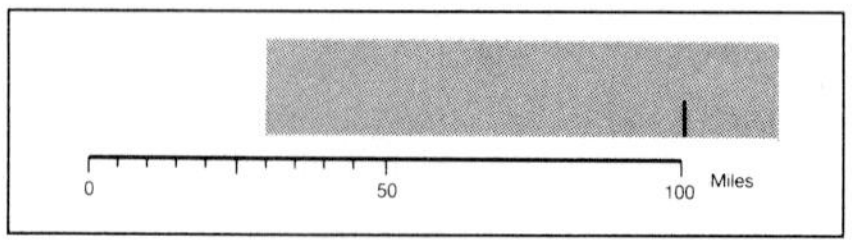

FIGURE 8

Determining Directions

Most of the maps in the atlas are drawn so that when oriented for normal reading, north is at the top of the map, south is at the bottom, west is at the left, and east is at the right. Most maps have a series of lines drawn across them–the lines of *latitude* and *longitude*. Lines of latitude, or *parallels* of latitude, are drawn east and west. Lines of longitude, or *meridians* of longitude, are drawn north and south (figure 9).

Parallels and meridians appear as either curved or straight lines. For example, in the section of the map of Europe (figure 10) the parallels of latitude appear as curved lines. The meridians of longitude are straight lines that come together toward the top of the map. Latitude and longitude lines help locate places on maps. Parallels of latitude are numbered in degrees north and south of the *Equator*. Meridians of longitude are numbered in degrees east and west of a line called the *Prime Meridian*, running through Greenwich, England, near London. Any place on earth can be located by the latitude and longitude lines running through it.

To determine directions or locations on the map, you must use the parallels and meridians. For example, suppose you want to know which is farther north, Bergen, Norway, or Stockholm, Sweden. The map (figure 10) shows that Stockholm is south of the 60° parallel of latitude and Bergen is north of it. Bergen is farther north than Stockholm. By looking at the meridians of longitude, you can determine which city is farther east. Bergen is approximately 5° east of the 0° meridian (Prime Meridian), and Stockholm is almost 20° east of it. Stockholm is farther east than Bergen.

FIGURE 10

Understanding Map Symbols

In a very real sense, the whole map is a symbol, representing the world or a part of it. It is a reduced representation of the earth; each of the world's features–cities, rivers, etc.–is represented on the map by a symbol. Map symbols may take the form of points, such as dots or squares (often used for cities, capital cities, or points of interest), or lines (roads, railroads, rivers). Symbols may also occupy an area, showing extent of coverage (terrain, forests, deserts). They seldom look like the feature they represent and therefore must be identified and interpreted. For instance, the maps in this atlas define political units by a colored line depicting their boundaries. Neither the colors nor the boundary lines are actually found on the surface of the earth, but because countries and states are such important political components of the world, strong symbols are used to represent them. The Map Symbols page in this atlas identifies the symbols used on the maps.

FIGURE 9

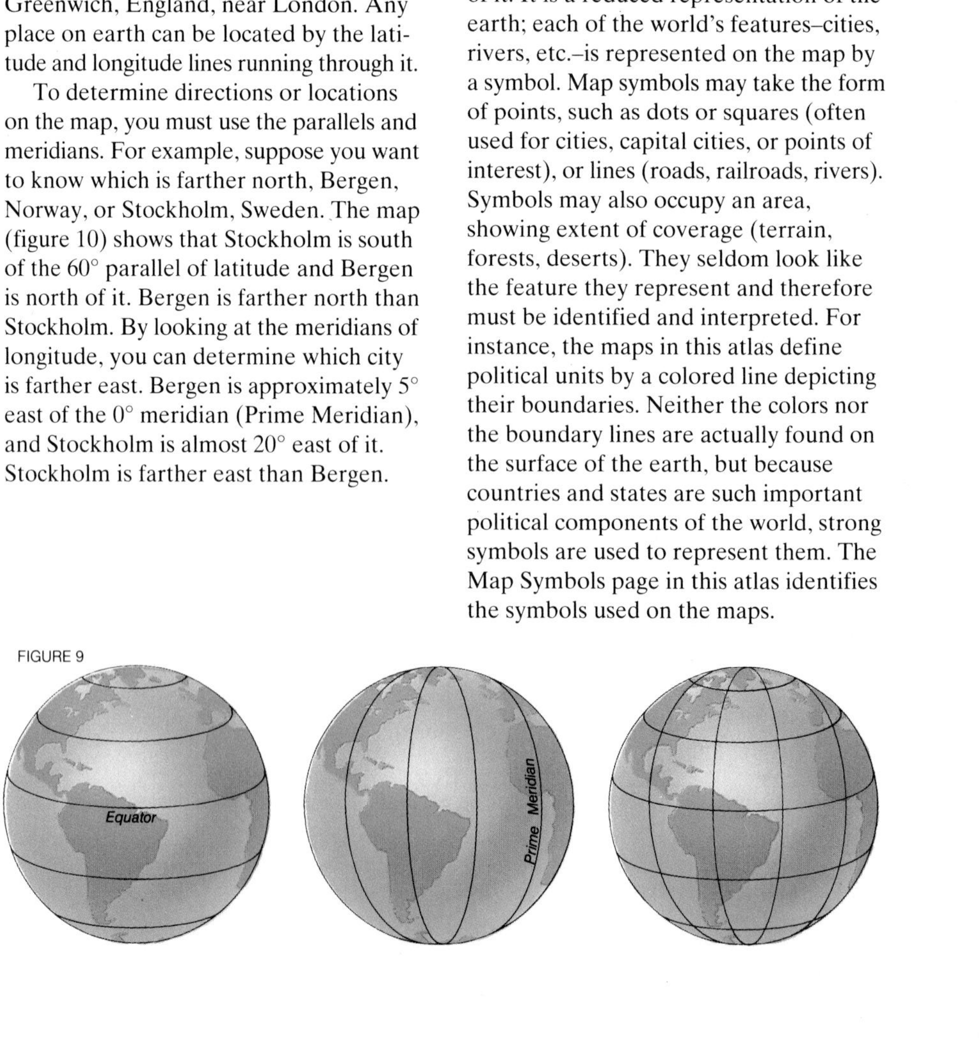

FLAGS OF THE WORLD

A simple piece of colored fabric, usually rectangular in shape, a flag embodies the fundamental human values of community and group identity. As symbols of a political entity, institution, office, or ideology, flags publicly communicate powerful messages and emotions: unity, loyalty, pride, honor, victory, submission, challenge, hope, and resolve.

The most important flags of the modern world are those that identify sovereign nations. Patriots express their love of country by hoisting flags; victorious armies humiliate their enemies by displaying captured flags; dictators use flags to help mold public opinion; insults to the flag may lead to punishment or, if the desecrators are foreign, to an international incident.

History of Flags

The date of the earliest flag is not known, but the first vexilloids (flaglike objects) came into use when people began to live in cities and to organize regular military forces. Archaeological records from the ancient Middle East, Egypt, China, and the Americas suggest that the use of flags was nearly universal among early civilizations. These first flags frequently consisted of a carved emblem—a sacred animal or some natural object—at the top of a pole, sometimes with ribbons attached below. Cloth flags may have been a Chinese invention, since woven silk was developed very early in the Far East.

The beginnings of modern flag design—the combination of colors and forms on cloth to convey certain ideas—may be seen in the development of heraldry during the 12th century in Europe and slightly later in Japan. Heraldry was the design of coats of arms to distinguish individuals, families, and institutions.

One of the most important developments in flag history has been the proliferation of national flags, which began in the late 18th century and continues today. The American and French revolutions of 1775 and 1789, respectively, associated specific designs and colors with the concepts of liberty, independence, democracy, nationalism, and mobilization of the masses. Since then, most of the great multinational empires have vanished. The organization of the world on the basis of countries characterized by a single nationality and ideology has spread from Europe to Latin America, Asia, Africa, the Pacific, and, most recently, the former Soviet Union and Yugoslavia. The old standard of a monarch or imperial regime representing many different peoples has given way to the national flag of a distinctive people with its own language, culture, territory, and aspirations.

Flag Symbolism

The design of each nation's flag carries unique symbolic meaning. Most flags feature such symbols as stripes, stars, animals, crosses, or other emblems. Even the colors chosen for a flag represent some geographic, ideological, or historical feature.

For example, the Union Jack of the United Kingdom combines the crosses of St. George, St. Andrew, and St. Patrick, the patron saints of England, Scotland, and Ireland, respectively. The five points of the star in the national flag of Somalia represent a claim to the five territories in which the Somalis live. The yellow-blue-red flag of Venezuela symbolizes the wealth of the New World (yellow) separated from Spain (red) by the blue ocean. The red of revolution and communism serves as the background for the national flag of China; its five gold stars reflect not only the old Chinese imperial color but also the five largest ethnic groups and "nationalities" (the largest representing the majority Han, the four others representing subnationalities).

As different as the national flags of the world are, cross-cultural borrowing of designs is very common. The red, white, and blue of the U.S. flag clearly were derived from British sources; the Continental Colors of 1776 featured the Union Jack in the top left quadrant. Even today, former French colonies in Africa fly flags similar to the French tricolor.

The evolution of some flag designs is a study in political history. For example, those who struggled against Spanish rule in Latin America achieved one of their early successes in Argentina. The blue-and-white flag adopted by that country (then called the United Provinces of La Plata) in 1816 was also flown by privateers who harassed Spanish ports and ships along the coasts of South and Central America. The same flag was adopted by the leaders of Central America after Spanish rule was thrown off in 1821. As individual republics emerged from the Central American federation (1825-38), they modified the flag but still retained its basic colors. The Revolutions of 1848 in Europe inspired Costa Rica to add a stripe of red through the center of the blue-and-white; Guatemala changed to vertical stripes; and Honduras, Nicaragua, and El Salvador added distinctive emblems on the central white stripe.

The struggle of the Arab countries for independence and unity is also represented in their flags. The first national flag (1947-51) of Cyrenaica was that of the conservative Sanusi religious sect; it was black with a white star and a crescent in the center. Stripes of red and green, symbolizing the Fezzan and Tripolitania, were added when they joined Cyrenaica as the independent country of Libya in 1951. A revolution there in 1969 replaced the monarchy, and the flag was altered to red-white-black, the recognized "Arab liberation colors." In 1971, Libya joined Egypt and Syria in the Confederation of Arab Republics and added its own emblem, the gold hawk of the Quraish tribe, to the center stripe. In 1977, angered by attempts of Egypt's President Anwar Sadat to negotiate peace with Israel, Libya again changed its flag. It chose a field of plain green, the fourth traditional Islamic color.

The flags of the world, shown in the following pages, thus form a kind of map of its sovereign states, political systems, peoples, and history.

Afghanistan

Albania

Algeria

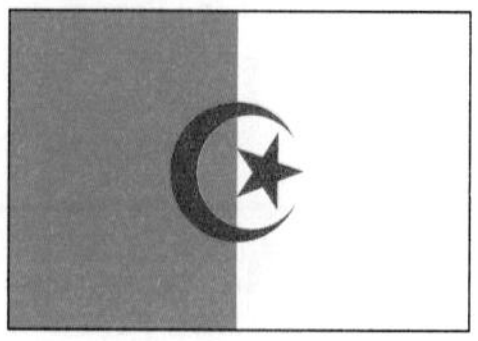

Andorra

Angola

Antigua and Barbuda

Argentina

Armenia

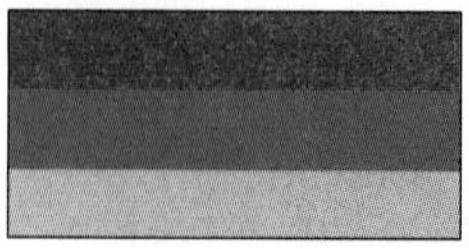

Australia

Austria

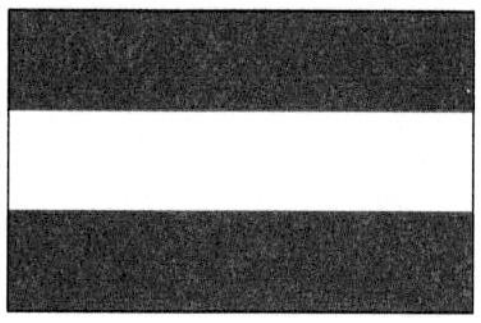

Azerbaijan

Bahamas

Bahrain

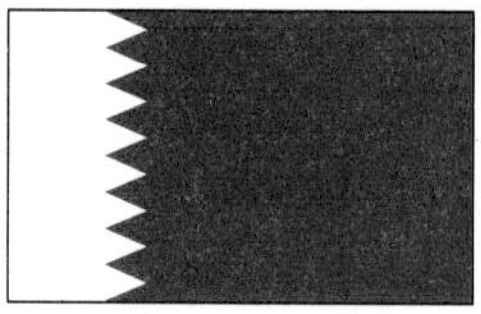

Bangladesh

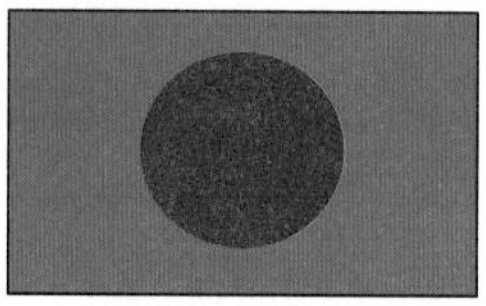

Barbados

Belarus

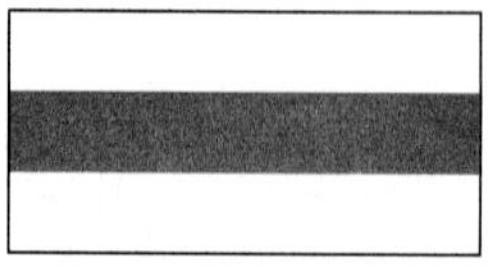

Belgium

Belize

Benin

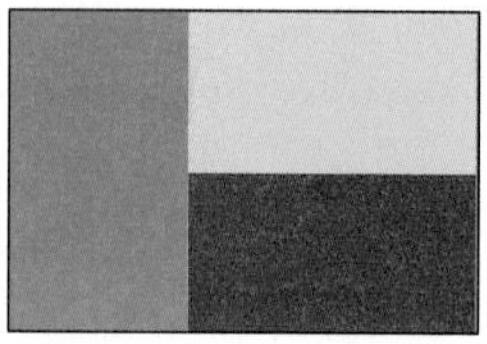

Bermuda

Bhutan

Bolivia

Bosnia and Herzegovina

Botswana

Brazil

Brunei

Bulgaria

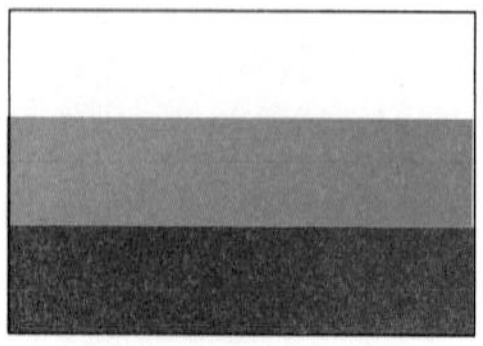

Burkina Faso

Burma (Myanmar)

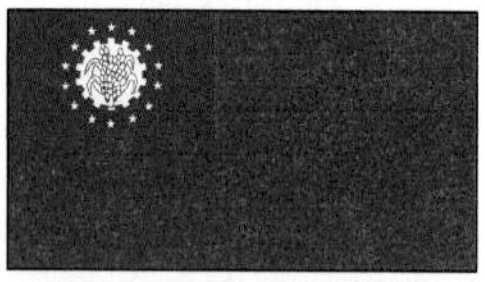

Burundi

Cambodia

Cameroon

Canada

Cape Verde

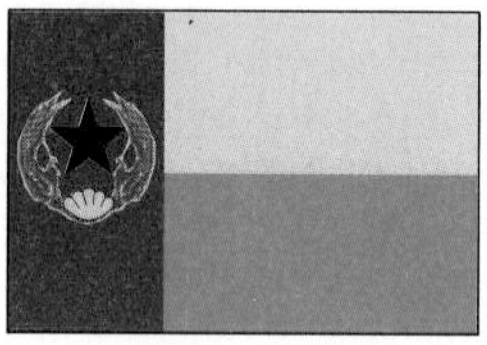

Central African Republic

Chad

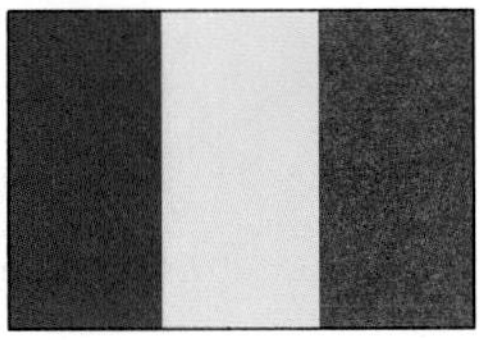

Chile

China

Colombia

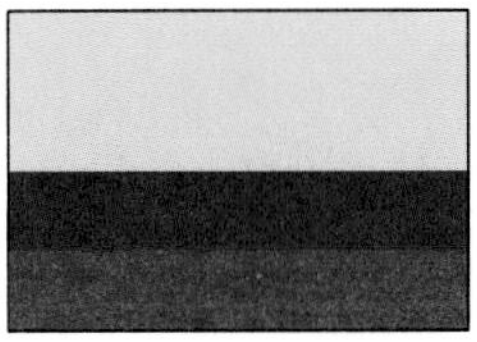

Comoros

Congo

Costa Rica

Croatia

Cuba

Cyprus

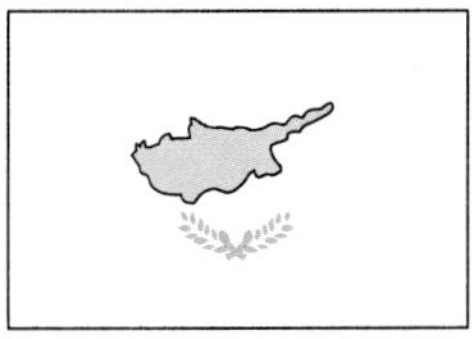

Czech Republic

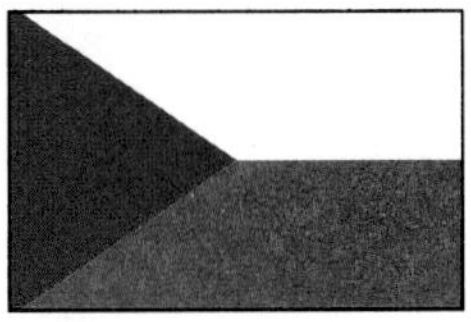

Denmark

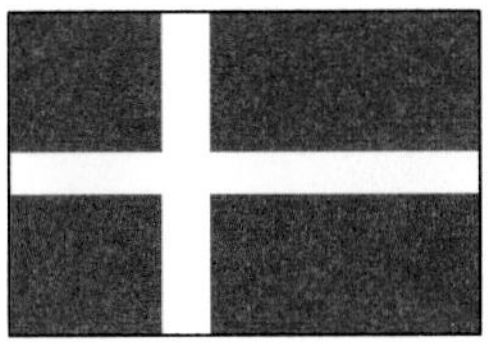

Djibouti

Dominica

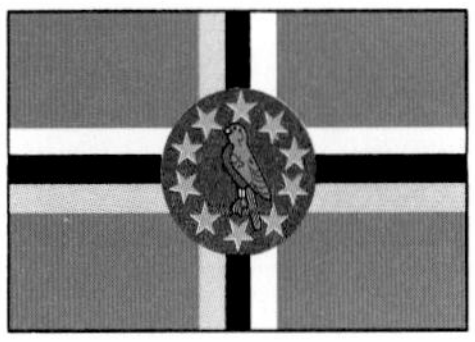

Dominican Republic

Ecuador

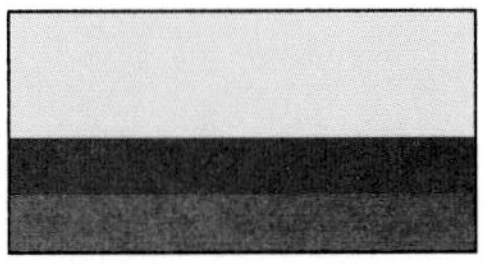

Egypt

El Salvador

Equatorial Guinea

Eritrea

Estonia

Ethiopia

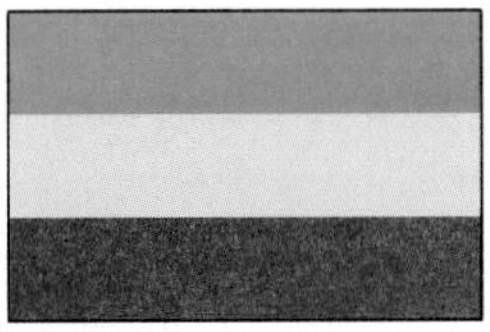

Fiji

Finland

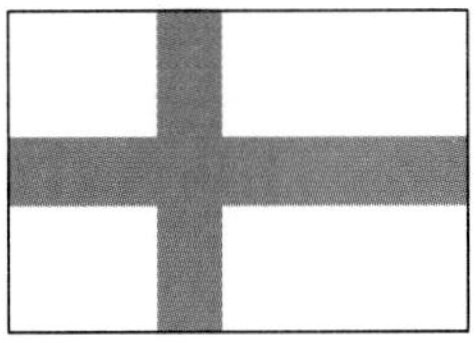

France

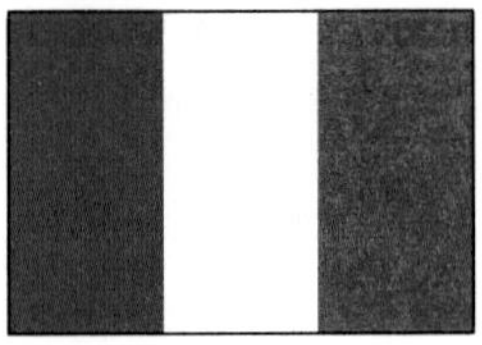

French Polynesia

Gabon

Gambia

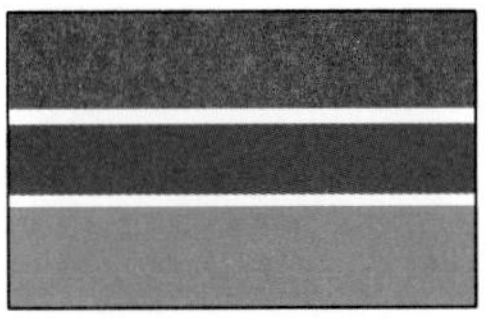

Georgia

Germany

Ghana

Greece

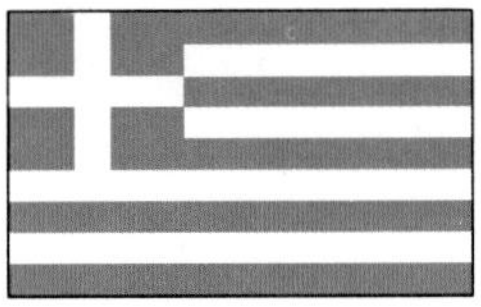

Grenada

Guatemala

Guinea

Guinea-Bissau

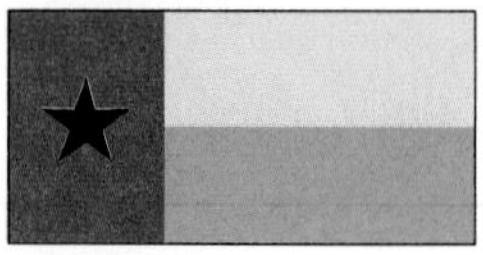

Guyana

Haiti

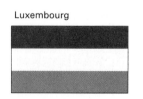

Honduras

Hong Kong

Hungary

Iceland

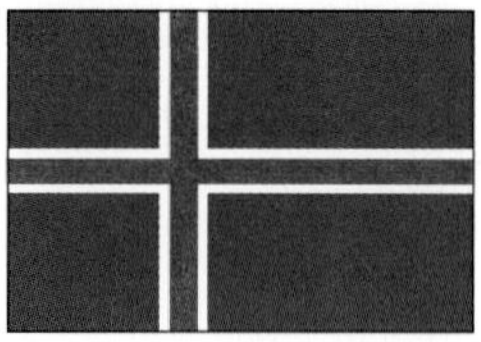

India

Indonesia

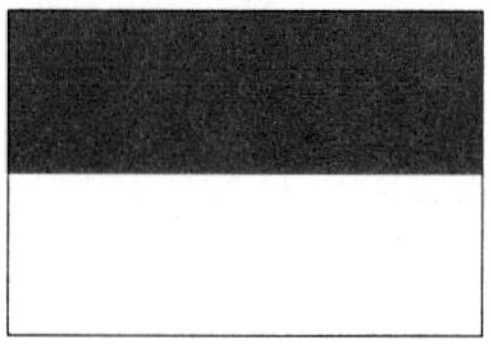

Iran

Iraq

Ireland

Israel

Italy

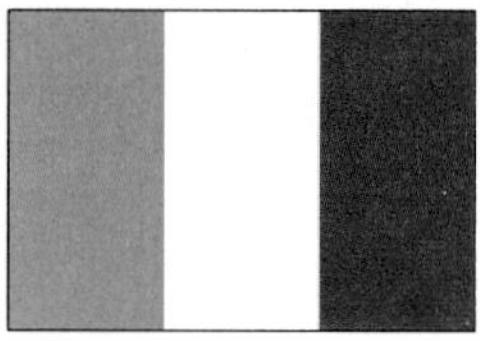

Ivory Coast

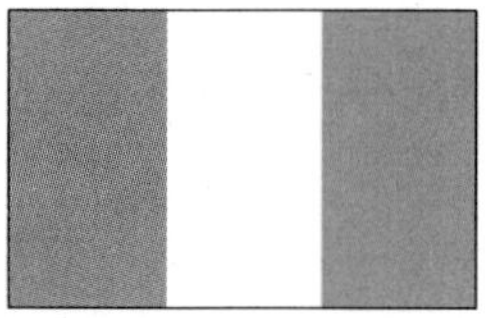

Jamaica

Japan

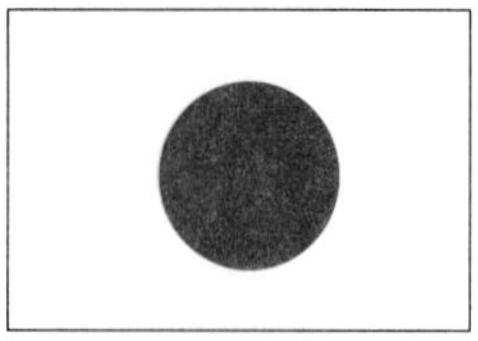

Jordan

Kazakhstan

Kenya

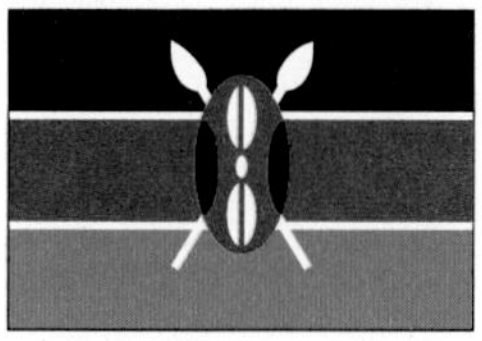

Kiribati

Korea, North

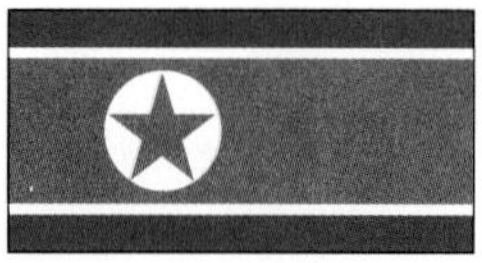

Korea, South

Kuwait

Kyrgyzstan

Laos

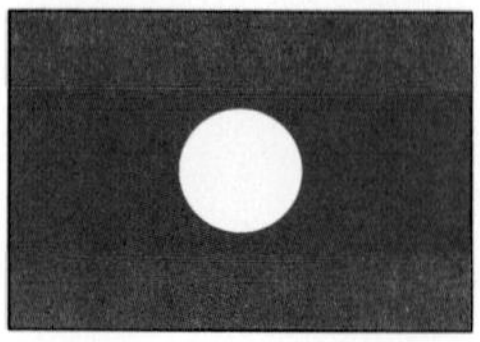

Latvia

Lebanon

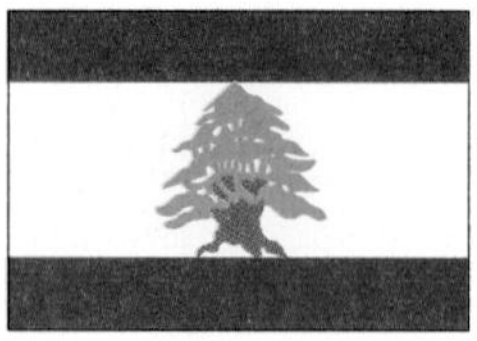

Lesotho

Liberia

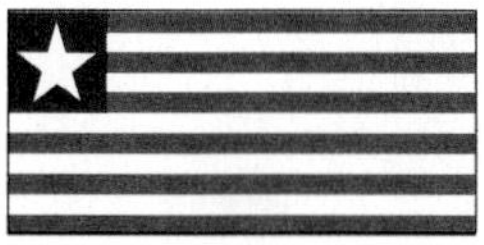

Libya

Liechtenstein

Lithuania

Luxembourg

Macedonia

Madagascar

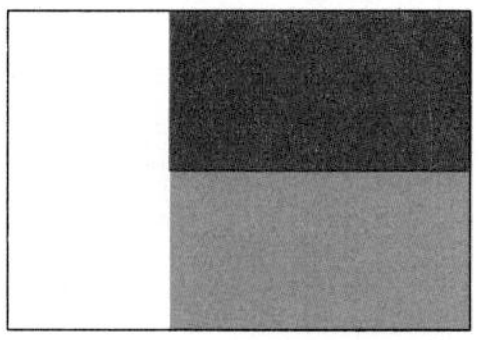

Malawi

Malaysia

Maldives

Mali

Malta

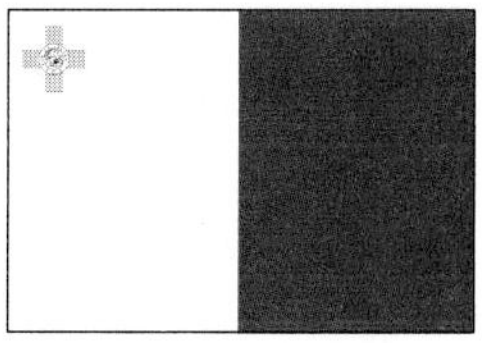

Marshall Islands

Mauritania

Mauritius

Mexico

Micronesia, Federated States of

Moldova

Monaco

Mongolia

Morocco

Mozambique

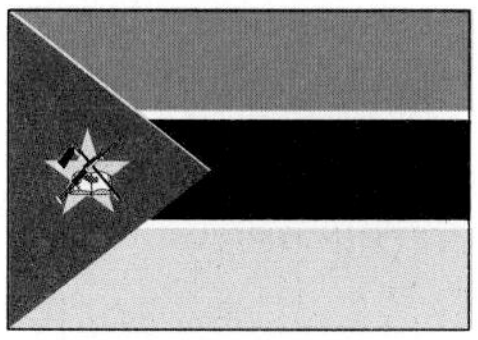

Namibia

Nauru

Nepal

Netherlands

New Zealand

Nicaragua

Niger

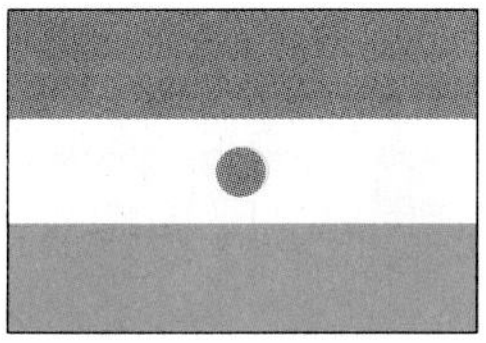

Nigeria

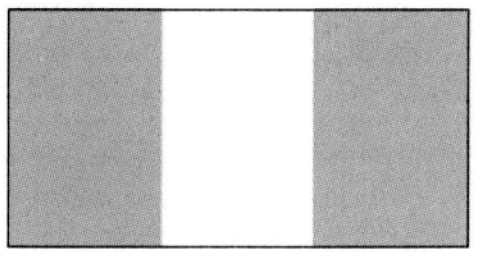

Northern Cyprus

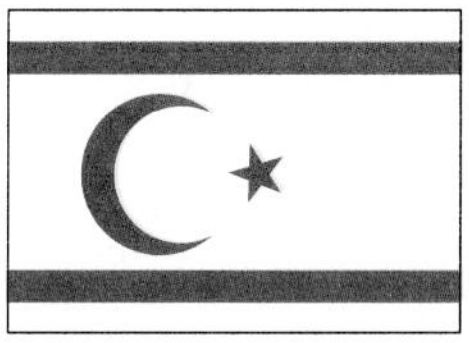

Northern Mariana Islands

Norway

Oman

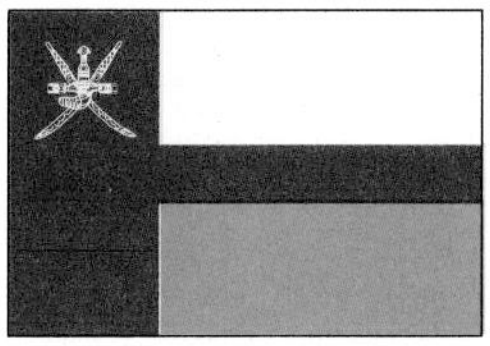

Pakistan

Palau

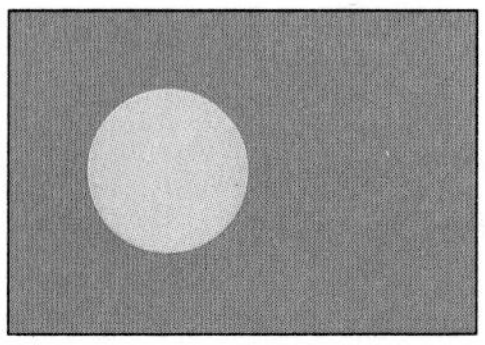

Panama

Papua New Guinea

Paraguay

Peru

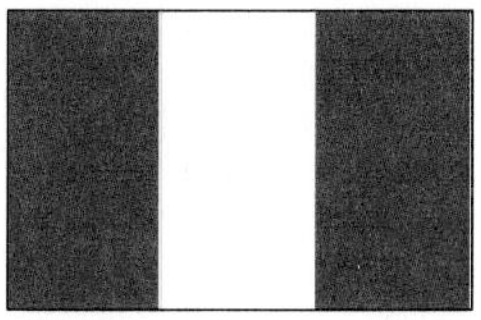

Philippines

Poland

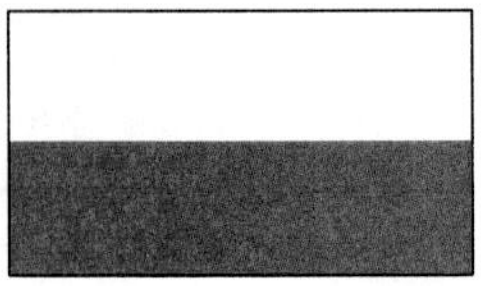

Portugal

Qatar

Romania

Russia

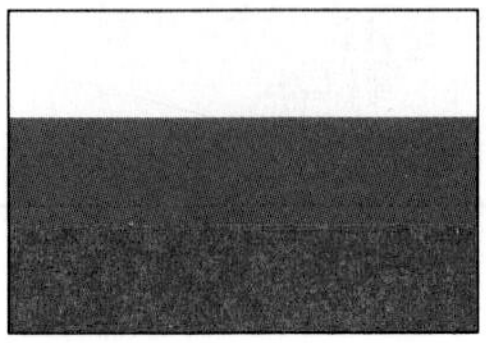

Rwanda

St. Kitts and Nevis

St. Lucia

St. Vincent and the Grenadines

San Marino

Sao Tome and Principe

Saudi Arabia

Senegal

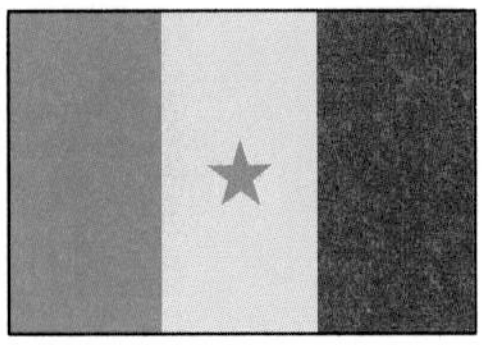

Seychelles

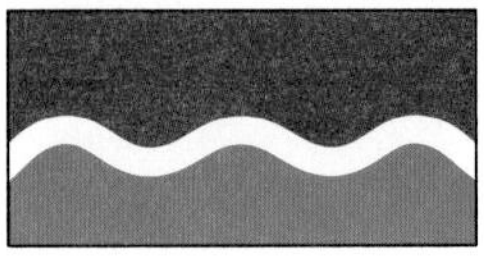

Sierra Leone

Singapore

Slovakia

Slovenia

Solomon Islands

Somalia

South Africa

Spain

Sri Lanka

Sudan

Suriname

Swaziland

Sweden

Switzerland

Syria

Taiwan

Tajikistan

Tanzania

Thailand

Togo

Tonga

Trinidad and Tobago

Tunisia

Turkey

Turkmenistan

Tuvalu

Uganda

Ukraine

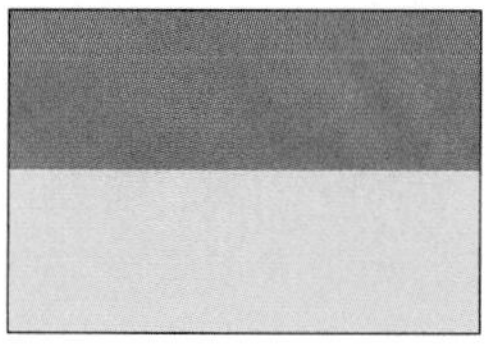

United Arab Emirates

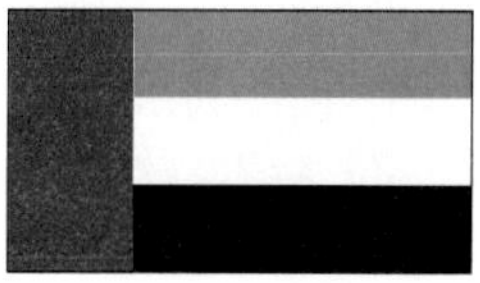

United Kingdom

United States

Uruguay

Uzbekistan

Vanuatu

Vatican City

Venezuela

Vietnam

Western Sahara

Western Samoa

Yemen

Yugoslavia

Zaire

Zambia

Zimbabwe

United Nations

Organization of American States

Council of Europe

Organization of African Unity

Olympics

WORLD TIME ZONES

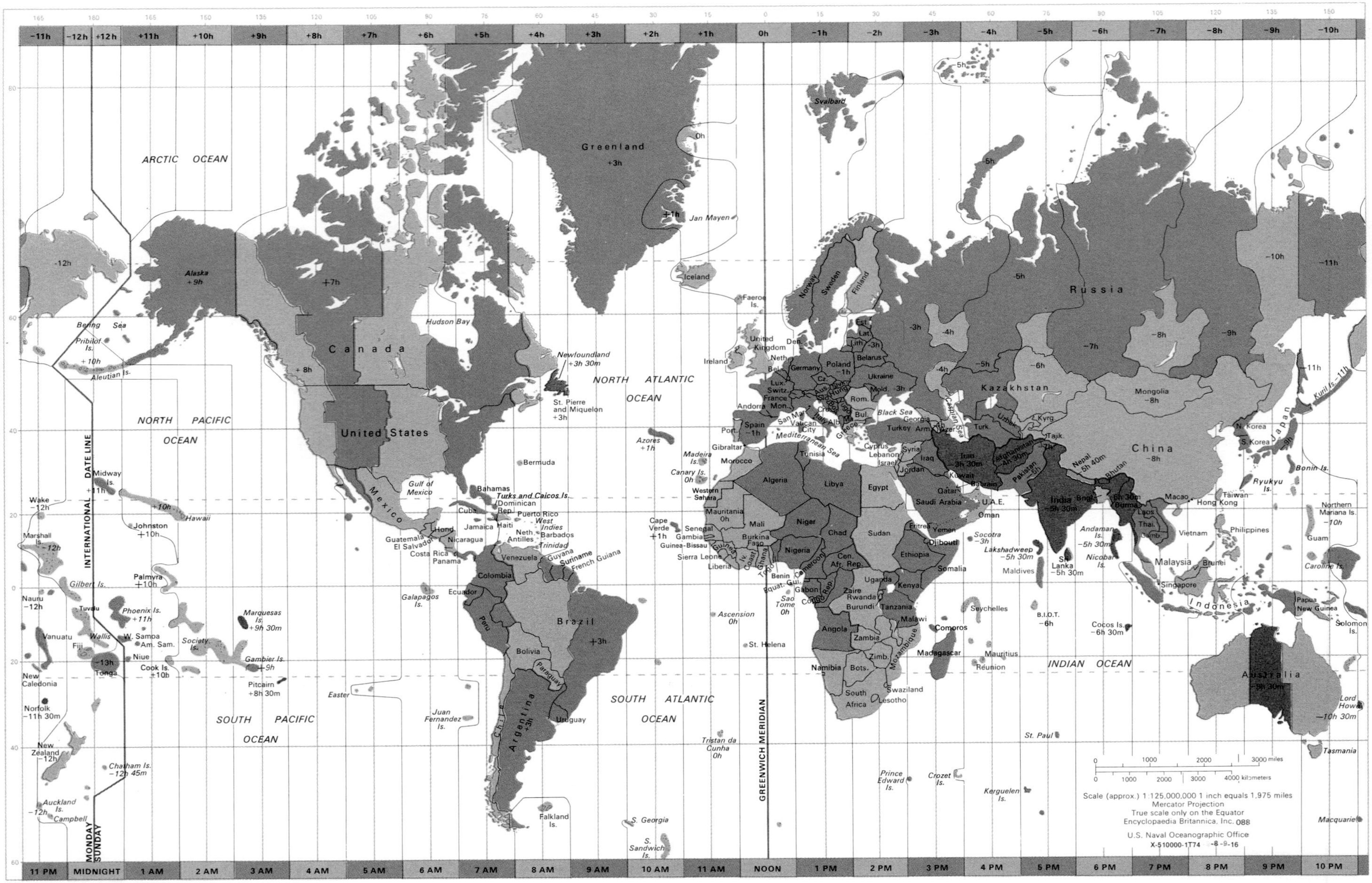

Time Zones

- Standard time zone of even-numbered hours from Greenwich time
- Standard time zone of odd-numbered hours from Greenwich time
- Time varies from the standard time zone by half an hour
- Time varies from the standard time zone by other than half an hour

h m — hours, minutes

The standard time zone system, fixed by international agreement and by law in each country, is based on a theoretical division of the globe into 24 zones of 15° longitude each. The mid-meridian of each zone fixes the hour for the entire zone. The zero time zone extends 7½° east and 7½° west of the Greenwich meridian, 0° longitude. Since the earth rotates toward the east, time zones to the west of Greenwich are earlier, to the east, later.

Plus and minus hours at the top of the map are added to or subtracted from local time to find Greenwich time. Local standard time can be determined for any area in the world by adding one hour for each time zone counted in an easterly direction from one's own, or by subtracting one hour for each zone counted in a westerly direction. To separate one day from the next, the 180th meridian has been designated as the international date line. On both sides of the line the time of day is the same, but west of the line it is one day later than it is to the east.

Countries that adhere to the international zone system adopt the zone applicable to their location. Some countries, however, establish time zones based on political boundaries, or adopt the time zone of a neighboring unit. For all or part of the year some countries also advance their time by one hour, thereby utilizing more daylight hours each day.

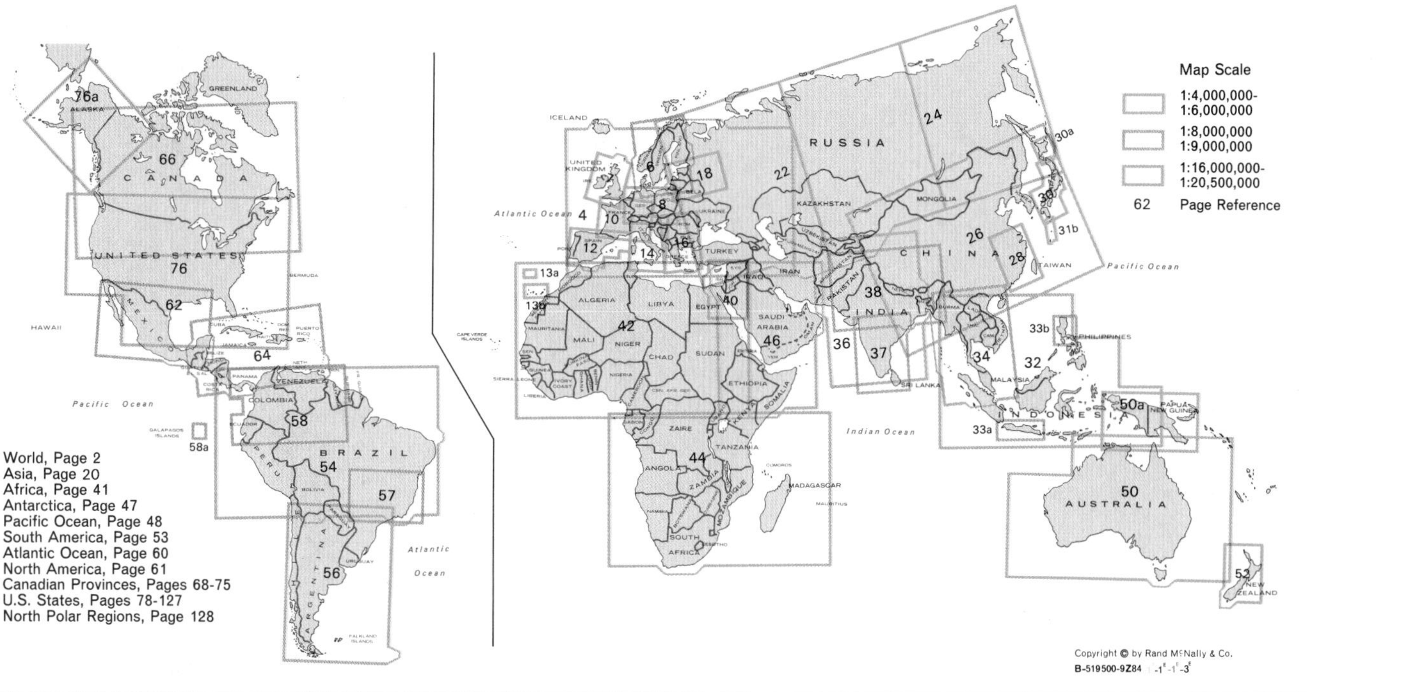

World, Page 2
Asia, Page 20
Africa, Page 41
Antarctica, Page 47
Pacific Ocean, Page 48
South America, Page 53
Atlantic Ocean, Page 60
North America, Page 61
Canadian Provinces, Pages 68-75
U.S. States, Pages 78-127
North Polar Regions, Page 128

World Maps Symbols

Inhabited Localities

The size of type indicates the relative economic and political importance of the locality

Écommoy	Lisieux	Rouen
Trouville	Orléans	PARIS
Bi'r Safājah °	Oasis	

Alternate Names

MOSKVA MOSCOW — Basel Bâle — English or second official language names are shown in reduced size lettering

Volgograd (Stalingrad) — Historical or other alternates in the local language are shown in parentheses

Urban Area (Area of continuous industrial, commercial, and residential development)

Capitals of Political Units

- BUDAPEST — Independent Nation
- Cayenne — Dependency (Colony, protectorate, etc.)
- Recife — State, Province, County, Oblast, etc.

Political Boundaries

International (First-order political unit)

- Demarcated and Undemarcated
- Disputed de jure
- Indefinite or Undefined
- Demarcation Line

Internal

- State, Province, etc. (Second-order political unit)
- MURCIA — Historical Region (No boundaries indicated)
- GALAPAGOS (Ecuador) — Administering Country

Transportation

- Primary Road
- Secondary Road
- Minor Road, Trail
- Railway
- Canal du Midi — Navigable Canal
- Bridge
- Tunnel
- TO MALMÖ — Ferry

Hydrographic Features

- Shoreline
- Undefined or Fluctuating Shoreline
- Amur — River, Stream
- Intermittent Stream
- Rapids, Falls
- Irrigation or Drainage Canal
- Reef
- The Everglades — Swamp
- RIMO GLACIER — Glacier
- L. Victoria — Lake, Reservoir
- Tuz Gölü — Salt Lake
- Intermittent Lake, Reservoir
- Dry Lake Bed
- (395) — Lake Surface Elevation

Topographic Features

- Matterhorn △ 4478 — Elevation Above Sea Level
- 76 ▽ — Elevation Below Sea Level
- Mount Cook ▲ 3764 — Highest Elevation in Country
- 133 ▼ — Lowest Elevation in Country
- Khyber Pass 1067 — Mountain Pass

Elevations are given in meters.
The highest and lowest elevations in a continent are underlined

- Sand Area
- Lava
- Salt Flat

State, Province Maps Symbols

- ✪ Capital
- ∘ County Seat
- ▲ Military Installation
- △ Point of Interest
- + Mountain Peak
- International Boundary
- State, Province Boundary
- County Boundary
- Railroad
- Road
- Urban Area

ARCTIC OCEAN
Beaufort Sea
GREENLAND
(Den.)
VICTORIA ISLAND
BAFFIN ISLAND
Baffin Bay
UNITED STATES
Arctic Circle
Mount McKinley
6194
Anchorage
Yellowknife
Godthåb
Reykjavik
ICELAND
Bering Sea
Gulf of Alaska
Juneau
Hudson Bay
C A N A D A
ROCKY MOUNTAINS
ALEUTIAN ISLANDS
Vancouver
Seattle
Winnipeg
NEWFOUNDLAND
IRELAND
Saint Lawrence
Montréal
Toronto
NORTH AMERICA
DETROIT
CHICAGO
NEW YORK
Washington
APPALACHIAN MOUNTAINS
ATLANTIC OCEAN
PORTUGAL
Denver
St. Louis
SAN FRANCISCO
UNITED STATES
AÇORES AZORES
(Port.)
P A C I F I C
LOS ANGELES
Phoenix
Mississippi
Atlanta
BERMUDA
(U.K.)
ARQUIPÉLAGO DA MADEIRA
(Port.)
Casablanca
MOROCCO
MIDWAY ISLANDS
(U.S.)
O C E A N
Houston
New Orleans
ISLAS CANARIAS
CANARY ISLANDS
(Sp.)
Gulf of Mexico
Miami
Monterrey
BAHAMAS
Tropic of Cancer
WESTERN SAHARA
HAWAIIAN ISLANDS
(U.S.)
Honolulu
La Habana
MEXICO
CUBA
Guadalajara
DOMINICAN REPUBLIC
HAITI
JAMAICA
CIUDAD DE MÉXICO
BELIZE
PUERTO RICO (U.S.)
MAURI-TANIA
GUADELOUPE (Fr.)
Caribbean Sea
GUATEMALA
HONDURAS
MARTINIQUE (Fr.)
CAPE VERDE
SENEGAL
EL SALVADOR
NICARAGUA
TRINIDAD AND TOBAGO
GAMBIA
GUINEA-BISSAU
CLIPPERTON
(Fr.)
COSTA RICA
Panamá
Caracas
GUINEA
PANAMA
VENEZUELA
SIERRA LEONE
GUYANA
Santa Fe de Bogotá
SURINAME
FRENCH GUIANA
LIBERIA
P O L Y N E S I A
COLOMBIA
Equator
Quito
ECUADOR
ARCHIPIÉLAGO DE COLÓN
GALAPAGOS ISLANDS
(Ec.)
Manaus
Amazon
Belém
Fortaleza
ANDES
PERU
B R A Z I L
Recife
TOKELAU ISLANDS
(N.Z.)
ÎLES MARQUISES
WALLIS AND FUTUNA
(Fr.)
W. SAMOA
AM. SAMOA
Lima
SOUTH AMERICA
Salvador
ATLANTIC OCEAN
FIJI
La Paz
Brasília
BOLIVIA
NIUE
(N.Z.)
COOK ISLANDS
(N.Z.)
FRENCH POLYNESIA
TONGA
PARAGUAY
Tropic of Capricorn
SÃO PAULO
RIO DE JANEIRO
PITCAIRN
(U.K.)
Antofagasta
Asunción
ISLA DE PASCUA
EASTER ISLAND
(Chile)
CHILE
International Date Line
Córdoba
Porto Alegre
URUGUAY
Santiago
P A C I F I C
BUENOS AIRES
Montevideo
Co. Aconcagua
6959
ARGENTINA
CHATHAM ISLAND
(N.Z.)
O C E A N
FALKLAND ISLANDS
(U.K.)
Punta Arenas
CABO DE HORNOS
CAPE HORN
SOUTH GEORGIA
(Falk. Is.)
SOUTH ORKNEY ISLANDS
(B.A.T.)
Antarctic Circle
Bellingshausen Sea
Weddell Sea
Ross Sea
Vinson Massif
4897
A N T A R

ARCTIC OCEAN
ZEML'A FRANCA-IOSIFA
NOVAJA ZEML'A
Barents Sea
Karskoje More
More Laptevych
NOVOSIBIRSKIJE OSTROVA
Arctic Circle
Noril'sk
Jenisej
Lena
Jakutsk
Anadyr'
Bering Sea
ALEUTIAN IS. (U.S.)
Petropavlovsk-Kamčatskij
Sea of Okhotsk
OSTROV SACHALIN
SWEDEN
FINLAND
Helsinki
Stockholm
SANKT-PETERBURG
Archangel'sk
Ob'
URAL'SKIJE GORY
R U S S I A
Nižnij Novgorod
Jekaterinburg
MOSKVA
Novosibirsk
Ozero Bajkal
ALTAI
Karaganda
K A Z A K H S T A N
MONGOLIA
Harbin
POLAND
Kijev
UKRAINE
MOLD.
GERMANY
ROM.
BUL.
ITALY
Roma
Black Sea
Gora El'brus 5633
Volga
Caspian Sea
Aral Sea
UZBEK.
Taškent
KYRG.
TURKMENISTAN
TAJIK.
GOBI
BEIJING (PEKING)
Sea of Japan
KOREA
SOUL
JAPAN
TŌKYŌ
ŌSAKA
Yellow Sea
Istanbul
TURKEY
GREECE
Mediterranean Sea
MALTA
SYRIA
LEB.
IRAQ
ISRAEL
JORDAN
Tehrān
IRAN
AFGHANISTAN
C H I N A
Xi'an
Wuhan
SHANGHAI
Chongqing
HIMALAYA
NEPAL
BHU.
Mount Everest 8848
PAKISTAN
DELHI
KUWAIT
QATAR
UNITED ARAB EMIRATES
SAUDI ARABIA
OMAN
LIBYA
AL-QĀHIRAH (CAIRO)
EGYPT
Red Sea
Karāchi
Tropic of Cancer
BNGL.
CALCUTTA
INDIA
BURMA
Guangzhou
HONG KONG (U.K.)
TAIWAN
International Date Line
P A C I F I C
O C E A N
NIGER
CHAD
Nile
Al-Kharṭūm
SUDAN
ERITREA
YEMEN
Adan
BOMBAY
Bay of Bengal
THAILAND
LAOS
South China Sea
VIETNAM
Philippine Sea
WAKE ISLAND (U.S.)
Arabian Sea
Madras
Krung Thep (Bangkok)
CAMB.
MANILA
PHILIPPINES
GUAM (U.S.)
NIGERIA
DJIBOUTI
ETHIOPIA
SOMALIA
SRI LANKA
Colombo
BRUNEI
M I C R O N E S I A
CAMEROON
CEN. AFR. REP.
MALDIVES
MALAYSIA
Singapore
UGANDA
KENYA
Muqdisho
GABON
CONGO
RWANDA
Lake Victoria
Nairobi
Equator
BORNEO
SULAWESI
IRIAN JAYA
PAPUA NEW GUINEA
SOLOMON ISLANDS
KIRIBATI
TUVALU
ZAIRE
Kinshasa
BURUNDI
Kilimanjaro 5895
SEYCHELLES
SUMATERA
INDONESIA
CHAGOS ARCHIPELAGO (B.I.O.T.)
TANZANIA
JAKARTA
JAWA
TIMOR
NEW GUINEA
Port Moresby
M E L A N E S I A
Luanda
CHRISTMAS ISLAND (Austl.)
ANGOLA
ZAMBIA
MALAWI
I N D I A N
O C E A N
Cairns
Coral Sea
VANUATU
FIJI
ZIMBABWE
MOZAMBIQUE
Mozambique Channel
MADAGASCAR
NAMIBIA
BOTSWANA
REUNION (Fr.)
MAURITIUS
Tropic of Capricorn
NEW CALEDONIA (Fr.)
Johannesburg
SWAZILAND
LESOTHO
Durban
A U S T R A L I A
Brisbane
SOUTH AFRICA
Cape Town
CAPE OF GOOD HOPE
Perth
Sydney
Melbourne
Mount Kosciusko 2230
Tasman Sea
NEW ZEALAND
Wellington
TASMANIA
ÎLES KERGUELEN (F.S.A.T.)
Antarctic Circle
ENDERBY LAND
WILKES LAND
A N T A R C T I C A
Copyright © by Rand McNally & Co.
Map prepared by Rand McNally & Co.
C-510000-264
Kilometers
Km.
Miles
Mi.
Robinson Projection

Europe

ALBANIA.................... G11
Amsterdam, 6,965,000 ('89) (1,860,000★) .... E 8
ANDORRA.................. G 8
Antwerpen, 497,748 ('87) (1,100,000★) .... E 8
Athínai (Athens), 885,737 ('81) (3,027,331★) ... H12
AUSTRIA.................... F10
Barcelona, 1,714,355 ('88) (4,040,000★) .... G 8
BELARUS.................... E13
Belfast, 303,800 ('87) (685,000★) .... E 6
BELGIUM.................... E 8
Beograd (Belgrade), 1,130,000 ('87) (1,400,000★) G12
Berlin, 3,352,848 ('89) (3,825,000★) E10
Bern, 134,393 ('90) (298,800★) .... F 9
Birmingham, 1,013,995 ('81) (2,675,000★) .... E 7
Bonn, 282,190 ('89) (570,000★) .... E 9
BOSNIA AND HERZEGOVINA........ G11
Bratislava, 444,482 ('91).......................... F11
Bremen, 535,058 ('89) (800,000★) .... E 9
Bruxelles, 136,920 ('87) (2,385,000★) .... E 8
București, 1,989,823 ('86) (2,275,000★) G13
Budapest, 2,016,132 ('90) (2,565,000★) F11
BULGARIA.................. G12
Cardiff, 262,313 ('81) (625,000★) .... E 7
Char'kov (Kharkov), 1,611,000 ('89) (1,940,000★) F15
CROATIA.................... F11
CZECH REPUBLIC...... F11
DENMARK.................. D 9
Dnepropetrovsk, 1,179,000 ('89) (1,600,000★) F14
Doneck, 1,110,000 ('89) (2,200,000★) F15
Dresden, 518,057 ('89) (670,000★) E10
Dublin, 502,749 ('86) (1,140,000★) .... E 6
Düsseldorf, 569,641 ('89) (1,190,000★) .... E 9
Edinburgh, 433,200 ('89) (630,000★) .... D 7
Essen, 620,594 ('89) (4,950,000★) .... E 9
ESTONIA.................... D12
FAEROE ISLANDS...... C 6
FINLAND.................... C13
Firenze, 425,835 ('87) (640,000★) G10
FRANCE..................... F 8
Frankfurt, 625,258 ('89) (1,855,000★) .... E 9
Gdańsk, 461,500 ('89) (909,000★) E11
Genève (Geneva), 165,404 ('90) (460,000★) .... F 9
Genova, 727,427 ('87) (805,000★) .... G 9
GERMANY.................. E10
Gibraltar, 30,077 ('88). H 6
Glasgow, 695,630 ('89) (1,800,000★) .... D 7
GREECE.................... H12
GUERNSEY................ F 7
Hamburg, 1,603,070 ('89) (2,225,000★) .... E 9
Helsinki, 490,034 ('88) (1,040,000★) C12
HUNGARY.................. F11
ICELAND.................... B 4
IRELAND.................... E 6
ISLE OF MAN............. E 7
İstanbul, 6,748,435 ('90) (7,000,000★) G13
ITALY........................ G10
JERSEY...................... F 7
Katowice, 365,800 ('89) (2,778,000★) E11
Kazan', 1,094,000 ('89) (1,140,000★) D17
Kijev (Kiev), 2,587,000 ('89) (2,900,000★) ... E14
København, 466,723 ('90) (1,685,000★) D10
Köln, 937,482 ('89) (1,760,000★) .... E 9
Kraków, 743,700 ('89) (828,000★) E11
LATVIA..................... D12
Leipzig, 545,307 ('89) (700,000★) E10
Leningrad *see* Sankt-Peterburg.................. D14
LIECHTENSTEIN........ F 9
Ljubljana, 233,200 ('87) (316,607▲) F10

★ Population of metropolitan area, including suburbs.

Kilometers 0 200 400 600 Km.
Miles 0 200 400 600 Mi.

1:16 000 000

Lisboa, 807,167 ('81) (2,250,000★) .... H 6
LITHUANIA D12
Liverpool, 538,809 ('81) (1,525,000★) .... E 7
Łódź, 851,500 ('89) (1,061,000★) E11
London, 6,574,009 ('81) (11,100,000★) .... E 7
LUXEMBOURG .... F 9
Lyon, 413,095 ('82) (1,275,000★) .... F 8
MACEDONIA G12
Madrid, 3,102,846 ('88) (4,650,000★) .... G 7
MALTA H10
Manchester, 437,612 ('81) (2,775,000★) .... E 7
Marseille, 874,436 ('82) (1,225,000★) .... G 9
Milano, 1,495,260 ('87) (3,750,000★) .... F 9
Minsk, 1,589,000 ('89) (1,650,000★) E13
MOLDOVA F13
MONACO .... G 9
Moskva (Moscow), 8,769,000 ('89) (13,100,000★) D15
München, 1,211,617 ('89) (1,955,000★) F10
Napoli, 1,204,211 ('87) (2,875,000★) G10
NETHERLANDS .... E 9
Nižnij Novgorod (Gor'kij), 1,438,000 ('89) (2,025,000★) D16
NORWAY .... C 9
Nürnberg, 480,078 ('89) (1,030,000★) F10
Odessa, 1,115,000 ('89) (1,185,000★) F14
Oslo, 452,415 ('87) (720,000★) D10
Paris, 2,078,900 ('87) (9,775,000★) .... F 8
POLAND E11
Porto, 327,368 ('81) (1,225,000★) .... G 6
PORTUGAL .... G 6
Praha, 1,215,656 ('90) (1,325,000★) E10
Reykjavík, 93,425 ('87) (137,941★) .... C 3
Rīga, 915,000 ('89) (1,005,000★) D12
Roma, 2,815,457 ('87) (3,175,000★) G10
ROMANIA F12
Rostov-na-Donu, 1,020,000 ('89) (1,165,000★) F15
Rotterdam, 576,300 ('89) (1,110,000★) .... E 8
RUSSIA D16
Samara, 1,257,000 ('89) (1,505,000★) E18
Sankt-Peterburg, 4,456,000 ('89) (5,825,000★) D14
SAN MARINO G10
Sarajevo, 341,200 ('87) (479,688▲) G11
Saratov, 905,000 ('89) (1,155,000★) E17
Sevilla, 663,132 ('88) (945,000★) .... H 6
's-Gravenhage (The Hague), 443,900 ('89) (770,000★) .... E 8
Skopje, 444,900 ('87) (547,214▲) G12
SLOVAKIA F11
SLOVENIA F10
Sofija, 1,119,152 ('86) (1,205,000★) G12
SPAIN .... H 7
Stockholm, 672,187 ('90) (1,449,972★) D11
SWEDEN C11
SWITZERLAND .... F 9
Tallinn, 482,000 .... D12
Thessaloníki, 406,413 ('81) (706,180★) G12
Tiranë, 255,700 ('87).. G11
Torino, 1,035,565 ('87) (1,550,000★) .... F 9
UKRAINE F14
UNITED KINGDOM ...... E 7
Valencia, 743,933 ('88) (1,270,000★) .... H 7
Valletta, 9,210 ('89) (215,000★) H10
Vilnius, 582,000 .... E12
Warszawa, 1,651,200 ('89) (2,323,000★) ... E12
Wien (Vienna), 1,482,800 ('88) (1,875,000★) F11
YUGOSLAVIA G11
Zagreb, 697,925 ('87).. F11
Zürich, 342,861 ('90) (860,000★) .... F 9

Scandinavia

Denmark
1990 ESTIMATE
Ålborg, 114,000
(155,019▲) . . . . H 7
Århus, 202,300
(261,437▲) . . . . H 8
Copenhagen *see*
København . . . . I 9
København (Copenhagen),
466,723
(1,685,000★) . . . . . . I 9
Odense, 140,100
(176,133▲) . . . . I 8

Finland
1988 ESTIMATE
Helsinki (Helsingfors),
490,034
(1,040,000★) F15
Lahti, 74,300
(108,000★) F15
Oulu, 98,582
(121,000★) D15
Tampere, 170,533
(241,000★) F14
Turku (Åbo), 160,456
(228,000★) F14

Norway
1987 ESTIMATE
Bergen, 209,320
(239,000★) . . . . F 5
Hammerfest,
7,208('83) A14
Oslo, 452,415
(720,000★) . . . . . . G 8
Stavanger, 94,200
(132,000★)('85) . . . . G 5
Trondheim, 135,010 . . E 8

Sweden
1990 ESTIMATE
Göteborg (Gothenburg),
431,840 (710,894★) H 8
Helsingborg, 108,359 H 9
Jönköping, 110,860 . . H10
Linköping, 120,562 . . G10

Malmö, 232,908
(445,000★) . . . . I 9
Norrköping, 119,921 G11
Örebro, 120,353 . . . . G10
Stockholm, 672,187
(1,449,972★) G12
Uppsala, 164,754 . . . . G11
Västerås, 118,386 . . G11

★ Population of metropolitan area, including suburbs.
▲ Population of entire district, including rural area.

Kilometers 0 100 200 300 Km.
Miles 0 100 200 300 Mi.

1:8 000 000

Conic Projection, Two Standard Parallels

Kilometers 0 50 100 150 Km.
Miles 0 50 100 150 Mi.
1:5 000 000

Ireland

1986 CENSUS

Cork, 133,271 (173,694★) . . . . . . J 4
Dublin (Baile Átha Cliath), 502,749 (1,140,000★) . . . . H 6
Galway, 47,104 . . . . . H 3
Limerick, 56,279 (76,557★) . . . . I 4
Waterford, 39,529 (41,054★) . . . . I 5

Isle of Man

1986 CENSUS

Douglas, 20,368 (28,500★) . . . . . . G 8

United Kingdom

England

1981 CENSUS

Birmingham, 1,013,995 (2,675,000★) I11
Blackpool, 146,297 (280,000★) . . . . . . H 9
Bournemouth, 142,829 (315,000★) K11
Bradford, 293,336 . . H11
Brighton, 134,581 (420,000★) K12
Bristol, 413,861 (630,000★) J10
Coventry, 318,718 (645,000★) I11
Derby, 218,026 (275,000★) I11
Kingston upon Hull, 322,144 (350,000★) H12
Leeds, 445,242 (1,540,000★) H11
Leicester, 324,394 (495,000★) I11
Liverpool, 538,809 (1,525,000★) H10
London, 6,574,009 (11,100,000★) J12
Manchester, 437,612 (2,775,000★) H10
Newcastle upon Tyne, 199,064 (1,300,000★) G11
Nottingham, 273,300 (655,000★) I11
Oxford, 113,847 (230,000★) J11
Plymouth, 238,583 (290,000★) . . . . . . K 8
Portsmouth, 174,218 (485,000★) K11
Preston, 166,675 (250,000★) H10
Reading, 194,727 (200,000★) J12
Sheffield, 470,685 (710,000★) H11
Southampton, 211,321 (415,000★) K11
Southend-on-Sea, 155,720 . . . . J13
Stoke-on-Trent, 272,446 (440,000★) H10
Sunderland, 195,064 G11
Teesside, 158,516 (580,000★) G11
Wolverhampton, 263,501 . . . . I10

Northern Ireland

1987 ESTIMATE

Bangor, 70,700 . . . . G 7
Belfast, 303,800 (685,000★) . . . . . . G 7
Londonderry, 97,500 (97,200★) . . . . . . G 5
Newtownabbey, 72,300 . . . . G 7

Scotland

1989 ESTIMATE

Aberdeen, 210,700 . . D10
Dundee, 172,540 . . . . E 9
Edinburgh, 433,200 (630,000★) . . . . . . F 9
Glasgow, 695,630 (1,800,000★) . . . . . . F 8
Greenock, 58,436 (101,000★)('81) . . F 8
Inverness, 38,204('81) D 8
Paisley, 84,330('81) . . F 8

Wales

1981 CENSUS

Cardiff, 262,313 (625,000★) . . . . . . J 9
Newport, 115,896 (310,000★) . . . . . . J 9
Swansea, 172,433 (275,000★) . . . . . . J 9

★ Population of metropolitan area, including suburbs.

Central Europe

Austria

1981 CENSUS

Graz, 243,166 (325,000★) H15
Innsbruck, 117,287 (185,000★) H11
Linz, 199,910 (335,000★) G14
Salzburg, 139,426 (220,000★) H13
Vienna *see* Wien G16
Villach, 52,692 (65,000★) I13
Wien (Vienna), 1,482,800 (1,875,000★)('88) .. G16

Belgium

1987 ESTIMATE

Antwerpen (Antwerp), 479,748 (1,100,000★) ...... D 4
Brugge, 117,755 (223,000★) .... D 3
Bruxelles (Brussel), 136,920 (2,385,000★) ...... E 4
Charleroi, 209,395 (480,000★) .... E 4
Gent (Gand), 233,856 (465,000★) .... D 3
Hasselt, 65,563 (290,000★) .... E 5
Liège, 200,891 (750,000★) .... E 5
Mons, 89,697 (242,000★) .... E 3

Czech Republic

1990 ESTIMATE

Brno, 392,285 (450,000★) F16
Hradec Králové, 101,302 (113,000★) E15
Liberec, 104,256 (175,000★) E15
Olomouc, 107,044 (126,000★) F17
Ostrava, 331,557 (760,000★) F18
Plzeň, 175,038 (210,000★) F13
Praha (Prague), 1,215,656 (1,325,000★) E14
Ústí nad Labem, 106,499 (115,000★) E14

Germany

1989 ESTIMATE

Aachen, 233,255 (535,000★) .... E 6
Augsburg, 247,731 (405,000★) G10
Berlin, 3,352,848 (3,825,000★) C13
Bielefeld, 311,946 (515,000★) .... C 8
Bochum, 389,087 .... D 7
Bonn, 282,190 (570,000★) .... E 7
Braunschweig, 253,794 (330,000★) C10
Bremen, 535,058 (800,000★) .... B 8
Bremerhaven, 126,934 (190,000★) .... B 8
Chemnitz, 311,765 (450,000★) E12
Cologne *see* Köln .... E 6
Dortmund, 587,328 .. D 7
Dresden, 518,057 (670,000★) D13
Duisburg, 527,447 .. D 6
Düsseldorf, 569,641 (1,190,000★) ...... D 6
Erfurt, 220,016 ...... E11
Essen, 620,594 (4,950,000★) ...... D 7
Frankfurt am Main, 625,258 (1,855,000★) ...... E 8
Gelsenkirchen, 287,255 .... D 7
Hagen, 210,640 .... D 7
Halle, 236,044 (475,000★) D11
Hamburg, 1,603,070 (2,225,000★) ...... B 9
Hannover, 498,495 (1,000,000★) ...... C 9
Karlsruhe, 265,100 (485,000★) .... F 8
Kiel, 240,675 (335,000★) A10
Köln (Cologne), 937,482 (1,760,000★) ...... E 6
Leipzig, 545,307 (700,000★) D12
Lübeck, 210,681 (260,000★) B10
Magdeburg, 290,579 (400,000★) C11

★ Population of metropolitan area, including suburbs.

Kilometers 0 50 100 150 Km.
Miles 0 50 100 150 Mi.

1:4 000 000

Mannheim, 300,468 (1,400,000★) . . . . . . F 8
Mönchengladbach, 252,910 (410,000★) D 6
München (Munich), 1,211,617 (1,955,000★) G11
Münster, 248,919 . . . . D 7
Nürnberg, 480,078 (1,030,000★) F11
Potsdam, 142,862 . . C13
Rostock, 253,990 . . . . A12
Saarbrücken, 188,467 (385,000★) . . . . F 6
Stuttgart, 562,658 (1,925,000★) . . . . . . G 9
Wiesbaden, 254,209 (795,000★) . . . . E 8
Wuppertal, 371,283 (830,000★) . . . . D 7

Hungary

1990 ESTIMATE

Budapest, 2,016,132 (2,565,000★) H19
Debrecen, 212,247 . . H21
Miskolc, 196,449 . . . . G20
Pécs, 170,119 . . . . . . I18
Szeged, 175,338 . . . . I20
Szombathely, 85,418 H16

Liechtenstein

1990 ESTIMATE

Vaduz, 4,874 . . . . . . H 9

Luxembourg

1985 ESTIMATE

Luxembourg, 76,130 (136,000★) . . . . F 6

Netherlands

1989 ESTIMATE

Amsterdam, 6,965,000 (1,860,000★) . . . . . . C 4
Eindhoven, 190,700 (379,377★) . . . . D 5
Groningen, 167,800 (206,781★) . . . . B 6
Rotterdam, 576,300 (1,110,000★) . . . . . . D 4
's-Gravenhage (The Hague), 443,900 (770,000★) . . . . C 4
Tilburg, 155,100 (224,934★) . . . . D 5
Utrecht, 230,700 (518,779★) . . . . C 5

Poland

1989 ESTIMATE

Białystok, 263,900 . . B23
Bydgoszcz, 377,900 B18
Gdańsk (Danzig), 461,500 (909,000★) A18
Gdynia, 250,200 . . . . A18
Katowice, 365,800 (2,778,000★) E19
Kielce, 211,100 . . . . . . E20
Kraków, 743,700 (828,000★) E19
łódź, 851,500 (1,061,000★) D19
Lublin, 339,500 (389,000★) D22
Poznań, 586,500 (672,000★) C16
Radom, 223,600 . . . . D21
Szczecin (Stettin), 409,500 (449,000★) B14
Toruń, 199,600 . . . . . . B18
Wałbrzych (Waldenburg), 141,400 (207,000★) E16
Warszawa (Warsaw), 1,651,200 (2,323,000★) C21
Wrocław (Breslau), 637,400 . . . . D17

Slovakia

1990 ESTIMATE

Bratislava, 442,999 . . G17
Košice, 237,099 . . . . G21

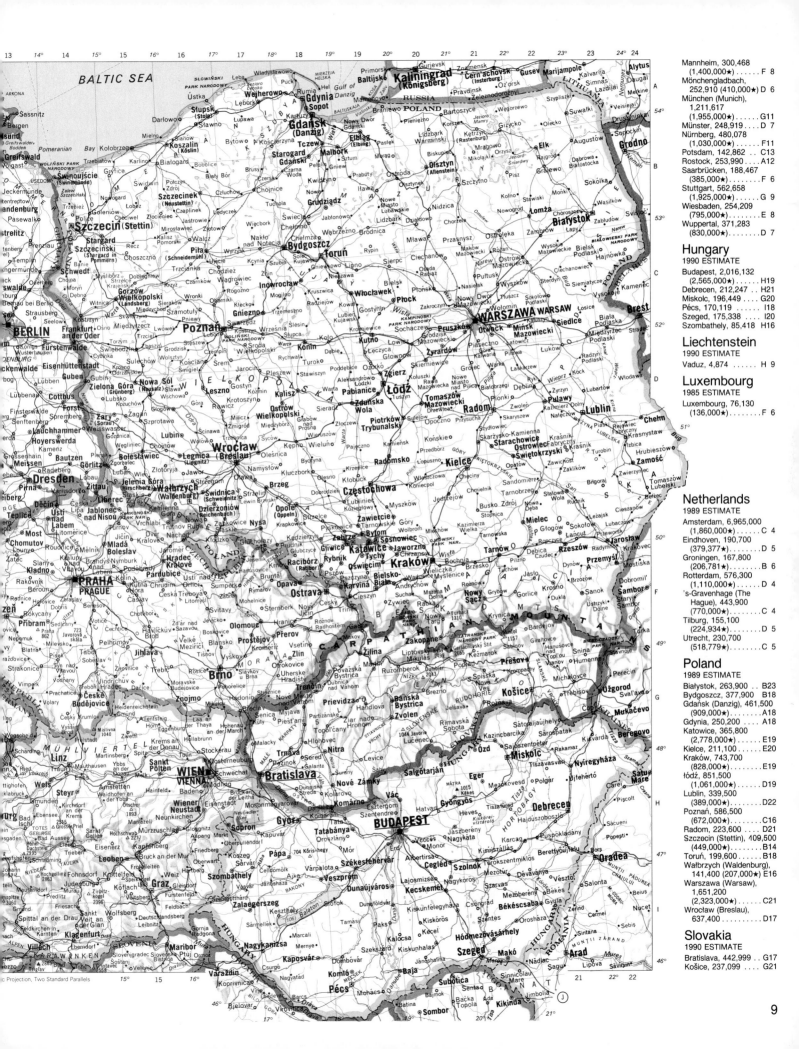

France

1982 CENSUS

Aix-en-Provence, 121,327 (126,552★) I12
Alès, 43,268 (70,180★) H11
Amiens, 131,332 (154,498★)........C 9
Angers, 136,038 (195,859★)........E 6
Angoulême, 46,197 (103,552★) ...... G 7
Bayonne, 41,381 (127,477★) .... I 5
Belfort, 51,206 (76,221★) E13
Besançon, 113,283 (120,772★)........E13
Béziers, 76,647 (81,347★) I10
Bordeaux, 208,159 (640,012★)........H 6
Boulogne-Billancourt, 102,582 ....D 9
Boulogne-sur-Mer, 47,653 (98,566★) .... B 8
Brest, 156,060 (201,145★)........D 2
Brive-la-Gaillarde, 51,511 (64,301★) .... G 8
Caen, 114,068 (183,526★)........C 6
Calais, 76,527 (100,823★)........B 8
Cannes, 72,259 (295,525★) I14
Chalon-sur-Saône, 56,194 (78,064★) F11
Chambéry, 53,427 (96,163★) G12
Cherbourg, 28,442 (85,485★) .... C 5
Cholet, 55,524 ...... E 6
Clermont-Ferrand, 147,361 (256,189★) G10
Compiègne, 40,384 (62,778★) .... C 9
Creil, 34,709 (82,505★) .... C 9
Dieppe, 35,957 (41,812★) .... C 8
Dijon, 140,942 (215,865★)........E12
Douai, 42,576 (202,366★)........B10
Dunkerque, 73,120 (195,705★)........A 9
Fontainebleau, 15,679 (35,629★) .... D 9
Grenoble, 156,637 (392,021★) G12
La Rochelle, 75,840 (102,143★)........F 5
Laval, 50,360 (55,984★) .... D 6
Le Havre, 199,388 (254,595★)........C 7
Le Mans, 147,697 (191,080★)........D 7
Lens, 38,244 (327,383★)........B 9
Lille, 168,424 (1,020,000★)...... B10
Limoges, 140,400 (171,689★) ...... G 8
Lorient, 62,554 (104,025★)........E 3
Lourdes, 17,425...... I 6
Lyon, 413,095 (1,275,000★)...... G11
Mâcon, 38,404 (47,274★) F11
Marseille, 874,436 (1,225,000★) J12
Maubeuge, 36,061 (105,714★)........B10
Meaux, 45,005 (55,797★) .... D 9
Melun, 35,005 (82,479★) .... D 9
Metz, 114,232 (186,437★)........C13
Montbéliard, 31,836 (128,194★)........E13
Montluçon, 49,912 (67,963★) .... F 9
Montpellier, 197,231 (221,307★) I10
Mulhouse, 112,157 (220,613★)........E14
Nancy, 96,317 (306,982★)........D13
Nantes, 240,539 (464,857★)........ E 5
Nevers, 43,013 (59,274★) E10
Nice, 337,085 (449,496★) I14
Nîmes, 124,220 (132,343★) I11
Niort, 58,203 (61,959★) .... F 6

Kilometers 0 50 100 150 Km.
Miles 0 50 100 150 Mi.

1 : 4 000 000

Orléans, 102,710
(220,478★) . . . . E 8
Paris, 2,078,900
(9,775,000★)('87) . . D 9
Pau, 83,790
(131,265★) . . . . I 6
Perpignan, 111,669
(137,915★) . . . . J 9
Poitiers, 79,350
(103,204★) . . . . F 7
Quimper, 56,907 . . . . D 2
Reims, 194,656
(199,388★) C11
Rennes, 117,234
(234,418★) . . . . D 5
Roanne, 48,705
(81,786★) F11
Roubaix, 101,602 . . . . B10
Rouen, 101,945
(379,879★) . . . . C 8
Saint-Brieuc, 48,563
(83,900★) . . . . D 4
Saint-Denis, 90,829 . . D 9
Saint-Étienne, 204,955
(317,228★) G11
Saint-Germain, 38,499 D 9
Saint-Malo, 46,347 . . D 4
Saint-Nazaire, 68,348
(130,271★) . . . . E 4
Saint-Quentin, 63,567
(71,887★) C10
Saint-Tropez, 4,961
(6,213▲) I13
Sedan, 23,477
(30,871★) C11
Strasbourg, 248,712
(400,000★) D14
Toulon, 179,423
(410,393★) I12
Toulouse, 347,995
(541,271★) . . . . I 8
Tourcoing, 96,908 . . B10
Tours, 132,209
(262,786★) . . . . E 7
Troyes, 63,581
(125,240★) D11
Valence, 66,356
(106,041★) H11
Valenciennes, 40,275
(349,505★) B10
Verdun, 21,516
(26,944★) C12
Versailles, 91,494 . . . . D 9
Vichy, 30,527
(63,501★) F10
Villeurbanne, 115,960 G11

Guernsey

1986 CENSUS

Saint Peter Port, 16,085
(36,000★) . . . . C 4

Jersey

1986 CENSUS

Saint Helier, 27,083
(46,500★) . . . . C 4

Liechtenstein

1990 ESTIMATE

Vaduz, 4,874 . . . . E16

Luxembourg

1985 ESTIMATE

Luxembourg, 76,130
(136,000★) C13

Monaco

1982 CENSUS

Monaco, 27,063
(87,000★) I14

Switzerland

1990 ESTIMATE

Basel (Bâle), 169,587
(575,000★) E14
Bern (Berne), 134,393
(298,800★) F14
Fribourg (Freiburg), 33,962
(56,800★) F14
Genève, 165,404
(460,000★) F13
Lausanne, 122,600
(259,900★) F13
Luzern, 59,115
(159,500★) E15
Neuchâtel, 32,509
(65,900★) F13
Sankt Gallen, 73,191
(125,000★) E16
Sankt Moritz,
5,335('87) F16
Schaffhausen, 33,956
(53,000★) E15
Thun, 37,707
(77,200★) F14
Winterthur, 85,174
(107,400★) E15
Zürich, 342,861
(860,000★) E15

★ Population of metropolitan area, including suburbs.
▲ Population of entire district, including rural area.

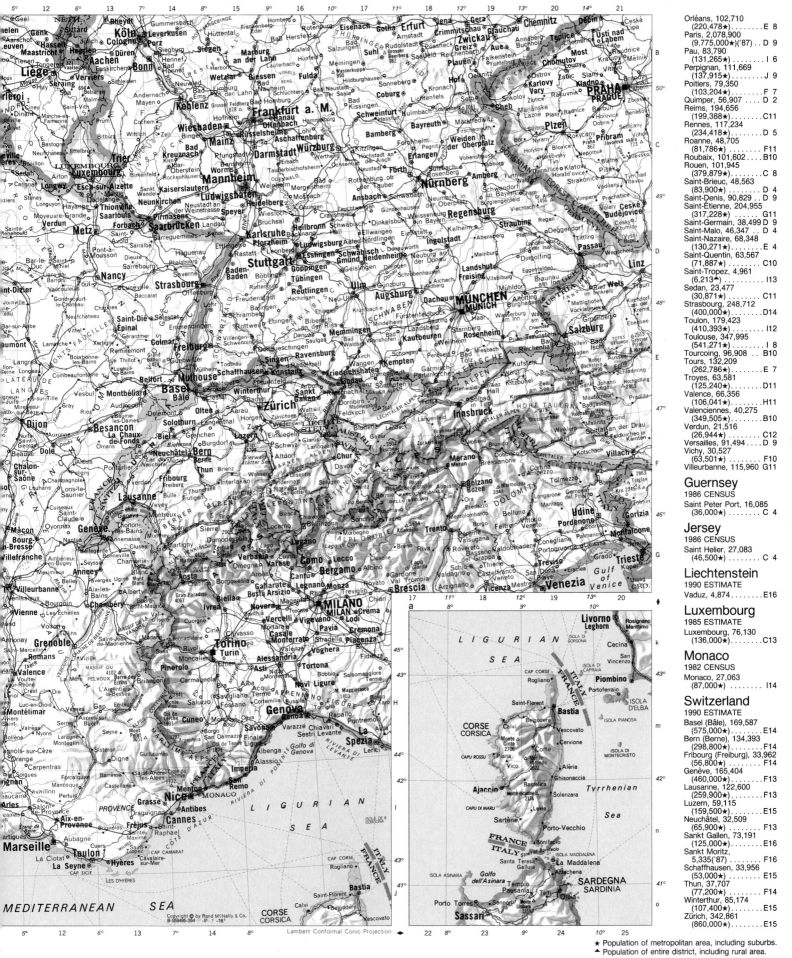

Spain and Portugal

Andorra
1986 CENSUS
Andorra, 18,463 .... C13

Gibraltar
1988 ESTIMATE
Gibraltar, 30,077 .... I 6

Portugal
1981 CENSUS
Almada, 42,607 .... G 2
Barreiro, 50,863 .... G 2
Beja, 19,643 .... G 4
Braga, 63,033 ...... D 3
Coimbra, 74,616 .... E 3
Covilhã, 21,807 ...... E 4
Évora, 34,851 ...... G 4
Faro, 27,974 .... H 4
Funchal, 44,111 .... m21
Guimarães, 21,947 .. D 3
Lisboa (Lisbon), 807,167 (2,250,000★) ...... G 2
Montijo, 23,017 ...... G 3
Porto, 327,368 (1,225,000★) ...... D 3
Póvoa de Varzim, 23,729 .... D 3
Santarém, 19,761 .... F 3
Setúbal, 77,885 .... G 3
Vila do Conde, 20,613 D 3
Vila Nova de Gaia, 62,469 .... D 3

Spain
1988 ESTIMATE
Albacete, 125,997 .. G10
Alcalá de Guadaira, 50,935 .... H 6
Alcalá de Henares, 150,021 .... E 8
Alcantarilla, 28,279 .. H10
Alcázar de San Juan, 26,258 .... F 8
Alcira, 40,575 ...... F11
Alcoy, 66,074 ...... G11
Algeciras, 99,528 .... I 6
Alicante, 261,051 .... G11
Almendralejo, 25,352 G 5
Almería, 157,644 .... I 9
Andújar, 32,300 (37,020▲) .... G 7
Antequera, 32,200 (41,284▲) .... H 7
Aranjuez, 37,694 .... E 8
Arcos de la Frontera, 19,600 (27,311▲) .. I 6
Arrecife, 36,297 ...... p27
Ávila, 45,092 .... E 7
Avilés, 87,811 (131,000★) .... B 6
Badajoz, 106,400 (122,407▲) ...... G 5
Badalona, 225,229 .. D14
Barcelona, 1,714,355 (4,040,000★) D14
Baza, 20,910 ...... H 9
Bilbao, 384,733 (985,000★) .... B 9
Burgos, 160,561 .... C 8
Burjasot, 35,011 .... F11
Cáceres, 71,598 .... F 5
Cádiz, 156,591 (240,000★) .... I 5
Cartagena, 70,000 (172,710▲) H11
Castellón de la Plana, 131,809 .... F11
Chiclana de la Frontera, 43,157 .... I 5
Ciudad Real, 56,300 G 8
Córdoba, 302,301 .. H 7
Coria del Río, 21,844 H 5
Cuenca, 42,222 ...... E 9
Don Benito, 24,500 (29,324▲) .... G 6
Durango, 27,425 .... B 9
Écija, 30,900 (35,836▲) .... H 6
Éibar, 34,355 ...... B 9
Elche, 158,300 (180,256▲) G11
Elda, 56,756 .... G11
El Ferrol del Caudillo, 86,503 (129,000★) B 3
El Puerto de Santa María, 49,900 (62,285▲) .. I 5
Gandía, 46,100 (52,646▲) G11
Gavá, 34,613 ...... D14
Gerona, 30,900 (68,902▲) D14
Getafe, 135,367 .... E 8
Gijón, 262,156 ...... B 6
Granada, 263,334 .... H 8
Granollers, 49,045 .. D14
Guadalajara, 61,309 .. E 8
Hospitalet, 278,449 .. D14
Huelva, 137,826 .... H 5
Huesca, 41,841 .... C11
Irún, 54,886 .... B10
Jaén, 106,435 ...... H 8

★ Population of metropolitan area, including suburbs.
▲ Population of entire district, including rural area.

Játiva, 23,755 ...... G11
Jerez de la Frontera, 156,200 (183,007▲) I 5
La Coruña, 248,862 .. B 3
La Línea, 60,956 .... I 6
Las Palmas de Gran Canaria, 319,000 (366,347▲) p25
León, 136,558 (159,000★) .... C 6
Lérida, 91,500 (109,795▲) D12
Linares, 58,622 ...... G 8
Logroño, 119,038 .... C 9
Lorca, 26,700 (66,437▲) H10
Los Palacios y Villafranca, 28,798 .... H 6
Lugo, 68,700 (78,795▲) .... B 4
Madrid, 3,102,846 (4,650,000★) ...... E 8
Málaga, 574,456 .... I 7
Manresa, 65,607 .... D13
Mataró, 100,817 .... D14
Mérida, 52,368 ...... G 5
Miranda de Ebro, 36,201 .... C 9
Morón de la Frontera, 29,048 .... H 6
Motril, 38,600 (45,901▲) .... I 8
Murcia, 149,800 (314,124▲) H10
Onteniente, 29,591 .. G11
Orense, 106,042 .... C 4
Oviedo, 168,900 (190,073▲) .... B 6
Palencia, 76,692 .... C 7
Palma [de Mallorca], 249,000 (314,608▲) F14
Pamplona, 180,598 .. C10
Plasencia, 33,613 .... E 5
Ponferrada, 33,900 (59,868▲) .... C 5
Pontevedra, 40,500 (68,223▲) .... C 3
Portugalete, 57,813 .. B 8
Prat de Llobregat, 64,193 .... D14
Puertollano, 52,284 .. G 7
Reus, 83,800 ...... D13
Sabadell, 189,489 .... D14
Sagunto, 19,600 (56,551▲) F11
Salamanca, 159,342 .. E 6
San Fernando, 81,975 I 5
Sanlúcar de Barrameda, 38,100 (54,690▲) .. I 5
San Sebastián, 177,622 (285,000★) B10
Santa Cruz de Tenerife, 215,228 .... p24
Santander, 166,800 (190,795▲) .... B 8
Santiago de Compostela, 68,800 (88,110▲) .. C 3
San Vicente de Baracaldo, 113,502 .... B 9
Segovia, 54,402 .... E 7
Sevilla, 663,132 (945,000★) .... H 6
Soria, 31,926 ...... D 9
Sueca, 24,667 ...... F11
Talavera de la Reina, 68,158 .... F 7
Tarragona, 63,500 (109,586▲) D13
Tarrasa, 161,410 .... D14
Teruel, 28,029 ...... E10
Toledo, 59,551 ...... F 7
Tomelloso, 28,386 .. F 9
Torrelavega, 28,900 (59,601▲) .... B 7
Torrente, 55,751 .... F11
Tudela, 26,618 ...... C10
Úbeda, 31,179 ...... G 8
Utrera, 36,300 (41,902▲) .... H 6
Valdepeñas, 25,568 .. G 8
Valencia, 743,933 (1,270,000★) F11
Valladolid, 331,461 .. D 7
Vall de Uxó, 27,853 .. F11
Vélez-Málaga, 32,200 (51,132▲) .... I 7
Vich, 28,873 .... D14
Vigo, 179,500 (271,128▲) .... C 3
Villanueva y Geltrú, 46,364 .... D13
Vitoria, 204,264 .... C 9
Zamora, 62,047 .... D 6
Zaragoza, 582,239 .. D11

Spanish North Africa

1988 ESTIMATE

Ceuta, 67,188 ...... J 6
Melilla, 55,717 ...... J 9

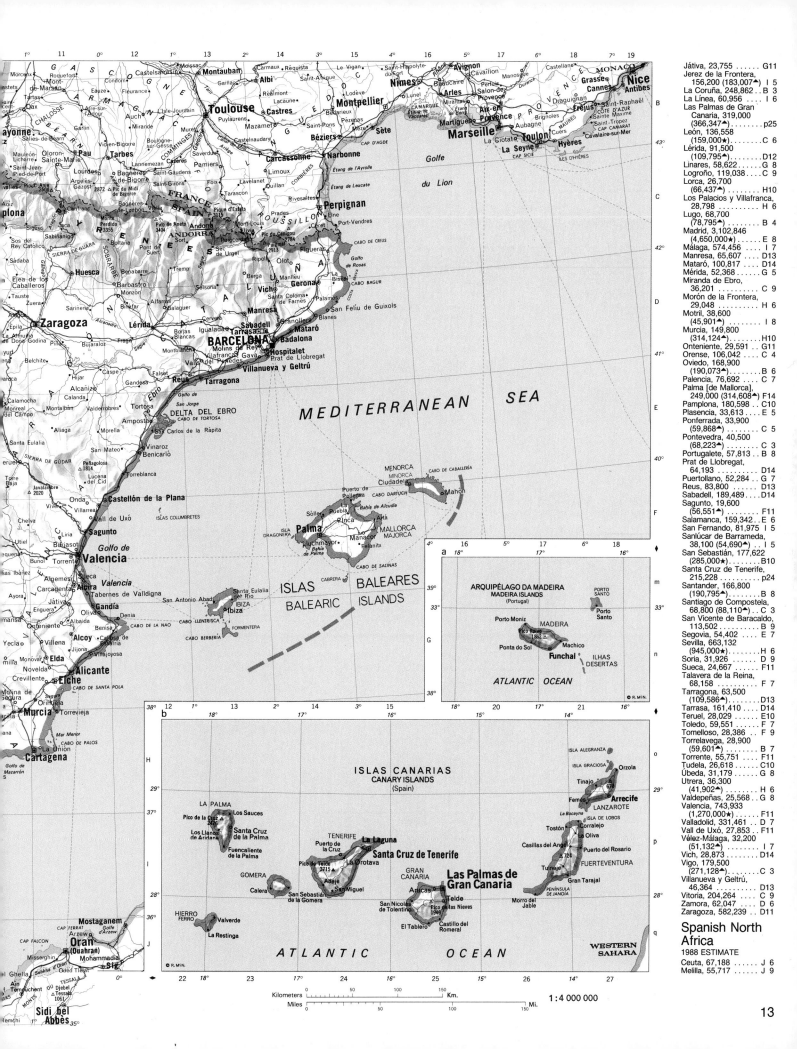

Bosnia and Herzegovina
1987 ESTIMATE

Banja Luka, 130,900 (193,890▲) E12
Mostar, 47,606('71) F12
Sarajevo, 341,200 (479,688▲) F13
Tuzla, 67,300 (129,967▲) E13
Zenica, 67,500 (144,869▲) E12

Croatia
1987 ESTIMATE

Osijek, 106,800 (162,490▲)('87) D13
Rijeka, 166,400 (199,282▲)('87) . . . . D 9
Sisak, 38,421('71) D11
Split, 191,074('87) F11
Zadar, 43,187('71) E10
Zagreb, 697,925('87) . . D10

Italy
1987 ESTIMATE

Acireale, 46,997 . . . . . . L10
Agrigento, 41,200 (54,600▲) . . . . L 8
Alcamo, 43,072 . . . . . . L 7
Alessandria, 76,100 (96,014▲) . . . . E 3
Altamura, 54,784 . . . . . . I11
Ancona, 104,409 . . . . . . F 8
Andria, 88,348 . . . . H11
Anzio, 30,806 . . . . H 7
Arezzo, 74,200 (91,681▲) . . . . F 6
Asti, 63,600 (75,459▲) E 3
Avellino, 56,407 . . . . I 9
Bagheria, 43,725 . . . . . . K 8
Bari, 362,524 (475,000★) H11
Barletta, 86,954 . . . . . . H11
Benevento, 54,400 (65,661▲) . . . . H 9
Bergamo, 118,959 (345,000★) . . . . D 4
Bisceglie, 47,771 . . . . . . H11
Bologna, 432,406 (525,000★) . . . . E 6
Bolzano (Bozen), 101,515 . . . . C 6
Brescia, 199,286 . . . . . . D 5
Brindisi, 92,280 . . . . I12
Busto Arsizio, 78,056 . . D 3
Cagliari, 220,574 (305,000★) . . . . J 4
Caltanissetta, 62,352 . . L 9
Carrara, 69,229 . . . . . . E 5
Caserta, 65,974 . . . . . . H 9
Castellammare [di Stabia], 68,491 . . . . I 9
Catania, 372,486 (550,000★) L10
Catanzaro, 102,558 . . . . K11
Cerignola, 53,463 . . . . H10
Cesena, 72,600 (90,012▲) . . . . E 7
Civitavecchia, 50,806 . . G 6
Como, 91,738 (165,000★) . . . . D 4
Cosenza, 106,026 (150,000★) J11
Cremona, 76,979 . . . . . D 5
Ferrara, 113,300 (143,950▲) . . . . E 6
Firenze (Florence), 425,835 (640,000★) . . . . F 6
Foggia, 155,051 . . . . . . H10
Forlì, 91,200 (110,482▲) E 7
Gela, 79,378 . . . . L 9
Genova (Genoa), 727,427 (805,000★) . . . . E 3
Grosseto, 56,400 (70,592▲) . . . . G 6
Iesi, 40,855 . . . . F 8
Imola, 48,200 (61,587▲) E 6
Imperia, 41,481 . . . . . . F 3
La Spezia, 108,937 (185,000★) . . . . E 4

★ Population of metropolitan area, including suburbs. ▲ Population of entire district, including rural area.

Kilometers 0 50 100 150 Km.
Miles 0 50 100 150 Mi.
1:4 000 000

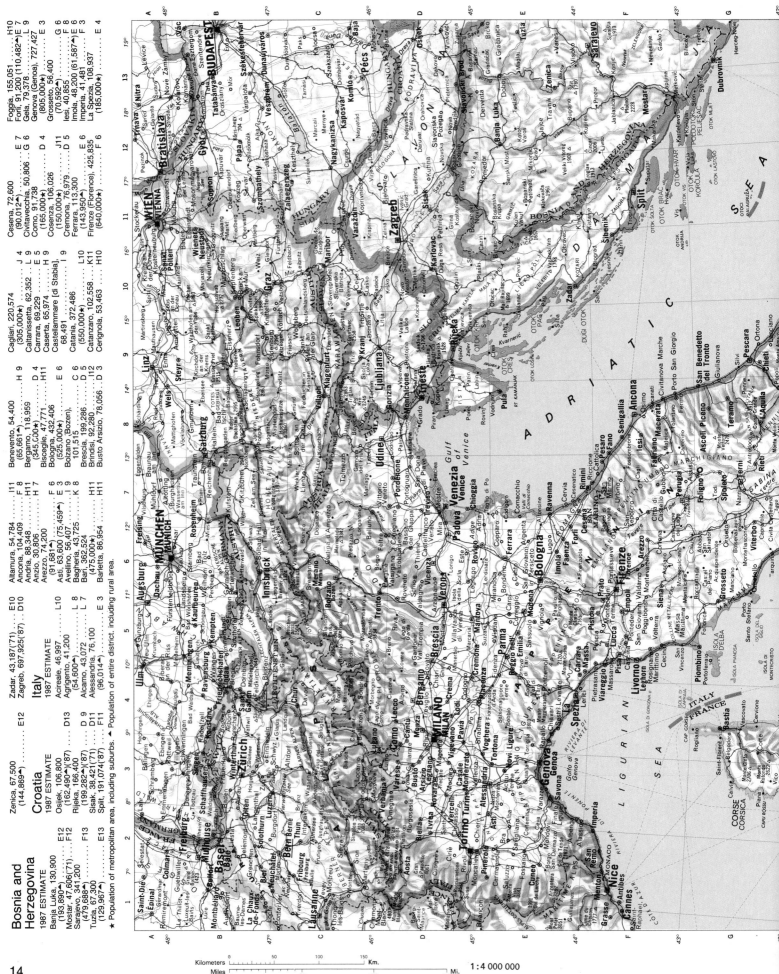

Latina, 67,800 (98,479▲) .... H 7
Lecce, 100,981 .... I13
Livorno (Leghorn), 174,065 .... F 5
Lucca, 88,024 .... F 5
Manfredonia, 57,707 .. H10
Marsala, 80,468 ...... L 7
Massa, 66,872 (145,000★) .... E 5
Messina, 268,896 .... K10
Mestre, 189,700 ...... D 7
Milano (Milan), 1,495,260 (3,750,000★) ...... D 4
Modena, 176,880 .... E 5
Molfetta, 64,519 ...... H11
Monza, 122,064 ...... D 4
Napoli (Naples), 1,204,211 (2,375,000★) .... I 9
Novara, 102,742 ...... D 3
Padova, 225,769 (270,000★) .... D 6
Palermo, 723,732 .... K 8
Parma, 175,842 ...... E 5
Pavia, 82,065 .... D 4
Perugia, 106,700 (146,713▲) .... F 7
Pesaro, 78,700 (90,336▲) .... F 7
Pescara, 131,027 .... G 9
Piacenza, 105,626 .... D 4
Pisa, 104,384 .... F 5
Pistoia, 76,800 (90,689▲) .... F 5
Pozzuoli, 65,000 ...... I 9
Prato, 164,595 (215,000★) .... F 6
Ragusa, 67,748 ...... M 9
Ravenna, 86,500 (136,016▲) .... E 7
Reggio di Calabria, 178,821 .... K10
Reggio nell'Emilia, 107,300 (130,086▲) .. E 5
Rimini, 114,600 (130,698▲) .... E 7
Roma (Rome), 2,815,457 (3,175,000★) ...... H 7
Salerno, 154,848 (250,000★) .... I 9
San Remo, 60,797 .... F 2
Sassari, 120,152 ...... I 3
Siracusa, 122,857 .... L10
Taranto, 244,997 ...... I12
Terni, 94,500 (111,157▲) .... G 7
Torino (Turin), 1,035,565 (1,550,000★) ...... D 2
Trento, 81,500 (100,202▲) .... C 6
Treviso, 85,083 ...... D 7
Trieste, 239,031 ...... D 8
Udine, 100,211 (126,000★) .... C 8
Varese, 88,353 ...... D 3
Venezia (Venice), 88,700 (420,000★) .... D 7
Verona, 259,151 ...... D 6
Vicenza, 110,449 ...... D 6

Malta

1989 ESTIMATE

Valletta, 9,210 (215,000★) .... N 9

San Marino

1988 ESTIMATE

San Marino, 2,777 .... F 7

Slovenia

1987 ESTIMATE

Ljubljana, 233,200 (316,607▲)('87) .... C 9
Maribor, 107,400 (187,651▲)('87) C10

Vatican City

1988 ESTIMATE

Vatican City, 766 ...... H 7

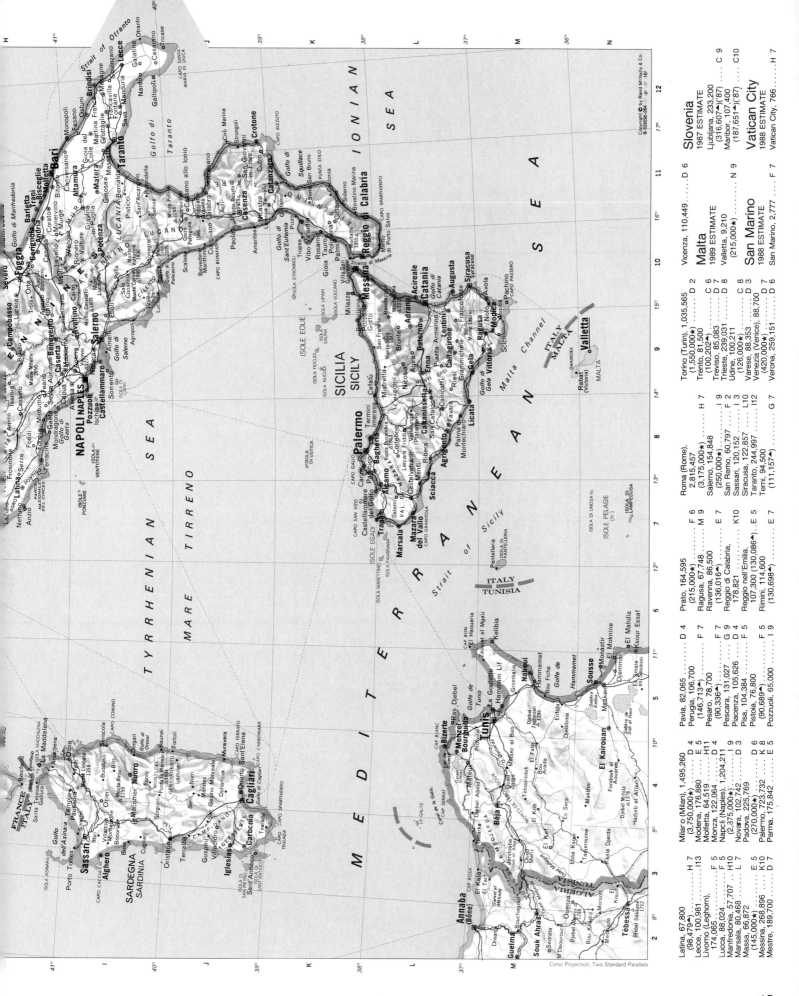

Albania

1987 ESTIMATE

Berat, 40,500 . . . . I 3
Durrës, 78,700 . . . . . . H 3
Elbasan, 78,300 . . . . . . H 4
Fier, 40,300('83) . . . . . . I 3
Korçë, 61,500 . . . . I 4
Shkodër, 76,300 . . . . G 3
Tiranë, 255,700 . . . . . . H 3
Vlorë, 67,700 . . . . I 3

Bosnia and Herzegovina

1987 ESTIMATE

Sarajevo, 341,200
(479,688▲) . . . . F 2
Zenica, 67,500
(144,869▲) . . . . E 1

Bulgaria

1986 ESTIMATE

Burgas, 186,369 . . . . G11
Dobrič, 110,471 . . . . . . F11
Gabrovo, 81,688 . . . . G 9
Haskovo, 89,273 . . . . H 9
Jambol, 92,321 . . . . . . G10
Pernik, 96,277 . . . . . . G 7
Pleven, 132,206 . . . . . . F 8
Plovdiv, 349,148 . . . . G 8
Ruse, 186,428 . . . . . . F 9
Sliven, 104,345 . . . . . . G10
Sofia *see* Sofija . . . . . . G 7
Sofija (Sofia), 1,119,152
(1,205,000★) . . . . . . G 7
Stara Zagora, 153,538 G 9
Šumen, 102,886 . . . . . . F10
Varna, 303,071 . . . . . . F11
Veliko Târnovo, 70,610 F 9
Vidin, 63,813 . . . . F 6
Vraca, 77,934 . . . . . . F 7

Greece

1981 CENSUS

Agrínion, 35,774
(45,087★) . . . . K 5
Athínai (Athens), 885,737
(3,027,331★) . . . . . . L 7
Iráklion, 102,398
(110,958★) . . . . N 9
Kalámai, 42,075
(43,235★) . . . . L 6
Kavállа, 56,375 . . . . . . I 8
Kérkira (Corfu), 33,561 J 3
Khaniá, 47,451
(61,976★) . . . . N 8
Lárisa, 102,048 . . . . . . J 6
Pátrai, 142,163
(154,596★) . . . . K 5
Piraiévs (Piraeus),
196,389 . . . . L 7
Ródhos (Rhodes),
40,392 . . . . M12
Thessaloníki (Salonika),
406,413 (706,180★) . . I 6
Vólos, 71,378
(107,407★) . . . . J 6

Macedonia

1987 ESTIMATE

Skopje, 444,900
(547,214▲) . . . . H 5

Moldova

1989 CENSUS

Bel'c', 159,000 . . . . . . B11
Bendery, 130,000 . . . . C13
Kišin'ov, 665,000 . . . . B12
Rybnica, 58,000('87) . . B13
Tiraspol', 182,000 . . . . C13

Romania

1986 ESTIMATE

Arad, 187,744 . . . . . . C 5
Bacău, 179,877 . . . . . . C10
Baia-Mare, 139,704 . . B 7
Brăila, 235,620 . . . . . . D11
Brașov, 351,493 . . . . D 9

★ Population of metropolitan area, including suburbs. ▲ Population of entire district, including rural area.

1:4 000 000

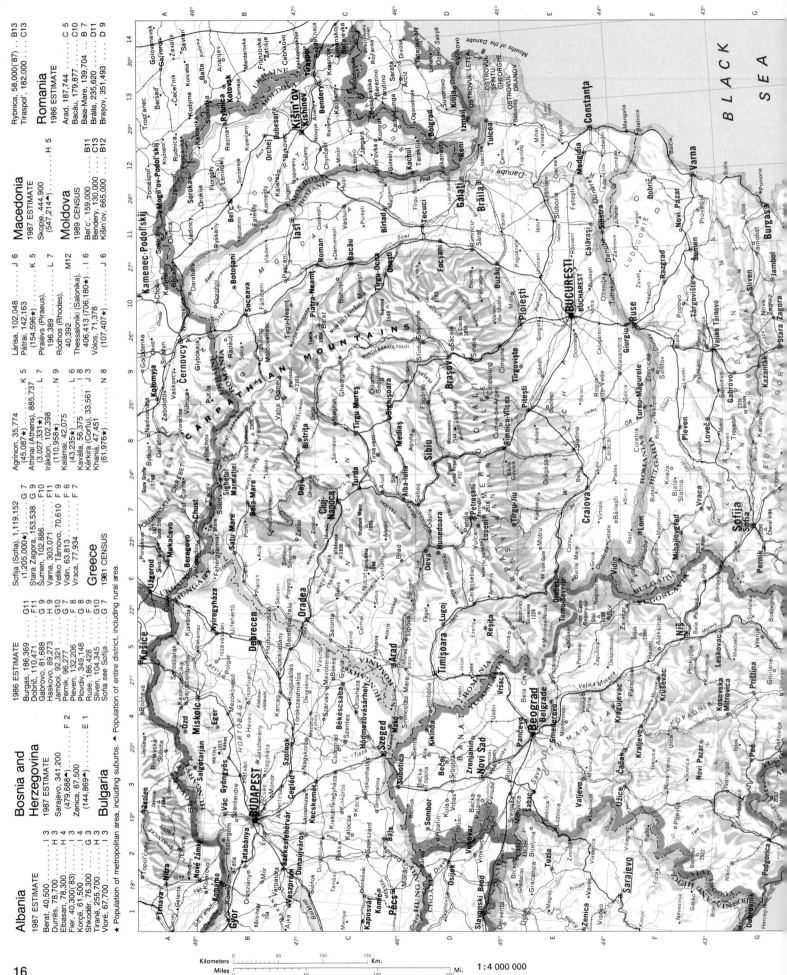

București (Bucharest), 1,989,823 (2,275,000★) E10
Buzău, 136,080 . . . . . . D10
Cluj-Napoca, 310,017 . . C 7
Constanța, 327,676 . . E12
Craiova, 281,044 . . . . E 7
Galați, 295,372 . . . . . . D12
Iași, 313,060 . . . . B11
Oradea, 213,846 . . . . B 5
Ploiești, 234,886 (310,000★) E10
Satu Mare, 130,082 . . B 6
Sibiu, 177,511 . . . . . . D 8
Timișoara, 325,272 . . . . D 5
Tîrgu Mureș, 158,998 . . C 8

Turkey

1990 CENSUS

Bursa, 838,323 . . . . . . I13
Denizli, 203,130 . . . . . . L13
İstanbul, 6,748,435 (7 000,000★) H12
İzmir, 2,553,209 (1,620,000★) K11
Manisa, 158,283 . . . . K11
Ödemiş, 511,110 . . . . K11

Yugoslavia

1987 ESTIMATE

Beograd (Belgrade), 1,130,000 (1,400,000★) . . . . . . E 4
Niš, 168,400 (240,219▲) F 5
Novi Sad, 176,000 (266,772▲) . . . . D 3
Pančevo, 62,700 . . . . E 4
Podgorica, 82,500 (145,163▲) . . . . G 3
Priština, 125,400 (244,830▲) . . . . G 5
Subotica, 100,500 (153,306▲) . . . . C 3
Zrenjanin, 65,400 (140,009▲) . . . . D 4

Baltic and Moscow Regions

Belarus

1989 CENSUS

Baranoviči, 159,000 .. H 9
Bobrujsk, 223,000 .. H12
Borisov, 144,000 .... G11
Brest, 258,000 ...... I 6
Gomel', 500,000 ...... I14
Grodno, 270,000 ...... H 6
Lida, 81,000('87) .... H 8
Minsk, 1,589,000 (1,650,000★) H10
Mogil'ov, 356,000 .... H13
Molodečno, 87,000('87) ...... G 9
Novopolock, 90,000('87) F11
Orša, 123,000 ...... G13
Pinsk, 119,000 ...... I 9
Polock, 80,000('87) .. F11
Rečica, 71,000('87) .. I13
Sluck, 55,000('87) .. H10
Svetlogorsk, 68,000('87) ...... G 3
Vitebsk, 350,000 .... F13
Žlobin, 52,000('87) I13

Estonia

1989 CENSUS

Kohtla-Järve, 78,000('87) B10
Narva, 81,000('87) .. B11
Pärnu, 53,000('87) .. C 7
Tallinn, 482,000 .... B 7
Tartu, 114,000 ...... C 9

Latvia

1989 CENSUS

Daugavpils, 127,000 .. F 9
Jelgava, 72,000('87) .. E 6
Jūrmala, 65,000('87) .. E 6
Liepāja, 114,000 .... E 4
Rēzekne, 35,620('79) E10
Rīga, 915,000 (1,005,000★) ...... E 7
Ventspils, 52,000('87) D 4

Lithuania

1989 CENSUS

Kaunas, 423,000 .... G 6
Klaipėda (Memel), 204,000 .... F 4
Panevėžys, 126,000 .. F 7
Šiauliai, 145,000 .... F 6
Vilnius, 582,000 .... G 8

Russia

1989 CENSUS

Aleksandrov, 66,000('87) E21
Aleksin, 72,000('87) .. G20
Balachna, 35,359('79) E26

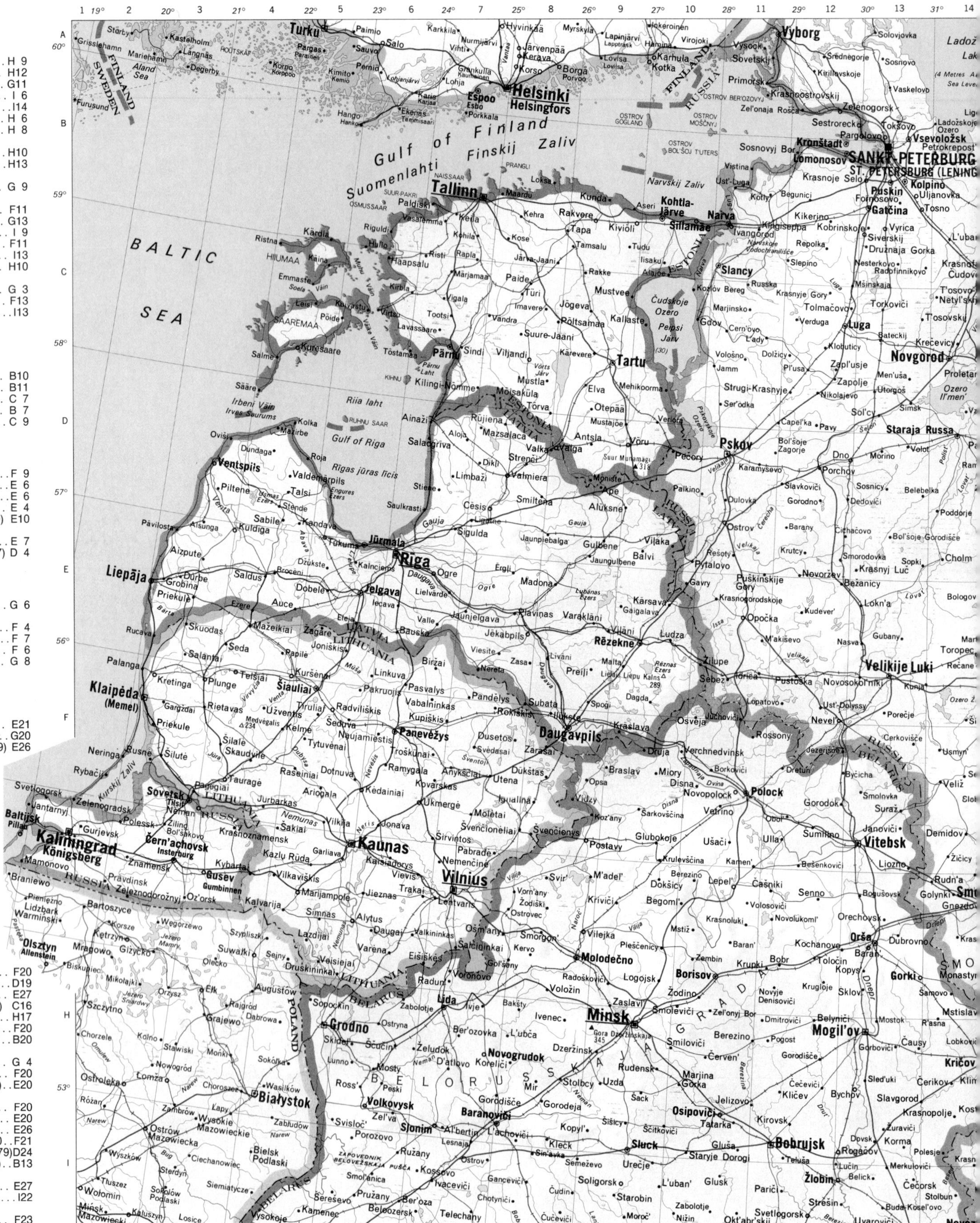

Balašicha, 136,000 .. F20
Bežeck, 30,711('79) .. D19
Bor, 65,000('87) E27
Boroviči, 64,000('87) C16
Br'ansk, 452,000 .... H17
Čechov, 57,000('87) .. F20
Čerepovec, 310,000 .. B20
Čern'achovsk, 36,361('79) ...... G 4
Chimki, 133,000 .... F20
Dmitrov, 64,000('87) .. E20
Domodedovo, 51,000('87) F20
Dubna, 64,000('87) .. E20
Dzeržinsk, 285,000 .. E26
Elektrostal', 153,000 .. F21
Furmanov, 44,430('79)D24
Gatčina, 81,000('87) .. B13
Gorki *see* Nižnij Novgorod E27
Gr'azi, 41,082('79) I22
Gus'-Chrustal'nyj, 75,000('87) F23
Ivanovo, 481,000 .... D23
Jarcevo, 40,908('79) .. F15
Jaroslavl', 633,000 .. D22
Jefremov, 58,000('87) H21
Jegorjevsk, 73,000('87) F22

★ Population of metropolitan area, including suburbs.

Kilometers 0 50 100 150 Km.
Miles 0 50 100 150 Mi.

1 : 4 000 000

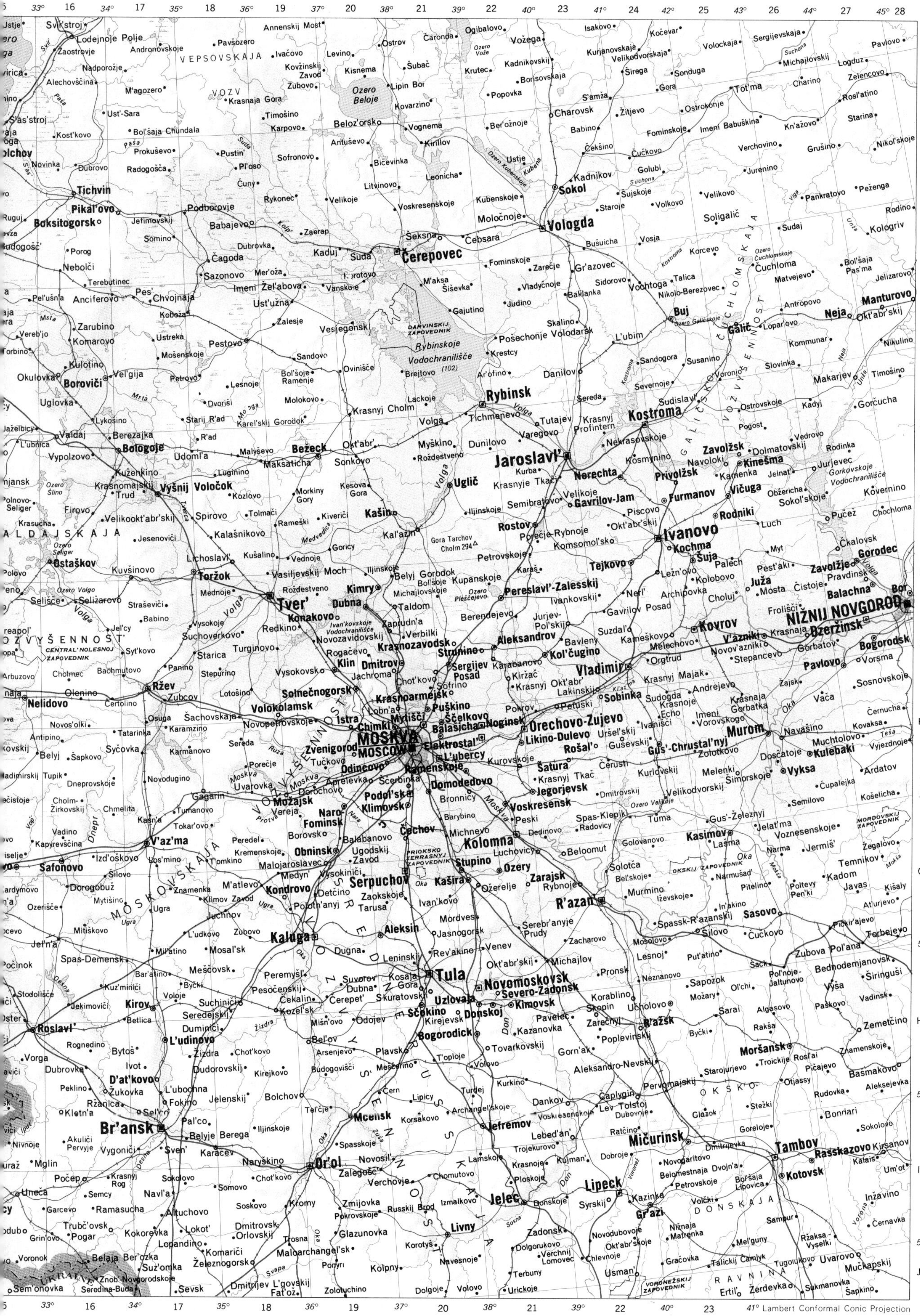

Jelec, 120,000 ...... I21
Kaliningrad (Königsberg), 401,000 .... G 3
Kaluga, 312,000 .... G19
Kasimov, 33,993('79) G24
Kašira, 43,867('79) .. G21
Kimovsk, 42,163('79) H21
Kimry, 61,000('87) .. E20
Kinešma, 105,000.... D25
Klimovsk, 57,000('87) F20
Klin, 95,000('87) E19
Klincy, 72,000('87).... I15
Kol'čugino, 43,686('79) E22
Kolomna, 162,000.... F21
Kolpino, 142,000 .... B13
Konakovo, 37,087('79) E19
Kostroma, 278,000 .. D23
Kotovsk, 36,000('74) .. I24
Kovrov, 160,000 .... E24
Kronštadt, 40,102('79) B12
Kulebaki, 48,302('79) F25
Leningrad *see* Sankt-Peterburg B13
Lipeck, 450,000 ...... I22
Livny, 51,000('87) I20
Lomonosov, 43,514('79) B12
L'ubercy, 165,000.... F20
L'udinovo, 40,339('79) H17
Luga, 37,680('79).... C12
Mcensk, 42,306('79) H19
Mičurinsk, 109,000.... I23
Moršansk, 51,000('87) H24
Moskva (Moscow), 8,769,000 (13,100,000★) F20
Murom, 124,000 .... F25
Mytišči, 154,000 .... F20
Naro-Fominsk, 60,000('87) F19
Nižnij Novgorod (Gorki), 1,438,000 (2,025,000★) E27
Novgorod, 229,000 .. C14
Novomoskovsk, 146,000 (365,000★) G21
Novozybkov, 41,344('79) I14
Obninsk, 100,000 .... F19
Odincovo, 125,000 .. F20
Orechovo-Zujevo, 137,000 (205,000★)........ F21
Or'ol, 337,000 ...... I19
Pavlovo, 72,000('87).. F26
Podol'sk, 210,000.... F20
Pskov, 204,000...... D11
Puškin, 97,000('87) .. B13
Puškino, 74,000('87) E20
Ramenskoje, 86,000('87) F21
Rasskazovo, 43,227('79) I24
R'azan', 515,000 .... G22
R'ažsk, 26,000('74) .. H23
Roslavl', 61,000('87) H15
Rybinsk, 252,000 .... C21
Ržev, 70,000('87).... E17
Safonovo, 56,000('87) F16
Sankt-Peterburg (Saint Petersburg), 4,456,000 (5,825,000★)...... B13
Ščelkovo, 109,000 .. F21
Ščokino, 70,000('87) G20
Sergijev Podad, 115,000 .... E21
Serpuchov, 144,000.. G20
Slancy, 42,253('79) .. B11
Smolensk, 341,000 .. G15
Sokol, 45,424('79) .. B23
Solnečnogorsk, 53,000('87) E19
Sovetsk (Tilsit), 40,091('79) ...... F 4
Stupino, 73,000('87) G21
Šuja, 72,000('87) E24
Tambov, 305,000 .... I24
Tichvin, 70,000('87) .. B16
Toržok, 51,000('87) .. D17
Tula, 540,000 (640,000★) G20
Tver', 451,000 ...... E18
Uglič, 39,872('79).... D21
Uzlovaja, 63,000('87) H21
V'az'ma, 57,000('87) F17
V'azniki, 45,916('79).. E25
Velikije Luki, 114,000 E13
Vičuga, 51,000('87) .. D24
Vladimir, 350,000 .... E23
Volchov, 51,000('87) B15
Vologda, 283,000.... B22
Voskresensk, 80,000('87) F21
Vyborg, 81,000('87).. A11
Vyksa, 60,000('87) .. F25
Vyšnij Voloček, 70,000('87) D17

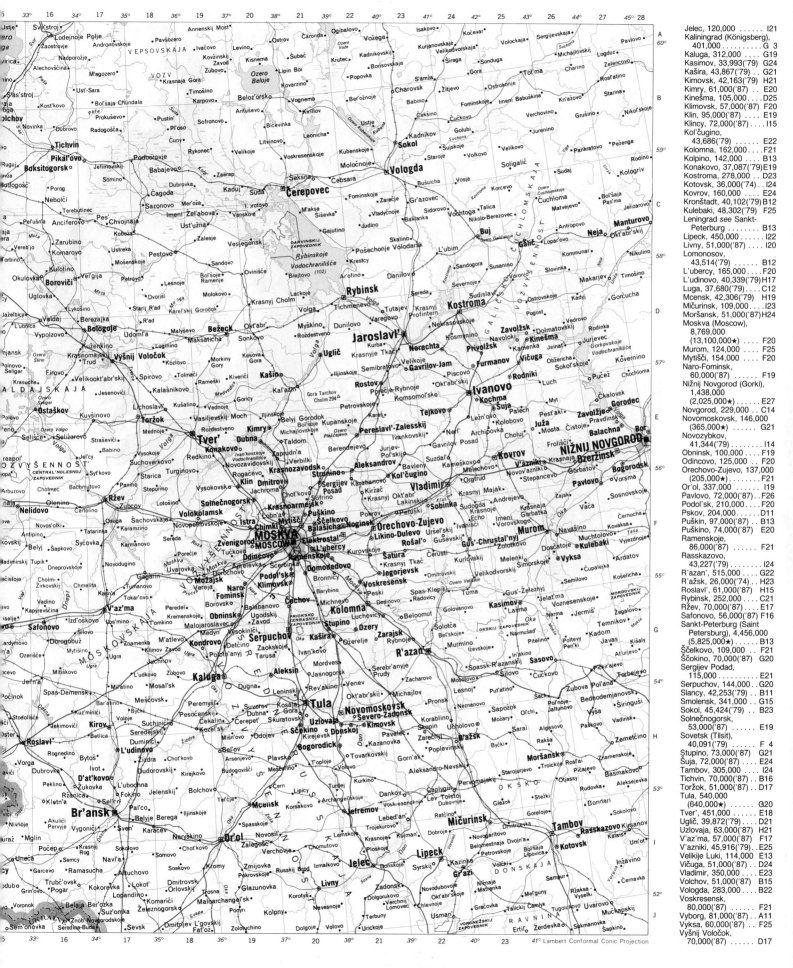

'Adan, 176,100 ('84) (318,000★) ....H 7
AFGHANISTAN...........F 9
Ahmadābād, 2,059,725 ('81) (2,400,000★) .. G10
Al Başrah, 616,700 ('85).........................F 7
Al-Kuwayt, 44,335 ('85) (1,375,000★) ....G 7
Alma-Ata, 1,128,000 ('89) (1,190,000★) E10
Al-Madīnah, 290,000 ('80)........................ G 6
'Ammān, 936,300 ('89) (1,450,000★) .... F 6
Ankara, 2,553,209 ('90) (2,670,000★) .... F 6
ARMENIA.................... F 7
Ar-Riyāḑ, 1,250,000 ('80)........................ G 7
Aščhabad, 398,000 ('89).........................F 8
AZERBAIJAN............. E 7
Baghdād, 3,841,268 ('87).........................F 7
Baku, 1,150,000 ('89) (2,020,000★) .... E 7
Bangalore, 2,476,355 ('81) (2,950,000★) H10
Bangkok see Krung Thep H13
BANGLADESH...........G12
Batumi, 136,000 ('89)..E 7
Bayrūt, 509,000 ('82) (1,675,000★) .... F 6
Beijing (Peking), 6,710,000 ('88) (6,450,000★) F14
BHUTAN.....................G12
Biškek, 616,000 ('89).. E10
Bombay, 8,243,405 ('81) (9,950,000★) H10
BRUNEI........................I14
BURMA...................... G12
Calcutta, 3,305,006 ('81) (11,100,000★) H11
CAMBODIA................ H13
Canton see Guangzhou G14
Celinograd, 277,000 ('89)........................ D10
Chabarovsk, 601,000 ('89).........................E16
Changchun, 1,822,000 ('88) (2,000,000▲) ...E15
Changsha, 1,230,000 ('88)........................ G14
Chengdu, 1,884,000 ('88) (2,960,000▲) F13
CHINA......................F12
Chongqing (Chungking), 2,502,000 ('88) (2,890,000▲) G13
Čita, 366,000 ('89)...... D14
Colombo, 683,000 ('86) (2,050,000★) I10
CYPRUS..................... F 6
CYPRUS, NORTH........F 6
Dacca see Dhaka ....:. G12
Dalian, 2,280,000 ('88) F15
Damascus see Dimashq ....F 6
Da Nang, 318,653 ('79)...........................H13
Delhi, 4,884,234 ('81) (7,200,000★) G10
Dhaka (Dacca), 2,365,695 ('81) (3,430,312★) .. G12
Dimashq (Damascus), 1,326,000 ('88) (1,950,000★) .... F 6
Dušanbe, 595,000 ('89).........................F 9
Eşfahān, 986,753 ('86) (1,175,000★) .... F 8
Frunze see Biškek E10
Fukuoka, 1,160,440 ('85) (1,750,000★) F16
Fuzhou, 910,000 ('88) (1,240,000▲) G14
George Town, 248,241 ('80) (495,000★) I13
GEORGIA.................. E 7
Guangzhou (Canton), 3,100,000 ('88) (3,420,000▲) G14
Hakodate, 319,194 ('85).........................E17
Ha Noi, 1,089,000 ('89) (1,500,000★) G13
Harbin, 2,710,000 ('88)..........................E15
Herāt, 177,300 ('88).... F 9
Hiroshima, 1,044,118 ('85) (1,575,000★) F16
HONG KONG............. G14
Hyderābād, 2,187,262 ('81) (2,750,000★) .. H10
INDIA........................ G10
INDONESIA................ I13
IRAN............................ F 8
IRAQ............................ F 7
Irkutsk, 626,000 ('89)..D13
Islāmābād, 204,364 ('81)..........................F10
ISRAEL........................ F 6
izmir, 2,553,209 ('90) (1,620,000★) .... F 5
Jakutsk, 187,000 ('89)..........C15
JAPAN........................F16
Jekateringbug, 1,367,000 ('89) (1,620,000★) ....D 9
Jerevan, 1,199,000 ('89) (1,315,000★) .... E 7
Jerusalem see Yerushalayim ....F 6
Jiddah, 1,300,000 ('80)......................... G 6
Jinan, 1,546,000 ('88) (2,140,000▲) F14
JORDAN..................... F 6
Kābol (Kabul), 1,424,400 ('88)............................F 9
Kānpur, 1,481,789 ('81) (1,875,000★) G11
Karāchi, 4,901,627 ('81) (5,300,000★) ....G 9
Kashi, 146,300 ('86) (194,500▲) F10
Kaţhmāņḑāū, 235,160 ('81) (320,000★) G11
KAZAKHSTAN............E 9
Kermān, 257,284 ('86)...........F 8
Konsomol'sk-na-Amure, 315,000 ('89).......... D16
KOREA, NORTH..........E15
KOREA, SOUTH..........F15
Krasnojarsk, 912,000 ('89)......................... D12
Krung Thep (Bangkok), 5,716,779 ('88) (6,450,000★) H13
Kuala Lumpur, 919,610 ('80) (1,475,000★) I13
Kuching, 72,555 ('80)... I14

Miles 0 200 400 600 800 1000 Mi.
Kilometers 0 400 800 1200 1600 Km.
1:40 000 000

Kunming, 1,310,000 ('88) (1,550,000▲) G13
KUWAIT .... G 7
Kyōto, 1,479,218 ('85) F16
KYRGYZSTAN E10
Kyzyl, 80,000 ('87) D12
Lahore, 2,707,215 ('81) (3,025,000★) F10
Lanzhou, 1,297,000 ('88) (1,420,000▲) F13
LAOS H13
LEBANON ....F 6
Lhasa, 84,400 ('86) (107,700▲) G12
MACAU G14
Madras, 3,276,622 ('81) (4,475,000★) H11
Makkah, 550,000 ('80) .... G 6
MALAYSIA I13
MALDIVES I10
Mandalay, 532,949 ('83) G12
Manila, 1,587,000 ('90) (6,800,000★) H15
Mashhad, 1,463,508 ('86) ....F 8
Masqaţ, 50,000 ('81)...G 8
Mawlamyine, 219,961 ('83) H12
MONGOLIA E13
Nāgpur, 1,219,461 ('81) (1,302,066★) G10
Nanjing, 2,390,000 ('88) F14
NEPAL G11
New Delhi, 273,036 ('81) G10
Novosibirsk, 1,436,000 ('89) (1,600,000★) .. D11
Ochotsk, 9,000 .... D17
OMAN .... G 8
Omsk, 1,148,000 ('89) (1,175,000★) D10
Ōsaka, 2,636,249 ('85) (1,645,000★) F16
PAKISTAN ....G 9
Patna, 776,371 ('81) (1,025,000★) G11
Peking see Beijing F14
Peshāwar, 506,896 ('81) (566,248★) F10
Petropavlovsk-Kamčatskij, 269,000 ('89) D18
PHILIPPINES H15
Phnum Penh, 700,000 ('86) H13
Pyŏngyang, 1,283,000 ('81) (1,600,000★) ...F15
QATAR ....G 8
Qingdao (Tsingtao), 1,300,000 ('88) F15
Quetta, 244,842 ('81) (285,719★) .... F 9
Quezon City, 1,632,000 ('90) H15
Rangoon see Yangon H12
Rāwalpindi, 457,091 ('81) (1,040,000★) F10
RUSSIA D10
Saigon see Thanh Pho Ho Chi Minh H13
Samarkand, 366,000 ('89) ....F 9
Şan'ā', 427,150 ('86)...H 7
SAUDI ARABIA .... G 7
Semipalatinsk, 334,000 ('89) D11
Sendai, 700,254 ('85) (1,175,000★) F17
Shanghai, 7,220,000 ('88) (9,300,000★) F15
Shenyang (Mukden), 3,910,000 ('88) (4,370,000▲) E15
Shīrāz, 848,289 ('86)...G 8
SINGAPORE I13
Sŏul, 10,522,000 ('89) (15,850,000★) F15
SRI LANKA I11
Srīnagar, 594,775 ('81) (606,002★) F10
SYRIA ....F 6
Tabrīz, 971,482 ('86)... F 7
T'aipei, 2,637,100 ('88) (6,130,000★) G15
TAIWAN G15
Taiyuan, 1,700,000 ('88) (1,980,000▲) F14
TAJIKISTAN F10
Taškent, 2,073,000 ('89) (2,325,000★) ....E 9
Tbilisi, 1,260,000 ('89) (1,460,000★) ....E 7
Tehrān, 6,042,584 ('86) (7,500,000★) ....F 8
THAILAND H13
Thanh Pho Ho Chi Minh (Saigon), 3,169,000 ('89) (3,100,000★) H13
Tianjin (Tientsin), 4,950,000 ('88) (5,540,000▲) F14
Tobol'sk, 82,000 ('87) .... D 9
Tōkyō, 8,354,615 ('85) (27,700,000★) F16
Tomsk, 502,000 ('89)..D11
TURKEY ....F 6
TURKMENISTAN ....F 9
Ulaanbaatar, 548,400 ('89) E13
UNITED ARAB EMIRATES .... G 8
Ürümqi, 1,060,000 ('88) E11
UZBEKISTAN .... E 9
Vārānasi, 708,647 ('81) (925,000★) G11
Verchojansk, 1,400 ..... C16
Viangchan, 377,409 ('85) H13
VIETNAM H13
Vladivostok, 648,000 ('89) E16
Wuhan, 3,570,000 ('88) F14
Xiamen, 343,700 ('86) (546,400▲) G14
Xi'an, 2,210,000 ('88) (2,580,000▲) F13
Yangon (Rangoon), 2,705,039 ('83) (2,800,000★) H12
YEMEN ....H 7
Yerevan see Jerevan ..E 7
Yerushalayim (Jerusalem), 493,500 ('89) (530,000★) .... F 6
Yokohama, 2,992,926 ('85) F16
Zhangjiakou, 500,000 ('88) (640,000▲) E14

★ Population of metropolitan area, including suburbs.
▲ Population of entire district, including rural area.

Northwest Asia

Armenia
1989 CENSUS
Jerevan, 1,199,000
(1,315,000★) . . . . . . I 6

Azerbaijan
1989 CENSUS
Baku, 1,150,000
(2,020,000★) . . . . . . I 7
Gjandža, 278,000 . . . . I 7
Sumgait, 231,000 . . . . I 7

Belarus
1989 CENSUS
Brest, 258,000 . . . . . . G 2
Gomel', 500,000 . . . . G 4
Grodno, 270,000 . . . . G 2
Minsk, 1,589,000
(1,650,000★) . . . . . . G 3
Mogil'ov, 356,000 . . . . G 4
Vitebsk, 350,000 . . . . F 4

Estonia
1989 CENSUS
Tallinn, 482,000 . . . . . . F 2

Georgia
1989 CENSUS
Kutaisi, 235,000 . . . . . . I 6
Tbilisi, 1,260,000
(1,460,000★) . . . . . . I 6

Kazakhstan
1989 CENSUS
Akt'ubinsk, 253,000 . . G 9
Alma-Ata, 1,128,000
(1,190,000★) I13
Čelinograd, 277,000 . . G12
Čimkent, 393,000 . . . . I11
Džambul, 307,000 . . . . I12
Karaganda, 614,000 . . H12
Pavlodar, 331,000 . . G13
Petropavlovsk,
241,000 . . . . G11
Semipalatinsk,
334,000 . . . . G14
Temirtau, 212,000 . . G12
Ural'sk, 200,000 . . . . G 8
Ust'-Kamenogorsk,
324,000 . . . . H14

Kyrgyzstan
1989 CENSUS
Biškek, 616,000 . . . . . . I12
Oš, 213,000 . . . . I12

Latvia
1989 CENSUS
Rīga, 915,000
(1,005,000★) . . . . . . F 2

Lithuania
1989 CENSUS
Kaunas, 423,000 . . . . G 2
Klaipėda, 204,000 . . . . F 2
Vilnius, 582,000 . . . . . . F 3

Moldova
1989 CENSUS
Bel'c', 131,000('81) . . H 3
Kišin'ov, 665,000 . . . . H 3
Tiraspol', 182,000 . . . . H 3

Russia
1989 CENSUS
Archangel'sk, 416,000 E 6
Astrachan', 509,000 . . H 7
Belgorod, 300,000 . . G 5
Br'ansk, 452,000 . . . . G 4
Čeboksary, 420,000 . . F 7
Čel'abinsk, 1,143,000
(1,325,000★) F10
Čerepovec, 310,000 . . F 5
Gor'kij *see* Nižnij
Novgorod . . . . F 6
Groznyj, 401,000 . . . . I 7
Ivanovo, 481,000 . . . . F 6
Iževsk, 635,000 . . . . . . F 8
Jaroslavl', 633,000 . . F 5
Jekaterinburg
(Sverdlovsk), 1,367,000
(1,620,000★) F10
Kaliningrad, 401,000 G 2
Kaluga, 312,000 . . . . G 5
Kazan', 1,094,000
(1,140,000★) . . . . . . F 7
Kirov, 441,000 . . . . . . F 7
Krasnodar, 620,000 . . H 5
Kurgan, 356,000 . . . . F11
Kursk, 424,000 . . . . . G 5
Leningrad *see*
Sankt-Peterburg . . F 4
Lipeck, 450,000 . . . . G 5
Machačkala, 315,000 . . I 7
Magnitogorsk,
440,000 . . . . G 9

★ Population of metropolitan area, including suburbs.

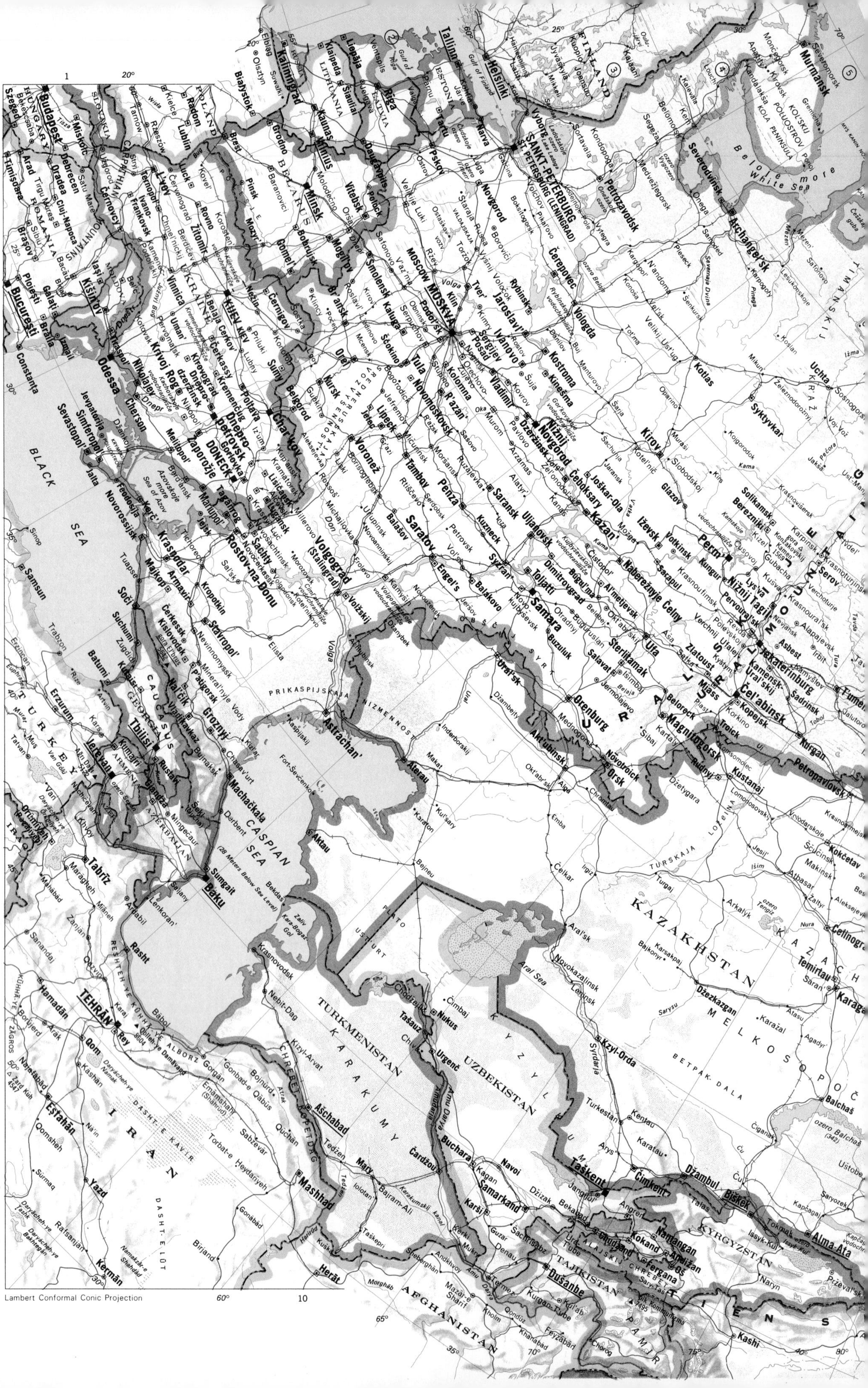

Lambert Conformal Conic Projection

Kilometers 0 200 400 600 Km.

Miles 0 200 400 600 Mi.

1:16 000 000

Moskva (Moscow), 8,769,000 (13,100,000★) .... F 5
Murmansk, 468,000 .. D 4
Naberežnyje Čelny, 501,000 .... F 8
Nižnij Novgorod (Gor'kij), 1,438,000 (2,025,000★) ...... F 6
Nižnij Tagil, 440,000 .. F 9
Orel, 337,000 ...... G 5
Orenburg, 547,000 .. G 9
Orsk, 271,000 ...... G 9
Penza, 543,000 .... G 7
Perm', 1,091,000 (1,160,000★) ...... F 9
Petrozavodsk, 270,000 .... E 4
R'azan', 515,000 .... G 5
Rostov-na-Donu, 1,020,000 (1,165,000★) ...... H 5
Samara, 1,257,000 (1,505,000★) ...... G 8
Sankt-Peterburg (St. Petersburg), 4,456,000 (5,825,000★) ...... F 4
Saransk, 312,000 .... G 7
Saratov, 905,000 (1,155,000★) ...... G 7
Smolensk, 341,000 .. G 4
Soči, 337,000 .... I 5
Stalingrad *see* Volgograd .... H 6
Stavropol', 318,000 .. H 6
Sverdlovsk *see* Jekaterinburg F10
Syktyvkar, 233,000 .. E 8
Taganrog, 291,000 .. H 5
Tambov, 305,000 .... G 6
Toljatti, 630,000 .... G 7
Tula, 540,000 (640,000★) ...... G 5
Tver' (Kalinin), 451,000 .... F 5
Ufa, 1,083,000 (1,100,000★) ...... G 9
Uljanovsk, 625,000 .. G 7
Vladikavkaz, 300,000 .. I 6
Vladimir, 350,000 .... F 6
Volgograd (Stalingrad), 999,000 (1,360,000★) ...... H 6
Vologda, 283,000 .... F 5
Volžskij, 269,000 .... H 6
Voronež, 887,000 .... G 5

Tajikistan
1989 CENSUS
Dušanbe, 595,000 .... J11

Turkmenistan
1989 CENSUS
Ašchabad, 398,000 .. J 9

Ukraine
1989 CENSUS
Čerkassy, 290,000 .. H 4
Černigov, 296,000 .. G 4
Char'kov, 1,611,000 (1,940,000★) ...... G 5
Cherson, 355,000 .... H 4
Dneprodzeržinsk, 282,000 .... H 4
Dnepropetrovsk, 1,179,000 (1,600,000★) ...... H 4
Doneck, 1,110,000 (2,200,000★) ...... H 5
Gorlovka, 337,000 (710,000★) ...... H 5
Jalta, 89,000('87) .... I 4
Kijev (Kiev), 2,587,000 (2,900,000★) ...... G 4
Krivoj Rog, 713,000 .. H 4
Lugansk, 497,000 .... H 5
L'vov, 790,000 ...... H 2
Mariupol' (Ždanov), 517,000 .... H 5
Nikolajev, 503,000 .. H 4
Odessa, 1,115,000 (1,185,000★) ...... H 4
Poltava, 315,000 .... H 4
Sevastopol', 356,000 .. I 4
Simferopol', 344,000 .. I 4
Sumy, 291,000 ...... G 4
Vinnica, 374,000 ...... H 3
Yalta *see* Jalta ...... I 4
Zaporožje, 884,000 .. H 5
Žitomir, 292,000 .... G 3

Uzbekistan
1989 CENSUS
Andižan, 293,000 .... I12
Buchara, 224,000 .... J10
Fergana, 200,000 .... I12
Namangan, 308,000 .. I12
Samarkand, 366,000 .. J11
Taškent, 2,073,000 (2,325,000★) I11

Northeast Asia

Russia

1989 CENSUS

Abakan, 154,000 .... G12
Ačinsk, 122,000 .... F12
Alapajevsk, 51,000('87) ...... F 6
Aldan, 20,000('74) .. F19
Alejsk, 31,390('79) .. G10
Aleksandrovsk-Sachalinskij, 20,000('74) G22
Angarsk, 266,000 .... G14
Anžero-Sudžensk, 108,000 .... F11
Arsenjev, 67,000('87) .. I20
Art'om, 73,000('87) .. I20
Art'omovsk, 17,000('79) G12
Asbest, 83,000('87) .. F 6
Asino, 31,329('79) ... F11
Balej, 25,000('79) G17
Barabinsk, 35,035('79) F 9
Barnaul, 602,000 (665,000★) G10
Belogorsk, 71,000('87) G19
Belovo, 118,000('87) G11
Berdsk, 77,000('87) .. G10
Berezniki, 201,000 .. F 5
Bijsk, 233,000 ...... G11
Bikin, 18,000('79) H20
Birobidžan, 82,000('87) H20
Blagoveščensk, 206,000 .... G19
Bogotol, 29,000('79) .. F11
Bolotnoje, 20,000('79) F10
Bratsk, 255,000 .... F14
Čel'abinsk, 1,143,000 (1,325,000★) ...... F 6
Čeremchovo, 73,000('87) G14
Černogorsk, 80,000('87) G12
Chabarovsk, 601,000 H21
Chanty-Mansijsk, 27,961('79) ...... E 7
Cholmsk, 50,000('87) H22
Čita, 366,000 ...... G16
Čusovoj, 59,000('87) F 5
Dudinka, 23,000('74) D11
Gorno-Altajsk, 39,917('79) G11
Gubacha, 32,461('79) F 5
Gusinoozersk, 18,000('79) G15
Igarka, 16,918('79) .. D11
Inta, 58,000('87) .... D 6
Irbit, 53,000('87) .... F 6
Irkutsk, 626,000 .... G14
Iskitim, 69,000('87) .. G10
Issyk-Kul', 64,000('87) I 9
Jakutsk, 187,000 .... E19
Jekaterinburg, 1,367,000 (1,620,000★) ...... F 6
Jenisejsk, 22,000('79) F12
Jurga, 92,000('87) .. F10
Južno-Sachalinsk, 157,000 .... H22
Kamen'-na-Obi, 40,684('79) G10
Kamensk-Ural'skij, 209,000 .... F 6
Kansk, 110,000 ...... F13
Karpinsk, 36,569('79) F 6
Kemerovo, 520,000 .. F11
Kirensk, 16,000('74) .. F15
Kisel'ovsk, 128,000 .. G11
Kizel, 40,157('79) .... F 5
Kolpaševo, 27,000('79) F10
Komsomol'sk-na-Amure, 315,000 .... G21
Kopejsk, 99,000('87) F 6
Korkino, 63,000('81) G 6
Korsakov, 43,348('79) H22
Krasnojarsk, 912,000 F12

★ Population of metropolitan area, including suburbs.

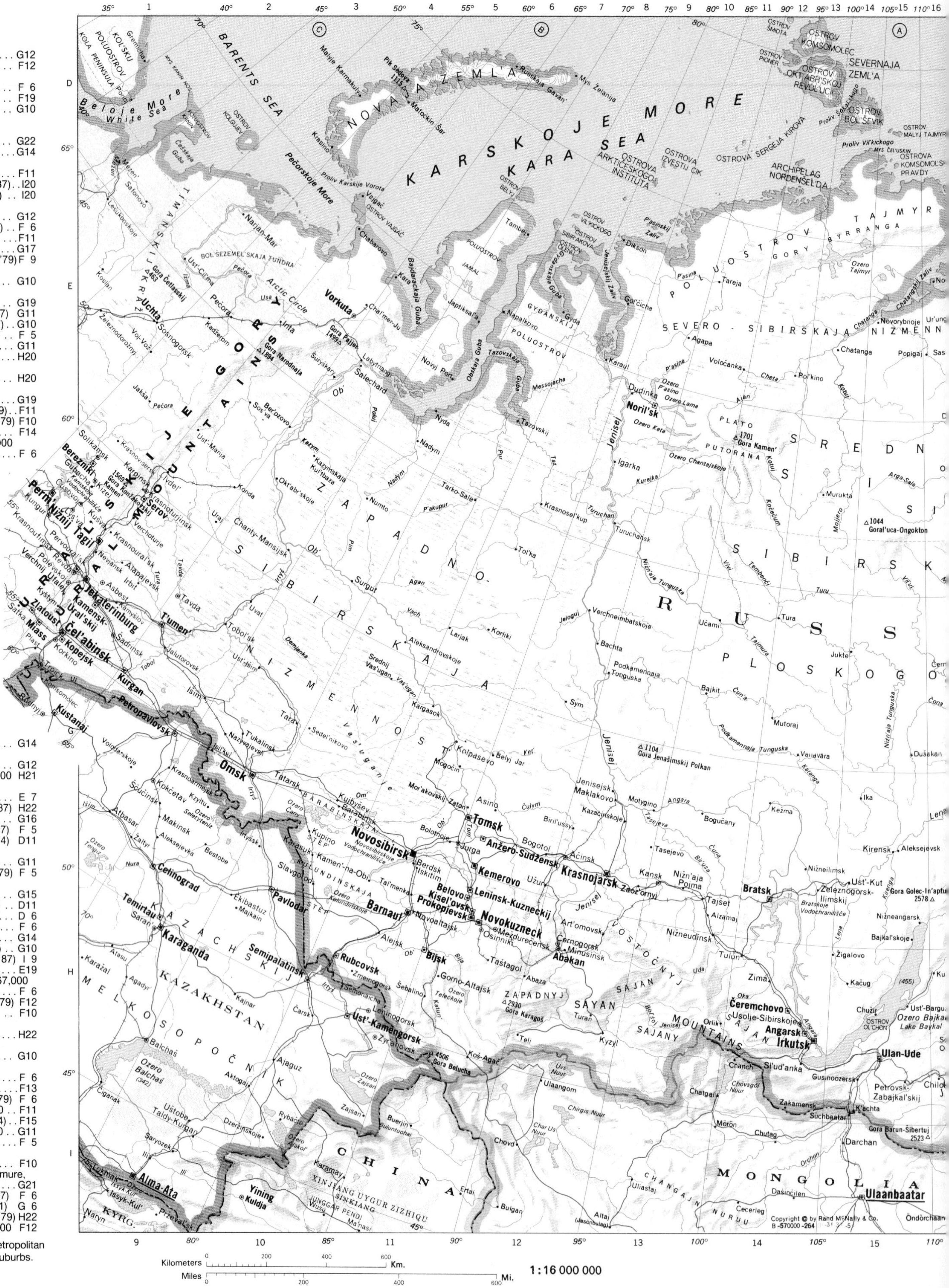

Krasnoturjinsk, 66,000('87) . . . . . . F 6
Krasnoufimsk, 40,027('79) . . . . . . F 5
Krasnoural'sk, 38,212('79) . . . . . . F 6
Kujbyšev, 51,000('87) F 9
Kungur, 83,000('87) . . F 5
Kupino, 19,000('79) . . G 9
Kurgan, 356,000 . . . . F 7
Kušva, 43,089('79) . . F 5
Kyštym, 39,701('79) . . F 6
Kyzyl, 80,000('87) . . G12
Leninsk-Kuzneckij, 165,000 . . . . G11
Lensk, 23,500('79) . . E16
Lesozavodsk, 38,573('79) H20
Lys'va, 77,000('87) . . F 5
Magadan, 152,000 . . F24
Meždurečensk, 107,000 . . . . G11
Miass, 168,000 . . . . . . G 6
Minusinsk, 72,000('87)G12
Mirnyj, 30,500('79) . . E16
Mogoča, 19,000('74) G17
Nachodka, 165,000 . . I20
Narjan-Mar, 18,000('74) . . . . . . D 4
Nevjansk, 31,946('79) F 6
Nikolajevsk-na-Amure, 33,795('79) G22
Nižneudinsk, 40,902('79) G13
Nižnij Tagil, 440,000 . . F 5
Noril'sk, 174,000 . . . . D11
Novoaltajsk, 51,000('87) G10
Novokuzneck, 600,000 . . . . G11
Novosibirsk, 1,436,000 (1,600,000★) F10
Ocha, 33,761('79) . . G22
Omsk, 1,148,000 (1,175,000★) . . . . . . F 8
Osinniki, 63,000('87) G11
Pečora, 58,000('81) . . D 5
Perm', 1,091,000 (1,160,000★) . . . . . . F 5
Pervoural'sk, 142,000 F 5
Petropavlovsk-Kamčatskij, 269,000 . . . . G25
Petrovsk-Zabajkal'skij, 30,000('74) G15
Polevskoj, 71,000('87) F 6
Poronajsk, 24,000('74)H22
Prokopjevsk, 274,000 (410,000★) G11
Rajčichinsk, 27,000('79) H19
Revda, 66,000('87) . . F 5
Rubcovsk, 172,000 . . G10
Šadrinsk, 87,000('87) F 6
Salechard, 26,000('74)D 7
Satka, 46,202('79) . . F 5
Serov, 104,000 . . . . . . F 6
Slavgorod, 33,000('74) . . . . . . G 9
Sl'ud'anka, 21,000('74) G14
Solikamsk, 110,000 . . F 5
Sovetskaja Gavan', 31,000('74) H22
Spassk-Dal'nij, 60,000('87) I20
Sučan, 45,628('79) I20
Surgut, 248,000 . . . . E 8
Sverdlovsk *see* Jekaterinburg . . . . . . F 6
Svobodnyj, 78,000('87) G19
Tajšet, 36,254('79) . . F13
Tal'menka, 22,000('79) G10
Tara, 24,000('74) . . . . F 8
Taštagol, 23,000('79) G11
Tatarsk, 29,190('79) . . F 9
Tavda, 46,115('79) . . F 7
Tobol'sk, 82,000('87) F 7
Tomsk, 502,000 . . . . F10
Troick, 91,000('87) . . G 6
Tulun, 56,000('87) . . G14
T'umen', 477,000 . . . . F 7
Tyndinskij, 56,000('85) F18
Uchta, 111,000 . . . . . . E 4
Uglegorsk, 18,000('79) H22
Ulan-Ude, 353,000 . . G15
Usolje-Sibirskoje, 107,000 . . . . G14
Ussurijsk, 162,000 . . . . I20
Ust'-Kut, 58,000('87) F15
Užur, 22,000('79) F11
V'azemskij, 19,000('79) H20
Vladivostok, 648,000 . . I20
Vorkuta, 116,000 . . . . D 6
Zaoz'ornyj, 26,000('79) F12
Zeja, 24,000('74) G19
Železnogorsk-Ilimskij, 30,000('79) F14
Zima, 51,000('87) G14
Zlatoust, 208,000 . . . . F 5

China, Japan, and Korea

Bhutan

1982 ESTIMATE

Thimphu, 12,000 .... F 4

China

1988 ESTIMATE

Andong, 579,800('86) C11
Anshan, 1,330,000 .. C11
Bangbu, 403,900 (612,600▲)('86) E10
Baoding, 423,200 (535,100▲)('86) D10
Baotou, 1,130,000 .. C 8
Beijing (Peking), 6,710,000 (6,450,000★) D10
Benxi, 860,000 ...... C11
Canton *see* Guangzhou ...... G 9
Changchun, 1,822,000 (2,000,000▲) C12
Changsha, 1,230,000 F 9
Changzhou, 522,700('86) E10
Chengdu, 1,884,000 (2,960,000▲) ...... E 7
Chongqing, 2,502,000 (2,890,000▲) ...... F 8
Dalian, 2,280,000 .... D11
Datong, 810,000 (1,040,000▲) ...... C 9
Fushun, 1,290,000 .. C11
Fuzhou, 910,000 (1,240,000▲) F10
Guangzhou (Canton), 3,100,000 (3,420,000▲) ...... G 9
Guiyang, 1,030,000 (1,430,000▲) ...... F 8
Handan, 870,000 (1,030,000▲) ...... D 9
Hanzhou, 1,290,000 E 11
Harbin, 2,710,000 .... B12
Hefei, 740,000 (930,000▲) E10
Hegang, 588,300('86) B13
Hengyang, 419,200 (601,300▲)('86) .... F 9
Hohhot, 670,000 (830,000▲) .... C 9
Huainan, 700,000 (1,110,000▲) E10
Huangshi, 451,900('86) E10
Jilin, 1,200,000 ...... C12
Jinan (Tsinan), 1,546,000 (2,140,000▲) D10
Jinzhou, 710,000 (810,000▲) C11
Jixi, 700,000 (820,000▲) B13
Kaifeng, 458,800 (629,100▲)('86) .... E 9
Kunming, 1,310,000 (1,550,000▲) ...... F 7
Lanzhou, 1,297,000 (1,420,000▲) ...... D 7
Lasa (Lhasa), 84,400 (107,700▲)('86) ..... F 5
Liuzhou, 680,000 .... G 8
Luoyang, 760,000 (1,090,000▲) ...... E 9
Mudanjiang, 650,000 C12
Nanchang, 1,090,000 (1,260,000▲) F10
Nanjing, 2,390,000 .. E10
Nanning, 720,000 (1,000,000▲) ...... G 8
Ningbo, 570,000 (1,050,000▲) F11
Peking *see* Beijing .. D10
Qingdao (Tsingtao), 1,300,000 .... D11
Shanghai, 7,220,000 (9,300,000★) E11
Shantou (Swatow), 560,000 (790,000▲) G10
Shenyang (Mukden), 3,910,000 (4,370,000▲) C11
Shijiazhuang, 1,220,000 .... D 9
Suzhou, 740,000 ...... E11
Taiyuan, 1,700,000 (1,980,000▲) ...... D 9
Tangshan, 1,080,000 (1,440,000▲) D10
Tianjin (Tientsin), 4,950,000 (5,540,000▲) D10
Ürümqi, 1,060,000 .. C 4
Wenzhou, 372,200 (530,600▲)('86) F11
Wuhan, 3,570,000 .. E 9
Wuhu, 396,000 (502,200▲)('86) E10
Wuxi, 880,000 ...... E11
Xi'an (Sian), 2,210,000 (2,580,000▲) ...... E 8
Xining, 620,000 ...... D 7
Xuzhou, 860,000 .... E10
Zhangjiakou (Kalgan), 500,000 (640,000▲) C 9

Kilometers 0 200 400 600 Km.
Miles 0 200 400 600 Mi.
1:16 000 000

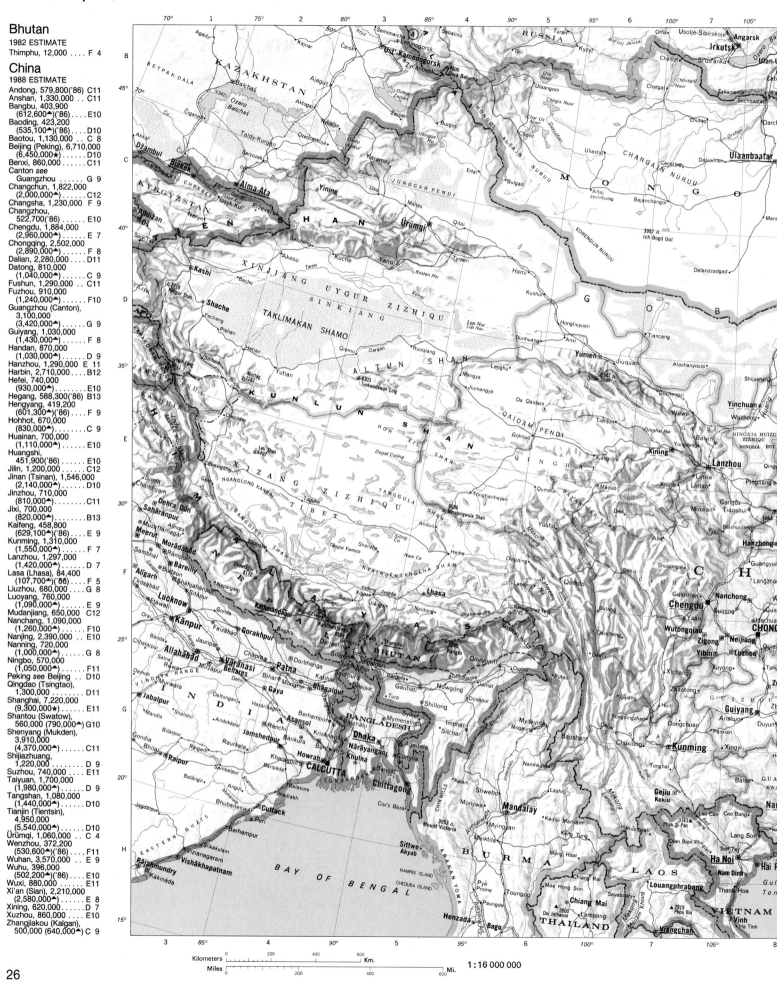

Zhengzhou, 1,150,000 (1,580,000▲) . . . . . E 9
Zibo, 840,000 (2,370,000▲) D10

Hong Kong
1986 CENSUS

Kowloon (Jiulong), 774,781 . . . . G 9
Victoria (Xianggang), 1,175,860 (4,770,000★) . . . . . G 9

Japan
1985 CENSUS

Asahikawa, 363,631 . . C15
Chiba, 788,930 . . . . . D15
Fukuoka, 1,160,440 (1,750,000★) E13
Hakodate, 319,194 . . C15
Hamamatsu, 514,118 E14
Himeji, 452,917 (660,000★) E13
Hiroshima, 1,044,118 (1,575,000★) E13
Kagoshima, 530,502 . . E13
Kanazawa, 430,481 . . D14
Kitakyūshū, 1,056,402 (1,525,000★) E13
Kōbe, 1,410,834 . . . . E14
Kumamoto, 555,719 . . E13
Kurashiki, 413,632 . . E13
Kyōto, 1,479,218 . . . . D14
Matsuyama, 426,658 E13
Nagasaki, 449,382 . . E12
Nagoya, 2,116,381 (4,800,000★) D14
Niigata, 475,630 . . . . D14
Okayama, 572,479 . . E13
Ōsaka, 2,636,249 (16,450,000★) E14
Sapporo, 1,542,979 (1,900,000★) C15
Sendai, 700,254 (1,175,000★) D15
Shizuoka, 468,362 (975,000★) E14
Tōkyō, 8,354,615 (27,700,000★) D14
Utsunomiya, 405,375 D14
Yokohama, 2,992,926 D14

Korea, North
1981 ESTIMATE

Ch'ŏngjin, 490,000 . . C12
Kaesŏng, 259,000 . . D12
Namp'o, 241,000 . . . . D12
P'yŏngyang, 1,283,000 (1,600,000★) D12
Sinŭiju, 305,000 . . . . C11
Wŏnsan, 398,000 . . . . D12

Korea, South
1989 ESTIMATE

Chŏnju, 426,473('85) D12
Inch'ŏn, 1,628,000 . . D12
Kwangju, 1,165,000 . . D12
Masan, 448,746 (625,000★)('85) D12
Pusan, 3,773,000 (3,800,000★) D12
Sŏul (Seoul), 10,522,000 (15,850,000★) D12
Taegu, 2,207,000 . . . . D12
Taejŏn, 1,041,000 . . D12

Macau
1987 ESTIMATE

Macau (Aomen), 429,000 . . . . G 9

Mongolia
1989 ESTIMATE

Ulaanbaatar (Ulan Bator), 548,400 . . . . B 8

Nepal
1981 CENSUS

Kāṭhmāṇḍau (Kathmandu), 235,160 (320,000★) . . . . F 4

Taiwan
1988 ESTIMATE

Kaohsiung, 1,342,797 (1,845,000★) G11
T'aichung, 715,107 . . G11
T'ainan, 656,927 . . . . G11
T'aipei, 2,637,100 (6,130,000★) F11

★ Population of metropolitan area, including suburbs.
▲ Population of entire district, including rural area.

Eastern and Southeastern China

China

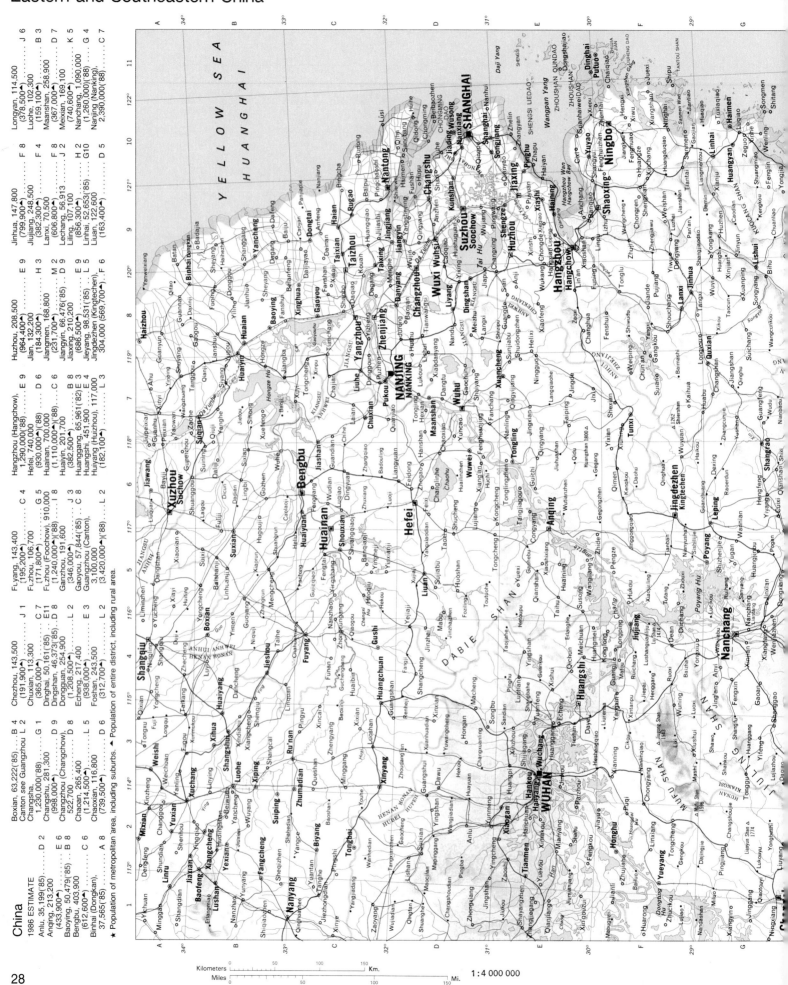

1986 ESTIMATE
Anlu, 35,199('85) . . . . . D 2
Anqing, 213,200 (433,900▲) . . . . E 6
Baoying, 50,479('85) . . B 8
Bengbu, 403,900 (612,600▲) . . . . C 6
Binhai (Dongkan), 37,565('85) . . . . A 8
Boxian, 63,222('85) . . . . B 4
Canton *see* Guangzhou L 2
Changsha, 1,230,000('88) . . . . . . G 1
Changshu, 281,300 (998,000▲) . . . . D 9
Changzhou (Changchow), 522,700 . . . . D 8
Chaoan, 265,400 (1,214,500▲) . . . . L 5
Chaoxian, 116,800 (739,500▲) . . . . D 6
Chezhou, 143,500 (191,900▲) . . . . J 1
Chuxian, 113,300 (365,000▲) . . . . C 7
Dinghai, 50,161('85) . . E11
Dingshan, 46,373('85) . . D 8
Dongguan, 254,900 (1,208,500▲) . . . . L 2
Echeng, 217,400 (938,000▲) . . . . E 3
Foshan, 243,500 (312,700▲) . . . . L 2
Fuyang, 143,400 (195,200▲) . . . . C 4
Fuzhou, 106,700 (171,800▲) . . . . G 5
Fuzhou (Foochow), 910,000 (1,240,000▲)('88) . . . . I 8
Ganzhou, 191,600 (346,000▲) . . . . J 3
Gaoyou, 57,844('85) . . C 8
Guangzhou (Canton), 3,100,000 (3,420,000▲)('88) . . . . L 2
Hangzhou (Hangchow), 1,290,000('88) . . . . . . E 9
Hefei, 740,000 (930,000▲)('88) . . . . D 6
Huainan, 700,000 (1,110,000▲)('88) . . . . C 6
Huaiyin, 201,700 (382,500▲) . . . . B 8
Huanggang, 65,961('82) E 3
Huangshi, 451,900 . . . . E 4
Huiyang (Huizhou), 117,000 (182,100▲) . . . . L 3
Huzhou, 208,500 (964,400▲) . . . . E 9
Jian, 132,200 (184,300▲) . . . . H 3
Jiangmen, 168,800 (231,700▲) . . . . M 2
Jiangyin, 66,476('85) . . D 9
Jiaxing, 210,200 (686,500▲) . . . . E 9
Jieyang, 98,531('85) . . L 5
Jingdezhen (Kingtechen), 304,000 (569,700▲) . . F 6
Jinhua, 147,800 (799,900▲) . . . . F 8
Jiujiang, 248,500 (382,300▲) . . . . F 4
Lanxi, 70,500 (606,800▲) . . . . F 8
Lechang, 56,913 . . . . . . J 2
Liling, 107,100 (856,300▲) . . . . H 2
Linhai, 52,653('85) G10
Liuan, 122,600 (163,400▲) . . . . D 5
Longyan, 114,500 (378,500▲) . . . . J 6
Luohe, 102,300 (159,100▲) . . . . B 3
Maanshan, 258,900 (367,000▲) . . . . D 7
Meixian, 169,100 (740,600▲) . . . . K 5
Nanchang, 1,090,000 (1,260,000)('88) . . . . G 4
Nanjing (Nanking), 2,390,000('88) . . . . . . C 7

★ Population of metropolitan area, including suburbs. ▲ Population of entire district, including rural area.

Kilometers 0 50 100 150 Km.
Miles 0 50 100 150 Mi.
1:4 000 000

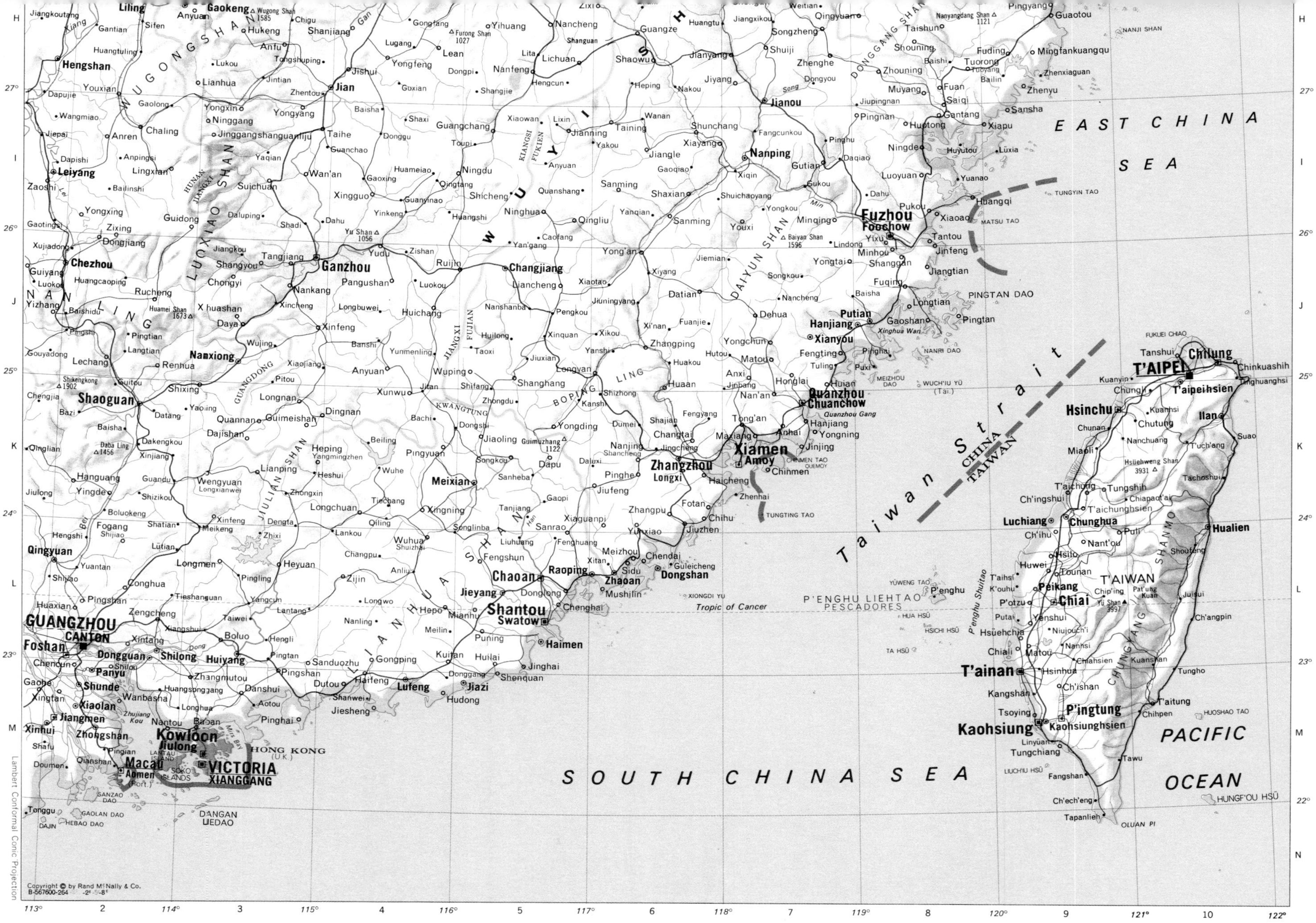

Nanping, 157,100 (420,800▲) . . . . I 7
Nantong, 308,800 (411,000▲) . . . . C 9
Nanyang, 199,400 (294,800▲) . . . . B 1
Ningbo, 570,000 (1,050,000▲)('88) F10
Pingxiang, 368,700 (1,286,700▲) . . . . . . H 2
Quanzhou, 157,000 (436,000▲) . . . . K 7
Shanghai, 7,220,000 (9,300,000★)('88) D10
Shantou (Swatow), 560,000 (790,000▲)('88) . . . . L 5
Shaoguan, 363,100 (344,892▲) . . . . K 2
Shaoxing, 167,100 (250,900▲) . . . . E 9
Suixian, 187,700 (1,281,600▲) . . . . . . D 2
Suzhou (Soochow), 740,000('88) . . . . D 9
Tongling, 182,900 (216,400▲) . . . . E 6
Wenzhou, 372,200 (530,600▲) . . . . G 9
Wuhan, 3,570,000('88) E 3
Wuhu, 396,000 (502,200▲) . . . . D 7
Wusong, 64,017('82) . . D10
Wuxi (Wuhsi), 880,000('88) . . . . D 9
Xiamen (Amoy), 343,700 (546,400▲) . . . . K 7
Xiangcheng, 363,200 (819,900▲) . . . . B 2
Xiangtan, 389,500 (511,100▲) . . . . H 1
Xinyang, 169,100 (234,200▲) . . . . C 3
Xuchang, 167,800 (247,200▲) . . . . A 2
Xuzhou (Süchow), 860,000('88) . . . . A 6
Yancheng, 258,400 (1,251,400▲) . . . . . . B 9
Yangzhou, 321,500 (417,300▲) . . . . C 8
Yanling, 52,679('82) . . C 8
Yueyang, 239,500 (411,300▲) . . . . F 2
Yuyao, 169,700 (772,700▲) E10
Zhangzhou (Longxi), 159,400 (310,400▲) K 6
Zhenjiang, 412,400 . . . . C 8
Zhongshan, 238,700 (1,059,700▲) . . . . . . M 2
Zhuzhou, 344,800 (499,600▲) . . . . H 2

Hong Kong

1986 CENSUS

Kowloon (Jiulong), 774,781 . . . . M 3
Victoria (Xianggang), 1,175,860 (4,770,000★) . . . . . . M 3

Macau

1987 ESTIMATE

Macau (Aomen), 429,000 . . . . M 2

Taiwan

1988 ESTIMATE

Changhua, 158,400 (206,603▲) . . . . K 9
Chiai, 254,875 . . . . L 9
Chilung, 348,541 . . . . . . J10
Hsinchu, 309,899 . . . . K 9
Kaohsiung, 1,342,797 (1,845,000★) . . . . . . M 9
Kaohsiunghsien, 276,259 . . . . M 9
P'ingtung, 167,600 (204,990▲) . . . . M 9
T'ainan, 656,927 . . . . . . L 9
T'aipei, 2,637,100 (6,130,000★) J10
T'aipeihsien, 506,220 . . J10

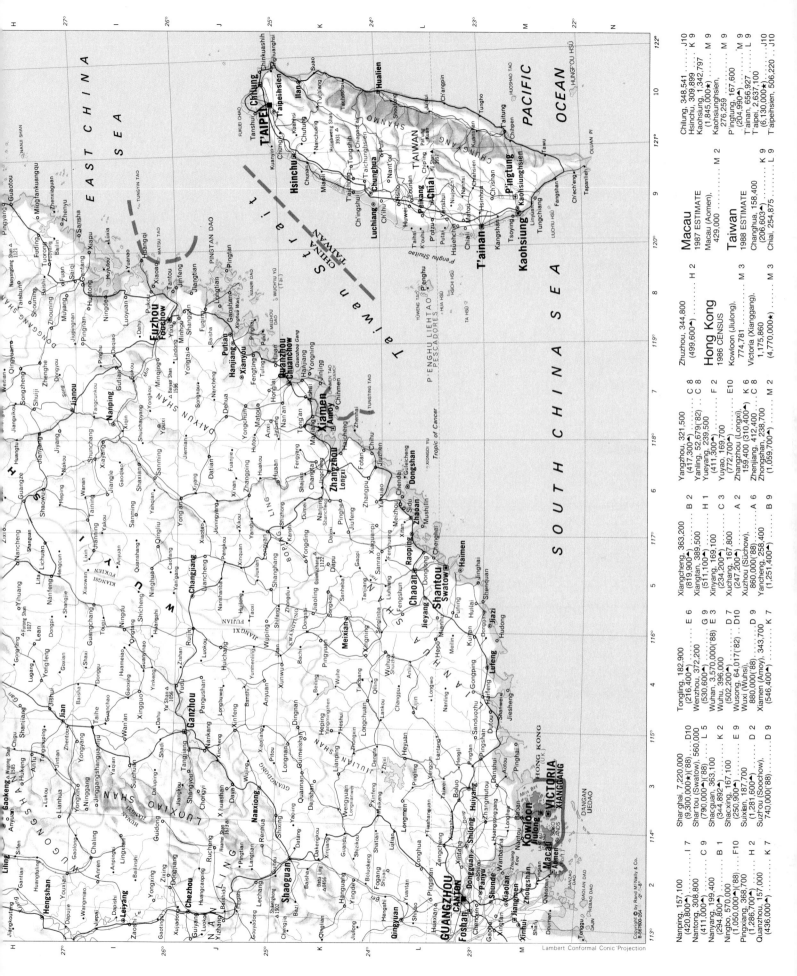

Japan

1985 CENSUS

Aizu-wakamatsu, 118,140 . . . E12
Akashi, 263,363 . . . H 7
Akita, 296,400 . . . C13
Amagasaki, 509,115 . . H 8
Aomori, 294,045 . . . B13
Asahikawa, 363,631 . . p20
Ashikaga, 167,656 . . . F12
Beppu, 134,775 . . . I 4
Chiba, 788,930 . . . G13
Chigasaki, 185,030 . . . G12
Chōshi, 87,883 . . . G13
Fuji, 214,448 (370,000★) . . . G11
Fujinomiya, 112,642 . . G11
Fujisawa, 328,387 . . . G12
Fukui, 250,261 . . . F 9
Fukuoka, 1,160,440 (1,750,000★) . . . I 3
Fukushima, 270,762 . . E13
Fukuyama, 360,261 . . H 6
Funabashi, 506,966 . . G13
Gifu, 411,743 . . . G 9
Hachinohe, 241,430 . . B14
Hachiōji, 426,654 . . . G12
Hakodate, 319,194 . . . r18
Hamamatsu, 514,118 . . H10
Handa, 92,883 . . . H 9
Higashiōsaka, 522,805 H 8
Hikone, 94,204 . . . G 9
Himeji, 452,917 (660,000★) . . . H 7
Hiratsuka, 229,990 . . . G12
Hirosaki, 134,800 (176,082▲) . . . B13
Hiroshima, 1,044,118 (1,575,000★) . . . H 5
Hitachi, 206,074 . . . F13
Hōfu, 118,067 . . . H 4
Ichinomiya, 257,388 . . G 9
Iizuka, 81,868 (110,000★) . . . I 3
Imabari, 125,115 . . . H 6
Ise, 105,455 . . . H 9
Isesaki, 112,459 . . . F12
Ishinomaki, 122,674 . . D14
Iwaki (Taira), 350,569 . . E13
Iwakuni, 111,833 . . . H 5
Kagoshima, 530,502 . . K 3
Kakogawa, 227,311 . . H 7
Kamaishi, 60,007 . . . C14
Kamakura, 175,495 . . . G12
Kanazawa, 430,481 . . . F 9
Kariya, 112,403 . . . H 9
Kashiwa, 273,128 . . . G12
Kasugai, 256,990 . . . G 9
Kawagoe, 285,437 . . . G12
Kawaguchi, 403,015 . . G12
Kawasaki, 1,088,624 . . G12
Kiryū, 131,267 . . . F12
Kishiwada, 185,731 . . . H 8
Kitakyūshū, 1,056,402 (1,525,000★) . . . I 3
Kitami, 107,281 . . . p21
Kōbe, 1,410,834 . . . H 8
Kōchi, 312,241 . . . I 6
Kōfu, 202,405 . . . G11
Komatsu, 106,041 . . . F 9
Kōriyama, 301,673 . . . E13
Kumagaya, 143,496 . . F12
Kumamoto, 555,719 . . J 3
Kurashiki, 413,632 . . . H 6
Kure, 226,488 . . . H 5
Kurume, 222,847 . . . I 3
Kushiro, 214,541 . . . q22
Kyōto, 1,479,218 . . . G 8
Maebashi, 277,319 . . . F12
Maizuru, 98,775 . . . G 8
Matsudo, 427,473 . . . G12
Matsue, 140,005 . . . G 6
Matsumoto, 197,340 . . F10
Matsusaka, 116,886 . . H 9
Matsuyama, 426,658 . . I 5
Mito, 228,985 . . . F13
Miyazaki, 279,114 . . . K 4
Morioka, 235,469 . . . C14
Muroran, 136,208 (195,000★) . . . q18
Nagahama, 55,531 . . . G 9
Nagano, 336,973 . . . F11
Nagaoka, 183,756 . . . E11
Nagasaki, 449,382 . . . J 2

★ Population of metropolitan area, including suburbs. ▲ Population of entire district, including rural area.

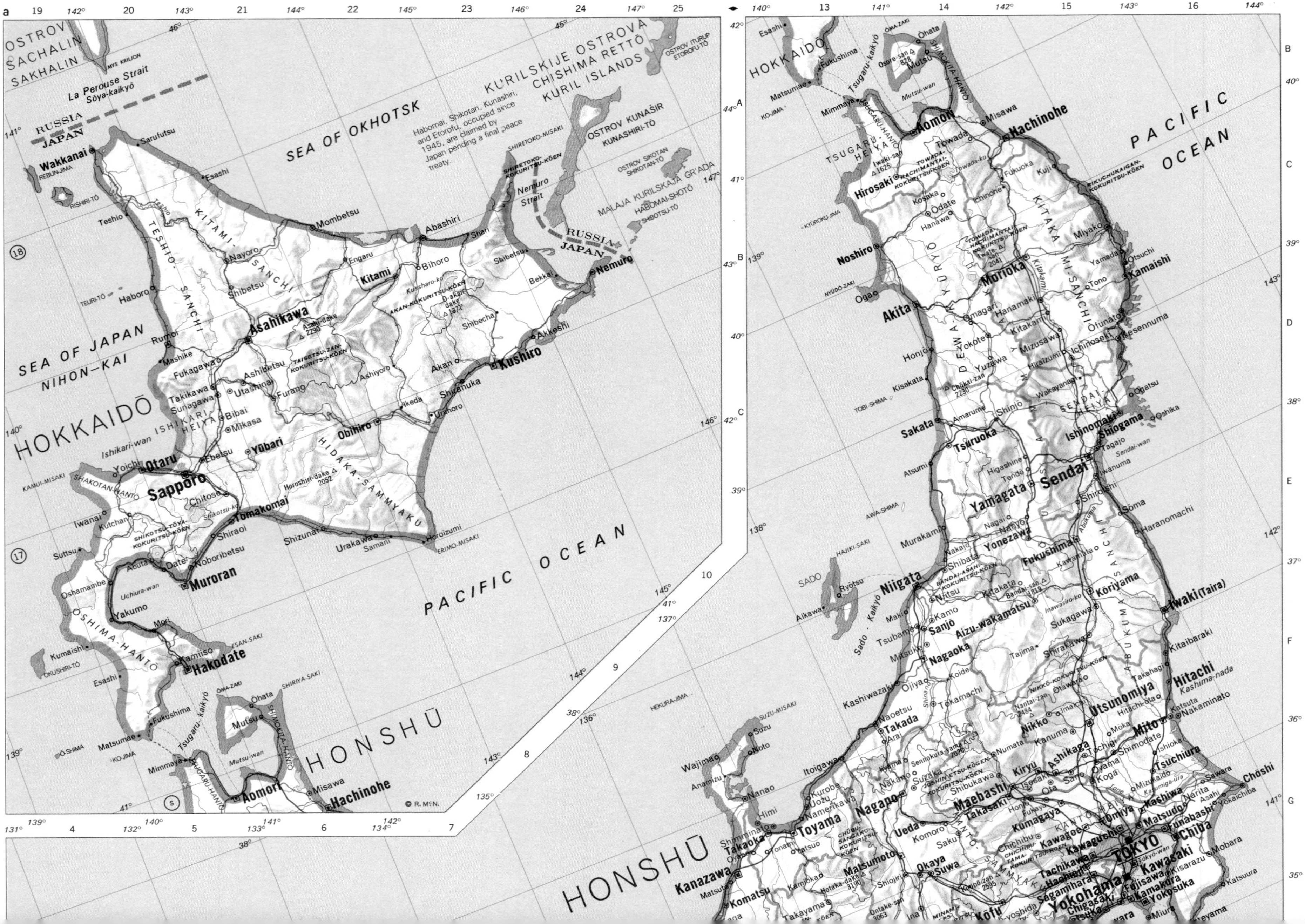

Kilometers 0 50 100 150 **Km.**
Miles 0 50 100 150 **Mi.**

1:4 000 000

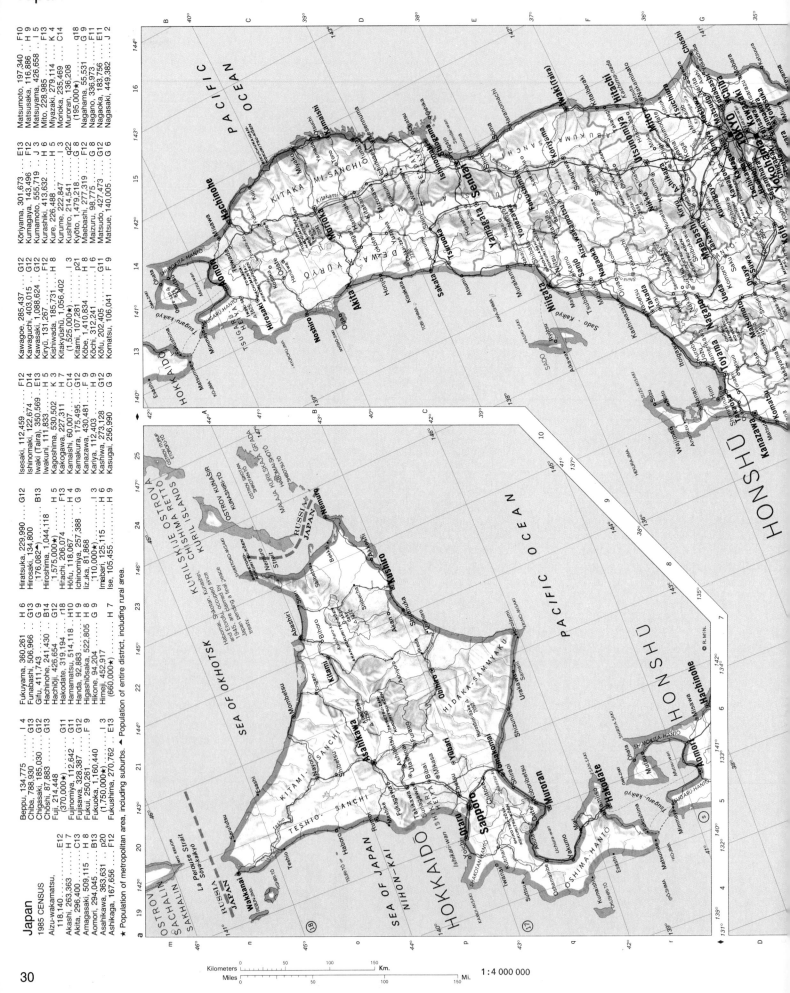

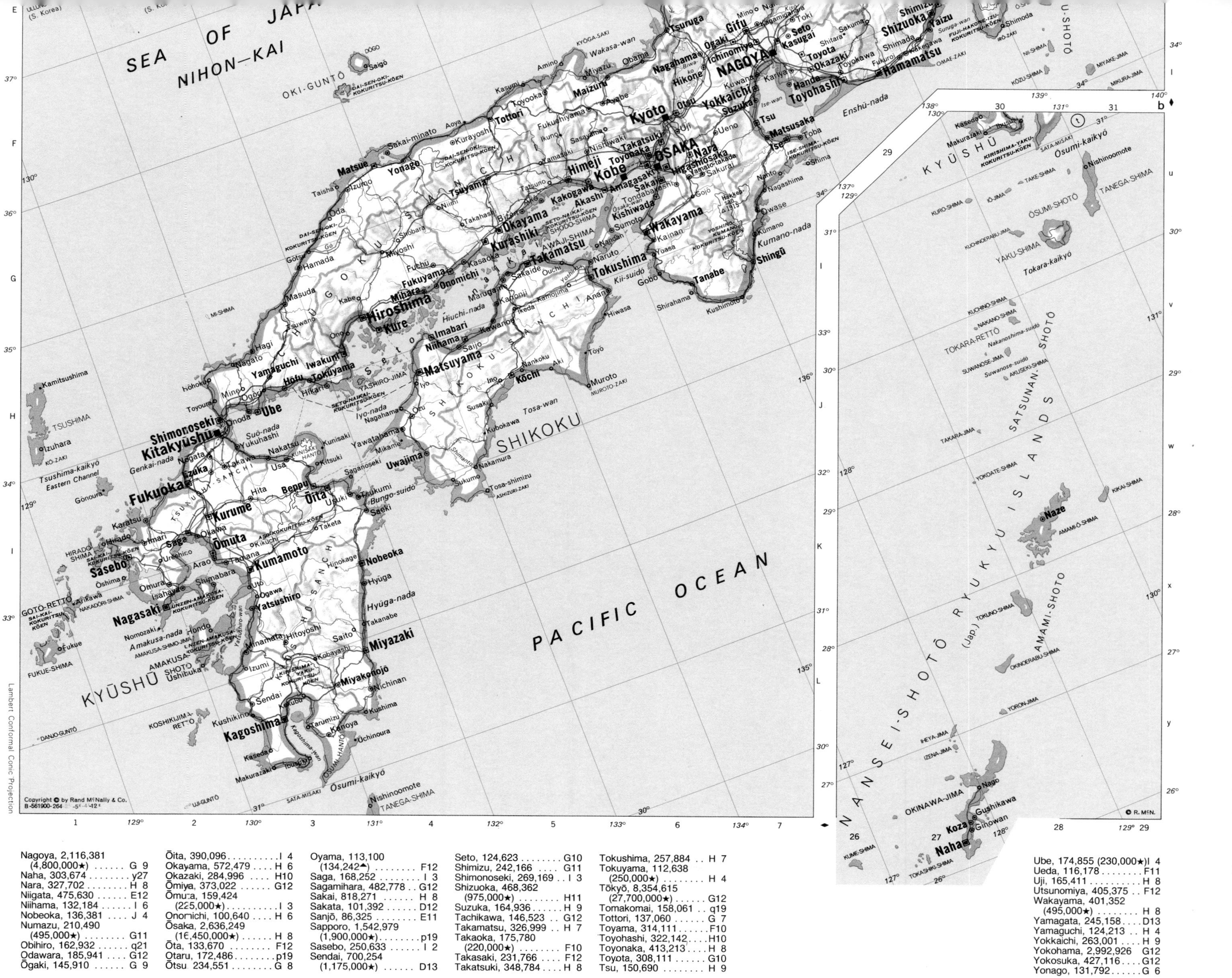

Lambert Conformal Conic Projection

Southeastern Asia

Brunei
1981 CENSUS
Bandar Seri Begawan, 22,777 (64,000★) .. E 5

Burma
1983 CENSUS
Bago, 150,528 ...... B 2
Henzada, 82,005 .... B 2
Mandalay, 532,949 .. A 2
Mawlamyine, 219,961 B 2
Monywa, 106,843 .... A 2
Pathein, 144,096 .... B 1
Pyè (Prome), 83,332 .. B 2
Sittwe (Akyab), 107,621 .... A 1
Yangon (Rangoon), 2,705,039 (2,800,000★) ...... B 2

Cambodia
1986 ESTIMATE
Phnum Pénh, 700,000 C 3

Indonesia
1980 CENSUS
Ambon, 111,914 (207,702▲) .... F 8
Balikpapan, 208,040 (279,852▲) .... F 6
Bandung, 1,633,000 (1,800,000★)('85) .. m13
Banjarmasin, 424,000('83) ...... F 5
Banjuwangi, 90,378 .. n17
Blitar, 78,503 (100,000★) n16
Bogor, 246,946 (560,000★) m13
Cilacap, 127,017 .... m14
Cirebon, 223,504 (275,000★) m14
Denpasar, 159,233 .. G 6
Dili, 6,890 (67,039▲) G 8
Garut, 145,624 ...... m13
Jakarta, 9,200,000 (10,000,000★)('89) m13
Jambi, 155,761 (230,046▲) .... F 3
Jember, 171,284 .... n16
Kediri, 176,261 (221,830▲) m16
Kudus, 154,478 ..... m15
Kupang, 84,587 .... H 7
Madiun, 150,562 (180,000★) m15
Magelang, 123,358 (160,000★) m15
Malang, 547,000('83) m16
Manado, 217,091 .... E 7
Medan, 2,110,000('85) E 2
Padang, 405,600 (657,000▲)('83) .... F 3
Pakanbaru, 186,199 .. E 3
Palembang, 874,000('83) ...... F 3
Pangkalpinang, 90,078 F 4
Pasuruan, 95,864 (125,000★) m16
Pekalongan, 132,413 (260,000★) m14
Pemalang, 72,663 .. m14
Pematangsiantar, 150,296 (175,000★) .... E 2
Pontianak, 343,000('83) ...... F 4
Probolinggo, 100,296 m16
Purwokerto, 143,787 m14
Salatiga, 85,740 .... m15
Samarinda, 182,473 (264,012▲) .... F 6
Semarang, 1,206,000('83) m15
Sukabumi, 109,898 (225,000★) m13
Surabaya, 2,345,000('85) m16
Surakarta, 491,000 (575,000★)('83) m15
Tanjungkarang-Telukbetung, 284,167 (375,000★) k12
Tasikmalaya, 192,267 m14
Tegal, 131,440 (340,000★) m14
Tual, 7,833 .... G 9
Tulungagung, 91,585 n15
Ujungpandang, 841,000('83) ...... G 6
Yogyakarta, 421,000 (510,000★)('83) m15

Laos
1975 ESTIMATE
Louangphrabang, 46,000 .... B 3
Paksé, 47,000 ...... B 4
Savannakhet, 53,000 B 3
Viangchan, 377,409('85) ...... B 3

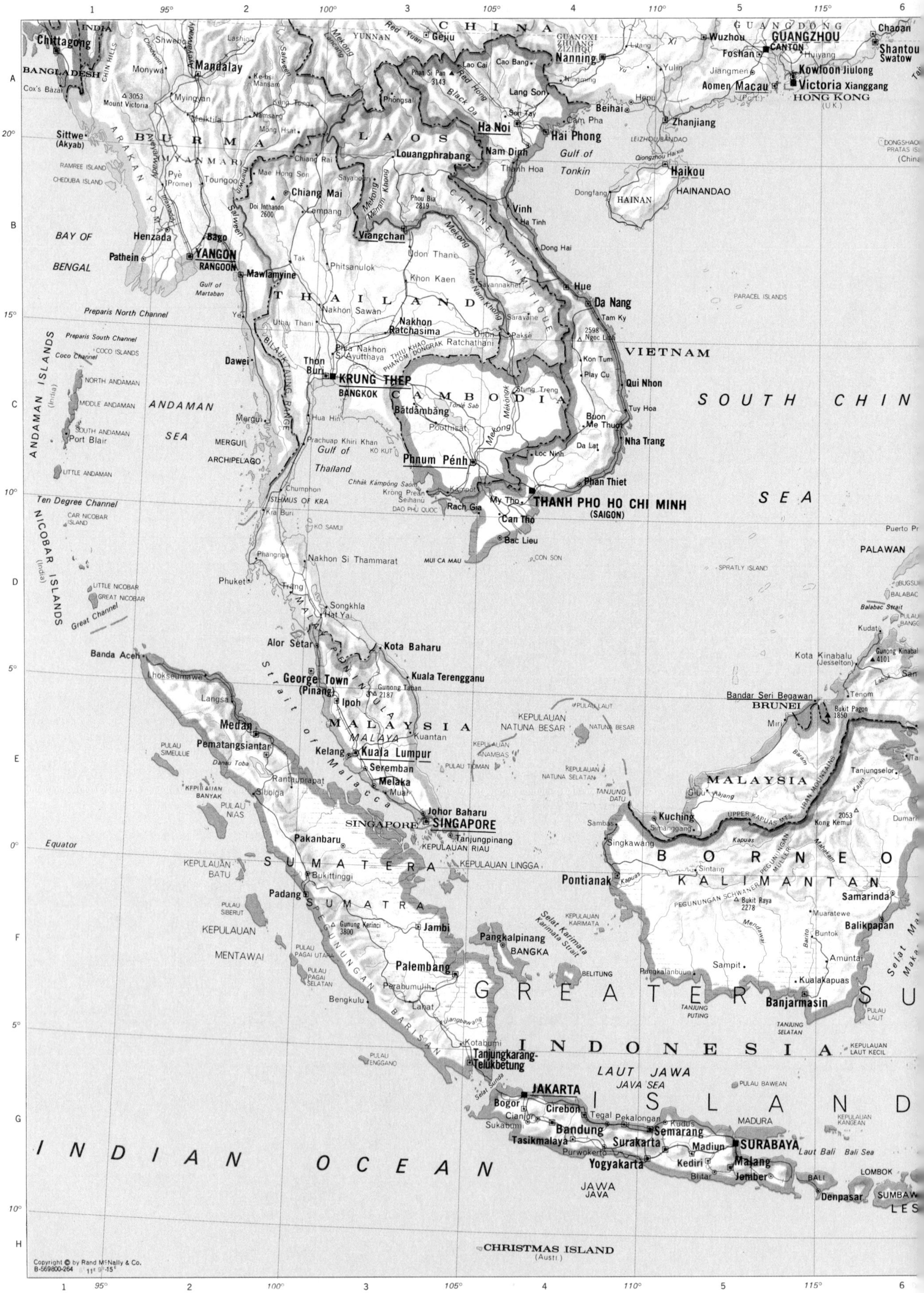

Kilometers 0 200 400 600 Km.
Miles 0 200 400 600 Mi.
1:16 000 000

★ Population of metropolitan area, including suburbs.
▲ Population of entire district, including rural area.

Malaysia
1980 CENSUS

Alor Setar, 69,435 .. D 3
George Town (Pinang), 248,241 (495,000★) D 3
Ipoh, 293,849 ...... E 3
Johor Baharu, 246,395 .... E 3
Kelang, 192,080 .... E 3
Kota Baharu, 167,872 D 3
Kuala Lumpur, 919,610 (1,475,000★) ...... E 3
Kuala Terengganu, 180,296 .... D 3
Kuantan, 131,547 .... E 3
Kuching, 72,555 .... E 5
Melaka, 87,494 ...... E 3
Sandakan, 70,420 .. D 6
Seremban, 132,911 .. E 3
Sibu, 85,231 .... E 5

Philippines
1990 CENSUS

Angeles, 236,000 .... q19
Bacolod, 364,000 .... C 7
Baguio, 183,000 .... p19
Batangas, 31,600 (184,000▲) r19
Cabanatuan, 75,700 (173,000▲) q19
Cavite, 92,000 (175,000★) q19
Cebu, 610,000 (720,000★) .... C 7
Cotabato, 127,000 .. D 7
Dagupan, 122,000 .. p19
Davao, 569,300 (850,000▲) .... D 8
Dumaguete, 80,000 .. D 7
Iloilo, 311,000 ...... C 7
Legaspi, 63,000 (121,000▲) r20
Lipa, 30,000 (160,000▲) r19
Lucena, 151,000 .... r19
Malalos, 95,699('80) .. q19
Manila, 1,587,000 (6,800,000★) q19
Naga, 115,000 ...... r20
Pasig, 318,853('84) .. q19
Puerto Princesa, 52,000 (92,000▲) .... D 6
Quezon City, 1,632,000 .... q19
San Fernando, 110,891('80) q19
San Pablo, 83,900 (161,000▲) q19
Tarlac, 38,205 (175,691▲)('80) q19
Zamboanga, 107,000 (444,000▲) .... D 7

Singapore
1989 ESTIMATE

Singapore, 2,685,400 (3,025,000★) ...... E 3

Thailand
1988 ESTIMATE

Bangkok *see* Krung Thep .... C 3
Chiang Mai, 164,030 B 2
Hat Yai, 138,046 .... D 3
Khon Kaen, 131,340 B 3
Krung Thep (Bangkok), 5,716,779 (6,450,000★) ...... C 3
Nakhon Ratchasima, 204,982 .... C 3
Nakhon Sawan, 105,220 .... B 3
Nakhon Si Thammarat, 72,407 .... D 2
Phitsanulok, 77,675 .. B 3
Songkhla, 84,433 .... D 3
Ubon Ratchathani, 100,374 .... B 3
Udon Thani, 81,202 .. B 3

Vietnam
1979 CENSUS

Can Tho, 182,856 .. C 4
Da Nang, 318,653 .. B 4
Hai Phong, 456,000 (1,279,067▲)('89) .. A 4
Ha Noi, 1,089,000 (1,500,000★)('89) .. A 4
Hue, 165,710 ...... B 4
My Tho, 101,493 .... C 4
Nam Dinh, 160,179 .. A 4
Nha Trang, 172,663 .. C 4
Phan Thiet, 75,241 .. C 4
Qui Nhon, 127,211 .. C 4
Rach Gia, 81,075 .... C 4
Saigon *see* Thanh Pho Ho Chi Minh .... C 4
Thanh Pho Ho Chi Minh (Saigon), 3,169,000 (3,300,000★)('89) .. C 4
Vinh, 159,753 ...... B 4

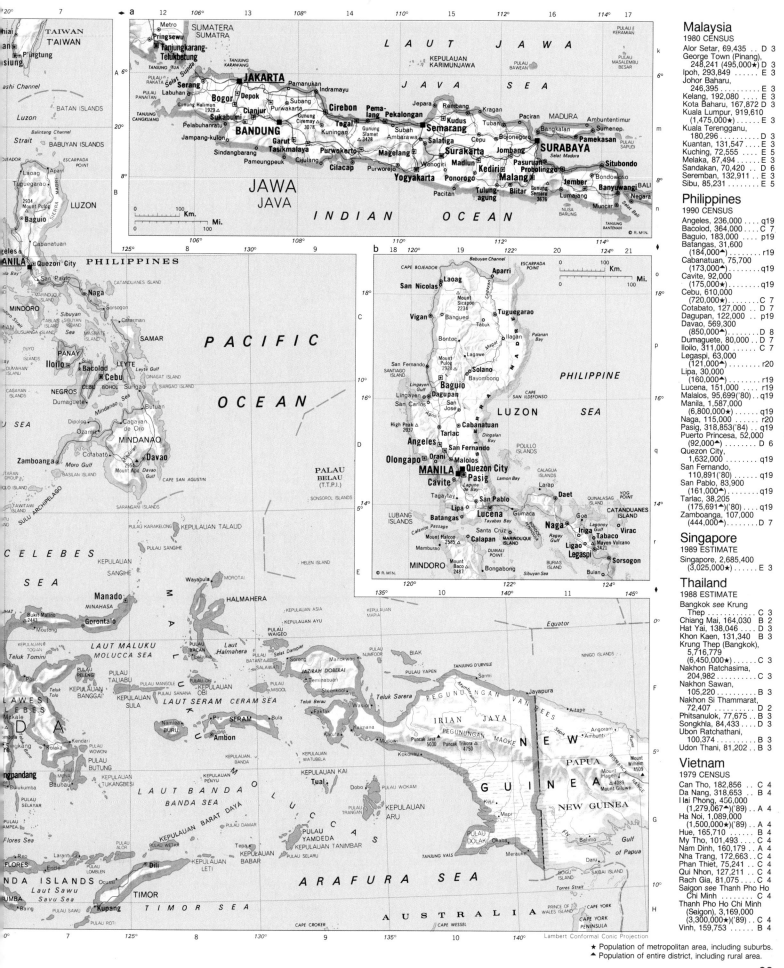

Burma, Thailand, and Indochina

Burma
1983 CENSUS

Bago, 150,528 . . . . F 4
Chauk, 51,437 . . . . D 3
Dawei, 69,882 . . . . G 5
Henzada, 82,005 . . . . . F 3
Mandalay, 532,949 . . . . C 4
Mawlamyine (Moulmein), 219,961 . . . . F 4
Maymyo, 63,782 . . . . . . C 4
Meiktila, 96,496 . . . . . . D 3
Mergui (Myeik), 88,600 H 5
Monywa, 106,843 . . . . C 3
Myingyan, 77,060 . . . . D 3
Myitkyinā, 56,427 . . . . B 4
Pakokku, 71,860 . . . . . . D 3
Pathein, 144,096 . . . . . . F 3
Pyè (Prome), 83,332 . . E 3
Rangoon *see* Yangon . . F 4
Sittwe (Akyab), 107,621 D 2
Thaton, 61,790 . . . . F 4
Toungoo, 65,861 . . . . . . E 4
Yangon (Rangoon), 2,705,039 (2,800,000★) . . . . F 4
Yenangyaung, 62,582 . . D 3

Cambodia
1986 ESTIMATE

Bătdâmbâng, 38,780('62) . . . . H 7
Kâmpóng Cham, 35,000('71) . . . . H 8
Kâmpóng Saôm, 53,000('81) . . . . I 7
Phnum Pénh (Phnom Penh), 700,000 . . . . I 8

Indonesia
1980 CENSUS

Banda Aceh, 71,868 . . L 3
Binjai, 71,444 . . . . M 5
Bukittinggi, 55,577 (70,691▲) . . . . O 6
Medan, 2,110,000('85) M 5
Padang, 405,600 (657,000▲)('83) . . . . O 6
Padangsidempuan, 56,984 . . . . N 5
Payakumbuh, 24,567 (78,789▲) . . . . O 6
Pekanbaru, 186,199 . . N 6
Pematangsiantar, 150,296 (175,000★) . . . . M 5
Rantauprapat, 25,043 M 5
Sibolga, 59,466 . . . . . . N 5
Singkawang, 58,693 . . N10
Tanjungpinang, 36,999 N 8
Tarutung, 5,522 . . . . . . M 5
Tebingtinggi, 69,569 (92,068▲) . . . . M 5

Laos
1975 ESTIMATE

Louangphrabang, 46,000 . . . . E 7
Pakxé, 47,000 . . . . G 8
Savannakhet, 53,000 . . F 8
Viangchan, 377,409('85) F 7

Malaysia
1980 CENSUS

Batu Pahat, 64,727 . . . . N 7
Butterworth, 77,982 . . L 6
George Town (Pinang), 248,241 (495,000★) . . L 6
Ipoh, 293,849 . . . . L 6
Johor Baharu, 246,395 N 7
Kelang, 192,080 . . . . . . M 6
Kota Baharu, 167,872 . . K 7
Kuala Lumpur, 919,610 (1,475,000★) . . . . . . M 6
Kuala Terengganu, 180,296 . . . . L 7
Kuantan, 131,547 . . . . . M 7
Kuching, 72,555 . . . . . . N11
Melaka, 87,494 . . . . M 7
Muar, 65,151 . . . . M 7
Seremban, 132,911 . . M 6
Taiping, 146,000 . . . . . . L 6

★ Population of metropolitan area, including suburbs. ▲ Population of entire district, including rural area.

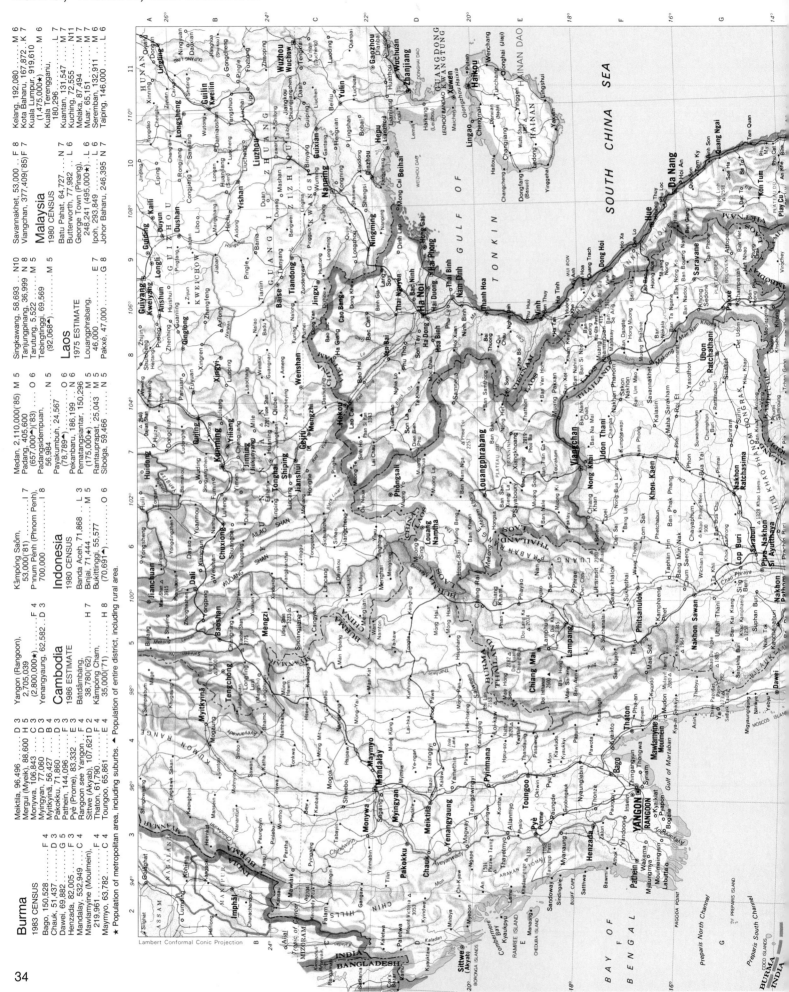

Singapore
1989 ESTIMATE
Singapore, 2,685,400 (3,025,000★) ...... N 7

Thailand
1988 ESTIMATE
Bangkok *see* Krung Thep .... H 6
Chiang Mai, 164,030 .. E 5
Hat Yai, 138,046 ...... K 6
Khon Kaen, 131,340 .. F 7
Krung Thep (Bangkok), 5,716,779 (6,450,000★) ...... H 6
Nakhon Ratchasima, 204,982 .... G 7
Nakhon Sawan, 105,220 .... G 6
Songkhla, 84,433 .... K 6
Ubon Ratchathani, 100,374 .... G 8

Vietnam
1979 CENSUS
Bien Hoa, 187,254 .... I 9
Can Tho, 182,856 ...... I 8
Da Nang, 318,653 .... F10
Hai Phong, 456,000 (1,279,067▲)('89)....D 9
Ha Noi, 1,089,000 (1,500,000★)('89)....D 8
Hon Gai, 114,573 .... D 9
Hue, 165,710 .... F 9
Long Xuyen, 112,485 .. I 8
Nam Dinh, 160,179.... D 9
Nha Trang, 172,663 .. H10
Qui Nhon, 127,211 .... H10
Rach Gia, 81,075 ...... I 8
Saigon *see* Thanh Pho Ho Chi Minh............ I 9
Thai Nguyen, 138,023 D 8
Thanh Pho Ho Chi Minh (Saigon), 3,169,000 (3,300,000★)('89) .... I 9
Vinh, 159,753 .... E 8

India and Pakistan

Afghanistan
1988 ESTIMATE
Herāt, 177,300 . . . . . . C 1
Kābol, 1,424,400 . . . . C 2

Bangladesh
1981 CENSUS
Chittagong, 980,000
(1,391,877★) . . . . . . E 7
Dhaka, 2,365,695
(3,430,312★) . . . . . . E 7
Nārāyanganj, 405,562 E 7

Bhutan
1982 ESTIMATE
Thimphu, 12,000 . . . . D 6

India
1981 CENSUS
Ahmadābād, 2,059,725
(2,400,000★) . . . . . . E 3
Bangalore, 2,476,355
(2,950,000★) . . . . . . G 4
Bombay, 8,243,405
(9,950,000★) . . . . . . F 3
Calcutta, 3,305,006
(11,100,000★) . . . . E 6
Delhi, 4,884,234
(7,200,000★) . . . . . . D 4
Hyderābād, 2,187,262
(2,750,000★) . . . . . . F 4
Kānpur, 1,481,789
(1,875,000★) . . . . . . D 5
Madras, 3,276,622
(4,475,000★) . . . . . . G 5
Nāgpur, 1,219,461
(1,302,066★) . . . . . . E 4
New Delhi, 273,036 . . D 4

Nepal
1981 CENSUS
Kāthmāndau, 235,160
(320,000★) . . . . D 6

Pakistan
1981 CENSUS
Islāmābād, 204,364 . . C 3
Karāchi, 4,901,627
(5,300,000★) . . . . . . E 2
Lahore, 2,707,215
(3,025,000★) . . . . . . C 3

Sri Lanka
1986 ESTIMATE
Colombo, 683,000
(2,050,000★) . . . . . . H 4

★ Population of metropolitan area, including suburbs.

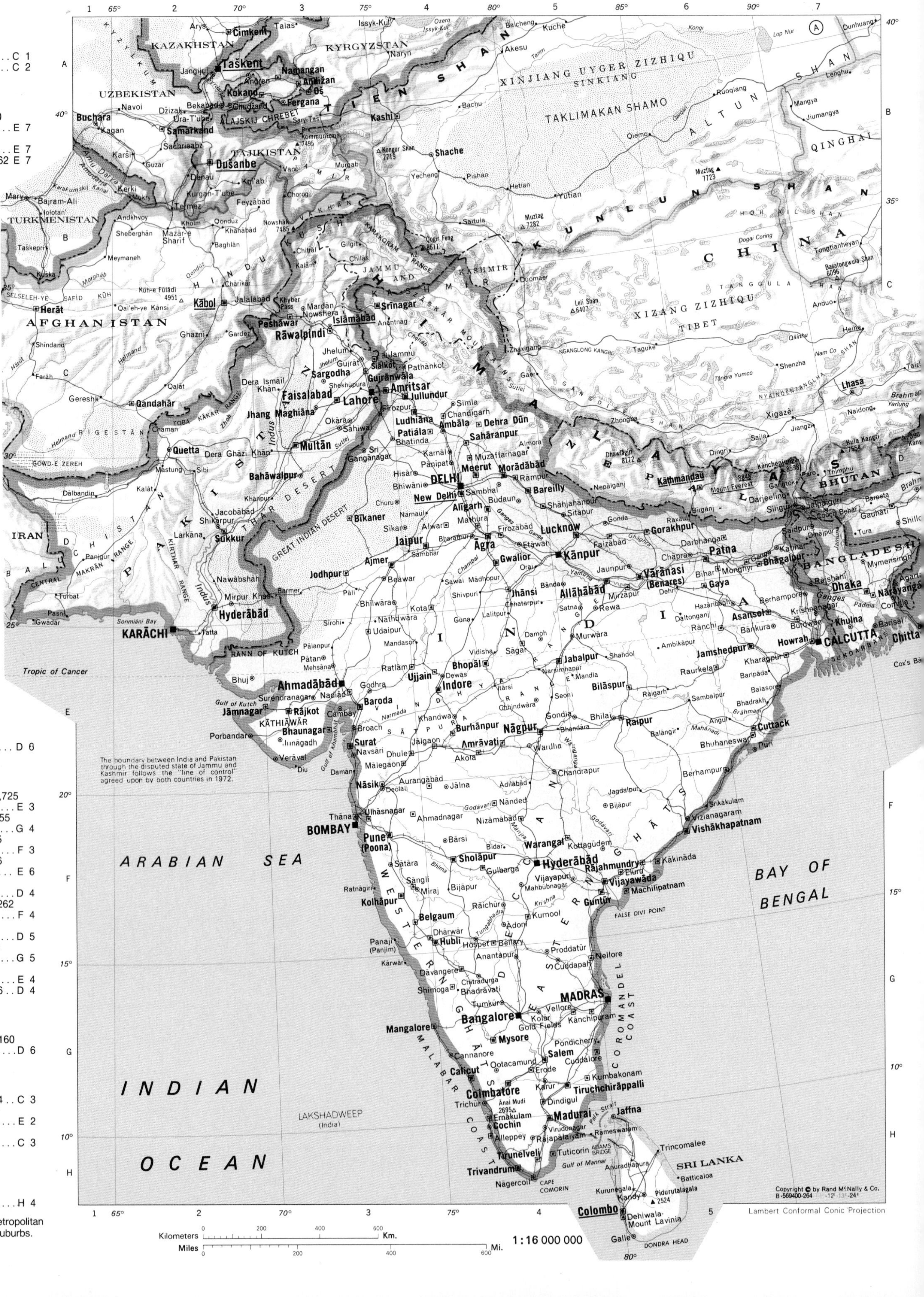

Southern India and Sri Lanka

Kilometers 0 100 200 300 Km.
Miles 0 100 200 300 Mi.

1:8 000 000

India

1981 CENSUS

Akola, 225,412 ...... B 4
Amrāvati, 261,404 .. B 4
Aurangābād, 284,607 (316,421★)........C 3
Bangalore, 2,476,355 (2,950,000★)...... F 4
Baroda, 734,473 (744,881★).........A 2
Belgaum, 274,430 (300,372★).........E 3
Bhāvnagar, 307,121 (308,642★).........B 2
Bhilai, 290,090 (490,214★).........B 6
Bhubaneswar, 219,211 ....B 8
Bombay, 8,243,405 (9,950,000★)......C 2
Calicut, 394,447 (546,058★) ...... G 3
Cochin, 513,249 (685,836★).........H 4
Coimbatore, 704,514 (965,000★) ...... G 4
Cuttack, 269,950 (327,412★).........B 8
Dhule, 210,759 ......B 3
Gulbarga, 221,325 .. D 4
Guntūr, 367,699 .... D 6
Hubli, 527,108 ...... E 3
Hyderābād, 2,187,262 (2,750,000★)......D 5
Indore, 829,327 (850,000★).........A 3
Kolhāpur, 340,625 (351,392★).........D 3
Madras, 3,276,622 (4,475,000★) ...... F 6
Madurai, 820,891 (960,000★).........H 5
Mālegaon, 245,883 .. B 3
Mysore, 441,754 (479,081★).........F 4
Nāgpur, 1,219,461 (1,302,066★)......B 5
Nāsik, 262,428 (429,034★).........C 2
Nellore, 237,065 .... E 5
Pondicherry, 162,636 (251,420★) ...... G 5
Pune (Poona), 1,203,351 (1,775,000★)......C 2
Raipur, 338,245 .... B 6
Salem, 361,394 (518,615★) ...... G 5
Sholāpur, 511,103 (514,860★).........D 3
Surat, 776,583 (913,806★).........B 2
Thāna, 309,897 .... C 2
Tiruchchirāppalli, 362,045 (609,548★) ...... G 5
Trivandrum, 483,086 (520,125★).........H 4
Ulhāsnagar, 273,668 C 2
Vijayawāda, 454,577 (543,008★).........D 6
Vishākhapatnam, 565,321 (603,630★).........D 7
Warangal, 335,150 .. C 5

Sri Lanka

1986 ESTIMATE

Colombo, 683,000 (2,050,000★) ...... I 5
Dehiwala-Mount Lavinia, 191,000 .... I 5
Kandy, 130,000 ...... I 6
Kotte, 104,000 ...... I 5

★ Population of metropolitan area, including suburbs.

Northern India and Pakistan

Afghanistan

1981 ESTIMATE

Baghlān, 41,000('82) B 3
Ghaznī, 31,196 . . . . . D 3
Jalālābād, 58,000('82) C 4
Kābol, 1,424,400('88) C 3
Khānābād, 27,482 . . B 3
Kholm, 28,788 . . . . . B 2
Mazār-e Sharīf,
130,600('88) . . . . . B 2
Meymaneh, 39,218 . . C 1
Qandahār,
225,500('88) . . . . . E 1
Sheberghān, 19,475 . . B 1

Bangladesh

1981 CENSUS

Barisāl, 172,905 . . . . . I14
Brāhmanbāria, 87,570 I14
Chittagong, 980,000
(1,391,877★) I14
Comilla, 184,132 . . . . I14
Dhaka, 2,365,695
(3,430,312★) I14
Jessore, 148,927 . . . . I13
Khulna, 648,359 . . . . . I13
Mymensingh, 190,991 H14
Nārāyanganj, 405,562 I14
Pābna, 109,065 . . . . H13
Rājshāhi, 253,740 . . . . H13
Rangpur, 153,174 . . . . H13
Saidpur, 126,608 . . . . H13
Sirājganj, 106,774 . . . . H13
Sylhet, 168,371 . . . . H14

Bhutan

1982 ESTIMATE

Thimphu, 12,000 . . . . G13

India

1981 CENSUS

Āgra, 694,191
(747,318★) . . . . . . G 8
Ahmadābād, 2,059,725
(2,400,000★) . . . . . . I 5
Ajmer, 375,593 . . . . . G 6
Alīgarh, 320,861 . . . . G 8
Allāhābād, 616,051
(650,070★) . . . . H 9
Alwar, 145,795 . . . . . . G 7
Amritsar, 594,844 . . . . E 6
Asansol, 183,375
(1,050,000★) I12
Bareilly, 386,734
(449,425★) . . . . F 8
Baroda, 734,473
(744,881★) . . . . I 5
Bhāgalpur, 225,062 . . H12
Bhātpāra, 260,761 . . . . I13
Bhāvnagar, 307,121
(308,642★) . . . . J 5
Bhilai, 290,090
(490,214★) . . . . J 9
Bhopāl, 671,018 . . . . . . I 7
Bhubaneswar, 219,211J11
Bikaner, 253,174
(287,712★) . . . . F 5
Calcutta, 3,305,006
(11,100,000★) I13
Chandīgarh, 373,789
(422,841★) . . . . E 7
Cuttack, 269,950
(327,412★) J11
Dehra Dūn, 211,416
(293,010★) . . . . E 8
Delhi, 4,884,234
(7,200,000★) . . . . . . F 7
Durgāpur, 311,798 . . . . I12
Gaya, 247,075 . . . . . . H11
Ghāziābād, 271,730
(287,170★) . . . . F 7
Gorakhpur, 290,814
(307,501★) G10
Gwalior, 539,015
(555,862★) . . . . . . G 8
Howrah, 744,429 . . . . I13
Indore, 829,327
(850,000★) . . . . I 6
Jabalpur, 614,162
(757,303★) . . . . I 8
Jaipur, 977,165
(1,025,000★) . . . . . . G 6
Jammu, 206,135
(223,361★) . . . . D 6
Jāmnagar, 277,615
(317,362★) . . . . I 4
Jamshedpur, 438,385
(669,580★) I12
Jhānsi, 246,172
(284,141★) . . . . H 8
Jodhpur, 506,345 . . . . G 5
Jullundur, 408,186
(441,552★) . . . . E 6
Kānpur, 1,481,789
(1,875,000★) . . . . . . G 9
Kota, 358,241 . . . . . . H 6
Lucknow, 895,721
(1,060,000★) . . . . . . G 9
Ludhiāna, 607,052 . . . E 6
Mathura, 147,493
(160,995★) . . . . G 7

★ Population of metropolitan area, including suburbs.

Kilometers 0 100 200 300 Km.
Miles 0 100 200 300 Mi.

1:8 000 000

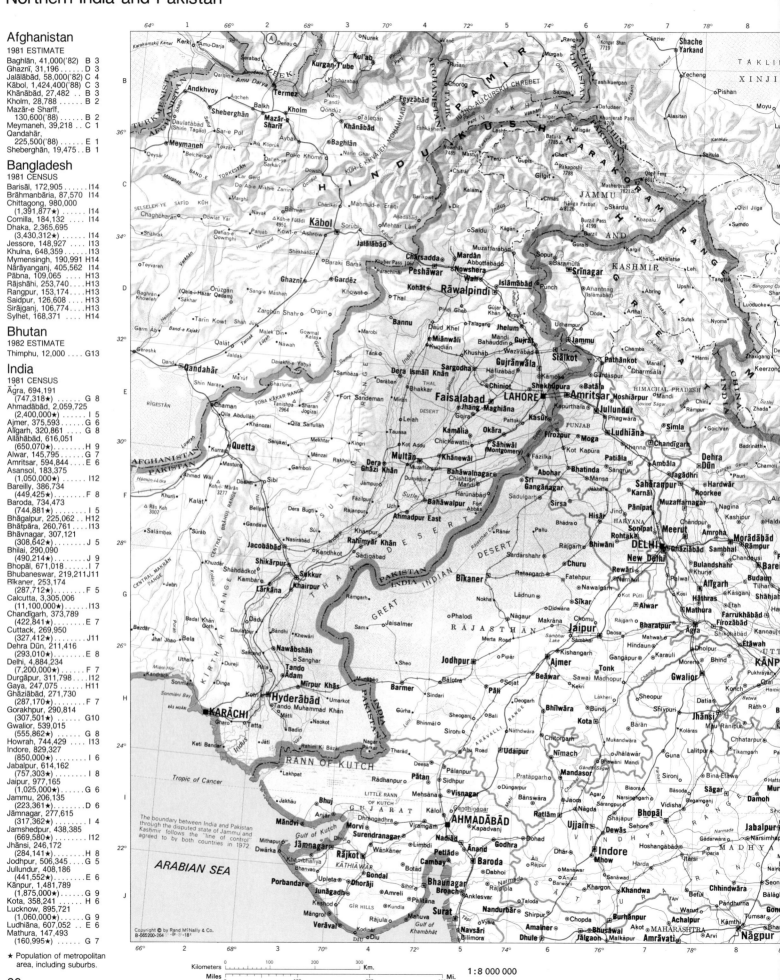

Meerut, 417,395 (536,615★) . . . . F 7
Morādābād, 330,051 (345,350★) . . . . F 8
Muzaffarnagar, 171,816 . . . . F 7
Muzaffarpur, 190,416 G11
Nāgpur, 1,219,461 (1,302,066★) . . . . . . J 8
New Delhi, 273,036 . . F 7
Patna, 776,371 (1,025,000★) H11
Raipur, 338,245 . . . . . . J 9
Rājkot, 445,076 . . . . . . I 4
Rānchī, 489,626 (502,771★) I11
Raurkela, 206,821 (322,610★) I11
Sāgar, 160,392 (207,479★) . . . . I 8
Sahāranpur, 295,355 F 7
Srīnagar, 594,775 (606,002★) . . . . C 6
Surat, 776,583 (913,806★) . . . . J 5
Ujjain, 278,454 (282,203★) . . . . I 6
Vārānasi (Benares), 708,647 (925,000★) H10

Nepal

1981 CENSUS

Bhaktapur, 48,472 . . G11
Birātnagar, 93,544 . . G12
Kathmāndau, 235,160 (320,000★) G11

Pakistan

1981 CENSUS

Bahāwalpur, 152,009 (180,263★) . . . . F 4
Chiniot, 105,559 . . . . E 5
Dera Ghāzi Khān, 102,007 . . . . E 4
Dera Ismāīl Khān, 64,358 (68,145★) . . . . E 4
Faisalabad, 1,104,209 E 5
Gujrānwāla, 600,993 (658,753★) . . . . D 6
Gujrāt, 155,058 . . . . . D 6
Hyderābād, 702,539 (800,000★) . . . . H 3
Islāmābād, 204,364 . . D 5
Jhang Maghiāna, 195,558 . . . . E 5
Karāchi, 4,901,627 (5,300,000★) . . . . . . H 2
Kasūr, 155,523 . . . . . E 6
Lahore, 2,707,215 (3,025,000★) . . . . . . E 6
Lārkāna, 123,890 . . . . G 3
Mardān, 141,842 (147,977★) . . . . C 5
Mīrpur Khās, 124,371 H 3
Multān, 696,316 (732,070★) . . . . E 4
Nawābshāh, 102,139 G 3
Okāra, 127,455 (153,483★) . . . . E 5
Peshāwar, 506,896 (566,248★) . . . . C 4
Quetta, 244,842 (285,719★) . . . . E 2
Rahīmyār Khān, 119,036 (132,635★) . . . . F 4
Rāwalpindi, 457,091 (1,040,000★) . . . . . . D 5
Sāhīwāl (Montgomery), 150,954 . . . . E 5
Sargodha, 231,895 (291,362★) . . . . E 5
Shekhūpura, 141,168 E 5
Siālkot, 258,147 (302,009★) . . . . D 6
Sukkur, 190,551 . . . . G 3
Wah, 122,335 . . . . . . D 5

Eastern Mediterranean Lands

Cyprus
1982 CENSUS
Lemesós (Limassol), 74,782 (107,161★) B 3
Nicosia, 48,221 (185,000★) . . . . . . B 3

Cyprus, North
1985 ESTIMATE
Nicosia, 37,400 . . . . B 3

Egypt
1986 CENSUS
Al-Iskandarīyah (Alexandria), 2,917,327 (3,350,000★) . . . . D 1
Al-Ismā'īlīyah (Ismailia), 212,567 (235,000★) D 3
Al-Jīzah (Giza), 1,870,508 . . . . . . D 2
Al-Qāhirah (Cairo), 6,052,836 (9,300,000★) . . . . D 2
As-Suways (Suez), 326,820 . . . . E 3
Asyūt, 273,191 . . . . F 2
Būr Sa'īd (Port Said), 399,793 . . . . D 3
Cairo *see* Al-Qāhirah D 2
Ṭanṭā, 334,505 . . . . D 2

Israel
1989 ESTIMATE
Be'er Sheva', 113,200 D 4
Ḥefa (Haifa), 222,600 (435,000★) . . . . . . C 4
Jerusalem *see* Yerushalayim . . . . D 4
Tel Aviv-Yafo, 317,800 (1,735,000★) . . . . C 4
Yerushalayim (Jerusalem), 493,500 (530,000★) D 4

Israeli Occupied Territories
1971 ESTIMATE
Ghazzah (Gaza), 118,272('67) . . . . D 4
Nābulus, 64,000 . . . . C 4

Jordan
1989 ESTIMATE
'Ammān, 936,300 (1,450,000★) . . . . D 4
Az-Zarqā', 318,055 . . C 5
Irbid, 167,785 . . . . . . C 4

Lebanon
1982 ESTIMATE
Bayrūt (Beirut), 509,000 (1,675,000★) . . . . C 4
Ṭarābulus (Tripoli), 198,000 . . . . B 4

Saudi Arabia
1980 ESTIMATE
Al-Madīnah (Medina), 290,000 . . . . G 6

Syria
1988 ESTIMATE
Al-Lādhiqīyah (Latakia), 249,000 . . . . B 4
Al-Qāmishlī, 126,236 A 7
Dayr az-Zawr, 112,000 . . . . B 7
Dimashq (Damascus), 1,326,000 (1,950,000★) . . . . C 5
Ḥalab (Aleppo), 1,261,000 (1,275,000★) . . . . A 5
Ḥamāh, 222,000 . . . B 5
Ḥimṣ (Homs), 447,000 B 5

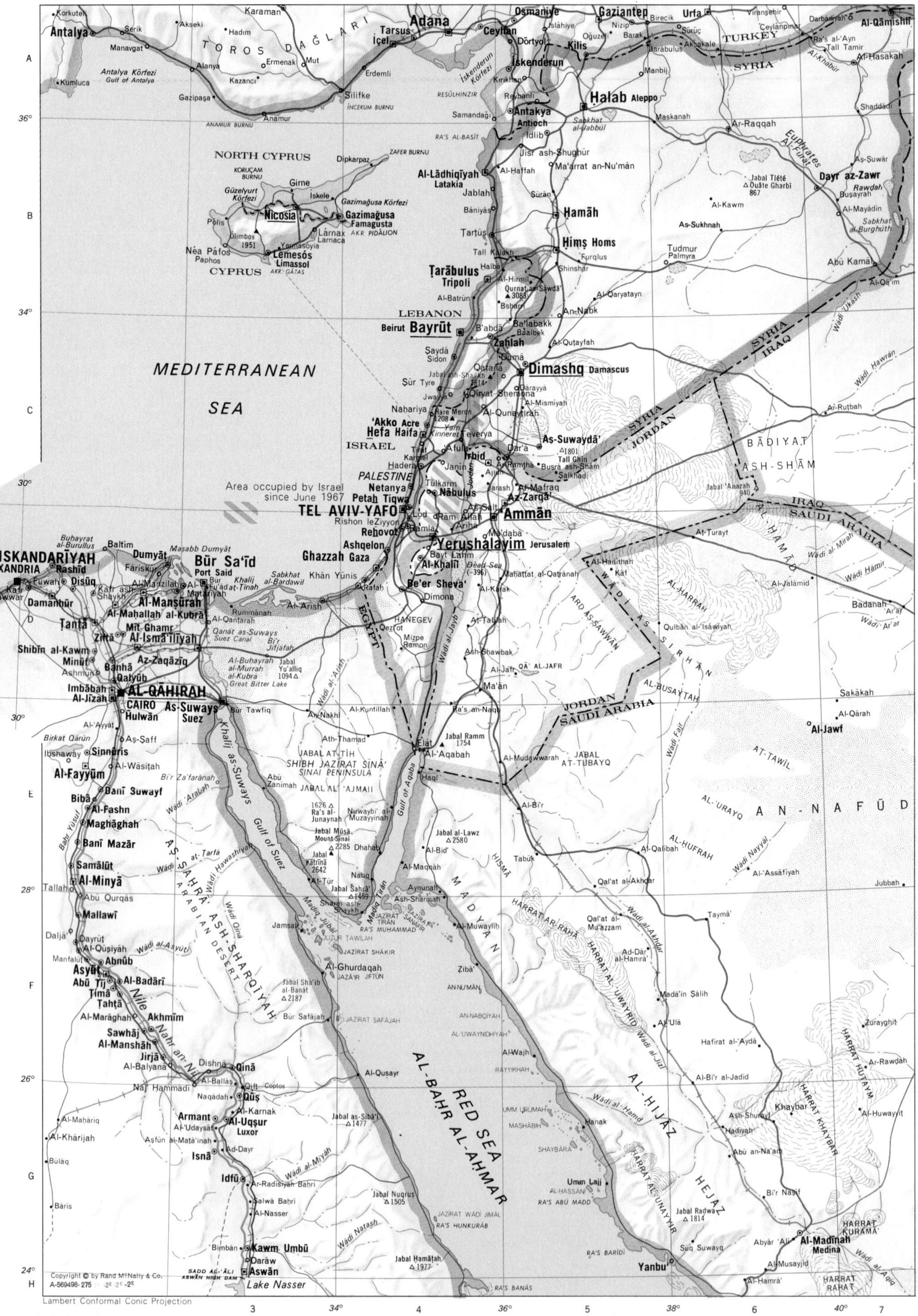

★ Population of metropolitan area, including suburbs.

Kilometers 0 100 200 300 Km.
Miles 0 100 200 300 Mi.

1: 6 000 000

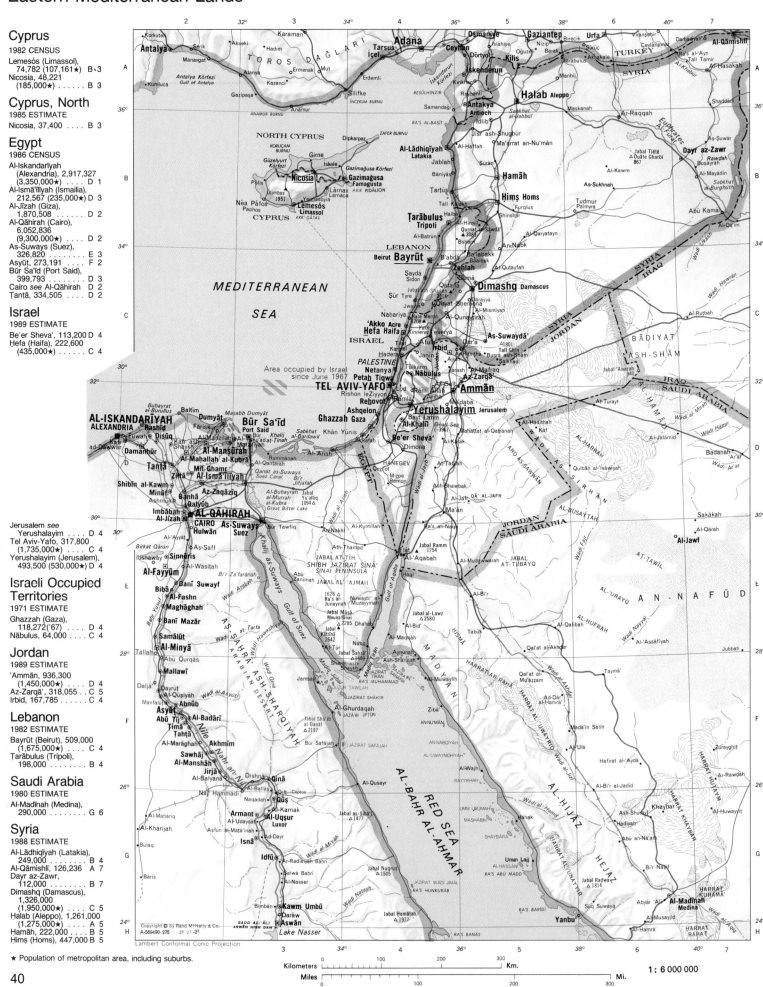

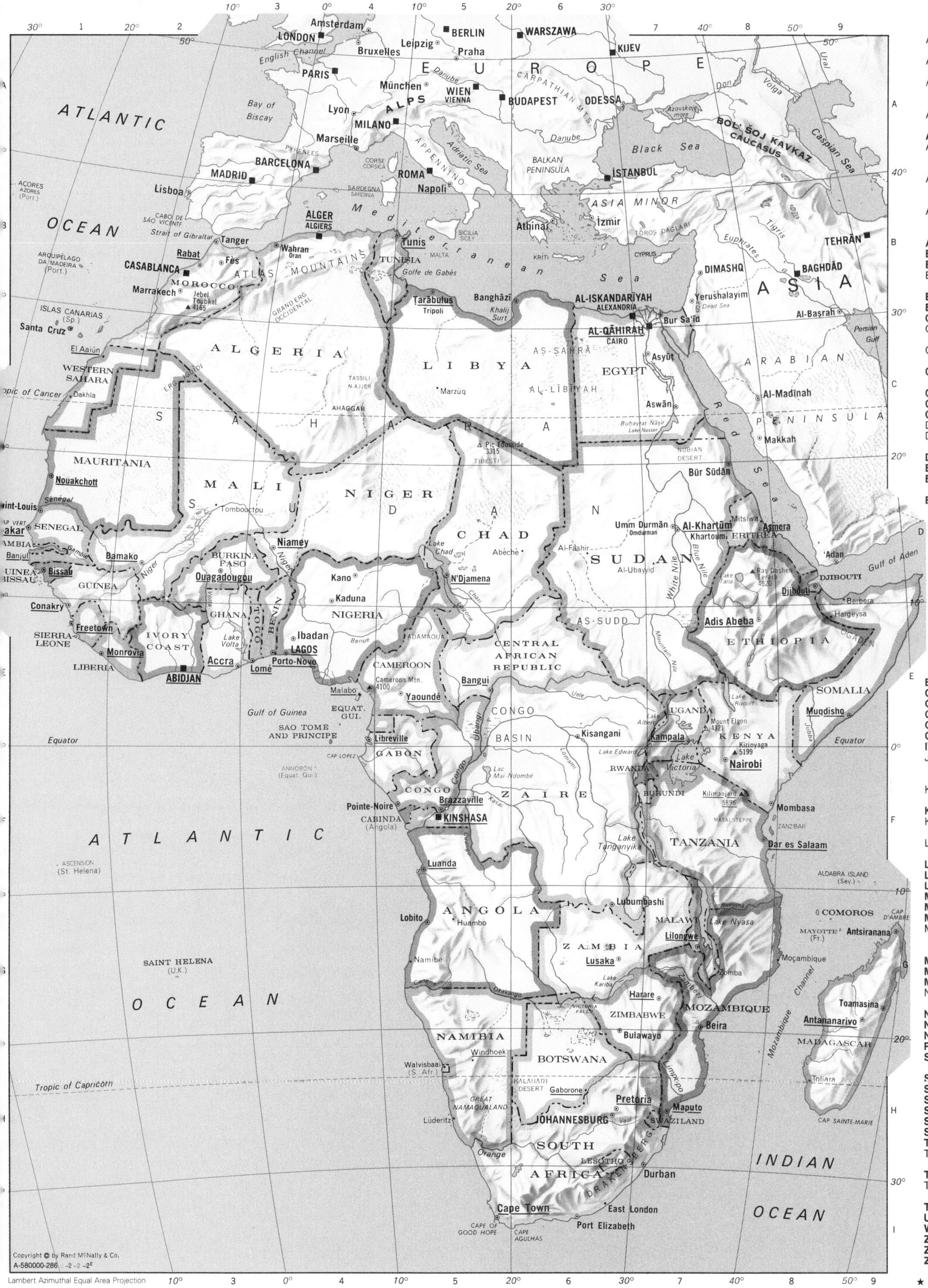

Abidjan, 1,950,000 ('83)..........E 3
Accra, 859,640 ('84) (1,250,000★)..........E 3
Adis Abeba (Addis Ababa), 1,686,300 ('88) (1,500,000★)..........E 7
Alger (Algiers), 1,507,241 ('87) (2,547,983★)...B 4
ALGERIA..........C 4
Al-Iskandarīyah (Alexandria), 2,917,327 ('86) (3,350,000★)..........B 6
Al-Kharṭūm (Khartoum), 476,218 ('83) (1,450,000★)..........D 7
Al-Qāhirah (Cairo), 6,052,836 ('86) (9,300,000★)..........B 7
ANGOLA..........G 5
BENIN..........E 4
BOTSWANA..........H 6
Brazzaville, 585,812 ('84)..........F 5
BURKINA FASO..........D 3
BURUNDI..........F 6
CAMEROON..........E 5
Cape Town, 776,617 ('85) (1,790,000★)..........I 5
Casablanca, 2,139,204 ('82) (2,475,000★)...B 3
CENTRAL AFRICAN REPUBLIC..........E 5
CHAD..........D 5
COMOROS..........G 8
CONGO..........F 5
Dakar, 1,447,642 ('88) D 2
Dar es Salaam, 1,300,000 ('84)..........F 7
DJIBOUTI..........D 8
EGYPT..........C 6
EQUATORIAL GUINEA..........E 4
ERITREA..........D 7
ETHIOPIA..........E 7
GABON..........F 5
GAMBIA..........D 2
GHANA..........E 3
GUINEA..........D 2
GUINEA-BISSAU..........D 2
IVORY COAST..........E 3
Johannesburg, 632,369 ('85) (3,650,000★)..........H 6
Kampala, 1,008,707 ('90)..........E 7
KENYA..........E 7
Kinshasa (Léopoldville), 3,000,000 ('86)..........F 5
Lagos, 1,213,000 ('87) (3,800,000★)..........E 4
LESOTHO..........H 6
LIBERIA..........E 3
LIBYA..........C 5
MADAGASCAR..........G 8
MALAWI..........G 7
MALI..........D 3
Maputo (Lourenço Marques), 1,069,727 ('89)..........H 7
MAURITANIA..........D 2
MOROCCO..........B 3
MOZAMBIQUE..........G 7
Nairobi, 1,505,000 ('90)..........F 7
NAMIBIA..........H 5
NIGER..........D 4
NIGERIA..........E 4
RWANDA..........F 6
SAO TOME AND PRINCIPE..........E 4
SENEGAL..........D 2
SIERRA LEONE..........E 2
SOMALIA..........E 8
SOUTH AFRICA..........I 6
SUDAN..........D 6
SWAZILAND..........H 7
TANZANIA..........F 7
Ṭarābulus (Tripoli), 990,697 ('84)..........B 5
TOGO..........E 4
Tunis, 596,654 ('84) (1,225,000★)..........B 5
TUNISIA..........B 4
UGANDA..........E 7
WESTERN SAHARA...C 2
ZAIRE..........F 6
ZAMBIA..........G 6
ZIMBABWE..........G 6

★ Population of metropolitan area, including suburbs.

Miles 0 200 400 600 800 1000 Mi.
Kilometers 0 400 800 1200 1600 Km.

1:40 000 000

Algeria
1987 CENSUS
Alger (Algiers), 1,507,241 (2,547,983★) . . . . . A 6
Annaba (Bône), 305,526 . . . . A 7
Batna, 181,601 . . . . . A 7
Blida, 170,935 . . . . . A 6
Constantine (Qacentina), 440,842 . . . . A 7
Oran (Wahran), 628,558 . . . . A 5
Sidi bel Abbès, 152,778 . . . . A 5
Skikda, 128,747 . . . . A 7

Benin
1984 ESTIMATE
Cotonou, 478,000 . . G 6
Porto-Novo, 164,000 G 6

Burkina Faso
1985 ESTIMATE
Bobo Dioulasso, 228,668 . . . . F 5
Ouagadougou, 441,514 . . . . F 5

Cameroon
1986 ESTIMATE
Douala, 1,029,731 . . H 7
Yaoundé, 653,670 . . H 8

Central African Republic
1984 ESTIMATE
Bangui, 473,817 . . . . H 9

Chad
1979 ESTIMATE
N'Djamena (Fort-Lamy), 303,000 . . . . F 9

Egypt
1986 CENSUS
Al-Fayyūm, 212,523 . . C12
Al-Iskandarīyah (Alexandria), 2,917,327 (3,350,000★) B11
Al-Manṣūrah, 316,870 (375,000★) B12
Al-Qāhirah (Cairo), 6,052,836 (9,300,000★) B12
Al-Uqṣur (Luxor), 125,404 . . . . C12
As-Suways (Suez), 326,820 . . . . C12
Aswān, 191,461 . . . . . . D12
Asyūṭ, 273,191 . . . . . . C12
Banī Suwayf, 151,813 C12
Būr Sa'īd (Port Said), 399,793 . . . . B12
Cairo *see* Al-Qāhirah B12
Qinā, 119,794 . . . . . . C12
Ṭanṭā, 334,505 . . . . . . B12

Equatorial Guinea
1983 CENSUS
Malabo, 31,630 . . . . . . H 7

Gambia
1983 CENSUS
Banjul, 44,536 (95,000★) . . . . F 2

Ghana
1984 CENSUS
Accra, 859,640 (1,250,000★) . . . . . . G 5
Cape Coast, 86,620 . . G 5
Kumasi, 348,880 (600,000★) . . . . . . G 5
Sekondi-Takoradi, 93,882 . . . . H 5
Tamale, 136,828 (168,091★) . . . . . . G 5

Guinea
1986 ESTIMATE
Conakry, 800,000 . . . G 3
Kankan, 100,000 . . . . F 4

Guinea-Bissau
1988 ESTIMATE
Bissau, 125,000 . . . . F 2

Ivory Coast
1983 ESTIMATE
Abidjan, 1,950,000 . . G 5
Bouaké, 275,000 . . . . G 4
Yamoussoukro, 80,000 . . . . G 4

★ Population of metropolitan area, including suburbs.

Kilometers 0 200 400 600 Km.
Miles 0 200 400 600 Mi.

1:16 000 000

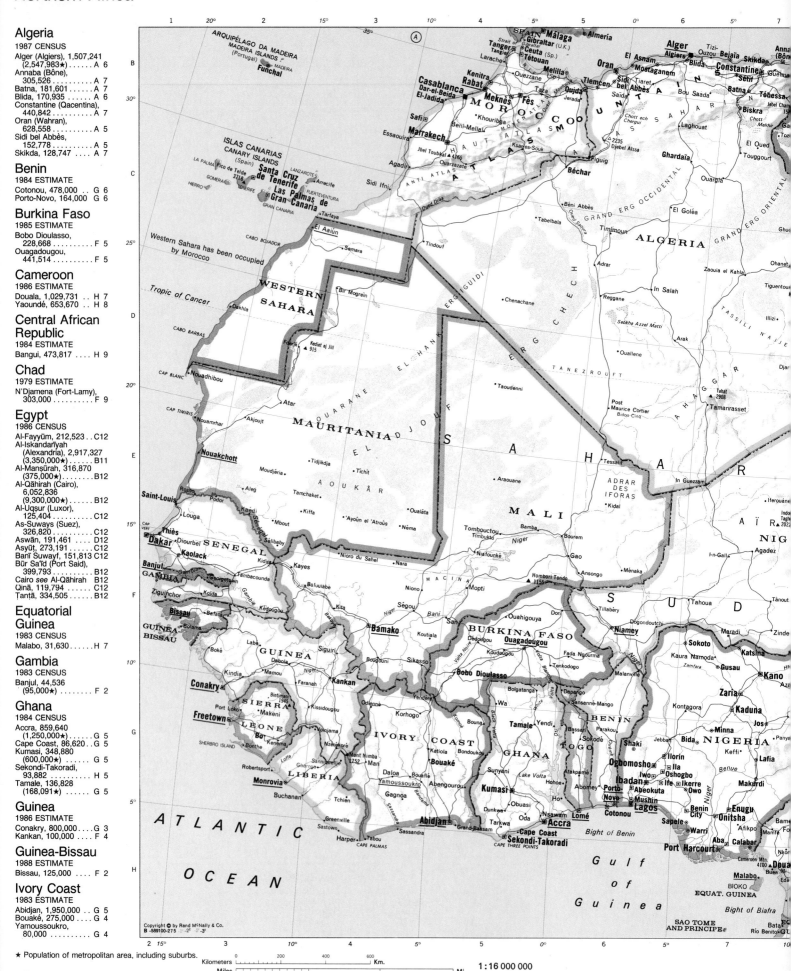

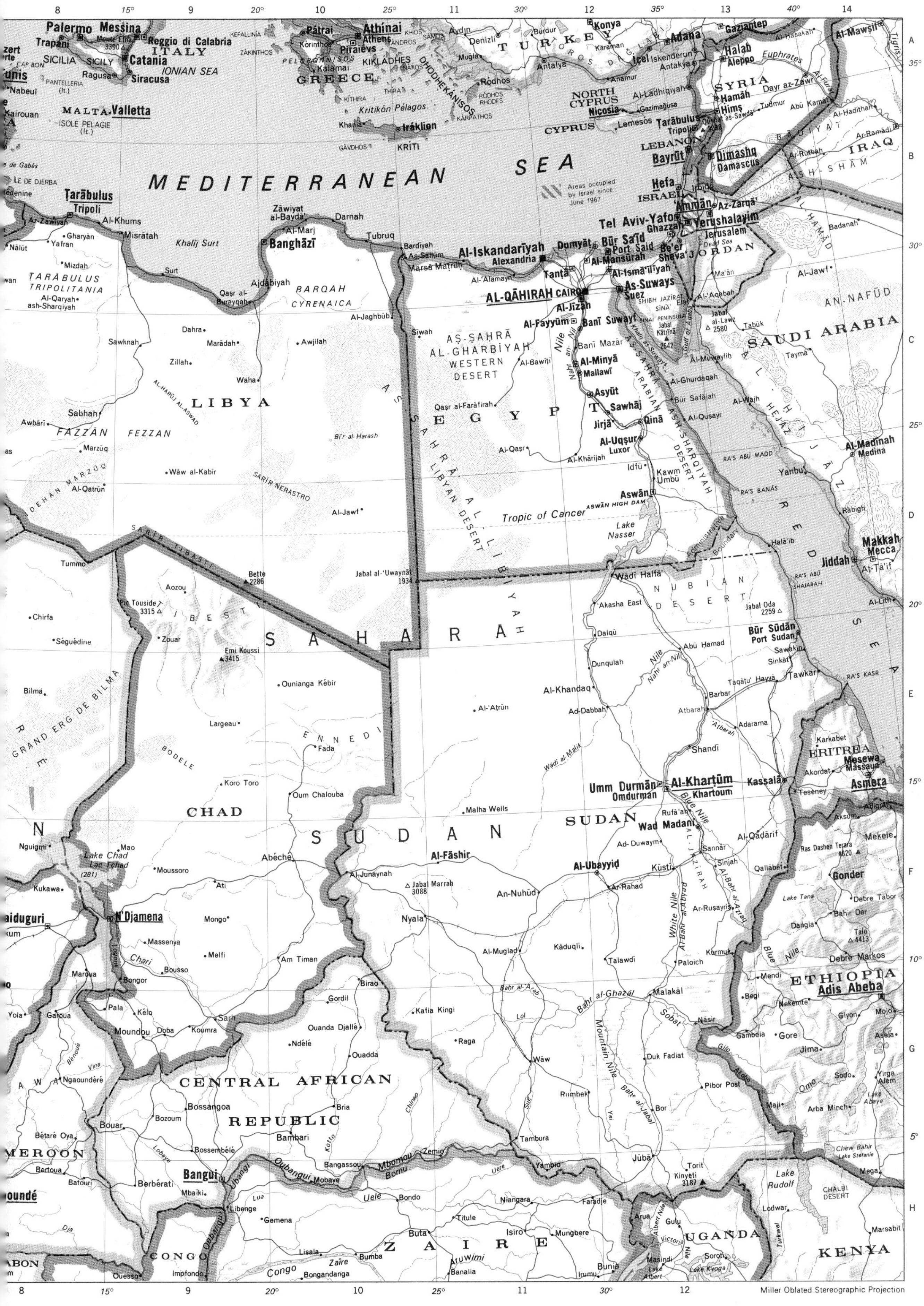

Liberia
1986 ESTIMATE
Monrovia, 465,000 .. G 3

Libya
1984 CENSUS
Banghāzī, 435,886 .. B10
Ṭarābulus (Tripoli), 990,697 .... B 8
Tripoli *see* Ṭarābulus B 8

Mali
1987 CENSUS
Bamako, 646,163 .... F 4
Tombouctou (Timbuktu), 31,925 .... E 5

Mauritania
1987 ESTIMATE
Nouakchott, 285,000 E 2

Morocco
1982 CENSUS
Casablanca (Dar-el-Beida), 2,139,204 (2,475,000★)...... B 4
Fès, 448,823 (535,000★)........ B 5
Marrakech, 439,728 (535,000★)........ B 4
Meknès, 319,783 (375,000★)........ B 4
Oujda, 260,082 ...... B 5
Rabat, 518,616 (980,000★)........ B 4
Safi, 197,309 ...... B 4
Tanger (Tangier), 266,346 (370,000★)........ A 4

Niger
1988 ESTIMATE
Niamey, 398,265 .... F 6

Nigeria
1987 ESTIMATE
Aba, 239,800 ...... G 7
Abeokuta, 341,300 .. G 6
Benin City, 183,200 .. G 7
Enugu, 252,500 .... G 7
Ibadan, 1,144,000 .. G 6
Ilorin, 380,000 ...... G 6
Iwo, 289,100 .... G 6
Kaduna, 273,200 .... F 7
Kano, 538,300 ...... F 7
Lagos, 1,213,000 (3,800,000★)...... G 6
Maiduguri, 255,100 .. F 8
Ogbomosho, 582,900 G 6
Onitsha, 298,200 .... G 7
Oshogbo, 380,800 .. G 6
Port Harcourt, 327,300 .... H 7
Zaria, 302,800 ...... F 7

Senegal
1988 CENSUS
Dakar, 1,447,642 .... F 2
Saint-Louis, 160,689 E 2

Sierra Leone
1985 CENSUS
Freetown, 469,776 (525,000★) ...... G 3

Sudan
1983 CENSUS
Al-Kharṭūm (Khartoum), 476,218 (1,450,000★)...... E12
Al-Ubayyiḍ, 140,000 .. F12
Būr Sūdān (Port Sudan), 206,727 .... E13
Khartoum *see* Al-Kharṭūm E12
Umm Durmān (Omdurman), 526,287 .... E12

Togo
1984 ESTIMATE
Lomé, 400,000 ...... G 6

Tunisia
1984 CENSUS
Bizerte, 94,509 ...... A 7
Sfax, 231,911 (310,000★)........ B 8
Tunis, 596,654 (1,225,000★)...... A 8

Western Sahara
1982 CENSUS
El Aaiún, 93,875 .... C 3

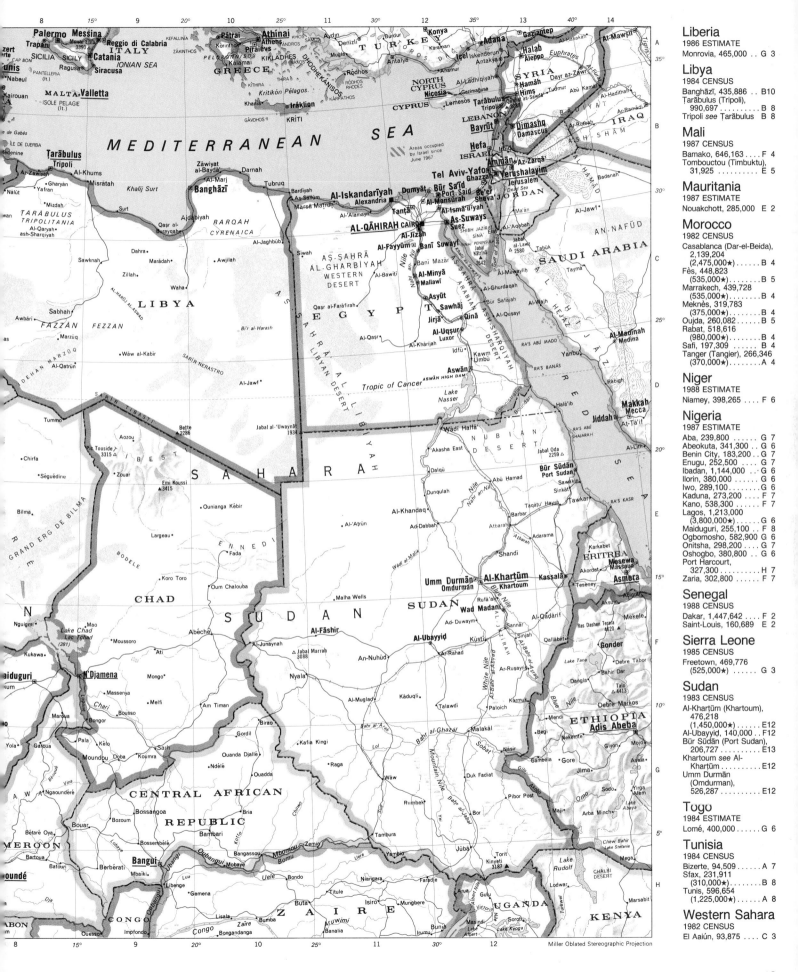

Southern Africa

Angola
1983 ESTIMATE
Benguela, 155,000 . . D 2
Huambo, 203,000 . . D 3
Lobito, 150,000 . . . . D 2
Luanda,
1,459,900('89) . . . . C 2
Namibe, 100,000('81) E 2

Botswana
1987 ESTIMATE
Gaborone, 107,677 . . F 5

Burundi
1986 ESTIMATE
Bujumbura, 273,000 B 5

Comoros
1990 ESTIMATE
Moroni, 23,432 . . . . D 8

Congo
1984 CENSUS
Brazzaville, 585,812 B 3
Pointe-Noire, 294,203 B 2

Gabon
1985 ESTIMATE
Libreville, 235,700 . . A 1
Port-Gentil, 124,400 . . B 1

Kenya
1990 ESTIMATE
Mombasa, 537,000 . . B 7
Nairobi, 1,505,000 . . B 7
Nakuru, 101,700('84) B 7

Lesotho
1986 CENSUS
Maseru, 109,382 . . . . G 5

Madagascar
1984 ESTIMATE
Antananarivo,
663,000('85) . . . . E 9
Antsiranana, 100,000 D 9
Fianarantsoa, 130,000 F 9
Mahajanga, 85,000 . . E 9
Toamasina, 100,000 E 9

Malawi
1987 CENSUS
Blantyre, 331,588 . . E 7
Lilongwe, 233,973 . . D 6
Zomba, 42,878 . . . . E 7

Mauritius
1987 ESTIMATE
Port Louis, 139,730
(420,000★) F11

Mayotte
1985 ESTIMATE
Dzaoudzi, 5,865
(6,979★) . . . . D 9

Mozambique
1989 ESTIMATE
Beira, 291,604 . . . . . . E 6
Maputo (Lourenço
Marques),
1,069,727 . . . . . . G 6
Xai-Xai, 51,620('86) . . G 6

Namibia
1988 ESTIMATE
Windhoek, 114,500 . . F 3

Reunion
1982 CENSUS
Saint-Denis, 84,400
(109,072▲) F11

Rwanda
1983 ESTIMATE
Kigali, 181,600 . . . . B 6

Sao Tome and Principe
1970 CENSUS
São Tomé, 17,380 . . A 1

Seychelles
1984 ESTIMATE
Victoria, 23,000 . . . . B11

★ Population of metropolitan area, including suburbs.
▲ Population of entire district, including rural area.

Miller Oblated Stereographic Projection

Kilometers 0 200 400 600 Km.
Miles 0 200 400 600 Mi.

1:16 000 000

Copyright © by Rand McNally & Co.
B-589200-264

Somalia
1984 ESTIMATE
Kismayu, 70,000 . . . . B 8

South Africa
1985 CENSUS
Bloemfontein, 104,381 (235,000★) . . . . . . G 5
Cape Town (Kaapstad), 776,617 (1,790,000★) . . . . H 3
Durban, 634,301 (1,550,000★) . . . . G 6
East London (Oos-Londen), 85,699 (320,000★) . . . . . . H 5
Germiston, 116,718 . . G 5
Johannesburg, 632,369 (3,650,000★) . . . . G 5
Kimberley, 74,061 (145,000★) . . . . . . G 4
King William's Town, 16,123 (48,300★) . . H 5
Klerksdorp, 48,947 (205,000★) . . . . . . G 5
Ladysmith, 25,102 (31,670★) . . . . . . G 5
Pietermaritzburg, 133,809 (230,000★) . . . . . . G 6
Port Elizabeth, 272,844 (690,000★) . . . . . . H 5
Potchefstroom, 43,766 (78,865★) . . . . . . G 5
Pretoria, 443,059 (960,000★) . . . . . . G 5
Springs, 68,235 . . . . G 5
Uitenhage, 54,987 . . H 5
Vereeniging, 60,584 (525,000★) . . . . . . G 5
Walvisbaai (Walvis Bay), 9,687 (16,607★) . . F 2
Welkom, 54,488 (215,000★) . . . . . . G 5

Swaziland
1986 CENSUS
Mbabane, 38,290 . . G 6

Tanzania
1984 ESTIMATE
Arusha, 69,000 . . . . B 7
Dar es Salaam, 1,300,000 . . . . . C 7
Mwanza, 110,611('78) B 6
Tanga, 121,000 . . . . C 7
Zanzibar, 133,000('85) C 7

Uganda
1990 ESTIMATE
Kampala, 1,008,707 . . A 6

Zaire
1984 CENSUS
Boma, 88,556 . . . . . . C 2
Bukavu, 171,064 . . . . B 5
Kalemie (Albertville), 70,694 . . . . C 5
Kananga (Luluabourg), 290,898 . . . . C 4
Kikwit, 146,784 . . . . C 3
Kinshasa (Léopoldville), 3,000,000('86) . . . . B 3
Kisangani (Stanleyville), 282,650 . . . . A 5
Kolwezi, 201,382 . . . . D 5
Likasi (Jadotville), 194,465 . . . . D 5
Lubumbashi (Élisabethville), 543,268 . . . . D 5
Matadi, 144,742 . . . . C 2
Mbandaka (Coquilhatville), 125,263 . . . . A 3
Mbuji-Mayi (Bakwanga), 423,363 . . . . C 4

Zambia
1980 CENSUS
Chingola, 130,872 . . D 5
Kabwe (Broken Hill), 127,420 . . . . D 5
Kitwe, 207,500 (283,962★) . . . . . . D 5
Livingstone, 61,296 . . E 5
Luanshya, 61,600 (113,422★) . . . . . . D 5
Lusaka, 535,830 . . . . E 5
Mufulira, 77,100 (138,824★) . . . . . . D 5
Ndola, 250,490 . . . . D 5

Zimbabwe
1983 ESTIMATE
Bulawayo, 429,000 . . F 5
Harare, 681,000 (890,000★) . . . . . . E 6

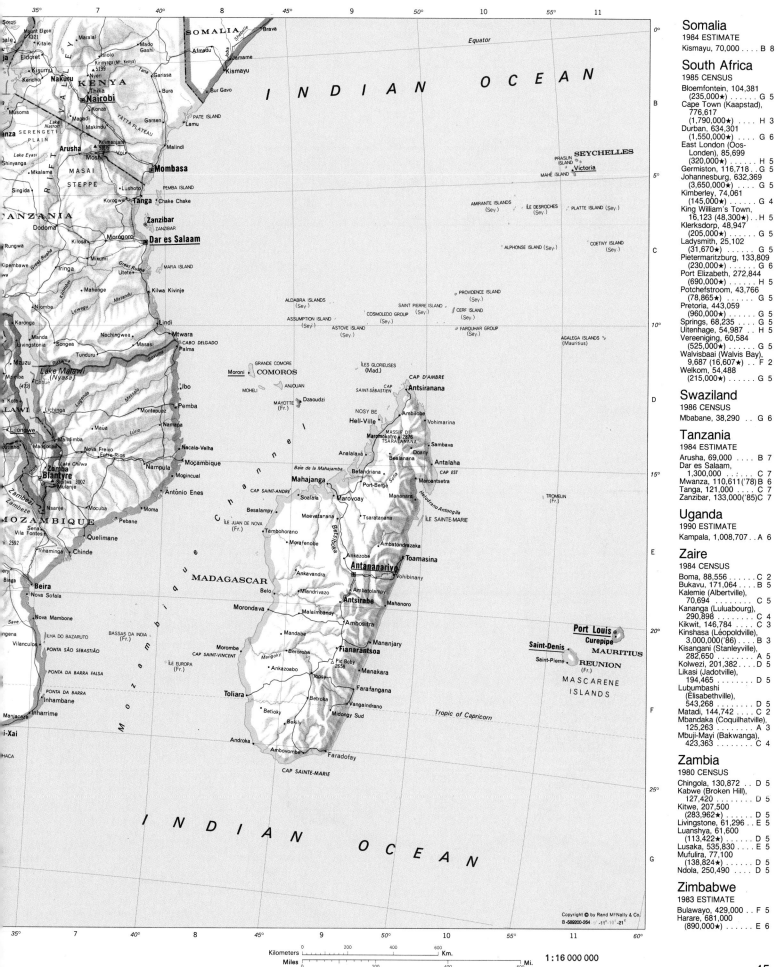

Eastern Africa and Middle East

Bahrain
1981 CENSUS
Al-Manāmah, 115,054 (224,643★) . . . . . . C 5

Djibouti
1976 ESTIMATE
Djibouti, 120,000 . . . F 3

Eritrea
1988 ESTIMATE
Asmara, 319,353 . . . E 2

Ethiopia
1988 ESTIMATE
Adis Abeba, 1,686,300 (1,500,000★) . . . . G 2
Asmera, 319,353 . . . E 2

Iran
1986 CENSUS
Esfahān, 986,753 (1,175,000★) . . . B 5
Shīrāz, 848,289 . . . C 5

Iraq
1985 ESTIMATE
Al-Basrah, 616,700 . . B 4
Baghdād, 3,841,268('87) . . . B 3

Kuwait
1985 CENSUS
Al-Kuwayt, 44,335 (1,375,000★) . . . C 4

Oman
1981 ESTIMATE
Masqat (Muscat), 50,000 . . . . D 6

Qatar
1986 CENSUS
Ad-Dawhah (Doha), 217,294 (310,000★) C 5

Saudi Arabia
1980 ESTIMATE
Al-Madīnah (Medina), 290,000 . . . . D 2
Ar-Riyād (Riyadh), 1,250,000 . . . . . . D 4
Jiddah, 1,300,000 . . D 2
Makkah (Mecca), 550,000 . . . . D 2

Somalia
1984 ESTIMATE
Muqdisho, 600,000 . . H 4

United Arab Emirates
1980 CENSUS
Abū Zaby, 242,975 . . D 5
Dubayy (Dubai), 265,702 . . . . C 6

Yemen
1984 ESTIMATE
'Adan (Aden), 176,100 (318,000★) . . . . . . F 4
Şan'ā', 427,150('86) E 3

★ Population of metropolitan area, including suburbs.

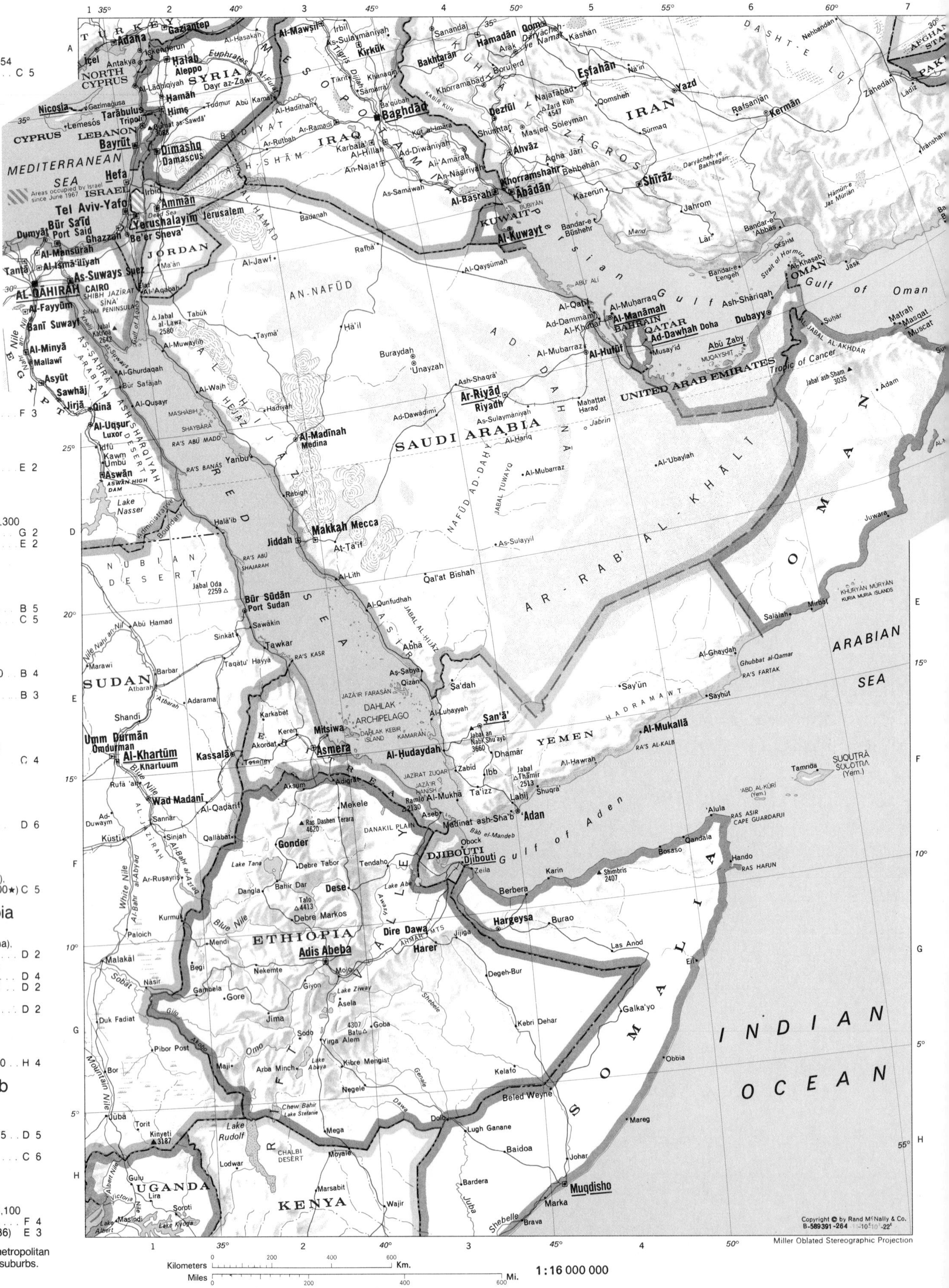

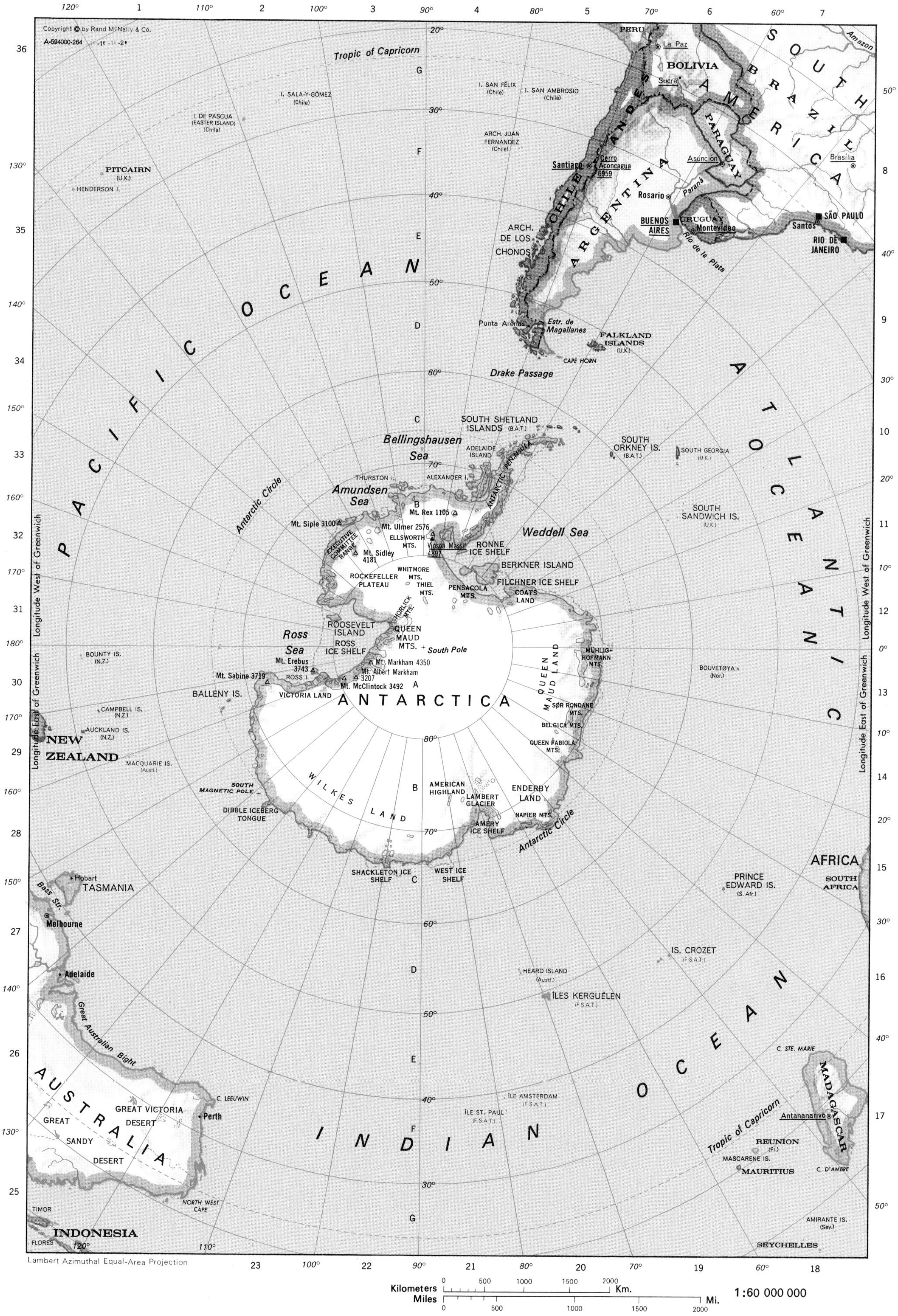
Copyright © by Rand McNally & Co.
A-594000-264
Tropic of Capricorn
PACIFIC OCEAN
ATLANTIC OCEAN
INDIAN OCEAN
ANTARCTICA
SOUTH AMERICA
BOLIVIA
La Paz
Sucre
PERU
BRAZIL
PARAGUAY
Asunción
Brasília
CHILE
ANDES
ARGENTINA
Santiago
Cerro Aconcagua 6959
Rosario
Paraná
BUENOS AIRES
URUGUAY
Montevideo
Río de la Plata
SÃO PAULO
Santos
RIO DE JANEIRO
Amazon
I. SALA-Y-GÓMEZ (Chile)
I. DE PASCUA (EASTER ISLAND) (Chile)
I. SAN FÉLIX (Chile)
I. SAN AMBROSIO (Chile)
ARCH. JUAN FERNÁNDEZ (Chile)
PITCAIRN (U.K.)
HENDERSON I.
ARCH. DE LOS CHONOS
Punta Arenas
Estr. de Magallanes
FALKLAND ISLANDS (U.K.)
CAPE HORN
Drake Passage
SOUTH SHETLAND ISLANDS (B.A.T.)
SOUTH ORKNEY IS. (B.A.T.)
SOUTH GEORGIA (U.K.)
SOUTH SANDWICH IS. (U.K.)
Bellingshausen Sea
ADELAIDE ISLAND
ALEXANDER I.
THURSTON I.
ANTARCTIC PENINSULA
Amundsen Sea
Antarctic Circle
Mt. Rex 1105
Mt. Siple 3100
Mt. Ulmer 2576
ELLSWORTH MTS.
Vinson Massif 4897
EXECUTIVE COMMITTEE RANGE
Mt. Sidley 4181
RONNE ICE SHELF
Weddell Sea
BERKNER ISLAND
WHITMORE MTS.
ROCKEFELLER PLATEAU
THIEL MTS.
PENSACOLA MTS.
FILCHNER ICE SHELF
COATS LAND
HORLICK MTS.
ROOSEVELT ISLAND
Ross Sea
ROSS ICE SHELF
QUEEN MAUD MTS.
South Pole
Mt. Erebus 3743
ROSS I.
Mt. Markham 4350
Mt. Albert Markham 3207
Mt. McClintock 3492
Mt. Sabine 3719
BALLENY IS.
VICTORIA LAND
QUEEN MAUD LAND
MÜHLIG-HOFMANN MTS.
SØR RONDANE MTS.
BELGICA MTS.
QUEEN FABIOLA MTS.
BOUVETØYA (Nor.)
BOUNTY IS. (N.Z.)
CAMPBELL IS. (N.Z.)
AUCKLAND IS. (N.Z.)
NEW ZEALAND
MACQUARIE IS. (Austl.)
SOUTH MAGNETIC POLE
DIBBLE ICEBERG TONGUE
WILKES LAND
AMERICAN HIGHLAND
LAMBERT GLACIER
ENDERBY LAND
NAPIER MTS.
AMERY ICE SHELF
SHACKLETON ICE SHELF
WEST ICE SHELF
AFRICA
SOUTH AFRICA
PRINCE EDWARD IS. (S. Afr.)
IS. CROZET (F.S.A.T.)
HEARD ISLAND (Austl.)
ÎLES KERGUÉLEN (F.S.A.T.)
ÎLE AMSTERDAM (F.S.A.T.)
ÎLE ST. PAUL (F.S.A.T.)
Hobart
TASMANIA
Bass Str.
Melbourne
Adelaide
Great Australian Bight
AUSTRALIA
C. LEEUWIN
Perth
GREAT VICTORIA DESERT
GREAT SANDY DESERT
NORTH WEST CAPE
TIMOR
INDONESIA
FLORES
C. STE. MARIE
MADAGASCAR
Antananarivo
C. D'AMBRE
REUNION (Fr.)
MASCARENE IS.
MAURITIUS
AMIRANTE IS. (Sey.)
SEYCHELLES
Longitude West of Greenwich
Longitude East of Greenwich
Lambert Azimuthal Equal-Area Projection
Kilometers
Miles
Km.
Mi.
1:60 000 000

Antarctica

Adelaide Island . . . . C 5
Albert Markham, Mount A29
Alexander Island . . . . B 5
American Highland . . B21
Amery Ice Shelf C20
Amsterdam, Île (island) F20
Amundsen Sea . . . . B 1
Antarctic Circle C34
Antarctic Peninsula . . B 6
Auckland Islands D29
Balleny Islands C29
Belgica Mountains . . B16
Bellingshausen Sea . . C 3
Berkner Island . . . . . . B 8
Bounty Islands D30
Bouvetøya (island) . . D13
Campbell Islands D29
Coats Land (region) . . B10
Crozet, Îles (islands) . . E18
Dibble Iceberg Tongue C26
Drake Passage . . . . D 5
Ellsworth Mountains B 3
Enderby Land (region) B18
Erebus, Mount B29
Executive Committee Range B35
Filchner Ice Shelf . . . . B 9
Heard Island D20
Horlick Mountains . . A35
Kerguélen, Îles (islands) E19
Lambert Glacier B20
Macquarie Islands . . D28
Markham, Mount A29
McClintock, Mount . . A28
Mühlighofmann Mountains B13
Napier Mountains . . C18
Pensacola Mountains A 7
Prince Edward Islands E16
Queen Fabiola Mountains B16
Queen Maud Land (region) B14
Queen Maud Mountains A33
Rex, Mount . . . . B 5
Rockefeller Plateau . . A35
Ronne Ice Shelf . . . . B 7
Roosevelt Island B32
Ross Ice Shelf A30
Ross Island B29
Ross Sea B31
Sabine, Mount B29
Saint Paul, Île (island) F21
Shackleton Ice Shelf C22
Sidley, Mount B36
Siple, Mount B36
Sør Rondane Mountains B15
South Georgia (island) . . . . D 9
South Magnetic Pole C26
South Orkney Islands . . . . D 8
South Pole . . . . A 1
South Sandwich Islands D10
South Shetland Islands . . . . C 5
Thiel Mountains . . . . A 3
Thurston Island . . . . B 2
Ulmer, Mount . . . . . . B 4
Victoria Land (region) B28
Vinson Massif (mountain) . . . . . . B 4
Weddell Sea . . . . . . B 8
West Ice Shelf C21
Whitmore Mountains A 2
Wilkes Land (region) B25

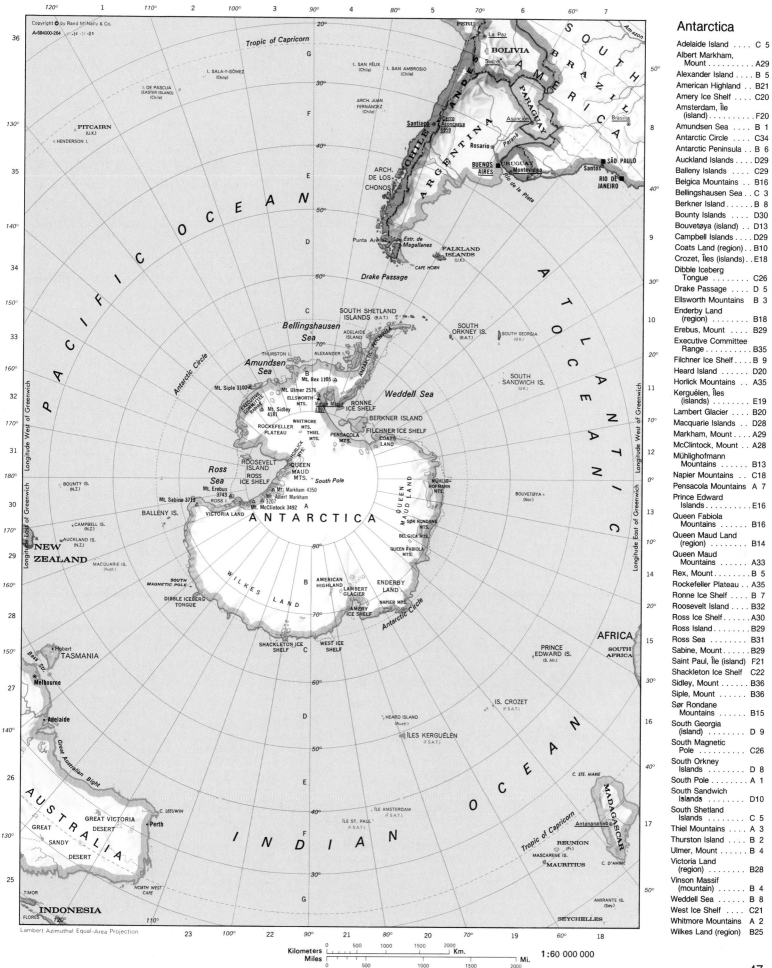

Pacific Ocean

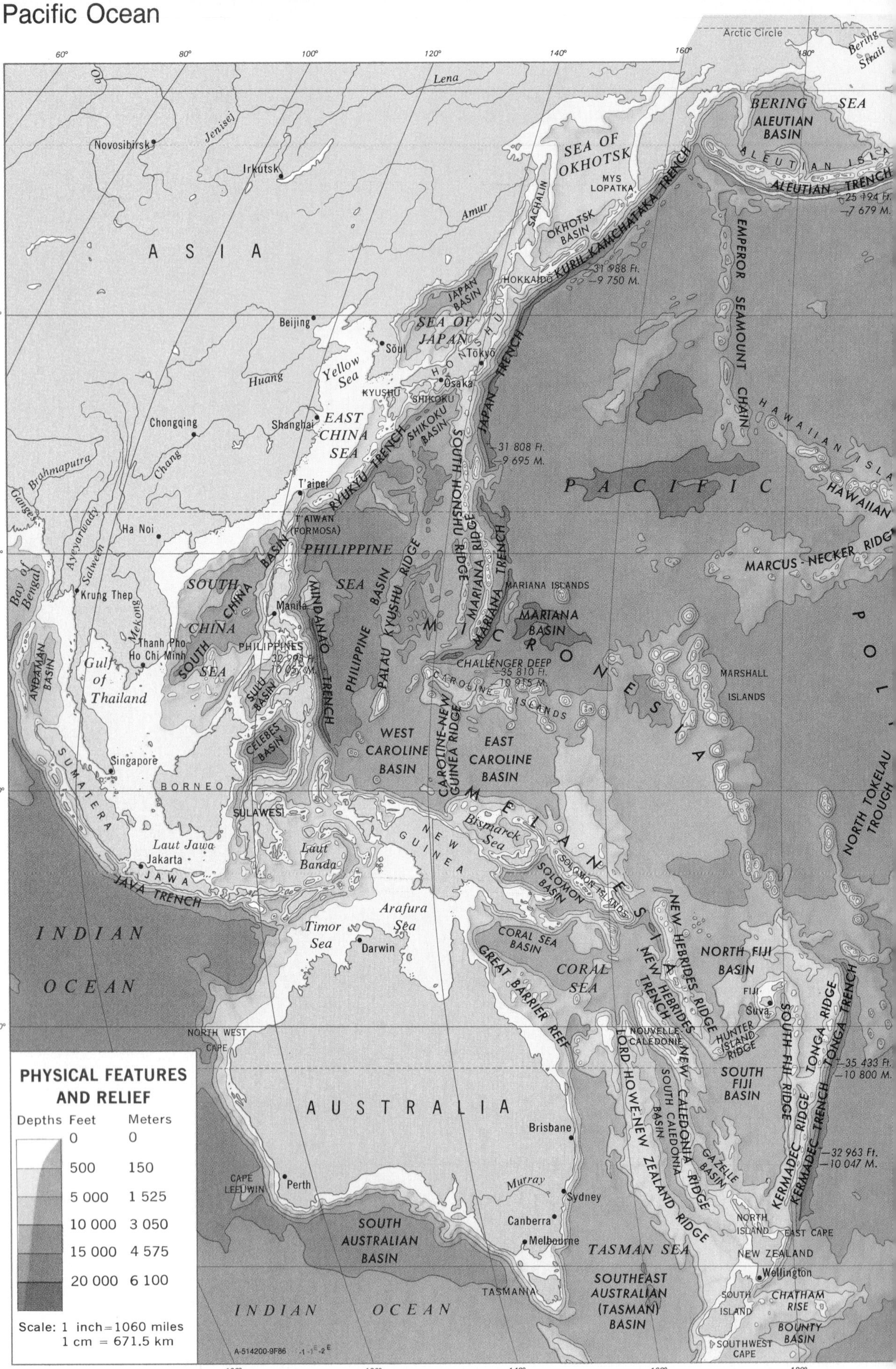

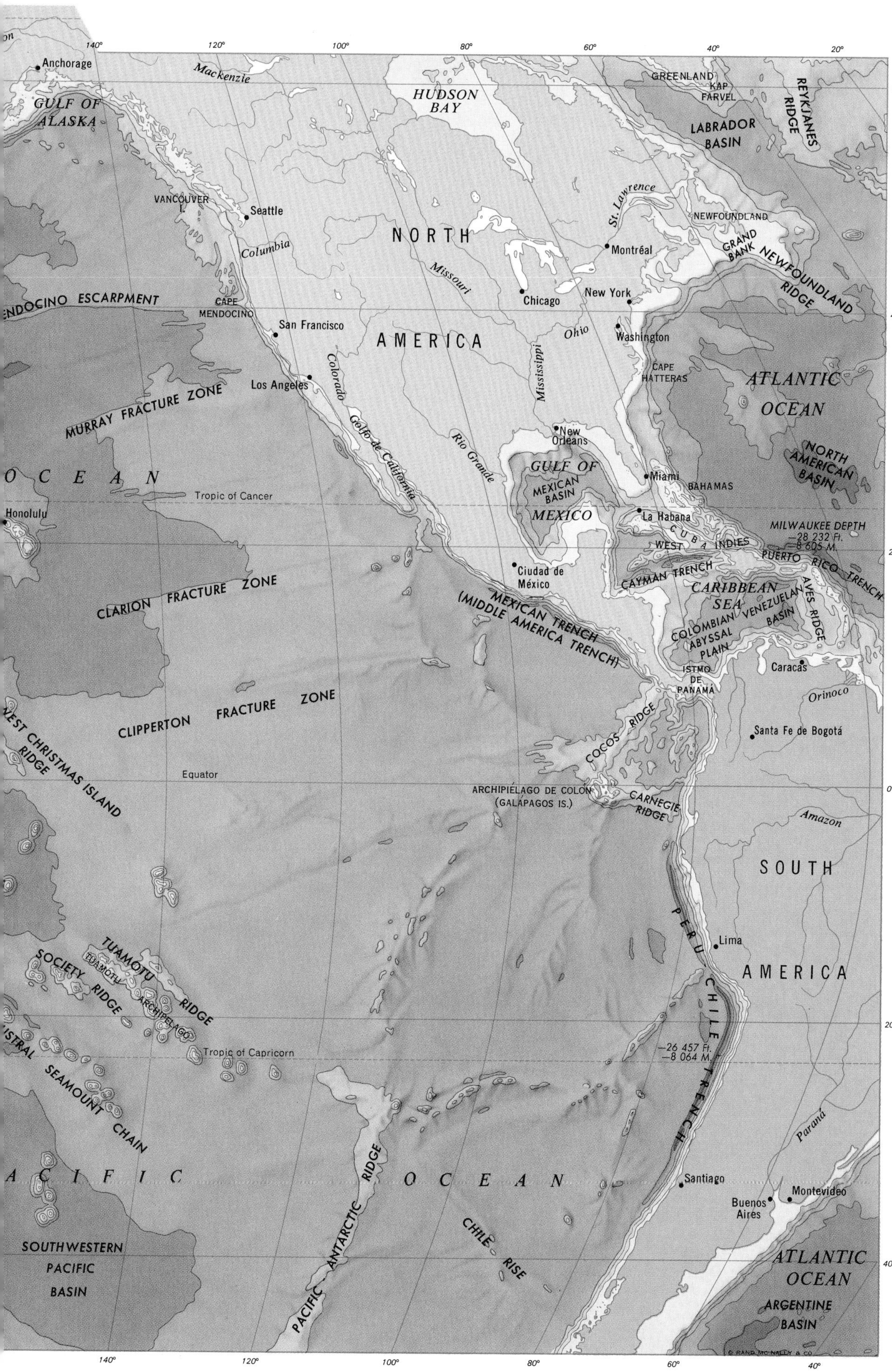

Anchorage
GULF OF ALASKA
Mackenzie
HUDSON BAY
GREENLAND
KAP FARVEL
REYKJANES RIDGE
LABRADOR BASIN
VANCOUVER I.
Seattle
St. Lawrence
NEWFOUNDLAND
NORTH
Columbia
Montréal
GRAND BANK
NEWFOUNDLAND RIDGE
Missouri
MENDOCINO ESCARPMENT
CAPE MENDOCINO
Chicago
New York
San Francisco
Ohio
Washington
AMERICA
Colorado
Mississippi
CAPE HATTERAS
ATLANTIC OCEAN
MURRAY FRACTURE ZONE
Los Angeles
Golfo de California
Rio Grande
New Orleans
NORTH AMERICAN BASIN
OCEAN
GULF OF MEXICO
MEXICAN BASIN
Miami
BAHAMAS
Tropic of Cancer
Honolulu
La Habana
CUBA
MILWAUKEE DEPTH
−28 232 Ft.
−8 605 M.
WEST INDIES
PUERTO RICO TRENCH
Ciudad de México
CAYMAN TRENCH
CARIBBEAN SEA
CLARION FRACTURE ZONE
MEXICAN TRENCH (MIDDLE AMERICA TRENCH)
COLOMBIAN ABYSSAL PLAIN
VENEZUELAN BASIN
AVES RIDGE
ISTMO DE PANAMÁ
Caracas
Orinoco
CLIPPERTON FRACTURE ZONE
WEST CHRISTMAS ISLAND RIDGE
COCOS RIDGE
Santa Fe de Bogotá
Equator
ARCHIPIÉLAGO DE COLÓN (GALÁPAGOS IS.)
CARNEGIE RIDGE
Amazon
SOUTH
PERU
Lima
AMERICA
TUAMOTU RIDGE
SOCIETY RIDGE
TUAMOTU ARCHIPELAGO
CHILE TRENCH
−26 457 Ft.
−8 064 M.
Tropic of Capricorn
AUSTRAL SEAMOUNT CHAIN
Paraná
PACIFIC OCEAN
PACIFIC ANTARCTIC RIDGE
Santiago
Buenos Aires
Montevideo
CHILE RISE
SOUTHWESTERN PACIFIC BASIN
ATLANTIC OCEAN
ARGENTINE BASIN
© RAND McNALLY & CO.
140°
120°
100°
80°
60°
40°
20°
0°

Australia

1989 ESTIMATE

Adelaide, 12,340 (1,036,747★) . . . . . . F 7
Albany, 14,958 . . . . . . G 3
Albury, 40,730 (66,530★) . . . . G 9
Alice Springs, 23,600 . . . . D 6
Ararat, 8,015('86) . . . . G 8
Armidale, 21,600 . . . . F10
Augusta, 933('86) . . . . F 3
Ballarat, 36,680 (80,090★) . . . . G 8
Barcaldine, 1,427('86) . . . . D 9
Bendigo, 32,050 (67,920★) . . . . G 8
Blackall, 1,497('86) . . D 9
Bombala, 1,458('86) . . G 9
Bordertown, 2,318('86) . . . . G 8
Bourke, 3,018('86) . . F 9
Bowen, 7,705('86) . . C 9
Brisbane, 744,828 (1,273,511★) E10
Broken Hill, 22,550 . . F 8
Broome, 5,778('86) . . C 4
Bunbury, 26,398 . . . . F 3
Bundaberg, 33,024 (45,161★) D10
Burketown, 232('86) . . . . C 7
Burnie, 20,665('86) . . H 9
Busselton, 7,784('86) . . . . F 3
Cairns, 42,839 (80,875★) . . . . C 9
Camooweal, 315('86) . . . . C 7
Canberra, 247,194 (271,362★)('86) . . . . G 9
Carnarvon, 6,847('86) . . . . D 2
Ceduna, 2,877('86) . . F 6
Cessnock, 43,870 . . . . F10
Charleville, 3,588('86) . . . . E 9
Charters Towers, 7,208('86) . . . . D 9
Cloncurry, 2,297('86) . . . . D 8
Coffs Harbour, 47,890 . . . . F10
Cooktown, 964('86) . . C 9
Coolgardie, 989('86) . . F 4
Cooma, 7,406('86) . . G 9
Croydon, 229('86) . . C 8
Cunnamulla, 1,697('86) . . . . E 9
Dampier, 2,201('86) . . D 3
Darwin, 63,900 (72,937★) . . . . B 6
Derby, 3,258('86) . . . . C 4
Devonport, 25,370 . . H 9
Dongara, 1,496('86) . . E 2
Dubbo, 32,230 . . . . . . F 9
Elizabeth, 29,998 . . . . F 7
Emerald, 5,982('86) . . D 9
Esperance, 6,440('86) . . . . F 4
Geelong, 13,190 (148,980★) . . . . . . G 8
Geraldton, 20,968 . . . . E 2
Gladstone, 22,033('86) D10
Glen Innes, 5,971('86) E10
Goondiwindi, 4,103('86) E10
Goulburn, 21,580 . . . . F 9
Grafton, 15,890 . . . . . . E10
Griffith, 13,630('86) . . F 9
Gympie, 10,772('86) . . E10
Halls Creek, 1,182('86) . . . . C 5
Hay, 2,961('86) . . . . . . F 8
Hobart, 47,280 (181,210★) . . . . H 9
Home Hill, 3,286('86) . . . . C 9
Horsham, 12,850 . . . . G 8
Hughenden, 1,791('86) . . . . D 8
Ingham, 5,202('86) . . C 9
Inverell, 9,693('86) . . E10
Ipswich, 75,283 . . . . . . E10
Kalgoorlie, 26,813 . . . . F 4
Kingaroy, 6,362('86) . . E10
Launceston, 32,150 (92,350★) . . . . H 9
Leonora, 1,004('86) . . E 4
Lismore, 39,450 . . . . E10
Longreach, 3,159('86) . . . . D 8
Mackay, 22,583 (50,885★) . . . . D 9
Maitland, 47,280 . . . . F10
Marble Bar, 332('86) D 3
Mareeba, 6,614('86) . . C 9
Marree, 300('76) . . . . E 7
Meekatharra, 1,018('86) . . . . E 3

★ Population of metropolitan area, including suburbs.

Kilometers 0 200 400 600 Km.
Miles 0 200 400 600 Mi.

1:16 000 000

Lambert Conformal Conic Projection

Melbourne, 55,300
(3,039,100★) . . . . . . G 8
Mildura, 20,512('86) . . F 8
Mitchell, 1,212('86) . . E 9
Moora, 1,469('86) . . . . F 3
Moree, 10,215('86) . . E 9
Morwell, 16,880 . . . . G 9
Mount Gambier, 22,194
(27,228★) . . . . G 8
Mount Isa, 24,023 . . D 7
Mount Magnet,
1,000('86) . . . . E 3
Mullewa, 758('86) . . . . E 3
Murwillumbah,
7,678('86) E10
Nambour, 9,579('86) E10
Naracoorte,
4,636('86) . . . . G 8
Newcastle, 130,940
(425,610★) F10
New Norfolk,
6,152('86) . . . . H 9
Normanton,
1,109('86) . . . . C 8
Norseman,
1,775('86) . . . . F 4
Northam, 6,377('86) . . F 3
Nyngan, 2,502('86) . . F 9
Onslow, 750('86) . . . . D 3
Oodnadatta, 200('76) E 7
Orange, 32,980 . . . . . . F 9
Pemberton, 802('86) . . F 3
Perth, 82,413
(1,158,387★) . . . . . . F 3
Peterborough,
2,239('86) . . . . F 7
Port Augusta,
15,752 . . . . F 7
Port Hedland,
13,069('86) . . . . D 3
Port Lincoln, 12,941 . . F 7
Port Macquarie,
22,884('86) F10
Port Pirie, 15,210 . . . . F 7
Quilpie, 780('86) . . . . E 8
Ravensthorpe,
299('86) . . . . F 3
Richmond, 704('86) . . D 8
Rockhampton, 58,890
(61,694★) D10
Roebourne,
1,269('86) . . . . D 3
Roma, 6,069('86) . . . . E 9
Saint George,
2,323('86) . . . . E 9
Sale, 13,800 . . . . G 9
Shepparton, 26,420
(39,700★) . . . . G 9
Smithton, 3,414('86) . . H 9
Southern Cross,
898('86) . . . . F 3
Swan Hill,
8,831('86) . . . . G 8
Sydney, 9,800
(3,623,550★) F10
Tamworth, 34,430 . . F10
Taree, 38,760 . . . . . . F10
Tennant Creek,
3,503('86) . . . . C 6
Tenterfield,
3,370('86) E10
Theodore, 576('86) . . D10
Toowoomba,
81,071 . . . . E10
Townsville, 83,339
(111,972★) . . . . C 9
Wagga Wagga,
52,180 . . . . G 9
Walgett, 2,151('86) . . E 9
Wangaratta, 16,320 . . G 9
Warrnambool,
24,480 . . . . G 8
Weipa, 2,406('86) . . . . B 8
Whyalla, 26,706 . . . . F 7
Wilcannia, 1,048('86) F 8
Wiluna, 279('86) . . . . E 4
Winton, 1,281('86) . . D 8
Wollongong, 174,770
(236,690★) F10
Woomera,
1,805('86) . . . . F 7
Wyndham,
1,329('86) . . . . C 5

Indonesia

1980 CENSUS

Jayapura, 60,641 . . . . k15
Kupang, 84,587 . . . . B 4
Sorong, 52,041 . . . . . . k13

Papua New Guinea

1987 ESTIMATE

Lae, 79,600 . . . . m16
Madang, 24,700 . . . . m16
Port Moresby,
152,100 . . . . m16
Rabaul, 14,954('80) . . k17
Wewak, 23,200 . . . . . . k15

New Zealand

1986 CENSUS

Alexandra, 4,842 . . . . F 2
Ashburton, 14,030 . . E 3
Auckland, 149,046 (850,000★) . . . . . . B 5
Blenheim, 18,308 (22,681★) . . . . . . D 4
Bluff, 2,537 . . . . G 2
Cambridge, 10,145 . . B 5
Christchurch, 168,200 (320,000★) . . . . . . E 4
Dannevirke, 5,873 . . D 6
Dargaville, 4,859 . . . . A 4
Devonport, 10,543 . . B 5
Dunedin, 76,964 (109,000★) . . . . . . F 3
Gisborne, 30,020 (32,238★) . . . . . . C 7
Gore, 8,594 (11,249★) G 2
Greymouth, 7,624 (11,261★) . . . . . . E 3
Hamilton, 94,511 (101,814★) . . . . . . B 5
Hastings, 37,658 . . . . C 6
Hawera, 4,151 (11,375★) . . . . . . C 5
Hokitika, 3,427 . . . . E 3
Huntly, 6,750 . . . . . . B 5
Invercargill, 48,197 (52,807★) . . . . . . G 2
Kaiapoi, 5,234 . . . . . . E 4
Kaikoura, 2,209 . . . . . E 4
Levin, 15,368 (18,962★) . . . . . . D 5
Lower Hutt, 63,862 . . D 5
Masterton, 18,511 (20,145★) . . . . . . D 5
Milton, 2,154 . . . . . . G 2
Morrinsville, 5,281 . . B 5
Motueka, 5,052 . . . . D 4
Murapara, 2,566 . . . . C 6
Napier, 49,428 (107,060★) . . . . . . C 6
Nelson, 34,274 (44,593★) . . . . . . D 4
New Plymouth, 36,865 (47,384★) . . . . . . C 5
Oamaru, 12,652 (14,247★) . . . . F 3
Opotiki, 3,719 . . . . . . C 6
Otaki, 4,407 . . . . . . D 5
Palmerston North, 60,503 (67,405★) . . . . . . D 5
Picton, 4,129 . . . . . . D 5
Port Chalmers, 2,871 F 3
Pukekohe, 9,398 (13,823★) . . . . . . B 5
Queenstown, 3,659 . . F 2
Richmond, 7,204 . . . . D 4
Rotorua, 40,597 (52,001★) . . . . . . C 6
Stratford, 5,528 . . . . C 5
Taihape, 2,472 . . . . C 5
Takapuna, 69,419 . . B 5
Taumarunui, 6,387 . . C 5
Taupo, 15,873 . . . . C 6
Tauranga, 41,611 (59,435★) . . . . . . B 6
Te Awamutu, 8,096 . . C 5
Te Kuiti, 4,787 . . . . C 5
Thames, 6,461 . . . . B 5
Timaru, 27,757 (28,621★) . . . . F 3
Tokoroa, 17,628 (18,193★) . . . . . . C 5
Waihi, 3,679 . . . . . . B 5
Waimate, 3,250 . . . . F 3
Waipukurau, 3,862 . . D 6
Wairoa, 5,094 . . . . . . C 6
Waitara, 6,482 . . . . C 5
Waiuku, 4,357 . . . . . . B 5
Wanaka, 1,710 . . . . . F 2
Wanganui, 38,084 (40,758★) . . . . . . C 5
Wellington, 137,495 (350,000★) . . . . . . D 5
Wellsford, 1,627 . . . . B 5
Westport, 4,660 . . . . D 3
Whakatane, 12,800 (15,954★) . . . . . . B 6
Whangarei, 40,179 (44,043★) . . . . . . A 5
Winton, 2,082 . . . . . . G 2

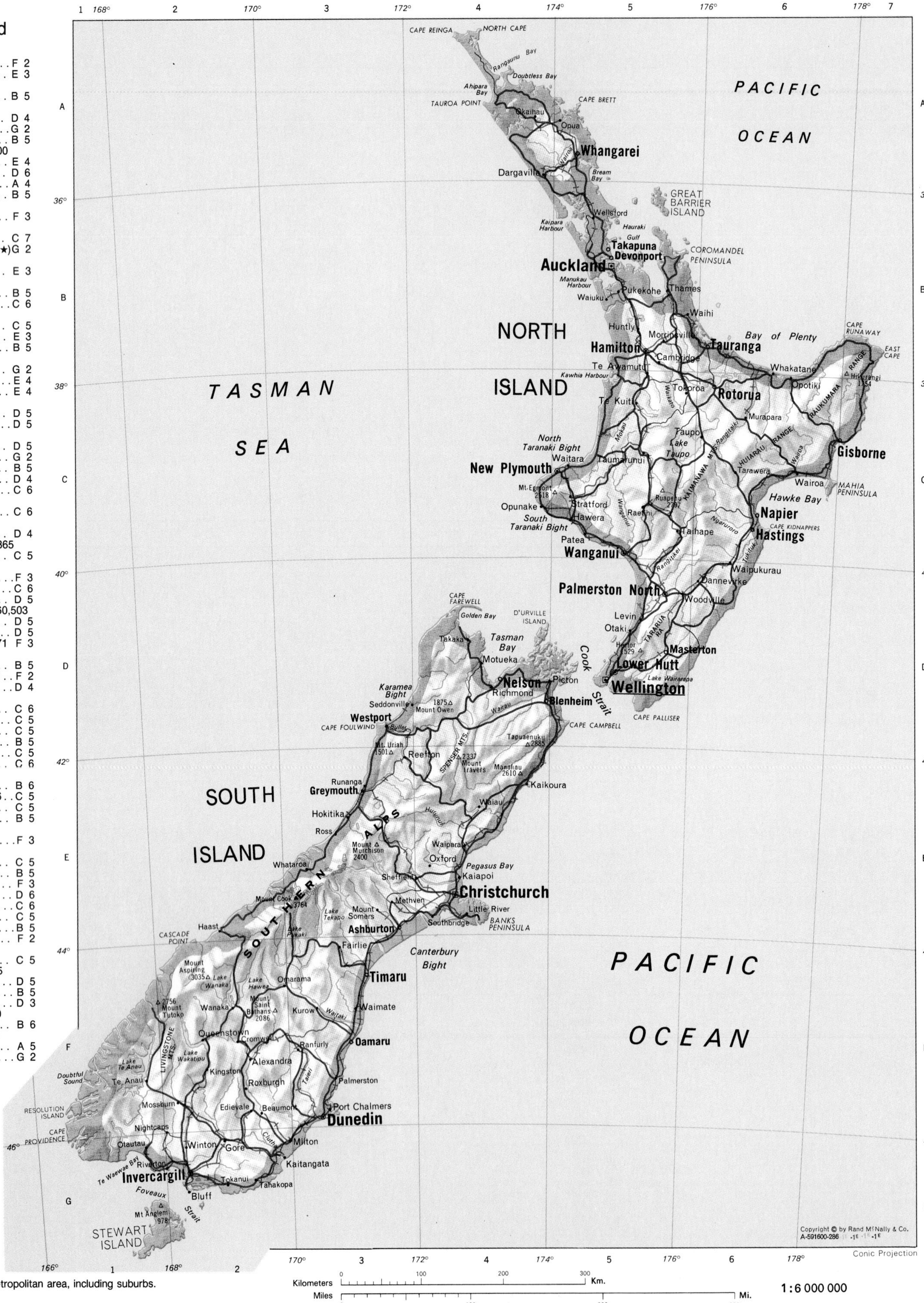

★ Population of metropolitan area, including suburbs.

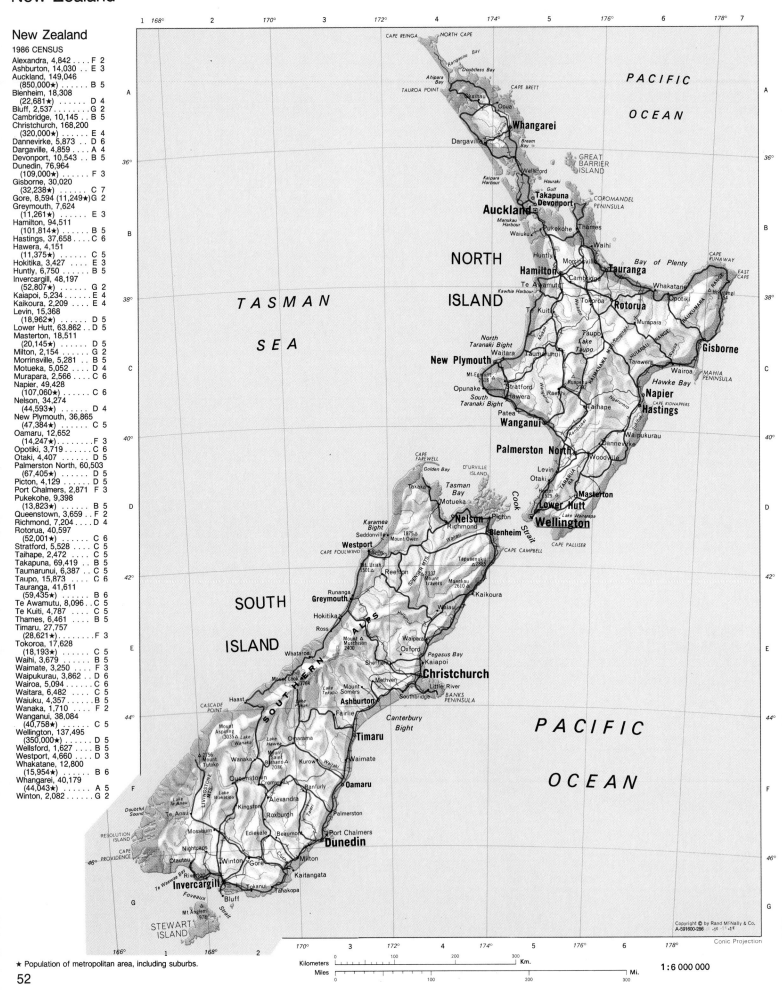

Antofagasta, 185,486 ('82)..........F 3
Arequipa, 108,023 ('81) (446,942★) ....E 3
ARGENTINA..........G 4
Asunción, 477,100 ('85) (700,000★) ....F 5
Barranquilla, 899,781 ('85) (1,140,000★) ....B 3
Belém, 1,116,578 ('85) (1,200,000★) ....D 6
Belo Horizonte, 2,114,429 ('85) (2,950,000★) ...E 6
Bogotá *see* Santa Fe de Bogotá..........C 3
BOLIVIA..........E 4
Brasília, 1,567,709 ('85)..........E 6
BRAZIL..........E 5
Buenos Aires, 2,922,829 ('80) (10,750,000★) G 5
Caracas, 1,816,901 ('81) (3,600,000★) ....B 4
Cartagena, 531,426 ('85)..........B 3
Cayenne, 38,091 ('82).C 5
Chiclayo, 213,095 ('81) (279,527★) ....D 3
CHILE..........G 3
Ciudad Bolívar, 182,941 ('81)..........C 4
COLOMBIA..........C 3
Concepción, 267,891 ('82) (675,000★) ....G 3
Cuzco, 89,563 ('81) (184,550★) ....E 3
ECUADOR..........D 3
FALKLAND ISLANDS...I 5
Fortaleza, 1,582,414 ('85) (1,825,000★) ....D 7
FRENCH GUIANA.......C 5
Georgetown, 78,500 ('83) (188,000★) ....C 5
Guayaquil, 1,572,615 ('87) (1,580,000★) ....D 3
GUYANA..........C 5
Iquitos, 178,738 ('81).. D 3
João Pessoa, 348,500 ('85) (550,000★) ..... D 7
La Paz, 992,592 ('85)..E 4
La Plata, 477,175 ('80)..........G 5
Lima, 371,122 ('81) (4,608,010★) ....E 3
Maceió, 482,195 ('85). D 7
Manaus, 809,914 ('85)D 5
Maracaibo, 890,643 ('81)..........B 3
Medellín, 1,468,089 ('85) (2,095,000★) ....C 3
Mendoza, 119,088 ('80) (650,000★) ....G 4
Montevideo, 1,251,647 ('85) (1,550,000★) .. G 5
Natal, 510,106 ('85).....D 7
PARAGUAY..........F 5
Paramaribo, 241,000 ('88) (296,000★) ....C 5
PERU..........E 3
Porto Alegre, 1,272,121 ('85) (2,600,000★) .. G 5
Quito, 1,137,705 ('87) (1,300,000★) ....D 3
Recife, 1,287,623 ('85) (2,625,000★) ....D 7
Rio Branco, 109,800 ('85) (145,486▲) ....D 4
Rio de Janeiro, 5,603,388 ('85) (10,150,000★) .F 6
Rosario, 938,120 ('80) (1,045,000★) ....G 4
Salta, 260,744 ('80).....F 4
Salvador, 1,804,438 ('85) (2,050,000★) ....E 7
San Miguel de Tucumán, 392,888 ('80) (525,000★) ....F 4
Santa Fe, 292,165 ('80)..........G 4
Santa Fe de Bogotá, 3,982,941 ('85) (4,260,000★) ....C 3
Santiago, 232,667 ('82) (4,100,000★) ....G 3
Santos, 460,100 ('85) (1,065,000★) ....F 6
São Luís, 227,900 ('85) (600,000★) ....D 6
São Paulo, 10,063,110 ('85) (15,175,000★) .F 6
Stanley, 1,200 ('86).......I 5
Sucre, 86,609 ('85)......E 4
SURINAME..........C 5
Teresina, 425,300 ('85) (525,000★) ....D 6
Trujillo, 202,469 ('81) (354,301★) ....D 3
URUGUAY..........G 5
Valparaíso, 265,355 ('82) (675,000★) ....G 3
VENEZUELA..........C 4
Vitória, 201,500 ('85) (735,000★) ....F 6

★ Population of metropolitan area, including suburbs.
▲ Population of entire district, including rural area.

Miles 0 200 400 600 800 1000 Mi.
Kilometers 0 400 800 1200 1600 Km.

1:40 000 000

Bolivia

1985 ESTIMATE

Cochabamba, 317,251 G 5
La Paz, 992,592 .... G 5
Oruro, 178,393 ..... G 5
Potosí, 113,380 .... G 5
Santa Cruz, 441,717 G 6
Sucre, 86,609 ...... G 5

Brazil

1985 ESTIMATE

Anápolis, 225,840 .. G 9
Aracaju, 360,013 .... F11
Araçatuba, 129,304 .. H 8
Bauru, 220,105...... H 9
Belém, 1,116,578 (1,200,000★) ...... D 9
Belo Horizonte, 2,114,429 (2,950,000★) G10
Brasília, 1,567,709 .. G 9
Campina Grande, 279,929 .... E11
Campinas, 841,016 (1,125,000★) ...... H 9
Campo Grande, 384,398 .... H 8
Campos, 187,900 (366,716▲) H10
Caruaru, 152,100 (190,794▲) E11
Cuiabá, 220,400 (279,651▲) ...... G 7
Feira de Santana, 278,600 (355,201▲) F11
Fortaleza, 1,582,414 (1,825,000★) D11
Goiânia, 923,333 (990,000★) ...... G 9
Governador Valadares, 192,300 (216,957▲) G10
João Pessoa, 348,500 (550,000★) E12
Juàzeiro do Norte, 159,806 .... E11
Juiz de Fora, 349,720 H10
Jundiaí, 268,900 (313,652▲) .... H 9
Maceió, 482,195 .... E11
Manaus, 809,914 .... D 6
Montes Claros, 183,500 (214,472▲) G10
Natal, 510,106 ...... E11
Niterói, 441,684 .... H10
Petrolina, 92,100 (225,000★) E10
Petrópolis, 170,300 .. H10
Piracicaba, 211,000 (252,079▲) .... H 9
Porto Velho, 152,700 (202,011▲) .... E 6
Presidente Prudente, 155,883 .... H 8
Recife, 1,287,623 (2,625,000★) E12
Ribeirão Prêto, 383,125 .... H 9
Rio de Janeiro, 5,603,388 (10,150,000★) H10
Salvador, 1,804,438 (2,050,000★) F11
Santarém, 120,800 (226,618▲) .... D 8
Santos, 460,100 (1,065,000★) ...... H 9
São Carlos, 140,383 H 9
São José do Rio Prêto, 229,221 .... H 9
São Luís, 227,900 (600,000★) D10
São Paulo, 10,063,110 (15,175,000★) .... H 9
Sorocaba, 327,468 .. H 9
Teresina, 425,300 (525,000★) E10
Uberaba, 244,875.... G 9
Uberlândia, 312,024 .. G 9
Vitória, 201,500 (735,000★) H10
Vitória da Conquista, 145,800 (198,150▲) F10
Volta Redonda, 219,267 (375,000★) H10

Colombia

1985 CENSUS

Armenia, 187,130 .... C 3
Barrancabermeja, 137,406 .... B 4
Barranquilla, 899,781 (1,140,000★) ...... A 4
Bogotá *see* Santa Fe de Bogotá .... C 4
Bucaramanga, 352,326 (550,000★) .... B 4
Buenaventura, 160,342 .... C 3
Buga, 82,992 ...... C 3
Cali, 1,350,565 (1,400,000★) ...... C 3
Cartagena, 531,426 .. A 3
Cúcuta, 379,478 (445,000★) .... B 4

Kilometers 0 200 400 600 Km.
Miles 0 200 400 600 Mi.

1:16 000 000

Ibagué, 292,965 .... C 3
Manizales, 299,352 (330,000★)........B 3
Medellín, 1,468,089 (2,095,000★)......B 3
Montería, 157,466 .. B 3
Neiva, 194,556 ......C 3
Palmira, 175,186 .... C 3
Pasto, 197,407 ......C 3
Pereira, 233,271 (390,000★)........C 3
Popayán, 141,964 .. C 3
Santa Fe de Bogotá, 3,982,941 (4,260,000★)......C 4
Santa Marta, 177,922 A 4
Tuluá, 99,721 ...... C 3
Valledupar, 142,771 .. A 4
Villavicencio, 178,685 C 4

Ecuador

1987 ESTIMATE

Ambato, 126,067 .... D 3
Cuenca, 201,490 .... D 3
Guayaquil, 1,572,615 (1,580,000★)......D 3
Machala, 144,396....D 3
Manta, 135,990 .... D 2
Portoviejo, 141,568 .. D 2
Quito, 1,137,705 (1,300,000★)......D 3

French Guiana

1982 CENSUS

Cayenne, 38,091 .... C 8

Guyana

1983 ESTIMATE

Georgetown, 78,500 (188,000★)........B 7

Peru

1981 CENSUS

Arequipa, 108,023 (446,942★) ...... G 4
Ayacucho, 57,432 (69,533★) .... F 4
Cajamarca, 62,259 .. E 3
Callao, 264,133......F 3
Cerro de Pasco, 55,597 (66,373★) .... F 3
Chiclayo, 213,095 (279,527★)........E 3
Chimbote, 223,341 .. E 3
Cuzco, 89,563 (184,550★)........F 4
Huancayo, 84,845 (164,954★)........F 3
Huánuco, 61,812 .... E 3
Ica, 114,786 .... F 3
Iquitos, 178,738 .... D 4
Lima, 371,122 (4,608,010★)......F 3
Piura, 144,609 (207,934★)........E 2
Sullana, 89,037......D 2
Tacna, 97,173 ...... G 4
Trujillo, 202,469 (354,301★)........E 3
Tumbes, 47,936 .... D 2
Vitarte, 145,504 .... F 3

Suriname

1988 ESTIMATE

Paramaribo, 241,000 (296,000★)........B 7

Venezuela

1981 CENSUS

Acarigua, 91,662 .... B 5
Barinas, 110,462 .... B 4
Barquisimeto, 497,635 A 5
Cabimas, 140,435 .. A 4
Calabozo, 61,995 ..... B 5
Caracas, 1,816,901 (3,600,000★)......A 5
Ciudad Bolívar, 182,941 ....B 6
Ciudad Guayana, 314,497 ....B 6
Ciudad Ojeda, 83,565 A 4
Cumaná, 179,814....A 6
El Tigre, 73,595 .... B 6
Maracaibo, 890,643.. A 4
Maracay, 322,560....A 5
Maturín, 154,976 .... B 6
Mérida, 143,209 .... B 4
Puerto Cabello, 71,759 .... A 5
Punto Fijo, 71,114 .. A 4
San Cristóbal, 198,793 ....B 4
Valencia, 616,224....A 5
Valera, 102,068 .... B 4

★ Population of metropolitan area, including suburbs.
▲ Population of entire district, including rural area.

Southern South America

Argentina
1980 CENSUS

Avellaneda, 334,145 . . C 5
Bahía Blanca, 223,818 D 4
Buenos Aires, 2,922,829 (10,750,000★) . . . . C 5
Catamarca, 78,799 (90,000★) . . . . B 3
Comodoro Rivadavia, 96,817 . . . . F 3
Concordia, 94,222 . . C 5
Córdoba, 993,055 (1,070,000★) . . . . . . C 4
Corrientes, 180,612 . . B 5
La Plata, 477,175 . . . . C 5
Mar del Plata, 414,696 . . . . D 5
Mendoza, 119,088 (650,000★) . . . . C 3
Paraná, 161,638 . . . . C 4
Posadas, 143,889 . . . B 5
Río Cuarto, 110,254 . . C 4
Rosario, 938,120 (1,045,000★) . . . . . . C 4
Salta, 260,744 . . . . . . A 3
San Isidro, 289,170 . . C 5
San Juan, 118,046 (300,000★) . . . . C 3
San Miguel de Tucumán, 392,888 (525,000★) B 3
Santa Fe, 292,165 . . C 4
Santiago del Estero, 148,758 (200,000★) B 4

Brazil
1985 ESTIMATE

Bauru, 220,105 . . . . . . A 7
Blumenau, 192,074 . . B 7
Campinas, 841,016 (1,125,000★) . . . . . . A 7
Caxias do Sul, 266,809 . . . . B 6
Curitiba, 1,279,205 (1,700,000★) . . . . . . B 7
Florianópolis, 178,400 (365,000★) . . . . B 7
Joinvile, 302,877 . . . . B 7
Jundiaí, 268,900 (313,652▲) . . . . A 7
Londrina, 296,400 (346,676▲) . . . . A 6
Maringá, 196,871 . . . . A 6
Pelotas, 210,300 (277,730▲) . . . . C 6
Piracicaba, 211,000 (252,079▲) . . . . A 7
Ponta Grossa, 223,154 . . . . B 6
Porto Alegre, 1,272,121 (2,600,000★) . . . . . . C 6
Presidente Prudente, 155,883 . . . . A 6
Ribeirão Prêto, 383,125 . . . . A 7
Rio Grande, 164,221 C 6
Santa Maria, 163,900 (196,827▲) . . . . B 6
Santos, 460,100 (1,065,000★) . . . . . . A 7
São Carlos, 140,383 A 7
São Paulo, 10,063,110 (15,175,000★) . . . . A 7
Sorocaba, 327,468 . . A 7

Chile
1982 CENSUS

Antofagasta, 185,486 A 2
Chillán, 118,163 . . . . D 2
Concepción, 267,891 (675,000★) . . . . D 2
Osorno, 95,286 . . . . . . E 2
Punta Arenas, 95,332 G 2
Rancagua, 139,925 . . C 2
Santiago, 232,667 (4,100,000★) . . . . . . C 2
Talca, 128,544 . . . . . . D 2
Talcahuano, 202,368 D 2
Temuco, 157,297 . . . . D 2
Valdivia, 100,046 . . . . D 2
Valparaíso, 265,355 (675,000★) . . . . C 2
Viña del Mar, 244,899 C 2

Falkland Islands
1986 ESTIMATE

Stanley, 1,200 . . . . . . G 5

Paraguay
1985 ESTIMATE

Asunción, 477,100 (700,000★) . . . . B 5

Uruguay
1985 CENSUS

Montevideo, 1,251,647 (1,550,000★) . . . . . . C 5
Paysandú, 76,191 . . . . C 5
Salto, 80,823 . . . . . . C 5

★ Population of metropolitan area, including suburbs.
▲ Population of entire district, including rural area.

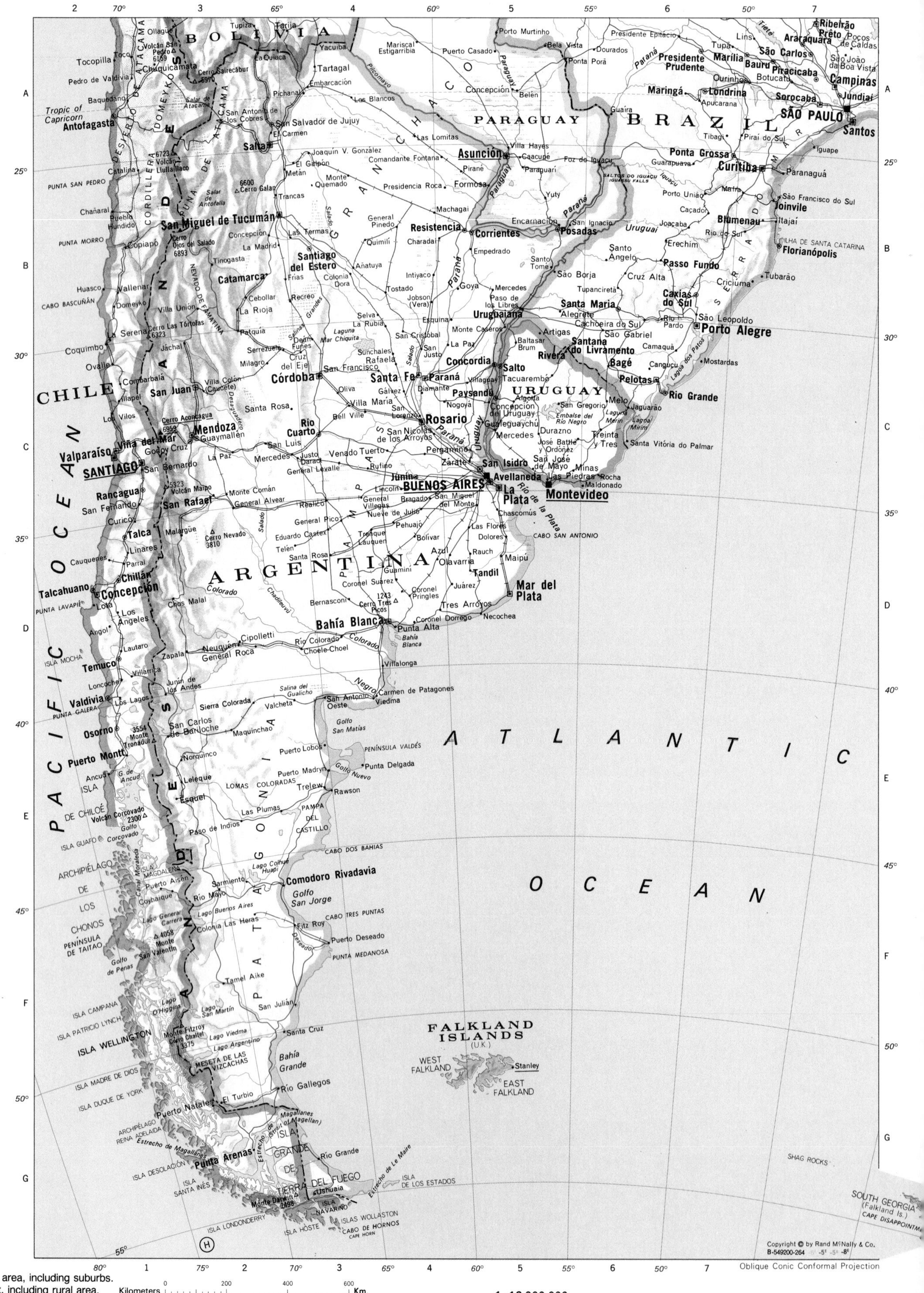

Kilometers 0 200 400 600 Km.
Miles 0 200 400 600 Mi.

1:16 000 000

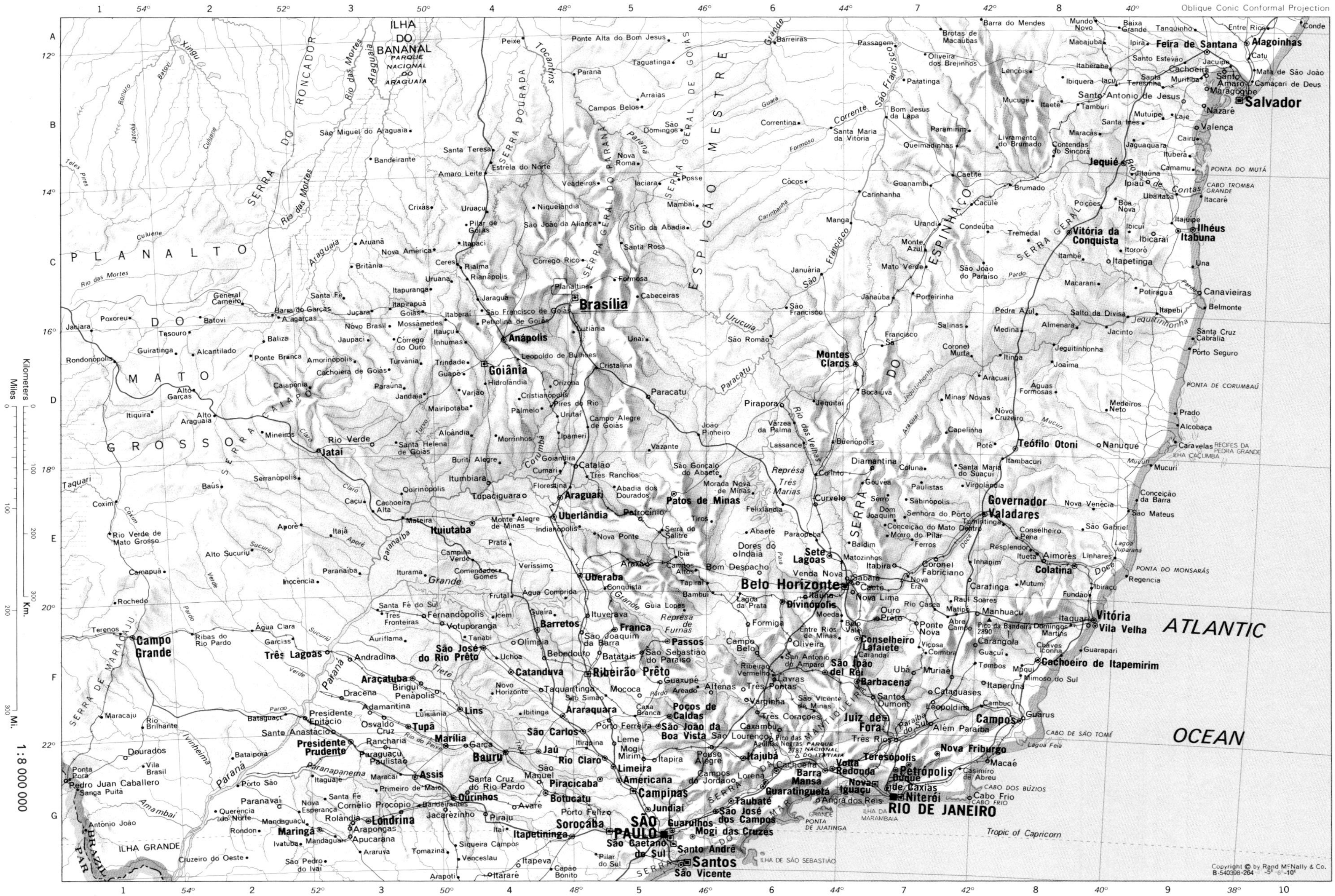

★ Population of metropolitan area, including suburbs. ▲ Population of entire district, including rural area.

Brazil

1985 ESTIMATE

Americana, 156,030 .. G 5
Anápolis, 225,840 .... D 4
Araçatuba, 129,304 .... F 3
Araraquara, 87,500 (145,042▲) .... F 4
Assis, 63,100 (74,238▲) G 3
Barbacena, 80,200 (99,337▲) .... F 7
Barra Mansa, 149,200 G 6
Bauru, 220,105 ...... G 4
Belo Horizonte, 2,114,429 (2,950,000★) ...... E 7
Brasília, 1,567,709 .... C 5
Cachoeiro de Itapemirim, 95,000 (138,156▲) .. F 8
Campinas, 841,016 (1,125,000★) ...... G 5
Campo Grande, 384,398 F 1
Campos, 187,900 (366,716▲) .... F 8
Conselheiro Lafaiete, 77,958 .... F 7
Divinópolis, 139,940 .. F 6
Duque de Caxias, 353,200 .... G 7
Feira de Santana, 278,600 (355,201▲) .... B 9
Franca, 182,820 ...... F 5
Goiânia, 923,333 (990,000★) .... D 4
Governador Valadares, 192,300 (216,957▲).. E 8
Guarulhos, 571,700 .. G 5
Itabuna, 142,200 (167,543▲) .... C 9
Itajubá, 61,500 (69,675▲) .... G 6
Itapetininga, 76,700 (105,512▲) .... G 4
Itaquari, 163,900 ...... F 8
Juiz de Fora, 349,720 .. F 7
Jundiaí, 268,900 (313,652▲) .... G 5
Limeira, 186,986 ...... G 5
Londrina, 296,400 (346,676▲) .... G 3
Maringá, 196,871 .... G 3
Mogi das Cruzes, 144,800 .... G 5
Montes Claros, 183,500 (214,472▲) .... D 7
Niterói, 441,684 ...... G 7
Nova Friburgo, 103,500 (143,529▲) .... G 7
Nova Iguaçu, 592,800 G 7
Petrópolis, 170,300 .... G 7
Piracicaba, 211,000 (252,079▲) .... G 5
Poços de Caldas, 100,004 .... F 5
Presidente Prudente, 155,883 .... G 3
Ribeirão Prêto, 383,125 F 5
Rio Claro, 129,859 .... G 5
Rio de Janeiro, 5,603,388 (10,150,000★) ...... G 7
Salvador, 1,804,438 (2,050,000★) ...... B 9
Santo André, 635,129 G 5
Santos, 460,100 (1,065,000★) ...... G 5
São Caetano do Sul, 171,005 .... G 5
São Cárlos, 140,383 .. G 5
São José do Rio Prêto, 229,221 .... F 4
São José dos Campos, 372,578 .... G 6
São Paulo, 10,063,110 (15,175,000★) ...... G 5
São Vicente, 239,778 .. G 5
Sete Lagoas, 121,418 .. E 6
Sorocaba, 327,468 .... G 5
Taubaté, 205,120 .... G 6
Uberaba, 244,875 .... E 5
Uberlândia, 312,024 .. E 4
Vitória, 201,500 (735,000★) .... F 8
Vitória da Conquista, 145,800 (198,150▲) C 8
Volta Redonda, 219,267 (375,000★) .... G 6

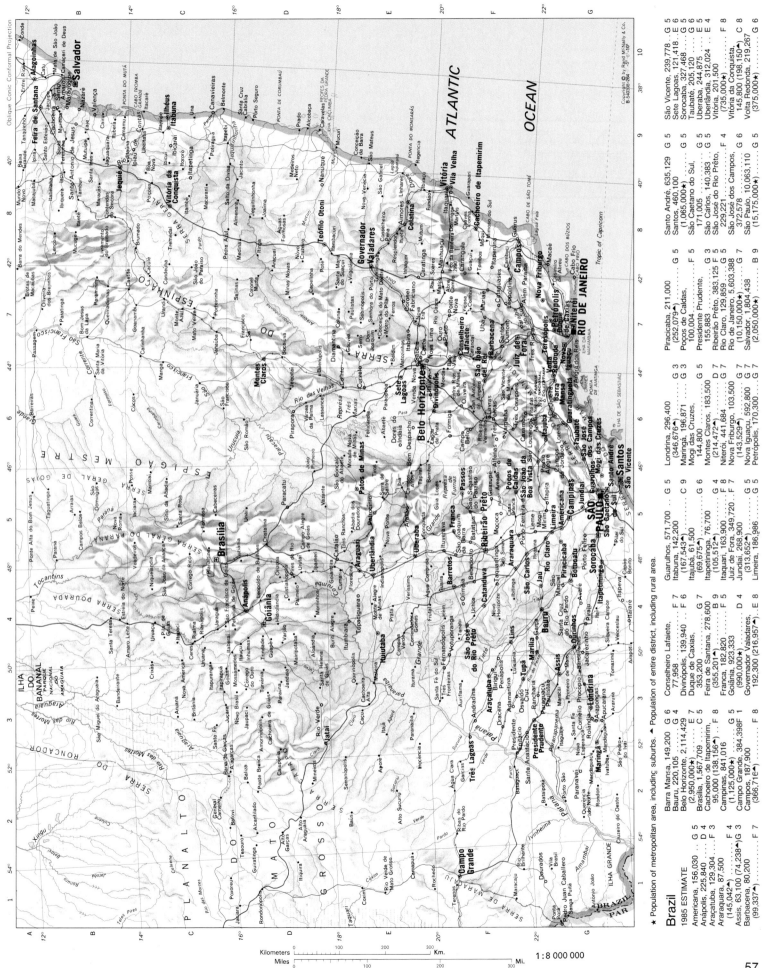

Colombia, Ecuador, Venezuela, and Guyana

Aruba
1987 ESTIMATE
Oranjestad, 19,800 .. A 7

Colombia
1985 CENSUS
Armenia, 187,130 .... E 5
Barrancabermeja, 137,406 .... D 6
Barranquilla, 899,781 (1,140,000★) ...... B 5
Bello, 212,861 ...... D 5
Bogotá *see* Santa Fe de Bogotá .... E 5
Bucaramanga, 352,326 (550,000★) .... D 6
Buenaventura, 160,342 .... F 4
Buga, 82,992 .... F 4
Cali, 1,350,565 (1,400,000★) ...... F 4
Cartagena, 531,426 .. B 5
Cartago, 97,791 .... E 5
Ciénaga, 56,860 .... B 5
Cúcuta, 379,478 (445,000★) .... D 6
Duitama, 56,390 .... E 6
Envigado, 91,391 .... D 5
Espinal, 37,563 ...... E 5
Facatativá, 44,331 .. E 5
Florencia, 66,430 .... G 5
Florida, 30,040 ...... F 4
Floridablanca, 143,824 .... D 6
Girardot, 70,078 .... E 5
Ibagué, 292,965 .... E 5
Ipiales, 45,419 ...... G 4
Itagüí, 137,623 ...... D 5
La Dorada, 48,572 .. E 5
Magangué, 49,160 .. C 5
Manizales, 299,352 (330,000★) .... E 5
Medellín, 1,468,089 (2,095,000★) ...... D 5
Montería, 157,466 .. C 5
Neiva, 194,556 ...... F 5
Ocaña, 51,443 ...... C 6
Palmira, 175,186 .... F 4
Pamplona, 34,213 .. D 6
Pasto, 197,407 ...... G 4
Pereira, 233,271 (390,000★) .... E 5
Planeta Rica, 24,238 C 5
Popayán, 141,964 .... F 4
Puerto Berrío, 21,414 D 5
Quibdó, 47,950 ...... E 4
Ríohacha, 46,667 .... B 6
Santa Fe de Bogotá, 3,982,941 (4,260,000★) ...... E 5
Santa Marta, 177,922 .... B 5
Santa Rosa de Cabal, 37,112 .... E 5
Sincelejo, 120,537 .. C 5
Sogamoso, 64,437 .. E 6
Soledad, 165,791 .... B 5
Tuluá, 99,721 ...... E 4
Tumaco, 45,456 .... G 3
Tunja, 93,792 ...... E 6
Valledupar, 142,771 .. B 6
Villavicencio, 178,685 E 6
Zipaquirá, 45,676 .... E 5

Ecuador
1987 ESTIMATE
Alfaro, 51,023('82) .... I 3
Ambato, 126,067 .... H 3
Babahoyo, 42,266('82) ...... H 3
Chone, 33,839('82) .. H 2
Cuenca, 201,490 ...... I 3
Esmeraldas, 120,387 G 3
Guayaquil, 1,572,615 (1,580,000★) ...... I 3
Ibarra, 53,428('82) .. G 3
Jipijapa, 27,146('82) .. H 2
Latacunga, 28,764('82) ...... H 3
Loja, 71,652('82) .... J 3
Machala, 144,396 .... I 3
Manta, 135,990 .... H 2
Milagro, 102,884 .... I 3
Portoviejo, 141,568 .. H 2
Quevedo, 67,023('82) ...... H 3
Quito, 1,137,705 (1,300,000★) ...... H 3
Riobamba, 75,455('82) ...... H 3
Santo Domingo de los Colorados, 104,059 H 3
Tulcán, 30,985('82) .. G 4

Guyana
1983 ESTIMATE
Georgetown, 78,500 (188,000★) D13
New Amsterdam, 20,000('82) D14

★ Population of metropolitan area, including suburbs.

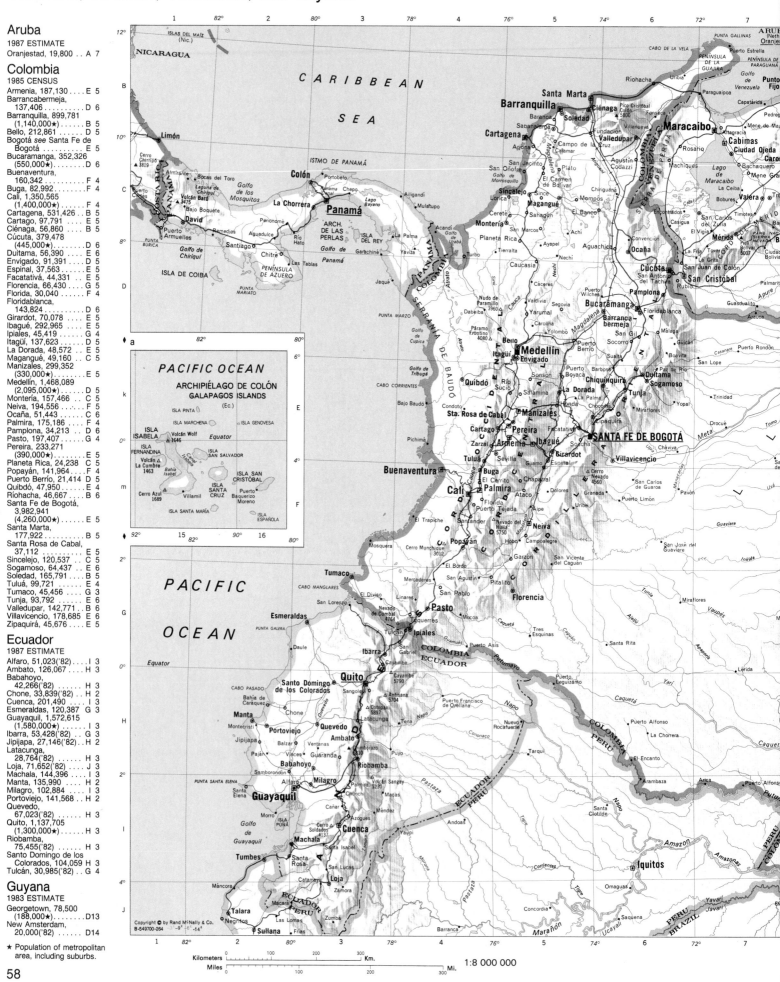

Netherlands Antilles
1981 CENSUS
Willemstad, 31,883 (130,000★) .... A 8

Panama
1990 CENSUS
Colón, 54,469 (96,000★) .... C 3
David, 65,635 ...... C 1
La Chorrera, 44,110 .. C 3
Panamá, 411,549 (770,000★) .... C 3
Puerto Armuelles, 12,562('80) ...... C 1
Santiago, 43,678 .... C 2

Trinidad and Tobago
1990 CENSUS
Arima, 29,695 ...... B12
Point Fortin, 6,538('80) B12
Port of Spain, 50,878 (370,000★) B12
San Fernando, 30,092 (75,000★) B12
Scarborough, 6,089('80) B12

Venezuela
1981 CENSUS
Acarigua, 91,662 .... C 8
Altagracia de Orituco, 31,582 .... C 9
Anaco, 43,607 ...... C10
Araure, 41,747 ...... C 8
Barcelona, 156,461 .. B10
Barinas, 110,462 .... C 7
Barquisimeto, 497,635 .... B 8
Cabimas, 140,435 .. B 7
Calabozo, 61,995 .... C 9
Cantaura, 21,236 .... C10
Caracas, 1,816,901 (3,600,000★) ...... B 9
Caripito, 18,172 .... B11
Carora, 58,694 ...... B 7
Carúpano, 64,579 .... B11
Ciudad Bolívar, 182,941 .... C11
Ciudad Guayana, 314,497 .... C11
Ciudad Ojeda (Lagunillas), 83,565 .... B 7
Coro, 96,339 .... B 8
Cumaná, 179,814 .... B10
El Tigre, 73,595 .... C10
El Tocuyo, 22,854 ... C 8
Guanare, 64,025 .... C 8
La Guaira, 21,815 .... B 9
Los Teques, 112,857 B 9
Machiques, 27,242 .. B 6
Maiquetía, 66,056 .... B 9
Maracaibo, 890,643 .. B 7
Maracay, 322,560 .... B 9
Maturín, 154,976 ... C11
Mérida, 143,209 .... C 7
Ocumare del Tuy, 40,666 .... B 9
Porlamar, 51,079 .... B11
Puerto Ayacucho, 28,248 .... E 9
Puerto Cabello, 71,759 .... B 8
Puerto la Cruz, 53,881 .... B10
Punto Fijo, 71,114 .. B 7
Rosario, 23,914 .... B 6
San Carlos, 37,892 .. C 8
San Carlos del Zulia, 31,437 .... C 7
San Cristóbal, 198,793 .... D 6
San Felipe, 57,526 .. B 8
San Fernando de Apure, 57,308 .... D 9
San José de Guanipa, 35,689 .... C10
San Juan de Colón, 23,447 .... C 6
San Juan de los Morros, 57,219 .... C 9
Tinaquillo, 28,168 .... C 8
Trujillo, 31,774 ...... C 7
Tucupita, 27,299 .... C11
Upata, 33,238 ...... C11
Valencia, 616,224 .... C 8
Valera, 102,068 .... C 7
Valle de la Pascua, 55,761 .... C 9
Yaritagua, 31,936 .... B 8
Zaraza, 24,562 ...... C10

Atlantic Ocean

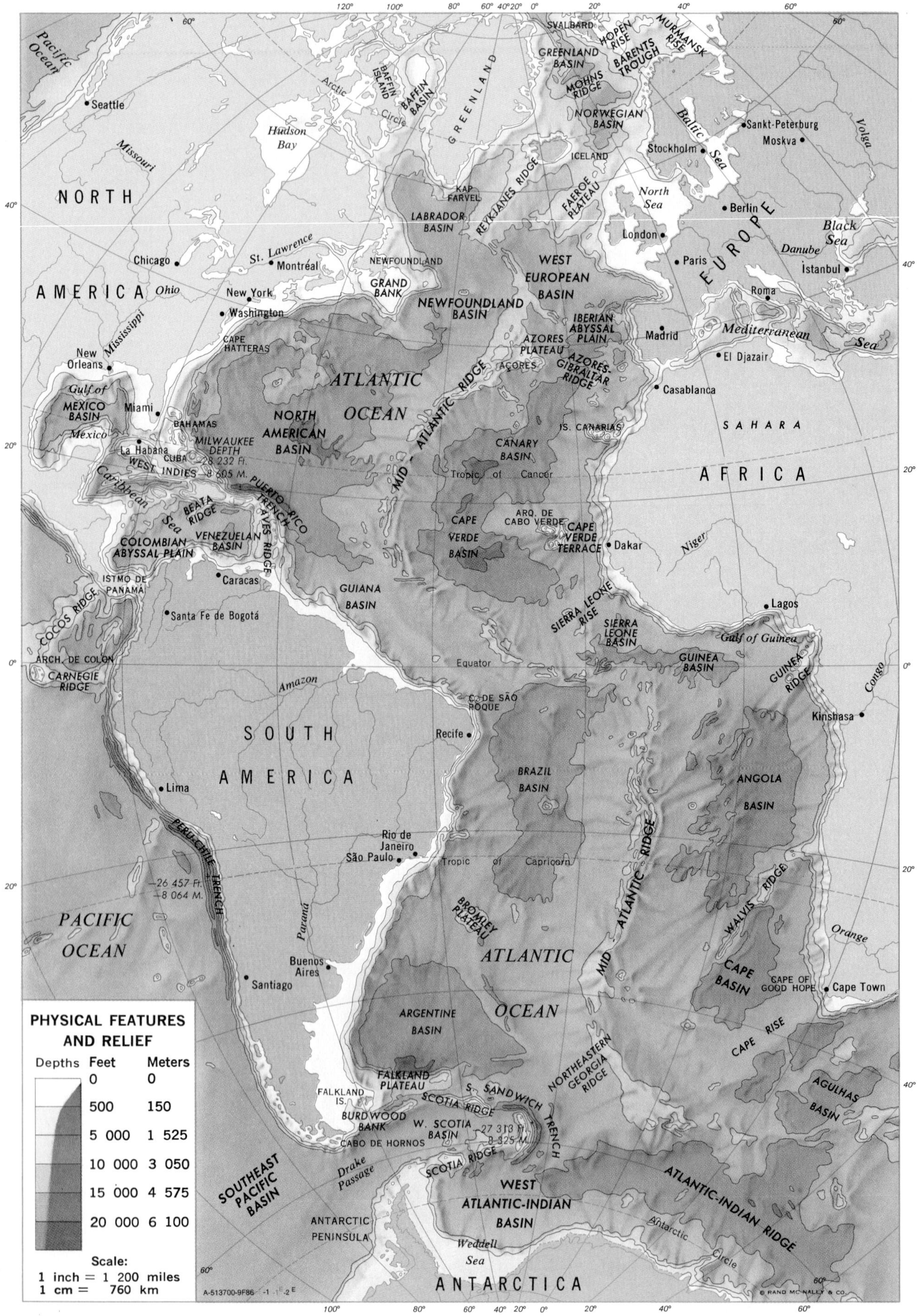

Atlanta, 394,017 ('90)..F12
BAHAMAS.................. G13
Baltimore, 736,014 ('90)..........................F13
BARBADOS................ H14
BELIZE........................H12
Boston, 574,283 ('90). E13
Calgary, 636,104 ('86) (671,326★) ....D 9
CANADA.....................D11
Chicago, 2,783,726 ('90)..........................E12
Ciudad de México (Mexico City), 8,831,079 ('80) (14,100,000★) H11
COSTA RICA.............. H12
CUBA.......................... G13
Dallas, 1,006,877 ('90) F11
Denver, 467,610 ('90)..F10
Detroit, 1,027,974 ('90)..........................E12
DOMINICAN REPUBLIC............... H13
EL SALVADOR........... H12
GREENLAND............. B16
Guadalajara, 1,626,152 ('80) (2,325,000★) .. H10
GUATEMALA............. H11
HAITI........................... H13
HONDURAS................ H12
Houston, 1,630,553 ('90)......................... G11
JAMAICA.................... H13
Kansas City, 435,146 ('90)..........................F11
La Habana (Havana), 2,036,800 ('87) (2,125,000★) G12
Los Angeles, 3,485,398 ('90)..........................F 9
Memphis, 610,337 ('90)..........................F11
MEXICO...................... G10
Miami, 358,548 ('90)... G12
Milwaukee, 628,088 ('90)..........................E12
Minneapolis, 368,383 ('90)..........................E11
Montréal, 1,015,420 ('86) (2,921,357★) E13
New Orleans, 496,938 ('90)......................... G11
New York, 7,322,564 ('90)..........................E13
NICARAGUA............... H12
Ottawa, 300,763 ('86) (819,263★) E13
PANAMA...................... I13
Philadelphia, 1,585,577 ('90)..........................F13
Phoenix, 900,013 ('90) F 9
PUERTO RICO............H14
San Antonio, 935,933 ('90)......................... G11
San Francisco, 723,959 ('90)..........................F 8
Santo Domingo, 1,313,172 ('81)......................... H13
Seattle, 516,259 ('90)..E 8
Toronto, 612,289 ('86) (3,427,168★) E13
TRINIDAD AND TOBAGO................... H14
UNITED STATES.........F11
Washington, 606,900 ('90)..........................F13

★ Population of metropolitan area, including suburbs.

Mexico

1980 CENSUS

Acámbaro, 38,224 . . G 9
Acapulco [de Juárez], 301,902 . . . . I10
Aguascalientes, 293,152 . . . . G 8
Ameca, 25,946 . . . . G 7
Apatzingán [de la Constitución], 55,522 . . . . H 8
Apizaco, 30,498 . . . . H10
Caborca, 33,696 . . . . B 3
Campeche, 128,434 H14
Celaya, 141,675 . . . . G 9
Chihuahua, 385,603 C 6
Chilpancingo [de los Bravos], 67,498 . . . . I10
Ciudad Acuña, 38,898 C 9
Ciudad Chetumal, 56,709 . . . . H15
Ciudad del Carmen, 72,489 . . . . H14
Ciudad de México (Mexico City), 8,831,079 (14,100,000★) H10
Ciudad de Valles, 65,609 . . . . G10
Ciudad Guzmán, 60,938 . . . . H 8
Ciudad Hidalgo, 32,311 . . . . H 9
Ciudad Juárez, 544,496 . . . . B 6
Ciudad Madero, 132,444 . . . . F11
Ciudad Mante, 70,647 F10
Ciudad Obregón, 165,572 . . . . D 5
Ciudad Victoria, 140,161 . . . . F10
Coatzacoalcos, 127,170 . . . . H12
Colima, 86,044 . . . . H 8
Córdoba, 99,972 . . . . H11
Cuernavaca, 192,770 H10
Culiacán, 304,826 . . E 6
Delicias, 65,504 . . . . C 7
Durango, 257,915 . . E 7
Empalme, 31,555 . . D 4
Ensenada, 120,483 . . B 1
Fresnillo, 56,066 . . . . F 8
Gómez Palacio, 116,967 . . . . E 8
Guadalajara, 1,626,152 (2,325,000★) . . . . G 8
Guadalupe, 370,524 . . E 9
Guanajuato, 48,981 . . G 9
Guaymas, 54,826 . . D 4
Hermosillo, 297,175 . . C 4
Hidalgo del Parral, 75,590 . . . . D 7
Iguala, 66,005 . . . . . . H10
Irapuato, 170,138 . . G 9
Jalapa Enríquez, 204,594 . . . . H11
Juchitán [de Zaragoza], 38,801 . . . . I12
La Barca, 20,889 . . G 8
Lagos de Moreno, 44,223 . . . . G 9
La Paz, 91,453 . . . . E 4
La Piedad [Cavadas], 47,441 . . . . G 8
León [de los Aldamas], 593,002 . . . . G 9
Los Mochis, 122,531 E 5
Manzanillo, 39,088 . . H 7
Matamoros, 188,745 E11
Matehuala, 41,550 . . F 9
Mazatlán, 199,830 . . F 6
Mérida, 400,142 . . . . G15
Mexicali, 341,559 (365,000★) . . . . . . A 2
Mexico City *see* Ciudad de México H10
Minatitlán, 106,765 . . I12
Monclova, 115,786 . . D 9
Montemorelos, 28,342 E10
Monterrey, 1,090,009 (2,015,000★) . . . . E 9
Morelia, 297,544 . . . . H 9
Navojoa, 62,901 . . . . D 5
Nogales, 65,603 . . . . B 4
Nueva Casas Grandes, 28,514 . . . . B 6
Nueva Rosita, 33,121 D 9
Nuevo Laredo, 201,731 . . . . D10
Oaxaca [de Juárez], 154,223 . . . . I11
Ocotlán, 48,931 . . . . G 8
Orizaba, 114,848 (215,000★) H11
Pachuca [de Soto], 110,351 . . . . G10
Papantla [de Olarte], 43,935 . . . . G11
Pátzcuaro, 32,902 . . H 9
Piedras Negras, 67,455 . . . . C 9
Poza Rica de Hidalgo, 166,799 . . . . G11

★ Population of metropolitan area, including suburbs.

San Diego
Tijuana
Mexicali
Yuma
San Luis Río Colorado
ARIZONA
NEW MEXICO
UNITED STATES
MEXICO
Tucson
El Paso
Ciudad Juárez
Nogales
Ensenada
Hermosillo
Chihuahua
Guaymas
Ciudad Obregón
Navojoa
Los Mochis
Culiacán
Mazatlán
Durango
Tepic
Guadalajara
Colima
Manzanillo
Delicias
Hidalgo del Parral
Gómez Palacio
Torreón
Golfo de California
BAJA CALIFORNIA
SIERRA MADRE OCCIDENTAL
La Paz
San José del Cabo
Tropic of Cancer
PACIFIC
OCEAN
ISLAS REVILLAGIGEDO (Mex.)
ISLAS MARÍAS
Copyright © by Rand McNally & Co.
Kilometers
Km.
Miles
Mi.
1:8 000 000

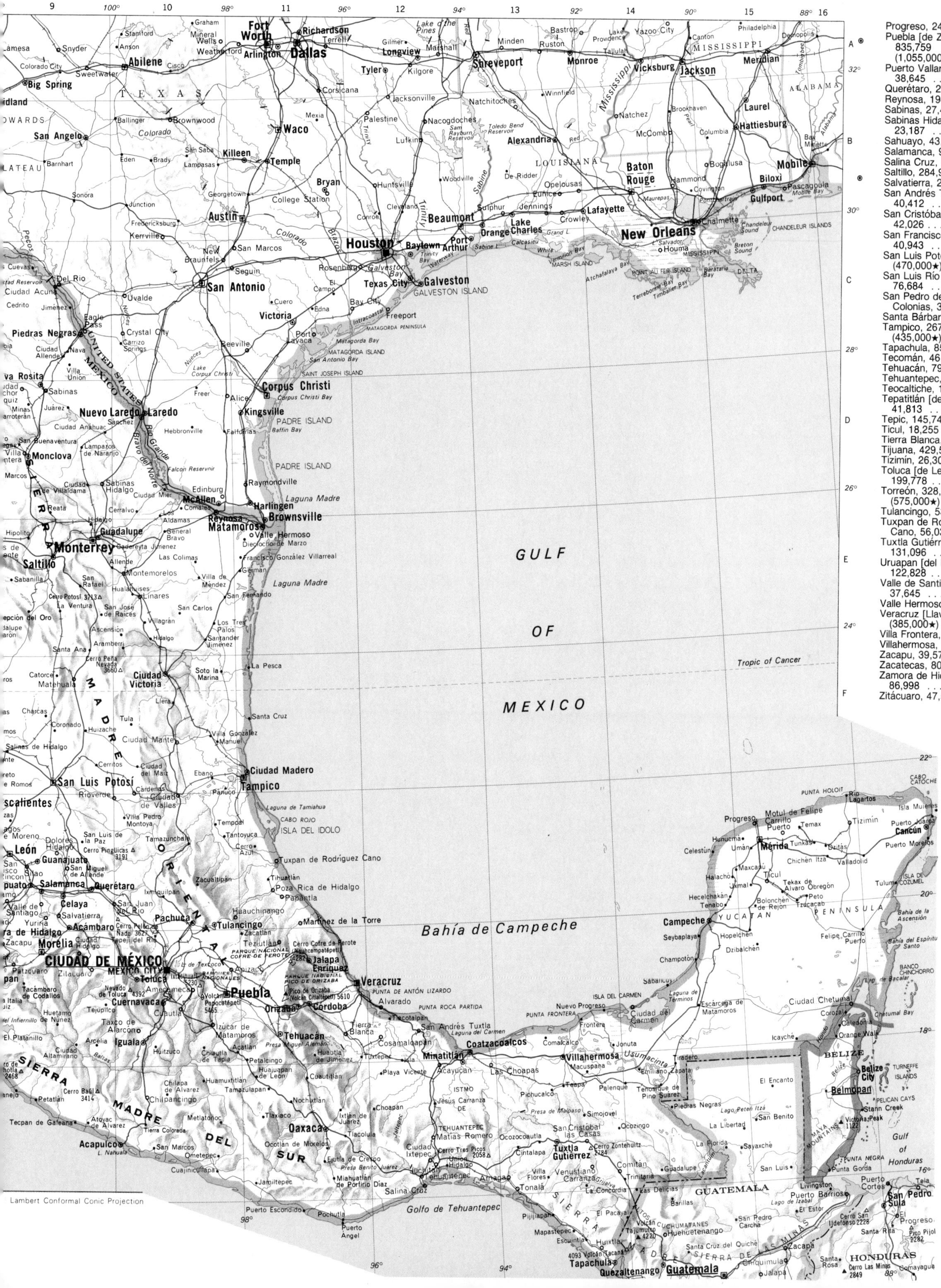

Progreso, 24,257 .. G15
Puebla [de Zaragoza], 835,759 (1,055,000★) H10
Puerto Vallarta, 38,645 .... G 7
Querétaro, 215,976 .. G 9
Reynosa, 194,693 .. D10
Sabinas, 27,413 .... D 9
Sabinas Hidalgo, 23,187 .... D 9
Sahuayo, 43,258 .... G 8
Salamanca, 96,703 .. G 9
Salina Cruz, 40,010 .. I12
Saltillo, 284,937 .... E 9
Salvatierra, 28,878 .. G 9
San Andrés Tuxtla, 40,412 .... H12
San Cristóbal las Casas, 42,026 .... I13
San Francisco del Rincón, 40,943 .... G 9
San Luis Potosí, 362,371 (470,000★) ...... F 9
San Luis Río Colorado, 76,684 ....A 2
San Pedro de las Colonias, 35,879 .. E 8
Santa Bárbara, 14,894D 7
Tampico, 267,957 (435,000★) F11
Tapachula, 85,766 .. J13
Tecomán, 46,371 .. H 8
Tehuacán, 79,547 .. H11
Tehuantepec, 22,019 I12
Teocaltiche, 16,559 .. G 8
Tepatitlán [de Morelos], 41,813 .... G 8
Tepic, 145,741 .... G 7
Ticul, 18,255 ...... G15
Tierra Blanca, 31,653 H11
Tijuana, 429,500 .... A 1
Tizimín, 26,305 .... G15
Toluca [de Lerdo], 199,778 .... H10
Torreón, 328,086 (575,000★) ...... E 8
Tulancingo, 53,400 .. G10
Tuxpan de Rodríguez Cano, 56,037 .... G11
Tuxtla Gutiérrez, 131,096 .... I13
Uruapan [del Progreso], 122,828 .... H 8
Valle de Santiago, 37,645 .... G 9
Valle Hermoso, 27,966E11
Veracruz [Llave], 284,822 (385,000★) H11
Villa Frontera, 32,568 D 9
Villahermosa, 158,216 I13
Zacapu, 39,570 .... H 9
Zacatecas, 80,088 .. F 8
Zamora de Hidalgo, 86,998 .... H 8
Zitácuaro, 47,520 .. H 9

Central America and the Caribbean

Antigua and Barbuda
1977 ESTIMATE
Saint Johns, 24,359 . . F17

Bahamas
1982 ESTIMATE
Nassau, 135,000 . . . . B 9

Barbados
1980 CENSUS
Bridgetown, 7,466
(115,000★) H18

Belize
1985 ESTIMATE
Belize City, 47,000 . . F 3
Belmopan, 4,500 . . . . F 3

Cayman Islands
1988 ESTIMATE
Georgetown, 13,700 E 7

Costa Rica
1988 ESTIMATE
Limón, 40,400
(62,600▲) . . . . I 6
San José, 278,600
(670,000★) . . . . . . J 5

Cuba
1987 ESTIMATE
Camagüey, 265,588 D 9
Guantánamo, 179,091 D10
Havana *see* La Habana . . . . C 6
Holguín, 199,861 . . . . D 9
La Habana (Havana), 2,036,800
(2,125,000★) . . . . C 6
Santa Clara, 182,349 C 8
Santiago de Cuba, 364,554 . . . . D10

Dominican Republic
1981 CENSUS
Santiago, 278,638 . . E 12
Santo Domingo, 1,313,172 . . . . . . E 13

El Salvador
1985 ESTIMATE
San Salvador, 462,652
(920,000★) . . . . . . H 3
Santa Ana, 137,879 . . H 3

Guadeloupe
1982 CENSUS
Basse-Terre, 13,656
(26,600★) F17

Guatemala
1989 ESTIMATE
Guatemala, 1,057,210
(1,400,000★) . . . . G 2

★ Population of metropolitan area, including suburbs.

ATLANTIC OCEAN
Tropic of Cancer
TURKS AND CAICOS ISLANDS
(U.K.)
CAICOS ISLANDS
TURKS ISLANDS
Grand Turk
Kew
Mouchoir Passage
Caicos Passage
Mayaguana Passage
Crooked Island Passage
GREAT INAGUA
LITTLE INAGUA
Matthew Town
SILVER BANK
MOUCHOIR BANK
AHAMAS
SAN SALVADOR (WATLING I.)
RUM CAY
LONG ISLAND
Deadmans Cay
SAMANA CAY
CROOKED ISLAND
ACKLINS ISLAND
MAYAGUANA
SALINA POINT
INDIES
HAITI
ÎLE DE LA TORTUE
Cap-Haïtien
Gonaïves
Golfe de la Gonâve
Saint-Marc
Port-au-Prince
Jérémie
Les Cayes
Jacmel
Pic de Macaya 2347
La Selle 2674
Windward Passage
Canal du Sud
POINTE L'ABACOU
HISPANIOLA
DOMINICAN REPUBLIC
Santo Domingo
Santiago
Puerto Plata
Montecristi
San Francisco de Macorís
La Vega
Pico Duarte 3175
Bonao
San Juan
Azua
Baní
San Pedro de Macorís
La Romana
Higüey
Enriquillo
ISLA BEATA
ISLA SAONA
Canal de la Mona
PUERTO RICO (U.S.)
San Juan
Arecibo
Mayagüez
Ponce
Caguas
Guayama
Cerro de Punta 1338
ISLA MONA
ISLA DE VIEQUES
VIRGIN ISLANDS (U.S.) (U.K.)
Charlotte Amalie
SAINT THOMAS
SAINT JOHN
TORTOLA
SAINT CROIX
Christiansted
Anegada Passage
ANGUILLA (U.K.)
SAINT MARTIN / SINT MAARTEN (Guad. and Neth. Ant.)
SAINT BARTHÉLEMY (Guad.)
SABA (Neth. Ant.)
SINT EUSTATIUS (Neth. Ant.)
SAINT CHRISTOPHER (SAINT KITTS)
NEVIS
Basseterre
SAINT KITTS AND NEVIS
BARBUDA
ANTIGUA AND BARBUDA
Saint Johns
MONTSERRAT (U.K.)
Plymouth
LEEWARD ISLANDS
LESSER ANTILLES
GRANDE-TERRE
Pointe-à-Pitre
GUADELOUPE (Fr.)
Basse-Terre
BASSE-TERRE
MARIE-GALANTE
Guadeloupe Passage
DOMINICA
Roseau
Dominica Channel
Montagne Pelée 1397
Fort-de-France
MARTINIQUE (Fr.)
Saint Lucia Channel
Castries
SAINT LUCIA
Saint Vincent Passage
Kingstown
SAINT VINCENT AND THE GRENADINES
GRENADINE IS.
WINDWARD ISLANDS
Bridgetown
BARBADOS
Saint George's
GRENADA
TOBAGO
Scarborough
TRINIDAD AND TOBAGO
Port of Spain
Arima
San Fernando
Point Fortin
Gulf of Paria
GALEOTA POINT
AN SEA
ANTILLES
ARUBA (Neth.)
Oranjestad
NETHERLANDS ANTILLES
BONAIRE
CURAÇAO
Willemstad
PUNTA GALLINAS
CABO DE LA VELA
PENÍNSULA DE LA GUAJIRA
PENÍNSULA DE PARAGUANÁ
Punto Fijo
Coro
Puerto Cumarebo
Golfo de Venezuela
Maracaibo
Lago de Maracaibo
Cabimas
Ciudad Ojeda
Riohacha
Santa Marta
Ciénaga
Valledupar
Pico Cristóbal Colón 5800
Barquisimeto
Valencia
Maracay
Puerto Cabello
La Guaira
Maiquetía
CARACAS
Los Teques
Barcelona
Puerto la Cruz
Cumaná
Carúpano
Maturín
Ciudad Guayana
Ciudad Bolívar
San Fernando de Apure
Mérida
Barinas
Valera
Cúcuta
San Cristóbal
Acarigua
Guanare
Calabozo
ISLA DE MARGARITA
ISLAS LOS ROQUES (Ven.)
ISLAS DE AVES (Ven.)
LA ORCHILA (Ven.)
LA BLANQUILLA (Ven.)
ISLAS LOS TESTIGOS (Ven.)
LLANOS
Orinoco
Apure
Lambert Conformal Conic Projection

Haiti
1987 ESTIMATE

Port-au-Prince, 797,000 (880,000★) E11

Honduras
1988 CENSUS

San Pedro Sula, 279,356 . . . . G 4
Tegucigalpa, 551,606 G 4

Jamaica
1987 ESTIMATE

Kingston, 646,400 (770,000★) . . . . . . E 9
Montego Bay, 70,265('82) . . . . . . E 9

Martinique
1982 CENSUS

Fort-de-France, 99,844 (116,017★) G17

Netherlands Antilles
1981 CENSUS

Willemstad, 31,883 (130,000★). . . . . H 13

Nicaragua
1985 ESTIMATE

León, 101,000. . . . . . H 4
Managua, 682,000 . . H 4

Panama
1990 CENSUS

Colón, 54,469 (96,000★). . . . . J 8
Panamá, 411,549 (770,000★) . . . . . . J 8

Puerto Rico
1980 CENSUS

Ponce, 161,739 (232,551★) E14
San Juan, 424,600 (1,775,260★) E14

Saint Lucia
1987 ESTIMATE

Castries, 53,933 . . . . G17

Saint Vincent and the Grenadines
1987 ESTIMATE

Kingstown, 19,028 (28,936★) H17

Trinidad and Tobago
1988 ESTIMATE

Port of Spain, 59,200 (370,000★) I17

ALBERTA....................F10
Alma, 25,923 ('86) (29,977★) G18
Baie-Comeau, 26,244 ('86) (33,047★) G19
Banff, 4,208 ('81).........F 9
Barrie, 48,287 ('86) (67,703★) H17
Bathurst, 14,683 ('86) (34,895★) G19
Belleville, 36,041 ('86) (87,530★) H17
Brandon, 38,708 ('86).G13
BRITISH COLUMBIA... F 8
Brockville, 20,880 ('86) (37,115★) H17
Calgary, 636,104 ('86) (671,326★) F10
Cambridge, 79,920 ('86)......................... H16
Campbell River, 15,370 ('81).........................F 7
Campbellton, 9,077 ('86) (17,418★) G19
CANADA.................... D13
Charlottetown, 15,776 ('86) (53,868★) G20
Chatham, 42,211 ('86) H16
Chicoutimi, 61,083 ('86) (158,468★) G18
Chilliwack, 41,337 ('86) (50,288★) .... G 8
Churchill, 1,186 ('81)... E14
Corner Brook, 22,719 ('86) (33,730★) G21
Cornwall, 46,425 ('86) (51,719★) G18
Dartmouth, 65,243 ('86)......................... H20
Dawson Creek, 10,544 ('86).........................E 8
Dolbeau, 8,554 ('86) (15,288★) G18
Drummondville, 36,020 ('86) (56,283★) G18
Edmonton, 573,982 ('86) (785,465★)...............F10
Edmundston, 11,497 ('86) (22,614★) G19
Eskimo Point, 1,189 ('86)......................... D14
Flin Flon, 7,591 ('86) (9,211★) F12
Fort McMurray, 34,949 ('86) (48,497★) E10
Fort Saint John, 13,355 ('86).........................E 8
Fredericton, 44,352 ('86) (65,768★)............... G19
Gander, 10,207 ('86) (10,899★) G22
Gaspé, 17,350 ('86).... G20
Granby, 38,508 ('86) (51,176★) G18
Grande-Prairie, 26,471 ('86).........................E 9
Grand Falls, 9,121 ('86) (25,612★) G21
Guelph, 78,235 ('86) (85,962★) H16
Halifax, 113,577 ('86) (295,990★) H20
Hamilton, 306,728 ('86) (557,029★) H17
Happy Valley-Goose Bay, 7,248 ('86)............... F20
Hull, 58,722 ('86)........ G17
Inuvik, 3,389 ('86)....... C 6
Jasper, 3,269 ('81).......F 9
Joliette, 16,845 ('86) (34,897★) G18
Jonquière, 58,467 ('86)......................... G18
Kamloops, 61,773 ('86).........................F 8
Kelowna, 61,213 ('86) (89,730★)............... G 9
Kenora, 9,621 ('86) (15,456★) G14
Kirkland Lake, 11,604 ('86)......................... G16
Kitchener, 150,604 ('86) (311,195★)............... H16
Kitimat, 11,196 ('86)..... F 7
Labrador City, 8,664 ('86) (11,301★) F19
La Tuque, 10,723 ('86) (13,468★) G18
Laval, 284,164 ('86).... G18
Lethbridge, 58,841 ('86)......................... G10
Lloydminster, 17,356 ('86).........................F11
London, 269,140 ('86) (342,302★) H16
MANITOBA..................F13
Matane, 13,243 ('86) (15,361★) G19
Medicine Hat, 41,804 ('86) (50,734★)...............F10
Midland, 12,092 ('86) (35,003★)............... H17
Moncton, 55,468 ('86) (102,084★) G20

★ Population of metropolitan area, including suburbs.

Kilometers 0 200 400 600 Km.
Miles 0 200 400 600 Mi.
1:16 000 000

Montréal, 1,015,420 ('86) (2,921,357★) G18
Moose Jaw, 35,073 ('86) (37,219★) F11
Nanaimo, 49,029 ('86) (60,420★) .... G 8
NEW BRUNSWICK..... G19
NEWFOUNDLAND.......F21
New Glasgow, 10,022 ('86) (38,737★) G20
Niagara Falls, 72,107 ('86)......................... H17
North Bay, 50,623 ('86) (57,422★) G17
NORTHWEST TERRITORIES.......... C13
NOVA SCOTIA........... G20
ONTARIO................... G16
Orillia, 24,077 ('86) (31,252★) H17
Oshawa, 123,651 ('86) (203,543★) H17
Ottawa, 300,763 ('86) (819,263★) G17
Owen Sound, 19,804 ('86) (27,364★) H16
Pembroke, 14,131 ('86) (22,560★) G17
Penticton, 23,588 ('86) (38,966★) .... G 9
Peterborough, 61,049 ('86) (87,083★) H17
Portage-la-Prairie, 13,198 ('86)......................... G13
Port Alberni, 18,241 ('86)......................... G 8
Prince Albert, 33,686 ('86) (40,841★) F11
PRINCE EDWARD ISLAND.................. G20
Prince George, 67,621 ('86)..........................F 8
Prince Rupert, 15,755 ('86) (17,581★) ....F 6
QUÉBEC......................F18
Québec, 164,580 ('86) (603,267★) G18
Rankin Inlet, 1,374 ('86)......................... D14
Red Deer, 54,425 ('86)F10
Regina, 175,064 ('86) (186,521★) F12
Saint-Hyacinthe, 38,603 ('86) (48,303★) G18
Saint-Jérôme, 23,316 ('86) (44,048★) G18
Saint John, 76,831 ('86) (121,265★) G19
Saint John's, 96,216 ('86) (161,901★) G22
Sarnia, 49,033 ('86) (85,700★) H16
SASKATCHEWAN.......F11
Saskatoon, 177,641 ('86) (200,665★) F11
Sault Sainte Marie, 80,905 ('86) (84,617★) G16
Selkirk, 10,013 ('86).... F13
Sept-Îles (Seven Islands), 25,637 ('86) (28,050★) F19
Shawinigan, 21,470 ('86) (61,965★) G18
Sherbrooke, 74,438 ('86) (129,960★) G18
Sorel, 19,522 ('86) (46,096★) G18
Sudbury, 88,717 ('86) (148,877★) G16
Summerside, 8,020 ('86) (15,614★) G20
Swift Current, 15,666 ('86)..........................F11
Sydney Mines, 8,063 ('86)......................... G20
Thetford Mines, 18,561 ('86) (31,940★) G18
Thunder Bay, 112,272 ('86) (122,217★) G15
Timmins, 46,657 ('86). G16
Toronto, 612,289 ('86) (3,427,168★) H17
Trail, 7,948 ('86) (20,257★) .... G 9
Trois-Rivières, 50,122 ('86) (128,888★) G18
Truro, 12,124 ('86) (41,516★) G20
Val-d'Or, 22,252 ('86) (27,178★) G17
Vancouver, 431,147 ('86) (1,380,729★) .... G 8
Victoria, 66,303 ('86) (255,547★) .... G 8
Whitehorse, 15,199 ('86).......................... D 5
Windsor, 193,111 ('86) (253,988★) H16
Winnipeg, 594,551 ('86) (625,304★) G13
Yellowknife, 11,753 ('86).......................... D10
YUKON....................... D 5

Alberta

1986 CENSUS

Airdrie, 10,390 . . . . . D 3
Athabasca, 1,970 . . . . B 4
Banff . . . . D 3
Barrhead, 3,991 . . . . B 3
Beaumont, 3,944 . . . . C 4
Beaverlodge, 1,808 . . B 1
Blackfalds, 1,688 . . . . C 4
Bonnyville, 5,470 . . . . B 5
Bow Island, 1,650 . . E 5
Brooks, 9,464 . . . . . . D 5
Calgary, 636,104
(671,326★) . . . . . . D 3
Camrose, 12,968 . . . . C 4
Canmore, 4,182 . . . . D 3
Cardston, 3,497 . . . . E 4
Carstairs, 1,629 . . . . D 3
Claresholm, 3,382 . . D 4
Coaldale, 4,796 . . . . E 4
Cochrane, 4,190 . . . . D 3
Cold Lake, 3,195 . . . . B 5
Coronation, 1,310 . . C 5
Crowsnest Pass,
6,912 . . . . E 3
Devon, 3,691 . . . . . . C 4
Didsbury, 3,184 . . . . D 3
Drayton Valley, 5,290 C 3
Drumheller, 6,366 . . D 4
Edmonton, 573,982
(785,465★) . . . . . . C 4
Edson, 7,323 . . . . . . C 2
Fairview, 2,998 . . . . A 1
Fort Chipewyan, 922 f 8
Fort Macleod, 3,123 E 4
Fort McMurray, 34,949
(48,497★) . . . . A 5
Fort Saskatchewan,
11,983 . . . . C 4
Fox Creek, 2,068 . . . . B 2
Gibbons, 2,335 . . . . C 4
Grand Centre, 3,655 B 5
Grande Cache, 3,646 C 1
Grande Prairie,
26,471 . . . . B 1
Grimshaw, 2,579 . . . . A 2
Hanna, 3,017 . . . . . . D 5
High Level, 3,004 . . . . F 7
High Prairie, 2,817 . . B 2
High River, 5,096 . . . . D 4
Hinton, 8,629 . . . . . . C 2
Innisfail, 5,535 . . . . . . C 4
Jasper . . . . C 1
Lac La Biche, 2,553 B 5
Lacombe, 6,080 . . . . C 4
La Crete, 689 . . . . . . f 7
Lake Louise, 688 . . . . D 2
Lamont, 1,576 . . . . . . C 4
Leduc, 13,126 . . . . . . C 4
Lethbridge, 58,841 . . E 4
Lloydminster, 17,354 C 5
Magrath, 1,637 . . . . . . E 4
Medicine Hat, 41,804
(50,734★) . . . . D 5
Morinville, 5,364 . . . . C 4
Nordegg, 53 . . . . C 2
Okotoks, 5,214 . . . . D 4
Olds, 4,871 . . . . D 3
Peace River, 6,288 . . A 2
Penhold, 1,580 . . . . . . C 4
Picture Butte, 1,576 . . E 4
Pincher Creek, 3,800 E 4
Ponoka, 5,473 . . . . . . C 4
Provost, 1,725 . . . . . . C 5
Raymond, 2,957 . . . . E 4
Redcliff, 3,834 . . . . . . D 5
Red Deer, 54,425 . . . C 4
Redwater, 1,982 . . . . C 4
Rimbey, 1,786 . . . . . . C 3
Rocky Mountain House,
5,182 . . . . C 3
Saint Albert, 36,710 . . C 4
Saint Paul, 5,030 . . . . B 5
Sherwood Park . . . . C 4
Slave Lake, 5,429 . . B 3
Smith, 251 . . . . B 3
Spruce Grove, 11,918 C 4
Stettler, 5,147 . . . . . . C 4
Stony Plain, 5,802 . . C 3
Strathmore, 3,544 . . D 4
Sundre, 1,712 . . . . . . D 3
Swan Hills, 2,403 . . . . B 3
Sylvan Lake, 3,937 . . C 3
Taber, 6,382 . . . . E 4
Three Hills, 2,528 . . . D 4
Valleyview, 1,987 . . . . B 2
Vegreville, 5,276 . . . . C 4
Vermilion, 3,879 . . . . C 5
Vulcan, 1,420 . . . . . . D 4
Wainwright, 4,665 . . C 5
Westlock, 4,532 . . . . B 4
Wetaskiwin, 10,071 . . C 4
Whitecourt, 5,737 . . B 3

★ Population of metropolitan area, including suburbs.

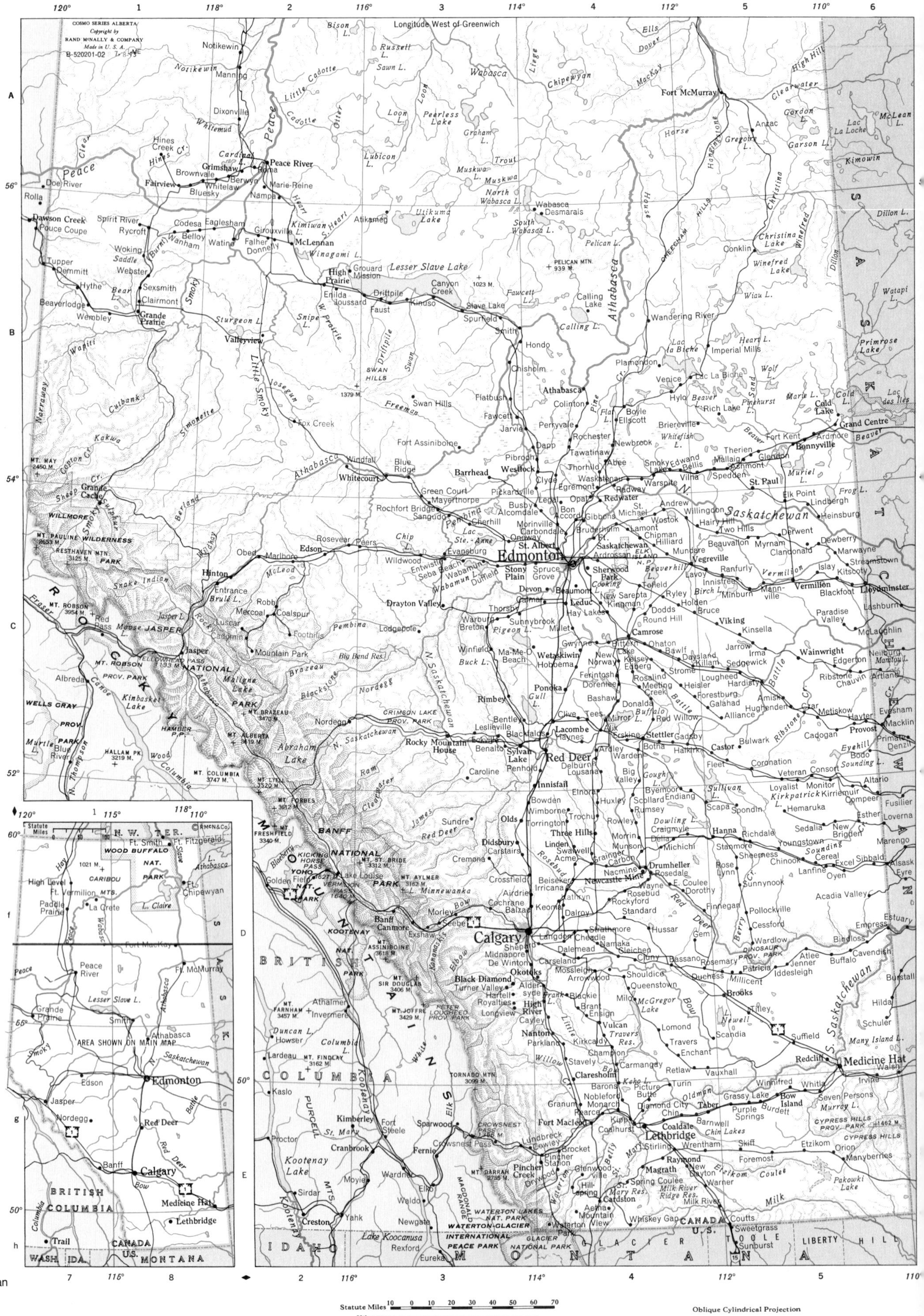

Statute Miles 10 0 10 20 30 40 50 60 70
Kilometers 10 0 10 20 40 60 80 100

Oblique Cylindrical Projection

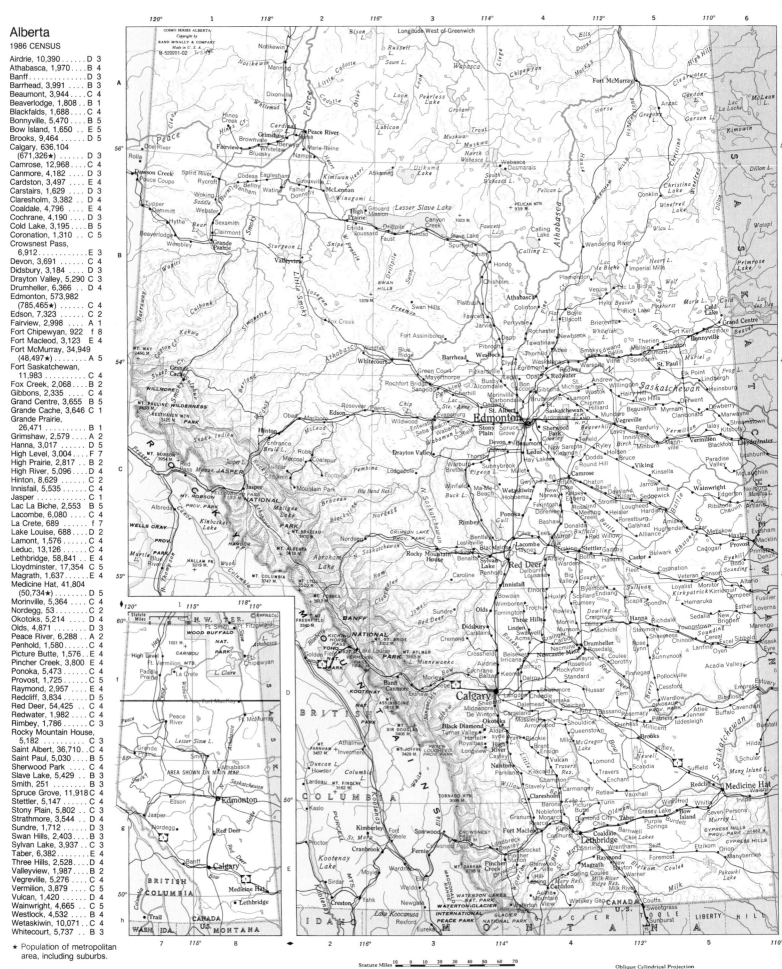

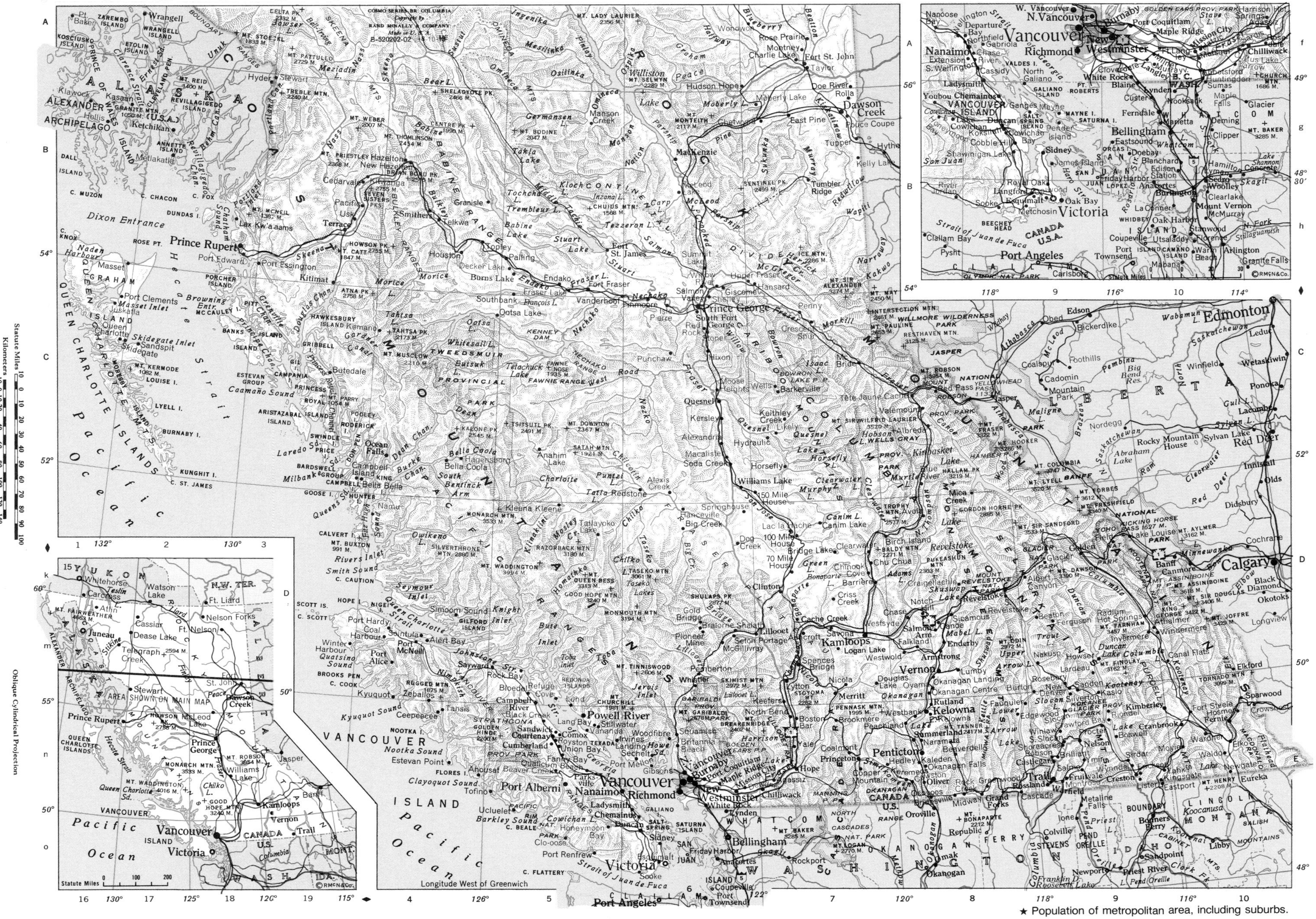

British Columbia

1986 CENSUS

★ Population of metropolitan area, including suburbs.

Armstrong, 2,706	D 8
Ashcroft, 1,914	D 7
Black Creek, 1,972	E 5
Burnaby, 145,161	E 6
Castlegar, 6,385	E 9
Chetwynd, 2,774	B 7
Chilliwack, 41,337 (50,288★)	E 7
Clearwater, 1,375	D 7
Colwood, 11,546	h12
Comox, 6,873	E 5
Courtenay, 9,631 (37,553★)	E 5
Cranbrook, 15,893	E10
Creston, 4,098	E 9
Dawson Creek, 10,544	B 7
Duncan, 4,039 (24,062★)	E 6
Elkford, 3,137	D10
Esquimalt, 15,972	E 6
Fernie, 5,188	E10
Fort Nelson, 3,729	m18
Fort Saint John, 13,355	A 7
Gibsons, 2,675	E 6
Golden, 3,584	D 9
Grand Forks, 3,282	E 8
Hope, 3,046	E 7
Kamloops, 61,773	D 7
Kelowna, 61,213 (89,730★)	E 8
Kimberley, 6,732	E 9
Kitimat, 11,196	B 3
Ladysmith, 4,393	E 6
Lake Cowichan, 2,170	g11
Langley, 16,557	f13
MacKenzie, 5,542	B 6
Matsqui, 51,449 (88,420★)	f13
Merritt, 6,180	D 7
Nanaimo, 49,029 (60,420★)	E 5
Nelson, 8,113	E 9
New Westminster, 39,972	E 6
North Vancouver, 35,698	E 6
Oak Bay, 17,065	h12
One Hundred Mile House, 1,692	D 7
Parksville, 5,828	E 5
Penticton, 23,588 (38,966★)	E 8
Port Alberni, 18,241 (26,134★)	E 5
Port Coquitlam, 29,115	E 6
Powell River, 12,440 (18,374★)	E 5
Prince George, 67,621	C 6
Prince Rupert, 15,755 (17,581★)	B 2
Qualicum Beach, 3,410	E 5
Quesnel, 8,358 (23,264★)	C 6
Revelstoke, 8,279	D 8
Richmond, 108,492	E 6
Rossland, 3,472	E 9
Sidney, 8,982	E 6
Smithers, 4,713	B 4
Sparwood, 4,540	E10
Summerland, 7,755	E 8
Terrace, 10,532 (17,390★)	B 3
Trail, 7,948 (20,257★)	E 9
Tumbler Ridge, 4,540	B 7
Vancouver, 431,147 (1,380,729★)	E 6
Vanderhoof, 3,505	C 5
Vernon, 20,241 (42,802★)	D 8
Victoria, 66,303 (255,547★)	E 6
West Vancouver, 36,266	f12
White Rock, 14,387	E 6
Williams Lake, 10,280 (33,556★)	C 6

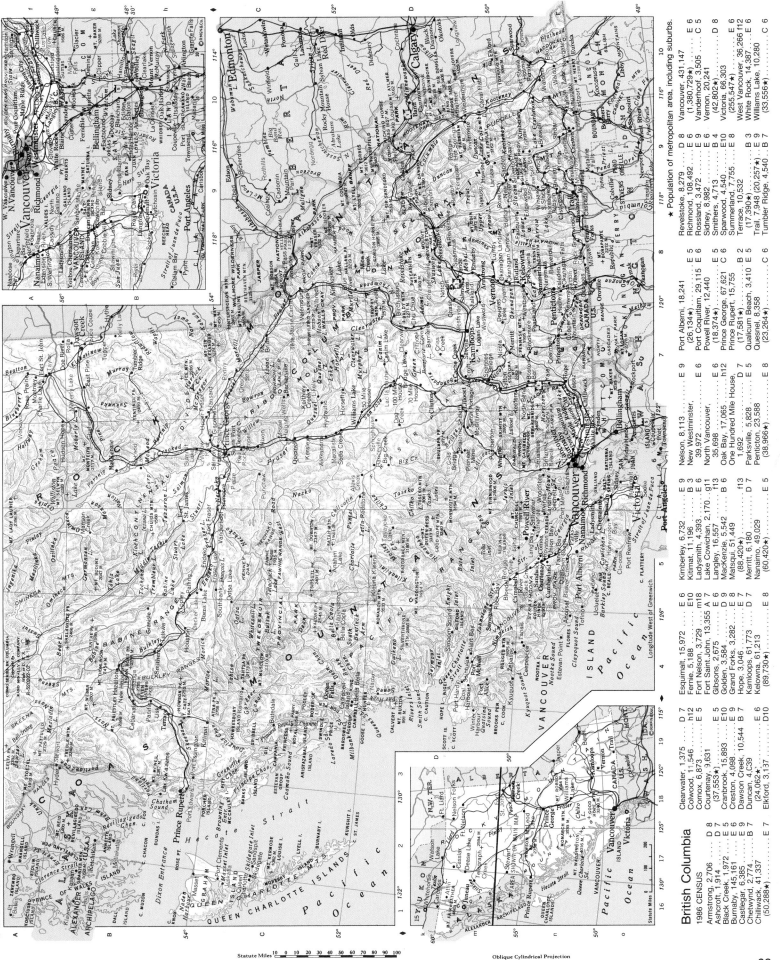

Manitoba

Manitoba

1986 CENSUS

Altona, 2,958 . . . . . . E 3
Arborg, 1,018 . . . . . . D 3
Ashern, 620 . . . . D 2
Beausejour, 2,535 . . D 3
Birch River, 509 . . . . C 1
Birtle, 850 . . . . D 1
Boissevain, 1,572 . . . E 1
Brandon, 38,708 . . . . E 2
Camperville, 588 . . . . D 1
Carberry, 1,544 . . . . E 2
Carman, 2,500 . . . . . . E 2
Churchill, 1,109 . . . . . . f 9
Cranberry Portage, 849 . . . . B 1
Cross Lake, 580 . . . . B 3
Crystal City, 487 . . . . E 2
Dauphin, 8,875 . . . . D 1
Deloraine, 1,134 . . . . E 1
Duck Bay, 559 . . . . . . C 1
Easterville, 675 . . . . C 2
East Selkirk, 572 . . . . D 3
Elkhorn, 534 . . . . E 1
Emerson, 725 . . . . . . E 3
Erickson, 565 . . . . . . D 2
Flin Flon, 7,591 (9,211★) . . . . B 1
Gilbert Plains, 816 . . D 1
Gillam, 1,909 . . . . . . A 4
Gimli, 1,681 . . . . D 3
Gladstone, 951 . . . . D 2
Glenboro, 719 . . . . . . E 2
Grandview, 941 . . . . D 1
Gretna, 503 . . . . E 3
Grunthal, 639 . . . . . . E 3
Hamiota, 815 . . . . . . D 1
Hartney, 523 . . . . . . E 1
Killarney, 2,318 . . . . E 2
Lac du Bonnet, 1,021 D 3
Leaf Rapids, 1,950 . . A 1
Lorette, 1,169 . . . . . . E 3
Lundar, 562 . . . . D 2
MacGregor, 854 . . . . E 2
Manitou, 856 . . . . . . E 2
McCreary, 578 . . . . . . D 2
Melita, 1,239 . . . . . . E 1
Minitonas, 559 . . . . . . C 1
Minnedosa, 2,520 . . D 2
Moose Lake, 541 . . . . C 1
Morden, 5,004 . . . . . . E 2
Morris, 1,613 . . . . . . E 3
Neepawa, 3,314 . . . . D 2
Niverville, 1,452 . . . . E 3
Norway House, 633 . . C 3
Notre Dame de Lourdes, 628 . . . . E 2
Pilot Mound, 819 . . . . E 2
Pine Falls, 831 . . . . . . D 3
Plum Coulee, 677 . . E 3
Portage la Prairie, 13,198 . . . . E 2
Powerview, 724 . . . . D 3
Reston, 616 . . . . E 1
Rivers, 1,157 . . . . . . D 1
Riverton, 635 . . . . . . D 3
Roblin, 1,913 . . . . . . D 1
Rossburn, 664 . . . . . . D 1
Russell, 1,669 . . . . . . D 1
Saint Adolphe, 1,059 E 3
Sainte Anne-des-Chênes, 1,402 . . . . E 3
Saint Claude, 610 . . E 2
Saint Jean Baptiste, 571 . . . . E 3
Saint Malo, 742 . . . . E 3
Saint Pierre-Jolys, 912 . . . . E 3
Sainte Rose du Lac, 1,030 . . . . D 2
Selkirk, 10,013 . . . . . . D 3
Shoal Lake, 832 . . . . D 1
Snow Lake, 1,837 . . . B 1
Somerset, 534 . . . . . . E 2
Souris, 1,751 . . . . . . E 1
South Indian Lake, 743 . . . . A 2
Steinbach, 7,473 . . . . E 3
Stonewall, 2,349 . . . . D 3
Swan River, 3,946 . . C 1
Teulon, 953 . . . . D 3
The Pas, 6,283 . . . . . C 1
Thompson, 14,701 . . B 3
Treherne, 762 . . . . . . E 2
Virden, 3,054 . . . . . . E 1
Wabowden, 571 . . . . B 2
Wawanesa, 502 . . . . . E 2
Winkler, 5,926 . . . . . . E 3
Winnipeg, 594,551 (625,304★) . . . . . . E 3
Winnipeg Beach, 548 D 3
Winnipegosis, 832 . . D 2

★ Population of metropolitan area, including suburbs.

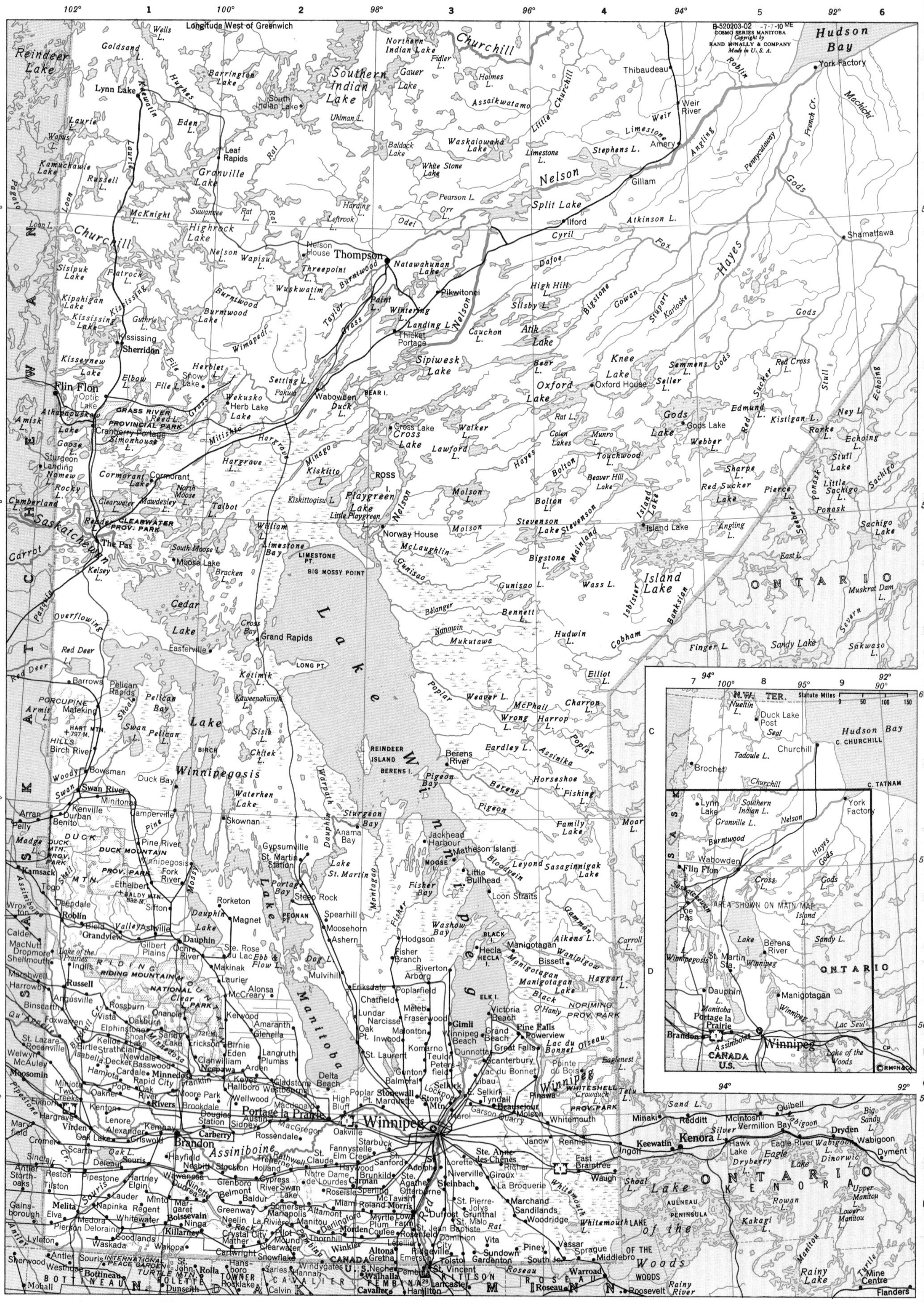

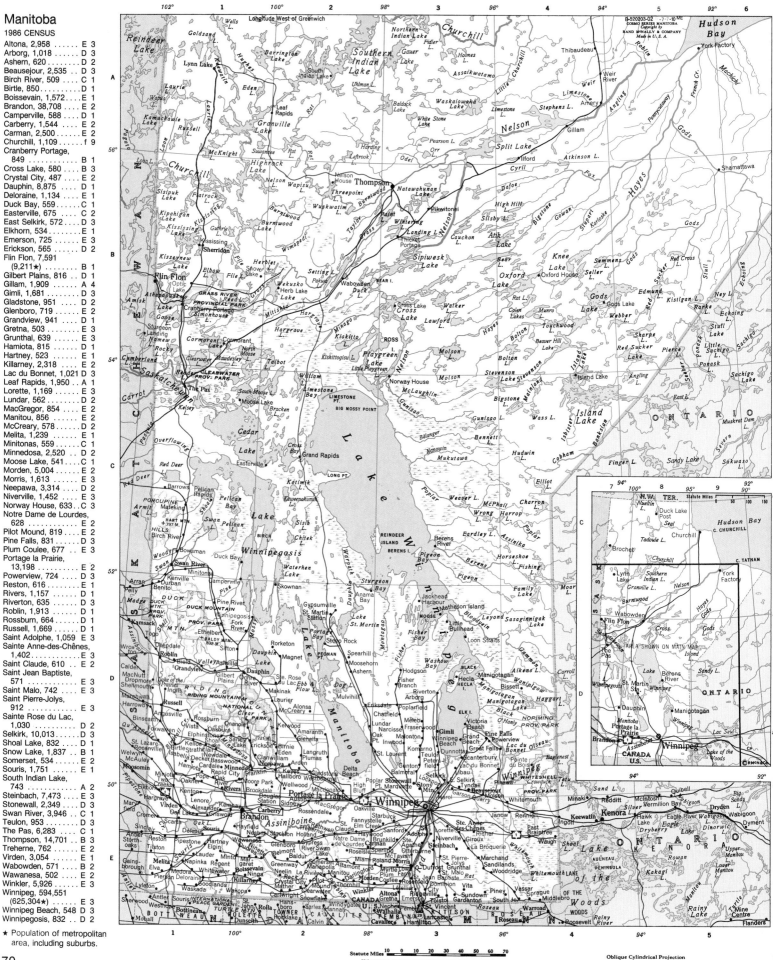

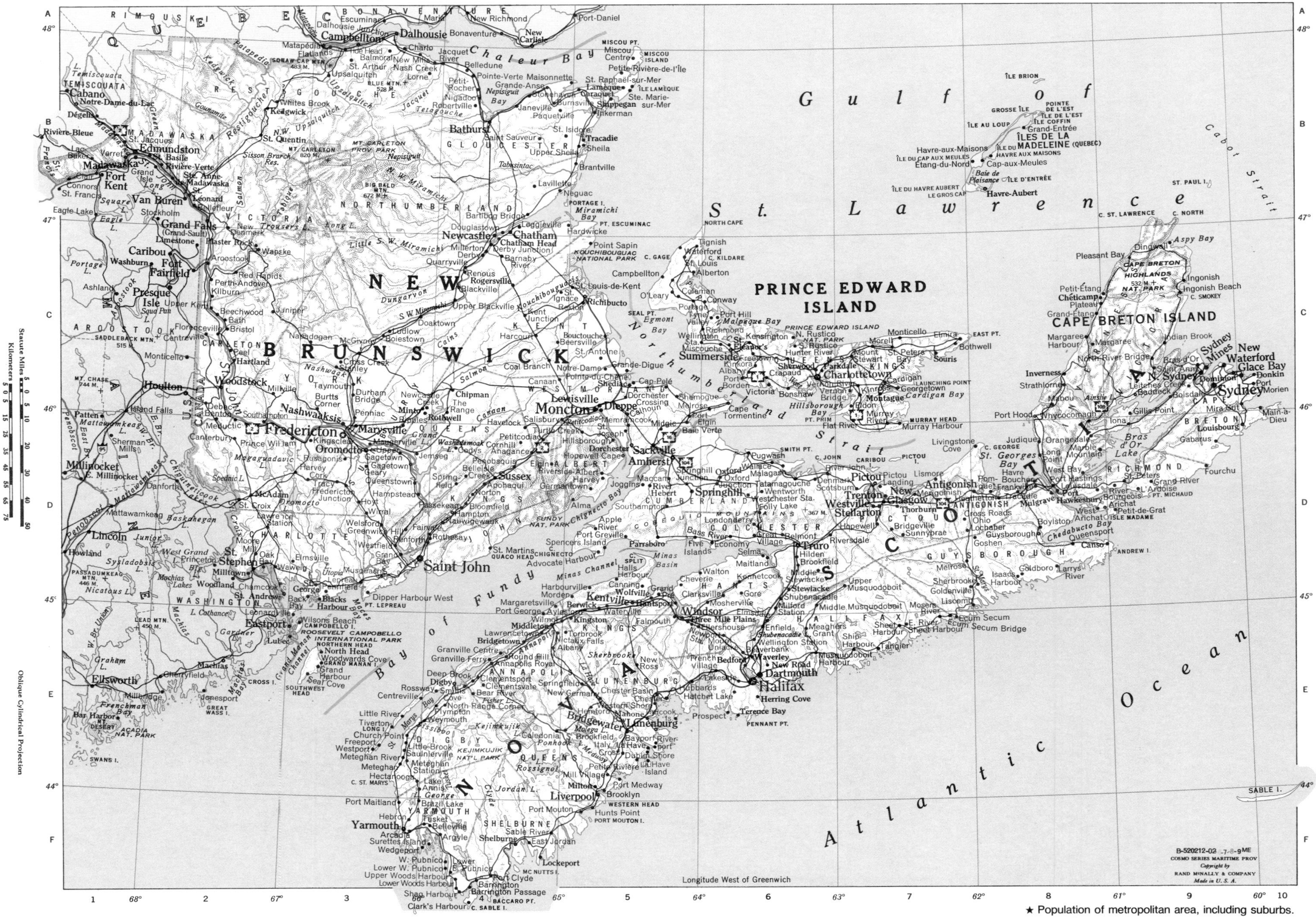

★ Population of metropolitan area, including suburbs.

New Brunswick

1986 CENSUS

- Bathurst, 14,683 (34,895★) . . . . B 4
- Blacks Harbour, 1,224 D 3
- Bouctouche, 2,420 . . . . C 5
- Campbellton, 9,077 (17,418★) . . . . A 3
- Caraquet, 4,493 . . . . . . B 5
- Chatham, 6,218 . . . . . . B 4
- Dalhousie, 5,363 . . . . . . A 3
- Dieppe, 9,084 . . . . C 5
- Edmundston, 11,497 (22,614★) . . . . B 1
- Fairvale, 4,660 . . . . D 4
- Fredericton, 44,352 (65,768★) . . . . D 3
- Grand Bay, 3,319 . . . . D 3
- Grand Falls (Grand-Sault), 6,209 . . . . B 2
- Hampton, 3,405 . . . . . . D 4
- Minto, 3,197 . . . . C 3
- Moncton, 55,468 (102,084★) . . . . C 5
- Newcastle, 5,804 . . . . C 4
- Oromocto, 9,656 . . . . . . D 3
- Sackville, 5,470 . . . . D 5
- Saint Basile, 3,306 . . . . B 1
- Saint Jacques, 2,310 . . B 1
- Saint John, 76,381 (121,265★) . . . . D 3
- Saint Quentin, 2,264 . . B 2
- Saint Stephen, 5,032 . . D 2
- Shediac, 4,370 . . . . . . C 5
- Shippegan, 2,801 . . . . . B 5
- Sussex, 4,114 . . . . D 4
- Tracadie, 2,444 . . . . . . B 5
- Woodstock, 4,549 . . . . . C 2

Nova Scotia

1986 CENSUS

- Amherst, 9,671 . . . . . . D 5
- Antigonish, 5,291 . . . . D 8
- Bedford, 8,010 . . . . E 6
- Berwick, 2,058 . . . . . . D 5
- Bridgewater, 6,617 . . . . E 5
- Canso, 1,285 . . . . D 8
- Chéticamp, 984 . . . . . . C 8
- Dartmouth, 65,243 . . . . E 6
- Digby, 2,525 . . . . E 4
- Dominion, 2,754 . . . . . . C 9
- Enfield, 1,775 . . . . E 6
- Glace Bay, 20,467 . . . . C10
- Halifax, 113,577 (295,990★) . . . . E 6
- Kentville, 5,208 . . . . . . D 5
- Liverpool, 3,295 . . . . . . E 5
- Lunenburg, 2,972 . . . . E 5
- New Glasgow, 10,022 (38,737★) . . . . D 7
- New Waterford, 8,326 C 9
- North Sydney, 7,472 . . C 9
- Pictou, 4,413 . . . . D 7
- Port Hawkesbury, 3,869 D 8
- Springhill, 4,712 . . . . . . D 5
- Stellarton, 5,259 . . . . . . D 7
- Sydney, 27,754 (119,470★) . . . . C 9
- Sydney Mines, 8,063 . . C 9
- Trenton, 3,083 . . . . D 7
- Truro, 12,124 (41,516★) D 6
- Westville, 4,271 . . . . . . D 7
- Windsor, 3,665 . . . . E 5
- Wolfville, 3,277 . . . . . . D 5
- Yarmouth, 7,617 . . . . . . F 3

Prince Edward Island

1986 CENSUS

- Charlottetown, 15,776 (53,868★) . . . . C 6
- Parkdale, 2,065 . . . . . . C 6
- Saint Eleanor's, 3,743 . . C 6
- Sherwood, 5,769 . . . . . . C 6
- Summerside, 8,020 (15,614★) . . . . C 6

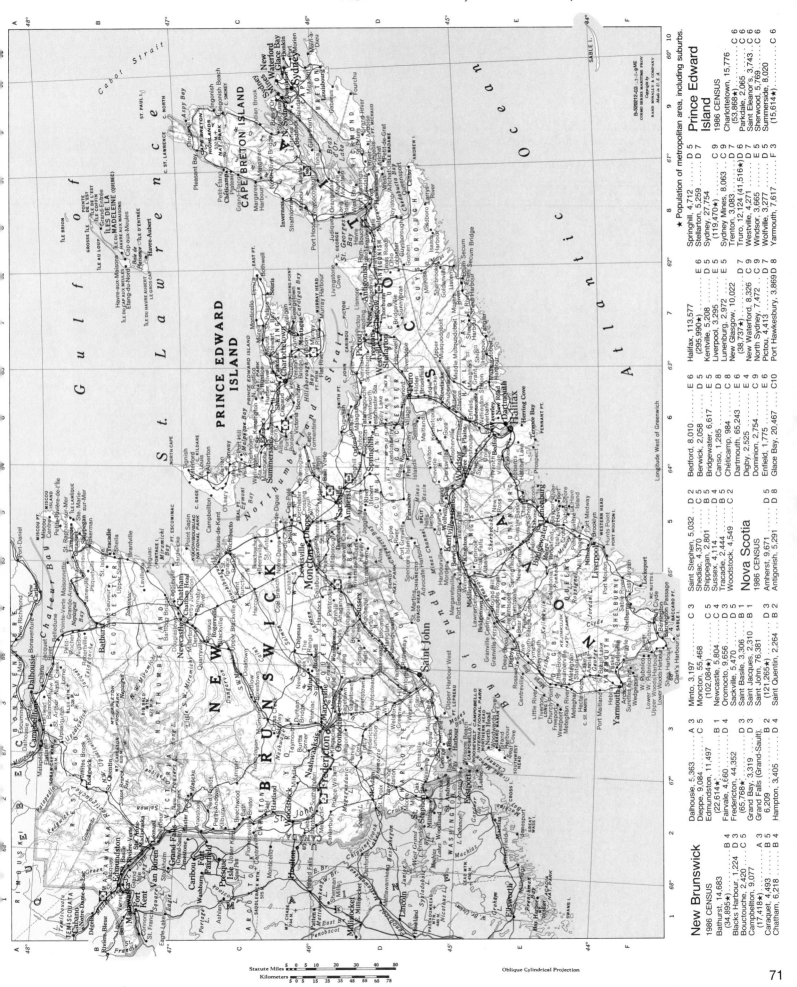

Newfoundland and Labrador

1986 CENSUS

Arnold's Cove, 1,117 E 4
Badger, 1,151 . . . . . . D 3
Baie Verte, 2,049 . . . . D 3
Bay Bulls, 1,114 . . . . E 5
Bay Roberts, 4,446 . . E 5
Bishop's Falls, 4,213 D 4
Bonavista, 4,605 . . . . D 5
Botwood, 3,916 . . . . D 4
Buchans, 1,281 . . . . D 3
Burgeo, 2,582 . . . . . . E 3
Burin, 2,892 . . . . E 4
Burnt Islands, 1,042 E 2
Carbonear, 5,337 (13,082★) . . . . E 5
Carmanville, 987 . . . . D 4
Cartwright, 674 . . . . B 3
Catalina, 1,211 . . . . . . D 5
Channel-Port-aux-Basques, 5,901 . . E 2
Clarenville, 2,967 . . . . D 4
Conception Bay South, 15,531 . . . . E 5
Corner Brook, 22,719 (33,730★) . . . . D 3
Cox's Cove, 999 . . . . D 2
Deer Lake, 4,233 . . . . D 3
Dunville, 1,833 . . . . . . E 5
Durrell, 1,060 . . . . . . D 4
Englee, 1,012 . . . . . . C 3
Fogo, 1,153 . . . . D 4
Fortune, 2,370 . . . . . . E 4
Gambo, 2,723 . . . . . . D 4
Gander, 10,207 . . . . . D 4
Glenwood, 1,038 . . . . D 4
Glovertown, 2,184 . . D 4
Grand Bank, 3,732 . . E 4
Grand Falls, 9,121 (25,612★) . . . . D 4
Hampden, 875 . . . . . . D 3
Happy Valley-Goose Bay, 7,248 . . . . B 1
Harbour Breton, 2,432 . . . . E 4
Harbour Grace, 3,053 E 5
Hare Bay, 1,436 . . . . D 4
Hermitage, 831 . . . . E 4
Isle-aux-Morts, 1,203 E 2
Joe Batt's Arm [-Barr'd Islands-Shoal Bay], 1,232 . . . . D 4
King's Point, 923 . . . . D 3
Labrador City, 8,664 (11,301★) . . . . h 8
Lark Harbour, 829 . . D 2
La Scie, 1,429 . . . . . . D 4
Lawn, 1,015 . . . . E 4
Lewisporte, 3,978 . . D 4
Lourdes, 937 . . . . . . D 2
Marystown, 6,660 . . E 4
Milltown [-Head of Bay d'Espoir], 1,276 . . E 4
Mount Pearl, 20,293 E 5
Musgrave Harbour, 1,527 . . . . D 5
Nain, 1,018 . . . . g 9
New Harbour, 957 . . E 5
Norris Arm, 1,127 . . D 4
Norris Point, 1,010 . . D 3
Pasadena, 3,268 . . . . D 3
Placentia, 2,016 . . . . E 5
Point Leamington, 850 . . . . D 4
Port au Port [West-Aguathuna-Felix Cove], 842 . . . . D 2
Pouch Cove, 1,576 . . E 5
Ramea, 1,380 . . . . . . E 3
Robert's Arm, 1,111 D 4
Rocky Harbour, 1,268 D 3
Roddickton, 1,223 . . C 3
Rose-Blanche [-Harbour le Cou], 967 . . . . E 2
Saint Alban's, 1,780 E 4
Saint Anthony, 3,182 C 4
Saint George's, 1,852 D 2
Saint John's, 96,216 (161,901★) . . . . . . E 5
Saint Lawrence, 1,841 . . . . E 4
Shoal Harbour, 1,049 D 4
Spaniard's Bay, 2,190 E 5
Springdale, 3,555 . . . . D 3
Stephenville, 7,994 . . D 2
Stephenville Crossing, 2,252 . . . . D 2
Summerford, 1,169 . . D 4
Torbay, 3,730 . . . . . . E 5
Trepassey, 1,460 . . . . E 5
Twillingate, 1,506 . . . . D 4
Upper Island Cove, 2,055 . . . . E 5
Victoria, 1,895 . . . . . . E 5
Wabana (Bell Island), 4,057 . . . . E 5
Wabush, 2,637 . . . . h 8
Wesleyville, 1,208 . . D 5
Whitbourne, 1,151 . . E 5
Windsor, 5,545 . . . . D 4
Witless Bay, 1,022 . . E 5

★ Population of metropolitan area, including suburbs.

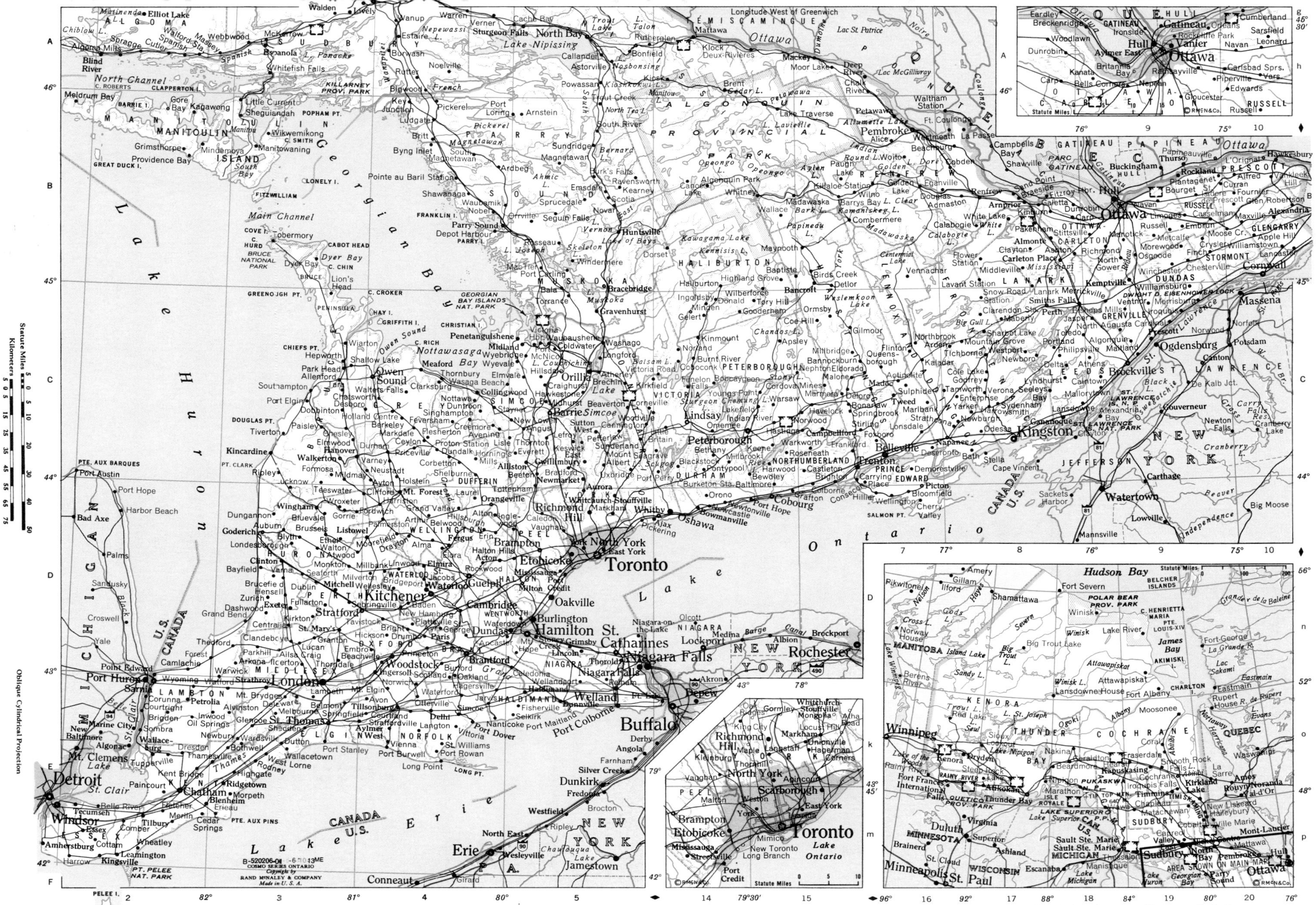

★ Population of metropolitan area, including suburbs.

Ontario

1986 CENSUS

Ajax, 36,550 . . . . D 6
Barrie, 48,287
(67,703★) . . . . C 5
Belleville, 36,041
(87,530★) . . . . C 7
Brampton, 188,498 . . . . D 5
Brantford, 76,146
(90,521★) . . . . D 4
Brockville, 20,880
(37,115★) . . . . C 9
Burlington, 116,675 . . . . D 5
Caledon, 29,666 . . . . . . D 5
Cambridge, 79,920 . . . . . D 4
Chatham, 42,211 . . . . . . E 2
Cornwall, 46,425
(51,719★) B10
East York, 101,085 . . . . D 5
Etobicoke, 302,973 . . . . D 5
Gloucester, 89,810 . . . . h12
Guelph, 78,235
(85,962★) . . . . D 4
Haileybury, 4,820
(14,781★) p20
Haldimand, 17,701 . . . . E 5
Halton Hills, 35,570 . . . . D 5
Hamilton, 306,728
(557,029★) . . . . D 5
Kanata, 27,519 . . . . . . B 9
Kingston, 55,050
(122,350★) . . . . C 8
Kitchener, 150,604
(311,195★) . . . . D 4
Lindsay, 14,455
(17,913★) . . . . C 6
London, 269,140
(342,302★) . . . . E 3
Markham, 114,597 . . . . D 5
Midland, 12,092
(35,003★) . . . . C 5
Milton, 32,037 . . . . D 5
Mississauga, 374,005 . . D 5
Nepean, 95,490 . . . . . . B 9
Newcastle, 34,073 . . . . D 6
Newmarket, 34,923 . . . . C 5
Niagara Falls, 72,107 . . D 5
North Bay, 50,623
(57,422★) . . . . A 5
North York, 556,297 . . D 5
Oakville, 87,107 . . . . . . D 5
Orillia, 24,077 (31,252★) C 5
Oshawa, 123,651
(203,543★) . . . . D 6
Ottawa, 300,763
(819,263★) . . . . B 9
Owen Sound, 19,804
(27,364★) . . . . C 4
Peterborough, 61,049
(87,083★) . . . . C 6
Pickering, 48,959 . . . . . D 5
Port Colborne, 18,281 . . E 5
Richmond Hill, 46,766 . . D 5
Saint Catharines, 123,455
(343,258★) . . . . D 5
Sarnia, 49,033
(85,700★) . . . . E 2
Sault Sainte Marie, 80,905
(84,617★) p18
Scarborough, 484,676 m15
Stoney Creek, 43,554 . . D 5
Stratford, 26,451 . . . . . . D 3
Sudbury, 88,717
(148,877★) . . . . A 4
Thunder Bay, 112,272
(122,217★) o17
Timmins, 46,657 . . . . . . o19
Toronto, 612,289
(3,427,168★) . . . . . . D 5
Vaughan, 65,058 . . . . . D 5
Waterloo, 58,718 . . . . . D 4
Welland, 45,054 . . . . . . E 5
Whitby, 45,819 . . . . . . D 6
Windsor, 193,111
(253,988★) . . . . E 1
Woodstock, 26,386 . . . . D 4
York, 135,401 . . . . D 5

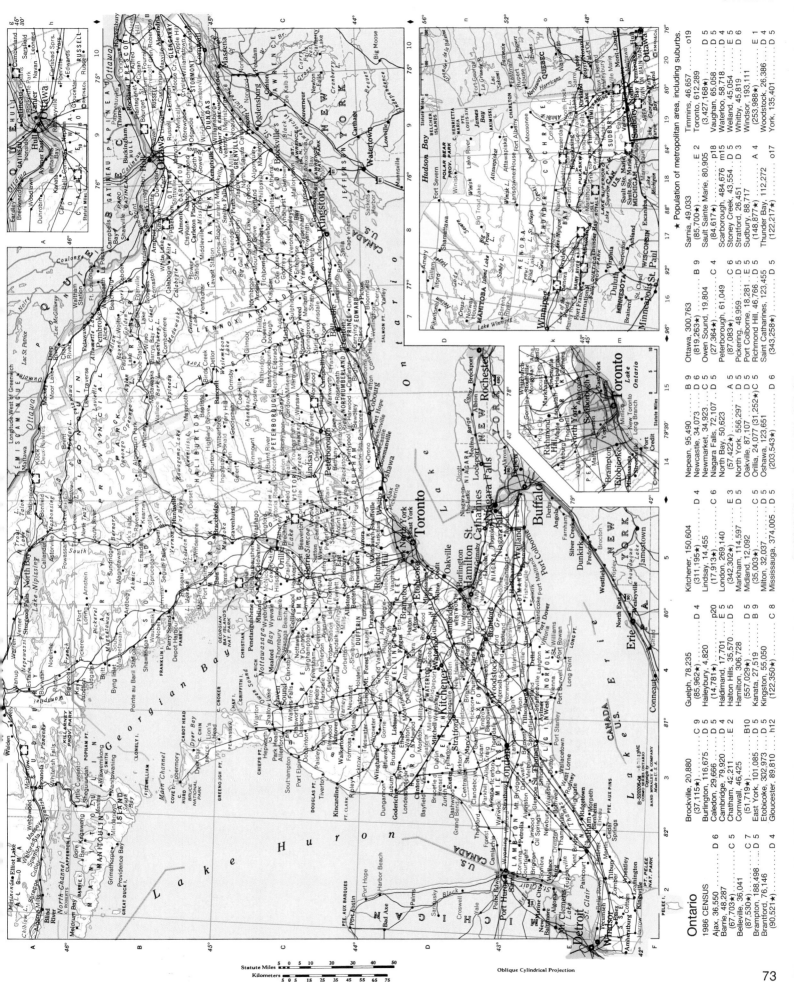

Quebec

1986 CENSUS

- Alma, 25,923 (29,977★) A 6
- Ancienne-Lorette, 13,747 . . . . C 6
- Anjou, 36,916 . . . . p19
- Aylmer East, 28,976 . . D 2
- Baie-Comeau, 26,244 (33,047★) k13
- Beaconsfield, 19,301 . . q19
- Beauport, 62,869. . . . . . n17
- Boucherville, 31,116 . . D 4
- Brossard, 57,441 . . . . . . q20
- Cap-de-la-Madeleine, 32,800 . . . . C 5
- Charlesbourg, 68,996 . . n17
- Châteauguay, 37,865 . . D 4
- Chicoutimi, 61,083 (158,468★) . . . . A 6
- Drummondville, 36,020 (56,283★) . . . . D 5
- Gaspé, 17,350 . . . . k14
- Gatineau, 81,244 . . . . . . D 2
- Granby, 38,508 (51,176★) . . . . D 5
- Grand-Mère, 14,582 . . C 5
- Hull, 58,722 . . . . D 2
- Joliette, 16,845 (34,897★) . . . . C 4
- Jonquière, 58,467 . . . . A 6
- Lachine, 34,906 . . . . . . D 4
- Lachute, 11,586 . . . . . . D 3
- LaSalle, 75,621 . . . . . . q19
- La Tuque, 10,723 (13,468★) . . . . B 5
- Laval, 284,164 . . . . D 4
- Lévis, 18,310 . . . . C 6
- Longueuil, 125,441 . . . . D 4
- Magog, 13,530 (18,738★) . . . . D 5
- Mascouche, 21,285 . . . . D 4
- Matane, 13,243 (15,361★) k13
- Montréal, 1,015,420 (2,921,357★) . . . . . . D 4
- Montréal-Nord, 90,303 . . p19
- Outremont, 23,080 . . . . p19
- Pierrefonds, 39,605 . . . . q19
- Pointe-Claire, 26,026 . . D 4
- Québec, 164,580 (603,267★) . . . . C 6
- Repentigny, 40,778 . . . . D 4
- Rimouski, 29,672 (46,210★) . . . . A 9
- Rivière-du-Loup, 13,321 (22,471★) . . . . B 8
- Rouyn, 17,319 (36,495★) k11
- Saint-Eustache, 32,226 D 4
- Sainte-Foy, 69,615 . . . . n17
- Saint-Hubert, 66,218 . . q20
- Saint-Hyacinthe, 38,603 (48,303★) . . . . D 5
- Saint-Jean-sur-Richelieu, 34,745 (59,958★). . . . D 4
- Saint-Jérôme, 23,316 (44,048★) . . . . D 3
- Saint-Laurent, 67,002 . . p19
- Salaberry-de-Valleyfield, 27,942 (38,797★). . . . D 3
- Sept-Îles (Seven Islands), 25,637 (28,050★) h13
- Shawinigan, 21,412 (61,965★) . . . . C 5
- Sherbrooke, 74,438 (129,960★) . . . . D 6
- Sorel, 19,522 (46,096★) C 4
- Terrebonne, 31,310 . . . D 4
- Thetford Mines, 18,561 (31,940★) . . . . C 6
- Trois-Rivières, 50,122 (128,888★) . . . . C 5
- Verdun, 60,246 . . . . . . q19
- Victoriaville, 21,587 (38,003★) . . . . C 6
- Ville Saint-Georges, 11,723 (21,022★) . . . . C 7

★ Population of metropolitan area, including suburbs.

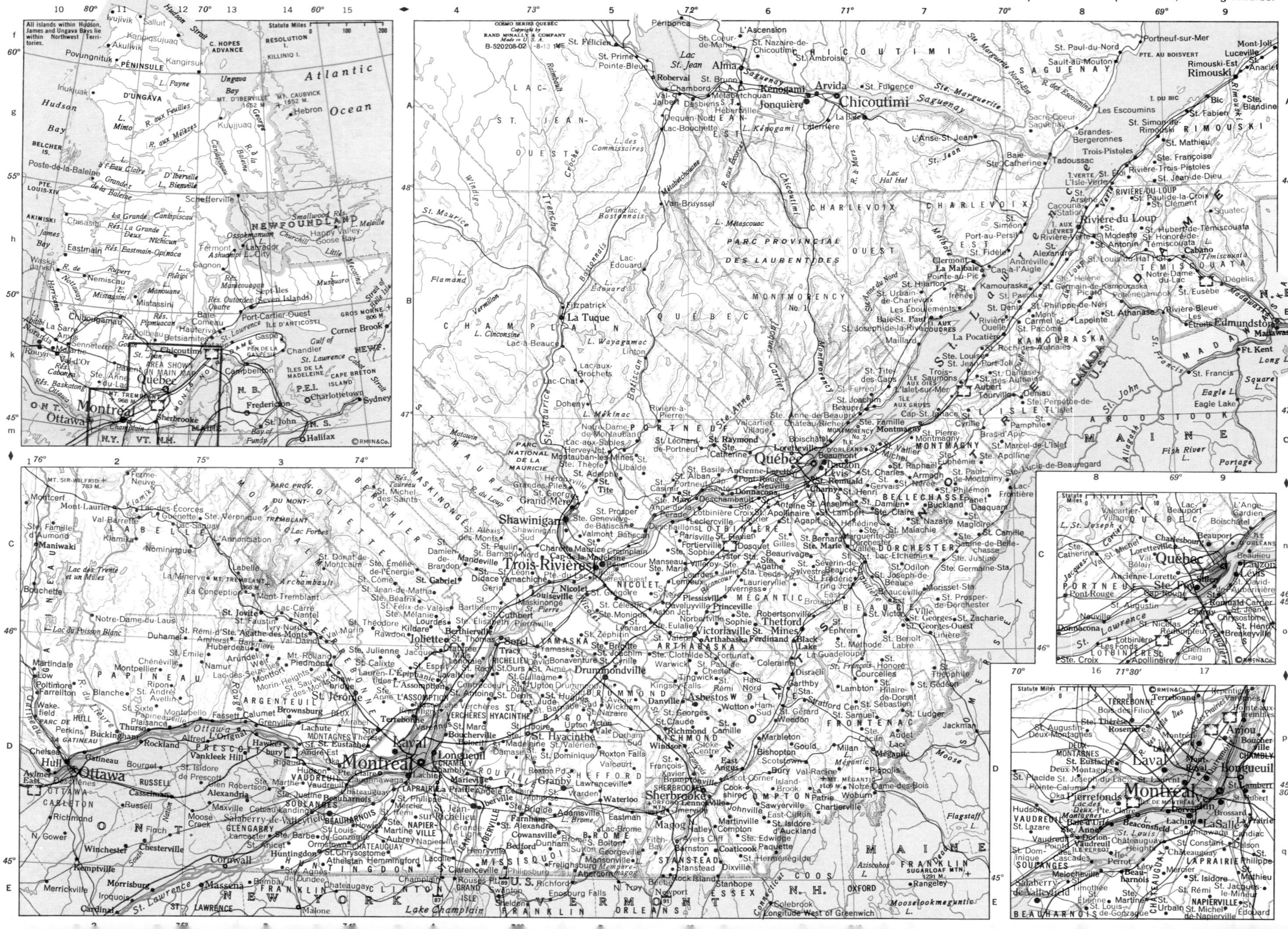

Oblique Cylindrical Projection

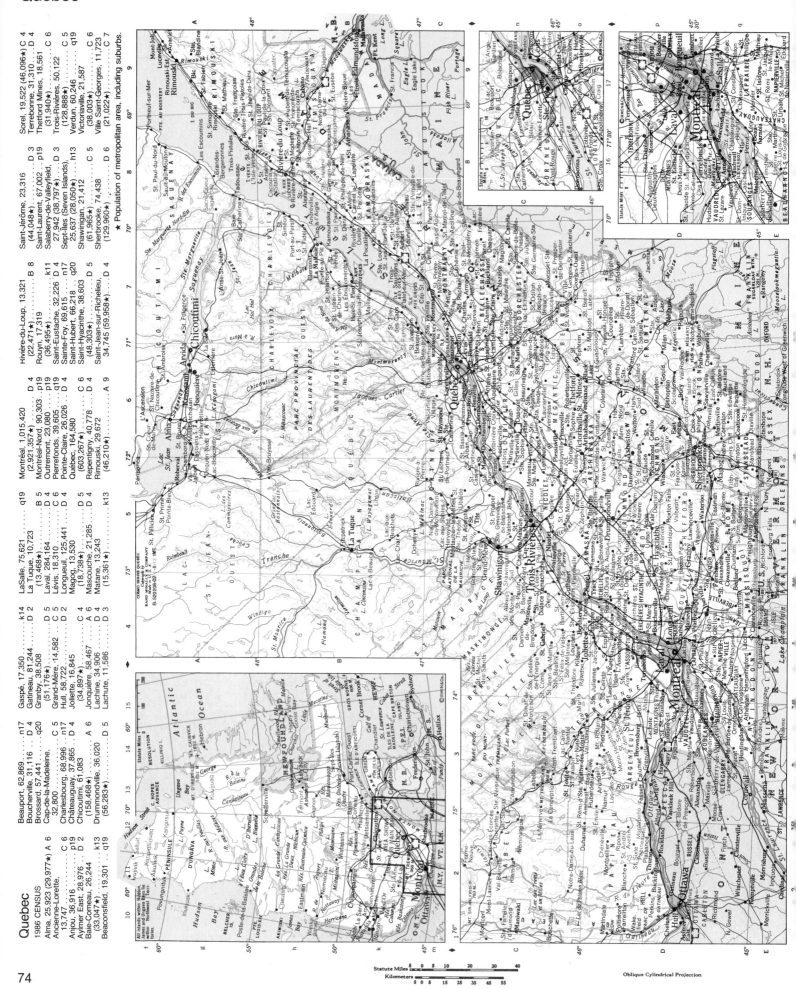

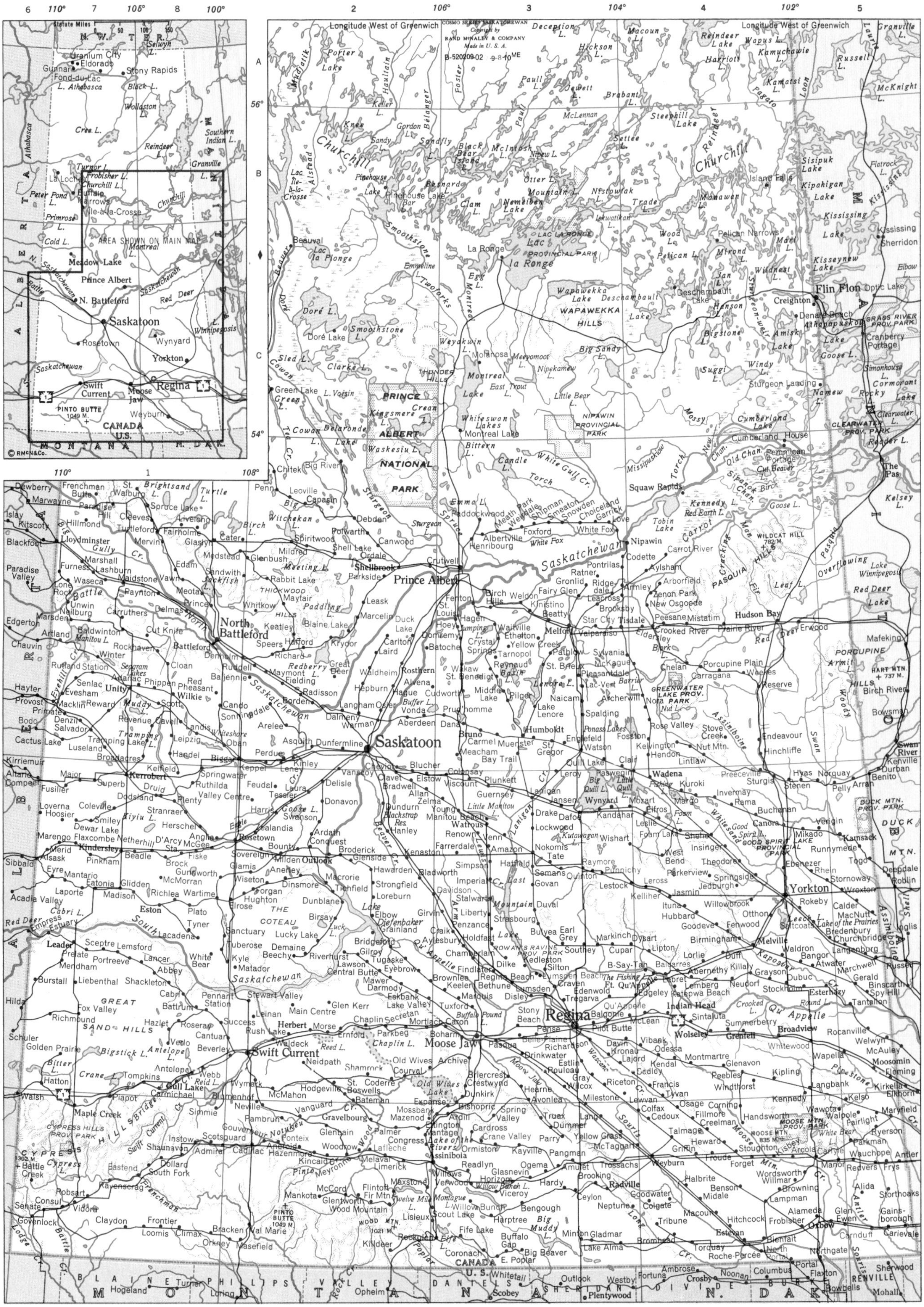

Statute Miles 10 0 10 20 30 40 50 60
Kilometers 10 0 10 20 40 60 80

Oblique Cylindrical Projection

Saskatchewan

1986 CENSUS

Assiniboia, 3,001 . . . . H 2
Balgonie, 901 . . . . . . G 3
Battleford, 3,833 . . . . E 1
Bienfait, 833 . . . . H 4
Biggar, 2,626 . . . . . . E 1
Birch Hills, 947 . . . . . . E 3
Broadview, 837 . . . . G 4
Buffalo Narrows, 1,183 . . . . m 7
Canora, 2,602 . . . . F 4
Carlyle, 1,172 . . . . . . H 4
Carnduff, 1,090 . . . . H 5
Carrot River, 1,101 . . D 4
Churchbridge, 1,035 G 5
Coronach, 1,006 . . . . H 3
Creighton, 1,620 . . . . C 5
Cudworth, 873 . . . . . . E 3
Cumberland House, 862 . . . . D 4
Dalmeny, 1,328 . . . . E 2
Davidson, 1,183 . . . . F 3
Delisle, 986 . . . . F 2
Esterhazy, 3,083 . . . . G 4
Estevan, 10,161 . . . . H 4
Eston, 1,383 . . . . F 1
Foam Lake, 1,535 . . F 4
Fort Qu'Appelle, 1,915 . . . . G 4
Gravelbourg, 1,305 . . H 2
Grenfell, 1,274 . . . . . . G 4
Gull Lake, 1,164 . . . . G 1
Herbert, 964 . . . . G 2
Hudson Bay, 2,133 . . . E 4
Humboldt, 5,089 . . . . E 3
Île-à-la-Crosse, 1,030 m 7
Indian Head, 1,886 . . G 4
Ituna, 902 . . . . F 4
Kamsack, 2,565 . . . . . F 5
Kelvington, 1,084 . . . . E 4
Kerrobert, 1,288 . . . . F 1
Kindersley, 4,912 . . . . F 1
Kipling, 1,033 . . . . . . G 4
La Loche, 1,623 . . . . . m 7
Langenburg, 1,371 . . G 5
Langham, 1,193 . . . . . E 2
Lanigan, 1,698 . . . . . . F 3
La Ronge, 2,696 . . . . B 3
Lashburn, 873 . . . . . . D 1
Leader, 1,130 . . . . G 1
Lloydminster (Alta. and Sask.), 17,356 . . . . D 1
Lumsden, 1,369 . . . . . G 3
Macklin, 1,131 . . . . . . E 1
Maidstone, 1,112 . . . . D 1
Maple Creek, 2,452 . . H 1
Meadow Lake, 3,976 n 7
Melfort, 6,078 . . . . . . E 3
Melville, 5,123 . . . . . . G 4
Moose Jaw, 35,073 (37,219★) . . . . G 3
Moosomin, 2,557 . . . G 5
Naicam, 902 . . . . E 3
Nipawin, 4,588 . . . . . . D 4
North Battleford, 14,876 (18,709★) . . . . E 1
Outlook, 2,137 . . . . . . F 2
Oxbow, 1,229 . . . . H 4
Pilot Butte, 1,387 . . . . G 3
Porcupine Plain, 918 E 4
Preeceville, 1,272 . . . F 4
Prince Albert, 33,686 (40,841★) . . . . D 3
Radville, 960 . . . . . . H 3
Redvers, 924 . . . . . . H 5
Regina, 175,064 (186,521★) . . . . . . G 3
Rocanville, 920 . . . . G 5
Rosetown, 2,663 . . . . F 1
Rosthern, 1,594 . . . . E 2
Saskatoon, 177,641 (200,665★) . . . . . . E 2
Shaunavon, 2,153 . . . H 1
Shellbrook, 1,238 . . . . D 2
Spiritwood, 1,025 . . . D 2
Strasbourg, 826 . . . . F 3
Swift Current, 15,666 G 2
Tisdale, 3,184 . . . . . . E 3
Unity, 2,471 . . . . E 1
Wadena, 1,602 . . . . . . F 4
Wakaw, 1,010 . . . . . . E 3
Warman, 2,455 . . . . . E 2
Watrous, 1,953 . . . . . F 3
Watson, 964 . . . . E 3
Weyburn, 10,153 . . . . H 4
Whitewood, 1,107 . . . G 4
Wilkie, 1,526 . . . . E 1
Wolseley, 896 . . . . . . G 4
Wynyard, 2,079 . . . . . F 3
Yorkton, 15,574 (18,525★) . . . . F 4

★ Population of metropolitan area, including suburbs.

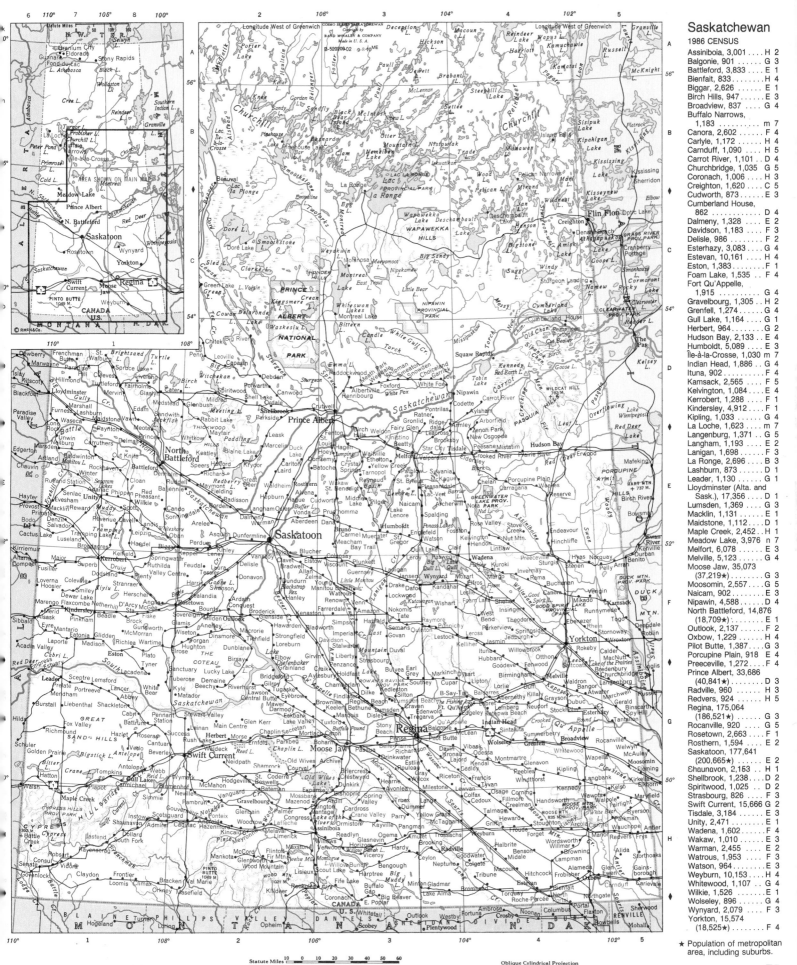

Akron, 223,019 ('90)...C10
ALABAMA..................E 9
ALASKA....................M19
Albany, 101,082 ('90)..C12
Albuquerque, 384,736 ('90)..........................D 5
Amarillo, 157,615 ('90)D 6
Anchorage, 226,338 ('90).........................M20
Annapolis, 33,187 ('90).........................D11
ARIZONA...................E 4
ARKANSAS................E 8
Atlanta, 394,017 ('90)..E10
Augusta, 21,325 ('90). C13
Austin, 465,622 ('90)...E 7
Baltimore, 736,014 ('90).........................D11
Baton Rouge, 219,531 ('90)..........................E 8
Billings, 81,151 ('90)....B 5
Birmingham, 265,968 ('90)..........................E 9
Bismarck, 49,256 ('90)B 6
Boise, 125,738 ('90)....C 3
Boston, 574,283 ('90). C12
Buffalo, 328,123 ('90). C11
CALIFORNIA..............D 2
Carson City, 40,443 ('90)......................... D 3
Charleston, 57,287 ('90)......................... D10
Charleston, 80,414 ('90)..........................E11
Charlotte, 395,934 ('90)......................... D10
Chattanooga, 152,466 ('90)......................... D 9
Cheyenne, 50,008 ('90)......................... C 6
Chicago, 2,783,726 ('90)......................... C 9
Cincinnati, 364,040 ('90)......................... D10
Cleveland, 505,616 ('90)......................... C10
COLORADO...............D 5
Colorado Springs, 281,140 ('90)......................... D 6
Columbia, 98,052 ('90)E10
Columbus, 178,681 ('90)..........................E10
Columbus, 632,910 ('90)......................... D10
Concord, 36,006 ('90). C12
CONNECTICUT..........C12
Dallas, 1,006,877 ('90) E 7
DELAWARE...............D11
Denver, 467,610 ('90). D 6
Des Moines, 193,187 ('90)......................... C 8
Detroit, 1,027,974 ('90)......................... C10
Dover, 27,630 ('90).....D11
El Paso, 515,342 ('90).E 5
FLORIDA...................F10
Fort Wayne, 173,072 ('90)......................... C 9
Fort Worth, 447,619 ('90)..........................E 7
Frankfort, 25,968 ('90)D10
Fresno, 354,202 ('90)..D 3
GEORGIA...................E10
Grand Rapids, 189,126 ('90)......................... C 9
Harrisburg, 52,376 ('90)......................... C11
Hartford, 139,739 ('90)......................... C12
Helena, 24,569 ('90).... B 4
Houston, 1,630,553 ('90)......................... F 7
IDAHO.......................C 4
ILLINOIS....................C 9
INDIANA....................C 9
Indianapolis, 731,327 ('90)......................... D 9
IOWA..........................C 8
Jackson, 196,637 ('90)E 8
Jacksonville, 635,230 ('90)..........................E10
Jefferson City, 35,481 ('90)......................... D 8
Juneau, 26,751 ('90)...N21
KANSAS....................D 7
Kansas City, 435,146 ('90)......................... D 8
KENTUCKY................D 9
Knoxville, 165,121 ('90)......................... D10
Las Vegas, 258,295 ('90)......................... D 3
Lincoln, 191,972 ('90)..C 7
Little Rock, 175,795 ('90)..........................E 8
Los Angeles, 3,485,398 ('90)..........................E 3
LOUISIANA.................E 8
Louisville, 269,063 ('90)......................... D 9
Madison, 191,262 ('90)......................... C 9
MAINE......................B13
MARYLAND...............D11

Kilometers 0 200 400 600 Km.
Miles 0 200 400 600 Mi.
1 : 16 000 000

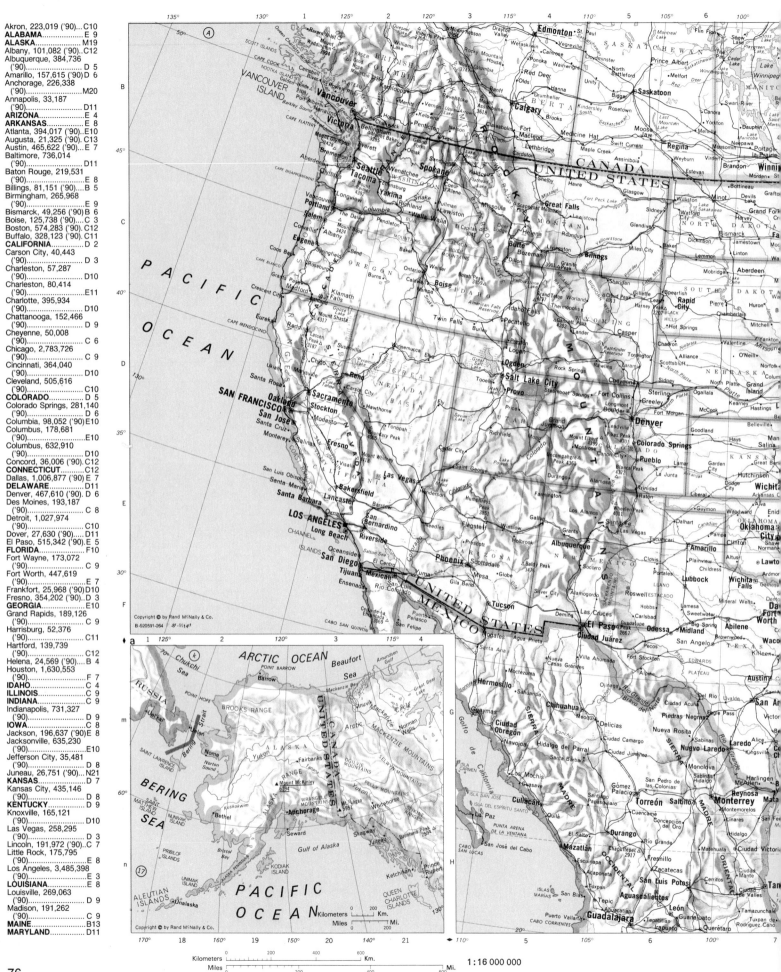

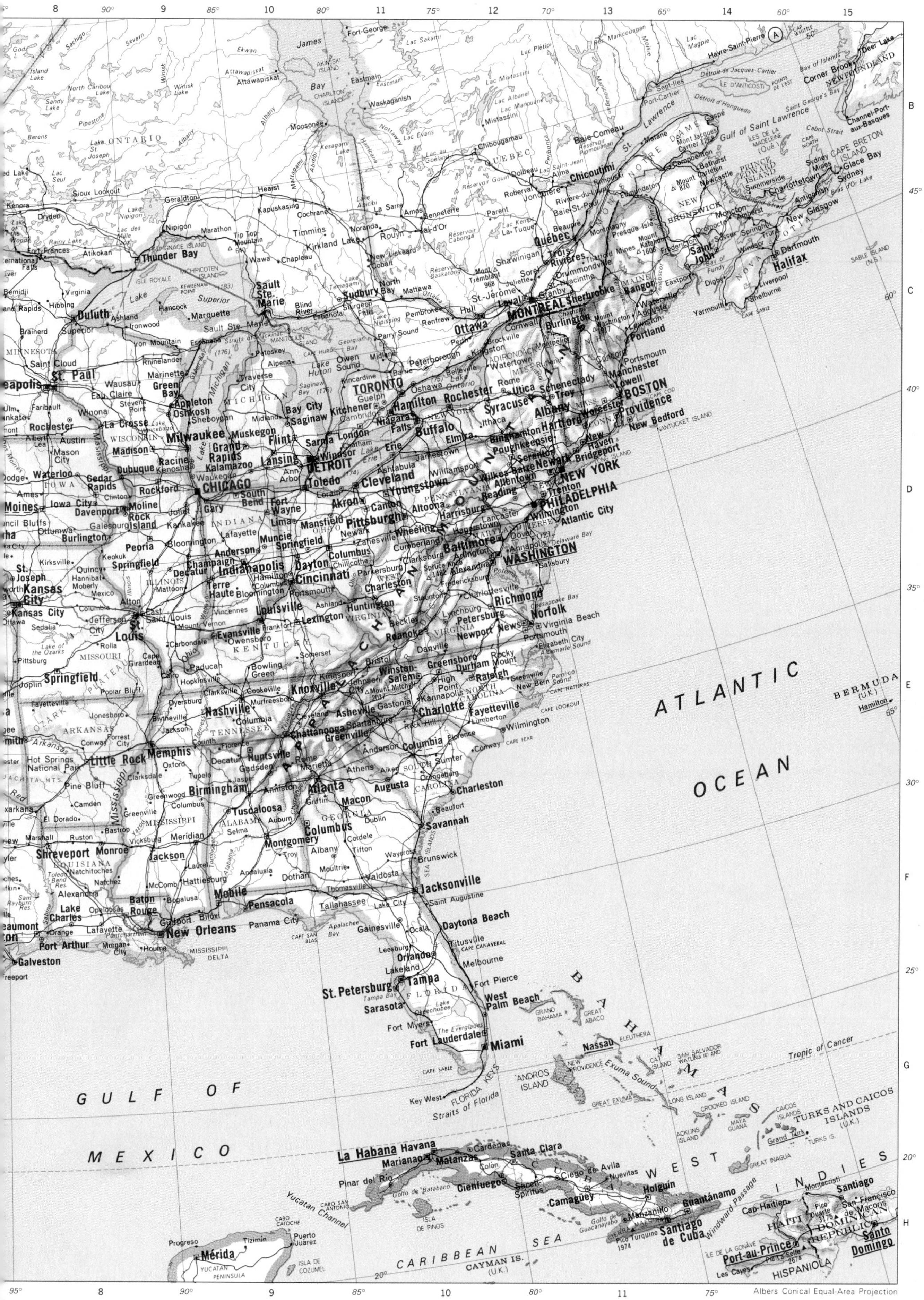
ATLANTIC
OCEAN
GULF OF
MEXICO
CARIBBEAN SEA
WEST INDIES
BAHAMAS
Tropic of Cancer
Straits of Florida
Yucatan Channel
Windward Passage
Gulf of Saint Lawrence
APPALACHIAN MOUNTAINS
BERMUDA (U.K.)
Hamilton
TURKS AND CAICOS ISLANDS (U.K.)
CAYMAN IS. (U.K.)
HISPANIOLA
HAITI
DOMINICAN REPUBLIC
NEWFOUNDLAND
NOVA SCOTIA
NEW BRUNSWICK
PRINCE EDWARD ISLAND
QUEBEC
ONTARIO
NEW YORK
WASHINGTON
PHILADELPHIA
BOSTON
TORONTO
MONTREAL
DETROIT
CHICAGO
Ottawa
Québec
Halifax
Pittsburgh
Baltimore
Cleveland
Cincinnati
Indianapolis
Milwaukee
St. Louis
Louisville
Nashville
Memphis
Atlanta
Charlotte
Richmond
Norfolk
Jacksonville
Tampa
Miami
New Orleans
Birmingham
Montgomery
Mobile
Charleston
Savannah
La Habana
Santiago de Cuba
Port-au-Prince
Santo Domingo
Mérida
Albers Conical Equal-Area Projection

MASSACHUSETTS.....C12
Memphis, 610,337 ('90)........................ D 8
Miami, 358,548 ('90)....F10
MICHIGAN................. C10
Milwaukee, 628,088 ('90)........................ C 9
Minneapolis, 368,383 ('90)........................ C 8
MINNESOTA.............. B 8
MISSISSIPPI................E 9
MISSOURI.................. D 8
Mobile, 196,278 ('90)...E 9
MONTANA...................B 5
Montgomery, 187,106 ('90).........................E 9
Montpelier, 8,247 ('90)C12
Nashville, 487,969 ('90)........................ D 9
NEBRASKA.................C 7
NEVADA.....................D 3
Newark, 275,221 ('90) C12
NEW HAMPSHIRE......C12
NEW JERSEY............C12
NEW MEXICO............ E 5
New Orleans, 496,938 ('90).........................F 8
NEW YORK................C11
New York, 7,322,564 ('90)........................ C12
Norfolk, 261,229 ('90). D11
NORTH CAROLINA.....D11
NORTH DAKOTA........ B 6
Oakland, 372,242 ('90)D 2
OHIO.......................... C10
OKLAHOMA................ D 7
Oklahoma City, 444,719 ('90)........................ D 7
Olympia, 33,840 ('90)..B 2
Omaha, 335,795 ('90). C 7
OREGON....................C 2
PENNSYLVANIA.........C11
Philadelphia, 1,585,577 ('90)........................ D11
Phoenix, 900,013 ('90) E 4
Pierre, 12,906 ('90)..... C 6
Pittsburgh, 369,879 ('90)........................ C11
Portland, 64,358 ('90). C12
Providence, 160,728 ('90)........................ C12
Raleigh, 207,951 ('90). D11
Rapid City, 54,523 ('90)........................ C 6
Reno, 133,850 ('90).... D 3
RHODE ISLAND..........C12
Richmond, 203,056 ('90)........................ D11
Rochester, 231,636 ('90)........................ C11
Sacramento, 369,365 ('90)........................ D 2
Saint Louis, 396,685 ('90)........................ D 8
Saint Paul, 272,235 ('90)........................ C 8
Saint Petersburg, 238,629 ('90).........................F10
Salem, 107,786 ('90)...C 2
Salt Lake City, 159,936 ('90)........................ C 4
San Antonio, 935,933 ('90).........................F 7
San Diego, 1,110,549 ('90).........................E 3
San Francisco, 723,959 ('90)........................ D 2
San Jose, 782,248 ('90)........................ D 2
Santa Fe, 55,859 ('90) D 5
Savannah, 137,560 ('90).........................E10
Seattle, 516,259 ('90)..B 2
Shreveport, 198,525 ('90).........................E 8
SOUTH CAROLINA..... E10
SOUTH DAKOTA........ C 7
Spokane, 177,196 ('90).........................B 3
Springfield, 105,227 ('90)........................ D 9
Syracuse, 163,860 ('90) C11
Tacoma, 176,664 ('90) B 2
Tallahassee, 124,773 ('90).........................E10
Tampa, 280,015 ('90)..F10
TENNESSEE............... D 9
TEXAS........................E 7
Toledo, 332,943 ('90)..C10
Topeka, 119,883 ('90).D 7
Trenton, 88,675 ('90).. C12
Tulsa, 367,302 ('90).... D 7
UNITED STATES........ D 7
UTAH..........................D 4
VERMONT.................. C12
VIRGINIA....................D11
WASHINGTON............ B 2
Washington, 606,900 ('90)........................ D11
WEST VIRGINIA......... D10
Wichita, 304,011 ('90). D 7
WISCONSIN................ C 9
WYOMING..................C 5

Alabama

1990 CENSUS

Alabaster, 14,732 .. B 3
Albertville, 14,507 .. A 3
Alexander City, 14,917 .... C 4
Andalusia, 9,269 .... D 3
Anniston, 26,623 .... B 4
Arab, 6,321 .... A 3
Athens, 16,901 .... A 3
Atmore, 8,046 ...... D 2
Attalla, 6,859 .... A 3
Auburn, 33,830 .... C 4
Bay Minette, 7,168 .. E 2
Bessemer, 33,497 .. B 3
Birmingham, 265,968 B 3
Bluff Park, 8,000('85) g 7
Boaz, 6,928 .... A 3
Brewton, 5,885 .... D 2
Center Point, 22,000('85) ...... f 7
Chickasaw, 6,649 .. E 1
Childersburg, 4,579 .. B 3
Clanton, 7,669 ...... C 3
Cullman, 13,367 .... A 3
Decatur, 48,761 ..... A 3
Demopolis, 7,512 .... C 2
Dothan, 53,589 .... D 4
Enterprise, 20,123 .. D 4
Eufaula, 13,220 .... D 4
Fairfield, 12,200 .... B 3
Fairhope, 8,485 .... E 2
Fayette, 4,909 ...... B 2
Florence, 36,426 .... A 2
Fort Payne, 11,838 .. A 4
Frisco City, 1,581 .. D 2
Fultondale, 6,400 .... f 7
Gadsden, 42,523 .... A 3
Gardendale, 9,251 .. B 3
Geneva, 4,681 ...... D 4
Greenville, 7,492 .... D 3
Guntersville, 7,038 .. A 3
Haleyville, 4,452 .... A 2
Hamilton, 5,787 .... A 2
Hartselle, 10,795 .... A 3
Homewood, 22,922 .. g 7
Hueytown, 15,280 .. g 6
Huntsville, 159,789 .. A 3
Irondale, 9,454 ...... f 7
Jackson, 5,819 ..... D 2
Jacksonville, 10,283 B 4
Jasper, 13,553 ...... B 2
Lanett, 8,985 ...... C 4
Leeds, 9,946 ...... B 3
Millbrook, 6,050 .... C 3
Mobile, 196,278 ..... E 1
Monroeville, 6,993 .. D 2
Montgomery, 187,106 C 3
Moundville, 1,348 .... C 2
Mountain Brook, 19,810 .... g 7
Muscle Shoals, 9,611 A 2
Northport, 17,366 ... B 2
Oneonta, 4,844 .... B 3
Opelika, 22,122 .... C 4
Opp, 6,985 .... D 3
Oxford, 9,362 ...... B 4
Ozark, 12,922 ...... D 4
Pelham, 9,765 ...... B 3
Pell City, 8,118 .... B 3
Phenix City, 25,312 .. C 4
Piedmont, 5,288 .... B 4
Pleasant Grove, 8,458 g 7
Prattville, 19,587 .... C 3
Prichard, 34,311 .... E 1
Rainbow City, 7,673 A 3
Roanoke, 6,362 .... B 4
Russellville, 7,812 .. A 2
Saraland, 11,751 .... E 1
Scottsboro, 13,786 .. A 3
Selma, 23,755 ...... C 2
Sheffield, 10,380 .... A 2
Spanish Fort, 3,415('80) .... E 2
Sylacauga, 12,520 .. B 3
Talladega, 18,175 .. B 3
Tallassee, 5,112 .... C 4
Tarrant, 8,046 ...... B 3
Theodore, 6,392('80) E 1
Tillmans Corner, 5,000('85) .... E 1
Troy, 13,051 .... D 4
Tuscaloosa, 77,759 .. B 2
Tuscumbia, 8,413 .. A 2
Tuskegee, 12,257 .... C 4
Vestavia Hills, 19,749 g 7
Warrior, 3,280 ...... B 3
Wetumpka, 4,670 .. C 3

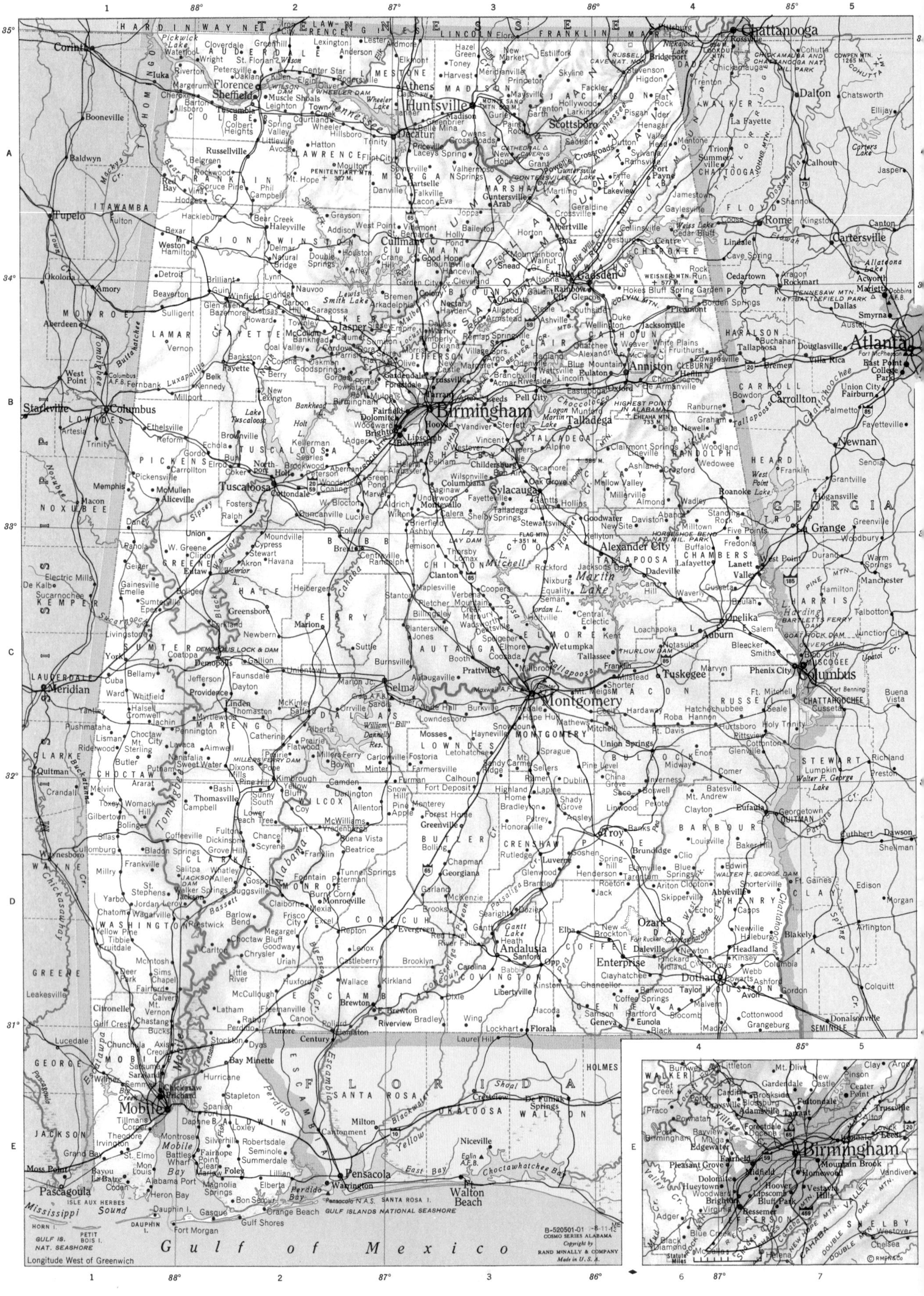

Statute Miles 5 0 5 10 20 30 40

Kilometers 5 0 5 15 25 35 45 55

Lambert Conformal Conic Projection

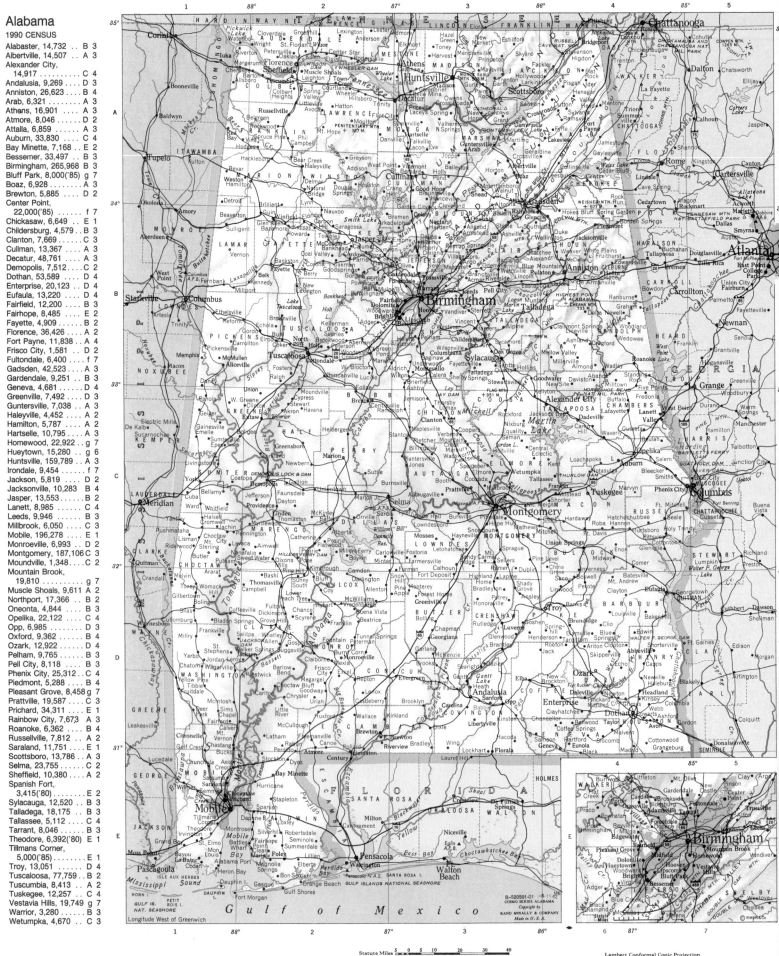

Alaska

1990 CENSUS

Akiachak, 400('83) . . . . C 7
Alakanuk, 544 . . . . C 7
Anchorage, 226,338 . . C10
Anderson, 628 . . . . C10
Angoon, 638 . . . . D13
Aniak, 540 . . . . C 8
Barrow, 3,469 . . . . A 8
Bethel, 4,674 . . . . C 7
Big Delta, 285('80) C10
Chevak, 598 . . . . C 6
Cold Bay, 148 . . . . E 7
College, 800('83) B10
Cordova, 2,110 . . . . . . C10
Craig, 1,260 . . . . D13
Delta Junction, 652 . . . . C10
Dillingham, 2,017 . . . . . . D 8
Emmonak, 642 . . . . C 7
Fairbanks, 30,843 . . . . C10
Fort Yukon, 580 . . . . . B10
Galena, 833 . . . . C 8
Gambell, 525 . . . . C 5
Glennallen, 511('80) f19
Haines, 1,238 . . . . D12
Healy, 334('80) C10
Homer, 3,660 . . . . D 9
Hoonah, 795 . . . . D12
Hooper Bay, 845 . . . . . C 6
Hydaburg, 384 . . . . D13
Juneau, 26,751 . . . . D13
Kake, 700 . . . . D13
Kenai, 6,327 . . . . C 9
Ketchikan, 8,263 . . . . . D13
Kiana, 385 . . . . B 7
King Cove, 451 . . . . E 7
King Salmon, 545('80) . D 8
Kipnuk, 371('80) . . . . . . C 7
Klawock, 722 . . . . D13
Kodiak, 6,365 . . . . D 9
Kotlik, 461 . . . . C 7
Kotzebue, 2,751 . . . . . . B 7
Kwethluk, 558 . . . . C 7
Kwigillingok, 354('80) . . D 7
Manokotak, 385 . . . . . . D 8
McGrath, 528 . . . . C 8
Metlakatla, 1,056('80) . . D13
Mountain Village, 674 . . C 7
Nenana, 393 . . . . C10
Nikishka, 1,109('80) g16
Ninilchik, 341('80) . . . . C 9
Nome, 3,500 . . . . C 6
Noorvik, 531 . . . . B 7
Nulato, 359 . . . . C 8
Old Harbor, 284 . . . . . . D 9
Palmer, 2,866 . . . . C10
Petersburg, 3,207 . . . . D13
Pilot Station, 463 . . . . . C 7
Point Hope, 639 . . . . . . B 6
Prudhoe Bay, 50('80) . . A10
Quinhagak, 501 . . . . . . D 7
Saint Marys, 441 . . . . . C 7
Saint Paul, 763 . . . . . . D 5
Sand Point, 878 . . . . . . D 7
Savoonga, 519 . . . . C 5
Selawik, 596 . . . . B 7
Seldovia, 316 . . . . D 9
Seward, 2,699 . . . . C10
Shishmaref, 456 . . . . . . B 6
Shungnak, 223 . . . . B 8
Sitka, 8,588 . . . . D12
Skagway, 692 . . . . D12
Soldotna, 3,482 . . . . . . g16
Stebbins, 400 . . . . C 7
Sterling, 919('80) g16
Tanana, 345 . . . . B 9
Togiak, 613 . . . . D 7
Tok, 589('80) C11
Tununak, 316 . . . . C 6
Unalakleet, 714 . . . . . . C 7
Unalaska, 3,089 . . . . . . E 6
Valdez, 4,068 . . . . C10
Wainwright, 492 . . . . . . A 8
Wasilla, 4,028 . . . . C10
Whittier, 243 . . . . C10
Wrangell, 2,479 . . . . . . D13
Yakutat, 534 . . . . D12

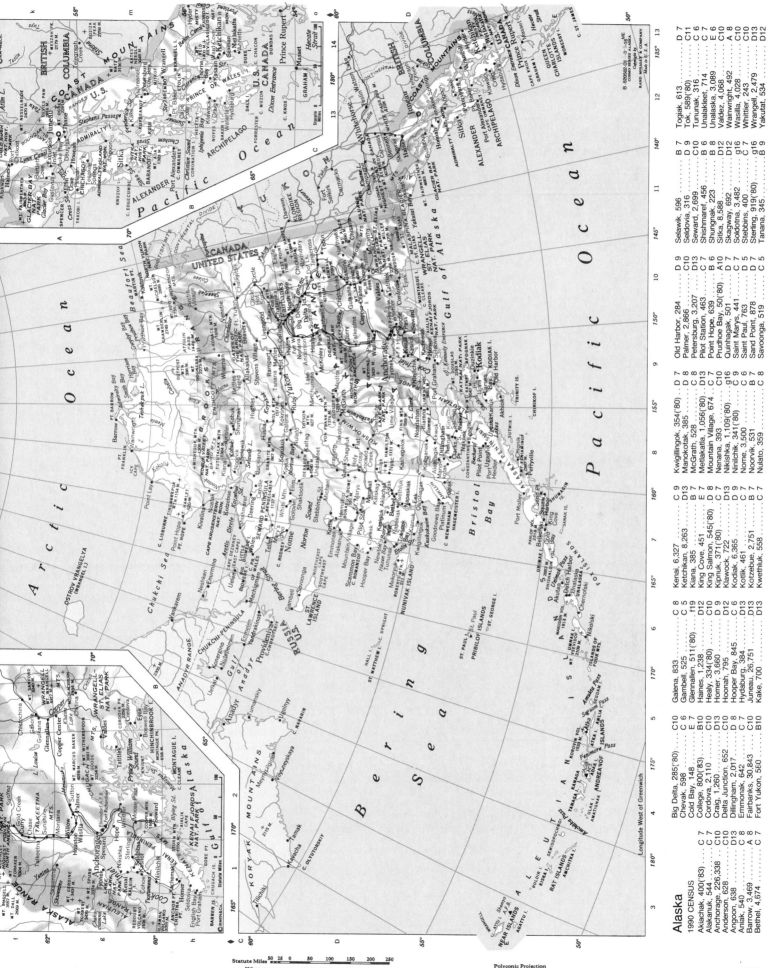

Arizona

1990 CENSUS

Ajo, 5,189('80) . . . . . E 3
Apache Junction, 18,100 . . . . m 9
Avondale, 16,169 . . . D 3
Bagdad, 2,331('80) . . C 2
Benson, 3,824 . . . . . F 5
Bisbee, 6,288 . . . . . . F 6
Black Canyon City, 850('86) . . . . C 3
Buckeye, 5,038 . . . . D 3
Bullhead City, 21,951 B 1
Camp Verde, 6,243 . . C 4
Casa Grande, 19,082 E 4
Casas Adobes, 12,155('86) . . . . . . E 5
Cashion, 3,014('80) . . m 8
Cave Creek, 2,925 . . D 4
Chandler, 90,533 . . . D 4
Chinle, 2,815('80) . . . A 6
Chino Valley, 4,837 . . C 3
Claypool, 2,362('80) D 5
Clifton, 2,840 . . . . . D 6
Coolidge, 6,927 . . . . E 4
Cottonwood, 5,918 . . C 3
Crane, 2,650('86) . . . E 1
Douglas, 12,822 . . . . F 6
Eagar, 4,025 . . . . . . C 6
El Mirage, 5,001 . . . . k 8
Eloy, 7,211 . . . . E 4
Flagstaff, 45,857 . . . . B 4
Florence, 7,510 . . . . D 4
Fort Defiance, 3,431('80) . . . . B 6
Ganado, 3,400('86) . . B 6
Gila Bend, 1,747 . . . . E 3
Gilbert, 29,188 . . . . . D 4
Glendale, 148,134 . . D 3
Globe, 6,062 . . . . . . D 5
Goodyear, 6,258 . . . . D 3
Grand Canyon, 1,348('80) . . . . A 3
Green Valley, 7,999('80) . . . . F 5
Guadalupe, 5,458 . . m 9
Holbrook, 4,686 . . . . C 5
Huachuca City, 1,782 F 5
Kayenta, 3,343('80) . . A 5
Kearny, 2,262 . . . . . . D 5
Kingman, 12,722 . . . . B 1
Lake Havasu City, 24,363 . . . . C 1
Lakeside-Pinetop, 2,422 . . . . C 6
Litchfield Park, 3,303 m 8
Mammoth, 1,845 . . . . E 5
Mesa, 288,091 . . . . . D 4
Miami, 2,018 . . . . . . D 5
Nogales, 19,489 . . . . F 5
Oracle, 2,484('80) . . E 5
Page, 6,598 . . . . A 4
Paradise Valley, 11,671 . . . . k 9
Parker, 2,897 . . . . . . C 1
Payson, 8,377 . . . . . . C 4
Peoria, 50,618 . . . . . . D 3
Phoenix, 900,013 . . . . D 3
Prescott, 26,455 . . . . C 3
Sacaton, 1,951('80) . . D 4
Safford, 7,359 . . . . . . E 6
Saint Johns, 3,294 . . C 6
San Carlos, 2,668('80) . . . . D 5
San Luis, 70('86) . . . . . E 3
San Manuel, 5,443('80) . . . . E 5
Scottsdale, 130,069 D 4
Sedona, 7,720 . . . . . . C 4
Sells, 1,864('80) . . . F 4
Show Low, 5,019 . . . C 5
Sierra Vista, 32,983 . . F 5
Snowflake, 3,679 . . . . C 5
Somerton, 5,282 . . . . E 1
South Tucson, 5,093 E 5
Sun City, 57,000 . . . . k 8
Superior, 3,468 . . . . D 4
Surprise, 7,122 . . . . . k 8
Taylor, 2,418 . . . . . . C 5
Tempe, 141,865 . . . . D 4
Thatcher, 3,763 . . . . E 6
Tolleson, 4,434 . . . . m 8
Tombstone, 1,220 . . F 5
Tuba City, 5,045('80) A 4
Tucson, 405,390 . . . . E 5
Twin Knolls, 5,210('86) . . . . m 9
Wickenburg, 4,515 . . D 3
Willcox, 3,122 . . . . . . E 6
Williams, 2,532 . . . . . B 3
Window Rock, 2,230('80) . . . . B 6
Winslow, 8,190 . . . . . C 5
Youngtown, 2,542 . . k 8
Yuma, 54,923 . . . . . . E 1

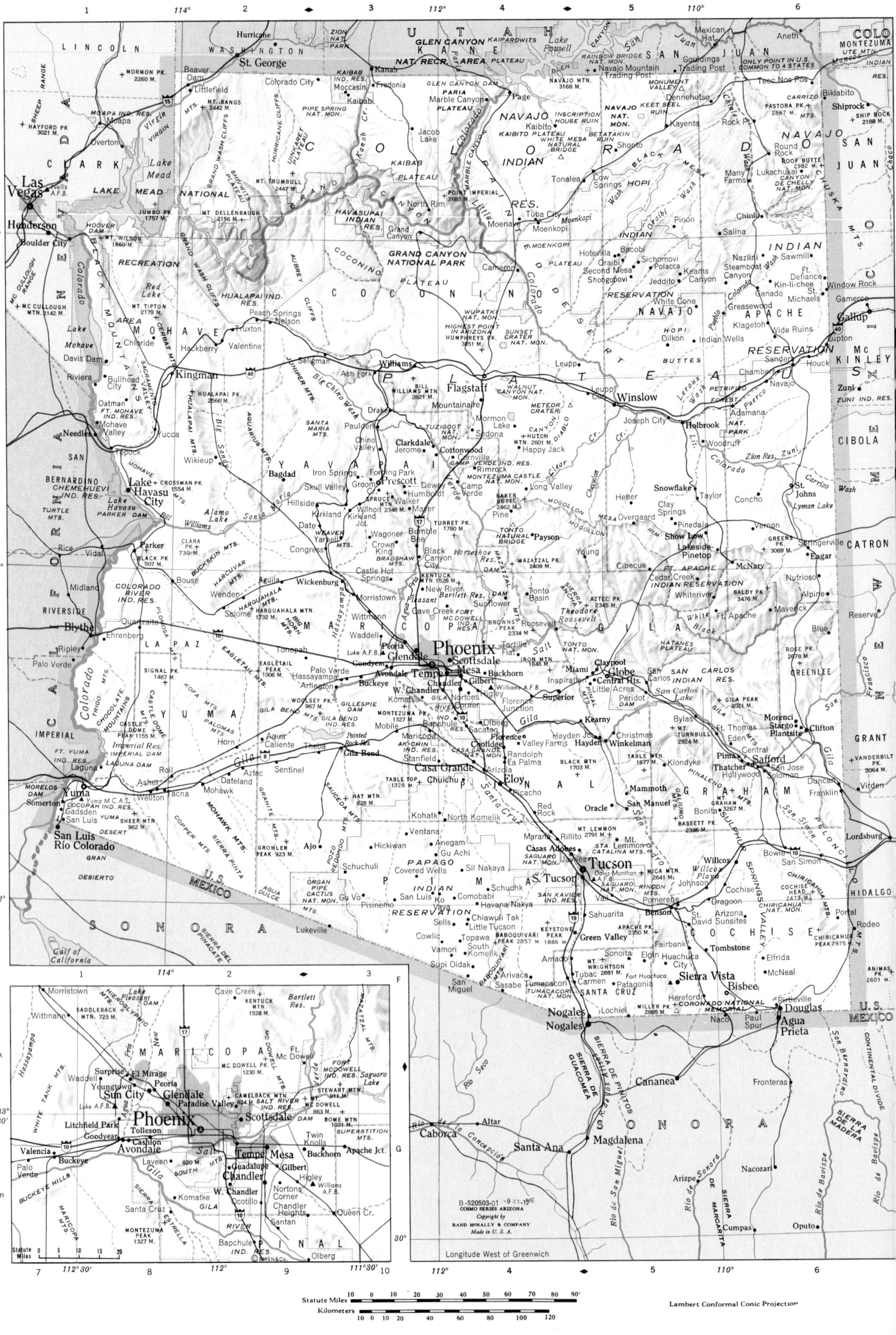

UTAH
NEVADA
CALIFORNIA
NEW MEXICO
SONORA
MEXICO
U.S.
Phoenix
Tucson
Flagstaff
Yuma
Prescott
Grand Canyon National Park
Lake Mead
Lake Havasu City
Kingman
Page
Winslow
Holbrook
Globe
Nogales
Douglas
Casa Grande
Mesa
Tempe
Scottsdale
Glendale
Chandler
MARICOPA
PINAL
Gulf of California
Statute Miles
Kilometers
Lambert Conformal Conic Projection
Longitude West of Greenwich
Copyright by RAND McNALLY & COMPANY
Made in U. S. A.

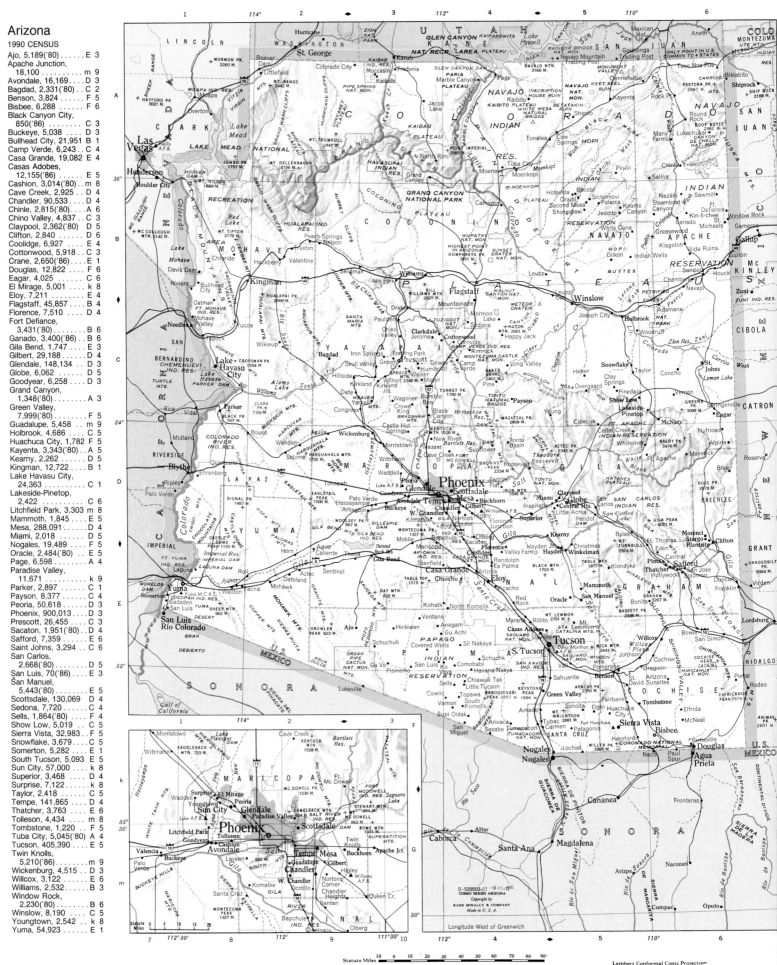

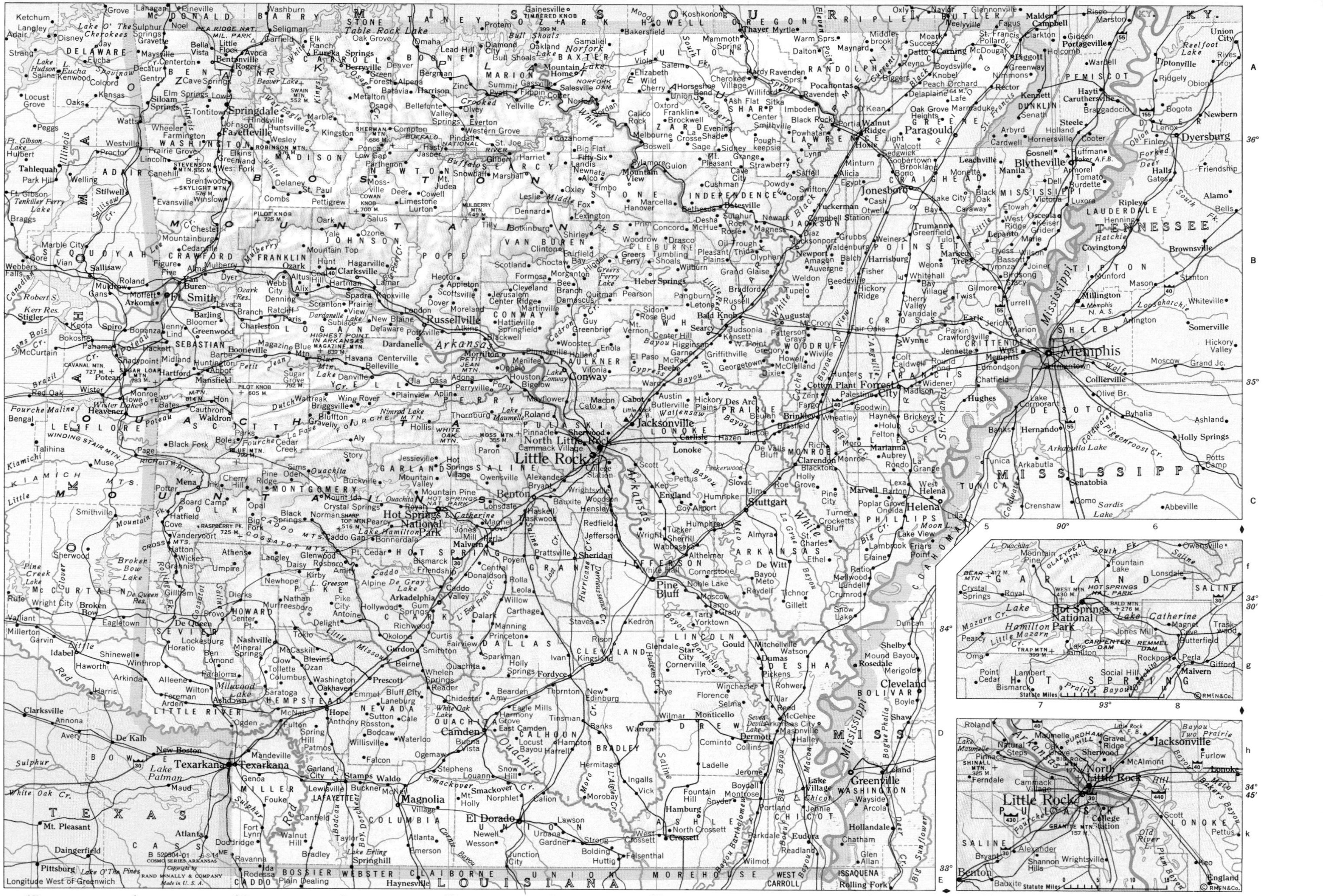

Arkansas

1990 CENSUS

Arkadelphia, 10,014	C 2
Ashdown, 5,150	D 1
Bald Knob, 2,653	B 4
Barling, 4,078	B 1
Batesville, 9,187	B 4
Beebe, 4,455	B 4
Benton, 18,177	C 3
Bentonville, 11,257	A 1
Berryville, 3,212	A 2
Blytheville, 22,906	B 6
Booneville, 3,804	B 2
Brinkley, 4,234	C 4
Bryant, 5,269	C 3
Cabot, 8,319	C 3
Camden, 14,380	D 3
Clarksville, 5,833	B 2
Conway, 26,481	B 3
Corning, 3,323	A 5
Crossett, 6,282	D 4
Dardanelle, 3,722	B 2
De Queen, 4,633	C 1
Dermott, 4,715	D 4
De Witt, 3,553	C 4
Dumas, 5,520	D 4
Earle, 3,393	B 5
El Dorado, 23,146	D 3
Eudora, 3,155	D 4
Eureka Springs, 1,900	A 2
Fayetteville, 42,099	A 1
Fordyce, 4,729	D 3
Forrest City, 13,364	B 5
Fort Smith, 72,798	B 1
Greenwood, 3,984	B 1
Harrisburg, 1,943	B 5
Harrison, 9,922	A 2
Heber Springs, 5,628	B 3
Helena, 7,491	C 5
Hope, 9,643	D 2
Hot Springs National Park, 32,462	C 2
Hoxie, 2,676	A 5
Jacksonville, 29,101	C 3
Jonesboro, 46,535	B 5
Lake Village, 2,791	D 4
Little Rock, 175,795	C 3
Lonoke, 4,022	C 4
Magnolia, 11,151	D 2
Malvern, 9,256	C 3
Marianna, 5,910	C 5
Marked Tree, 3,100	B 5
McGehee, 4,997	D 4
Mena, 5,475	C 1
Monticello, 8,116	D 4
Morrilton, 6,551	B 3
Mountain Home, 9,027	A 3
Mountain View, 2,439	B 3
Nashville, 4,639	D 2
Newport, 7,459	B 4
North Little Rock, 61,741	C 3
Osceola, 8,930	B 6
Ozark, 3,330	B 2
Paragould, 18,540	A 5
Paris, 3,674	B 2
Piggott, 3,777	A 5
Pine Bluff, 57,140	C 3
Pocahontas, 6,151	A 5
Prescott, 3,673	D 2
Rogers, 24,692	A 1
Russellville, 21,260	B 2
Searcy, 15,180	B 4
Sherwood, 18,893	C 3
Siloam Springs, 8,151	A 1
Smackover, 2,232	D 3
Springdale, 29,941	A 1
Stuttgart, 10,420	C 4
Texarkana, 22,631	D 1
Trumann, 6,304	B 5
Tuckerman, 2,020	B 4
Van Buren, 14,979	B 1
Walnut Ridge, 4,388	A 5
Warren, 6,455	D 3
West Helena, 9,695	C 5
West Memphis, 28,259	B 5
Wynne, 8,187	B 5

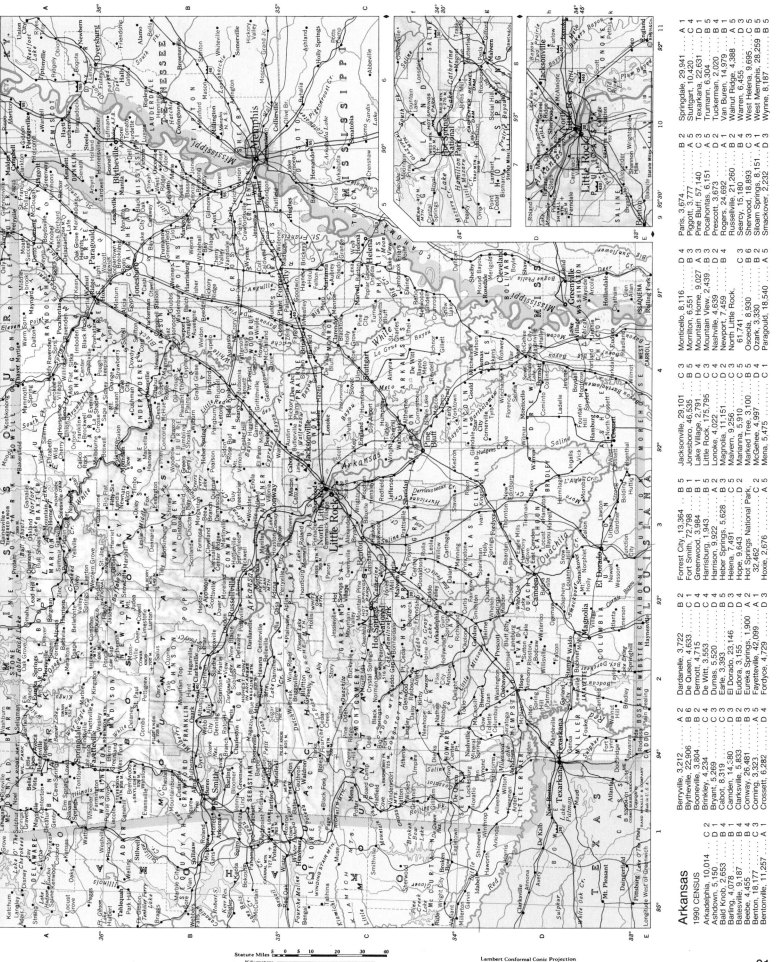

California

1990 CENSUS

- Alameda, 76,459 . . . . h 8
- Alhambra, 82,106 . . m12
- Anaheim, 266,406 . . F 5
- Antioch, 62,195 . . . . h 9
- Bakersfield, 174,820 E 4
- Berkeley, 102,724 . . D 2
- Beverly Hills, 31,971 m12
- Burbank, 93,643 . . . . E 4
- Calexico, 18,633 . . . . F 6
- Chico, 40,079 . . . . . . C 3
- Chula Vista, 135,163 F 5
- Compton, 90,454 . . . . n12
- Concord, 111,348 . . . h 8
- Costa Mesa, 96,357 . . n13
- Daly City, 92,311 . . . . h 8
- Davis, 46,209 . . . . . . C 3
- Downey, 91,444 . . . . n12
- East Los Angeles, 126,379 . . . . m12
- El Cajon, 88,693 . . . . F 5
- El Centro, 31,384 . . . . F 6
- Escondido, 108,635 . . F 5
- Eureka, 27,025 . . . . B 1
- Fairfield, 77,211 . . . . C 2
- Fremont, 173,339 . . . D 2
- Fresno, 354,202 . . . . D 4
- Fullerton, 114,144 . . n13
- Garden Grove, 143,050 . . . . n13
- Glendale, 180,038 . . m12
- Hayward, 111,498 . . h 8
- Huntington Beach, 181,519 . . . . F 4
- Indio, 36,793 . . . . . . F 5
- Inglewood, 109,602 . . n12
- Irvine, 110,330 . . . . . . n13
- Lancaster, 97,291 . . . E 4
- Lompoc, 37,649 . . . . E 3
- Long Beach, 429,433 F 4
- Los Angeles, 3,485,398 . . . . E 4
- Marysville, 12,324 . . C 3
- Menlo Park, 28,040 . . k 8
- Merced, 56,216 . . . . D 3
- Modesto, 164,730 . . D 3
- Monterey, 31,954 . . D 3
- Napa, 61,842 . . . . . . C 2
- Newport Beach, 66,643 . . . . n13
- Norwalk, 94,279 . . . . n12
- Oakland, 372,242 . . D 2
- Oceanside, 128,398 . . F 5
- Ontario, 133,179 . . . . E 5
- Orange, 110,658 . . . . n13
- Oxnard, 142,216 . . . . E 4
- Palm Springs, 40,181 F 5
- Palo Alto, 55,900 . . . . D 2
- Pasadena, 131,591 . . E 4
- Pomona, 131,723 . . . . E 5
- Redding, 66,462 . . . . B 2
- Redwood City, 66,072 . . . . D 2
- Richmond, 87,425 . . D 2
- Riverside, 226,505 . . F 5
- Sacramento, 369,365 C 3
- Salinas, 108,777 . . . . D 3
- San Bernardino, 164,164 . . . . E 5
- San Clemente, 41,100 F 5
- San Diego, 1,110,549 F 5
- San Francisco, 723,959 . . . . D 2
- San Jose, 782,248 . . D 3
- San Juan Capistrano, 26,183 . . . . F 5
- San Luis Obispo, 41,958 . . . . E 3
- San Mateo, 85,486 . . D 2
- Santa Ana, 293,742 . . F 5
- Santa Barbara, 85,571 . . . . E 4
- Santa Clara, 93,613 D 2
- Santa Cruz, 49,040 . . D 2
- Santa Maria, 61,284 E 3
- Santa Monica, 86,905 m12
- Santa Rosa, 113,313 C 2
- Simi Valley, 100,217 E 4
- South Gate, 86,284 . . n12
- South Lake Tahoe, 21,586 . . . . C 4
- Stockton, 210,943 . . D 3
- Sunnyvale, 117,229 . . k 8
- Torrance, 133,107 . . n12
- Tulare, 33,249 . . . . . D 4
- Turlock, 42,198 . . . . D 3
- Vallejo, 109,199 . . . . C 2
- Ventura (San Buenaventura), 92,575 . . . . E 4
- Visalia, 75,636 . . . . . . D 4
- West Covina, 96,086 m13
- Westminster, 78,118 n12
- Whittier, 77,671 . . . . F 4
- Yuba City, 27,437 . . C 3

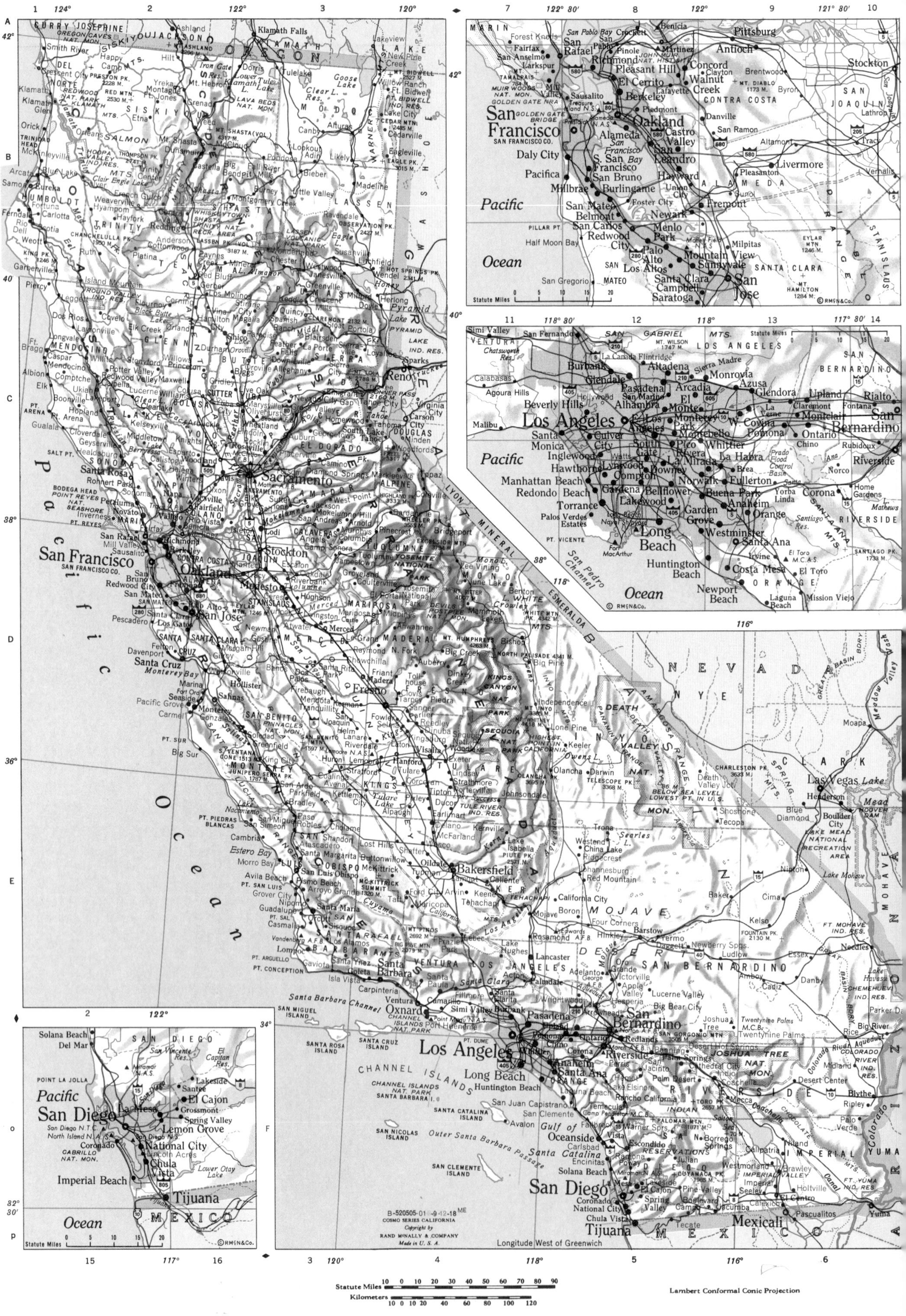

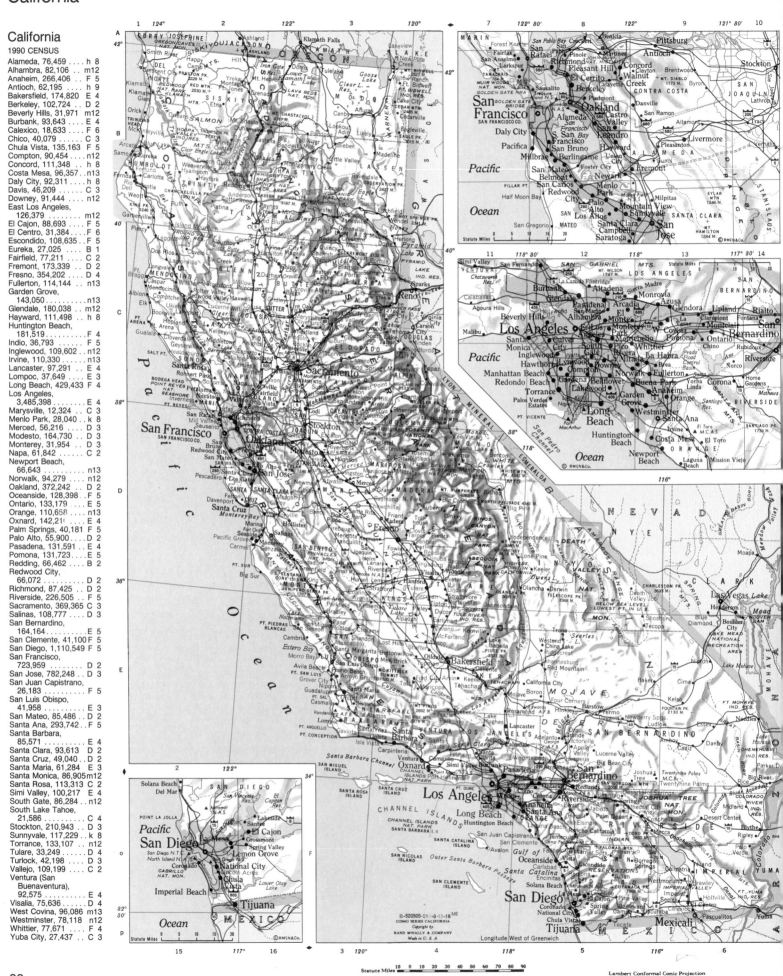

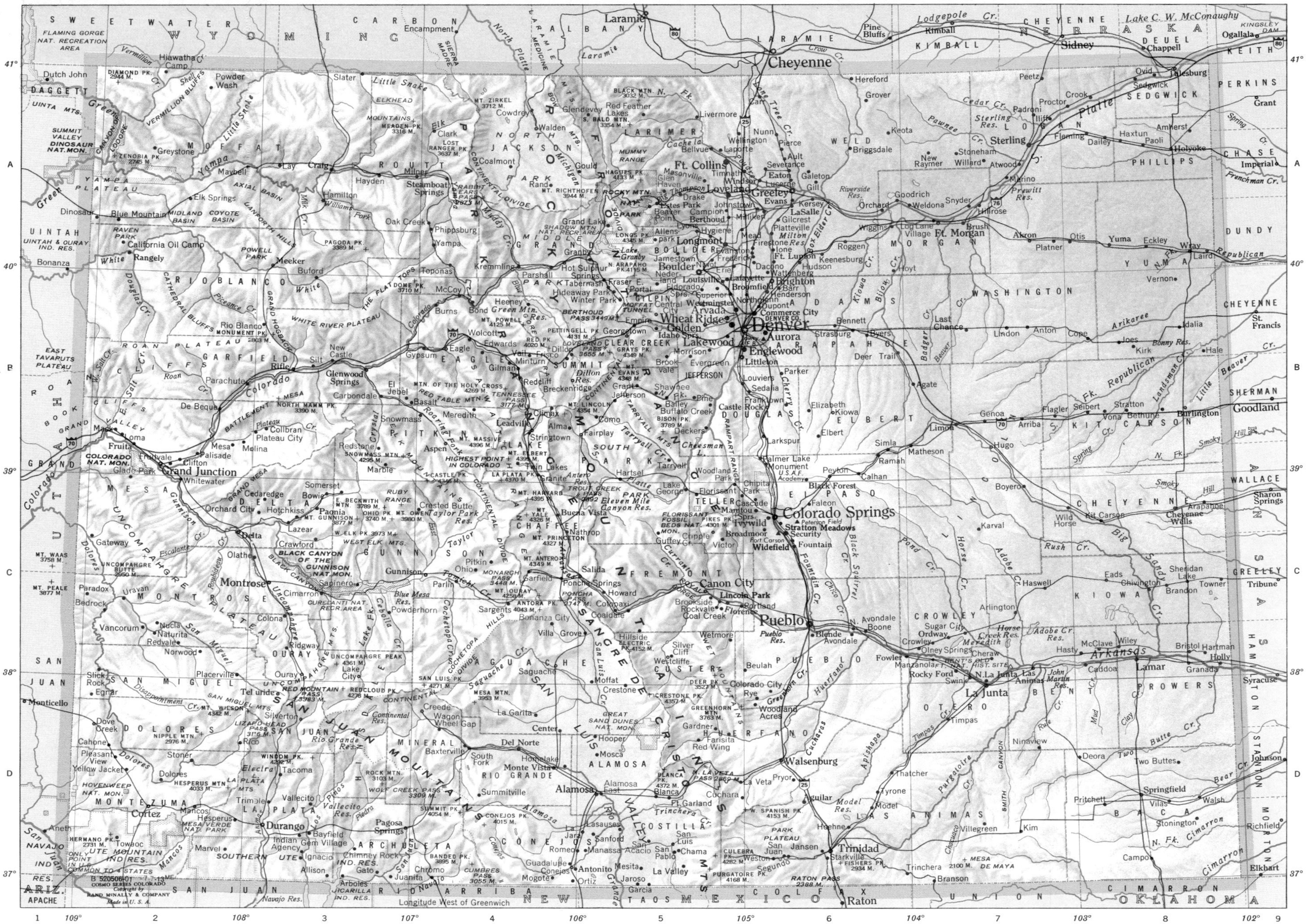
Statute Miles 5 0 5 10 20 30 40 50
Kilometers 5 0 5 15 25 35 45 55 65 75
Lambert Conformal Conic Projection
Longitude West of Greenwich
Copyright by RAND McNALLY & COMPANY Made in U. S. A.

Colorado

1990 CENSUS

Alamosa, 7,579 ...... D 5
Applewood, 8,130('85) B 5
Arvada, 89,235 ...... B 5
Aspen, 5,049 .... B 4
Aurora, 222,103 ..... B 6
Berthoud, 2,990 ..... A 5
Boulder, 83,312 ..... A 5
Breckenridge, 1,285 .. B 4
Brighton, 14,203 ..... B 6
Broomfield, 24,638 ... B 5
Brush, 4,165 .... A 7
Buena Vista, 1,752 ... C 4
Burlington, 2,941 ..... B 8
Canon City, 12,687 ... C 5
Carbondale, 3,004 .... B 3
Castle Rock, 8,708 .... B 6
Central City, 335 ..... B 5
Colorado Springs, 281,140 .... C 6
Commerce City, 16,466 B 6
Cortez, 7,284 .... D 2
Craig, 8,091 .... A 3
Dacono, 2,228 .... A 6
Delta, 3,789 .... C 2
Denver, 467,610 .... B 6
Durango, 12,430 ...... D 3
Eaton, 1,959 .... A 6
Englewood, 29,387 .... B 6
Estes Park, 3,184 .... A 5
Evans, 5,877 .... A 6
Florence, 2,990 ...... C 5
Fort Collins, 87,758 .... A 5
Fort Lupton, 5,159 ..... A 6
Fort Morgan, 9,068 ..... A 7
Fountain, 9,984 ...... C 6
Fruita, 4,045 .... B 2
Glenwood Springs, 6,561 .... B 3
Golden, 13,116 .... B 5
Grand Junction, 29,034 B 2
Greeley, 60,536 .... A 6
Gunnison, 4,636 ...... C 4
Holyoke, 1,931 ...... A 8
Idaho Springs, 1,834 .. B 5
Julesburg, 1,295 ...... A 8
Lafayette, 14,548 ..... B 5
La Junta, 7,637 .... D 7
Lakewood, 126,481 .... B 5
Lamar, 8,343 .... C 8
La Salle, 1,783 ...... A 6
Las Animas, 2,481 ..... C 7
Leadville, 2,629 .... B 4
Limon, 1,831 .... B 7
Littleton, 33,685 ...... B 6
Longmont, 51,555 ..... A 5
Louisville, 12,361 ...... B 5
Loveland, 37,352 ...... A 5
Manitou Springs, 4,535 C 6
Meeker, 2,098 .... A 3
Monte Vista, 4,324 .... D 4
Montrose, 8,854 .... C 3
Northglenn, 27,195 .... B 6
Orchard City, 2,218 ... C 3
Ouray, 644 .... C 3
Pagosa Springs, 1,207 D 3
Pueblo, 98,640 .... C 6
Rangely, 2,278 ...... A 2
Rifle, 4,636 .... B 3
Rocky Ford, 4,162 .... C 7
Salida, 4,737 .... C 5
Springfield, 1,475 .... D 8
Steamboat Springs, 6,695 .... A 4
Sterling, 10,362 ...... A 7
Telluride, 1,309 ...... D 3
Trinidad, 8,580 ...... D 6
Vail, 3,659 .... B 4
Walsenburg, 3,300 .... D 6
Westminster, 74,625 .. B 5
Wheat Ridge, 29,419 .. B 5
Widefield, 12,112('85) .. C 6
Windsor, 5,062 .... A 6
Woodland Park, 4,610 C 5
Wray, 1,998 .... A 8
Yuma, 2,719 .... A 8

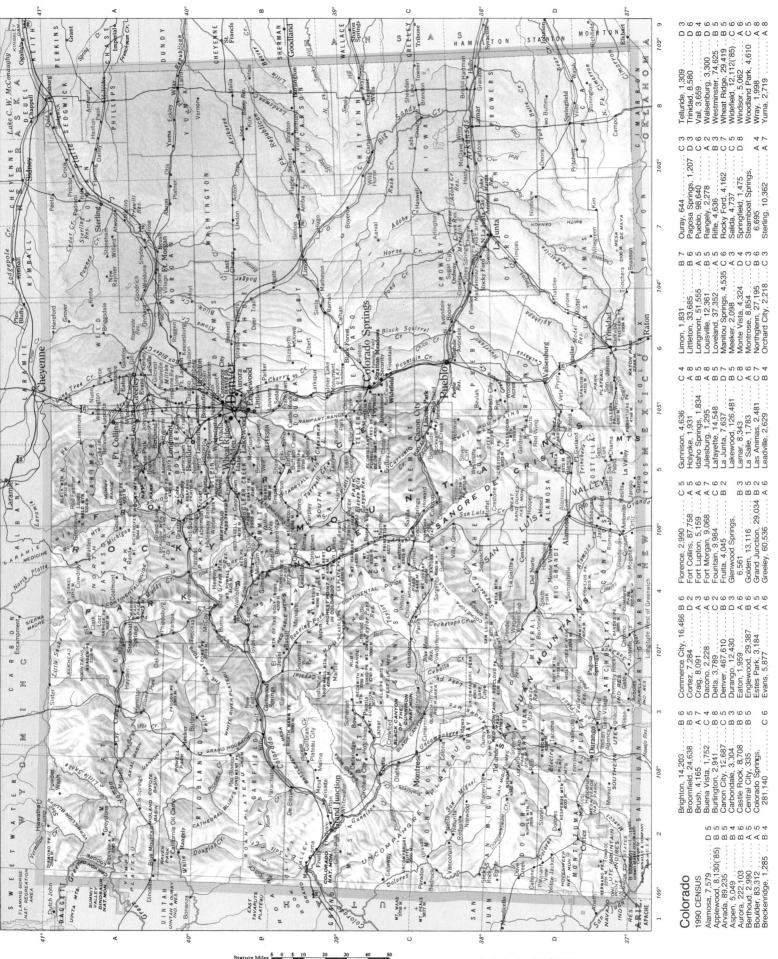

Connecticut

1990 CENSUS

- Ansonia, 18,403 . . . . . . D 3
- Bethel, 8,755 (17,541▲) D 2
- Bloomfield, 7,120 (19,483▲) . . . . B 5
- Branford, 5,438 (27,603▲) . . . . D 4
- Bridgeport, 141,686 . . E 3
- Bristol, 60,640 . . . . C 4
- Cheshire, 5,722 (25,684▲) . . . . D 4
- Clinton, 11,195('87) . . . . D 5
- Coventry, 3,769 (10,063▲) . . . . B 6
- Danbury, 65,585 . . . . . . D 2
- Danielson, 4,441 . . . . . . B 8
- Derby, 12,199 . . . . D 3
- East Hartford, 50,452 . . B 5
- East Haven, 26,144 . . . D 4
- Enfield, 8,454 (45,532▲) B 5
- Fairfield, 52,400 . . . . . . E 2
- Glastonbury, 7,049 (27,901▲) . . . . C 5
- Greenwich, 58,000 . . . . E 1
- Groton, 9,837 . . . . D 7
- Hamden, 53,100 . . . . . . D 4
- Hartford, 139,739 . . . . B 5
- Harwinton, 3,293 (5,228▲) . . . . B 3
- Jewett City, 3,349 . . . . C 8
- Manchester, 51,000 . . B 5
- Meriden, 59,479 . . . . . . C 4
- Middlebury, 4,140 (6,145▲) . . . . C 3
- Middletown, 42,762 . . . . C 5
- Milford, 48,168 . . . . . . E 3
- Mystic, 2,333('80) . . . . D 8
- Naugatuck, 30,625 . . . . D 3
- New Britain, 75,491 . . C 4
- New Fairfield, 4,600 (12,911▲) . . . . D 2
- New Haven, 130,474 . . D 4
- Newington, 29,800 . . . . C 5
- New London, 28,540 . . D 7
- New Milford, 5,186 (23,629▲) . . . . C 2
- North Branford, 6,600 (12,996▲) . . . . D 4
- North Haven, 22,700 . . D 4
- Norwalk, 78,331 . . . . . . E 2
- Norwich, 37,391 . . . . . . C 7
- Orange, 13,300 . . . . . . D 3
- Putnam, 6,850 (9,031▲) B 8
- Ridgefield, 6,066 (20,919▲) . . . . D 2
- Shelton, 35,418 . . . . . . D 3
- Simsbury, 5,488 (22,023▲) . . . . B 4
- Southington, 40,700 . . C 4
- South Windsor, 10,800 (22,090▲) . . . . B 5
- Stafford Springs, 4,100 B 6
- Stamford, 108,056 . . . . E 1
- Stratford, 50,400 . . . . . . E 3
- Thomaston, 3,590 (6,947▲) . . . . C 3
- Torrington, 33,687 . . . . B 3
- Trumbull, 33,200 . . . . . . E 3
- Wallingford, 41,400 . . . . D 4
- Waterbury, 108,961 . . C 3
- Watertown, 5,920 (20,456▲) . . . . C 3
- West Hartford, 59,100 B 4
- West Haven, 54,021 . . D 4
- Westport, 25,300 . . . . . . E 2
- Wethersfield, 26,500 . . C 5
- Willimantic, 14,600('87) C 7
- Wilton, 7,200 (15,989▲) E 2
- Windsor, 17,517 (27,817▲) . . . . B 5
- Windsor Locks, 12,190('80) . . . . B 5
- Wolcott, 6,070 (13,700▲) . . . . C 4
- Woodbridge, 7,700 (7,924▲) . . . . D 3

▲ Population of entire town (township), including rural area.

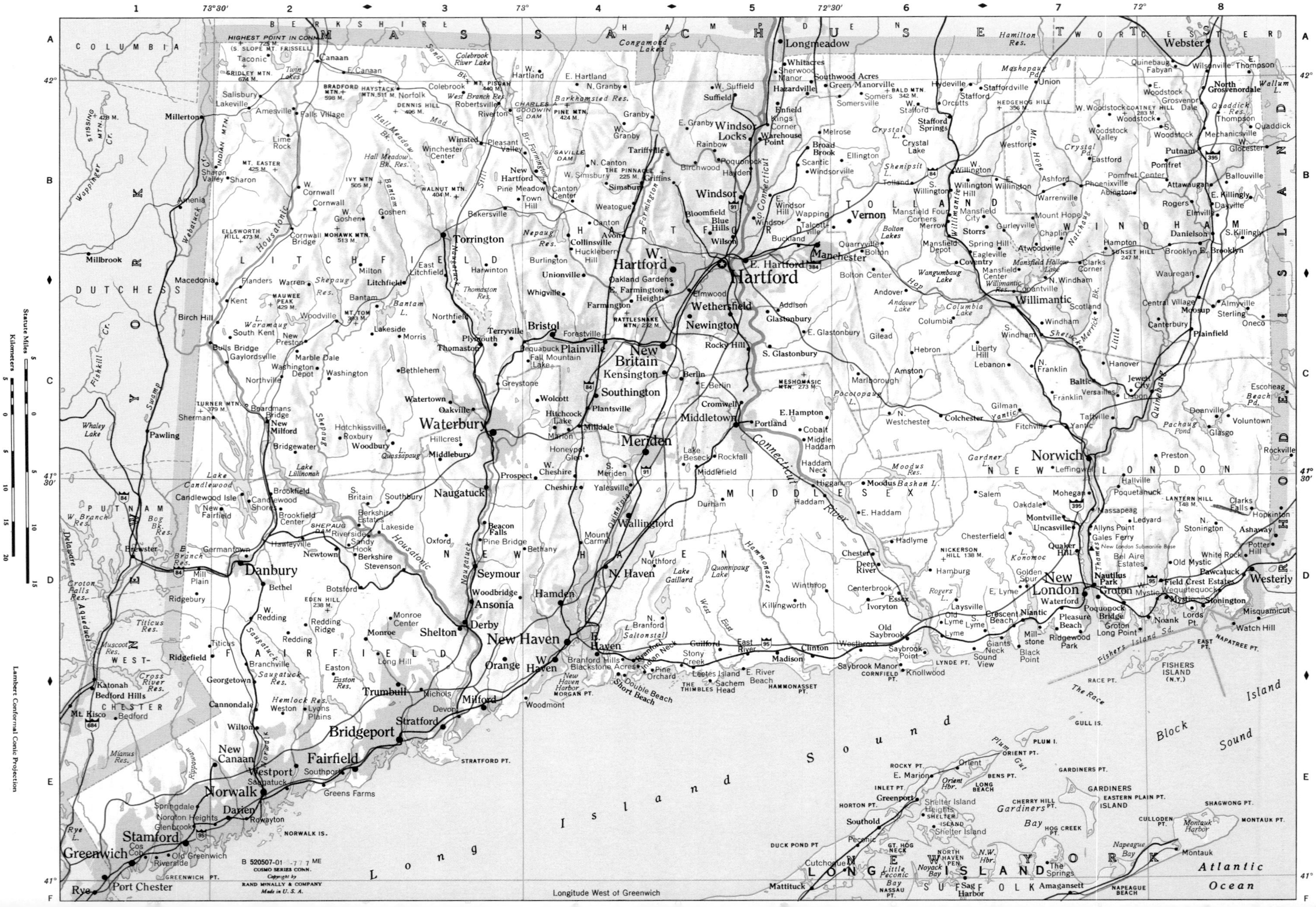

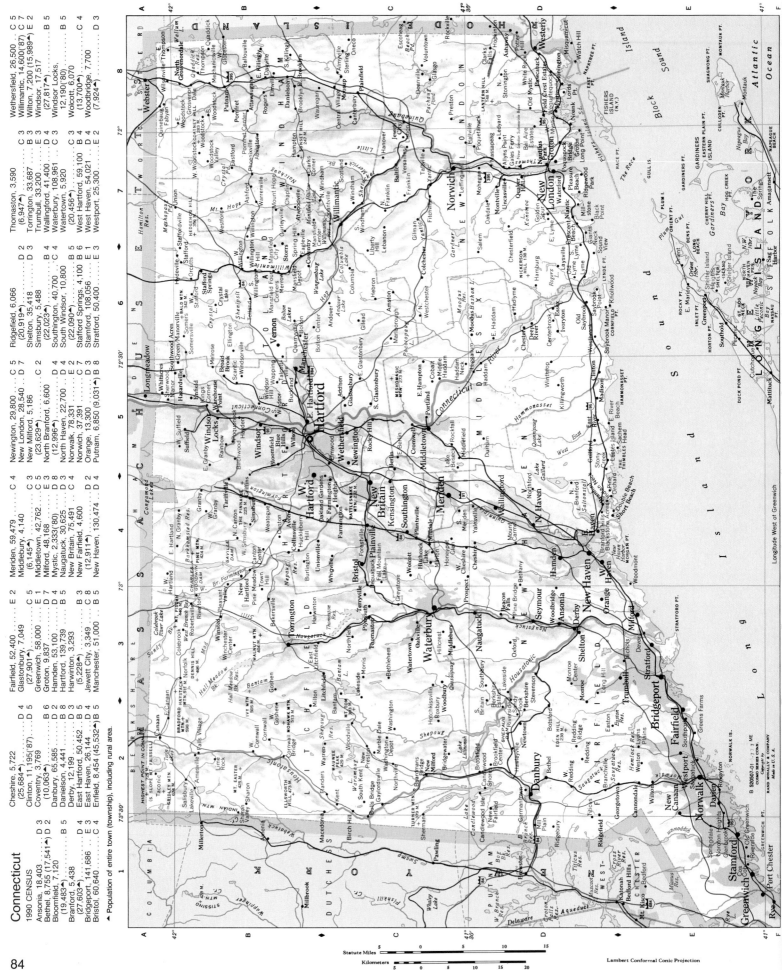

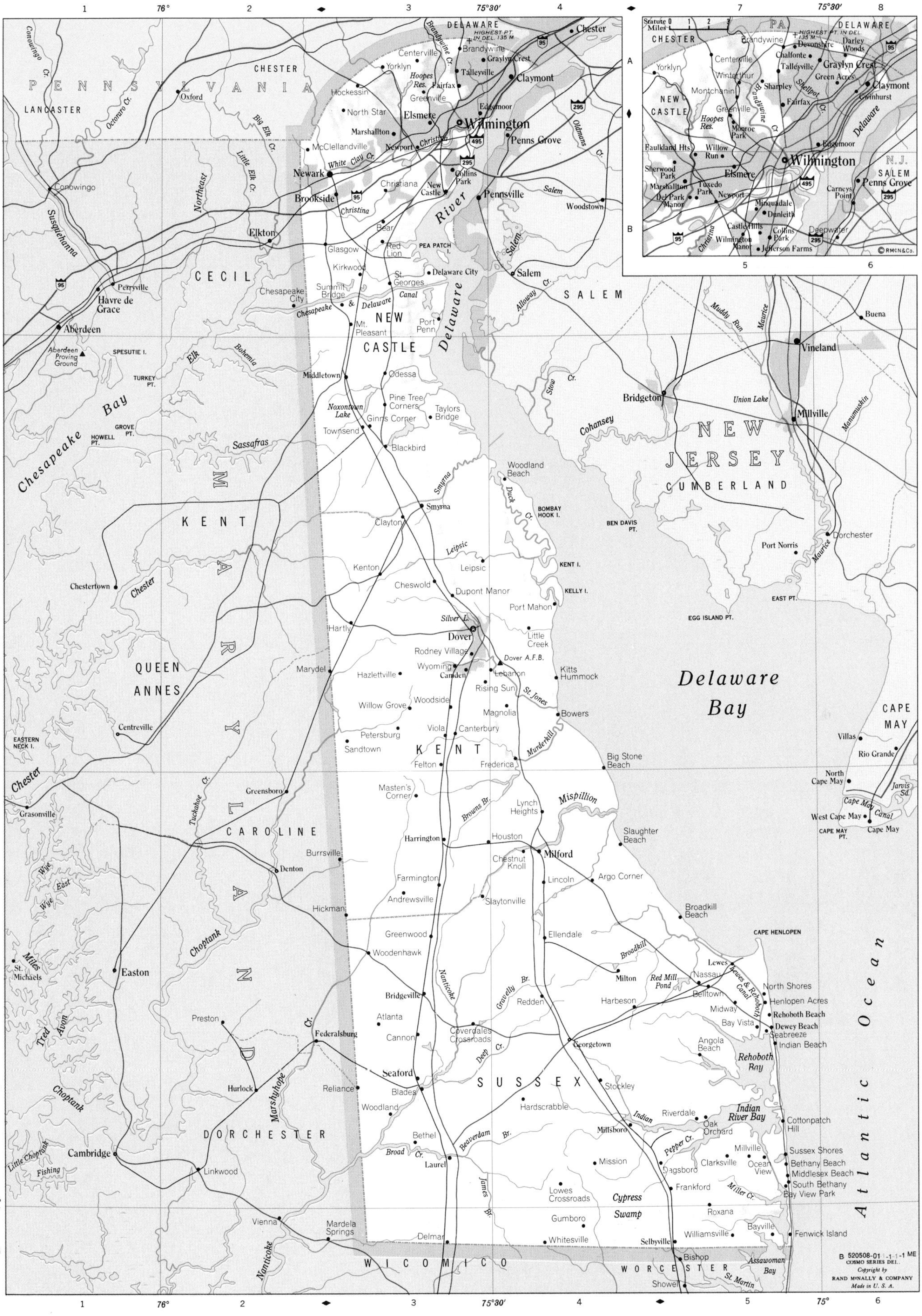

Statute Miles 5 0 5 10 15
Kilometers 5 0 5 10 15 20

Lambert Conformal Conic Projection

Delaware

1990 CENSUS

Bear, 1,200('88) .... B 3
Bethany Beach, 326 F 5
Blades, 834 .... F 3
Bridgeville, 1,210 .... F 3
Broadkill Beach, 390('88) .... E 5
Brookside, 7,450('88) B 3
Camden, 1,899 .... D 3
Canterbury, 500('88) D 3
Castle Hills, 1,475('88) i 7
Chalfonte, 1,740('88) h 7
Cheswold, 321 ......D 3
Christiana, 500('88).. B 3
Clarksville, 500('88) .. F 5
Claymont, 15,100('88) A 4
Clayton, 1,163 ...... C 3
Collins Park, 2,100('88)........ B 3
Dagsboro, 398 ...... F 5
Darley Woods, 1,220('88)........ h 8
Delaware City, 1,682 B 3
Delmar, 962 .... G 3
Del Park Manor, 1,550('88) .... i 7
Devonshire, 2,120('88)h 7
Dewey Beach, 204 .. F 5
Dover, 27,630 ...... D 3
Dunleith, 2,600('88) .. i 7
Dupont Manor, 1,059('80)........ D 3
Edgemoor, 5,400('88) A 3
Ellendale, 313 ...... E 4
Elsmere, 5,935 ...... B 3
Fairfax, 2,075('88) .. A 3
Faulkland Heights, 1,300('88) .... i 7
Felton, 683 .... D 3
Frankford, 591 ...... F 5
Frederica, 761 ...... D 4
Georgetown, 3,732 .. F 4
Graylyn Crest, 4,380('88)........ A 3
Green Acres, 1,140('88)........ h 8
Greenville, 800('88) .. a 3
Greenwood, 578 .... E 3
Gumboro, 200('88) .. g 4
Gwinhurst, 1,340('88) h 8
Harbeson, 500('88) .. f 4
Harrington, 2,311 .... E 8
Hockessin, 2,430('88) A 3
Houston, 487 ...... E 3
Jefferson Farms, 3,130('88) .... i 7
Kenton, 232 .... D 3
Kirkwood, 350('88) .. b 3
Laurel, 3,226 ...... F 3
Lebanon, 130('88) .. d 4
Leipsic, 236 .... D 3
Lewes, 2,295 ...... E 5
Lincoln, 500('88) .... e 4
Little Creek, 167 .... D 4
Marshallton, 1,765('88)........ B 3
Middletown, 3,834 .. C 3
Midway, 500('88) .... f 5
Milford, 6,040 ...... E 4
Millsboro, 1,643 .... F 4
Milton, 1,417 ...... E 4
Minquadale, 790('88).. i 7
Monroe Park, 1,000('88)........ h 7
Montchanin, 500('88) h 7
Newark, 25,098 .... B 3
New Castle, 4,837 .. B 3
Newport, 1,240 .... B 3
North Star, 1,030('88) A 3
Oak Orchard, 350('88) f 5
Ocean View, 606 .... F 5
Odessa, 303 ...... C 3
Port Penn, 300('88) .. b 3
Rehoboth Beach, 1,234 .... F 5
Rising Sun, 540('88) D 3
Rodney Village, 1,100('88)........ D 3
Saint Georges, 500('88) .... B 3
Seabreeze, 350('88).. F 5
Seaford, 5,689 ...... F 3
Selbyville, 1,335 .... G 5
Sharpley, 1,250('88).. h 7
Sherwood Park, 2,000('88) .... i 7
Silview, 1,500('88) .. B 3
Smyrna, 5,231 ...... C 3
Talleyville, 6,880('88) A 3
Townsend, 322 .... C 3
Tuxedo Park, 1,300('88) .... i 7
Willow Run, 1,600('88) i 7
Wilmington, 71,529 .. B 3
Wilmington Manor, 1,235('88) .... i 7
Wyoming, 977 ...... D 3
Yorklyn, 600('88).... A 3

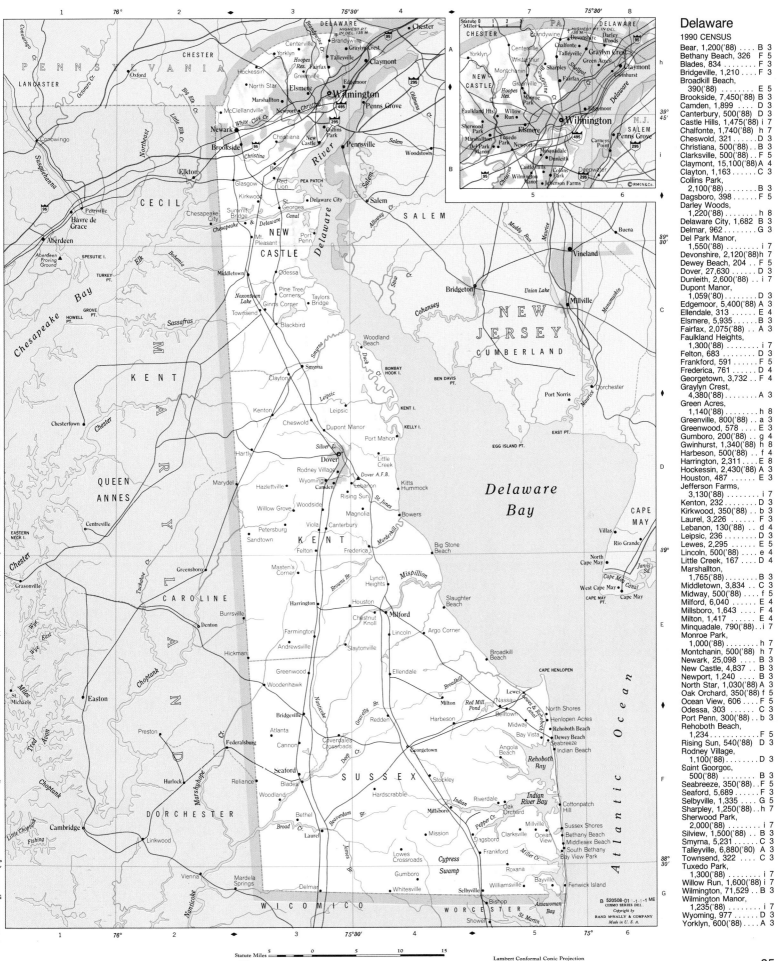

Florida

1990 CENSUS

Altamonte Springs, 34,879 .... D 5
Bartow, 14,716 .... E 5
Belle Glade, 16,177 .. F 6
Boca Raton, 61,492 .. F 6
Boynton Beach, 46,194 .... F 6
Bradenton, 43,779 .. E 4
Brandon, 36,300 .... E 4
Brownsville, 18,058('80) s13
Cape Canaveral, 8,014 .... D 6
Cape Coral, 74,991 .. F 5
Carol City, 52,800 .. s13
Clearwater, 98,784 .. E 4
Cocoa, 17,722 ...... D 6
Coral Gables, 40,091 G 6
Cutler Ridge, 20,886('80) s13
Davie, 47,217 ...... F 6
Daytona Beach, 61,921 .... C 5
Deerfield Beach, 46,325 .... F 6
De Land, 16,491 .... C 5
Delray Beach, 47,181 F 6
Dunedin, 34,012 .... D 4
Fort Lauderdale, 149,377 .... F 6
Fort Myers, 45,206 .. F 5
Fort Pierce, 36,830 .. E 6
Fort Walton Beach, 21,471 .... u15
Gainesville, 84,770 .. C 4
Hallandale, 30,996 .. G 6
Hialeah, 188,004 .... G 6
Hollywood, 121,697 .. F 6
Homestead, 26,866 .. G 6
Jacksonville, 635,230 B 5
Kendall, 53,100 ...... s13
Key Largo, 7,447('80) G 6
Key West, 24,832 .. H 5
Kissimmee, 30,050 .. D 5
Lake City, 10,005 .. B 4
Lakeland, 70,576 .... D 5
Lake Worth, 28,564 .. F 6
Largo, 65,674 ...... E 4
Lauderdale Lakes, 27,341 .... r13
Lealman, 19,873('80) p10
Leesburg, 14,903 .... D 5
Leisure City, 17,905('80) s13
Margate, 42,985 .... F 6
Melbourne, 59,646 .. D 6
Merritt Island, 44,300 D 6
Miami, 358,548 .... G 6
Miami Beach, 92,639 G 6
Miramar, 40,663 .... s13
Naples, 19,505 ...... F 5
New Smyrna Beach, 16,543 .... C 6
North Fort Myers, 17,200('83) ...... F 5
North Miami, 49,998 G 6
North Miami Beach, 35,359 .... s13
Oakland Park, 26,326 r13
Ocala, 42,045 ...... C 4
Orlando, 164,693 .... D 5
Ormond Beach, 29,721 .... C 5
Palm Bay, 62,632 .. D 6
Panama City, 34,378 u16
Pembroke Pines, 65,452 .... r13
Pensacola, 58,165 .. u14
Pine Hills, 35,600 .... D 5
Pinellas Park, 43,426 E 4
Plantation, 66,692 .... r13
Plant City, 22,754 .. D 4
Pompano Beach, 72,411 .... F 6
Port Charlotte, 43,300 F 4
Port Orange, 35,317 C 6
Riviera Beach, 27,639 F 6
Saint Augustine, 11,692 .... C 5
Saint Petersburg, 238,629 .... E 4
Sanford, 32,387 .... D 5
Sarasota, 50,961 .... E 4
Sebring, 8,900 ...... E 5
South Miami Heights, 18,000('83) s13
Sweetwater Creek, 18,000('83) p10
Tallahassee, 124,773 B 2
Tampa, 280,015 .... E 4
Tarpon Springs, 17,906 .... D 4
Titusville, 39,394 .... D 6
Venice, 16,922 ...... E 4
Vero Beach, 17,350 .. E 6
West Palm Beach, 67,643 .... F 6
West Pensacola, 30,200 .... u14
Winter Haven, 24,725 D 5
Winter Park, 22,242 D 5

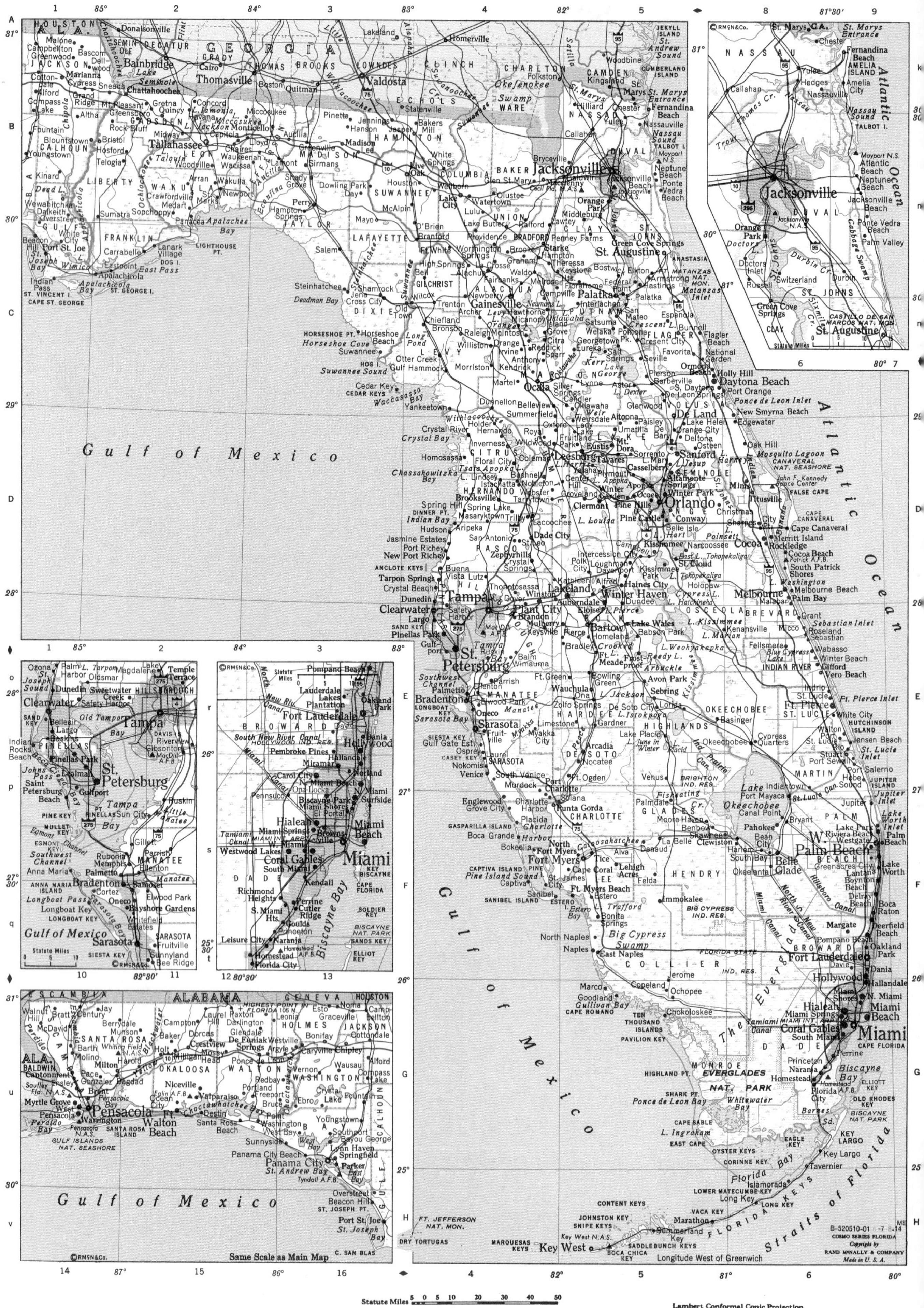

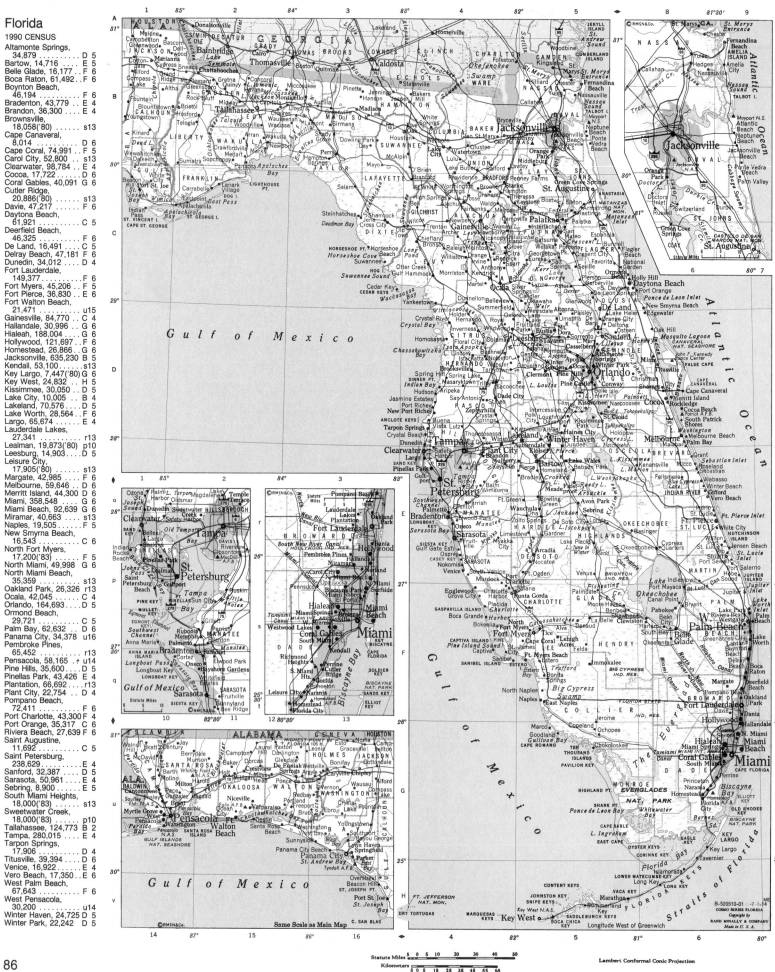

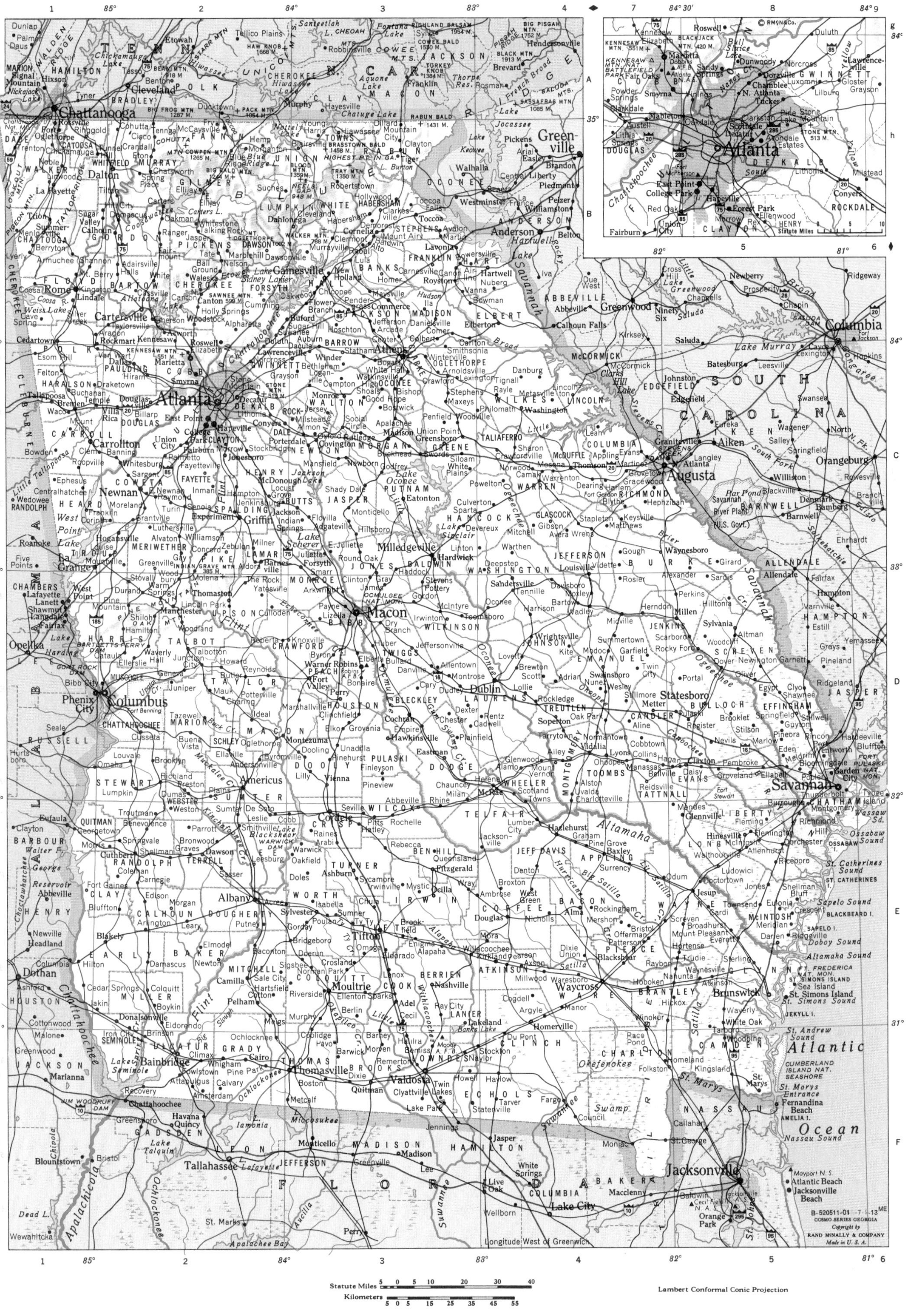

Georgia

1990 CENSUS

Adel, 5,093 . . . . E 3
Albany, 78,122 . . . . . E 2
Americus, 16,512 . . . . D 2
Athens, 45,734 . . . . C 3
Atlanta, 394,017 . . . . C 2
Augusta, 44,639 . . . . C 5
Bainbridge, 10,712 . . F 2
Blakely, 5,595 . . . . . . E 2
Brunswick, 16,433 . . E 5
Buford, 8,771 . . . . . . B 2
Cairo, 9,035 . . . . F 2
Calhoun, 7,135 . . . . . . B 2
Camilla, 5,008 . . . . . . E 2
Carrollton, 16,029 . . . C 1
Cartersville, 12,035 . . B 2
Cedartown, 7,978 . . B 1
Chamblee, 7,668 . . . . h 8
Cochran, 4,390 . . . . D 3
College Park, 20,457 C 2
Columbus, 178,681 . . D 2
Conyers, 7,380 . . . . C 2
Cordele, 10,321 . . . . E 3
Covington, 10,026 . . C 3
Dalton, 21,761 . . . . . . B 2
Dawson, 5,295 . . . . . . E 2
Decatur, 17,336 . . . . C 2
Dock Junction, 6,189('80) . . . . E 5
Doraville, 7,626 . . . . . . h 8
Douglas, 10,464 . . . . E 4
Douglasville, 11,635 C 2
Dublin, 16,312 . . . . . . D 4
Dunwoody, 7,840('85) h 8
Eastman, 5,153 . . . . D 3
East Point, 34,402 . . C 2
Elberton, 5,682 . . . . . B 4
Fair Oaks, 8,486('80) h 7
Fitzgerald, 8,612 . . . . E 3
Forest Park, 16,925 . . h 8
Fort Oglethorpe, 5,880 . . . . B 1
Fort Valley, 8,198 . . D 3
Gainesville, 17,885 . . B 3
Garden City, 7,410 . . D 5
Griffin, 21,347 . . . . . . C 2
Hapeville, 5,483 . . . . C 2
Hardwick, 8,800('85) C 3
Hinesville, 21,603 . . . . E 5
Jesup, 8,958 . . . . . . E 5
Kennesaw, 8,936 . . . . B 2
Lafayette, 6,313 . . . . B 1
La Grange, 25,597 . . C 1
Lawrenceville, 16,848 C 3
Lithia Springs, 9,145('80) . . . . h 7
Mableton, 21,390('85) h 7
Macon, 106,612 . . . . D 3
Marietta, 44,129 . . . . C 2
Martinez, 16,472('80) C 4
Milledgeville, 17,727 C 3
Monroe, 9,759 . . . . . . C 3
Moultrie, 14,865 . . . . E 3
Newnan, 12,497 . . . . C 2
North Atlanta, 21,340('85) . . . . . . h 8
North Druid Hills, 4,900('85) . . . . h 8
Pendley Hills, 5,400('85) . . . . h 8
Perry, 9,452 . . . . D 3
Quitman, 5,292 . . . . . . F 3
Rome, 30,326 . . . . . . B 1
Roswell, 47,923 . . . . B 2
Saint Simons Island, 6,566('80) . . . . E 5
Sandersville, 6,290 . . D 4
Sandy Springs, 21,120('85) . . . . . . h 8
Savannah, 137,560 . . D 5
Scottdale, 8,770('80) h 8
Smyrna, 30,981 . . . . . C 2
Statesboro, 15,854 . . D 5
Stone Mountain, 6,494 . . . . C 2
Swainsboro, 7,361 . . . D 4
Sylvester, 5,702 . . . . . E 3
Thomaston, 9,127 . . . D 2
Thomasville, 17,457 . . F 3
Thomson, 6,862 . . . . . C 4
Tifton, 14,215 . . . . . . E 3
Toccoa, 8,266 . . . . . . B 3
Tucker, 22,250('85) . . h 8
Union City, 8,375 . . . . C 2
Valdosta, 39,806 . . . . F 3
Vidalia, 11,078 . . . . . . D 4
Warner Robins, 43,726 . . . . D 3
Waycross, 16,410 . . E 4
Waynesboro, 5,701 . . C 4
Winder, 7,373 . . . . . . C 3

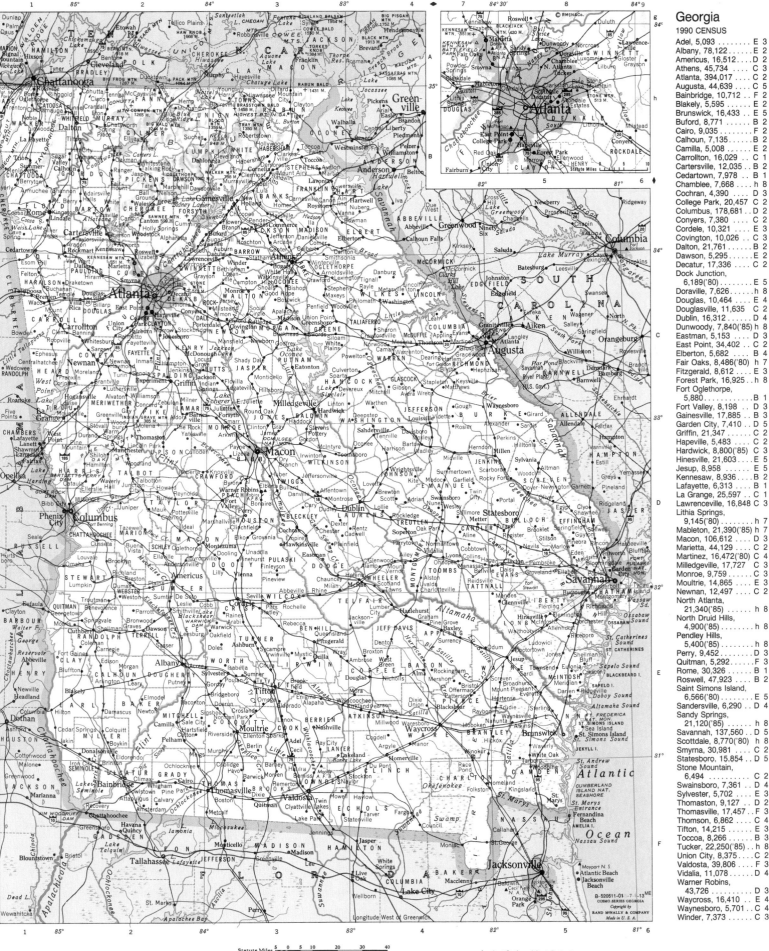

Hawaii

1990 CENSUS

Aiea, 8,906 . . . . B 4
Anahola, 1,181 . . . . . . A 2
Captain Cook, 2,595 . . D 6
Ewa, 3,780 . . . . B 3
Ewa Beach, 14,315 . . . B 3
Halawa Heights, 7,000('83) g10
Haleiwa, 2,442 . . . . B 3
Haliimaile, 841 . . . . C 5
Hana, 683 . . . . C 6
Hanamaulu, 3,611 . . . . B 2
Hanapepe, 1,395 . . . . . . B 2
Hauula, 3,479 . . . . B 4
Hawi, 924 . . . . C 6
Hilo, 37,808 . . . . D 6
Holualoa, 3,834 . . . . . . D 6
Honokaa, 2,186 . . . . . . C 6
Honolulu, 365,272 . . . . B 4
Honomu, 532 . . . . D 6
Kaaawa, 1,138 . . . . f10
Kahaluu, 3,068 . . . . g10
Kahuku, 2,063 . . . . B 4
Kahului, 16,889 . . . . . . C 5
Kailua, 36,818 . . . . B 4
Kailua Kona, 9,126 . . . . D 6
Kalaheo, 3,592 . . . . . . B 2
Kamuela (Waimea), 5,972 . . . . C 6
Kaneohe, 35,448 . . . . . . B 4
Kapaa, 8,149 . . . . A 2
Kapaau, 1,083 . . . . C 6
Kaumakani, 803 . . . . . . B 2
Kaunakakai, 2,658 . . . . B 4
Keaau, 1,584 . . . . D 6
Kealakekua, 1,453 . . . . D 6
Kealia, 700('83) . . . . . . A 2
Kekaha, 3,506 . . . . B 2
Keokea, 900('83) . . . . . . C 5
Kihei, 11,107 . . . . C 5
Kilauea, 1,685 . . . . A 2
Koloa, 1,791 . . . . B 2
Kula, 1,300('83) . . . . . . C 5
Kurtistown, 910 . . . . . . D 6
Lahaina, 9,073 . . . . C 5
Laie, 5,577 . . . . B 4
Lanai City, 2,400 . . . . . C 5
Lawai, 1,787 . . . . B 2
Lihue, 5,536 . . . . B 2
Lower Paia, 1,500('80) C 5
Maili, 6,059 . . . . g 9
Makaha, 7,990 . . . . g 9
Makakilo City, 9,828 . . g 9
Makawao, 5,405 . . . . . . C 5
Makaweli, 565 . . . . B 2
Maunaloa, 405 . . . . B 4
Maunawili, 4,847 . . . . . . g10
Mililani Town, 29,359 . . g 9
Naalehu, 1,027 . . . . . . D 6
Nanakuli, 9,575 . . . . . . B 3
Paauilo, 620 . . . . C 6
Pacific Palisades, 10,000('83) g10
Pahala, 1,520 . . . . D 6
Pahoa, 1,027 . . . . D 7
Paia, 2,091 . . . . C 5
Papaikou, 1,634 . . . . . . D 6
Pearl City, 30,993 . . . . B 4
Pepeekeo, 1,813 . . . . . . D 6
Poipu, 975 . . . . B 2
Puhi, 1,210 . . . . B 2
Pukalani, 5,879 . . . . . . C 5
Sunset Beach, 800('83) f 9
Volcano, 1,516 . . . . . . D 6
Wahiawa, 17,386 . . . . . . B 3
Waialua, 3,943 . . . . B 3
Waianae, 8,758 . . . . . . B 3
Waikapu, 729 . . . . C 5
Wailua, 2,018 . . . . A 2
Wailuku, 10,688 . . . . . . C 5
Waimanalo, 3,508 . . . . B 4
Waimea, 600('83) . . . . . . f 9
Waimea, 1,840 . . . . B 2
Waipahu, 31,435 . . . . . . B 3
Waipio Acres, 5,304 . . . g 9
Whitmore Village, 3,373 f 9

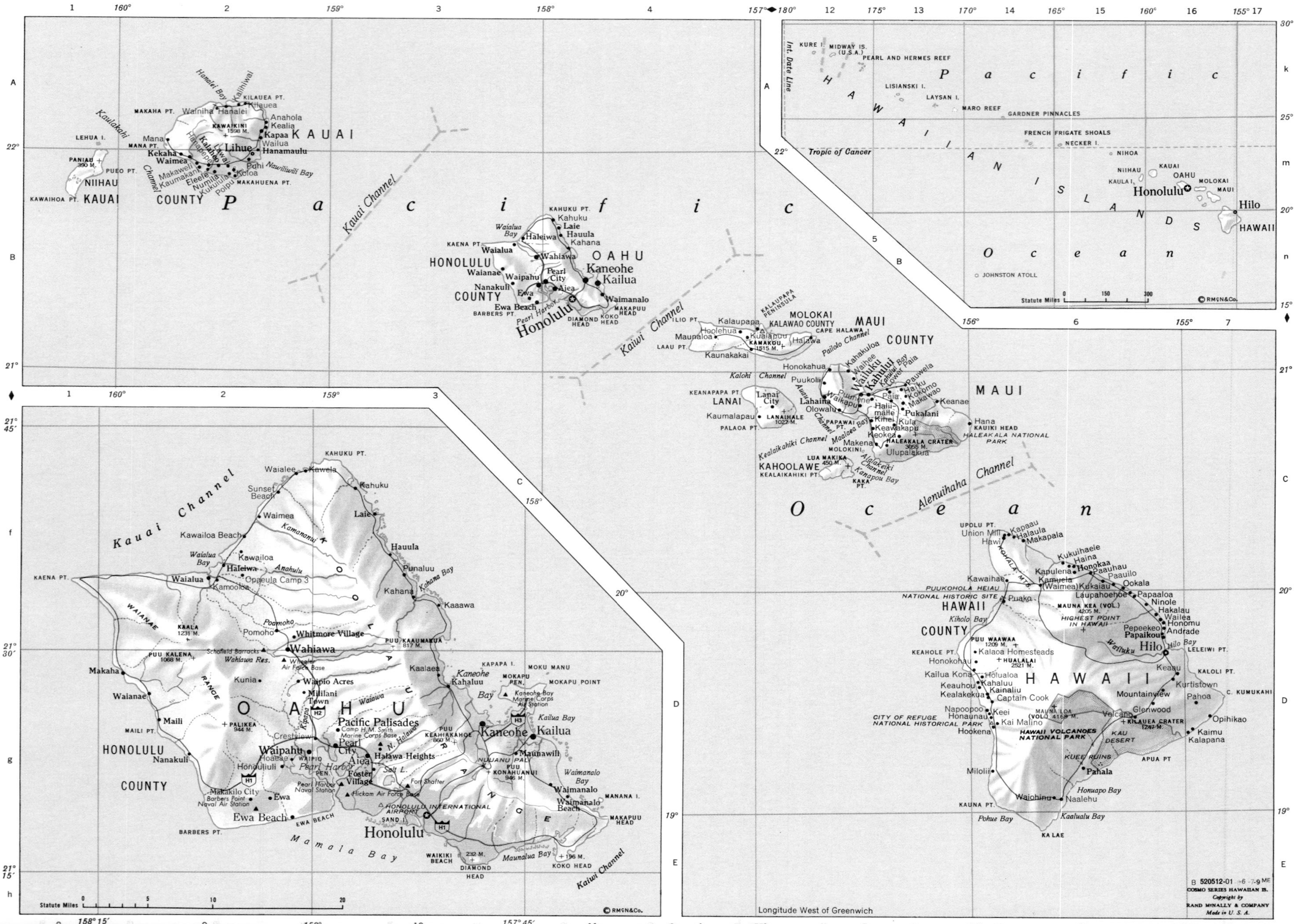

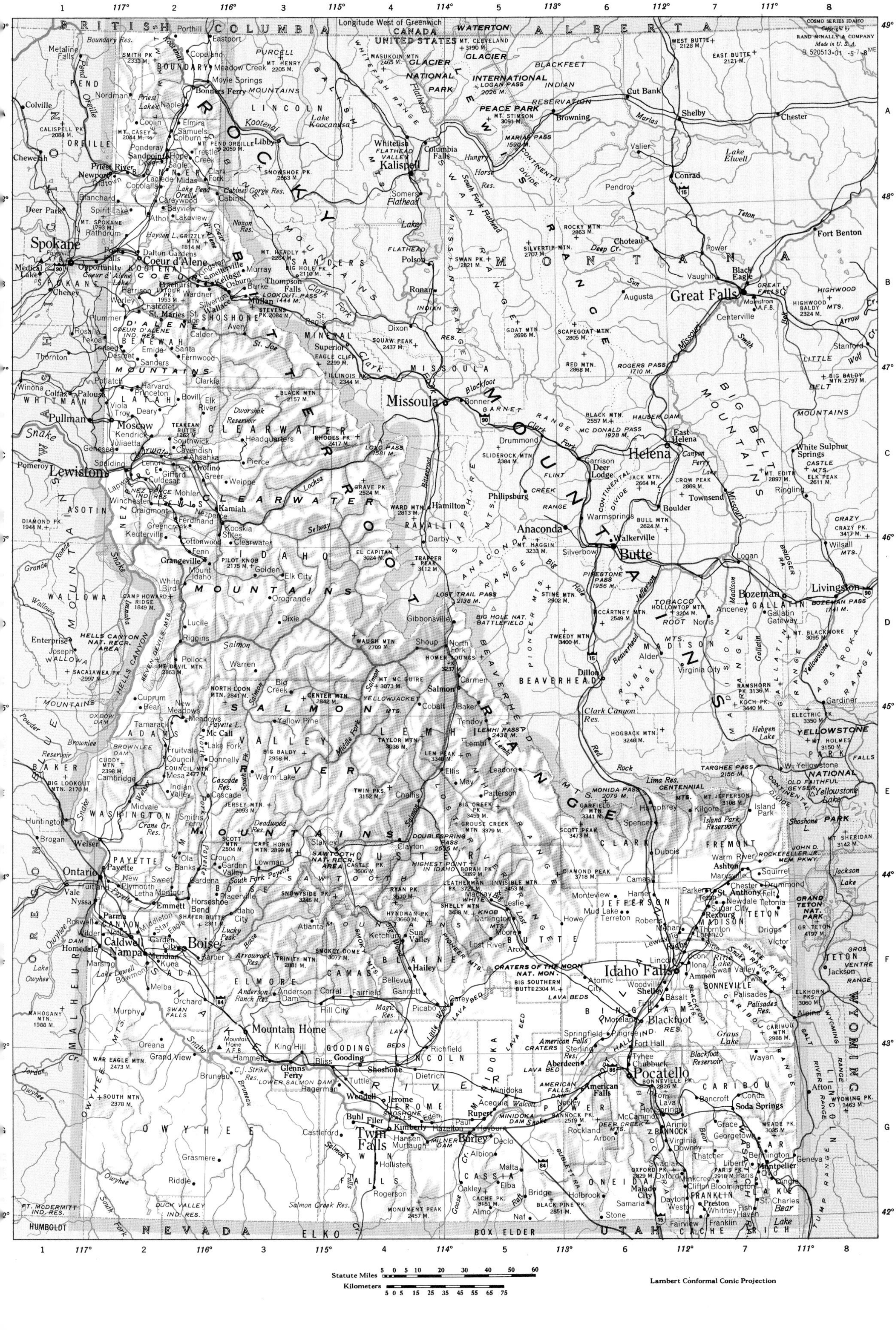

Lambert Conformal Conic Projection

Idaho

1990 CENSUS

Aberdeen, 1,406 . . . . G 6
American Falls, 3,757 G 6
Ammon, 5,002 . . . . . F 7
Arco, 1,016 . . . . F 5
Ashton, 1,114 . . . . . . E 7
Bellevue, 1,275. . . . . F 4
Blackfoot, 9,646 . . . . F 6
Boise, 125,738 . . . . . F 2
Bonners Ferry, 2,193 A 2
Buhl, 3,516 . . . . G 4
Burley, 8,702 . . . . . . G 5
Caldwell, 18,400 . . . . F 2
Cascade, 877 . . . . . . E 2
Chubbuck, 7,791. . . . G 6
Coeur d'Alene,
24,563 . . . . B 2
Cottonwood, 822. . . . C 2
Council, 831 . . . . E 2
Dalton Gardens,
1,951. . . . . B 2
Eagle, 3,327 . . . . F 2
Emmett, 4,601 . . . . . F 2
Filer, 1,511 . . . . G 4
Fort Hall, 900('83) . . F 6
Fruitland, 2,400 . . . . . F 2
Garden City, 6,369 . . F 2
Genesee, 725 . . . . C 2
Glenns Ferry, 1,304. . G 3
Gooding, 2,820 . . . . G 4
Grace, 973 . . . . G 7
Grangeville, 3,226 . . D 2
Hailey, 3,687 . . . . . . F 4
Hansen, 848 . . . . . . G 4
Heyburn, 2,714 . . . . G 5
Homedale, 1,963 . . . . F 2
Idaho Falls, 43,929 . . F 6
Inkom, 769 . . . . G 6
Iona, 1,049 . . . . F 7
Jerome, 6,529 . . . . . . G 4
Kamiah, 1,157 . . . . . . C 2
Kellogg, 2,591 . . . . . B 2
Ketchum, 2,523 . . . . F 4
Kimberly, 2,367 . . . . G 4
Kingston, 1,000('83) B 2
Kuna, 1,955 . . . . F 2
Lapwai, 932. . . . . C 2
Lewiston, 28,082. . . . C 1
Malad City, 1,946 . . G 6
Marsing, 798 . . . . . . F 2
McCall, 2,005 . . . . . . E 2
Meridian, 9,596 . . . . F 2
Middleton, 1,851 . . . . F 2
Montpelier, 2,656. . . . G 7
Moscow, 18,519 . . . . C 2
Mountain Home,
7,913. . . . . F 3
Mullan, 821 . . . . B 3
Nampa, 28,365. . . . . F 2
New Plymouth, 1,313 F 2
Orofino, 2,868 . . . . . C 2
Osburn, 1,579 . . . . . B 3
Parma, 1,597 . . . . . . F 2
Paul, 901 . . . . G 5
Payette, 5,592 . . . . . E 2
Pierce, 746 . . . . C 3
Pocatello, 46,080. . . . G 6
Post Falls, 7,349. . . . B 2
Potlatch, 790 . . . . . . C 2
Preston, 3,710. . . . . . G 7
Priest River, 1,560 . . A 2
Rathdrum, 2,000 . . . . B 2
Rexburg, 14,302 . . . . F 7
Rigby, 2,681. . . . . F 7
Rupert, 5,455 . . . . . . G 5
Saint Anthony, 3,010 F 7
Saint Maries, 2,442 . . B 2
Salmon, 2,941 . . . . . . D 5
Sandpoint, 5,203 . . . . A 2
Shelley, 3,536 . . . . . . F 6
Shoshone, 1,249 . . . . G 4
Shoup, 10('83). . . . . . D 4
Soda Springs, 3,111 G 7
Spirit Lake, 790 . . . . B 2
Sugar City, 1,275. . . . F 7
Sun Valley, 938 . . . . F 4
Troy, 699 . . . . C 2
Twin Falls, 27,591 . . G 4
Ucon, 895. . . . . F 7
Wallace, 1,010. . . . . . B 3
Weippe, 532. . . . . C 3
Weiser, 4,571 . . . . . . E 2
Wendell, 1,963. . . . . G 4
Wilder, 1,232 . . . . . . F 2

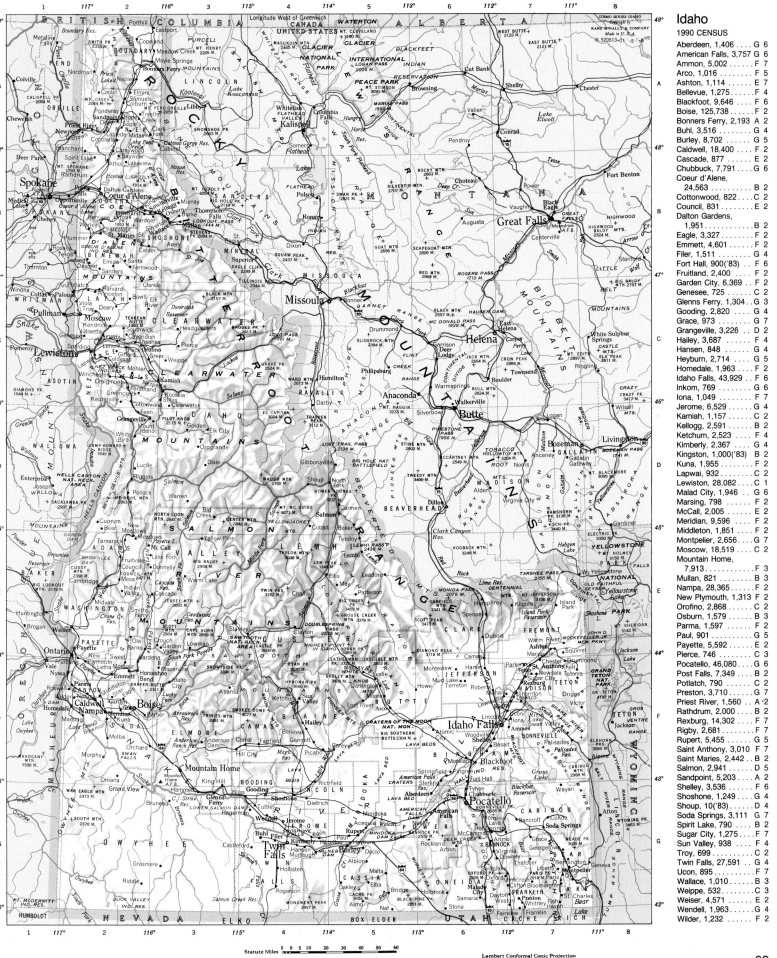

Illinois

1990 CENSUS

Addison, 32,058 .... k 8
Alton, 32,905 ...... E 3
Arlington Heights, 75,460 .... A 5
Aurora, 99,581...... B 5
Belleville, 42,785 .... E 4
Berwyn, 45,426 .... k 9
Bloomington, 51,972 C 4
Bolingbrook, 40,843.. k 8
Bourbonnais, 13,934 B 6
Brookfield, 18,876 .. k 9
Burbank, 27,600 .... k 9
Cahokia, 17,550 .... E 3
Cairo, 4,846 .... F 4
Calumet City, 37,840 B 6
Canton, 13,922 .... C 3
Carbondale, 27,033 .. F 4
Centralia, 14,274 .... E 4
Champaign, 63,502 .. C 5
Charleston, 20,398 .. D 5
Chicago, 2,783,726.. B 6
Chicago Heights, 33,072 .... B 6
Cicero, 67,436...... B 6
Danville, 33,828 .... C 6
Decatur, 83,885 .... D 5
De Kalb, 34,925 .... B 5
Des Plaines, 53,223.. A 6
Dixon, 15,144 ...... B 4
Downers Grove, 46,858 .... B 5
East Saint Louis, 40,944 .... E 3
Elgin, 77,010 .... A 5
Elk Grove Village, 33,429 .... h 9
Elmhurst, 42,029.... B 6
Evanston, 73,233.... A 6
Freeport, 25,840 .... A 4
Galena, 3,647 ...... A 3
Galesburg, 33,530 .. C 3
Glenview, 37,093 ... h 9
Granite City, 32,862.. E 3
Gurnee, 13,701 .... h 9
Hanover Park, 32,895 k 8
Harvey, 29,771 .... B 6
Highland Park, 30,575 A 6
Hoffman Estates, 46,561 .... h 8
Jacksonville, 19,324 D 3
Joliet, 76,836 ...... B 5
Kankakee, 27,575 .. B 6
Kewanee, 12,969.... B 4
Lake Forest, 17,836 A 6
Lansing, 28,086 .... B 6
La Salle, 9,717...... B 4
Lincoln, 15,418 .... C 4
Lombard, 39,408 .... k 8
Macomb, 19,952 .... C 3
Marion, 14,545...... F 5
Mattoon, 18,441 .... D 5
Moline, 43,202 ...... B 3
Monmouth, 9,489 .. C 3
Mount Prospect, 53,170 .... A 6
Mount Vernon, 16,988 E 5
Naperville, 85,351 .. B 5
Nauvoo, 1,108....... C 2
Niles, 28,284 .... h 9
Normal, 40,023 .... C 5
Northbrook, 32,308 .. h 9
North Chicago, 34,978 .... A 6
Oak Lawn, 56,182 ... B 6
Oak Park, 53,648 .. B 6
Ottawa, 17,451 .... B 5
Palatine, 39,253 .... A 5
Park Ridge, 36,175 .. B 6
Pekin, 32,254 ...... C 4
Peoria, 113,504 .... C 4
Peru, 9,302 .... B 4
Pontiac, 11,428 .... C 5
Quincy, 39,681...... D 2
Rockford, 139,426 .. A 4
Rock Island, 40,552.. B 3
Salem, 7,470 ...... E 5
Schaumburg, 68,586 h 8
Skokie, 59,432...... A 6
Springfield, 105,227.. D 4
Sterling, 15,132 .... B 4
Streator, 14,121 .... B 5
Taylorville, 11,133 .. D 4
Tinley Park, 37,121 .. k 9
Urbana, 36,344 .... C 5
Vandalia, 6,114 .... E 4
Waukegan, 69,392 .. A 6
Wheaton, 51,464 .... B 5
Zion, 19,775........ A 6

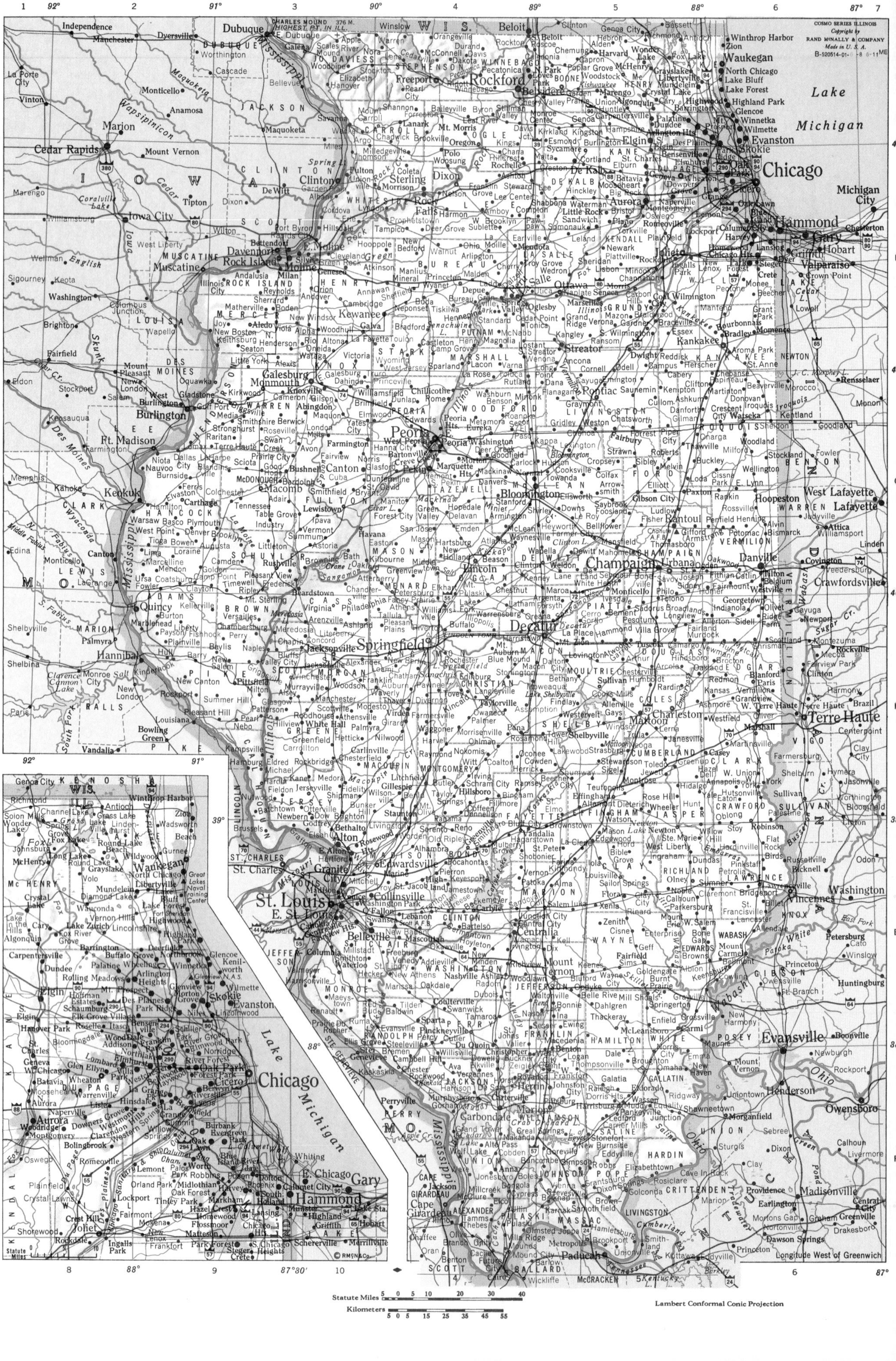

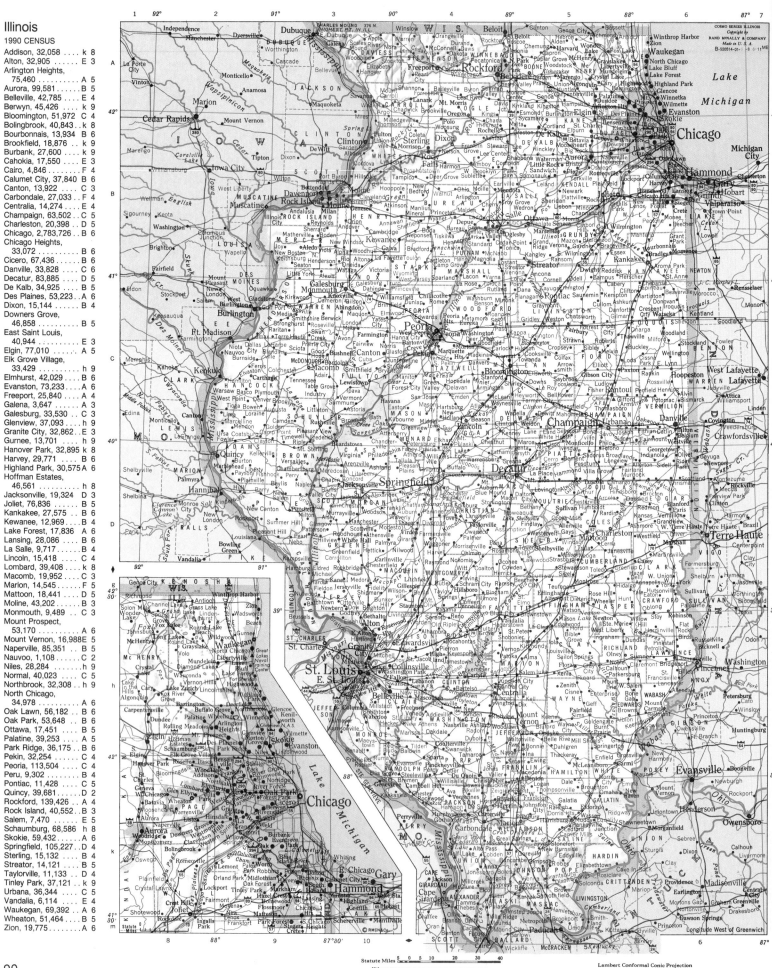

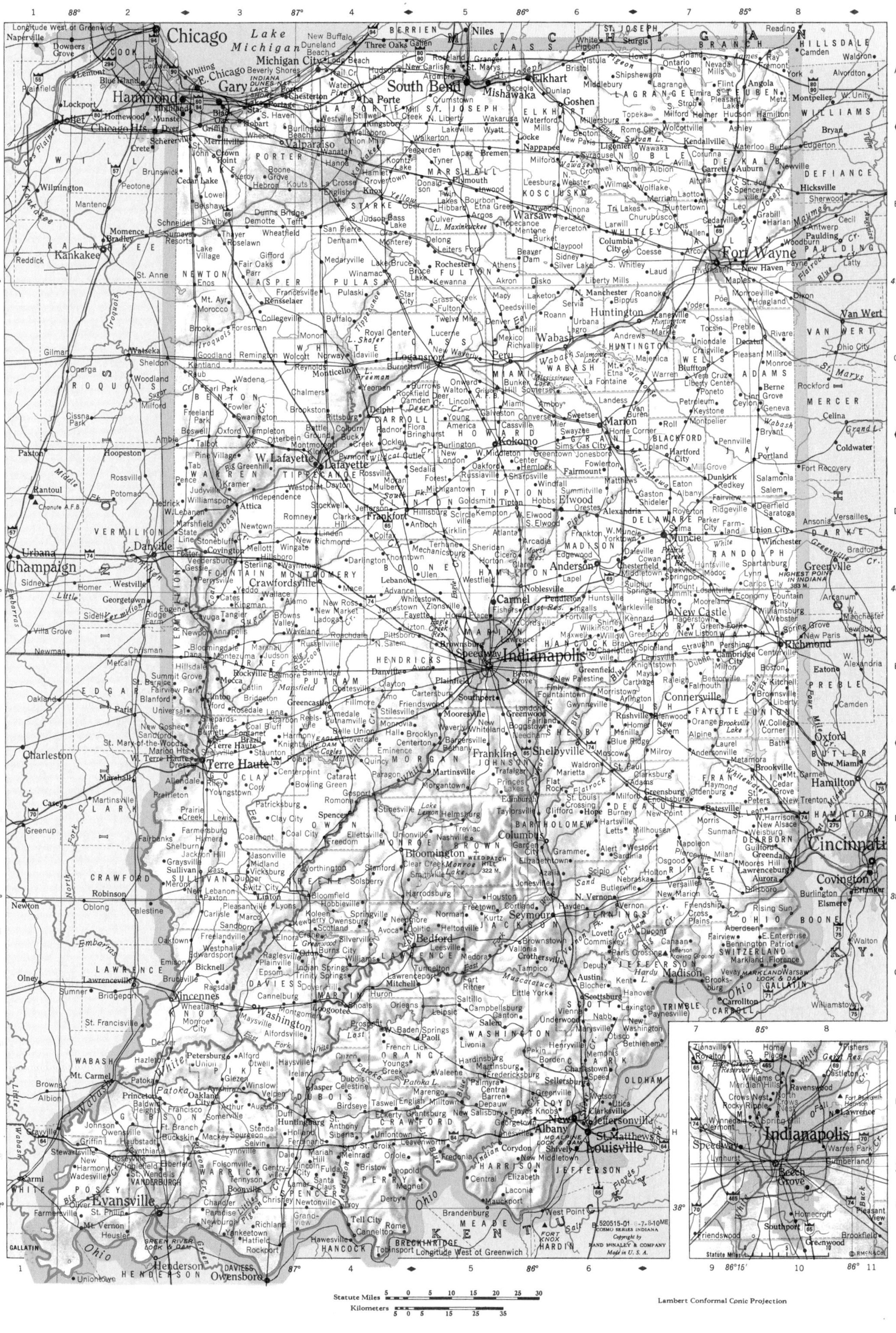

Indiana

1990 CENSUS

Anderson, 59,459 .. D 6
Auburn, 9,379 ...... B 7
Bedford, 13,817 .... G 5
Beech Grove, 13,383 E 5
Bloomington, 60,633 F 4
Bluffton, 9,020 ...... C 7
Boonville, 6,724 .... H 3
Brazil, 7,640 .... E 3
Brownsburg, 7,628 .. E 5
Carmel, 25,380 .... E 5
Cedar Lake, 8,885 .. B 3
Chesterton, 9,124 .. A 3
Clarksville, 19,833 .. H 6
Columbus, 31,802 .. F 6
Connersville, 15,550 E 7
Corydon, 2,661 ...... H 5
Crawfordsville, 13,584 D 4
Crown Point, 17,728 B 3
Decatur, 8,644 ...... C 8
Dyer, 10,923 ...... A 2
East Chicago, 33,892 A 3
Elkhart, 43,627 .... A 6
Elwood, 9,494 .... D 6
Evansville, 126,272 .. I 2
Fort Wayne, 173,072 B 7
Frankfort, 14,754 .... D 4
Franklin, 12,907 .... F 5
French Lick, 2,087 .. G 4
Gary, 116,646 ...... A 3
Gas City, 6,296 .... D 6
Goshen, 23,797 .... A 6
Greencastle, 8,984 .. E 4
Greenfield, 11,657 .. E 6
Greensburg, 9,286 .. F 7
Greenwood, 26,265 .. E 5
Griffith, 17,916 ...... A 3
Hammond, 84,236 .. A 2
Hartford City, 6,960 .. D 7
Highland, 23,696 .... A 3
Hobart, 21,822 ...... A 3
Huntington, 16,389 .. C 7
Indianapolis, 731,327 E 5
Jasper, 10,030 ...... H 4
Jeffersonville, 21,841 H 6
Kendallville, 7,773 .. B 7
Kokomo, 44,962 .... D 5
Lafayette, 43,764 .. D 4
Lake Station, 13,899 A 3
La Porte, 21,507 .... A 4
Lawrence, 26,763 .. E 5
Lebanon, 12,059 .... D 5
Linton, 5,814 ...... F 3
Logansport, 16,812 .. C 5
Madison, 12,006 .... G 7
Marion, 32,618 ...... C 6
Martinsville, 11,677 .. F 5
Merrillville, 27,257 .. B 3
Michigan City, 33,822 A 4
Mishawaka, 42,608 .. A 5
Mount Vernon, 7,217 I 2
Muncie, 71,035 .... D 7
Munster, 19,949 .... A 2
New Albany, 36,322 H 6
New Castle, 17,753 .. E 7
New Haven, 9,320 .. B 7
Noblesville, 17,655 .. D 6
Peru, 12,843 ...... C 5
Plainfield, 10,433 .... E 5
Plymouth, 8,303 .... B 5
Portage, 29,060 .... A 3
Portland, 6,483 ...... D 8
Princeton, 8,127 .... H 2
Richmond, 38,705 .. E 8
Rockville, 2,706 .... E 3
Rushville, 5,533 .... E 7
Schererville, 19,926 . B 3
Seymour, 15,576 .... G 6
Shelbyville, 15,336 .. F 6
South Bend, 105,511 A 5
South Haven, 6,679('80) .... A 3
Speedway, 13,092 .. E 5
Tell City, 8,088 ...... I 4
Terre Haute, 57,483 .. F 3
Valparaiso, 24,414 .. B 3
Vincennes, 19,859 .. G 2
Wabash, 12,127 .... C 6
Warsaw, 10,968 .... B 6
Washington, 10,838 G 3
West Lafayette, 25,907 .... D 4

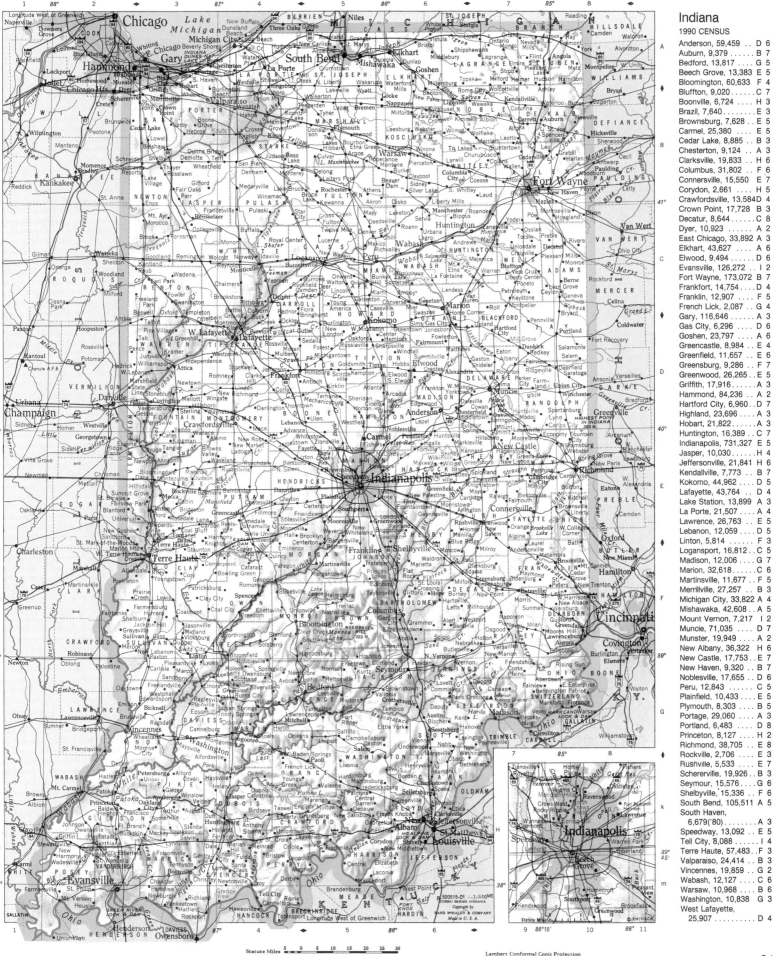

Iowa

1990 CENSUS

Place, population	Grid
Algona, 6,015	A 3
Altoona, 7,191	C 4
Amana, 540('87)	C 6
Ames, 47,198	B 4
Anamosa, 5,100	B 6
Ankeny, 18,482	C 4
Atlantic, 7,432	C 2
Bettendorf, 28,132	C 7
Boone, 12,392	B 4
Burlington, 27,208	D 6
Camanche, 4,436	C 7
Carroll, 9,579	B 3
Cedar Falls, 34,298	B 5
Cedar Rapids, 108,751	C 6
Centerville, 5,936	D 5
Chariton, 4,616	C 4
Charles City, 7,878	A 5
Cherokee, 6,026	B 2
Clarinda, 5,104	D 2
Clear Lake, 8,183	A 4
Clinton, 29,201	C 7
Clive, 7,462	e 8
Coralville, 10,347	C 6
Council Bluffs, 54,315	C 2
Creston, 7,911	C 3
Davenport, 95,333	C 7
Decorah, 8,063	A 6
Denison, 6,604	B 2
Des Moines, 193,187	C 4
Dubuque, 57,546	B 7
Estherville, 6,720	A 3
Evansdale, 4,638	B 5
Fairfield, 9,768	C 6
Forest City, 4,430	A 4
Fort Dodge, 25,894	B 3
Fort Madison, 11,618	D 6
Glenwood, 4,571	C 2
Grinnell, 8,902	C 5
Hampton, 4,133	B 4
Harlan, 5,148	C 2
Hiawatha, 4,986	B 6
Humboldt, 4,438	B 3
Independence, 5,972	B 6
Indianola, 11,340	C 4
Iowa City, 59,738	C 6
Iowa Falls, 5,424	B 4
Jefferson, 4,292	B 3
Keokuk, 12,451	D 6
Knoxville, 8,232	C 4
Le Mars, 8,454	B 1
Manchester, 5,137	B 6
Maquoketa, 6,111	B 7
Marion, 20,403	B 6
Marshalltown, 25,178	B 5
Mason City, 29,040	A 4
Mount Pleasant, 8,027	D 6
Muscatine, 22,881	C 6
Nevada, 6,009	B 4
New Hampton, 3,660	A 5
Newton, 14,789	C 4
Oelwein, 6,493	B 6
Orange City, 4,940	B 1
Oskaloosa, 10,632	C 5
Ottumwa, 24,488	C 5
Pella, 9,270	C 5
Perry, 6,652	C 3
Red Oak, 6,264	D 2
Sheldon, 4,937	A 2
Shenandoah, 5,572	D 2
Sioux Center, 5,074	A 1
Sioux City, 80,505	B 1
Spencer, 11,066	A 2
Spirit Lake, 3,871	A 2
Storm Lake, 8,769	B 2
Urbandale, 23,500	C 4
Vinton, 5,103	B 5
Washington, 7,074	C 6
Waterloo, 66,467	B 5
Waukon, 4,019	A 6
Waverly, 8,539	B 5
Webster City, 7,894	B 4
West Branch, 1,908	C 6
West Des Moines, 31,702	C 4
Windsor Heights, 5,190	e 8

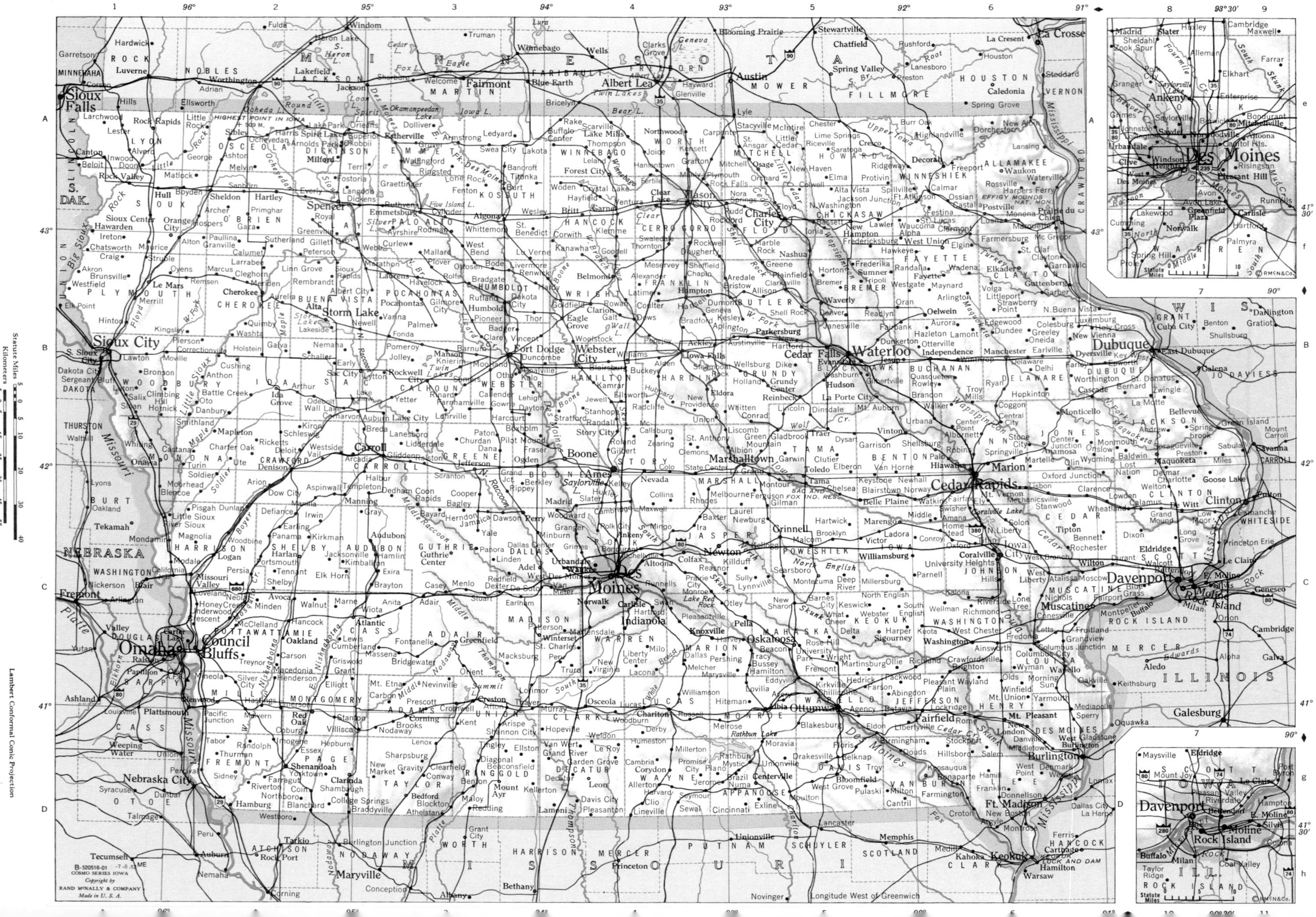

Statute Miles 5 0 5 10 20 30 40
Kilometers 5 0 5 15 25 35 45 55
Lambert Conformal Conic Projection
B-520516-01 COSMO SERIES IOWA
Copyright by RAND McNALLY & COMPANY Made in U. S. A.
Longitude West of Greenwich

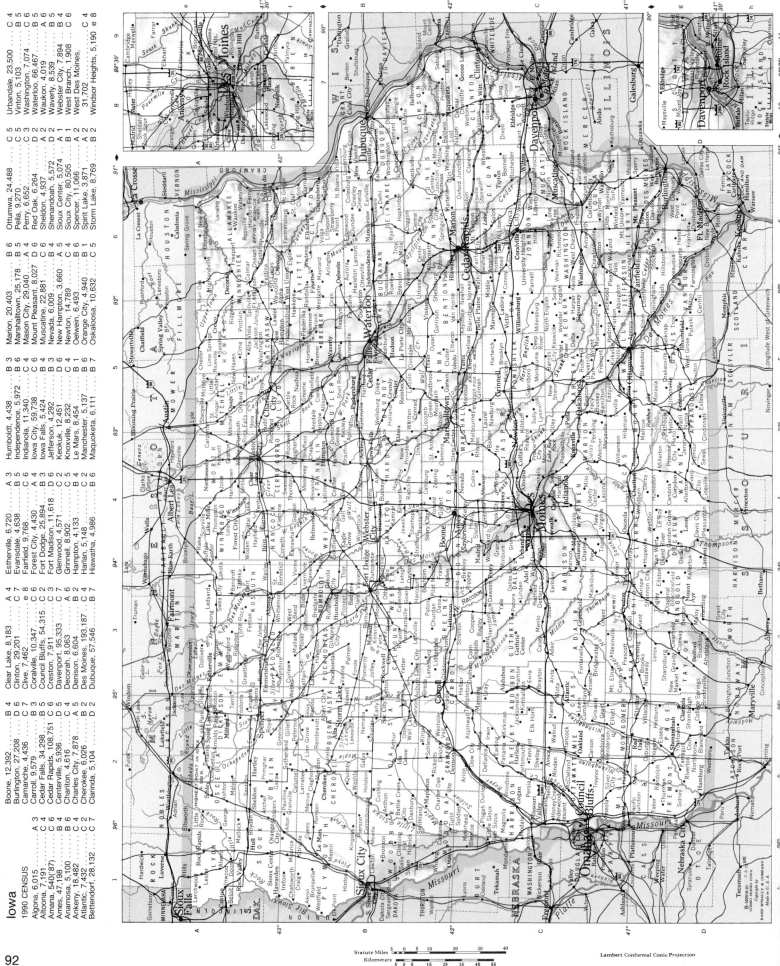

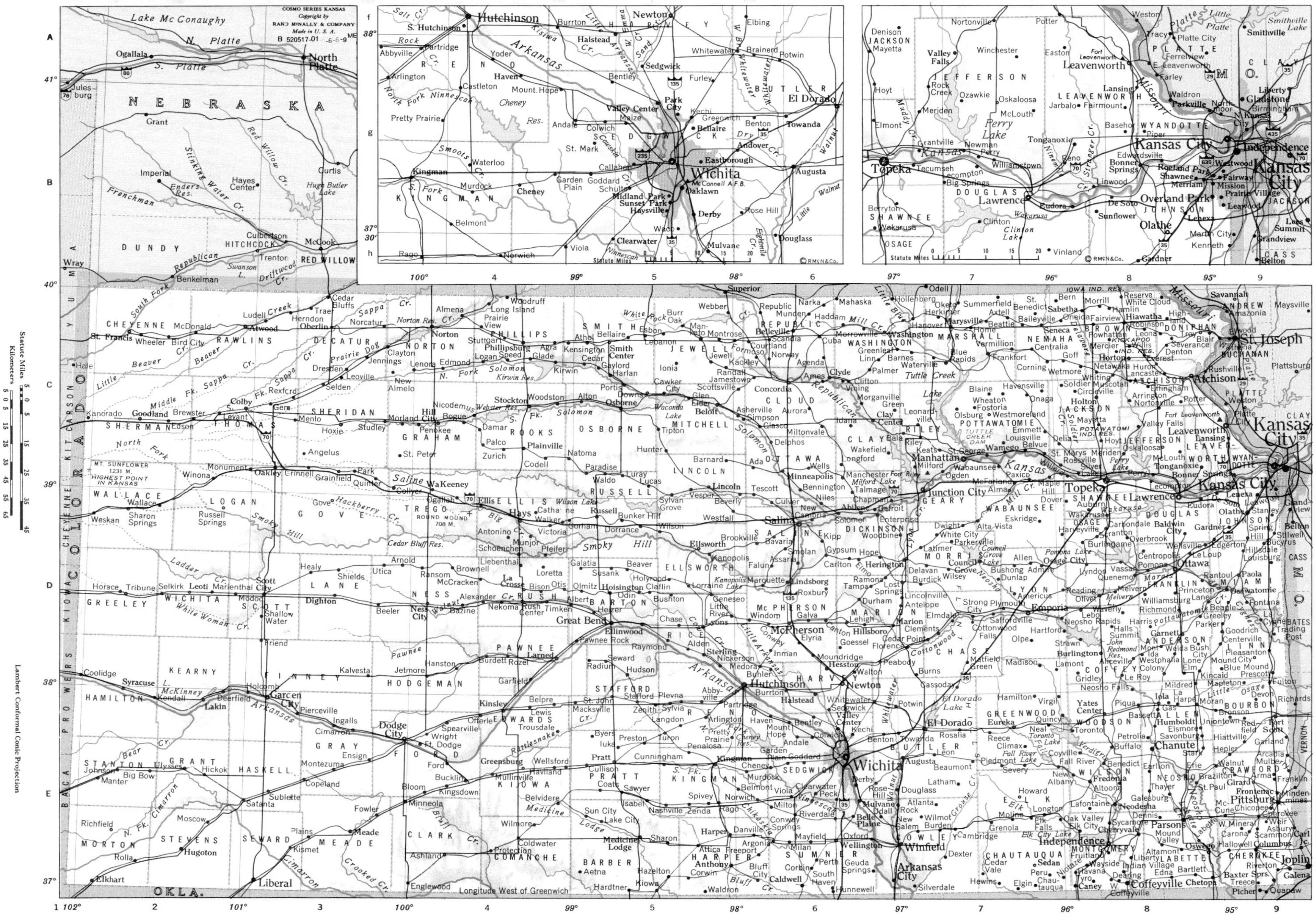
COSMO SERIES KANSAS
Copyright by RAND McNALLY & COMPANY
Made in U. S. A.
B 520517-01 -6-6-9
NEBRASKA
OKLA.
Longitude West of Greenwich
Statute Miles
Kilometers
Lambert Conformal Conic Projection

Kansas

1990 CENSUS

Abilene, 6,242 . . . . D 6
Andover, 4,047 . . . . . . g12
Arkansas City, 12,762 . . E 6
Atchison, 10,656 . . . . . . C 8
Augusta, 7,876 . . . . E 7
Baldwin City, 2,961 . . . D 8
Baxter Springs, 4,351 . . E 9
Beloit, 4,066 . . . . C 5
Bonner Springs, 6,413 C 9
Burlington, 2,735 . . . . . D 8
Chanute, 9,483 . . . . . . E 8
Clay Center, 4,613 . . . . C 6
Coffeyville, 12,917 . . . . E 8
Colby, 5,396 . . . . C 2
Columbus, 3,268 . . . . . . E 9
Concordia, 6,167 . . . . . . C 6
Derby, 14,699 . . . . E 6
Dodge City, 21,129 . . . . E 3
Edwardsville, 3,979 . . . . k16
El Dorado, 11,504 . . . . E 7
Emporia, 25,512 . . . . . . D 7
Eudora, 3,006 . . . . D 8
Eureka, 2,974 . . . . E 7
Fairway, 4,173 . . . . k16
Fort Scott, 8,362 . . . . . . E 9
Fredonia, 2,599 . . . . E 8
Galena, 3,308 . . . . E 9
Garden City, 24,097 . . E 3
Garnett, 3,210 . . . . D 8
Goodland, 4,983 . . . . . . C 2
Great Bend, 15,427 . . . . D 5
Hays, 17,767 . . . . D 4
Haysville, 8,364 . . . . . . g12
Herington, 2,685 . . . . . . D 7
Hiawatha, 3,603 . . . . . . C 8
Hoisington, 3,182 . . . . D 5
Holton, 3,196 . . . . C 8
Hugoton, 3,179 . . . . E 2
Hutchinson, 39,308 . . . . D 6
Independence, 9,942 . . . E 8
Iola, 6,351 . . . . E 8
Junction City, 20,604 . . C 7
Kansas City, 149,767 . . C 9
Kingman, 3,196 . . . . E 5
Lansing, 7,120 . . . . C 9
Larned, 4,490 . . . . D 4
Lawrence, 65,608 . . . . . D 8
Leavenworth, 38,495 . . C 9
Leawood, 19,693 . . . . . D 9
Lenexa, 34,034 . . . . . . D 9
Liberal, 16,573 . . . . E 3
Lindsborg, 3,076 . . . . . . D 6
Lyons, 3,688 . . . . D 5
Manhattan, 37,712 . . . . C 7
Marysville, 3,359 . . . . . . C 7
McPherson, 12,422 . . . . D 6
Merriam, 11,821 . . . . . . k16
Mission, 9,504 . . . . m16
Mulvane, 4,674 . . . . E 6
Neodesha, 2,837 . . . . . . E 8
Newton, 16,700 . . . . . . D 6
Norton, 3,017 . . . . C 4
Olathe, 63,352 . . . . D 9
Osawatomie, 4,590 . . . . D 9
Ottawa, 10,667 . . . . D 8
Overland Park, 111,790 m16
Paola, 4,698 . . . . D 9
Park City, 5,050 . . . . . . g12
Parsons, 11,924 . . . . . . E 8
Phillipsburg, 2,828 . . . . C 4
Pittsburg, 17,775 . . . . . . E 9
Prairie Village, 23,186 . . m16
Pratt, 6,687 . . . . E 5
Roeland Park, 7,706 . . k16
Russell, 4,781 . . . . D 5
Salina, 42,303 . . . . D 6
Scott City, 3,785 . . . . . . D 3
Shawnee, 37,993 . . . . . . k16
Topeka, 119,883 . . . . . . C 8
Ulysses, 5,474 . . . . E 2
Valley Center, 3,624 . . E 6
Wamego, 3,706 . . . . C 7
Wellington, 8,411 . . . . . . E 6
Wichita, 304,011 . . . . . . E 6
Winfield, 11,931 . . . . . . E 7

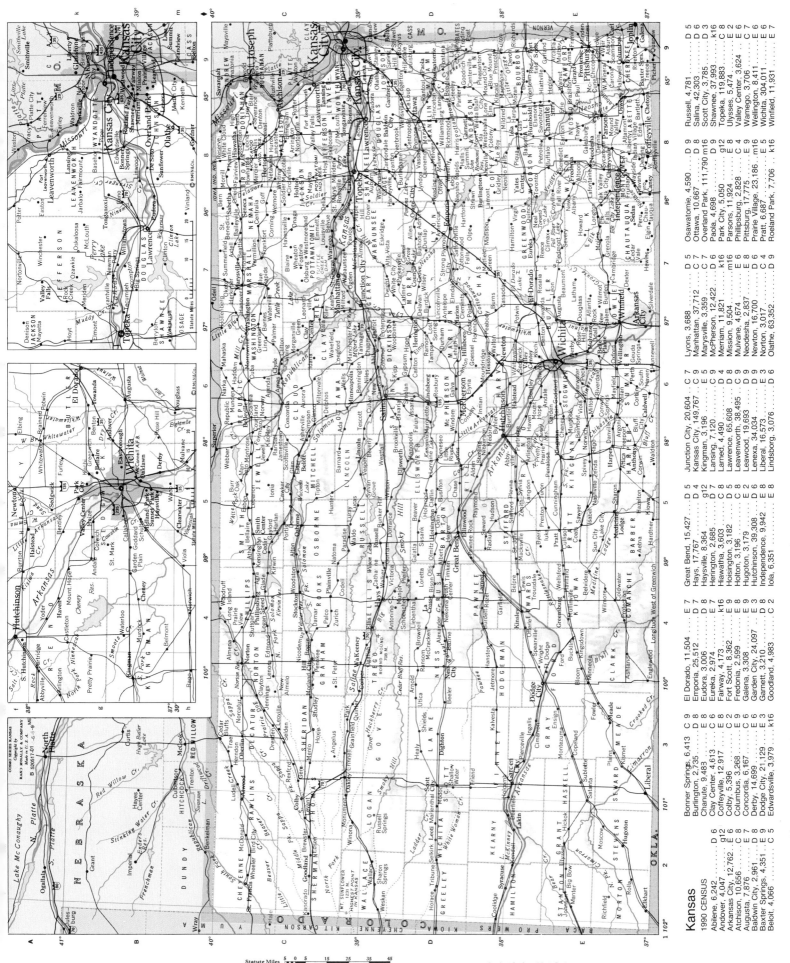

Kentucky

1990 CENSUS

Alexandria, 5,592 .... B 5
Ashland, 23,622 ...... B 7
Barbourville, 3,658 .... D 6
Bardstown, 6,801 .... C 4
Bellevue, 6,997 ...... h13
Benton, 3,899 .... f 9
Berea, 9,126 .... C 5
Bowling Green, 40,641 D 3
Campbellsville, 9,577 .. C 4
Carrollton, 3,715 ...... B 4
Cave City, 1,953 ...... C 4
Central City, 4,979 .... C 2
Columbia, 3,845 ...... C 4
Corbin, 7,419 .... D 5
Covington, 43,264 .... A 5
Cumberland, 3,112 .... D 7
Cynthiana, 6,497 ...... B 5
Danville, 12,420 ...... C 5
Dayton, 6,576 .... h14
Edgewood, 8,143 ...... h13
Elizabethtown, 18,167 C 4
Elsmere, 6,847 ...... B 5
Erlanger, 15,979 ...... A 5
Flatwoods, 7,799 ...... B 7
Florence, 18,624 ...... A 5
Fort Mitchell, 7,438 .... h13
Fort Thomas, 16,032 .. h14
Fort Wright, 6,570 .... h13
Frankfort, 25,968 ...... B 5
Franklin, 7,607 .... D 3
Georgetown, 11,414 .. B 5
Glasgow, 12,351 ...... C 4
Greenville, 4,689 ...... C 2
Harrodsburg, 7,335 .... C 5
Hazard, 5,416 .... C 6
Henderson, 25,945 .... C 2
Hopkinsville, 29,809 .. D 2
Independence, 10,444 .. B 5
Jeffersontown, 23,221 B 4
Lawrenceburg, 5,911 .. B 5
Lebanon, 5,695 ...... C 4
Leitchfield, 4,965 ...... C 3
Lexington, 225,366 .... B 5
London, 5,757 .... C 5
Louisville, 269,063 .... B 4
Ludlow, 4,736 .... h13
Madisonville, 16,200 .. C 2
Mayfield, 9,935 .... f 9
Maysville, 7,169 ...... B 6
Middlesboro, 11,328 .. D 6
Monticello, 5,357 ...... D 5
Morehead, 8,357 ...... B 6
Morganfield, 3,776 .... C 2
Mount Sterling, 5,362 .. B 6
Mount Washington, 5,226 .... B 4
Murray, 14,439 .... f 9
Newport, 18,871 ...... A 5
Nicholasville, 13,603 .. C 5
Owensboro, 53,549 .. C 2
Paducah, 27,256 ...... e 9
Paintsville, 4,354 ...... C 7
Paris, 8,730 .... B 5
Pikeville, 6,324 ...... C 7
Prestonsburg, 3,558 .. C 7
Princeton, 6,940 ...... C 2
Providence, 4,123 .... C 2
Radcliff, 19,772 ...... C 4
Richmond, 21,155 .... C 5
Russell, 4,014 .... B 7
Russellville, 7,454 .... D 3
Saint Matthews, 15,800 B 4
Scottsville, 4,278 ...... D 3
Shelbyville, 6,238 ...... B 4
Shepherdsville, 4,805 .. C 4
Shively, 15,535 ...... B 4
Somerset, 10,733 .... C 5
Taylor Mill, 5,530 ...... k14
Tompkinsville, 2,861 .. D 4
Valley Station, 20,000('84) g11
Versailles, 7,269 ...... B 5
Williamsburg, 5,493 .... D 5
Wilmore, 4,215 ...... C 5
Winchester, 15,799 .... C 5

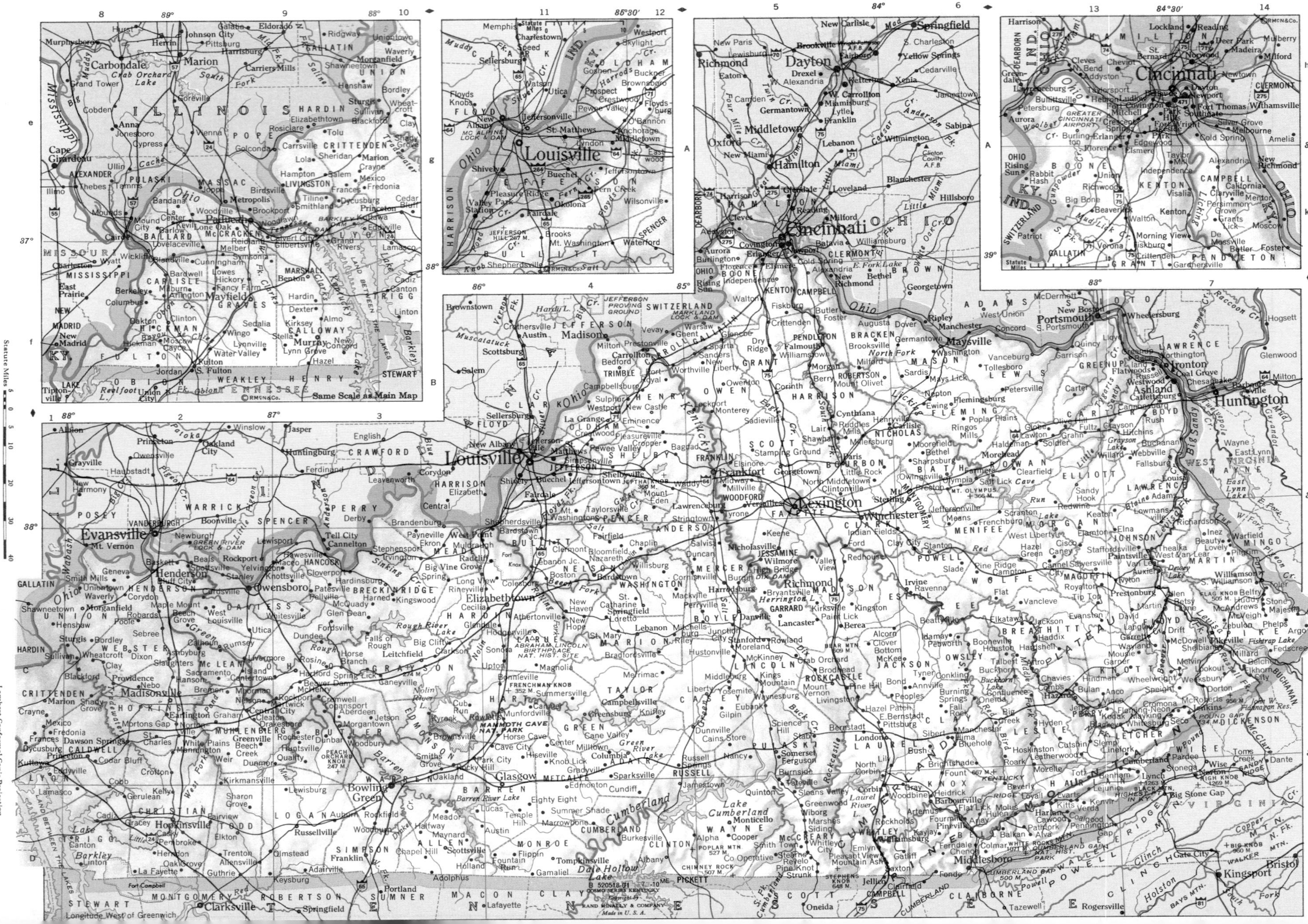
Statute Miles
Kilometers
Lambert Conformal Conic Projection
Same Scale as Main Map

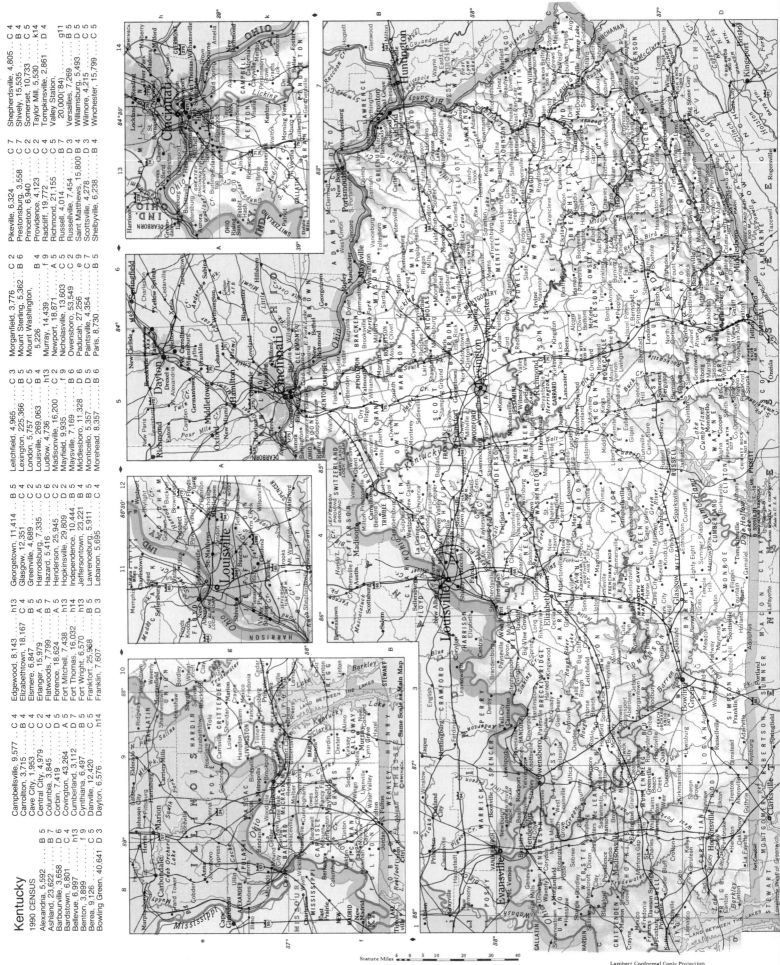

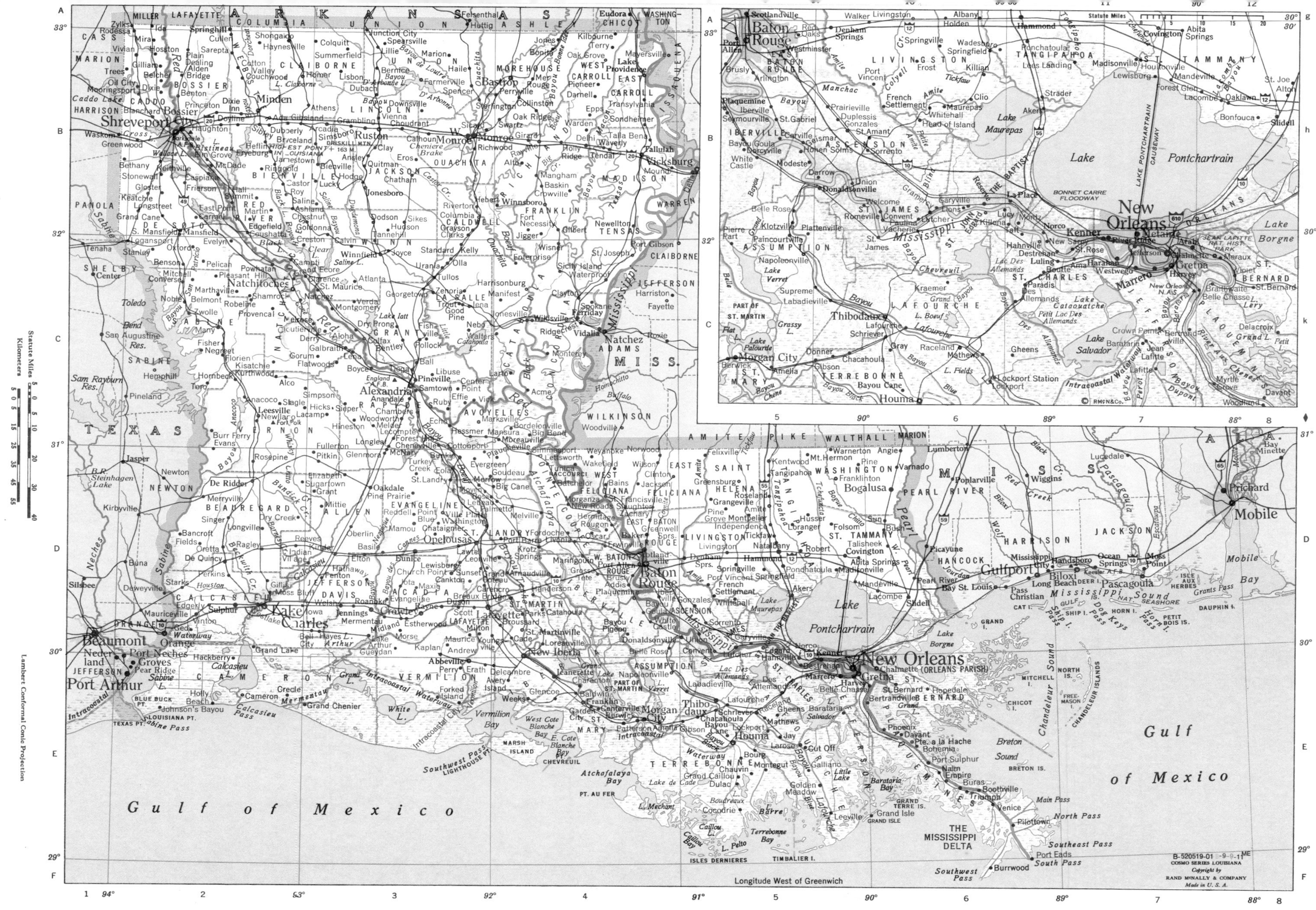

Louisiana

1990 CENSUS

Abbeville, 11,187 . . . . . E 3
Alexandria, 49,188 . . . C 3
Arabi, 10,248('80) k11
Baker, 13,233 . . . . D 4
Bastrop, 13,916 . . . . . . B 4
Baton Rouge, 219,531 D 4
Berwick, 4,375 . . . . E 4
Bogalusa, 14,280 . . . . . D 6
Bossier City, 52,721 . . B 2
Breaux Bridge, 5,515 . . D 4
Bunkie, 5,044 . . . . D 3
Chalmette, 31,850 . . . . E 6
Church Point, 4,677 . . . D 3
Covington, 7,691 . . . . . . D 5
Crowley, 13,983 . . . . . . D 3
Cut Off, 5,049('80) . . . . E 5
Denham Springs, 8,381 D 5
De Ridder, 9,868 . . . . . . D 2
Donaldsonville, 7,949 . . D 4
Eunice, 11,162 . . . . D 3
Ferriday, 4,111 . . . . C 4
Franklin, 9,004 . . . . E 4
Gonzales, 7,003 . . . . . . D 5
Grambling, 5,484 . . . . . . B 3
Gretna, 17,208 . . . . E 5
Hammond, 15,871 . . . . . D 5
Harahan, 9,927 . . . . k11
Harvey, 15,000 . . . . E 5
Houma, 96,982 . . . . E 5
Jeanerette, 6,205 . . . . . E 4
Jefferson, 15,550('80) . . k11
Jena, 2,626 . . . . C 3
Jennings, 11,305 . . . . . . D 3
Jonesboro, 4,305 . . . . B 3
Kaplan, 4,535 . . . . D 3
Kenner, 72,033 . . . . . . E 5
Lafayette, 94,440 . . . . . D 3
Lake Charles, 70,580 . . D 2
Lake Providence, 5,380 B 4
La Place, 16,112('80) . . . h11
Leesville, 7,638 . . . . . . C 2
Lutcher, 3,907 . . . . D 5
Mandeville, 7,083 . . . . D 5
Mansfield, 5,389 . . . . . . B 2
Marksville, 5,526 . . . . . . C 3
Marrero, 36,671 . . . . E 5
Metairie, 149,428 . . . . . . k11
Minden, 13,661 . . . . B 2
Monroe, 54,909 . . . . B 3
Morgan City, 14,531 . . . E 4
Moss Bluff, 7,004('80) D 2
Natchitoches, 16,609 . . C 2
New Iberia, 31,828 . . . . D 4
New Orleans, 496,938 E 5
Oakdale, 6,832 . . . . . . D 3
Opelousas, 18,151 . . . D 3
Patterson, 4,736 . . . . . . E 4
Pineville, 12,251 . . . . . . C 3
Plaquemine, 7,186 . . . . D 4
Ponchatoula, 5,425 . . . . D 5
Port Allen, 6,277 . . . . . . D 4
Raceland, 6,302('80) . . E 5
Rayne, 8,502 . . . . D 3
Rayville, 4,411 . . . . B 4
Reserve, 7,288('80) h10
River Ridge, 17,146('80) k11
Ruston, 20,027 . . . . . . B 3
Saint Martinville, 7,137 D 4
Scotlandville,
15,113('80) . . . . D 4
Shreveport, 198,525 . . B 2
Slidell, 24,124 . . . . D 6
Springhill, 5,668 . . . . . . A 2
Sulphur, 20,125 . . . . . . D 2
Tallulah, 8,526 . . . . B 4
Thibodaux, 14,035 . . . . E 5
Vidalia, 4,953 . . . . C 4
Ville Platte, 9,037 . . . . D 3
Violet, 6,000 . . . . k12
Westlake, 5,007 . . . . D 2
West Monroe, 14,096 . . B 3
Westwego, 11,218 . . . . k11
Winnfield, 6,138 . . . . . . C 3
Winnsboro, 5,755 . . . . . B 4
Zachary, 9,036 . . . . D 4

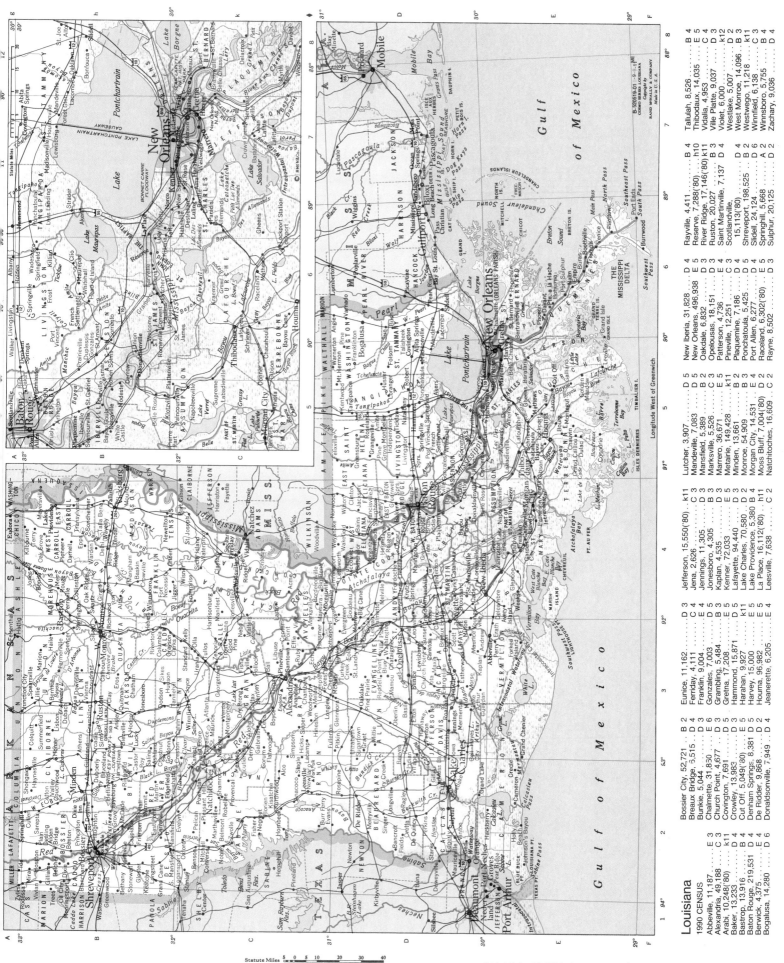

Maine

1990 CENSUS

Auburn, 24,309 .... D 2
Augusta, 21,325 .... D 3
Bangor, 33,181 .... D 4
Bar Harbor, 2,685 (4,443▲) .... D 4
Bath, 9,799 .... E 3
Belfast, 6,355 ..... D 3
Berwick, 2,378 (5,995▲) .... E 2
Biddeford, 20,710 .. E 2
Brewer, 9,021 ...... D 4
Bridgton, 1,639 (4,307▲) .... D 2
Brunswick, 10,990 (20,906▲) .... E 3
Bucksport, 2,853 (4,825▲) .... D 4
Calais, 3,963 ...... C 5
Camden, 3,743 (5,060▲) .... D 3
Caribou, 9,415 ...... B 5
Dexter, 3,118 (4,419▲) .... C 3
Dixfield, 1,725 (2,574▲) .... D 2
Dover-Foxcroft, 2,974 (4,657▲) .... C 3
Eastport, 1,965 .... D 6
Ellsworth, 5,975 .... D 4
Fairfield, 3,169 (6,718▲) .... D 3
Farmingdale, 2,014 (2,918▲) .... D 3
Farmington, 3,583 (7,436▲) .... D 2
Fort Fairfield, 2,282 (3,998▲) .... B 5
Fort Kent, 2,375 (4,268▲) .... A 4
Fryeburg, 1,644 (2,968▲) .... D 2
Gardiner, 6,746 .... D 3
Gorham, 4,052 (11,856▲) .... E 2
Hallowell, 2,534 .... D 3
Hampden, 2,300 (5,974▲) .... D 4
Houlton, 5,730 (6,613▲) .... B 5
Kennebunk, 3,294 (8,004▲) .... E 2
Kennebunkport, 1,685 (3,356▲) .... E 2
Kittery, 5,465 (9,372▲) .... E 2
Lewiston, 39,757 .... D 2
Lincoln, 3,524 (5,587▲) .... C 4
Livermore Falls, 2,441 (3,455▲) .... D 2
Madawaska, 4,165 (4,803▲) .... A 4
Madison, 2,788 (4,725▲) .... D 3
Mexico, 3,207 (3,344▲) .... D 2
Milford, 1,688 (2,884▲) .... D 4
Milo, 2,255 (2,600▲) C 4
Newport, 1,748 (3,036▲) .... D 3
Norway, 2,653 (4,754▲) .... D 2
Oakland, 3,387 (5,595▲) .... D 3
Old Town, 8,317 .... D 4
Pittsfield, 3,117 (4,190▲) .... D 3
Portland, 64,358 .... E 2
Presque Isle, 10,550 B 5
Richmond, 1,578 (3,072▲) .... D 3
Rockland, 7,972 .... D 3
Rumford, 6,256 (7,078▲) .... D 2
Saco, 15,181 ...... E 2
Sanford, 10,268 (20,463▲) .... E 2
Scarborough, 2,280 (12,518▲) .... E 2
Skowhegan, 6,517 (8,725▲) .... D 3
South Berwick, 2,120 (5,877▲) .... E 2
South Portland, 23,163 .... E 2
Thomaston, 2,348 (3,306▲) .... D 3
Topsham, 4,657 (8,746▲) .... E 3
Waterville, 17,173 .. D 3
Westbrook, 16,121 .. E 2
Wilton, 2,262 (4,242▲) .... D 2
Winslow, 5,903 (7,997▲) .... D 3
Winthrop, 3,264 (5,968▲) .... D 3
Yarmouth, 2,981 (7,862▲) .... E 2
York, 3,130 (9,818▲) E 2

▲ Population of entire town (township), including rural area.

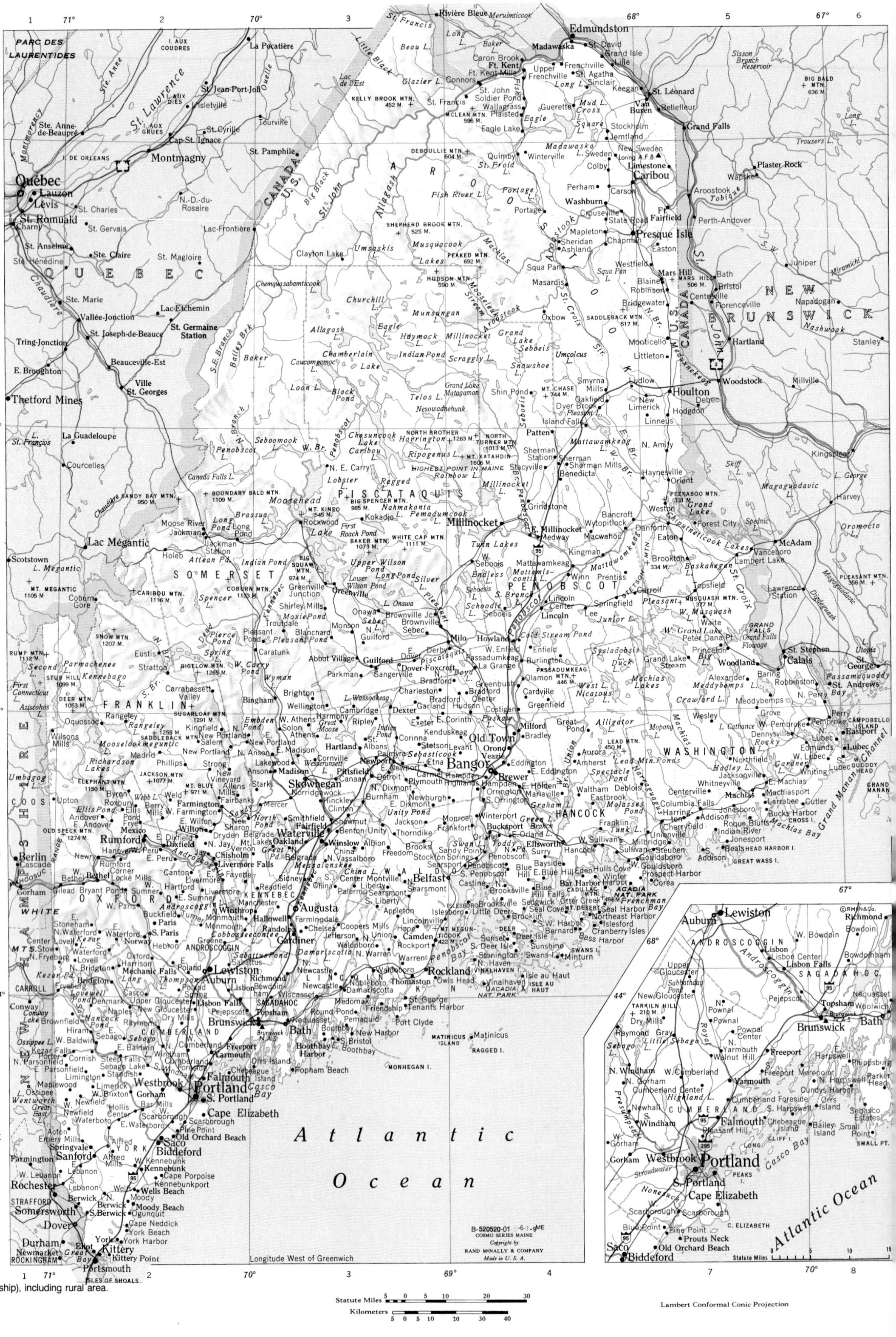

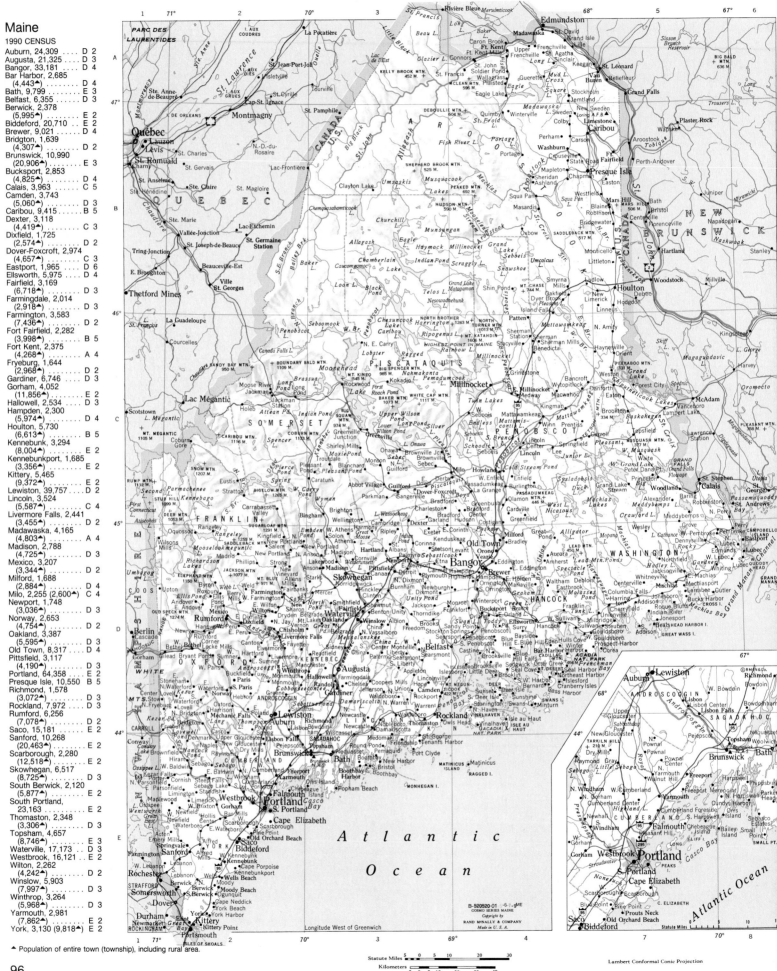

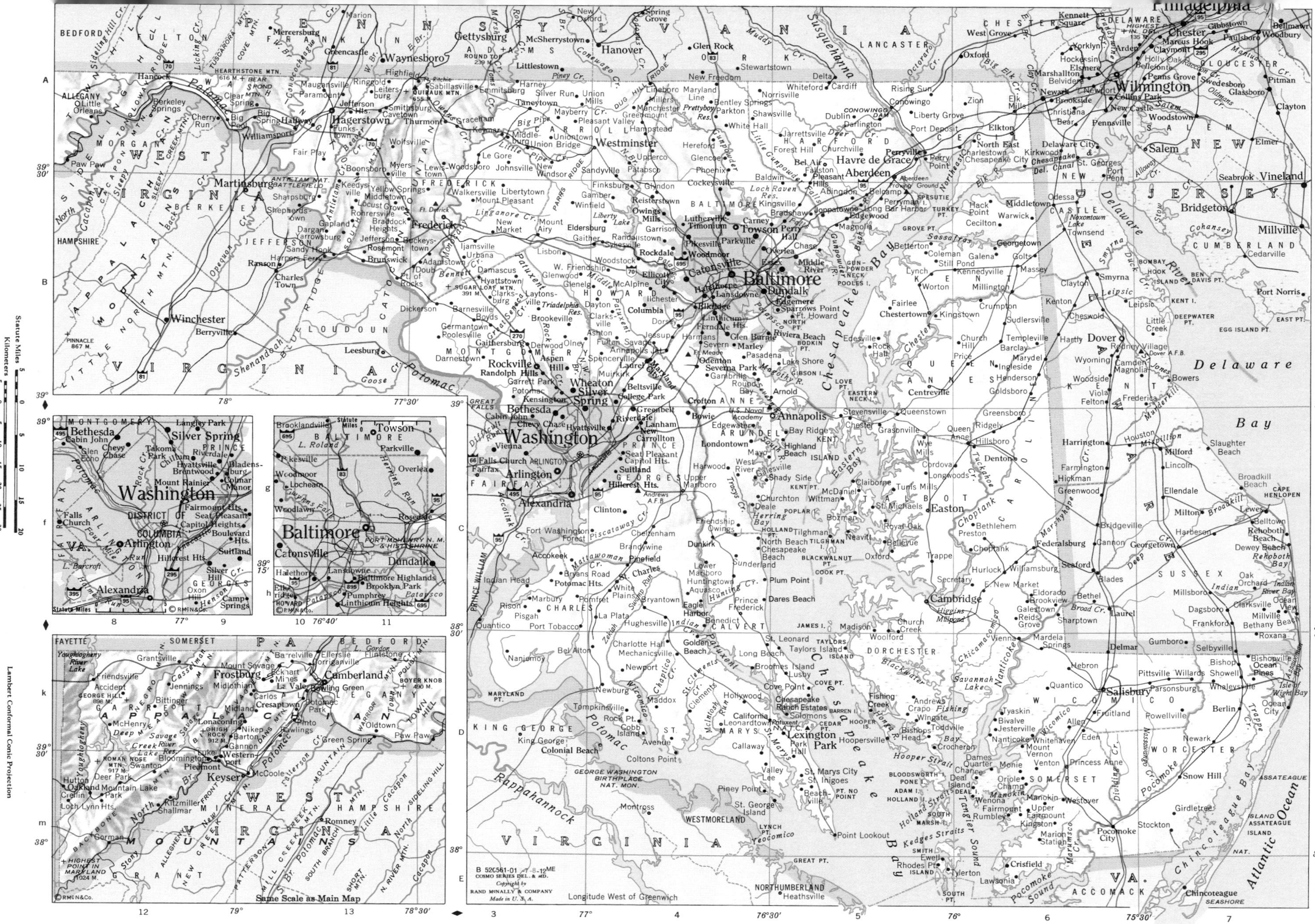

Maryland

1990 CENSUS

Aberdeen, 13,087	A 5
Annapolis, 33,187	C 5
Baltimore, 736,014	B 4
Bel Air, 8,860	A 5
Beltsville, 7,670('88)	B 4
Bethesda, 62,936	C 3
Bladensburg, 8,064	f 9
Bowie, 37,589	C 4
Brunswick, 5,117	B 2
Calverton, 7,649('80)	B 4
Cambridge, 11,514	C 5
Catonsville, 35,200	B 4
Chevy Chase, 8,559	C 3
Chillum, 12,500('88)	f 9
Clinton, 7,570('88)	C 4
College Park, 21,927	C 4
Columbia, 75,883	B 4
Crofton, 12,009('80)	B 4
Cumberland, 23,706	k13
Dundalk, 65,800	B 4
Easton, 9,372	C 5
Edgemere, 7,410('88)	B 5
Edgewood, 19,455('80)	B 5
Elkton, 9,073	A 6
Essex, 40,872	B 5
Fallston, 5,572('80)	A 5
Frederick, 40,148	B 3
Frostburg, 8,075	k13
Gaithersburg, 39,542	B 3
Germantown, 760('88)	B 3
Glen Burnie, 32,700	B 4
Greenbelt, 21,096	C 4
Hagerstown, 35,445	A 2
Halethorpe, 20,163	B 4
Halfway, 2,000('88)	A 2
Havre de Grace, 8,952	A 5
Hyattsville, 13,864	C 4
Langley Park, 9,150('88)	f 9
Lanham, 5,000('88)	C 4
Lansdowne, 9,430('88)	B 4
Laurel, 19,438	B 4
La Vale, 5,000('88)	k13
Lutherville-Timonium, 16,871('80)	B 4
Lynne Acres, 5,910('88)	B 4
Middle River, 24,616	B 5
Mount Rainier, 7,954	f 9
Oakland, 1,741	m12
Ocean City, 5,146	D 7
Odenton, 6,590('88)	B 4
Olney, 9,500('88)	B 3
Overlea, 3,320('88)	B 5
Owings Mills, 9,526('80)	B 4
Oxon Hill, 3,730('88)	f 9
Parkville, 31,617	B 4
Perry Hall, 10,285('88)	B 5
Pikesville, 16,280	B 4
Pocomoke City, 3,922	D 6
Potomac, 25,370	B 3
Randallstown, 18,680('88)	B 4
Reisterstown, 19,385('80)	B 4
Rockville, 44,835	B 3
Rosedale, 11,390('88)	g11
Salisbury, 20,592	D 6
Seat Pleasant, 5,359	C 4
Severn, 20,147('80)	B 4
Severna Park, 21,253('80)	B 4
Sharpsburg, 659	B 2
Silver Spring, 76,200	C 3
Snow Hill, 2,217	D 7
Suitland, 35,400	C 4
Takoma Park, 16,700	f 8
Towson, 49,445	B 4
Westminster, 13,068	A 4
Wheaton, 58,300	B 3
Woodmoor, 8,630('88)	B 4

District of Columbia

1990 CENSUS

Washington, 606,900	C 3

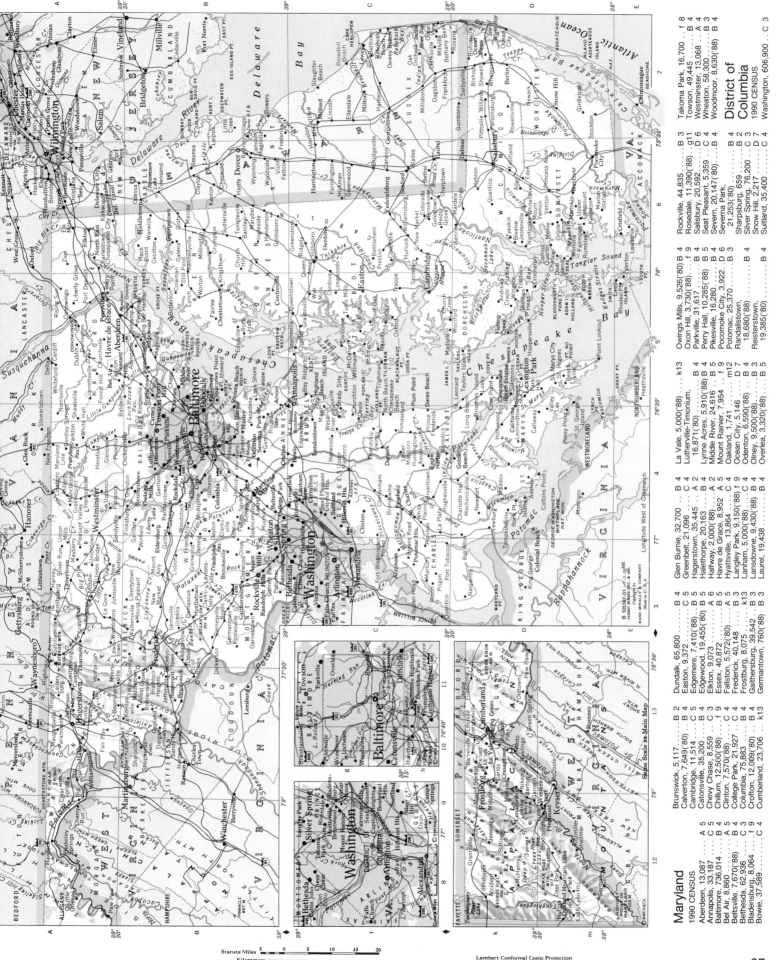

Massachusetts

1990 CENSUS

Amherst, 17,773 (35,228▲) .... B 2
Arlington, 44,630 ..... B 5
Attleboro, 38,383 .... C 5
Belmont, 24,720 ...... g11
Beverly, 38,195 ...... A 6
Boston, 574,283 ...... B 5
Braintree, 33,836 ..... B 5
Brockton, 92,788 ...... B 5
Brookline, 54,718 .... B 5
Burlington, 23,302 ...... f11
Cambridge, 95,802 .... B 5
Chelmsford, 32,383 ... A 5
Chelsea, 28,710 ...... B 5
Chicopee, 56,632 .... B 2
Concord, 4,680 (17,076▲) .... B 5
Danvers, 24,174 ...... A 6
Dedham, 23,782 ...... B 5
Everett, 35,701 ...... g11
Fall River, 92,703 .... C 5
Fitchburg, 41,194 .... A 4
Framingham, 64,989 .. B 5
Gardner, 20,125 ...... A 4
Gloucester, 28,716 .... A 6
Greenfield, 14,198 (18,666▲) .... A 2
Haverhill, 51,418 ...... A 5
Holyoke, 43,704 ...... B 2
Hyannis, 9,900 ...... C 7
Lawrence, 70,207 .... A 5
Leominster, 38,145 .... A 4
Lexington, 28,974 .... B 5
Lowell, 103,439 ...... A 5
Lynn, 81,245 .... B 6
Malden, 53,884 ...... B 5
Marblehead, 20,126('80) B 6
Marlborough, 31,813 .. B 4
Medford, 57,407 ...... B 5
Melrose, 28,150 ...... B 5
Methuen, 40,300 ...... A 5
Milford, 25,200 ...... B 4
Milton, 25,725 .... B 5
Nantucket, 3,229 (6,012▲) .... D 7
Natick, 30,100 .... B 5
Needham, 27,557 ...... g11
New Bedford, 99,922 .. C 6
Newburyport, 16,317 .. A 6
Newton, 82,585 ...... B 5
North Adams, 16,797 .. A 1
Northampton, 29,289 .. B 2
North Andover, 20,129('87) .... A 5
North Attleboro, 24,200 C 5
Norwood, 28,700 ...... B 5
Peabody, 47,039 ...... A 6
Pittsfield, 48,622 ...... B 1
Plymouth, 7,232 (45,608▲) .... C 6
Quincy, 84,985 ...... B 5
Randolph, 30,093 .... B 5
Reading, 22,539 ...... A 5
Revere, 42,786 ...... g11
Salem, 38,091 .... A 6
Saugus, 25,549 ...... B 5
Shrewsbury, 23,400 .... B 4
Somerville, 76,210 .... B 5
Springfield, 156,983 .. B 2
Stoneham, 22,203 .... g11
Stoughton, 27,800 .... B 5
Taunton, 49,832 ...... C 5
Vineyard Haven, 1,704('80) .... D 6
Wakefield, 24,825 .... B 5
Waltham, 57,878 ...... B 5
Watertown, 33,284 .... g11
Wellesley, 26,615 .... B 5
Westfield, 38,372 .... B 2
West Springfield, 27,537 B 2
Weymouth, 54,063 .... B 6
Winchester, 20,701('80) g11
Winthrop, 19,294('80) .. B 6
Woburn, 35,943 ...... B 5
Worcester, 169,759 .... B 4

▲ Population of entire town (township), including rural area.

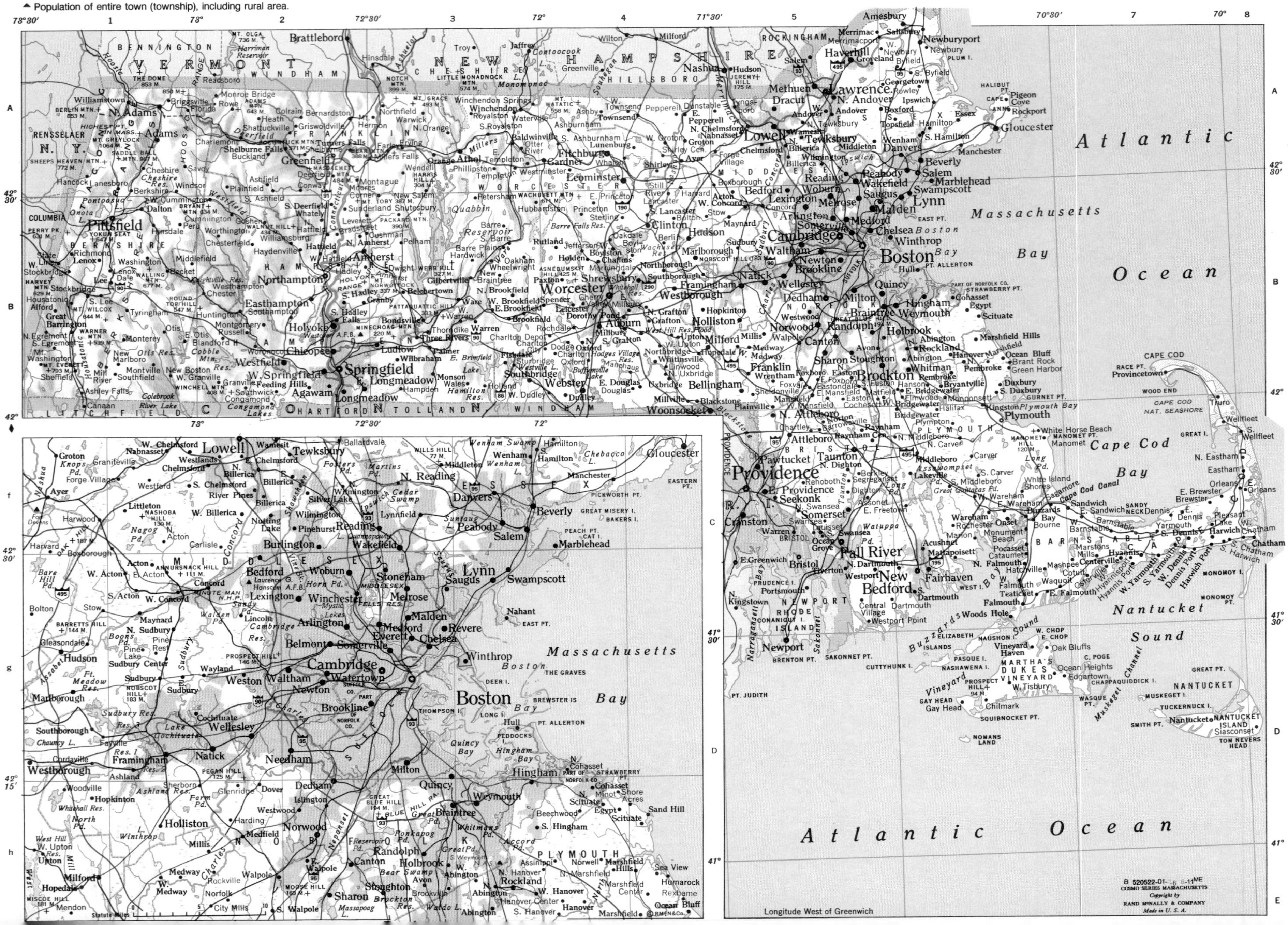

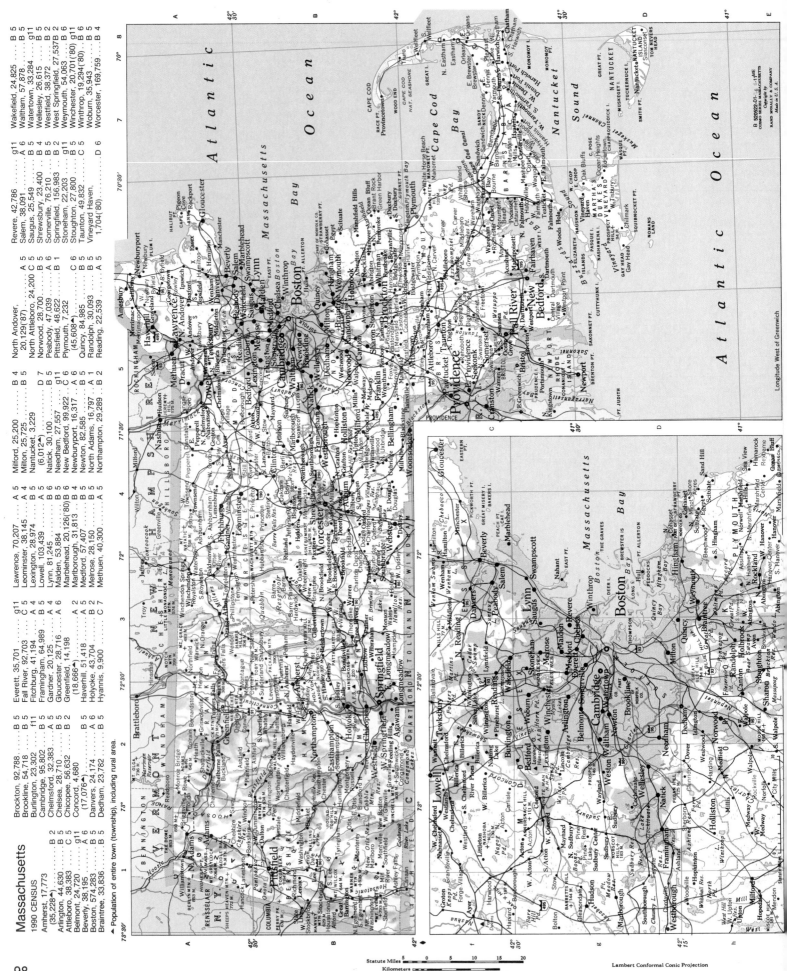

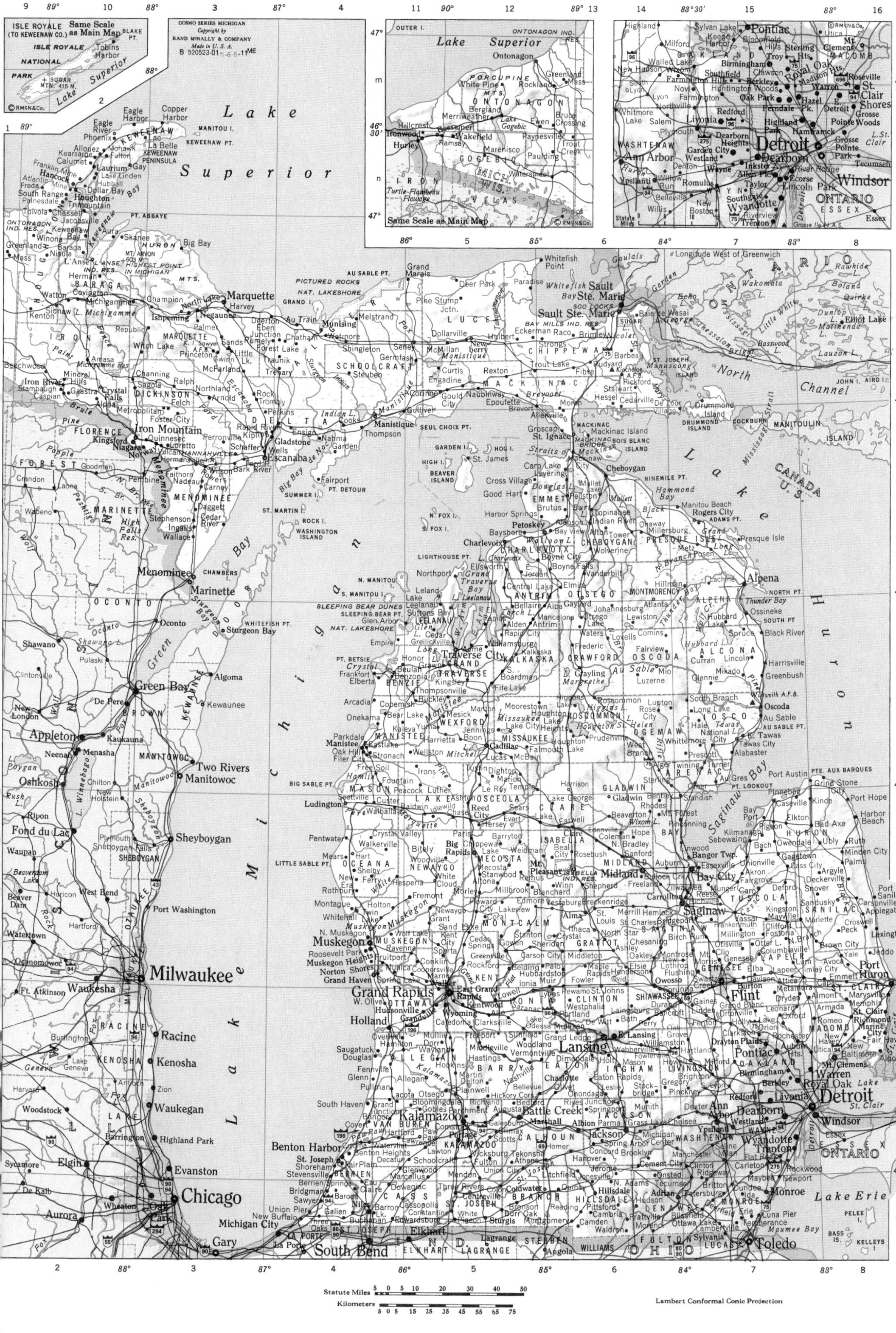

Michigan

1990 CENSUS

Adrian, 22,097 . . . . . G 6
Albion, 10,066 . . . . . . F 6
Allen Park, 31,092 . . p15
Alpena, 11,354. . . . . .C 7
Ann Arbor, 109,592 . . F 7
Auburn Heights, 17,076 . . . . F 7
Bangor Township, 17,494('88) . . . . . . E 7
Battle Creek, 53,540 F 5
Bay City, 38,936 . . . . E 7
Beecher, 17,178('80) E 7
Benton Harbor, 12,818 . . . . F 4
Berkley, 16,960 . . . . F 7
Big Rapids, 12,603 . . E 5
Birmingham, 19,997 . . F 7
Burton, 27,617 . . . . . E 7
Cadillac, 10,104 . . . . D 5
Cheboygan, 4,999 . . . C 6
Clawson, 13,874 . . . . o15
Coldwater, 9,607 . . . . G 5
Dearborn, 89,286 . . . . F 7
Dearborn Heights, 60,838 . . . . p15
Detroit, 1,027,974 . . F 7
Drayton Plains, 18,000('88) . . . . . . F 7
East Detroit, 35,283 . . .p16
East Lansing, 50,677 F 6
Escanaba, 13,659 . . C 3
Farmington Hills, 74,652 . . . . o15
Ferndale, 25,084 . . . . P15
Flint, 140,761 . . . . . . E 7
Garden City, 31,846 . .p15
Grand Haven, 11,951 E 4
Grand Rapids, 189,126 . . . . .F 5
Grosse Pointe Woods, 17,715 . . . . p16
Hamtramck, 18,372 . . p15
Hazel Park, 20,051 . . p15
Highland, 750('88) . . o14
Highland Park, 20,121 p15
Holland, 30,745 . . . . F 4
Houghton, 7,498 . . . . A 2
Inkster, 30,772 . . . . . . p15
Iron Mountain, 8,525 C 2
Ironwood, 6,849 . . . . n11
Jackson, 37,446 . . . . F 6
Kalamazoo, 80,277 . . F 5
Kentwood, 37,826 . . F 5
Lansing, 127,321 . . . . F 6
Lincoln Park, 41,832 p15
Livonia, 100,850 . . . . F 7
Ludington, 8,507 . . . . E 4
Mackinaw City, 875 . . C 6
Madison Heights, 32,196 . . . . o15
Manistee, 6,734 . . . . D 4
Marquette, 21,977 . . B 3
Menominee, 9,398 . . C 3
Midland, 38,053 . . . . E 6
Monroe, 22,902 . . . . G 7
Mount Clemens, 18,405 . . . . F 8
Mount Pleasant, 23,285 . . . . E 6
Muskegon, 40,283 . . E 4
Niles, 12,458 . . . . . . G 4
Norton Shores, 21,755 . . . . E 4
Novi, 32,998 . . . . p15
Oak Park, 30,462 . . . . p15
Owosso, 16,322 . . . . E 6
Petoskey, 6,056 . . . . C 6
Pontiac, 71,166 . . . . F 7
Portage, 41,042 . . . . F 5
Port Huron, 33,694 . . F 8
Redford, 54,387 . . . . F 7
Romulus, 22,897 . . . . p15
Roseville, 51,412 . . . . o16
Royal Oak, 65,410 . . F 7
Saginaw, 69,512 . . . . E 7
Saint Clair Shores, 68,107 . . . . p16
Sault Sainte Marie, 14,689 . . . . B 6
Southfield, 75,728 . . o15
Southgate, 30,771 . . p15
Sterling Heights, 117,810. . . . . .o15
Sturgis, 10,130 . . . . G 5
Taylor, 70,811 . . . . . . p15
Traverse City, 15,155 D 5
Trenton, 20,586 . . . . F 7
Troy, 72,884. . . . . . . .o15
Walker, 17,279. . . . . . E 5
Warren, 144,864 . . . . F 7
Wayne, 19,899 . . . . . .p15
Westland, 84,724 . . . F 7
Wyandotte, 30,938 . . F 7
Wyoming, 63,891 . . . F 5
Ypsilanti, 24,846 . . . . F 7

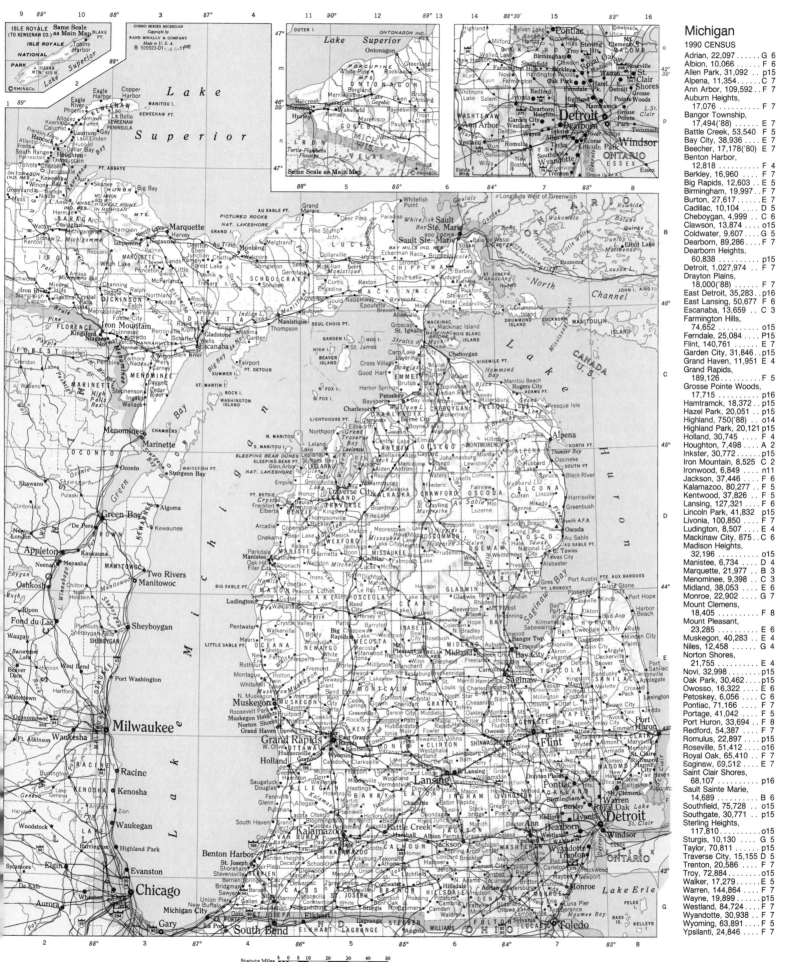

Minnesota

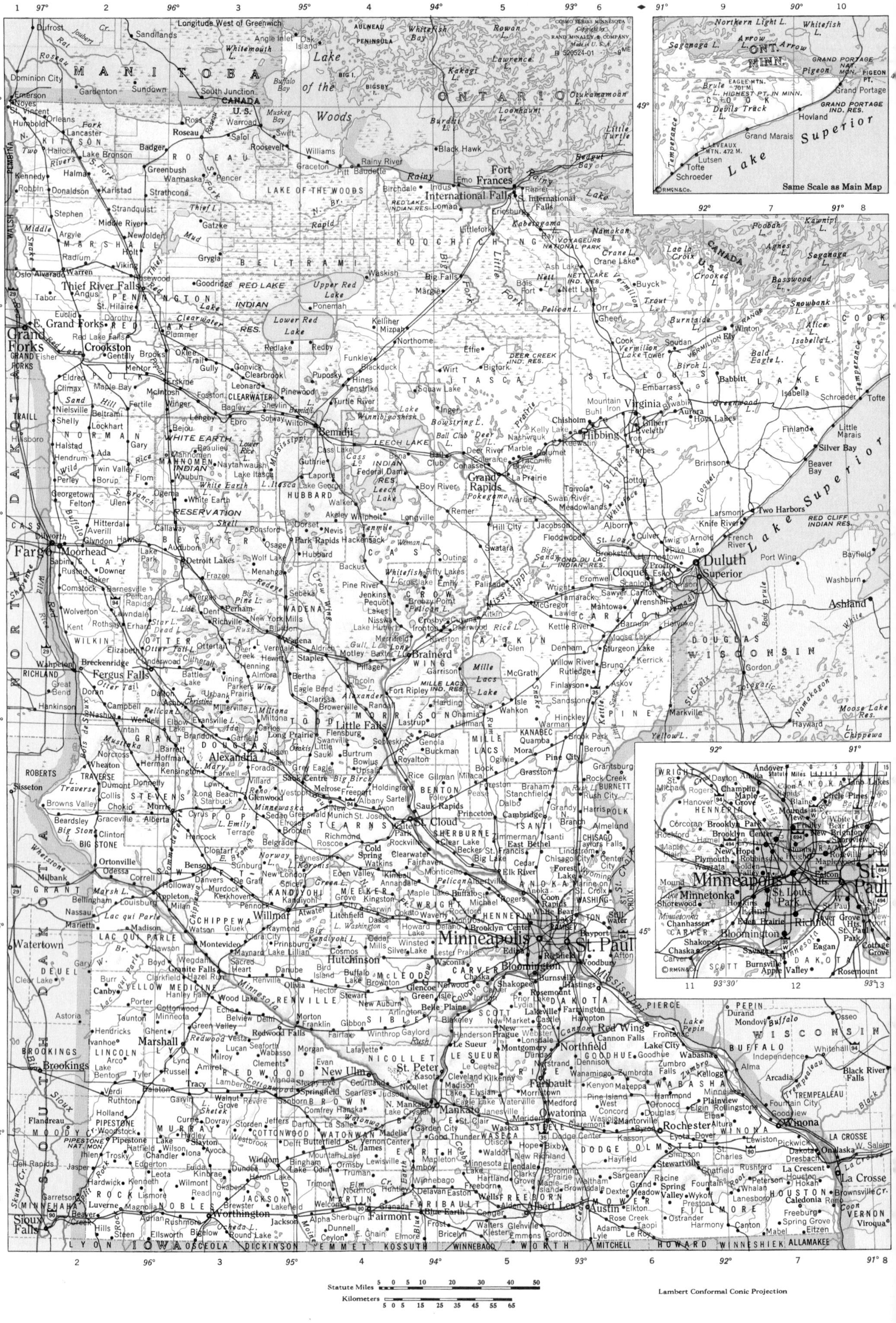

Statute Miles 5 0 5 10 20 30 40 50

Kilometers 5 0 5 15 25 35 45 55 65

Lambert Conformal Conic Projection

Minnesota

1990 CENSUS

Albert Lea, 18,310 .. G 5
Alexandria, 7,838 .... E 3
Andover, 15,216 .... m12
Anoka, 17,192 ...... E 5
Apple Valley, 34,598 n12
Austin, 21,907 ...... G 6
Bemidji, 11,245 .... C 4
Blaine, 38,975 ...... m12
Bloomington, 86,335 F 5
Brainerd, 12,353 .... D 4
Brooklyn Center, 28,887 .... E 5
Brooklyn Park, 56,381 .... m12
Burnsville, 51,288 .... F 5
Champlin, 16,849 .. m12
Chisholm, 5,290 .... C 6
Cloquet, 10,885 .... D 6
Columbia Heights, 18,910 .... m12
Coon Rapids, 52,978 E 5
Cottage Grove, 22,935 .... n13
Crookston, 8,119 .... C 2
Crystal, 23,788 .... m12
Detroit Lakes, 6,635 D 3
Duluth, 85,493 ...... D 6
Eagan, 47,409 ...... n12
East Bethel, 8,050 ... E 5
East Grand Forks, 8,658 .... C 2
Eden Prairie, 39,311 .. n12
Edina, 46,070 ...... F 5
Ely, 3,968 .... C 7
Fairmont, 11,265 .... G 4
Faribault, 17,085 .... F 5
Fergus Falls, 12,362 D 2
Fridley, 28,335 ...... m12
Golden Valley, 20,971 n12
Grand Marais, 1,171 k 9
Grand Rapids, 7,976 C 5
Hastings, 15,445 .... F 6
Hibbing, 18,046 .... C 6
Hopkins, 16,534 .... n12
Hutchinson, 11,523 .. F 4
International Falls, 8,325 .... B 5
Inver Grove Heights, 22,477 .... n12
Lakeville, 24,854 .... F 5
Litchfield, 6,041 .... E 4
Little Falls, 7,232 .... E 4
Mankato, 31,477 .... F 5
Maple Grove, 38,736 m12
Maplewood, 30,954 .. n12
Marshall, 12,023 .... F 3
Minneapolis, 368,383 F 5
Minnetonka, 48,370 .. n12
Montevideo, 5,499 .. F 3
Moorhead, 32,295 .. D 2
Morris, 5,613 ...... E 3
Mound, 9,634 ...... n11
Mounds View, 12,541 m12
New Brighton, 22,207 m12
New Hope, 21,853 .. m12
New Ulm, 13,132 .... F 4
Northfield, 14,684 .. F 5
North Mankato, 10,164 .... F 4
North St. Paul, 12,376 .... m13
Owatonna, 19,386 .. F 5
Pipestone, 4,554 .... G 2
Plymouth, 50,889 .. m12
Prior Lake, 11,482 .. F 5
Ramsey, 12,408 .... E 5
Red Wing, 15,134 .. F 6
Redwood Falls, 4,859 F 3
Richfield, 35,710 .... F 5
Robbinsdale, 14,396 m12
Rochester, 70,745 .. F 6
Roseville, 33,485 .... m12
Saint Cloud, 48,812 .. E 4
Saint Louis Park, 43,787 .... n12
Saint Paul, 272,235 .. F 5
Saint Peter, 9,421 .. F 5
Shakopee, 11,739 .. F 5
Shoreview, 24,587 .. m12
South St. Paul, 20,197 .... n12
Stillwater, 13,882 .... E 6
Thief River Falls, 8,010 .... B 2
Virginia, 9,410 ...... C 6
Waseca, 8,385 ...... F 5
West Saint Paul, 19,248 .... n12
White Bear Lake, 24,704 .... E 5
Willmar, 17,531 .... E 3
Winona, 25,399 .... F 7
Woodbury, 20,075 .. F 6
Worthington, 9,977 .. G 3

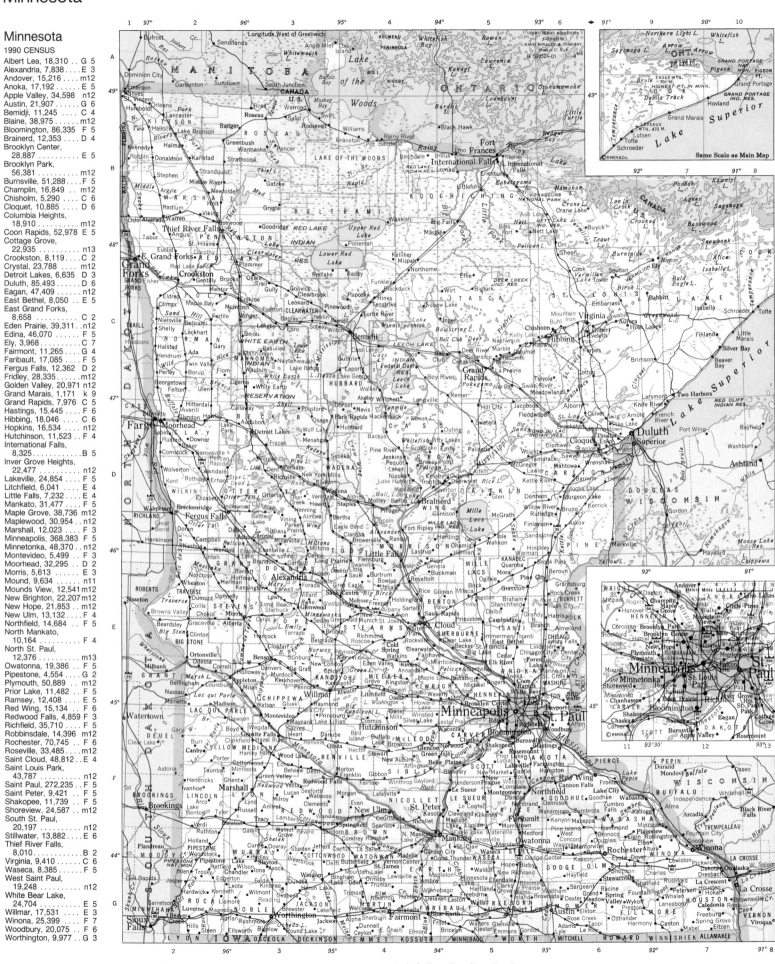

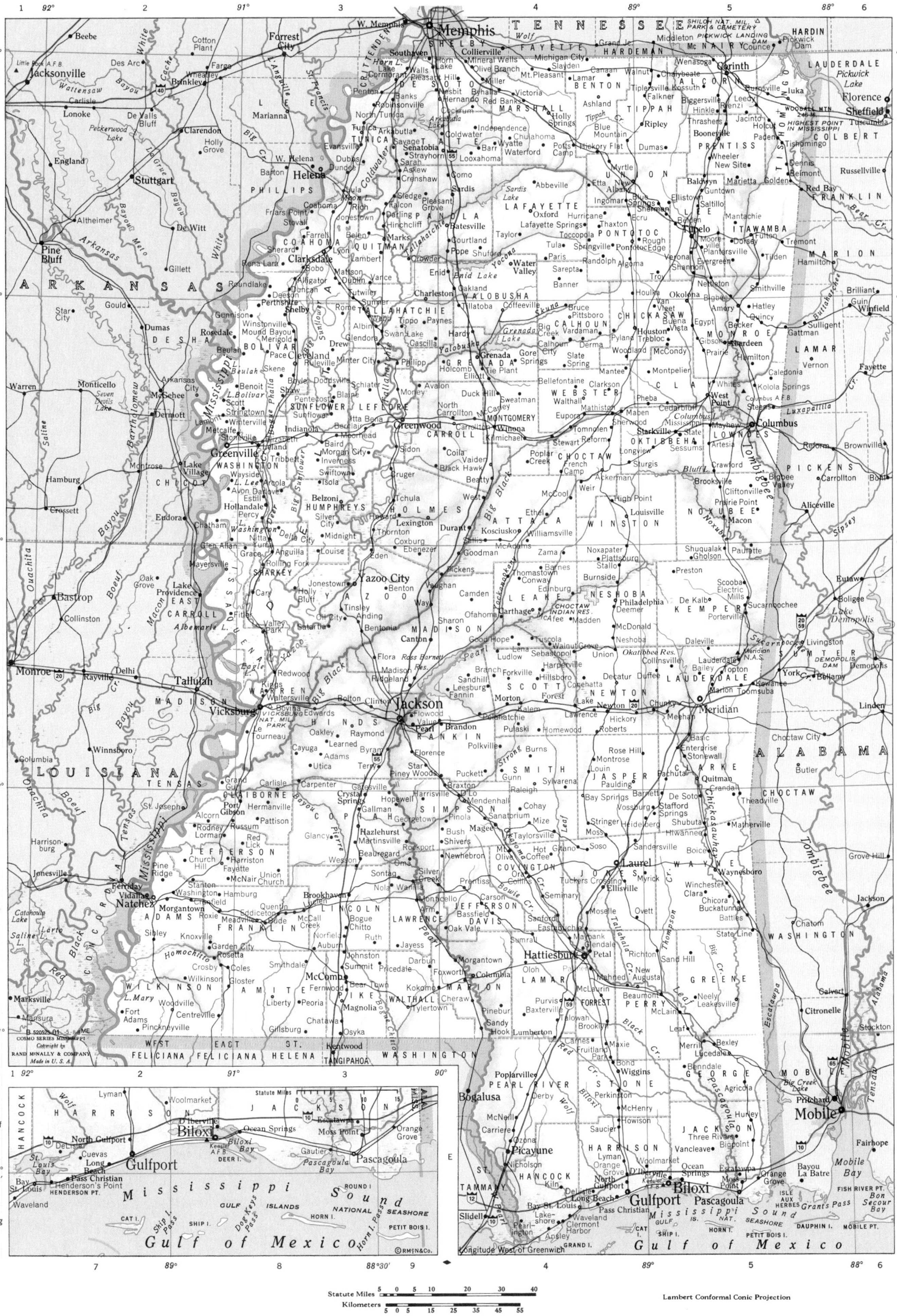

Mississippi

1990 CENSUS

Aberdeen, 6,837 .... B 5
Amory, 7,093 ...... B 5
Baldwyn, 3,204 .... A 5
Batesville, 6,403 .... A 4
Bay Saint Louis, 8,063 .... E 4
Belzoni, 2,536 ...... B 3
Biloxi, 46,319 ...... E 5
Booneville, 7,955 .... A 5
Brandon, 11,077 ..... C 4
Brookhaven, 10,243 D 3
Canton, 10,062 .... C 3
Carthage, 3,819 .... C 4
Charleston, 2,328 .. A 3
Clarksdale, 19,717 .. A 3
Cleveland, 15,384 .. B 3
Clinton, 21,847 ..... C 3
Columbia, 6,815 .... D 4
Columbus, 23,799 .. B 5
Corinth, 11,820 ...... A 5
Crystal Springs, 5,643D 3
D'Iberville, 6,566 .... E 5
Durant, 2,838 .... B 4
Ellisville, 3,634 ...... D 4
Escatawpa, 5,367('80)E 5
Forest, 5,060 .... C 4
Fulton, 3,387 .... A 5
Gautier, 10,088 ...... f 8
Greenville, 45,226 .. B 2
Greenwood, 18,906 . B 3
Grenada, 10,864 .... B 4
Gulfport, 40,775 .... E 4
Hattiesburg, 41,882 . D 4
Hazlehurst, 4,221 .... D 3
Hernando, 3,125 .... A 4
Hollandale, 3,576 .... B 3
Holly Springs, 7,261 A 4
Horn Lake, 9,069 .... A 3
Houston, 3,903 .... B 4
Indianola, 11,809 .... B 3
Itta Bena, 2,377 .... B 3
Iuka, 3,122 .... A 5
Jackson, 196,637 ... C 3
Kosciusko, 6,986 .... B 4
Laurel, 18,827 ...... D 4
Leland, 6,366 .... B 3
Lexington, 2,227 .... B 3
Long Beach, 15,804 .. g 7
Louisville, 7,169 ..... B 4
Magee, 3,607 ...... D 4
McComb, 11,591 ..... D 3
Meridian, 41,036 .... C 5
Mississippi State, 4,600('81) .... B 5
Morgantown, 3,288('80) .... D 2
Morton, 3,212 ...... C 4
Moss Point, 17,837 .. E 5
Mound Bayou, 2,222 B 3
Natchez, 19,460 .... D 2
New Albany, 6,775 .. A 4
Newton, 3,701 ...... C 4
North Gulfport, 6,660('80) .... E 4
Ocean Springs, 14,658 .... E 5
Okolona, 3,267 .... B 5
Orange Grove, 3,000('81) .... E 5
Oxford, 9,984 ...... A 4
Palmer, 2,765('80) ... D 4
Pascagoula, 25,899 .. E 5
Pass Christian, 5,557 E 4
Pearl, 19,588 ...... C 3
Petal, 7,883 .... D 4
Philadelphia, 6,758 .. C 4
Picayune, 10,633 .... E 4
Pontotoc, 4,570 .... A 4
Quitman, 2,736 .... C 5
Ridgeland, 11,714 ... C 3
Ripley, 5,371 ...... A 5
Rolling Fork, 2,444 .. C 3
Rosedale, 2,595 .... B 2
Ruleville, 3,245 ..... B 3
Senatobia, 4,772 .... A 4
Southaven, 17,949 .. A 3
Starkville, 18,458 .... B 5
Tupelo, 30,685 ...... A 5
Vicksburg, 20,908 ... C 3
Water Valley, 3,610 .. A 4
Waveland, 5,369 .... E 4
Waynesboro, 5,143 .. D 5
West Point, 8,489 ... B 5
Wiggins, 3,185 ...... E 4
Winona, 5,705 ...... B 4
Yazoo City, 12,427 .. C 3

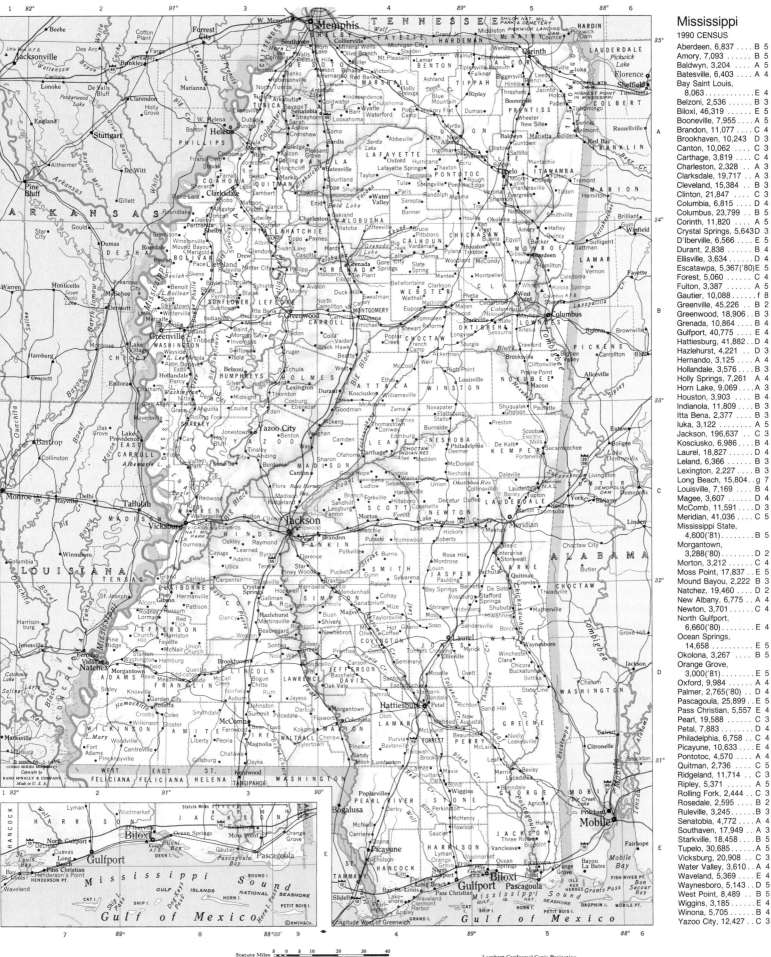

Missouri

1990 CENSUS

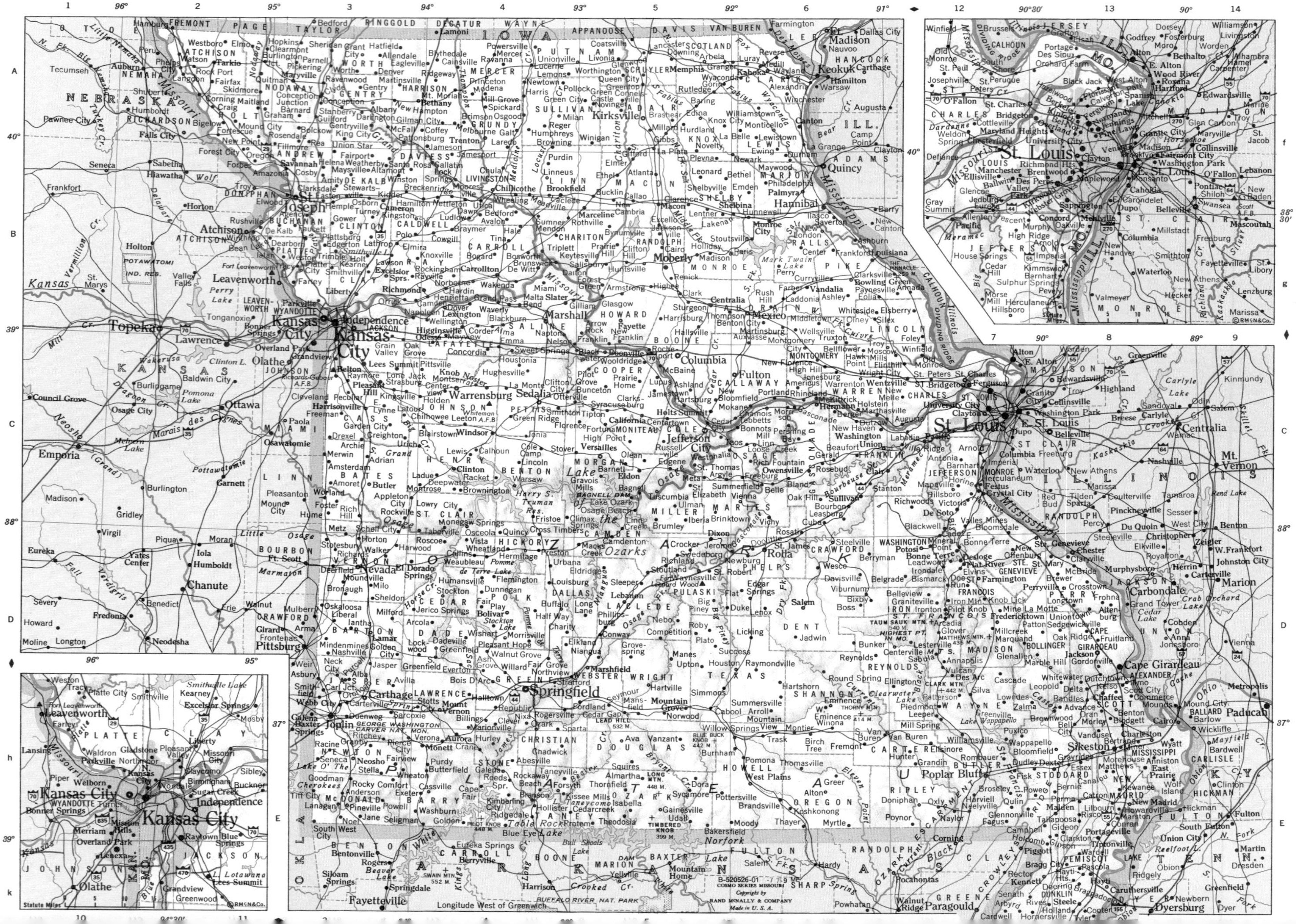

Statute Miles
Kilometers
Lambert Conformal Conic Projection
Longitude West of Greenwich

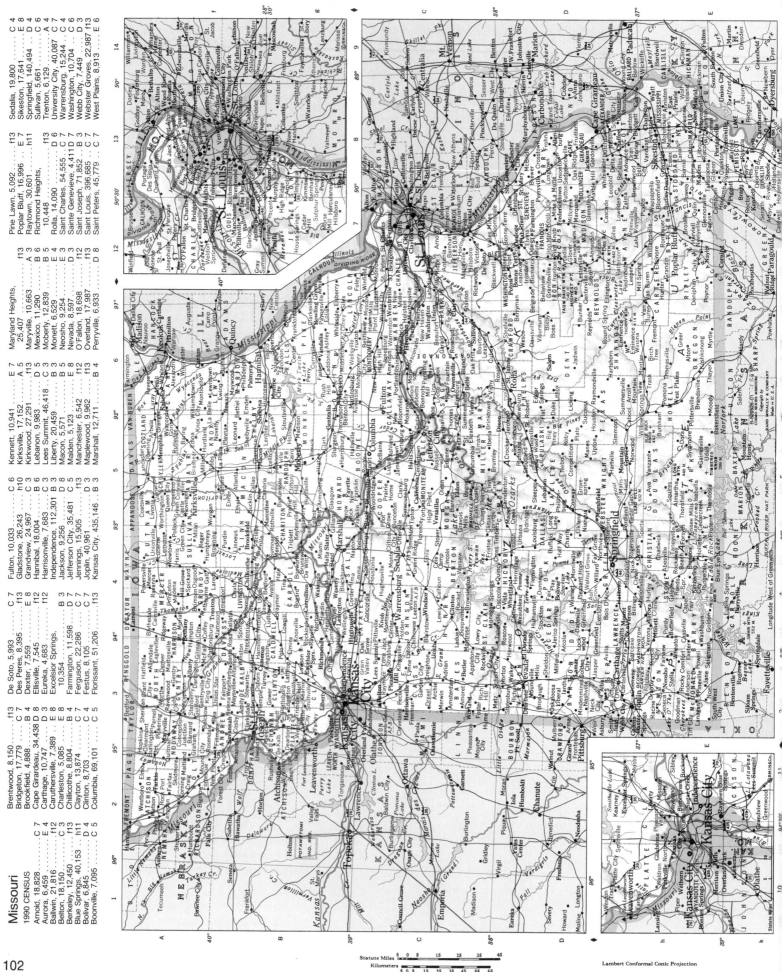

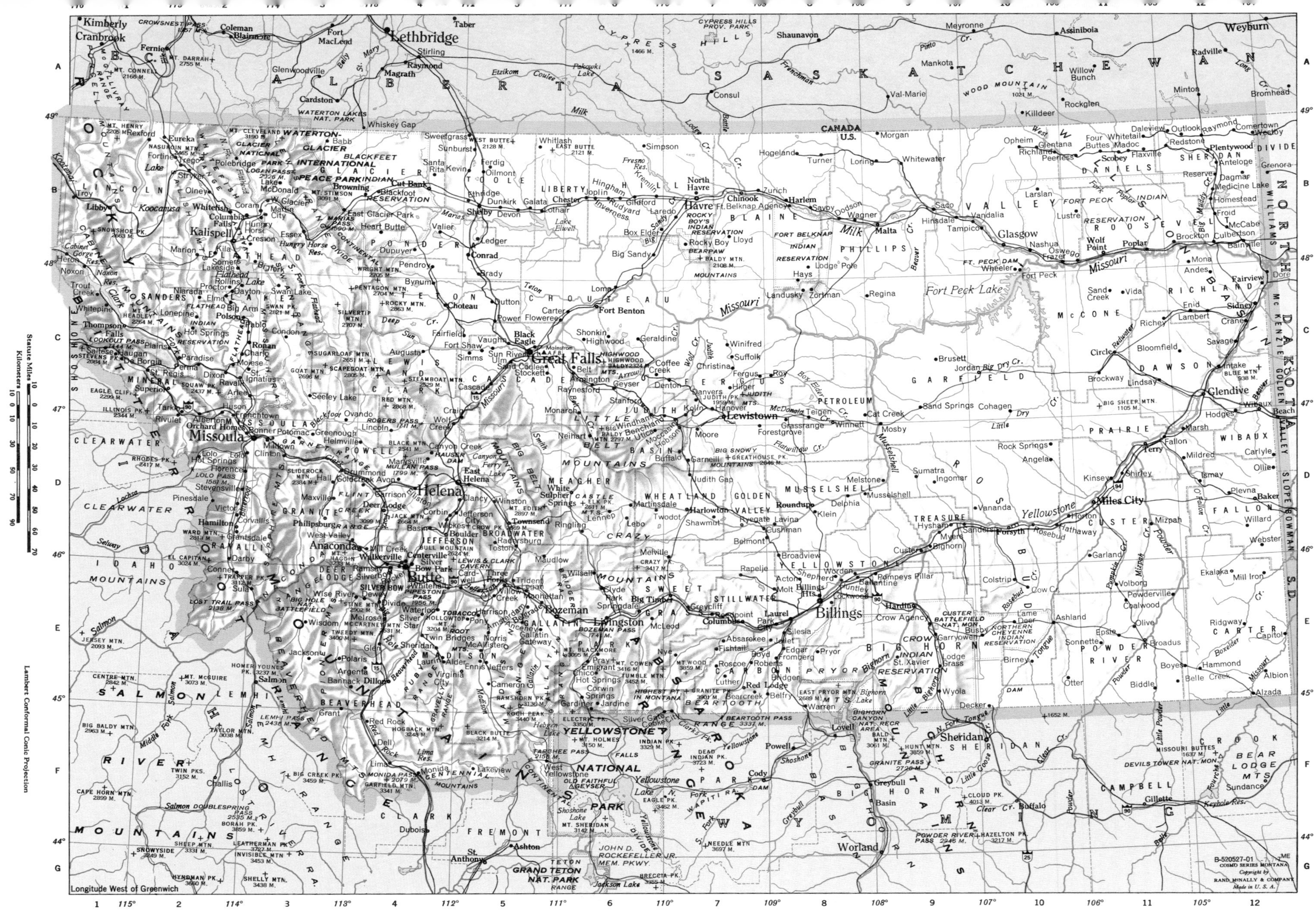

Montana

1990 CENSUS

Anaconda, 10,278 .... D 4
Baker, 1,818 .... D12
Belgrade, 3,411 ...... E 5
Belt, 571 .... C 6
Bigfork, 1,080('80) .... B 2
Big Sandy, 740 ...... B 6
Big Timber, 1,557 .... E 7
Billings, 81,151 ...... E 8
Billings Heights, 8,480('80) .... E 8
Boulder, 1,316 .... D 4
Bozeman, 22,660 .... E 5
Bridger, 692 .... E 8
Broadus, 572 .... E11
Browning, 1,170 ...... B 3
Butte, 33,336 .... E 4
Cascade, 729 .... C 5
Chester, 942 .... B 6
Chinook, 1,512 .... B 7
Choteau, 1,741 ...... C 4
Circle, 805 .... C11
Colstrip, 1,476('80) E10
Columbia Falls, 2,942 . B 2
Columbus, 1,573 ...... E 7
Conrad, 2,891 .... B 5
Culbertson, 796 ...... B12
Cut Bank, 3,329 ...... B 4
Deer Lodge, 3,378 .... D 4
Dillon, 3,991 .... E 4
East Helena, 1,538 .... D 5
Ennis, 773 .... E 5
Eureka, 1,043 .... B 1
Fairview, 869 .... C12
Forsyth, 2,178 .... D10
Fort Benton, 1,660 .... C 6
Glasgow, 3,572 ...... B10
Glendive, 4,802 ...... C12
Great Falls, 55,097 .... C 5
Hamilton, 2,737 ...... D 2
Hardin, 2,940 .... E 9
Harlem, 882 .... B 8
Harlowton, 1,049 ...... D 7
Havre, 10,201 .... B 7
Helena, 24,569 .... D 4
Kalispell, 11,917 ...... B 2
Laurel, 5,686 .... E 8
Lewistown, 6,051 .... C 7
Libby, 2,532 .... B 1
Livingston, 6,701 ...... E 6
Lockwood, 2,300('89) .. E 8
Lolo, 2,418('80) .... D 2
Malta, 2,340 .... B 9
Manhattan, 1,034 .... E 5
Miles City, 8,461 ...... D11
Missoula, 42,918 ...... D 2
Orchard Homes, 4,500('89) .... D 2
Philipsburg, 925 ...... D 3
Plains, 992 .... C 2
Plentywood, 2,136 .... B12
Polson, 3,283 .... C 2
Poplar, 881 .... B11
Red Lodge, 1,958 .... E 7
Ronan, 1,547 .... C 2
Roundup, 1,808 ...... D 8
Saint Ignatius, 778 .... C 2
Scobey, 1,154 .... B11
Shelby, 2,763 .... B 5
Sidney, 5,217 .... C12
Stevensville, 1,221 .... D 2
Superior, 881 .... C 2
Terry, 659 .... D11
Thompson Falls, 1,319 C 1
Three Forks, 1,203 .... E 5
Townsend, 1,635 .... D 5
Troy, 953 .... B 1
Vaughn, 2,270('80) .... C 5
Walkerville, 605 ...... D 4
West Yellowstone, 913 F 5
Whitefish, 4,368 ...... B 2
Whitehall, 1,067 ...... E 4
White Sulphur Springs, 963 .... D 6
Wibaux, 628 .... D12
Wolf Point, 2,880 .... B11

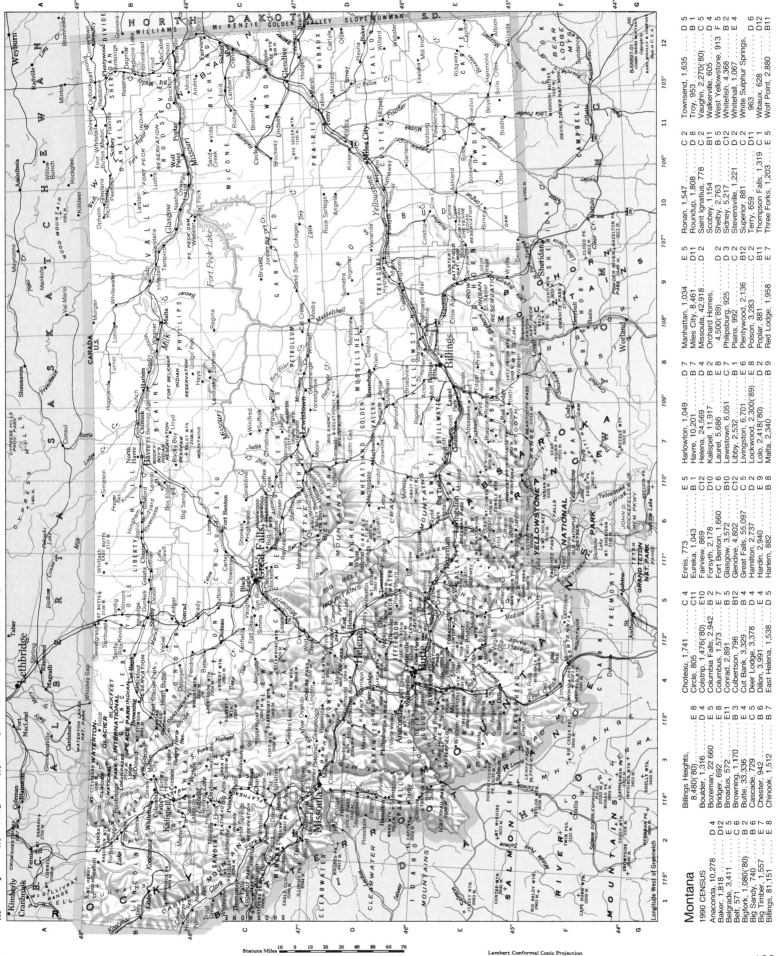

Nebraska

1990 CENSUS

- Ainsworth, 1,870 . . . . . . B 6
- Albion, 1,916 . . . . C 7
- Alliance, 9,765 . . . . B 3
- Alma, 1,226 . . . . D 6
- Ashland, 2,136 . . . . C 9
- Atkinson, 1,380 . . . . . . B 7
- Auburn, 3,443 . . . . D10
- Aurora, 3,810 . . . . D 7
- Bayard, 1,196 . . . . C 2
- Beatrice, 12,354 . . . . . . D 9
- Bellevue, 30,982 . . . . . . C10
- Blair, 6,860 . . . . C 9
- Bridgeport, 1,581 . . . . . C 2
- Broken Bow, 3,778 . . . . . C 6
- Central City, 2,868 . . . . C 7
- Chadron, 5,588 . . . . B 3
- Columbus, 19,480 . . . . . C 8
- Cozad, 3,823 . . . . D 6
- Creighton, 1,223 . . . . . . B 8
- Crete, 4,841 . . . . D 9
- Dakota City, 1,470 . . . . B 9
- David City, 2,522 . . . . . . C 8
- Elkhorn, 1,398 . . . . g12
- Fairbury, 4,335 . . . . D 8
- Falls City, 4,769 . . . . . . D10
- Fremont, 23,680 . . . . . . C 9
- Fullerton, 1,452 . . . . . . C 8
- Geneva, 2,310 . . . . D 8
- Gering, 7,946 . . . . C 2
- Gibbon, 1,525 . . . . D 7
- Gordon, 1,803 . . . . B 3
- Gothenburg, 3,232 . . . . . D 5
- Grand Island, 39,386 . . . D 7
- Gretna, 2,249 . . . . C 9
- Hartington, 1,583 . . . . . . B 8
- Hastings, 22,837 . . . . D 7
- Hebron, 1,765 . . . . D 8
- Holdrege, 5,671 . . . . D 6
- Imperial, 2,007 . . . . D 4
- Kearney, 24,396 . . . . D 6
- Kimball, 2,574 . . . . C 2
- La Vista, 9,840 . . . . . . g12
- Lexington, 6,601 . . . . . . D 6
- Lincoln, 191,972 . . . . . . D 9
- Loup City, 1,104 . . . . . . C 7
- Madison, 2,135 . . . . C 8
- McCook, 8,112 . . . . D 5
- Milford, 1,886 . . . . D 8
- Minden, 2,749 . . . . D 7
- Mitchell, 1,743 . . . . C 2
- Nebraska City, 6,547 . . D10
- Neligh, 1,742 . . . . B 7
- Norfolk, 21,476 . . . . . . B 8
- North Bend, 1,249 . . . . . C 9
- North Platte, 22,605 . . C 5
- Ogallala, 5,095 . . . . C 4
- Omaha, 335,795 . . . . . . C10
- O'Neill, 3,852 . . . . B 7
- Ord, 2,481 . . . . C 7
- Papillion, 10,372 . . . . . . C 9
- Pierce, 1,615 . . . . B 8
- Plainview, 1,333 . . . . . . B 8
- Plattsmouth, 6,412 . . . . D10
- Ralston, 6,236 . . . . g12
- Saint Paul, 2,009 . . . . . . C 7
- Schuyler, 4,052 . . . . C 8
- Scottsbluff, 13,711 . . . . C 2
- Seward, 5,634 . . . . D 8
- Sidney, 5,959 . . . . C 3
- South Sioux City, 9,677 B 9
- Stanton, 1,549 . . . . C 8
- Superior, 2,397 . . . . D 7
- Sutton, 1,353 . . . . D 8
- Syracuse, 1,646 . . . . D 9
- Tecumseh, 1,702 . . . . . D 9
- Tekamah, 1,852 . . . . C 9
- Valentine, 2,826 . . . . B 5
- Valley, 1,775 . . . . C 9
- Wahoo, 3,681 . . . . C 9
- Waverly, 1,869 . . . . D 9
- Wayne, 5,142 . . . . B 8
- West Point, 3,250 . . . . . C 9
- Wilber, 1,527 . . . . D 9
- Wymore, 1,611 . . . . D 9
- York, 7,884 . . . . D 8

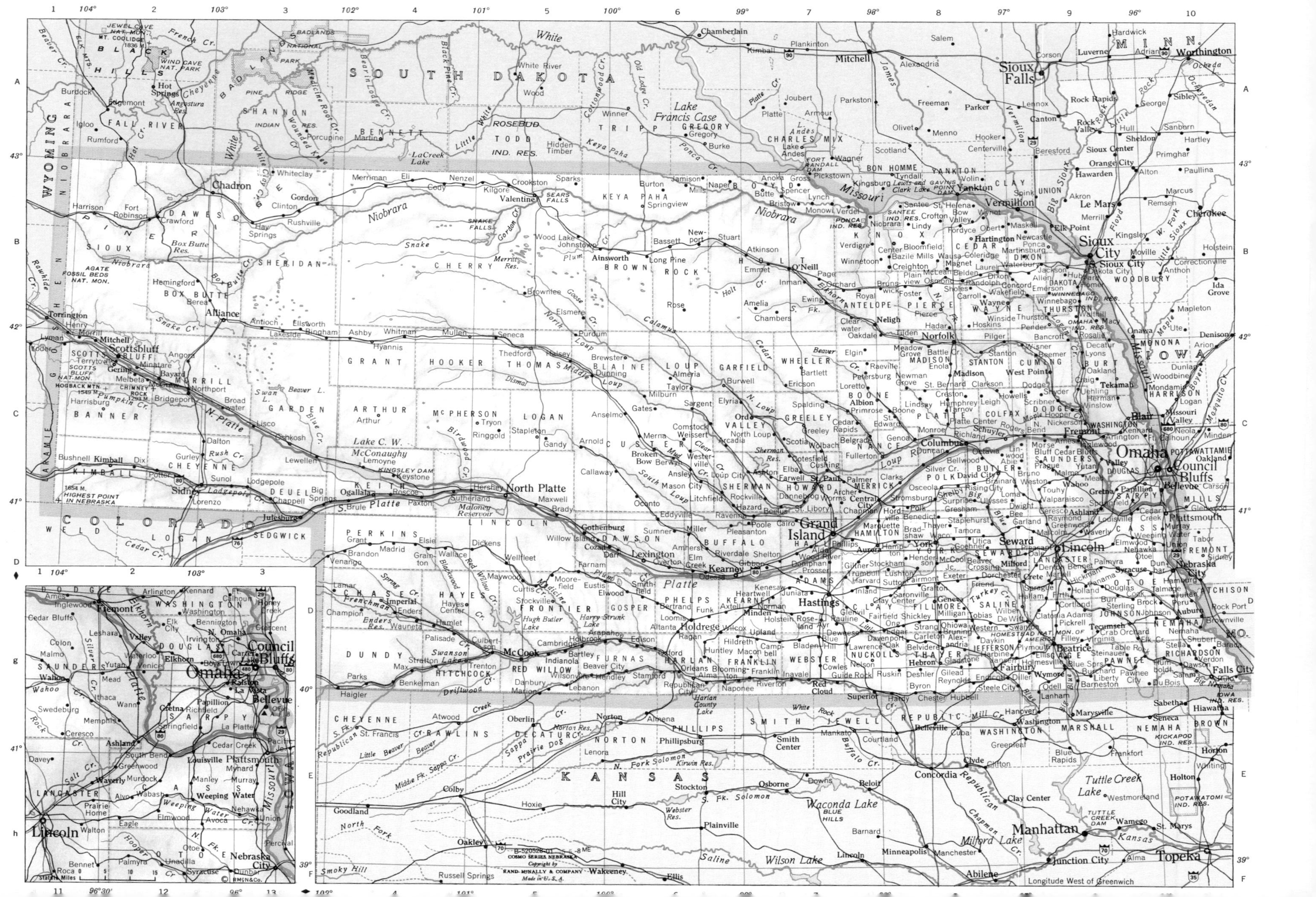

Statute Miles 5 0 5 10 20 30 40 50 60

Kilometers 5 0 5 15 35 55 75 95

Lambert Conformal Conic Projection

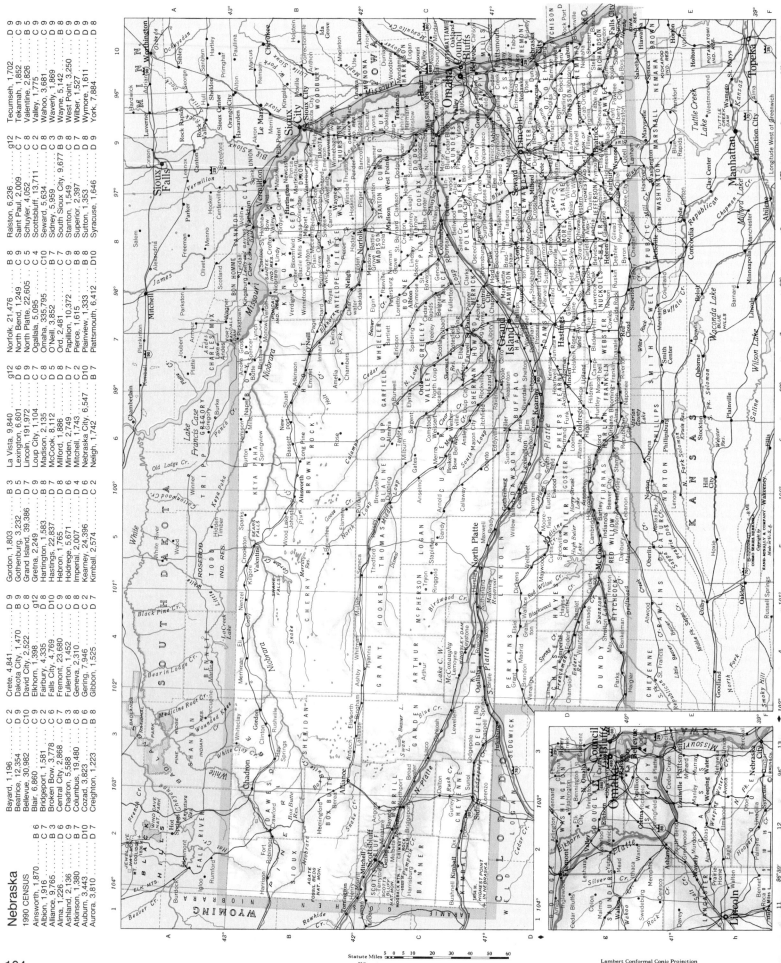

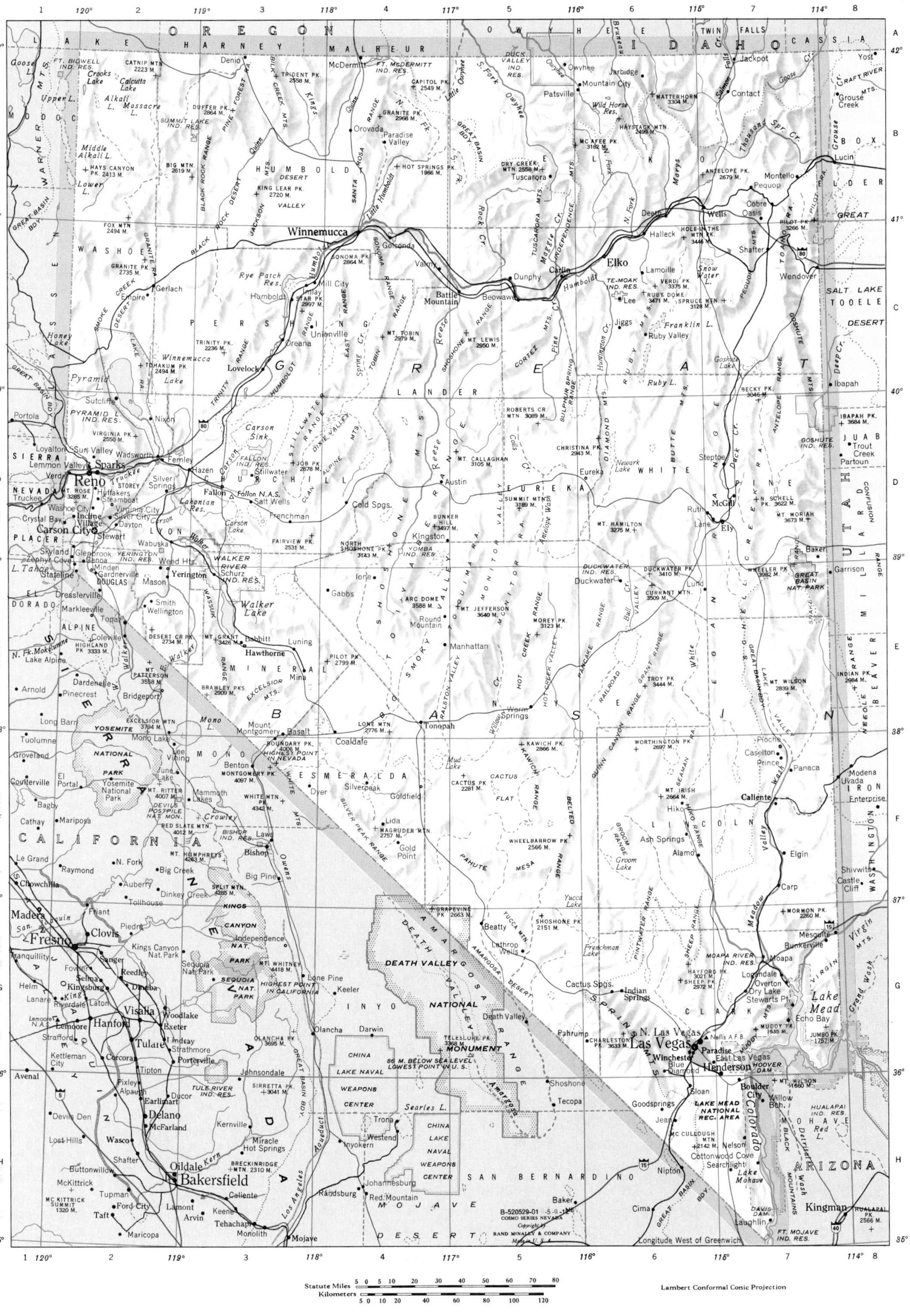

Nevada

1990 CENSUS

Alamo, 400('89) . . . . F 6
Austin, 370('89) . . . . D 4
Babbitt, 1,800('77) . . E 3
Battle Mountain, 2,749('80) . . . . C 5
Beatty, 1,200('89) . . G 5
Beowawe, 250('89) . . C 5
Blue Diamond, 420('89) . . . . G 6
Boulder City, 12,567 H 7
Bunkerville, 300('89) G 7
Caliente, 1,111 . . . . . F 7
Carlin, 2,220 . . . . . . C 5
Carson City, 40,443 D 2
Crystal Bay, 1,200('89) . . . . D 1
Dayton, 600('89) . . . . D 2
Dresslerville, 180('89) E 2
East Las Vegas, 6,449('80) . . . . G 6
Echo Bay, 120('89) . . G 7
Elko, 14,736 . . . . C 6
Ely, 4,756 . . . . D 7
Empire, 300('89) . . . . C 2
Eureka, 650('89) . . . . D 6
Fallon, 6,438 . . . . D 3
Fernley, 1,680('89) . . D 2
Gabbs, 667 . . . . E 4
Gardnerville, 3,700('89) . . . . E 2
Genoa, 190('89) . . . . D 2
Gerlach, 200('89) . . . . C 2
Glenbrook, 400('89) . . D 2
Golconda, 200('89) . . . C 4
Goldfield, 600('89) . . . F 4
Goodsprings, 150('89)H 6
Hawthorne, 3,741('80)E 3
Henderson, 64,942 . . G 7
Huffakers, 150('77) . . D 2
Imlay, 250('89) . . . . . . C 3
Incline Village, 4,500('89) . . . . D 2
Indian Springs, 1,200('89) . . . . G 6
Jackpot, 570('89) . . . . B 7
Jean, 150('89) . . . . . . H 6
Lamoille, 110('89) . . . C 6
Las Vegas, 258,295 G 6
Lathrop Wells, 350('89) . . . . G 5
Laughlin, 140('89) . . . H 7
Lemmon Valley, 4,100('89) . . . . D 2
Logandale, 500('89) . . G 7
Lovelock, 2,069 . . . . . C 3
Lund, 330('89) . . . . . . E 6
Mason, 400('89) . . . . . E 2
McDermitt, 250('89) . . B 4
McGill, 1,419('80) . . . . D 7
Mesquite, 1,871 . . . . . G 7
Mina, 400('89) . . . . . . E 3
Minden, 1,700('89) . . E 2
Montello, 200('89) . . B 7
Mountain City, 110('89) . . . . B 6
Nixon, 150('89) . . . . . D 2
North Las Vegas, 47,707 . . . . G 6
Overton, 1,111('80) . . G 7
Owyhee, 790('89) . . . B 5
Pahrump, 1,300('89) G 6
Panaca, 700('89) . . . . F 7
Paradise, 124,682 . . G 6
Paradise Valley, 150('89) . . . . B 4
Pioche, 830('89) . . . . F 7
Reno, 133,850 . . . . . . D 2
Round Mountain, 210('89) . . . . E 4
Ruth, 550('89) . . . . . . D 6
Schurz, 330('89) . . . . . E 3
Searchlight, 430('89) H 7
Silver City, 100('89) . . D 2
Silverpeak, 190('89) . . F 4
Silver Springs, 420('89) . . . . D 2
Skyland, 660('89) . . . . D 2
Sparks, 53,367 . . . . D 2
Stateline, 1,500('89) . . E 2
Steamboat, 450('89) D 2
Sunrise Manor, 95,362 . . . . G 6
Sun Valley, 8,822('80)D 2
Tonopah, 1,952('80) E 4
Verdi, 1,140('89) . . . . D 2
Virginia City, 920('89) D 2
Wadsworth, 510('89) D 2
Washoe City, 400('89)D 2
Weed Heights, 230('89) . . . . E 2
Wellington, 280('89) . . E 2
Wells, 1,256 . . . . B 7
Winchester, 19,728('80) . . . . . . G 6
Winnemucca, 6,134 . . C 4
Yerington, 2,367 . . . . E 2
Zephyr Cove, 1,700('89) . . . . E 2

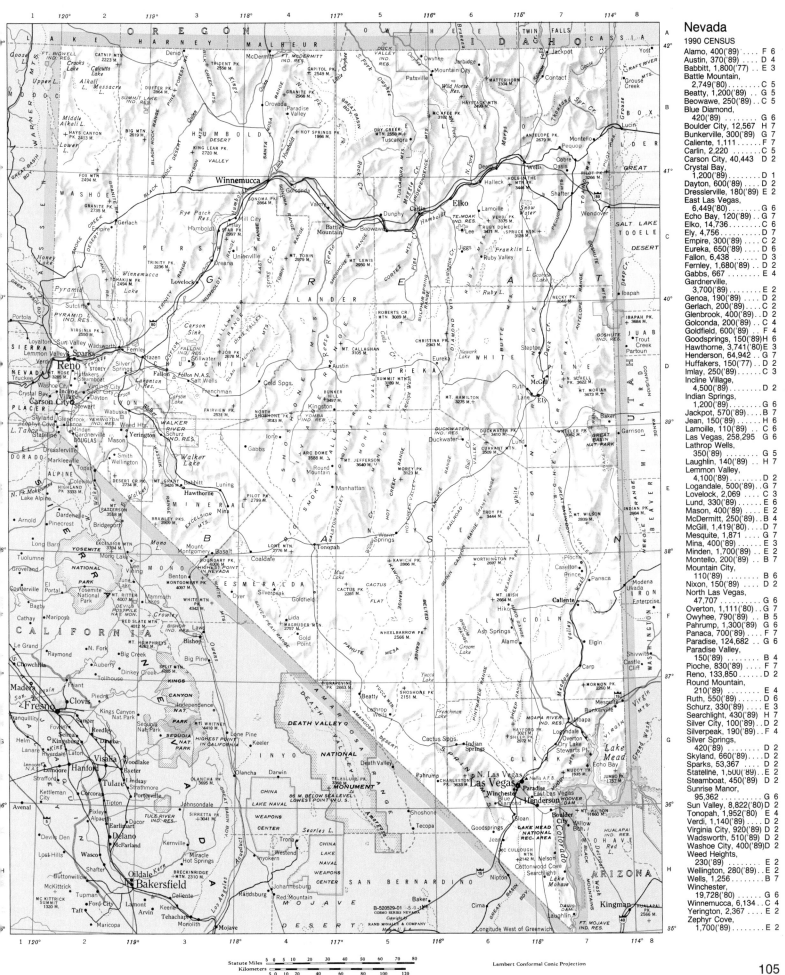

New Hampshire

New Hampshire

1990 CENSUS

Alton, 975 (3,286▲) . . D 4
Amherst, 850 (9,068▲) . . . . E 3
Antrim, 1,142 (2,360▲) . . . . D 3
Ashland, 1,479 (1,915▲) . . . . C 3
Bedford, 1,400 (12,563▲) . . . . E 3
Berlin, 11,824 . . . . . . B 4
Bristol, 1,258 (2,537▲) . . . . C 3
Charlestown, 1,294 (4,630▲) . . . . D 2
Claremont, 13,902 . . D 2
Colebrook, 1,131 (2,444▲) . . . . g 7
Concord, 36,006 . . . . D 3
Conway, 1,781 (7,940▲) . . . . C 4
Derry, 12,248 (29,603▲) . . . . E 4
Dover, 25,042 . . . . . . D 5
Durham, 8,448 (11,818▲) . . . . D 5
Enfield, 1,581 (3,979▲) . . . . C 2
Epping, 1,384 (5,162▲) . . . . D 4
Exeter, 8,947 (12,481▲) . . . . E 5
Farmington, 3,284 (5,739▲) . . . . D 4
Franklin, 8,304 . . . . . . D 3
Goffstown, 2,700 (14,621▲) . . . . D 3
Gorham, 2,180 (3,173▲) . . . . B 4
Greenville, 1,447 (2,231▲) . . . . E 3
Hampton, 6,779 (12,278▲) . . . . E 5
Hanover, 6,861 (9,212▲) . . . . C 2
Henniker, 1,538 (4,151▲) . . . . D 3
Hinsdale, 1,546 (3,936▲) . . . . E 2
Hooksett, 1,868 (8,767▲) . . . . D 4
Hudson, 6,248 (19,530▲) . . . . E 4
Jaffrey, 2,684 (5,361▲) . . . . E 2
Keene, 22,430 . . . . . . E 2
Laconia, 15,743 . . . . C 4
Lancaster, 2,134 (3,522▲) . . . . B 3
Lebanon, 12,183 . . . . C 2
Lisbon, 1,151 (1,664▲) . . . . B 3
Littleton, 4,480 (5,827▲) . . . . B 3
Manchester, 99,567 . . E 4
Marlborough, 1,184 (1,927▲) . . . . E 2
Meredith, 1,202 (4,837▲) . . . . C 3
Merrimack, 1,300 (22,156▲) . . . . E 4
Milford, 6,269 (11,795▲) . . . . E 3
Milton, 1,000 (3,691▲) D 5
Nashua, 79,662 . . . . . . E 4
New London, 1,335 (3,180▲) . . . . D 3
Newmarket, 3,749 (7,157▲) . . . . D 5
Newport, 4,388 (6,110▲) . . . . D 2
Northfield, 1,375 (4,263▲) . . . . D 3
North Hampton, 1,000 (3,637▲) . . . . E 5
Peterborough, 2,100 (5,239▲) . . . . E 3
Pittsfield, 1,584 (3,701▲) . . . . D 4
Plaistow, 1,850 (7,316▲) . . . . E 4
Plymouth, 3,628 (5,811▲) . . . . C 3
Portsmouth, 25,925 . . D 5
Raymond, 1,192 (8,713▲) . . . . D 4
Rochester, 26,630 . . D 5
Rollinsford, 1,173 (2,645▲) . . . . D 5
Rye, 835 (4,612▲) . . D 5
Salem, 12,000 (25,746▲) . . . . E 4
Somersworth, 11,249 D 5
Tilton, 1,380 (3,240▲) D 3
Troy, 1,318 (2,097▲) E 2
Whitefield, 1,005 (1,909▲) . . . . B 3
Winchester, 1,732 (4,038▲) . . . . E 2
Wolfeboro, 2,000 (4,807▲) . . . . C 4

▲ Population of entire town (township), including rural area.

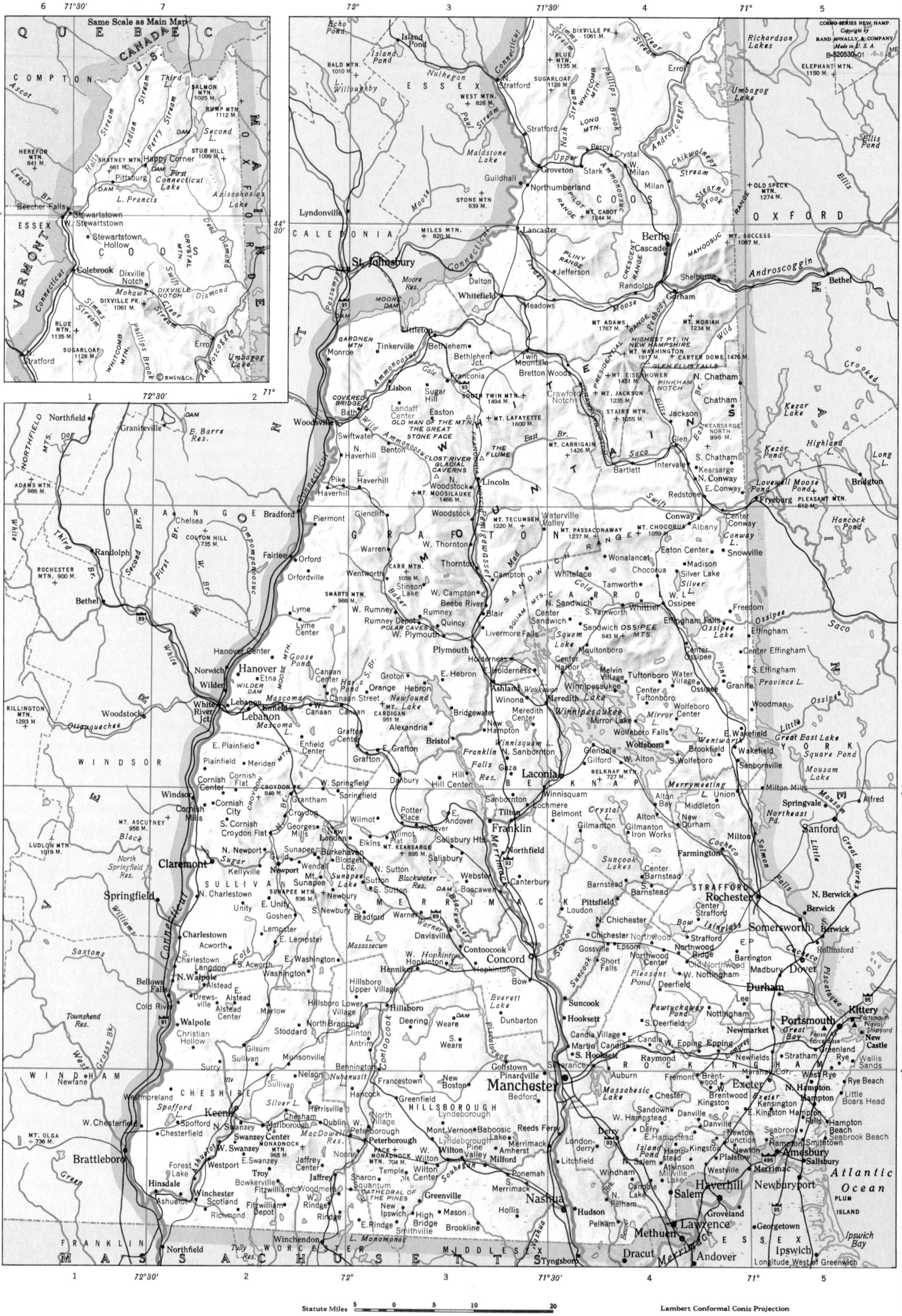

Statute Miles 5 0 5 10 20
Kilometers 5 0 5 10 15 20 25

Lambert Conformal Conic Projection

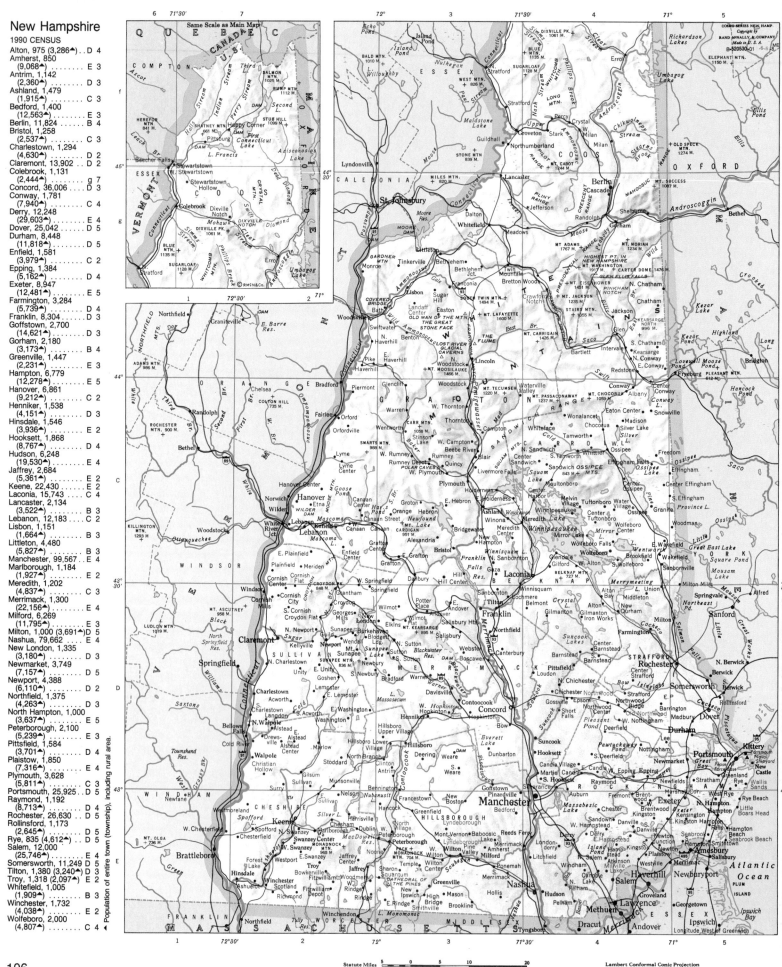

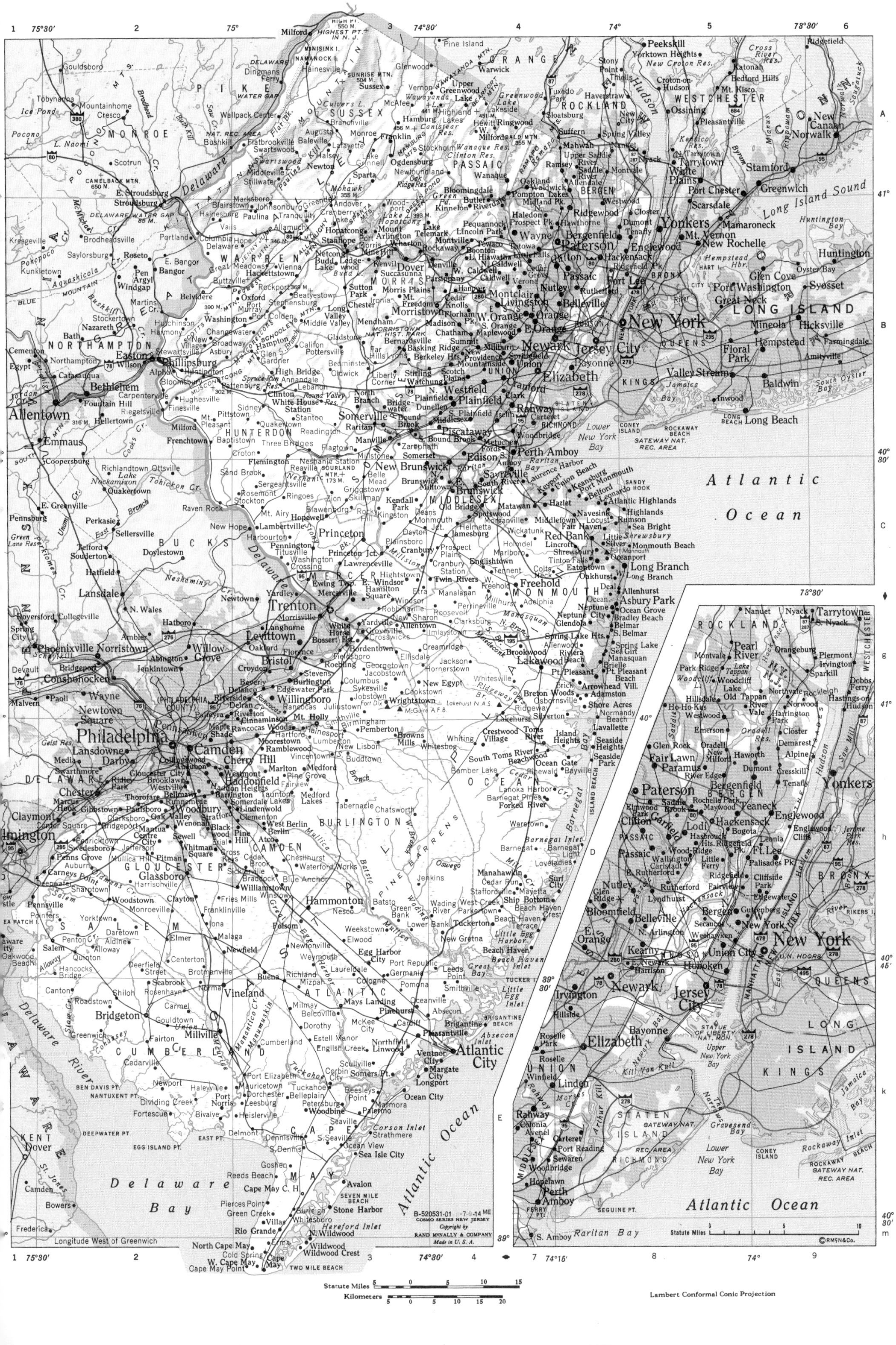

New Jersey

1990 CENSUS

Asbury Park, 16,799 C 4
Atlantic City, 37,986 E 4
Bayonne, 61,444 .... B 4
Belleville, 34,213 .... B 4
Bergenfield, 24,458 .. B 4
Bloomfield, 45,061 .. h 8
Brick [Township], 64,800('89) ...... C 4
Bridgeton, 18,942 .. E 2
Camden, 87,492 .... D 2
Cape May, 4,668 .... F 3
Carteret, 19,025 .... B 4
Cherry Hill, 69,319 .. D 2
Cliffside Park, 20,393 h 9
Clifton, 71,742 ...... B 4
Cranford, 22,624 .... B 4
Dover, 15,115 ...... B 3
East Brunswick, 43,548 .... C 4
East Orange, 73,552 B 4
Edison, 88,680 ...... B 4
Elizabeth, 110,002 .. B 4
Englewood, 24,850 .. B 5
Ewing Township, 34,185 .... C 3
Fair Lawn, 30,548 .. h 8
Fort Lee, 31,997 .... B 5
Freehold, 10,742 .... C 4
Garfield, 26,727 .... h 8
Glassboro, 15,614 .. D 2
Hackensack, 37,049 B 4
Hackettstown, 8,120 B 3
Hammonton, 12,208 D 3
Hazlet, 23,013('80) .. C 4
Hillside, 21,044 ...... k 8
Hoboken, 33,397 .... k 8
Irvington, 59,774 .... k 8
Jersey City, 228,537 B 4
Kearny, 34,874 ...... h 8
Lakewood, 26,095 .. C 4
Linden, 36,701 ...... k 8
Livingston, 26,609 .. B 4
Lodi, 22,355 .... h 8
Long Branch, 28,658 C 5
Lyndhurst, 20,326('80)h 8
Maple Shade, 20,525('80) ...... D 2
Maplewood, 21,756 .. B 4
Middletown, 21,300('85) ...... C 4
Millburn, 18,630 .... B 4
Millville, 25,992 ...... E 2
Montclair, 37,729 .... B 4
Morristown, 16,189 .. B 4
Neptune, 29,800 .... C 4
Newark, 275,221 .... B 4
New Brunswick, 41,711 .... C 4
North Bergen, 48,414 h 8
North Brunswick, 31,287 .... C 4
North Plainfield, 18,820 .... B 4
Nutley, 27,099 ...... B 4
Ocean [Township], 24,700('86) ...... C 4
Orange, 29,925 .... B 4
Paramus, 25,067 .... h 8
Passaic, 58,041 .... B 4
Paterson, 140,891 .. B 4
Pennsauken, 34,733 D 2
Pennsville, 12,467('80) ...... D 1
Perth Amboy, 41,967 B 4
Phillipsburg, 15,757 .. B 2
Piscataway, 43,800 .. B 4
Plainfield, 46,567 .... B 4
Princeton, 12,016 .. C 3
Rahway, 25,325 .... B 4
Red Bank, 10,636 .. C 4
Ridgewood, 24,152 .. B 4
Roselle, 20,314 .... k 7
Sayreville, 34,986 .. C 4
Scotch Plains, 20,774('80) ...... B 4
Somerset, 21,731('80)B 3
Somerville, 11,632 .. B 3
South Plainfield, 20,489 .... B 4
Summit, 19,757 .... B 4
Sussex, 2,201 ...... A 3
Teaneck, 37,825 .... h 8
Trenton, 88,675 .... C 3
Union City, 58,012 .. h 8
Vineland, 54,780 .... E 2
Wayne, 47,025 ...... B 4
Westfield, 28,870 .... B 4
West New York, 38,125 .... h 8
West Orange, 39,103 B 4
Willingboro, 36,291 .. C 3
Woodbine, 2,678 .... E 3
Woodbridge [Township], 95,100('86) ...... B 4

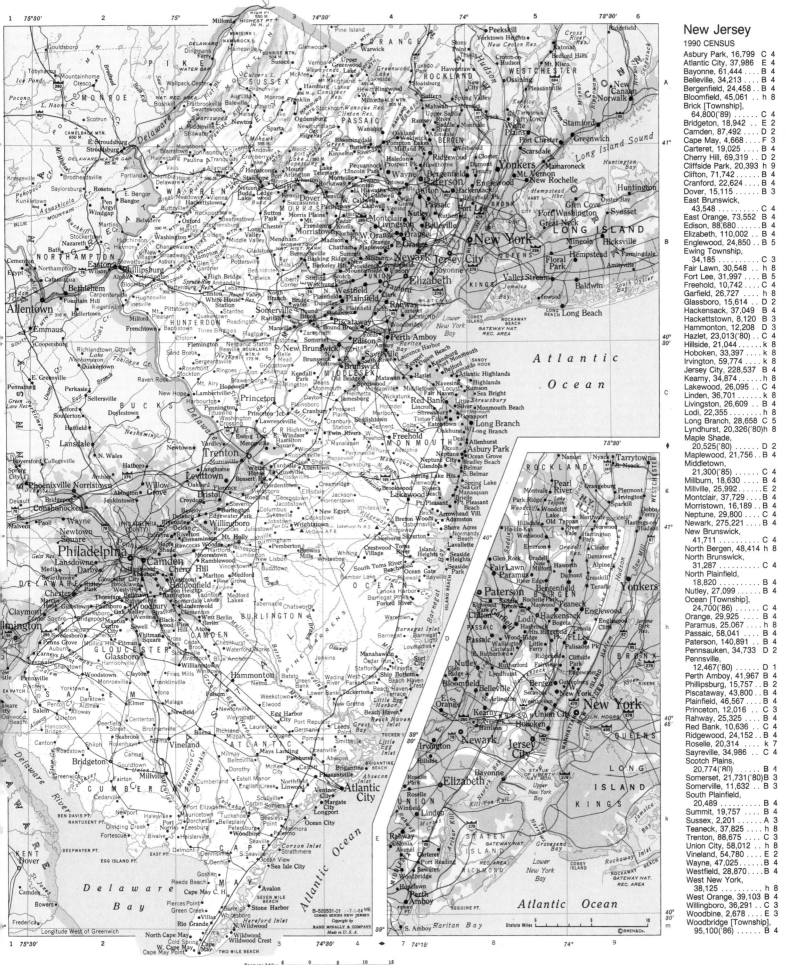

New Mexico

1990 CENSUS

Alameda, 5,900('87) B 3
Alamogordo, 27,596 E 4
Albuquerque, 384,736 B 3
Anthony, 3,285('80) . . F 3
Armijo, 14,600('87) . . k 7
Artesia, 10,610 . . . . . E 5
Aztec, 5,479 . . . . A 2
Bayard, 2,598 . . . . . . E 1
Belen, 6,547 . . . . C 3
Bernalillo, 5,960 . . . . B 3
Bloomfield, 5,214 . . . . A 2
Carlsbad, 24,952 . . . . E 5
Carrizozo, 1,075 . . . . D 4
Cedar Crest,
1,200('87) . . . . k 8
Central, 1,835 . . . . . . E 1
Chama, 1,048 . . . . A 3
Chimayo, 1,993('80) A 4
Clayton, 2,484 . . . . . . A 6
Clovis, 30,954 . . . . . . C 6
Crownpoint,
1,134('80) . . . . B 1
Deming, 10,970 . . . . E 2
Dona Ana, 950('87) . . E 3
Dulce, 1,648('80) . . . . A 2
Espanola, 8,389 . . . . B 3
Eunice, 2,676 . . . . . . E 6
Farmington, 33,997 . . A 1
Five Points,
4,200('87) . . . . B 3
Fort Sumner, 1,269 . . C 5
Fort Wingate,
950('87) . . . . B 1
Gallup, 19,154 . . . . . . B 1
Grants, 8,626 . . . . . . B 2
Hagerman, 961 . . . . D 5
Hatch, 1,136 . . . . E 2
Hobbs, 29,115 . . . . . . E 6
Hurley, 1,534 . . . . . . E 1
Isleta, 1,246('80) . . . . C 3
Jal, 2,156 . . . . E 6
Jemez Pueblo,
1,503('80) . . . . B 3
Kirtland, 2,358('80) . . A 1
La Luz, 1,194('80) . . D 4
La Mesa, 900('87) . . . E 3
Las Cruces, 62,126 . . E 3
Las Vegas, 14,753 . . B 4
Lordsburg, 2,951 . . . E 1
Los Alamos,
11,039('80) . . . . . . B 3
Los Lunas, 6,013 . . . . C 3
Los Ranchos de
Albuquerque, 3,955 B 3
Loving, 1,243 . . . . . . E 5
Lovington, 9,322 . . . . E 6
Magdalena, 861 . . . . C 2
Mescalero, 1,259('80) D 4
Mesilla, 1,975 . . . . . . E 3
Milan, 1,911 . . . . B 2
Moriarty, 1,399 . . . . . C 3
Mountainair, 926 . . . . C 3
Mountain View,
2,300('87) . . . . C 3
Paradise Hills,
5,096('80) . . . . B 3
Portales, 10,690 . . . . C 6
Questa, 1,707 . . . . . . A 4
Ranchos de Taos,
1,411('80) . . . . A 4
Raton, 7,372 . . . . . . A 5
Rio Rancho, 32,505 . . B 3
Roswell, 44,654 . . . . D 5
Ruidoso, 4,600 . . . . D 4
Ruidoso Downs, 920 D 4
San Felipe Pueblo,
1,465('80) . . . . B 3
Santa Cruz, 975('87) B 3
Santa Fe, 55,859 . . . . B 4
Santa Rosa, 2,263 . . C 5
Santo Domingo Pueblo,
2,082('80) . . . . B 3
Shiprock, 7,237('80) A 1
Silver City, 10,683 . . E 1
Socorro, 8,159 . . . . . C 3
Springer, 1,262 . . . . . A 5
Sunland Park, 8,179 F 3
Taos, 4,065 . . . . A 4
Taos Pueblo,
1,030('87) . . . . A 4
Tesuque, 1,014('80) B 4
Texico, 966 . . . . C 6
Thoreau, 1,099('80) . . B 1
Tierra Amarilla,
900('87) . . . . A 3
Tohatchi, 1,011('80) . . B 1
Truth or Consequences
(Hot Springs), 6,221 D 2
Tucumcari, 6,831 . . . . B 6
Tularosa, 2,615 . . . . D 3
Tyrone, 950('87) . . . . E 1
University Park,
4,353('80) . . . . E 3
Zuni, 5,551('80) . . . . B 1

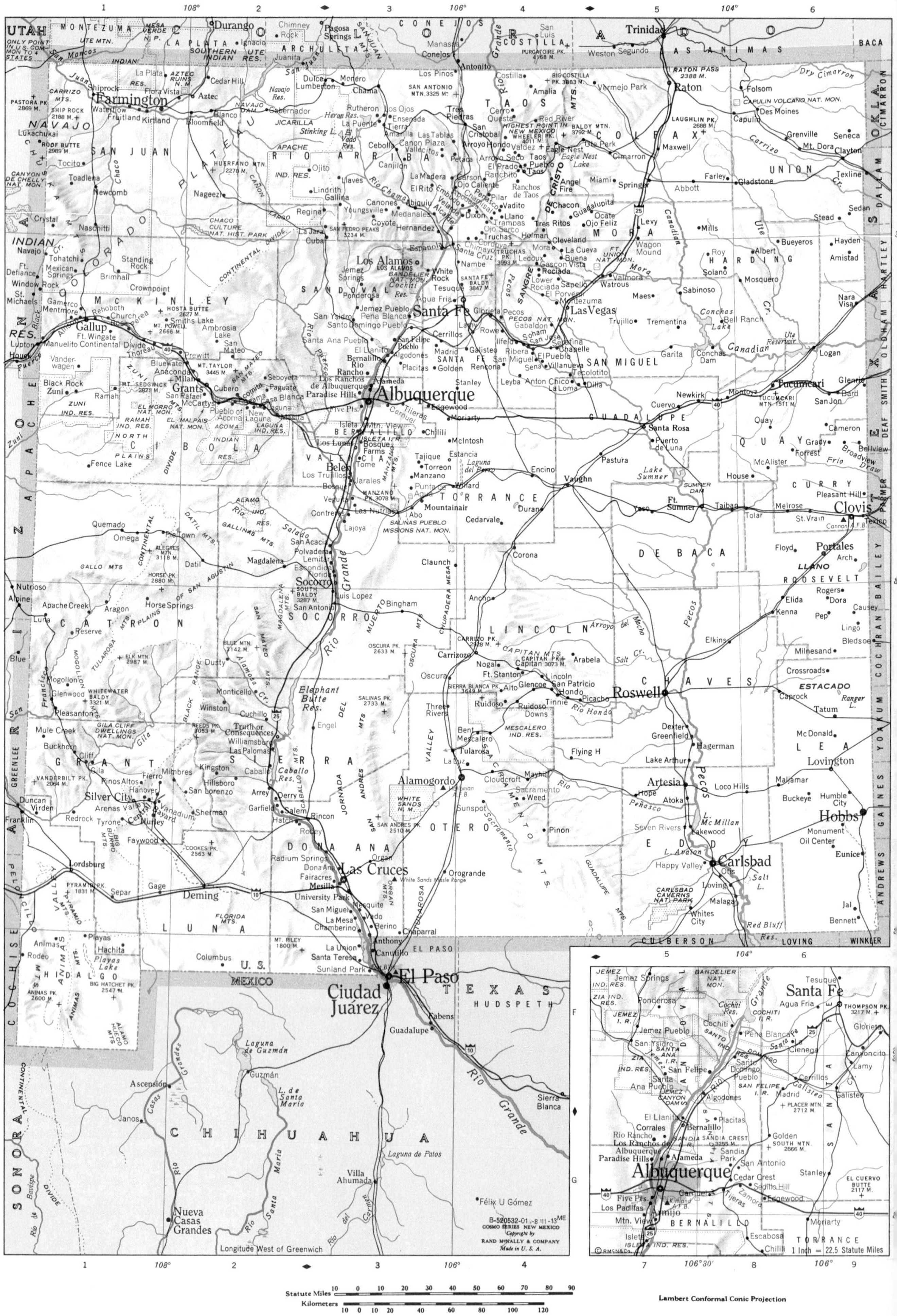

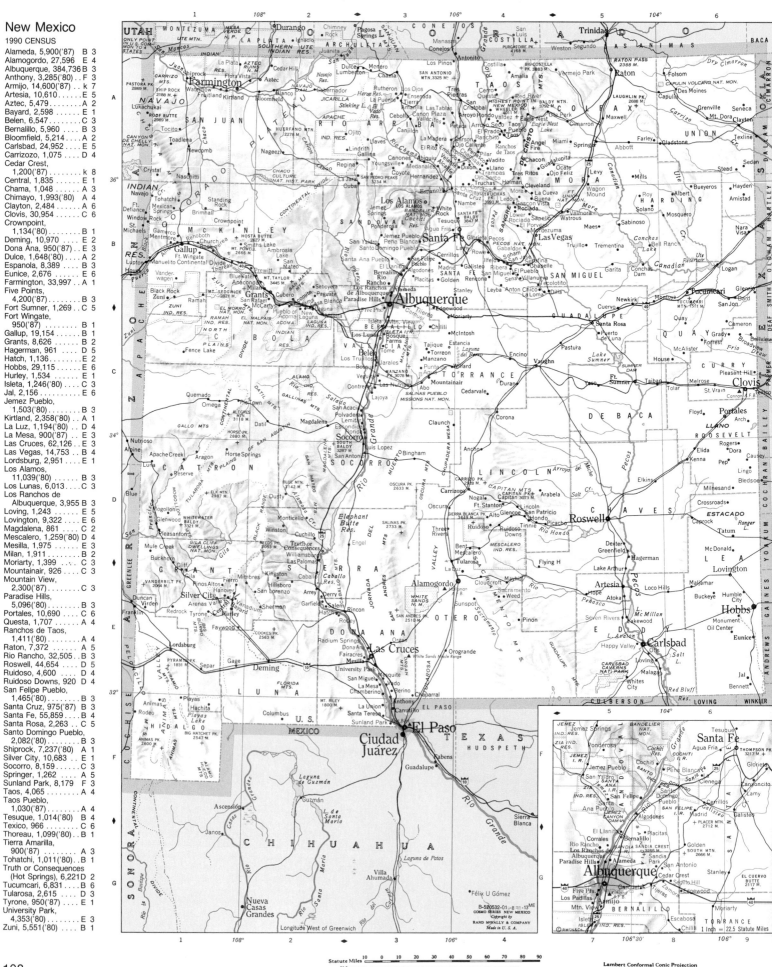

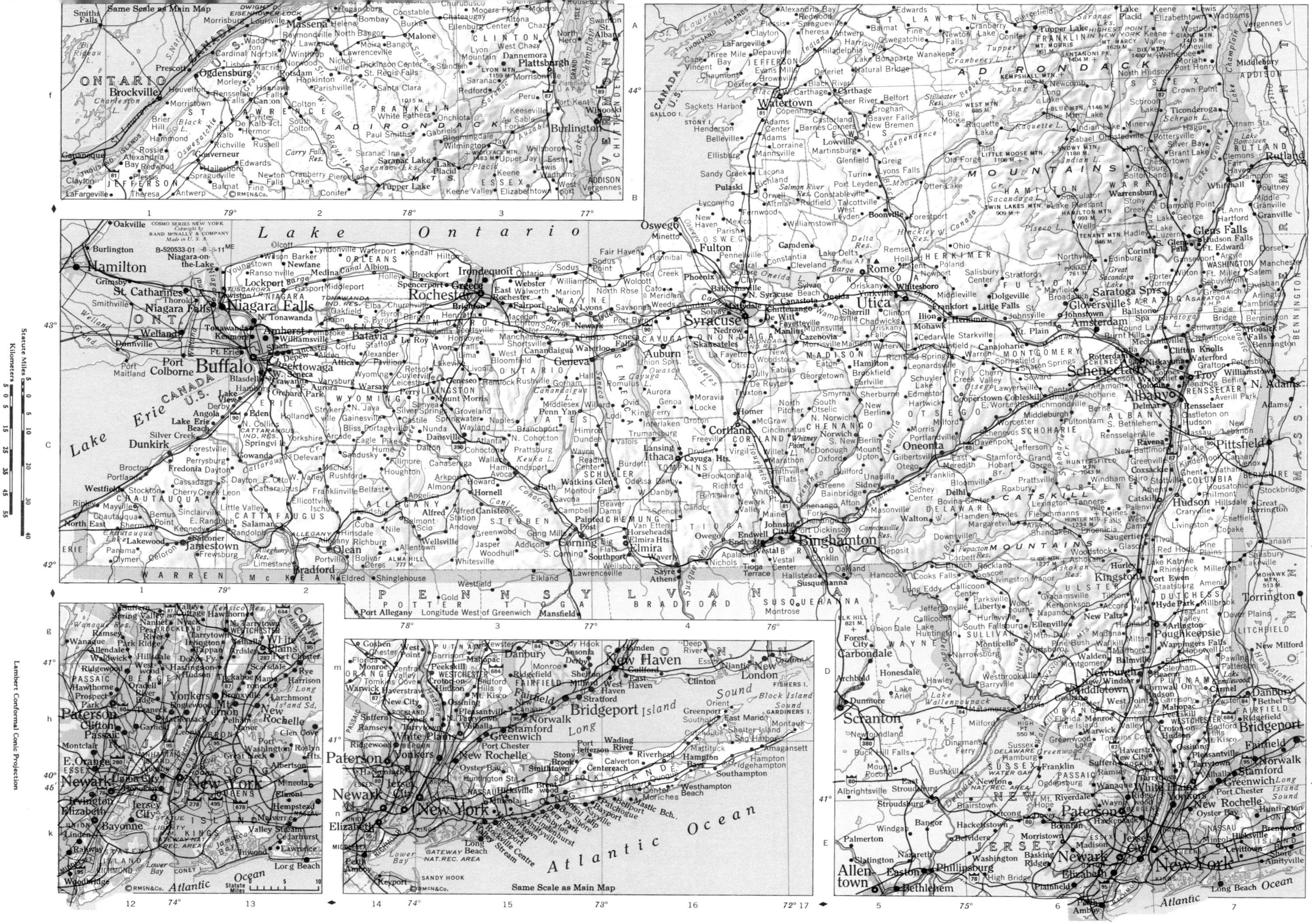

New York

1990 CENSUS

Albany, 101,082 . . . . . . C 7
Amherst, 45,600 . . . . . . C 2
Amityville, 9,286 . . . . . . E 7
Amsterdam, 20,714 . . . . C 6
Auburn, 31,258 . . . . C 4
Batavia, 16,310 . . . . . . C 2
Bay Shore, 33,000 . . . . . E 7
Binghamton, 53,008 . . . . C 5
Brentwood, 45,218 . . . . E 7
Brighton, 34,455 . . . . . . B 3
Buffalo, 328,123 . . . . . . C 2
Centereach, 26,720 . . . . n15
Central Islip, 42,600 . . . . n15
Cheektowaga, 84,387 . . C 2
Cooperstown, 2,180 . . . . C 6
Corning, 11,933 . . . . . . C 3
Cortland, 19,801 . . . . . . C 4
Deer Park, 28,840 . . . . . n15
Depew, 17,673 . . . . . . C 2
Dunkirk, 13,989 . . . . . . C 1
Elmira, 33,724 . . . . C 4
Elmont, 28,612 . . . . k13
Freeport, 39,894 . . . . . . n15
Fulton, 12,929 . . . . B 4
Gates, 30,000 . . . . B 3
Geneva, 14,143 . . . . C 4
Glen Cove, 24,149 . . . . . h13
Glens Falls, 15,023 . . . . B 7
Gloversville, 16,656 . . . . B 6
Greece, 64,600 . . . . B 3
Harrison, 23,308 . . . . . . h13
Hempstead, 49,453 . . . . n15
Hicksville, 40,174 . . . . . . E 7
Hyde Park, 2,550('80) . . D 7
Irondequoit, 52,322 . . . . B 3
Ithaca, 29,541 . . . . C 4
Jamestown, 34,681 . . . . C 1
Kenmore, 17,180 . . . . . . C 2
Kingston, 23,095 . . . . . . D 6
Lackawanna, 20,585 . . . C 2
Lake Placid, 2,485 . . . . A 7
Levittown, 53,286 . . . . E 7
Lindenhurst, 26,879 . . . . n15
Lockport, 24,426 . . . . . . B 2
Long Beach, 33,510 . . . E 7
Massena, 11,719 . . . . . . f10
Middletown, 24,160 . . . . D 6
Mineola, 18,994 . . . . . . E 7
Mount Vernon, 67,153 . . h13
Newburgh, 26,454 . . . . . D 6
New City, 33,673 . . . . . D 6
New Rochelle, 67,265 . . E 7
New York, 7,322,564 . . E 7
Niagara Falls, 61,840 . . B 1
North Tonawanda,
34,989 . . . . B 2
Ogdensburg, 13,521 . . . . f 9
Olean, 16,946 . . . . C 2
Oneonta, 13,954 . . . . . . C 5
Ossining, 22,582 . . . . . . D 7
Oswego, 19,195 . . . . . . B 4
Palmyra, 3,566 . . . . B 3
Peekskill, 19,536 . . . . . D 7
Plattsburgh, 21,255 . . . . f11
Port Chester, 24,728 . . E 7
Poughkeepsie, 28,844 D 7
Rochester, 231,636 . . . B 3
Rockville Centre, 24,727 n15
Rome, 44,350 . . . . B 5
Rotterdam, 21,228 . . . . C 6
Saratoga Springs,
25,001 . . . . B 7
Schenectady, 65,566 . . C 7
Spring Valley, 21,802 . . g12
Syracuse, 163,860 . . . . B 4
Ticonderoga, 2,770 . . . . B 7
Tonawanda, 17,284 . . . . B 2
Troy, 54,269 . . . . C 7
Utica, 68,637 . . . . B 5
Valley Stream, 33,946 . . n15
Watertown, 29,429 . . . . B 5
West Point, 8,105('80) D 7
West Seneca, 47,866 . . C 2
White Plains, 48,718 . . D 7
Yonkers, 188,082 . . . . E 7

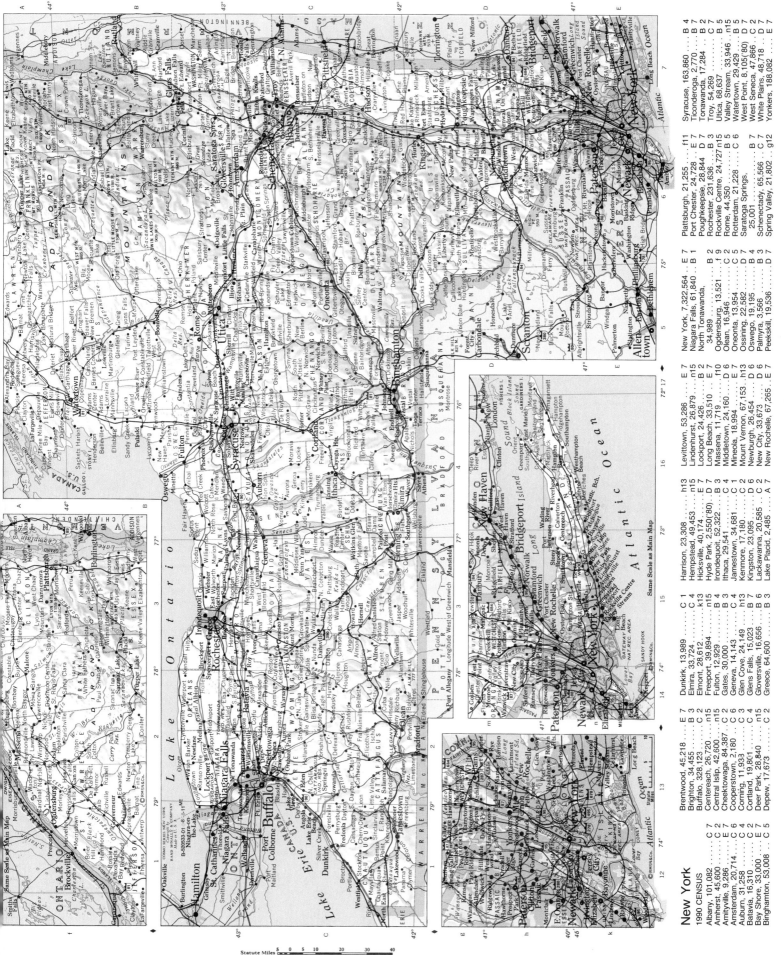

North Carolina

1990 CENSUS

Ahoskie, 4,391	A 6
Albemarle, 14,939	B 2
Archdale, 6,913	B 3
Asheboro, 16,362	B 3
Asheville, 61,607	f10
Bessemer City, 4,698	B 1
Boone, 12,915	A 1
Brevard, 5,388	f10
Burlington, 39,498	A 3
Carrboro, 11,553	B 3
Cary, 43,858	B 4
Chapel Hill, 38,719	B 3
Charlotte, 395,934	B 2
Cherryville, 4,756	B 1
Clemmons, 6,020	A 2
Clinton, 8,204	C 4
Concord, 27,347	B 2
Dunn, 8,336	B 4
Durham, 136,611	B 4
Eden, 15,238	A 3
Edenton, 5,268	A 6
Elizabeth City, 14,292	A 6
Farmville, 4,392	B 5
Fayetteville, 75,695	B 4
Forest City, 7,475	B 1
Garner, 14,967	B 4
Gastonia, 54,732	B 1
Goldsboro, 40,709	B 5
Graham, 10,426	A 3
Greensboro, 183,521	A 3
Greenville, 44,972	B 5
Hamlet, 6,196	C 3
Havelock, 20,268	C 6
Henderson, 15,655	A 4
Hendersonville, 7,284	f10
Hickory, 28,301	B 1
High Point, 69,496	B 2
Hope Mills, 8,184	C 4
Jacksonville, 30,013	C 5
Kannapolis, 29,696	B 2
Kernersville, 10,836	A 2
Kings Mountain, 8,763	B 1
Kinston, 25,295	B 5
Laurinburg, 11,643	C 3
Lenoir, 14,192	B 1
Lexington, 16,581	B 2
Lincolnton, 6,847	B 1
Lumberton, 18,601	C 3
Matthews, 13,651	B 2
Mint Hill, 11,567	B 2
Monroe, 16,127	C 2
Mooresville, 9,317	B 2
Morehead City, 6,046	C 6
Morganton, 15,085	B 1
Mount Airy, 7,156	A 2
Mount Olive, 4,582	B 4
Nags Head, 1,838	B 7
New Bern, 17,363	B 5
Newton, 9,304	B 1
Oxford, 7,913	A 4
Plymouth, 4,328	B 6
Raleigh, 207,951	B 4
Reidsville, 12,183	A 3
Roanoke Rapids, 15,722	A 5
Rockingham, 9,399	C 3
Rocky Mount, 48,997	B 5
Roxboro, 7,332	A 4
Salisbury, 23,087	B 2
Sanford, 14,475	B 3
Selma, 4,600	B 4
Shelby, 14,669	B 1
Smithfield, 7,540	B 4
Southern Pines, 9,129	B 3
Spring Lake, 7,524	B 4
Statesville, 17,567	B 2
Tarboro, 11,037	B 5
Thomasville, 15,915	B 2
Washington, 9,075	B 5
Waynesville, 6,758	f10
Whiteville, 5,078	C 4
Williamston, 5,503	B 5
Wilmington, 55,530	C 5
Wilson, 36,930	B 5
Winston-Salem, 143,485	A 2

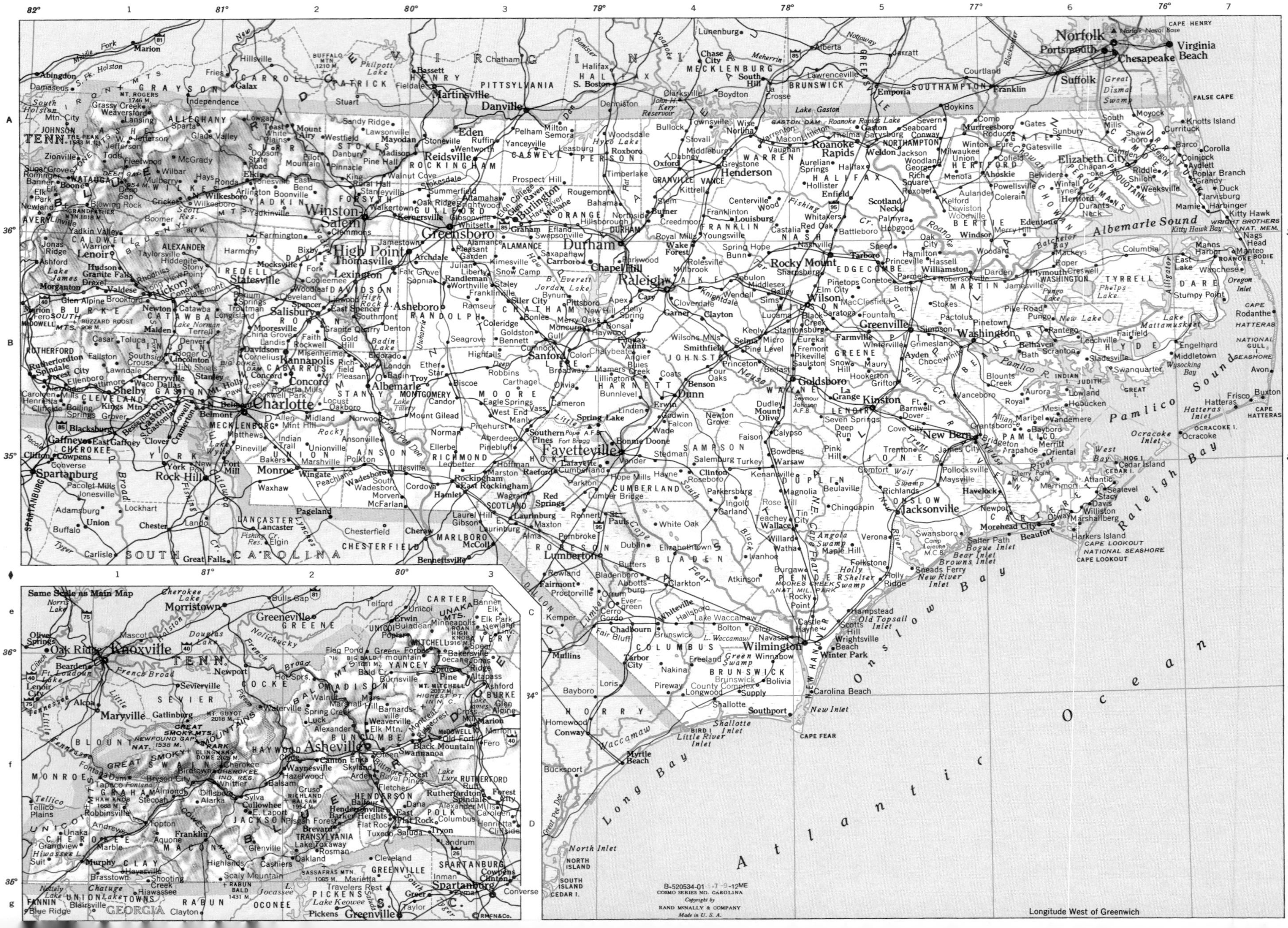

Statute Miles 5 0 5 10 20 30 40

Kilometers 5 0 5 15 25 35 45 55

Lambert Conformal Conic Projection

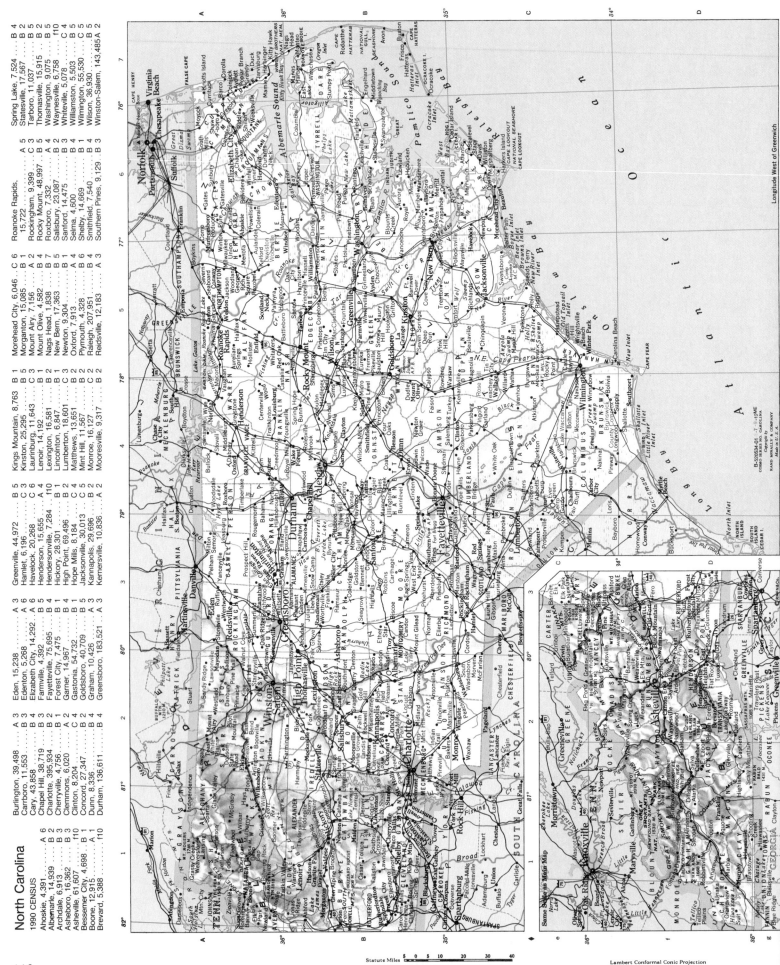

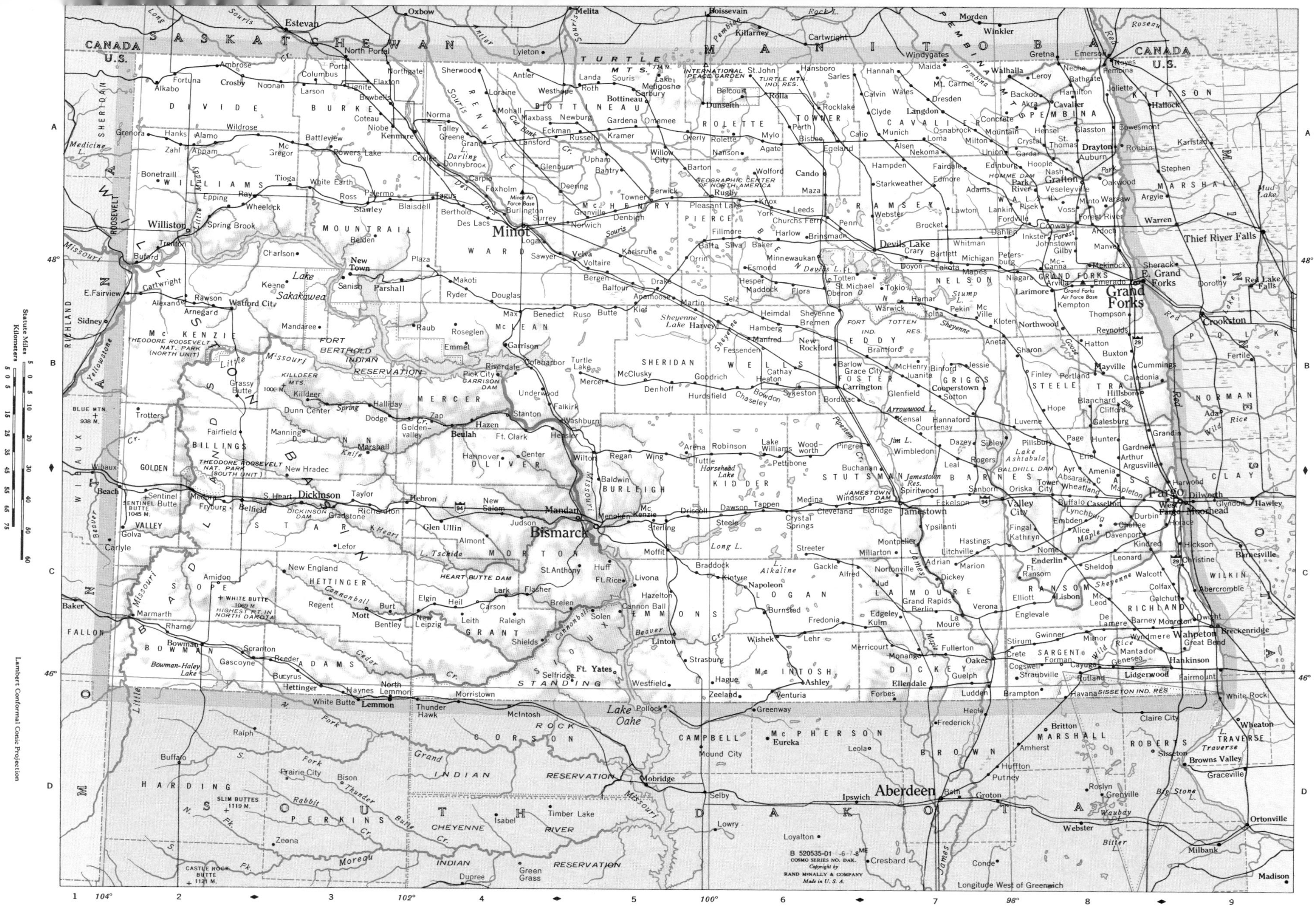

North Dakota

1990 CENSUS

- Ashley, 1,052 .... C 6
- Beach, 1,205 .... C 1
- Belfield, 887 .... C 2
- Beulah, 3,363 .... B 4
- Bismarck, 49,256 .... C 5
- Bottineau, 2,598 ...... A 5
- Bowman, 1,741 .... C 2
- Burlington, 995 .... A 4
- Cando, 1,564 .... A 6
- Carrington, 2,267 .... B 6
- Casselton, 1,601 ...... C 8
- Cavalier, 1,508 .... A 8
- Center, 826 .... B 4
- Cooperstown, 1,247 .. B 7
- Crosby, 1,312 .... A 2
- Devils Lake, 7,782 .... A 7
- Dickinson, 16,097 .... C 3
- Drayton, 961 .... A 8
- Dunseith, 723 .... A 5
- Edgeley, 680 .... C 7
- Elgin, 765 .... C 4
- Ellendale, 1,798 ...... C 7
- Enderlin, 997 .... C 8
- Fargo, 74,111 .... C 9
- Fessenden, 655 ...... B 6
- Garrison, 1,530 .... B 4
- Glen Ullin, 927 .... C 4
- Grafton, 4,840 .... A 8
- Grand Forks, 49,425 .. B 8
- Gwinner, 585 .... C 8
- Hankinson, 1,038 .... C 9
- Harvey, 2,263 .... B 6
- Hatton, 800 .... B 8
- Hazen, 2,818 .... B 4
- Hebron, 888 .... C 3
- Hettinger, 1,574 ...... D 3
- Hillsboro, 1,488 .... B 8
- Jamestown, 15,571 ... C 7
- Kenmare, 1,214 .... A 3
- Killdeer, 722 .... B 3
- Lakota, 898 .... A 7
- La Moure, 970 .... C 7
- Langdon, 2,241 .... A 7
- Larimore, 1,464 ...... B 8
- Lidgerwood, 799 ...... C 8
- Linton, 1,410 .... C 5
- Lisbon, 2,177 .... C 8
- Mandan, 15,177 .... C 5
- Mayville, 2,092 .... B 8
- Milnor, 651 .... C 8
- Minot, 34,544 .... A 4
- Mohall, 931 .... A 4
- Mott, 1,019 .... C 3
- Napoleon, 930 .... C 6
- New England, 663 .... C 3
- New Rockford, 1,604 .. B 6
- New Salem, 909 ...... C 4
- New Town, 1,388 .... B 3
- Northwood, 1,166 .... B 8
- Oakes, 1,775 .... C 7
- Park River, 1,725 .... A 8
- Parshall, 943 .... B 3
- Ray, 603 .... A 2
- Richardton, 625 ...... C 3
- Rolla, 1,286 .... A 6
- Rugby, 2,909 .... A 6
- Stanley, 1,371 .... A 3
- Steele, 762 .... C 6
- Surrey, 856 .... A 4
- Thompson, 930 .... B 8
- Tioga, 1,278 .... A 3
- Towner, 669 .... A 5
- Turtle Lake, 681 ...... B 5
- Underwood, 976 ...... B 4
- Valley City, 7,163 .... C 8
- Velva, 968 .... A 5
- Wahpeton, 8,751 ..... C 9
- Walhalla, 1,131 ...... A 8
- Washburn, 1,506 ...... B 5
- Watford City, 1,784 ... B 2
- West Fargo, 12,287 ... C 9
- Westhope, 578 .... A 4
- Williston, 13,131 ...... A 2
- Wilton, 728 .... B 5
- Wishek, 1,171 .... C 6

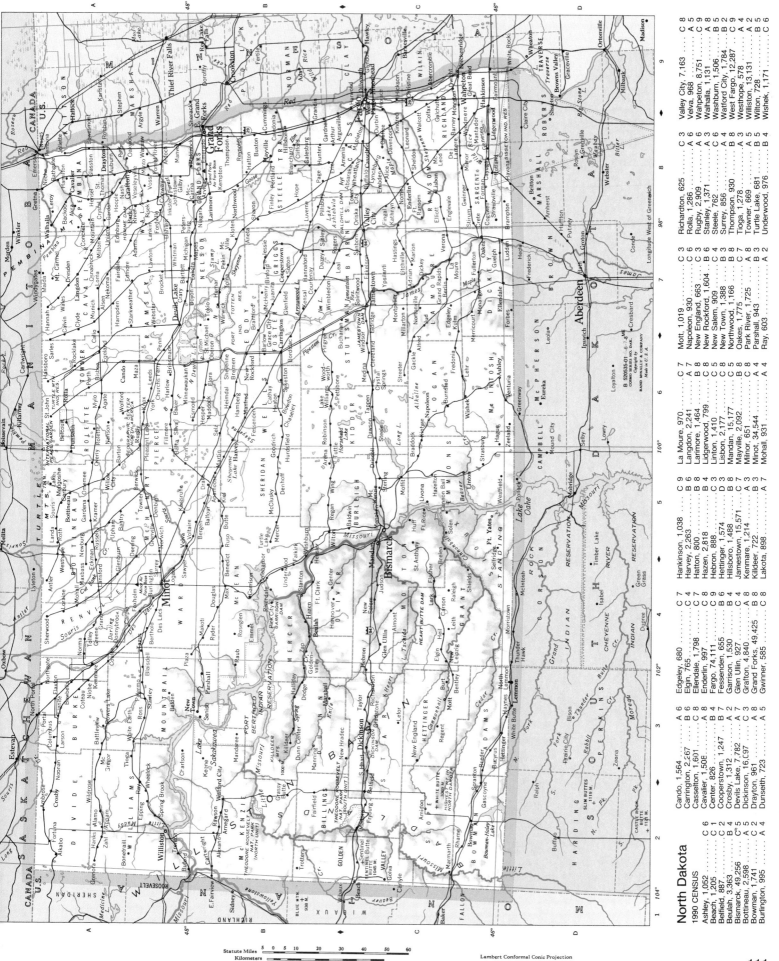

Ohio

1990 CENSUS

Akron, 223,019 . . . . . . A 4
Alliance, 23,376 . . . . . . B 4
Ashland, 20,079 . . . . . . B 3
Ashtabula, 21,633 . . . . . A 5
Athens, 21,265 . . . . . . C 3
Austintown, 23,300 . . . . A 5
Barberton, 27,623 . . . . A 4
Beavercreek, 33,626 . . C 1
Bellefontaine, 12,142 . . B 2
Boardman, 38,596 . . . . A 5
Bowling Green, 28,176 A 2
Brook Park, 22,865 . . . . h 9
Brunswick, 28,230 . . . . A 4
Canton, 84,161 . . . . . . B 4
Chillicothe, 21,923 . . . . C 3
Cincinnati, 364,040 . . . . C 1
Cleveland, 505,616 . . . . A 4
Cleveland Heights, 54,052 . . . . A 4
Columbus, 632,910 . . . . C 2
Cuyahoga Falls, 48,950 A 4
Dayton, 182,044 . . . . . . C 1
Defiance, 16,768 . . . . . . A 1
Delaware, 20,030 . . . . B 2
East Cleveland, 33,096 g 9
Eastlake, 21,161 . . . . . . A 4
East Liverpool, 13,654 B 5
Elyria, 56,746 . . . . A 3
Euclid, 54,875 . . . . A 4
Fairborn, 31,300 . . . . . . C 1
Fairfield, 39,729 . . . . . . n12
Findlay, 35,703 . . . . . . A 2
Fostoria, 14,983 . . . . . . A 2
Fremont, 17,648 . . . . . . A 2
Garfield Heights, 31,739 h 9
Greenville, 12,863 . . . . B 1
Hamilton, 61,368 . . . . . . C 1
Ironton, 12,751 . . . . . . D 3
Kent, 28,835 . . . . A 4
Kettering, 60,569 . . . . . C 1
Lakewood, 59,718 . . . . A 4
Lancaster, 34,507 . . . . C 3
Lima, 45,549 . . . . B 1
Lorain, 71,245 . . . . A 3
Mansfield, 50,627 . . . . . B 3
Maple Heights, 27,089 . . h 9
Marietta, 15,026 . . . . . . C 4
Marion, 34,075 . . . . . . B 2
Massillon, 31,007 . . . . B 4
Medina, 19,231 . . . . . . A 4
Mentor, 47,358 . . . . . . A 4
Middletown, 46,022 . . . . C 1
Mount Vernon, 14,550 B 3
Newark, 44,389 . . . . . . B 3
New Philadelphia, 15,698 . . . . B 4
Niles, 21,128 . . . . A 5
North Olmsted, 34,204 h 9
Norwalk, 14,731 . . . . . . A 3
Norwood, 23,674 . . . . . . o13
Oxford, 18,937 . . . . C 1
Parma, 87,876 . . . . A 4
Parma Heights, 21,448 h 9
Piqua, 20,612 . . . . B 1
Portsmouth, 22,676 . . D 3
Reynoldsburg, 25,748 . . C 3
Salem, 12,233 . . . . B 5
Sandusky, 29,764 . . . . A 3
Shaker Heights, 30,831 A 4
South Euclid, 23,866 . . g 9
Springfield, 70,487 . . . . C 2
Steubenville, 22,125 . . B 5
Stow, 27,702 . . . . A 4
Strongsville, 35,308 . . . . A 4
Tiffin, 18,604 . . . . A 2
Toledo, 332,943 . . . . . . A 2
Upper Arlington, 34,128 B 2
Urbana, 11,353 . . . . . . B 2
Warren, 50,793 . . . . . . A 5
Westerville, 30,269 . . . . B 3
Whitehall, 20,572 . . . . m11
Wooster, 22,191 . . . . . . B 4
Xenia, 24,664 . . . . C 2
Youngstown, 95,732 . . A 5
Zanesville, 26,778 . . . . C 4

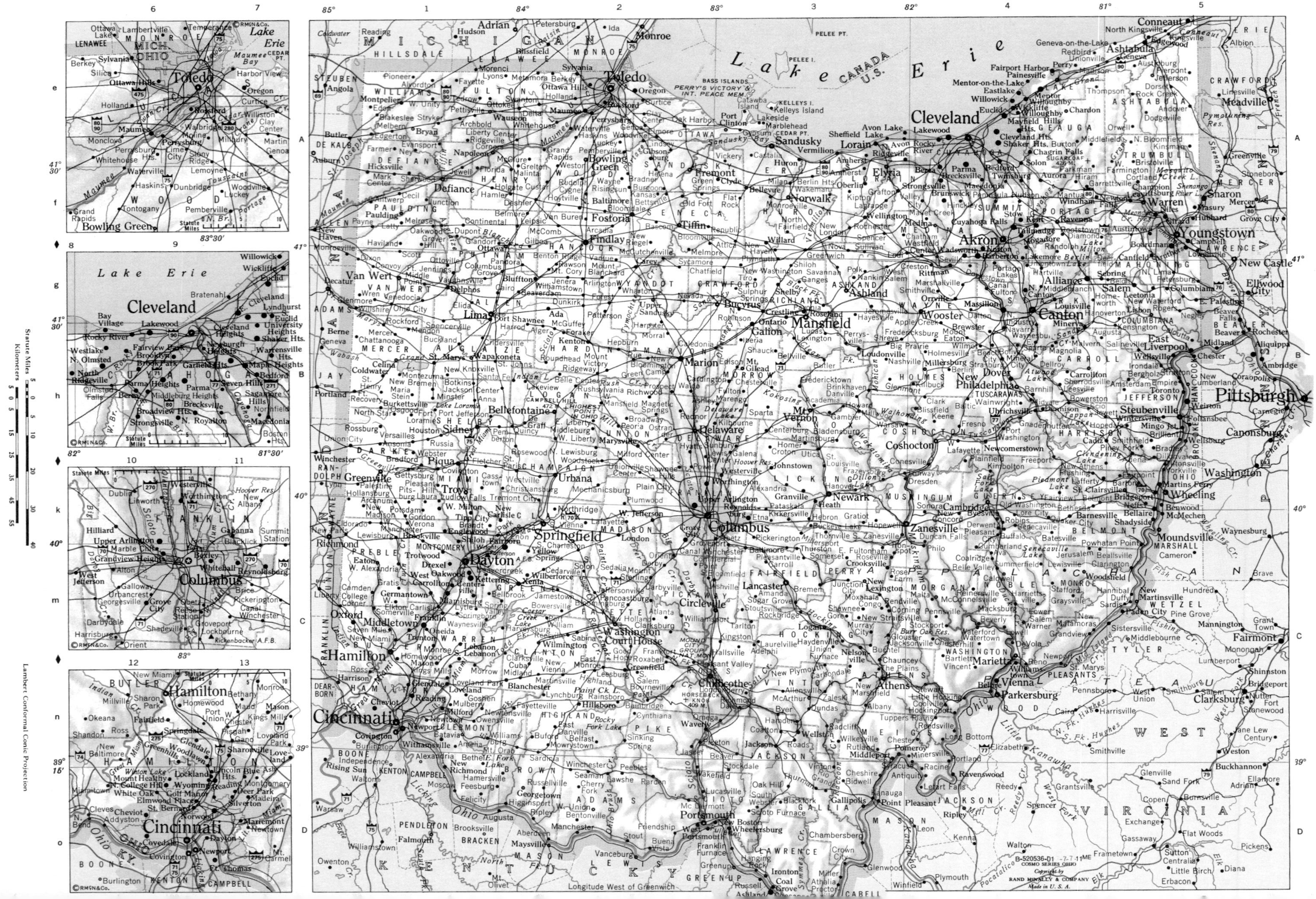

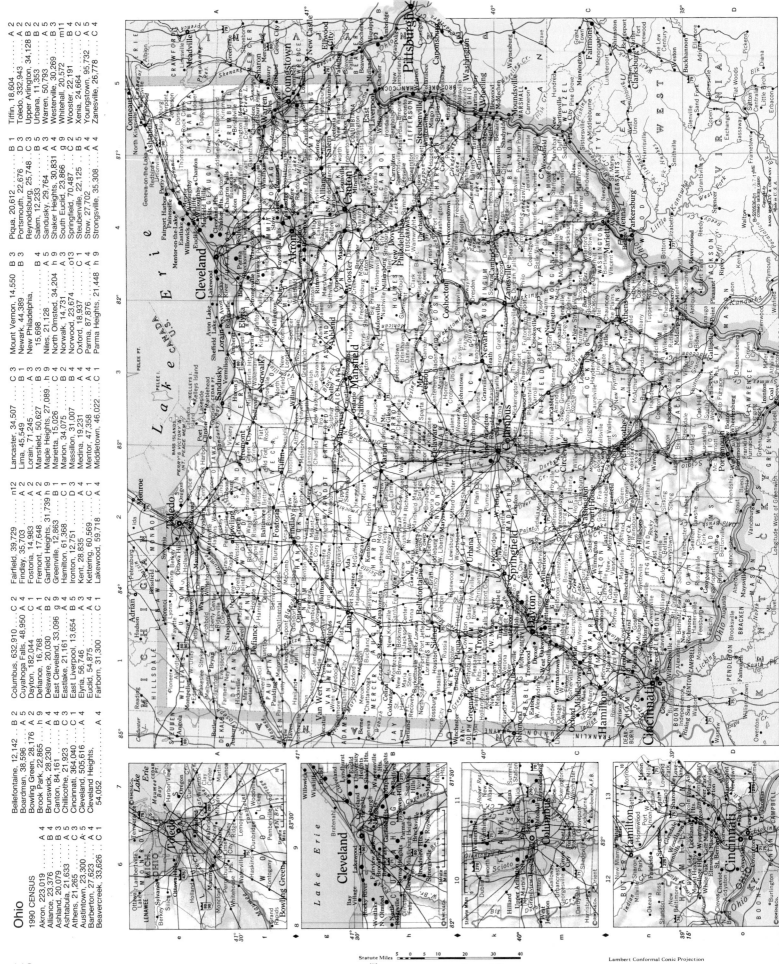

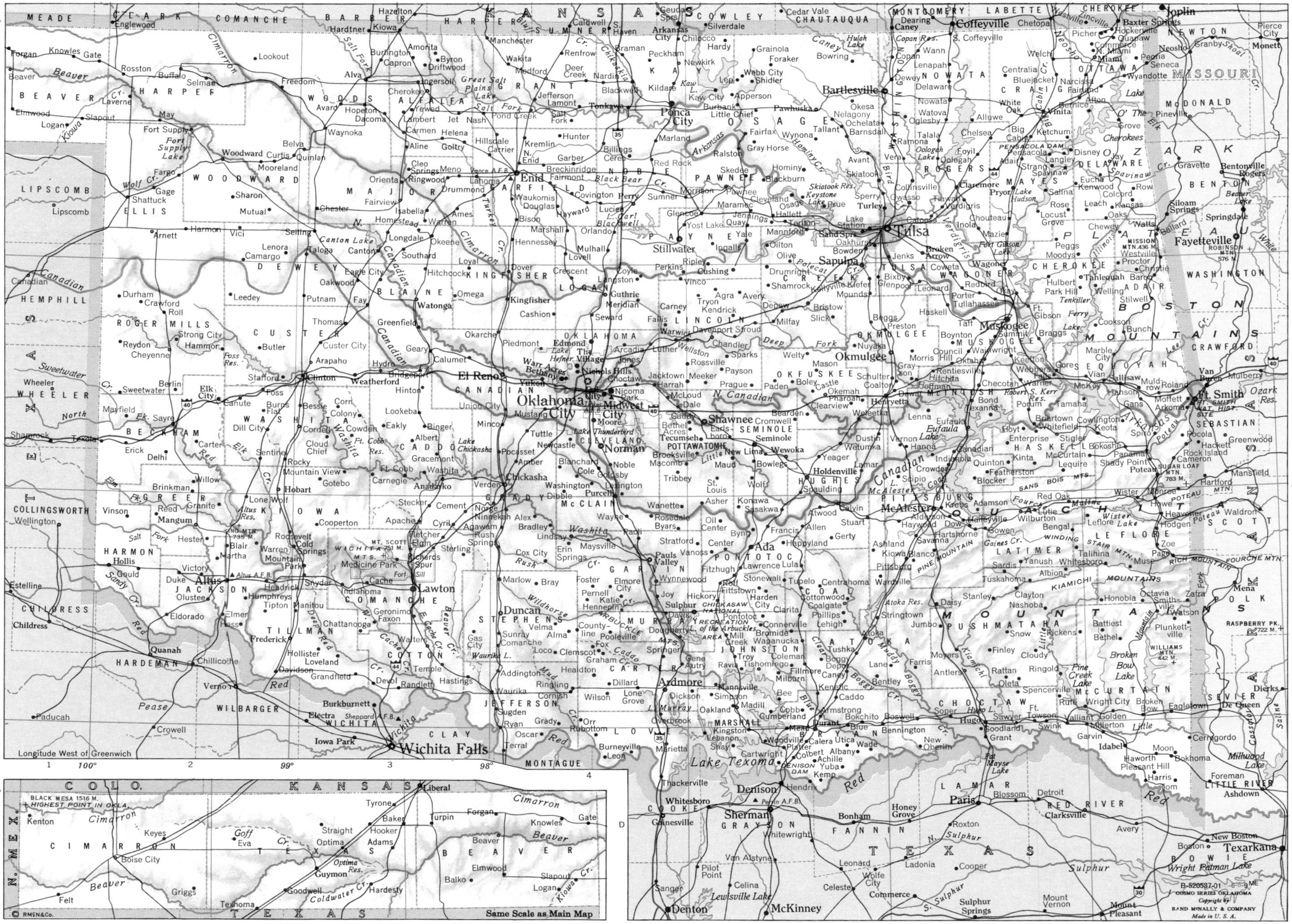

Statute Miles 5 0 5 10 20 30 40

Kilometers 5 0 5 15 25 35 45 55

Lambert Conformal Conic Projection

Oklahoma

1990 CENSUS

Ada, 15,820	C	5
Altus, 21,910	C	2
Alva, 5,495	A	3
Anadarko, 6,586	B	3
Ardmore, 23,079	C	4
Atoka, 3,298	C	5
Bartlesville, 34,256	A	6
Bethany, 20,075	B	4
Bixby, 9,502	B	6
Blackwell, 7,538	A	4
Bristow, 4,062	B	5
Broken Arrow, 58,043	A	6
Broken Bow, 3,961	C	7
Checotah, 3,290	B	6
Chickasha, 14,988	B	4
Choctaw, 8,545	B	4
Claremore, 13,280	A	6
Clinton, 9,298	B	3
Collinsville, 3,612	A	6
Coweta, 6,159	B	6
Cushing, 7,218	B	5
Del City, 23,928	B	4
Dewey, 3,326	A	6
Duncan, 21,732	C	4
Durant, 12,823	D	5
Edmond, 52,315	B	4
Elk City, 10,428	B	2
El Reno, 15,414	B	4
Enid, 45,309	A	4
Frederick, 5,221	C	2
Guthrie, 10,518	B	4
Guymon, 7,803	e	9
Harrah, 4,206	B	4
Henryetta, 5,872	B	6
Hobart, 4,305	B	2
Holdenville, 4,792	B	5
Hugo, 5,978	C	6
Idabel, 6,957	D	7
Jenks, 7,493	A	6
Kingfisher, 4,095	B	4
Lawton, 80,561	C	3
Lindsay, 2,947	C	4
Madill, 3,069	C	5
Mangum, 3,344	C	2
Marlow, 4,416	C	4
McAlester, 16,370	C	6
McLoud, 2,493	B	4
Miami, 13,142	A	7
Midwest City, 52,267	B	4
Moore, 40,318	B	4
Muskogee, 37,708	B	6
Mustang, 10,434	B	4
Nichols Hills, 4,020	B	4
Noble, 4,710	B	4
Norman, 80,071	B	4
Nowata, 3,896	A	6
Oklahoma City, 444,719	B	4
Okmulgee, 13,441	B	6
Owasso, 11,151	A	6
Pauls Valley, 6,150	C	4
Perry, 4,978	A	4
Ponca City, 26,359	A	4
Poteau, 7,210	B	7
Pryor, 8,327	A	6
Purcell, 4,784	B	4
Sallisaw, 7,122	B	7
Sand Springs, 15,346	A	5
Sapulpa, 18,074	B	5
Seminole, 7,071	B	5
Shawnee, 26,017	B	5
Skiatook, 4,910	A	5
Stillwater, 36,676	A	4
Sulphur, 4,824	C	5
Tahlequah, 10,398	B	7
Tecumseh, 5,750	B	5
The Village, 10,353	B	4
Tonkawa, 3,127	A	4
Tulsa, 367,302	A	6
Vinita, 5,804	A	6
Wagoner, 6,894	B	6
Warr Acres, 9,288	B	4
Weatherford, 10,124	B	3
Wewoka, 4,050	B	5
Woodward, 12,340	A	2
Yukon, 20,935	B	4

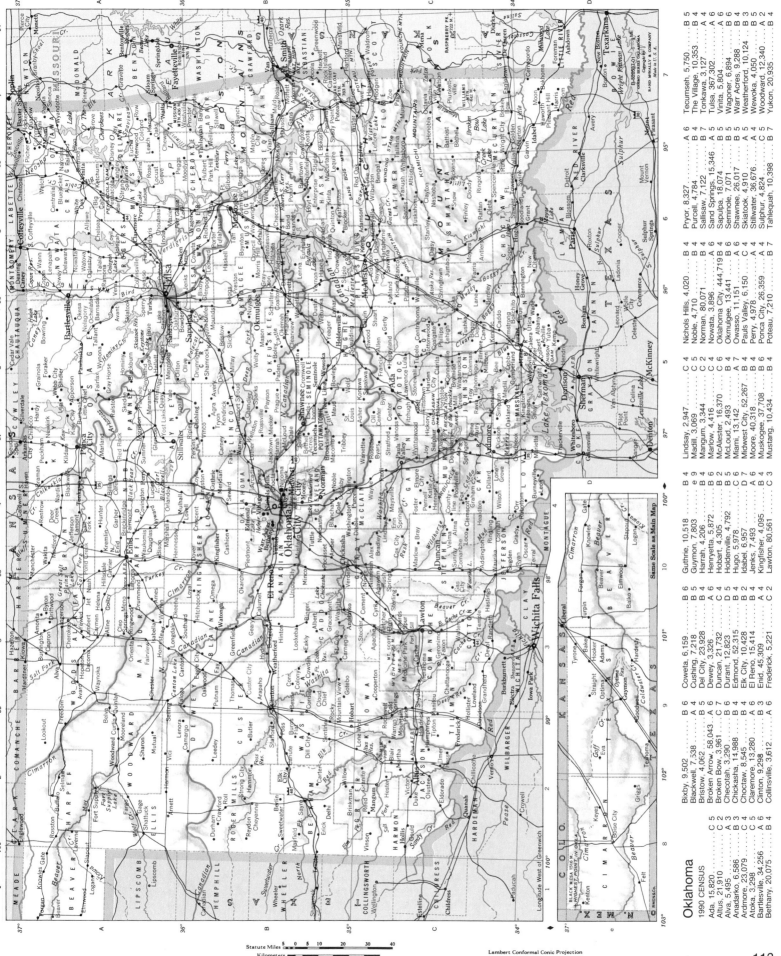

Oregon

1990 CENSUS

- Albany, 29,462 . . . . . . C 3
- Aloha, 10,000('82) h12
- Altamont, 19,805('80) . . E 5
- Ashland, 16,234 . . . . . . E 4
- Astoria, 10,069 . . . . . . A 3
- Baker, 9,140 . . . . C 9
- Beaverton, 53,310 . . . . B 4
- Bend, 20,469 . . . . C 5
- Brookings, 4,400 . . . . . . E 2
- Burns, 2,913 . . . . D 7
- Canby, 8,983 . . . . B 4
- Central Point, 7,509 . . . E 4
- Coos Bay, 15,076 . . . . D 2
- Coquille, 4,121 . . . . D 2
- Cornelius, 6,148 . . . . . . g11
- Corvallis, 44,757 . . . . . . C 3
- Cottage Grove, 7,402 . . D 3
- Dallas, 9,422 . . . . C 3
- Eugene, 112,669 . . . . . . C 3
- Florence, 5,162 . . . . . . D 2
- Forest Grove, 13,559 . . B 3
- Gladstone, 10,152 . . . . . B 4
- Grants Pass, 17,488 . . . E 3
- Green, 3,897('80) . . . . D 3
- Gresham, 68,235 . . . . . B 4
- Hermiston, 10,040 . . . . B 7
- Hillsboro, 37,520 . . . . . B 4
- Hood River, 4,632 . . . . B 5
- Independence, 4,425 . . C 3
- John Day, 1,836 . . . . . . C 8
- Junction City, 3,670 . . . C 3
- Keizer, 21,884 . . . . C 3
- Klamath Falls, 17,737 . . E 5
- La Grande, 11,766 . . . . B 8
- Lake Oswego, 30,576 . . B 4
- Lakeview, 2,526 . . . . . . E 6
- Lebanon, 10,950 . . . . . C 4
- Lincoln City, 5,892 . . . . C 3
- McMinnville, 17,894 . . . B 3
- Medford, 46,951 . . . . . . E 4
- Metzger, 5,544('80) h12
- Milton-Freewater, 5,533 B 8
- Milwaukie, 18,692 . . . . B 4
- Molalla, 3,651 . . . . B 4
- Monmouth, 6,288 . . . . C 3
- Mount Angel, 2,778 . . . . B 4
- Myrtle Creek, 3,063 . . . D 3
- Myrtle Point, 2,712 . . . D 2
- Newberg, 13,086 . . . . . B 4
- Newport, 8,437 . . . . . . C 2
- North Albany, 4,499('80) k11
- North Bend, 9,614 . . . . D 2
- Nyssa, 2,629 . . . . D 9
- Oak Grove, 11,640('80) B 4
- Oakridge, 3,063 . . . . . . D 4
- Ontario, 9,392 . . . . C10
- Oregon City, 14,698 . . B 4
- Parkrose, 21,108('80) . . B 4
- Pendleton, 15,126 . . . . B 8
- Portland, 437,319 . . . . C 4
- Prineville, 5,355 . . . . . . C 6
- Redmond, 7,163 . . . . . . C 5
- Reedsport, 4,796 . . . . D 2
- River Road, 10,370('80) C 3
- Roseburg, 17,032 . . . . D 3
- Saint Helens, 7,535 . . . . B 4
- Salem, 107,786 . . . . . . C 4
- Sandy, 4,152 . . . . B 4
- Scappoose, 3,529 . . . . B 4
- Seaside, 5,359 . . . . B 3
- Silverton, 5,635 . . . . . . C 4
- Springfield, 44,683 . . . . C 4
- Stayton, 5,011 . . . . C 4
- Sutherlin, 5,020 . . . . . . D 3
- Sweet Home, 6,850 . . C 4
- The Dalles, 11,060 . . . . B 5
- Tigard, 29,344 . . . . h12
- Tillamook, 4,001 . . . . . B 3
- Toledo, 3,174 . . . . C 3
- Tri City, 3,439('80) . . . . E 3
- Umatilla, 3,046 . . . . B 7
- West Linn, 16,367 . . . . B 4
- Wilsonville, 7,106 . . . . . h12
- Winston, 3,773 . . . . . . D 3
- Woodburn, 13,404 . . . . B 4

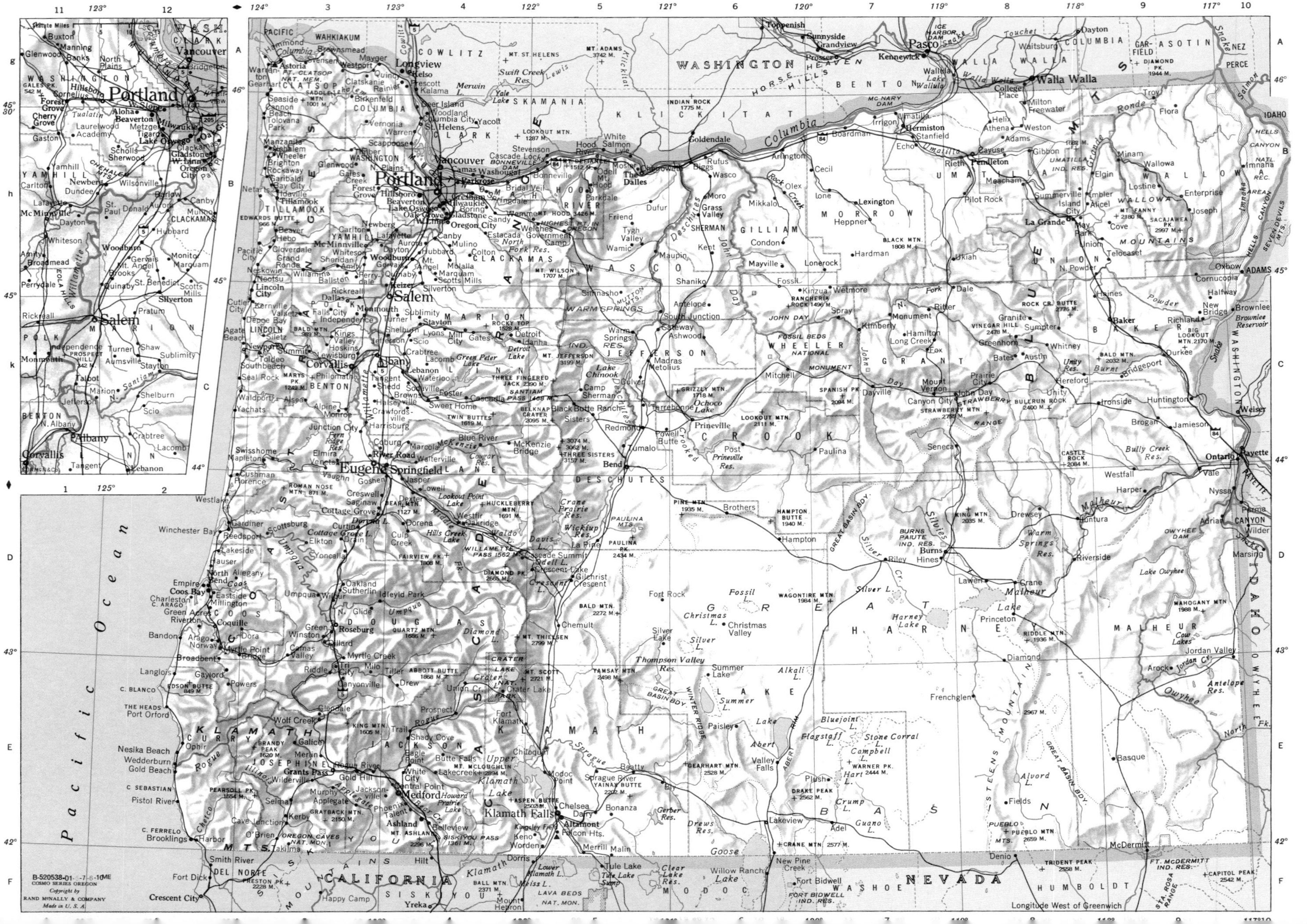

Lambert Conformal Conic Projection

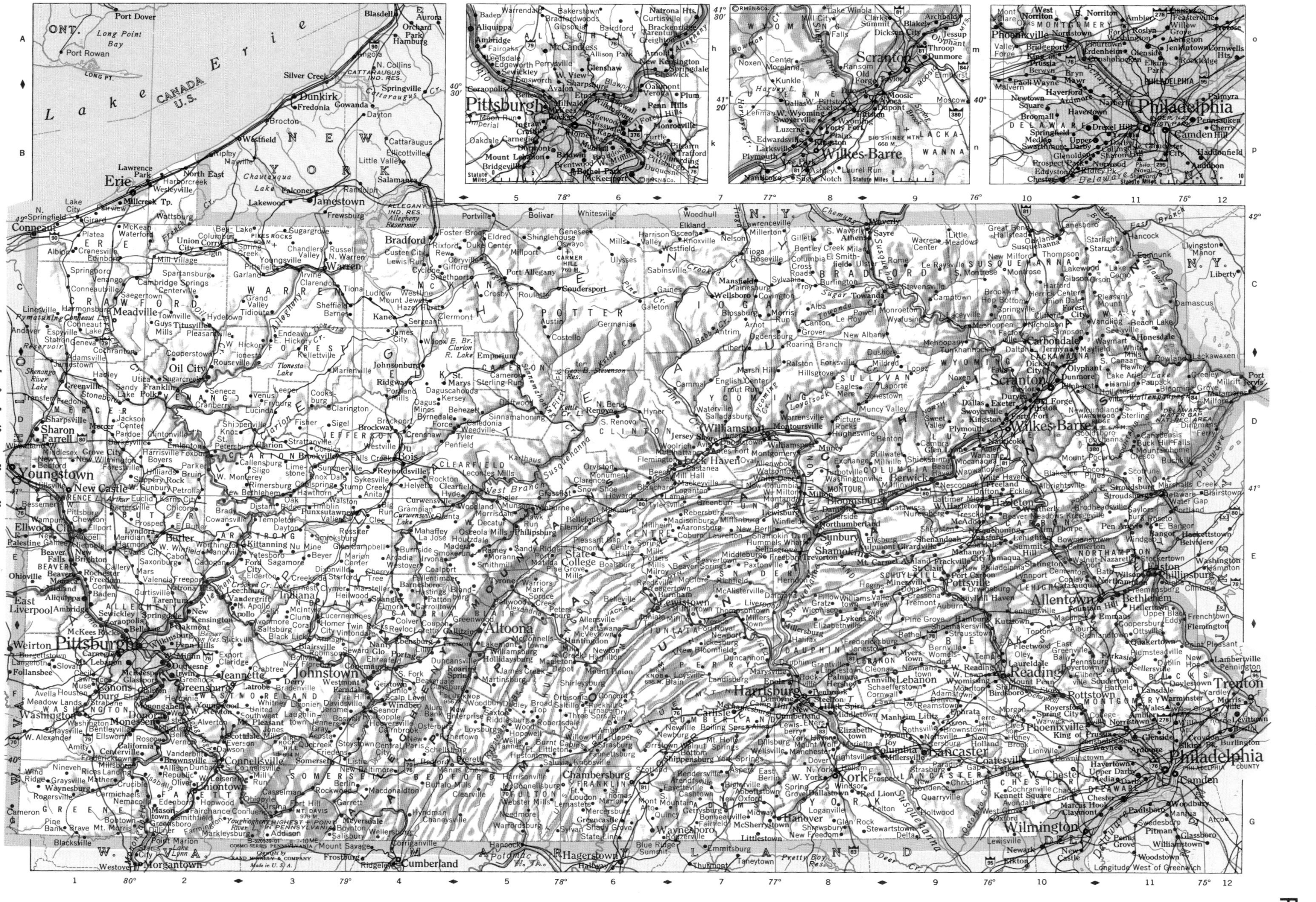

Pennsylvania

1990 CENSUS

Abington Township, 59,300 .... o21
Aliquippa, 13,374 .... E 1
Allentown, 105,090 .... E11
Altoona, 51,881 ...... E 5
Baldwin, 21,923 ...... k13
Beaver Falls, 10,687 .. E 1
Bethel Park, 33,823 .... k14
Bethlehem, 71,428 .... E11
Bloomsburg, 12,439 .. E 9
Bradford, 9,625 ...... C 4
Brentwood, 10,823 .... k14
Broomall, 10,930 ...... p20
Butler, 15,714 .... E 2
Carbondale, 10,664 .... C10
Carlisle, 18,419 ...... F 7
Chambersburg, 16,647 G 6
Chester, 41,856 ...... G11
Clairton, 9,656 .... F 2
Coatesville, 11,038 .... G10
Connellsville, 9,229 .... F 2
Du Bois, 8,286 ...... D 4
Dunmore, 15,403 .... D10
Easton, 26,276 ...... E11
Ephrata, 12,133 ...... F 9
Erie, 108,718 .... B 1
Gettysburg, 7,025 .... G 7
Greensburg, 16,318 .... F 2
Hanover, 14,399 ...... G 8
Harrisburg, 52,376 .... F 8
Haverford Township, 51,800 .... o20
Hazleton, 24,730 ...... E10
Hershey, 13,249('80) .. F 8
Indiana, 15,174 ...... E 3
Jeannette, 11,221 .... F 2
Johnstown, 28,134 .... F 4
Kingston, 14,507 ...... D10
Lancaster, 55,551 .... F 9
Lansdale, 16,362 ...... F11
Latrobe, 9,265 .... F 3
Lebanon, 24,800 ...... F 9
Levittown, 17,420('84)..F12
Lewistown, 9,341 .... E 6
Lock Haven, 9,230 .... D 7
McCandless, 28,781 .. h13
McKeesport, 26,016 .. F 2
Meadville, 14,318 .... C 1
Middletown, 9,254 .... F 8
Millcreek Township, 46,100 .... B 1
Monroeville, 29,169 .... k14
Mount Lebanon, 33,362 F 1
Munhall, 13,158 ...... k14
Nanticoke, 12,267 .... D10
Natrona Heights, 12,200 E 2
New Castle, 28,334 .. D 1
New Kensington, 15,894 E 2
Norristown, 30,749 .... F11
Oil City, 11,949 ...... D 2
Penn Hills, 51,430 .... k14
Philadelphia, 1,585,577 G11
Phoenixville, 15,066 .... F10
Pittsburgh, 369,879 .... F 1
Plum, 25,609 .... k14
Pottstown, 21,831 .... F10
Pottsville, 16,603 ...... E 9
Punxsutawney, 6,782 .. E 4
Reading, 78,380 ...... F10
Scranton, 81,805 ...... D10
Sharon, 17,493 .... D 1
Springfield, 24,160 .... p20
State College, 38,923 .. E 6
Uniontown, 12,034 .... G 2
Upper Darby, 86,100 .. G11
Warminster, 36,900 .... F11
Warren, 11,122 .... C 3
Washington, 15,864 .... F 1
Waynesboro, 9,578 .... G 6
West Chester, 18,041 .. G10
West Mifflin, 23,644 .. F 2
Wilkes-Barre, 47,523 .. D10
Wilkinsburg, 21,080 .... F 2
Williamsport, 31,933 .. D 7
York, 42,192 .... G 8

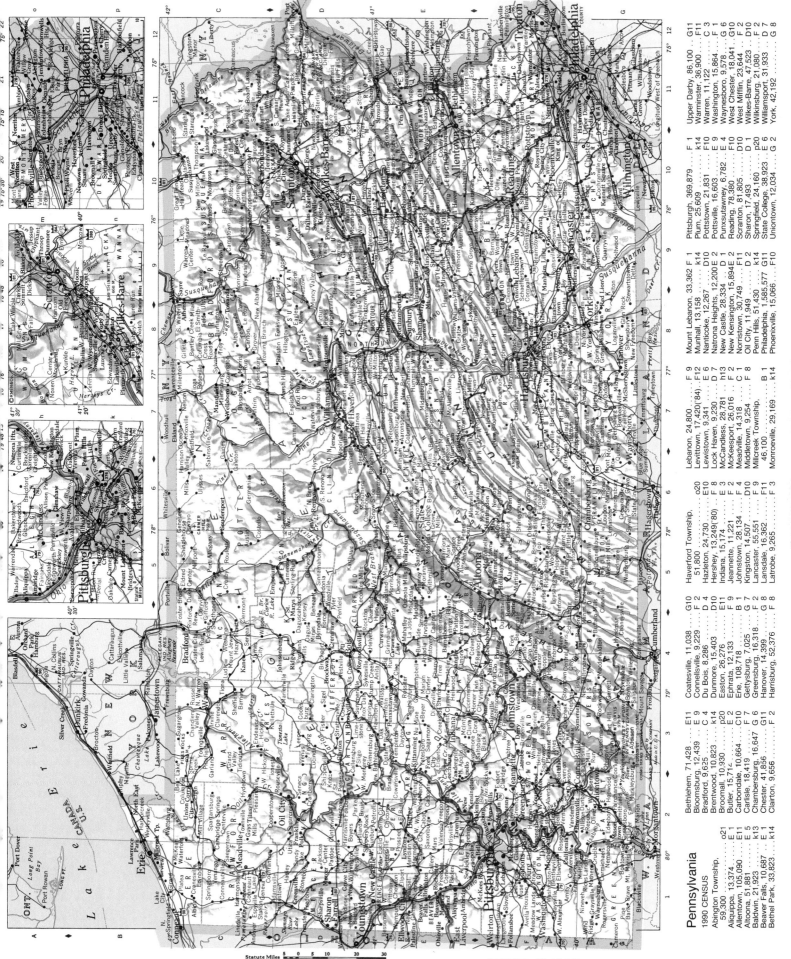

Rhode Island

Rhode Island

1990 CENSUS

Abbott Run Valley, 1,050('87) .... B 4
Adamsville, 600('87) E 6
Albion, 1,600('87) .. B 4
Allenton, 600('87) ... E 4
Anthony, 2,980('87) .. D 3
Arnold Mills, 600('87) B 4
Ashton, 820('87) .... B 4
Barrington, 16,174('80) ...... D 5
Berkeley, 830('87) .. B 4
Block Island, 620('87) h 7
Branch Village, 400('87) .... B 3
Bristol, 20,128('80) .. D 5
Burdickville, 500('87) F 2
Carolina, 650('87) ... F 2
Central Falls, 17,637 B 4
Charlestown, 1,500 (6,478▲) .... F 2
Chepachet, 900('87) B 2
Common Fence Point, 860('87) .... D 6
Coventry, 6,980 (31,083▲) .... D 3
Cranston, 76,060 .... C 4
Davisville, 500('87) .. E 4
Diamond Hill, 810('87) B 4
East Greenwich, 10,211('87) ...... D 4
East Matunuck, 500('87) .... F 3
East Providence, 50,380 .... C 4
Esmond, 4,320('87) .. B 4
Forestdale, 530('87) B 3
Glendale, 700('87) .. B 2
Greenville, 7,576('80) C 3
Harmony, 820('87) .. B 3
Harris, 1,050('87) ... D 3
Hope, 270('87) ...... D 3
Hopkinton, 550 (6,873▲) .... F 1
Island Park, 1,240('87) .... E 6
Jamestown, 4,040('87) .... F 5
Johnston, 26,800 .... C 4
Kenyon, 400('87) .... F 2
Kingston, 5,479('80) .. F 3
La Fayette, 640('87) E 4
Little Compton, 500 (3,339▲) .... E 6
Lonsdale, 3,850('87) B 4
Manville, 3,030('87) .. B 4
Mapleville, 1,300('87) B 2
Matunuck, 550('87) .. G 3
Middletown, 3,350 (19,460▲) .... E 5
Mount View, 610('87) D 4
Narragansett, 3,342 (14,985▲) .... F 4
Newport, 28,227 .... F 5
North Kingstown, 2,750 (23,786▲) .... E 4
North Providence, 32,090 .... C 4
Oakland, 600('87) .. B 2
Pascoag, 3,807('80) B 2
Pawtucket, 72,644 .. C 4
Peace Dale, 3,100('87) .... F 3
Plum Beach, 400('87) E 4
Portsmouth, 3,540 (16,857▲) .... E 6
Primrose, 500('87) .. B 3
Providence, 160,728 C 4
Quidnessett, 3,300('87) .... E 4
Quidnick, 2,300('87) D 3
Quonochontaug, 1,500('87) .... G 2
Saunderstown, 400('87) .... E 4
Saylesville, 3,510('87) B 4
Shannock, 950('87) .. F 2
Shores Acres, 410('87) .... E 4
Slatersville, 2,330('87) A 3
South Hopkinton, 900('87) .... F 1
Tiverton, 7,653 (14,312▲) .... D 6
Union Village, 2,150('87) .... B 3
Usquepaug, 400('87) F 3
Valley Falls, 10,892('80) ...... B 4
Wakefield, 3,450('87) F 3
Warren, 10,640('87) .. D 5
Warwick, 85,427 .... D 4
Westerly, 16,477 (21,605▲) .... F 1
West Kingston, 1,150('87) .... F 3
West Warwick, 29,268 .... D 3
Woonsocket, 43,877 A 3
Yorktown Manor, 2,520('87) .... C 3

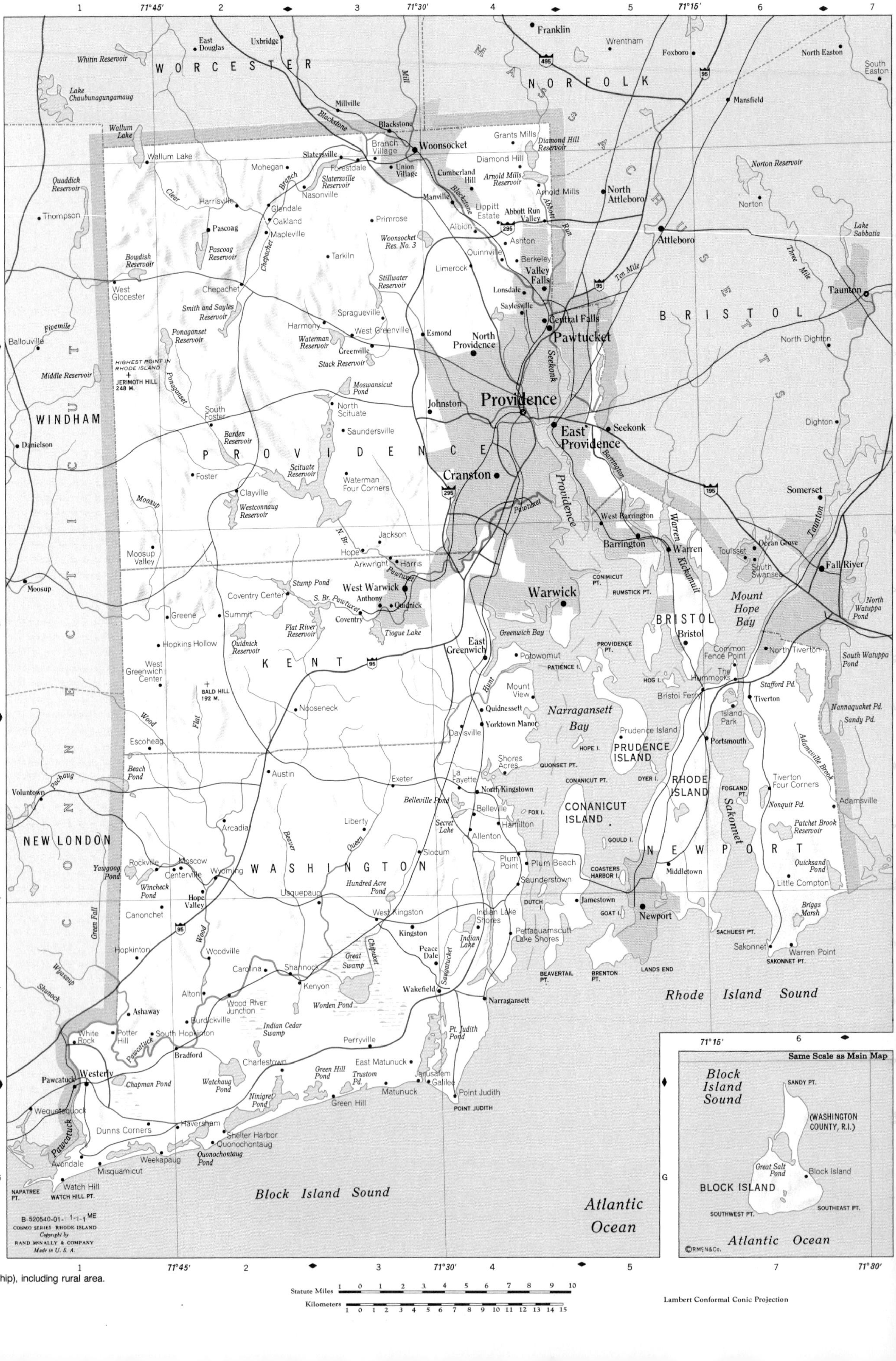

▲ Population of entire town (township), including rural area.

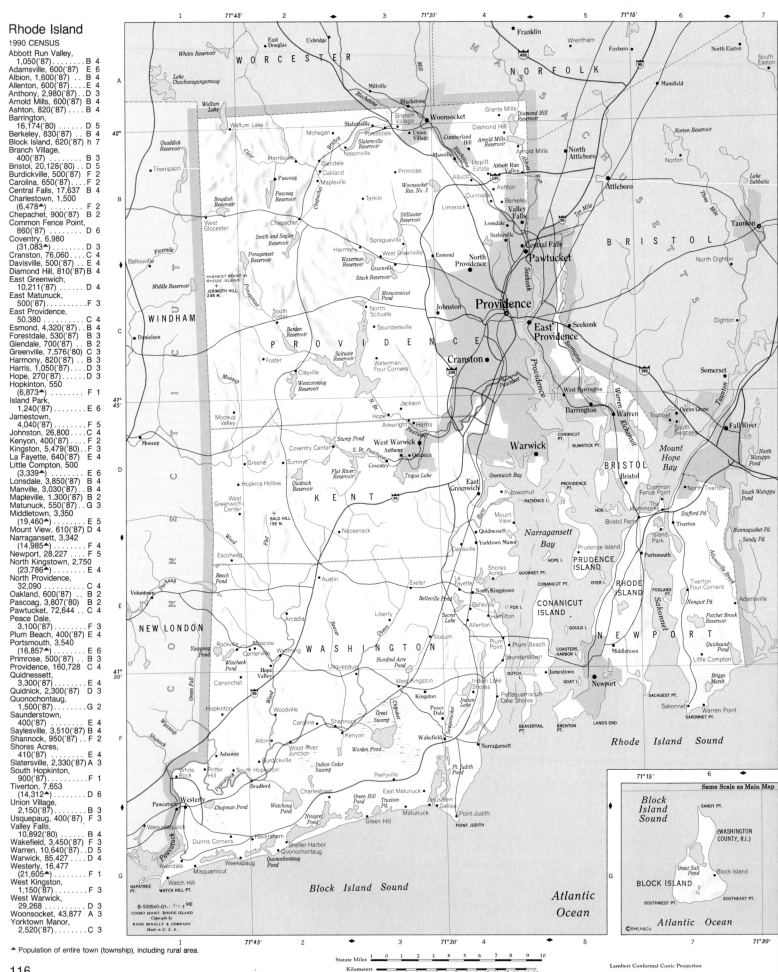

South Carolina

1990 CENSUS

Abbeville, 5,778 . . . . . . C 3
Aiken, 19,872 . . . . D 4
Allendale, 4,410 . . . . . E 5
Anderson, 26,184 . . . . B 2
Bamberg, 3,843 . . . . . E 5
Barnwell, 5,255 . . . . . . E 5
Batesburg, 4,082 . . . . . D 4
Beaufort, 9,576 . . . . . . G 6
Belton, 4,646 . . . . B 3
Bennettsville, 9,345 . . . . B 8
Bishopville, 3,560 . . . . . C 7
Camden, 6,696 . . . . . . C 6
Cayce, 11,163 . . . . D 5
Charleston, 80,414 . . . . F 8
Cheraw, 5,505 . . . . B 8
Chester, 7,158 . . . . B 5
Clemson, 11,096 . . . . B 2
Clinton, 7,987 . . . . C 4
Clover, 3,422 . . . . A 5
Columbia, 98,052 . . . . C 5
Conway, 9,819 . . . . . . D 9
Cowpens, 2,176 . . . . . . A 4
Darlington, 7,311 . . . . . . C 8
Denmark, 3,762 . . . . . . E 5
Dillon, 6,829 . . . . C 9
Easley, 15,195 . . . . B 2
East Gaffney, 4,092('80) A 4
Florence, 29,813 . . . . . . C 8
Forest Acres, 7,197 . . C 6
Fort Mill, 4,930 . . . . . . A 6
Fountain Inn, 4,388 . . . . B 3
Gaffney, 13,145 . . . . . . A 4
Georgetown, 9,517 . . . . E 9
Goose Creek, 24,692 . . F 7
Greenville, 58,282 . . . . B 3
Greenwood, 20,807 . . C 3
Greer, 10,322 . . . . B 3
Hanahan, 13,176 . . . . . . F 7
Hartsville, 8,372 . . . . . . C 7
Hilton Head Island, 23,694 . . . . G 6
Honea Path, 3,841 . . . . C 3
Irmo, 11,280 . . . . C 5
Isle of Palms, 3,680 . . . . k12
James Island, 24,124('80) k12
Kingstree, 3,858 . . . . . . D 8
Ladson, 13,246('80) . . F 7
Lake City, 7,153 . . . . . . D 8
Lancaster, 8,914 . . . . . . B 6
Laurens, 9,694 . . . . . . C 3
Liberty, 3,228 . . . . B 2
Manning, 4,428 . . . . . . D 7
Marion, 7,658 . . . . C 9
Mauldin, 11,587 . . . . . . B 3
Moncks Corner, 5,607 E 7
Mount Pleasant, 30,108 F 8
Mullins, 5,910 . . . . C 9
Myrtle Beach, 24,848 . . D10
Newberry, 10,542 . . . . C 4
North Augusta, 15,351 D 4
North Charleston, 70,218 . . . . F 8
North Myrtle Beach, 8,636 . . . . D10
Orangeburg, 13,739 . . E 6
Pickens, 3,042 . . . . B 2
Rock Hill, 41,643 . . . . . . B 5
Saint Andrews, 9,908('80) . . . . F 7
Saint Andrews, 20,245('80) . . . . C 5
Seneca, 7,726 . . . . B 2
Simpsonville, 11,708 . . B 3
Spartanburg, 43,467 . . B 4
Summerville, 22,519 . . E 7
Sumter, 41,943 . . . . . . D 7
Union, 9,836 . . . . B 4
Walhalla, 3,755 . . . . . . B 1
Walterboro, 5,492 . . . . . . F 6
West Columbia, 10,588 D 5
Williamston, 3,876 . . . . B 3
Williston, 3,099 . . . . . . E 5
Woodruff, 4,365 . . . . . . B 3
York, 6,709 . . . . B 5

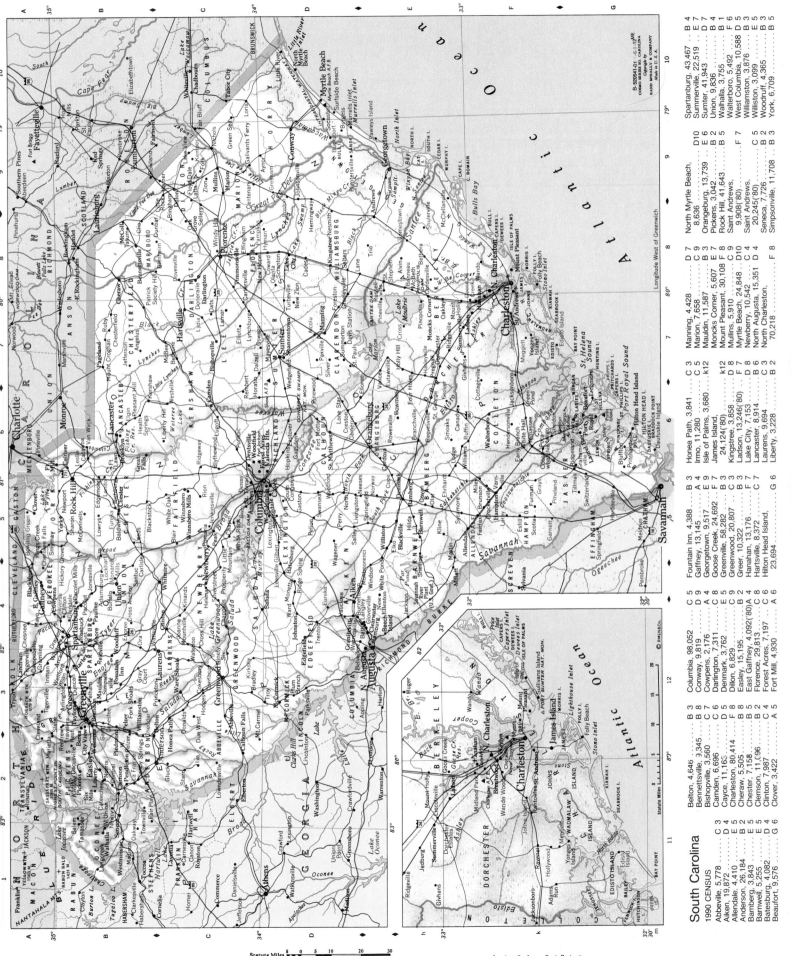

South Dakota

1990 CENSUS

Aberdeen, 24,927 . . . . B 7
Alcester, 843 . . . . D 9
Arlington, 908 . . . . C 8
Armour, 854 . . . . D 7
Belle Fourche, 4,335 . . C 2
Beresford, 1,849 . . . . . D 9
Box Elder, 2,680 . . . . . C 2
Brandon, 3,543 . . . . . . D 9
Britton, 1,394 . . . . B 8
Brookings, 16,270 . . . . C 9
Burke, 756 . . . . D 6
Canton, 2,787 . . . . D 9
Centerville, 887 . . . . D 9
Chamberlain, 2,347 . . . . D 6
Clark, 1,292 . . . . C 8
Clear Lake, 1,247 . . . . C 9
Custer, 1,741 . . . . D 2
Deadwood, 1,830 . . . . C 2
Dell Rapids, 2,484 . . . . D 9
De Smet, 1,172 . . . . . . C 8
Edgemont, 906 . . . . D 2
Elk Point, 1,423 . . . . . . E 9
Eureka, 1,197 . . . . B 6
Faulkton, 809 . . . . B 6
Flandreau, 2,311 . . . . . . C 9
Fort Pierre, 1,854 . . . . C 5
Freeman, 1,293 . . . . . . D 8
Garretson, 924 . . . . D 9
Gettysburg, 1,510 . . . . C 6
Gregory, 1,384 . . . . . . D 6
Groton, 1,196 . . . . B 7
Hartford, 1,262 . . . . D 9
Highmore, 835 . . . . C 6
Hot Springs, 4,325 . . . . D 2
Howard, 1,156 . . . . C 8
Huron, 12,448 . . . . C 7
Ipswich, 965 . . . . B 6
Kadoka, 736 . . . . D 4
Lake Andes, 846 . . . . . D 7
Lake Preston, 663 . . . . C 8
Lead, 3,632 . . . . C 2
Lemmon, 1,614 . . . . . . B 3
Lennox, 1,767 . . . . D 9
Madison, 6,257 . . . . C 8
Marion, 831 . . . . D 8
Martin, 1,151 . . . . D 4
McLaughlin, 780 . . . . . . B 5
Menno, 768 . . . . D 8
Milbank, 3,879 . . . . B 9
Miller, 1,678 . . . . C 7
Mitchell, 13,798 . . . . . . D 7
Mobridge, 3,768 . . . . . . B 5
North Sioux City, 2,019 E 9
Onida, 761 . . . . C 5
Parker, 984 . . . . D 8
Parkston, 1,572 . . . . . . D 8
Philip, 1,077 . . . . C 4
Pierre, 12,906 . . . . C 5
Platte, 1,311 . . . . D 7
Presho, 654 . . . . D 5
Rapid City, 54,523 . . . . C 2
Redfield, 2,770 . . . . . . C 7
Saint Francis, 815 . . . . D 5
Salem, 1,289 . . . . D 8
Scotland, 968 . . . . D 8
Selby, 707 . . . . B 5
Sioux Falls, 100,814 . . D 9
Sisseton, 2,181 . . . . . . B 8
Spearfish, 6,966 . . . . . C 2
Springfield, 834 . . . . . . E 8
Sturgis, 5,330 . . . . C 2
Tyndall, 1,201 . . . . E 8
Valley Springs, 739 . . . D 9
Vermillion, 10,034 . . . . E 9
Volga, 1,263 . . . . C 9
Wagner, 1,462 . . . . D 7
Wall, 834 . . . . D 3
Watertown, 17,592 . . . . C 8
Webster, 2,017 . . . . B 8
Wessington Springs, 1,083 . . . . C 7
Whitewood, 891 . . . . . . C 2
Winner, 3,354 . . . . D 6
Woonsocket, 766 . . . . C 7
Yankton, 12,703 . . . . . . E 8

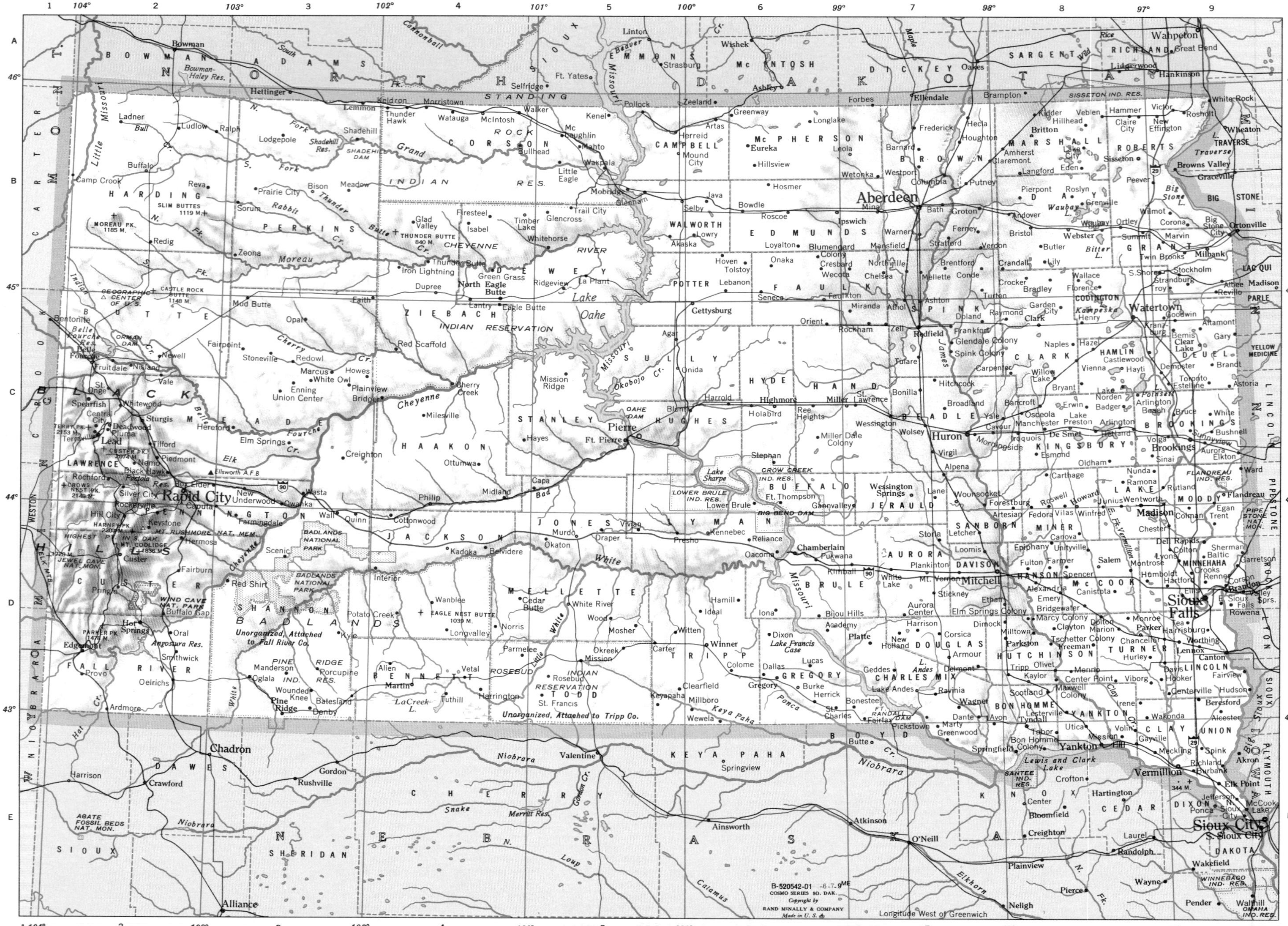

Statute Miles 5 0 5 10 20 30 40 50 60
Kilometers 5 0 5 15 25 35 45 55 65 75

Lambert Conformal Conic Projection

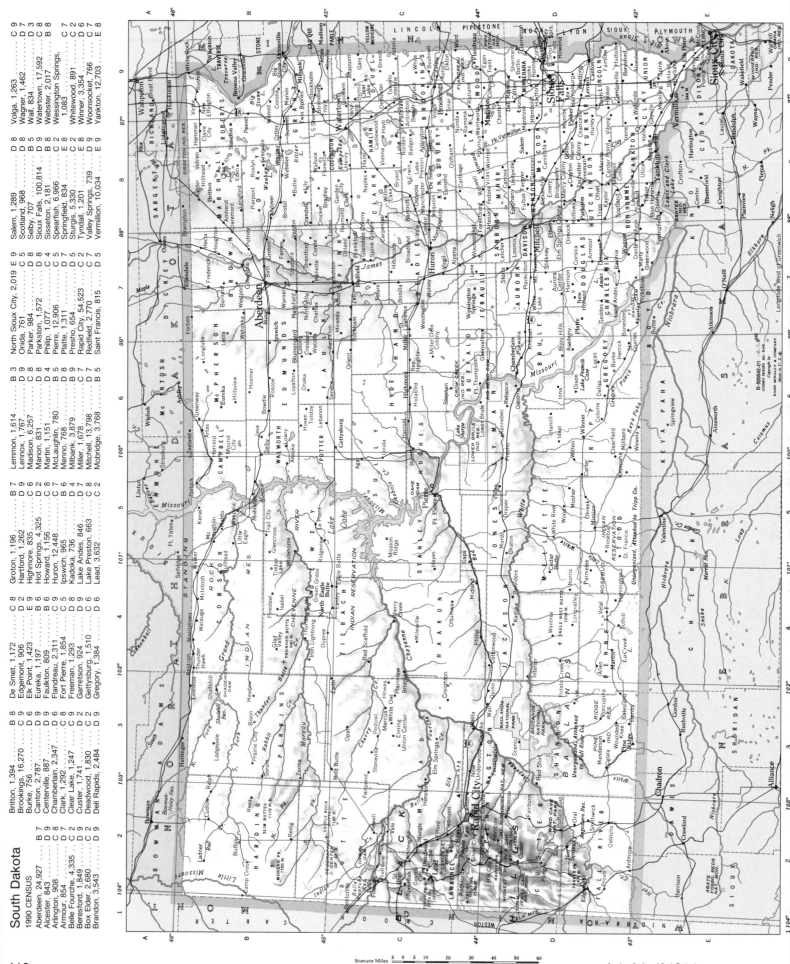

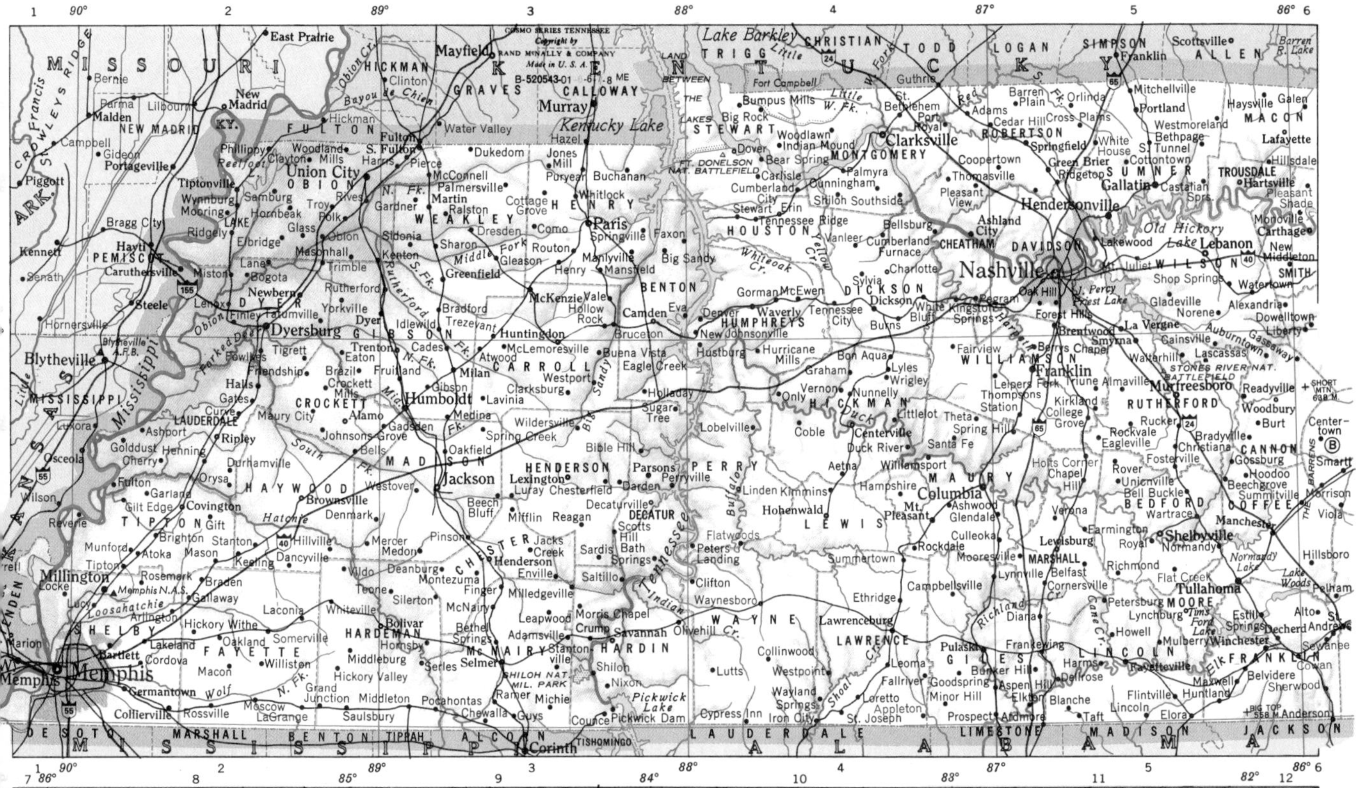

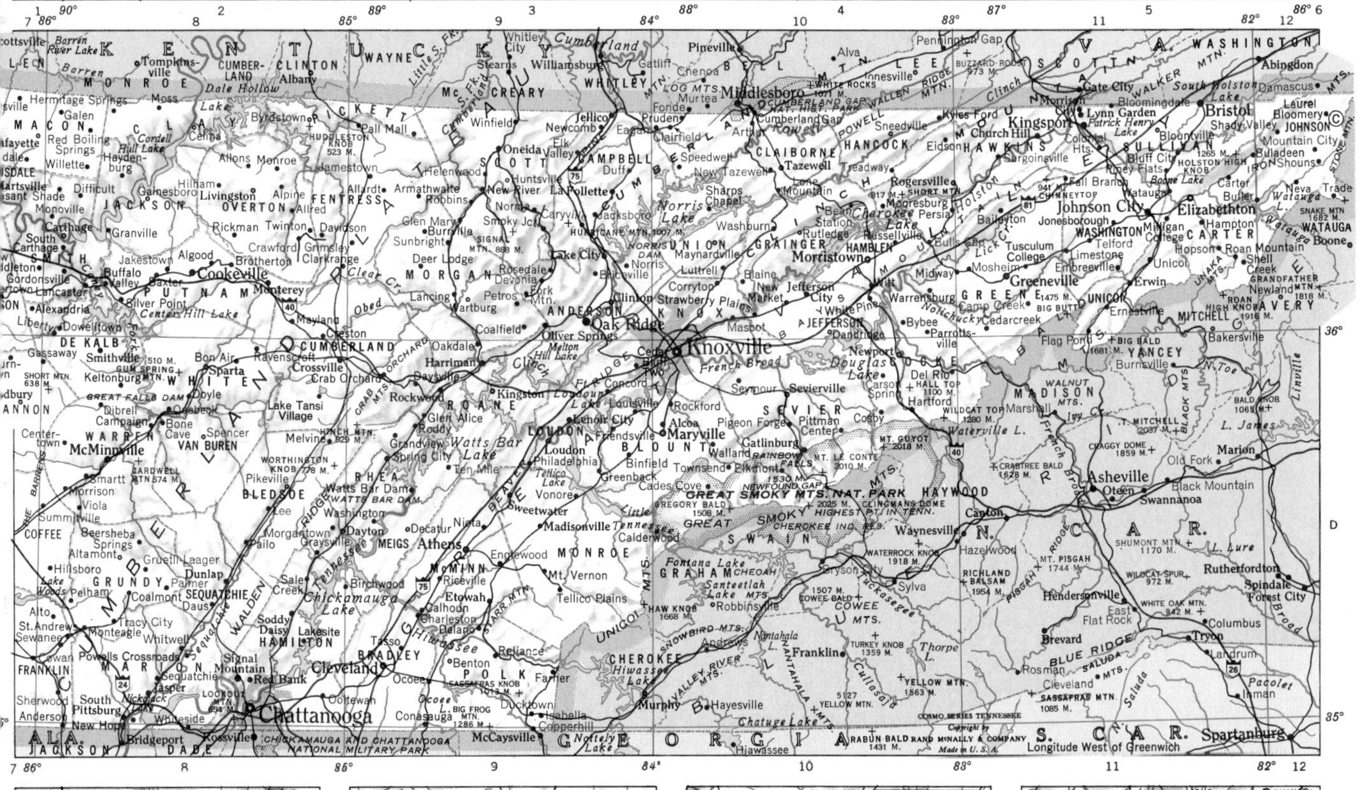

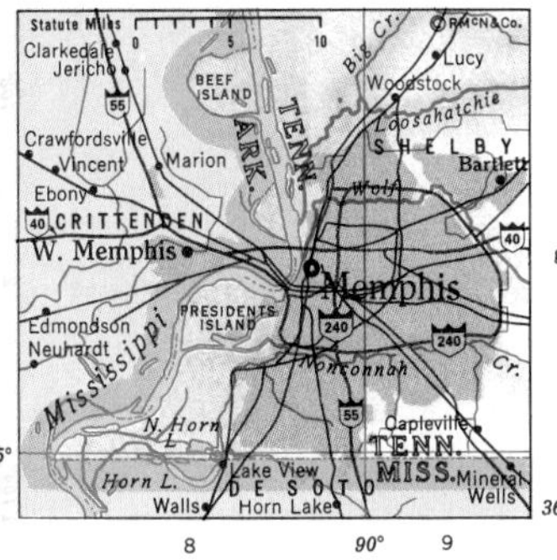

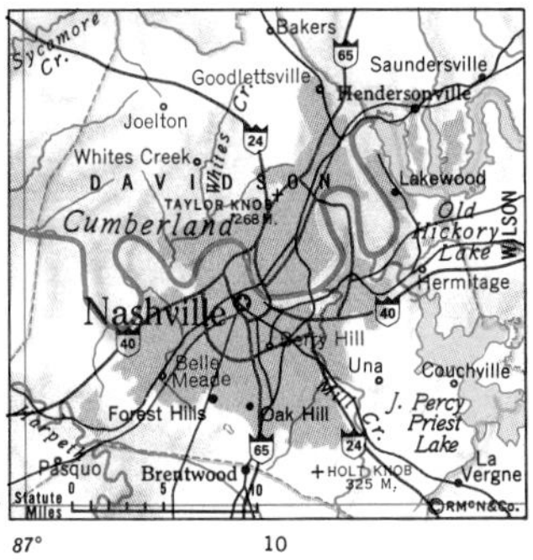

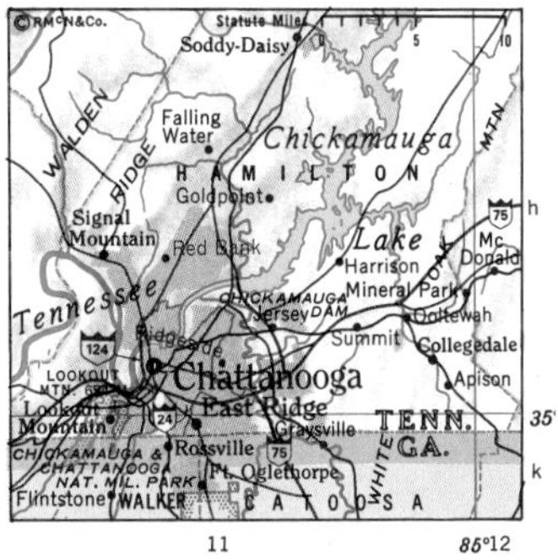

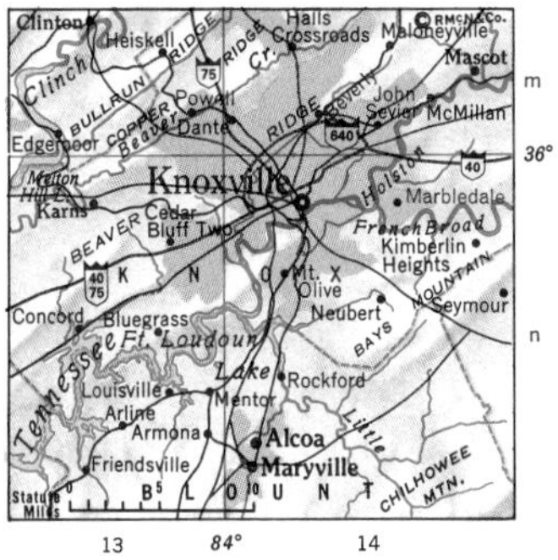

Statute Miles 5 0 5 10 20 30 40

Kilometers 5 0 5 15 25 35 45 55

Lambert Conformal Conic Projection

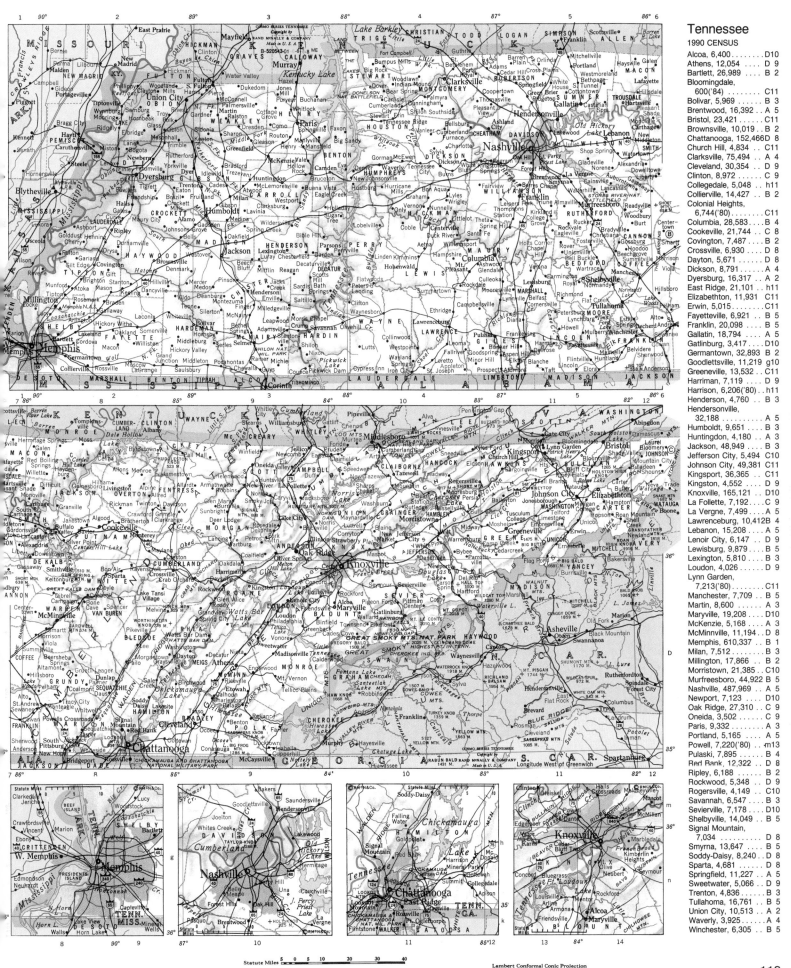

Tennessee

1990 CENSUS

Alcoa, 6,400 . . . . D10
Athens, 12,054 . . . . D 9
Bartlett, 26,989 . . . . B 2
Bloomingdale,
600('84) C11
Bolivar, 5,969 . . . . . . B 3
Brentwood, 16,392 . . A 5
Bristol, 23,421 . . . . . . C11
Brownsville, 10,019 . . B 2
Chattanooga, 152,466 D 8
Church Hill, 4,834 . . C11
Clarksville, 75,494 . . A 4
Cleveland, 30,354 . . D 9
Clinton, 8,972 . . . . . . C 9
Collegedale, 5,048 . . h11
Collierville, 14,427 . . B 2
Colonial Heights,
6,744('80) C11
Columbia, 28,583 . . . . B 4
Cookeville, 21,744 . . C 8
Covington, 7,487 . . . . B 2
Crossville, 6,930 . . . . D 8
Dayton, 5,671 . . . . . . D 8
Dickson, 8,791 . . . . . . A 4
Dyersburg, 16,317 . . A 2
East Ridge, 21,101 . . h11
Elizabethton, 11,931 C11
Erwin, 5,015 . . . . C11
Fayetteville, 6,921 . . B 5
Franklin, 20,098 . . . . B 5
Gallatin, 18,794 . . . . A 5
Gatlinburg, 3,417 . . . . D10
Germantown, 32,893 B 2
Goodlettsville, 11,219 g10
Greeneville, 13,532 . . C11
Harriman, 7,119 . . . . D 9
Harrison, 6,206('80) . . h11
Henderson, 4,760 . . B 3
Hendersonville,
32,188 . . . . A 5
Humboldt, 9,651 . . . . B 3
Huntingdon, 4,180 . . A 3
Jackson, 48,949 . . . . B 3
Jefferson City, 5,494 C10
Johnson City, 49,381 C11
Kingsport, 36,365 . . C11
Kingston, 4,552 . . . . D 9
Knoxville, 165,121 . . D10
La Follette, 7,192 . . . . C 9
La Vergne, 7,499 . . . . A 5
Lawrenceburg, 10,412 B 4
Lebanon, 15,208 . . . . A 5
Lenoir City, 6,147 . . D 9
Lewisburg, 9,879 . . . . B 5
Lexington, 5,810 . . . . B 3
Loudon, 4,026 . . . . . . D 9
Lynn Garden,
7,213('80) C11
Manchester, 7,709 . . B 5
Martin, 8,600 . . . . . . A 3
Maryville, 19,208 . . . . D10
McKenzie, 5,168 . . . . A 3
McMinnville, 11,194 . . D 8
Memphis, 610,337 . . B 1
Milan, 7,512 . . . . B 3
Millington, 17,866 . . B 2
Morristown, 21,385 . . C10
Murfreesboro, 44,922 B 5
Nashville, 487,969 . . A 5
Newport, 7,123 . . . . D10
Oak Ridge, 27,310 . . C 9
Oneida, 3,502 . . . . . . C 9
Paris, 9,332 . . . . A 3
Portland, 5,165 . . . . A 5
Powell, 7,220('80) . . m13
Pulaski, 7,895 . . . . . . B 4
Red Bank, 12,322 . . D 8
Ripley, 6,188 . . . . . . B 2
Rockwood, 5,348 . . D 9
Rogersville, 4,149 . . C10
Savannah, 6,547 . . . . B 3
Sevierville, 7,178 . . . . D10
Shelbyville, 14,049 . . B 5
Signal Mountain,
7,034 . . . . D 8
Smyrna, 13,647 . . . . B 5
Soddy-Daisy, 8,240 . . D 8
Sparta, 4,681 . . . . . . D 8
Springfield, 11,227 . . A 5
Sweetwater, 5,066 . . D 9
Trenton, 4,836 . . . . . . B 3
Tullahoma, 16,761 . . B 5
Union City, 10,513 . . A 2
Waverly, 3,925 . . . . . . A 4
Winchester, 6,305 . . B 5

Texas

1990 CENSUS

Abilene, 106,654 . . . . C 3
Alice, 19,788 . . . . . . F 3
Alvin, 19,220 . . . . . . E 5
Amarillo, 157,615 . . . B 2
Arlington, 261,721 . . n 9
Austin, 465,622 . . . . D 4
Bay City, 18,170 . . . . E 5
Baytown, 63,850 . . . . E 5
Beaumont, 114,323 . . D 5
Beeville, 13,547 . . . . E 4
Big Spring, 23,093 . . C 2
Borger, 15,675 . . . . . B 2
Brownsville, 98,962 . . G 4
Brownwood, 18,387 D 3
Bryan, 55,002 . . . . . . D 4
Cleburne, 22,205 . . . . C 4
College Station,
 52,456 . . . . D 4
Conroe, 27,610 . . . . D 5
Copperas Cove,
 24,079 . . . . D 4
Corpus Christi,
 257,453 . . . . F 4
Corsicana, 22,911 . . C 4
Dallas, 1,006,877 . . . C 4
Del Rio, 30,705 . . . . E 2
Denison, 21,505 . . . . C 4
Denton, 66,270 . . . . C 4
Duncanville, 35,748 . . n10
Eagle Pass, 20,651 . . E 2
Edinburg, 29,885 . . . . F 3
El Paso, 515,342 . . . . o11
Farmers Branch,
 24,250 . . . . n10
Fort Worth, 447,619 C 4
Galveston, 59,070 . . E 5
Garland, 180,650 . . . . n10
Grand Prairie, 99,616 n10
Greenville, 23,071 . . C 4
Harlingen, 48,735 . . . F 4
Hereford, 14,745 . . . . B 1
Houston, 1,630,553 . . E 5
Huntsville, 27,925 . . D 5
Irving, 155,037 . . . . . . n10
Kerrville, 17,384 . . . . D 3
Killeen, 63,535 . . . . . D 4
Kingsville, 25,276 . . . . F 4
Lake Jackson, 22,776 E 5
La Porte, 27,910 . . . . r14
Laredo, 122,899 . . . . F 3
Lewisville, 46,521 . . C 4
Longview, 70,311 . . C 5
Lubbock, 186,206 . . C 2
Lufkin, 30,206 . . . . . . D 5
Marshall, 23,682 . . . . C 5
McAllen, 84,021 . . . . F 3
Mesquite, 101,484 . . n10
Midland, 89,443 . . . . D 1
Mineral Wells, 14,870 C 3
Mission, 28,653 . . . . F 3
Missouri City, 36,176 r14
Nacogdoches, 30,872 D 5
New Braunfels,
 27,334 . . . . E 3
North Richland Hills,
 45,895 . . . . n 9
Odessa, 89,699 . . . . D 1
Orange, 19,381 . . . . . D 6
Palestine, 18,042 . . . . D 5
Pampa, 19,959 . . . . . B 2
Paris, 24,699 . . . . . . C 5
Pasadena, 119,363 . . r14
Pecos, 12,069 . . . . . . D 1
Pharr, 32,921 . . . . . . F 3
Plainview, 21,700 . . . B 2
Plano, 128,713 . . . . . C 4
Port Arthur, 58,724 . . E 6
Richardson, 74,840 . . n10
Rosenberg, 20,183 . . E 5
San Angelo, 84,474 . . D 2
San Antonio, 935,933 E 3
San Benito, 20,125 . . F 4
San Marcos, 28,743 E 4
Seguin, 18,853 . . . . . E 4
Sherman, 31,601 . . . . C 4
Temple, 46,109 . . . . D 4
Texarkana, 31,656 . . C 5
Texas City, 40,822 . . E 5
Tyler, 75,450 . . . . . . C 5
University Park,
 22,259 . . . . n10
Uvalde, 14,729 . . . . . . E 3
Victoria, 55,076 . . . . E 4
Waco, 103,590 . . . . . D 4
Waxahachie, 18,168 C 4
Weslaco, 21,877 . . . . F 4
Wichita Falls, 96,259 C 3

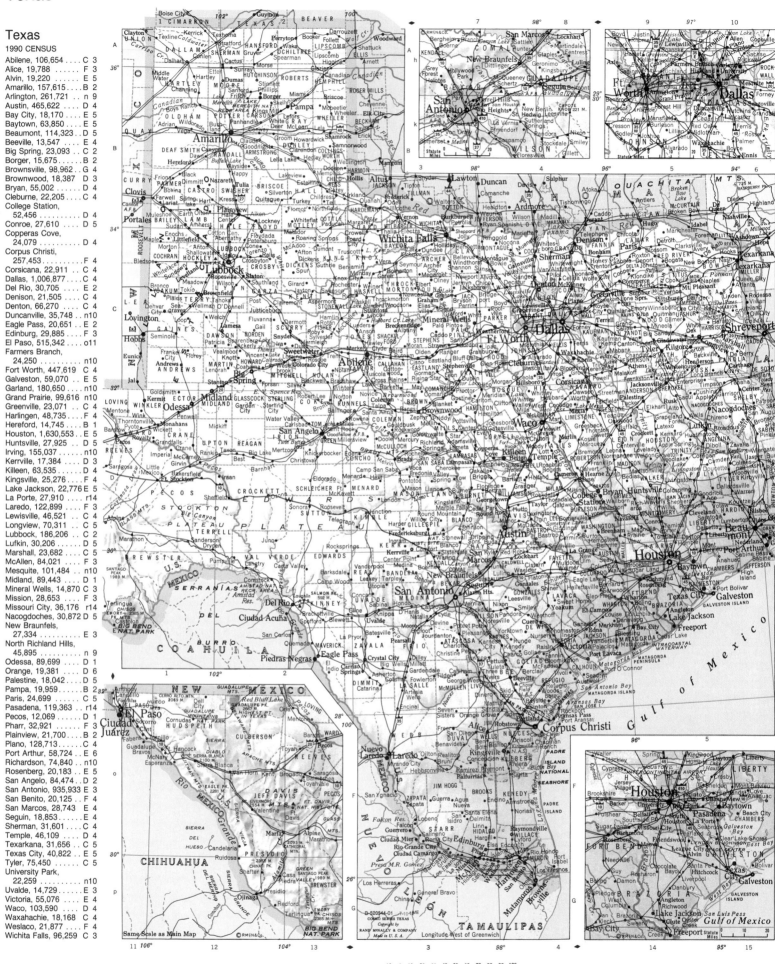

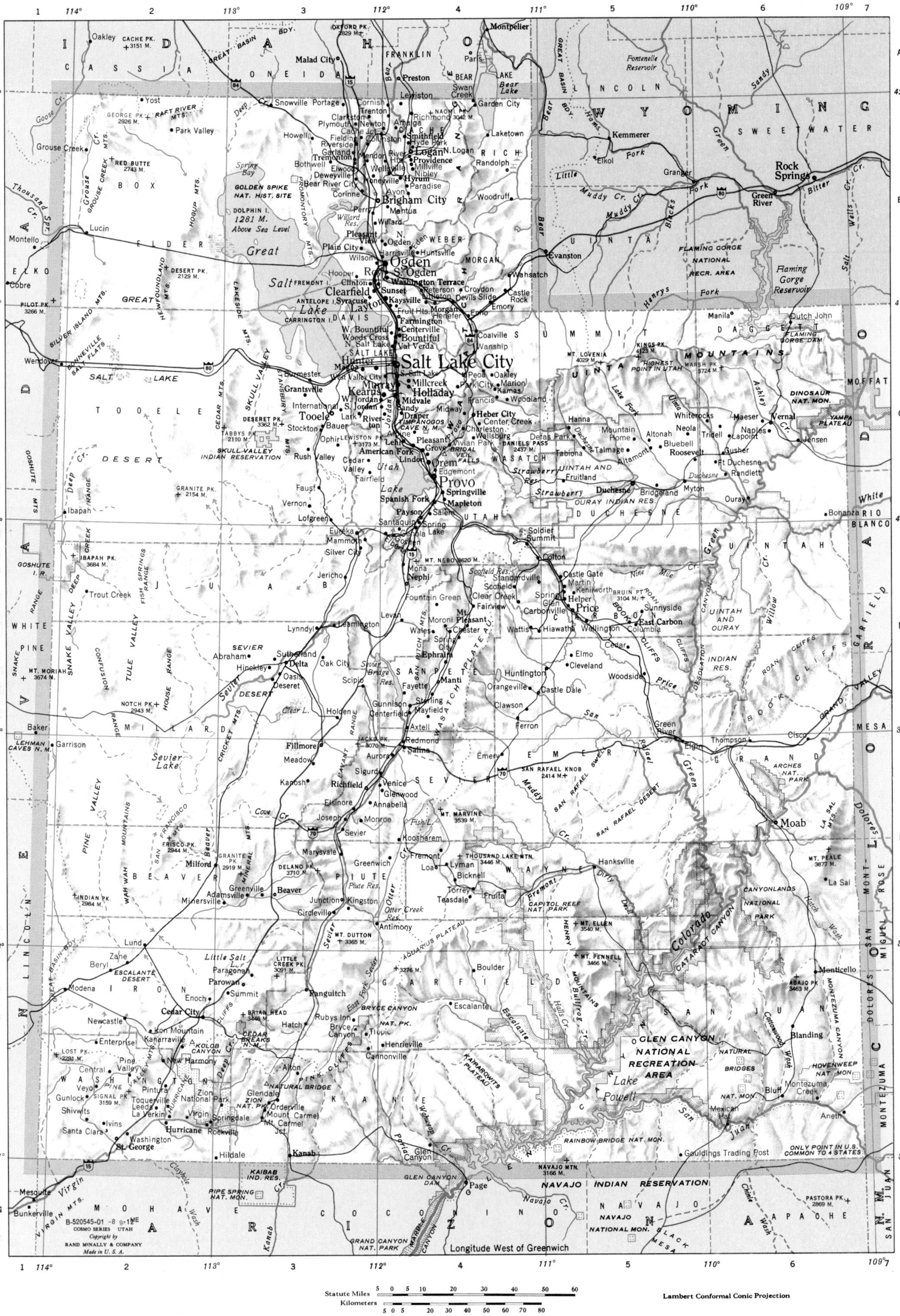

Utah

1990 CENSUS

Alpine, 3,492 . . . . . . C 4
American Fork, 15,696 . . . . C 4
Beaver, 1,998 . . . . . . E 3
Blanding, 3,162 . . . . F 6
Bountiful, 36,659 . . . . C 4
Brigham City, 15,644 B 3
Castle Dale, 1,704 . . D 4
Cedar City, 13,443 . . F 2
Centerville, 11,500 . . C 4
Clearfield, 21,435 . . . B 3
Clinton, 7,945 . . . . . . B 3
Delta, 2,998 . . . . D 3
Draper, 7,257 . . . . C 4
Duchesne, 1,308 . . . . C 5
East Carbon, 1,270 . . D 5
Ephraim, 3,363 . . . . D 4
Farmington, 9,028 . . C 4
Ferron, 1,606 . . . . . . D 4
Fillmore, 1,956 . . . . . . E 3
Fruit Heights, 3,900 . . B 4
Grantsville, 4,500 . . . . C 3
Heber City, 4,782 . . . C 4
Helper, 2,148 . . . . . . D 5
Holladay, 26,200 . . . . C 4
Huntington, 1,875 . . D 5
Hurricane, 3,915 . . . . F 2
Hyrum, 4,829 . . . . . . B 4
Kanab, 3,289 . . . . . . F 3
Kaysville, 13,961 . . . . B 4
Kearns, 17,000('80) . . C 4
Layton, 41,784 . . . . . . B 4
Lehi, 8,475 . . . . C 4
Lindon, 3,818 . . . . . . C 4
Logan, 32,762 . . . . . . B 4
Maeser, 1,850('80) . . C 6
Magna, 8,600('80) . . . C 3
Manti, 2,268 . . . . D 4
Mapleton, 3,572 . . . . C 4
Midvale, 11,886 . . . . C 4
Millcreek, 28,500 . . . . C 4
Moab, 3,971 . . . . E 6
Monticello, 1,806 . . . . F 6
Morgan, 2,023 . . . . . . B 4
Mount Pleasant, 2,092 . . . . D 4
Murray, 31,282 . . . . C 4
Nephi, 3,515 . . . . D 4
North Logan, 3,768 . . B 4
North Ogden, 11,668 B 4
North Salt Lake, 6,474 . . . . C 4
Ogden, 63,909 . . . . . . B 4
Orem, 67,561 . . . . . . C 4
Panguitch, 1,444 . . . . F 3
Park City, 4,468 . . . . C 4
Parowan, 1,873 . . . . F 3
Payson, 9,510 . . . . . . C 4
Plain City, 2,722 . . . . B 3
Pleasant Grove, 13,476 . . . . C 4
Price, 8,712 . . . . D 5
Providence, 3,344 . . B 4
Provo, 86,835 . . . . . . C 4
Richfield, 5,593 . . . . E 3
Richmond, 1,955 . . . . B 4
Riverton, 11,261 . . . C 4
Roosevelt, 3,915 . . . . C 5
Roy, 24,603 . . . . B 3
Saint George, 28,502 F 2
Salem, 2,284 . . . . . . C 4
Salina, 1,943 . . . . . . E 4
Salt Lake City, 159,936 . . . . C 4
Sandy, 75,058 . . . . . . C 4
Santaquin, 2,386 . . . . D 4
Smithfield, 5,566 . . . . B 4
South Jordan, 12,220 C 3
South Ogden, 12,105 B 4
Spanish Fork, 11,272 C 4
Springville, 13,950 . . C 4
Sunset, 5,128 . . . . . . B 4
Syracuse, 4,658 . . . . B 3
Tooele, 13,887 . . . . . . C 3
Tremonton, 4,264 . . B 3
Val Verda, 6,500('80) C 4
Vernal, 6,644 . . . . . . C 6
Washington, 4,198 . . F 2
Washington Terrace, 8,189 . . . . B 4
Wellsville, 2,206 . . . . B 4
Wendover, 1,127 . . . . C 1
West Bountiful, 4,477 C 4
West Jordan, 42,892 C 4
West Valley City, 86,976 . . . . C 4
Woods Cross, 5,384 C 4

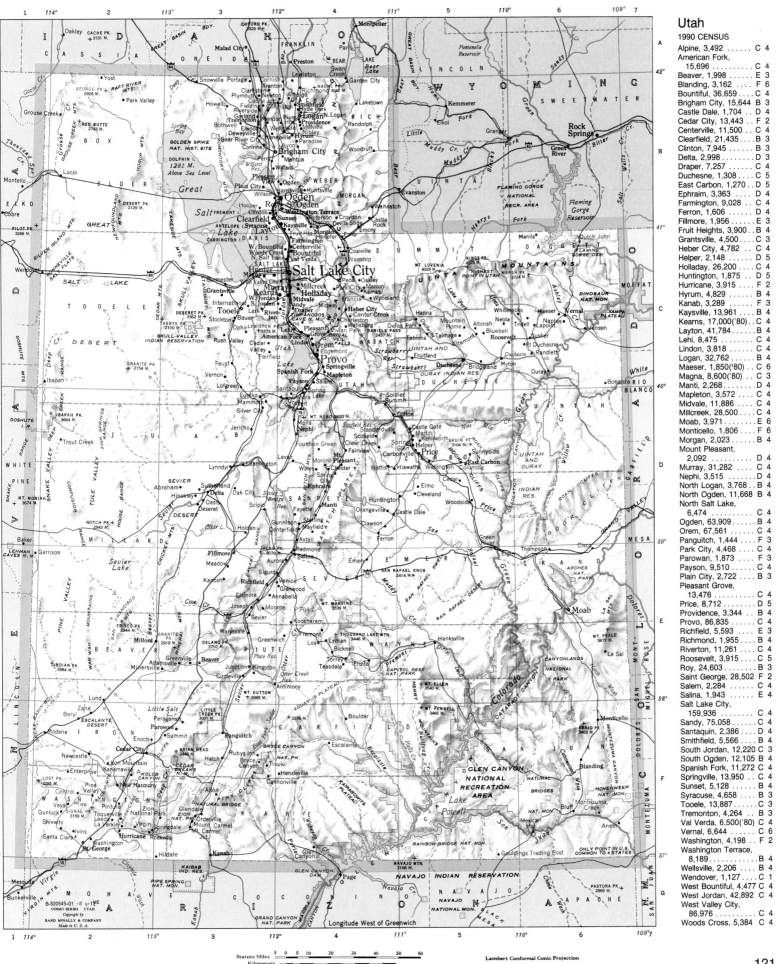

Vermont

Vermont

1990 CENSUS

Arlington, 700 (2,299▲) . . . . E 2
Barre, 9,482 . . . . C 4
Barton, 908 . . . . B 4
Bellows Falls, 3,313 . . E 4
Bennington, 9,349 (16,451▲) . . . . F 2
Bethel, 1,016 (1,866▲) . . . . D 3
Bradford, 672 . . . . . . D 4
Brandon, 1,925 (4,223▲) . . . . D 2
Brattleboro, 8,596 (12,241▲) . . . . F 3
Bristol, 1,801 . . . . C 2
Burlington, 39,127 . . C 2
Castleton, 600 (4,278▲) . . . . D 2
Chester, 550 (2,832▲) E 3
Chester Depot, 500 . . E 3
Derby Line, 855 . . . . A 4
Dorset, 550 (1,918▲) E 2
East Arlington, 600 . . E 2
East Barre, 700 . . . . C 4
East Middlebury, 500 D 2
East Montpelier, 600 (2,239▲) . . . . C 4
Enosburg Falls, 1,350 B 3
Essex, 800 (16,498▲) B 2
Essex Junction, 8,396 C 2
Fair Haven, 2,887 . . D 2
Forest Dale, 350 . . . . D 2
Gilman, 500 . . . . C 5
Graniteville, 500 . . . . . C 4
Hardwick, 1,400 (2,964▲) . . . . B 4
Hartford, 500 (9,404▲) . . . . D 4
Hydeville, 450 . . . . . . D 2
Jericho, 1,300 (4,302▲) . . . . B 3
Johnson, 1,470 . . . . B 3
Ludlow, 1,123 . . . . . . E 3
Lyndonville, 1,255 . . B 4
Manchester, 561 . . . . E 2
Middlebury, 5,591 (8,034▲) . . . . C 2
Milton, 1,578 . . . . . . B 2
Montpelier, 8,247 . . . C 3
Morrisville, 1,984 . . . . B 3
Newport, 4,434 . . . . B 4
North Bennington, 1,520 . . . . F 2
North Clarendon, 500 D 3
Northfield, 1,889 . . . . C 3
Northfield Falls, 600 . . C 3
North Springfield, 750 E 3
North Troy, 723 . . . . B 4
Norwich, 1,000 (3,093▲) . . . . D 4
Orleans, 806 . . . . . . B 4
Pittsford, 650 (2,919▲) . . . . D 2
Plainfield, 600 (1,302▲) . . . . C 4
Poultney, 1,731 . . . . . D 2
Proctor, 1,979 . . . . . D 2
Proctorsville, 480 . . . . E 3
Putney, 1,100 (2,352▲) . . . . F 3
Quechee, 550 . . . . . . D 4
Randolph, 2,200 (4,764▲) . . . . D 3
Richford, 1,425 . . . . . B 3
Richmond, 650 (3,729▲) . . . . C 3
Riverton, 150 . . . . . . C 3
Rochester, 500 (1,181▲) . . . . D 3
Rutland, 18,230 . . . . . D 3
Saint Albans, 7,339 . . B 2
Saint Johnsbury, 7,150 (7,608▲) . . . . C 4
Saxtons River, 541 . . E 3
Shaftsbury, 700 (3,368▲) . . . . E 2
South Burlington, 12,809 . . . . C 2
South Royalton, 700 D 3
Springfield, 5,603 (9,579▲) . . . . E 4
Stamford, 400 (773▲) F 2
Stowe, 450 . . . . C 3
Swanton, 2,360 . . . . B 2
Vergennes, 2,578 . . C 2
Wallingford, 1,141 (2,184▲) . . . . E 3
Warren, 350 (1,172▲) C 3
Waterbury, 1,702 . . . . C 3
Waterbury Center, 500 . . . . C 3
Websterville, 600 . . . . C 4
West Pawlet, 350 . . E 2
West Rutland, 2,448 D 2
Williamstown, 650 (2,839▲) . . . . C 3
Wilmington, 550 (1,968▲) . . . . F 3
Windsor, 3,714 . . . . . . E 4
Winooski, 6,649 . . . . C 2
Woodstock, 1,037 . . D 3

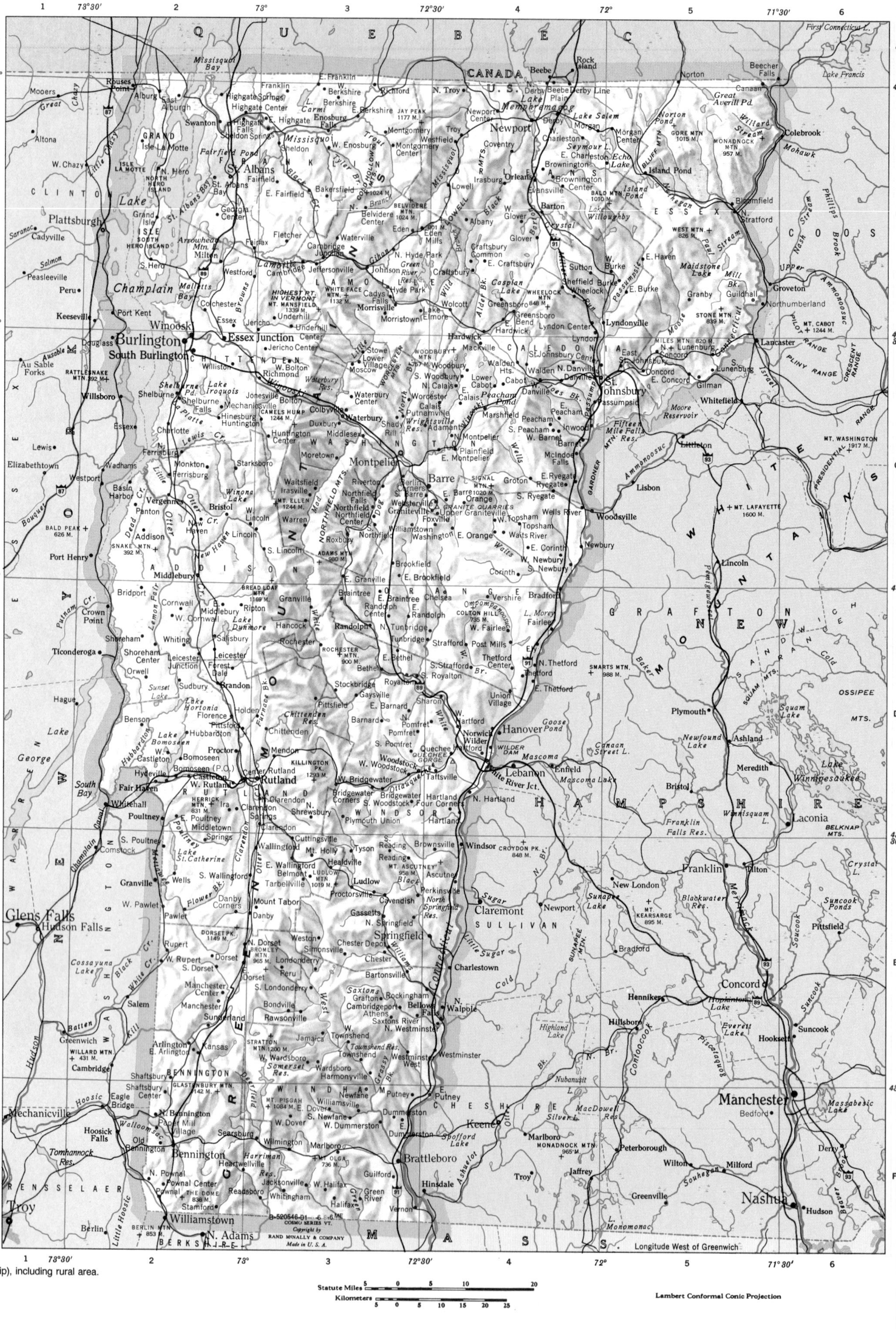

▲ Population of entire town (township), including rural area.

Statute Miles 5 0 5 10 20

Kilometers 5 0 5 10 15 20 25

Lambert Conformal Conic Projection

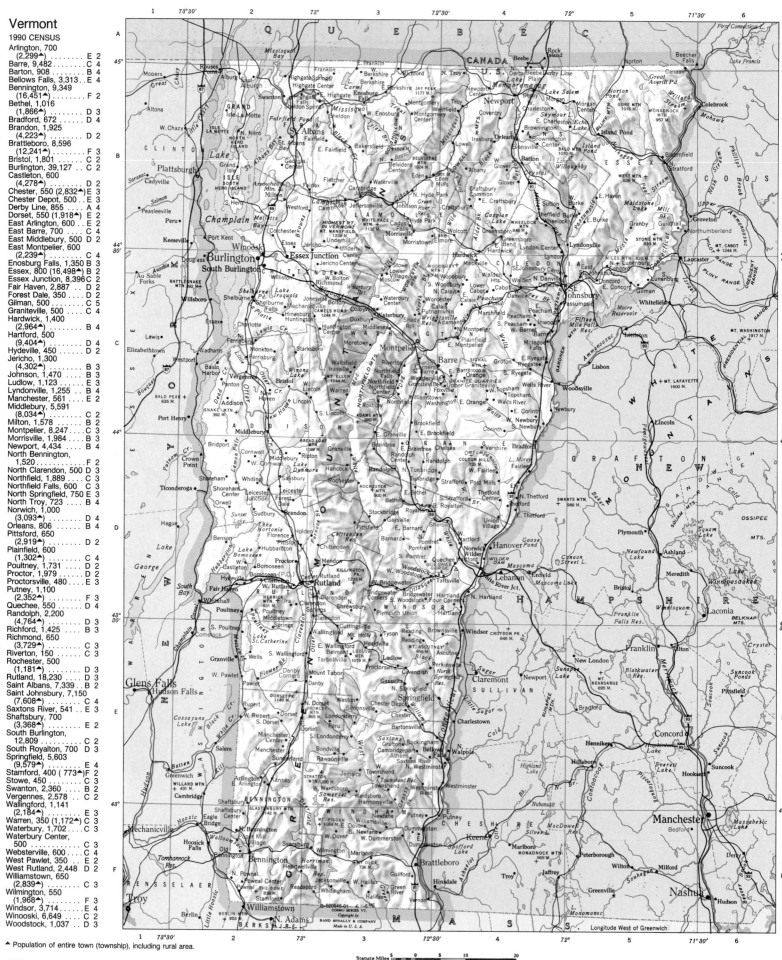

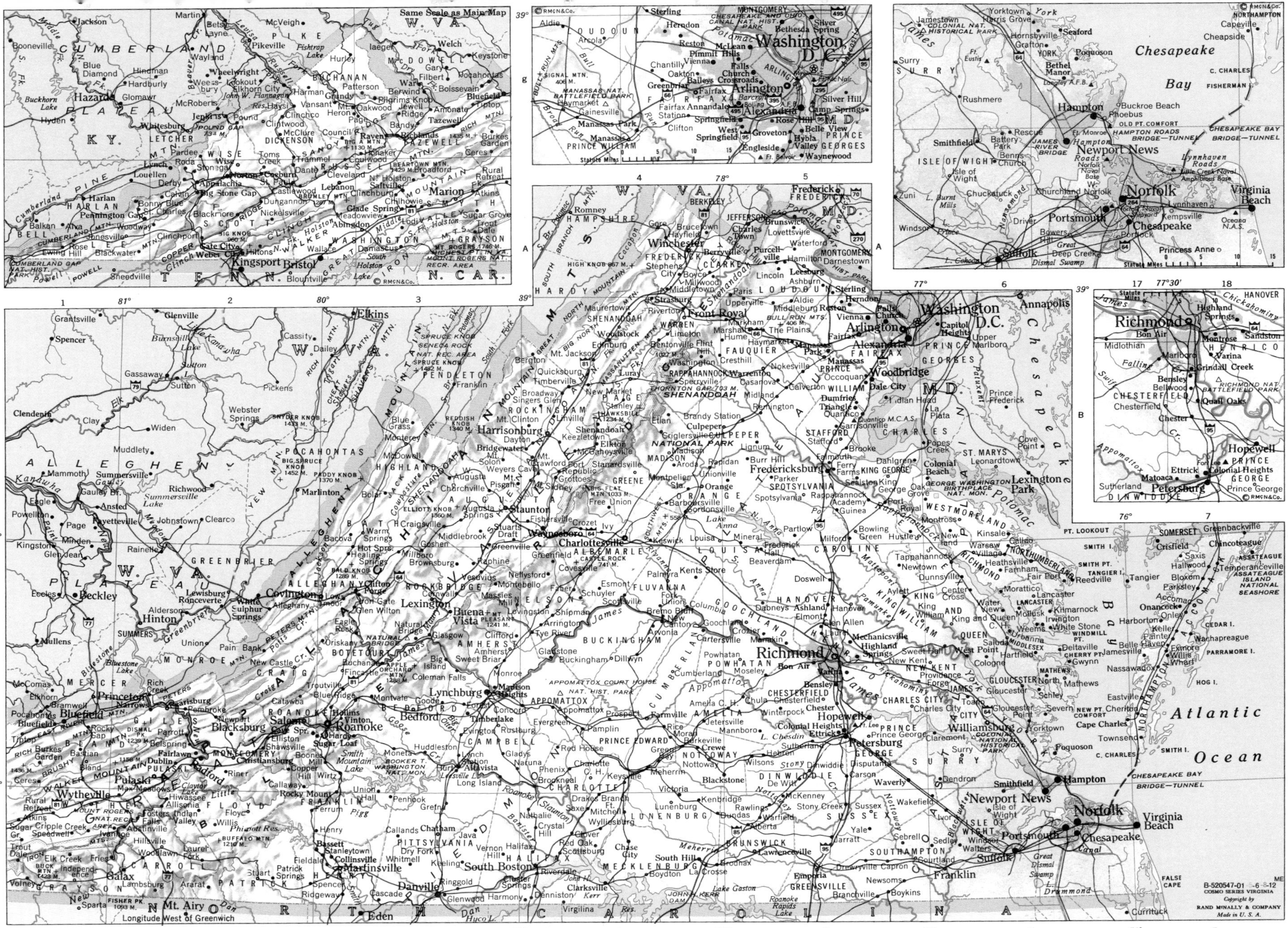

Virginia

1990 CENSUS

- Alexandria, 111,183 .. B 5
- Annandale, 38,000 .... g12
- Appomattox, 1,707 .... C 4
- Arlington, 170,936 .... B 5
- Bedford, 6,073 ..... C 3
- Big Stone Gap, 4,748 .. f 9
- Blacksburg, 34,590 .... C 2
- Bluefield, 5,363 ...... C 1
- Bristol, 18,426 .... f 9
- Buena Vista, 6,406 .... C 3
- Cave Spring, 15,200 .. C 2
- Charlottesville, 40,341 .. B 4
- Chesapeake, 151,976 .. D 6
- Chincoteague, 3,572 .. C 7
- Christiansburg, 15,004 C 2
- Clifton Forge, 4,679 .. C 3
- Colonial Heights, 16,064 C 5
- Covington, 6,991 ...... C 3
- Culpeper, 8,581 ..... B 5
- Dale City, 47,170 ...... B 5
- Danville, 53,056 ...... D 3
- Emporia, 5,306 .... D 5
- Engleside, 24,058('80) .. g12
- Fairfax, 19,622 .... B 5
- Falls Church, 9,578 .... g12
- Farmville, 6,046 ...... C 4
- Franklin, 7,864 .... D 6
- Fredericksburg, 19,027 B 5
- Front Royal, 11,880 .. B 4
- Galax, 6,670 .... D 2
- Greenbriar, 6,200 ..... g12
- Groveton, 6,300 ...... g12
- Hampton, 133,793 .... C 6
- Harrisonburg, 30,707 .. B 4
- Herndon, 16,139 ...... B 5
- Highland Springs, 4,230 C 5
- Hollins, 12,295('80) .... C 3
- Hopewell, 23,101 ..... C 5
- Leesburg, 16,202 .... A 5
- Lexington, 6,959 ...... C 3
- Lynchburg, 66,049 .... C 3
- Madison Heights, 14,146('80) .... C 3
- Manassas, 27,957 .... B 5
- Manassas Park, 6,734 B 5
- Marion, 6,630 .... f10
- Martinsville, 16,162 .... D 3
- McLean, 24,000 ...... g12
- Mechanicsville, 2,969('80) .... C 5
- Newport News, 170,045 D 6
- Norfolk, 261,229 ...... D 6
- Norton, 4,247 .... f 9
- Oakton, 12,500 .... g12
- Petersburg, 38,386 ... C 5
- Poquoson, 11,005 .... C 6
- Portsmouth, 103,907 .. D 6
- Pulaski, 9,985 .... C 2
- Radford, 15,940 ...... C 2
- Reston, 48,556 ...... B 5
- Richlands, 4,456 ...... e10
- Richmond, 203,056 .... C 5
- Roanoke, 96,397 ..... C 3
- Salem, 23,756 .... C 2
- Shenandoah, 2,213 .... B 4
- South Boston, 6,997 .. D 4
- Springfield, 15,000 .... g12
- Staunton, 24,461 ..... B 3
- Sterling, 16,080('80) .. A 5
- Suffolk, 52,141 ...... D 6
- Sugar Loaf, 2,000 .... C 3
- Tazewell, 4,176 ...... e10
- Timberlake, 8,700 .... C 3
- Vienna, 14,852 ...... B 5
- Vinton, 7,665 .... C 3
- Virginia Beach, 393,069 D 7
- Waynesboro, 18,549 .. B 4
- Waynewood, 5,000 .... g12
- West Springfield, 18,000 g12
- Williamsburg, 11,530 .. C 6
- Winchester, 21,947 .... A 4
- Woodbridge, 26,401 .. B 5
- Wytheville, 8,038 ...... D 1
- Yorktown, 270 .... C 6

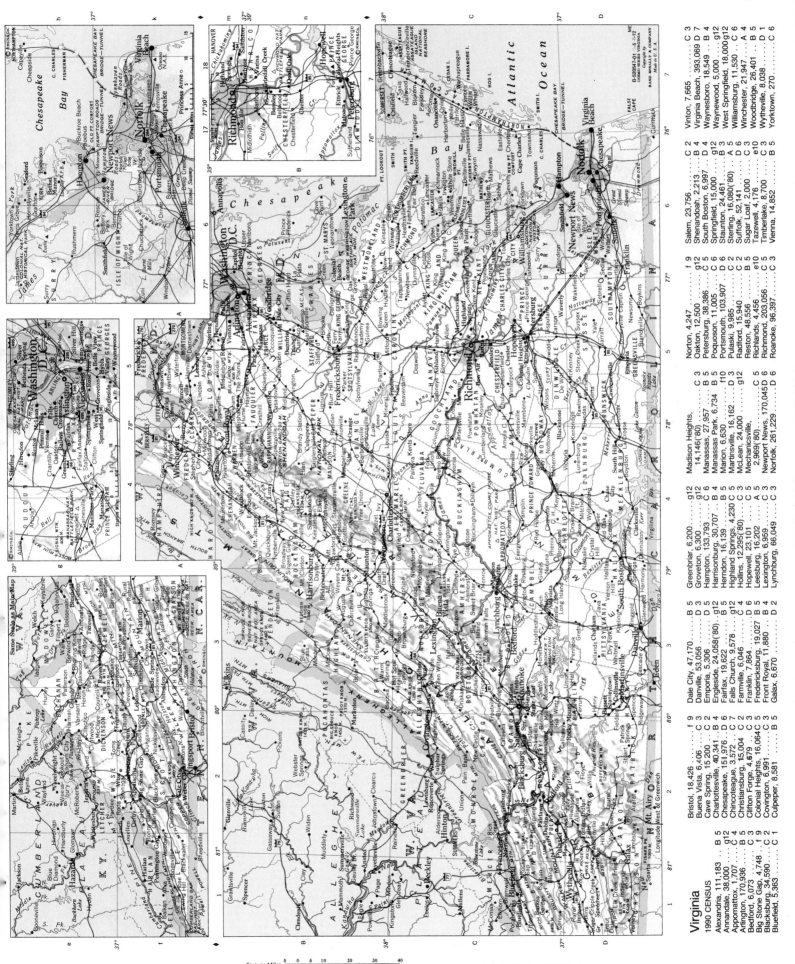

Washington

1990 CENSUS

- Aberdeen, 16,565 .... C 2
- Anacortes, 11,451 .... A 3
- Auburn, 33,102 .... B 3
- Bellevue, 86,874 .... e11
- Bellingham, 52,179 .... A 3
- Bonney Lake, 7,494 .. B 3
- Bothell, 12,345 .... B 3
- Bremerton, 38,142 .... B 3
- Camas, 6,442 .... D 3
- Centralia, 12,101 .... C 3
- Chehalis, 6,527 .... C 3
- Cheney, 7,723 .... B 8
- Clarkston, 6,753 .... C 8
- College Place, 6,308 .. C 7
- Colville, 4,360 .... A 8
- Coulee Dam, 1,087 .... B 7
- Des Moines, 17,283 .. B 3
- Edmonds, 30,744 .... B 3
- Ellensburg, 12,361 .... C 5
- Enumclaw, 7,227 .... B 4
- Ephrata, 5,349 .... B 6
- Everett, 69,961 .... B 3
- Ferndale, 5,398 .... A 3
- Fircrest, 5,258 .... f10
- Goldendale, 3,319 .... D 5
- Grandview, 7,169 .... C 6
- Hoquiam, 8,972 .... C 2
- Issaquah, 7,786 .... B 3
- Kelso, 11,820 .... C 3
- Kennewick, 42,155 .... C 6
- Kent, 37,960 .... B 3
- Kirkland, 40,052 .... B 3
- Lacey, 19,279 .... B 3
- Lakewood Center, 62,000 .... B 3
- Longview, 31,499 .... C 3
- Lynden, 5,709 .... A 3
- Lynnwood, 28,695 .... B 3
- Marysville, 10,328 .... A 3
- Medical Lake, 3,664 .. B 8
- Mercer Island, 20,816 .. B 3
- Montesano, 3,064 .... C 2
- Moses Lake, 11,235 .. B 6
- Mount Vernon, 17,647 A 3
- Oak Harbor, 17,176 .. A 3
- Olympia, 33,840 .... B 3
- Omak, 4,117 .... A 6
- Othello, 4,638 .... C 6
- Parkland, 27,300 .... f11
- Parkwater, 4,300('91) .. g14
- Pasco, 20,337 .... C 6
- Port Angeles, 17,710 .. A 2
- Port Orchard, 4,984 .. B 3
- Port Townsend, 7,001 A 3
- Prosser, 4,476 .... C 6
- Pullman, 23,478 .... C 8
- Puyallup, 23,875 .... B 3
- Quincy, 3,738 .... B 6
- Redmond, 35,800 .... e11
- Renton, 41,688 .... B 3
- Richland, 32,315 .... C 6
- Richmond Beach, 6,700('91) .... B 3
- Richmond Highlands, 27,900 .... B 3
- Riverton Heights, 14,182 f11
- Seattle, 516,259 .... B 3
- Sedro Woolley, 6,031 .. A 3
- Selah, 5,113 .... C 5
- Shelton, 7,241 .... B 2
- Snohomish, 6,499 .... B 3
- Spokane, 177,196 .... B 8
- Steilacoom, 5,728 .... f10
- Sumner, 6,281 .... B 3
- Sunnyside, 11,238 .... C 5
- Tacoma, 176,664 .... B 3
- Toppenish, 7,419 .... C 5
- Tukwila, 11,874 .... f11
- Tumwater, 9,976 .... B 3
- Vancouver, 46,380 .... D 3
- Walla Walla, 26,478 .. C 7
- Wenatchee, 21,756 .... B 5
- White Center, 18,000('91) e11
- Yakima, 54,827 .... C 5

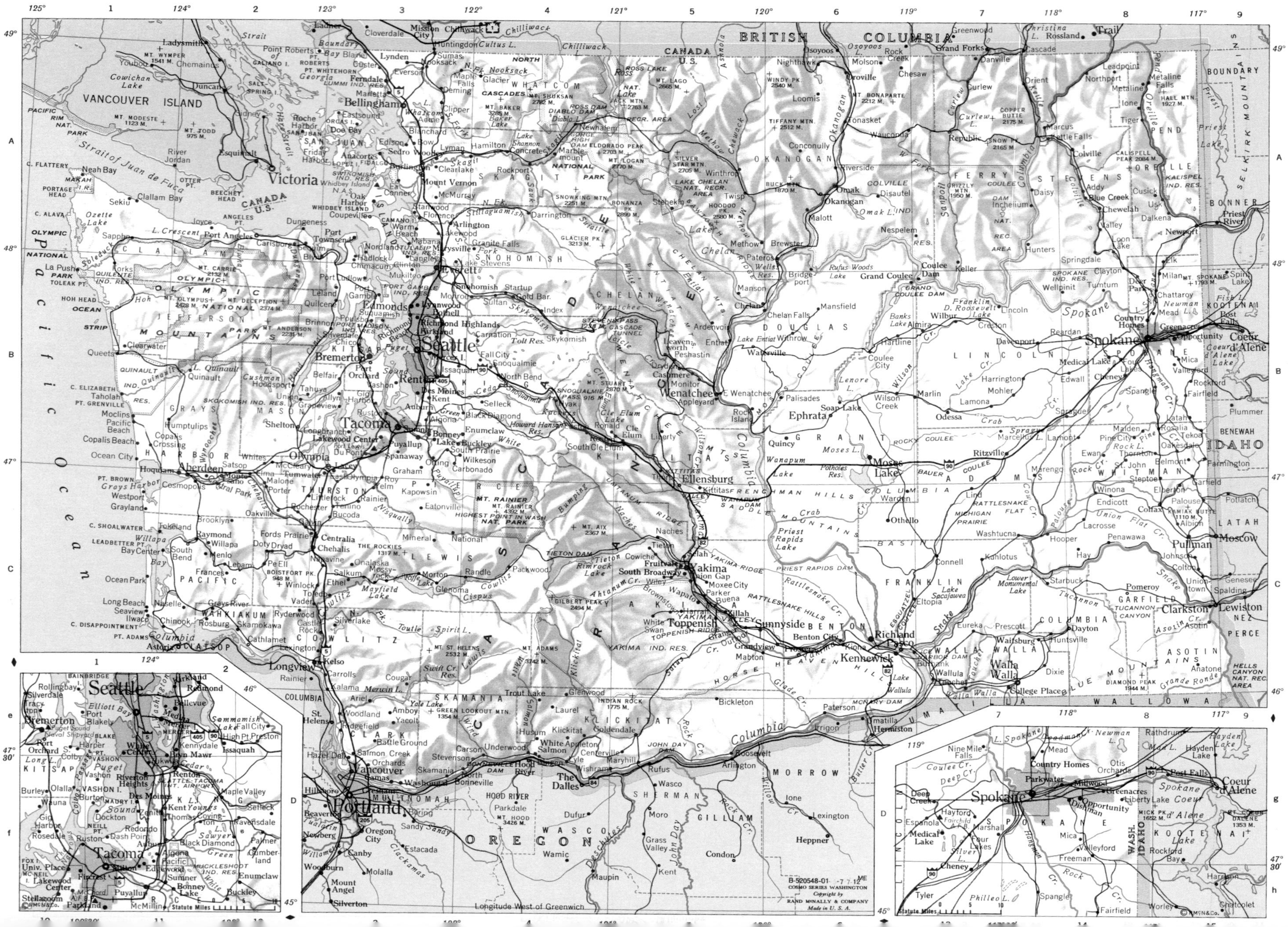

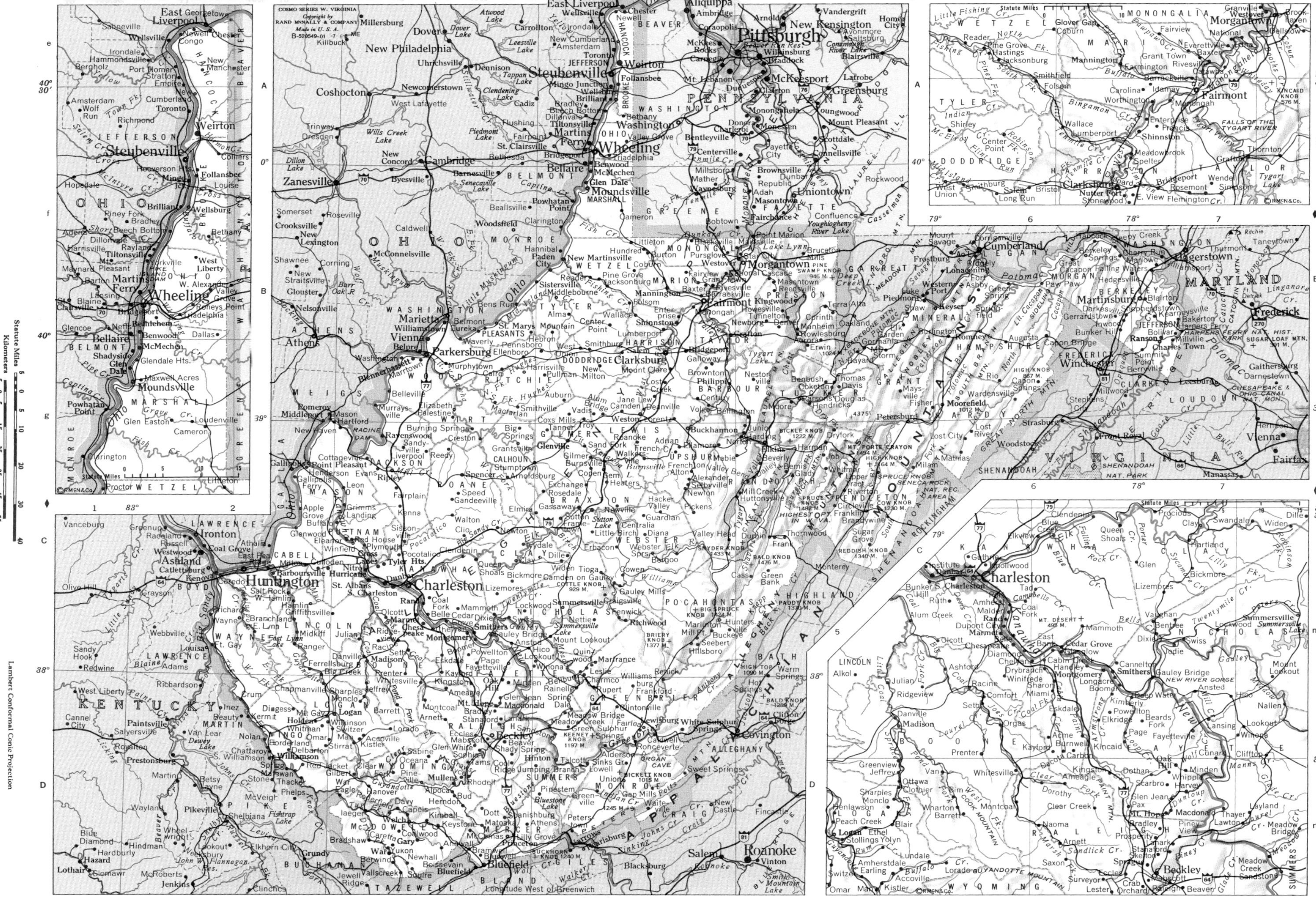

West Virginia

1990 CENSUS

Ansted, 1,643 . . . . C 3
Barboursville, 2,774 . . C 2
Beckley, 18,296 . . . . . . D 3
Belington, 1,850 . . . . . . B 5
Benwood, 1,669 . . . . . . f 8
Bluefield, 12,756 . . . . . D 3
Bridgeport, 6,739 . . . . B 4
Buckhannon, 5,909 . . . . C 4
Ceredo, 1,916 . . . . C 2
Charleston, 57 287 . . . . C 3
Charles Town, 3,122 . . B 7
Chesapeake, 1,896 . . . . C 3
Chester, 2,905 . . . . A 4
Clarksburg, 18,059 . . . . B 4
Dunbar, 8,697 . . . . C 3
Elkins, 7,420 . . . . C 5
Fairmont, 20,210 . . . . . B 4
Fayetteville, 2,132 . . . . C 3
Follansbee, 3,339 . . . . A 4
Gary, 1,355 . . . . D 3
Glenville, 1,923 . . . . C 4
Grafton, 5,524 . . . . B 4
Harpers Ferry, 308 . . . . . B 7
Hinton, 3,433 . . . . D 4
Huntington, 54,844 . . . . C 2
Hurricane, 4,461 . . . . C 2
Kenova, 3,748 . . . . C 2
Keyser, 5,870 . . . . B 6
Kingwood, 3,243 . . . . B 5
Lewisburg, 3,598 . . . . . . D 4
Logan, 2,206 . . . . D 3
Madison, 3,051 . . . . C 3
Mannington, 2,184 . . . . B 4
Marmet, 1,879 . . . . C 3
Martinsburg, 14,073 . . . B 7
McMechen, 2,130 . . . . B 4
Milton, 2,242 . . . . C 2
Montgomery, 2,449 . . . . C 3
Moorefield, 2,148 . . . . B 6
Morgantown, 25,879 . . . B 5
Moundsville, 10,753 . . . B 4
Mullens, 2,006 . . . . D 3
New Martinsville, 6,705 B 4
Nitro, 6,851 . . . . C 3
Nutter Fort, 1,819 . . . . k10
Oak Hill, 6,812 . . . . D 3
Oceana, 1,791 . . . . D 3
Paden City, 2,862 . . . . B 4
Parkersburg, 33,862 . . . B 3
Parsons, 1,453 . . . . B 5
Petersburg, 2,360 . . . . B 5
Philippi, 3,132 . . . . B 4
Point Pleasant, 4,996 . . C 2
Princeton, 7,043 . . . . . . D 3
Rainelle, 1,681 . . . . D 4
Rand, 2,400('86) . . . . . . C 3
Ranson, 2,890 . . . . B 7
Ravenswood, 4,189 . . C 3
Richwood, 2,808 . . . . . . C 4
Ripley, 3,023 . . . . C 3
Romney, 1,966 . . . . . . B 6
Ronceverte, 1,754 . . . . D 4
Saint Albans, 11,194 . . C 3
Saint Marys, 2,148 . . . . B 3
Salem, 2,063 . . . . B 4
Shinnston, 2,543 . . . . . . B 4
Sistersville, 1,797 . . . . B 4
South Charleston,
13,645 . . . . C 3
Spencer, 2,279 . . . . . . C 3
Stonewood, 1,996 . . . . k10
Summersville, 2,906 . . . C 4
Terra Alta, 1,713 . . . . . B 5
Vienna, 10,862 . . . . . . B 3
War, 1,081 . . . . D 3
Weirton, 22,124 . . . . . . A 4
Welch, 3,028 . . . . D 3
Wellsburg, 3,385 . . . . . A 4
Weston, 4,994 . . . . B 4
Westover, 4,201 . . . . . . B 5
Wheeling, 34,882 . . . . . A 4
White Sulphur Springs,
2,779 . . . . D 4
Williamson, 4,154 . . . . D 2
Williamstown, 2,774 . . B 3

Wisconsin

1990 CENSUS

Allouez, 14,431 .... h 9
Antigo, 8,276 ...... C 4
Appleton, 65,695 .... D 5
Ashland, 8,695 ...... B 3
Ashwaubenon, 16,376 D 5
Baraboo, 9,203 .... E 4
Beaver Dam, 14,196 E 5
Beloit, 35,573 ...... F 4
Brookfield, 35,184 .. m11
Brown Deer, 12,236 m12
Burlington, 8,855 .... F 5
Cedarburg, 9,895 .... E 6
Chippewa Falls, 12,727 .... D 2
Cudahy, 18,659 .... F 6
De Pere, 16,569 .... D 5
Eau Claire, 56,856 .. D 2
Fond du Lac, 37,757 E 5
Fort Atkinson, 10,227 F 5
Franklin, 21,855 ...... n11
Germantown, 13,658 E 5
Glendale, 14,088 .... m12
Grafton, 9,340 ...... E 6
Green Bay, 96,466 .. D 6
Greendale, 15,128 .. F 6
Greenfield, 33,403 .. n11
Hayward, 1,897 .... B 2
Howard, 9,874 ...... D 5
Hudson, 6,378 ...... D 1
Janesville, 52,133 .. F 4
Kaukauna, 11,982 .. D 5
Kenosha, 80,352 .... F 6
La Crosse, 51,003 .. E 2
Lake Geneva, 5,979 .. F 5
Little Chute, 9,207 .. D 5
Madison, 191,262 .. E 4
Manitowoc, 32,520 .. D 6
Marinette, 11,843 .. C 6
Marshfield, 19,291 .. D 3
Menasha, 14,711 .... D 5
Menomonee Falls, 26,840 .... E 5
Menomonie, 13,547 .. D 2
Mequon, 18,885 .... E 6
Merrill, 9,860 .... C 4
Middleton, 13,289 .. E 4
Milwaukee, 628,088 .. E 6
Monona, 8,637 ...... E 4
Monroe, 10,241 .... F 4
Muskego, 16,813 .... F 5
Neenah, 23,219 .... D 5
New Berlin, 33,592 .. n11
New London, 6,658 .. D 5
Oak Creek, 19,513 .. n12
Oconomowoc, 10,993 E 5
Oconto, 4,474 ...... D 6
Onalaska, 11,284 .... E 2
Oshkosh, 55,006 .... D 5
Park Falls, 3,104 .. C 3
Platteville, 9,708 .... F 3
Portage, 8,640 ...... E 4
Port Washington, 9,338 .... E 6
Prairie du Chien, 5,659 .... E 2
Racine, 84,298 ...... F 6
Reedsburg, 5,834 .. E 3
Rhinelander, 7,427 .. C 4
Rice Lake, 7,998 .... C 2
River Falls, 10,610 .. D 1
Saint Francis, 9,245 .. n12
Shawano, 7,598 .... D 5
Sheboygan, 49,676 .. E 6
Shorewood, 14,116 .. E 6
South Milwaukee, 20,958 .... F 6
Stevens Point, 23,006 D 4
Stoughton, 8,786 .... F 4
Sturgeon Bay, 9,176 D 6
Sun Prairie, 15,333 .. E 4
Superior, 27,134 .... B 1
Tomah, 7,570 ...... E 3
Two Rivers, 13,030 .. D 6
Watertown, 19,142 .. E 5
Waukesha, 56,958 .. F 5
Waupun, 8,207 ...... E 5
Wausau, 37,060 .... D 4
Wauwatosa, 49,366 m12
West Allis, 63,221 .. m11
West Bend, 23,916 .. E 5
Weston, 8,775('80) .. D 4
Whitefish Bay, 14,272 m12
Whitewater, 12,636 .. F 5
Wisconsin Dells, 2,393 .... E 4
Wisconsin Rapids, 18,245 .... D 4

Statute Miles 5 0 5 10 20 30 40
Kilometers 5 0 5 15 25 35 45 55

Lambert Conformal Conic Projection

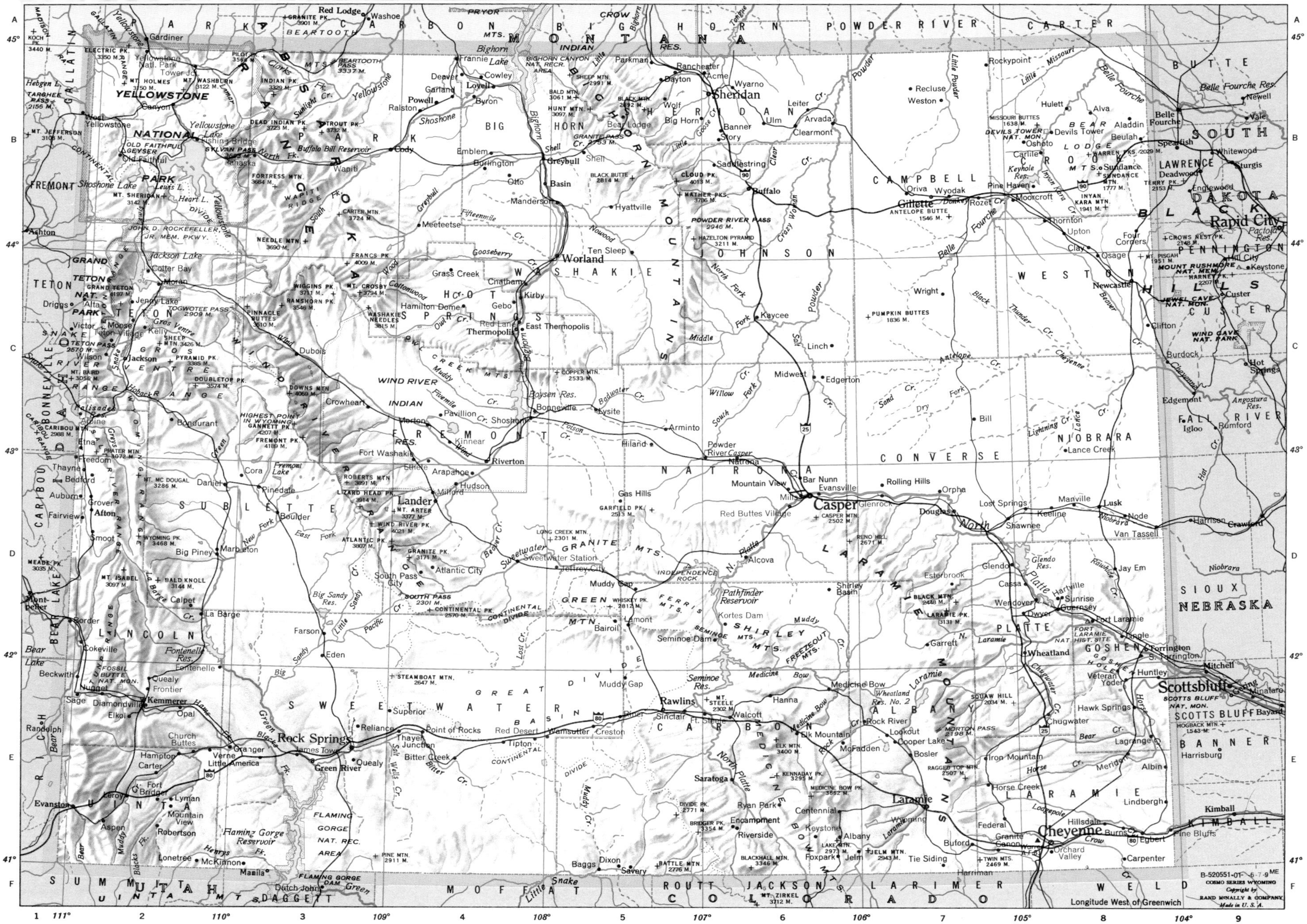

Statute Miles 5 0 5 10 20 30 40 50
Kilometers 5 0 5 15 25 35 45 55 65 75

Lambert Conformal Conic Projection

Wyoming

1990 CENSUS

Afton, 1,394 . . . . D 2
Baggs, 272 . . . . E 5
Basin, 1,180 . . . . B 4
Big Piney, 454 . . . . D 2
Buffalo, 3,302 . . . . B 6
Burns, 254 . . . . E 8
Byron, 470 . . . . B 4
Casper, 46,742 . . . . . . D 6
Cheyenne, 50,008 . . . . E 8
Chugwater, 192 . . . . . . E 8
Cody, 7,897 . . . . B 3
Cokeville, 493 . . . . D 2
Cowley, 477 . . . . B 4
Dayton, 565 . . . . B 5
Diamondville, 864 . . . . E 2
Douglas, 5,076 . . . . D 7
Dubois, 895 . . . . C 3
Edgerton, 247 . . . . C 6
Elk Mountain, 174 . . . . E 6
Encampment, 490 . . . . E 6
Evanston, 10,903 . . . . . E 2
Evansville, 1,403 . . . . . D 6
Fort Laramie, 243 . . . . D 8
Freedom, 450('91) . . . . D 2
Gillette, 17,635 . . . . . . B 7
Glendo, 195 . . . . D 7
Glenrock, 2,153 . . . . . . D 7
Green River, 12,711 . . E 3
Greybull, 1,789 . . . . . . B 4
Guernsey, 1,155 . . . . . . D 8
Hanna, 1,076 . . . . E 6
Hudson, 392 . . . . D 4
Hulett, 429 . . . . B 8
Jackson, 4,472 . . . . . . C 2
James Town, 280('91) E 3
Kaycee, 256 . . . . C 6
Kemmerer, 3,020 . . . . . E 2
La Barge, 493 . . . . D 2
Lander, 7,023 . . . . D 4
Laramie, 26,687 . . . . . . E 7
Lingle, 473 . . . . D 8
Lovell, 2,131 . . . . B 4
Lusk, 1,504 . . . . D 8
Lyman, 1,896 . . . . E 2
Marbleton, 634 . . . . . . D 2
Medicine Bow, 389 . . . E 6
Meeteetse, 368 . . . . . . B 4
Midwest, 495 . . . . C 6
Mills, 1,574 . . . . D 6
Moorcroft, 768 . . . . B 8
Mountain View, 1,189 . . E 2
Newcastle, 3,003 . . . . . C 8
Osage, 350('91) . . . . . . C 8
Pine Bluffs, 1,054 . . . . E 8
Pinedale, 1,181 . . . . . . D 3
Powell, 5,292 . . . . B 4
Ranchester, 676 . . . . . . B 5
Rawlins, 9,380 . . . . E 5
Reliance, 500('91) . . . . E 3
Riverton, 9,202 . . . . C 4
Rock River, 190 . . . . . . E 7
Rock Springs, 19,050 . . E 3
Saratoga, 1,969 . . . . . . E 6
Sheridan, 13,900 . . . . . . B 6
Shoshoni, 497 . . . . C 4
Sinclair, 500 . . . . E 5
South Torrington, 300('91) . . . . D 8
Story, 700('91) . . . . B 6
Sundance, 1,139 . . . . . . B 8
Superior, 273 . . . . E 4
Ten Sleep, 311 . . . . . . B 5
Teton Village, 250('91) C 2
Thayne, 267 . . . . D 1
Thermopolis, 3,247 . . . . C 4
Torrington, 5,651 . . . . . . D 8
Upton, 980 . . . . B 8
Wamsutter, 240 . . . . . . E 5
West Laramie, 2,000('91) . . . . E 7
Wheatland, 3,271 . . . . D 8
Wilson, 500('91) . . . . . . C 2
Worland, 5,742 . . . . B 5
Yellowstone National Park, 400('91) . . . . B 2

North Polar Regions

Anchorage, 226,338 ('90)........................C27
Archangel'sk, 416,000 ('89)..........................C 8
BELGIUM.............................D12
Berlin, 3,352,848 ('89) (3,825,000★) D11
CANADA..........................D22
Chicago, 2,783,726 ('90)............................E21
CHINA..............................F 2
Churchill, 1,186 ('81)...D22
DENMARK........................D11
Dublin, 502,749 ('86) (1,140,000★) D13
Dutch Harbor, 20 ('81)D29
Edmonton, 573,982 ('86) (785,465★) D24
ESTONIA.........................C10
FAEROE ISLANDS..... C13
Fairbanks, 30,843 ('90)............................C27
FINLAND..........................C10
FRANCE...........................E12
Gander, 10,207 ('86) (10,899★) E18
GERMANY........................D11
Godthåb, 12,217 ('90).C18
GREENLAND.............. B17
Hammerfest, 7,208 ('83).......................... B10
Happy Valley-Goose Bay, 7,248 ('86)................D19
Helsinki, 490,034 ('88) (1,040,000★) C10
ICELAND..........................C14
Igarka, 16,918 ('79).....C 4
IRELAND..........................D13
JAPAN...............................F35
Jekaterinburg, 1,367,000 ('89) (1,620,000★) .. D 6
Juneau, 26,751 ('90)...D26
Kijev (Kiev), 2,587,000 ('89) (2,900,000★) .. D 9
KOREA, NORTH..........E36
KOREA, SOUTH..........F36
LATVIA..............................C10
LITHUANIA.......................C10
Leningrad, 4,456,000 ('89) (5,825,000★) ....D 9
LUXEMBOURG............E12
Magadan, 152,000 ('89)..........................D33
MONGOLIA................. E 2
Moskva (Moscow), 8,769,000 ('89) (13,100,000★) ....D 9
Murmansk, 468,000 ('89)...........................C 9
NETHERLANDS.......... D12
New York, 7,322,564 ('90)............................E20
Nižnij Novgorod (Gorky), 1,438,000 ('89) (2,025,000★) ....D 8
Nome, 3,500 ('90)....... C29
Noril'sk, 174,000 ('89).C 4
NORWAY.........................C12
Novosibirsk, 1,436,000 ('89) (1,600,000★) .. D 4
Ōsaka, 2,636,249 ('85) (16,450,000★) F35
Oslo, 452,415 ('87) (720,000★) D11
Ottawa, 300,763 ('86) (819,263★) E20
Paris, 2,078,900 ('87) (9,775,000★) E12
POLAND.......................D11
Québec, 164,580 ('86) (603,267★) E20
Reykjavík, 93,425 ('87) (137,941★) C15
RUSSIA.......................C 4
Saint John's, 96,216 ('86) (161,901★) E18
Sankt-Peterburg, 4,456,000 ('89) (5,825,000★) ....D 9
Seattle, 516,259 ('90)..E25
Shenyang (Mukden), 3,910,000 ('88) (4,370,000▲) E36
Sŏul (Seoul), 10,522,000 ('89) (15,850,000★) .F36
Stockholm, 672,187 ('90) (1,449,972★) D11
SWEDEN.........................C11
Thule, 551 ('90)..........B19
Tōkyō, 8,354,615 ('85) (27,700,000★) F35
UKRAINE........................E 9
Ulaanbaatar (Ulan Bator), 548,400 ('89)...........E 2
UNITED KINGDOM..... D13
UNITED STATES.........F22
Vancouver, 431,147 ('86) (1,380,729★) E25
Vladivostok, 648,000 ('89)............................E35
Vorkuta, 116,000 ('89)C 6
Warszawa, 1,651,200 ('89) (2,323,000★) .. D10
Winnipeg, 594,551 ('86) (625,304★) E22

Kilometers 0 500 1000 1500 2000 Km.
Miles 0 500 1000 1500 2000 Mi.

1:60 000 000

★ Population of metropolitan area, including suburbs.
▲ Population of entire district, including rural area.

ıdex to World Reference Maps

ıtroduction to the Index

ıs universal index includes in a single alphabetical list approximately 38,000 names of features that ɔear on the reference maps. Each name is followed by the name of the country or continent in ich it is located, a map-reference key and a page reference.

ımes The names of cities appear in the index in regular type. The names of all other features ɔear in *italics*, followed by descriptive terms (hill, mtn., state) to indicate their nature.

Names that appear in shortened versions on the maps due to space limitations are spelled out in in the index. The portions of these names omitted from the maps are enclosed in brackets — for ample, Acapulco [de Juárez].

Abbreviations of names on the maps have been standardized as much as possible. Names that abbreviated on the maps are generally spelled out in full in the index.

Country names and names of features that extend beyond the boundaries of one country are owed by the name of the continent in which each is located. Country designations follow the nes of all other places in the index. The locations of places in the United States, Canada, and the ted Kingdom are further defined by abbreviations that indicate the state, province, or political ision in which each is located.

All abbreviations used in the index are defined in the List of Abbreviations below.

ıhabetization Names are alphabetized in the order of the letters of the English alphabet. Spanish and *ch*, for example, are not treated as distinct letters. Furthermore, diacritical marks are regarded in alphabetization — German or Scandinavian *ä* or *ö* are treated as *a* or *o*.

The names of physical features may appear inverted, since they are always alphabetized under proper, not the generic, part of the name, thus: 'Gibraltar, Strait of'. Otherwise every entry, whether consisting of one word or more, is alphabetized as a single continuous entity. 'Lakeland', for example, appears after 'La Crosse' and before 'La Salle'. Names beginning with articles (Le Havre, Den Helder, Al Manṣūrah) are not inverted. Names beginning 'St.', 'Ste.' and 'Sainte' are alphabetized as though spelled 'Saint'.

In the case of identical names, towns are listed first, then political divisions, then physical features. Entries that are completely identical are listed alphabetically by country name.

Map-Reference Keys and Page References The map-reference keys and page references are found in the last two columns of each entry.

Each map-reference key consists of a letter and number. The letters appear along the sides of the maps. Lowercase letters indicate reference to inset maps. Numbers appear across the tops and bottoms of the maps.

Map reference keys for point features, such as cities and mountain peaks, indicate the locations of the symbols. For extensive areal features, such as countries or mountain ranges, locations are given for the approximate centers of the features. Those for linear features, such as canals and rivers, are given for the locations of the names.

Names of some important places or features that are omitted from the maps due to space limitations are included in the index. Each of these places is identified by an asterisk (*) preceding the map-reference key.

The page number generally refers to the main map for the country in which the feature is located. Page references to two-page maps always refer to the left-hand page.

st of Abbreviations

g.	Afghanistan
'.	Africa
., U.S.	Alaska, U.S.
, U.S.	Alabama, U.S.
).	Albania
j.	Algeria
a., Can.	Alberta, Can.
ı. Sam.	American Samoa
ch.	anchorage
d.	Andorra
g.	Angola
t.	Antarctica
tig.	Antigua and Barbuda
, U.S.	Arkansas, U.S.
g.	Argentina
m.	Armenia
s.	Austria
stl.	Australia
., U.S.	Arizona, U.S.
er.	Azerbaijan
	bay, gulf, inlet, lagoon
h.	Bahamas
hr.	Bahrain
rb.	Barbados
A.T.	British Antarctic Territory
C., Can.	British Columbia, Can.
i.	Burundi
l.	Belgium
la.	Belarus
r.	Bermuda
u.	Bhutan
.O.T.	British Indian Ocean Territory
gl.	Bangladesh
l.	Bolivia
ph.	Bophuthatswana
s.	Bosnia and Herzegovina
ts.	Botswana
az.	Brazil
J.	Brunei
Vir. Is.	British Virgin Islands
l.	Bulgaria
rkina	Burkina Faso
	cape, point
., U.S.	California, U.S.
m.	Cameroon
mb.	Cambodia
n.	Canada
y. Is.	Cayman Islands
n. Afr. Rep.	Central African Republic
rist. I.	Christmas Island
	cliff, escarpment
	county, parish
., U.S.	Colorado, U.S.
l.	Colombia
m.	Comoros
nt.	continent
R.	Costa Rica
at.	crater
ɔ.	Croatia
, U.S.	Connecticut, U.S.

ctry.	country
C.V.	Cape Verde
Cyp.	Cyprus
Czech.	Czech Republic
D.C., U.S.	District of Columbia, U.S.
De., U.S.	Delaware, U.S.
Den.	Denmark
dep.	dependency, colony
depr.	depression
dept.	department, district
des.	desert
Dji.	Djibouti
Dom.	Dominica
Dom. Rep.	Dominican Republic
Ec.	Ecuador
El Sal.	El Salvador
Eng., U.K.	England, U.K.
Eq. Gui.	Equatorial Guinea
Erit.	Eritrea
est.	estuary
Est.	Estonia
Eth.	Ethiopia
Eur.	Europe
Faer. Is.	Faeroe Islands
Falk. Is.	Falkland Islands
Fin.	Finland
Fl., U.S.	Florida, U.S.
for.	forest, moor
Fr.	France
Fr. Gu.	French Guiana
Fr. Poly.	French Polynesia
F.S.A.T.	French Southern and Antarctic Territory
Ga., U.S.	Georgia, U.S.
Gam.	Gambia
Geor.	Georgia
Ger.	Germany
Gib.	Gibraltar
Grc.	Greece
Gren.	Grenada
Grnld.	Greenland
Guad.	Guadeloupe
Guat.	Guatemala
Gui.	Guinea
Gui.-B.	Guinea-Bissau
Guy.	Guyana
Hi., U.S.	Hawaii, U.S.
hist.	historic site, ruins
hist. reg.	historic region
H.K.	Hong Kong
Hond.	Honduras
Hung.	Hungary
i.	island
Ia., U.S.	Iowa, U.S.
I.C.	Ivory Coast
Ice.	Iceland
ice	ice feature, glacier
Id., U.S.	Idaho, U.S.
Il., U.S.	Illinois, U.S.
In., U.S.	Indiana, U.S.
Indon.	Indonesia
I. of Man	Isle of Man
Ire.	Ireland

is.	islands
Isr.	Israel
Isr. Occ.	Israeli Occupied Territories
Jam.	Jamaica
Jord.	Jordan
Kaz.	Kazakhstan
Kir.	Kiribati
Ks., U.S.	Kansas, U.S.
Kuw.	Kuwait
Ky., U.S.	Kentucky, U.S.
Kyrg.	Kyrgyzstan
l.	lake, pond
La., U.S.	Louisiana, U.S.
Lat.	Latvia
Leb.	Lebanon
Leso.	Lesotho
Lib.	Liberia
Liech.	Liechtenstein
Lith.	Lithuania
Lux.	Luxembourg
Ma., U.S.	Massachusetts, U.S.
Mac.	Macedonia
Madag.	Madagascar
Malay.	Malaysia
Mald.	Maldives
Man., Can.	Manitoba, Can.
Marsh. Is.	Marshall Islands
Mart.	Martinique
Maur.	Mauritania
May.	Mayotte
Md., U.S.	Maryland, U.S.
Me., U.S.	Maine, U.S.
Mex.	Mexico
Mi., U.S.	Michigan, U.S.
Micron.	Federated States of Micronesia
Mid. Is.	Midway Islands
mil.	military installation
Mn., U.S.	Minnesota, U.S.
Mo., U.S.	Missouri, U.S.
Mol.	Moldova
Mon.	Monaco
Mong.	Mongolia
Monts.	Montserrat
Mor.	Morocco
Moz.	Mozambique
Mrts.	Mauritius
Ms., U.S.	Mississippi, U.S.
Mt., U.S.	Montana, U.S.
mth.	river mouth or channel
mtn.	mountain
mts.	mountains
Mwi.	Malawi
N.A.	North America
N.B., Can.	New Brunswick, Can.
N.C., U.S.	North Carolina, U.S.
N. Cal.	New Caledonia
N. Cyp.	North Cyprus
N.D., U.S.	North Dakota, U.S.
Ne., U.S.	Nebraska, U.S.
Neth.	Netherlands
Neth. Ant.	Netherlands Antilles
Newf., Can.	Newfoundland, Can.

N.H., U.S.	New Hampshire, U.S.
Nic.	Nicaragua
Nig.	Nigeria
N. Ire., U.K.	Northern Ireland, U.K.
N.J., U.S.	New Jersey, U.S.
N. Kor.	North Korea
N.M., U.S.	New Mexico, U.S.
N. Mar. Is.	Northern Mariana Islands
Nmb.	Namibia
Nor.	Norway
Norf. I.	Norfolk Island
N.S., Can.	Nova Scotia, Can.
Nv., U.S.	Nevada, U.S.
N.W. Ter., Can.	Northwest Territories, Can.
N.Y., U.S.	New York, U.S.
N.Z.	New Zealand
Oc.	Oceania
Oh., U.S.	Ohio, U.S.
Ok., U.S.	Oklahoma, U.S.
Ont., Can.	Ontario, Can.
Or., U.S.	Oregon, U.S.
Pa., U.S.	Pennsylvania, U.S.
Pak.	Pakistan
Pan.	Panama
Pap. N. Gui.	Papua New Guinea
Para.	Paraguay
P.E.I., Can.	Prince Edward Island, Can.
pen.	peninsula
Phil.	Philippines
Pit.	Pitcairn
pl.	plain, flat
plat.	plateau, highland
Pol.	Poland
Port.	Portugal
P.R.	Puerto Rico
prov.	province, region
Que., Can.	Quebec, Can.
reg.	physical region
res.	reservoir
Reu.	Reunion
rf.	reef, shoal
R.I., U.S.	Rhode Island, U.S.
Rom.	Romania
Rw.	Rwanda
S.A.	South America
S. Afr.	South Africa
Sask., Can.	Saskatchewan, Can.
Sau. Ar.	Saudi Arabia
S.C., U.S.	South Carolina, U.S.
sci.	scientific station
Scot., U.K.	Scotland, U.K.
S.D., U.S.	South Dakota, U.S.
Sen.	Senegal
Sey.	Seychelles
Sing.	Singapore
S. Kor.	South Korea
S.L.	Sierra Leone
Slo.	Slovenia
Slov.	Slovakia
S. Mar.	San Marino
Sol. Is.	Solomon Islands

Som.	Somalia
Sp. N. Afr.	Spanish North Africa
Sri L.	Sri Lanka
state	state, republic, canton
St. Hel.	St. Helena
St. K./N	St. Kitts and Nevis
St. Luc.	St. Lucia
stm.	stream (river, creek)
S. Tom./P.	Sao Tome and Principe
St. P./M.	St. Pierre and Miquelon
strt.	strait, channel, sound
St. Vin.	St. Vincent and the Grenadines
Sud.	Sudan
Sur.	Suriname
sw.	swamp, marsh
Swaz.	Swaziland
Swe.	Sweden
Switz.	Switzerland
Tai.	Taiwan
Taj.	Tajikistan
Tan.	Tanzania
T./C. Is.	Turks and Caicos Islands
ter.	territory
Thai.	Thailand
Tn., U.S.	Tennessee, U.S.
Tok.	Tokelau
Trin.	Trinidad and Tobago
Tun.	Tunisia
Tur.	Turkey
Turk.	Turkmenistan
Tx., U.S.	Texas, U.S.
U.A.E.	United Arab Emirates
Ug.	Uganda
U.K.	United Kingdom
Ukr.	Ukraine
Ur.	Uruguay
U.S.	United States
Ut., U.S.	Utah, U.S.
Uzb.	Uzbekistan
Va., U.S.	Virginia, U.S.
val.	valley, watercourse
Vat.	Vatican City
Ven.	Venezuela
Viet.	Vietnam
V.I.U.S.	Virgin Islands (U.S.)
vol.	volcano
Vt., U.S.	Vermont, U.S.
Wa., U.S.	Washington, U.S.
Wal./F.	Wallis and Futuna
Wi., U.S.	Wisconsin, U.S.
W. Sah.	Western Sahara
W. Sam.	Western Samoa
wtfl.	waterfall
W.V., U.S.	West Virginia, U.S.
Wy., U.S.	Wyoming, U.S.
Yugo.	Yugoslavia
Yukon, Can.	Yukon Territory, Can.
Zam.	Zambia
Zimb.	Zimbabwe

Index

A

Name — Map Ref — Page

Aachen, Ger. E6 8
Aalen, Ger. G10 8
Aalst, Bel. E4 8
Äänekoski, Fin. E15 6
Aarau, Switz. E15 10
Aarschot, Bel. E4 8
Aba, China E7 26
Aba, Nig. G7 42
Ābādān, Iran B4 46
Abaeté, Braz. E6 57
Abajo Peak, mtn., Ut., U.S. F6 121
Abakan, Russia G12 24
Abancay, Peru F4 54
Abashiri, Japan o22 30a
Abasolo, Mex. E7 62
Abaya, Lake, l., Eth. G2 46
Abaza, Russia G12 24
Abbadia San Salvatore, Italy G6 14
Abbaye, Point, c., Mi., U.S. B2 99
Abbeville, Fr. B8 10
Abbeville, Al., U.S. D4 78
Abbeville, Ga., U.S. E3 87
Abbeville, La., U.S. E3 95
Abbeville, S.C., U.S. C3 117
Abbeville, co., S.C., U.S. C2 117
Abbotsford, Wi., U.S. D3 126
Abbottābād, Pak. C5 38
Abbott Butte, mtn., Or., U.S. E4 114
Abbott Run, stm., U.S. B4 116
Abbott Run Valley, R.I., U.S. B4 116
'Abd al-Kūrī, i., Yemen F5 46
Abe, Lake, l., Afr. F3 46
Abéché, Chad F10 42
Abéjar, Spain D9 12
Abengourou, I.C. G5 42
Abeokuta, Nig. G6 42
Aberayron, Wales, U.K. I8 7
Aberdeen, Scot., U.K. D10 7
Aberdeen, Id., U.S. G6 89
Aberdeen, Md., U.S. A5 97
Aberdeen, Ms., U.S. B5 101
Aberdeen, N.C., U.S. B3 110
Aberdeen, Oh., U.S. D2 112
Aberdeen, S.D., U.S. B7 118
Aberdeen, Wa., U.S. C2 124
Aberdeen Lake, l., N.W. Ter., Can. D13 66
Aberdeen Proving Ground, mil., Md., U.S. A5 97
Abernathy, Tx., U.S. C2 120
Abert, Lake, l., Or., U.S. E6 114
Abert Rim, clf, Or., U.S. E6 114
Aberystwyth, Wales, U.K. I8 7
Abhā, Sau. Ar. E3 46
Abidjan, I.C. G5 42
Abilene, Ks., U.S. D6 93
Abilene, Tx., U.S. C3 120
Abingdon, Il., U.S. C3 90
Abingdon, Md., U.S. B5 97
Abingdon, Va., U.S. f10 123
Abington, Ma., U.S. B6 98
Abington [Township], Pa., U.S. o21 115
Abisko, Swe. B12 6
Abita Springs, La., U.S. D5 95
Abitibi, stm., Ont., Can. o19 73
Abitibi, Lake, l., Can. G17 66
Abohar, India E6 38
Abomey, Benin G6 42
Aborigen, Pik, mtn., Russia E23 24
Abraham Lake, res., Alta., Can. C2 68
Abraham Lincoln Birthplace National Historic Site, hist., Ky., U.S. C4 94
Abrantes, Port. F3 12
Absaroka Range, mts., U.S. F7 127
Absarokee, Mt., U.S. E7 103
Absecon, N.J., U.S. E4 107
Absecon Inlet, b., N.J., U.S. E4 107
Abū 'Alī, i., Sau. Ar. C4 46
Abu Dhabi see Abū Ẓaby, U.A.E. D5 46
Abū Ḥamad, Sudan E12 42
Abū Kamāl, Syria B7 40
Abukuma-sanchi, mts., Japan E13 30
Abū Madd, Ra's, c., Sau. Ar. D2 46
Abunã, Braz. E5 54
Abū Shajarah, Ra's, c., Sudan D13 42
Abū Ẓaby, U.A.E. D5 46
Academia, Oh., U.S. B3 112
Acadia, co., La., U.S. D3 95
Acadia National Park, Me., U.S. D4 96
Acajutla, El Sal. H3 64
Acámbaro, Mex. G9 62
Acaponeta, Mex. F7 62
Acapulco [de Juárez], Mex. I10 62
Acarai Mountains, mts., S.A. C7 54
Acaraú, Braz. D10 54
Acarigua, Ven. C8 58
Acatlán [de Osorio], Mex. H10 62
Acayucan, Mex. I12 62
Accomack, co., Va., U.S. C7 123
Accoville, W.V., U.S. D3 125
Accra, Ghana G5 42
Acerra, Italy I9 14
Achaguas, Ven. D8 58
Achalpur, India B4 37
Acheng, China B12 26
Achí, Col. C5 58
Achill Island, i., Ire. H2 7
Achtubinsk, Russia H7 22
Ačinsk, Russia F12 24
Acireale, Italy L10 14
Ackerman, Ms., U.S. B4 101
Ackley, Ia., U.S. B4 92
Acklins Island, i., Bah. C10 64
Acoma Indian Reservation, N.M., U.S. C2 108
Aconcagua, Cerro, mtn., Arg. C2 56
Açores (Azores), is., Port. D11 2
Acquapendente, Italy G6 14
Acqui Terme, Italy E3 14
Acre, stm., S.A. E5 54
Acri, Italy J11 14
Acton, Ma., U.S. B5 98
Acton Vale, Que., Can. D5 74
Acushnet, Ma., U.S. C6 98
Acworth, Ga., U.S. B2 87
Ada, Mn., U.S. C2 100
Ada, Oh., U.S. B2 112
Ada, Ok., U.S. C5 113
Ada, co., Id., U.S. F2 89
Ada, Mount, mtn., Ak., U.S. m22 79
Adair, Ia., U.S. C3 92
Adair, Ok., U.S. A6 113
Adair, co., Ia., U.S. C3 92
Adair, co., Ky., U.S. C4 94
Adair, co., Mo., U.S. A5 102
Adair, co., Ok., U.S. B7 113
Adair, Cape, c., N.W. Ter., Can. B18 66
Adairsville, Ga., U.S. B2 87
Adairville, Ky., U.S. D3 94
Adak Island, i., Ak., U.S. E4 79
Adak Naval Station, mil., Ak., U.S. E4 79
Ādam, Oman D6 46
Adamantina, Braz. F3 57
Adamawa, mts., Afr. G8 42
Adam Island, i., Md., U.S. D5 97
Adams, Ma., U.S. A1 98
Adams, Mn., U.S. G6 100
Adams, N.Y., U.S. B4 109
Adams, Wi., U.S. E4 126
Adams, co., Co., U.S. B6 83
Adams, co., Id., U.S. E2 89
Adams, co., Il., U.S. D2 90
Adams, co., In., U.S. C8 91
Adams, co., Ia., U.S. C3 92
Adams, co., Ms., U.S. D2 101
Adams, co., Ne., U.S. D7 104
Adams, co., N.D., U.S. C3 111
Adams, co., Oh., U.S. D2 112
Adams, co., Pa., U.S. G7 115
Adams, co., Wa., U.S. B7 124
Adams, co., Wi., U.S. D4 126
Adams, Mount, mtn., N.H., U.S. B4 106
Adams, Mount, mtn., Wa., U.S. C4 124
Adams Bridge, rf., Asia H5 37
Adams Point, c., Mi., U.S. C7 99
Adams Run, S.C., U.S. k11 117
Adamstown, Pa., U.S. F9 115
Adamsville, Al., U.S. f7 78
Adamsville, R.I., U.S. E6 116
Adamsville, Tn., U.S. B3 119
Adamsville Brook, stm., R.I., U.S. E6 116
'Adan (Aden), Yemen F4 46
Adana, Tur. H15 4
Adapazarı, Tur. G14 4
Adarama, Sudan E12 42
Ad-Dabbah, Sudan E12 42
Ad-Dahnā, des., Sau. Ar. D4 46
Ad-Dammām, Sau. Ar. C5 46
Ad-Dawādimī, Sau. Ar. D3 46
Ad-Dawḥah (Doha), Qatar C5 46
Addis, La., U.S. D4 95
Addis Ababa see Adis Abeba, Eth. G2 46
Addison, Al., U.S. A2 78
Addison, Ct., U.S. C5 84
Addison, Il., U.S. k8 90
Addison, N.Y., U.S. C3 109
Addison, co., Vt., U.S. C2 122
Ad-Dīwānīyah, Iraq B3 46
Ad-Duwaym, Sudan F12 42
Addyston, Oh., U.S. o12 112
Adel, Ga., U.S. E3 87
Adel, Ia., U.S. C3 92
Adelaide, Austl. F7 50
Adelaide Peninsula, pen., N.W. Ter., Can. C13 66
Adelanto, Ca., U.S. E5 82
Aden, Gulf of, b. F4 46
Aden see 'Adan, Yemen F4 46
Adieu, Cape, c., Austl. F6 50
Adige, stm., Italy D7 14
Adigrat, Eth. F2 46
Ādilābād, India C5 37
Adimi, Russia H21 24
Adirondack Mountains, mts., N.Y., U.S. A6 109
Adis Abeba, Eth. G2 46
Admiralty Bay, b., Ak., U.S. A9 79
Admiralty Inlet, b., N.W. Ter., Can. B15 66
Admiralty Island, i., Ak., U.S. m22 79
Admiralty Islands, is., Pap. N. Gui. k16 50a
Adobe Acres, N.M., U.S. *B3 108
Adobe Creek Reservoir, res., Co., U.S. C7 83
Adolfo López Mateos, Presa, res., Mex. E6 62
Ādoni, India E4 37
Adour, stm., Fr. I7 10
Adra, Spain I8 12
Adrano, Italy L9 14
Adrar, Alg. C5 42
Adria, Italy D7 14
Adrian, Ga., U.S. D4 87
Adrian, Mi., U.S. G6 99
Adrian, Mn., U.S. G3 100
Adrian, Mo., U.S. C3 102
Adriatic Sea, Eur. G11 4
Advance, Mo., U.S. D8 102
Adyča, stm., Russia D21 24
Aegean Sea J8 16
Afars and Issas see Djibouti, ctry., Afr. F3 46
Afghanistan, ctry., Asia C1 36
Afikpo, Nig. G7 42
Åfjord, Nor. E8 6
Afmadu, Som. A8 44
Afognak Island, i., Ak., U.S. D9 79
Africa D6 41
Afton, Ia., U.S. C3 92
Afton, Mn., U.S. F6 100
Afton, Ok., U.S. A7 113
Afton, Wy., U.S. D2 127
'Afula, Isr. C4 40
Afyon, Tur. H14 4
Agadez, Niger E7 42
Agadir, Mor. B4 42
Agalega Islands, is., Mrts. D11 44
Agalta, Cordillera de, mts., Hond. G5 64
Agapa, Russia C11 24
Agartala, India I14 38
Agate Fossil Beds National Monument, Ne., U.S. B2 104
Agattu Island, i., Ak., U.S. E2 79
Agawam, Ma., U.S. B2 98
Agen, Fr. H7 10
Agency, Ia., U.S. D5 92
Agency, Mo., U.S. B3 102
Āghā Jārī, Iran B4 46
Agira, Italy L9 14
Agnone, Italy H9 14
Agoura Hills, Ca., U.S. m11 82
Āgra, India G8 38
Ágreda, Spain D10 12
Ağrı Dağı (Mount Ararat), mtn., Tur. H16 4
Agrigento, Italy L8 14
Agrínion, Grc. K5 16
Agropoli, Italy I9 14
Agua Caliente, Mex. F7 62
Agua Caliente Grande, Mex. D5 62
Aguachica, Col. C6 58
Água Clara, Braz. F2 57
Agua Fria, N.M., U.S. B3 108
Agua Fria, stm., Az., U.S. D3 80
Agua Prieta, Mex. B5 62
Aguascalientes, Mex. G8 62
Águas Formosas, Braz. D8 57
Águeda, Port. E3 12
Aguila, Az., U.S. D2 80
Aguilar, Spain H7 12
Águilas, Spain H10 12
Agulhas, Cape, c., S. Afr. H3 44
Agustín Codazzi, Col. B6 58
Agustín Codazzi, Col. I11 64
Ahaggar, mts., Alg. D7 42
Ahipara Bay, b., N.Z. A4 52
Ahklun Mountains, mts., Ak., U.S. D7 79
Ahlen, Ger. D7 8
Ahmadābād, India I5 38
Ahmadnagar, India C3 37
Ahmadpur East, Pak. F4 38
Ahmar Mountains, mts., Eth. G3 46
Ahoskie, N.C., U.S. A6 110
Ahtanum Creek, stm., Wa., U.S. C5 124
Ahu, China A7 28
Ahuacatlán, Mex. G7 62
Ahvāz, Iran B4 46
Ahvenanmaa (Åland), is., Fin. F12 6
Aialik, Cape, c., Ak., U.S. D10 79
Aichach, Ger. G11 8
Aiea, Hi., U.S. B4 88
Aihun, China A12 26
Aijal, India I15 38
Aiken, S.C., U.S. D4 117
Aiken, co., S.C., U.S. D4 117
Ailsa Craig, Ont., Can. D3 73
Aim, Russia F20 24
Aimorés, Braz. E8 57
Ainslie Lake, l., N.S., Can. C8 71
Ainsworth, Ne., U.S. B6 104
Aipe, Col. F5 58
Aïr, mts., Niger E7 42
Airdrie, Alta., Can. D3 68
Aire-sur-l'Adour, Fr. I6 10
Air Force Island, i., N.W. Ter., Can. C18 66
Air Park West, Ne., U.S. *D9 104
Aisne, stm., Fr. C10 10
Aïssa, Djebel, mtn., Alg. B5 42
Aitape, Pap. N. Gui. k15 50a
Aitkin, Mn., U.S. D5 100
Aitkin, co., Mn., U.S. D5 100
Aix, Mount, mtn., Wa., U.S. C4 124
Aix-en-Provence, Fr. I12 10
Aix-la-Chapelle see Aachen, Ger. E6 8
Aix-les-Bains, Fr. G12 10
Aizu-wakamatsu, Japan E12 30
Ajaccio, Fr. n23 11a
Ajaguz, Kaz. H10 24
Ajan, Russia F21 24
Ajan, stm., Russia C13 24
Ajax, Ont., Can. D6 73
Ajdābiyah, Libya B10 42
Ajjer, Tassili n', plat., Alg. C7 42
'Ajlūn, Jord. C4 40
Ajmer, India G6 38
Ajo, Az., U.S. E3 80
Ajo, Cabo de, c., Spain B8 12
Ajon, Ostrov, i., Russia D27 24
Ajtos, Bul. G11 16
Akademii, Zaliv, b., Russia G21 24
Akaltara, India A7 37
Akan, Japan p22 30a
'Akasha East, Sudan D12 42
Akashi, Japan H7 30
Akçakale, Tur. A6 40
Ak-Chin Indian Reservation, Az., U.S. E3 80
Akesu, China C3 26
Akharnaí, Grc. K7 16
Akhisar, Tur. H13 4
Akiachak, Ak., U.S. C7 79
Akimiski Island, i., N.W. Ter., Can. F16 66
Akita, Japan C13 30
Akjoujt, Maur. E3 42
'Akko (Acre), Isr. C4 40
Aklavik, N.W. Ter., Can. C6 66
Akō, Japan H7 30
Akobo, stm., Afr. G12 42
Akola, India B4 37
Akordat, Erit. E2 46
Akot, India B4 37
Akpatok Island, i., N.W. Ter., Can. D19 66
Akron, Co., U.S. A7 83
Akron, In., U.S. B5 91
Akron, Ia., U.S. B1 92
Akron, N.Y., U.S. B2 109
Akron, Oh., U.S. A4 112
Akron, Pa., U.S. F9 115
Aksaray, Tur. H14 4
Akşehir, Tur. H14 4
Aksum, Eth. F2 46
Aktau, Kaz. I8 22
Akt'ubinsk, Kaz. G9 22
Akureyri, Ice. B4 4
Ål, Nor. F7 6
Alabama, state, U.S. C3 78
Alabama, stm., Al., U.S. D2 78
Alabaster, Al., U.S. B3 78
Alachua, Fl., U.S. C4 86
Alachua, co., Fl., U.S. C4 86
Alagoinhas, Braz. B9 57
Alagón, Spain D10 12
Alajuela, C.R. I5 64
Alakanuk, Ak., U.S. C7 79
Alalakeiki Channel, strt., Hi., U.S. C5 88
Al-'Alamayn, Egypt B11 42
Alamance, co., N.C., U.S. B3 110
Al-'Amārah, Iraq B4 46
Alameda, Ca., U.S. h8 82
Alameda, N.M., U.S. B3 108
Alameda, co., Ca., U.S. D3 82
Alameda Naval Air Station, mil., Ca., U.S. h8 82
Alamito Creek, stm., Tx., U.S. p12 120
Alamo, Ga., U.S. D4 87
Alamo, Nv., U.S. F6 105
Alamo, Tn., U.S. B2 119
Alamo, Tx., U.S. F3 120
Alamogordo, N.M., U.S. E4 108
Alamo Heights, Tx., U.S. E3 120
Alamo Hueco Mountains, mts., N.M., U.S. F1 108
Alamo Indian Reservation, N.M., U.S. C2 108
Alamo Lake, res., Az., U.S. C2 80
Alamosa, Co., U.S. D5 83
Alamosa, co., Co., U.S. D5 83
Alamosa, stm., Co., U.S. D4 83
Alamosa Creek, stm., N.M., U.S. D2 108
Alamosa East, Co., U.S. D5 83
Alanäs, Swe. D10 6
Alanya, Tur. A3 40
Alapaha, Ga., U.S. E3 87
Alapaha, stm., U.S. E3 87
Al-'Aqabah, Jord. E4 40
Alaşehir, Tur. K12 16
Alashanyouqi, China C7 26
Alaska, state, U.S. C9 79
Alaska, Gulf of, b., Ak., U.S. D10 79
Alaska Peninsula, pen., Ak., U.S. D8 79
Alaska Range, mts., Ak., U.S. C9 79
Alassio, Italy E3 14
Alatna, stm., Ak., U.S. B9 79
Al-'Aṭrūn, Sudan E11 42
Alava, Cape, c., Wa., U.S. A1 124
Alazeja, stm., Russia C24 24
Alba, Italy E3 14
Albacete, Spain G10 12
Alba de Tormes, Spain E6 12
Albaida, Spain G11 12
Albanel, Lac, l., Que., Can. F18 66
Albania, ctry., Eur. G11 4
Albano Laziale, Italy H7 14
Albany, Austl. G3 50
Albany, Ga., U.S. E2 87
Albany, Il., U.S. B3 90
Albany, In., U.S. D7 91
Albany, Ky., U.S. D4 94
Albany, La., U.S. g10 95
Albany, Mn., U.S. E4 100
Albany, Mo., U.S. A3 102
Albany, N.Y., U.S. C7 109
Albany, Or., U.S. C3 114
Albany, Tx., U.S. C3 120
Albany, Wi., U.S. F4 126
Albany, co., N.Y., U.S. C6 109
Albany, co., Wy., U.S. E7 127
Albany, stm., Ont., Can. o18 73
Al-Baṣrah, Iraq B4 46
Albatross Bay, b., Austl. B8 50
Al-Batrūn, Leb. B4 40
Al-Bawītī, Egypt C11 42
Albemarle, N.C., U.S. B2 110
Albemarle, co., Va., U.S. C4 123
Albemarle Lake, l., Ms., U.S. C2 101
Albemarle Sound, strt., N.C., U.S. A6 110
Albenga, Italy E3 14
Albergaria-a-Velha, Port. E3 12
Albert, Fr. B9 10
Albert, Lake, l., Afr. A6 44
Alberta, prov., Can. C4 68
Alberta, Mount, mtn., Alta., Can. C2 68
Albert City, Ia., U.S. B3 92
Albert Lea, Mn., U.S. G5 100
Albert Nile, stm., Ug. H12 42
Alberton, P.E.I., Can. C5 71
Albertson, N.Y., U.S. k13 109
Albertville, Fr. G13 10
Albertville, Al., U.S. A3 78
Albertville, Mn., U.S. E5 100
Albertville see Kalemie, Zaire C5 44
Albi, Fr. I9 10
Albia, Ia., U.S. C5 92
Albino, Italy D4 14
Albion, Il., U.S. E5 90
Albion, In., U.S. B7 91
Albion, Mi., U.S. F6 99
Albion, Ne., U.S. C7 104
Albion, N.Y., U.S. B2 109
Albion, Pa., U.S. C1 115
Albion, R.I., U.S. B4 116
Albion, Wa., U.S. C8 124
Alborán, Isla de, i., Spain J8 12
Ålborg, Den. H7 6
Alborz, Reshteh-ye Kūhhā-ye, mts., Iran J8 22
Albufeira, Port. H3 12
Albuñol, Spain I8 12
Albuquerque, N.M., U.S. B3 108
Alburquerque, Spain F4 12
Alburtis, Pa., U.S. F10 115
Albury, Austl. G9 50
Alcácer do Sal, Port. G3 12
Alcalá de Guadaira, Spain H6 12
Alcalá de Henares, Spain E8 12
Alcalá la Real, Spain H8 12
Alcalde, N.M., U.S. A3 108
Alcamo, Italy L7 14
Alcañices, Spain D5 12
Alcañiz, Spain D11 12
Alcântara, Braz. D10 54
Alcántara, Spain F5 12
Alcantarilla, Spain H10 12
Alcaraz, Spain G9 12
Alcázar de San Juan, Spain F8 12
Alcester, S.D., U.S. D9 118
Alcira, Spain F11 12
Alcoa, Tn., U.S. D10 119
Alcobaça, Braz. D9 57
Alcobaça, Port. F3 12
Alcolu, S.C., U.S. D7 117
Alcona, co., Mi., U.S. D7 99
Alconchel, Spain G4 12
Alcorn, co., Ms., U.S. A5 101
Alcoy, Spain G11 12
Aldabra Islands, atoll, Sey. C9 44
Aldan, Russia F19 24
Aldan, stm., Russia E20 24
Aldanskoje Nagorje, plat., Russia F19 24
Alden, Ia., U.S. B4 92
Alden, Mn., U.S. G5 100
Alden, N.Y., U.S. C2 109
Alder Brook, stm., Vt., U.S. B4 122
Aldershot, Eng., U.K. J12 7
Alderson, W.V., U.S. D4 125
Aldrich, Al., U.S. B3 78
Aledo, Il., U.S. B3 90
Aleg, Maur. E3 42
Alegres Mountain, mtn., N.M., U.S. C2 108
Alegrete, Braz. B5 56
Alejsk, Russia G10 24
Aleksandrov, Russia E21 18
Aleksandrovsk-Sachalinskij, Russia G22 24
Aleksejevsk, Russia F15 24
Aleksin, Russia G20 18
Além Paraíba, Braz. F7 57
Alençon, Fr. D7 10
Alenuihaha Channel, strt., Hi., U.S. C5 88
Aleppo see Ḥalab, Syria A5 40
Alert Bay, B.C., Can. D4 69
Alès, Fr. H11 10
Alessandria, Italy E3 14
Alessano, Italy J13 14
Ålesund, Nor. E6 6
Aleutian Islands, is., Ak., U.S. E3 79
Aleutian Range, mts., Ak., U.S. D9 79
Aleutka, Russia H24 24
Alevina, Mys, c., Russia F24 24
Alex, Ok., U.S. C4 11
Alexander, co., Il., U.S. F4 9
Alexander, co., N.C., U.S. B1 11
Alexander, Lake, l., Mn., U.S. D4 10
Alexander Archipelago, is., Ak., U.S. D12 79
Alexander Bay, S. Afr. G3 4
Alexander City, Al., U.S. C4 7
Alexander Island, i., Ant. B6 4
Alexandra, N.Z. F2 5
Alexandretta, Gulf of see İskenderun Körfezi, b., Tur. A4 4
Alexandria, Ont., Can. B10 7
Alexandria, In., U.S. D6 9
Alexandria, Ky., U.S. B5 9
Alexandria, La., U.S. C3 9
Alexandria, Mn., U.S. E3 10
Alexandria, Tn., U.S. A5 11
Alexandria, Va., U.S. B5 12
Alexandria see Al-Iskandarīyah, Egypt B11 4
Alexandroúpolis, Grc. I9 1
Alexis, Il., U.S. B3 9
Alfalfa, co., Ok., U.S. A3 11
Alfaro, Ec. I3 5
Alfaro, Spain C10 1
Alfarrás, Spain D12 1
Al-Fāshir, Sudan F11 4
Al-Fayyūm, Egypt C12 4
Alfeld, Ger. D9
Alfenas, Braz. F6 5
Alfred, Ont., Can. B10 7
Alfred, N.Y., U.S. C3 10
Algarve, hist. reg., Port. H3 1
Algeciras, Spain I6 1
Algemesí, Spain F11 1
Alger (Algiers), Alg. A6 4
Alger, Oh., U.S. B2 11
Alger, co., Mi., U.S. B4 9
Algeria, ctry., Afr. C6 4
Al-Ghaydah, Yemen E5 4
Alghero, Italy I3 1
Al-Ghurdaqah, Egypt C12 4
Algiers see Alger, Alg. A6 4
Algoma, Wi., U.S. D6 12
Algona, Ia., U.S. A3 9
Algona, Wa., U.S. B3 12
Algonac, Mi., U.S. F8 9
Algonquin, Il., U.S. A5 9
Algonquin Provincial Park, Ont., Can. B6 7
Algood, Tn., U.S. C8 11
Algorta, Ur. C5 5
Al-Ḥadīthah, Iraq B3 4
Al-Haffah, Syria B5 4
Al-Ḥamād, pl., Sau. Ar. B2 4
Alhama de Granada, Spain H8 1
Alhambra, Ca., U.S. m12 8
Al-Ḥarīq, Sau. Ar. D4 4
Al-Harūj al-Aswad, hills, Libya C9 4
Al-Ḥasakah, Syria A7 4
Alhaurín el Grande, Spain I7 1
Al-Hawrah, Yemen F4 4
Al-Hijāz (Hejaz), reg., Sau. Ar. C2 4
Al-Hillah, Iraq B3 4
Al-Hirmil, Leb. B5 4
Al-Ḥudaydah, Yemen F3 4
Al-Hufūf, Sau. Ar. C4 4
Aliaga, Spain E11 1
Alicante, Spain G11 1
Alice, Tx., U.S. F3 12
Alice Lake, l., Mn., U.S. C7 10
Alice Springs, Austl. D6 5
Aliceville, Al., U.S. B1 7
Alīgarh, India G8 3
Alijos, Escollos, Mex. E2 6
Alingsås, Swe. H9
Alīpur Duār, India G13 3
Aliquippa, Pa., U.S. E1 11
Al-Iskandarīyah (Alexandria), Egypt B11 4
Al-Ismā'īlīyah, Egypt B12 4
Aliwal North, S. Afr. H5 4
Alix, Alta., Can. C4 6
Al-Jabal al-Akhḍar, mts., Oman D6 4
Al-Jafr, Jord. D5 4
Al-Jaghbūb, Libya C10 4
Al-Jawf, Libya D10 4

Name	Map Ref	Page
-Jawf, Sau. Ar.	C2	46
-Jazīrah, reg., Sudan	F12	42
jezur, Port.	H3	12
-Jīzah, Egypt	B12	42
-Junaynah, Sudan	F10	42
justrel, Port.	H3	12
kali Lake, l., Nv., U.S.	B2	105
kali Lake, l., Or., U.S.	E6	114
kaline Lake, l., N.D., U.S.	C6	111
-Karak, Jord.	D4	40
-Kawm, Syria	B6	40
-Khābūr, stm., Syria	A7	40
-Khalīl, Isr. Occ.	D4	40
-Khandaq, Sudan	E12	42
-Khārijah, Egypt	C12	42
-Kharṭūm (Khartoum), Sudan	E12	42
-Khaṣab, Oman	C6	46
-Khubar, Sau. Ar.	C5	46
-Khums, Libya	B8	42
kmaar, Neth.	C4	8
-Kuwayt, Kuw.	C4	46
lach-Jun', Russia	E21	24
-Lādhiqīyah (Latakia), Syria	B4	40
lagash, stm., Me., U.S.	B3	96
lagash Lake, l., Me., U.S.	B3	96
lāhābād, India	H9	38
lamakee, co., Ia., U.S.	A6	92
lan, Sask., Can.	F2	75
lanche, Fr.	G9	10
lanmyo, Burma	E3	34
lardt, Tn., U.S.	C9	119
latoona Lake, res., Ga., U.S.	B2	87
legan, Mi., U.S.	F5	99
legan, co., Mi., U.S.	F5	99
legany, N.Y., U.S.	C2	109
legany, co., Md., U.S.	k13	97
legany, co., N.Y., U.S.	C2	109
legany Indian Reservation, N.Y., U.S.	C2	109
leghany, co., N.C., U.S.	A1	110
leghany, co., Va., U.S.	C2	123
legheny, co., Pa., U.S.	E2	115
legheny, stm., U.S.	E2	115
legheny Reservoir, res., U.S.	B4	115
lemands, Lac Des, l., La., U.S.	E5	95
len, Ok., U.S.	C5	113
len, co., In., U.S.	B7	91
len, co., Ks., U.S.	E8	93
len, co., Ky., U.S.	D3	94
len, co., La., U.S.	D3	95
len, co., Oh., U.S.	B1	112
len, Mount, mtn., Ak., U.S.	C11	79
lendale, N.J., U.S.	A4	107
lendale, S.C., U.S.	E5	117
lendale, co., S.C., U.S.	F5	117
len Park, Mi., U.S.	p15	99
lenton, R.I., U.S.	E4	116
lenton, Wi., U.S.	E5	126
lentown, Pa., U.S.	E11	115
lentsteig, Aus.	G15	8
leppey, India	H4	37
ler, stm., Ger.	C9	8
lerton, Point, c., Ma., U.S.	B6	98
lgäuer Alpen, mts., Eur.	H10	8
liance, Ne., U.S.	B3	104
liance, Oh., U.S.	B4	112
ligator, stm., N.C., U.S.	B6	110
ligator Lake, l., Me., U.S.	D4	96
lison, Ia., U.S.	B5	92
lison, Pa., U.S.	G2	115
lison Park, Pa., U.S.	h14	115
liston [Beeton Tecumseth and Tottenham], Ont., Can.	C5	73
-Līth, Sau. Ar.	D3	46
louez, Wi., U.S.	h9	126
loway Creek, stm., N.J., U.S.	D2	107
-Luḥayyah, Yemen	E3	46
lumette Lake, l., Can.	B7	73
lyn, Wa., U.S.	B3	124
ma, Que., Can.	A6	74
ma, Ar., U.S.	B1	81
ma, Ga., U.S.	E4	87
ma, Ks., U.S.	C7	93
ma, Mi., U.S.	E6	99
ma, Ne., U.S.	D6	104
ma, Wi., U.S.	D2	126
ma-Ata, Kaz.	I9	24
mada, Port.	G2	12
-Madīnah (Medina), Sau. Ar.	D2	46
-Mafraq, Jord.	C5	40
magro, Spain	G8	12
-Manāmah, Bahr.	C5	46
manor, Lake, l., Ca., U.S.	B3	82
mansa, Spain	G10	12
-Manṣūrah, Egypt	B12	42
-Marj, Libya	B10	42
mas, Pico das, mtn., Braz.	F10	54
-Maṣīrah, i., Oman	D6	46
-Mawṣil, Iraq	A3	46
-Mayādīn, Syria	B7	40
mazán, Spain	D9	12
melo, Neth.	C6	8
menara, Braz.	D8	57
mendralejo, Spain	G5	12
mería, Spain	I9	12
metjevsk, Russia	G8	22
-Minyā, Egypt	C12	42
mirante, Pan.	J6	64
-Mismīyah, Syria	C5	40
modóvar, Port.	H3	12
modóvar del Campo, Spain	G7	12
mont, Mi., U.S.	F7	99
monte, Ont., Can.	B8	73
monte, Spain	H5	12
mora, India	F8	38
-Mubarraz, Sau. Ar.	C4	46
-Mubarraz, Sau. Ar.	D4	46
-Muglad, Sudan	F11	42
-Muḥarraq, Bahr.	C5	46
-Mukallā, Yemen	F4	46
-Mukhā, Yemen	F3	46
-Muwayliḥ, Sau. Ar.	C2	46
nwick, Eng., U.K.	F11	7
ɔândia, Braz.	D4	57
oha, Or., U.S.	h12	114
or, Pulau, i., Indon.	G7	32
Álora, Spain	I7	12
Alor Setar, Malay.	K6	34
Aloysius, Mount, mtn., Austl.	E5	50
Alpena, Mi., U.S.	C7	99
Alpena, co., Mi., U.S.	D7	99
Alpharetta, Ga., U.S.	B2	87
Alphonse Island, i., Sey.	C10	44
Alpiarça, Port.	F3	12
Alpine, Az., U.S.	D6	80
Alpine, Tx., U.S.	D1	120
Alpine, Ut., U.S.	C4	121
Alpine, co., Ca., U.S.	C4	82
Alps, mts., Eur.	F9	4
Al-Qaḍārif, Sudan	F13	42
Al-Qāhirah (Cairo), Egypt	B12	42
Al-Qāmishlī, Syria	A7	40
Al-Qaryah ash-Sharqīyah, Libya	B8	42
Al-Qaryatayn, Syria	B5	40
Al-Qaṣr, Egypt	C11	42
Al-Qaṭīf, Sau. Ar.	C4	46
Al-Qaṭrūn, Libya	D8	42
Al-Qayṣūmah, Sau. Ar.	C4	46
Al-Qunayṭirah, Syria	C4	40
Al-Qunfudhah, Sau. Ar.	E3	46
Al-Quṣayr, Egypt	C12	42
Al-Quṭayfah, Syria	C5	40
Alsace, hist. reg., Fr.	E14	10
Alsasua, Spain	C9	12
Alsfeld, Ger.	E9	8
Alta, Nor.	B14	6
Alta, Ia., U.S.	B2	92
Altadena, Ca., U.S.	m12	82
Altagracia, Ven.	B7	58
Altagracia de Orituco, Ven.	C9	58
Altai, mts., Asia	B4	26
Altaj (Jesönbulag), Mong.	B6	26
Altamaha, stm., Ga., U.S.	E4	87
Altamira, Braz.	D8	54
Altamont, Il., U.S.	D5	90
Altamont, Ks., U.S.	E8	93
Altamont, Or., U.S.	E5	114
Altamont, Tn., U.S.	D8	119
Altamonte Springs, Fl., U.S.	D5	86
Altamura, Italy	I11	14
Altar, Mex.	B4	62
Altar, Desierto de, des., Mex.	B3	62
Altata, Mex.	E6	62
Altavista, Va., U.S.	C3	123
Altdorf, Switz.	F15	10
Altenburg, Ger.	E12	8
Altheimer, Ar., U.S.	C4	81
Altiplano, plat., S.A.	G5	54
Alto, Ga., U.S.	B3	87
Alto, N.M., U.S.	D4	108
Alto Araguaia, Braz.	D2	57
Alton, Il., U.S.	E3	90
Alton, Ia., U.S.	B2	92
Alton, Mo., U.S.	E6	102
Alton, N.H., U.S.	D4	106
Altona, Man., Can.	E3	70
Alton Bay, N.H., U.S.	D4	106
Altoona, Al., U.S.	A3	78
Altoona, Fl., U.S.	D5	86
Altoona, Ia., U.S.	C4	92
Altoona, Pa., U.S.	E5	115
Altoona, Wi., U.S.	D2	126
Alto Parnaíba, Braz.	E9	54
Altötting, Ger.	G12	8
Altun Shan, mts., China	D4	26
Alturas, Ca., U.S.	B3	82
Altus, Ok., U.S.	C2	113
Altus Air Force Base, mil., Ok., U.S.	C2	113
Altus Reservoir, res., Ok., U.S.	C2	113
Al-'Ubaylah, Sau. Ar.	D5	46
Al-Ubayyiḍ, Sudan	F12	42
'Alula, Som.	F5	46
Alum Bank, Pa., U.S.	F4	115
Alum Creek, stm., Oh., U.S.	k11	112
Al-Uqṣur (Luxor), Egypt	C12	42
Alva, Fl., U.S.	F5	86
Alva, Ok., U.S.	A3	113
Alvarado, Mex.	H12	62
Alvarado, Tx., U.S.	C4	120
Álvaro Obregón, Presa, res., Mex.	D5	62
Älvdalen, Swe.	F10	6
Alvin, Tx., U.S.	E5	120
Alvinston, Ont., Can.	E3	73
Älvkarleby, Swe.	F11	6
Alvord Lake, l., Or., U.S.	E8	114
Älvsbyn, Swe.	D13	6
Al-Wajh, Sau. Ar.	C2	46
Alwar, India	G7	38
Alzamaj, Russia	F13	24
Ama, La., U.S.	k11	95
Amadeus, Lake, l., Austl.	D6	50
Amadjuak Lake, l., N.W. Ter., Can.	C18	66
Amador, co., Ca., U.S.	C3	82
Amagansett, N.Y., U.S.	n16	109
Amagasaki, Japan	H8	30
Amakusa-nada, Japan	J2	30
Amakusa-shotō, is., Japan	J3	30
Åmål, Swe.	G9	6
Amalāpuram, India	D7	37
Amalfi, Italy	I9	14
Amalner, India	J6	38
Amambaí, stm., Braz.	G1	57
Amambaí, Serra de, mts., S.A.	H7	54
Amami-Ō-shima, i., Japan	w29	31b
Amami-shotō, is., Japan	x29	31b
Amana, Ia., U.S.	C6	92
Amantea, Italy	J11	14
Amares, Port.	D3	12
Amargosa, stm., U.S.	D5	82
Amargosa Desert, des., U.S.	G5	105
Amargosa Range, mts., U.S.	G5	105
Amarillo, Tx., U.S.	B2	120
Amatignak Island, i., Ak., U.S.	E4	79
Amazon (Solimões) (Amazonas), stm., S.A.	D7	54
Ambāla, India	E7	38
Ambarčik, Russia	D26	24
Ambāsamudram, India	H4	37
Ambato, Ec.	H3	58
Ambatolampy, Madag.	E9	44
Ambatondrazaka, Madag.	E9	44
Amberg, Ger.	F11	8
Ambérieu-en-Bugey, Fr.	G1	10
Ambert, Fr.	G10	10
Ambikāpur, India	I10	38
Ambilobe, Madag.	D9	44
Amble, Eng., U.K.	F11	7
Ambler, Pa., U.S.	F11	115
Amboise, Fr.	E7	10
Ambon, Indon.	F8	32
Ambositra, Madag.	F9	44
Ambovombe, Madag.	G9	44
Amboy, Il., U.S.	B4	90
Ambre, Cap d', c., Madag.	D9	44
Ambridge, Pa., U.S.	E1	115
Ambrières, Fr.	D6	10
Ambriz, Ang.	C2	44
Āmbūr, India	F5	37
Amchitka Island, i., Ak., U.S.	E3	79
Amchitka Pass, strt., Ak., U.S.	E4	79
Ameca, Mex.	G7	62
Amecameca [de Juárez], Mex.	H10	62
Amelia, La., U.S.	E4	95
Amelia, Oh., U.S.	C1	112
Amelia, co., Va., U.S.	C4	123
Amelia Court House, Va., U.S.	C5	123
Amelia Island, i., Fl., U.S.	k9	86
American, stm., Ca., U.S.	C3	82
Americana, Braz.	G5	57
American Falls, Id., U.S.	G6	89
American Falls Dam, Id., U.S.	G6	89
American Falls Reservoir, res., Id., U.S.	F5	89
American Fork, Ut., U.S.	C4	121
American Highland, plat., Ant.	B20	47
American Samoa, dep., Oc.	G1	2
Americus, Ga., U.S.	D2	87
Americus, Ks., U.S.	D7	93
Amersfoort, Neth.	C5	8
Amery, Wi., U.S.	C1	126
Ames, Ia., U.S.	B4	92
Amesbury, Ma., U.S.	A6	98
Amfilokhía, Grc.	K5	16
Ámfissa, Grc.	K6	16
Amga, Russia	E20	24
Amga, stm., Russia	E20	24
Amgun', stm., Russia	G21	24
Amherst, Ma., U.S.	B2	98
Amherst, N.H., U.S.	E3	106
Amherst, N.Y., U.S.	C2	109
Amherst, Oh., U.S.	A3	112
Amherst, Va., U.S.	C3	123
Amherst, Wi., U.S.	D4	126
Amherst, co., Va., U.S.	C3	123
Amherstburg, Ont., Can.	E1	73
Amherstdale, W.V., U.S.	n12	125
Amiens, Fr.	C9	10
Amīndīvi Islands, is., India	G2	37
Amirante Islands, is., Sey.	C10	44
Amisk Lake, l., Sask., Can.	C4	75
Amistad National Recreation Area, Tx., U.S.	E2	120
Amistad Reservoir, res., N.A.	C9	62
Amite, La., U.S.	D5	95
Amite, co., Ms., U.S.	D3	101
Amite, stm., La., U.S.	D5	95
Amity, Or., U.S.	B3	114
Amityville, N.Y., U.S.	E7	109
Amlia Island, i., Ak., U.S.	E5	79
'Ammān, Jord.	D4	40
Ämmänsaari, Fin.	D17	6
Ammon, Id., U.S.	F7	89
Ammonoosuc, stm., N.H., U.S.	B3	106
Amo, stm., Asia	G13	38
Amory, Ms., U.S.	B5	101
Amos, Que., Can.	k11	74
Amot, Nor.	G6	6
Amoy see Xiamen, China	K7	28
Amposta, Spain	E12	12
Amrāvati, India	B4	37
Amreli, India	J4	38
Amritsar, India	E6	38
Amroha, India	F8	38
Amsterdam, Neth.	C4	8
Amsterdam, N.Y., U.S.	C6	109
Amstetten, Aus.	G14	8
Am Timan, Chad	F10	42
Amu Darya (Amudarja), stm., Asia	I10	22
Amukta Pass, strt., Ak., U.S.	E5	79
Amundsen Gulf, b., N.W. Ter., Can.	B8	66
Amundsen Sea, Ant.	B1	47
Amuntai, Indon.	F6	32
Amur (Heilongjiang), stm., Asia	G21	24
An, Burma	E3	34
Anabar, stm., Russia	C16	24
Anaco, Ven.	C10	58
Anacoco, La., U.S.	C2	95
Anaconda, Mt., U.S.	D4	103
Anaconda Range, mts., Mt., U.S.	E3	103
Anacortes, Wa., U.S.	A3	124
Anacostia, stm., U.S.	C4	97
Anacostia, Northwest Branch, stm., Md., U.S.	B3	97
Anadarko, Ok., U.S.	B3	113
Anadyr', Russia	E29	24
Anadyr', stm., Russia	E29	24
Anadyrskij Zaliv, b., Russia	E30	24
Anagni, Italy	H8	14
Anaheim, Ca., U.S.	F5	82
Anahola, Hi., U.S.	A2	88
Anahuac, Tx., U.S.	E5	120
Ānai Mudi, mtn., India	G4	37
Anakāpalle, India	D7	37
Analalava, Madag.	D9	44
Ana María, Golfo de, b., Cuba	D8	64
Anambas, Kepulauan, is., Indon.	M9	34
Anamosa, Ia., U.S.	B6	92
Anamur, Tur.	H14	4
Anamur Burnu, c., Tur.	A3	40
Anan, Japan	I7	30
Ānand, India	I5	38
Anantapur, India	E4	37
Anantnāg (Islāmābād), India	D6	38
Anápolis, Braz.	D4	57
Anastasia Island, i., Fl., U.S.	C5	86
Añatuya, Arg.	B4	56
'Anazah, Jabal, mtn., Asia	C6	40
Ancaster, Ont., Can.	D4	73
Ancha, Sierra, mts., Az., U.S.	D4	80
Anchang, China	E9	28
Anchorage, Ak., U.S.	C10	79
Anchorage, Ky., U.S.	g11	94
Anchor Point, Ak., U.S.	D9	79
Anchor Point, c., Ak., U.S.	h15	79
Ancienne-Lorette, Que., Can.	C6	74
Anclote Keys, is., Fl., U.S.	D4	86
Ancona, Italy	F8	14
Ancud, Chile	E2	56
Ancud, Golfo de, b., Chile	E2	56
Andalucía, hist. reg., Spain	H7	12
Andalusia, Al., U.S.	D3	78
Andalusia, Il., U.S.	B3	90
Andaman Islands, is., India	H2	34
Andaman Sea, Asia	I3	34
Andermatt, Switz.	F15	10
Andernach, Ger.	E7	8
Anderson, Ak., U.S.	C10	79
Anderson, Ca., U.S.	B2	82
Anderson, In., U.S.	D6	91
Anderson, Mo., U.S.	E3	102
Anderson, S.C., U.S.	B2	117
Anderson, co., Ks., U.S.	D8	93
Anderson, co., Ky., U.S.	C4	94
Anderson, co., S.C., U.S.	B2	117
Anderson, co., Tn., U.S.	C9	119
Anderson, co., Tx., U.S.	D5	120
Anderson, stm., N.W. Ter., Can.	C7	66
Anderson, stm., In., U.S.	H4	91
Anderson, Mount, mtn., Wa., U.S.	B2	124
Anderson Ranch Reservoir, res., Id., U.S.	F3	89
Andes, mts., S.A.	F4	53
Andes, Lake, l., S.D., U.S.	D7	118
Andhra Pradesh, state, India	D5	37
Andižan, Uzb.	I12	22
Andkhvoy, Afg.	B1	38
Andong, China	C11	26
Andong, S. Kor.	D12	26
Andorra, And.	C13	12
Andorra, ctry., Eur.	G8	4
Andover, Ks., U.S.	g12	93
Andover, Ma., U.S.	A5	98
Andover, Mn., U.S.	m12	100
Andover, Oh., U.S.	A5	112
Andover Lake, res., Ct., U.S.	C6	84
Andradina, Braz.	F3	57
Andreanof Islands, is., Ak., U.S.	E4	79
Andrew, co., Mo., U.S.	B3	102
Andrew Island, i., N.S., Can.	D9	71
Andrews, In., U.S.	C6	91
Andrews, N.C., U.S.	f9	110
Andrews, S.C., U.S.	E8	117
Andrews, Tx., U.S.	C1	120
Andrews, co., Tx., U.S.	C1	120
Andrews Air Force Base, mil., Md., U.S.	C4	97
Andria, Italy	H11	14
Androka, Madag.	G8	44
Ándros, i., Grc.	L8	16
Androscoggin, co., Me., U.S.	D2	96
Androscoggin, stm., Me., U.S.	D2	96
Androscoggin Lake, l., Me., U.S.	D2	96
Andros Island, i., Bah.	B8	64
Andros Town, Bah.	B9	64
Andújar, Spain	G7	12
Anduo, China	D14	38
Anegada Passage, strt., N.A.	E16	64
Anfeng, China	C9	28
Anfu, China	H3	28
Ang'angxi, China	B11	26
Angara, stm., Russia	F13	24
Angarsk, Russia	G14	24
Ånge, Swe.	E10	6
Ángel, Salto (Angel Falls), wtfl, Ven.	E11	58
Ángel de la Guarda, Isla, i., Mex.	C3	62
Angeles, Phil.	q19	32
Angeles Point, c., Wa., U.S.	A2	124
Angel Falls see Ángel, Salto, wtfl, Ven.	E11	58
Ängelholm, Swe.	H9	6
Angelina, co., Tx., U.S.	D5	120
Angels Camp, Ca., U.S.	C3	82
Angermünde, Ger.	B13	8
Angers, Fr.	E6	10
Angerville, Fr.	D8	10
Angicos, Braz.	E11	54
Angier, N.C., U.S.	B4	110
Ângk Tasaôm, Camb.	I8	34
Angleton, Tx., U.S.	E5	120
Angmagssalik, Grnld.	C25	66
Angol, Chile	D2	56
Angola, In., U.S.	A8	91
Angola, N.Y., U.S.	C1	109
Angola, ctry., Afr.	D3	44
Angola Swamp, sw., N.C., U.S.	C5	110
Angoon, Ak., U.S.	D13	79
Angostura Reservoir, res., S.D., U.S.	D2	118
Angoulême, Fr.	G7	10
Angra dos Reis, Braz.	G6	57
Anguilla, Ms., U.S.	C3	101
Anguilla, dep., N.A.	E16	64
Anguille, Cape, c., Newf., Can.	E2	72
Angul, India	J11	38
Anhai, China	K7	28
Anhui, prov., China	E10	26
Aniak, Ak., U.S.	C8	79
Animas, stm., U.S.	D3	83
Animas Mountains, mts., N.M., U.S.	F1	108
Animas Peak, mtn., N.M., U.S.	F2	108
Animas Valley, val., N.M., U.S.	F1	108
Anita, Ia., U.S.	C3	92
Anjār, India	I4	38
Anji, China	E8	28
Anjiang, China	F9	26
Anjou, Que., Can.	p19	74
Anjouan, i., Com.	D8	44
Ankang, China	E8	26
Ankara, Tur.	H14	4
Ankavandra, Madag.	E9	44
Ankazoabo, Madag.	F8	44
Ankazobe, Madag.	E9	44
Ankeny, Ia., U.S.	C4	92
Anklesvar, India	B2	37
Anlong, China	B8	34
Anlu, China	D2	28
Ann, Cape, c., Ma., U.S.	A6	98
Anna, Il., U.S.	F4	90
Anna, Oh., U.S.	B1	112
Anna, Lake, res., Va., U.S.	B5	123
Annaba (Bône), Alg.	A7	42
Annaberg-Buchholz, Ger.	E12	8
An-Nabk, Syria	B5	40
An-Nafūd, des., Sau. Ar.	C3	46
An-Najaf, Iraq	B3	46
Anna Maria, Fl., U.S.	p10	86
Anna Maria Island, i., Fl., U.S.	q10	86
Annandale, Mn., U.S.	E4	100
Annandale, Va., U.S.	g12	123
Annapolis, Md., U.S.	C5	97
Annapolis, stm., N.S., Can.	E4	71
Annapolis Junction, Md., U.S.	B4	97
Annapolis Royal, N.S., Can.	E4	71
Annapurna, mtn., Nepal	F10	38
Ann Arbor, Mi., U.S.	F7	99
Anna Regina, Guy.	D13	58
An-Nāṣirīyah, Iraq	B4	46
Annawan, Il., U.S.	B4	90
Anne Arundel, co., Md., U.S.	B4	97
Annecy, Fr.	G13	10
Annemasse, Fr.	F13	10
Annette, Ak., U.S.	n24	79
Anniston, Al., U.S.	B4	78
Annobón, i., Eq. Gui.	B1	44
Annonay, Fr.	G11	10
An-Nuhūd, Sudan	F11	42
Annville, Pa., U.S.	F8	115
Anoka, Mn., U.S.	E5	100
Anoka, co., Mn., U.S.	E5	100
Anqing, China	E6	28
Anren, China	I2	28
Ansbach, Ger.	F10	8
Anshan, China	C11	26
Anshun, China	A8	34
Anson, Me., U.S.	D3	96
Anson, Tx., U.S.	C3	120
Anson, co., N.C., U.S.	B2	110
Ansonia, Ct., U.S.	D3	84
Ansonia, Oh., U.S.	B1	112
Ansted, W.V., U.S.	C3	125
Antakya, Tur.	H15	4
Antalaha, Madag.	D10	44
Antalya, Tur.	H14	4
Antalya, Gulf of see Antalya Körfezi, b., Tur.	A2	40
Antalya Körfezi, b., Tur.	A2	40
Antananarivo, Madag.	E9	44
Antarctica	A18	47
Antarctic Peninsula, pen., Ant.	C6	47
Antelope, co., Ne., U.S.	B7	104
Antelope Creek, stm., Wy., U.S.	C7	127
Antelope Island, i., Ut., U.S.	B3	121
Antelope Peak, mtn., Nv., U.S.	B7	105
Antelope Range, mts., Nv., U.S.	D7	105
Antelope Reservoir, res., Or., U.S.	E9	114
Antelope Wash, val., Nv., U.S.	D5	105
Antequera, Spain	H7	12
Antero, Mount, mtn., Co., U.S.	C4	83
Antero Reservoir, res., Co., U.S.	C5	83
Anthon, Ia., U.S.	B2	92
Anthony, Fl., U.S.	C4	86
Anthony, Ks., U.S.	E5	93
Anthony, N.M., U.S.	F3	108
Anthony, R.I., U.S.	D3	116
Anthony, Tx., U.S.	o11	120
Anthony Creek, stm., W.V., U.S.	D4	125
Anti Atlas, mts., Mor.	B4	42
Antibes, Fr.	I14	10
Anticosti, Île d', i., Que., Can.	k14	74
Antietam National Battlefield, hist., Md., U.S.	B2	97
Antigo, Wi., U.S.	C4	126
Antigua and Barbuda, ctry., N.A.	F17	64
Antioch, Ca., U.S.	h9	82
Antioch, Il., U.S.	A5	90
Antioch see Antakya, Tur.	H15	4
Antisana, vol., Ec.	H3	58
Antlers, Ok., U.S.	C6	113
Antofagasta, Chile	A2	56
Antofalla, Salar de, pl., Arg.	B3	56
Anton, Tx., U.S.	C1	120
Antongila, Helodrano, b., Madag.	E9	44
António Enes, Moz.	E7	44
Antônio João, Braz.	G1	57
Antonito, Co., U.S.	D5	83
Antora Peak, mtn., Co., U.S.	C4	83
Antrim, N.H., U.S.	D3	106
Antrim, co., Mi., U.S.	C5	99
Antrodoco, Italy	G8	14
Antsirabe, Madag.	E9	44
Antsiranana, Madag.	D9	44
Antwerp, Oh., U.S.	A1	112
Antwerp see Antwerpen, Bel.	D4	8
Antwerpen (Antwerp), Bel.	D4	8
Anuradhapura, Sri L.	H6	37
Anxi, China	C6	26
Anxi, China	J7	28
Anyang, China	D9	26
Anyi, China	G4	28
Anyuan, China	H2	28
Anyuan, China	J4	28
Anžero-Sudžensk, Russia	F11	24
Anzio, Italy	H7	14
Anžu, Ostrova, is., Russia	B23	24
Aoíz, Spain	C10	12
Aomori, Japan	B13	30
Aóös (Vijosë), stm., Eur.	J4	16
Aôral, Phnum, mtn., Camb.	H8	34
Aosta, Italy	D2	14
Aoukâr, reg., Maur.	E4	42
Aozou, Chad	D9	42
Apache, Ok., U.S.	C3	113
Apache, co., Az., U.S.	B6	80
Apache Junction, Az., U.S.	m9	80
Apache Peak, mtn., Az., U.S.	F5	80
Apalachee Bay, b., Fl., U.S.	B2	86
Apalachicola, Fl., U.S.	C2	86
Apalachicola, stm., Fl., U.S.	B1	86
Apalachicola Bay, b., Fl., U.S.	C2	86
Apaporis, stm., S.A.	H7	58
Aparri, Phil.	B7	32
Apatzingán [de la Constitución], Mex.	H8	62
Apeldoorn, Neth.	C5	8
Apennines see Appennino, mts., Italy	F7	14
Apex, N.C., U.S.	B4	110

Name	Map Ref	Page
Apishapa, stm., Co., U.S.	D6	83
Apizaco, Mex.	H10	62
Aplington, Ia., U.S.	B5	92
Apo, Mount, mtn., Phil.	D8	32
Apolda, Ger.	D11	8
Apollo, Pa., U.S.	E2	115
Apopka, Fl., U.S.	D5	86
Apopka, Lake, l., Fl., U.S.	D5	86
Aporé, Braz.	E2	57
Apostle Islands, is., Wi., U.S.	A3	126
Apostle Islands National Lakeshore, Wi., U.S.	A3	126
Appalachia, Va., U.S.	f9	123
Appalachian Mountains, mts., N.A.	D10	76
Appanoose, co., Ia., U.S.	D5	92
Appennino (Apennines), mts., Italy	F7	14
Appiano, Italy	C6	14
Apple, stm., Wi., U.S.	C1	126
Apple Creek, Oh., U.S.	B4	112
Applegate, Or., U.S.	E3	114
Applegate, stm., Or., U.S.	E3	114
Appleton, Mn., U.S.	E2	100
Appleton, Wi., U.S.	D5	126
Appleton City, Mo., U.S.	C3	102
Apple Valley, Ca., U.S.	E5	82
Apple Valley, Mn., U.S.	n12	100
Applewood, Co., U.S.	*B5	83
Appleyard, Wa., U.S.	B5	124
Appling, co., Ga., U.S.	E4	87
Appomattox, Va., U.S.	C4	123
Appomattox, co., Va., U.S.	C4	123
Appomattox, stm., Va., U.S.	C4	123
Appomattox Court House National Historical Park, Va., U.S.	C4	123
Apua Point, c., Hi., U.S.	D6	88
Apucarana, Braz.	G3	57
Apure, stm., Ven.	D9	58
Apurímac, stm., Peru	F4	54
Aqaba, Gulf of, b.	E4	40
Āqcheh, Afg.	B2	38
Āq Koprük, Afg.	B2	38
Aquarius Mountains, mts., Az., U.S.	C2	80
Aquidauana, Braz.	H7	54
Arab, Al., U.S.	A3	78
'Arab, Bahr al-, stm., Sudan	G11	42
Arabelo, Ven.	E10	58
Arabi, La., U.S.	k11	95
Arabian Desert see Sharqīyah, Aṣ-Ṣaḥrā' al-, des., Egypt	C12	42
Arabian Sea	E17	2
Aracaju, Braz.	F11	54
Aracati, Braz.	D11	54
Araçatuba, Braz.	F3	57
Aracena, Spain	H5	12
Araçuaí, Braz.	D7	57
Arad, Rom.	C5	16
Arafura Sea	G9	32
Arago, Cape, c., Or., U.S.	D2	114
Aragon, Ga., U.S.	B1	87
Aragón, hist. reg., Spain	D11	12
Araguacema, Braz.	E9	54
Aragua de Barcelona, Ven.	C10	58
Araguari, Braz.	E4	57
Arak, Alg.	C6	42
Arāk, Iran	B4	46
Arakan Yoma, mts., Burma	E3	34
Aral Sea, Asia	H10	22
Arambaza, Col.	I6	58
Aranda de Duero, Spain	D8	12
Arandas, Mex.	G8	62
Ārani, India	F5	37
Aran Island, i., Ire.	G4	7
Aran Islands, is., Ire.	H3	7
Aranjuez, Spain	E8	12
Aransas, co., Tx., U.S.	E4	120
Aransas Bay, b., Tx., U.S.	E4	120
Aransas Pass, Tx., U.S.	F4	120
Aranyaprathet, Thai.	H7	34
Arao, Japan	I3	30
Arapaho, Ok., U.S.	B3	113
Arapahoe, Ne., U.S.	D6	104
Arapahoe, co., Co., U.S.	B6	83
Arapiraca, Braz.	E11	54
Arapongas, Braz.	G3	57
Araraquara, Braz.	F4	57
Ararat, Austl.	G8	50
Ararat, Mount see Ağrı Dağı, mtn., Tur.	H16	4
Arauca, Col.	D7	58
Araure, Ven.	C8	58
Arāvalli Range, mts., India	H5	38
Araxá, Braz.	E5	57
Araya, Punta de, c., Ven.	B10	58
Arba Minch, Eth.	G2	46
Arbois, Fr.	F12	10
Arbon, Switz.	E16	10
Arborg, Man., Can.	D3	70
Arbroath, Scot., U.K.	E10	7
Arbuckle, Lake, l., Fl., U.S.	E5	86
Arbuckle Mountains, mts., Ok., U.S.	C4	113
Arbuckles, Lake of the, res., Ok., U.S.	C5	113
Arcachon, Fr.	H5	10
Arcade, Ca., U.S.	*C3	82
Arcade, Ga., U.S.	B3	87
Arcade, N.Y., U.S.	C2	109
Arcadia, Ca., U.S.	m12	82
Arcadia, Fl., U.S.	E5	86
Arcadia, In., U.S.	D5	91
Arcadia, La., U.S.	B3	95
Arcadia, Mo., U.S.	D7	102
Arcadia, S.C., U.S.	B4	117
Arcadia, Wi., U.S.	D2	126
Arcanum, Oh., U.S.	C1	112
Arcata, Ca., U.S.	B1	82
Arc Dome, mtn., Nv., U.S.	E4	105
Archangel'sk, Russia	E6	22
Archbald, Pa., U.S.	m18	115
Archbold, Oh., U.S.	A1	112
Archdale, N.C., U.S.	B3	110
Archer, Fl., U.S.	C4	86
Archer, co., Tx., U.S.	C3	120
Archer City, Tx., U.S.	C3	120
Arches National Park, Ut., U.S.	E6	121
Archidona, Spain	H7	12
Archie, Mo., U.S.	C3	102
Archuleta, co., Co., U.S.	D3	83
Arcis-sur-Aube, Fr.	D11	10
Arco, Id., U.S.	F5	89
Arco de Baúlhe, Port.	D4	12
Arcola, Il., U.S.	D5	90
Arcos de la Frontera, Spain	I6	12
Arctic Bay, N.W. Ter., Can.	B15	66
Arctic Ocean	A32	128
Arda, stm., Eur.	H9	16
Ardabīl, Iran	J7	22
Årdalstangen, Nor.	F6	6
Ardennes, reg., Eur.	E5	8
Ardlussa, Scot., U.K.	E7	7
Ardmore, Al., U.S.	A3	78
Ardmore, In., U.S.	A5	91
Ardmore, Ok., U.S.	C4	113
Ardmore, Tn., U.S.	B5	119
Ardsley, N.Y., U.S.	g13	109
Åre, Swe.	E9	6
Arecibo, P.R.	E14	64
Arena, Point, c., Ca., U.S.	C2	82
Arena, Punta, c., Mex.	F5	62
Arenac, co., Mi., U.S.	D7	99
Arenas de San Pedro, Spain	E6	12
Arendal, Nor.	G7	6
Arequipa, Peru	G4	54
Arès, Fr.	H5	10
Arévalo, Spain	D7	12
Arezzo, Italy	F6	14
Arganda, Spain	E8	12
Arga-Sala, stm., Russia	D15	24
Argelès-Gazost, Fr.	I7	10
Argenta, Italy	E6	14
Argenta, Il., U.S.	D5	90
Argentan, Fr.	D6	10
Argentat, Fr.	G8	10
Argentera, mtn., Italy	E2	14
Argentina, ctry., S.A.	C4	56
Argentino, Lago, l., Arg.	G2	56
Argenton-sur-Creuse, Fr.	F8	10
Argonne, reg., Fr.	C12	10
Árgos, Grc.	L6	16
Argos, In., U.S.	B5	91
Argostólion, Grc.	K4	16
Argun' (Ergun), stm., Asia	A11	26
Argyle, Mn., U.S.	B2	100
Argyle, Wi., U.S.	F4	126
Århus, Den.	H8	6
Ariano Irpino, Italy	H10	14
Arica, Chile	G4	54
Arica, Col.	I7	58
Arichat, N.S., Can.	D8	71
Arid, Cape, c., Austl.	F4	50
Arīḥā (Jericho), Jord.	D4	40
Arikaree, stm., U.S.	B8	83
Arima, Trin.	I17	64
Arinos, stm., Braz.	F7	54
Aripuanã, stm., Braz.	E7	54
Ariquemes, Braz.	E6	54
Arismendi, Ven.	C8	58
Aristazabal Island, i., B.C., Can.	C3	69
Ariton, Al., U.S.	D4	78
Arizona, state, U.S.	C4	80
Arizona Sunsites, Az., U.S.	F6	80
Arizpe, Mex.	B4	62
Arjay, Ky., U.S.	D6	94
Arjeplog, Swe.	C11	6
Arjona, Col.	B5	58
Arkabutla Lake, res., Ms., U.S.	A4	101
Arkadelphia, Ar., U.S.	C2	81
Arkansas, co., Ar., U.S.	C4	81
Arkansas, state, U.S.	C3	81
Arkansas, stm., U.S.	D8	76
Arkansas City, Ks., U.S.	E6	93
Arklow, Ire.	I6	7
Arkoma, Ok., U.S.	B7	113
Arkonam, India	F5	37
Arktičeskogo Instituta, Ostrova, is., Russia	B10	24
Arles, Fr.	I11	10
Arlington, Ga., U.S.	E2	87
Arlington, Ma., U.S.	B5	98
Arlington, Mn., U.S.	F4	100
Arlington, Ne., U.S.	C9	104
Arlington, N.Y., U.S.	D7	109
Arlington, N.C., U.S.	A2	110
Arlington, Oh., U.S.	B2	112
Arlington, S.C., U.S.	B3	117
Arlington, S.D., U.S.	C8	118
Arlington, Tn., U.S.	B2	119
Arlington, Tx., U.S.	n9	120
Arlington, Vt., U.S.	E2	122
Arlington, Va., U.S.	B5	123
Arlington, Wa., U.S.	A3	124
Arlington, co., Va., U.S.	g12	123
Arlington, Lake, res., Tx., U.S.	n9	120
Arlington Heights, Il., U.S.	A5	90
Arma, Ks., U.S.	E9	93
Armada, Mi., U.S.	F8	99
Armagh, Que., Can.	C7	74
Armavir, Russia	H6	22
Armenia, Col.	E5	58
Armenia, ctry., Asia	I6	22
Armentières, Fr.	B9	10
Armidale, Austl.	F10	50
Armijo, N.M., U.S.	k7	108
Armour, S.D., U.S.	D7	118
Armstrong, B.C., Can.	D8	69
Armstrong, Ia., U.S.	A3	92
Armstrong, co., Pa., U.S.	E2	115
Armstrong, co., Tx., U.S.	B2	120
Armstrong, Mount, mtn., Yukon, Can.	D6	66
Armstrong Creek, stm., W.V., U.S.	m13	125
Arnaudville, La., U.S.	D4	95
Arnedo, Spain	C9	12
Arnett, W.V., U.S.	D3	125
Arnhem, Neth.	D5	8
Arnhem, Cape, c., Austl.	B7	50
Arnhem Land, reg., Austl.	B6	50
Árnissa, Grc.	I5	16
Arno, stm., Italy	F5	14
Arnold, Mn., U.S.	D6	100
Arnold, Mo., U.S.	C7	102
Arnold, Ne., U.S.	C5	104
Arnold, Pa., U.S.	h14	115
Arnold Mills, R.I., U.S.	B4	116
Arnold Mills Reservoir, res., R.I., U.S.	B4	116
Arnold's Cove, Newf., Can.	E4	72
Arnolds Park, Ia., U.S.	A2	92
Arnprior, Ont., Can.	B8	73
Arnsberg, Ger.	D8	8
Arnstadt, Ger.	E10	8
Arona, Italy	D3	14
Aroostook, co., Me., U.S.	B4	96
Arpajon, Fr.	D9	10
Ar-Rab' al-Khālī, des., Asia	D5	46
Arrah, India	H11	38
Ar-Rahad, Sudan	F12	42
Ar-Ramadi, Iraq	B3	46
Ar-Ramthā, Jord.	C4	40
Arran, Island of, i., Scot., U.K.	F7	7
Ar-Raqqah, Syria	B6	40
Arras, Fr.	B9	10
Arrecife, Spain	C3	42
Arriaga, Mex.	I13	62
Ar-Riyāḍ (Riyadh), Sau. Ar.	D4	46
Arronches, Port.	F4	12
Arrowhead Mountain Lake, res., Vt., U.S.	B2	122
Arrowrock Reservoir, res., Id., U.S.	F3	89
Arrowwood Lake, res., N.D., U.S.	B7	111
Arroyo de la Luz, Spain	F5	12
Arroyo Grande, Ca., U.S.	E3	82
Ar-Ruṣayriṣ, Sudan	F12	42
Ar-Ruṭbah, Iraq	C7	40
Arsenjev, Russia	I20	24
Árta, Grc.	J4	16
Artá, Spain	F15	12
Artemisa, Cuba	C6	64
Artemus, Ky., U.S.	D6	94
Artenay, Fr.	D8	10
Arter, Mount, mtn., Wy., U.S.	D4	127
Artesia, N.M., U.S.	E5	108
Arthabaska, Que., Can.	C6	74
Arthur, Ont., Can.	D4	73
Arthur, Il., U.S.	D5	90
Arthur, co., Ne., U.S.	C4	104
Arthur, Lake, l., La., U.S.	D3	95
Arthur, Lake, res., Pa., U.S.	E1	115
Arthur Kill, stm., N.J., U.S.	k8	107
Arthurs Town, Bah.	B10	64
Artigas, Ur.	C5	56
Art'om, Russia	I20	24
Art'omovsk, Russia	G12	24
Artvin, Tur.	G16	4
Aru, Kepulauan, is., Indon.	G9	32
Arua, Ug.	H12	42
Aruanã, Braz.	C3	57
Aruba, dep., N.A.	H13	64
Arunachal Pradesh, ter., India	F16	38
Aruppukkottai, India	H5	37
Arusha, Tan.	B7	44
Aruwimi, stm., Zaire	A5	44
Arvada, Co., U.S.	B5	83
Arvi, India	B5	37
Arvidsjaur, Swe.	D12	6
Arvika, Swe.	G9	6
Arvin, Ca., U.S.	E4	82
Arvon, Mount, mtn., Mi., U.S.	B2	99
Arvonia, Va., U.S.	C4	123
Arzachena, Italy	H4	14
Arzignano, Italy	D6	14
Arzúa, Spain	C3	12
Asadābād, Afg.	C4	38
Asahi-dake, mtn., Japan	p20	30a
Asahikawa, Japan	p20	30a
Asansol, India	I12	38
Asbestos, Que., Can.	D6	74
Asbury Park, N.J., U.S.	C4	107
Ascensión, Mex.	E10	62
Ascension, co., La., U.S.	D5	95
Ascensión, Bahía de la, b., Mex.	H16	62
Aščhabad, Turk.	J9	22
Aschaffenburg, Ger.	F9	8
Aschersleben, Ger.	D11	8
Asciano, Italy	F6	14
Ascoli Piceno, Italy	G8	14
Ascoli Satriano, Italy	H10	14
Aseb, Erit.	F3	46
Asela, Eth.	G2	46
Åsele, Swe.	D11	6
Åsen, Nor.	E8	6
Asenovgrad, Bul.	G8	16
Ashaway, R.I., U.S.	F1	116
Ashburn, Ga., U.S.	E3	87
Ashburton, N.Z.	E3	52
Ashcroft, B.C., Can.	D7	69
Ashdown, Ar., U.S.	D1	81
Ashe, co., N.C., U.S.	A1	110
Asheboro, N.C., U.S.	B3	110
Ashepoo, stm., S.C., U.S.	F6	117
Ashern, Man., Can.	D2	70
Asherton, Tx., U.S.	E3	120
Asheville, N.C., U.S.	f10	110
Ash Flat, Ar., U.S.	A4	81
Ashford, Eng., U.K.	J13	7
Ashford, Al., U.S.	D4	78
Ashford, W.V., U.S.	m12	125
Ash Grove, Mo., U.S.	D4	102
Ashibetsu, Japan	p20	30a
Ashikaga, Japan	F12	30
Ashizuri-zaki, c., Japan	J6	30
Ashkhabad see Aščhabad, Turk.	J9	22
Ashland, Al., U.S.	B4	78
Ashland, Il., U.S.	D3	90
Ashland, Ks., U.S.	E4	93
Ashland, Ky., U.S.	B7	94
Ashland, Me., U.S.	B4	96
Ashland, Ma., U.S.	g10	98
Ashland, Mo., U.S.	C5	102
Ashland, Ne., U.S.	C9	104
Ashland, N.H., U.S.	C3	106
Ashland, Oh., U.S.	B3	112
Ashland, Or., U.S.	E4	114
Ashland, Pa., U.S.	E9	115
Ashland, Va., U.S.	C5	123
Ashland, Wi., U.S.	B3	126
Ashland, co., Oh., U.S.	B3	112
Ashland, co., Wi., U.S.	B3	126
Ashland, Mount, mtn., Or., U.S.	E4	114
Ashland City, Tn., U.S.	A4	119
Ashland Reservoir, res., Ma., U.S.	h10	98
Ashley, In., U.S.	A7	91
Ashley, N.D., U.S.	C6	111
Ashley, Oh., U.S.	B3	112
Ashley, Pa., U.S.	n17	115
Ashley, co., Ar., U.S.	D4	81
Ashley, stm., S.C., U.S.	F7	117
Ashley Creek, stm., Ut., U.S.	C6	121
Ashmore, Il., U.S.	D5	90
Ashokan Reservoir, res., N.Y., U.S.	D6	109
Ashqelon, Isr.	D4	40
Ash-Shaqrā', Sau. Ar.	C4	46
Ash-Shāriqah, U.A.E.	C6	46
Ash-Shawbak, Jord.	D4	40
Ashtabula, Oh., U.S.	A5	112
Ashtabula, co., Oh., U.S.	A5	112
Ashtabula, Lake, res., N.D., U.S.	B8	111
Ashton, Id., U.S.	E7	89
Ashton, Il., U.S.	B4	90
Ashton, Md., U.S.	B3	97
Ashton, R.I., U.S.	B4	116
Ashuanipi Lake, l., Newf., Can.	h8	72
Ashuelot, stm., N.H., U.S.	E2	106
Ashville, Al., U.S.	B3	78
Ashville, Oh., U.S.	C3	112
Ashwaubenon, Wi., U.S.	D5	126
Asia	D12	20
Asia, Kepulauan, is., Indon.	E9	32
Asia Minor, reg., Tur.	H14	4
Asino, Russia	F11	24
'Asīr, reg., Sau. Ar.	E3	46
Asir, Ras, c., Som.	F5	46
Askham, S. Afr.	G4	44
Askvoll, Nor.	F5	6
Asmara see Asmera, Erit.	E2	46
Asmera, Erit.	E2	46
Asotin, Wa., U.S.	C8	124
Asotin, co., Wa., U.S.	C8	124
Asotin Creek, stm., Wa., U.S.	C8	124
Aspang Markt, Aus.	H16	8
Aspen, Co., U.S.	B4	83
Aspen Butte, mtn., Or., U.S.	E4	114
Aspermont, Tx., U.S.	C2	120
Aspinwall, Pa., U.S.	k14	115
Aspiring, Mount, mtn., N.Z.	F2	52
Aspres-sur-Buëch, Fr.	H12	10
Aspy Bay, b., N.S., Can.	C9	71
Assabet, stm., Ma., U.S.	g9	98
Aṣ-Ṣabyā, Sau. Ar.	E3	46
As-Sallūm, Egypt	B11	42
As-Salṭ, Jord.	C4	40
Assam, state, India	G15	38
As-Samāwah, Iraq	B4	46
Assateague Island, i., U.S.	D7	97
Assateague Island National Seashore, U.S.	D7	97
Assawoman Bay, b., Md., U.S.	D7	97
Assen, Neth.	C6	8
Assiniboine, stm., Can.	E2	70
Assiniboine, Mount, mtn., Can.	D3	68
Assis, Braz.	G3	57
Assisi, Italy	F7	14
As-Sulaymānīyah, Iraq	A4	46
As-Sulaymānīyah, Sau. Ar.	D4	46
As-Sulayyil, Sau. Ar.	D4	46
Assumption, Il., U.S.	D4	90
Assumption, co., La., U.S.	E4	95
Assumption Island, i., Sey.	C9	44
Aṣ-Ṣuwār, Syria	B7	40
As-Suwaydā', Syria	C5	40
As-Suways (Suez), Egypt	C12	42
Asti, Italy	E3	14
Astorga, Spain	C5	12
Astoria, Il., U.S.	C3	90
Astoria, Or., U.S.	A3	114
Astove Island, i., Sey.	D9	44
Astrachan', Russia	H7	22
Astrakhan see Astrachan', Russia	H7	22
Astudillo, Spain	C7	12
Asunción, Para.	B5	56
Aswān, Egypt	D12	42
Aswān High Dam, Egypt	D12	42
Asyūṭ, Egypt	C12	42
Atacama, Desierto de, des., Chile	A3	56
Atacama, Puna de, plat., S.A.	A3	56
Atacama, Salar de, pl., Chile	A3	56
Ataco, Col.	F5	58
Atakpamé, Togo	G6	42
Atami, Japan	G12	30
Atar, Maur.	D3	42
Atascadero, Ca., U.S.	E3	82
Atascosa, co., Tx., U.S.	E3	120
'Aṭbarah, Sudan	E12	42
'Aṭbarah (Atbara), stm., Afr.	E12	42
Atchafalaya, stm., La., U.S.	D4	95
Atchafalaya Bay, b., La., U.S.	E4	95
Atchison, Ks., U.S.	C8	93
Atchison, co., Ks., U.S.	C8	93
Atchison, co., Mo., U.S.	A2	102
Ateca, Spain	D10	12
Aterau, Kaz.	H8	22
Athabasca, Alta., Can.	B4	68
Athabasca, stm., Alta., Can.	f8	68
Athabasca, Lake, l., Can.	m7	75
Athena, Or., U.S.	B8	114
Athenry, Ire.	H4	7
Athens, Ont., Can.	C9	73
Athens, Al., U.S.	A3	78
Athens, Ga., U.S.	C3	87
Athens, Il., U.S.	D4	90
Athens, Mi., U.S.	F5	99
Athens, N.Y., U.S.	C7	109
Athens, Oh., U.S.	C3	112
Athens, Pa., U.S.	C8	115
Athens, Tn., U.S.	D9	119
Athens, Tx., U.S.	C5	120
Athens, W.V., U.S.	D3	125
Athens, Wi., U.S.	C3	126
Athens, co., Oh., U.S.	C3	112
Athens see Athínai, Grc.	L7	16
Athínai (Athens), Grc.	L7	16
Athlone, Ire.	H5	7
Athol, Ma., U.S.	A3	98
Ati, Chad	F9	42
Atienza, Spain	D9	12
Atik Lake, l., Man., Can.	B4	70
Atikonak Lake, l., Newf., Can.	h8	72
Atka Island, i., Ak., U.S.	E5	79
Atkins, Ar., U.S.	B3	81
Atkins, Va., U.S.	D1	123
Atkinson, Il., U.S.	B3	90
Atkinson, Ne., U.S.	B7	104
Atkinson, N.H., U.S.	E4	106
Atkinson, co., Ga., U.S.	E4	87
Atlanta, Ga., U.S.	C2	87
Atlanta, Il., U.S.	C4	90
Atlanta, In., U.S.	D5	91
Atlanta, Mi., U.S.	C6	99
Atlanta, Tx., U.S.	C5	120
Atlantic, Ia., U.S.	C2	92
Atlantic, N.C., U.S.	C6	110
Atlantic, co., N.J., U.S.	E3	107
Atlantic Beach, Fl., U.S.	m9	86
Atlantic City, N.J., U.S.	E4	107
Atlantic Highlands, N.J., U.S.	C4	107
Atlantic Ocean	G11	2
Atlantic Peak, mtn., Wy., U.S.	D3	127
Atlas Mountains, mts., Afr.	B5	42
Atlas Saharien, mts., Alg.	B6	42
Atmore, Al., U.S.	D2	78
Atna Peak, mtn., B.C., Can.	C3	69
Atoka, Ok., U.S.	C5	113
Atoka, Tn., U.S.	B2	119
Atoka, co., Ok., U.S.	C5	113
Atoka Reservoir, res., Ok., U.S.	C5	113
Atotonilco el Alto, Mex.	G8	62
Atrato, stm., Col.	D4	58
Aṭ-Ṭafīlah, Jord.	D4	40
Aṭ-Ṭā'if, Sau. Ar.	D3	46
Attala, co., Ms., U.S.	B4	101
Attalla, Al., U.S.	A3	78
Attawapiskat, stm., Ont., Can.	n18	73
Attica, In., U.S.	D3	91
Attica, Ks., U.S.	E5	93
Attica, N.Y., U.S.	C2	109
Attica, Oh., U.S.	A3	112
Attleboro, Ma., U.S.	C5	98
Attopeu, Laos	G9	34
Attow, Ben, mtn., Scot., U.K.	D7	7
Attu Island, i., Ak., U.S.	E2	79
Āttūr, India	G5	37
Atwater, Ca., U.S.	D3	82
Atwater, Mn., U.S.	E4	100
Atwood, Ont., Can.	D3	73
Atwood, Il., U.S.	D5	90
Atwood, Ks., U.S.	C2	93
Atwood, Tn., U.S.	B3	119
Atwood Lake, res., Oh., U.S.	B4	112
Auau Channel, strt., Hi., U.S.	C5	88
Aubagne, Fr.	I12	10
Aube, stm., Fr.	D11	10
Auberry, Ca., U.S.	D4	82
Aubigny-sur-Nère, Fr.	E9	10
Aubin, Fr.	H9	10
Auburn, Al., U.S.	C4	78
Auburn, Ca., U.S.	C3	82
Auburn, Ga., U.S.	B3	87
Auburn, Il., U.S.	D4	90
Auburn, In., U.S.	B7	91
Auburn, Ks., U.S.	D8	93
Auburn, Ky., U.S.	D3	94
Auburn, Me., U.S.	D2	96
Auburn, Ma., U.S.	B4	98
Auburn, Mi., U.S.	E6	99
Auburn, Ne., U.S.	D10	104
Auburn, N.Y., U.S.	C4	109
Auburn, Wa., U.S.	B3	124
Auburndale, Fl., U.S.	D5	86
Auburn Heights, Mi., U.S.	F7	99
Aubusson, Fr.	G9	10
Auch, Fr.	I7	10
Aucilla, stm., Fl., U.S.	B3	86
Auckland, N.Z.	B5	52
Audincourt, Fr.	E13	10
Audrain, co., Mo., U.S.	B6	102
Audubon, Ia., U.S.	C3	92
Audubon, N.J., U.S.	D2	107
Audubon, co., Ia., U.S.	C2	92
Aue, Ger.	E12	
Auglaize, co., Oh., U.S.	B1	112
Auglaize, stm., Oh., U.S.	A1	112
Au Gres, Mi., U.S.	D7	99
Augsburg, Ger.	G10	
Augusta, Italy	L10	14
Augusta, Ar., U.S.	B4	81
Augusta, Ga., U.S.	C5	87
Augusta, Ks., U.S.	E7	93
Augusta, Ky., U.S.	B6	94
Augusta, Me., U.S.	D3	96
Augusta, Mi., U.S.	F5	99
Augusta, Wi., U.S.	D2	126
Augusta, co., Va., U.S.	B3	123
Augustus, Mount, mtn., Austl.	D3	50
Aulander, N.C., U.S.	A5	110
Auld, Lake, l., Austl.	D4	50
Aulneau Peninsula, pen., Ont., Can.	E4	70
Ault, Co., U.S.	A6	83
Aumont-Aubrac, Fr.	H10	10
Aumsville, Or., U.S.	k12	114
Aurangābād, India	C3	37
Auray, Fr.	E4	10
Aurelia, Ia., U.S.	B2	92
Aurich, Ger.	B7	
Auriflama, Braz.	F3	57
Aurillac, Fr.	H9	10
Aurora, Ont., Can.	C5	73
Aurora, Co., U.S.	B6	83
Aurora, Il., U.S.	B5	90
Aurora, In., U.S.	F8	91
Aurora, Mn., U.S.	C6	100
Aurora, Mo., U.S.	E4	102
Aurora, Ne., U.S.	D7	104
Aurora, Oh., U.S.	A4	112
Aurora, S.D., U.S.	C9	118
Aurora, Ut., U.S.	E4	121
Aurora, co., S.D., U.S.	D7	118
Aus, Nmb.	G3	44
Au Sable, Mi., U.S.	D7	99
Au Sable, stm., Mi., U.S.	D6	99
Ausable, stm., N.Y., U.S.	f11	109
Au Sable Forks, N.Y., U.S.	f11	109
Au Sable Point, c., Mi., U.S.	D7	99
Au Sable Point, c., Mi., U.S.	B4	99
Auschwitz see Oświęcim, Pol.	E19	
Austell, Ga., U.S.	h7	87
Austin, In., U.S.	G6	91
Austin, Mn., U.S.	G6	100

Name | Map Ref | Page

ıstin, Nv., U.S. D4 105
ıstin, Tx., U.S. D4 120
ıstin, co., Tx., U.S. E4 120
ıstin, Lake, l., Austl. E3 50
ıstin Channel, strt., N.W. Ter., Can. A12 66
ıstintown, Oh., U.S. A5 112
ıstinville, Va., U.S. D2 123
ıstralia, ctry., Oc. D6 50
ıstralian Capital Territory, ter., Austl. G9 50
ıstria, ctry., Eur. F10 4
ıtauga, co., Al., U.S. C3 78
ıtaugaville, Al., U.S. C3 78
ıtlán de Navarro, Mex. H7 62
ıtun, Fr. F11 10
ıxerre, Fr. E10 10
ıxier, Ky., U.S. C7 94
ıxi-le-Château, Fr. B9 10
ıxonne, Fr. E12 10
ıxvasse, Mo., U.S. B6 102
ıyán Tepuy, mtn., Ven. E11 58
ızances, Fr. F9 10
va, Mo., U.S. E5 102
vallon, Fr. E10 10
valon, Ca., U.S. F4 82
valon, Pa., U.S. h13 115
valon, Lake, res., N.M., U.S. E5 108
valon Peninsula, pen., Newf., Can. E5 72
varé, Braz. G4 57
veiro, Port. E3 12
vella, Pa., U.S. F1 115
vellaneda, Arg. C5 56
vellino, Italy I9 14
venal, Ca., U.S. E3 82
very, co., N.C., U.S. e11 110
ves, Islas de, is., Ven. A9 58
vesnes, Fr. B10 10
vesta, Swe. F11 6
vezzano, Italy G8 14
viemore, Scot., U.K. D9 7
vignon, Fr. I11 10
vila, Spain E7 12
vilés, Spain B6 12
villa, In., U.S. B7 91
vis, Pa., U.S. D7 115
vispa, Cerro, mtn., Ven. G10 58
viston, Il., U.S. E4 90
viz, Port. F4 12
voca, Ia., U.S. C2 92
voca, Pa., U.S. m18 115
vola, Italy M10 14
von, Ct., U.S. B4 84
von, Il., U.S. C3 90
von, Ma., U.S. B5 98
von, Mn., U.S. E4 100
von, N.Y., U.S. C3 109
von, Oh., U.S. A3 112
vondale, Az., U.S. D3 80
vondale, Co., U.S. C6 83
vondale, Pa., U.S. G10 115
vondale Estates, Ga., U.S. h8 87
von Lake, Ia., U.S. e8 92
von Lake, Oh., U.S. A3 112
vonmore, Pa., U.S. E3 115
von Park, Fl., U.S. E5 86
voyelles, co., La., U.S. C3 95
vranches, Fr. D5 10
waji-shima, i., Japan H7 30
wash, stm., Eth. F3 46
wbārī, Libya C8 42
we, Loch, l., Scot., U.K. E7 7
wjilah, Libya C10 42
xiós (Vardar), stm., Eur. I6 16
xis, Al., U.S. E1 78
xtell, Ne., U.S. D6 104
yabe, Japan G8 30
yacucho, Peru F4 54
yamonte, Spain H4 12
yapel, Col. C5 58
yaviri, Peru F4 54
ybak, Afg. B3 38
yden, N.C., U.S. B5 110
ydin, Tur. H13 4
yer, Ma., U.S. A4 98
yers Cliff, Que., Can. D5 74
yeyarwady (Irrawaddy), stm., Burma G3 34
yion Óros, pen., Grc. I8 16
yios Nikólaos, Grc. N9 16
ylesbury, Eng., U.K. J12 7
ylesford, N.S., Can. D5 71
ylmer, Mount, mtn., Alta., Can. D3 68
ylmer East, Que., Can. D2 74
ylmer Lake, l., N.W. Ter., Can. D11 66
ylmer West, Ont., Can. E4 73
yora, Spain F10 12
Ayoûn el 'Atroûs, Maur. E4 42
yr, Scot., U.K. F8 7
yre, Point of, c., I. of Man G8 7
yu, Kepulauan, is., Indon. E9 32
yvalık, Tur. J10 16
zambuja, Port. F3 12
zamgarh, India G10 38
zare, Nig. F8 42
zerbaijan, ctry., Asia I7 22
ziscohos Lake, l., Me., U.S. C1 96
zle, Tx., U.S. n9 120
zogues, Ec. I3 58
zores see Açores, is., Port. D11 2
zov, Sea of see Azovskoje more, Eur. H5 22
zovskoje more (Sea of Azov), Eur. H5 22
ztec, N.M., U.S. A2 108
ztec Peak, mtn., Az., U.S. D5 80
ztec Ruins National Monument, N.M., U.S. A1 108
zua, Dom. Rep. E12 64
zuaga, Spain G6 12
zuero, Península de, pen., Pan. K7 64
zul, Arg. D5 56
zur, Côte d', Fr. I14 10
zusa, Ca., U.S. m13 82
z-Zaqāzīq, Egypt D2 40
Az-Zarqā', Jord. C5 40
Az-Zāwiyah, Libya B8 42
Azzel Matti, Sebkha, pl., Alg. C6 42

B

Ba, stm., Viet. H10 34
Babaeski, Tur. H11 16
Babahoyo, Ec. H3 58
Babar, Kepulauan, is., Indon. G8 32
Babb Creek, stm., Pa., U.S. C7 115
Babbitt, Mn., U.S. C7 100
Babbitt, Nv., U.S. E3 105
B'abdā, Leb. C4 40
Bāb el-Mandeb see Mandeb, Bāb el-, strt. F3 46
Babine, stm., B.C., Can. B4 69
Babine Lake, l., B.C., Can. B5 69
Babine Range, mts., B.C., Can. B4 69
Bābol, Iran J8 22
Baboquivari Mountains, mts., Az., U.S. F4 80
Baboquivari Peak, mtn., Az., U.S. F4 80
Babuyan Islands, is., Phil. B7 32
Babylon, N.Y., U.S. n15 109
Baca, co., Co., U.S. D8 83
Bacabal, Braz. D10 54
Bacan, Pulau, i., Indon. F8 32
Bacău, Rom. C10 16
Bac Can, Viet. C8 34
Bacerac, Mex. B5 62
Bachaquero, Ven. C7 58
Bachta, Russia E11 24
Bachu, China D2 26
Back, stm., N.W. Ter., Can. C13 66
Back, stm., S.C., U.S. h12 117
Backbone Mountain, mtn., U.S. m12 97
Backnang, Ger. G9 8
Bac Lieu, Viet. J8 34
Bac Ninh, Viet. D9 34
Bacolod, Phil. C7 32
Bacon, co., Ga., U.S. E4 87
Baconton, Ga., U.S. E2 87
Bacoor, Phil. q19 33b
Bad, stm., S.D., U.S. C5 118
Bad, stm., Wi., U.S. B3 126
Badagara, India G3 37
Badajia, China B9 28
Badajoz, Spain G5 12
Badalona, Spain D14 12
Badanah, Sau. Ar. B3 46
Bad Aussee, Aus. H13 8
Bad Axe, Mi., U.S. E8 99
Baddeck, N.S., Can. C9 71
Bad Doberan, Ger. A11 8
Bad Ems, Ger. E7 8
Baden, Aus. G16 8
Baden, Ont., Can. D4 73
Baden, Switz. E15 10
Baden, Pa., U.S. E1 115
Baden-Baden, Ger. G8 8
Badgastein, Aus. H13 8
Badger, Newf., Can. D3 72
Bad Hersfeld, Ger. E9 8
Bad Homburg [vor der Höhe], Ger. E8 8
Bad Honnef, Ger. E7 8
Badin, N.C., U.S. B2 110
Badin Lake, res., N.C., U.S. B2 110
Bad Ischl, Aus. H13 8
Bad Kissingen, Ger. E10 8
Bad Kreuznach, Ger. F7 8
Badlands, hills, S.D., U.S. D3 118
Badlands, reg., U.S. C2 111
Badlands National Park, S.D., U.S. D3 118
Bad Lauterberg, Ger. D10 8
Bad Nauheim, Ger. E8 8
Bad Neustadt an der Saale, Ger. E10 8
Bad Oldesloe, Ger. B10 8
Bad Reichenhall, Ger. H12 8
Bad River Indian Reservation, Wi., U.S. B3 126
Bad Salzungen, Ger. E10 8
Bad Schwartau, Ger. B10 8
Bad Segeberg, Ger. B10 8
Bad Tölz, Ger. H11 8
Badulla, Sri L. I6 37
Badwater Creek, stm., Wy., U.S. C5 127
Bad Wildungen, Ger. D9 8
Bad Wörishofen, Ger. G10 8
Baena, Spain H7 12
Baeza, Spain H8 12
Bafatá, Gui.-B. F3 42
Baffin Bay, b., N.A. B14 61
Baffin Bay, b., Tx., U.S. E4 120
Baffin Island, i., N.W. Ter., Can. C18 66
Bafwasende, Zaire A5 44
Bagaha, India G11 38
Bāgalkot, India D3 37
Bagansiapiapi, Indon. M6 34
Bağarası, Tur. L11 16
Bagdad, Az., U.S. C2 80
Bagdad, Fl., U.S. u14 86
Bagdad see Baghdād, Iraq B3 46
Bagdarin, Russia G16 24
Bagé, Braz. C6 56
Baggs, Wy., U.S. E5 127
Baghdād, Iraq B3 46
Bagheria, Italy K8 14
Baghlān, Afg. B3 38
Baghrān Khowleh, Afg. D1 38
Bagley, Mn., U.S. C3 100
Bagnères-de-Bigorre, Fr. I7 10
Bagnères-de-Luchon, Fr. J7 10
Bagnols-sur-Cèze, Fr. H11 10
Bago, Burma F4 34
Baguio, Phil. p19 32
Bahamas, ctry., N.A. B9 64
Bahāwalnagar, Pak. F5 38
Bahāwalpur, Pak. F4 38
Bahía, Islas de la, is., Hond. F4 64
Bahía Blanca, Arg. D4 56
Bahía de Caráquez, Ec. H2 58
Bahía Kino, Mex. C4 62
Bahir Dar, Eth. F2 46
Bahraich, India G9 38
Bahrain, ctry., Asia C5 46
Baia-Mare, Rom. B7 16
Bai Bung, Muy, c., Viet. J8 34
Baicheng, China B11 26
Baicheng, China C3 26
Baidoa, Som. H3 46
Baie-Comeau, Que., Can. k13 74
Baie-d'Urfé, Que., Can. q19 74
Baie-Saint-Paul, Que., Can. B7 74
Baie Verte, Newf., Can. D3 72
Baigneux-les-Juifs, Fr. E11 10
Baiju, China B9 28
Bailén, Spain G8 12
Bailey, co., Tx., U.S. B1 120
Bailey Island, Me., U.S. g8 96
Bailey Island, i., S.C., U.S. k11 117
Baileys Crossroads, Va., U.S. g12 123
Bainbridge, Ga., U.S. F2 87
Bainbridge, In., U.S. E4 91
Bainbridge, Oh., U.S. C2 112
Bainbridge Island, i., Wa., U.S. e10 124
Bain-de-Bretagne, Fr. E5 10
Baing, Indon. H7 32
Baird, Tx., U.S. C3 120
Bairdford, Pa., U.S. h14 115
Baird Inlet, b., Ak., U.S. C7 79
Baird Mountains, mts., Ak., U.S. B7 79
Bais, Fr. D6 10
Baise, China C9 34
Baishuijiang, China E8 26
Baiyin, China D7 26
Baiyunebo, China C9 26
Baja, Hung. I18 8
Baja, Punta, c., Mex. C4 62
Baja California, pen., Mex. D3 62
Bajanchongor, Mong. B7 26
Bajkal, Ozero (Lake Baykal), l., Russia G15 24
Bajkal'skoje, Russia F15 24
Bajkit, Russia E13 24
Bajkonyr, Kaz. H11 22
Bajo Baudó, Col. E4 58
Baker, La., U.S. D4 95
Baker, Mt., U.S. D12 103
Baker, Or., U.S. C9 114
Baker, co., Fl., U.S. B4 86
Baker, co., Ga., U.S. E2 87
Baker, co., Or., U.S. C9 114
Baker, stm., N.H., U.S. C3 106
Baker, Mount, mtn., Wa., U.S. A4 124
Baker Air Force Base, mil., Ar., U.S. B6 81
Baker Butte, mtn., Az., U.S. C4 80
Baker Island, i., Ak., U.S. n22 79
Baker Lake, N.W. Ter., Can. D13 66
Baker Lake, l., Me., U.S. B3 96
Baker Lake, res., Wa., U.S. A4 124
Bakersfield, Ca., U.S. E4 82
Bakers Island, i., Ma., U.S. f12 98
Bakerstown, Pa., U.S. h14 115
Bakhtarān, Iran B4 46
Bakhtegān, Daryācheh-ye, l., Iran C5 46
Bakır, stm., Tur. J11 16
Bakoye, stm., Afr. F4 42
Baku, Azer. I7 22
Balabac Island, i., Phil. D6 32
Balabac Strait, strt., Asia D6 32
Ba'labakk (Baalbek), Leb. B5 40
Balachna, Russia E26 18
Bālāghāt, India J9 38
Bālāghāt Range, mts., India C4 37
Balaguer, Spain D12 12
Balakovo, Russia G7 22
Balallan, Scot., U.K. C6 7
Balāngīr, India B7 37
Balašicha, Russia F20 18
Balasore, India J12 38
Balašov, Russia G6 22
Balaton, Mn., U.S. F3 100
Balaton, l., Hung. I17 8
Balbriggan, Ire. H6 7
Balcarres, Sask., Can. G4 75
Balchaš, Ozero, l., Kaz. H9 24
Bald Eagle Lake, l., Mn., U.S. m12 100
Bald Eagle Lake, l., Mn., U.S. C7 100
Baldhill Dam, N.D., U.S. B7 111
Bald Knob, Ar., U.S. B4 81
Bald Knoll, mtn., Wy., U.S. D2 127
Bald Mountain, mtn., Or., U.S. D5 114
Bald Mountain, mtn., Or., U.S. C9 114
Bald Mountain, mtn., Wy., U.S. B5 127
Bald Mountains, mts., N.C., U.S. f10 110
Baldwin, Fl., U.S. B5 86
Baldwin, Ga., U.S. B3 87
Baldwin, La., U.S. E4 95
Baldwin, Mi., U.S. E5 99
Baldwin, Pa., U.S. k14 115
Baldwin, S.C., U.S. B5 117
Baldwin, Wi., U.S. D1 126
Baldwin, co., Al., U.S. E2 78
Baldwin, co., Ga., U.S. C3 87
Baldwin City, Ks., U.S. D8 93
Baldwinsville, N.Y., U.S. B4 109
Baldwinville, Ma., U.S. A3 98
Baldwyn, Ms., U.S. A5 101
Baldy Mountain, mtn., B.C., Can. D7 69
Baldy Mountain, mtn., Man., Can. D1 70
Baldy Mountain, mtn., Mt., U.S. B7 103
Baldy Mountain, mtn., N.M., U.S. A4 108
Baldy Peak, mtn., Az., U.S. D6 80
Baleares, Islas (Balearic Islands), is., Spain F14 12
Balearic Islands see Baleares, Islas, is., Spain E15 12
Baleine, Rivière à la, stm., Que., Can. g13 74
Balej, Russia G17 24
Balfate, Hond. G4 64
Balfour, N.C., U.S. f10 110
Bali, i., Indon. G5 32
Bali, Laut (Bali Sea), Indon. G6 32
Balıkesir, Tur. H13 4
Balikpapan, Indon. F6 32
Balimo, Pap. N. Gui. G11 32
Balingen, Ger. G8 8
Balintang Channel, strt., Phil. B7 32
Baliza, Braz. D2 57
Balkan Mountains see Stara Planina, mts., Eur. G8 16
Balkh, Afg. B2 38
Balkhash, Lake see Balchaš, Ozero, l., Kaz. H9 24
Ball, La., U.S. C3 95
Ballachulish, Scot., U.K. E7 7
Ballālpur, India C5 37
Ballarat, Austl. G8 50
Ballard, co., Ky., U.S. e8 94
Ball Club Lake, l., Mn., U.S. C5 100
Ballenas, Canal de, strt., Mex. C3 62
Ball Ground, Ga., U.S. B2 87
Ballia, India H11 38
Ballina, Ire. G3 7
Ballinger, Tx., U.S. D3 120
Ballinrobe, Ire. H3 7
Ball Mountain Lake, res., Vt., U.S. E3 122
Ballston Spa, N.Y., U.S. B7 109
Ballwin, Mo., U.S. f12 102
Bally, Pa., U.S. F10 115
Ballycastle, N. Ire., U.K. F6 7
Ballymena, N. Ire., U.K. G6 7
Ballyshannon, Ire. G4 7
Balmoral, N.B., Can. B3 71
Balmoral, Scot., U.K. D9 7
Balmville, N.Y., U.S. D6 109
Balovale, Zam. D4 44
Balrāmpur, India G10 38
Balsam Lake, Wi., U.S. C1 126
Balsam Lake, l., Wi., U.S. C1 126
Balsas, Braz. E9 54
Baltasar Brum, Ur. C5 56
Baltic, Ct., U.S. C7 84
Baltic, S.D., U.S. D9 118
Baltic Sea, Eur. H12 6
Baltijsk, Russia G2 18
Baltijskaja Kosa, spit, Eur. A19 8
Baltimore, Ire. J3 7
Baltimore, Md., U.S. B4 97
Baltimore, Oh., U.S. C3 112
Baltimore, co., Md., U.S. B4 97
Baltimore Highlands, Md., U.S. h11 97
Baluchistan, hist. reg., Asia D1 36
Bālurghāt, India H13 38
Balygyčan, Russia E24 24
Balzar, Ec. H3 58
Bamako, Mali F4 42
Bambana, stm., Nic. H6 64
Bambari, Cen. Afr. Rep. G10 42
Bamberg, Ger. F10 8
Bamberg, S.C., U.S. E5 117
Bamberg, co., S.C., U.S. E5 117
Bamenda, Cam. G8 42
Bāmīān, Afg. C2 38
Banalia, Zaire A5 44
Banana, Zaire C2 44
Bananal, Ilha do, i., Braz. F8 54
Banana River, b., Fl., U.S. D6 86
Banās, Ra's, c., Egypt D13 42
Banbridge, N. Ire., U.K. G6 7
Banbury, Eng., U.K. I11 7
Bancroft, Ont., Can. B7 73
Bancroft, Ia., U.S. A3 92
Bānda, India H9 38
Banda, Kepulauan, is., Indon. F8 32
Banda, Laut (Banda Sea), Indon. G8 32
Banda Aceh, Indon. D2 32
Bandama, stm., I.C. G4 42
Bandar Beheshtī, Iran C7 46
Bandar-e 'Abbās, Iran C6 46
Bandar-e Būshehr, Iran C5 46
Bandar-e Lengeh, Iran C5 46
Bandar Seri Begawan, Bru. E5 32
Banded Peak, mtn., Co., U.S. D4 83
Bandeira, Pico da, mtn., Braz. F8 57
Bandelier National Monument, N.M., U.S. B3 108
Bandera, co., Tx., U.S. E3 120
Banderas, Bahía de, b., Mex. G7 62
Bandırma, Tur. G13 4
Bandon, Ire. J4 7
Bandon, Or., U.S. D2 114
Bandundu, Zaire B3 44
Bandung, Indon. m13 32
Banes, Cuba D10 64
Banff, Scot., U.K. D10 7
Banff National Park, Alta., Can. D2 68
Bangalore, India F4 37
Bangassou, Cen. Afr. Rep. H10 42
Banggai, Kepulauan, is., Indon. F7 32
Banggi, Pulau, i., Malay. D6 32
Banghāzī, Libya B10 42
Bangil, Indon. m16 33a
Bangka, i., Indon. F4 32
Bangkalan, Indon. m16 33a
Bangkinang, Indon. N6 34
Bangkok see Krung Thep, Thai. H6 34
Bangladesh, ctry., Asia E6 36
Bangor, N. Ire., U.K. G7 7
Bangor, Wales, U.K. H8 7
Bangor, Me., U.S. D4 96
Bangor, Mi., U.S. F4 99
Bangor, Pa., U.S. E11 115
Bangor, Wi., U.S. E3 126
Bangor Township, Mi., U.S. E7 99
Bangs, Tx., U.S. D3 120
Bangs, Mount, mtn., Az., U.S. A2 80
Bangui, Cen. Afr. Rep. H9 42
Bangweulu, Lake, l., Zam. D5 44
Baní, Dom. Rep. E12 64
Banī Mazār, Egypt C12 42
Banister, stm., Va., U.S. D4 123
Banī Suwayf, Egypt C12 42
Bāniyās, Syria B4 40
Banja Luka, Bos. E12 14
Banjarmasin, Indon. F5 32
Banjul, Gam. F2 42
Bankhead Lake, res., Al., U.S. B2 78
Banks, co., Ga., U.S. B3 87
Banks Island, i., B.C., Can. C2 69
Banks Island, i., N.W. Ter., Can. B8 66
Banks Lake, res., Wa., U.S. B6 124
Banks Strait, strt., Austl. H9 50
Bānkura, India I12 38
Bann, stm., N. Ire., U.K. G6 7
Banner, co., Ne., U.S. C2 104
Banner Elk, N.C., U.S. A1 110
Banning, Ca., U.S. F5 82
Bannock, co., Id., U.S. G6 89
Bannock Peak, mtn., Id., U.S. F6 89
Bannock Range, mts., Id., U.S. G6 89
Bannu, Pak. D4 38
Baños de Cerrato, Spain D7 12
Ban Pak Phraek, Thai. J6 34
Ban Phak Phang, Thai. F6 34
Ban Pong, Thai. H5 34
Banská Bystrica, Slov. G19 8
Bānswāra, India I6 38
Bantam, stm., Ct., U.S. B3 84
Bantam Lake, l., Ct., U.S. C3 84
Bantry, Ire. J3 7
Banyak, Kepulauan, is., Indon. M4 34
Banyuwangi, Indon. n17 33a
Baoding, China D10 26
Baofeng, China B2 28
Bao Ha, Viet. C8 34
Baoji, China E8 26
Baoshan, China B5 34
Baotou, China C8 26
Baoying, China B8 28
Ba'qūbah, Iraq B3 46
Baquedano, Chile A3 56
Baraboo, Wi., U.S. E4 126
Baraboo, stm., Wi., U.S. E3 126
Baracoa, Cuba D10 64
Baraga, Mi., U.S. B2 99
Baraga, co., Mi., U.S. B2 99
Barakī Barak, Afg. D3 38
Baram, stm., Malay. E5 32
Bārāmati, India C3 37
Bārāmūla, India C6 38
Bārān, India H7 38
Baranagar, India I13 38
Baranoa, Col. B5 58
Baranof Island, i., Ak., U.S. m22 79
Baranoviči, Bela. H9 18
Barataria, La., U.S. E5 95
Barataria Bay, b., La., U.S. E6 95
Barat Daya, Kepulauan, is., Indon. G8 32
Barbacena, Braz. F7 57
Barbados, ctry., N.A. H18 64
Barbar, Sudan E12 42
Barbas, Cabo, c., W. Sah. D2 42
Barbastro, Spain C12 12
Barbate de Franco, Spain I6 12
Barber, co., Ks., U.S. E5 93
Barbers Point, c., Hi., U.S. B3 88
Barbers Point Naval Air Station, mil., Hi., U.S. g9 88
Barberton, Oh., U.S. A4 112
Barbezieux, Fr. G6 10
Barbosa, Col. E6 58
Barbour, co., Al., U.S. D4 78
Barbour, co., W.V., U.S. B4 125
Barboursville, W.V., U.S. C2 125
Barbourville, Ky., U.S. D6 94
Barbuda, i., Antig. F17 64
Barcaldine, Austl. D9 50
Barcellona Pozzo di Gotto, Italy K10 14
Barcelona, Spain D14 12
Barcelona, Ven. B10 58
Barcelos, Braz. D6 54
Barcelos, Port. D3 12
Barcroft, Lake, res., Va., U.S. g12 123
Barden Reservoir, res., R.I., U.S. C2 116
Bardera, Som. H3 46
Bardīyah, Libya B11 42
Bardstown, Ky., U.S. C4 94
Bardufoss, Nor. B12 6
Bardwell, Ky., U.S. f9 94
Bardwell Lake, res., Tx., U.S. C4 120
Bareilly, India F8 38
Barents Sea, Eur. B8 128
Barfleur, Fr. C5 10
Bargersville, In., U.S. E5 91
Bar Harbor, Me., U.S. D4 96
Bari, Italy H11 14
Barīkowṭ, Afg. C4 38
Barillas, Guat. G2 64
Barinas, Ven. C7 58
Barinitas, Ven. C7 58
Baripāda, India J12 38
Barisāl, Bngl. I14 38
Barisan, Pegunungan, mts., Indon. F3 32
Barito, stm., Indon. F5 32
Barker Heights, N.C., U.S. f10 110
Barkhamsted Reservoir, res., Ct., U.S. B3 84
Barkley, Lake, res., U.S. f10 94
Barkley Sound, strt., B.C., Can. E5 69
Barkly Tableland, plat., Austl. C7 50
Bark Point, c., Wi., U.S. B2 126
Barksdale Air Force Base, mil., La., U.S. B2 95
Bar-le-Duc, Fr. D12 10
Barlee, Lake, l., Austl. E3 50
Barletta, Italy H11 14
Barling, Ar., U.S. B1 81
Barlow, Ky., U.S. e8 94
Barmer, India H4 38
Barmouth, Wales, U.K. I8 7
Barnaul, Russia G10 24
Barnegat Bay, b., N.J., U.S. D4 107
Barnegat Inlet, b., N.J., U.S. D4 107
Barnes, co., N.D., U.S. B7 111
Barnesboro, Pa., U.S. E4 115
Barnes Sound, strt., Fl., U.S. G6 86
Barnesville, Ga., U.S. C2 87
Barnesville, Mn., U.S. D2 100
Barnesville, Oh., U.S. C4 112
Barneville-Carteret, Fr. C5 10
Barnhart, Mo., U.S. C7 102
Barnsdall, Ok., U.S. A5 113
Barnsley, Eng., U.K. H11 7
Barnstable, Ma., U.S. C7 98
Barnstable, co., Ma., U.S. C7 98
Barnstaple, Eng., U.K. J8 7
Barnwell, S.C., U.S. E5 117
Barnwell, co., S.C., U.S. E5 117
Baroda, India I5 38
Barpeta, India G14 38
Barqah (Cyrenaica), reg., Libya B10 42
Barques, Pointe aux, c., Mi., U.S. D8 99
Barquisimeto, Ven. B8 58
Barra, Braz. F10 54
Barra, Ponta da, c., Moz. F7 44
Barrackville, W.V., U.S. B4 125
Barra do Corda, Braz. E9 54
Barra Falsa, Ponta da, c., Moz. F7 44

Name	Map Ref	Page
Barra Mansa, Braz.	G6	57
Barrancabermeja, Col.	D6	58
Barranca del Cobre, Parque Nacional, Mex.	D6	62
Barrancas, Ven.	C11	58
Barrancos, Port.	G5	12
Barranquilla, Col.	B5	58
Barras, Braz.	D10	54
Barrax, Spain	F9	12
Barre, Vt., U.S.	C4	122
Barre, Lake, l., La., U.S.	E5	95
Barre Falls Reservoir, res., Ma., U.S.	B4	98
Barreiras, Braz.	B6	57
Barreiro, Port.	G2	12
Barreiros, Braz.	E11	54
Barrême, Fr.	I13	10
Barren, co., Ky., U.S.	D4	94
Barren, stm., Ky., U.S.	C3	94
Barren Island, i., Md., U.S.	D5	97
Barren Islands, is., Ak., U.S.	h15	79
Barren River Lake, res., Ky., U.S.	D3	94
Barretos, Braz.	F4	57
Barrett, W.V., U.S.	D3	125
Barrhead, Alta., Can.	B3	68
Barrie, Ont., Can.	C5	73
Barrie Island, i., Ont., Can.	B2	73
Barrière, B.C., Can.	D7	69
Barrington, Il., U.S.	A5	90
Barrington, N.J., U.S.	D2	107
Barrington, R.I., U.S.	D5	116
Barrington, stm., R.I., U.S.	C5	116
Barron, Wi., U.S.	C2	126
Barron, co., Wi., U.S.	C2	126
Barron Lake, Mi., U.S.	G4	99
Barrow, Ak., U.S.	A8	79
Barrow, co., Ga., U.S.	B3	87
Barrow, Point, c., Ak., U.S.	A8	79
Barrow Creek, Austl.	D6	50
Barrow-in-Furness, Eng., U.K.	G9	7
Barrow Island, i., Austl.	D3	50
Barrow Strait, strt., N.W. Ter., Can.	B14	66
Barry, Il., U.S.	D2	90
Barry, co., Mi., U.S.	F5	99
Barry, co., Mo., U.S.	E4	102
Barrys Bay, Ont., Can.	B7	73
Bārsi, India	C3	37
Barstow, Ca., U.S.	E5	82
Bar-sur-Aube, Fr.	D11	10
Barth, Ger.	A12	8
Bartholomew, co., In., U.S.	F6	91
Bartholomew, Bayou, stm., U.S.	D4	81
Bartica, Guy.	D13	58
Bartlesville, Ok., U.S.	A6	113
Bartlett, N.H., U.S.	B4	106
Bartlett, Tn., U.S.	B2	119
Bartlett, Tx., U.S.	D4	120
Bartlett Reservoir, res., Az., U.S.	D4	80
Bartletts Ferry Dam, U.S.	C4	78
Barton, Oh., U.S.	B5	112
Barton, Vt., U.S.	B4	122
Barton, co., Ks., U.S.	D5	93
Barton, co., Mo., U.S.	D3	102
Barton, stm., Vt., U.S.	B4	122
Bartonville, Il., U.S.	C4	90
Bartow, Fl., U.S.	E5	86
Bartow, co., Ga., U.S.	B2	87
Barú, Volcán, vol., Pan.	J6	64
Bāruni, India	H11	38
Baruun Urt, Mong.	B9	26
Barvas, Scot., U.K.	C6	7
Basalt, Co., U.S.	B3	83
Basankusu, Zaire	A3	44
Basatongwula Shan, mtn., China	D14	38
Bascuñán, Cabo, c., Chile	B2	56
Basehor, Ks., U.S.	k16	93
Basel (Bâle), Switz.	E14	10
Bashan Lake, l., Ct., U.S.	D6	84
Bashaw, Alta., Can.	C4	68
Bashi Channel, strt., Asia	G11	26
Basilan Island, i., Phil.	D7	32
Basildon, Eng., U.K.	J13	7
Basile, La., U.S.	D3	95
Basin, Wy., U.S.	B4	127
Basingstoke, Eng., U.K.	J11	7
Basīrhāt, India	I13	38
Basīt, Ra's al-, c., Syria	B4	40
Baskahegan Lake, l., Me., U.S.	C5	96
Baskatong, Réservoir, res., Que., Can.	G17	66
Basking Ridge, N.J., U.S.	B3	107
Basoko, Zaire	A4	44
Basra see Al-Baṣrah, Iraq	B4	46
Bassano, Alta., Can.	D4	68
Bassano del Grappa, Italy	D6	14
Bassari, Togo	G6	42
Bassas da India, rf., Reu.	F7	44
Basse-Terre, Guad.	F17	64
Basseterre, St. K./N.	F16	64
Basse-Terre, i., Guad.	F17	64
Bassett, Ne., U.S.	B6	104
Bassett, Va., U.S.	D3	123
Bassett Peak, mtn., Az., U.S.	E5	80
Bass Islands, is., Oh., U.S.	A3	112
Bass Lake, In., U.S.	B4	91
Bass Strait, strt., Austl.	G9	50
Basswood Lake, l., Mn., U.S.	B7	100
Basti, India	G10	38
Bastogne, Bel.	E5	8
Bastrop, La., U.S.	B4	95
Bastrop, Tx., U.S.	D4	120
Bastrop, co., Tx., U.S.	D4	120
Bastuträsk, Swe.	D13	6
Bata, Eq. Gui.	H7	42
Bataan Peninsula, pen., Phil.	q19	33b
Batabanó, Golfo de, b., Cuba	C6	64
Batagaj, Russia	D20	24
Bataguaçu, Braz.	F2	57
Bataiporã, Braz.	G2	57
Batāla, India	E6	38
Batalha, Port.	F3	12
Batamaj, Russia	E19	24
Batang, China	E6	26
Batangas, Phil.	r19	33b
Batan Islands, is., Phil.	A7	32
Batanta, Pulau, i., Indon.	F9	32
Batatais, Braz.	F5	57
Batavia, Il., U.S.	B5	90
Batavia, N.Y., U.S.	C2	109
Batavia, Oh., U.S.	C1	112
Batchelor Bay, b., N.C., U.S.	B6	110
Bătdâmbâng, Camb.	H7	34
Batepito, Mex.	B5	62
Bates, co., Mo., U.S.	C3	102
Batesburg, S.C., U.S.	D4	117
Batesville, Ar., U.S.	B4	81
Batesville, In., U.S.	F7	91
Batesville, Ms., U.S.	A4	101
Bath, N.B., Can.	C2	71
Bath, Ont., Can.	C8	73
Bath, Eng., U.K.	J10	7
Bath, Me., U.S.	E3	96
Bath, N.Y., U.S.	C3	109
Bath, Pa., U.S.	E11	115
Bath, S.C., U.S.	D4	117
Bath, co., Ky., U.S.	B6	94
Bath, co., Va., U.S.	B3	123
Bathurst, N.B., Can.	B4	71
Bathurst, Cape, c., N.W. Ter., Can.	B7	66
Bathurst Inlet, N.W. Ter., Can.	C11	66
Bathurst Inlet, b., N.W. Ter., Can.	C11	66
Bathurst Island, i., Austl.	B6	50
Bathurst Island, i., N.W. Ter., Can.	A12	66
Batiscan, stm., Que., Can.	B5	74
Batna, Alg.	A7	42
Baton Rouge, La., U.S.	D4	95
Batouri, Cam.	H8	42
Batsto, stm., N.J., U.S.	D3	107
Batten Kill, stm., U.S.	E2	122
Batticaloa, Sri L.	I6	37
Battle, stm., Can.	F10	66
Battle Creek, Ia., U.S.	B2	92
Battle Creek, Mi., U.S.	F5	99
Battle Creek, Ne., U.S.	C8	104
Battle Ground, In., U.S.	C4	91
Battle Ground, Wa., U.S.	D3	124
Battle Lake, Mn., U.S.	D3	100
Battle Mountain, Nv., U.S.	C5	105
Battle Mountain, mtn., Wy., U.S.	E5	127
Batu, mtn., Eth.	G2	46
Batu, Kepulauan, is., Indon.	O5	34
Batumi, Geor.	I6	22
Batu Pahat, Malay.	N7	34
Baturité, Braz.	D11	54
Baubau, Indon.	G7	32
Bauchi, Nig.	F7	42
Baud, Fr.	E3	10
Baudette, Mn., U.S.	B4	100
Bauld, Cape, c., Newf., Can.	C4	72
Baume-les-Dames, Fr.	E13	10
Baunei, Italy	I4	14
Bauru, Braz.	G4	57
Baús, Braz.	E2	57
Bautzen, Ger.	D14	8
Bawean, Pulau, i., Indon.	G5	32
Baxley, Ga., U.S.	E4	87
Baxter, Ia., U.S.	C4	92
Baxter, Mn., U.S.	D4	100
Baxter, Tn., U.S.	C8	119
Baxter, co., Ar., U.S.	A3	81
Baxter Springs, Ks., U.S.	E9	93
Bay, Ar., U.S.	B5	81
Bay, co., Fl., U.S.	u16	86
Bay, co., Mi., U.S.	E6	99
Bay, Laguna de, l., Phil.	q19	33b
Bayamo, Cuba	D9	64
Bayan Har Shan, mts., China	E6	26
Bayard, Ne., U.S.	C2	104
Bayard, N.M., U.S.	E1	108
Bayberry, N.Y., U.S.	*B4	109
Bayboro, N.C., U.S.	B6	110
Bay Bulls, Newf., Can.	E5	72
Bay City, Mi., U.S.	E7	99
Bay City, Or., U.S.	B3	114
Bay City, Tx., U.S.	E5	120
Bay de Verde, Newf., Can.	D5	72
Bayerische Alpen, mts., Eur.	H11	8
Bayeux, Fr.	C6	10
Bayfield, Ont., Can.	D3	73
Bayfield, Co., U.S.	D3	83
Bayfield, Wi., U.S.	B3	126
Bayfield, co., Wi., U.S.	B2	126
Bayındır, Tur.	K11	16
Baykonur see Bajkonyr, Kaz.	H11	22
Baylor, co., Tx., U.S.	C3	120
Bay Mills Indian Reservation, Mi., U.S.	B6	99
Bay Minette, Al., U.S.	E2	78
Bayo, Spain	B3	12
Bayona, Spain	C3	12
Bayonne, Fr.	I5	10
Bayonne, N.J., U.S.	B4	107
Bayou Bodcau Reservoir, res., La., U.S.	B2	95
Bayou D'Arbonne Lake, res., La., U.S.	B3	95
Bayou George, Fl., U.S.	u16	86
Bayou Goula, La., U.S.	D4	95
Bayou La Batre, Al., U.S.	E1	78
Bay Point, c., S.C., U.S.	G7	117
Bayport, Mn., U.S.	E6	100
Bayport, N.Y., U.S.	n15	109
Bayramıç, Tur.	J10	16
Bayreuth, Ger.	F11	8
Bay Ridge, Md., U.S.	C5	97
Bay Roberts, Newf., Can.	E5	72
Bayrūt (Beirut), Leb.	C4	40
Bays, Lake of, l., Ont., Can.	B5	73
Bay Saint Louis, Ms., U.S.	E4	101
Bay Shore, N.Y., U.S.	E7	109
Bayshore Gardens, Fl., U.S.	q10	86
Bayside, Wi., U.S.	m12	126
Bay Springs, Ms., U.S.	D4	101
Bayt Laḥm, Isr. Occ.	D4	40
Baytown, Tx., U.S.	E5	120
Bayview, Al., U.S.	f7	78
Bay Village, Oh., U.S.	h9	112
Baza, Spain	H9	12
Bazaruto, Ilha do, i., Moz.	F7	44
Bazas, Fr.	H6	10
Be, Nosy, i., Madag.	D9	44
Beach, Il., U.S.	h9	90
Beach, N.D., U.S.	C1	111
Beachburg, Ont., Can.	B8	73
Beach City, Oh., U.S.	B4	112
Beach Haven Inlet, b., N.J., U.S.	D4	107
Beach Pond, res., U.S.	C8	84
Beachville, Ont., Can.	D4	73
Beachwood, N.J., U.S.	D4	107
Beachy Head, c., Eng., U.K.	K13	7
Beacon, N.Y., U.S.	D7	109
Beacon Falls, Ct., U.S.	D3	84
Beaconsfield, Que., Can.	q19	74
Beadle, co., S.D., U.S.	C7	118
Beagle Gulf, b., Austl.	B6	50
Bealanana, Madag.	D9	44
Beale, Cape, c., B.C., Can.	E5	69
Beale Air Force Base, mil., Ca., U.S.	C3	82
Bear, De., U.S.	B3	85
Bear, stm., U.S.	B3	121
Bear Creek, Al., U.S.	A2	78
Bear Creek, stm., U.S.	E2	93
Bear Creek, stm., Or., U.S.	E4	114
Bear Creek, stm., Wy., U.S.	E8	127
Bearden, Ar., U.S.	D3	81
Beardstown, Il., U.S.	C3	90
Bear Inlet, b., N.C., U.S.	C5	110
Bear Lake, co., Id., U.S.	G7	89
Bear Lake, l., U.S.	A4	121
Bear Lake, l., Wi., U.S.	C2	126
Bear Lodge Mountains, mts., Wy., U.S.	B8	127
Bear Mountain, mtn., Or., U.S.	D4	114
Bearpaw Mountains, mts., Mt., U.S.	B7	103
Bear River, N.S., Can.	E4	71
Bear River City, Ut., U.S.	B3	121
Beartooth Pass, Wy., U.S.	B3	127
Beartooth Range, mts., U.S.	E7	103
Bear Town, Ms., U.S.	D3	101
Beasain, Spain	B9	12
Beas de Segura, Spain	G9	12
Beata, Isla, i., Dom. Rep.	F12	64
Beatrice, Ne., U.S.	D9	104
Beatton, stm., B.C., Can.	E8	66
Beatty, Nv., U.S.	G5	105
Beattyville, Ky., U.S.	C6	94
Beaucaire, Fr.	I11	10
Beaufort, N.C., U.S.	C6	110
Beaufort, S.C., U.S.	G6	117
Beaufort, co., N.C., U.S.	B5	110
Beaufort, co., S.C., U.S.	G6	117
Beaufort Marine Corps Air Station, mil., S.C., U.S.	F6	117
Beaufort Sea, N.A.	B7	61
Beaufort West, S. Afr.	H4	44
Beaugency, Fr.	E8	10
Beauharnois, Que., Can.	D4	74
Beau Lake, l., Me., U.S.	A3	96
Beauly, Scot., U.K.	D8	7
Beaumont, Alta., Can.	C4	68
Beaumont, Ms., U.S.	D5	101
Beaumont, Tx., U.S.	D5	120
Beaumont-sur-Sarthe, Fr.	D7	10
Beaune, Fr.	E11	10
Beauport, Que., Can.	n17	74
Beaupré, Que., Can.	B7	74
Beaupréau, Fr.	E5	10
Beauregard, co., La., U.S.	D2	95
Beausejour, Man., Can.	D3	70
Beauvais, Fr.	C9	10
Beauval, Sask., Can.	B2	75
Beauvoir-sur-Niort, Fr.	F6	10
Beaver, Ok., U.S.	A1	113
Beaver, Pa., U.S.	E1	115
Beaver, Ut., U.S.	E3	121
Beaver, W.V., U.S.	D3	125
Beaver, co., Ok., U.S.	e10	113
Beaver, co., Pa., U.S.	E1	115
Beaver, co., Ut., U.S.	E2	121
Beaver, stm., Can.	D7	66
Beaver, stm., Can.	B2	75
Beaver, stm., U.S.	A2	113
Beaver, stm., N.Y., U.S.	B6	109
Beaver, stm., R.I., U.S.	E2	116
Beaver, stm., Ut., U.S.	E2	121
Beaverbank, N.S., Can.	E6	71
Beaver Brook, stm., U.S.	E4	106
Beaver City, Ne., U.S.	D6	104
Beavercreek, Oh., U.S.	C1	112
Beaver Creek, stm., U.S.	E4	104
Beaver Creek, stm., U.S.	C8	127
Beaver Creek, stm., N.D., U.S.	C5	111
Beaver Creek, stm., N.D., U.S.	C1	111
Beaver Creek, stm., Ok., U.S.	C3	113
Beaver Creek, stm., Tn., U.S.	m13	119
Beaver Creek, stm., Wy., U.S.	D4	127
Beaverdale, Pa., U.S.	F4	115
Beaver Dam, Ky., U.S.	C3	94
Beaver Dam, Wi., U.S.	E5	126
Beaverdam Branch, stm., De., U.S.	F3	85
Beaverdam Lake, res., Wi., U.S.	E5	126
Beaver Falls, Pa., U.S.	E1	115
Beaverhead, co., Mt., U.S.	E3	103
Beaverhead, stm., Mt., U.S.	E4	103
Beaverhead Mountains, mts., U.S.	D5	89
Beaverhill Lake, l., Alta., Can.	C4	68
Beaver Island, i., Mi., U.S.	C5	99
Beaver Lake, res., Ar., U.S.	A2	81
Beaverlodge, Alta., Can.	B1	68
Beaver Meadows, Pa., U.S.	E10	115
Beaver Run Reservoir, res., Pa., U.S.	F2	115
Beavertail Point, c., R.I., U.S.	F4	116
Beaverton, Mi., U.S.	E6	99
Beaverton, Or., U.S.	B4	114
Beāwar, India	G6	38
Bebedouro, Braz.	F4	57
Bécancour, Que., Can.	C5	74
Bečej, Yugo.	D4	16
Becerreá, Spain	C4	12
Béchar, Alg.	B5	42
Becharof Lake, l., Ak., U.S.	D8	79
Beckemeyer, Il., U.S.	E4	90
Becker, Mn., U.S.	E5	100
Becker, co., Mn., U.S.	D3	100
Beckham, co., Ok., U.S.	B2	113
Beckley, W.V., U.S.	D3	125
Beckum, Ger.	D8	8
Becky Peak, mtn., Nv., U.S.	D7	105
Bédarieux, Fr.	I10	10
Bedford, Que., Can.	D5	74
Bedford, Eng., U.K.	I12	7
Bedford, In., U.S.	G5	91
Bedford, Ia., U.S.	D3	92
Bedford, Ky., U.S.	B4	94
Bedford, Ma., U.S.	B5	98
Bedford, N.H., U.S.	E3	106
Bedford, Oh., U.S.	A4	112
Bedford, Pa., U.S.	F4	115
Bedford, Va., U.S.	C3	123
Bedford, co., Pa., U.S.	G4	115
Bedford, co., Tn., U.S.	B5	119
Bedford, co., Va., U.S.	C3	123
Bedford Hills, N.Y., U.S.	D7	109
Bee, co., Tx., U.S.	E4	120
Beebe, Que., Can.	D5	74
Beebe, Ar., U.S.	B4	81
Beecher, Il., U.S.	B6	90
Beecher, Mi., U.S.	*E7	99
Beech Fork, stm., Ky., U.S.	C4	94
Beech Grove, In., U.S.	E5	91
Beech Island, S.C., U.S.	E4	117
Beemer, Ne., U.S.	C9	104
Bee Ridge, Fl., U.S.	q11	86
Beersheba see Be'er Sheva', Isr.	D4	40
Be'er Sheva', Isr.	D4	40
Beeton (part of Alliston Beeton Tecumseth and Tottenham), Ont., Can.	C5	73
Beeville, Tx., U.S.	E4	120
Befale, Zaire	A4	44
Befandriana, Madag.	E9	44
Beggs, Ok., U.S.	B5	113
Begi, Eth.	G1	46
Behbehān, Iran	B5	46
Behm Canal, strt., Ak., U.S.	n24	79
Bei, stm., China	G9	26
Bei'an, China	B12	26
Beihai, China	D10	34
Beijing (Peking), China	D10	26
Beijing Shih, China	C10	26
Beipiao, China	C11	26
Beira, Moz.	E6	44
Beirut see Bayrūt, Leb.	C4	40
Beja, Port.	G4	12
Béja, Tun.	M4	14
Bejaïa, Alg.	A7	42
Béjar, Spain	E6	12
Békéscsaba, Hung.	I21	8
Bekily, Madag.	F9	44
Bela, India	H9	38
Bel Air, Md., U.S.	A5	97
Belaja Cerkov', Ukr.	H4	22
Belalcázar, Spain	G6	12
Bel Alton, Md., U.S.	D4	97
Belampalli, India	C5	37
Belarus, ctry., Eur.	G3	22
Bela Vista, Braz.	A5	56
Belaya Tserkov' see Belaja Cerkov', Ukr.	H4	22
Belcamp, Md., U.S.	B5	97
Belcherāgh, Afg.	C1	38
Belcher Islands, is., N.W. Ter., Can.	E17	66
Belchertown, Ma., U.S.	B3	98
Belchite, Spain	D11	12
Belcourt, N.D., U.S.	A6	111
Belden, Ms., U.S.	A5	101
Belding, Mi., U.S.	E5	99
Beled Weyne, Som.	H4	46
Belém, Braz.	D9	54
Belén, Para.	A5	56
Belen, N.M., U.S.	C3	108
Belfair, Wa., U.S.	B3	124
Belfast, N. Ire., U.K.	G7	7
Belfast, Me., U.S.	D3	96
Belfield, N.D., U.S.	C2	111
Belford, N.J., U.S.	C4	107
Belfort, Fr.	E13	10
Belfry, Ky., U.S.	C7	94
Belgaum, India	E3	37
Belgium, Wi., U.S.	E6	126
Belgium, ctry., Eur.	E8	4
Belgorod, Russia	G5	22
Belgrade, Mn., U.S.	E3	100
Belgrade, Mt., U.S.	E5	103
Belgrade see Beograd, Yugo.	E4	16
Belhaven, N.C., U.S.	B6	110
Belin, Fr.	H6	10
Belington, W.V., U.S.	B5	125
Belitung, i., Indon.	F4	32
Belize, ctry., N.A.	F3	64
Belize City, Belize	F3	64
Belknap, co., N.H., U.S.	C3	106
Belknap Crater, crat., Or., U.S.	C5	114
Bell, co., Ky., U.S.	D6	94
Bell, co., Tx., U.S.	D4	120
Bellac, Fr.	F8	10
Bella Coola, stm., B.C., Can.	C4	69
Bellaire, Ks., U.S.	g12	93
Bellaire, Mi., U.S.	D5	99
Bellaire, Oh., U.S.	C5	112
Bellaire, Tx., U.S.	r14	120
Bellamy, Al., U.S.	C1	78
Bellary, India	E4	37
Bellavista, Peru	E3	54
Bella Vista, Ar., U.S.	A1	81
Bellbrook, Oh., U.S.	C1	112
Belle, Mo., U.S.	C6	102
Belle, W.V., U.S.	C3	125
Belle, stm., La., U.S.	k9	95
Belleair, Fl., U.S.	p10	86
Belle Bay, b., Newf., Can.	E4	72
Belle Chasse, La., U.S.	E6	95
Bellefontaine, Oh., U.S.	B2	112
Bellefonte, Pa., U.S.	E6	115
Belle Fourche, S.D., U.S.	C2	118
Belle Fourche, stm., U.S.	C3	118
Belle Fourche Reservoir, res., S.D., U.S.	C2	118
Bellegarde, Fr.	F12	10
Belle Glade, Fl., U.S.	F6	86
Belle Isle, Fl., U.S.	D5	86
Belle Isle, i., Newf., Can.	C4	72
Belle Isle, Strait of, strt., Newf., Can.	C3	72
Belle Meade, Tn., U.S.	g10	119
Belle Plaine, Ia., U.S.	C5	92
Belle Plaine, Ks., U.S.	E6	93
Belle Plaine, Mn., U.S.	F5	100
Belle River, Ont., Can.	E2	73
Belle Rose, La., U.S.	D4	95
Belle Vernon, Pa., U.S.	F2	115
Belleview, Fl., U.S.	C4	86
Belle View, Va., U.S.	g12	123
Belleville, Ont., Can.	C7	73
Belleville, Il., U.S.	E4	90
Belleville, Ks., U.S.	C6	93
Belleville, Mi., U.S.	p15	99
Belleville, N.J., U.S.	B4	107
Belleville, Pa., U.S.	E6	115
Belleville, Wi., U.S.	F4	126
Belleville Pond, l., R.I., U.S.	E4	116
Bellevue, Id., U.S.	F4	89
Bellevue, Ia., U.S.	B7	92
Bellevue, Ky., U.S.	h13	94
Bellevue, Mi., U.S.	F5	99
Bellevue, Ne., U.S.	C10	104
Bellevue, Oh., U.S.	A3	112
Bellevue, Pa., U.S.	F1	115
Bellevue, Wa., U.S.	e11	124
Belley, Fr.	G12	10
Bellflower, Ca., U.S.	n12	82
Bellingham, Ma., U.S.	B5	98
Bellingham, Wa., U.S.	A3	124
Bellingshausen Sea, Ant.	B4	47
Bellinzona, Switz.	F16	10
Bell Island, i., Newf., Can.	C4	72
Bellmawr, N.J., U.S.	D2	107
Bello, Col.	D5	58
Bellows Falls, Vt., U.S.	E4	122
Bell Peninsula, pen., N.W. Ter., Can.	D16	66
Bellport, N.Y., U.S.	n16	109
Bells, Tn., U.S.	B2	119
Bells Creek, stm., W.V., U.S.	m13	125
Belluno, Italy	C7	14
Bell Ville, Arg.	C4	56
Bellville, Oh., U.S.	B3	112
Bellville, Tx., U.S.	E4	120
Bellwood, Il., U.S.	k9	90
Bellwood, Pa., U.S.	E5	115
Bellwood, Va., U.S.	n18	123
Belmar, N.J., U.S.	C4	107
Belmond, Ia., U.S.	B4	92
Belmont, Ont., Can.	E3	73
Belmont, Ca., U.S.	h8	82
Belmont, Ma., U.S.	g11	98
Belmont, Ms., U.S.	A5	101
Belmont, N.H., U.S.	D4	106
Belmont, N.C., U.S.	B1	110
Belmont, W.V., U.S.	B3	125
Belmont, Wi., U.S.	F3	126
Belmont, co., Oh., U.S.	C4	112
Belmonte, Braz.	C9	57
Belmonte, Port.	E4	12
Belmonte, Spain	E5	12
Belmonte, Spain	F9	12
Belmopan, Belize	F3	64
Belmullet, Ire.	G2	7
Bel-Nor, Mo., U.S.	f13	102
Belo, Madag.	E8	44
Beloeil, Que., Can.	D4	74
Belogorsk, Russia	G19	24
Belo Horizonte, Braz.	E7	57
Beloit, Ks., U.S.	C5	93
Beloit, Oh., U.S.	B5	112
Beloit, Wi., U.S.	F4	126
Beloit North, Wi., U.S.	*F4	126
Beloje, Ozero, l., Russia	A20	18
Beloje more (White Sea), Russia	D5	22
Belorado, Spain	C8	12
Beloreck, Russia	G9	22
Belorussia see Belarus, ctry., Eur.	G3	22
Belovo, Russia	G11	24
Belpre, Oh., U.S.	C4	112
Belt, Mt., U.S.	C6	103
Belted Range, mts., Nv., U.S.	F5	105
Belton, Mo., U.S.	C3	102
Belton, S.C., U.S.	B3	117
Belton, Tx., U.S.	D4	120
Belton Lake, res., Tx., U.S.	D4	120
Beltrami, co., Mn., U.S.	B3	100
Beltsville, Md., U.S.	B4	97
Belucha, Gora, mtn., Asia	H11	24
Belvedere, S.C., U.S.	D4	117
Belvedere Marittimo, Italy	J10	14
Belvidere, Il., U.S.	A5	90
Belvidere, N.J., U.S.	B2	107
Belyj, Ostrov, i., Russia	C8	24
Belyj Jar, Russia	F11	24
Belzoni, Ms., U.S.	B3	101
Bement, Il., U.S.	D5	90
Bemidji, Mn., U.S.	C4	100
Bemidji, Lake, l., Mn., U.S.	C4	100
Benabarre, Spain	C12	12
Bena-Dibele, Zaire	B4	44
Benavente, Port.	G3	12
Benavente, Spain	C6	12
Benavides, Tx., U.S.	F3	120
Benbrook Lake, res., Tx., U.S.	n9	120
Bend, Or., U.S.	C5	114
Ben Davis Point, c., N.J., U.S.	E2	107
Bendeleben, Mount, mtn., Ak., U.S.	B7	79
Bendigo, Austl.	G8	50
Benedict, Md., U.S.	C4	97
Benedito Leite, Braz.	E10	54
Benevento, Italy	H9	14
Benewah, co., Id., U.S.	B2	89
Bengal, Bay of, b., Asia	F6	36
Bengbu, China	C6	28
Benghazi see Banghāzī, Libya	B10	42
Bengkalis, Indon.	N7	34
Bengkulu, Indon.	F3	32
Benguela, Ang.	D2	44
Benham, Ky., U.S.	D7	94
Ben Hill, co., Ga., U.S.	E3	87
Beni, stm., Bol.	F5	54
Béni Abbès, Alg.	B5	42
Benicarló, Spain	E12	12
Benicia, Ca., U.S.	C2	82
Beni-Mellal, Mor.	B4	42
Benin, ctry., Afr.	G6	42
Benin, Bight of, Afr.	G6	42
Benin City, Nig.	G7	42

Name — Map Ref — Page

enisa, Spain G12 12
enito Juárez, Presa, res., Mex. I12 62
enjamin Constant, Braz. D4 54
enjamín Hill, Mex. B4 62
enkelman, Ne., U.S. D4 104
enld, Il., U.S. D4 90
ennett, Co., U.S. B6 83
ennett, co., S.D., U.S. D4 118
ennettsville, S.C., U.S. B8 117
ennington, Ne., U.S. g12 104
ennington, N.H., U.S. D3 106
ennington, Vt., U.S. F2 122
ennington, co., Vt., U.S. E2 122
enoit, Ms., U.S. B2 101
énoué (Benue), stm., Afr. G8 42
ensenville, Il., U.S. B6 90
ensheim, Ger. F8 8
ensley, Va., U.S. C5 123
enson, Az., U.S. F5 80
enson, Mn., U.S. E3 100
enson, N.C., U.S. B4 110
enson, co., N.D., U.S. A6 111
ent, co., Co., U.S. D7 83
entley, Alta., Can. C3 68
entleyville, Pa., U.S. F1 115
enton, Ar., U.S. C3 81
enton, Il., U.S. E5 90
enton, Ks., U.S. E6 93
enton, Ky., U.S. f9 94
enton, La., U.S. B2 95
enton, Pa., U.S. D9 115
enton, Tn., U.S. B7 119
enton, Wi., U.S. F3 126
enton, co., Ar., U.S. A1 81
enton, co., In., U.S. C3 91
enton, co., Ia., U.S. B5 92
enton, co., Mn., U.S. E4 100
enton, co., Ms., U.S. A4 101
enton, co., Mo., U.S. C4 102
enton, co., Or., U.S. C3 114
enton, co., Tn., U.S. A3 119
enton, co., Wa., U.S. C6 124
enton City, Wa., U.S. C6 124
enton Harbor, Mi., U.S. F4 99
enton Heights, Mi., U.S. F4 99
entonville, Ar., U.S. A1 81
en Treang, Viet. I9 34
ent's Old Fort National Historic Site, hist., Co., U.S. C7 83
enue (Bénoué), stm., Afr. G7 42
enwood, W.V., U.S. f8 125
enxi, China C11 26
enzie, co., Mi., U.S. D4 99
eograd (Belgrade), Yugo. E4 16
eowawe, Nv., U.S. C5 105
eppu, Japan I4 30
erau, Teluk, b., Indon. F9 32
erbera, Som. F4 46
erbérati, Cen. Afr. Rep. H9 42
erchtesgaden, Ger. H13 8
erck, Fr. B8 10
erdigest'ach, Russia E19 24
erdsk, Russia G10 24
erea, Ky., U.S. C5 94
erea, Oh., U.S. A4 112
erea, S.C., U.S. B3 117
erens, stm., Can. F13 66
erens, stm., Can. C3 70
eresford, S.D., U.S. D9 118
erg, Nor. B11 6
erga, Spain C13 12
ergama, Tur. J11 16
ergamo, Italy D4 14
ergen, Nor. F5 6
ergen, co., N.J., U.S. A4 107
ergen [auf Rügen], Ger. A13 8
ergenfield, N.J., U.S. B4 107
ergen op Zoom, Neth. D4 8
ergerac, Fr. H7 10
ergland, Mi., U.S. m12 99
ergstrom Air Force Base, mil., Tx., U.S. D4 120
erhampore, India H13 38
erhampur, India C8 37
eringovskij, Russia E29 24
ering Sea D30 128
ering Strait, strt. m18 76a
erja, Spain I9 12
erkåk, Nor. E7 6
erkeley, Ca., U.S. D2 82
erkeley, Mo., U.S. f13 102
erkeley, R.I., U.S. B4 116
erkeley, co., S.C., U.S. E8 117
erkeley, co., W.V., U.S. B6 125
erkeley Heights, N.J., U.S. B4 107
erkeley Springs, W.V., U.S. B6 125
erkley, Mi., U.S. F7 99
erkner Island, i., Ant. B8 47
erks, co., Pa., U.S. F9 115
erkshire, co., Ma., U.S. B1 98
erkshire Hills, hills, Ma., U.S. B1 98
erlin, Ger. C13 8
erlin, Ct., U.S. C5 84
erlin, Md., U.S. D7 97
erlin, N.H., U.S. B4 106
erlin, N.J., U.S. D3 107
erlin, Pa., U.S. G4 115
erlin, Wi., U.S. E5 126
erlin Lake, res., Oh., U.S. A4 112
ermeo, Spain B9 12
ermuda, dep., N.A. E14 76
ern (Berne), Switz. F14 10
ernalillo, N.M., U.S. B3 108
ernalillo, co., N.M., U.S. C3 108
ernardsville, N.J., U.S. B3 107
ernasconi, Arg. D4 56
ernau bei Berlin, Ger. C13 8
ernay, Fr. C7 10
ernburg, Ger. D11 8
erne, In., U.S. C8 91
ernice, La., U.S. B3 95
ernie, Mo., U.S. E8 102
ernier Island, i., Austl. D2 50
ernina, Piz, mtn., Eur. F16 10
eroroha, Madag. F9 44
erre, Étang de, b., Fr. I12 10

Berrien, co., Ga., U.S. E3 87
Berrien, co., Mi., U.S. F4 99
Berrien Springs, Mi., U.S. G4 99
Berry, Al., U.S. B2 78
Berryessa, Lake, res., Ca., U.S. C2 82
Berry Hill, Tn., U.S. g10 119
Berry Islands, is., Bah. B9 64
Berryville, Ar., U.S. A2 81
Berryville, Va., U.S. A5 123
Berthierville, Que., Can. C4 74
Berthoud, Co., U.S. A5 83
Berthoud Pass, Co., U.S. B5 83
Bertie, co., N.C., U.S. A5 110
Bertoua, Cam. H8 42
Bertrand, Mo., U.S. E8 102
Bertrand, Ne., U.S. D6 104
Berwick, Ia., U.S. e8 92
Berwick, La., U.S. E4 95
Berwick, Me., U.S. E2 96
Berwick, Pa., U.S. D9 115
Berwick-upon-Tweed, Eng., U.K. F10 7
Berwyn, Alta., Can. A2 68
Berwyn, Il., U.S. k9 90
Berwyn, Pa., U.S. o20 115
Besalampy, Madag. E8 44
Besançon, Fr. E13 10
Beskid Mountains, mts., Eur. F19 8
Bessemer, Al., U.S. B3 78
Bessemer, Mi., U.S. n11 99
Bessemer, Pa., U.S. E1 115
Bessemer City, N.C., U.S. B1 110
Best'ach, Russia E19 24
Betanzos, Spain B3 12
Bétaré Oya, Cam. G8 42
Betatakin Ruin, hist., Az., U.S. A5 80
Bethalto, Il., U.S. E3 90
Bethany, Ct., U.S. D4 84
Bethany, Il., U.S. D5 90
Bethany, Mo., U.S. A3 102
Bethany, Ok., U.S. B4 113
Bethany, W.V., U.S. A4 125
Bethany Beach, De., U.S. F5 85
Bethel, Ak., U.S. C7 79
Bethel, Ct., U.S. D2 84
Bethel, Me., U.S. D2 96
Bethel, N.C., U.S. B5 110
Bethel, Oh., U.S. D1 112
Bethel, Vt., U.S. D3 122
Bethel Park, Pa., U.S. k14 115
Bethel Springs, Tn., U.S. B3 119
Bethesda, Md., U.S. C3 97
Bethesda, Oh., U.S. B4 112
Bethlehem, S. Afr. G5 44
Bethlehem, Ct., U.S. C3 84
Bethlehem, N.H., U.S. B3 106
Bethlehem, Pa., U.S. E11 115
Bethlehem see Bayt Laḥm, Jord. D4 40
Béthune, Fr. B9 10
Beticos, Sistemas, mts., Spain H9 12
Betioky, Madag. F8 44
Betong, Malay. M6 34
Betroka, Madag. F9 44
Betsiboka, stm., Madag. E9 44
Betsie, Point, c., Mi., U.S. D4 99
Betsy Layne, Ky., U.S. C7 94
Bette, mtn., Libya D9 42
Bettendorf, Ia., U.S. C7 92
Bettiah, India G11 38
Betūl, India B4 37
Betzdorf, Ger. E7 8
Beulah, Co., U.S. C6 83
Beulah, N.D., U.S. B4 111
Beulah, Lake, l., Ms., U.S. B3 101
Beulaville, N.C., U.S. C5 110
B. Everett Jordan Lake, res., N.C., U.S. B3 110
Beverley, Austl. F3 50
Beverley, Eng., U.K. H12 7
Beverley Head, c., Newf., Can. D2 72
Beverly, Ma., U.S. A6 98
Beverly, N.J., U.S. C3 107
Beverly, Oh., U.S. C4 112
Beverly, W.V., U.S. C5 125
Beverly Hills, Ca., U.S. m12 82
Beverly Shores, In., U.S. A4 91
Bexar, co., Tx., U.S. E3 120
Bexley, Oh., U.S. m11 112
Beypore, India G3 37
Bežeck, Russia D19 18
Béziers, Fr. I10 10
Bhadrakh, India J12 38
Bhadrāvati, India F3 37
Bhāgalpur, India H12 38
Bhakkar, Pak. E4 38
Bhaktapur, Nepal G11 38
Bhandāra, India B5 37
Bharatpur, India G7 38
Bhatinda, India E6 38
Bhātpāra, India I13 38
Bhāvnagar, India J5 38
Bhilai, India B6 37
Bhīlwāra, India H6 38
Bhīma, stm., India D4 37
Bhīmavaram, India D6 37
Bhind, India G8 38
Bhiwandi, India C2 37
Bhiwāni, India F7 38
Bhopāl, India I7 38
Bhubaneswar, India J11 38
Bhuj, India I3 38
Bhusāwal, India B3 37
Bhutan, ctry., Asia D7 36
Bia, Phou, mtn., Laos E7 34
Biafra, Bight of, Afr. H7 42
Biak, i., Indon. F10 32
Biała Podlaska, Pol. C23 8
Białystok, Pol. B23 8
Biarritz, Fr. I5 10
Biasca, Switz. F15 10
Bibai, Japan p19 30a
Bibb, co., Al., U.S. C2 78
Bibb, co., Ga., U.S. D3 87
Biberach an der Riss, Ger. G9 8
Bic, Que., Can. A9 74
Bic, Île du, i., Que., Can. A9 74
Biche, Lac la, l., Alta., Can. B4 68
Bicknell, In., U.S. G3 91
Bida, Nig. G7 42
Bīdar, India D4 37

Biddeford, Me., U.S. E2 96
Bideford, Eng., U.K. J8 7
Bidwell, Mount, mtn., Ca., U.S. B3 82
Biel [Bienne], Switz. E14 10
Bielefeld, Ger. C8 8
Bieler Lake, l., N.W. Ter., Can. B18 66
Bielersee, l., Switz. E14 10
Biella, Italy D3 14
Bielsko-Biała, Pol. F19 8
Bien Hoa, Viet. I9 34
Bienville, co., La., U.S. B2 95
Bienville, Lac, l., Que., Can. g12 74
Big, stm., Mo., U.S. c7 102
Biga, Tur. I11 16
Bigadiç, Tur. J12 16
Big Bald, mtn., Ga., U.S. B2 87
Big Bald Mountain, mtn., N.B., Can. B3 71
Big Baldy, mtn., Id., U.S. E3 89
Big Baldy Mountain, mtn., Mt., U.S. D6 103
Big Bay De Noc, b., Mi., U.S. C4 99
Big Bear City, Ca., U.S. E5 82
Big Belt Mountains, mts., Mt., U.S. D5 103
Big Bend, Wi., U.S. n11 126
Big Bend Dam, S.D., U.S. C6 118
Big Bend National Park, Tx., U.S. E1 120
Big Birch Lake, l., Mn., U.S. E4 100
Big Black, stm., Me., U.S. B3 96
Big Black, stm., Ms., U.S. C3 101
Big Blue, stm., In., U.S. E6 91
Big Burro Mountains, mts., N.M., U.S. E1 108
Big Cabin Creek, stm., Ok., U.S. A6 113
Big Coal, stm., W.V., U.S. C3 125
Big Costilla Peak, mtn., N.M., U.S. A4 108
Big Creek, stm., Tn., U.S. e8 119
Big Creek Lake, res., Al., U.S. E1 78
Big Creek Peak, mtn., Id., U.S. E5 89
Big Cypress Indian Reservation, Fl., U.S. F5 86
Big Cypress Swamp, sw., Fl., U.S. F5 86
Big Darby Creek, stm., Oh., U.S. C2 112
Big Delta, Ak., U.S. C10 79
Big Duke Dam, N.C., U.S. B2 110
Big Eau Pleine, stm., Wi., U.S. D3 126
Big Eau Pleine Reservoir, res., Wi., U.S. D4 126
Big Escambia Creek, stm., U.S. D2 78
Big Flats, N.Y., U.S. C4 109
Bigfork, Mt., U.S. B2 103
Big Fork, stm., Mn., U.S. B5 100
Biggs, Ca., U.S. C3 82
Big Hatchet Peak, mtn., N.M., U.S. F1 108
Big Hole, stm., Mt., U.S. E4 103
Big Hole National Battlefield, hist., Mt., U.S. E3 103
Big Horn, co., Mt., U.S. E9 103
Big Horn, co., Wy., U.S. B4 127
Bighorn Canyon National Recreation Area, U.S. F8 103
Bighorn Lake, res., U.S. E8 103
Bighorn Mountains, mts., U.S. B5 127
Big Horn Mountains, mts., Az., U.S. D2 80
Big Kandiyohi Lake, l., Mn., U.S. F4 100
Big Lake, Mn., U.S. E5 100
Big Lake, Tx., U.S. D2 120
Big Lake, l., Me., U.S. C5 96
Biglerville, Pa., U.S. G7 115
Big Lookout Mountain, mtn., Or., U.S. C9 114
Big Lost, stm., Id., U.S. F5 89
Big Mossy Point, c., Man., Can. C2 70
Big Mountain, mtn., Nv., U.S. B2 105
Big Muddy, stm., Il., U.S. F4 90
Big Nemaha, stm., Ne., U.S. D10 104
Big Otter, stm., Va., U.S. C3 123
Big Pine Lake, l., Mn., U.S. D3 100
Big Pine Mountain, mtn., Ca., U.S. E4 82
Big Piney, Wy., U.S. D2 127
Big Piney, stm., Mo., U.S. D5 102
Bigpoint, Ms., U.S. E5 101
Big Rapids, Mi., U.S. E5 99
Big Rib, stm., Wi., U.S. C3 126
Big River, Sask., Can. D2 75
Big Sable Point, c., Mi., U.S. D4 99
Big Sandy, Mt., U.S. B6 103
Big Sandy, Tx., U.S. C5 120
Big Sandy, stm., U.S. C2 125
Big Sandy, stm., Az., U.S. C2 80
Big Sandy, stm., Tn., U.S. B3 119
Big Sandy, stm., Wy., U.S. D3 127
Big Sandy Creek, stm., W.V., U.S. C3 125
Big Sandy Lake, l., Mn., U.S. D5 100
Big Sandy Reservoir, res., Wy., U.S. D3 127
Big Sheep Mountain, mtn., Mt., U.S. C11 103
Big Sioux, stm., U.S. E9 118
Big Smoky Valley, val., Nv., U.S. E4 105
Big Snowy Mountains, mts., Mt., U.S. D7 103
Big Southern Butte, mtn., Id., U.S. F5 89
Big South Fork, stm., Ky., U.S. k13 94
Big Spring, Tx., U.S. C2 120
Big Stone, co., Mn., U.S. E2 100
Big Stone City, S.D., U.S. B9 118
Big Stone Gap, Va., U.S. f9 123
Big Stone Lake, l., U.S. E2 100
Big Sunflower, stm., Ms., U.S. B3 101
Big Thompson, stm., Co., U.S. A5 83
Big Timber, Mt., U.S. E7 103
Big Trout Lake, l., Ont., Can. n17 73
Big Walnut Creek, stm., Oh., U.S. m11 112
Big Wood, stm., Id., U.S. F4 89
Bihać, Bos. E10 14
Bihār, India H11 38
Bihār, state, India H11 38
Biharamulo, Tan. B6 44
Bihoro, Japan p22 30a
Bija, stm., Russia G11 24
Bijāpur, India C6 37
Bijāpur, India D3 37

Bijsk, Russia G11 24
Bīkaner, India F5 38
Bikin, Russia H20 24
Bikoro, Zaire B3 44
Bilāspur, India I10 38
Bilauktaung Range, mts., Asia G5 34
Bilbao, Spain B9 12
Bilimora, India B2 37
Bilk Creek Mountains, mts., Nv., U.S. B3 105
Billerica, Ma., U.S. A5 98
Billings, Mo., U.S. D4 102
Billings, Mt., U.S. E8 103
Billings, co., N.D., U.S. B2 111
Billings Heights, Mt., U.S. E8 103
Bill Williams, stm., Az., U.S. C1 80
Bill Williams Mountain, mtn., Az., U.S. B3 80
Bilma, Niger E8 42
Biloxi, Ms., U.S. E5 101
Biloxi, stm., Ms., U.S. E4 101
Biloxi Bay, b., Ms., U.S. f8 101
Biltmore Forest, N.C., U.S. f10 110
Bimini Islands, is., Bah. B8 64
Bīna-Etāwa, India H8 38
Bindura, Zimb. E6 44
Binéfar, Spain D12 12
Binga, Monte, mtn., Afr. E6 44
Bingamon Creek, stm., W.V., U.S. k10 125
Bingen, Ger. F7 8
Bingen, Wa., U.S. D4 124
Binger, Ok., U.S. B3 113
Bingham, Me., U.S. C3 96
Bingham, co., Id., U.S. F6 89
Binghamton, N.Y., U.S. C5 109
Binhai (Dongkan), China A8 28
Binjai, Indon. M5 34
Bintimani, mtn., S.L. G3 42
Biograd, Cro. F10 14
Bioko, i., Eq. Gui. H7 42
Bīr, India C3 37
Birao, Cen. Afr. Rep. F10 42
Birātnagar, Nepal G12 38
Birch, stm., W.V., U.S. C4 125
Birch Island, i., Man., Can. C2 70
Birch Lake, l., Mn., U.S. C7 100
Birch River, Man., Can. C1 70
Birch Run, Mi., U.S. E7 99
Birchwood City, Md., U.S. *f9 97
Birchy Bay, Newf., Can. D4 72
Bird Creek, stm., Ok., U.S. A6 113
Bird Island, Mn., U.S. F4 100
Bird Island, i., N.C., U.S. D4 110
Birdsboro, Pa., U.S. F10 115
Birdum, Austl. C6 50
Birecik, Tur. A5 40
Bīrganj, Nepal G11 38
Birigui, Braz. F3 57
Biril'ussy, Russia F12 24
Bīrjand, Iran K9 22
Birkenfeld, Ger. F7 8
Birkenhead, Eng., U.K. H9 7
Bîrlad, Rom. C11 16
Birmingham, Eng., U.K. I11 7
Birmingham, Al., U.S. B3 78
Birmingham, Mi., U.S. F7 99
Birmitrapur, India I11 38
Bir Mogreïn, Maur. C3 42
Birobidžan, Russia H20 24
Biron, Wi., U.S. D4 126
Birr, Ire. H5 7
Bi'r Safājah, Egypt C12 42
Birtle, Man., Can. D1 70
Bisbee, Az., U.S. F6 80
Biscarrosse, Fr. H5 10
Biscay, Bay of, b., Eur. G7 4
Biscayne, Key, i., Fl., U.S. s13 86
Biscayne Bay, b., Fl., U.S. G6 86
Biscayne National Monument, Fl., U.S. G6 86
Biscayne Park, Fl., U.S. s13 86
Bisceglie, Italy H11 14
Bischofshofen, Aus. H13 8
Biscoe, N.C., U.S. B3 110
Bishnupur, India I12 38
Bishop, Ca., U.S. D4 82
Bishop, Tx., U.S. F4 120
Bishop Auckland, Eng., U.K. G11 7
Bishop's Falls, Newf., Can. D4 72
Bishopville, S.C., U.S. C7 117
Biškek (Bishkek), Kyrg. I12 22
Biskra, Alg. B7 42
Bismarck, Il., U.S. C6 90
Bismarck, Mo., U.S. D7 102
Bismarck, N.D., U.S. C5 111
Bismarck Archipelago, is., Pap. N. Gui. m16 50a
Bismarck Range, mts., Pap. N. Gui. m15 50a
Bison Peak, mtn., Co., U.S. B5 83
Bissau, Gui.-B. F2 42
Bistineau, Lake, res., La., U.S. B2 95
Bistrița, Rom. B8 16
Bitola, Mac. H5 16
Bitonto, Italy H11 14
Bitter Creek, stm., Wy., U.S. E4 127
Bitterfeld, Ger. D12 8
Bitterfontein, S. Afr. H3 44
Bitter Lake, l., S.D., U.S. B8 118
Bitterroot, stm., Mt., U.S. D2 103
Bitterroot Range, mts., U.S. B3 89
Bitti, Italy I4 14
Biwabik, Mn., U.S. C6 100
Biwa-ko, l., Japan G9 30
Bixby, Ok., U.S. B6 113
Biyang, China C2 28
Bizen, Japan H7 30
Bizerte, Tun. L4 14
Bjelovar, Cro. D11 14
Black (Lixian) (Da), stm., Asia D8 34
Black, stm., Az., U.S. D5 80
Black, stm., Ar., U.S. B4 81
Black, stm., La., U.S. C4 95
Black, stm., Mi., U.S. E8 99
Black, stm., N.Y., U.S. B4 109
Black, stm., N.C., U.S. C4 110
Black, stm., S.C., U.S. D8 117
Black, stm., Vt., U.S. B4 122
Black, stm., Vt., U.S. E3 122

Black, stm., Wi., U.S. D3 126
Blackall, Austl. D9 50
Black Bear Creek, stm., Ok., U.S. A4 113
Blackbeard Island, i., Ga., U.S. E5 87
Blackburn, Eng., U.K. H10 7
Blackburn, Mount, mtn., Ak., U.S. C11 79
Black Butte, mtn., Mt., U.S. F5 103
Black Butte Lake, res., Ca., U.S. C2 82
Black Canyon, val., Co., U.S. C3 83
Black Canyon City, Az., U.S. C3 80
Black Canyon of the Gunnison National Monument, Co., U.S. C3 83
Black Creek, B.C., Can. E5 69
Black Creek, Wi., U.S. D5 126
Black Creek, stm., U.S. B1 108
Black Creek, stm., S.C., U.S. B7 117
Black Diamond, Alta., Can. D3 68
Black Diamond, Wa., U.S. B4 124
Blackduck, Mn., U.S. C4 100
Black Eagle, Mt., U.S. C5 103
Black Earth, Wi., U.S. E4 126
Blackfalds, Alta., Can. C4 68
Blackfeet Indian Reservation, Mt., U.S. B4 103
Blackfoot, Id., U.S. F6 89
Blackfoot, stm., Mt., U.S. C3 103
Blackfoot Mountains, mts., Id., U.S. F7 89
Blackfoot Reservoir, res., Id., U.S. G7 89
Blackford, co., In., U.S. D7 91
Black Forest, Co., U.S. C6 83
Black Forest see Schwarzwald, mts., Ger. G8 8
Blackhall Mountain, mtn., Wy., U.S. E6 127
Black Hawk, S.D., U.S. C2 118
Black Hawk, co., Ia., U.S. B5 92
Black Hills, mts., U.S. C2 118
Blackjack Mountain, mtn., Ga., U.S. h8 87
Black Lake, Que., Can. C6 74
Black Lake, l., Mi., U.S. C6 99
Black Lake, l., N.Y., U.S. f9 109
Black Lick, Pa., U.S. F3 115
Blacklick Estates, Oh., U.S. *m11 112
Black Mesa, mtn., Ok., U.S. e8 113
Black Mingo Creek, stm., S.C., U.S. D9 117
Blackmore, Mount, mtn., Mt., U.S. E6 103
Black Mountain, N.C., U.S. f10 110
Black Mountain, mtn., U.S. D7 94
Black Mountain, mtn., Az., U.S. E4 80
Black Mountain, mtn., Co., U.S. A5 83
Black Mountain, mtn., Id., U.S. C3 89
Black Mountain, mtn., Mt., U.S. D4 103
Black Mountain, mtn., Or., U.S. B7 114
Black Mountain, mtn., Wy., U.S. B5 127
Black Mountain, mtn., Wy., U.S. D7 127
Black Mountains, mts., Az., U.S. B1 80
Black Peak, mtn., Az., U.S. C1 80
Black Pine Peak, mtn., Id., U.S. G5 89
Blackpool, Eng., U.K. H9 7
Black Range, mts., N.M., U.S. D2 108
Black River Falls, Wi., U.S. D3 126
Black Rock, Ar., U.S. A4 81
Black Rock, N.M., U.S. B1 108
Black Rock Desert, des., Nv., U.S. B3 105
Black Rock Range, mts., Nv., U.S. B3 105
Blacksburg, S.C., U.S. A4 117
Blacksburg, Va., U.S. C2 123
Black Sea G14 4
Blacks Fork, stm., U.S. E3 127
Blacks Harbour, N.B., Can. D3 71
Blackshear, Ga., U.S. E4 87
Blackstone, Ma., U.S. B4 98
Blackstone, Va., U.S. C5 123
Blackstone, stm., R.I., U.S. B4 116
Black Thunder Creek, stm., Wy., U.S. C8 127
Blackville, N.B., Can. C4 71
Blackville, S.C., U.S. E5 117
Black Volta (Volta Noire), stm., Afr. G5 42
Blackwalnut Point, c., Md., U.S. C5 97
Black Warrior, stm., Al., U.S. C2 78
Blackwater, stm., Fl., U.S. u15 86
Blackwater, stm., Md., U.S. D5 97
Blackwater, stm., N.H., U.S. D3 106
Blackwater, stm., Va., U.S. D6 123
Blackwater Reservoir, res., N.H., U.S. D3 106
Blackwell, Ok., U.S. A4 113
Blackwood, N.J., U.S. D2 107
Bladen, co., N.C., U.S. C4 110
Bladenboro, N.C., U.S. C4 110
Bladensburg, Md., U.S. f9 97
Blades, De., U.S. F3 85
Blagoevgrad, Bul. G7 16
Blagoveščensk, Russia G19 24
Blaine, Me., U.S. B5 96
Blaine, Mn., U.S. m12 100
Blaine, Tn., U.S. C10 119
Blaine, Wa., U.S. A3 124
Blaine, co., Id., U.S. F4 89
Blaine, co., Mt., U.S. B7 103
Blaine, co., Ne., U.S. C6 104
Blaine, co., Ok., U.S. B3 113
Blaine Lake, Sask., Can. E2 75
Blair, Ne., U.S. C9 104
Blair, Ok., U.S. C2 113
Blair, W.V., U.S. n12 125
Blair, Wi., U.S. D2 126
Blair, co., Pa., U.S. E5 115
Blair Athol, Austl. D9 50
Blairstown, Ia., U.S. C5 92
Blairsville, Pa., U.S. F3 115
Blake Island, i., Wa., U.S. e11 124
Blakely, Ga., U.S. E2 87
Blakely, Pa., U.S. m18 115
Blake Point, c., Mi., U.S. h10 99
Blanc, Cap, c., Afr. D2 42
Blanc, Mont (Monte Bianco), mtn., Eur. G13 10
Blanca Peak, mtn., Co., U.S. D5 83
Blanchard, La., U.S. B2 95
Blanchard, Ok., U.S. B4 113
Blanchard, stm., Oh., U.S. A1 112

Name	Map Ref	Page
Blanchardville, Wi., U.S.	F4	126
Blanchester, Oh., U.S.	C2	112
Blanco, Tx., U.S.	D3	120
Blanco, co., Tx., U.S.	D3	120
Blanco, Cape, c., Or., U.S.	E2	114
Bland, Mo., U.S.	C6	102
Bland, co., Va., U.S.	C1	123
Blanding, Ut., U.S.	F6	121
Blandinsville, Il., U.S.	C3	90
Blanes, Spain	D14	12
Blangkedjeren, Indon.	M4	34
Blangy-sur-Bresle, Fr.	C8	10
Blanquilla, Isla, i., Ven.	B10	58
Blantyre, Mwi.	E7	44
Blasdell, N.Y., U.S.	C2	109
Blawnox, Pa., U.S.	k14	115
Blaye-et-Sainte-Luce, Fr.	G6	10
Bleckley, co., Ga., U.S.	D3	87
Bled, Slo.	C9	14
Bledsoe, co., Tn., U.S.	D8	119
Blende, Co., U.S.	C6	83
Blenheim, Ont., Can.	E3	73
Blenheim, N.Z.	D4	52
Blennerhassett, W.V., U.S.	B3	125
Bléré, Fr.	E7	10
Blida, Alg.	A6	42
Blind, stm., La., U.S.	h10	95
Blind River, Ont., Can.	A2	73
Blissfield, Mi., U.S.	G7	99
Blitar, Indon.	n16	32
Block Island, R.I., U.S.	h7	116
Block Island, i., R.I., U.S.	h7	116
Block Island Sound, strt., U.S.	G2	116
Bloemfontein, S. Afr.	G5	44
Bloemhof, S. Afr.	G5	44
Blois, Fr.	E8	10
Blood Mountain, mtn., Ga., U.S.	B3	87
Bloodsworth Island, i., Md., U.S.	D5	97
Bloodvein, stm., Can.	D3	70
Bloody Foreland, c., Ire.	F4	7
Bloomer, Wi., U.S.	C2	126
Bloomfield, Ont., Can.	D7	73
Bloomfield, Ct., U.S.	B5	84
Bloomfield, In., U.S.	F4	91
Bloomfield, Ia., U.S.	D5	92
Bloomfield, Ky., U.S.	C4	94
Bloomfield, Mo., U.S.	E8	102
Bloomfield, Ne., U.S.	B8	104
Bloomfield, N.J., U.S.	h8	107
Bloomfield, N.M., U.S.	A2	108
Bloomfield Hills, Mi., U.S.	o15	99
Bloomingdale, Ga., U.S.	D5	87
Bloomingdale, Il., U.S.	k8	90
Bloomingdale, N.J., U.S.	A4	107
Bloomingdale, Tn., U.S.	C11	119
Blooming Prairie, Mn., U.S.	G5	100
Bloomington, Il., U.S.	C4	90
Bloomington, In., U.S.	F4	91
Bloomington, Mn., U.S.	F5	100
Bloomington, Tx., U.S.	E4	120
Bloomington, Wi., U.S.	F3	126
Bloomington, Lake, res., Il., U.S.	C5	90
Bloomsburg, Pa., U.S.	E9	115
Bloomville, Oh., U.S.	A2	112
Blora, Indon.	m15	33a
Blossburg, Pa., U.S.	C7	115
Blossom, Tx., U.S.	C5	120
Blount, co., Al., U.S.	B3	78
Blount, co., Tn., U.S.	D10	119
Blountstown, Fl., U.S.	B1	86
Blountsville, Al., U.S.	A3	78
Blountville, Tn., U.S.	C11	119
Blowing Rock, N.C., U.S.	A1	110
Bludenz, Aus.	H9	8
Blue, stm., Co., U.S.	B4	83
Blue, stm., In., U.S.	H5	91
Blue, stm., Mo., U.S.	k10	102
Blue, stm., Ok., U.S.	C5	113
Blue Ash, Oh., U.S.	o13	112
Blue Buck Point, c., La., U.S.	E2	95
Blue Creek, W.V., U.S.	m13	125
Blue Creek, stm., W.V., U.S.	m13	125
Blue Cypress Lake, l., Fl., U.S.	E6	86
Blue Diamond, Nv., U.S.	G6	105
Blue Earth, Mn., U.S.	G4	100
Blue Earth, co., Mn., U.S.	G4	100
Blue Earth, stm., Mn., U.S.	G4	100
Bluefield, Va., U.S.	C1	123
Bluefield, W.V., U.S.	D3	125
Bluefields, Nic.	H6	64
Blue Grass, Ia., U.S.	C7	92
Blue Hill, Me., U.S.	D4	96
Blue Hill, Ne., U.S.	D7	104
Blue Hill Range, hills, Ma., U.S.	h11	98
Blue Hills, Ct., U.S.	B5	84
Blue Island, Il., U.S.	B6	90
Bluejoint Lake, l., Or., U.S.	E7	114
Blue Lake, Ca., U.S.	B2	82
Blue Mesa Reservoir, res., Co., U.S.	C3	83
Blue Mound, Il., U.S.	D4	90
Blue Mountain, Ms., U.S.	A4	101
Blue Mountain, mtn., Mt., U.S.	C12	103
Blue Mountain, mtn., N.M., U.S.	D2	108
Blue Mountain, mtn., Pa., U.S.	F6	115
Blue Mountain Lake, res., Ar., U.S.	B2	81
Blue Mountain Peak, mtn., Jam.	E9	64
Blue Nile (Al-Bahr al-Azraq), stm., Afr.	F12	42
Blue Point, Me., U.S.	g7	96
Blue Rapids, Ks., U.S.	C7	93
Blue Ridge, Ga., U.S.	B2	87
Blue Ridge, Va., U.S.	C3	123
Blue Ridge, mtn., U.S.	E10	76
Blue Ridge Summit, Pa., U.S.	G7	115
Blue Springs, Mo., U.S.	h11	102
Bluestone, stm., W.V., U.S.	D3	125
Bluestone Lake, res., U.S.	D4	125
Bluewell, W.V., U.S.	D3	125
Bluff City, Tn., U.S.	C11	119
Bluff Creek, stm., Ok., U.S.	A4	113
Bluff Lake, res., Ms., U.S.	B5	101
Bluff Park, Al., U.S.	g7	78
Bluffs, Il., U.S.	D3	90
Bluffton, In., U.S.	C7	91
Bluffton, Oh., U.S.	B2	112
Bluffton, S.C., U.S.	G6	117
Blumenau, Braz.	B7	56
Bly, Or., U.S.	E5	114
Blying Sound, strt., Ak., U.S.	h17	79
Blyth, Ont., Can.	D3	73
Blyth, Eng., U.K.	F11	7
Blythe, Ca., U.S.	F6	82
Blytheville, Ar., U.S.	B6	81
Bø, Nor.	B10	6
Bø, Nor.	G7	6
Bo, S.L.	G3	42
Boaco, Nic.	H5	64
Boalsburg, Pa., U.S.	E6	115
Boa Nova, Braz.	C8	57
Boardman, Oh., U.S.	A5	112
Boardman, Or., U.S.	B7	114
Boa Vista, Braz.	C6	54
Boavita, Col.	D6	58
Boaz, Al., U.S.	A3	78
Bobbili, India	C7	37
Bobbio, Italy	E4	14
Bobcaygeon, Ont., Can.	C6	73
Böblingen, Ger.	G9	8
Bobo Dioulasso, Burkina	F5	42
Bobrujsk, Bela.	H12	18
Bobtown, Pa., U.S.	G2	115
Bobures, Ven.	C7	58
Boby, Pic, mtn., Madag.	F9	44
Boca Chica Key, i., Fl., U.S.	H5	86
Boca Ciega Bay, b., Fl., U.S.	p10	86
Bôca do Acre, Braz.	E5	54
Boca Grande, Fl., U.S.	F4	86
Boca Raton, Fl., U.S.	F6	86
Bocas del Toro, Pan.	J6	64
Bocholt, Ger.	D6	8
Bochum, Ger.	D7	8
Bodajbo, Russia	F16	24
Bodega Head, c., Ca., U.S.	C2	82
Bodele, reg., Chad	E9	42
Boden, Swe.	D13	6
Bodensee, l., Eur.	H9	8
Bodhan, India	C4	37
Bodie Island, i., N.C., U.S.	B7	110
Bodināyakkanūr, India	G4	37
Bodkin Point, c., Md., U.S.	B5	97
Bodø, Nor.	C10	6
Boende, Zaire	B4	44
Boën-sur-Lignon, Fr.	G10	10
Boerne, Tx., U.S.	E3	120
Boeuf, stm., La., U.S.	C4	95
Boeuf, Lake, l., La., U.S.	k10	95
Bogale, Burma	F3	34
Bogalusa, La., U.S.	D6	95
Bogart, Ga., U.S.	C3	87
Bogata, Tx., U.S.	C5	120
Bogenfels, Nmb.	G3	44
Boger City, N.C., U.S.	B1	110
Bognes, Nor.	B10	6
Bogor, Indon.	m13	32
Bogorodick, Russia	H21	18
Bogorodsk, Russia	E26	18
Bogota, N.J., U.S.	h8	107
Bogotá see Santa Fe de Bogotá, Col.	E5	58
Bogotol, Russia	F11	24
Bogra, Bngl.	H13	38
Bogučany, Russia	F13	24
Bogue Chitto, Ms., U.S.	D3	101
Bogue Chitto, stm., U.S.	D5	95
Bogue Inlet, b., N.C., U.S.	C5	110
Bogue Phalia, stm., Ms., U.S.	B3	101
Bo Hai, b., China	D10	26
Bohain-en-Vermandois, Fr.	C10	10
Bohemia see Čechy, hist. reg., Czech.	F14	8
Bohemian Forest, mts., Eur.	F12	8
Bohol, i., Phil.	D7	32
Boiano, Italy	H9	14
Boigu, i., Austl.	A8	50
Boiling Springs, N.C., U.S.	B1	110
Boiling Springs, Pa., U.S.	F7	115
Bois Blanc Island, i., Mi., U.S.	C6	99
Bois Brule, stm., Wi., U.S.	B2	126
Boischâtel, Que., Can.	C6	74
Bois-des-Filion, Que., Can.	p19	74
Bois de Sioux, stm., Mn., U.S.	E2	100
Boise, Id., U.S.	F2	89
Boise, co., Id., U.S.	F3	89
Boise City, Ok., U.S.	e8	113
Boissevain, Man., Can.	E1	70
Boissevain, Va., U.S.	e10	123
Boistfort Peak, mtn., Wa., U.S.	C2	124
Boizenburg, Ger.	B10	8
Bojador, Cabo, c., W. Sah.	C3	42
Bojeador, Cape, c., Phil.	B7	32
Bojnūrd, Iran	J9	22
Bojonegoro, Indon.	m15	33a
Boké, Gui.	F3	42
Boketu, China	B11	26
Boknafjorden, Nor.	G5	6
Boksitogorsk, Russia	B16	18
Bokungu, Zaire	B4	44
Bolama, Gui.-B.	F2	42
Bolbec, Fr.	C7	10
Bolesławiec, Pol.	D15	8
Boley, Ok., U.S.	B5	113
Bolgatanga, Ghana	F5	42
Boli, China	B13	26
Bolingbrook, Il., U.S.	k8	90
Bolívar, Arg.	D4	56
Bolivar, Mo., U.S.	D4	102
Bolivar, Oh., U.S.	B4	112
Bolivar, Tn., U.S.	B3	119
Bolivar, W.V., U.S.	B7	125
Bolivar, co., Ms., U.S.	B3	101
Bolívar, Cerro, mtn., Ven.	D11	58
Bolivar, Lake, l., Ms., U.S.	B3	101
Bolívar, Pico, mtn., Ven.	C7	58
Bolivia, ctry., S.A.	G5	54
Bollène, Fr.	H11	10
Bollinger, co., Mo., U.S.	D7	102
Bollnäs, Swe.	F11	6
Bollullos par del Condado, Spain	H5	12
Bolobo, Zaire	B3	44
Bologna, Italy	E6	14
Bologoje, Russia	D17	18
Bolotnoje, Russia	F10	24
Bolsena, Italy	G6	14
Bol'šereck, Russia	G25	24
Bol'ševik, Russia	E23	24
Bol'ševik, Ostrov, i., Russia	B14	24
Bol'šoj An'uj, stm., Russia	D26	24
Bol'šoj Begičev, Ostrov, i., Russia	C16	24
Bol'šoj L'achovskij, Ostrov, i., Russia	C22	24
Bolton, Eng., U.K.	H10	7
Bolton, Ms., U.S.	C3	101
Bolton Lakes, l., Ct., U.S.	B6	84
Bolton Landing, N.Y., U.S.	B7	109
Bolzano (Bozen), Italy	C6	14
Boma, Zaire	C2	44
Bombala, Austl.	G9	50
Bombarral, Port.	F2	12
Bombay, India	C2	37
Bombay Hook Island, i., De., U.S.	C4	85
Bom Despacho, Braz.	E6	57
Bom Jesus da Lapa, Braz.	B7	57
Bomoseen, Lake, l., Vt., U.S.	D2	122
Bomu (Mbomou), stm., Afr.	H10	42
Bon, Cap, c., Tun.	A8	42
Bon Accord, Alta., Can.	C4	68
Bon Air, Va., U.S.	C5	123
Bonaire, Ga., U.S.	D3	87
Bonaire, i., Neth. Ant.	H13	64
Bonanza Peak, mtn., Wa., U.S.	A5	124
Bonao, Dom. Rep.	E12	64
Bonaparte, Mount, mtn., Wa., U.S.	A6	124
Bonaparte Archipelago, is., Austl.	B5	50
Bonarbridge, Scot., U.K.	D8	7
Bonasila Dome, mtn., Ak., U.S.	C7	79
Bonaventure, Que., Can.	A4	71
Bonavista, Newf., Can.	D5	72
Bonavista, Cape, c., Newf., Can.	D5	72
Bonavista Bay, b., Newf., Can.	G22	66
Bonavista Bay, b., Newf., Can.	D5	72
Bond, co., Il., U.S.	E4	90
Bondeno, Italy	E6	14
Bondo, Zaire	H10	42
Bondoukou, I.C.	G5	42
Bondowoso, Indon.	m16	33a
Bondsville, Ma., U.S.	B3	98
Bonduel, Wi., U.S.	D5	126
Bondurant, Ia., U.S.	C4	92
Bone, Teluk, b., Indon.	F7	32
Bone Lake, l., Wi., U.S.	C1	126
Bongandanga, Zaire	A4	44
Bongor, Chad	F9	42
Bonham, Tx., U.S.	C4	120
Bon Homme, co., S.D., U.S.	D8	118
Bonifati, Capo, c., Italy	J10	14
Bonifay, Fl., U.S.	u16	86
Bonita Springs, Fl., U.S.	F5	86
Bonn, Ger.	E7	8
Bonneauville, Pa., U.S.	G7	115
Bonne Bay, b., Newf., Can.	D3	72
Bonner, co., Id., U.S.	A2	89
Bonners Ferry, Id., U.S.	A2	89
Bonner Springs, Ks., U.S.	C9	93
Bonnet Carre Floodway, La., U.S.	h11	95
Bonne Terre, Mo., U.S.	D7	102
Bonneval, Fr.	D8	10
Bonneville, Fr.	F13	10
Bonneville, co., Id., U.S.	F7	89
Bonneville Dam, U.S.	B4	114
Bonneville Peak, mtn., Id., U.S.	F6	89
Bonneville Salt Flats, pl., Ut., U.S.	C2	121
Bonney Lake, Wa., U.S.	B3	124
Bonnie Doone, N.C., U.S.	B4	110
Bonny Reservoir, res., Co., U.S.	B8	83
Bonnyville, Alta., Can.	B5	68
Bono, Ar., U.S.	B5	81
Bonorva, Italy	I3	14
Bon Secour, Al., U.S.	E2	78
Bonthe, S.L.	G3	42
Booker, Tx., U.S.	A2	120
Booker T. Washington National Monument, Va., U.S.	C3	123
Boomer, W.V., U.S.	C3	125
Boone, Ia., U.S.	B4	92
Boone, N.C., U.S.	A1	110
Boone, co., Ar., U.S.	A2	81
Boone, co., Il., U.S.	A5	90
Boone, co., In., U.S.	D4	91
Boone, co., Ia., U.S.	B3	92
Boone, co., Ky., U.S.	B5	94
Boone, co., Mo., U.S.	B5	102
Boone, co., Ne., U.S.	C7	104
Boone, co., W.V., U.S.	C3	125
Boone, stm., Ia., U.S.	B4	92
Boone Lake, res., Tn., U.S.	C11	119
Booneville, Ar., U.S.	B2	81
Booneville, Ms., U.S.	A5	101
Boonsboro, Md., U.S.	A2	97
Boonton, N.J., U.S.	B4	107
Boonville, In., U.S.	H3	91
Boonville, Mo., U.S.	C5	102
Boonville, N.Y., U.S.	B5	109
Boonville, N.C., U.S.	A2	110
Boothbay Harbor, Me., U.S.	E3	96
Boothia, Gulf of, b., N.W. Ter., Can.	B14	66
Boothia Peninsula, pen., N.W. Ter., Can.	B14	66
Booths Creek, stm., W.V., U.S.	h11	125
Boothville, La., U.S.	E6	95
Booué, Gabon	B2	44
Boquete, Pan.	J6	64
Boquillas del Carmen, Mex.	C8	62
Bor, Russia	E27	18
Bor, Sudan	G12	42
Boraha, Nosy, i., Madag.	E9	44
Borah Peak, mtn., Id., U.S.	E5	89
Borås, Swe.	H9	6
Bordeaux, Fr.	H6	10
Borden, co., Tx., U.S.	C2	120
Borden Peninsula, pen., N.W. Ter., Can.	B16	66
Bordentown, N.J., U.S.	C3	107
Bordertown, Austl.	G8	50
Borgå (Porvoo), Fin.	F15	6
Borgarnes, Ice.	C3	4
Borger, Tx., U.S.	B2	120
Borgne, Lake, b., La., U.S.	D6	95
Borgo, Italy	C6	14
Borgo San Dalmazzo, Italy	E2	14
Borgosesia, Italy	D3	14
Borgo Val di Taro, Italy	E4	14
Borisov, Bela.	G11	18
Borja, Spain	D10	12
Borjas Blancas, Spain	D12	12
Borken, Ger.	D6	8
Borlänge, Swe.	F10	6
Borlu, Tur.	K12	16
Borneo (Kalimantan), i., Asia	E5	32
Bornholm, i., Den.	I10	6
Bornova, Tur.	K11	16
Borogoncy, Russia	E20	24
Boron, Ca., U.S.	E5	82
Boronga Islands, is., Burma	E2	34
Borovići, Russia	C16	18
Borrego Springs, Ca., U.S.	F5	82
Bort-les-Orgues, Fr.	G9	10
Borūjerd, Iran	B4	46
Borz'a, Russia	G17	24
Bosa, Italy	I3	14
Bosanska Gradiška, Bos.	D12	14
Bosanska Krupa, Bos.	E11	14
Bosanski Novi, Bos.	D11	14
Bosanski Petrovac, Bos.	E11	14
Bosaso, Som.	F4	46
Boscobel, Wi., U.S.	E3	126
Boshan, China	D10	26
Bosnia and Herzegovina, ctry., Eur.	E12	14
Bosporus see İstanbul Boğazı, strt., Tur.	H13	16
Bosque, co., Tx., U.S.	D4	120
Bossangoa, Cen. Afr. Rep.	G9	42
Bossembélé, Cen. Afr. Rep.	G9	42
Bossier, co., La., U.S.	B2	95
Bossier City, La., U.S.	B2	95
Bosten Hu, l., China	C4	26
Boston, Eng., U.K.	I12	7
Boston, Ga., U.S.	F3	87
Boston, Ma., U.S.	B5	98
Boston Bay, b., Ma., U.S.	B6	98
Boston Mountains, mts., Ar., U.S.	B2	81
Boswell, In., U.S.	C3	91
Boswell, Ok., U.S.	C6	113
Boswell, Pa., U.S.	F3	115
Botād, India	I4	38
Boteti, stm., Bots.	F4	44
Botetourt, co., Va., U.S.	C3	123
Bothell, Wa., U.S.	B3	124
Bothnia, Gulf of, b., Eur.	E12	6
Bothwell, Ont., Can.	E3	73
Botkins, Oh., U.S.	B1	112
Botoșani, Rom.	B10	16
Botswana, ctry., Afr.	F4	44
Bottenhavet (Selkämeri), b., Eur.	F12	6
Bottenviken (Perämeri), b., Eur.	D14	6
Bottineau, N.D., U.S.	A5	111
Bottineau, co., N.D., U.S.	A4	111
Botucatu, Braz.	G4	57
Botwood, Newf., Can.	D4	72
Bouaflé, I.C.	G4	42
Bouaké, I.C.	G4	42
Bouar, Cen. Afr. Rep.	G9	42
Bou Arada, Tun.	M4	14
Boucherville, Que., Can.	D4	74
Bouctouche, N.B., Can.	C5	71
Boudreaux, Lake, l., La., U.S.	E5	95
Bou Ficha, Tun.	M5	14
Bougainville Reef, rf., Austl.	C9	50
Bougouni, Mali	F4	42
Bouillon, Bel.	F5	8
Boulder, Co., U.S.	A5	83
Boulder, Mt., U.S.	D4	103
Boulder, co., Co., U.S.	A5	83
Boulder City, Nv., U.S.	H7	105
Boulevard Heights, Md., U.S.	f9	97
Boulogne-Billancourt, Fr.	D9	10
Boulogne-sur-Gesse, Fr.	I7	10
Boulogne-sur-Mer, Fr.	B8	10
Bouna, I.C.	G5	42
Boundary, co., Id., U.S.	A2	89
Boundary Bay, b., Wa., U.S.	A3	124
Boundary Peak, mtn., Nv., U.S.	F3	105
Bound Brook, N.J., U.S.	B3	107
Bountiful, Ut., U.S.	C4	121
Bourbeuse, stm., Mo., U.S.	C6	102
Bourbon, In., U.S.	B5	91
Bourbon, Mo., U.S.	C6	102
Bourbon, co., Ks., U.S.	E9	93
Bourbon, co., Ky., U.S.	B5	94
Bourbonnais, Il., U.S.	B6	90
Bourbonnais, hist. reg., Fr.	F9	10
Bourbonne-les-Bains, Fr.	E12	10
Bourem, Mali	E5	42
Bourg, La., U.S.	E5	95
Bourganeuf, Fr.	G8	10
Bourg-en-Bresse, Fr.	F12	10
Bourges, Fr.	E9	10
Bourg-Lastic, Fr.	G9	10
Bourgogne, hist. reg., Fr.	E11	10
Bourgoin, Fr.	G12	10
Bourg-Saint-Andéol, Fr.	H11	10
Bourg-Saint-Maurice, Fr.	G13	10
Bourke, Austl.	F9	50
Bournemouth, Eng., U.K.	K11	7
Bou Saâda, Alg.	A6	42
Bouse, Az., U.S.	D2	80
Boussac, Fr.	F9	10
Bousso, Chad	F9	42
Boutte, La., U.S.	k11	95
Bøvågen, Nor.	F5	6
Bovalino Marina, Italy	K11	14
Bovec, Slo.	C8	14
Bøverdal, Nor.	F7	6
Bovey, Mn., U.S.	C5	100
Bovina, Tx., U.S.	B1	120
Bow, N.H., U.S.	D3	106
Bow, stm., Alta., Can.	D4	68
Bowden, Alta., Can.	D4	68
Bowdish Reservoir, res., R.I., U.S.	B1	116
Bowdon, Ga., U.S.	C1	87
Bowen, Austl.	C9	50
Bowie, Az., U.S.	E6	80
Bowie, Md., U.S.	C4	97
Bowie, Tx., U.S.	C4	120
Bowie, co., Tx., U.S.	C5	120
Bow Island, Alta., Can.	E5	68
Bow Lake, l., N.H., U.S.	D4	106
Bowling Green, Fl., U.S.	E5	86
Bowling Green, Ky., U.S.	D3	94
Bowling Green, Mo., U.S.	B6	102
Bowling Green, Oh., U.S.	A2	112
Bowling Green, S.C., U.S.	A5	117
Bowling Green, Va., U.S.	B5	123
Bowman, Ga., U.S.	B3	87
Bowman, N.D., U.S.	C2	111
Bowman, S.C., U.S.	E6	117
Bowman, co., N.D., U.S.	C2	111
Bowman Creek, stm., Pa., U.S.	m16	115
Bowman-Haley Lake, res., N.D., U.S.	C2	111
Bowron, stm., B.C., Can.	C7	69
Bowstring Lake, l., Mn., U.S.	C5	100
Box Butte, co., Ne., U.S.	B2	104
Box Butte Reservoir, res., Ne., U.S.	B2	104
Box Elder, S.D., U.S.	C2	118
Box Elder, co., Ut., U.S.	B2	121
Boxford, Ma., U.S.	A6	98
Boxian, China	B4	28
Boyce, La., U.S.	C3	95
Boyceville, Wi., U.S.	C1	126
Boyd, Tx., U.S.	C4	120
Boyd, co., Ky., U.S.	B7	94
Boyd, co., Ne., U.S.	B7	104
Boyden, Ia., U.S.	A2	92
Boyd Lake, l., Me., U.S.	C4	96
Boyer, stm., Ia., U.S.	C2	92
Boyertown, Pa., U.S.	F10	115
Boykins, Va., U.S.	D5	123
Boyle, Alta., Can.	B4	68
Boyle, Ire.	H4	7
Boyle, Ms., U.S.	B3	101
Boyle, co., Ky., U.S.	C5	94
Boyne City, Mi., U.S.	C6	99
Boynton Beach, Fl., U.S.	F6	86
Boysen Reservoir, res., Wy., U.S.	C4	127
Boys Town, Ne., U.S.	g12	104
Bozburun, Tur.	M12	16
Boz Dağ, mtn., Tur.	L13	16
Bozeman, Mt., U.S.	E5	103
Bozeman Pass, Mt., U.S.	E6	103
Bozoum, Cen. Afr. Rep.	G9	42
Bra, Italy	E2	14
Bracciano, Italy	G7	14
Bracebridge, Ont., Can.	B5	73
Bräcke, Swe.	E10	6
Bracken, co., Ky., U.S.	B5	94
Brackenridge, Pa., U.S.	h15	115
Brackettville, Tx., U.S.	E2	120
Braddock, Pa., U.S.	k14	115
Braddock Heights, Md., U.S.	B2	97
Braddock Point, c., S.C., U.S.	G6	117
Bradenton, Fl., U.S.	E4	86
Bradenville, Pa., U.S.	F3	115
Bradford, Eng., U.K.	H11	7
Bradford, Ar., U.S.	B4	81
Bradford, Oh., U.S.	B1	112
Bradford, Pa., U.S.	C4	115
Bradford, R.I., U.S.	F2	116
Bradford, Tn., U.S.	A3	119
Bradford, Vt., U.S.	D4	122
Bradford, co., Fl., U.S.	C4	86
Bradford, co., Pa., U.S.	C8	115
Bradford [West Gwillimbury], Ont., Can.	C5	73
Bradfordwoods, Pa., U.S.	h13	115
Bradley, Il., U.S.	B6	90
Bradley, Me., U.S.	D4	96
Bradley, W.V., U.S.	D3	125
Bradley, co., Ar., U.S.	D3	81
Bradley, co., Tn., U.S.	D9	119
Bradley Beach, N.J., U.S.	C4	107
Bradner, Oh., U.S.	A2	112
Bradshaw, Md., U.S.	B5	97
Bradshaw Mountains, mts., Az., U.S.	C3	80
Brady, Tx., U.S.	D3	120
Braga, Port.	D3	12
Bragado, Arg.	D4	56
Bragança, Port.	D5	12
Braham, Mn., U.S.	E5	100
Brāhmanbāria, Bngl.	I14	38
Brāhmani, stm., India	J11	38
Brahmaputra (Yarlung), stm., Asia	G15	38
Braich y Pwll, c., Wales, U.K.	I8	7
Braidwood, Il., U.S.	B5	90
Brăila, Rom.	D11	16
Brainerd, Mn., U.S.	D4	100
Braintree, Ma., U.S.	B5	98
Brake, Ger.	B8	8
Brampton, Ont., Can.	D5	73
Bramsche, Ger.	C7	8
Bramwell, W.V., U.S.	D3	125
Branch, co., Mi., U.S.	G5	99
Branch, stm., R.I., U.S.	B3	116
Branch, stm., Wi., U.S.	h10	126
Branch Lake, l., Me., U.S.	D4	96
Branch Village, R.I., U.S.	B3	116
Branchville, S.C., U.S.	E6	117
Branco, stm., Braz.	C6	54
Brandberg, mtn., Nmb.	F2	44
Brandbu, Nor.	F8	6
Brandenburg, Ger.	C12	8
Brandenburg, Ky., U.S.	C3	94
Brandon, Man., Can.	E2	70
Brandon, Fl., U.S.	E4	86
Brandon, Ms., U.S.	C4	101
Brandon, S.C., U.S.	B3	117
Brandon, S.D., U.S.	D9	118
Brandon, Vt., U.S.	D2	122
Brandon, Wi., U.S.	E5	126
Brandvlei, S. Afr.	H4	44
Brandy Peak, mtn., Or., U.S.	E3	114
Brandywine, Md., U.S.	C4	97
Brandywine Creek, stm., U.S.	A3	85
Branford, Ct., U.S.	D4	84
Branford Hills, Ct., U.S.	D4	84
Br'ansk, Russia	H17	18
Branson, Mo., U.S.	E4	102
Brantford, Ont., Can.	D4	73
Brantley, Al., U.S.	D3	78
Brantley, co., Ga., U.S.	E4	87
Brantôme, Fr.	G7	10
Brant Rock, Ma., U.S.	B6	98
Brantville, N.B., Can.	B5	71
Bras d'Or Lake, l., N.S., Can.	D9	71
Brasília, Braz.	C5	57
Brașov, Rom.	D9	16

Name — Map Ref — Page

Brasstown Bald, mtn., Ga., U.S. B3 87
Brassua Lake, res., Me., U.S. C3 96
Bratenahl, Oh., U.S. g9 112
Bratislava, Slov. G17 8
Bratsk, Russia F14 24
Bratskoje Vodochranilišče, res., Russia F14 24
Brattleboro, Vt., U.S. F3 122
Braunau [am Inn], Aus. G13 8
Braunschweig, Ger. C10 8
Brava, Som. H3 46
Brava, Costa, Spain D15 12
Bravo del Norte (Rio Grande), stm., N.A. F6 76
Brawley, Ca., U.S. F6 82
Brawley Peaks, mts., Nv., U.S. E3 105
Braxton, co., W.V., U.S. C4 125
Bray, Ire. H6 7
Bray, Ok., U.S. C4 113
Bray Island, i., N.W. Ter., Can. C17 66
Braymer, Mo., U.S. B4 102
Brazeau, stm., Alta., Can. C2 68
Brazil, In., U.S. E3 91
Brazil, ctry., S.A. E7 54
Brazoria, Tx., U.S. r14 120
Brazoria, co., Tx., U.S. E5 120
Brazos, co., Tx., U.S. D4 120
Brazos, stm., Tx., U.S. D4 120
Brazzaville, Congo B3 44
Brčko, Bos. E2 16
Brea, Ca., U.S. n13 82
Breakenridge, Mount, mtn., B.C., Can. E7 69
Breathitt, co., Ky., U.S. C6 94
Breaux Bridge, La., U.S. D4 95
Brebes, Indon. m14 33a
Breckenridge, Co., U.S. B4 83
Breckenridge, Mi., U.S. E6 99
Breckenridge, Mn., U.S. D2 100
Breckenridge, Tx., U.S. C3 120
Breckinridge, co., Ky., U.S. C3 94
Brecksville, Oh., U.S. A4 112
Brecon Beacons National Park, Wales, U.K. J9 7
Breda, Neth. D4 8
Bredstedt, Ger. A8 8
Breese, Il., U.S. E4 90
Bréhal, Fr. D5 10
Brekstad, Nor. E7 6
Bremen, Ger. B8 8
Bremen, Ga., U.S. C1 87
Bremen, In., U.S. B5 91
Bremen, Oh., U.S. C3 112
Bremer, co., Ia., U.S. B5 92
Bremerhaven, Ger. B8 8
Bremerton, Wa., U.S. B3 124
Bremond, Tx., U.S. D4 120
Brenham, Tx., U.S. D4 120
Brenner Pass, Eur. B6 14
Breno, Italy D5 14
Brent, Al., U.S. C2 78
Brent, Fl., U.S. u14 86
Brenton Point, c., R.I., U.S. F5 116
Brentwood, Ca., U.S. h9 82
Brentwood, Md., U.S. f9 97
Brentwood, Mo., U.S. f13 102
Brentwood, N.Y., U.S. E7 109
Brentwood, Pa., U.S. k14 115
Brentwood, S.C., U.S. k11 117
Brentwood, Tn., U.S. A5 119
Brescia, Italy D5 14
Breslau see Wrocław, Pol. D17 8
Bressanone, Italy C6 14
Bressuire, Fr. F6 10
Brest, Bela. I6 18
Brest, Fr. D2 10
Bretagne, hist. reg., Fr. D3 10
Breton Islands, is., La., U.S. E6 95
Breton Sound, strt., La., U.S. E6 95
Brevard, N.C., U.S. f10 110
Brevard, co., Fl., U.S. E6 86
Brevoort Lake, l., Mi., U.S. B6 99
Brewer, Me., U.S. D4 96
Brewster, Ma., U.S. C7 98
Brewster, N.Y., U.S. D7 109
Brewster, Oh., U.S. B4 112
Brewster, Wa., U.S. A6 124
Brewster, co., Tx., U.S. E1 120
Brewster Islands, is., Ma., U.S. g12 98
Brewton, Al., U.S. D2 78
Brežice, Slo. D10 14
Bria, Cen. Afr. Rep. G10 42
Brian Boru Peak, mtn., B.C., Can. B4 69
Briançon, Fr. H13 10
Brian Head, mtn., Ut., U.S. F3 121
Briare, Fr. E9 10
Briceville, Tn., U.S. C9 119
Brick [Township], N.J., U.S. C4 107
Bricquebec, Fr. C5 10
Bridal Veil Falls, wtfl, Ut., U.S. C4 121
Bridgehampton, N.Y., U.S. n16 109
Bridgeport, Al., U.S. A4 78
Bridgeport, Ct., U.S. E3 84
Bridgeport, Il., U.S. E6 90
Bridgeport, Mi., U.S. E7 99
Bridgeport, Ne., U.S. C2 104
Bridgeport, Oh., U.S. B5 112
Bridgeport, Pa., U.S. o20 115
Bridgeport, Tx., U.S. C4 120
Bridgeport, Wa., U.S. B6 124
Bridgeport, W.V., U.S. B4 125
Bridger, Mt., U.S. E8 103
Bridger Peak, mtn., Wy., U.S. E5 127
Bridger Range, mts., Mt., U.S. E6 103
Bridgeton, Mo., U.S. C7 102
Bridgeton, N.J., U.S. E2 107
Bridgetown, Barb. H18 64
Bridgetown, N.S., Can. E4 71
Bridgeville, De., U.S. F3 85
Bridgeville, Pa., U.S. k13 115
Bridgewater, Ma., U.S. C6 98
Bridgewater, N.J., U.S. B3 107
Bridgewater, Va., U.S. B4 123
Bridgman, Mi., U.S. G4 99
Bridgton, Me., U.S. D2 96
Bridgwater, Eng., U.K. J9 7
Bridlington, Eng., U.K. G12 7
Briec, Fr. D2 10
Brielle, N.J., U.S. C4 107
Brienne-le-Château, Fr. D11 10
Brienz, Switz. F15 10
Brig, Switz. F14 10
Brigantine, N.J., U.S. E4 107
Brigantine Beach, N.J., U.S. E4 107
Brigden, Ont., Can. E2 73
Briggs Marsh, sw., R.I., U.S. F6 116
Brigham City, Ut., U.S. B3 121
Brighton, Ont., Can. C7 73
Brighton, Eng., U.K. K12 7
Brighton, Al., U.S. B3 78
Brighton, Co., U.S. B6 83
Brighton, Il., U.S. D3 90
Brighton, Ia., U.S. C6 92
Brighton, Mi., U.S. F7 99
Brighton, N.Y., U.S. B3 109
Brighton, Tn., U.S. B2 119
Brighton Indian Reservation, Fl., U.S. E5 86
Brihuega, Spain E9 12
Brilliant, Al., U.S. A2 78
Brilliant, Oh., U.S. B5 112
Brillion, Wi., U.S. D5 126
Brilon, Ger. D8 8
Brimfield, Il., U.S. C4 90
Brindisi, Italy I12 14
Brinkley, Ar., U.S. C4 81
Brinnon, Wa., U.S. B3 124
Brioude, Fr. G10 10
Brisbane, Austl. E10 50
Briscoe, co., Tx., U.S. B2 120
Bristol, N.B., Can. C2 71
Bristol, Eng., U.K. J10 7
Bristol, Ct., U.S. C4 84
Bristol, In., U.S. A6 91
Bristol, N.H., U.S. C3 106
Bristol, R.I., U.S. D5 116
Bristol, Tn., U.S. C11 119
Bristol, Vt., U.S. C2 122
Bristol, Va., U.S. f9 123
Bristol, co., Ma., U.S. C5 98
Bristol, co., R.I., U.S. D5 116
Bristol Bay, b., Ak., U.S. D7 79
Bristol Channel, strt., U.K. J8 7
Bristol [Township], Pa., U.S. F12 115
Bristow, Ok., U.S. B5 113
British Columbia, prov., Can. C6 69
British Honduras see Belize, ctry., N.A. F3 64
British Indian Ocean Territory, dep., Afr. G17 2
British Mountains, mts., N.A. C5 66
British Solomon Islands see Solomon Islands, ctry., Oc. G23 2
Britstown, S. Afr. H4 44
Britt, Ia., U.S. A4 92
Brittany see Bretagne, hist. reg., Fr. D3 10
Britton, S.D., U.S. B8 118
Brive-la-Gaillarde, Fr. G8 10
Briviesca, Spain C8 12
Brno, Czech. F16 8
Broach, India B2 37
Broad, stm., S.C., U.S. C5 117
Broad Brook, Ct., U.S. B5 84
Broadford, Scot., U.K. D7 7
Broadkill, stm., De., U.S. E4 85
Broadkill Beach, De., U.S. E5 85
Broad Law, mtn., Scot., U.K. F9 7
Broad Run, stm., Va., U.S. g11 123
Broadus, Mt., U.S. E11 103
Broadview Heights, Oh., U.S. h9 112
Broadwater, co., Mt., U.S. D5 103
Broadway, N.C., U.S. B3 110
Broadway, Va., U.S. B4 123
Brockport, N.Y., U.S. B3 109
Brockton, Ma., U.S. B5 98
Brockton Reservoir, res., Ma., U.S. h11 98
Brockville, Ont., Can. C9 73
Brockway, Pa., U.S. D4 115
Brodeur Peninsula, pen., N.W. Ter., Can. B15 66
Brodhead, Ky., U.S. C5 94
Brodhead, Wi., U.S. F4 126
Brodheadsville, Pa., U.S. E11 115
Broken Arrow, Ok., U.S. A6 113
Broken Bow, Ne., U.S. C6 104
Broken Bow, Ok., U.S. C7 113
Broken Bow Lake, res., Ok., U.S. C7 113
Broken Hill, Austl. F8 50
Brokopondo, Sur. B8 54
Brome, Lac, l., Que., Can. D5 74
Bromptonville, Que., Can. D6 74
Bromsgrove, Eng., U.K. I10 7
Bronlund Peak, mtn., B.C., Can. E7 66
Brønnøysund, Nor. D9 6
Bronson, Mi., U.S. G5 99
Bronte, Italy L9 14
Bronx, co., N.Y., U.S. E7 109
Bronxville, N.Y., U.S. h13 109
Brook, In., U.S. C3 91
Brooke, co., W.V., U.S. A4 125
Brookfield, N.S., Can. D6 71
Brookfield, Ct., U.S. D2 84
Brookfield, Il., U.S. k9 90
Brookfield, Mo., U.S. B4 102
Brookfield, Va., U.S. *B5 123
Brookfield, Wi., U.S. m11 126
Brookfield Center, Ct., U.S. D2 84
Brookhaven, Ms., U.S. D3 101
Brookhaven, W.V., U.S. h11 125
Brookings, Or., U.S. E2 114
Brookings, S.D., U.S. C9 118
Brookings, co., S.D., U.S. C9 118
Brookland, Ar., U.S. B5 81
Brooklandville, Md., U.S. g10 97
Brooklet, Ga., U.S. D5 87
Brookline, Ma., U.S. B5 98
Brooklyn, N.S., Can. E5 71
Brooklyn, Ct., U.S. B8 84
Brooklyn, In., U.S. E5 91
Brooklyn, Ia., U.S. C5 92
Brooklyn, Mi., U.S. F6 99
Brooklyn, Ms., U.S. D4 101
Brooklyn, Oh., U.S. h9 112
Brooklyn, S.C., U.S. B6 117
Brooklyn, Wi., U.S. F4 126
Brooklyn Center, Mn., U.S. E5 100
Brooklyn Park, Md., U.S. h11 97
Brooklyn Park, Mn., U.S. m12 100
Brookneal, Va., U.S. C4 123
Brook Park, Oh., U.S. h9 112
Brookport, Il., U.S. F5 90
Brooks, Alta., Can. D5 68
Brooks, Ky., U.S. g11 94
Brooks, co., Ga., U.S. F3 87
Brooks, co., Tx., U.S. F3 120
Brooks Air Force Base, mil., Tx., U.S. k7 120
Brookshire, Tx., U.S. E5 120
Brookside, Al., U.S. f7 78
Brookside, De., U.S. B3 85
Brooks Range, mts., Ak., U.S. B9 79
Brookston, In., U.S. C4 91
Brooksville, Fl., U.S. D4 86
Brooksville, Ky., U.S. B5 94
Brooksville, Ms., U.S. B5 101
Brookville, In., U.S. F8 91
Brookville, Oh., U.S. C1 112
Brookville, Pa., U.S. D3 115
Brookville Lake, res., In., U.S. E7 91
Brookwood, Al., U.S. B2 78
Brookwood, N.J., U.S. C4 107
Broomall, Pa., U.S. p20 115
Broome, Austl. C4 50
Broome, co., N.Y., U.S. C5 109
Broomfield, Co., U.S. B5 83
Broons, Fr. D4 10
Brossard, Que., Can. q20 74
Brou, Fr. D8 10
Broussard, La., U.S. D4 95
Broward, co., Fl., U.S. F6 86
Browerville, Mn., U.S. D4 100
Brown, co., Il., U.S. D3 90
Brown, co., In., U.S. F5 91
Brown, co., Ks., U.S. C8 93
Brown, co., Mn., U.S. F4 100
Brown, co., Ne., U.S. B6 104
Brown, co., Oh., U.S. D2 112
Brown, co., S.D., U.S. B7 118
Brown, co., Tx., U.S. D3 120
Brown, co., Wi., U.S. D6 126
Brown, Point, c., Wa., U.S. C1 124
Brown City, Mi., U.S. E8 99
Brown Deer, Wi., U.S. m12 126
Brownfield, Tx., U.S. C1 120
Browning, Mt., U.S. B3 103
Brownlee Dam, U.S. E2 89
Brownlee Reservoir, res., U.S. C10 114
Browns, stm., Vt., U.S. B2 122
Browns Branch, stm., De., U.S. E3 85
Brownsburg, Que., Can. D3 74
Brownsburg, In., U.S. E5 91
Brownsdale, Mn., U.S. G6 100
Browns Inlet, b., N.C., U.S. C5 110
Browns Mills, N.J., U.S. D3 107
Browns Peak, mtn., Az., U.S. D4 80
Brownstown, In., U.S. G5 91
Browns Valley, Mn., U.S. E2 100
Brownsville, Fl., U.S. s13 86
Brownsville, Ky., U.S. C3 94
Brownsville, Or., U.S. C4 114
Brownsville, Pa., U.S. F2 115
Brownsville, Tn., U.S. B2 119
Brownsville, Tx., U.S. G4 120
Brownton, Mn., U.S. F4 100
Brownville Junction, Me., U.S. C3 96
Brownwood, Tx., U.S. D3 120
Brownwood, Lake, res., Tx., U.S. D3 120
Broxton, Ga., U.S. E4 87
Bruay-en-Artois, Fr. B9 10
Bruce, Ms., U.S. B4 101
Bruce, Wi., U.S. C2 126
Bruce, Mount, mtn., Austl. D3 50
Bruce National Park, Ont., Can. B3 73
Bruce Peninsula, pen., Ont., Can. B3 73
Bruceton, Tn., U.S. A3 119
Bruchsal, Ger. F8 8
Bruck an der Leitha, Aus. H16 8
Bruck an der Mur, Aus. H15 8
Bruderheim, Alta., Can. C4 68
Brugge, Bel. D3 8
Bruin Point, mtn., Ut., U.S. D5 121
Brule, co., S.D., U.S. D6 118
Brule, stm., U.S. C5 126
Brule Lake, l., Mn., U.S. k9 100
Brundidge, Al., U.S. D4 78
Bruneau, stm., U.S. G3 89
Brunei, ctry., Asia E5 32
Brunico, Italy C6 14
Brunkeberg, Nor. G7 6
Bruno, Sask., Can. E3 75
Brunsbüttel, Ger. B9 8
Brunswick, Ga., U.S. E5 87
Brunswick, Me., U.S. E3 96
Brunswick, Md., U.S. B2 97
Brunswick, Mo., U.S. B4 102
Brunswick, Oh., U.S. A4 112
Brunswick, co., N.C., U.S. C4 110
Brunswick, co., Va., U.S. D5 123
Brunswick Naval Air Station, mil., Me., U.S. E3 96
Brush, Co., U.S. A7 83
Brushy Mountains, mts., N.C., U.S. B1 110
Brus Laguna, Hond. G5 64
Brusly, La., U.S. D4 95
Brussels, Ont., Can. D3 73
Brussels see Bruxelles, Bel. E4 8
Bruxelles (Brussel), Bel. E4 8
Bryan, Oh., U.S. A1 112
Bryan, Tx., U.S. D4 120
Bryan, co., Ga., U.S. D5 87
Bryan, co., Ok., U.S. D5 113
Bryans Road, Md., U.S. C3 97
Bryant, Ar., U.S. C3 81
Bryantville, Ma., U.S. B6 98
Bryce Canyon National Park, Ut., U.S. F3 121
Bryn Mawr, Wa., U.S. e11 124
Bryson City, N.C., U.S. f9 110
Brzeg, Pol. E17 8
Bsharrī, Leb. B5 40
Būbiyān, i., Kuw. C4 46
Bucaramanga, Col. D6 58
Buccaneer Archipelago, is., Austl. C4 50
Buchanan, Lib. G3 42
Buchanan, Ga., U.S. C1 87
Buchanan, Mi., U.S. G4 99
Buchanan, Va., U.S. C3 123
Buchanan, co., Ia., U.S. B6 92
Buchanan, co., Mo., U.S. B3 102
Buchanan, co., Va., U.S. e9 123
Buchan Gulf, b., N.W. Ter., Can. B18 66
Buchans, Newf., Can. D3 72
Buchara, Uzb. J10 22
Bucharest see București, Rom. E10 16
Buchholz, Ger. B9 8
Buckatunna, Ms., U.S. D5 101
Bückeburg, Ger. C9 8
Buckeye, Az., U.S. D3 80
Buckeye Lake, Oh., U.S. C3 112
Buckhannon, W.V., U.S. C4 125
Buck Hill Falls, Pa., U.S. D11 115
Buckhorn Lake, res., Ky., U.S. C6 94
Buckingham, Que., Can. D2 74
Buckingham, co., Va., U.S. C4 123
Buckley, Wa., U.S. B3 124
Bucklin, Ks., U.S. E4 93
Bucklin, Mo., U.S. B5 102
Buck Mountain, mtn., Wa., U.S. A6 124
Buckner, Mo., U.S. h11 102
Bucks, co., Pa., U.S. F11 115
Buckskin Mountains, mts., Az., U.S. C2 80
Bucksport, Me., U.S. D4 96
Bucksport, S.C., U.S. D9 117
București (Bucharest), Rom. E10 16
Bucyrus, Oh., U.S. B3 112
Buda, Tx., U.S. D4 120
Budapest, Hung. H19 8
Budaun, India F8 38
Budd Lake, l., N.J., U.S. B3 107
Buddusò, Italy I4 14
Bude, Eng., U.K. K8 7
Bude, Ms., U.S. D3 101
Buea, Cam. H7 42
Buechel, Ky., U.S. B4 94
Buena, N.J., U.S. D3 107
Buena, Wa., U.S. C5 124
Buena Park, Ca., U.S. n12 82
Buena Vista, Bol. G6 54
Buena Vista, Co., U.S. C4 83
Buena Vista, Fl., U.S. D4 86
Buena Vista, Ga., U.S. D2 87
Buena Vista, Va., U.S. C3 123
Buena Vista, co., Ia., U.S. B2 92
Buenópolis, Braz. D6 57
Buenos Aires, Arg. C5 56
Buffalo, Ia., U.S. C7 92
Buffalo, Mn., U.S. E5 100
Buffalo, Mo., U.S. D4 102
Buffalo, N.Y., U.S. C2 109
Buffalo, Ok., U.S. A2 113
Buffalo, S.C., U.S. B4 117
Buffalo, Tx., U.S. D5 120
Buffalo, W.V., U.S. C3 125
Buffalo, Wi., U.S. D2 126
Buffalo, Wy., U.S. B6 127
Buffalo, co., Ne., U.S. D6 104
Buffalo, co., S.D., U.S. C6 118
Buffalo, co., Wi., U.S. D2 126
Buffalo, stm., Ar., U.S. B3 81
Buffalo, stm., Mn., U.S. D2 100
Buffalo, stm., Tn., U.S. B4 119
Buffalo, stm., Wi., U.S. D2 126
Buffalo Bill Reservoir, res., Wy., U.S. B3 127
Buffalo Center, Ia., U.S. A4 92
Buffalo Creek, stm., U.S. f8 125
Buffalo Creek, stm., W.V., U.S. h10 125
Buffalo Creek, stm., W.V., U.S. n12 125
Buffalo Grove, Il., U.S. h9 90
Buffalo Lake, Mn., U.S. F4 100
Buffalo Lake, l., Alta., Can. C4 68
Buffalo Lake, l., N.W. Ter., Can. D9 66
Buffalo Lake, res., Tx., U.S. B1 120
Buffalo Lake, res., Wi., U.S. E4 126
Buffumville Lake, res., Ma., U.S. B4 98
Buford, Ga., U.S. B2 87
Bug, stm., Eur. E12 4
Buga, Col. F4 58
Bugøynes, Nor. B17 6
Bugsuk Island, i., Phil. D6 32
Bugul'ma, Russia G8 22
Buhl, Id., U.S. G4 89
Buhl, Mn., U.S. C6 100
Buhler, Ks., U.S. D6 93
Buies Creek, N.C., U.S. B4 110
Buj, Russia C24 18
Bujalance, Spain H7 12
Bujaraloz, Spain D11 12
Bujumbura, Bdi. B5 44
Bukačača, Russia G17 24
Bukama, Zaire C5 44
Bukavu, Zaire B5 44
Bukittinggi, Indon. F3 32
Bukoba, Tan. B6 44
Bukovina, hist. reg., Eur. B9 16
Bula, Indon. F9 32
Bulan, Ky., U.S. C6 94
Bulandshahr, India F7 38
Bulawayo, Zimb. F5 44
Buldan, Tur. K12 16
Buldāna, India B4 37
Bulgan, Mong. B5 26
Bulgaria, ctry., Eur. G12 4
Bulkley, stm., B.C., Can. B4 69
Bull Creek, stm., S.D., U.S. B2 118
Bulle, Switz. F14 10
Bullfinch, Austl. F3 50
Bullfrog Creek, stm., Ut., U.S. F5 121
Bullhead City, Az., U.S. B1 80
Bull Island, i., S.C., U.S. G6 117
Bull Island, i., S.C., U.S. D9 117
Bull Island, i., S.C., U.S. F8 117
Bullitt, co., Ky., U.S. C4 94
Bull Mountain, mtn., Mt., U.S. D8 103
Bulloch, co., Ga., U.S. D5 87
Bullock, co., Al., U.S. C4 78
Bullock Creek, Mi., U.S. E6 99
Bull Run, stm., Va., U.S. g11 123
Bullrun Rock, mtn., Or., U.S. C8 114
Bulls Bay, b., S.C., U.S. F8 117
Bulls Gap, Tn., U.S. C10 119
Bull Shoals, Ar., U.S. A3 81
Bull Shoals Lake, res., U.S. A3 81
Bully Creek Reservoir, res., Or., U.S. C9 114
Bulsār, India B2 37
Bulukumba, Indon. G7 32
Bumba, Zaire A4 44
Bumping, stm., Wa., U.S. C4 124
Buna, Tx., U.S. D6 120
Bunbury, Austl. F3 50
Buncombe, co., N.C., U.S. f10 110
Buncrana, Ire. F5 7
Bundaberg, Austl. D10 50
Būndi, India H6 38
Bundoran, Ire. G4 7
Bungo-suidō, strt., Japan I5 30
Bunia, Zaire A6 44
Bunker Hill, Il., U.S. D4 90
Bunker Hill, In., U.S. C5 91
Bunker Hill, W.V., U.S. B6 125
Bunker Hill, W.V., U.S. m12 125
Bunker Hill, mtn., Nv., U.S. D4 105
Bunkerville, Nv., U.S. G7 105
Bunkie, La., U.S. D3 95
Bunnell, Fl., U.S. C5 86
Buñol, Spain F11 12
Buntok, Indon. F5 32
Buolkalach, Russia C17 24
Buon Me Thuot, Viet. H10 34
Buor-Chaja, Guba, b., Russia C20 24
Buor-Chaja, Mys, c., Russia C20 24
Bura, Kenya B7 44
Burao, Som. G4 46
Buras, La., U.S. E6 95
Buraydah, Sau. Ar. C3 46
Burbank, Ca., U.S. E4 82
Burbank, Il., U.S. k9 90
Burbank, Wa., U.S. C7 124
Burdickville, R.I., U.S. F2 116
Burdur, Tur. H14 4
Burdwān, India I12 38
Bureau, co., Il., U.S. B4 90
Bureinskij Chrebet, mts., Russia G20 24
Bureja, stm., Russia G20 24
Burfjord, Nor. B13 6
Burgas, Bul. G11 16
Bur Gavo, Som. B8 44
Burgaw, N.C., U.S. C5 110
Burg [bei Magdeburg], Ger. C11 8
Burgdorf, Switz. E14 10
Burgeo, Newf., Can. E3 72
Burgettstown, Pa., U.S. F1 115
Burghausen, Ger. G12 8
Burghūth, Sabkhat al-, l., Syria B7 40
Burgin, China B4 26
Burgin, Ky., U.S. C5 94
Burglengenfeld, Ger. F12 8
Burgos, Spain C8 12
Burgsteinfurt, Ger. C7 8
Burgundy see Bourgogne, hist. reg., Fr. E11 10
Burhaniye, Tur. J10 16
Burhānpur, India B4 37
Burica, Punta, c., N.A. J6 64
Burin, Newf., Can. E4 72
Burin Peninsula, pen., Newf., Can. E4 72
Buriram, Thai. G7 34
Burjasot, Spain F11 12
Burkburnett, Tx., U.S. B3 120
Burke, S.D., U.S. D6 118
Burke, co., Ga., U.S. C4 87
Burke, co., N.C., U.S. B1 110
Burke, co., N.D., U.S. A3 111
Burke Channel, strt., B.C., Can. C4 69
Burkesville, Ky., U.S. D4 94
Burketown, Austl. C7 50
Burkina Faso, ctry., Afr. F5 42
Burk's Falls, Ont., Can. B5 73
Burleigh, co., N.D., U.S. C5 111
Burleson, Tx., U.S. n9 120
Burleson, co., Tx., U.S. D4 120
Burley, Id., U.S. G5 89
Burlingame, Ca., U.S. h8 82
Burlingame, Ks., U.S. D8 93
Burlington, Ont., Can. D5 73
Burlington, Co., U.S. B8 83
Burlington, Ia., U.S. D6 92
Burlington, Ks., U.S. D8 93
Burlington, Ky., U.S. A5 94
Burlington, Ma., U.S. f11 98
Burlington, N.J., U.S. C3 107
Burlington, N.C., U.S. A3 110
Burlington, N.D., U.S. A4 111
Burlington, Vt., U.S. C2 122
Burlington, Wa., U.S. A3 124
Burlington, Wi., U.S. F5 126
Burlington, co., N.J., U.S. D3 107
Burlington Beach, In., U.S. B3 91
Burlington Junction, Mo., U.S. A2 102
Burma, ctry., Asia A2 32
Burnaby, B.C., Can. E6 69
Burnet, Tx., U.S. D3 120
Burnet, co., Tx., U.S. D3 120
Burnett, co., Wi., U.S. C1 126
Burney, Ca., U.S. B3 82
Burnham, Pa., U.S. E6 115
Burnie, Austl. H9 50
Burns, Or., U.S. D7 114
Burns, Tn., U.S. A4 119
Burns, Wy., U.S. E8 127
Burns Flat, Ok., U.S. B2 113
Burnside, Ky., U.S. D5 94
Burns Lake, B.C., Can. B5 69
Burns Paiute Indian Reservation, Or., U.S. D7 114
Burnsville, Mn., U.S. F5 100
Burnsville, Ms., U.S. A5 101
Burnsville, N.C., U.S. f10 110
Burnsville Lake, res., W.V., U.S. C4 125
Burnt Islands, Newf., Can. E2 72
Burnt Mills, Lake, l., Va., U.S. k14 123
Burntside Lake, l., Mn., U.S. C6 100
Burntwood, stm., Man., Can. B2 70
Burravoe, Scot., U.K. A11 7
Burr Oak, Mi., U.S. G5 99
Burr Oak Reservoir, res., Oh., U.S. C3 112

Name — Map Ref — Page

Burrton, Ks., U.S. D6 93
Bursa, Tur. G13 4
Būr Sa'īd (Port Said), Egypt B12 42
Būr Sūdān (Port Sudan), Sudan E13 42
Burt, co., Ne., U.S. C9 104
Burt Lake, l., Mi., U.S. C6 99
Burton, Mi., U.S. F7 99
Burton, Oh., U.S. A4 112
Burton upon Trent, Eng., U.K. I11 7
Burtts Corner, N.B., Can. C3 71
Buru, i., Indon. F8 32
Burundi, ctry., Afr. B5 44
Burwell, Ne., U.S. C6 104
Burwick, Scot., U.K. C10 7
Bury Saint Edmunds, Eng., U.K. I13 7
Busalla, Italy E3 14
Buşayrah, Syria B7 40
Bushnell, Fl., U.S. D4 86
Bushnell, Il., U.S. C3 90
Bush River, b., Md., U.S. B5 97
Buşrá ash-Shām, Syria C5 40
Busselton, Austl. F3 50
Busto Arsizio, Italy D3 14
Busuanga Island, i., Phil. C7 32
Buta, Zaire H10 42
Butare, Rw. B5 44
Butehaqi, China B11 26
Bute Inlet, b., B.C., Can. D5 69
Butler, Al., U.S. C1 78
Butler, Ga., U.S. D2 87
Butler, In., U.S. B8 91
Butler, Ky., U.S. B5 94
Butler, Mo., U.S. C3 102
Butler, N.J., U.S. B4 107
Butler, Oh., U.S. B3 112
Butler, Pa., U.S. E2 115
Butler, Wi., U.S. m11 126
Butler, co., Al., U.S. D3 78
Butler, co., Ia., U.S. B5 92
Butler, co., Ks., U.S. E7 93
Butler, co., Ky., U.S. C3 94
Butler, co., Mo., U.S. E7 102
Butler, co., Ne., U.S. C8 104
Butler, co., Oh., U.S. C1 112
Butler, co., Pa., U.S. E2 115
Butner, N.C., U.S. A4 110
Buttahatchee, stm., U.S. B5 101
Butte, Mt., U.S. E4 103
Butte, co., Ca., U.S. C3 82
Butte, co., Id., U.S. F5 89
Butte, co., S.D., U.S. C2 118
Butte des Morts, Lake, l., Wi., U.S. D5 126
Butte Mountains, mts., Nv., U.S. D6 105
Butternut Lake, l., Wi., U.S. C5 126
Butterworth, Malay. L6 34
Butt of Lewis, c., Scot., U.K. C6 7
Buttonwillow, Ca., U.S. E4 82
Butts, co., Ga., U.S. C3 87
Butuan, Phil. D8 32
Butung, Pulau, i., Indon. F7 32
Bützow, Ger. B11 8
Buxtehude, Ger. B9 8
Buxton, N.C., U.S. B7 110
Büyükmenderes, stm., Tur. L11 16
Buzançais, Fr. F8 10
Buzău, Rom. D10 16
Búzi, stm., Moz. F6 44
Buzuluk, Russia G8 22
Buzzards Bay, Ma., U.S. C6 98
Buzzards Bay, b., Ma., U.S. C6 98
Byam Channel, strt., N.W. Ter., Can. A11 66
Byam Martin Island, i., N.W. Ter., Can. A12 66
Bydgoszcz, Pol. B18 8
Byers, Co., U.S. B6 83
Byesville, Oh., U.S. C4 112
Byhalia, Ms., U.S. A4 101
Bylas, Az., U.S. D5 80
Bylot Island, i., N.W. Ter., Can. B17 66
Byng, Ok., U.S. C5 113
Byrdstown, Tn., U.S. C8 119
Byron, Ga., U.S. D3 87
Byron, Il., U.S. A4 90
Byron, Mn., U.S. F6 100
Byron, Wy., U.S. B4 127
Byrranga, Gory, mts., Russia B14 24
Bytantaj, stm., Russia D20 24
Bytom (Beuthen), Pol. E18 8
Byxelkrok, Swe. H11 6

C

Caacupé, Para. B5 56
Cabaiguán, Cuba C8 64
Caballo Mountains, mts., N.M., U.S. E2 108
Caballo Reservoir, res., N.M., U.S. E2 108
Cabanatuan, Phil. q19 32
Cabano, Que., Can. B9 74
Cabarrus, co., N.C., U.S. B2 110
Cabbage Swamp, sw., Fl., U.S. m9 86
Cabell, co., W.V., U.S. C2 125
Cabeza del Buey, Spain G6 12
Cabimas, Ven. B7 58
Cabin Creek, W.V., U.S. m13 125
Cabin Creek, stm., W.V., U.S. m13 125
Cabinda, Ang. C2 44
Cabinda, dept., Ang. C2 44
Cabinet Gorge Reservoir, res., U.S. B1 103
Cabinet Mountains, mts., Mt., U.S. B1 103
Cabin John, Md., U.S. C3 97
Cabo Frio, Braz. G7 57
Cabonga, Réservoir, res., Que., Can. k11 74
Cabool, Mo., U.S. D5 102
Caborca, Mex. B3 62
Cabot, Ar., U.S. C3 81
Cabot, Mount, mtn., N.H., U.S. A4 106
Cabot Head, c., Ont., Can. B3 73
Cabot Strait, strt., Can. G21 66
Cabra, Spain H7 12
Cabri, Sask., Can. G1 75
Cabrillo National Monument, Ca., U.S. o15 82
Cabrobó, Braz. E11 54
Cabruta, Ven. D9 58
Çaçador, Braz. B6 56
Čačak, Yugo. F4 16
Cacapon, stm., W.V., U.S. B6 125
Cáceres, Braz. G7 54
Cáceres, Col. D5 58
Cáceres, Spain F5 12
Cache, Ok., U.S. C3 113
Cache, co., Ut., U.S. B4 121
Cache, stm., Ar., U.S. C4 81
Cache, stm., Il., U.S. F4 90
Cache Bay, Ont., Can. A5 73
Cache Creek, B.C., Can. D7 69
Cache la Poudre, stm., Co., U.S. A5 83
Cache Mountain, mtn., Ak., U.S. B10 79
Cache Peak, mtn., Id., U.S. G5 89
Cachimbo, Serra do, mts., Braz. E7 54
Cachoeira, Braz. B9 57
Cachoeira do Sul, Braz. C6 56
Cachoeiro de Itapemirim, Braz. F8 57
Cacólo, Ang. D3 44
Caconda, Ang. D3 44
Cactus Flat, pl., Nv., U.S. F5 105
Cactus Peak, mtn., Nv., U.S. F5 105
Caddo, Ok., U.S. C5 113
Caddo, co., La., U.S. B2 95
Caddo, co., Ok., U.S. B3 113
Caddo, stm., Ar., U.S. C2 81
Caddo Creek, stm., Ok., U.S. C4 113
Caddo Lake, res., U.S. B2 95
Cader Idris, mtn., Wales, U.K. I9 7
Cadillac, Fr. H6 10
Cadillac, Mi., U.S. D5 99
Cadillac Mountain, mtn., Me., U.S. D4 96
Cádiz, Spain I5 12
Cadiz, Ky., U.S. D2 94
Cadiz, Oh., U.S. B4 112
Cádiz, Golfo de, b., Eur. I4 12
Cadott, Wi., U.S. D2 126
Caen, Fr. C6 10
Caernarvon, Wales, U.K. H8 7
Caesar Creek Lake, res., Oh., U.S. C2 112
Caeté, Braz. E7 57
Cagayan de Oro, Phil. D7 32
Çagayan Islands, is., Phil. D7 32
Çagda, Russia F20 24
Cagles Mill Lake, res., In., U.S. F4 91
Cagli, Italy F7 14
Cagliari, Italy J4 14
Caguas, P.R. E14 64
Cahaba, stm., Al., U.S. C2 78
Caha Mountains, mts., Ire. J3 7
Cahirciveen, Ire. J2 7
Cahokia, Il., U.S. E3 90
Cahore Point, c., Ire. I6 7
Cahors, Fr. H8 10
Caiapó, Serra, mts., Braz. D2 57
Caibarién, Cuba C8 64
Caicara, Ven. D9 58
Caicos Islands, is., T./C. Is. D12 64
Caicos Passage, strt., N.A. C11 64
Caillou Bay, b., La., U.S. E5 95
Caillou Lake, l., La., U.S. E5 95
Cairnbrook, Pa., U.S. F4 115
Cairngorm Mountains, mts., Scot., U.K. D9 7
Cairns, Austl. C9 50
Cairo, Ga., U.S. F2 87
Cairo, Il., U.S. F4 90
Cairo, Ne., U.S. D7 104
Cairo see Al-Qāhirah, Egypt B12 42
Caiundo, Ang. E3 44
Cajamarca, Peru E3 54
Çajàzeiras, Braz. E11 54
Čakovec, Cro. C11 14
Calabar, Nig. H7 42
Calabozo, Ven. C9 58
Calahorra, Spain C10 12
Calais, Fr. B8 10
Calais, Me., U.S. C5 96
Calais, Pas de (Strait of Dover), strt., Eur. K14 7
Calamar, Col. B5 58
Calamian Group, is., Phil. C6 32
Calamocha, Spain E10 12
Calamus, stm., Ne., U.S. B6 104
Calanda, Spain E11 12
Calapan, Phil. r19 33b
Călărași, Rom. E11 16
Calatayud, Spain D10 12
Calaveras, co., Ca., U.S. C3 82
Calcasieu, co., La., U.S. D2 95
Calcasieu, stm., La., U.S. D2 95
Calcasieu Lake, l., La., U.S. E2 95
Calcasieu Pass, strt., La., U.S. E2 95
Calçoene, Braz. C8 54
Calcutta, India I13 38
Calcutta, Oh., U.S. B5 112
Calcutta Lake, l., Nv., U.S. B2 105
Caldas da Rainha, Port. F2 12
Calderwood, Tn., U.S. D10 119
Caldron Falls Reservoir, res., Wi., U.S. C5 126
Caldwell, Id., U.S. F2 89
Caldwell, Ks., U.S. E6 93
Caldwell, N.J., U.S. B4 107
Caldwell, Oh., U.S. C4 112
Caldwell, Tx., U.S. D4 120
Caldwell, co., Ky., U.S. C2 94
Caldwell, co., La., U.S. B3 95
Caldwell, co., Mo., U.S. B3 102
Caldwell, co., N.C., U.S. B1 110
Caldwell, co., Tx., U.S. E4 120
Caledon, Ont., Can. D5 73
Caledonia, Mi., U.S. F5 99
Caledonia, Mn., U.S. G7 100
Caledonia, Ms., U.S. B5 101
Caledonia, N.Y., U.S. C3 109
Caledonia, co., Vt., U.S. C4 122
Calera, Al., U.S. B3 78
Calera, Ok., U.S. D5 113
Calexico, Ca., U.S. F6 82
Calgary, Alta., Can. D3 68
Calhoun, Ga., U.S. B2 87
Calhoun, Ky., U.S. C2 94
Calhoun, co., Al., U.S. B4 78
Calhoun, co., Ar., U.S. D3 81
Calhoun, co., Fl., U.S. B1 86
Calhoun, co., Ga., U.S. E2 87
Calhoun, co., Il., U.S. D3 90
Calhoun, co., Ia., U.S. B3 92
Calhoun, co., Mi., U.S. F5 99
Calhoun, co., Ms., U.S. B4 101
Calhoun, co., S.C., U.S. D6 117
Calhoun, co., Tx., U.S. E4 120
Calhoun, co., W.V., U.S. C3 125
Calhoun City, Ms., U.S. B4 101
Calhoun Falls, S.C., U.S. C2 117
Cali, Col. F4 58
Calico Rock, Ar., U.S. A3 81
Calicut, India G3 37
Caliente, Nv., U.S. F7 105
California, Mo., U.S. C5 102
California, Pa., U.S. F2 115
California, state, U.S. D4 82
California, Golfo de, b., Mex. D4 62
California Aqueduct, Ca., U.S. E4 82
Calimere, Point, c., India G5 37
Calipatria, Ca., U.S. F6 82
Calispell Peak, mtn., Wa., U.S. A8 124
Calistoga, Ca., U.S. C2 82
Calitri, Italy I10 14
Callac, Fr. D3 10
Callaghan, Mount, mtn., Nv., U.S. D5 105
Callahan, co., Tx., U.S. C3 120
Callao, Peru F3 54
Callaway, co., Mo., U.S. C6 102
Calling Lake, l., Alta., Can. B4 68
Callosa de Ensarriá, Spain G11 12
Calloway, co., Ky., U.S. f9 94
Calmar, Alta., Can. C4 68
Calmar, Ia., U.S. A6 92
Caloosahatchee, stm., Fl., U.S. F5 86
Caltagirone, Italy L9 14
Caltanissetta, Italy L9 14
Calumet, Que., Can. D3 74
Calumet, Mi., U.S. A2 99
Calumet, co., Wi., U.S. D5 126
Calumet, Lake, l., Il., U.S. k9 90
Calumet City, Il., U.S. B6 90
Calunda, Ang. D4 44
Calvert, Tx., U.S. D4 120
Calvert, co., Md., U.S. C4 97
Calvert City, Ky., U.S. e9 94
Calverton, Md., U.S. *B4 97
Calverton Park, Mo., U.S. f13 102
Calvinia, S. Afr. H3 44
Camacho, Mex. E8 62
Camacupa, Ang. D3 44
Camaguán, Ven. C9 58
Camagüey, Cuba D9 64
Camaná, Peru G4 54
Camanche, Ia., U.S. C7 92
Camano Island, i., Wa., U.S. A3 124
Camapuã, Braz. E1 57
Camaquã, Braz. C6 56
Camas, Spain H5 12
Camas, Wa., U.S. D3 124
Camas, co., Id., U.S. F4 89
Ca Mau, Viet. J8 34
Cambados, Spain C3 12
Cambay, India I5 38
Cambodia (Kampuchea), ctry., Asia C3 32
Cambrai, Fr. B10 10
Cambria, Ca., U.S. E3 82
Cambria, Wi., U.S. E4 126
Cambria, co., Pa., U.S. E4 115
Cambrian Mountains, mts., Wales, U.K. I9 7
Cambridge, Ont., Can. D4 73
Cambridge, Eng., U.K. I13 7
Cambridge, Il., U.S. B3 90
Cambridge, Ia., U.S. C4 92
Cambridge, Md., U.S. C5 97
Cambridge, Ma., U.S. B5 98
Cambridge, Mn., U.S. E5 100
Cambridge, Ne., U.S. D5 104
Cambridge, N.Y., U.S. B7 109
Cambridge, Oh., U.S. B4 112
Cambridge, Wi., U.S. F4 126
Cambridge Bay, N.W. Ter., Can. C11 66
Cambridge City, In., U.S. E7 91
Cambridge Reservoir, res., Ma., U.S. g10 98
Cambridge Springs, Pa., U.S. C1 115
Cambuci, Braz. F8 57
Camden, Al., U.S. D2 78
Camden, Ar., U.S. D3 81
Camden, De., U.S. D3 85
Camden, In., U.S. C4 91
Camden, Me., U.S. D3 96
Camden, N.J., U.S. D2 107
Camden, N.Y., U.S. B5 109
Camden, Oh., U.S. C1 112
Camden, S.C., U.S. C6 117
Camden, Tn., U.S. A3 119
Camden, co., Ga., U.S. F5 87
Camden, co., Mo., U.S. C5 102
Camden, co., N.J., U.S. D3 107
Camden, co., N.C., U.S. A6 110
Camdenton, Mo., U.S. D5 102
Camelback Mountain, mtn., Az., U.S. k9 80
Cameron, Az., U.S. B4 80
Cameron, La., U.S. E2 95
Cameron, Mo., U.S. B3 102
Cameron, Tx., U.S. D4 120
Cameron, W.V., U.S. B4 125
Cameron, Wi., U.S. C2 126
Cameron, co., La., U.S. E2 95
Cameron, co., Pa., U.S. D5 115
Cameron, co., Tx., U.S. F4 120
Cameron Highlands, Malay. L6 34
Cameron Hills, hills, Can. E9 66
Cameroon, ctry., Afr. G8 42
Cameroon Mountain, mtn., Cam. H7 42
Cametá, Braz. D9 54
Camilla, Ga., U.S. E2 87
Camino, Ca., U.S. C3 82
Camiranga, Braz. D9 54
Camissombo, Ang. C4 44
Cam Lo, Viet. F9 34
Cammack Village, Ar., U.S. C3 81
Camooweal, Austl. C7 50
Camorta Island, i., India J2 34
Camp, co., Tx., U.S. C5 120
Campana, Isla, i., Chile F1 56
Campanero, Cerro, mtn., Ven. E10 58
Campbell, Ca., U.S. k8 82
Campbell, Fl., U.S. D5 86
Campbell, Mo., U.S. E7 102
Campbell, Oh., U.S. A5 112
Campbell, co., Ky., U.S. B5 94
Campbell, co., S.D., U.S. B5 118
Campbell, co., Tn., U.S. C9 119
Campbell, co., Va., U.S. C3 123
Campbell, co., Wy., U.S. B7 127
Campbellford, Ont., Can. C7 73
Campbell Hill, hill, Oh., U.S. B2 112
Campbell Lake, l., Or., U.S. E7 114
Campbellsburg, In., U.S. G5 91
Campbellsburg, Ky., U.S. B4 94
Campbells Creek, stm., W.V., U.S. m13 125
Campbellsport, Wi., U.S. E5 126
Campbellsville, Ky., U.S. C4 94
Campbellton, N.B., Can. A3 71
Campbellton, Newf., Can. D4 72
Campbeltown, Scot., U.K. F7 7
Campeche, Mex. H14 62
Campeche, Bahía de, b., Mex. H13 62
Camperville, Man., Can. D1 70
Camp Hill, Al., U.S. C4 78
Camp Hill, Pa., U.S. F8 115
Camp H. M. Smith Marine Corps Base, mil., Hi., U.S. g10 88
Camp Howard Ridge, mtn., Id., U.S. D2 89
Campina Grande, Braz. E11 54
Campinas, Braz. G5 57
Camp Lejeune Marine Corps Base, mil., N.C., U.S. C5 110
Campoalegre, Col. F5 58
Campo Alegre de Goiás, Braz. D5 57
Campobasso, Italy H9 14
Campobello Island, i., N.B., Can. E3 71
Campo Belo, Braz. F6 57
Campo de Criptana, Spain F8 12
Campo de la Cruz, Col. B5 58
Campo Grande, Braz. F1 57
Campo Maior, Braz. D10 54
Campos, Braz. F8 57
Campos do Jordão, Braz. G6 57
Camp Pendleton Marine Corps Base, mil., Ca., U.S. F5 82
Camp Point, Il., U.S. C2 90
Camp Springs, Md., U.S. f9 97
Campti, La., U.S. C2 95
Campton, N.H., U.S. C3 106
Camp Verde, Az., U.S. C4 80
Camp Verde Indian Reservation, Az., U.S. C4 80
Cam Ranh, Viet. I10 34
Camrose, Alta., Can. C4 68
Canaan, Ct., U.S. A2 84
Canaan, N.H., U.S. C2 106
Canaan, stm., N.B., Can. C4 71
Canada, ctry., N.A. D14 66
Canada Bay, b., Newf., Can. C3 72
Canada Falls Lake, res., Me., U.S. C2 96
Canadensis, Pa., U.S. D11 115
Canadian, Tx., U.S. B2 120
Canadian, co., Ok., U.S. B3 113
Canadian, stm., U.S. D6 76
Canajoharie, N.Y., U.S. C6 109
Çanakkale, Tur. G13 4
Çanakkale Boğazı (Dardanelles), strt., Tur. I10 16
Canal Flats, B.C., Can. D10 69
Canal Fulton, Oh., U.S. B4 112
Canal Winchester, Oh., U.S. C3 112
Canandaigua, N.Y., U.S. C3 109
Canandaigua Lake, l., N.Y., U.S. C3 109
Cananea, Mex. B4 62
Cañar, Ec. I3 58
Canarias, Islas (Canary Islands), is., Spain p24 136
Canary Islands see Canarias, Islas, is., Spain p24 136
Cañas, C.R. I5 64
Canastota, N.Y., U.S. B5 109
Canaveral, Cape, c., Fl., U.S. D6 86
Canaveral National Seashore, Fl., U.S. D6 86
Canavieiras, Braz. C9 57
Canberra, Austl. G9 50
Canby, Mn., U.S. F2 100
Canby, Or., U.S. B4 114
Cancale, Fr. D5 10
Cancon, Fr. H7 10
Cancún, Mex. G16 62
Candeleda, Spain E6 12
Candiac, Que., Can. q19 74
Candle Lake, l., Sask., Can. D3 75
Candler, co., Ga., U.S. D4 87
Candlewood, Lake, l., Ct., U.S. D1 84
Candlewood Isle, Ct., U.S. D2 84
Candlewood Shores, Ct., U.S. D2 84
Cando, N.D., U.S. A6 111
Candor, N.C., U.S. B3 110
Cane, stm., La., U.S. C2 95
Cañete, Spain E10 12
Caney, Ks., U.S. E8 93
Caney, stm., Ok., U.S. A5 113
Caney Creek, stm., Tx., U.S. r14 120
Caney Fork, stm., Tn., U.S. C8 119
Canfield, Oh., U.S. A5 112
Canfranc, Spain C11 12
Cangas de Onís, Spain B6 12
Cangombe, Ang. D3 44
Canguçu, Braz. C6 56
Cangzhou, China D10 26
Caniapiscau, stm., Que., Can. g13 74
Caniapiscau, Lac, l., Que., Can. F19 66
Canicattì, Italy L8 14
Canistear Reservoir, res., N.J., U.S. A4 107
Canisteo, N.Y., U.S. C3 109
Canisteo, stm., N.Y., U.S. C3 109
Canistota, S.D., U.S. D8 118
Cañitas, Mex. F8 62
Çankırı, Tur. G14 4
Canmore, Alta., Can. D3 68
Cannanore, India G3 37
Cannelton, In., U.S. I4 91
Cannes, Fr. I14 10
Canning, N.S., Can. D5 71
Cannon, co., Tn., U.S. B5 119
Cannon, stm., Mn., U.S. F5 100
Cannon Air Force Base, mil., N.M., U.S. C6 108
Cannonball, stm., N.D., U.S. C5 111
Cannon Beach, Or., U.S. B3 114
Cannondale, Ct., U.S. E2 84
Cannon Falls, Mn., U.S. F6 100
Cannonsburg, Ky., U.S. B7 94
Cannonsville Reservoir, res., N.Y., U.S. C5 109
Canon, Ga., U.S. B3 87
Canon City, Co., U.S. C5 83
Canonsburg, Pa., U.S. F1 115
Canosa [di Puglia], Italy H11 14
Cantábrica, Cordillera, mts., Spain B7 12
Cantalejo, Spain D8 12
Cantanhede, Port. E3 12
Cantaura, Ven. C10 58
Canterbury, Eng., U.K. J14 7
Canterbury, De., U.S. D3 85
Canterbury Bight, N.Z. F3 52
Can Tho, Viet. I8 34
Canton, Ct., U.S. B4 84
Canton, Ga., U.S. B2 87
Canton, Il., U.S. C3 90
Canton, Ks., U.S. D6 93
Canton, Ma., U.S. B5 98
Canton, Ms., U.S. C3 101
Canton, Mo., U.S. A6 102
Canton, N.Y., U.S. f9 109
Canton, N.C., U.S. f10 110
Canton, Oh., U.S. B4 112
Canton, Ok., U.S. A3 113
Canton, Pa., U.S. C8 115
Canton, S.D., U.S. D9 118
Canton, Tx., U.S. C5 120
Canton see Guangzhou, China L2 28
Canton Lake, res., Ok., U.S. A3 113
Cantonment, Fl., U.S. u14 86
Cantù, Italy D4 14
Canutillo, Tx., U.S. o11 120
Canyon, Tx., U.S. B2 120
Canyon, co., Id., U.S. F2 89
Canyon City, Or., U.S. C8 114
Canyon de Chelly National Monument, Az., U.S. A6 80
Canyon Ferry Lake, res., Mt., U.S. D5 103
Canyon Lake, Tx., U.S. E3 120
Canyon Lake, res., Tx., U.S. E3 120
Canyonlands National Park, Ut., U.S. E6 121
Canyonville, Or., U.S. E3 114
Cao Bang, Viet. C9 34
Capac, Mi., U.S. F8 99
Cap-à-l'Aigle, Que., Can. B7 74
Cap-aux-Meules, Que., Can. B8 71
Cap-de-la-Madeleine, Que., Can. C5 74
Cape Breton Highlands National Park, N.S., Can. C9 71
Cape Breton Island, i., N.S., Can. C9 71
Cape Broyle, Newf., Can. E5 72
Cape Canaveral, Fl., U.S. D6 86
Cape Charles, Va., U.S. C6 123
Cape Coast, Ghana G5 42
Cape Cod Bay, b., Ma., U.S. C7 98
Cape Cod Canal, Ma., U.S. C6 98
Cape Cod National Seashore, Ma., U.S. C7 98
Cape Coral, Fl., U.S. F5 86
Cape Dorset, N.W. Ter., Can. D17 66
Cape Elizabeth, Me., U.S. E2 96
Cape Fear, stm., N.C., U.S. C4 110
Cape Girardeau, Mo., U.S. D8 102
Cape Girardeau, co., Mo., U.S. D8 102
Cape Hatteras National Seashore, N.C., U.S. B7 110
Cape Horn Mountain, mtn., Id., U.S. E3 89
Cape Island, i., S.C., U.S. E9 117
Cape Lookout National Seashore, N.C., U.S. C6 110
Cape May, N.J., U.S. F3 107
Cape May, co., N.J., U.S. E3 107
Cape May Court House, N.J., U.S. E3 107
Capers Inlet, b., S.C., U.S. k12 117
Capers Island, i., S.C., U.S. G6 117
Capers Island, i., S.C., U.S. F8 117
Cape Sable Island, i., N.S., Can. F4 71
Cape Town (Kaapstad), S. Afr. H3 44
Cape Verde, ctry., Afr. E11 2
Cape York Peninsula, pen., Austl. B8 50
Cap-Haïtien, Haiti E11 64
Capim, stm., Braz. D9 54
Capitan, N.M., U.S. D4 108
Capitan Mountains, mts., N.M., U.S. D4 108
Capitan Peak, mtn., N.M., U.S. D4 108
Capitol Heights, Ia., U.S. e8 92
Capitol Heights, Md., U.S. C4 97
Capitol Peak, mtn., Nv., U.S. B4 105
Capitol Reef National Park, Ut., U.S. E4 121
Čapljina, Bos. F12 14
Cap-Pelé, N.B., Can. C5 71
Capreol, Ont., Can. p19 73
Capri, Italy I9 14
Caprivi Strip, hist. reg., Nmb. E4 44
Cap-Rouge, Que., Can. n17 74
Cap-Saint-Ignace, Que., Can. B7 74
Captain Cook, Hi., U.S. D6 88
Captieux, Fr. H6 10
Captiva, Fl., U.S. F4 86
Captiva Island, i., Fl., U.S. F4 86
Capua, Italy H9 14
Capulin Volcano National Monument, N.M., U.S. A6 108
Caquetá (Japurá), stm., S.A. D5 54
Çara, Russia F17 24
Cara, stm., Russia F17 24
Caracaraí, Braz. C6 54

Name	Map Ref	Page
aracas, Ven.	B9	58
arajás, Serra dos, mts., Braz.	E8	54
arangola, Braz.	F7	57
araquet, N.B., Can.	B5	71
aratasca, Laguna de, b., Hond.	G6	64
aratinga, Braz.	E7	57
arauari, Braz.	D5	54
aravaca, Spain	G10	12
aravelas, Braz.	D9	57
araway, Ar., U.S.	B5	81
arballo, Spain	B3	12
arberry, Man., Can.	E2	70
arbon, co., Mt., U.S.	E7	103
arbon, co., Pa., U.S.	E10	115
arbon, co., Ut., U.S.	D5	121
arbon, co., Wy., U.S.	E5	127
arbondale, Co., U.S.	B3	83
arbondale, Il., U.S.	F4	90
arbondale, Ks., U.S.	D8	93
arbondale, Pa., U.S.	C10	115
arbonear, Newf., Can.	E5	72
arboneras de Guadazaon, Spain	F10	12
arbon Hill, Al., U.S.	B2	78
arbonia, Italy	J3	14
arcagente, Spain	F11	12
arcassonne, Fr.	I9	10
arcross, Yukon, Can.	D6	66
árdenas, Cuba	C7	64
árdenas, Mex.	F10	62
ardiff, Wales, U.K.	J9	7
ardigan, Wales, U.K.	I8	7
ardigan Bay, b., P.E.I., Can.	C7	71
ardigan Bay, b., Wales, U.K.	I8	7
ardinal, Ont., Can.	C9	73
ardington, Oh., U.S.	B3	112
ardston, Alta., Can.	E4	68
ardwell, Mo., U.S.	E7	102
ardžou, Turk.	J10	22
arencro, La., U.S.	D3	95
arentan, Fr.	C5	10
aretta, W.V., U.S.	D3	125
arey, Id., U.S.	F5	89
arey, Oh., U.S.	B2	112
arey, Lake, l., Austl.	E4	50
aribbean Sea	G10	64
ariboo Mountains, mts., B.C., Can.	C7	69
aribou, Me., U.S.	B5	96
aribou, co., Id., U.S.	G7	89
aribou Island, i., N.S., Can.	D7	71
aribou Lake, l., Me., U.S.	C3	96
aribou Mountain, mtn., Id., U.S.	F7	89
aribou Mountains, mts., Alta., Can.	f7	68
aribou Range, mts., Id., U.S.	F7	89
arignan, Fr.	C12	10
ariñena, Spain	D10	12
arinhanha, Braz.	C7	57
arini, Italy	K8	14
aripito, Ven.	B11	58
arl Blackwell, Lake, res., Ok., U.S.	A4	113
arleton, Mi., U.S.	F7	99
arleton, Mount, mtn., N.B., Can.	B3	71
arleton Place, Ont., Can.	B8	73
arlin, Nv., U.S.	C5	105
arlinville, Il., U.S.	D4	90
arlisle, Eng., U.K.	G10	7
arlisle, Ar., U.S.	C4	81
arlisle, In., U.S.	G3	91
arlisle, Ia., U.S.	C4	92
arlisle, Ky., U.S.	B5	94
arlisle, Oh., U.S.	C1	112
arlisle, Pa., U.S.	F7	115
arlisle, co., Ky., U.S.	f8	94
arl Junction, Mo., U.S.	D3	102
arlow, Ire.	I6	7
arlsbad, Ca., U.S.	F5	82
arlsbad, N.M., U.S.	E5	108
arlsbad Caverns National Park, N.M., U.S.	E5	108
arlstadt, N.J., U.S.	h8	107
arlton, Mn., U.S.	D6	100
arlton, Or., U.S.	B3	114
arlton, co., Mn., U.S.	D6	100
arlyle, Il., U.S.	E4	90
arlyle Lake, res., Il., U.S.	E4	90
armacks, Yukon, Can.	D5	66
armagnola, Italy	E2	14
arman, Man., Can.	E2	70
armanville, Newf., Can.	D4	72
armarthen, Wales, U.K.	J8	7
armaux, Fr.	H9	10
armel, Ca., U.S.	D3	82
armel, In., U.S.	E5	91
armel, N.Y., U.S.	D7	109
armel Head, c., Wales, U.K.	H8	7
armen, Isla, i., Mex.	E4	62
armen, Isla del, i., Mex.	H14	62
armen de Patagones, Arg.	E4	56
armi, Il., U.S.	E5	90
armi, Lake, l., Vt., U.S.	B3	122
armona, Spain	H6	12
arnarvon, Austl.	D2	50
arnarvon, S. Afr.	H4	44
arnation, Wa., U.S.	B4	124
arndonagh, Ire.	F5	7
arnegie, Ok., U.S.	B3	113
arnegie, Pa., U.S.	F1	115
arnegie, Lake, l., Austl.	E4	50
arneys Point, N.J., U.S.	D2	107
arniche, Alpi, mts., Eur.	C8	14
ar Nicobar Island, i., India	J2	34
arnsore Point, c., Ire.	I6	7
aro, Mi., U.S.	E7	99
arol City, Fl., U.S.	s13	86
aroleen, N.C., U.S.	B1	110
arolina, Braz.	E9	54
arolina, Col.	D5	58
arolina, R.I., U.S.	F2	116
arolina, W.V., U.S.	k10	125
arolina Beach, N.C., U.S.	C5	110
aroline, co., Md., U.S.	C6	97
aroline, co., Va., U.S.	C5	123
aroní, stm., Ven.	D11	58
arora, Ven.	B7	58
Carpathian Mountains, mts., Eur.	F12	4
Carpații Meridionali, mts., Rom.	D8	16
Carpentaria, Gulf of, b., Austl.	B7	50
Carpenter Dam, Ar., U.S.	g7	81
Carpentersville, Il., U.S.	A5	90
Carpentras, Fr.	H12	10
Carpi, Italy	E5	14
Carpinteria, Ca., U.S.	E4	82
Carquefou, Fr.	E5	10
Carrabelle, Fl., U.S.	C2	86
Carrara, Italy	E5	14
Carrauntoohill, mtn., Ire.	I3	7
Carrboro, N.C., U.S.	B3	110
Carreta, Punta, c., Peru	F3	54
Carrickfergus, N. Ire., U.K.	G7	7
Carrickmacross, Ire.	H6	7
Carrie, Mount, mtn., Wa., U.S.	B2	124
Carriere, Ms., U.S.	E4	101
Carrier Mills, Il., U.S.	F5	90
Carrillo, Mex.	D8	62
Carrington, N.D., U.S.	B6	111
Carrington Island, i., Ut., U.S.	C3	121
Carrión de los Condes, Spain	C7	12
Carrizo Creek, stm., U.S.	A1	120
Carrizo Mountain, mtn., N.M., U.S.	D4	108
Carrizo Mountains, mts., U.S.	A6	80
Carrizo Springs, Tx., U.S.	*E3	120
Carrizozo, N.M., U.S.	D4	108
Carroll, Ia., U.S.	B3	92
Carroll, co., Ar., U.S.	A2	81
Carroll, co., Ga., U.S.	C1	87
Carroll, co., Il., U.S.	A4	90
Carroll, co., In., U.S.	C4	91
Carroll, co., Ia., U.S.	B3	92
Carroll, co., Ky., U.S.	B4	94
Carroll, co., Md., U.S.	A3	97
Carroll, co., Ms., U.S.	B4	101
Carroll, co., Mo., U.S.	B4	102
Carroll, co., N.H., U.S.	C4	106
Carroll, co., Oh., U.S.	B4	112
Carroll, co., Tn., U.S.	B3	119
Carroll, co., Va., U.S.	D2	123
Carrollton, Al., U.S.	B1	78
Carrollton, Ga., U.S.	C1	87
Carrollton, Il., U.S.	D3	90
Carrollton, Ky., U.S.	B4	94
Carrollton, Mi., U.S.	E7	99
Carrollton, Mo., U.S.	B4	102
Carrollton, Oh., U.S.	B4	112
Carrolltown, Pa., U.S.	E4	115
Carrot, stm., Can.	D4	75
Carry Falls Reservoir, res., N.Y., U.S.	f10	109
Čarsk, Kaz.	H10	24
Carson, Ia., U.S.	C2	92
Carson, Wa., U.S.	D4	124
Carson, co., Tx., U.S.	B2	120
Carson, stm., Nv., U.S.	D2	105
Carson City, Mi., U.S.	E6	99
Carson City, Nv., U.S.	D2	105
Carson Lake, l., Nv., U.S.	D3	105
Carson Sink, l., Nv., U.S.	D3	105
Carson Spring, Tn., U.S.	D10	119
Carstairs, Alta., Can.	D3	68
Carswell Air Force Base, mil., Tx., U.S.	n9	120
Cartagena, Col.	B5	58
Cartagena, Spain	H11	12
Cartago, Col.	E5	58
Cartago, C.R.	J6	64
Carter, co., Ky., U.S.	B6	94
Carter, co., Mo., U.S.	E7	102
Carter, co., Mt., U.S.	E12	103
Carter, co., Ok., U.S.	C4	113
Carter, co., Tn., U.S.	C11	119
Carteret, N.J., U.S.	B4	107
Carteret, co., N.C., U.S.	C6	110
Carter Lake, Ia., U.S.	C2	92
Carter Mountain, mtn., Wy., U.S.	B3	127
Carters Lake, res., Ga., U.S.	B2	87
Cartersville, Ga., U.S.	B2	87
Carterville, Il., U.S.	F4	90
Carterville, Mo., U.S.	D3	102
Carthage, Il., U.S.	C2	90
Carthage, In., U.S.	E6	91
Carthage, Ms., U.S.	C4	101
Carthage, Mo., U.S.	D3	102
Carthage, N.Y., U.S.	B5	109
Carthage, N.C., U.S.	B3	110
Carthage, Tn., U.S.	C8	119
Carthage, Tx., U.S.	C5	120
Cartier Island, i., Austl.	B4	50
Cartwright, Newf., Can.	B3	72
Cartwright, Ok., U.S.	D5	113
Caruaru, Braz.	E11	54
Carúpano, Ven.	B11	58
Caruthersville, Mo., U.S.	E8	102
Carver, Ma., U.S.	C6	98
Carver, Mn., U.S.	F5	100
Carver, co., Mn., U.S.	F5	100
Carville, La., U.S.	h9	95
Cary, Il., U.S.	A5	90
Cary, N.C., U.S.	B4	110
Caryville, Tn., U.S.	C9	119
Casablanca (Dar-el-Beida), Mor.	B4	42
Casacalenda, Italy	I19	14
Casa Grande, Az., U.S.	E4	80
Casa Grande National Monument, Az., U.S.	E4	80
Casale Monferrato, Italy	D3	14
Casarano, Italy	I13	14
Casas Adobes, Az., U.S.	E5	80
Casas Ibáñez, Spain	F10	12
Cascade, Co., U.S.	C6	83
Cascade, Id., U.S.	E2	89
Cascade, Ia., U.S.	B6	92
Cascade, Mt., U.S.	C5	103
Cascade, co., Mt., U.S.	C5	103
Cascade Locks, Or., U.S.	B5	114
Cascade Range, mts., N.A.	C2	76
Cascade Reservoir, res., Id., U.S.	E3	89
Cascade Tunnel, Wa., U.S.	B4	124
Cascais, Port.	G2	12
Cascina, Italy	F5	14
Casco Bay, b., Me., U.S.	E3	96
Caserta, Italy	H9	14
Caseville, Mi., U.S.	E7	99
Casey, Il., U.S.	D6	90
Casey, co., Ky., U.S.	C5	94
Casey, Mount, mtn., Id., U.S.	A2	89
Casey Key, i., Fl., U.S.	E4	86
Cashion, Az., U.S.	m8	80
Cashmere, Wa., U.S.	B5	124
Cashton, Wi., U.S.	E3	126
Casigua, Ven.	C6	58
Caspe, Spain	D11	12
Casper, Wy., U.S.	D6	127
Casper Mountain, mtn., Wy., U.S.	D6	127
Caspian, Mi., U.S.	B2	99
Caspian Lake, l., Vt., U.S.	B4	122
Caspian Sea	G17	4
Cass, co., Il., U.S.	D3	90
Cass, co., In., U.S.	C5	91
Cass, co., Ia., U.S.	C3	92
Cass, co., Mi., U.S.	G4	99
Cass, co., Mn., U.S.	D4	100
Cass, co., Mo., U.S.	C3	102
Cass, co., Ne., U.S.	D9	104
Cass, co., N.D., U.S.	C8	111
Cass, co., Tx., U.S.	C5	120
Cass, stm., Mi., U.S.	E7	99
Cassai (Kasai), stm., Afr.	C4	44
Cassano allo Ionio, Italy	J11	14
Cass City, Mi., U.S.	E7	99
Casselberry, Fl., U.S.	D5	86
Casselman, Ont., Can.	B9	73
Casselman, stm., U.S.	k12	97
Casselton, N.D., U.S.	C8	111
Cassia, co., Id., U.S.	G5	89
Cassiar, B.C., Can.	m17	69
Cassinga, Ang.	E3	44
Cassino, Italy	H8	14
Cass Lake, Mn., U.S.	C4	100
Cass Lake, l., Mn., U.S.	C4	100
Cassopolis, Mi., U.S.	G4	99
Cassville, Ga., U.S.	B2	87
Cassville, Mo., U.S.	E4	102
Cassville, Wi., U.S.	F3	126
Castalia, Oh., U.S.	A3	112
Castanea, Pa., U.S.	D7	115
Castanheira de Pêra, Port.	E3	12
Castel del Piano, Italy	G6	14
Castelfranco Veneto, Italy	D6	14
Castellammare del Golfo, Italy	K7	14
Castellammare [di Stabia], Italy	I9	14
Castellane, Fr.	I13	10
Castellón de la Plana, Spain	F11	12
Castelnaudary, Fr.	I8	10
Castelo Branco, Port.	F4	12
Castelsarrasin, Fr.	H8	10
Castelvetrano, Italy	L7	14
Castets, Fr.	I5	10
Castiglione del Lago, Italy	F7	14
Castilla, Peru	E2	54
Castilla la Nueva, hist. reg., Spain	F8	12
Castillo de San Marcos National Monument, Fl., U.S.	n9	86
Castine, Me., U.S.	D4	96
Castle Air Force Base, mil., Ca., U.S.	D3	82
Castlebar, Ire.	H3	7
Castleberry, Al., U.S.	D2	78
Castle Dale, Ut., U.S.	D4	121
Castle Dome Mountains, mts., Az., U.S.	D1	80
Castle Dome Peak, mtn., Az., U.S.	D1	80
Castlegar, B.C., Can.	E9	69
Castle Hayne, N.C., U.S.	C5	110
Castle Hills, De., U.S.	i7	85
Castle Mountain, mtn., Yukon, Can.	D5	66
Castle Mountains, mts., Mt., U.S.	D6	103
Castle Peak, mtn., Co., U.S.	B4	83
Castle Peak, mtn., Id., U.S.	E4	89
Castle Point, Mo., U.S.	f13	102
Castle Rock, Co., U.S.	B6	83
Castle Rock, Wa., U.S.	C3	124
Castle Rock, mtn., Or., U.S.	C8	114
Castle Rock Lake, res., Wi., U.S.	E4	126
Castleton, Vt., U.S.	D2	122
Castletown, I. of Man	G8	7
Castletown Berehaven, Ire.	J3	7
Castlewood, Va., U.S.	f9	123
Castor, Alta., Can.	C5	68
Castor, stm., Mo., U.S.	D7	102
Castres, Fr.	I9	10
Castries, St. Luc.	G17	64
Castro, co., Tx., U.S.	B1	120
Castro Daire, Port.	E4	12
Castro del Río, Spain	H7	12
Castropol, Spain	B4	12
Castro Valley, Ca., U.S.	h8	82
Castrovillari, Italy	J11	14
Castroville, Tx., U.S.	E3	120
Castuera, Spain	G6	12
Caswell, co., N.C., U.S.	A3	110
Catacamas, Hond.	G5	64
Cataguases, Braz.	F7	57
Catahoula, co., La., U.S.	C4	95
Catahoula Lake, l., La., U.S.	C3	95
Catalão, Braz.	E5	57
Catalina, Newf., Can.	D5	72
Catalina, Chile	B3	56
Catamarca, Arg.	B3	56
Catamayo, Ec.	I3	58
Catanduanes Island, i., Phil.	C7	32
Catanduva, Braz.	F4	57
Catania, Italy	L10	14
Catanzaro, Italy	K11	14
Cataouatche, Lake, l., La., U.S.	k11	95
Catarman, Phil.	C7	32
Catasauqua, Pa., U.S.	E11	115
Catastrophe, Cape, c., Austl.	F7	50
Cataumet, Ma., U.S.	C6	98
Catawba, co., N.C., U.S.	B1	110
Catawba, stm., S.C., U.S.	B6	117
Catawba, South Fork, stm., N.C., U.S.	B1	110
Catawissa, Pa., U.S.	E9	115
Catete, Ang.	C2	44
Cathance, Lake, l., Me., U.S.	D5	96
Cathcart, S. Afr.	H5	44
Cathedral City, Ca., U.S.	F5	82
Cathedral of the Pines, N.H., U.S.	E3	106
Catherine, Lake, res., Ar., U.S.	C3	81
Cat Island, i., Bah.	B10	64
Cat Island, i., Ma., U.S.	f12	98
Cat Island, i., Ms., U.S.	E4	101
Cat Island, i., S.C., U.S.	E9	117
Catlettsburg, Ky., U.S.	B7	94
Catlin, Il., U.S.	C6	90
Catnip Mountain, mtn., Nv., U.S.	B2	105
Catoche, Cabo, c., Mex.	G16	62
Cato Island, i., Austl.	D11	50
Catonsville, Md., U.S.	B4	97
Catoosa, Ok., U.S.	A6	113
Catoosa, co., Ga., U.S.	B1	87
Catorce, Mex.	F9	62
Catron, co., N.M., U.S.	D1	108
Catskill, N.Y., U.S.	C7	109
Catskill Mountains, mts., N.Y., U.S.	C6	109
Catt, Mount, mtn., B.C., Can.	B3	69
Cattaraugus, co., N.Y., U.S.	C2	109
Cattaraugus Creek, stm., N.Y., U.S.	C2	109
Cattaraugus Indian Reservation, N.Y., U.S.	C2	109
Cattolica, Italy	F7	14
Catus, Fr.	H8	10
Caubvick, Mount (Mont d'Iberville), mtn., Can.	f9	72
Cauca, stm., Col.	D5	58
Caucasia, Col.	C5	58
Caucasus, mts., Eur.	I6	22
Caucomgomoc Lake, l., Me., U.S.	B3	96
Caudry, Fr.	B10	10
Caulonia, Italy	K11	14
Caúngula, Ang.	C3	44
Čaunskaja Guba, b., Russia	D27	24
Cauquenes, Chile	D2	56
Caura, stm., Ven.	D10	58
Caussade, Fr.	H8	10
Cauvery, stm., India	G5	37
Cavalaire-sur-Mer, Fr.	I13	10
Cavalier, N.D., U.S.	A8	111
Cavalier, co., N.D., U.S.	A7	111
Cavan, Ire.	G5	7
Cave City, Ar., U.S.	B4	81
Cave City, Ky., U.S.	C4	94
Cave Creek, Az., U.S.	D4	80
Cave Junction, Or., U.S.	E3	114
Cave Point, c., Wi., U.S.	D6	126
Cave Run Lake, res., Ky., U.S.	B6	94
Cave Spring, Ga., U.S.	B1	87
Cave Spring, Va., U.S.	C2	123
Cavetown, Md., U.S.	A2	97
Caviana, Ilha, i., Braz.	C8	54
Cavite, Phil.	q19	33b
Cawood, Ky., U.S.	D6	94
Cawston, B.C., Can.	E8	69
Caxambu, Braz.	F6	57
Caxias, Braz.	D10	54
Caxias do Sul, Braz.	B6	56
Caxito, Ang.	C2	44
Cayambe, Ec.	G3	58
Cayambe, vol., Ec.	H4	58
Cayce, S.C., U.S.	D5	117
Cayenne, Fr. Gu.	C8	54
Cayman Brac, i., Cay. Is.	E8	64
Cayman Islands, dep., N.A.	E7	64
Cayuga, In., U.S.	E3	91
Cayuga, co., N.Y., U.S.	C4	109
Cayuga Heights, N.Y., U.S.	C4	109
Cayuga Lake, l., N.Y., U.S.	C4	109
Cazenovia, N.Y., U.S.	C5	109
Cazères, Fr.	I8	10
Cazin, Bos.	E10	14
Cazorla, Spain	H8	12
Čeboksary, Russia	F7	22
Cebollar, Arg.	B3	56
Cebreros, Spain	E7	12
Cebu, Phil.	C7	32
Cebu, i., Phil.	C7	32
Čecerleg, Mong.	B7	26
Čechov, Russia	F20	18
Čechy, hist. reg., Czech.	F14	8
Cecil, co., Md., U.S.	A6	97
Cecil Field Naval Air Station, mil., Fl., U.S.	B5	86
Cecilia, Ky., U.S.	C4	94
Cecina, Italy	F5	14
Cedar, co., Ia., U.S.	C6	92
Cedar, co., Mo., U.S.	D4	102
Cedar, co., Ne., U.S.	B8	104
Cedar, stm., U.S.	C6	92
Cedar, stm., Ne., U.S.	B7	104
Cedar, stm., Wa., U.S.	B4	124
Cedar Bluff, Al., U.S.	A4	78
Cedar Bluff Reservoir, res., Ks., U.S.	D4	93
Cedar Bluff Two, Tn., U.S.	D9	119
Cedar Breaks National Monument, Ut., U.S.	F3	121
Cedarburg, Wi., U.S.	E6	126
Cedar City, Ut., U.S.	F2	121
Cedar Creek, stm., N.J., U.S.	D4	107
Cedar Creek, stm., N.D., U.S.	C3	111
Cedar Creek, stm., Oh., U.S.	e7	112
Cedar Creek Lake, res., Tx., U.S.	C4	120
Cedar Crest, N.M., U.S.	k8	108
Cedaredge, Co., U.S.	C3	83
Cedar Falls, Ia., U.S.	B5	92
Cedar Grove, N.J., U.S.	B4	107
Cedar Grove, W.V., U.S.	C3	125
Cedar Grove, Wi., U.S.	E6	126
Cedar Hill, Mo., U.S.	g12	102
Cedar Hill, Tx., U.S.	n10	120
Cedarhurst, N.Y., U.S.	k13	109
Cedar Island, i., N.C., U.S.	C6	110
Cedar Island, i., S.C., U.S.	E9	117
Cedar Island, i., Va., U.S.	C7	123
Cedar Key, Fl., U.S.	C3	86
Cedar Keys, is., Fl., U.S.	C3	86
Cedar Lake, In., U.S.	B3	91
Cedar Lake, res., Man., Can.	C1	70
Cedar Lake, res., Il., U.S.	F4	90
Cedar Mountain, mtn., Ca., U.S.	B3	82
Cedar Point, c., Md., U.S.	D5	97
Cedar Point, c., Oh., U.S.	A3	112
Cedar Point, c., Oh., U.S.	e7	112
Cedar Rapids, Ia., U.S.	C6	92
Cedar Springs, Mi., U.S.	E5	99
Cedartown, Ga., U.S.	B1	87
Cedar Vale, Ks., U.S.	E7	93
Cedarville, Oh., U.S.	C2	112
Cedros, Isla, i., Mex.	C2	62
Ceduna, Austl.	F6	50
Cefalù, Italy	K9	14
Čegdomyn, Russia	G20	24
Cegléd, Hung.	H19	8
Cehegín, Spain	G10	12
Çela, Ang.	D3	44
Čel'abinsk, Russia	F10	22
Celano, Italy	G8	14
Celanova, Spain	C4	12
Celaya, Mex.	G9	62
Cele, China	B9	38
Celebes Sea, Asia	E7	32
Celebes see Sulawesi, i., Indon.	F7	32
Celina, Oh., U.S.	B1	112
Celina, Tn., U.S.	C8	119
Celina, Tx., U.S.	C4	120
Celinograd, Kaz.	G8	24
Celje, Slo.	C10	14
Celle, Ger.	C10	8
Cement, Ok., U.S.	C3	113
Cementon, Pa., U.S.	E10	115
Centennial Mountains, mts., Id., U.S.	E7	89
Center, Co., U.S.	D4	83
Center, N.D., U.S.	B4	111
Center, Tx., U.S.	D5	120
Centerbrook, Ct., U.S.	D6	84
Centerburg, Oh., U.S.	B3	112
Centereach, N.Y., U.S.	n15	109
Centerfield, Ut., U.S.	D4	121
Center Hill Lake, res., Tn., U.S.	C8	119
Center Moriches, N.Y., U.S.	n16	109
Center Mountain, mtn., Id., U.S.	D3	89
Center Point, Al., U.S.	f7	78
Center Point, Ia., U.S.	B6	92
Centerville, In., U.S.	E8	91
Centerville, Ia., U.S.	D5	92
Centerville, La., U.S.	E4	95
Centerville, Ma., U.S.	C7	98
Centerville, Oh., U.S.	C1	112
Centerville, Pa., U.S.	F2	115
Centerville, S.D., U.S.	D9	118
Centerville, Tn., U.S.	B4	119
Centerville, Ut., U.S.	C4	121
Cento, Italy	E6	14
Central, N.M., U.S.	E1	108
Central, S.C., U.S.	B2	117
Central, Cordillera, mts., Bol.	G6	54
Central, Cordillera, mts., Col.	E5	58
Central, Cordillera, mts., Peru	E3	54
Central, Massif, mts., Fr.	G10	10
Central, Planalto, plat., Braz.	G9	54
Central, Sistema, mts., Spain	E6	12
Central African Republic, ctry., Afr.	G10	42
Central City, Co., U.S.	B5	83
Central City, Il., U.S.	E4	90
Central City, Ia., U.S.	B6	92
Central City, Ky., U.S.	C2	94
Central City, Ne., U.S.	C7	104
Central City, Pa., U.S.	F4	115
Central Falls, R.I., U.S.	B4	116
Central Heights, Az., U.S.	D5	80
Centralia, Il., U.S.	E4	90
Centralia, Mo., U.S.	B5	102
Centralia, Wa., U.S.	C3	124
Central Islip, N.Y., U.S.	n15	109
Central Lake, Mi., U.S.	C5	99
Central Makrān Range, mts., Pak.	D1	36
Central Park, Wa., U.S.	C2	124
Central Point, Or., U.S.	E4	114
Central Square, N.Y., U.S.	B4	109
Central Valley, Ca., U.S.	B2	82
Central Valley, N.Y., U.S.	D6	109
Central Village, Ct., U.S.	C8	84
Centre, Al., U.S.	A4	78
Centre, co., Pa., U.S.	E6	115
Centre Hall, Pa., U.S.	E6	115
Centreville, Al., U.S.	C2	78
Centreville, Il., U.S.	E3	90
Centreville, Md., U.S.	B5	97
Centreville, Mi., U.S.	G5	99
Centreville, Ms., U.S.	D2	101
Centuria, Wi., U.S.	C1	126
Century, Fl., U.S.	u14	86
Cepu, Indon.	m15	33a
Ceram Sea see Seram, Laut, Indon.	F8	32
Cerbat Mountains, mts., Az., U.S.	B1	80
Ceredo, W.V., U.S.	C2	125
Čeremchovo, Russia	G14	24
Čerepovec, Russia	B20	18
Ceres, Ca., U.S.	D3	82
Ceresco, Ne., U.S.	C9	104
Céret, Fr.	J9	10
Cereté, Col.	C5	58
Cerf Island, i., Sey.	C10	44
Cerignola, Italy	H10	14
Cérilly, Fr.	F9	10
Čerkassy, Ukr.	H4	22
Čerkessk, Russia	I6	22
Čern'achovsk, Russia	G4	18
Černigov, Ukr.	G4	22
Černobyl' (Chernobyl), Ukr.	G4	22
Černogorsk, Russia	G12	24
Černovcy, Ukr.	H3	22
Černyševskij, Russia	E16	24
Cerralvo, Isla, i., Mex.	E5	62
Cerritos, Mex.	F9	62
Cerro de Pasco, Peru	F3	54
Cerro Gordo, Il., U.S.	D5	90
Cerro Gordo, co., Ia., U.S.	A4	92
Čerskij, Russia	D26	24
Čerskogo, Chrebet, mts., Russia	E23	24
Cervera del Río Alhama, Spain	C10	12
Cervera de Pisuerga, Spain	C7	12
Cervia, Italy	E7	14
Cesena, Italy	E7	14
Cesenatico, Italy	E7	14
České Budějovice, Czech.	G14	8
Cessnock, Austl.	F10	50
Ceuta, Sp. N. Afr.	A4	42
Ceyhan, Tur.	A4	40
Ceylânpınar, Tur.	A7	40
Ceylon see Sri Lanka, ctry., Asia	H5	36
Chabanais, Fr.	G7	10
Chabarovsk, Russia	H21	24

Name	Map Ref	Page
Chachoengsao, Thai.	H6	34
Chaco, stm., N.M., U.S.	A1	108
Chaco Culture National Historic Park, N.M., U.S.	A2	108
Chacon, Cape, c., Ak., U.S.	n24	79
Chad, ctry., Afr.	E9	42
Chad, Lake (Lac Tchad), l., Afr.	F8	42
Chadbourn, N.C., U.S.	C4	110
Chadds Ford, Pa., U.S.	G10	115
Chadileuvú, stm., Arg.	D3	56
Chadron, Ne., U.S.	B3	104
Chadwicks, N.Y., U.S.	B5	109
Chaffee, Mo., U.S.	D8	102
Chaffee, co., Co., U.S.	C4	83
Chaffin, Ma., U.S.	B4	98
Chaghcharān, Afg.	C1	38
Chagny, Fr.	F11	10
Chagos Archipelago, is., B.I.O.T.	G17	2
Chagrin Falls, Oh., U.S.	A4	112
Chaibāsā, India	I11	38
Chaîne Annamitique, mts., Asia	F9	34
Chakachamna Lake, l., Ak., U.S.	g15	79
Chake Chake, Tan.	C7	44
Chalais, Fr.	G7	10
Chalbi Desert, des., Kenya	H2	46
Chalcuapa, El Sal.	H3	64
Chaleur Bay, b., Can.	B4	71
Chalfonte, De., U.S.	h7	85
Chālisgaon, India	B3	37
Chalk River, Ont., Can.	A7	73
Challans, Fr.	F5	10
Challis, Id., U.S.	E4	89
Chalmette, La., U.S.	E6	95
Chalonnes-sur-Loire, Fr.	E6	10
Châlons-sur-Marne, Fr.	D11	10
Chalon-sur-Saône, Fr.	F11	10
Châlus, Fr.	G7	10
Cham, Ger.	F12	8
Chama, N.M., U.S.	A3	108
Chama, Rio, stm., N.M., U.S.	A3	108
Chaman, Pak.	E2	38
Chambal, stm., India	G7	38
Chamberlain, S.D., U.S.	D6	118
Chamberlain Lake, l., Me., U.S.	B3	96
Chamberlin, Mount, mtn., Ak., U.S.	B10	79
Chambers, co., Al., U.S.	C4	78
Chambers, co., Tx., U.S.	E5	120
Chambersburg, Pa., U.S.	G6	115
Chambers Island, i., Wi., U.S.	C6	126
Chambéry, Fr.	G12	10
Chambi, Jebel, mtn., Tun.	A7	42
Chamblee, Ga., U.S.	h8	87
Chambly, Que., Can.	D4	74
Chambon-sur-Voueize, Fr.	F9	10
Chamisal, N.M., U.S.	A4	108
Chamonix-Mont-Blanc, Fr.	G13	10
Champagne, hist. reg., Fr.	D11	10
Champagnole, Fr.	F12	10
Champaign, Il., U.S.	C5	90
Champaign, co., Il., U.S.	C5	90
Champaign, co., Oh., U.S.	B2	112
Champassak, Laos	G8	34
Champion, Oh., U.S.	A5	112
Champlain, Lake, l., N.A.	C12	76
Champlin, Mn., U.S.	m12	100
Chāmrājnagar Rāmasamudram, India	G4	37
Chañaral, Chile	B2	56
Chance, Md., U.S.	D6	97
Chanch, Mong.	A7	26
Chanchelulla Peak, mtn., Ca., U.S.	B2	82
Chandalar, stm., Ak., U.S.	B10	79
Chandausi, India	F8	38
Chandeleur Islands, is., La., U.S.	E7	95
Chandeleur Sound, strt., La., U.S.	E6	95
Chandīgarh, India	E7	38
Chandler, Que., Can.	k14	74
Chandler, Az., U.S.	D4	80
Chandler, In., U.S.	H3	91
Chandler, Ok., U.S.	B5	113
Chandler, Tx., U.S.	C5	120
Chandler Heights, Az., U.S.	m9	80
Chāndpur, Bngl.	I14	38
Chāndpur, India	F8	38
Chandrapur, India	C5	37
Chandyga, Russia	E21	24
Chang (Yangtze), stm., China	E10	26
Changajn Nuruu, mts., Mong.	B6	26
Changchun, China	C12	26
Changde, China	F9	26
Changhua, Tai.	K9	28
Changjiang, China	J5	28
Changli, China	D10	26
Changsha, China	G1	28
Changshu, China	D9	28
Changzhi, China	D9	26
Changzhou (Changchow), China	D8	28
Chanhassen, Mn., U.S.	n11	100
Chanka, Ozero (Xingkathu), l., Asia	I20	24
Channahon, Il., U.S.	B5	90
Channapatna, India	F4	37
Channel Islands, is., Eur.	C4	10
Channel Islands National Park, Ca., U.S.	F4	82
Channel Lake, Il., U.S.	H8	90
Channel-Port-aux-Basques, Newf., Can.	E2	72
Channelview, Tx., U.S.	r14	120
Chantada, Spain	C4	12
Chantajskoje, Ozero, l., Russia	D12	24
Chanthaburi, Thai.	H7	34
Chantilly, Va., U.S.	g12	123
Chantrey Inlet, b., N.W. Ter., Can.	C13	66
Chanute, Ks., U.S.	E8	93
Chanute Air Force Base, mil., Il., U.S.	C5	90
Chaoan, China	L5	28
Chao Phraya, stm., Thai.	G6	34
Chapala, Lago de, l., Mex.	G8	62
Chaparral, Col.	F5	58
Chapčeranga, Russia	H16	24
Chapel Hill, N.C., U.S.	B3	110
Chapel Hill, Tn., U.S.	B5	119
Chaplin, stm., Ky., U.S.	C4	94
Chaplin Lake, l., Sask., Can.	G2	75
Chapman, Ks., U.S.	D6	93
Chapman Pond, l., R.I., U.S.	F1	116
Chapmanville, W.V., U.S.	D2	125
Chappaquiddick Island, i., Ma., U.S.	D7	98
Chappell, Ne., U.S.	C3	104
Chāpra, India	H11	38
Chapultepec, mtn., Mex.	F8	62
Charadai, Arg.	B5	56
Charcas, Mex.	F9	62
Chardon, Oh., U.S.	A4	112
Chardzhou see Čardžou, Turk.	J10	22
Charenton, La., U.S.	E4	95
Chari, stm., Afr.	F9	42
Chārīkār, Afg.	C3	38
Chariton, Ia., U.S.	C4	92
Chariton, co., Mo., U.S.	B4	102
Chariton, stm., U.S.	A5	102
Charity, Guy.	D13	58
Char'kov, Ukr.	G5	22
Charleroi, Bel.	E4	8
Charleroi, Pa., U.S.	F2	115
Charles, co., Md., U.S.	C3	97
Charles, stm., Ma., U.S.	B5	98
Charles, Cape, c., Va., U.S.	C6	123
Charles A. Goodwin Dam, Ct., U.S.	B3	84
Charlesbourg, Que., Can.	n17	74
Charles City, Ia., U.S.	A5	92
Charles City, co., Va., U.S.	C5	123
Charles Island, i., N.W. Ter., Can.	D18	66
Charles Mill Lake, res., Oh., U.S.	B3	112
Charles Mix, co., S.D., U.S.	D7	118
Charles Mound, hill, Il., U.S.	A3	90
Charleston, Ar., U.S.	B1	81
Charleston, Il., U.S.	D5	90
Charleston, Ms., U.S.	A3	101
Charleston, Mo., U.S.	E8	102
Charleston, Or., U.S.	D2	114
Charleston, S.C., U.S.	F8	117
Charleston, Tn., U.S.	D9	119
Charleston, W.V., U.S.	C3	125
Charleston, co., S.C., U.S.	F8	117
Charleston Air Force Base, mil., S.C., U.S.	k11	117
Charleston Naval Shipyard, mil., S.C., U.S.	k12	117
Charleston Peak, mtn., Nv., U.S.	G6	105
Charlestown, In., U.S.	H6	91
Charlestown, N.H., U.S.	D2	106
Charlestown, R.I., U.S.	F2	116
Charles Town, W.V., U.S.	B7	125
Charleville, Austl.	E9	50
Charleville-Mézières, Fr.	C11	10
Charlevoix, Mi., U.S.	C5	99
Charlevoix, co., Mi., U.S.	C5	99
Charlevoix, Lake, l., Mi., U.S.	C5	99
Charlo, N.B., Can.	B3	71
Charlotte, Mi., U.S.	F6	99
Charlotte, N.C., U.S.	B2	110
Charlotte, Tn., U.S.	A4	119
Charlotte, Tx., U.S.	E3	120
Charlotte, co., Fl., U.S.	F5	86
Charlotte, co., Va., U.S.	C4	123
Charlotte Amalie, V.I.U.S.	E15	64
Charlotte Hall, Md., U.S.	D4	97
Charlotte Harbor, Fl., U.S.	F4	86
Charlotte Harbor, b., Fl., U.S.	F4	86
Charlottenberg, Swe.	G9	6
Charlottesville, Va., U.S.	B4	123
Charlottetown, P.E.I., Can.	C6	71
Charlton, co., Ga., U.S.	F4	87
Charmco, W.V., U.S.	C4	125
Charmes, Fr.	D13	10
Charny, Que., Can.	C6	74
Charolles, Fr.	F11	10
Chārsadda, Pak.	C4	38
Charters Towers, Austl.	D9	50
Chartres, Fr.	D8	10
Char Us Nuur, l., Mong.	B5	26
Chascomús, Arg.	D5	56
Chase, B.C., Can.	D8	69
Chase, Md., U.S.	B5	97
Chase, co., Ks., U.S.	D7	93
Chase, co., Ne., U.S.	D4	104
Chase City, Va., U.S.	D4	123
Chase Field Naval Air Station, mil., Tx., U.S.	E4	120
Chaska, Mn., U.S.	F5	100
Chassahowitzka Bay, b., Fl., U.S.	D4	86
Chassell, Mi., U.S.	B2	99
Chatanbulag, Mong.	C8	26
Chatanga, Russia	C14	24
Chatanga, stm., Russia	C14	24
Chatangskij Zaliv, b., Russia	C15	24
Châteaubriant, Fr.	E5	10
Château-du-Loir, Fr.	E7	10
Châteaudun, Fr.	D8	10
Château-Gontier, Fr.	E6	10
Châteauguay, Que., Can.	D4	74
Château-Landon, Fr.	D9	10
Châteaulin, Fr.	D2	10
Châteaumeillant, Fr.	F9	10
Châteauneuf-sur-Charente, Fr.	G6	10
Châteauneuf-sur-Loire, Fr.	E9	10
Château-Renault, Fr.	E7	10
Château-Richer, Que., Can.	C6	74
Châteauroux, Fr.	F8	10
Château-Thierry, Fr.	C10	10
Châtellerault, Fr.	F7	10
Chatfield, Mn., U.S.	G6	100
Chatgal, Mong.	A7	26
Chatham, N.B., Can.	B4	71
Chatham, Ont., Can.	E2	73
Chatham, Eng., U.K.	J13	7
Chatham, Il., U.S.	D4	90
Chatham, La., U.S.	B3	95
Chatham, Ma., U.S.	C8	98
Chatham, N.J., U.S.	B4	107
Chatham, N.Y., U.S.	C7	109
Chatham, Va., U.S.	D3	123
Chatham, co., Ga., U.S.	E5	87
Chatham, co., N.C., U.S.	B3	110
Chatham Strait, strt., Ak., U.S.	m22	79
Châtillon, Italy	D2	14
Châtillon-Coligny, Fr.	E9	10
Châtillon-sur-Indre, Fr.	F8	10
Châtillon-sur-Seine, Fr.	E11	10
Chatom, Al., U.S.	D1	78
Chatsworth, Ga., U.S.	B2	87
Chatsworth, Il., U.S.	C5	90
Chatsworth Reservoir, res., Ca., U.S.	m11	82
Chattahoochee, Fl., U.S.	B2	86
Chattahoochee, co., Ga., U.S.	D2	87
Chattahoochee, stm., U.S.	E1	87
Chattanooga, Tn., U.S.	D8	119
Chattaroy, W.V., U.S.	D2	125
Chattooga, co., Ga., U.S.	B1	87
Chattooga, stm., U.S.	B1	117
Chatuge Lake, res., U.S.	g9	110
Chatyrka, Russia	E29	24
Chaudière, stm., Que., Can.	C7	74
Chau Doc, Viet.	I8	34
Chauk, Burma	D3	34
Chaumont, Fr.	D12	10
Chauncey, Oh., U.S.	C3	112
Chauny, Fr.	C10	10
Chautauqua, co., Ks., U.S.	E7	93
Chautauqua, co., N.Y., U.S.	C1	109
Chautauqua Lake, l., N.Y., U.S.	C1	109
Chauvigny, Fr.	F7	10
Chauvin, La., U.S.	E5	95
Chavakkad, India	G4	37
Chaves, Port.	D4	12
Chaves, co., N.M., U.S.	D5	108
Cháviva, Col.	E6	58
Chbukha Dzong, Bhu.	G13	38
Cheaha Mountain, mtn., Al., U.S.	B4	78
Cheat, Shavers Fork, stm., W.V., U.S.	B5	125
Cheatham, co., Tn., U.S.	A4	119
Chebanse, Il., U.S.	C6	90
Cheboygan, Mi., U.S.	C6	99
Cheboygan, co., Mi., U.S.	C6	99
Chech, Erg, des., Afr.	C5	42
Checotah, Ok., U.S.	B6	113
Chedabucto Bay, b., N.S., Can.	D8	71
Cheduba Island, i., Burma	E2	34
Cheektowaga, N.Y., U.S.	C2	109
Cheeseman Lake, res., Co., U.S.	B5	83
Chehalem Mountains, mts., Or., U.S.	h12	114
Chehalis, Wa., U.S.	C3	124
Chehalis, stm., Wa., U.S.	C2	124
Cheju-do, i., S. Kor.	E12	26
Chelan, Wa., U.S.	B5	124
Chelan, co., Wa., U.S.	B4	124
Chelan, Lake, l., Wa., U.S.	A5	124
Chelan Mountains, mts., Wa., U.S.	A5	124
Chełm, Pol.	D23	8
Chełmno, Pol.	B18	8
Chelmsford, Eng., U.K.	J13	7
Chelmsford, Ma., U.S.	A5	98
Chelsea, Que., Can.	D2	74
Chelsea, Al., U.S.	g7	78
Chelsea, Ma., U.S.	B5	98
Chelsea, Mi., U.S.	F6	99
Chelsea, Ok., U.S.	A6	113
Cheltenham, Eng., U.K.	J10	7
Cheltenham, Md., U.S.	C4	97
Chelva, Spain	F11	12
Chelyabinsk see Čel'abinsk, Russia	F10	22
Chelyan, W.V., U.S.	C3	125
Chemehuevi Indian Reservation, Ca., U.S.	E6	82
Chemnitz, Ger.	E12	8
Chemquasabamticook Lake (Ross Lake), l., Me., U.S.	B3	96
Chemung, co., N.Y., U.S.	C4	109
Chemung, stm., Pa., U.S.	C8	115
Chemung Lake, l., Ont., Can.	C6	73
Chenāb, stm., Asia	E5	38
Chenachane, Alg.	C6	42
Chenango, co., N.Y., U.S.	C5	109
Chenango, stm., N.Y., U.S.	C5	109
Chenango Bridge, N.Y., U.S.	C5	109
Chenes, River Aux, b., La., U.S.	k12	95
Chénéville, Que., Can.	D2	74
Cheney, Ks., U.S.	E6	93
Cheney, Wa., U.S.	B8	124
Cheney Reservoir, res., Ks., U.S.	E6	93
Cheneyville, La., U.S.	C3	95
Chengde, China	C10	26
Chengdu, China	E7	26
Chengutu, Zimb.	E6	44
Chenoa, Il., U.S.	C5	90
Chenoweth, Or., U.S.	B5	114
Chepachet, R.I., U.S.	B2	116
Chepachet, stm., R.I., U.S.	B2	116
Chepo, Pan.	J8	64
Chequamegon Bay, b., Wi., U.S.	B3	126
Cheraw, S.C., U.S.	B8	117
Cherbourg, Fr.	C5	10
Chergui, Chott ech, l., Alg.	B6	42
Cherkassy see Čerkassy, Ukr.	H4	22
Chernigov see Černigov, Ukr.	G4	22
Chernobyl see Černobyl', Ukr.	G4	22
Cherokee, Al., U.S.	A2	78
Cherokee, Ia., U.S.	B2	92
Cherokee, Ks., U.S.	E9	93
Cherokee, Ok., U.S.	A3	113
Cherokee, co., Al., U.S.	A4	78
Cherokee, co., Ga., U.S.	B2	87
Cherokee, co., Ia., U.S.	B2	92
Cherokee, co., Ks., U.S.	E9	93
Cherokee, co., N.C., U.S.	f8	110
Cherokee, co., Ok., U.S.	B6	113
Cherokee, co., S.C., U.S.	A4	117
Cherokee, co., Tx., U.S.	D5	120
Cherokee Indian Reservation, N.C., U.S.	f9	110
Cherokee Lake, res., Tn., U.S.	C10	119
Cherokees, Lake O' The, res., Ok., U.S.	A7	113
Cherokee Village, Ar., U.S.	A4	81
Cherry, co., Ne., U.S.	B4	104
Cherry Creek, stm., S.D., U.S.	C3	118
Cherry Hill, N.J., U.S.	D2	107
Cherry Point, c., Va., U.S.	C6	123
Cherry Point Marine Corps Air Station, mil., N.C., U.S.	C6	110
Cherryvale, Ks., U.S.	E8	93
Cherry Valley, Ar., U.S.	B5	81
Cherry Valley, Il., U.S.	A5	90
Cherryville, N.C., U.S.	B1	110
Cherson, Ukr.	H4	22
Chesaning, Mi., U.S.	E6	99
Chesapeake, Oh., U.S.	D3	112
Chesapeake, Va., U.S.	D6	123
Chesapeake, W.V., U.S.	C3	125
Chesapeake and Delaware Canal, U.S.	B3	85
Chesapeake Bay, b., U.S.	D11	76
Chesapeake Bay Bridge-Tunnel, Va., U.S.	D7	123
Chesapeake Beach, Md., U.S.	C4	97
Chesapeake City, Md., U.S.	A6	97
Chesdin, Lake, res., Va., U.S.	C5	123
Cheshire, Ct., U.S.	D4	84
Cheshire, co., N.H., U.S.	E2	106
Cheshire Reservoir, res., Ma., U.S.	A1	98
Chesley, Ont., Can.	C3	73
Chesnee, S.C., U.S.	A4	117
Chester, Eng., U.K.	H10	7
Chester, Ca., U.S.	B3	82
Chester, Ct., U.S.	D6	84
Chester, Ga., U.S.	D3	87
Chester, Il., U.S.	F4	90
Chester, Md., U.S.	C5	97
Chester, Mt., U.S.	B6	103
Chester, N.H., U.S.	E4	106
Chester, N.Y., U.S.	D6	109
Chester, Pa., U.S.	G11	115
Chester, S.C., U.S.	B5	117
Chester, Vt., U.S.	E3	122
Chester, Va., U.S.	C5	123
Chester, W.V., U.S.	A4	125
Chester, co., Pa., U.S.	G10	115
Chester, co., S.C., U.S.	B5	117
Chester, co., Tn., U.S.	B3	119
Chester, stm., Md., U.S.	B5	97
Chester Basin, N.S., Can.	E5	71
Chester Depot, Vt., U.S.	E3	122
Chesterfield, In., U.S.	D6	91
Chesterfield, S.C., U.S.	B7	117
Chesterfield, co., S.C., U.S.	B7	117
Chesterfield, co., Va., U.S.	C5	123
Chesterfield, Îles, is., N. Cal.	C11	50
Chesterfield Inlet, N.W. Ter., Can.	D14	66
Chesterfield Inlet, b., N.W. Ter., Can.	D14	66
Chesterton, In., U.S.	A3	91
Chestertown, Md., U.S.	B5	97
Chesterville, Ont., Can.	B9	73
Chesuncook Lake, l., Me., U.S.	C3	96
Cheswick, Pa., U.S.	h14	115
Cheswold, De., U.S.	D3	85
Cheta, stm., Russia	C13	24
Chetac, Lake, l., Wi., U.S.	C2	126
Chetco, stm., Or., U.S.	E2	114
Chetek, Wi., U.S.	C2	126
Chetek, Lake, l., Wi., U.S.	C2	126
Chetopa, Ks., U.S.	E8	93
Chetumal Bay, b., N.A.	H15	62
Chetwynd, B.C., Can.	B7	69
Chevak, Ak., U.S.	C6	79
Cheval Blanc, Pointe du, c., Haiti	E11	64
Cheviot, Oh., U.S.	C1	112
Chevreuil, Point, c., La., U.S.	E4	95
Chevy Chase, Md., U.S.	C3	97
Chewack, stm., Wa., U.S.	A5	124
Chew Bahir (Lake Stefanie), l., Afr.	H2	46
Chewelah, Wa., U.S.	A8	124
Cheyenne, Ok., U.S.	B2	113
Cheyenne, Wy., U.S.	E8	127
Cheyenne, co., Co., U.S.	C8	83
Cheyenne, co., Ks., U.S.	C2	93
Cheyenne, co., Ne., U.S.	C2	104
Cheyenne, stm., U.S.	C4	118
Cheyenne, Dry Fork, stm., Wy., U.S.	C7	127
Cheyenne River Indian Reservation, S.D., U.S.	B4	118
Cheyenne Wells, Co., U.S.	C8	83
Chezhou, China	J1	28
Chhatarpur, India	H8	38
Chhindwāra, India	I8	38
Chi, stm., Thai.	G8	34
Chiai, Tai.	L9	28
Chiali, Tai.	L9	28
Chiang Khan, Thai.	F6	34
Chiang Mai, Thai.	E5	34
Chiang Rai, Thai.	E5	34
Chiari, Italy	D4	14
Chiavari, Italy	E4	14
Chiavenna, Italy	C4	14
Chiba, Japan	G13	30
Chiblow Lake, l., Ont., Can.	A1	73
Chibougamau, Que., Can.	k12	74
Chibuto, Moz.	F6	44
Chicago, Il., U.S.	B6	90
Chicago Heights, Il., U.S.	B6	90
Chicago Sanitary and Ship Canal, Il., U.S.	k8	90
Chicamacomico, stm., Md., U.S.	D6	97
Chicapa, stm., Afr.	C4	44
Chichagof Island, i., Ak., U.S.	m22	79
Chīchāwatni, Pak.	E5	38
Chichén Itzá, Mex.	G15	62
Chichibu, Japan	G12	30
Chickahominy, stm., Va., U.S.	C5	123
Chickamauga, Ga., U.S.	B1	87
Chickamauga and Chattanooga National Military Park, U.S.	k11	119
Chickamauga Dam, Tn., U.S.	h11	119
Chickamauga Lake, res., Tn., U.S.	D8	119
Chickasaw, Al., U.S.	E1	78
Chickasaw, co., Ia., U.S.	A5	92
Chickasaw, co., Ms., U.S.	B5	101
Chickasawhay, stm., Ms., U.S.	D5	101
Chickasaw National Recreation Area, Ok., U.S.	C5	113
Chickasha, Ok., U.S.	B4	113
Chickasha, Lake, res., Ok., U.S.	B3	113
Chickwolnepy Stream, stm., N.H., U.S.	A4	106
Chiclana de la Frontera, Spain	I5	12
Chiclayo, Peru	E3	54
Chico, Ca., U.S.	C3	82
Chicoa, Moz.	E6	44
Chicopee, Ga., U.S.	B3	87
Chicopee, Ma., U.S.	B2	98
Chicora, Pa., U.S.	E2	115
Chicot, Lake, l., Ar., U.S.	D4	81
Chicot Island, i., La., U.S.	E6	95
Chicoutimi, Que., Can.	A6	74
Chicoutimi, stm., Que., Can.	A6	74
Chidambaram, India	G5	37
Chidley, Cape, c., Can.	D20	66
Chiefland, Fl., U.S.	C4	86
Chieri, Italy	D2	14
Chieti, Italy	G9	14
Chifeng, China	C10	26
Chigasaki, Japan	G12	30
Chignecto, Cape, c., N.S., Can.	D5	71
Chignecto Bay, b., Can.	D5	71
Ch'ihu, Tai.	L9	28
Chihuahua, Mex.	C6	62
Chikaskia, stm., U.S.	A4	113
Chik Ballāpur, India	F4	37
Chikmagalūr, India	F3	37
Chilakalūrupet, India	D6	37
Chilapa de Alvarez, Mex.	I10	62
Chilās, Pak.	C6	38
Childersburg, Al., U.S.	B3	78
Childress, Tx., U.S.	B2	120
Childress, co., Tx., U.S.	B2	120
Chile, ctry., S.A.	C2	56
Chilete, Peru	E3	54
Chilhowie, Va., U.S.	f10	123
Chililabombwe (Bancroft), Zam.	D5	44
Chilka Lake, l., India	C8	37
Chilko, stm., B.C., Can.	D6	69
Chilko Lake, l., B.C., Can.	D5	69
Chillán, Chile	D2	56
Chillicothe, Il., U.S.	C4	90
Chillicothe, Mo., U.S.	B4	102
Chillicothe, Oh., U.S.	C3	112
Chilliwack, B.C., Can.	E7	69
Chillum, Md., U.S.	f9	97
Chiloé, Isla de, i., Chile	E2	56
Chilok, Russia	G16	24
Chiloquin, Or., U.S.	E5	114
Chilpancingo [de los Bravos], Mex.	I10	62
Chilton, Wi., U.S.	D5	126
Chilton, co., Al., U.S.	C3	78
Chilung, Tai.	J10	28
Chilwa, Lake, l., Afr.	E7	44
Chimacum, Wa., U.S.	A3	124
Chimayo, N.M., U.S.	A4	108
Chimborazo, vol., Ec.	H3	58
Chimbote, Peru	E3	54
Chimkent see Čimkent, Kaz.	I11	22
Chimki, Russia	F20	18
Chimney Rock, mtn., Ne., U.S.	C2	104
China, ctry., Asia	D7	26
China Grove, N.C., U.S.	B2	110
China Lake, l., Me., U.S.	D3	96
Chinandega, Nic.	H4	64
Chincha Alta, Peru	F3	54
Chincilla de Monte Aragón, Spain	G10	12
Chincoteague, Va., U.S.	C7	123
Chincoteague Bay, b., U.S.	D7	97
Chinde, Moz.	E7	44
Chindwinn, stm., Burma	C3	34
Chingleput, India	F5	37
Chingola, Zam.	D5	44
Ch'ingshui, Tai.	K9	28
Chin Hills, hills, Burma	D2	34
Chinhoyi, Zimb.	E6	44
Chiniot, Pak.	E5	38
Chinitna Point, c., Ak., U.S.	h15	79
Chinju, S. Kor.	D12	26
Chinko, stm., Cen. Afr. Rep.	G10	42
Chinkuashih, Tai.	J10	28
Chinle, Az., U.S.	A6	80
Chinmen Tao, i., Tai.	K7	28
Chino, Ca., U.S.	F5	82
Chinon, Fr.	E7	10
Chinook, Mt., U.S.	B7	103
Chinook, Wa., U.S.	C2	124
Chinook, Lake, res., Or., U.S.	C5	114
Chino Valley, Az., U.S.	C3	80
Chinshan, Tai.	J10	28
Chioggia, Italy	D7	14
Chipata, Zam.	D6	44
Chipita Park, Co., U.S.	C6	83
Chipley, Fl., U.S.	u16	86
Chipman, N.B., Can.	C4	71
Chipola, stm., Fl., U.S.	B1	86
Chippewa, co., Mi., U.S.	B6	99
Chippewa, co., Mn., U.S.	E3	100
Chippewa, co., Wi., U.S.	C2	126
Chippewa, stm., Mn., U.S.	E3	100
Chippewa, stm., Wi., U.S.	D2	126
Chippewa, Lake, l., Wi., U.S.	C2	126
Chippewa Falls, Wi., U.S.	D2	126
Chipuxet, stm., R.I., U.S.	F3	116
Chiquimula, Guat.	G3	64
Chiquinquirá, Col.	E6	58
Chīrāla, India	E6	37
Chirfa, Niger	D8	42
Chirgis Nuur, l., Mong.	B5	26
Chiricahua Mountains, mts., Az., U.S.	E6	80
Chiricahua National Monument, Az., U.S.	F6	80
Chiricahua Peak, mtn., Az., U.S.	F6	80
Chiriguaná, Col.	C6	58
Chirikof Island, i., Ak., U.S.	D8	79
Chiriquí, Golfo, b., Pan.	K6	64
Chiriquí, Laguna de, b., Pan.	J7	64
Chirripó, Cerro, mtn., C.R.	J6	64
Chisago, co., Mn., U.S.	E6	100
Chisago City, Mn., U.S.	E6	100
Chisholm, Me., U.S.	D2	96
Chisholm, Mn., U.S.	C6	100
Chishtiān Mandi, Pak.	F5	38
Chisos Mountains, mts., Tx., U.S.	E1	120
Chitato, Ang.	C4	44
Chitembo, Ang.	D3	44
Chitina, stm., Ak., U.S.	g19	79
Chitipa, Mwi.	C6	44
Chitorgarh, India	H6	38
Chitose, Japan	q19	30
Chitradurga, India	E4	37
Chitrāl, Pak.	C4	38
Chitré, Pan.	K7	64
Chittagong, Bngl.	I14	38

Name	Map Ref	Page
hittenango, N.Y., U.S.	B5	109
hittenden, co., Vt., U.S.	C2	122
hittenden Reservoir, res., Vt., U.S.	D3	122
hittoor, India	F5	37
hiusi, Italy	F6	14
hivasso, Italy	D2	14
hoapan, Mex.	I12	62
hocolate Mountains, mts., U.S.	F6	82
hocontá, Col.	E6	58
hoctaw, Ok., U.S.	B4	113
hoctaw, co., Al., U.S.	C1	78
hoctaw, co., Ms., U.S.	B4	101
hoctaw, co., Ok., U.S.	C6	113
hoctawhatchee Bay, b., Fl., U.S.	u15	86
hoctaw Indian Reservation, Ms., U.S.	C4	101
hoele-Choel, Arg.	D3	56
holet, Fr.	E6	10
holmsk, Russia	H22	24
holuteca, Hond.	H4	64
homa, Zam.	E5	44
homutov, Czech.	E13	8
hon Buri, Thai.	H6	34
hone, Ec.	H2	58
h'ŏngjin, N. Kor.	C12	26
h'ŏngju, S. Kor.	D12	26
hongmingdao, i., China	D10	28
hongqing, China	F8	26
hŏnju, S. Kor.	D12	26
honos, Archipiélago de los, is., Chile	F2	56
honuu, Russia	D22	24
hoptank, stm., Md., U.S.	C6	97
hōshi, Japan	G13	30
hos Malal, Arg.	D2	56
hoteau, Mt., U.S.	C4	103
houteau, Ok., U.S.	A6	113
houteau, co., Mt., U.S.	C6	103
hovd, Mong.	B5	26
hövsgöl Nuur, l., Mong.	A7	26
howan, co., N.C., U.S.	A6	110
howan, stm., N.C., U.S.	A6	110
howchilla, Ca., U.S.	D3	82
hrisman, Il., U.S.	D6	90
hristanshåb, Grnld.	C22	66
hristchurch, N.Z.	E4	52
hristian, co., Il., U.S.	D4	90
hristian, co., Ky., U.S.	D2	94
hristian, co., Mo., U.S.	E4	102
hristian, Cape, c., N.W. Ter., Can.	B19	66
hristiana, De., U.S.	B3	85
hristiana, Pa., U.S.	G9	115
hristiansburg, Va., U.S.	C2	123
hristian Sound, strt., Ak., U.S.	n22	79
hristiansted, V.I.U.S.	F15	64
hristina, stm., Alta., Can.	A5	68
hristina, stm., De., U.S.	B3	85
hristina, Lake, l., Mn., U.S.	D3	100
hristina Peak, mtn., Nv., U.S.	D6	105
hristmas, Fl., U.S.	D5	86
hristmas Island, dep., Oc.	H4	32
hristmas Lake, l., Or., U.S.	D6	114
hristopher, Il., U.S.	F4	90
hroma, stm., Russia	C22	24
hrzanów, Pol.	E19	8
hubbuck, Id., U.S.	G6	89
hugach Islands, is., Ak., U.S.	h16	79
hugach Mountains, mts., Ak., U.S.	g18	79
hūgoku-sanchi, mts., Japan	H5	30
hugwater, Wy., U.S.	E8	127
hugwater Creek, stm., Wy., U.S.	E8	127
hukai, Malay.	L7	34
hukchi Sea	C30	128
hula Vista, Ca., U.S.	F5	82
hulucanas, Peru	E2	54
humphon, Thai.	I5	34
hum Saeng, Thai.	G6	34
hunchi, Ec.	I3	58
h'unch'ŏn, S. Kor.	D12	26
hunchula, Al., U.S.	E1	78
h'ungju, S. Kor.	D12	26
hungking see Chongqing, China	F8	26
hungli, Tai.	K10	28
hungyang Shanmo, mts., Tai.	L10	28
huŏr Phnum Krâvanh, mts., Asia	H7	34
hupadera Mesa, mtn., N.M., U.S.	D3	108
hupaderos, Mex.	F8	62
huquicamata, Chile	A3	56
hur, Switz.	F16	10
hurch Hill, Tn., U.S.	C11	119
hurchill, Man., Can.	f9	70
hurchill, co., Nv., U.S.	D3	105
hurchill, stm., Can.	E13	66
hurchill, stm., Newf., Can.	h9	72
hurchill, Cape, c., Man., Can.	f9	70
hurchill, Mount, mtn., B.C., Can.	E6	69
hurchill Falls, wtfl, Newf., Can.	h8	72
hurchill Lake, l., Sask., Can.	m7	75
hurchill Lake, l., Me., U.S.	B3	96
hurch Point, La., U.S.	D3	95
hurch Rock, N.M., U.S.	B1	108
hurohton, Md., U.S.	C4	97
hurchville, N.Y., U.S.	B3	109
huru, India	F6	38
hurubusco, In., U.S.	B7	91
huruguara, Ven.	B8	58
huska Mountains, mts., Az., U.S.	A6	80
hutag, Mong.	B7	26
huxian, China	C7	28
huxiong, China	B6	34
hužir, Russia	G15	24
anjur, Indon.	G4	32
becue, Az., U.S.	C5	80
binong, Indon.	m13	33a
bola, co., N.M., U.S.	C1	108
bolo Creek, stm., Tx., U.S.	h7	120
cero, Il., U.S.	B6	90
cero, In., U.S.	D5	91
echanów, Pol.	C20	8
ego de Avila, Cuba	D8	64
empozuelos, Spain	E8	12
Ciénaga, Col.	B5	58
Cienfuegos, Cuba	C7	64
Cieszyn, Pol.	F18	8
Cieza, Spain	G10	12
Cifuentes, Spain	E9	12
Cikampek, Indon.	m13	33a
Cilacap, Indon.	m14	33a
Cilleruelo de Bezana, Spain	C8	12
Cimarron, Ks., U.S.	E3	93
Cimarron, N.M., U.S.	A5	108
Cimarron, co., Ok., U.S.	e8	113
Cimkent, Kaz.	I11	22
Çınarcık, Tur.	I13	16
Cincinnati, Oh., U.S.	C1	112
Çine, Tur.	L12	16
Ciney, Bel.	E5	8
Cinnaminson, N.J., U.S.	D3	107
Cipa, stm., Russia	F17	24
Cipolletti, Arg.	D3	56
Circle, Ak., U.S.	B11	79
Circle, Mt., U.S.	C11	103
Circle Pines, Mn., U.S.	m12	100
Circleville, Oh., U.S.	C3	112
Cirebon, Indon.	m14	32
Cirencester, Eng., U.K.	J11	7
Ciriè, Italy	D2	14
Cirò Marina, Italy	J12	14
Cisco, Tx., U.S.	C3	120
Cispus, stm., Wa., U.S.	C4	124
Cissna Park, Il., U.S.	C6	90
Cistierna, Spain	C6	12
Čita, Russia	G16	24
Citra, Fl., U.S.	C4	86
Citronelle, Al., U.S.	D1	78
Citrus, co., Fl., U.S.	D4	86
Città di Castello, Italy	F7	14
City of Refuge National Historical Park, Hi., U.S.	D5	88
City View, S.C., U.S.	B3	117
Ciudad, Mex.	F7	62
Ciudad Acuña, Mex.	C9	62
Ciudad Altamirano, Mex.	H9	62
Ciudad Bolívar, Ven.	C11	58
Ciudad Bolivia, Ven.	C7	58
Ciudad Camargo, Mex.	D7	62
Ciudad Chetumal, Mex.	H15	62
Ciudad del Carmen, Mex.	H14	62
Ciudad del Maíz, Mex.	F10	62
Ciudad de México (Mexico City), Mex.	H10	62
Ciudad de Nutrias, Ven.	C8	58
Ciudad de Valles, Mex.	G10	62
Ciudadela, Spain	E15	12
Ciudad Guayana, Ven.	C11	58
Ciudad Guzmán, Mex.	H8	62
Ciudad Hidalgo, Mex.	H9	62
Ciudad Ixtepec, Mex.	I12	62
Ciudad Jiménez, Mex.	D7	62
Ciudad Juárez, Mex.	B6	62
Ciudad Madero, Mex.	F11	62
Ciudad Mante, Mex.	F10	62
Ciudad Melchor Múzquiz, Mex.	D9	62
Ciudad Obregón, Mex.	D5	62
Ciudad Ojeda (Lagunillas), Ven.	B7	58
Ciudad Piar, Ven.	D11	58
Ciudad Real, Spain	G8	12
Ciudad Rodrigo, Spain	E5	12
Ciudad Victoria, Mex.	F10	62
Civita Castellana, Italy	G7	14
Civitanova Marche, Italy	F8	14
Civitavecchia, Italy	G6	14
Civray, Fr.	F7	10
C.J. Strike Reservoir, res., Id., U.S.	G3	89
Clackamas, Or., U.S.	h12	114
Clackamas, co., Or., U.S.	B4	114
Clacton-on-Sea, Eng., U.K.	J14	7
Claflin, Ks., U.S.	D5	93
Claiborne, co., La., U.S.	B2	95
Claiborne, co., Ms., U.S.	D3	101
Claiborne, co., Tn., U.S.	C10	119
Claiborne, Lake, res., La., U.S.	B3	95
Clair, N.B., Can.	B1	71
Claire, Lake, l., Alta., Can.	f8	68
Clair Engle Lake, res., Ca., U.S.	B2	82
Clairton, Pa., U.S.	F2	115
Clallam, co., Wa., U.S.	B1	124
Clallam Bay, Wa., U.S.	A1	124
Clamecy, Fr.	E10	10
Clam Lake, l., Wi., U.S.	C1	126
Clan Alpine Mountains, mts., Nv., U.S.	D4	105
Clanton, Al., U.S.	C3	78
Clanwilliam, S. Afr.	H3	44
Clara City, Mn., U.S.	F3	100
Clara Peak, mtn., Az., U.S.	C2	80
Clare, Mi., U.S.	E6	99
Clare, co., Mi., U.S.	E6	99
Claremont, Ca., U.S.	m13	82
Claremont, N.H., U.S.	D2	106
Claremont, N.C., U.S.	B1	110
Claremont, mtn., Ca., U.S.	C3	82
Claremore, Ok., U.S.	A6	113
Claremorris, Ire.	H3	7
Clarence, Ia., U.S.	C6	92
Clarence, Mo., U.S.	B5	102
Clarence Strait, strt., Ak., U.S.	n23	79
Clarendon, Ar., U.S.	C4	81
Clarendon, Tx., U.S.	B2	120
Clarendon, co., S.C., U.S.	D7	117
Clarendon, stm., Vt., U.S.	E2	122
Clarendon Hills, Il., U.S.	k9	90
Clarenville, Newf., Can.	D4	72
Claresholm, Alta., Can.	D4	68
Claridge, Pa., U.S.	F2	115
Clarinda, Ia., U.S.	D2	92
Clarines, Ven.	C10	58
Clarion, Ia., U.S.	B4	92
Clarion, Pa., U.S.	D3	115
Clarion, co., Pa., U.S.	D3	115
Clarion, stm., Pa., U.S.	D3	115
Clarión, Isla, i., Mex.	H2	62
Clarissa, Mn., U.S.	D4	100
Clark, N.J., U.S.	B4	107
Clark, S.D., U.S.	C8	118
Clark, co., Ar., U.S.	C2	81
Clark, co., Id., U.S.	E6	89
Clark, co., Il., U.S.	D6	90
Clark, co., In., U.S.	H6	91
Clark, co., Ks., U.S.	E4	93
Clark, co., Ky., U.S.	C5	94
Clark, co., Mo., U.S.	A6	102
Clark, co., Nv., U.S.	G6	105
Clark, co., Oh., U.S.	C2	112
Clark, co., S.D., U.S.	C8	118
Clark, co., Wa., U.S.	D3	124
Clark, co., Wi., U.S.	D3	126
Clark, Lake, l., Ak., U.S.	C9	79
Clark, Point, c., Ont., Can.	C3	73
Clarkdale, Az., U.S.	C3	80
Clarkdale, Ga., U.S.	h7	87
Clarke, co., Al., U.S.	D2	78
Clarke, co., Ga., U.S.	C3	87
Clarke, co., Ia., U.S.	D4	92
Clarke, co., Ms., U.S.	C5	101
Clarke, co., Va., U.S.	A4	123
Clarkesville, Ga., U.S.	B3	87
Clarkfield, Mn., U.S.	F3	100
Clark Fork, stm., U.S.	C1	103
Clarks, La., U.S.	B3	95
Clarks, stm., Ky., U.S.	f9	94
Clarksburg, Md., U.S.	B3	97
Clarksburg, W.V., U.S.	B4	125
Clarksdale, Ms., U.S.	A3	101
Clarks Grove, Mn., U.S.	G5	100
Clark's Harbour, N.S., Can.	F4	71
Clarks Hill, In., U.S.	D4	91
Clarkson, Ky., U.S.	C3	94
Clarkson, Ne., U.S.	C8	104
Clarks Summit, Pa., U.S.	m18	115
Clarkston, Ga., U.S.	h8	87
Clarkston, Mi., U.S.	F7	99
Clarkston, Ut., U.S.	B3	121
Clarkston, Wa., U.S.	C8	124
Clarksville, Ar., U.S.	B2	81
Clarksville, De., U.S.	F5	85
Clarksville, In., U.S.	H6	91
Clarksville, Ia., U.S.	B5	92
Clarksville, Tn., U.S.	A4	119
Clarksville, Tx., U.S.	C5	120
Clarksville, Va., U.S.	D4	123
Clarkton, Mo., U.S.	E8	102
Clarkton, N.C., U.S.	C4	110
Clatskanie, Or., U.S.	A3	114
Clatsop, co., Or., U.S.	A3	114
Claude, Tx., U.S.	B2	120
Clausthal-Zellerfeld, Ger.	D10	8
Clawson, Mi., U.S.	o15	99
Claxton, Ga., U.S.	D5	87
Clay, Ky., U.S.	C2	94
Clay, co., Al., U.S.	B4	78
Clay, co., Ar., U.S.	A5	81
Clay, co., Fl., U.S.	B5	86
Clay, co., Ga., U.S.	E2	87
Clay, co., Il., U.S.	E5	90
Clay, co., In., U.S.	F3	91
Clay, co., Ia., U.S.	A2	92
Clay, co., Ks., U.S.	C6	93
Clay, co., Ky., U.S.	C6	94
Clay, co., Mn., U.S.	D2	100
Clay, co., Ms., U.S.	B5	101
Clay, co., Mo., U.S.	B3	102
Clay, co., Ne., U.S.	D7	104
Clay, co., N.C., U.S.	f9	110
Clay, co., S.D., U.S.	E8	118
Clay, co., Tn., U.S.	C8	119
Clay, co., Tx., U.S.	C3	120
Clay, co., W.V., U.S.	C3	125
Clay Center, Ks., U.S.	C6	93
Clay Center, Ne., U.S.	D7	104
Clay City, Il., U.S.	E5	90
Clay City, In., U.S.	F3	91
Clay City, Ky., U.S.	C6	94
Clay Creek, stm., S.D., U.S.	D8	118
Claymont, De., U.S.	A4	85
Clayoquot Sound, strt., B.C., Can.	E4	69
Claypool, Az., U.S.	D5	80
Claysburg, Pa., U.S.	F5	115
Claysville, Pa., U.S.	F1	115
Clayton, Al., U.S.	D4	78
Clayton, De., U.S.	C3	85
Clayton, Ga., U.S.	B3	87
Clayton, In., U.S.	E4	91
Clayton, La., U.S.	C4	95
Clayton, Mo., U.S.	f13	102
Clayton, N.J., U.S.	D2	107
Clayton, N.M., U.S.	A6	108
Clayton, N.Y., U.S.	A4	109
Clayton, N.C., U.S.	B4	110
Clayton, Ok., U.S.	C6	113
Clayton, co., Ga., U.S.	C2	87
Clayton, co., Ia., U.S.	B6	92
Claytor Lake, res., Va., U.S.	C2	123
Clear, stm., R.I., U.S.	B2	116
Clear Boggy Creek, stm., Ok., U.S.	C5	113
Clear Creek, co., Co., U.S.	B5	83
Clear Creek, stm., Tn., U.S.	C9	119
Clear Creek, stm., Wy., U.S.	B6	127
Cleare, Cape, c., Ak., U.S.	D10	79
Clearfield, Ky., U.S.	B6	94
Clearfield, Pa., U.S.	D5	115
Clearfield, Ut., U.S.	B3	121
Clearfield, co., Pa., U.S.	D5	115
Clear Fork, stm., W.V., U.S.	D3	125
Clear Fork, stm., W.V., U.S.	n13	125
Clearlake, Ca., U.S.	C2	82
Clear Lake, Ia., U.S.	A4	92
Clear Lake, S.D., U.S.	C9	118
Clearlake, Wa., U.S.	A3	124
Clear Lake, Wi., U.S.	C1	126
Clear Lake, l., Ia., U.S.	A4	92
Clear Lake, l., Ut., U.S.	D3	121
Clear Lake, res., Ca., U.S.	C2	82
Clear Lake Reservoir, res., Ca., U.S.	B3	82
Clear Lake Shores, Tx., U.S.	r15	120
Clear Stream, stm., N.H., U.S.	g7	106
Clearwater, B.C., Can.	D7	69
Clearwater, Fl., U.S.	E4	86
Clearwater, Ks., U.S.	E6	93
Clearwater, S.C., U.S.	E4	117
Clearwater, co., Id., U.S.	C3	89
Clearwater, co., Mn., U.S.	C3	100
Clearwater, stm., Can.	A5	68
Clearwater, stm., Id., U.S.	C2	89
Clearwater, stm., Mn., U.S.	C3	100
Clearwater Lake, res., Mo., U.S.	D7	102
Clearwater Mountains, mts., Id., U.S.	C2	89
Cleburne, Tx., U.S.	C4	120
Cleburne, co., Al., U.S.	B4	78
Cleburne, co., Ar., U.S.	B3	81
Cle Elum, Wa., U.S.	B5	124
Cle Elum, stm., Wa., U.S.	B4	124
Cle Elum Lake, res., Wa., U.S.	B4	124
Clementon, N.J., U.S.	D3	107
Clemmons, N.C., U.S.	A2	110
Clemson, S.C., U.S.	B2	117
Clendenin, W.V., U.S.	C3	125
Clendening Lake, res., Oh., U.S.	B4	112
Cleona, Pa., U.S.	F9	115
Clermont, Que., Can.	B7	74
Clermont, Fr.	C9	10
Clermont, Fl., U.S.	D5	86
Clermont, co., Oh., U.S.	C1	112
Clermont-Ferrand, Fr.	G10	10
Cles, Italy	C6	14
Cleveland, Al., U.S.	A3	78
Cleveland, Ga., U.S.	B3	87
Cleveland, Mn., U.S.	F5	100
Cleveland, Ms., U.S.	B3	101
Cleveland, N.C., U.S.	B2	110
Cleveland, Oh., U.S.	A4	112
Cleveland, Ok., U.S.	A5	113
Cleveland, Tn., U.S.	D9	119
Cleveland, Tx., U.S.	D5	120
Cleveland, Wi., U.S.	k10	126
Cleveland, co., Ar., U.S.	D3	81
Cleveland, co., N.C., U.S.	B1	110
Cleveland, co., Ok., U.S.	B4	113
Cleveland, Mount, mtn., Mt., U.S.	B3	103
Cleveland Heights, Oh., U.S.	A4	112
Cleves, Oh., U.S.	o12	112
Clewiston, Fl., U.S.	F6	86
Clifden, Ire.	H2	7
Cliff Island, i., Me., U.S.	g7	96
Clifford, Ont., Can.	D4	73
Cliffside, N.C., U.S.	B1	110
Cliffside Park, N.J., U.S.	h9	107
Clifton, Az., U.S.	D6	80
Clifton, Co., U.S.	B2	83
Clifton, Il., U.S.	C6	90
Clifton, N.J., U.S.	B4	107
Clifton, S.C., U.S.	B4	117
Clifton, Tn., U.S.	B4	119
Clifton, Tx., U.S.	D4	120
Clifton Forge, Va., U.S.	C3	123
Clifton Knolls, N.Y., U.S.	C7	109
Clifton Springs, N.Y., U.S.	C3	109
Clinch, co., Ga., U.S.	F4	87
Clinch, stm., U.S.	D9	119
Clinchco, Va., U.S.	e9	123
Clinch Mountain, mtn., U.S.	C10	119
Clingmans Dome, mtn., U.S.	D10	119
Clinton, B.C., Can.	D7	69
Clinton, Ont., Can.	D3	73
Clinton, Ar., U.S.	B3	81
Clinton, Ct., U.S.	D5	84
Clinton, Il., U.S.	C5	90
Clinton, In., U.S.	E3	91
Clinton, Ia., U.S.	C7	92
Clinton, Ky., U.S.	f9	94
Clinton, La., U.S.	D4	95
Clinton, Me., U.S.	D3	96
Clinton, Md., U.S.	C4	97
Clinton, Ma., U.S.	B4	98
Clinton, Mi., U.S.	F7	99
Clinton, Ms., U.S.	C3	101
Clinton, Mo., U.S.	C4	102
Clinton, N.Y., U.S.	B5	109
Clinton, N.C., U.S.	C4	110
Clinton, Ok., U.S.	B3	113
Clinton, S.C., U.S.	C4	117
Clinton, Tn., U.S.	C9	119
Clinton, Ut., U.S.	B3	121
Clinton, Wa., U.S.	B3	124
Clinton, Wi., U.S.	F5	126
Clinton, co., Il., U.S.	E4	90
Clinton, co., In., U.S.	D4	91
Clinton, co., Ia., U.S.	C7	92
Clinton, co., Ky., U.S.	D4	94
Clinton, co., Mi., U.S.	F6	99
Clinton, co., Mo., U.S.	B3	102
Clinton, co., N.Y., U.S.	f11	109
Clinton, co., Oh., U.S.	C2	112
Clinton, co., Pa., U.S.	D6	115
Clinton, Lake, res., Il., U.S.	C5	90
Clinton-Colden Lake, l., N.W. Ter., Can.	D11	66
Clinton Lake, res., Ks., U.S.	m15	93
Clinton Reservoir, res., N.J., U.S.	A4	107
Clintonville, Wi., U.S.	D5	126
Clintwood, Va., U.S.	e9	123
Clio, Al., U.S.	D4	78
Clio, Mi., U.S.	E7	99
Clio, S.C., U.S.	B8	117
Clive, Ia., U.S.	e8	92
Clogher Head, c., Ire.	H6	7
Cloncurry, Austl.	D8	50
Clonmel, Ire.	I5	7
Cloppenburg, Ger.	C8	8
Cloquet, Mn., U.S.	D6	100
Cloquet, stm., Mn., U.S.	C6	100
Closter, N.J., U.S.	B5	107
Clothier, W.V., U.S.	n12	125
Cloud, co., Ks., U.S.	C6	93
Cloudcroft, N.M., U.S.	E4	108
Cloud Peak, mtn., Wy., U.S.	B5	127
Clover, S.C., U.S.	A5	117
Cloverdale, Al., U.S.	A2	78
Cloverdale, Ca., U.S.	C2	82
Cloverdale, In., U.S.	E4	91
Cloverport, Ky., U.S.	C3	94
Clovis, Ca., U.S.	D4	82
Clovis, N.M., U.S.	C6	108
Cluj-Napoca, Rom.	C7	16
Cluny, Fr.	F11	10
Cluses, Fr.	F13	10
Clusone, Italy	D4	14
Clute, Tx., U.S.	r14	120
Clutha, stm., N.Z.	G2	52
Clyde, N.W. Ter., Can.	B19	66
Clyde, Ks., U.S.	C6	93
Clyde, N.Y., U.S.	B4	109
Clyde, N.C., U.S.	f10	110
Clyde, Oh., U.S.	A3	112
Clyde, Tx., U.S.	C3	120
Clyde, stm., Scot., U.K.	F9	7
Clyde, Firth of, est., Scot., U.K.	F7	7
Clymer, Pa., U.S.	E3	115
Coachella, Ca., U.S.	F5	82
Coachella Canal, Ca., U.S.	F6	82
Coacoyole, Mex.	E6	62
Coahoma, Tx., U.S.	C2	120
Coahoma, co., Ms., U.S.	A3	101
Coal, co., Ok., U.S.	C5	113
Coal, stm., W.V., U.S.	C3	125
Coal Branch, N.B., Can.	C4	71
Coal City, Il., U.S.	B5	90
Coalcomán de Matamoros, Mex.	H8	62
Coal Creek, stm., Ok., U.S.	B6	113
Coaldale, Alta., Can.	E4	68
Coal Fork, W.V., U.S.	C3	125
Coal Fork, stm., W.V., U.S.	m13	125
Coalgate, Ok., U.S.	C5	113
Coal Grove, Oh., U.S.	D3	112
Coal Hill, Ar., U.S.	B2	81
Coalhurst, Alta., Can.	E4	68
Coalinga, Ca., U.S.	D3	82
Coalmont, Tn., U.S.	D8	119
Coalville, Ut., U.S.	C4	121
Coalwood, W.V., U.S.	D3	125
Coari, Braz.	D6	54
Coasters Harbor Island, i., R.I., U.S.	E5	116
Coast Mountains, mts., N.A.	E6	66
Coast Ranges, mts., U.S.	C2	76
Coatepeque, Guat.	G2	64
Coatesville, Pa., U.S.	G10	115
Coaticook, Que., Can.	D6	74
Coats, N.C., U.S.	B4	110
Coats Island, i., N.W. Ter., Can.	D16	66
Coats Land, reg., Ant.	B10	47
Coatzacoalcos, Mex.	H12	62
Cobalt, Ont., Can.	p19	73
Cobb, co., Ga., U.S.	C2	87
Cobb, stm., Mn., U.S.	G5	100
Cobble Mountain Reservoir, res., Ma., U.S.	B2	98
Cobbosseecontee Lake, l., Me., U.S.	D3	96
Cobden, Ont., Can.	B8	73
Cobden, Il., U.S.	F4	90
Cobequid Mountains, mts., N.S., Can.	D5	71
Cobham, stm., Can.	C4	70
Cobija, Bol.	F5	54
Cobleskill, N.Y., U.S.	C6	109
Cobourg, Ont., Can.	D6	73
Cóbuè, Moz.	D6	44
Cobun Creek, stm., W.V., U.S.	h11	125
Coburg, Ger.	E10	8
Coburg, Or., U.S.	C3	114
Coburg Island, i., N.W. Ter., Can.	A17	66
Cochabamba, Bol.	G5	54
Cocheco, stm., N.H., U.S.	D5	106
Cochin, India	H4	37
Cochise, co., Az., U.S.	F5	80
Cochise Head, mtn., Az., U.S.	E6	80
Cochiti Indian Reservation, N.M., U.S.	h8	108
Cochiti Reservoir, res., N.M., U.S.	B3	108
Cochituate, Ma., U.S.	g10	98
Cochituate, Lake, l., Ma., U.S.	g10	98
Cochran, Ga., U.S.	D3	87
Cochran, co., Tx., U.S.	C1	120
Cochrane, Alta., Can.	D3	68
Cochrane, Ont., Can.	o19	73
Cochranton, Pa., U.S.	C1	115
Cocke, co., Tn., U.S.	D10	119
Cockeysville, Md., U.S.	B4	97
Cockrell Hill, Tx., U.S.	n10	120
Coco, stm., N.A.	G6	64
Coco, Isla del, i., C.R.	B1	54
Cocoa, Fl., U.S.	D6	86
Cocoa Beach, Fl., U.S.	D6	86
Coco Channel, strt., Asia	H2	34
Coco Islands, is., Burma	G2	34
Coconino, co., Az., U.S.	B3	80
Cocopah Indian Reservation, Az., U.S.	E1	80
Côcos, Braz.	C6	57
Cocula, Mex.	G8	62
Cod, Cape, c., Ma., U.S.	C7	98
Codajás, Braz.	D6	54
Coden, Al., U.S.	E1	78
Codigoro, Italy	E7	14
Codington, co., S.D., U.S.	C8	118
Codogno, Italy	D4	14
Codroipo, Italy	D7	14
Cody, Wy., U.S.	B3	127
Coeburn, Va., U.S.	f9	123
Coen, Austl.	B8	50
Coetivy Island, i., Sey.	C11	44
Coeur d'Alene, Id., U.S.	B2	89
Coeur d'Alene, stm., Id., U.S.	B2	89
Coeur d'Alene Indian Reservation, Id., U.S.	B2	89
Coeur d'Alene Lake, res., Id., U.S.	B2	89
Coeur d'Alene Mountains, mts., Id., U.S.	B2	89
Coffee, co., Al., U.S.	D3	78
Coffee, co., Ga., U.S.	E4	87
Coffee, co., Tn., U.S.	B5	119
Coffeeville, Ms., U.S.	B4	101
Coffey, co., Ks., U.S.	D8	93
Coffeyville, Ks., U.S.	E8	93
Coffs Harbour, Austl.	F10	50
Coggon, Ia., U.S.	B6	92
Cognac, Fr.	G6	10
Cohansey, stm., N.J., U.S.	E2	107
Cohasset, Ma., U.S.	B6	98
Cohasset, Mn., U.S.	C5	100
Cohocton, stm., N.Y., U.S.	C3	109
Cohoes, N.Y., U.S.	C7	109
Cohoon, Lake, res., Va., U.S.	k14	123
Cohutta Mountain, mtn., Ga., U.S.	B2	87
Coiba, Isla de, i., Pan.	K7	64
Coimbatore, India	G4	37
Coimbra, Braz.	F7	57
Coimbra, Port.	E3	12
Çoín, Spain	I7	12
Čojbalsan, Mong.	B9	26
Cokato, Mn., U.S.	E4	100
Coke, co., Tx., U.S.	D2	120

Name — Map Ref — Page

Cokeville, Wy., U.S. D2 127
Čokurdach, Russia C23 24
Colatina, Braz. E8 57
Colbert, Ok., U.S. D5 113
Colbert, co., Al., U.S. A2 78
Colborne, Ont., Can. C7 73
Colby, Ks., U.S. C2 93
Colby, Wi., U.S. D3 126
Colchester, Eng., U.K. J13 7
Colchester, Ct., U.S. C6 84
Colchester, Il., U.S. C3 90
Colcord, Ok., U.S. A7 113
Cold, stm., N.H., U.S. C4 106
Cold, stm., N.H., U.S. D2 106
Cold Bay, Ak., U.S. E7 79
Cold Lake, Alta., Can. B5 68
Cold Spring, Ky., U.S. A5 94
Cold Spring, Mn., U.S. E4 100
Coldwater, Ont., Can. C5 73
Coldwater, Ks., U.S. E4 93
Coldwater, Mi., U.S. G5 99
Coldwater, Ms., U.S. A4 101
Coldwater, Oh., U.S. B1 112
Coldwater, stm., Ms., U.S. A3 101
Coldwater Creek, stm., U.S. e9 113
Cole, co., Mo., U.S. C5 102
Colebrook, N.H., U.S. g7 106
Colebrook River Lake, res., Ct., U.S. A3 84
Cole Camp, Mo., U.S. C4 102
Coleen, stm., Ak., U.S. B11 79
Coleman, Mi., U.S. E6 99
Coleman, Tx., U.S. D3 120
Coleman, Wi., U.S. C5 126
Coleman, co., Tx., U.S. D3 120
Coleraine, N. Ire., U.K. F6 7
Coleraine, Mn., U.S. C5 100
Coles, co., Il., U.S. D5 90
Colesberg, S. Afr. H5 44
Colfax, Ca., U.S. C3 82
Colfax, Il., U.S. C5 90
Colfax, In., U.S. D4 91
Colfax, Ia., U.S. C4 92
Colfax, La., U.S. C3 95
Colfax, Wa., U.S. C8 124
Colfax, Wi., U.S. D2 126
Colfax, co., Ne., U.S. C8 104
Colfax, co., N.M., U.S. A5 108
Colhué Huapi, Lago, l., Arg. F3 56
Colima, Mex. H8 62
Colima, Nevado de, mtn., Mex. H8 62
Colinas, Braz. E10 54
Coll, i., Scot., U.K. E6 7
College, Ak., U.S. B10 79
Collegedale, Tn., U.S. h11 119
College Park, Ga., U.S. C2 87
College Park, Md., U.S. C4 97
College Place, Wa., U.S. C7 124
College Station, Ar., U.S. C3 81
College Station, Tx., U.S. D4 120
Collegeville, In., U.S. C3 91
Collegeville, Pa., U.S. F11 115
Colleton, co., S.C., U.S. F6 117
Collier, co., Fl., U.S. F5 86
Collier Bay, b., Austl. C4 50
Colliers, W.V., U.S. f8 125
Collierville, Tn., U.S. B2 119
Collin, co., Tx., U.S. C4 120
Collingdale, Pa., U.S. p20 115
Collingswood, N.J., U.S. D2 107
Collingsworth, co., Tx., U.S. B2 120
Collingwood, Ont., Can. C4 73
Collins, Ms., U.S. D4 101
Collins Park, De., U.S. B3 85
Collinsville, Al., U.S. A4 78
Collinsville, Ct., U.S. B4 84
Collinsville, Il., U.S. E4 90
Collinsville, Ms., U.S. C5 101
Collinsville, Ok., U.S. A6 113
Collinsville, Va., U.S. D3 123
Collinwood, Tn., U.S. B4 119
Collooney, Ire. G4 7
Colmar, Fr. D14 10
Colmar Manor, Md., U.S. f9 97
Colmenar, Spain I7 12
Colmenar de Oreja, Spain E8 12
Colmenar Viejo, Spain E8 12
Colo, Ia., U.S. B4 92
Cologne see Köln, Ger. E6 8
Coloma, Mi., U.S. F4 99
Colomb-Béchar see Béchar, Alg. B5 42
Colombia, ctry., S.A. C4 54
Colombo, Sri L. I5 37
Colón, Cuba C7 64
Colón, Pan. J8 64
Colon, Mi., U.S. G5 99
Colon, Archipiélago de (Galapagos Islands), is., Ec. m15 58a
Colonia Dora, Arg. B4 56
Colonia Las Heras, Arg. F3 56
Colonial Beach, Va., U.S. B6 123
Colonial Heights, Tn., U.S. C11 119
Colonial Heights, Va., U.S. C5 123
Colonial National Historical Park, Va., U.S. C6 123
Colonia Vicente Guerrero, Mex. B1 62
Colonie, N.Y., U.S. C7 109
Coloradas, Lomas, hills, Arg. E3 56
Colorado, co., Tx., U.S. E4 120
Colorado, state, U.S. B5 83
Colorado, stm., Arg. D4 56
Colorado, stm., N.A. E4 76
Colorado, stm., Tx., U.S. D3 120
Colorado City, Az., U.S. A3 80
Colorado City, Co., U.S. D6 83
Colorado City, Tx., U.S. C2 120
Colorado City, Lake, res., Tx., U.S. C2 120
Colorado National Monument, Co., U.S. B2 83
Colorado River Aqueduct, Ca., U.S. F6 82
Colorado River Indian Reservation, U.S. D1 80
Colorado Springs, Co., U.S. C6 83
Colotlán, Mex. F8 62
Colquitt, Ga., U.S. E2 87
Colquitt, co., Ga., U.S. E3 87
Colstrip, Mt., U.S. E10 103
Colton, S.D., U.S. D9 118
Coltons Point, Md., U.S. D4 97
Columbia, Al., U.S. D4 78
Columbia, Il., U.S. E3 90
Columbia, Ky., U.S. C4 94
Columbia, Md., U.S. B4 97
Columbia, Ms., U.S. D4 101
Columbia, Mo., U.S. C5 102
Columbia, N.C., U.S. B6 110
Columbia, Pa., U.S. F9 115
Columbia, S.C., U.S. C5 117
Columbia, Tn., U.S. B4 119
Columbia, co., Ar., U.S. D2 81
Columbia, co., Fl., U.S. B4 86
Columbia, co., Ga., U.S. C4 87
Columbia, co., N.Y., U.S. C7 109
Columbia, co., Or., U.S. B3 114
Columbia, co., Pa., U.S. D9 115
Columbia, co., Wa., U.S. C7 124
Columbia, co., Wi., U.S. E4 126
Columbia, stm., N.A. G8 66
Columbia, Mount, mtn., Can. C2 68
Columbia City, In., U.S. B7 91
Columbia City, Or., U.S. B4 114
Columbia Falls, Mt., U.S. B2 103
Columbia Heights, Mn., U.S. m12 100
Columbia Lake, res., Ct., U.S. C6 84
Columbia Mountains, mts., B.C., Can. C7 69
Columbiana, Al., U.S. B3 78
Columbiana, Oh., U.S. B5 112
Columbiana, co., Oh., U.S. B5 112
Columbiaville, Mi., U.S. E7 99
Columbus, Ga., U.S. D2 87
Columbus, In., U.S. F6 91
Columbus, Ks., U.S. E9 93
Columbus, Ms., U.S. B5 101
Columbus, Mt., U.S. E7 103
Columbus, Ne., U.S. C8 104
Columbus, N.M., U.S. F2 108
Columbus, N.C., U.S. f10 110
Columbus, Oh., U.S. C2 112
Columbus, Tx., U.S. E4 120
Columbus, Wi., U.S. E4 126
Columbus, co., N.C., U.S. C4 110
Columbus Air Force Base, mil., Ms., U.S. B5 101
Columbus Grove, Oh., U.S. B1 112
Columbus Junction, Ia., U.S. C6 92
Columbus Lake, res., Ms., U.S. B5 101
Colusa, Ca., U.S. C2 82
Colusa, co., Ca., U.S. C2 82
Colver, Pa., U.S. E4 115
Colville, Wa., U.S. A8 124
Colville, stm., Ak., U.S. B9 79
Colville, stm., Wa., U.S. A8 124
Colville Indian Reservation, Wa., U.S. A6 124
Colvos Passage, strt., Wa., U.S. f10 124
Colwich, Ks., U.S. E6 93
Colwood, B.C., Can. h12 69
Comacchio, Italy E7 14
Comal, co., Tx., U.S. E3 120
Comanche, Ok., U.S. C4 113
Comanche, Tx., U.S. D3 120
Comanche, co., Ks., U.S. E4 93
Comanche, co., Ok., U.S. C3 113
Comanche, co., Tx., U.S. D3 120
Comandante Fontana, Arg. B5 56
Comayagua, Hond. G4 64
Combahee, stm., S.C., U.S. F6 117
Combarbalá, Chile C2 56
Combeaufontaine, Fr. E12 10
Comber, Ont., Can. E2 73
Combermere Bay, b., Burma E2 34
Combined Locks, Wi., U.S. h9 126
Combourg, Fr. D5 10
Combs, Ky., U.S. C6 94
Comer, Ga., U.S. B3 87
Comfort, Tx., U.S. E3 120
Comilla, Bngl. I14 38
Comitán [de Domínguez], Mex. I13 62
Comite, stm., La., U.S. D4 95
Commentry, Fr. F9 10
Commerce, Ga., U.S. B3 87
Commerce, Ok., U.S. A7 113
Commerce, Tx., U.S. C5 120
Commerce City, Co., U.S. B6 83
Committee Bay, b., N.W. Ter., Can. C15 66
Common Fence Point, R.I., U.S. D6 116
Como, Italy D4 14
Como, Ms., U.S. A4 101
Como, Lago di, l., Italy C4 14
Comodoro Rivadavia, Arg. F3 56
Comorin, Cape, c., India H4 37
Comoros, ctry., Afr. D8 44
Comox, B.C., Can. E5 69
Compiègne, Fr. C9 10
Compton, Que., Can. D6 74
Compton, Ca., U.S. n12 82
Comstock, Mi., U.S. F5 99
Çon, stm., Viet. E8 34
Čona, stm., Russia E16 24
Conakry, Gui. G3 42
Conanicut Island, i., R.I., U.S. E5 116
Conanicut Point, c., R.I., U.S. E5 116
Concarneau, Fr. E3 10
Conceição do Araguaia, Braz. E9 54
Concepción, Arg. B3 56
Concepción, Bol. G6 54
Concepción, Chile D2 56
Concepción, Para. A5 56
Concepción, Laguna, l., Bol. G6 54
Concepción, Volcán, vol., Nic. I5 64
Concepción del Oro, Mex. E9 62
Concepción del Uruguay, Arg. C5 56
Conception, Point, c., Ca., U.S. E3 82
Conception Bay, b., Newf., Can. E5 72
Conception Bay South, Newf., Can. E5 72
Conchas Lake, res., N.M., U.S. B5 108
Conches, Fr. D7 10
Concho, co., Tx., U.S. D3 120
Concho, stm., Tx., U.S. D2 120
Conchos, stm., Mex. C7 62
Concord, Ca., U.S. h8 82
Concord, Ma., U.S. B5 98
Concord, Mi., U.S. F6 99
Concord, Mo., U.S. g13 102
Concord, N.H., U.S. D3 106
Concord, N.C., U.S. B2 110
Concord, stm., Ma., U.S. A5 98
Concordia, Arg. C5 56
Concordia, Mex. F6 62
Concordia, Ks., U.S. C6 93
Concordia, Mo., U.S. C4 102
Concordia, co., La., U.S. C4 95
Concrete, Wa., U.S. A4 124
Condé, Fr. D6 10
Condom, Fr. I7 10
Condon, Or., U.S. B6 114
Condoto, Col. E4 58
Conecuh, co., Al., U.S. D2 78
Conecuh, stm., U.S. D3 78
Conegliano, Italy D7 14
Conejos, co., Co., U.S. D4 83
Conejos, stm., Co., U.S. D4 83
Conejos Peak, mtn., Co., U.S. D4 83
Conemaugh, Pa., U.S. F4 115
Conemaugh River Lake, res., Pa., U.S. F3 115
Confolens, Fr. F7 10
Congamond Lakes, l., U.S. A4 84
Congaree, stm., S.C., U.S. D6 117
Congaree Swamp National Monument, S.C., U.S. D6 117
Congo, ctry., Afr. B2 44
Congo (Zaïre), stm., Afr. C2 44
Congress, Az., U.S. C3 80
Conimicut Point, c., R.I., U.S. D5 116
Conitaca, Mex. E6 62
Conklin, N.Y., U.S. C5 109
Conn, Lough, l., Ire. G3 7
Connaught, hist. reg., Ire. H3 7
Conneaut, Oh., U.S. A5 112
Conneaut Creek, stm., Oh., U.S. A5 112
Conneaut Lake, l., Pa., U.S. C1 115
Connecticut, state, U.S. C5 84
Connecticut, stm., U.S. C12 76
Connell, Wa., U.S. C7 124
Connellsville, Pa., U.S. F2 115
Connemara, reg., Ire. H3 7
Connersville, In., U.S. E7 91
Conover, N.C., U.S. B1 110
Conowingo, Md., U.S. A5 97
Conrad, Ia., U.S. B5 92
Conrad, Mt., U.S. B5 103
Conroe, Tx., U.S. D5 120
Conselheiro Lafaiete, Braz. F7 57
Conshohocken, Pa., U.S. F11 115
Con Son, is., Viet. J9 34
Consort, Alta., Can. C5 68
Constance, Lake see Bodensee, l., Eur. H9 8
Constanța, Rom. E12 16
Constantina, Spain H6 12
Constantine (Qacentina), Alg. A7 42
Constantine, Mi., U.S. G5 99
Constantine, Cape, c., Ak., U.S. D8 79
Consuegra, Spain F8 12
Contai, India J12 38
Contas, Rio de, stm., Braz. C9 57
Content Keys, is., Fl., U.S. H5 86
Continental, Oh., U.S. A1 112
Continental Peak, mtn., Wy., U.S. D4 127
Continental Reservoir, res., Co., U.S. D3 83
Contoocook, N.H., U.S. D3 106
Contoocook, stm., N.H., U.S. D3 106
Contra Costa, co., Ca., U.S. D3 82
Contrecoeur, Que., Can. D4 74
Contres, Fr. E8 10
Contwoyto Lake, l., N.W. Ter., Can. C10 66
Convención, Col. C6 58
Conversano, Italy I12 14
Converse, In., U.S. C6 91
Converse, S.C., U.S. B4 117
Converse, co., Wy., U.S. C7 127
Convoy, Oh., U.S. B1 112
Conway, Ar., U.S. B3 81
Conway, Fl., U.S. D5 86
Conway, Mo., U.S. D5 102
Conway, N.H., U.S. C4 106
Conway, N.C., U.S. A5 110
Conway, Pa., U.S. E1 115
Conway, S.C., U.S. D9 117
Conway, co., Ar., U.S. B3 81
Conway, Lake, res., Ar., U.S. B3 81
Conway Lake, l., N.H., U.S. C4 106
Conway Springs, Ks., U.S. E6 93
Conyers, Ga., U.S. C2 87
Cooch Behār, India G13 38
Cook, Mn., U.S. C6 100
Cook, co., Ga., U.S. E3 87
Cook, co., Il., U.S. B6 90
Cook, co., Mn., U.S. k9 100
Cook, Cape, c., B.C., Can. D4 69
Cook, Mount, mtn., N.Z. E3 52
Cooke, co., Tx., U.S. C4 120
Cookes Peak, mtn., N.M., U.S. E2 108
Cookeville, Tn., U.S. C8 119
Cook Inlet, b., Ak., U.S. D9 79
Cook Islands, dep., Oc. H2 2
Cook Point, c., Md., U.S. C5 97
Cookshire, Que., Can. D6 74
Cookson, Ok., U.S. B7 113
Cookstown, N. Ire., U.K. G6 7
Cook Strait, strt., N.Z. D5 52
Cooktown, Austl. C9 50
Cooleemee, N.C., U.S. B2 110
Coolgardie, Austl. F4 50
Coolidge, Az., U.S. E4 80
Coolidge, Ga., U.S. E3 87
Cooma, Austl. G9 50
Coonoor, India G4 37
Coon Rapids, Ia., U.S. C3 92
Coon Rapids, Mn., U.S. E5 100
Coon Valley, Wi., U.S. E2 126
Cooper, Tx., U.S. C5 120
Cooper, co., Mo., U.S. C5 102
Cooper, stm., S.C., U.S. F8 117
Cooper Mountain, mtn., Ak., U.S. g17 79
Coopersburg, Pa., U.S. F11 115
Cooperstown, N.Y., U.S. C6 109
Cooperstown, N.D., U.S. B7 111
Coopersville, Mi., U.S. E5 99
Coos, co., N.H., U.S. A4 106
Coos, co., Or., U.S. D2 114
Coos, stm., Or., U.S. D2 114
Coosa, co., Al., U.S. C3 78
Coosa, stm., U.S. C3 78
Coosada, Al., U.S. C3 78
Coosawhatchie, stm., S.C., U.S. F5 117
Coos Bay, Or., U.S. D2 114
Copalis Beach, Wa., U.S. B1 124
Copan, Ok., U.S. A6 113
Copan Reservoir, res., Ok., U.S. A6 113
Copenhagen see København, Den. I9 6
Copiah, co., Ms., U.S. D3 101
Copiapó, Chile B2 56
Coplay, Pa., U.S. E10 115
Copparo, Italy E6 14
Copper, stm., Ak., U.S. C11 79
Copperas Cove, Tx., U.S. D4 120
Copper Butte, mtn., Wa., U.S. A7 124
Coppermine, N.W. Ter., Can. C9 66
Coppermine, stm., N.W. Ter., Can. C10 66
Copper Mountain, mtn., Wy., U.S. C5 127
Copper Mountains, mts., Az., U.S. E2 80
Coquille, Or., U.S. D2 114
Coquimbo, Chile B2 56
Coral Gables, Fl., U.S. G6 86
Coral Harbour, N.W. Ter., Can. D16 66
Coral Sea, Oc. B10 50
Coralville, Ia., U.S. C6 92
Coralville Lake, res., Ia., U.S. C5 92
Corantijn (Corentyne), stm., S.A. E14 58
Coraopolis, Pa., U.S. E1 115
Corato, Italy H11 14
Corbeil-Essonnes, Fr. D9 10
Corbigny, Fr. E10 10
Corbin, Ky., U.S. D5 94
Corcoran, Ca., U.S. D4 82
Corcoran, Mn., U.S. m11 100
Corcovado, Golfo, b., Chile E2 56
Corcovado, Volcán, vol., Chile E2 56
Corcubión, Spain C2 12
Cordele, Ga., U.S. E3 87
Cordell, Ok., U.S. B3 113
Cordell Hull Lake, res., Tn., U.S. C8 119
Cordes, Fr. H8 10
Córdoba, Arg. C4 56
Córdoba, Mex. H11 62
Córdoba, Spain H7 12
Cordova, Al., U.S. B2 78
Cordova, Ak., U.S. C10 79
Cordova, N.M., U.S. A4 108
Cordova, N.C., U.S. C3 110
Cordova Peak, mtn., Ak., U.S. C10 79
Corentyne (Corantijn), stm., S.A. E14 58
Corfu see Kérkira, Grc. J3 16
Coria, Spain F5 12
Coria del Río, Spain H5 12
Corigliano Calabro, Italy J11 14
Coringa Islets, is., Austl. C9 50
Corinna, Me., U.S. D3 96
Corinne, Ut., U.S. B3 121
Corinne Key, i., Fl., U.S. G6 86
Corinth, Ms., U.S. A5 101
Corinth, N.Y., U.S. B7 109
Corinth see Kórinthos, Grc. L6 16
Corinto, Braz. E6 57
Cork, Ire. J4 7
Corlay, Fr. D3 10
Corleone, Italy L8 14
Corleto Perticara, Italy I11 14
Çorlu, Tur. H11 16
Cormorant Lake, l., Man., Can. B1 70
Cornelia, Ga., U.S. B3 87
Cornélio Procópio, Braz. G3 57
Cornelius, N.C., U.S. B2 110
Cornelius, Or., U.S. g11 114
Cornell, Wi., U.S. C2 126
Corner Brook, Newf., Can. D3 72
Cornersville, Tn., U.S. B5 119
Cornfield Point, c., Ct., U.S. D6 84
Cornie Bayou, stm., U.S. D3 81
Corning, Ar., U.S. A5 81
Corning, Ca., U.S. C2 82
Corning, Ia., U.S. D3 92
Corning, N.Y., U.S. C3 109
Cornish, Me., U.S. E2 96
Corn Islands, is., Nic. H6 64
Corno Grande, mtn., Italy G8 14
Cornville, Az., U.S. C4 80
Cornwall, Ont., Can. B10 73
Cornwall, Pa., U.S. F9 115
Cornwallis Island, i., N.W. Ter., Can. A14 66
Cornwall on Hudson, N.Y., U.S. D6 109
Coro, Ven. B8 58
Corocoro, Bol. G5 54
Coroico, Bol. G5 54
Coromandel Coast, India F6 37
Coromandel Peninsula, pen., N.Z. B5 52
Corona, Ca., U.S. F5 82
Coronado, Ca., U.S. F5 82
Coronado National Memorial, Az., U.S. F5 80
Coronation, Alta., Can. C5 68
Coronation Gulf, b., N.W. Ter., Can. C10 66
Coronation Island, i., Ak., U.S. n22 79
Coronel Dorrego, Arg. D4 56
Coronel Fabriciano, Braz. E7 57
Coronel Pringles, Arg. D4 56
Coronel Suárez, Arg. D4 56
Coropuna, Nevado, mtn., Peru G4 54
Corpus Christi, Tx., U.S. F4 120
Corpus Christi Naval Air Station, mil., Tx., U.S. F4 120
Corral de Almaguer, Spain F8 12
Correctionville, Ia., U.S. B2 92
Correggio, Italy E5 14
Corrente, stm., Braz. B7 57
Corrib, Lough, l., Ire. H3 7
Corrientes, Arg. B5 56
Corrientes, Cabo, c., Col. E4 58
Corrientes, Cabo, c., Cuba D5 64
Corrientes, Cabo, c., Mex. G7 62
Corrigan, Tx., U.S. D5 120
Corriganville, Md., U.S. k13 97
Corry, Pa., U.S. C2 115
Corse (Corsica), i., Fr. m19 11
Corsica, S.D., U.S. D7 118
Corsica see Corse, i., Fr. m19 11
Corsicana, Tx., U.S. C4 120
Corson, co., S.D., U.S. B4 118
Corson Inlet, b., N.J., U.S. E3 107
Cortemilia, Italy E3 14
Cortez, Co., U.S. D2 83
Cortez, Fl., U.S. q10 86
Cortez Mountains, mts., Nv., U.S. C5 105
Cortina d'Ampezzo, Italy C7 14
Cortland, Il., U.S. B5 90
Cortland, N.Y., U.S. C4 109
Cortland, Oh., U.S. A5 112
Cortland, co., N.Y., U.S. C4 109
Çorum, Tur. G14 4
Corumbá, Braz. G7 54
Corumbá, stm., Braz. E4 57
Corunna, Mi., U.S. F6 99
Corvallis, Or., U.S. C3 114
Corydon, In., U.S. H5 91
Corydon, Ia., U.S. D4 92
Corydon, Ky., U.S. C2 94
Coryell, co., Tx., U.S. D4 120
Cosamaloapan [de Carpio], Mex. H12 62
Cosenza, Italy J11 14
Coshocton, Oh., U.S. B4 112
Coshocton, co., Oh., U.S. B4 112
Cosmoledo Group, is., Sey. C9 44
Cosmopolis, Wa., U.S. C2 124
Cosmos, Mn., U.S. F4 100
Cosne-sur-Loire, Fr. E9 10
Cossatot, stm., Ar., U.S. C1 81
Costa Mesa, Ca., U.S. n13 82
Costa Rica, Mex. C4 62
Costa Rica, ctry., N.A. I5 64
Costilla, co., Co., U.S. D5 83
Cotabato, Phil. D7 32
Coteau-Landing, Que., Can. D3 74
Cotentin, pen., Fr. C5 10
Cotonou, Benin G6 42
Cotopaxi, vol., Ec. H3 58
Cottage Grove, Mn., U.S. n13 100
Cottage Grove, Or., U.S. D3 114
Cottage Grove Reservoir, res., Or., U.S. D3 114
Cottam, Ont., Can. E2 73
Cottbus, Ger. D14 8
Cotter, Ar., U.S. A3 81
Cottiennes, Alpes (Alpi Cozie), mts., Eur. H13 10
Cottle, co., Tx., U.S. B2 120
Cottleville, Mo., U.S. f12 102
Cotton, co., Ok., U.S. C3 113
Cottondale, Al., U.S. B2 78
Cotton Plant, Ar., U.S. B4 81
Cottonport, La., U.S. C3 95
Cotton Valley, La., U.S. B2 95
Cottonwood, Al., U.S. D4 78
Cottonwood, Az., U.S. C3 80
Cottonwood, Ca., U.S. B2 82
Cottonwood, Id., U.S. C2 89
Cottonwood, Mn., U.S. F3 100
Cottonwood, co., Mn., U.S. F3 100
Cottonwood, stm., Ks., U.S. D7 93
Cottonwood, stm., Mn., U.S. F3 100
Cottonwood Creek, stm., Wy., U.S. C4 127
Cottonwood Falls, Ks., U.S. D7 93
Cotuit, Ma., U.S. C7 98
Cotulla, Tx., U.S. E3 120
Coudersport, Pa., U.S. C5 115
Cougar Reservoir, res., Or., U.S. C4 114
Couhé, Fr. F7 10
Coulee Creek, stm., Wa., U.S. g13 124
Coulee Dam, Wa., U.S. B7 124
Coulee Dam National Recreation Area, Wa., U.S. A7 124
Coulommiers, Fr. D10 10
Coulterville, Il., U.S. E4 90
Counce, Tn., U.S. B3 119
Council, Id., U.S. E2 89
Council Bluffs, Ia., U.S. C2 92
Council Grove, Ks., U.S. D7 93
Council Grove Lake, res., Ks., U.S. D7 93
Council Mountain, mtn., Id., U.S. E2 89
Country Homes, Wa., U.S. B8 124
Coupeville, Wa., U.S. A3 124
Courtenay, B.C., Can. E5 69
Courte Oreilles, Lac, l., Wi., U.S. C2 126
Courtland, Ont., Can. E4 73
Courtland, Al., U.S. A2 78
Courtland, Va., U.S. D5 123
Coushatta, La., U.S. B2 95
Coutances, Fr. C5 10
Coutras, Fr. G6 10
Cove Creek, stm., Ut., U.S. E3 121
Covedale, Oh., U.S. o12 112
Coventry, Eng., U.K. I11 7
Coventry, Ct., U.S. B6 84
Coventry, R.I., U.S. D3 116
Cove Point, c., Md., U.S. D5 97
Covilhã, Port. E4 12
Covina, Ca., U.S. m13 82
Covington, Ga., U.S. C3 87
Covington, In., U.S. D3 91
Covington, Ky., U.S. A5 94
Covington, La., U.S. D5 95
Covington, Oh., U.S. B1 112
Covington, Tn., U.S. B2 119
Covington, Va., U.S. C3 123
Covington, co., Al., U.S. D3 78
Covington, co., Ms., U.S. D4 101
Cowan, Tn., U.S. B5 119
Cowan, Lake, l., Austl. F4 50
Cowansville, Que., Can. D5 74
Cowarts, Al., U.S. D4 78
Cow Creek, stm., Wa., U.S. C7 124
Cowee Mountains, mts., N.C., U.S. f9 110
Cowen, Mount, mtn., Mt., U.S. E6 103
Coweta, Ok., U.S. B6 113
Coweta, co., Ga., U.S. C2 87
Cow Head, Newf., Can. D3 72
Cowichan Bay, B.C., Can. g12 69

Name | Map Ref | Page

ow Lakes, l., Or., U.S. D9 114
owley, Wy., U.S. B4 127
owley, co., Ks., U.S. E7 93
owlington, Ok., U.S. B7 113
owlitz, co., Wa., U.S. C2 124
owlitz, stm., Wa., U.S. C3 124
owpasture, stm., Va., U.S. B3 123
owpen Mountain, mtn., Ga., U.S. B2 87
owpens, S.C., U.S. A4 117
oxim, Braz. E1 57
oxsackie, N.Y., U.S. C7 109
ox's Bāzār, Bngl. J14 38
ox's Cove, Newf., Can. D2 72
oyhaique, Chile F2 56
ozad, Ne., U.S. D6 104
ozumel, Isla de, i., Mex. G16 62
rab Creek, stm., Wa., U.S. C6 124
rab Creek, stm., Wa., U.S. B7 124
rab Orchard, Ky., U.S. C5 94
rab Orchard, Tn., U.S. D9 119
rab Orchard, W.V., U.S. n13 125
rab Orchard Lake, res., Il., U.S. F4 90
rabtree, Pa., U.S. F3 115
rabtree Mills, Que., Can. D4 74
radock, S. Afr. H5 44
rafton, Pa., U.S. k13 115
raig, Ak., U.S. D13 79
raig, Co., U.S. A3 83
raig, co., Ok., U.S. A6 113
raig, co., Va., U.S. C2 123
raig Air Force Base, mil., Al., U.S. C3 78
raig Creek, stm., Va., U.S. C2 123
raighead, co., Ar., U.S. B5 81
raigsville, Va., U.S. B3 123
raigsville, W.V., U.S. C4 125
railsheim, Ger. F10 8
raiova, Rom. E7 16
ramerton, N.C., U.S. B1 110
ranberry Lake, l., N.Y., U.S. A6 109
ranberry Portage, Man., Can. B1 70
ranbrook, B.C., Can. E10 69
randall, Tx., U.S. n10 120
randon, Wi., U.S. C5 126
rane, Az., U.S. *E1 80
rane, Mo., U.S. E4 102
rane, Tx., U.S. D1 120
rane, co., Tx., U.S. D1 120
rane Creek, stm., Oh., U.S. e7 112
rane Creek Reservoir, res., Id., U.S. E2 89
rane Lake, l., Il., U.S. C3 90
rane Lake, l., Mn., U.S. B6 100
rane Mountain, mtn., Or., U.S. E6 114
rane Prairie Reservoir, res., Or., U.S. D5 114
ranford, N.J., U.S. B4 107
ranston, R.I., U.S. C4 116
raon, Fr. E6 10
raponne, Fr. G10 10
rater Lake, l., Or., U.S. E4 114
rater Lake National Park, Or., U.S. E4 114
raters of the Moon National Monument, Id., U.S. F5 89
ratéus, Braz. E10 54
rato, Braz. E11 54
rauford, Cape, c., N.W. Ter., Can. B16 66
raven, co., N.C., U.S. B5 110
rawford, Ga., U.S. C3 87
rawford, Ms., U.S. B5 101
rawford, Ne., U.S. B2 104
rawford, co., Ar., U.S. B1 81
rawford, co., Ga., U.S. D3 87
rawford, co., Il., U.S. D6 90
rawford, co., In., U.S. H4 91
rawford, co., Ia., U.S. B2 92
rawford, co., Ks., U.S. E9 93
rawford, co., Mi., U.S. D6 99
rawford, co., Mo., U.S. D6 102
rawford, co., Oh., U.S. B3 112
rawford, co., Pa., U.S. C1 115
rawford, co., Wi., U.S. E3 126
rawford Lake, l., Me., U.S. C5 96
rawford Notch State Park, N.H., U.S. B4 106
rawfordsville, Ar., U.S. B5 81
rawfordsville, In., U.S. D4 91
rawfordville, Fl., U.S. B2 86
razy Mountains, mts., Mt., U.S. D6 103
razy Peak, mtn., Mt., U.S. D6 103
razy Woman Creek, stm., Wy., U.S. B6 127
real Springs, Il., U.S. F5 90
ree, stm., Sask., Can. E11 66
reedmoor, N.C., U.S. A4 110
reek, co., Ok., U.S. B5 113
ree Lake, l., Sask., Can. m7 75
reemore, Ont., Can. C4 73
reighton, Ne., U.S. B8 104
reighton, Pa., U.S. h14 115
reil, Fr. C9 10
rema, Italy D4 14
remona, Italy D5 14
renshaw, Ms., U.S. A3 101
renshaw, co., Al., U.S. D3 78
reola, Al., U.S. E1 78
res, Cro. E9 14
resaptown, Md., U.S. k13 97
rescent, Ok., U.S. B4 113
rescent, Or., U.S. D5 114
rescent, Lake, l., Wa., U.S. A2 124
rescent City, Ca., U.S. B1 82
rescent City, Fl., U.S. C5 86
rescent Lake, l., Fl., U.S. C5 86
rescent Lake, l., Or., U.S. D5 114
rescent Springs, Ky., U.S. h13 94
resco, Ia., U.S. A5 92
resskill, N.J., U.S. h9 107
resson, Pa., U.S. F4 115
ressona, Pa., U.S. E9 115
rest, Fr. H12 10
rested Butte, Co., U.S. C4 83
rest Hill, Il., U.S. k8 90
restline, Oh., U.S. B3 112
Creston, B.C., Can. E9 69
Creston, Ia., U.S. C3 92
Creston, Oh., U.S. B4 112
Crestone Peak, mtn., Co., U.S. D5 83
Crestview, Fl., U.S. u15 86
Crestview, Hi., U.S. g10 88
Crestwood, Ky., U.S. B4 94
Crestwood Village, N.J., U.S. D4 107
Creswell, Or., U.S. D3 114
Crete, Il., U.S. B6 90
Crete, Ne., U.S. D9 104
Crete see Kríti, i., Grc. N8 16
Creve Coeur, Il., U.S. C4 90
Crevillente, Spain G11 12
Crewe, Eng., U.K. H10 7
Crewe, Va., U.S. C4 123
Criciúma, Braz. B7 56
Cricket, N.C., U.S. A1 110
Cridersville, Oh., U.S. B1 112
Crikvenica, Cro. D9 14
Crimea see Krymskij poluostrov, pen., Ukr. H4 22
Crimmitschau, Ger. E12 8
Crisfield, Md., U.S. E6 97
Crisp, co., Ga., U.S. E3 87
Cristalândia, Braz. F9 54
Cristalina, Braz. D5 57
Cristianópolis, Braz. D4 57
Cristóbal Colón, Pico, mtn., Col. B6 58
Crittenden, Ky., U.S. B5 94
Crittenden, co., Ar., U.S. B5 81
Crittenden, co., Ky., U.S. e9 94
Črivitz, Wi., U.S. C6 126
Črnomelj, Slo. D10 14
Croatia, ctry., Eur. D10 14
Crocker, Mo., U.S. D5 102
Crockett, Ca., U.S. g8 82
Crockett, Tx., U.S. D5 120
Crockett, co., Tn., U.S. B2 119
Crockett, co., Tx., U.S. D2 120
Crofton, Ky., U.S. C2 94
Crofton, Md., U.S. B4 97
Crofton, Ne., U.S. B8 104
Croix, Lac la, l., Mn., U.S. B6 100
Croker, Cape, c., Ont., Can. C4 73
Croker Island, i., Austl. B6 50
Cromarty, Scot., U.K. D8 7
Cromona, Ky., U.S. C7 94
Cromwell, Ct., U.S. C5 84
Crook, co., Or., U.S. C6 114
Crook, co., Wy., U.S. B8 127
Crooked, stm., Or., U.S. C6 114
Crooked Creek, stm., U.S. E3 93
Crooked Creek, stm., Pa., U.S. C7 115
Crooked Creek Lake, res., Pa., U.S. E3 115
Crooked Island, i., Bah. C10 64
Crooked Island Passage, strt., Bah. C10 64
Crooked Lake, l., Fl., U.S. E5 86
Crooked Lake, l., Mn., U.S. B7 100
Crooks, S.D., U.S. D9 118
Crooks Lake, l., Nv., U.S. B2 105
Crookston, Mn., U.S. C2 100
Crooksville, Oh., U.S. C3 112
Crosby, Mn., U.S. D5 100
Crosby, N.D., U.S. A2 111
Crosby, Tx., U.S. r14 120
Crosby, co., Tx., U.S. C2 120
Crosby, Mount, mtn., Wy., U.S. C3 127
Crosbyton, Tx., U.S. C2 120
Cross, co., Ar., U.S. B5 81
Cross Bay, b., Man., Can. C2 70
Cross City, Fl., U.S. C3 86
Cross Creek, stm., W.V., U.S. f8 125
Crossett, Ar., U.S. D4 81
Crossfield, Alta., Can. D3 68
Cross Island, i., Me., U.S. D5 96
Cross Lake, Man., Can. B3 70
Crosslake, Mn., U.S. D4 100
Cross Lake, l., Me., U.S. A4 96
Cross Lake, res., La., U.S. B2 95
Cross Lanes, W.V., U.S. C3 125
Crossman Peak, mtn., Az., U.S. C1 80
Cross Plains, Tn., U.S. A5 119
Cross Plains, Tx., U.S. C3 120
Cross Plains, Wi., U.S. E4 126
Cross Sound, strt., Ak., U.S. k21 79
Crossville, Al., U.S. A4 78
Crossville, Il., U.S. E5 90
Crossville, Tn., U.S. D8 119
Croswell, Mi., U.S. E8 99
Crothersville, In., U.S. G6 91
Crotone, Italy J12 14
Croton-on-Hudson, N.Y., U.S. D7 109
Crouse, N.C., U.S. B1 110
Crow, stm., Mn., U.S. F4 100
Crow Agency, Mt., U.S. E9 103
Crow Creek, stm., U.S. A6 83
Crow Creek Indian Reservation, S.D., U.S. C6 118
Crowder, Ms., U.S. A3 101
Crowell, Tx., U.S. C3 120
Crow Indian Reservation, Mt., U.S. E9 103
Crowley, La., U.S. D3 95
Crowley, Tx., U.S. n9 120
Crowley, co., Co., U.S. C7 83
Crowley, Lake, res., Ca., U.S. D4 82
Crowleys Ridge, mtn., U.S. B5 81
Crown Point, In., U.S. B3 91
Crown Point, La., U.S. k11 95
Crownpoint, N.M., U.S. B1 108
Crown Prince Frederick Island, i., N.W. Ter., Can. B15 66
Crow Peak, mtn., Mt., U.S. D5 103
Crowsnest Pass, Alta., Can. E3 68
Crowsnest Pass, Can. E3 68
Crow Wing, co., Mn., U.S. D4 100
Crow Wing, stm., Mn., U.S. D4 100
Croydon, Austl. C8 50
Crozet, Va., U.S. B4 123
Crozon, Fr. D2 10
Cruces, Cuba C7 64
Crump Lake, l., Or., U.S. E7 114
Cruz Alta, Braz. B6 56
Cruz del Eje, Arg. C4 56
Cruzeiro do Sul, Braz. E4 54
Crystal, Mn., U.S. m12 100
Crystal, stm., Co., U.S. B3 83
Crystal Bay, Nv., U.S. D1 105
Crystal Bay, b., Fl., U.S. D4 86
Crystal Beach, Fl., U.S. D4 86
Crystal City, Man., Can. E2 70
Crystal City, Mo., U.S. C7 102
Crystal City, Tx., U.S. E3 120
Crystal Falls, Mi., U.S. B2 99
Crystal Lake, Ct., U.S. B6 84
Crystal Lake, Fl., U.S. u16 86
Crystal Lake, Il., U.S. A5 90
Crystal Lake, l., Ct., U.S. B6 84
Crystal Lake, l., Mi., U.S. D4 99
Crystal Lake, l., N.H., U.S. D4 106
Crystal Lake, l., Vt., U.S. B4 122
Crystal Lawns, Il., U.S. k8 90
Crystal Pond, res., Ct., U.S. B7 84
Crystal River, Fl., U.S. D4 86
Crystal Springs, Ms., U.S. D3 101
Cuando (Kwando), stm., Afr. E4 44
Cuangar, Ang. E3 44
Cuango, Ang. C3 44
Cuango (Kwango), stm., Afr. C3 44
Cuanza, stm., Ang. C3 44
Cuauhtémoc, Mex. C6 62
Cuautla, Mex. H10 62
Cuba, Port. G4 12
Cuba, Il., U.S. C3 90
Cuba, Mo., U.S. C6 102
Cuba, N.M., U.S. A3 108
Cuba, N.Y., U.S. C2 109
Cuba, ctry., N.A. D8 64
Cuba City, Wi., U.S. F3 126
Cubango (Okavango), stm., Afr. E3 44
Cubero, N.M., U.S. B2 108
Cucharas, Mex. F7 62
Cucharas, stm., Co., U.S. D6 83
Cudahy, Wi., U.S. F6 126
Cuddalore, India G5 37
Cuddapah, India E5 37
Cuddy Mountain, mtn., Id., U.S. E2 89
Čudskoje Ozero (Peipsi Järv), l., Eur. C10 18
Cuéllar, Spain D7 12
Cuenca, Ec. I3 58
Cuenca, Spain E9 12
Cuencamé [de Ceniceros], Mex. E8 62
Cuernavaca, Mex. H10 62
Cuero, Tx., U.S. E4 120
Cuers, Fr. I13 10
Cuervos, Mex. A2 62
Cuevas del Almanzora, Spain H10 12
Cuglieri, Italy I3 14
Cuiabá, Braz. G7 54
Cuiseaux, Fr. F12 10
Cuíto, stm., Ang. E3 44
Cuíto-Cuanavale, Ang. E3 44
Cuivre, West Fork, stm., Mo., U.S. B6 102
Čukotskij, Mys, c., Russia E31 24
Čukotskij Poluostrov, pen., Russia D30 24
Culberson, co., Tx., U.S. o12 120
Culbertson, Mt., U.S. B12 103
Culbertson, Ne., U.S. D5 104
Culebra Peak, mtn., Co., U.S. D5 83
Culiacán, Mex. E6 62
Cullen, La., U.S. B2 95
Cullman, Al., U.S. A3 78
Cullman, co., Al., U.S. A3 78
Culloden, W.V., U.S. C2 125
Cullowhee, N.C., U.S. f9 110
Čul'man, Russia F18 24
Culpeper, Va., U.S. B4 123
Culpeper, co., Va., U.S. B5 123
Culver, In., U.S. B5 91
Culver City, Ca., U.S. m12 82
Culvers Lake, l., N.J., U.S. A3 107
Čulym, Russia F10 24
Cumalı, Tur. M11 16
Cumaná, Ven. B10 58
Cumanacoa, Ven. B11 58
Cumbal, Nevado de, mtn., Col. G4 58
Cumberland, B.C., Can. E5 69
Cumberland, Ky., U.S. D7 94
Cumberland, Md., U.S. k13 97
Cumberland, Wi., U.S. C2 126
Cumberland, co., Il., U.S. D5 90
Cumberland, co., Ky., U.S. D4 94
Cumberland, co., Me., U.S. E2 96
Cumberland, co., N.J., U.S. E2 107
Cumberland, co., N.C., U.S. C4 110
Cumberland, co., Pa., U.S. F7 115
Cumberland, co., Tn., U.S. D8 119
Cumberland, co., Va., U.S. C4 123
Cumberland, stm., U.S. D4 94
Cumberland, Lake, res., Ky., U.S. D5 94
Cumberland Center, Me., U.S. g7 96
Cumberland Foreside, Me., U.S. E2 96
Cumberland Gap, U.S. D6 94
Cumberland Gap National Historical Park, U.S. D6 94
Cumberland Hill, R.I., U.S. B4 116
Cumberland Island National Seashore, Ga., U.S. F5 87
Cumberland Islands, is., Austl. D9 50
Cumberland Lake, l., Sask., Can. C4 75
Cumberland Peninsula, pen., N.W. Ter., Can. C19 66
Cumberland Sound, strt., N.W. Ter., Can. C19 66
Cumbres Pass, Co., U.S. D4 83
Čumikan, Russia G21 24
Cuming, co., Ne., U.S. C9 104
Cumming, Ga., U.S. B2 87
Cumnock, Scot., U.K. F8 7
Čuna, stm., Russia F13 24
Čun'a, stm., Russia E13 24
Cunani, Braz. C8 54
Cunene, stm., Afr. E2 44
Cuneo, Italy E2 14
Cunnamulla, Austl. E9 50
Cunningham, Ky., U.S. f9 94
Cupar, Sask., Can. G3 75
Curaçao, i., Neth. Ant. H13 64
Curecanti National Recreation Area, Co., U.S. C3 83
Curepipe, Mrts. F11 44
Curiapo, Ven. C12 58
Curicó, Chile C2 56
Curitiba, Braz. B7 56
Curlew Creek, stm., Wa., U.S. A7 124
Curlew Lake, l., Wa., U.S. A7 124
Curralinho, Braz. D9 54
Currant Mountain, mtn., Nv., U.S. E6 105
Current, stm., U.S. A5 81
Currituck, co., N.C., U.S. A6 110
Curry, co., N.M., U.S. C6 108
Curry, co., Or., U.S. E2 114
Curtis, Ne., U.S. D5 104
Curtisville, Pa., U.S. E2 115
Curvelo, Braz. E6 57
Curwensville, Pa., U.S. E4 115
Curwensville Lake, res., Pa., U.S. E4 115
Curwood, Mount, mtn., Mi., U.S. B2 99
Cushing, Ok., U.S. B5 113
Cushman, Lake, res., Wa., U.S. B2 124
Cusseta, Ga., U.S. D2 87
Custer, S.D., U.S. D2 118
Custer, co., Co., U.S. C5 83
Custer, co., Id., U.S. E4 89
Custer, co., Mt., U.S. D11 103
Custer, co., Ne., U.S. C6 104
Custer, co., Ok., U.S. B2 113
Custer, co., S.D., U.S. D2 118
Custer Battlefield National Monument, Mt., U.S. E9 103
Cut Bank, Mt., U.S. B4 103
Cut Bank Creek, stm., N.D., U.S. A4 111
Cutchogue, N.Y., U.S. m16 109
Cuthbert, Ga., U.S. E2 87
Cutler Ridge, Fl., U.S. s13 86
Cut Off, La., U.S. E5 95
Cutro, Italy J11 14
Cuttack, India J11 38
Cuttyhunk Island, i., Ma., U.S. D6 98
Cuxhaven, Ger. B8 8
Cuyahoga, co., Oh., U.S. A4 112
Cuyahoga, stm., Oh., U.S. A4 112
Cuyahoga Falls, Oh., U.S. A4 112
Cuyama, stm., Ca., U.S. E4 82
Cuyamaca Peak, mtn., Ca., U.S. F5 82
Cuyo Islands, is., Phil. C7 32
Cuyuni, stm., S.A. D13 58
Cuzco, Peru F4 54
C.W. McConaughy, Lake, res., Ne., U.S. C4 104
Cyclades see Kikládhes, is., Grc. L8 16
Cynthiana, In., U.S. H2 91
Cynthiana, Ky., U.S. B5 94
Cypress Creek, stm., Tx., U.S. r14 120
Cypress Hills Provincial Park, Sask., Can. H1 75
Cypress Lake, l., Fl., U.S. D5 86
Cypress Quarters, Fl., U.S. E6 86
Cypress Swamp, sw., U.S. F4 85
Cyprus, ctry., Asia B3 40
Cyril, Ok., U.S. C3 113
Czech Republic, ctry., Eur. F11 4
Częstochowa, Pol. E19 8

D

Dabeiba, Col. D4 58
Dabhoi, India I5 38
Dabie Shan, mts., China D4 28
Dabola, Gui. F3 42
Dacca see Dhaka, Bngl. I14 38
Dachaidan, China B16 38
Dachau, Ger. G11 8
Dacono, Co., U.S. A6 83
Dacula, Ga., U.S. C3 87
Dadanawa, Guy. F13 58
Dade, co., Fl., U.S. G6 86
Dade, co., Ga., U.S. B1 87
Dade, co., Mo., U.S. D4 102
Dade City, Fl., U.S. D4 86
Dadeville, Al., U.S. C4 78
Dādra and Nagar Haveli, ter., India B2 37
Dādu, Pak. G2 38
Daet, Phil. q20 33b
Daggett, co., Ut., U.S. C6 121
Dagsboro, De., U.S. F5 85
Dagupan, Phil. p19 33b
Dahan-e Qowmghī, Afg. C2 38
Da Hinggan Ling, mts., China C11 26
Dahlak Archipelago, is., Erit. E3 46
Dahlak Kebir Island, i., Erit. E3 46
Dahlonega, Ga., U.S. B3 87
Dahomey see Benin, ctry., Afr. G6 42
Dahra, Libya C9 42
Dahy, Nafūd ad-, des., Sau. Ar. D4 46
Daimiel, Spain F8 12
Daingerfield, Tx., U.S. C5 120
Dairen see Dalian, China D11 26
Dakar, Sen. F2 42
Dakhla, W. Sah. D2 42
Dakota, co., Mn., U.S. F5 100
Dakota, co., Ne., U.S. B9 104
Dakota City, Ia., U.S. B3 92
Dakota City, Ne., U.S. B9 104
Dalandzadgad, Mong. C7 26
Da Lat, Viet. I10 34
Dālbandin, Pak. D1 36
Dalby, Austl. E10 50
Dale, In., U.S. H4 91
Dale, co., Al., U.S. D4 78
Dale City, Va., U.S. B5 123
Dale Hollow Lake, res., U.S. C8 119
Daleville, Al., U.S. D4 78
Daleville, In., U.S. D6 91
Dalhart, Tx., U.S. A1 120
Dalhousie, N.B., Can. A3 71
Dalhousie, Cape, c., N.W. Ter., Can. B7 66
Dali, China B6 34
Dalian, China D11 26
Dall, Mount, mtn., Ak., U.S. f15 79
Dallam, co., Tx., U.S. A1 120
Dallas, Ga., U.S. C2 87
Dallas (part of Melcher), Ia., U.S. C4 92
Dallas, N.C., U.S. B1 110
Dallas, Or., U.S. C3 114
Dallas, Pa., U.S. D10 115
Dallas, Tx., U.S. C4 120
Dallas, co., Al., U.S. C2 78
Dallas, co., Ar., U.S. D3 81
Dallas, co., Ia., U.S. C3 92
Dallas, co., Mo., U.S. D4 102
Dallas, co., Tx., U.S. C4 120
Dallas Center, Ia., U.S. C4 92
Dallas City, Il., U.S. C2 90
Dallas Naval Air Station, mil., Tx., U.S. n9 120
Dallastown, Pa., U.S. G8 115
Dall Island, i., Ak., U.S. n23 79
Dalmacija, hist. reg., Eur. F11 14
Dalmatia see Dalmacija, hist. reg., Eur. F11 14
Daloa, I.C. G4 42
Dalqū, Sudan D12 42
Dalton, Ga., U.S. B2 87
Dalton, Ma., U.S. B1 98
Dalton, Oh., U.S. B4 112
Dalton, Pa., U.S. C10 115
Daltonganj, India H11 38
Dalton Gardens, Id., U.S. B2 89
Dalwallinu, Austl. F3 50
Daly City, Ca., U.S. h8 82
Damān, India B2 37
Damān, ter., India B2 37
Damar, Pulau, i., Indon. G8 32
Damariscotta, Me., U.S. D3 96
Damariscotta Lake, l., Me., U.S. D3 96
Damascus, Md., U.S. B3 97
Damascus, Va., U.S. f10 123
Damascus see Dimashq, Syria C5 40
Damāvand, Qolleh-ye, mtn., Iran J8 22
Damba, Ang. C3 44
Damoh, India I8 38
Dampar, Tasek, l., Malay. M7 34
Dampier, Austl. D3 50
Dampier, Selat, strt., Indon. F9 32
Dampier Archipelago, is., Austl. D3 50
Dan, stm., U.S. D3 123
Dana, In., U.S. E3 91
Danakil Plain, pl., Erit. F3 46
Da Nang, Viet. F10 34
Danbury, Ct., U.S. D2 84
Danbury, Tx., U.S. r14 120
Dand, Afg. E1 38
Dandridge, Tn., U.S. C10 119
Dane, co., Wi., U.S. E4 126
Dangla, Eth. F2 46
Dania, Fl., U.S. F6 86
Daniels, co., Mt., U.S. B11 103
Danielson, Ct., U.S. B8 84
Daniels Pass, Ut., U.S. C4 121
Danilov, Russia C23 18
Danlí, Hond. G4 64
Dannemora, N.Y., U.S. f11 109
Dansville, N.Y., U.S. C3 109
Dante, Va., U.S. f9 123
Danube, stm., Eur. G13 4
Danube, Mouths of the, mth., Eur. D13 16
Danvers, Il., U.S. C4 90
Danvers, Ma., U.S. A6 98
Danville, Que., Can. D5 74
Danville, Ar., U.S. B2 81
Danville, Ca., U.S. h9 82
Danville, Il., U.S. C6 90
Danville, In., U.S. E4 91
Danville, Ia., U.S. D6 92
Danville, Ky., U.S. C5 94
Danville, Oh., U.S. B3 112
Danville, Pa., U.S. E8 115
Danville, Va., U.S. D3 123
Danyang, China C8 28
Danzig, Gulf of, b., Eur. A19 8
Danzig see Gdańsk, Pol. A18 8
Daocheng, China F7 26
Dapango, Togo F6 42
Daphne, Al., U.S. E2 78
Dar'ā, Syria C5 40
Darakht-e Yaḥyá, Afg. E3 38
Dārayyā, Syria C5 40
Darbāsīyah, Syria A7 40
Darbhanga, India G11 38
Darby, Mt., U.S. D2 103
Darby, Pa., U.S. G11 115
Darchan, Mong. B8 26
Dardanelle, Ar., U.S. B2 81
Dardanelle Lake, res., Ar., U.S. B2 81
Dardanelles see Çanakkale Boğazı, strt., Tur. I10 16
Dare, co., N.C., U.S. B7 110
Dar es Salaam, Tan. C7 44
Dargaville, N.Z. A4 52
Dari, China E6 26
Darien, Ct., U.S. E2 84
Darien, Ga., U.S. E5 87
Darien, Wi., U.S. F5 126
Dariganga, Mong. B9 26
Darjeeling, India G13 38
Darke, co., Oh., U.S. B1 112
Darley Woods, De., U.S. h8 85
Darling, stm., Austl. F9 50
Darling, Lake, res., N.D., U.S. A4 111
Darling Range, mts., Austl. F3 50
Darlington, Eng., U.K. G11 7
Darlington, In., U.S. D4 91
Darlington, Md., U.S. A5 97
Darlington, S.C., U.S. C8 117
Darlington, Wi., U.S. F3 126
Darlington, co., S.C., U.S. C8 117
Darmstadt, Ger. F8 8
Darnah, Libya B10 42
Daroca, Spain D10 12
Darrah, Mount, mtn., Can. E3 68
Darrington, Wa., U.S. A4 124
Dartmoor National Park, Eng., U.K. K9 7
Dartmouth, Eng., U.K. K9 7
Daru, Pap. N. Gui. G11 32
Darwin, Austl. B6 50
Dašinčilen, Mong. B7 26
Dassel, Mn., U.S. E4 100
Datia, India H8 38
Datil Mountains, mts., N.M., U.S. C2 108
D'at'kovo, Russia H17 18
Datong, China C9 26
Datu, Tanjung, c., Asia M10 34
Dāūd Khel, Pak. D4 38
Daufuskie Island, i., S.C., U.S. G6 117
Daugavpils, Lat. F9 18

Name Map Ref Page

Daulatābād (Shirin Tagāo), Afg. B1 38
Daule, Ec. G2 58
Dauphin, Man., Can. D1 70
Dauphin, co., Pa., U.S. F8 115
Dauphin, stm., Man., Can. D2 70
Dauphin Island, Al., U.S. E1 78
Dauphin Island, i., Al., U.S. E1 78
Dauphin Lake, l., Man., Can. D2 70
Dāvangere, India E3 37
Davao, Phil. D8 32
Davao Gulf, b., Phil. D8 32
Daveluyville, Que., Can. C5 74
Davenport, Fl., U.S. D5 86
Davenport, Ia., U.S. C7 92
Davenport, Ok., U.S. B5 113
Davenport, Wa., U.S. B7 124
David, Pan. J6 64
David City, Ne., U.S. C8 104
Davidson, N.C., U.S. B2 110
Davidson, co., N.C., U.S. B2 110
Davidson, co., Tn., U.S. A5 119
Davidsville, Pa., U.S. F4 115
Davie, Fl., U.S. F6 86
Davie, co., N.C., U.S. B2 110
Daviess, co., In., U.S. G3 91
Daviess, co., Ky., U.S. C2 94
Daviess, co., Mo., U.S. B3 102
Davis, Ca., U.S. C3 82
Davis, Ok., U.S. C4 113
Davis, W.V., U.S. B5 125
Davis, co., Ia., U.S. D5 92
Davis, co., Ut., U.S. C3 121
Davis, Mount, mtn., Pa., U.S. G3 115
Davis Creek, stm., W.V., U.S. m12 125
Davis Dam, U.S. H7 105
Davis Islands, is., Fl., U.S. p11 86
Davis Lake, l., Or., U.S. E5 114
Davis-Monthan Air Force Base, mil., Az., U.S. E5 80
Davison, Mi., U.S. E7 99
Davison, co., S.D., U.S. D7 118
Davis Strait, strt., N.A. C21 66
Davisville, R.I., U.S. E4 116
Davos, Switz. F16 10
Dawa (Daua), stm., Afr. H3 46
Dawei, Burma G5 34
Dawes, co., Ne., U.S. B2 104
Daws Island, i., S.C., U.S. G6 117
Dawson, Ga., U.S. E2 87
Dawson, Mn., U.S. F2 100
Dawson, co., Ga., U.S. B2 87
Dawson, co., Mt., U.S. C11 103
Dawson, co., Ne., U.S. D6 104
Dawson, co., Tx., U.S. C1 120
Dawson, Mount, mtn., B.C., Can. D9 69
Dawson Creek, B.C., Can. B7 69
Dawson Springs, Ky., U.S. C2 94
Dax, Fr. I5 10
Day, co., S.D., U.S. B8 118
Dayr az-Zawr, Syria B7 40
Daysland, Alta., Can. C4 68
Dayton, In., U.S. D4 91
Dayton, Ia., U.S. B3 92
Dayton, Ky., U.S. h14 94
Dayton, Md., U.S. B4 97
Dayton, Mn., U.S. m12 100
Dayton, Nv., U.S. D2 105
Dayton, Oh., U.S. C1 112
Dayton, Or., U.S. B3 114
Dayton, Tn., U.S. D8 119
Dayton, Tx., U.S. D5 120
Dayton, Va., U.S. B4 123
Dayton, Wa., U.S. C8 124
Dayton, Wy., U.S. B5 127
Daytona Beach, Fl., U.S. C5 86
Da Yunhe, China E10 26
Dayville, Ct., U.S. B8 84
De Aar, S. Afr. H4 44
Dead, North Branch, stm., Me., U.S. C2 96
Dead, South Branch, stm., Me., U.S. C2 96
Dead Creek, stm., Vt., U.S. C2 122
Dead Diamond, stm., N.H., U.S. g7 106
Dead Indian Peak, mtn., Wy., U.S. B3 127
Dead Lake, l., Mn., U.S. D3 100
Dead Lakes, l., Fl., U.S. B1 86
Deadman Bay, b., Fl., U.S. C3 86
Deadman Creek, stm., Wa., U.S. g14 124
Deadmans Cay, Bah. C10 64
Dead Sea, l., Asia D4 40
Deadwood, S.D., U.S. C2 118
Deadwood Reservoir, res., Id., U.S. E3 89
Deaf Smith, co., Tx., U.S. B1 120
Deale, Md., U.S. C4 97
Deal Island, Md., U.S. D6 97
Deal Island, i., Md., U.S. D6 97
Dean, stm., B.C., Can. C4 69
Dean Channel, strt., B.C., Can. C4 69
Deán Funes, Arg. C4 56
Dearborn, Mi., U.S. F7 99
Dearborn, co., In., U.S. F7 91
Dearborn Heights, Mi., U.S. p15 99
Dearg, Beinn, mtn., Scot., U.K. D8 7
Dease Strait, strt., N.W. Ter., Can. C11 66
Death Valley, val., Ca., U.S. D5 82
Death Valley National Monument, U.S. D5 82
Deauville, Fr. C7 10
De Baca, co., N.M., U.S. C5 108
De Bary, Fl., U.S. D5 86
Debauch Mountain, mtn., Ak., U.S. C8 79
Dębica, Pol. E21 8
Debrecen, Hung. H21 8
Debre Markos, Eth. F2 46
Debre Tabor, Eth. F2 46
De Cade, Lake, l., La., U.S. E5 95
Decatur, Al., U.S. A3 78
Decatur, Ar., U.S. A1 81
Decatur, Ga., U.S. C2 87
Decatur, Il., U.S. D5 90
Decatur, In., U.S. C8 91
Decatur, Mi., U.S. F5 99
Decatur, Ms., U.S. C4 101
Decatur, Ne., U.S. B9 104
Decatur, Tn., U.S. D9 119
Decatur, Tx., U.S. C4 120
Decatur, co., Ga., U.S. F2 87
Decatur, co., In., U.S. F6 91
Decatur, co., Ia., U.S. D4 92
Decatur, co., Ks., U.S. C3 93
Decatur, co., Tn., U.S. B3 119
Decatur, Lake, res., Il., U.S. D5 90
Decaturville, Tn., U.S. B3 119
Decazeville, Fr. H9 10
Deccan, plat., India E4 37
Deception, Mount, mtn., Wa., U.S. B2 124
Decherd, Tn., U.S. B5 119
Děčín, Czech. E14 8
Decize, Fr. F10 10
Deckerville, Mi., U.S. E8 99
Decorah, Ia., U.S. A6 92
Dedham, Ma., U.S. B5 98
Dédougou, Burkina F5 42
Dedovsk, Russia F20 18
Deep, stm., N.C., U.S. B3 110
Deep Creek, stm., Ut., U.S. C2 121
Deep Creek, stm., Ut., U.S. B3 121
Deep Creek, stm., Ut., U.S. F3 121
Deep Creek, stm., Wa., U.S. g13 124
Deep Creek Lake, res., Md., U.S. K12 97
Deep Creek Mountains, mts., Id., U.S. G6 89
Deep Fork, stm., Ok., U.S. B5 113
Deep Inlet, b., Newf., Can. g10 72
Deep Red Creek, stm., Ok., U.S. C3 113
Deep River, Ont., Can. A7 73
Deep River, Ct., U.S. D6 84
Deer Creek, stm., Oh., U.S. C2 112
Deer Creek Indian Reservation, Mn., U.S. C5 100
Deerfield, Il., U.S. h9 90
Deerfield, Ks., U.S. E2 93
Deerfield, Ma., U.S. A2 98
Deerfield, Mi., U.S. G7 99
Deerfield, Wi., U.S. E4 126
Deerfield, stm., U.S. A2 98
Deerfield Beach, Fl., U.S. F6 86
Deer Island, pen., Ma., U.S. g12 98
Deer Island, i., Ms., U.S. f8 101
Deer Isle, i., Me., U.S. D4 96
Deer Lake, Newf., Can. D3 72
Deer Lake, l., Newf., Can. D3 72
Deer Lake, l., Mn., U.S. C5 100
Deer Lodge, Mt., U.S. D4 103
Deer Lodge, co., Mt., U.S. E3 103
Deer Park, N.Y., U.S. n15 109
Deer Park, Oh., U.S. o13 112
Deer Park, Wa., U.S. B8 124
Deer Peak, mtn., Co., U.S. C5 83
Deer River, Mn., U.S. C5 100
Deesa, India H5 38
Defiance, Oh., U.S. A1 112
Defiance, co., Oh., U.S. A1 112
Defiance, Mount, mtn., Or., U.S. B5 114
De Forest, Wi., U.S. E4 126
De Funiak Springs, Fl., U.S. u15 86
Degeh-Bur, Eth. G3 46
Dégelis, Que., Can. B9 74
Deggendorf, Ger. G12 8
De Graff, Oh., U.S. B2 112
De Gray Lake, res., Ar., U.S. C2 81
Dehiwala-Mount Lavinia, Sri L. I5 37
Dehra Dūn, India E8 38
Dehri, India H11 38
Dehu, India C2 37
Dehui, China C12 26
Dej, Rom. B7 16
Deje, Swe. G9 6
De Kalb, Il., U.S. B5 90
De Kalb, Ms., U.S. C5 101
De Kalb, Tx., U.S. C5 120
De Kalb, co., Al., U.S. A4 78
De Kalb, co., Ga., U.S. C2 87
De Kalb, co., Il., U.S. B5 90
De Kalb, co., In., U.S. B7 91
De Kalb, co., Mo., U.S. B3 102
De Kalb, co., Tn., U.S. D8 119
Dekese, Zaire B4 44
Delafield, Wi., U.S. m11 126
Delanco, N.J., U.S. C3 107
De Land, Fl., U.S. C5 86
Delano, Ca., U.S. E4 82
Delano, Mn., U.S. E5 100
Delano Peak, mtn., Ut., U.S. E3 121
Delaronde Lake, l., Sask., Can. C2 75
Delavan, Il., U.S. C4 90
Delavan, Wi., U.S. F5 126
Delaware, Oh., U.S. B2 112
Delaware, co., In., U.S. D7 91
Delaware, co., Ia., U.S. B6 92
Delaware, co., N.Y., U.S. C5 109
Delaware, co., Oh., U.S. B2 112
Delaware, co., Ok., U.S. A7 113
Delaware, co., Pa., U.S. G11 115
Delaware, state, U.S. D3 85
Delaware, stm., U.S. G11 115
Delaware, stm., Ks., U.S. C8 93
Delaware, East Branch, stm., N.Y., U.S. C5 109
Delaware Bay, b., U.S. D11 76
Delaware City, De., U.S. B3 85
Delaware Lake, res., Oh., U.S. B3 112
Delaware Water Gap, N.J., U.S. B2 107
Delaware Water Gap National Recreation Area, U.S. B2 107
Delbarton, W.V., U.S. D2 125
Delcambre, La., U.S. E4 95
Del City, Ok., U.S. B4 113
Delémont, Switz. E14 10
De Leon, Tx., U.S. C3 120
De Leon Springs, Fl., U.S. C5 86
Delft, Neth. C4 8
Delfzijl, Neth. B6 8
Delgado, Cabo, c., Moz. D8 44
Delhi, India F7 38
Delhi, La., U.S. B4 95
Delhi, N.Y., U.S. C6 109
Delicias, Mex. C7 62
De Lisle, Ms., U.S. E4 101
Delitzsch, Ger. D12 8
Dellenbaugh, Mount, mtn., Az., U.S. A2 80
Dell Rapids, S.D., U.S. D9 118
Del Mar, Ca., U.S. o15 82
Delmar, De., U.S. G3 85
Delmar, Md., U.S. D6 97
Delmar, N.Y., U.S. C7 109
Delmenhorst, Ger. B8 8
Delnice, Cro. D9 14
Del Norte, Co., U.S. D4 83
Del Norte, co., Ca., U.S. B2 82
De-Longa, Ostrova, is., Russia B23 24
Deloraine, Man., Can. E1 70
Del Park Manor, De., U.S. i7 85
Delphi, In., U.S. C4 91
Delphos, Oh., U.S. B1 112
Delran, N.J., U.S. C3 107
Delray Beach, Fl., U.S. F6 86
Del Rio, Tx., U.S. E2 120
Delson, Que., Can. q19 74
Delta, Co., U.S. C2 83
Delta, Oh., U.S. A2 112
Delta, Ut., U.S. D3 121
Delta, co., Co., U.S. C3 83
Delta, co., Mi., U.S. C3 99
Delta, co., Tx., U.S. C5 120
Delta, reg., Ms., U.S. B3 101
Delta Junction, Ak., U.S. C10 79
Delta Peak, mtn., B.C., Can. A3 69
Delta Reservoir, res., N.Y., U.S. B5 109
Deltaville, Va., U.S. C6 123
Deltona, Fl., U.S. D5 86
Demarest, N.J., U.S. h9 107
Deming, N.M., U.S. E2 108
Demirci, Tur. J12 16
Demirköy, Tur. H11 16
Demmin, Ger. B13 8
Demopolis, Al., U.S. C2 78
Demorest, Ga., U.S. B3 87
Demotte, In., U.S. B3 91
Denain, Fr. B10 10
Denali National Park, Ak., U.S. C9 79
Denare Beach, Sask., Can. C4 75
Denham Springs, La., U.S. D5 95
Den Helder, Neth. C4 8
Denia, Spain G12 12
Denison, Ia., U.S. B2 92
Denison, Tx., U.S. C4 120
Denison Dam, U.S. D5 113
Denizli, Tur. H13 4
Denmark, S.C., U.S. E5 117
Denmark, Wi., U.S. D6 126
Denmark, ctry., Eur. D9 4
Denmark Strait, strt. C15 128
Dennehotso, Az., U.S. A6 80
Dennis, Ma., U.S. C7 98
Dennison, Oh., U.S. B4 112
Dennis Port, Ma., U.S. C7 98
Denny Terrace, S.C., U.S. C5 117
Denpasar, Indon. G6 32
Dent, co., Mo., U.S. D6 102
Denton, Md., U.S. C6 97
Denton, N.C., U.S. B2 110
Denton, Tx., U.S. C4 120
Denton, co., Tx., U.S. C4 120
D'Entrecasteaux Islands, is., Pap. N. Gui. m17 50a
Dentsville, S.C., U.S. C6 117
Denver, Co., U.S. B6 83
Denver, Ia., U.S. B5 92
Denver, Pa., U.S. F9 115
Denver, co., Co., U.S. B6 83
Denver City, Tx., U.S. C1 120
Denville, N.J., U.S. B4 107
Deoghar, India H12 38
Deolāli, India C2 37
Deoria, India G10 38
De Pere, Wi., U.S. D5 126
Depew, N.Y., U.S. C2 109
Depoe Bay, Or., U.S. C2 114
Depok, Indon. m13 33a
Deposit, N.Y., U.S. C5 109
Depue, Il., U.S. B4 90
Deqin, China F6 26
De Queen, Ar., U.S. C1 81
De Queen Reservoir, res., Ar., U.S. C1 81
De Quincy, La., U.S. D2 95
Dera Ghāzi Khān, Pak. E4 38
Dera Ismāīl Khān, Pak. E4 38
Derby, Austl. C4 50
Derby, Eng., U.K. I11 7
Derby, Ct., U.S. D3 84
Derby, Ks., U.S. E6 93
Derby, Vt., U.S. B4 122
Derby Line, Vt., U.S. A4 122
Derg, Lough, l., Ire. I4 7
De Ridder, La., U.S. D2 95
Derma, Ms., U.S. B4 101
Dermott, Ar., U.S. D4 81
Dernieres, Isles, is., La., U.S. E5 95
Derry, N.H., U.S. E4 106
Derry, Pa., U.S. F3 115
Derval, Fr. E5 10
Derventa, Bos. E12 14
Derwood, Md., U.S. B3 97
Desaguadero, stm., Arg. C3 56
Des Allemands, La., U.S. E5 95
Des Arc, Ar., U.S. C4 81
Desbiens, Que., Can. A6 74
Descartes, Fr. F7 10
Deschaillons [-sur-Saint-Laurent], Que., Can. C5 74
Deschambault, Que., Can. C6 74
Deschambault Lake, l., Sask., Can. C4 75
Deschutes, co., Or., U.S. D5 114
Deschutes, stm., Or., U.S. B6 114
Dese, Eth. F2 46
Deseado, stm., Arg. F3 56
Deseret Peak, mtn., Ut., U.S. C3 121
Deseronto, Ont., Can. C7 73
Desert Creek Peak, mtn., Nv., U.S. E2 105
Desert Hot Springs, Ca., U.S. F5 82
Desert Peak, mtn., Ut., U.S. B2 121
Desert Valley, val., Nv., U.S. B3 105
Desha, Ar., U.S. B4 81
Desha, co., Ar., U.S. D4 81
Deshler, Ne., U.S. D8 104
Deshler, Oh., U.S. A2 112
Des Lacs, stm., N.D., U.S. A4 111
Desloge, Mo., U.S. D7 102
De Smet, S.D., U.S. C8 118
Des Moines, Ia., U.S. C4 92
Des Moines, Wa., U.S. B3 124
Des Moines, co., Ia., U.S. D6 92
Des Moines, stm., U.S. D5 92
Desolación, Isla, i., Chile G2 56
De Soto, Il., U.S. F4 90
De Soto, Ia., U.S. C3 92
De Soto, Ks., U.S. D9 93
De Soto, Mo., U.S. C7 102
De Soto, co., Fl., U.S. E5 86
De Soto, co., La., U.S. B2 95
De Soto, co., Ms., U.S. A3 101
Despard, W.V., U.S. k10 125
Des Peres, Mo., U.S. f13 102
Des Plaines, Il., U.S. A6 90
Des Plaines, stm., U.S. k8 90
Desroches, Île, i., Sey. C10 44
Dessau, Ger. D12 8
Destin, Fl., U.S. u15 86
Destrehan, La., U.S. E5 95
Desvres, Fr. B8 10
Detmold, Ger. D8 8
Detour, Point, c., Mi., U.S. C4 99
Detroit, Mi., U.S. F7 99
Detroit Lake, res., Or., U.S. C4 114
Detroit Lakes, Mn., U.S. D3 100
Deuel, co., Ne., U.S. C3 104
Deuel, co., S.D., U.S. C9 118
Deutsche Bucht, b., Ger. A7 8
Deutschlandsberg, Aus. I15 8
Deux-Montagnes, Que., Can. p19 74
Deux Montagnes, Lac des, l., Que., Can. q19 74
Deva, Rom. D6 16
Devakottai, India H5 37
De Valls Bluff, Ar., U.S. C4 81
Deventer, Neth. C6 8
DeView, Bayou, stm., Ar., U.S. B4 81
Devil's Island see Diable, Île du, i., Fr. Gu. B8 54
Devils Lake, N.D., U.S. A7 111
Devils Lake, l., N.D., U.S. A6 111
Devils Paw, mtn., Ak., U.S. k23 79
Devils Postpile National Monument, Ca., U.S. D4 82
Devils Tower National Monument, Wy., U.S. B8 127
Devil Track Lake, l., Mn., U.S. k9 100
Devine, Tx., U.S. E3 120
DeVola, Oh., U.S. C4 112
Devon, Alta., Can. C4 68
Devon Island, i., N.W. Ter., Can. A15 66
Devonport, Austl. H9 50
Devonport, N.Z. B5 52
Devonshire, De., U.S. h7 85
Dewa-kyūryō, hills, Japan C13 30
Dewar, Ok., U.S. B6 113
Dewās, India I7 38
Dewees Inlet, b., S.C., U.S. k12 117
Dewees Island, i., S.C., U.S. F8 117
Dewey, Az., U.S. C3 80
Dewey, Ok., U.S. A6 113
Dewey, co., Ok., U.S. B2 113
Dewey, co., S.D., U.S. B4 118
Dewey Beach, De., U.S. F5 85
Dewey Lake, res., Ky., U.S. C7 94
Deweyville, Tx., U.S. D6 120
De Witt, Ar., U.S. C4 81
De Witt, Ia., U.S. C7 92
De Witt, Mi., U.S. F6 99
De Witt, N.Y., U.S. B4 109
De Witt, co., Il., U.S. C4 90
De Witt, co., Tx., U.S. E4 120
Dexter, Ia., U.S. C3 92
Dexter, Me., U.S. C3 96
Dexter, Mi., U.S. F7 99
Dexter, Mo., U.S. E8 102
Dexter, N.M., U.S. D5 108
Dexter, Lake, l., Fl., U.S. C5 86
Dezfūl, Iran B4 46
Dezhou, China D10 26
Dhaka, Bngl. I14 38
Dhamār, Yemen F3 46
Dhamtari, India B6 37
Dhānbād, India I12 38
Dhār, India I6 38
Dharmapuri, India F5 37
Dharmavaram, India E4 37
Dhārwār, India E3 37
Dhawlāgiri, mtn., Nepal F10 38
Dhodhekánisos (Dodecanese), is., Grc. M10 16
Dholpur, India G7 38
Dhorāji, India J4 38
Dhrol, India I4 38
Dhubri, India G13 38
Dhule, India B3 37
Diable, Île du, i., Fr. Gu. B8 54
Diablo, Canyon, val., Az., U.S. C4 80
Diablo, Mount, mtn., Ca., U.S. h9 82
Diablo Dam, Wa., U.S. A4 124
Diablo Lake, res., Wa., U.S. A4 124
Diablo Range, mts., Ca., U.S. D3 82
Diamante, Arg. C4 56
Diamantina, Braz. E7 57
Diamantino, Braz. F7 54
Diamond Head, crat., Hi., U.S. B4 88
Diamond Hill, R.I., U.S. B4 116
Diamond Hill Reservoir, res., R.I., U.S. A4 116
Diamond Lake, Il., U.S. h9 90
Diamond Lake, l., Or., U.S. D4 114
Diamond Mountains, mts., Nv., U.S. D6 105
Diamond Peak, mtn., Co., U.S. A2 83
Diamond Peak, mtn., Id., U.S. E5 89
Diamond Peak, mtn., Or., U.S. D4 114
Diamond Peak, mtn., Wa., U.S. C8 124
Diamondville, Wy., U.S. E2 127
Diaz, Ar., U.S. B4 81
Dibaya, Zaire C4 44
D'Iberville, Ms., U.S. E5 101
Diboll, Tx., U.S. D5 120
Dibrugarh, India G16 38
Dickens, co., Tx., U.S. C2 120
Dickenson, co., Va., U.S. e9 123
Dickerson, Md., U.S. B3 97
Dickey, co., N.D., U.S. C7 111
Dickeyville, Wi., U.S. F3 126
Dickinson, N.D., U.S. C3 111
Dickinson, co., Ia., U.S. A2 92
Dickinson, co., Ks., U.S. D6 93
Dickinson, co., Mi., U.S. B3 99
Dickinson Dam, N.D., U.S. C3 111
Dickson, Ok., U.S. C5 113
Dickson, Tn., U.S. A4 119
Dickson, co., Tn., U.S. A4 119
Dickson City, Pa., U.S. D10 115
Didsbury, Alta., Can. D3 68
Die, Fr. H12 10
Dieburg, Ger. F8 8
Dieciocho de Marzo, Mex. E11 62
Diefenbaker, Lake, res., Sask., Can. F2 75
Diégo-Suarez see Antsiranana, Madag. D9 44
Dien Bien Phu, Viet. D7 34
Diepholz, Ger. C8 8
Dieppe, N.B., Can. C5 71
Dieppe, Fr. C8 10
Dierks, Ar., U.S. C1 81
Dieuze, Fr. D13 10
Digboi, India G16 38
Dighton, Ks., U.S. D3 93
Digne, Fr. H13 10
Digoin, Fr. F10 10
Dijon, Fr. E12 10
Dike, Ia., U.S. B5 92
Dikson, Russia C10 24
Dili, Indon. G8 32
Dillard, Or., U.S. D3 114
Dill City, Ok., U.S. B2 113
Dilley, Tx., U.S. E3 120
Dillingen [an der Donau], Ger. G10 8
Dillingham, Ak., U.S. D8 79
Dillon, Mt., U.S. E4 103
Dillon, S.C., U.S. C9 117
Dillon, co., S.C., U.S. C9 117
Dillon Lake, res., Oh., U.S. B3 112
Dillon Reservoir, res., Co., U.S. B4 83
Dillonvale, Oh., U.S. B5 112
Dillsboro, In., U.S. F7 91
Dillsburg, Pa., U.S. F7 115
Dilolo, Zaire D4 44
Dilworth, Mn., U.S. D2 100
Dimāpur, India H15 38
Dimashq (Damascus), Syria C5 40
Dimitrovgrad, Bul. G9 16
Dimitrovgrad, Russia G7 22
Dimmit, co., Tx., U.S. E3 120
Dimmitt, Tx., U.S. B1 120
Dimona, Isr. D4 40
Dimondale, Mi., U.S. F6 99
Dinagat Island, i., Phil. C8 32
Dinājpur, Bngl. H13 38
Dinan, Fr. D4 10
Dinant, Bel. E4 8
Dinara, mts., Eur. F11 14
Dinard, Fr. D4 10
Dinaric Alps see Dinara, mts., Eur. F11 14
Dindigul, India G4 37
Dinghai, China E11 28
Dingle, Ire. I2 7
Dingmans Ferry, Pa., U.S. D12 115
Dingolfing, Ger. G12 8
Dingqing, China E16 38
Dingri, China F12 38
Dingshan, China D8 28
Dingwall, Scot., U.K. D8 7
Dinh Lap, Viet. D9 34
Dinner Point, c., Fl., U.S. D4 86
Dinosaur National Monument, U.S. C6 121
Dinuba, Ca., U.S. D4 82
Dinwiddie, co., Va., U.S. C5 123
Diourbel, Sen. F2 42
Dipkarpaz, N. Cyp. B4 40
Dipolog, Phil. D7 32
Dire Dawa, Eth. G3 46
Diriamba, Nic. I4 64
Dirico, Ang. E4 44
Dirk Hartog Island, i., Austl. E2 50
Dirty Devil, stm., Ut., U.S. E5 121
Disappointment, Cape, c., Falk. Is. G9 56
Disappointment, Cape, c., Wa., U.S. C1 124
Disappointment, Lake, l., Austl. D4 50
Disentis, Switz. F15 10
Dishman, Wa., U.S. g14 124
Disko, i., Grnld. C22 66
Disko Bugt, b., Grnld. C22 66
Dismal, stm., Ne., U.S. C5 104
Disraëli, Que., Can. D6 74
District of Columbia, dept., U.S. f8 97
Diu, India J4 38
Diu, ter., India J4 38
Divernon, Il., U.S. D4 90
Divide, co., N.D., U.S. A2 111
Divide Peak, mtn., Wy., U.S. E5 127
Divinópolis, Braz. F6 57
Divisor, Serra do, plat., S.A. E4 54
Dix, stm., Ky., U.S. C5 94
Dixfield, Me., U.S. D2 96
Dixie, co., Fl., U.S. C3 86
Dixie Valley, val., Nv., U.S. D4 105
Dixon, Ca., U.S. C3 82
Dixon, Il., U.S. B4 90
Dixon, Mo., U.S. D5 102
Dixon, N.M., U.S. A4 108
Dixon, co., Ne., U.S. B9 104
Dixon Entrance, strt., N.A. F6 66
Dixonville, Pa., U.S. E3 115
Diyarbakır, Tur. H16 4
Dja, stm., Afr. H8 42
Djakarta see Jakarta, Indon. m13 33a
Djambala, Congo B2 44
Djanet, Alg. D7 42
Djebel Abiod, Tun. M4 14
Djebibina, Tun. M5 14
Djemmal, Tun. N5 14
Djerba, Île de, i., Tun. B8 42
Djerid, Chott, sw., Tun. B7 42
Djibouti, Dji. F3 46

Name Map Ref Page
'bouti, ctry., Afr. F3 46
nitrija Lapteva, Proliv, strt., Russia C22 24
nitrov, Russia E20 18
iepr, stm., Eur. H4 22
ieprodzeržinsk, Ukr. H4 22
iepropetrovsk, Ukr. H4 22
iestr, stm., Eur. H3 22
iieper see Dnepr, stm., Eur. H4 22
iiester see Dnestr, stm., Eur. H3 22
io, Russia D12 18
Āb-e Mīkh-e Zarrīn, Afg. C2 38
aktown, N.B., Can. C3 71
any, Madag. D9 44
ba, Chad E9 42
bbiaco, Italy C7 14
bbs Ferry, N.Y., U.S. g13 109
beln, Ger. D13 8
berai, Jazirah, pen., Indon. F9 32
bo, Indon. G9 32
boj, Bos. E2 16
brič, Bul. F11 16
bruš, Bela. I14 18
bson, N.C., U.S. A2 110
ce, stm., Braz. E8 57
cena, Al., U.S. f7 78
ck Junction, Ga., U.S. *E5 87
ctors Lake, l., Fl., U.S. m8 86
ddridge, co., W.V., U.S. B4 125
decanese see Dhodhekánisos, is., Grc. M10 16
dge, Ne., U.S. C9 104
dge, co., Ga., U.S. D3 87
dge, co., Mn., U.S. G6 100
dge, co., Ne., U.S. C9 104
dge, co., Wi., U.S. E5 126
dge Center, Mn., U.S. F6 100
dge City, Ks., U.S. E3 93
dgeville, Wi., U.S. F3 126
doma, Tan. C7 44
erun, Ga., U.S. E3 87
e Run, Mo., U.S. D7 102
etinchem, Neth. D6 8
g, stm., Vt., U.S. C3 122
gai Coring, l., China C13 38
g Island, i., Fl., U.S. C2 86
g Keys Pass, strt., Ms., U.S. g8 101
g Lake, l., Man., Can. D2 70
gondoutchi, Niger F6 42
ha see Ad-Dawḥah, Qatar C5 46
had, India I6 38
iran, Lake, l., Eur. H6 16
kka, Nor. F8 6
kkum, Neth. B5 8
lak, Pulau, i., Indon. G10 32
lbeau, Que., Can. k12 74
l-de-Bretagne, Fr. D5 10
lgeville, N.Y., U.S. B6 109
lianova, Italy J4 14
lisie, Congo B2 44
llar Bay, Mi., U.S. A2 99
lo, Som. H3 46
lomite, Al., U.S. B3 78
lomites see Dolomiti, mts., Italy C6 14
lomiti, mts., Italy C6 14
lores, Arg. D5 56
lores, Col. F5 58
lores, Co., U.S. D2 83
lores, co., Co., U.S. D2 83
lores, stm., U.S. E7 121
lores Hidalgo, Mex. G9 62
lphin and Union Strait, strt., N.W. Ter., Can. C9 66
lphin Island, i., Ut., U.S. B3 121
lton, Il., U.S. k9 90
mbås, Nor. E7 6
me Mountain, mtn., Az., U.S. k9 80
me Peak, mtn., Co., U.S. B3 83
meyko, Chile B2 56
meyko, Cordillera, mts., Chile A3 56
mfront, Fr. D6 10
minica, ctry., N.A. G17 64
minica Channel, strt., N.A. G17 64
minican Republic, ctry., N.A. E12 64
minion, Cape, c., N.W. Ter., Can. C18 66
modedovo, Russia F20 18
modossola, Italy C3 14
mžale, Slo. C9 14
n, stm., Russia H6 22
na Ana, N.M., U.S. E3 108
na Ana, co., N.M., U.S. E2 108
naldsonville, La., U.S. D4 95
nalsonville, Ga., U.S. E2 87
naueschingen, Ger. H8 8
nauwörth, Ger. G10 8
n Benito, Spain G6 12
ncaster, Eng., U.K. H11 7
ndo, Ang. C2 44
ndra Head, c., Sri L. J6 37
neck, Ukr. H5 22
negal Bay, b., Ire. G4 7
neraile, S.C., U.S. C8 117
netsk see Doneck, Ukr. H5 22
nga, stm., Nig. G8 42
ngara, Austl. E2 50
ngchuan, China A7 34
ngfang, China H8 26
ngfang (Basuo), China E10 34
ngguan, China L2 28
nghai Dao, i., China D11 34
ng Hoi, Viet. F9 34
ngshan, China L6 28
ngtai, China C9 28
ngting Hu, l., China F1 28
niphan, Mo., U.S. E7 102
niphan, Ne., U.S. D7 104
niphan, co., Ks., U.S. C8 93
nkey Creek, stm., Wy., U.S. B7 127
nkin, N.S., Can. C10 71
nley, co., Tx., U.S. B2 120
nna, Tx., U.S. F3 120
nnacona, Que., Can. C6 74
nnellson, Ia., U.S. D6 92
nner Pass, Ca., U.S. C3 82
nora, Pa., U.S. F2 115
Donskoj, Russia H21 18
Dooly, co., Ga., U.S. D3 87
Doonerak, Mount, mtn., Ak., U.S. B9 79
Door, co., Wi., U.S. D6 126
Dora, Al., U.S. B2 78
Doraville, Ga., U.S. h8 87
Dorcheat, Bayou, stm., U.S. B2 95
Dorchester, N.B., Can. D5 71
Dorchester, Eng., U.K. K10 7
Dorchester, Ne., U.S. D8 104
Dorchester, co., Md., U.S. D5 97
Dorchester, co., S.C., U.S. E7 117
Dorchester, Cape, c., N.W. Ter., Can. C17 66
Dordogne, stm., Fr. H8 10
Dordrecht, Neth. D4 8
Doré Lake, l., Sask., Can. C2 75
Dorena Lake, res., Or., U.S. D3 114
Dores do Indaiá, Braz. E6 57
Dorgali, Italy I4 14
Dori, Burkina F5 42
Dorion-Vaudreuil, Que., Can. q18 74
Dormont, Pa., U.S. k13 115
Dornbirn, Aus. H9 8
Dorothy Pond, Ma., U.S. B4 98
Dorr, Mi., U.S. F5 99
Dorset, Vt., U.S. E2 122
Dorsey, Md., U.S. B4 97
Dortmund, Ger. D7 8
Dorton, Ky., U.S. C7 94
Dorval, Que., Can. q19 74
Dos Bahías, Cabo, c., Arg. E3 56
Dothan, Al., U.S. D4 78
Douai, Fr. B10 10
Douala, Cam. H7 42
Douarnenez, Fr. D2 10
Double Beach, Ct., U.S. D4 84
Doublespring Pass, Id., U.S. E5 89
Double Springs, Al., U.S. A2 78
Doubletop Peak, mtn., Wy., U.S. C2 127
Doubs, stm., Eur. E12 10
Dougherty, co., Ga., U.S. E2 87
Douglas, I. of Man G8 7
Douglas, Az., U.S. F6 80
Douglas, Ga., U.S. E4 87
Douglas, Mi., U.S. F4 99
Douglas, Wy., U.S. D7 127
Douglas, co., Co., U.S. B6 83
Douglas, co., Ga., U.S. C2 87
Douglas, co., Il., U.S. D5 90
Douglas, co., Ks., U.S. D8 93
Douglas, co., Mn., U.S. E3 100
Douglas, co., Mo., U.S. E5 102
Douglas, co., Ne., U.S. C9 104
Douglas, co., Nv., U.S. E2 105
Douglas, co., Or., U.S. D3 114
Douglas, co., S.D., U.S. D7 118
Douglas, co., Wa., U.S. B6 124
Douglas, co., Wi., U.S. B2 126
Douglas, Mount, mtn., Ak., U.S. D9 79
Douglas Channel, strt., B.C., Can. C3 69
Douglas Lake, l., Mi., U.S. C6 99
Douglas Lake, res., Tn., U.S. D10 119
Douglass, Ks., U.S. E7 93
Douglastown, N.B., Can. B4 71
Douglasville, Ga., U.S. C2 87
Dourada, Serra, plat., Braz. B4 57
Dourados, Braz. G1 57
Douro (Duero), stm., Eur. D4 12
Dousman, Wi., U.S. E5 126
Dove Creek, Co., U.S. D2 83
Dover, Eng., U.K. J14 7
Dover, Ar., U.S. B2 81
Dover, De., U.S. D3 85
Dover, Fl., U.S. D4 86
Dover, Ma., U.S. h10 98
Dover, N.H., U.S. D5 106
Dover, N.J., U.S. B3 107
Dover, Oh., U.S. B4 112
Dover, Pa., U.S. F8 115
Dover, Tn., U.S. A4 119
Dover, Strait of (Pas de Calais), strt., Eur. J14 7
Dover Air Force Base, mil., De., U.S. D4 85
Dover-Foxcroft, Me., U.S. C3 96
Dover Plains, N.Y., U.S. D7 109
Dowagiac, Mi., U.S. G4 99
Dowlat Yār, Afg. C1 38
Downers Grove, Il., U.S. B5 90
Downey, Ca., U.S. n12 82
Downey, Id., U.S. G6 89
Downingtown, Pa., U.S. F10 115
Downpatrick, N. Ire., U.K. G7 7
Downpatrick Head, c., Ire. G3 7
Downs, Ks., U.S. C5 93
Downs Mountain, mtn., Wy., U.S. C3 127
Downton, Mount, mtn., B.C., Can. C5 69
Dows, Ia., U.S. B4 92
Dowshī, Afg. C3 38
Doylestown, Oh., U.S. B4 112
Doylestown, Pa., U.S. F11 115
Doyline, La., U.S. B2 95
Drâa, Oued, val., Afr. C4 42
Dracena, Braz. F3 57
Drachten, Neth. B6 8
Dracut, Ma., U.S. A5 98
Draguignan, Fr. I13 10
Drain, Or., U.S. D3 114
Drake Passage, strt. D6 47
Drake Peak, mtn., Or., U.S. E6 114
Dráma, Grc. H8 16
Drammen, Nor. G8 6
Draper, Ut., U.S. C4 121
Drau (Drava), stm., Eur. C8 14
Drava (Drau), stm., Eur. D13 14
Drayton, Ont., Can. D4 73
Drayton, N.D., U.S. A8 111
Drayton, S.C., U.S. B4 117
Drayton Plains, Mi., U.S. F7 99
Drayton Valley, Alta., Can. C3 68
Dresden, Ont., Can. E2 73
Dresden, Ger. D13 8
Dresden, Oh., U.S. B3 112
Dresden, Tn., U.S. A3 119
Dresslerville, Nv., U.S. E2 105
Dreux, Fr. D8 10
Drew, Ms., U.S. B3 101
Drew, co., Ar., U.S. D4 81
Drews Reservoir, res., Or., U.S. E6 114
Drexel, Mo., U.S. C3 102
Drexel, N.C., U.S. B1 110
Drexel, Oh., U.S. C1 112
Drift, Ky., U.S. C7 94
Driggs, Id., U.S. F7 89
Driskill Mountain, hill, La., U.S. B3 95
Drogheda, Ire. H6 7
Drumheller, Alta., Can. D4 68
Drum Island, i., S.C., U.S. k12 117
Drummond, Lake, l., Va., U.S. D6 123
Drummond Island, i., Mi., U.S. C7 99
Drummondville, Que., Can. D5 74
Drumright, Ok., U.S. B5 113
Družina, Russia D23 24
Drybranch, W.V., U.S. m13 125
Dry Cimarron, stm., U.S. A6 108
Dry Creek Mountain, mtn., Nv., U.S. B5 105
Dryden, Ont., Can. o16 73
Dryden, N.Y., U.S. C4 109
Dry Fork, stm., Mo., U.S. D6 102
Dry Fork, stm., W.V., U.S. D3 125
Dry Fork, stm., W.V., U.S. B5 125
Dry Ridge, Ky., U.S. B5 94
Dry Tortugas, is., Fl., U.S. H5 86
Duarte, Pico, mtn., Dom. Rep. E12 64
Dubach, La., U.S. B3 95
Dubai see Dubayy, U.A.E. C6 46
Dubawnt, stm., N.W. Ter., Can. D12 66
Dubawnt Lake, l., N.W. Ter., Can. D12 66
Du Bay, Lake, res., Wi., U.S. D4 126
Dubayy (Dubai), U.A.E. C6 46
Dubbo, Austl. F9 50
Dublin (Baile Átha Cliath), Ire. H6 7
Dublin, Ga., U.S. D4 87
Dublin, In., U.S. E7 91
Dublin, N.H., U.S. E2 106
Dublin, Oh., U.S. k10 112
Dublin, Pa., U.S. F11 115
Dublin, Tx., U.S. C3 120
Dublin, Va., U.S. C2 123
Dubna, Russia E20 18
Dubois, In., U.S. H4 91
Du Bois, Pa., U.S. D4 115
Dubois, Wy., U.S. C3 127
Dubois, co., In., U.S. H4 91
Duboistown, Pa., U.S. D7 115
Dubrovnik, Cro. G13 14
Dubuque, Ia., U.S. B7 92
Dubuque, co., Ia., U.S. B7 92
Duchesne, Ut., U.S. C5 121
Duchesne, co., Ut., U.S. C5 121
Duchesne, stm., Ut., U.S. C5 121
Duchess, Austl. D7 50
Duck, stm., Tn., U.S. B4 119
Duck Bay, Man., Can. C1 70
Duck Creek, stm., Oh., U.S. C4 112
Duck Creek, stm., Wi., U.S. h9 126
Duck Lake, Sask., Can. E2 75
Duck Lake, l., Me., U.S. C4 96
Duck Mountain Provincial Park, Sask., Can. F5 75
Duck Valley Indian Reservation, U.S. B5 105
Duckwater Indian Reservation, Nv., U.S. E6 105
Duckwater Peak, mtn., Nv., U.S. E6 105
Dudelange, Lux. F6 8
Dudinka, Russia D11 24
Dudley, Ma., U.S. B4 98
Duenweg, Mo., U.S. D3 102
Duero (Douro), stm., Eur. D5 12
Due West, S.C., U.S. C3 117
Duffer Peak, mtn., Nv., U.S. B3 105
Dufour Spitze, mtn., Eur. G14 10
Duga Resa, Cro. D10 14
Dugdemona, stm., La., U.S. B3 95
Dugger, In., U.S. F3 91
Duida, Cerro, mtn., Ven. F10 58
Duifken Point, c., Austl. B8 50
Duisburg, Ger. D6 8
Duke Island, i., Ak., U.S. n24 79
Dukes, co., Ma., U.S. D6 98
Duk Fadiat, Sudan G12 42
Dulce, N.M., U.S. A2 108
Dulgalach, stm., Russia D20 24
Duluth, Ga., U.S. B2 87
Duluth, Mn., U.S. D6 100
Dūmā, Syria C5 40
Dumaguete, Phil. D7 32
Dumaran Island, i., Phil. C6 32
Dumaring, Indon. E6 32
Dumas, Ar., U.S. D4 81
Dumas, Tx., U.S. B2 120
Dumbarton, Scot., U.K. F8 7
Dumfries, Scot., U.K. F9 7
Dumfries, Va., U.S. B5 123
Dumont, Ia., U.S. B5 92
Dumont, N.J., U.S. B5 107
Dumyāṭ, Egypt B12 42
Dunaújváros, Hung. I18 8
Dunbar, Pa., U.S. G2 115
Dunbar, W.V., U.S. C3 125
Duncan, B.C., Can. E6 69
Duncan, Az., U.S. E6 80
Duncan, Ok., U.S. C4 113
Duncan, S.C., U.S. B3 117
Duncan Falls, Oh., U.S. C4 112
Duncan Lake, res., B.C., Can. D9 69
Duncannon, Pa., U.S. F7 115
Duncansville, Pa., U.S. F5 115
Duncanville, Tx., U.S. n10 120
Dundalk, Ont., Can. C4 73
Dundalk, Ire. G6 7
Dundalk, Md., U.S. B4 97
Dundas, Ont., Can. D5 73
Dundas Peninsula, pen., N.W. Ter., Can. B10 66
Dundee, S. Afr. G6 44
Dundee, Scot., U.K. E9 7
Dundee, Fl., U.S. D5 86
Dundee, Il., U.S. A5 90
Dundee, Mi., U.S. G7 99
Dundee, N.Y., U.S. C4 109
Dundee, Or., U.S. h11 114
Dundy, co., Ne., U.S. D4 104
Dunedin, N.Z. F3 52
Dunedin, Fl., U.S. D4 86
Dunellen, N.J., U.S. B4 107
Dunfermline, Scot., U.K. E9 7
Dungarvan, Ire. I5 7
Dungeness, stm., Wa., U.S. A2 124
Dungun, Malay. L7 34
Dunham, Que., Can. D5 74
Dunhua, China C12 26
Dunhuang, China C5 26
Dunkard Creek, stm., U.S. B4 125
Dunkerque, Fr. A9 10
Dunkerton, Ia., U.S. B5 92
Dunkirk, In., U.S. D7 91
Dunkirk, N.Y., U.S. C1 109
Dunkirk, Oh., U.S. B2 112
Dunklin, co., Mo., U.S. E7 102
Dunkwa, Ghana G5 42
Dún Laoghaire, Ire. H6 7
Dunlap, Il., U.S. C4 90
Dunlap, In., U.S. A6 91
Dunlap, Ia., U.S. C2 92
Dunlap, Tn., U.S. D8 119
Dunleith, De., U.S. i7 85
Dunloup Creek, stm., W.V., U.S. n13 125
Dunmore, Pa., U.S. D10 115
Dunmore, Lake, l., Vt., U.S. D2 122
Dunn, N.C., U.S. B4 110
Dunn, co., N.D., U.S. B3 111
Dunn, co., Wi., U.S. D2 126
Dunnellon, Fl., U.S. C4 86
Dunnville, Ont., Can. E5 73
Dunqulah, Sudan E12 42
Duns, Scot., U.K. F10 7
Dunseith, N.D., U.S. A5 111
Dunsmuir, Ca., U.S. B2 82
Duntou, China F8 28
Dunville, Newf., Can. E5 72
Dunwoody, Ga., U.S. h8 87
Duomaer, China E2 26
Du Page, co., Il., U.S. B5 90
Du Page, stm., Il., U.S. k8 90
Duplin, co., N.C., U.S. C5 110
Dupont, Co., U.S. B6 83
Dupont, Pa., U.S. n18 115
Dupont City, W.V., U.S. m12 125
Dupont Manor, De., U.S. B1 41
Dupont Manor, De., U.S. D3 85
Duque de Caxias, Braz. G7 57
Duque de York, Isla, i., Chile G1 56
Duquesne, Pa., U.S. F2 115
Du Quoin, Il., U.S. E4 90
Durand, Il., U.S. A4 90
Durand, Mi., U.S. F6 99
Durand, Wi., U.S. D2 126
Durango, Mex. E7 62
Durango, Spain B9 12
Durango, Co., U.S. D3 83
Durant, Ia., U.S. C7 92
Durant, Ms., U.S. B4 101
Durant, Ok., U.S. D5 113
Durazno, Ur. C5 56
Durban, S. Afr. G6 44
Đurđevac, Cro. C12 14
Düren, Ger. E6 8
Durg, India B6 37
Durgāpur, India I12 38
Durham, Ont., Can. C4 73
Durham, Eng., U.K. G11 7
Durham, Ca., U.S. C3 82
Durham, Ct., U.S. D5 84
Durham, N.H., U.S. D5 106
Durham, N.C., U.S. B4 110
Durham, co., N.C., U.S. A4 110
Durness, Scot., U.K. C8 7
Durrell, Newf., Can. D4 72
Durrës, Alb. H3 16
Dursunbey, Tur. J12 16
D'Urville, Tanjung, c., Indon. F10 32
Duryea, Pa., U.S. D10 115
Dušanbe, Taj. J11 22
Dušekan, Russia E15 24
Dushan, China B9 34
Dushanbe see Dušanbe, Taj. J11 22
Duson, La., U.S. D3 95
Düsseldorf, Ger. D6 8
Dutchess, co., N.Y., U.S. D7 109
Dutch Island, i., R.I., U.S. F4 116
Dutton, Ont., Can. E3 73
Dutton, Mount, mtn., Ut., U.S. E3 121
Duval, co., Fl., U.S. B5 86
Duval, co., Tx., U.S. F3 120
Duxbury, Ma., U.S. B6 98
Duyun, China A9 34
Dwight, Il., U.S. B5 90
Dwight D. Eisenhower Lock, N.Y., U.S. f9 109
Dworshak Reservoir, res., Id., U.S. C3 89
Dyer, In., U.S. A2 91
Dyer, Tn., U.S. A3 119
Dyer, co., Tn., U.S. A2 119
Dyer, Cape, c., N.W. Ter., Can. C20 66
Dyer Island, i., R.I., U.S. E5 116
Dyersburg, Tn., U.S. A2 119
Dyersville, Ia., U.S. B6 92
Dyess Air Force Base, mil., Tx., U.S. C3 120
Dysart, Ia., U.S. B5 92
Džalinda, Russia G18 24
Džambul, Kaz. I12 22
Dzaoudzi, May. D9 44
Džardžan, Russia D18 24
Dzavchan, stm., Mong. B5 26
Dzeržinsk, Russia E26 18
Dzeržinskoje, Kaz. H10 24
Džezkazgan, Kaz. H11 22
Dzhambul see Džambul, Kaz. I12 22
Dzierżoniów (Reichenbach), Pol. E16 8
Džugdžur, Chrebet, mts., Russia F21 24

E

Eads, Co., U.S. C8 83
Eagan, Mn., U.S. n12 100
Eagar, Az., U.S. C6 80
Eagle, Co., U.S. B4 83
Eagle, Id., U.S. F2 89
Eagle, Ne., U.S. h12 104
Eagle, Wi., U.S. F5 126
Eagle, co., Co., U.S. B4 83
Eagle, stm., Newf., Can. B2 72
Eagle Creek Reservoir, res., In., U.S. E5 91
Eagle Grove, Ia., U.S. B4 92
Eagle Key, i., Fl., U.S. G6 86
Eagle Lake, Me., U.S. A4 96
Eagle Lake, Mn., U.S. F5 100
Eagle Lake, Tx., U.S. E4 120
Eagle Lake, l., Ca., U.S. B3 82
Eagle Lake, l., Me., U.S. A4 96
Eagle Lake, l., Me., U.S. B3 96
Eagle Lake, l., Ms., U.S. C3 101
Eagle Lake, l., Wi., U.S. C4 126
Eagle Mountain, mtn., Mn., U.S. k9 100
Eagle Mountain Lake, res., Tx., U.S. m9 120
Eagle Nest Lake, l., N.M., U.S. A4 108
Eagle Pass, Tx., U.S. E2 120
Eagle Peak, mtn., Ca., U.S. B3 82
Eagle Point, Or., U.S. E4 114
Eagle River, Wi., U.S. C4 126
Eagletail Mountains, mts., Az., U.S. D2 80
Eagletail Peak, mtn., Az., U.S. D2 80
Eagletown, Ok., U.S. C7 113
Earle, Ar., U.S. B5 81
Earlham, Ia., U.S. C3 92
Earlimart, Ca., U.S. E4 82
Earlington, Ky., U.S. C2 94
Earlville, Il., U.S. B5 90
Earlville, Ia., U.S. B6 92
Early, Ia., U.S. B2 92
Early, co., Ga., U.S. E2 87
Earth, Tx., U.S. B1 120
Easley, S.C., U.S. B2 117
East, stm., Ct., U.S. D5 84
East, stm., N.Y., U.S. k13 109
East, stm., Wi., U.S. h9 126
East Alton, Il., U.S. E3 90
East Angus, Que., Can. D6 74
East Arlington, Vt., U.S. E2 122
East Aurora, N.Y., U.S. C2 109
East Bangor, Pa., U.S. E11 115
East Bank, W.V., U.S. m13 125
East Barre, Vt., U.S. C4 122
East Baton Rouge, co., La., U.S. D4 95
East Bay, b., Fl., U.S. u16 86
East Bay, b., Tx., U.S. R15 120
East Beckwith Mountain, mtn., Co., U.S. C3 83
East Berlin, Ct., U.S. C5 84
East Berlin, Pa., U.S. G8 115
East Bernard, Tx., U.S. E4 120
East Bernstadt, Ky., U.S. C5 94
East Bethel, Mn., U.S. E5 100
East Billerica, Ma., U.S. f11 98
Eastborough, Ks., U.S. g12 93
Eastbourne, Eng., U.K. K13 7
East Brady, Pa., U.S. E2 115
East Branch Clarion River Lake, res., Pa., U.S. C4 115
East Brewton, Al., U.S. D2 78
East Bridgewater, Ma., U.S. B6 98
East Brimfield Lake, res., Ma., U.S. B3 98
East Brooklyn, Ct., U.S. B8 84
East Broughton, Que., Can. C6 74
East Brunswick, N.J., U.S. C4 107
East Butte, mtn., Mt., U.S. B5 103
East Cache Creek, stm., Ok., U.S. C3 113
East Cape, c., Fl., U.S. G5 86
East Carbon, Ut., U.S. D5 121
East Carroll, co., La., U.S. B4 95
East Chicago, In., U.S. A3 91
East China Sea, Asia E12 26
East Chop, c., Ma., U.S. D6 98
East Cleveland, Oh., U.S. g9 112
East Cote Blanche Bay, b., La., U.S. E4 95
East Dennis, Ma., U.S. C7 98
East Derry, N.H., U.S. E4 106
East Detroit, Mi., U.S. p16 99
East Douglas, Ma., U.S. B4 98
East Dubuque, Il., U.S. A3 90
Eastend, Sask., Can. H1 75
Easter Island see Pascua, Isla de, i., Chile H5 2
Eastern Bay, b., Md., U.S. C5 97
Eastern Channel see Tsushima-kaikyō, strt., Japan I2 30
Eastern Ghāts, mts., India F5 37
Eastern Neck Island, i., Md., U.S. B5 97
Eastern Point, c., Ma., U.S. f13 98
Easterville, Man., Can. C2 70
East Falkland, i., Falk. Is. G5 56
East Falmouth, Ma., U.S. C6 98
East Feliciana, co., La., U.S. D4 95
East Flat Rock, N.C., U.S. f10 110
East Fork, stm., Wy., U.S. D3 127
East Fork Lake, res., Oh., U.S. C1 112
East Gaffney, S.C., U.S. A4 117
East Galesburg, Il., U.S. C3 90
East Granby, Ct., U.S. B5 84
East Grand Forks, Mn., U.S. C2 100
East Grand Rapids, Mi., U.S. F5 99
East Greenville, Pa., U.S. F10 115
East Greenwich, R.I., U.S. D4 116
East Gwillimbury, Ont., Can. C5 73
East Hampstead, N.H., U.S. E4 106
East Hampton, Ct., U.S. C5 84
Easthampton, Ma., U.S. B2 98
East Hanover, N.J., U.S. *B4 107
East Hartford, Ct., U.S. B5 84
East Hartland, Ct., U.S. B4 84
East Haven, Ct., U.S. D4 84
East Helena, Mt., U.S. D5 103
East Jordan, Mi., U.S. C5 99
Eastlake, Oh., U.S. A4 112
East Lake Tohopekaliga, l., Fl., U.S. D5 86
Eastland, Tx., U.S. C3 120
Eastland, co., Tx., U.S. C3 120
East Lansing, Mi., U.S. F6 99
East Las Vegas, Nv., U.S. G6 105
East Liverpool, Oh., U.S. B5 112
East London (Oos-Londen), S. Afr. H5 44

Name — Map Ref — Page
East Longmeadow, Ma., U.S. B2 98
East Los Angeles, Ca., U.S. m12 82
East Lyme, Ct., U.S. D7 84
East Lynn Lake, res., W.V., U.S. C2 125
Eastmain, stm., Que., Can. F17 66
Eastmain-Opinaca, Réservoir, res., Que., Can. h11 74
Eastman, Que., Can. D5 74
Eastman, Ga., U.S. D3 87
East Matunuck, R.I., U.S. F3 116
East Middlebury, Vt., U.S. D2 122
East Millinocket, Me., U.S. C4 96
East Moline, Il., U.S. B3 90
East Montpelier, Vt., U.S. C4 122
East Naples, Fl., U.S. F5 86
East Newnan, Ga., U.S. C2 87
East Nishnabotna, stm., Ia., U.S. C2 92
East Norriton, Pa., U.S. o20 115
East Olympia, Wa., U.S. C3 124
Easton, Md., U.S. C5 97
Easton, Pa., U.S. E11 115
Easton Reservoir, res., Ct., U.S. E2 84
East Orange, N.J., U.S. B4 107
East Orleans, Ma., U.S. C8 98
Eastover, S.C., U.S. D6 117
East Palatka, Fl., U.S. C5 86
East Palestine, Oh., U.S. B5 112
East Pass, strt., Fl., U.S. C2 86
East Pea Ridge, W.V., U.S. C2 125
East Peoria, Il., U.S. C4 90
East Pepperell, Ma., U.S. A4 98
East Petersburg, Pa., U.S. F9 115
East Pittsburgh, Pa., U.S. k14 115
Eastpoint, Fl., U.S. C2 86
East Point, Ga., U.S. C2 87
East Point, c., P.E.I., Can. C8 71
East Point, c., Ma., U.S. B6 98
East Point, c., N.J., U.S. E2 107
Eastport, Newf., Can. D5 72
Eastport, Me., U.S. D6 96
East Prairie, Mo., U.S. E8 102
East Providence, R.I., U.S. C4 116
East Pryor Mountain, mtn., Mt., U.S. E8 103
East Quogue, N.Y., U.S. n16 109
East Range, mts., Nv., U.S. C4 105
East Ridge, Tn., U.S. h11 119
East River, Ct., U.S. D5 84
East Rochester, N.Y., U.S. B3 109
East Rockingham, N.C., U.S. C3 110
East Rutherford, N.J., U.S. h8 107
East Saint Louis, Il., U.S. E3 90
East Selkirk, Man., Can. D3 70
Eastsound, Wa., U.S. A3 124
East Spencer, N.C., U.S. B2 110
East Stroudsburg, Pa., U.S. D11 115
East Tawas, Mi., U.S. D7 99
East Troy, Wi., U.S. F5 126
East Vestal, N.Y., U.S. C4 109
East View, W.V., U.S. k10 125
East Walker, stm., U.S. E2 105
East Walpole, Ma., U.S. h11 98
East Wareham, Ma., U.S. C6 98
East Washington, Pa., U.S. F1 115
East Wenatchee, Wa., U.S. B5 124
East Windsor, N.J., U.S. C3 107
East York, Ont., Can. D5 73
Eaton, Co., U.S. A6 83
Eaton, In., U.S. D7 91
Eaton, Oh., U.S. C1 112
Eaton, co., Mi., U.S. F6 99
Eaton Rapids, Mi., U.S. F6 99
Eatonton, Ga., U.S. C3 87
Eatontown, N.J., U.S. C4 107
Eatonville, Wa., U.S. C3 124
Eau Claire, Wi., U.S. D2 126
Eau Claire, co., Wi., U.S. D2 126
Eau Claire, stm., Wi., U.S. D2 126
Eau Claire, Lac à l', l., Que., Can. g11 74
Eauze, Fr. I7 10
Ebano, Mex. F10 62
Ebba Ksour, Tun. N3 14
Ebbw Vale, Wales, U.K. J9 7
Ebensburg, Pa., U.S. F4 115
Eberndorf, Aus. I14 8
Eberswalde, Ger. C13 8
Ebetsu, Japan p19 30a
Ebingen, Ger. G9 8
Ebinur Hu, l., China B3 26
Eboli, Italy I10 14
Ebolowa, Cam. H8 42
Ebro, stm., Spain E12 12
Ebro, Delta del, Spain E12 12
Eccles, W.V., U.S. n13 125
Echo Bay, Nv., U.S. G7 105
Echo Lake, l., Me., U.S. D3 96
Echo Lake, l., Vt., U.S. B5 122
Echols, co., Ga., U.S. F4 87
Écija, Spain H6 12
Eckernförde, Ger. A9 8
Eckhart Mines, Md., U.S. k13 97
Eckville, Alta., Can. C3 68
Eclectic, Al., U.S. C3 78
Eclipse Sound, strt., N.W. Ter., Can. B17 66
Écommoy, Fr. E7 10
Econfina, stm., Fl., U.S. B3 86
Economy, Pa., U.S. *h13 115
Écorces, Rivière aux, stm., Que., Can. A6 74
Ecorse, Mi., U.S. p15 99
Ecru, Ms., U.S. A4 101
Ector, co., Tx., U.S. D1 120
Ecuador, ctry., S.A. D3 54
Ed, Swe. G8 6
Edcouch, Tx., U.S. F4 120
Eddy, co., N.M., U.S. E5 108
Eddy, co., N.D., U.S. B7 111
Eddystone, Pa., U.S. p20 115
Eddyville, Ia., U.S. C5 92
Eddyville, Ky., U.S. e9 94
Ede, Neth. C5 8
Edéa, Cam. H8 42
Eden, Ga., U.S. D5 87
Eden, Md., U.S. D6 97
Eden, N.Y., U.S. C2 109
Eden, N.C., U.S. A3 110
Eden, Tx., U.S. D3 120
Edenderry, Ire. H5 7
Eden Prairie, Mn., U.S. n12 100
Edenton, N.C., U.S. A6 110
Eden Valley, Mn., U.S. E4 100
Edgar, Ne., U.S. D8 104
Edgar, Wi., U.S. D4 126
Edgar, co., Il., U.S. D6 90
Edgard, La., U.S. D5 95
Edgartown, Ma., U.S. D6 98
Edgecombe, co., N.C., U.S. B5 110
Edgecumbe, Cape, c., Ak., U.S. m21 79
Edgefield, S.C., U.S. D4 117
Edgefield, co., S.C., U.S. D4 117
Edgeley, N.D., U.S. C7 111
Edgemere, Md., U.S. B5 97
Edgemont, S.D., U.S. D2 118
Edgemoor, De., U.S. A3 85
Edgerton, Ks., U.S. D8 93
Edgerton, Mn., U.S. G2 100
Edgerton, Oh., U.S. A1 112
Edgerton, Wi., U.S. F4 126
Edgerton, Wy., U.S. C6 127
Edgewater, Al., U.S. f7 78
Edgewater, Fl., U.S. D6 86
Edgewater, Md., U.S. C4 97
Edgewater, N.J., U.S. h9 107
Edgewater Park, N.J., U.S. C3 107
Edgewood, In., U.S. D6 91
Edgewood, Ia., U.S. B6 92
Edgewood, Ky., U.S. h13 94
Edgewood, Md., U.S. B5 97
Edgewood, N.M., U.S. B3 108
Edgewood, Oh., U.S. A5 112
Edgewood, Pa., U.S. k14 115
Edgewood, Wa., U.S. f11 124
Edgeworth, Pa., U.S. h13 115
Edina, Mn., U.S. F5 100
Edina, Mo., U.S. A5 102
Edinboro, Pa., U.S. C1 115
Edinburg, Il., U.S. D4 90
Edinburg, Tx., U.S. F3 120
Edinburg, Va., U.S. B4 123
Edinburgh, Scot., U.K. F9 7
Edinburgh, In., U.S. F6 91
Edirne, Tur. G13 4
Edison, Ga., U.S. E2 87
Edison, N.J., U.S. B4 107
Edisto, stm., S.C., U.S. E6 117
Edisto Island, i., S.C., U.S. F7 117
Edith, Mount, mtn., Mt., U.S. D5 103
Edjeleh, Alg. C7 42
Edmond, Ok., U.S. B4 113
Edmonds, Wa., U.S. B3 124
Edmondson Heights, Md., U.S. *g10 97
Edmonson, co., Ky., U.S. C3 94
Edmonton, Alta., Can. C4 68
Edmonton, Ky., U.S. D4 94
Edmore, Mi., U.S. E5 99
Edmunds, co., S.D., U.S. B6 118
Edmundston, N.B., Can. B1 71
Edna, Tx., U.S. E4 120
Edon, Oh., U.S. A1 112
Édouard, Lac, l., Que., Can. B5 74
Edremit, Tur. J11 16
Edrengijn Nuruu, mts., Mong. C6 26
Edsbyn, Swe. F10 6
Edson, Alta., Can. C2 68
Edson Butte, mtn., Or., U.S. E2 114
Eduardo Castex, Arg. D4 56
Edward, Lake, l., Afr. B5 44
Edwards, Ms., U.S. C3 101
Edwards, co., Il., U.S. E5 90
Edwards, co., Ks., U.S. E4 93
Edwards, co., Tx., U.S. E2 120
Edwards Air Force Base, mil., Ca., U.S. E5 82
Edwardsburg, Mi., U.S. G4 99
Edwards Butte, mtn., Or., U.S. B3 114
Edwardsville, Il., U.S. E4 90
Edwardsville, Ks., U.S. k16 93
Edwardsville, Pa., U.S. n17 115
Eel, stm., Ca., U.S. B2 82
Eel, stm., In., U.S. F3 91
Eel, stm., In., U.S. C6 91
Effigy Mounds National Monument, Ia., U.S. A6 92
Effingham, Il., U.S. D5 90
Effingham, co., Ga., U.S. D5 87
Effingham, co., Il., U.S. D5 90
Efland, N.C., U.S. A3 110
Egan Range, mts., Nv., U.S. E7 105
Eganville, Ont., Can. B7 73
Egede og Rothes Fjord, Grnld. C25 66
Egedesminde, Grnld. C22 66
Eger, Hung. H20 8
Egersund, Nor. G5 6
Eggenfelden, Ger. G12 8
Egg Harbor City, N.J., U.S. D3 107
Egg Island Point, c., N.J., U.S. E2 107
Égletons, Fr. G9 10
Eglin Air Force Base, mil., Fl., U.S. u15 86
Egmont, Mount, mtn., N.Z. C5 52
Egmont Bay, b., P.E.I., Can. C5 71
Egmont Channel, strt., Fl., U.S. p10 86
Egmont Key, i., Fl., U.S. p10 86
Egvekinot, Russia D29 24
Egypt, ctry., Afr. C11 42
Egypt, Lake of, res., Il., U.S. F5 90
Ehingen, Ger. G9 8
Ehrenberg, Az., U.S. D1 80
Éibar, Spain B9 12
Eichstätt, Ger. G11 8
Eidsvoll, Nor. F8 6
Eielson Air Force Base, mil., Ak., U.S. C10 79
Eifel, mts., Ger. E6 8
Eighty Mile Beach, Austl. C4 50
Eil, Som. G4 46
Eilenburg, Ger. D12 8
Eindhoven, Neth. D5 8
Einsiedeln, Switz. E15 10
Eirunepé, Braz. E5 54
Eisenach, Ger. E10 8
Eisenberg, Ger. E11 8
Eisenerz, Aus. H14 8
Eisenhower, Mount, mtn., N.H., U.S. B4 106
Eisenhüttenstadt, Ger. C14 8
Eisenstadt, Aus. H16 8
Eisleben, Ger. D11 8
Ejea de los Caballeros, Spain C10 12
Ekiatapskij Chrebet, mts., Russia D29 24
Ekimčan, Russia G20 24
Ekwan, stm., Ont., Can. F16 66
El Aaiún, W. Sah. C3 42
Elaine, Ar., U.S. C5 81
El Asnam, Alg. A6 42
Elat, Isr. E4 40
El Avión, Mex. E6 62
Elâzığ, Tur. H15 4
Elba, Al., U.S. D3 78
Elba, Isola d', i., Italy G5 14
El Banco, Col. C6 58
El Barco de Valdeorras, Spain C5 12
Elbasan, Alb. H4 16
El Baúl, Ven. C8 58
Elbe (Labe), stm., Eur. B9 8
Elberfeld, In., U.S. H3 91
Elbert, co., Co., U.S. B6 83
Elbert, co., Ga., U.S. B4 87
Elbert, Mount, mtn., Co., U.S. B4 83
Elberta, Ga., U.S. D3 87
Elberton, Ga., U.S. B4 87
Elbeuf, Fr. C8 10
Elbląg (Elbing), Pol. A19 8
El Bonillo, Spain G9 12
El Bordo, Col. F4 58
Elbow, stm., Alta., Can. D3 68
Elbow Lake, Mn., U.S. E3 100
El'brus, gora (Mount Elbrus), mtn., Russia I6 22
El Burgo de Osma, Spain D8 12
Elburn, Il., U.S. B5 90
Elburz Mountains see Alborz, Reshteh-ye Kūhhā-ye, mts., Iran J8 22
El Cajon, Ca., U.S. F5 82
El Callao, Ven. D12 58
El Campo, Tx., U.S. E4 120
El Capitan, mtn., Mt., U.S. D2 103
El Capitan Reservoir, res., Ca., U.S. o16 82
El Carmen, Arg. A3 56
El Carmen de Bolívar, Col. C5 58
El Centro, Ca., U.S. F6 82
El Cerrito, Col. F4 58
El Cerrito, Ca., U.S. h8 82
Elche, Spain G11 12
Elche de la Sierra, Spain G9 12
El Cozón, Mex. B3 62
El Cuervo Butte, mtn., N.M., U.S. k9 108
Elda, Spain G11 12
El Desemboque, Mex. C3 62
El Diviso, Col. G3 58
El Djouf, des., Afr. D4 42
Eldon, Ia., U.S. D5 92
Eldon, Mo., U.S. C5 102
Eldora, Ia., U.S. B4 92
Eldorado, Mex. E6 62
El Dorado, Ar., U.S. D3 81
Eldorado, Il., U.S. F5 90
El Dorado, Ks., U.S. E7 93
Eldorado, Tx., U.S. D2 120
El Dorado, co., Ca., U.S. C3 82
Eldorado Peak, mtn., Wa., U.S. A4 124
Eldorado Springs, Co., U.S. B5 83
El Dorado Springs, Mo., U.S. D3 102
Eldoret, Kenya A7 44
Eldridge, Ia., U.S. C7 92
Eleanor, W.V., U.S. C3 125
Electra, Tx., U.S. C3 120
Electra Lake, res., Co., U.S. D3 83
Electric Peak, mtn., Co., U.S. C5 83
Electric Peak, mtn., Mt., U.S. E6 103
Elektrostal', Russia F21 18
El Encanto, Col. H6 58
Elephant Butte Reservoir, res., N.M., U.S. D2 108
El Estor, Guat. G3 64
Eleuthera, i., Bah. B9 64
Eleven Mile Canyon Reservoir, res., Co., U.S. C5 83
Eleven Point, stm., U.S. A4 81
Elevsís, Grc. K7 16
El Fahs, Tun. M4 14
El Ferrol del Caudillo, Spain B3 12
El Galpón, Arg. B4 56
Elgin, Scot., U.K. D9 7
Elgin, Il., U.S. A5 90
Elgin, Ia., U.S. B6 92
Elgin, Mn., U.S. F6 100
Elgin, Ne., U.S. C7 104
Elgin, N.D., U.S. C4 111
Elgin, Ok., U.S. C3 113
Elgin, Or., U.S. B9 114
Elgin, S.C., U.S. B6 117
Elgin, Tx., U.S. D4 120
El Goléa, Alg. B6 42
El Golfo de Santa Clara, Mex. B2 62
Elgon, Mount, mtn., Afr. A6 44
El Hank, clf, Afr. D4 42
El Haouaria, Tun. L6 14
Elida, Oh., U.S. B1 112
Elisabethville see Lubumbashi, Zaire D5 44
Elizabeth, Austl. F7 50
Elizabeth, Co., U.S. B6 83
Elizabeth, N.J., U.S. B4 107
Elizabeth, W.V., U.S. B3 125
Elizabeth, Cape, c., Wa., U.S. B1 124
Elizabeth City, N.C., U.S. A6 110
Elizabeth Islands, is., Ma., U.S. D6 98
Elizabeth Reef, atoll, Austl. E11 50
Elizabethton, Tn., U.S. C11 119
Elizabethtown, Ky., U.S. C4 94
Elizabethtown, N.C., U.S. C4 110
Elizabethtown, Pa., U.S. F8 115
Elizabethville, Pa., U.S. E8 115
El-Jadida, Mor. B4 42
El Jebel, Co., U.S. B3 83
Ełk, Pol. B22 8
Elk, co., Ks., U.S. E7 93
Elk, co., Pa., U.S. D4 115
Elk, stm., U.S. A2 78
Elk, stm., Co., U.S. A4 83
Elk, stm., Ks., U.S. E7 93
Elk, stm., W.V., U.S. C3 125
Elk, stm., Wi., U.S. C3 126
Elkader, Ia., U.S. B6 92
El Kairouan, Tun. N5 14
Elk City, Id., U.S. D3 89
Elk City, Ok., U.S. B2 113
Elk City Lake, res., Ks., U.S. E7 93
Elk Creek, stm., Ok., U.S. B2 113
Elk Creek, stm., S.D., U.S. C3 118
El Kef, Tun. M3 14
Elkford, B.C., Can. D10 69
Elk Grove, Ca., U.S. C3 82
Elk Grove Village, Il., U.S. h9 90
Elkhart, In., U.S. A6 91
Elkhart, Ks., U.S. E2 93
Elkhart, Tx., U.S. D5 120
Elkhart, co., In., U.S. A6 91
Elkhart, stm., In., U.S. B6 91
Elkhart Lake, Wi., U.S. E5 126
Elkhead Mountains, mts., Co., U.S. A3 83
Elkhorn, Man., Can. E1 70
Elk Horn, Ia., U.S. C2 92
Elkhorn, Ne., U.S. g12 104
Elkhorn, Wi., U.S. F5 126
Elkhorn, stm., Ne., U.S. B7 104
Elkhorn City, Ky., U.S. C7 94
Elkhorn Peaks, mts., Id., U.S. F7 89
Elkin, N.C., U.S. A2 110
Elkins, Ar., U.S. A1 81
Elkins, W.V., U.S. C5 125
Elkland, Pa., U.S. C7 115
Elk Mills, Md., U.S. A6 97
Elk Mound, Wi., U.S. D2 126
Elk Mountain, Wy., U.S. E6 127
Elk Mountain, mtn., N.M., U.S. D1 108
Elk Mountain, mtn., Wy., U.S. E6 127
Elk Mountains, mts., U.S. D1 118
Elk Mountains, mts., Co., U.S. B3 83
Elko, Nv., U.S. C6 105
Elko, co., Nv., U.S. B6 105
Elk Peak, mtn., Mt., U.S. D6 103
Elk Point, Alta., Can. C5 68
Elk Point, S.D., U.S. E9 118
Elk Rapids, Mi., U.S. D5 99
El Krib, Tun. M4 14
Elkridge, Md., U.S. B4 97
Elk River, Mn., U.S. E5 100
Elkton, Ky., U.S. D2 94
Elkton, Md., U.S. A6 97
Elkton, Mi., U.S. E7 99
Elkton, S.D., U.S. C9 118
Elkton, Va., U.S. B4 123
Elkview, W.V., U.S. m13 125
Elkville, Il., U.S. F4 90
Ellaville, Ga., U.S. D2 87
Ellen, Mount, mtn., Ut., U.S. E5 121
Ellendale, De., U.S. E4 85
Ellendale, N.D., U.S. C7 111
Ellensburg, Wa., U.S. C5 124
Ellenton, Fl., U.S. E4 86
Ellenville, N.Y., U.S. D6 109
Ellerbe, N.C., U.S. B3 110
Ellerslie, Md., U.S. k13 97
Ellesmere Island, i., N.W. Ter., Can. A21 128
Ellettsville, In., U.S. F4 91
Ellice Islands see Tuvalu, ctry., Oc. G24 2
Ellicott City, Md., U.S. B4 97
Ellijay, Ga., U.S. B2 87
Ellington, Ct., U.S. B6 84
Ellington, Mo., U.S. D7 102
Ellinwood, Ks., U.S. D5 93
Elliot Lake, Ont., Can. A2 73
Elliott, Ms., U.S. B4 101
Elliott, co., Ky., U.S. B6 94
Elliott Bay, b., Wa., U.S. e11 124
Elliott Key, i., Fl., U.S. G6 86
Ellis, Ks., U.S. D4 93
Ellis, co., Ks., U.S. D4 93
Ellis, co., Ok., U.S. A2 113
Ellis, co., Tx., U.S. C4 120
Ellis, stm., N.H., U.S. B4 106
Elliston, Va., U.S. C2 123
Ellisville, Ms., U.S. D4 101
Ellisville, Mo., U.S. f12 102
Ellon, Scot., U.K. D10 7
Elloree, S.C., U.S. D6 117
Ellport, Pa., U.S. E1 115
Ellsworth, Ks., U.S. D5 93
Ellsworth, Me., U.S. D4 96
Ellsworth, Pa., U.S. F1 115
Ellsworth, Wi., U.S. D1 126
Ellsworth, co., Ks., U.S. D5 93
Ellsworth Air Force Base, mil., S.D., U.S. C2 118
Ellwangen, Ger. G10 8
Ellwood City, Pa., U.S. E1 115
Elm, stm., N.D., U.S. B8 111
Elma, Ia., U.S. A5 92
Elma, Wa., U.S. C2 124
El Mahdia, Tun. N6 14
El Manteco, Ven. D11 58
Elm City, N.C., U.S. B5 110
Elm Creek, Ne., U.S. D6 104
El Médano, Mex. E4 62
Elmendorf Air Force Base, mil., Ak., U.S. C10 79
Elm Grove, Wi., U.S. m11 126
Elmhurst, Il., U.S. B6 90
Elmhurst, Pa., U.S. D10 115
Elmira, N.Y., U.S. C4 109
El Mirage, Az., U.S. k8 80
Elmira Heights, N.Y., U.S. C4 109
El Moknine, Tun. N5 14
Elmont, N.Y., U.S. k13 109
Elmora, Pa., U.S. E4 115
Elmore, Mn., U.S. G4 100
Elmore, Oh., U.S. A2 112
Elmore, co., Al., U.S. C3 78
Elmore, co., Id., U.S. F3 89
El Morro National Monument, N.M., U.S. B1 108
Elmsdale, N.S., Can. E6 71
Elmshorn, Ger. B9 8
Elm Springs, Ar., U.S. A1 81
Elmvale, Ont., Can. C5 73
Elmwood, Il., U.S. C3 90
Elmwood, Wi., U.S. D1 126
Elmwood Park, Il., U.S. k9 90
Elmwood Park, N.J., U.S. h8 107
Elmwood Place, Oh., U.S. o13 112
Elne, Fr. J9 10
Elnora, In., U.S. G3 91
Eloise, Fl., U.S. E5 86
Elon College, N.C., U.S. A3 110
Elora, Ont., Can. D4 73
Elorza, Ven. D8 58
El Oued, Alg. B7 42
Eloy, Az., U.S. E4 80
El Palmar, Ven. D12 58
El Paso, Il., U.S. C4 90
El Paso, Tx., U.S. o11 120
El Paso, co., Co., U.S. C6 83
El Paso, co., Tx., U.S. o11 120
El Pilar, Ven. B11 58
El Pital, Cerro, mtn., N.A. G3 64
El Portal, Fl., U.S. s13 86
El Prado, N.M., U.S. A4 108
El Progreso, Hond. G4 64
El Puente del Arzobispo, Spain F6 12
El Puerto de Santa María, Spain I5 12
El Quelite, Mex. F6 62
El Reno, Ok., U.S. B4 113
Elrose, Sask., Can. F1 75
Elroy, Wi., U.S. E3 126
Elsa, Yukon, Can. D5 66
Elsa, Tx., U.S. F3 120
Elsah, Il., U.S. E3 90
El Salto, Mex. F7 62
El Salvador, ctry., N.A. H3 64
El Sauce, Nic. H4 64
El Sauzal, Mex. B1 62
Elsberry, Mo., U.S. B7 102
Elsie, Mi., U.S. E6 99
Elsinore, Ut., U.S. E3 121
Elsmere, De., U.S. B3 85
Elsmere, Ky., U.S. B5 94
El Socorro, Ven. C10 58
El Sombrero, Ven. C9 58
Elspe, Ger. D8 8
Elsterwerda, Ger. D13 8
El Tigre, Col. F8 58
El Tigre, Ven. C10 58
El Tocuyo, Ven. C8 58
Elton, La., U.S. D3 95
El Toro Marine Corps Air Station, mil., Ca., U.S. n13 82
El Trapiche, Col. F4 58
El Triunfo, Mex. F4 62
El Turbio, Arg. G2 56
Elūru, India D6 37
El Vado Reservoir, res., N.M., U.S. A3 108
Elvas, Port. G4 12
Elverum, Nor. F8 6
El Vigía, Ven. C7 58
Elvins, Mo., U.S. D7 102
Elwell, Lake, res., Mt., U.S. B5 103
Elwha, stm., Wa., U.S. A2 124
Elwood, In., U.S. D6 91
Elwood, Ks., U.S. C9 93
Elwood, Ne., U.S. D6 104
Ely, Eng., U.K. I13 7
Ely, Mn., U.S. C7 100
Ely, Nv., U.S. D7 105
Elyria, Oh., U.S. A3 112
Elysburg, Pa., U.S. E8 115
Emanuel, co., Ga., U.S. D4 87
Embarcación, Arg. A4 56
Embarras, stm., Il., U.S. E6 90
Embarrass, stm., Wi., U.S. D5 126
Embro, Ont., Can. D4 73
Embrun, Fr. H13 10
Emden, Ger. B7 8
Emerald, Austl. D9 50
Emerson, Man., Can. E3 70
Emerson, Ga., U.S. B2 87
Emerson, Ne., U.S. B9 104
Emerson, N.J., U.S. h8 107
Emery, co., Ut., U.S. E5 121
Emet, Tur. J13 16
Emily, Mn., U.S. D5 100
Emily, Lake, l., Mn., U.S. E3 100
Eminence, Ky., U.S. B4 94
Emmaus, Pa., U.S. E11 115
Emmen, Neth. C6 8
Emmendingen, Ger. G7 8
Emmet, co., Ia., U.S. A3 92
Emmet, co., Mi., U.S. C6 99
Emmetsburg, Ia., U.S. A3 92
Emmett, Id., U.S. F2 89
Emmiganūru, India E4 37
Emmitsburg, Md., U.S. A3 97
Emmonak, Ak., U.S. C7 79
Emmons, co., N.D., U.S. C5 111
Emory Peak, mtn., Tx., U.S. E1 120
Empalme, Mex. D4 62
Empangeni, S. Afr. G6 44
Empedrado, Arg. B5 56
Empire, La., U.S. E6 95
Empire, Nv., U.S. C2 105
Empoli, Italy F5 14
Emporia, Ks., U.S. D7 93
Emporia, Va., U.S. D5 123
Emporium, Pa., U.S. D5 115
Empty Quarter see Ar-Rab' al-Khālī, des., Asia D5 46
Emsdetten, Ger. C7 8
Emsworth, Pa., U.S. h13 115
Encampment, Wy., U.S. E6 127
Encarnación, Para. B5 56
Encinitas, Ca., U.S. F5 82
Encontrados, Ven. C6 58
Ende, Indon. G7 32
Enderby, B.C., Can. D8 69
Enderby Land, reg., Ant. C18 47
Enderlin, N.D., U.S. C8 111
Enders Reservoir, res., Ne., U.S. D4 104
Endicott, N.Y., U.S. C4 109
Endicott Mountains, mts., Ak., U.S. B9 79
Endless Lake, l., Me., U.S. C4 96
Endwell, N.Y., U.S. C4 109
Enfida, Tun. M5 14
Enfield (Thompsonville), Ct., U.S. B5 84

Name | Map Ref | Page
field, N.H., U.S. C2 106
field, N.C., U.S. A5 110
gel's, Russia G7 22
ggano, Pulau, i., Indon. G3 32
gland, Ar., U.S. C4 81
gland, ter., U.K. I11 7
gland Air Force Base, mil., La., U.S. C3 95
glee, Newf., Can. C3 72
gleside, Va., U.S. g12 123
glewood, Co., U.S. B6 83
glewood, Fl., U.S. F4 86
glewood, N.J., U.S. B5 107
glewood, Oh., U.S. C1 112
glewood, Tn., U.S. D9 119
glewood Cliffs, N.J., U.S. h9 107
glish, In., U.S. H5 91
glish Bāzār, India H13 38
glish Channel (La Manche), strt., Eur. B5 10
guera, Spain G11 12
id, Ok., U.S. A4 113
id Lake, res., Ms., U.S. A4 101
igma, Ga., U.S. E3 87
ka, N.C., U.S. f10 110
khuizen, Neth. C5 8
köping, Swe. G11 6
melen, Russia D30 24
na, Italy L9 14
nadai Lake, l., N.W. Ter., Can. D12 66
nedi, plat., Chad E10 42
nis, Ire. I4 7
nis, Mt., U.S. E5 103
nis, Tx., U.S. C4 120
niskillen, N. Ire., U.K. G5 7
och, Ut., U.S. F2 121
ola, Pa., U.S. F8 115
on, Oh., U.S. *C2 112
oree, S.C., U.S. B4 117
oree, stm., S.C., U.S. B3 117
osburg Falls, Vt., U.S. B3 122
riquillo, Dom. Rep. F12 64
schede, Neth. C6 8
senada, Mex. B1 62
shi, China E8 26
shū-nada, Japan H10 30
sley, Fl., U.S. u14 86
tebbe, Ug. A6 44
terprise, Al., U.S. D4 78
terprise, Ks., U.S. D6 93
terprise, Or., U.S. B9 114
terprise, Ut., U.S. F2 121
terprise, W.V., U.S. B4 125
tiat, stm., Wa., U.S. B5 124
tiat, Lake, l., Wa., U.S. B5 124
tiat Mountains, mts., Wa., U.S. B5 124
traygues, Fr. H9 10
tre-Rios, Moz. D7 44
ugu, Nig. G7 42
umclaw, Wa., U.S. B4 124
vigado, Col. D5 58
la Hills, hills, Or., U.S. h11 114
ernay, Fr. C10 10
hraim, Ut., U.S. D4 121
hrata, Pa., U.S. F9 115
hrata, Wa., U.S. B6 124
ila, Spain D10 12
inal, Fr. D13 10
ping, N.H., U.S. D4 106
worth, Ia., U.S. B7 92
uatorial Guinea, ctry., Afr. H7 42
aclea, Italy D7 14
ath, La., U.S. E3 95
ath, co., Tx., U.S. C3 120
dek, Tur. I11 16
demli, Tur. A4 40
ebus, Mount, mtn., Ant. B29 47
echim, Braz. B6 56
furt, Ger. E11 8
chsen Lake, l., N.W. Ter., Can. B16 66
ck, Ok., U.S. B2 113
ckson, Man., Can. D2 70
e, Co., U.S. A5 83
e, Il., U.S. B3 90
e, Ks., U.S. E8 93
e, Mi., U.S. G7 99
e, Pa., U.S. B1 115
e, co., N.Y., U.S. C2 109
e, co., Oh., U.S. A3 112
e, co., Pa., U.S. C1 115
e, Lake, l., N.A. C10 76
e Canal, N.Y., U.S. B5 109
imo-misaki, c., Japan r21 30a
n, Ont., Can. D4 73
n, Tn., U.S. A4 119
trea, ctry., Afr. E2 46
angen, Ger. F11 8
anger, Ky., U.S. A5 94
ian, China C9 26
ling, Lake, res., Ar., U.S. D2 81
melo, S. Afr. G5 44
menak, Tur. A3 40
ākulam, India H4 37
ne, Lower Lough, l., N. Ire., U.K. G5 7
née, Fr. D6 10
odo, India G4 37
rigal, mtn., Ire. F4 7
ai, China B5 26
win, N.C., U.S. B4 110
win, Tn., U.S. C11 119
zgebirge (Krušné hory), mts., Eur. E12 8
zincan, Tur. H15 4
zurum, Tur. H16 4
ashi, Japan A13 30
bjerg, Den. I7 6
calante, Ut., U.S. F4 121
calante, stm., Ut., U.S. F4 121
calón, Mex. D7 62
calon, Ca., U.S. D3 82
cambia, co., Al., U.S. D2 78
cambia, co., Fl., U.S. u14 86
cambia, stm., Fl., U.S. u14 86
canaba, Mi., U.S. C3 99
canaba, stm., Mi., U.S. B3 99
Escarpada Point, c., Phil. B7 32
Escatawpa, Ms., U.S. E5 101
Escatawpa, stm., U.S. D5 101
Esch-sur-Alzette, Lux. F5 8
Eschwege, Ger. D10 8
Escondido, Ca., U.S. F5 82
Escoumins, Rivière des, stm., Que., Can. A8 74
Escuinapa [de Hidalgo], Mex. F7 62
Escuintla, Guat. G2 64
Escuintla, Mex. J13 62
Escuminac, Point, c., N.B., Can. B5 71
Eşfahān, Iran B5 46
Eshkāshem, Afg. B4 38
Eskilstuna, Swe. G11 6
Eskimo Lakes, l., N.W. Ter., Can. C6 66
Eskimo Point, N.W. Ter., Can. D14 66
Eskişehir, Tur. H14 4
Eşme, Tur. K12 16
Esmeralda, co., Nv., U.S. F4 105
Esmeraldas, Ec. G3 58
Esmond, R.I., U.S. B4 116
Espalion, Fr. H9 10
Espanola, Ont., Can. A3 73
Espanola, N.M., U.S. B3 108
Esparto, Ca., U.S. C2 82
Espelkamp, Ger. C8 8
Esperance, Austl. F4 50
Espinal, Col. E5 58
Espinhaço, Serra do, mts., Braz. C7 57
Espinho, Port. D3 12
Espíritu Santo, Bahía del, b., Mex. H16 62
Espíritu Santo, Isla del, i., Mex. E4 62
Espoo (Esbo), Fin. F15 6
Espy, Pa., U.S. D9 115
Esquel, Arg. E2 56
Esquimalt, B.C., Can. E6 69
Esquina, Arg. B5 56
Essaouira, Mor. B4 42
Essen, Ger. D7 8
Essendon, Mount, mtn., Austl. D4 50
Essequibo, stm., Guy. E13 58
Es Sers, Tun. M4 14
Essex, Ont., Can. E2 73
Essex, Ct., U.S. D6 84
Essex, Ia., U.S. D2 92
Essex, Md., U.S. B5 97
Essex, Ma., U.S. A6 98
Essex, Vt., U.S. B2 122
Essex, co., Ma., U.S. A5 98
Essex, co., N.J., U.S. B4 107
Essex, co., N.Y., U.S. B7 109
Essex, co., Vt., U.S. B5 122
Essex, co., Va., U.S. C6 123
Essex Junction, Vt., U.S. C2 122
Essexville, Mi., U.S. E7 99
Esslingen, Ger. G9 8
Es Smala es Souassi, Tun. N5 14
Est, Cap, c., Madag. E10 44
Est, Pointe de l', c., Que., Can. G20 66
Estacada, Or., U.S. B4 114
Estaca de Bares, Punta de la, c., Spain B4 12
Estacado, Llano, pl., U.S. C1 120
Estados, Isla de los, i., Arg. G4 56
Estancia, N.M., U.S. C3 108
Estcourt, S. Afr. G5 44
Este, Italy D6 14
Estelí, Nic. H4 64
Estella, Spain C9 12
Estelline, S.D., U.S. C9 118
Estepona, Spain I6 12
Esternay, Fr. D10 10
Estero Bay, b., Ca., U.S. E3 82
Estero Bay, b., Fl., U.S. F5 86
Estero Island, i., Fl., U.S. F5 86
Estes Park, Co., U.S. A5 83
Estherville, Ia., U.S. A3 92
Estherwood, La., U.S. D3 95
Estill, S.C., U.S. F5 117
Estill, co., Ky., U.S. C6 94
Estill Springs, Tn., U.S. B5 119
Estonia, ctry., Eur. C9 18
Estremoz, Port. G4 12
Esztergom, Hung. H18 8
Etah, Grnld. B20 128
Etah, India G8 38
Étampes, Fr. D9 10
Étang-du-Nord, Que., Can. B8 71
Étaples, Fr. B8 10
Etāwah, India G8 38
Ethel, W.V., U.S. n12 125
Ethiopia, ctry., Afr. G2 46
Etna, Pa., U.S. k14 115
Etna, Monte, vol., Italy L9 14
Etobicoke, Ont., Can. D5 73
Etolin Island, i., Ak., U.S. m23 79
Etolin Strait, strt., Ak., U.S. C6 79
Etoshapan, pl., Nmb. E3 44
Etowah, Tn., U.S. D9 119
Etowah, co., Al., U.S. A3 78
Etowah, stm., Ga., U.S. B2 87
Ettelbruck, Lux. F6 8
Ettlingen, Ger. G8 8
Ettrick, Va., U.S. C5 123
Eu, Fr. B8 10
Eucla, Austl. F5 50
Euclid, Oh., U.S. A4 112
Eudora, Ar., U.S. D4 81
Eudora, Ks., U.S. D8 93
Eufaula, Al., U.S. D4 78
Eufaula, Ok., U.S. B6 113
Eufaula Lake, res., Ok., U.S. B6 113
Eugene, Or., U.S. C3 114
Eugenia, Punta, c., Mex. D2 62
Eunice, La., U.S. D3 95
Eunice, N.M., U.S. E6 108
Euphrates (Al-Furāt), stm., Asia A2 46
Eupora, Ms., U.S. B4 101
Eureka, Ca., U.S. B1 82
Eureka, Il., U.S. C4 90
Eureka, Ks., U.S. E7 93
Eureka, Mo., U.S. f12 102
Eureka, Mt., U.S. B1 103
Eureka, Nv., U.S. D6 105
Eureka, S.C., U.S. B5 117
Eureka, S.D., U.S. B6 118
Eureka, co., Nv., U.S. D5 105
Eureka Springs, Ar., U.S. A2 81
Europa, Île, i., Reu. F8 44
Europa Point, c., Gib. I6 12
Europe E11 4
Euskirchen, Ger. E6 8
Eustis, Fl., U.S. D5 86
Eutaw, Al., U.S. C2 78
Eutin, Ger. A10 8
Eutsuk Lake, l., B.C., Can. C4 69
Evangeline, co., La., U.S. D3 95
Evans, Co., U.S. A6 83
Evans, Ga., U.S. C4 87
Evans, W.V., U.S. C3 125
Evans, co., Ga., U.S. D5 87
Evans, Lac, l., Que., Can. F17 66
Evans, Mount, mtn., Co., U.S. B5 83
Evansburg, Alta., Can. C3 68
Evans City, Pa., U.S. E1 115
Evansdale, Ia., U.S. B5 92
Evans Strait, strt., N.W. Ter., Can. D16 66
Evanston, Il., U.S. A6 90
Evanston, Wy., U.S. E2 127
Evansville, Il., U.S. E4 90
Evansville, In., U.S. I2 91
Evansville, Wi., U.S. F4 126
Evansville, Wy., U.S. D6 127
Evart, Mi., U.S. E5 99
Evarts, Ky., U.S. D6 94
Eveleth, Mn., U.S. C6 100
Everard, Lake, l., Austl. F7 50
Everest, Mount, mtn., Asia G12 38
Everett, Ma., U.S. g11 98
Everett, Pa., U.S. F5 115
Everett, Wa., U.S. B3 124
Everett Lake, res., N.H., U.S. D3 106
Everglades National Park, Fl., U.S. G5 86
Evergreen, Al., U.S. D3 78
Evergreen, Co., U.S. B5 83
Evergreen Park, Il., U.S. k9 90
Everly, Ia., U.S. A2 92
Everson, Wa., U.S. A3 124
Evesham, Eng., U.K. I11 7
Evje, Nor. G6 6
Évora, Port. G4 12
Évreux, Fr. C8 10
Évros (Marica) (Meriç), stm., Eur. H10 16
E.V. Spence Reservoir, res., Tx., U.S. D2 120
Évvoia, i., Grc. K7 16
Ewa, Hi., U.S. B3 88
Ewa Beach, Hi., U.S. B3 88
Ewa Beach, Hi., U.S. g9 88
Ewing Township, N.J., U.S. C3 107
Ewo, Congo B2 44
Excelsior Mountain, mtn., Ca., U.S. C4 82
Excelsior Mountains, mts., Nv., U.S. E3 105
Excelsior Springs, Mo., U.S. B3 102
Executive Committee Range, mts., Ant. B36 47
Exeter, Ont., Can. D3 73
Exeter, Eng., U.K. K9 7
Exeter, Ca., U.S. D4 82
Exeter, Ne., U.S. D8 104
Exeter, N.H., U.S. E5 106
Exeter, Pa., U.S. D10 115
Exeter, stm., N.H., U.S. E5 106
Exeter Sound, strt., N.W. Ter., Can. C20 66
Exira, Ia., U.S. C3 92
Exmore, Va., U.S. C7 123
Exmouth, Eng., U.K. K9 7
Exmouth Gulf, b., Austl. D2 50
Experiment, Ga., U.S. C2 87
Exploits, stm., Newf., Can. D3 72
Exploits, Bay of, b., Newf., Can. D4 72
Export, Pa., U.S. F2 115
Exuma Sound, strt., Bah. B9 64
Eyasi, Lake, l., Tan. B6 44
Eylar Mountain, mtn., Ca., U.S. D3 82
Eymoutiers, Fr. G8 10
Eyota, Mn., U.S. G6 100
Eyre (North), Lake, l., Austl. E7 50
Eyre (South), Lake, l., Austl. E7 50
Eyre Peninsula, pen., Austl. F7 50

F

Fabens, Tx., U.S. o11 120
Fabius, stm., Mo., U.S. A6 102
Fabriano, Italy F7 14
Facatativá, Col. E5 58
Factoryville, Pa., U.S. C10 115
Fada, Chad E10 42
Fada Ngourma, Burkina F6 42
Faddejevskij, Ostrov, i., Russia B22 24
Faenza, Italy E6 14
Faeroe Islands, dep., Eur. C6 4
Fagernes, Nor. F7 6
Fagersta, Swe. F10 6
Fairacres, N.M., U.S. E3 108
Fairbank, Ia., U.S. B5 92
Fairbanks, Ak., U.S. C10 79
Fair Bluff, N.C., U.S. C3 110
Fairborn, Oh., U.S. C1 112
Fairburn, Ga., U.S. C2 87
Fairbury, Il., U.S. C5 90
Fairbury, Ne., U.S. D8 104
Fairchance, Pa., U.S. G2 115
Fairchild Air Force Base, mil., Wa., U.S. g13 124
Fairdale, Ky., U.S. B4 94
Fairfax, Ca., U.S. C2 82
Fairfax, De., U.S. A3 85
Fairfax, Ia., U.S. C6 92
Fairfax, Mn., U.S. F4 100
Fairfax, Mo., U.S. A2 102
Fairfax, Ok., U.S. A5 113
Fairfax, S.C., U.S. F5 117
Fairfax, Va., U.S. B5 123
Fairfax, co., Va., U.S. B5 123
Fairfield, Al., U.S. B3 78
Fairfield, Ca., U.S. C2 82
Fairfield, Ct., U.S. E2 84
Fairfield, Il., U.S. E5 90
Fairfield, Ia., U.S. C6 92
Fairfield, Me., U.S. D3 96
Fairfield, Mt., U.S. C5 103
Fairfield, Oh., U.S. n12 112
Fairfield, Tx., U.S. D4 120
Fairfield, co., Ct., U.S. D2 84
Fairfield, co., Oh., U.S. C3 112
Fairfield, co., S.C., U.S. C5 117
Fairfield Bay, Ar., U.S. B3 81
Fairfield Pond, l., Vt., U.S. B3 122
Fair Grove, Mo., U.S. D4 102
Fair Grove, N.C., U.S. B2 110
Fairhaven, Ma., U.S. C6 98
Fair Haven, Mi., U.S. F8 99
Fair Haven, N.J., U.S. C4 107
Fair Haven, Vt., U.S. D2 122
Fairhope, Al., U.S. E2 78
Fair Isle, i., Scot., U.K. B11 7
Fairland, In., U.S. E6 91
Fairland, Ok., U.S. A7 113
Fair Lawn, N.J., U.S. h8 107
Fairlawn, Va., U.S. C2 123
Fairlea, W.V., U.S. D4 125
Fairmont, Il., U.S. C6 90
Fairmont, Mn., U.S. G4 100
Fairmont, Ne., U.S. D8 104
Fairmont, N.C., U.S. C3 110
Fairmont, W.V., U.S. B4 125
Fairmount, Ga., U.S. B2 87
Fairmount, In., U.S. D6 91
Fairmount Heights, Md., U.S. f9 97
Fair Oaks, Ga., U.S. h7 87
Fairoaks, Pa., U.S. h13 115
Fair Plain, Mi., U.S. F4 99
Fairport, N.Y., U.S. B3 109
Fairport Harbor, Oh., U.S. A4 112
Fairvale, N.B., Can. D4 71
Fairview, Alta., Can. A1 68
Fairview, Mt., U.S. C12 103
Fairview, N.J., U.S. h8 107
Fairview, Ok., U.S. A3 113
Fairview, Pa., U.S. B1 115
Fairview, Tn., U.S. B4 119
Fairview, Ut., U.S. D4 121
Fairview Heights, Il., U.S. E3 90
Fairview Park, In., U.S. E3 91
Fairview Park, Oh., U.S. g9 112
Fairview Peak, mtn., Nv., U.S. D3 105
Fairview Peak, mtn., Or., U.S. D4 114
Fairway, Ks., U.S. k16 93
Fairweather, Mount, mtn., N.A. E5 66
Faisalabad, Pak. E5 38
Faison, N.C., U.S. B4 110
Faizābād, India G10 38
Fakenham, Eng., U.K. I13 7
Fakfak, Indon. F9 32
Falaise, Fr. D6 10
Falam, Burma C2 34
Falconer, N.Y., U.S. C1 109
Falcon Heights, Mn., U.S. n12 100
Falcon Heights, Or., U.S. E5 114
Falcon Reservoir, res., N.A. D10 62
Falfurrias, Tx., U.S. F3 120
Falher, Alta., Can. B2 68
Falkenberg, Swe. H9 6
Falkensee, Ger. C13 8
Falkenstein, Ger. E12 8
Falkland Islands (Islas Malvinas), dep., S.A. G5 56
Falköping, Swe. G9 6
Falkville, Al., U.S. A3 78
Fall, stm., Ks., U.S. E7 93
Fall Branch, Tn., U.S. C11 119
Fallbrook, Ca., U.S. F5 82
Fall City, Wa., U.S. B4 124
Fall Creek, Wi., U.S. D2 126
Falling Creek, stm., Va., U.S. n17 123
Falling Rock Creek, stm., W.V., U.S. m13 125
Fall Mountain Lake, Ct., U.S. C4 84
Fallon, Nv., U.S. D3 105
Fallon, co., Mt., U.S. D12 103
Fallon Indian Reservation, Nv., U.S. D3 105
Fallon Naval Air Station, mil., Nv., U.S. D3 105
Fall River, Ma., U.S. C5 98
Fall River, Wi., U.S. E4 126
Fall River, co., S.D., U.S. D2 118
Fall River Lake, res., Ks., U.S. E7 93
Falls, co., Tx., U.S. D4 120
Falls Church, Va., U.S. g12 123
Falls City, Ne., U.S. D10 104
Falls City, Or., U.S. C3 114
Falls Creek, Pa., U.S. D4 115
Fallston, Md., U.S. A5 97
Falmouth, N.S., Can. E5 71
Falmouth, Eng., U.K. K7 7
Falmouth, Ky., U.S. B5 94
Falmouth, Me., U.S. E2 96
Falmouth, Ma., U.S. C6 98
Falmouth, Va., U.S. B5 123
False Cape, c., Fl., U.S. D6 86
False Cape, c., Va., U.S. D7 123
False Divi Point, c., India E6 37
Falset, Spain D12 12
Falun, Swe. F10 6
Famagusta see Gazimağusa, N. Cyp. B3 40
Famatina, Nevado de, mts., Arg. B3 56
Fancy Farm, Ky., U.S. f9 94
Fangcheng, China B1 28
Fannin, co., Ga., U.S. B2 87
Fannin, co., Tx., U.S. C4 120
Fanny, Mount, mtn., Or., U.S. B9 114
Fano, Italy F8 14
Faradje, Zaire H11 42
Faradofay, Madag. G9 44
Farafangana, Madag. F9 44
Farāh, Afg. C1 36
Faranah, Gui. F3 42
Farasān, Jazā'ir, is., Sau. Ar. E3 46
Farewell, Cape, c., N.Z. D4 52
Fargo, Ga., U.S. F4 87
Fargo, N.D., U.S. C9 111
Faribault, Mn., U.S. F5 100
Faribault, co., Mn., U.S. G4 100
Farīdpur, Bngl. I13 38
Färjestaden, Swe. H11 6
Farley, Ia., U.S. B6 92
Farmer City, Il., U.S. C5 90
Farmers Branch, Tx., U.S. n10 120
Farmersburg, In., U.S. F3 91
Farmerville, La., U.S. B3 95
Farmingdale, Me., U.S. D3 96
Farmington, Ar., U.S. A1 81
Farmington, Ct., U.S. C4 84
Farmington, Il., U.S. C3 90
Farmington, Ia., U.S. D6 92
Farmington, Me., U.S. D2 96
Farmington, Mi., U.S. p15 99
Farmington, Mn., U.S. F5 100
Farmington, Mo., U.S. D7 102
Farmington, N.H., U.S. D4 106
Farmington, N.M., U.S. A1 108
Farmington, Ut., U.S. C4 121
Farmington, stm., Ct., U.S. B4 84
Farmington Hills, Mi., U.S. o15 99
Farmland, In., U.S. D7 91
Farmville, N.C., U.S. B5 110
Farmville, Va., U.S. C4 123
Farnham, Que., Can. D5 74
Faro, Braz. D7 54
Faro, Port. H4 12
Faro, Punta del, c., Italy K10 14
Fårösund, Swe. H12 6
Farquhar Group, is., Sey. D10 44
Farrell, Pa., U.S. D1 115
Farrukhābād, India G8 38
Fartak, Ra's, c., Yemen E5 46
Farvel, Kap, c., Grnld. E24 66
Farwell, Mi., U.S. E6 99
Farwell, Tx., U.S. B1 120
Fasano, Italy I12 14
Fatehpur, India H9 38
Fatehpur, India G6 38
Faulk, co., S.D., U.S. B6 118
Faulkland Heights, De., U.S. i7 85
Faulkner, co., Ar., U.S. B3 81
Faulkton, S.D., U.S. B6 118
Fauquier, co., Va., U.S. B5 123
Fauske, Nor. C10 6
Favara, Italy L8 14
Faverges, Fr. G13 10
Fawnie Nose, mtn., B.C., Can. C5 69
Fayette, Al., U.S. B2 78
Fayette, Ia., U.S. B6 92
Fayette, Ms., U.S. D2 101
Fayette, Mo., U.S. B5 102
Fayette, Oh., U.S. A1 112
Fayette, co., Al., U.S. B3 78
Fayette, co., Ga., U.S. C2 87
Fayette, co., Il., U.S. D5 90
Fayette, co., In., U.S. E7 91
Fayette, co., Ia., U.S. B6 92
Fayette, co., Ky., U.S. B5 94
Fayette, co., Oh., U.S. C2 112
Fayette, co., Pa., U.S. G2 115
Fayette, co., Tn., U.S. B2 119
Fayette, co., Tx., U.S. E4 120
Fayette, co., W.V., U.S. C3 125
Fayetteville, Ar., U.S. A1 81
Fayetteville, Ga., U.S. C2 87
Fayetteville, N.C., U.S. B4 110
Fayetteville, Pa., U.S. G6 115
Fayetteville, Tn., U.S. B5 119
Fayetteville, W.V., U.S. C3 125
Fāzilka, India E6 38
Fazzān (Fezzan), reg., Libya C8 42
Fdérik, Maur. D3 42
Fear, Cape, c., N.C., U.S. D5 110
Feather, stm., Ca., U.S. C3 82
Fécamp, Fr. C7 10
Federalsburg, Md., U.S. C6 97
Feeding Hills, Ma., U.S. B2 98
Fehmarn Belt, strt., Eur. A11 8
Feijó, Braz. E4 54
Feira de Santana, Braz. B9 57
Felanitx, Spain F15 12
Feldbach, Aus. I15 8
Feldkirch, Aus. H9 8
Feldkirchen in Kärnten, Aus. I14 8
Félix Gómez, Mex. C4 62
Felletin, Fr. G9 10
Fellsmere, Fl., U.S. E6 86
Felton, Ca., U.S. D2 82
Felton, De., U.S. D3 85
Feltre, Italy C6 14
Femundsenden, Nor. F8 6
Fence, stm., Mi., U.S. B2 99
Fence Lake, l., Wi., U.S. C4 126
Fenelon Falls, Ont., Can. C6 73
Fengcheng, China G4 28
Fengzhen, China C9 26
Fenimore Pass, strt., Ak., U.S. E4 79
Fennimore, Wi., U.S. F3 126
Fennville, Mi., U.S. F4 99
Fenton, Mi., U.S. F7 99
Fentress, co., Tn., U.S. C9 119
Fenwick Island, i., S.C., U.S. k11 117
Fenyang, China D9 26
Feodosija, Ukr. H5 22
Fer, Point au, c., La., U.S. E4 95
Ferdinand, In., U.S. H4 91
Fergana, Uzb. I12 22
Fergus, Ont., Can. D4 73
Fergus, co., Mt., U.S. C7 103
Fergus Falls, Mn., U.S. D2 100
Ferguson, Ky., U.S. C5 94
Ferguson, Mo., U.S. C7 102
Ferme-Neuve, Que., Can. C2 74
Fermo, Italy F8 14
Fermont, Que., Can. h13 74
Fermoy, Ire. I4 7
Fernandina Beach, Fl., U.S. B5 86
Fernando de Noronha, Ilha, i., Braz. D12 54
Fernandópolis, Braz. F3 57
Fernando Póo see Bioko, i., Eq. Gui. H7 42
Fernán-Núñez, Spain H7 12
Fern Creek, Ky., U.S. g11 94
Ferndale, Ca., U.S. B1 82
Ferndale, Md., U.S. B4 97
Ferndale, Mi., U.S. P15 99
Ferndale, Pa., U.S. F4 115
Ferndale, Wa., U.S. A3 124
Fernie, B.C., Can. E10 69
Fernley, Nv., U.S. D2 105

Name — Map Ref — Page

Fern Ridge Lake, res., Or., U.S. C3 114
Fernwood, Id., U.S. B2 89
Fernwood, Ms., U.S. D3 101
Ferrara, Italy E6 14
Ferreira do Alentejo, Port. G3 12
Ferrelo, Cape, c., Or., U.S. E2 114
Ferriday, La., U.S. C4 95
Ferris, Tx., U.S. C4 120
Ferris Mountains, mts., Wy., U.S. D5 127
Ferron, Ut., U.S. D4 121
Ferrum, Va., U.S. D2 123
Ferry, co., Wa., U.S. A7 124
Ferry Farms, Va., U.S. B5 123
Ferryland, Newf., Can. E5 72
Ferry Point, c., N.J., U.S. k7 107
Fertile, Mn., U.S. C2 100
Fès, Mor. B5 42
Feshi, Zaire C3 44
Fessenden, N.D., U.S. B6 111
Festus, Mo., U.S. C7 102
Fethiye, Tur. M13 16
Feuilles, Rivière aux, stm., Que., Can. g12 74
Feurs, Fr. G11 10
Feyzābād, Afg. B4 38
Fez see Fès, Mor. B5 42
Fianarantsoa, Madag. F9 44
Ficksburg, S. Afr. G5 44
Fidalgo Island, i., Wa., U.S. A3 124
Fidenza, Italy E5 14
Fieldale, Va., U.S. D3 123
Fields, Lake, l., Fl., U.S. B3 86
Fields, Lake, l., La., U.S. k10 95
Fier, Alb. I3 16
Fifteenmile Creek, stm., Wy., U.S. B4 127
Fifteen Mile Falls Reservoir, res., U.S. C5 122
Figeac, Fr. H9 10
Figueira da Foz, Port. E3 12
Figueras, Spain C14 12
Figuig, Mor. B5 42
Fiji, ctry., Oc. H1 2
Filchner Ice Shelf, Ant. B9 47
Filer, Id., U.S. G4 89
Fillmore, Ca., U.S. E4 82
Fillmore, Ut., U.S. E3 121
Fillmore, co., Mn., U.S. G6 100
Fillmore, co., Ne., U.S. D8 104
Finale Ligure, Italy E3 14
Findlay, Il., U.S. D5 90
Findlay, Oh., U.S. A2 112
Finisterre, Cabo de, c., Spain C2 12
Finland, ctry., Eur. C13 4
Finland, Gulf of, b., Eur. G16 6
Finlay, stm., B.C., Can. E7 66
Finley, Tn., U.S. A2 119
Finney, co., Ks., U.S. D3 93
Finn Mountain, mtn., Ak., U.S. C8 79
Finse, Nor. F6 6
Finspång, Swe. G10 6
Finsterwalde, Ger. D13 8
Fiorenzuola d'Arda, Italy E4 14
Fircrest, Wa., U.S. f10 124
Firebaugh, Ca., U.S. D3 82
Firenze (Florence), Italy F6 14
Firenzuola, Italy E6 14
Firestone, Co., U.S. A6 83
Firminy, Fr. G11 10
Fīrozābād, India G8 38
Fīrozpur, India E6 38
First Connecticut Lake, l., N.H., U.S. f7 106
Fish, stm., Al., U.S. E2 78
Fish, stm., Me., U.S. A4 96
Fish Creek, stm., W.V., U.S. g8 125
Fisher, Il., U.S. C5 90
Fisher, co., Tx., U.S. C2 120
Fisher Bay, b., Man., Can. D3 70
Fishermans Island, i., Va., U.S. h15 123
Fishers, In., U.S. E5 91
Fishers Island, i., N.Y., U.S. m16 109
Fishers Peak, mtn., Co., U.S. D6 83
Fisher Strait, strt., N.W. Ter., Can. D16 66
Fishersville, Va., U.S. B4 123
Fishing Bay, b., Md., U.S. D5 97
Fishing Creek, Md., U.S. D5 97
Fishing Creek, stm., N.C., U.S. A5 110
Fishing Creek, stm., S.C., U.S. B5 117
Fishing Creek, stm., W.V., U.S. B4 125
Fishing Creek Reservoir, res., S.C., U.S. B6 117
Fishkill, N.Y., U.S. D7 109
Fish Lake, l., Ut., U.S. E4 121
Fish River Lake, l., Me., U.S. B4 96
Fishtrap Lake, res., Ky., U.S. C7 94
Fiskdale, Ma., U.S. B3 98
Fitchburg, Ma., U.S. A4 98
Fitzgerald, Ga., U.S. E3 87
Fitz Roy, Arg. F3 56
Fitzroy, stm., Austl. C4 50
Fitzroy, Monte (Cerro Chaltel), mtn., S.A. F2 56
Fitzroy Crossing, Austl. C5 50
Fitzwilliam, N.H., U.S. E2 106
Fitzwilliam Island, i., Ont., Can. B3 73
Five Island Lake, l., Ia., U.S. A3 92
Fivemile Creek, stm., Wy., U.S. C4 127
Five Points, N.M., U.S. B3 108
Flagler, co., Fl., U.S. C5 86
Flagler Beach, Fl., U.S. C5 86
Flagstaff, Az., U.S. B4 80
Flagstaff Lake, l., Or., U.S. E7 114
Flambeau, stm., Wi., U.S. C3 126
Flamborough Head, c., Eng., U.K. G12 7
Flaming Gorge Dam, Ut., U.S. C6 121
Flaming Gorge National Recreation Area, U.S. E3 127
Flaming Gorge Reservoir, res., U.S. E3 127
Flanagan, Il., U.S. C5 90
Flandreau, S.D., U.S. C9 118
Flandreau Indian Reservation, S.D., U.S. C9 118
Flat, stm., Mi., U.S. E5 99
Flat, stm., N.C., U.S. A4 110
Flat, stm., R.I., U.S. E2 116
Flat Brook, stm., N.J., U.S. A3 107
Flathead, co., Mt., U.S. B2 103
Flathead, South Fork, stm., Mt., U.S. C3 103
Flathead Indian Reservation, Mt., U.S. C2 103
Flathead Lake, l., Mt., U.S. C2 103
Flathead Valley, val., Mt., U.S. C2 103
Flat Lake, l., La., U.S. k9 95
Flat Lick, Ky., U.S. D6 94
Flatonia, Tx., U.S. E4 120
Flat River, Mo., U.S. D7 102
Flat River Reservoir, res., R.I., U.S. D3 116
Flat Rock, Mi., U.S. F7 99
Flat Rock, N.C., U.S. f10 110
Flatrock, stm., In., U.S. F6 91
Flattery, Cape, c., Wa., U.S. A1 124
Flatwoods, Ky., U.S. B7 94
Fleetwood, Eng., U.K. H9 7
Fleetwood, Pa., U.S. F10 115
Flekkefjord, Nor. G6 6
Fleming, co., Ky., U.S. B6 94
Fleming-Neon, Ky., U.S. C7 94
Flemingsburg, Ky., U.S. B6 94
Flemington, N.J., U.S. B3 107
Flemington, Pa., U.S. D7 115
Flensburg, Ger. A9 8
Flers, Fr. D6 10
Fletcher, N.C., U.S. f10 110
Fletcher, Ok., U.S. C3 113
Fleurance, Fr. I7 10
Flinders, stm., Austl. C8 50
Flinders Island, i., Austl. G9 50
Flin Flon, Man., Can. B1 70
Flint, Wales, U.K. H9 7
Flint, Mi., U.S. E7 99
Flint, stm., Ga., U.S. E2 87
Flint City, Al., U.S. A3 78
Flint Creek Range, mts., Mt., U.S. D3 103
Flint Run, stm., W.V., U.S. k9 125
Flippin, Ar., U.S. A3 81
Flomaton, Al., U.S. D2 78
Flora, Il., U.S. E5 90
Flora, In., U.S. C4 91
Flora, Ms., U.S. C3 101
Florac, Fr. H10 10
Florala, Al., U.S. D3 78
Floral City, Fl., U.S. D4 86
Florence, Al., U.S. A2 78
Florence, Az., U.S. D4 80
Florence, Co., U.S. C5 83
Florence, Ks., U.S. D7 93
Florence, Ky., U.S. A5 94
Florence, Ms., U.S. C3 101
Florence, N.J., U.S. C3 107
Florence, Or., U.S. D2 114
Florence, S.C., U.S. C8 117
Florence, co., S.C., U.S. C8 117
Florence, co., Wi., U.S. C5 126
Florence see Firenze, Italy F6 14
Florenceville, N.B., Can. C2 71
Florencia, Col. G5 58
Flores, i., Indon. G7 32
Flores, Laut (Flores Sea), Indon. G6 32
Floresville, Tx., U.S. E3 120
Florham Park, N.J., U.S. B4 107
Floriano, Braz. E10 54
Florianópolis, Braz. B7 56
Florida, Col. F4 58
Florida, Cuba D8 64
Florida, N.Y., U.S. D6 109
Florida, state, U.S. E5 86
Florida, Cape, c., Fl., U.S. G6 86
Florida, Straits of, strt., N.A. B7 64
Florida Bay, b., Fl., U.S. H6 86
Floridablanca, Col. D6 58
Florida City, Fl., U.S. G6 86
Florida Keys, is., Fl., U.S. H6 86
Florida Mountains, mts., N.M., U.S. E2 108
Florida State Indian Reservation, Fl., U.S. F5 86
Florien, La., U.S. C2 95
Florissant, Mo., U.S. f13 102
Florissant Fossil Beds National Monument, Co., U.S. C5 83
Florø, Nor. F5 6
Flossmoor, Il., U.S. k9 90
Flovilla, Ga., U.S. C3 87
Flower Brook, stm., Vt., U.S. E2 122
Flowery Branch, Ga., U.S. B3 87
Flowood, Ms., U.S. C3 101
Floyd, co., Ga., U.S. B1 87
Floyd, co., In., U.S. H6 91
Floyd, co., Ia., U.S. A5 92
Floyd, co., Ky., U.S. C7 94
Floyd, co., Tx., U.S. B2 120
Floyd, co., Va., U.S. D2 123
Floyd, stm., Ia., U.S. B1 92
Floydada, Tx., U.S. C2 120
Floyds Fork, stm., Ky., U.S. B4 94
Floyds Knobs, In., U.S. H6 91
Flushing, Mi., U.S. E7 99
Flushing, Oh., U.S. B4 112
Flushing see Vlissingen, Neth. D3 8
Fluvanna, co., Va., U.S. C4 123
Fly, stm. m15 50a
Foard, co., Tx., U.S. B3 120
Foça, Tur. K10 16
Focşani, Rom. D11 16
Fogang (Shijiao), China L2 28
Foggia, Italy H10 14
Fogland Point, c., R.I., U.S. E6 116
Fogo, Newf., Can. D4 72
Fogo, Cape, c., Newf., Can. D5 72
Fogo Island, i., Newf., Can. D4 72
Fohnsdorf, Aus. H14 8
Foix, Fr. J8 10
Foley, Al., U.S. E2 78
Foley, Mn., U.S. E5 100
Foley Island, i., N.W. Ter., Can. C17 66
Foligno, Italy G7 14
Folkestone, Eng., U.K. J14 7
Folkston, Ga., U.S. F4 87
Follansbee, W.V., U.S. A4 125
Follonica, Italy G5 14
Folly Beach, S.C., U.S. F8 117
Folly Island, i., S.C., U.S. F8 117
Folsom, Ca., U.S. C3 82
Fonda, Ia., U.S. B3 92
Fond du Lac, Wi., U.S. E5 126
Fond du Lac, co., Wi., U.S. E5 126
Fond du Lac Indian Reservation, Mn., U.S. D6 100
Fondi, Italy H8 14
Fondouk el Aouareb, Tun. N4 14
Fonni, Italy I4 14
Fonseca, Col. B6 58
Fonseca, Golfo de, b., N.A. H4 64
Fontainebleau, Fr. D9 10
Fontana, Ca., U.S. m14 82
Fontana, Wi., U.S. F5 126
Fontana Lake, res., N.C., U.S. f9 110
Fontanelle, Ia., U.S. C3 92
Fonte Boa, Braz. D5 54
Fontenay-le-Comte, Fr. F6 10
Fontenelle Reservoir, res., Wy., U.S. D2 127
Fontur, c., Ice. B5 4
Foochow see Fuzhou, China I8 28
Footville, Wi., U.S. F4 126
Foraker, Mount, mtn., Ak., U.S. f16 79
Forbach, Fr. C13 10
Forbach, Ger. G8 8
Forbes, Mount, mtn., Alta., Can. D2 68
Forcalquier, Fr. I12 10
Forchheim, Ger. F11 8
Ford, co., Il., U.S. C5 90
Ford, co., Ks., U.S. E4 93
Ford, stm., Mi., U.S. C3 99
Ford City, Ca., U.S. E4 82
Ford City, Pa., U.S. E2 115
Førde, Nor. F5 6
Fordoche, La., U.S. D4 95
Fords Prairie, Wa., U.S. C2 124
Fordyce, Ar., U.S. D3 81
Forel, Mont, mtn., Grnld. C25 66
Foreman, Ar., U.S. D1 81
Forest, Ont., Can. D2 73
Forest, Ms., U.S. C4 101
Forest, Oh., U.S. B2 112
Forest, co., Pa., U.S. C3 115
Forest, co., Wi., U.S. C5 126
Forest, stm., N.D., U.S. A8 111
Forest Acres, S.C., U.S. C6 117
Forestburg, Alta., Can. C4 68
Forest City, Ia., U.S. A4 92
Forest City, N.C., U.S. B1 110
Forest City, Pa., U.S. C11 115
Forestdale, R.I., U.S. B3 116
Forest Dale, Vt., U.S. D2 122
Forest Glen, La., U.S. h12 95
Forest Grove, Or., U.S. B3 114
Forest Hill, Md., U.S. A5 97
Forest Hills, Pa., U.S. k14 115
Forest Knolls, Ca., U.S. g7 82
Forest Lake, Mn., U.S. E6 100
Forest Park, Ga., U.S. h8 87
Forest Park, Il., U.S. k9 90
Forest Park, La., U.S. *B3 95
Forest Park, Oh., U.S. *n12 112
Forfar, Scot., U.K. E10 7
Forillon, Parc National de, Que., Can. k14 74
Fork Creek, stm., W.V., U.S. m12 125
Forked Deer, stm., Tn., U.S. B2 119
Forkland, Al., U.S. C2 78
Forks, Wa., U.S. B1 124
Forlì, Italy E7 14
Formia, Italy H8 14
Formiga, Braz. F6 57
Formosa, Arg. B5 56
Formosa, Braz. C5 57
Formosa, Serra, plat., Braz. F8 54
Formosa see Taiwan, i., Asia L9 28
Forney, Tx., U.S. C4 120
Fornovo di Taro, Italy E5 14
Forrest, Austl. F5 50
Forrest, Il., U.S. C5 90
Forrest, co., Ms., U.S. D4 101
Forrest City, Ar., U.S. B5 81
Forrester Island, i., Ak., U.S. n23 79
Forreston, Il., U.S. A4 90
Forsayth, Austl. C8 50
Forst, Ger. D14 8
Forsyth, Ga., U.S. C3 87
Forsyth, Il., U.S. D5 90
Forsyth, Mo., U.S. E4 102
Forsyth, Mt., U.S. D10 103
Forsyth, co., Ga., U.S. B2 87
Forsyth, co., N.C., U.S. A2 110
Fortaleza, Braz. D11 54
Fort Apache Indian Reservation, Az., U.S. D5 80
Fort-Archambault see Sarh, Chad G9 42
Fort Ashby, W.V., U.S. B6 125
Fort Atkinson, Wi., U.S. F5 126
Fort Augustus, Scot., U.K. D8 7
Fort Beaufort, S. Afr. H5 44
Fort Belknap Indian Reservation, Mt., U.S. B8 103
Fort Belvoir, mil., Va., U.S. g12 123
Fort Bend, co., Tx., U.S. E5 120
Fort Benjamin Harrison, mil., In., U.S. k10 91
Fort Benning, mil., Ga., U.S. D2 87
Fort Benton, Mt., U.S. C6 103
Fort Berthold Indian Reservation, N.D., U.S. B3 111
Fort Bidwell Indian Reservation, Ca., U.S. B3 82
Fort Bliss, mil., Tx., U.S. o11 120
Fort Bragg, Ca., U.S. C2 82
Fort Bragg, mil., N.C., U.S. B3 110
Fort Branch, In., U.S. H2 91
Fort Calhoun, Ne., U.S. C9 104
Fort Campbell, mil., U.S. A4 119
Fort Carson, mil., Co., U.S. C6 83
Fort Chipewyan, Alta., Can. f8 68
Fort Clatsop National Memorial, hist., Or., U.S. A3 114
Fort Cobb, Ok., U.S. B3 113
Fort Cobb Reservoir, res., Ok., U.S. B3 113
Fort Collins, Co., U.S. A5 83
Fort Coulonge, Que., Can. B8 73
Fort Davis, Tx., U.S. o13 120
Fort Davis National Historic Site, hist., Tx., U.S. o13 120
Fort Defiance, Az., U.S. B6 80
Fort-de-France, Mart. G17 64
Fort Deposit, Al., U.S. D3 78
Fort Detrick, mil., Md., U.S. B3 97
Fort Devens, mil., Ma., U.S. f9 98
Fort Dix, mil., N.J., U.S. C3 107
Fort Dodge, Ia., U.S. B3 92
Fort Donelson National Battlefield, Tn., U.S. A4 119
Fort Edward, N.Y., U.S. B7 109
Fort Erie, Ont., Can. E6 73
Fortescue, stm., Austl. D3 50
Fort Eustis, mil., Va., U.S. h14 123
Fort Fairfield, Me., U.S. B5 96
Fort Frances, Ont., Can. o16 73
Fort Franklin, N.W. Ter., Can. C8 66
Fort Gaines, Ga., U.S. E1 87
Fort Gay, W.V., U.S. C2 125
Fort Gibson, Ok., U.S. B6 113
Fort Gibson Lake, res., Ok., U.S. A6 113
Fort Good Hope, N.W. Ter., Can. C7 66
Fort Gordon, mil., Ga., U.S. C4 87
Fort Greely, mil., Ak., U.S. C10 79
Forth, Firth of, est., Scot., U.K. E10 7
Fort Hall, Id., U.S. F6 89
Fort Hall Indian Reservation, Id., U.S. F6 89
Fort Hood, mil., Tx., U.S. D4 120
Fort Howard, Md., U.S. B5 97
Fort Huachuca, mil., Az., U.S. F5 80
Fortín Coronel Eugenio Garay, Para. H6 54
Fort Jackson, mil., S.C., U.S. C6 117
Fort Jefferson National Monument, Fl., U.S. H4 86
Fort Kent, Me., U.S. A4 96
Fort Knox, mil., Ky., U.S. B4 94
Fort-Lamy see N'Djamena, Chad F9 42
Fort Laramie, Wy., U.S. D8 127
Fort Laramie National Historic Site, hist., Wy., U.S. D8 127
Fort Lauderdale, Fl., U.S. F6 86
Fort Lawn, S.C., U.S. B6 117
Fort Leavenworth, mil., Ks., U.S. C9 93
Fort Lee, N.J., U.S. B5 107
Fort Lee, mil., Va., U.S. C5 123
Fort Leonard Wood, mil., Mo., U.S. D5 102
Fort Lewis, mil., Wa., U.S. B3 124
Fort Liard, N.W. Ter., Can. D8 66
Fort Loramie, Oh., U.S. B1 112
Fort Loudon, Pa., U.S. G6 115
Fort Loudoun Lake, res., Tn., U.S. D9 119
Fort Lupton, Co., U.S. A6 83
Fort MacArthur, mil., Ca., U.S. n12 82
Fort Macleod, Alta., Can. E4 68
Fort Madison, Ia., U.S. D6 92
Fort Matanzas National Monument, Fl., U.S. C5 86
Fort McClellan, mil., Al., U.S. B4 78
Fort McDermitt Indian Reservation, U.S. B4 105
Fort McDowell Indian Reservation, Az., U.S. D4 80
Fort McHenry National Monument And Historic Shrine, Md., U.S. g11 97
Fort McMurray, Alta., Can. A5 68
Fort Meade, Fl., U.S. E5 86
Fort Meade, mil., Md., U.S. B4 97
Fort Meadow Reservoir, res., Ma., U.S. g9 98
Fort Mill, S.C., U.S. A6 117
Fort Mitchell, Al., U.S. C4 78
Fort Mitchell, Ky., U.S. h13 94
Fort Mojave Indian Reservation, U.S. C1 80
Fort Monmouth, mil., N.J., U.S. C4 107
Fort Monroe, mil., Va., U.S. h15 123
Fort Morgan, Co., U.S. A7 83
Fort Myer, mil., Va., U.S. g12 123
Fort Myers, Fl., U.S. F5 86
Fort Myers Beach, Fl., U.S. F5 86
Fort Nelson, B.C., Can. m18 69
Fort Norman, N.W. Ter., Can. D7 66
Fort Oglethorpe, Ga., U.S. B1 87
Fort Ord, mil., Ca., U.S. D3 82
Fort Payne, Al., U.S. A4 78
Fort Peck Indian Reservation, Mt., U.S. B11 103
Fort Peck Lake, res., Mt., U.S. C9 103
Fort Pierce, Fl., U.S. E6 86
Fort Pierce Inlet, b., Fl., U.S. E6 86
Fort Pierre, S.D., U.S. C5 118
Fort Plain, N.Y., U.S. C6 109
Fort Polk, mil., La., U.S. C2 95
Fort Portal, Ug. A6 44
Fort Providence, N.W. Ter., Can. D9 66
Fort Randall Dam, S.D., U.S. D7 118
Fort Recovery, Oh., U.S. B1 112
Fort Reliance, N.W. Ter., Can. D11 66
Fort Resolution, N.W. Ter., Can. D10 66
Fortress Mountain, mtn., Wy., U.S. B3 127
Fort Richardson, mil., Ak., U.S. C10 79
Fort Riley, mil., Ks., U.S. C7 93
Fort Ritchie, mil., Md., U.S. A3 97
Fort Rucker, mil., Al., U.S. D4 78
Fort Saint James, B.C., Can. B5 69
Fort Saint John, B.C., Can. A7 69
Fort Sam Houston, mil., Tx., U.S. k7 120
Fort Sandeman, Pak. E3 38
Fort Saskatchewan, Alta., Can. C4 68
Fort Scott, Ks., U.S. E9 93
Fort Shafter, mil., Hi., U.S. g10 88
Fort Shawnee, Oh., U.S. B1 112
Fort Sheridan, mil., Il., U.S. h9 90
Fort Sill, mil., Ok., U.S. C3 113
Fort Simpson, N.W. Ter., Can. D8 66
Fort Smith, N.W. Ter., Can. D10 66
Fort Smith, Ar., U.S. B1 81
Fort Stewart, mil., Ga., U.S. D5 87
Fort Stockton, Tx., U.S. D1 120
Fort Sumner, N.M., U.S. C5 108
Fort Sumter National Monument, S.C., U.S. k12 117
Fort Supply Lake, res., Ok., U.S. A2 113
Fort Thomas, Ky., U.S. h14 94
Fort Totten, N.D., U.S. B7 111
Fort Totten Indian Reservation, N.D., U.S. B7 111
Fortuna, Ca., U.S. B1 82
Fortune, Newf., Can. E4 72
Fortune Bay, b., Newf., Can. E4 72
Fort Union National Monument, N.M., U.S. B5 108
Fort Valley, Ga., U.S. D3 87
Fort Vermilion, Alta., Can. f7 68
Fortville, In., U.S. E6 91
Fort Wainwright, mil., Ak., U.S. C10 79
Fort Walton Beach, Fl., U.S. u15 86
Fort Washington Forest, Md., U.S. C4 97
Fort Wayne, In., U.S. B7 91
Fort William, Scot., U.K. E7 7
Fort Wingate, N.M., U.S. B1 108
Fort Worth, Tx., U.S. C4 120
Fort Wright, Ky., U.S. h13 94
Forty Fort, Pa., U.S. D10 115
Fort Yukon, Ak., U.S. B10 79
Fort Yuma Indian Reservation, Ca., U.S. F6 82
Foshan, China L2 28
Fossano, Italy E2 14
Fossil Butte National Monument, Wy., U.S. E2 127
Fossil Lake, l., Or., U.S. D6 114
Fossombrone, Italy F7 14
Foss Reservoir, res., Ok., U.S. B2 113
Fosston, Mn., U.S. C3 100
Foster, Or., U.S. C4 114
Foster, co., N.D., U.S. B6 111
Foster Village, Hi., U.S. g10 88
Fostoria, Oh., U.S. A2 112
Fougamou, Gabon B2 44
Fougères, Fr. D5 10
Fouke, Ar., U.S. D2 81
Foula, i., Scot., U.K. A10 7
Foumban, Cam. G8 42
Fountain, Co., U.S. C6 83
Fountain, co., In., U.S. D3 91
Fountain City, In., U.S. E8 91
Fountain City, Wi., U.S. D2 126
Fountain Hill, Pa., U.S. E11 115
Fountain Inn, S.C., U.S. B3 117
Fountain Peak, mtn., Ca., U.S. E6 82
Fountain Place, La., U.S. *D4 95
Fourche LaFave, stm., Ar., U.S. C2 81
Fourche Maline, stm., Ok., U.S. C6 113
Fourmies, Fr. B11 10
Four Mountains, Islands of, is., Ak., U.S. E6 79
Four Oaks, N.C., U.S. B4 110
Fowler, Ca., U.S. D4 82
Fowler, Co., U.S. C6 83
Fowler, In., U.S. C3 91
Fowler, Mi., U.S. E6 99
Fowlerville, Mi., U.S. F6 99
Fox, stm., Man., Can. B4 70
Fox, stm., U.S. B5 90
Fox, stm., U.S. A6 102
Fox, stm., Mi., U.S. B4 99
Fox, stm., Wi., U.S. D5 126
Foxboro, Ont., Can. C7 73
Foxboro, Ma., U.S. B5 98
Fox Creek, Alta., Can. B2 68
Foxe Basin, b., N.W. Ter., Can. C17 66
Foxe Channel, strt., N.W. Ter., Can. D16 66
Foxe Peninsula, pen., N.W. Ter., Can. D17 66
Fox Island, i., R.I., U.S. E4 116
Fox Island, i., Wa., U.S. f10 124
Fox Islands, is., Ak., U.S. E6 79
Fox Lake, Il., U.S. A5 90
Fox Lake, Wi., U.S. E5 126
Fox Lake, l., Il., U.S. h8 90
Fox Mountain, mtn., Nv., U.S. B2 105
Fox Point, Wi., U.S. E6 126
Fox River Grove, Il., U.S. h8 90
Foxworth, Ms., U.S. D4 101
Foz do Cunene, Ang. E2 44
Foz do Iguaçu, Braz. B6 56
Frackville, Pa., U.S. E9 115
Fraga, Spain D12 12
Framingham, Ma., U.S. B5 98
Franca, Braz. F5 57
Francavilla Fontana, Italy I12 14
France, ctry., Eur. F8 4
Francesville, In., U.S. C4 91
Franceville, Gabon B2 44
Francis, Lake, l., N.H., U.S. f7 106
Francis Case, Lake, res., S.D., U.S. D6 118
Francistown, Bots. F5 44
Francofonte, Italy L9 14
Franconia, N.H., U.S. B3 106
Franconia Notch, N.H., U.S. B3 106
Francs Peak, mtn., Wy., U.S. C3 127
Frankenberg, Ger. E13 8
Frankenberg-Eder, Ger. D8 8
Frankenmuth, Mi., U.S. E7 99
Frankford, Ont., Can. C7 73
Frankford, De., U.S. F5 85
Frankfort, Il., U.S. m9 90
Frankfort, In., U.S. D4 91
Frankfort, Ks., U.S. C7 93
Frankfort, Ky., U.S. B5 94
Frankfort, Mi., U.S. D4 99
Frankfort, N.Y., U.S. B5 109
Frankfort, Oh., U.S. C2 112
Frankfurt am Main, Ger. E8 8
Frankfurt an der Oder, Ger. C14 8
Franklin, Ga., U.S. C1 87
Franklin, In., U.S. F5 91
Franklin, Ky., U.S. D3 94
Franklin, La., U.S. E4 95
Franklin, Ma., U.S. B5 98
Franklin, Ne., U.S. D7 104
Franklin, N.H., U.S. D3 106
Franklin, N.J., U.S. A3 107
Franklin, N.C., U.S. f9 110
Franklin, Oh., U.S. C1 112
Franklin, Pa., U.S. D2 115
Franklin, Tn., U.S. B5 119
Franklin, Tx., U.S. D4 120
Franklin, Va., U.S. D6 123
Franklin, W.V., U.S. C5 125

Name	Map Ref	Page
Franklin, Wi., U.S.	n11	126
Franklin, co., Al., U.S.	A2	78
Franklin, co., Ar., U.S.	B2	81
Franklin, co., Fl., U.S.	C2	86
Franklin, co., Ga., U.S.	B3	87
Franklin, co., Id., U.S.	G7	89
Franklin, co., Il., U.S.	E4	90
Franklin, co., In., U.S.	F7	91
Franklin, co., Ia., U.S.	B4	92
Franklin, co., Ks., U.S.	D8	93
Franklin, co., Ky., U.S.	B5	94
Franklin, co., La., U.S.	B4	95
Franklin, co., Me., U.S.	C2	96
Franklin, co., Ma., U.S.	A2	98
Franklin, co., Ms., U.S.	D3	101
Franklin, co., Mo., U.S.	C6	102
Franklin, co., Ne., U.S.	D7	104
Franklin, co., N.Y., U.S.	f10	109
Franklin, co., N.C., U.S.	A4	110
Franklin, co., Oh., U.S.	B2	112
Franklin, co., Pa., U.S.	G6	115
Franklin, co., Tn., U.S.	B5	119
Franklin, co., Tx., U.S.	C5	120
Franklin, co., Vt., U.S.	B2	122
Franklin, co., Va., U.S.	D3	123
Franklin, co., Wa., U.S.	C6	124
Franklin, Point, c., Ak., U.S.	A8	79
Franklin Bay, b., N.W. Ter., Can.	C7	66
Franklin D. Roosevelt Lake, res., Wa., U.S.	B7	124
Franklin Falls Reservoir, res., N.H., U.S.	C3	106
Franklin Grove, Il., U.S.	B4	90
Franklin Lake, l., N.W. Ter., Can.	C13	66
Franklin Lake, l., Nv., U.S.	C6	105
Franklin Mountains, mts., N.W. Ter., Can.	D8	66
Franklin Park, Il., U.S.	k9	90
Franklin Park, Pa., U.S.	*h13	115
Franklin Strait, strt., N.W. Ter., Can.	B13	66
Franklinton, La., U.S.	D5	95
Franklinton, N.C., U.S.	A4	110
Franklinville, N.Y., U.S.	C2	109
Frankston, Tx., U.S.	C5	120
Frankton, In., U.S.	D6	91
Frascati, Italy	H7	14
Fraser, stm., B.C., Can.	E7	69
Fraser, stm., Newf., Can.	g9	72
Fraser, Mount, mtn., Can.	C8	69
Fraserburgh, Scot., U.K.	D10	7
Fraser Lake, B.C., Can.	B5	69
Fraser Plateau, plat., B.C., Can.	D6	69
Frauenfeld, Switz.	E15	10
Frazee, Mn., U.S.	D3	100
Frazeysburg, Oh., U.S.	B3	112
Frazier Park, Ca., U.S.	E4	82
Fr'azino, Russia	F21	18
Frederic, Wi., U.S.	C1	126
Frederica, De., U.S.	D4	85
Fredericia, Den.	I7	6
Frederick, Co., U.S.	A6	83
Frederick, Md., U.S.	B3	97
Frederick, Ok., U.S.	C2	113
Frederick, co., Md., U.S.	B3	97
Frederick, co., Va., U.S.	A4	123
Fredericksburg, Ia., U.S.	B5	92
Fredericksburg, Tx., U.S.	D3	120
Fredericksburg, Va., U.S.	B5	123
Frederick Sound, strt., Ak., U.S.	m23	79
Fredericktown, Mo., U.S.	D7	102
Fredericktown, Oh., U.S.	B3	112
Fredericktown, Pa., U.S.	F1	115
Fredericton, N.B., Can.	D3	71
Fredericton Junction, N.B., Can.	D3	71
Frederikshåb, Grnld.	D23	66
Frederikshavn, Den.	H8	6
Fredonia, Az., U.S.	A3	80
Fredonia, Ks., U.S.	E8	93
Fredonia, N.Y., U.S.	C1	109
Fredonia, Wi., U.S.	E6	126
Fredrikstad, Nor.	G8	6
Freeborn, co., Mn., U.S.	G5	100
Freeburg, Il., U.S.	E4	90
Freedom, Pa., U.S.	E1	115
Freedom, Wy., U.S.	D2	127
Freehold, N.J., U.S.	C4	107
Freeland, Mi., U.S.	E6	99
Freeland, Pa., U.S.	D10	115
Freelandville, In., U.S.	G3	91
Freel Peak, mtn., Ca., U.S.	C4	82
Freels, Cape, c., Newf., Can.	D5	72
Freels, Cape, c., Newf., Can.	E5	72
Freeman, S.D., U.S.	D8	118
Freeman, Lake, l., In., U.S.	C4	91
Freemansburg, Pa., U.S.	E11	115
Freemason Island, i., La., U.S.	E7	95
Freeport, Bah.	A8	64
Freeport, Il., U.S.	A4	90
Freeport, Me., U.S.	E2	96
Freeport, N.Y., U.S.	n15	109
Freeport, Pa., U.S.	E2	115
Freeport, Tx., U.S.	E5	120
Freer, Tx., U.S.	F3	120
Freestone, co., Tx., U.S.	D4	120
Freetown, S.L.	G3	42
Freetown, In., U.S.	G5	91
Freezeout Mountains, mts., Wy., U.S.	D6	127
Fregenal de la Sierra, Spain	G5	12
Freiberg, Ger.	E13	8
Freiburg [im Breisgau], Ger.	H7	8
Freising, Ger.	G11	8
Freistadt, Aus.	G14	8
Freital, Ger.	D13	8
Fréjus, Fr.	I13	10
Fremont, Ca., U.S.	D2	82
Fremont, In., U.S.	A8	91
Fremont, Ia., U.S.	C5	92
Fremont, Mi., U.S.	E5	99
Fremont, Ne., U.S.	C9	104
Fremont, N.C., U.S.	B5	110
Fremont, Oh., U.S.	A2	112
Fremont, co., Co., U.S.	C5	83
Fremont, co., Id., U.S.	E7	89
Fremont, co., Ia., U.S.	D2	92
Fremont, co., Wy., U.S.	C4	127
Fremont, stm., Ut., U.S.	E4	121
Fremont Island, i., Ut., U.S.	B3	121
Fremont Lake, l., Wy., U.S.	D3	127
Fremont Peak, mtn., Wy., U.S.	C3	127
French Broad, stm., U.S.	D10	119
Frenchburg, Ky., U.S.	C6	94
French Creek, stm., Pa., U.S.	C2	115
French Frigate Shoals, rf., Hi., U.S.	m14	88
French Guiana, dep., S.A.	C8	54
French Lick, In., U.S.	G4	91
Frenchman Bay, b., Me., U.S.	D4	96
Frenchman Creek, stm., U.S.	D4	104
Frenchman Hills, hills, Wa., U.S.	C6	124
Frenchman Lake, l., Nv., U.S.	G6	105
French Polynesia, dep., Oc.	G3	2
French Settlement, La., U.S.	D5	95
Freshfield, Mount, mtn., Can.	D2	68
Fresnillo, Mex.	F8	62
Fresno, Ca., U.S.	D4	82
Fresno, co., Ca., U.S.	D4	82
Fresno Reservoir, res., Mt., U.S.	B6	103
Freudenstadt, Ger.	G8	8
Frewsburg, N.Y., U.S.	C1	109
Fria, Cape, c., Nmb.	E2	44
Friars Point, Ms., U.S.	A3	101
Frías, Arg.	B3	56
Fribourg (Freiburg), Switz.	F14	10
Friday Harbor, Wa., U.S.	A2	124
Fridley, Mn., U.S.	m12	100
Friedberg, Aus.	H16	8
Friedrichshafen, Ger.	H9	8
Friend, Ne., U.S.	D8	104
Friendsville, Tn., U.S.	D9	119
Fries, Va., U.S.	D2	123
Friesland, hist. reg., Neth.	B5	8
Frio, co., Tx., U.S.	E3	120
Frio, stm., Tx., U.S.	E3	120
Frio, Cabo, c., Braz.	G7	57
Friona, Tx., U.S.	B1	120
Fripps Island, i., S.C., U.S.	G7	117
Frisco, Co., U.S.	B4	83
Frisco City, Al., U.S.	D2	78
Frisco Peak, mtn., Ut., U.S.	E2	121
Frissell, Mount, mtn., U.S.	A2	84
Fritch, Tx., U.S.	B2	120
Fritzlar, Ger.	D9	8
Friza, Proliv, strt., Russia	H23	24
Frobisher Bay, b., N.W. Ter., Can.	D19	66
Frobisher Lake, l., Sask., Can.	m7	75
Frohnleiten, Aus.	H15	8
Frontenac, Ks., U.S.	E9	93
Frontier, co., Ne., U.S.	D5	104
Front Range, mts., Co., U.S.	A5	83
Front Royal, Va., U.S.	B4	123
Frosinone, Italy	H8	14
Frostburg, Md., U.S.	k13	97
Frostproof, Fl., U.S.	E5	86
Fruita, Co., U.S.	B2	83
Fruit Heights, Ut., U.S.	B4	121
Fruitland, Id., U.S.	F2	89
Fruitland, Md., U.S.	D6	97
Fruitland, N.M., U.S.	A1	108
Fruitland Park, Fl., U.S.	D5	86
Fruitport, Mi., U.S.	E4	99
Fruitvale, B.C., Can.	E9	69
Fruitvale, Co., U.S.	B2	83
Fruitvale, Wa., U.S.	C5	124
Fruitville, Fl., U.S.	E4	86
Frunze see Biškek, Kyrg.	I12	22
Frutigen, Switz.	F14	10
Fryeburg, Me., U.S.	D2	96
Fuchū, Japan	H6	30
Fuencaliente, Spain	G7	12
Fuente de Cantos, Spain	G5	12
Fuente-obejuna, Spain	G6	12
Fuerteventura, i., Spain	p27	13b
Fuji, Japan	G11	30
Fuji, Mount see Fuji-san, vol., Japan	G11	30
Fujian, prov., China	F10	26
Fujin, China	B13	26
Fujinomiya, Japan	G11	30
Fuji-san (Fujiyama), vol., Japan	G11	30
Fujisawa, Japan	G12	30
Fujiyama see Fuji-san, vol., Japan	G11	30
Fuji-yoshida, Japan	G11	30
Fukagawa, Japan	p20	30a
Fukaya, Japan	F12	30
Fukuchiyama, Japan	G8	30
Fukue, Japan	J1	30
Fukui, Japan	F9	30
Fukuoka, Japan	I3	30
Fukushima, Japan	E13	30
Fukushima, Japan	r18	30a
Fukuyama, Japan	H6	30
Fūlādī, Kūh-e, mtn., Afg.	C2	38
Fulda, Ger.	E9	8
Fulda, Mn., U.S.	G3	100
Fullerton, Ca., U.S.	n13	82
Fullerton, Ne., U.S.	C8	104
Fulton, Il., U.S.	B3	90
Fulton, Ky., U.S.	f9	94
Fulton, Md., U.S.	B4	97
Fulton, Ms., U.S.	A5	101
Fulton, Mo., U.S.	C6	102
Fulton, N.Y., U.S.	B4	109
Fulton, co., Ar., U.S.	A4	81
Fulton, co., Ga., U.S.	C2	87
Fulton, co., Il., U.S.	C3	90
Fulton, co., In., U.S.	B5	91
Fulton, co., Ky., U.S.	f8	94
Fulton, co., N.Y., U.S.	B6	109
Fulton, co., Oh., U.S.	A1	112
Fulton, co., Pa., U.S.	G5	115
Fultondale, Al., U.S.	f7	78
Funabashi, Japan	G13	30
Funchal, Port.	n21	13a
Fundación, Col.	B5	58
Fundy, Bay of, b., Can.	D4	71
Fundy National Park, N.B., Can.	D4	71
Funkstown, Md., U.S.	A2	97
Fuquay-Varina, N.C., U.S.	B4	110
Furano, Japan	p20	30a
Furmanov, Russia	D24	18
Furnace Brook, stm., Vt., U.S.	D3	122
Furnas, co., Ne., U.S.	D6	104
Furnas, Reprêsa de, res., Braz.	F5	57
Furneaux Group, is., Austl.	H9	50
Furqlus, Syria	B5	40
Fürstenfeld, Aus.	H16	8
Fürstenfeldbruck, Ger.	G11	8
Fürstenwalde, Ger.	C14	8
Fürth, Ger.	F10	8
Furth im Wald, Ger.	F12	8
Furudal, Swe.	F10	6
Fushun, China	C11	26
Füssen, Ger.	H10	8
Fuxian, China	D11	26
Fuxian, China	D8	26
Fuxinshi, China	C11	26
Fuyang, China	C4	28
Fuzhou, China	G5	28
Fuzhou (Foochow), China	I8	28
Fyffe, Al., U.S.	A4	78

G

Name	Map Ref	Page
Gabbs, Nv., U.S.	E4	105
Gabès, Tun.	B8	42
Gabès, Golfe de, b., Tun.	B8	42
Gabon, ctry., Afr.	B2	44
Gaborone, Bots.	F5	44
Gabriel Strait, strt., N.W. Ter., Can.	D19	66
Gabriola, B.C., Can.	f12	69
Gabrovo, Bul.	G9	16
Gadag, India	E3	37
Gäddede, Swe.	D10	6
Gadsden, Al., U.S.	A3	78
Gadsden, co., Fl., U.S.	B2	86
Gaeta, Italy	H8	14
Gaffney, S.C., U.S.	A4	117
Gafsa, Tun.	B7	42
Gage, co., Ne., U.S.	D9	104
Gagetown, N.B., Can.	D3	71
Gagliano del Capo, Italy	J13	14
Gagnoa, I.C.	G4	42
Gahanna, Oh., U.S.	k11	112
Gaillac, Fr.	I8	10
Gaillard, Lake, l., Ct., U.S.	D5	84
Gaines, co., Tx., U.S.	C1	120
Gainesboro, Tn., U.S.	C8	119
Gaines Creek, stm., Ok., U.S.	C6	113
Gainesville, Fl., U.S.	C4	86
Gainesville, Ga., U.S.	B3	87
Gainesville, Mo., U.S.	E5	102
Gainesville, Tx., U.S.	C4	120
Gainesville, Va., U.S.	g11	123
Gairdner, Lake, l., Austl.	F7	50
Gaithersburg, Md., U.S.	B3	97
Galán, Cerro, mtn., Arg.	B3	56
Galapagos Islands see Coloón, Archipiélago de, is., Ec.	m15	58a
Galashiels, Scot., U.K.	F10	7
Galați, Rom.	D12	16
Galatia, Il., U.S.	F5	90
Galatina, Italy	I13	14
Galax, Va., U.S.	D2	123
Galena, Ak., U.S.	C8	79
Galena, Il., U.S.	A3	90
Galena, Ks., U.S.	E9	93
Galeota Point, c., Trin.	I17	64
Galera, Punta, c., Chile	D2	56
Galera, Punta, c., Ec.	G2	58
Galesburg, Il., U.S.	C3	90
Galesburg, Mi., U.S.	F5	99
Gales Ferry, Ct., U.S.	D7	84
Galesville, Md., U.S.	C4	97
Galesville, Wi., U.S.	D2	126
Galeton, Pa., U.S.	C6	115
Galič, Russia	C25	18
Galicia, hist. reg., Eur.	F21	8
Galicia, hist. reg., Spain	B3	12
Galilee, Sea of see Kinneret, Yam, l., Isr.	C4	40
Galion, Oh., U.S.	B3	112
Galisteo Creek, stm., N.M., U.S.	k8	108
Galiuro Mountains, mts., Az., U.S.	E5	80
Galka'yo, Som.	G4	46
Gallant, Al., U.S.	B3	78
Gallarate, Italy	D3	14
Gallatin, Mo., U.S.	B4	102
Gallatin, Tn., U.S.	A5	119
Gallatin, co., Il., U.S.	F5	90
Gallatin, co., Ky., U.S.	B5	94
Gallatin, co., Mt., U.S.	E5	103
Gallatin, stm., Mt., U.S.	E5	103
Gallatin Range, mts., Mt., U.S.	E5	103
Gallaway, Tn., U.S.	B2	119
Galle, Sri L.	I6	37
Gallia, co., Oh., U.S.	D3	112
Galliano, La., U.S.	E5	95
Gallinas, Punta, c., Col.	A7	58
Gallinas Mountains, mts., N.M., U.S.	C2	108
Gallipoli, Italy	I12	14
Gallipoli see Gelibolu, Tur.	I10	16
Gallipolis, Oh., U.S.	D3	112
Gallitzin, Pa., U.S.	F4	115
Gällivare, Swe.	C13	6
Gallo Mountains, mts., N.M., U.S.	C1	108
Galloo Island, i., N.Y., U.S.	B4	109
Galloway, Mull of, c., Scot., U.K.	G8	7
Gallup, N.M., U.S.	B1	108
Galt, Ca., U.S.	C3	82
Galtür, Aus.	I10	8
Galty Mountains, mts., Ire.	I4	7
Galva, Il., U.S.	B3	90
Galva, Ks., U.S.	D6	93
Galveston, In., U.S.	C5	91
Galveston, Tx., U.S.	E5	120
Galveston, co., Tx., U.S.	E5	120
Galveston Bay, b., Tx., U.S.	E5	120
Galveston Island, i., Tx., U.S.	E5	120
Gálvez, Arg.	C4	56
Galway, Ire.	H3	7
Gambela, Eth.	G1	46
Gambell, Ak., U.S.	C5	79
Gambia, ctry., Afr.	F2	42
Gambia (Gambie), stm., Afr.	F2	42
Gambier, Oh., U.S.	B3	112
Gambo, Newf., Can.	D4	72
Gambrills, Md., U.S.	B4	97
Gamleby, Swe.	H11	6
Ganado, Az., U.S.	B6	80
Ganado, Tx., U.S.	E4	120
Gananoque, Ont., Can.	C8	73
Ganda, Ang.	D2	44
Gandak, stm., Asia	G11	38
Gander, Newf., Can.	D4	72
Gander, stm., Newf., Can.	D4	72
Ganderkesee, Ger.	B8	8
Gander Lake, l., Newf., Can.	D4	72
Gandesa, Spain	D12	12
Gāndhinagar, India	I5	38
Gāndhi Sāgar, res., India	H6	38
Gandia, Spain	G11	12
Gangāpur, India	G7	38
Gangāwati, India	E4	37
Gangdisê Shan, mts., China	E10	38
Ganges, B.C., Can.	g12	69
Ganges (Ganga) (Padma), stm., Asia	I13	38
Ganges, Mouths of the, mth., Asia	J13	38
Gang Mills, N.Y., U.S.	C3	109
Gangtok, India	G13	38
Gangu, China	E8	26
Gannat, Fr.	F10	10
Gannett Peak, mtn., Wy., U.S.	C3	127
Gansu, prov., China	D7	26
Gantt, S.C., U.S.	B3	117
Gantt Lake, res., Al., U.S.	D3	78
Ganzhou, China	J3	28
Ganzi, China	E7	26
Gao, Mali	E5	42
Gaokeng, China	H2	28
Gaoyou, China	C8	28
Gaozhou, China	D11	34
Gap, Fr.	H13	10
Gap, Pa., U.S.	G9	115
Gar, China	E9	38
Garanhuns, Braz.	E11	54
Garber, Ok., U.S.	A4	113
Garberville, Ca., U.S.	B2	82
Garça, Braz.	G4	57
Garda, Lago di, l., Italy	D5	14
Gardelegen, Ger.	C11	8
Garden, co., Ne., U.S.	C3	104
Gardena, Ca., U.S.	n12	82
Garden City, Ga., U.S.	D5	87
Garden City, Id., U.S.	F2	89
Garden City, Ks., U.S.	E3	93
Garden City, Mi., U.S.	p15	99
Garden City, Mo., U.S.	C3	102
Gardendale, Al., U.S.	B3	78
Garden Grove, Ca., U.S.	n13	82
Garden Island, i., Mi., U.S.	C5	99
Garden Plain, Ks., U.S.	E6	93
Garden Reach, India	I13	38
Gardēz, Afg.	D3	38
Gardiner, Me., U.S.	D3	96
Gardiner, Mt., U.S.	E6	103
Gardiner, Or., U.S.	D2	114
Gardiners Island, i., N.Y., U.S.	m16	109
Gardner, Il., U.S.	B5	90
Gardner, Ks., U.S.	D9	93
Gardner, Ma., U.S.	A4	98
Gardner Canal, strt., B.C., Can.	C3	69
Gardner Lake, l., Ct., U.S.	C6	84
Gardner Lake, l., Me., U.S.	D5	96
Gardner Pinnacles, Hi., U.S.	k14	88
Gardnerville, Nv., U.S.	E2	105
Gardone Val Trompia, Italy	D5	14
Garfield, N.J., U.S.	h8	107
Garfield, co., Co., U.S.	B2	83
Garfield, co., Mt., U.S.	C9	103
Garfield, co., Ne., U.S.	C6	104
Garfield, co., Ok., U.S.	A4	113
Garfield, co., Ut., U.S.	F4	121
Garfield, co., Wa., U.S.	C8	124
Garfield Heights, Oh., U.S.	h9	112
Garfield Mountain, mtn., Mt., U.S.	F4	103
Garfield Peak, mtn., Wy., U.S.	D5	127
Garibaldi, Or., U.S.	B3	114
Garibaldi, Mount, mtn., B.C., Can.	E6	69
Garies, S. Afr.	H3	44
Garissa, Kenya	B7	44
Garland, N.C., U.S.	C4	110
Garland, Tx., U.S.	n10	120
Garland, Ut., U.S.	B3	121
Garland, co., Ar., U.S.	C2	81
Garlin, Fr.	I6	10
Garm Āb, Afg.	D1	38
Garmisch-Partenkirchen, Ger.	H11	8
Garnavillo, Ia., U.S.	B6	92
Garner, Ia., U.S.	A4	92
Garner, N.C., U.S.	B4	110
Garnet Range, mts., Mt., U.S.	D3	103
Garnett, Ks., U.S.	D8	93
Garnish, Newf., Can.	E4	72
Garonne, stm., Eur.	H6	10
Garoua, Cam.	G8	42
Garrard, co., Ky., U.S.	C5	94
Garretson, S.D., U.S.	D9	118
Garrett, In., U.S.	B7	91
Garrett, co., Md., U.S.	k12	97
Garrett Park, Md., U.S.	B3	97
Garrettsville, Oh., U.S.	A4	112
Garrison, Ky., U.S.	B6	94
Garrison, Md., U.S.	B4	97
Garrison, N.D., U.S.	B4	111
Garrison Dam, N.D., U.S.	B4	111
Garrovillas, Spain	F5	12
Garry Lake, l., N.W. Ter., Can.	C12	66
Garsen, Kenya	B8	44
Garut, Indon.	m13	33a
Garvin, co., Ok., U.S.	C4	113
Gary, In., U.S.	A3	91
Gary, W.V., U.S.	D3	125
Garysburg, N.C., U.S.	A5	110
Garyville, La., U.S.	D5	95
Garza, co., Tx., U.S.	C2	120
Garza-Little Elm Reservoir, res., Tx., U.S.	C4	120
Garzón, Col.	F5	58
Gas City, In., U.S.	D6	91
Gasconade, co., Mo., U.S.	C6	102
Gasconade, stm., Mo., U.S.	C6	102
Gascoyne, stm., Austl.	E3	50
Gasparilla Island, i., Fl., U.S.	F4	86
Gaspé, Que., Can.	k14	74
Gaspésie, Péninsule de la, pen., Que., Can.	k13	74
Gassaway, W.V., U.S.	C4	125
Gassville, Ar., U.S.	A3	81
Gaston, In., U.S.	D7	91
Gaston, N.C., U.S.	A5	110
Gaston, S.C., U.S.	D5	117
Gaston, co., N.C., U.S.	B1	110
Gaston, Lake, res., U.S.	A5	110
Gaston Dam, N.C., U.S.	A5	110
Gastonia, N.C., U.S.	B1	110
Gátas, Akrotírion, c., Cyp.	B3	40
Gatčina, Russia	B13	18
Gate City, Va., U.S.	f9	123
Gates, N.Y., U.S.	*B3	109
Gates, Tn., U.S.	B2	119
Gates, co., N.C., U.S.	A6	110
Gateshead, Eng., U.K.	G11	7
Gateshead Island, i., N.W. Ter., Can.	B12	66
Gates of the Arctic National Park, Ak., U.S.	B9	79
Gatesville, Tx., U.S.	D4	120
Gatineau, Que., Can.	D2	74
Gatineau, stm., Que., Can.	D2	74
Gatineau, Parc de la, Que., Can.	D2	74
Gatlinburg, Tn., U.S.	D10	119
Gaucín, Spain	I6	12
Gauhāti, India	G14	38
Gauley, stm., W.V., U.S.	C3	125
Gauley Bridge, W.V., U.S.	C3	125
Gautier, Ms., U.S.	f8	101
Gauting, Ger.	G11	8
Gavá, Spain	D14	12
Gavins Point Dam, U.S.	B8	104
Gävle, Swe.	F11	6
Gavrilov-Jam, Russia	D22	18
Gawler Ranges, mts., Austl.	F7	50
Gaya, India	H11	38
Gay Head, c., Ma., U.S.	D6	98
Gaylord, Mi., U.S.	C6	99
Gaylord, Mn., U.S.	F4	100
Gayndah, Austl.	E10	50
Gaza see Ghazzah, Isr. Occ.	D4	40
Gaziantep, Tur.	H15	4
Gazimağusa, N. Cyp.	B3	40
Gazimağusa Körfezi, b., N. Cyp.	B4	40
Gbarnga, Lib.	G4	42
Gdańsk (Danzig), Pol.	A18	8
Gdynia, Pol.	A18	8
Gearhart, Or., U.S.	A3	114
Gearhart Mountain, mtn., Or., U.S.	E6	114
Geary, N.B., Can.	D3	71
Geary, Ok., U.S.	B3	113
Geary, co., Ks., U.S.	D7	93
Geauga, co., Oh., U.S.	A4	112
Gebze, Tur.	I13	16
Gediz, stm., Tur.	K11	16
Geel, Bel.	D4	8
Geelong, Austl.	G8	50
Ge'ermu, China	B16	38
Geesthacht, Ger.	B10	8
Geilo, Nor.	F7	6
Geislingen, Ger.	G9	8
Geistown, Pa., U.S.	F4	115
Geist Reservoir, res., In., U.S.	E6	91
Gejiu (Kokiu), China	C7	34
Gela, Italy	L9	14
Gelibolu, Tur.	I10	16
Gelibolu Yarımadası (Gallipoli Peninsula), pen., Tur.	I10	16
Gelsenkirchen, Ger.	D7	8
Gem, co., Id., U.S.	E2	89
Gembloux, Bel.	E4	8
Gemena, Zaire	H9	42
Gemlik, Tur.	I13	16
Gemona del Friuli, Italy	C8	14
Genale (Juba), stm., Afr.	G3	46
General Alvear, Arg.	C3	56
General Bravo, Mex.	E10	62
General Carneiro, Braz.	C2	57
General Levalle, Arg.	C4	56
General Pico, Arg.	D4	56
General Pinedo, Arg.	B4	56
General Roca, Arg.	D3	56
General Villegas, Arg.	D4	56
Genesee, Id., U.S.	C2	89
Genesee, Mi., U.S.	E7	99
Genesee, co., Mi., U.S.	E7	99
Genesee, co., N.Y., U.S.	B2	109
Genesee, stm., N.Y., U.S.	C2	109
Geneseo, Il., U.S.	B3	90
Geneseo, N.Y., U.S.	C3	109
Geneva, Al., U.S.	D4	78
Geneva, Il., U.S.	B5	90
Geneva, In., U.S.	C8	91
Geneva, Ne., U.S.	D8	104
Geneva, N.Y., U.S.	C4	109
Geneva, Oh., U.S.	A5	112
Geneva, co., Al., U.S.	D4	78
Geneva, Lake, l., Eur.	F13	10
Geneva, Lake, l., Wi., U.S.	F5	126
Geneva see Genève, Switz.	F13	10
Geneva-on-the-Lake, Oh., U.S.	A5	112
Genève, Switz.	F13	10
Genk, Bel.	E5	8
Genkai-nada, Japan	I3	30
Genoa, Il., U.S.	A5	90
Genoa, Ne., U.S.	C8	104
Genoa, Nv., U.S.	D2	105
Genoa, Oh., U.S.	A2	112
Genoa City, Wi., U.S.	F5	126
Genoa see Genova, Italy	E3	14
Genola, Ut., U.S.	D4	121
Genova (Genoa), Italy	E3	14
Genova, Golfo di, b., Italy	E3	14
Gent (Gand), Bel.	D3	8
Genteng, Indon.	n17	33a
Genthin, Ger.	C12	8
Gentry, Ar., U.S.	A1	81
Gentry, co., Mo., U.S.	A3	102
Geographe Bay, b., Austl.	F3	50
George, S. Afr.	H4	44
George, Ia., U.S.	A2	92
George, co., Ms., U.S.	E5	101
George, stm., Que., Can.	g13	74
George, Cape, c., N.S., Can.	D8	71
George, Lake, l., Ug.	B6	44

Name | Map Ref | Page

George, Lake, l., Fl., U.S. C5 86
George, Lake, l., N.Y., U.S. B7 109
George Air Force Base, mil., Ca., U.S. E5 82
George B. Stevenson Reservoir, res., Pa., U.S. D6 115
George Peak, mtn., Ut., U.S. B2 121
Georgetown, P.E.I., Can. C7 71
Georgetown, Cay. Is. E7 64
Georgetown, Gam. F3 42
Georgetown, Guy. D13 58
George Town (Pinang), Malay. L6 34
Georgetown, Ca., U.S. C3 82
Georgetown, Co., U.S. B5 83
Georgetown, Ct., U.S. D2 84
Georgetown, De., U.S. F4 85
Georgetown, Ga., U.S. E1 87
Georgetown, Il., U.S. D6 90
Georgetown, In., U.S. H6 91
Georgetown, Ky., U.S. B5 94
Georgetown, Ma., U.S. A6 98
Georgetown, Oh., U.S. D2 112
Georgetown, S.C., U.S. E9 117
Georgetown, Tx., U.S. D4 120
Georgetown, co., S.C., U.S. E9 117
George Washington Birthplace National Monument, Va., U.S. B6 123
George Washington Carver National Monument, Mo., U.S. E3 102
George West, Tx., U.S. E3 120
Georgia, ctry., Asia I6 22
Georgia, state, U.S. D3 87
Georgia, Strait of, strt., N.A. B2 76
Georgiana, Al., U.S. D3 78
Georgian Bay, b., Ont., Can. B3 73
Georgina, stm., Austl. D7 50
Gera, Ger. E12 8
Gerald, Mo., U.S. C6 102
Geraldine, Al., U.S. A4 78
Geral do Paranã, Serra, hills, Braz. C5 57
Geraldton, Austl. E2 50
Geraldton, Ont., Can. o18 73
Gérardmer, Fr. D13 10
Gerber Reservoir, res., Or., U.S. E5 114
Gerdine, Mount, mtn., Ak., U.S. C9 79
Gereshk, Afg. E1 38
Gérgal, Spain H9 12
Gering, Ne., U.S. C2 104
Gerlach, Nv., U.S. C2 105
Germantown, Il., U.S. E4 90
Germantown, Md., U.S. B3 97
Germantown, Oh., U.S. C1 112
Germantown, Tn., U.S. B2 119
Germantown, Wi., U.S. E5 126
Germany, ctry., Eur. E10 4
Germiston, S. Afr. G5 44
Gerona, Spain D14 12
Geronimo, Ok., U.S. C3 113
Gervais, Or., U.S. B4 114
Geseke, Ger. D8 8
Getafe, Spain E8 12
Gettysburg, Pa., U.S. G7 115
Gettysburg, S.D., U.S. C6 118
Ghāghra, stm., Asia G10 38
Ghana, ctry., Afr. G5 42
Ghanzi, Bots. F4 44
Gharbīyah, Aş-Şahrā' al- (Western Desert), des., Egypt C11 42
Ghardaïa, Alg. B6 42
Gharyān, Libya B8 42
Ghāt, Libya D8 42
Għawdex, i., Malta M9 14
Ghazāl, Bahr al-, stm., Sudan G12 42
Ghāziābād, India F7 38
Ghāzīpur, India H10 38
Ghaznī, Afg. D3 38
Ghazzah (Gaza), Isr. Occ. D4 40
Ghedi, Italy D5 14
Gheen, Mn., U.S. C6 100
Ghent see Gent, Bel. D3 8
Ghīn, Tall, mtn., Syria C5 40
Ghudāmis, Libya B7 42
Giants Neck, Ct., U.S. D7 84
Gibbon, Mn., U.S. F4 100
Gibbon, Ne., U.S. D7 104
Gibbons, Alta., Can. C4 68
Gibbstown, N.J., U.S. D2 107
Gibeon, Nmb. G3 44
Gibraltar, Gib. I6 12
Gibraltar, dep., Eur. H6 4
Gibraltar, Strait of (Estrecho de Gibraltar), strt. J6 12
Gibraltar Point, c., Eng., U.K. H13 7
Gibsland, La., U.S. B2 95
Gibson, Ga., U.S. C4 87
Gibson, co., In., U.S. H2 91
Gibson, co., Tn., U.S. A3 119
Gibsonburg, Oh., U.S. A2 112
Gibson City, Il., U.S. C5 90
Gibson Desert, des., Austl. D4 50
Gibsonia, Pa., U.S. h14 115
Gibson Island, i., Md., U.S. B5 97
Gibsons, B.C., Can. E6 69
Gibsonton, Fl., U.S. p11 86
Gibsonville, N.C., U.S. A3 110
Giddings, Tx., U.S. D4 120
Gideon, Mo., U.S. E8 102
Gien, Fr. E9 10
Giessen, Ger. E8 8
Gifford, Fl., U.S. E6 86
Gifford, Il., U.S. C5 90
Gifu, Japan G9 30
Gig Harbor, Wa., U.S. B3 124
Gihon, stm., Vt., U.S. B3 122
Gijón, Spain B6 12
Gila, co., Az., U.S. D5 80
Gila, stm., U.S. E4 76
Gila Bend, Az., U.S. E3 80
Gila Bend Indian Reservation, Az., U.S. D3 80
Gila Bend Mountains, mts., Az., U.S. D2 80
Gila Cliff Dwellings National Monument, N.M., U.S. D1 108
Gila Mountains, mts., Az., U.S. D6 80
Gila Peak, mtn., Az., U.S. D6 80
Gila River Indian Reservation, Az., U.S. D4 80
Gilbert, Az., U.S. D4 80
Gilbert, Ia., U.S. B4 92
Gilbert, La., U.S. B4 95
Gilbert, Mn., U.S. C6 100
Gilbert Islands see Kiribati, ctry., Oc. G24 2
Gilbert Peak, mtn., Wa., U.S. C4 124
Gilbert Plains, Man., Can. D1 70
Gilbertsville, Ky., U.S. f9 94
Gilbertsville, Pa., U.S. F10 115
Gilbertville, Ia., U.S. B5 92
Gilbués, Braz. E9 54
Gilchrist, Or., U.S. D5 114
Gilchrist, co., Fl., U.S. C4 86
Gilcrest, Co., U.S. A6 83
Giles, co., Tn., U.S. B4 119
Giles, co., Va., U.S. C2 123
Gilford Island, i., B.C., Can. D4 69
Gilgit, Pak. C6 38
Gillam, Man., Can. A4 70
Gillespie, Il., U.S. D4 90
Gillespie, co., Tx., U.S. D3 120
Gillespie Dam, Az., U.S. D3 80
Gillett, Ar., U.S. C4 81
Gillett, Wi., U.S. D5 126
Gillette, Wy., U.S. B7 127
Gilliam, co., Or., U.S. B6 114
Gilman, Il., U.S. C5 90
Gilman, Vt., U.S. C5 122
Gilmanton, N.H., U.S. D4 106
Gilmer, Tx., U.S. C5 120
Gilmer, co., Ga., U.S. B2 87
Gilmer, co., W.V., U.S. C4 125
Gilo, stm., Eth. G1 46
Gilpin, co., Co., U.S. B5 83
Gilroy, Ca., U.S. D3 82
Gil'uj, stm., Russia G19 24
Giluwe, Mount, mtn., Pap. N. Gui. m15 50a
Gimli, Man., Can. D3 70
Ginosa, Italy I11 14
Ginowan, Japan y27 31b
Gioia del Colle, Italy I11 14
Gioia Tauro, Italy K10 14
Girard, Il., U.S. D4 90
Girard, Ks., U.S. E9 93
Girard, Oh., U.S. A5 112
Girard, Pa., U.S. B1 115
Girardot, Col. E5 58
Girardville, Pa., U.S. E9 115
Giridih, India H12 38
Girifalco, Italy K11 14
Girne, N. Cyp. B3 40
Girwa, stm., Asia F9 38
Gisborne, N.Z. C7 52
Gisenyi, Rw. B5 44
Gisors, Fr. C8 10
Giugliano [in Campania], Italy I9 14
Giulianova, Italy G8 14
Giurgiu, Rom. F9 16
Givet, Fr. B11 10
Givors, Fr. G11 10
Giyon, Eth. G2 46
Giza see Al-Jīzah, Egypt B12 42
Gižiga, Russia E26 24
Gižiginskaja Guba, b., Russia E25 24
Gjandža, Azer. I7 22
Gjirokastër, Alb. I4 16
Gjoa Haven, N.W. Ter., Can. C13 66
Glacier, co., Mt., U.S. B3 103
Glacier Bay, b., Ak., U.S. k21 79
Glacier Bay National Park, Ak., U.S. D12 79
Glacier National Park, B.C., Can. D9 69
Glacier National Park, Mt., U.S. B2 103
Glacier Peak, mtn., Wa., U.S. A4 124
Gladbrook, Ia., U.S. B5 92
Glade Creek, stm., Wa., U.S. C6 124
Glade Creek, stm., W.V., U.S. n13 125
Glade Creek, stm., W.V., U.S. n14 125
Glades, co., Fl., U.S. F5 86
Glade Spring, Va., U.S. f10 123
Gladewater, Tx., U.S. C5 120
Gladstone, Austl. D10 50
Gladstone, Man., Can. D2 70
Gladstone, Mi., U.S. C4 99
Gladstone, Mo., U.S. h10 102
Gladstone, Or., U.S. B4 114
Gladwin, Mi., U.S. E6 99
Gladwin, co., Mi., U.S. D6 99
Glåma, stm., Nor. F8 6
Glarner Alpen, mts., Switz. F15 10
Glarus, Switz. E16 10
Glascock, co., Ga., U.S. C4 87
Glasford, Il., U.S. C4 90
Glasgow, Scot., U.K. F8 7
Glasgow, Ky., U.S. C4 94
Glasgow, Mo., U.S. B5 102
Glasgow, Mt., U.S. B10 103
Glasgow, Va., U.S. C3 123
Glasgow, W.V., U.S. m13 125
Glassboro, N.J., U.S. D2 107
Glasscock, co., Tx., U.S. D2 120
Glassport, Pa., U.S. F2 115
Glastonbury, Ct., U.S. C5 84
Glauchau, Ger. E12 8
Glazier Lake, l., Me., U.S. A3 96
Glazov, Russia F8 22
Gleason, Tn., U.S. A3 119
Gleisdorf, Aus. H15 8
Glen Allan, Ms., U.S. B2 101
Glen Allen, Va., U.S. C5 123
Glenboro, Man., Can. E2 70
Glenbrook, Nv., U.S. D2 105
Glen Burnie, Md., U.S. B4 97
Glen Canyon Dam, Az., U.S. A4 80
Glen Canyon National Recreation Area, U.S. F5 121
Glencoe, Ont., Can. E3 73
Glencoe, Al., U.S. B4 78
Glencoe, Il., U.S. A6 90
Glencoe, Mn., U.S. F4 100
Glen Cove, N.Y., U.S. h13 109
Glendale, Az., U.S. D3 80
Glendale, Ca., U.S. m12 82
Glendale, Ms., U.S. D4 101
Glendale, Oh., U.S. C1 112
Glendale, Or., U.S. E3 114
Glendale, R.I., U.S. B2 116
Glendale, S.C., U.S. B4 117
Glen Dale, W.V., U.S. B4 125
Glendale, Wi., U.S. m12 126
Glendale Heights, W.V., U.S. g8 125
Glendive, Mt., U.S. C12 103
Glendo, Wy., U.S. D7 127
Glendora, Ca., U.S. m13 82
Glendo Reservoir, res., Wy., U.S. D8 127
Glenelg, Md., U.S. B4 97
Glen Ellis Falls, wtfl, N.H., U.S. B4 106
Glen Ellyn, Il., U.S. k8 90
Glenham, N.Y., U.S. D7 109
Glen Innes, Austl. E10 50
Glen Jean, W.V., U.S. D3 125
Glen Lake, l., Mi., U.S. D5 99
Glen Lyon, Pa., U.S. D9 115
Glenmora, La., U.S. D3 95
Glenn, co., Ca., U.S. C2 82
Glennallen, Ak., U.S. f19 79
Glenns Ferry, Id., U.S. G3 89
Glennville, Ga., U.S. E5 87
Glenolden, Pa., U.S. p20 115
Glenpool, Ok., U.S. B5 113
Glen Raven, N.C., U.S. A3 110
Glen Ridge, N.J., U.S. h8 107
Glen Rock, N.J., U.S. h8 107
Glen Rock, Pa., U.S. G8 115
Glenrock, Wy., U.S. D7 127
Glen Rose, Tx., U.S. C4 120
Glens Falls, N.Y., U.S. B7 109
Glen Ullin, N.D., U.S. C4 111
Glenview, Il., U.S. h9 90
Glenview Naval Air Station, mil., Il., U.S. h9 90
Glenville, Mn., U.S. G5 100
Glenville, W.V., U.S. C4 125
Glenwood, Newf., Can. D4 72
Glenwood, Ar., U.S. C2 81
Glenwood, Ga., U.S. D4 87
Glenwood, Ia., U.S. C2 92
Glenwood, Mn., U.S. E3 100
Glenwood, Va., U.S. D3 123
Glenwood City, Wi., U.S. C1 126
Glenwood Springs, Co., U.S. B3 83
Glidden, Ia., U.S. B3 92
Glide, Or., U.S. D3 114
Glina, Cro. D11 14
Glittertinden, mtn., Nor. F7 6
Gliwice (Gleiwitz), Pol. E18 8
Globe, Az., U.S. D5 80
Gloggnitz, Aus. H15 8
Gloster, Ms., U.S. D2 101
Gloucester, Ont., Can. h12 73
Gloucester, Eng., U.K. J10 7
Gloucester, Ma., U.S. A6 98
Gloucester, Va., U.S. C6 123
Gloucester, co., N.J., U.S. D2 107
Gloucester, co., Va., U.S. C6 123
Gloucester City, N.J., U.S. D2 107
Gloucester Point, Va., U.S. C6 123
Glouster, Oh., U.S. C3 112
Glover Island, i., Newf., Can. D3 72
Gloversville, N.Y., U.S. B6 109
Glovertown, Newf., Can. D4 72
Gloverville, S.C., U.S. E4 117
Gluck, S.C., U.S. C2 117
Glücksburg, Ger. A9 8
Glückstadt, Ger. B9 8
Glyndon, Md., U.S. B4 97
Glyndon, Mn., U.S. D2 100
Glynn, co., Ga., U.S. E5 87
Gmünd, Aus. G14 8
Gmunden, Aus. H13 8
Gnadenhutten, Oh., U.S. B4 112
Gnarp, Swe. E11 6
Gniezno, Pol. C17 8
Gnjilane, Yugo. G5 16
Gō, stm., Japan H5 30
Goa, ter., India E2 37
Goat Island, i., R.I., U.S. F5 116
Goat Mountain, mtn., Mt., U.S. C3 103
Goat Rock Dam, U.S. C4 78
Goba, Eth. G3 46
Gobabis, Nmb. F3 44
Gobi, des., Asia C7 26
Gobles, Mi., U.S. F5 99
Godāvari, stm., India D6 37
Goddard, Ks., U.S. E6 93
Goderich, Ont., Can. D3 73
Godfrey, Il., U.S. E3 90
Godhavn, Grnld. C22 66
Godhra, India I5 38
Godoy Cruz, Arg. C3 56
Gods, stm., Man., Can. A5 70
Gods Lake, l., Man., Can. B4 70
Godthåb, Grnld. D22 66
Godwin Austen see K2, mtn., Asia C7 38
Goéland, Lac au, l., Que., Can. G17 66
Goélands, Lac aux, l., Que., Can. E20 66
Goff Creek, stm., Ok., U.S. e9 113
Goffstown, N.H., U.S. D3 106
Gogebic, co., Mi., U.S. n12 99
Gogebic, Lake, l., Mi., U.S. m12 99
Goiana, Braz. G9 54
Goiânia, Braz. D4 57
Goiás, Braz. C3 57
Gojra, Pak. E5 38
Gokāk, India D3 37
Gökçeada, i., Tur. I9 16
Gol'čiha, Russia C10 24
Golconda, Il., U.S. F5 90
Golconda, Nv., U.S. C4 105
Gold Bar, Wa., U.S. B4 124
Gold Beach, Or., U.S. E2 114
Golden, B.C., Can. D9 69
Golden, Co., U.S. B5 83
Golden City, Mo., U.S. D3 102
Goldendale, Wa., U.S. D5 124
Golden Gate Bridge, Ca., U.S. h7 82
Golden Gate National Recreation Area, Ca., U.S. h7 82
Golden Hinde, mtn., B.C., Can. E5 69
Golden Meadow, La., U.S. E5 95
Golden Spike National Historic Site, hist., Ut., U.S. B3 121
Golden Valley, Mn., U.S. n12 100
Golden Valley, co., Mt., U.S. D7 103
Golden Valley, co., N.D., U.S. B2 111
Goldfield, Ia., U.S. B4 92
Goldfield, Nv., U.S. F4 105
Gold Hill, Or., U.S. E3 114
Goldsboro, N.C., U.S. B5 110
Goldsby, Ok., U.S. B4 113
Goldthwaite, Tx., U.S. D3 120
Goleta, Ca., U.S. E4 82
Golf Manor, Oh., U.S. o13 112
Goliad, Tx., U.S. E4 120
Goliad, co., Tx., U.S. E4 120
Golspie, Scot., U.K. D9 7
Gomati, stm., India G9 38
Gombe, stm., Tan. B6 44
Gomel', Bela. I14 18
Gomera, i., Spain C2 42
Gómez Palacio, Mex. E8 62
Gonābād, Iran K9 22
Gonaïves, Haiti E11 64
Gonam, Russia F20 24
Gonam, stm., Russia F28 24
Gonâve, Golfe de la, b., Haiti E11 64
Gonâve, Île de la, i., Haiti E11 64
Gonda, India G9 38
Gondal, India J4 38
Gonder, Eth. F2 46
Gondia, India B6 37
Gondomar, Port. D3 12
Gondrecourt-le-Château, Fr. D12 10
Gönen, Tur. I11 16
Gōnoura, Japan I2 30
Gonzales, Ca., U.S. D3 82
Gonzales, La., U.S. D5 95
Gonzales, Tx., U.S. E4 120
Gonzales, co., Tx., U.S. E4 120
Gonzalez, Fl., U.S. u14 86
Goochland, co., Va., U.S. C5 123
Goode, Mount, mtn., Ak., U.S. g18 79
Goodfellow Air Force Base, mil., Tx., U.S. D2 120
Good Hope, Cape of, c., S. Afr. H3 44
Good Hope Mountain, mtn., B.C., Can. D5 69
Goodhue, co., Mn., U.S. F6 100
Gooding, Id., U.S. G4 89
Gooding, co., Id., U.S. F4 89
Goodland, In., U.S. C3 91
Goodland, Ks., U.S. C2 93
Goodlettsville, Tn., U.S. g10 119
Goodman, Ms., U.S. C4 101
Goodman, Mo., U.S. E3 102
Good Pine, La., U.S. C3 95
Goodsprings, Nv., U.S. H6 105
Goodview, Mn., U.S. F7 100
Goodwater, Al., U.S. B3 78
Goodwell, Ok., U.S. e9 113
Goodyear, Az., U.S. D3 80
Goole, Eng., U.K. H12 7
Goondiwindi, Austl. E10 50
Goose, stm., N.D., U.S. B8 111
Goose Bay, b., Newf., Can. B1 72
Gooseberry Creek, stm., Wy., U.S. B4 127
Goose Creek, S.C., U.S. F7 117
Goose Creek, stm., U.S. G5 89
Goose Creek, stm., Va., U.S. C3 123
Goose Creek Reservoir, res., S.C., U.S. k11 117
Goose Lake, l., U.S. B3 82
Goose Pond, l., N.H., U.S. C2 106
Göppingen, Ger. G9 8
Gorakhpur, India G10 38
Gorda, Punta, c., Cuba C6 64
Gordil, Cen. Afr. Rep. G10 42
Gordo, Al., U.S. B2 78
Gordon, Ga., U.S. D3 87
Gordon, Ne., U.S. B3 104
Gordon, co., Ga., U.S. B2 87
Gordonsville, Tn., U.S. C8 119
Gordonsville, Va., U.S. B4 123
Gore, Eth. G2 46
Gore, N.Z. G2 52
Gore, Ok., U.S. B6 113
Gore Bay, Ont., Can. B2 73
Gore Point, c., Ak., U.S. h16 79
Gore Range, mts., Co., U.S. B4 83
Goreville, Il., U.S. F5 90
Gorey, Ire. I6 7
Gorgān, Iran J8 22
Gorge High Dam, Wa., U.S. A4 124
Gorham, Me., U.S. E2 96
Gorham, N.H., U.S. B4 106
Gorinchem, Neth. D4 8
Gorizia, Italy D8 14
Gorki, Bela. G13 18
Gorki see Nižnij Novgorod, Russia E27 18
Gorkovskoje Vodochranilišče, res., Russia D26 18
Görlitz, Ger. B13 8
Gorlovka, Ukr. H5 22
Gorman, Tx., U.S. C3 120
Gornja Radgona, Slo. C10 14
Gorno-Altajsk, Russia G11 24
Gorodec, Russia E26 18
Gorontalo, Indon. E7 32
Gort, Ire. H4 7
Gorzów Wielkopolski (Landsberg an der Warthe), Pol. C15 8
Goshen, In., U.S. A6 91
Goshen, N.Y., U.S. D6 109
Goshen, Oh., U.S. C1 112
Goshen, co., Wy., U.S. D8 127
Goshute Indian Reservation, U.S. D7 105
Goshute Lake, l., Nv., U.S. C7 105
Goshute Mountains, mts., Nv., U.S. C7 105
Goslar, Ger. D10 8
Gosper, co., Ne., U.S. D6 104
Gosport, In., U.S. F4 91
Göteborg (Gothenburg), Swe. H8 6
Gotemba, Japan G11 30
Gotha, Ger. E10 8
Gothenburg, Ne., U.S. D5 104
Gothenburg see Göteborg, Swe. H8 6
Gotland, i., Swe. H12 6
Gotō-rettō, is., Japan J1 30
Göttingen, Ger. D9 8
Gouda, Neth. C4 8
Gouin, Réservoir, res., Que., Can. k12 74
Goulburn, Austl. F9 50
Goulburn Islands, is., Austl. B6 50
Gould, Ar., U.S. D4 81
Goulding, Fl., U.S. u14 86
Gould Island, i., R.I., U.S. E5 116
Goulds, Fl., U.S. s13 86
Gourdon, Fr. H8 10
Gouré, Niger F8 42
Gourin, Fr. D3 10
Gournay-en-Bray, Fr. C8 10
Gouverneur, N.Y., U.S. f9 109
Gove, co., Ks., U.S. D3 93
Governador Valadares, Braz. E8 57
Governors Harbour, Bah. B9 64
Govind Balabh Pant Sāgar, res., India H10 38
Govind Sāgar, res., India E7 38
Gowanda, N.Y., U.S. C2 109
Gower, Mo., U.S. B3 102
Gowmal (Gumal), stm., Asia D3 38
Gowmal Kalay, Afg. D3 38
Gowrie, Ia., U.S. B3 92
Goya, Arg. B5 56
Gozo see Għawdex, i., Malta M9 14
Graaff-Reinet, S. Afr. H4 44
Grabill, In., U.S. B8 91
Grace, Id., U.S. G7 89
Graceville, Fl., U.S. u16 86
Graceville, Mn., U.S. E2 100
Gracewood, Ga., U.S. C4 87
Gracias a Dios, Cabo, c., N.A. G6 64
Gradaús, Braz. E8 54
Gradaús, Serra dos, plat., Braz. E8 54
Grado, Italy D8 14
Grady, co., Ga., U.S. F2 87
Grady, co., Ok., U.S. C4 113
Graettinger, Ia., U.S. A3 92
Grafton, Austl. E10 50
Grafton, Il., U.S. E3 90
Grafton, Ma., U.S. B4 98
Grafton, N.D., U.S. A8 111
Grafton, Oh., U.S. A3 112
Grafton, Va., U.S. h15 123
Grafton, W.V., U.S. B4 125
Grafton, Wi., U.S. E6 126
Grafton, co., N.H., U.S. C3 106
Grafton, Cape, c., Austl. C9 50
Graham, N.C., U.S. A3 110
Graham, Tx., U.S. C3 120
Graham, co., Az., U.S. E5 80
Graham, co., Ks., U.S. C4 93
Graham, co., N.C., U.S. f9 110
Graham, Lake, res., Tx., U.S. C3 120
Graham, Mount, mtn., Az., U.S. E6 80
Graham Island, i., B.C., Can. C1 69
Graham Lake, l., Me., U.S. D4 96
Graham Moore, Cape, c., N.W. Ter., Can. B17 66
Grahamstown, S. Afr. H5 44
Grahn, Ky., U.S. B6 94
Grainger, co., Tn., U.S. C10 119
Grain Valley, Mo., U.S. B3 102
Grajaú, Braz. E9 54
Gramat, Fr. H8 10
Grambling, La., U.S. B3 95
Gramercy, La., U.S. h10 95
Grammichele, Italy L9 14
Grampian Mountains, mts., Scot., U.K. E8 7
Granada, Col. F6 58
Granada, Nic. I5 64
Granada, Spain H8 12
Granard, Ire. H5 7
Granbury, Tx., U.S. C4 120
Granby, Que., Can. D5 74
Granby, Co., U.S. A5 83
Granby, Ct., U.S. B4 84
Granby, Mo., U.S. E3 102
Granby, Lake, res., Co., U.S. A5 83
Gran Canaria, i., Spain p25 13
Gran Chaco, pl., S.A. A4 56
Grand, co., Co., U.S. A4 83
Grand, co., Ut., U.S. E6 121
Grand, stm., Ont., Can. D4 73
Grand, stm., Mi., U.S. E5 99
Grand, stm., Mo., U.S. A3 102
Grand, stm., Oh., U.S. A4 112
Grand, stm., S.D., U.S. B4 118
Grandas, Spain B5 12
Grand Bahama, i., Bah. A8 64
Grand Bank, Newf., Can. E4 72
Grand-Bassam, I.C. G5 42
Grand Bay, N.B., Can. D3 71
Grand Bay, Al., U.S. E1 78
Grand Bend, Ont., Can. D3 73
Grand Blanc, Mi., U.S. F7 99
Grand Caillou, La., U.S. E5 95
Grand Canal, Ire. H5 7
Grand Canal see Da Yunhe, China E10 26
Grand Canyon, Az., U.S. A3 80
Grand Canyon, val., Az., U.S. A3 80
Grand Canyon National Park, Az., U.S. B3 80
Grand Cayman, i., Cay. Is. E7 64
Grand Centre, Alta., Can. B5 68
Grand Coteau, La., U.S. D3 95
Grand Coulee, Wa., U.S. B6 124
Grand Coulee Dam, Wa., U.S. B6 124
Grande, stm., Bol. G6 54
Grande, stm., Braz. E3 57
Grande, Bahía, b., Arg. G3 56
Grande, Boca, mth., Ven. C12 58
Grande, Ilha, i., Braz. G6 57
Grande, Ilha, i., Braz. G1 57
Grande, Rio (Bravo del Norte), stm., N.A. F7 76
Grande-Anse, N.B., Can. B4 71
Grande Cache, Alta., Can. C1 68
Grande Comore, i., Com. D8 44
Grande de Matagalpa, stm., Nic. H5 64
Grande de Santiago, Río, stm., Mex. G7 62
Grande do Gurupá, Ilha, i., Braz. D8 54
Grand-Entrée, Que., Can. B8 71
Grande Prairie, Alta., Can. B1 68
Grand Erg de Bilma, des., Niger E8 42
Grand Erg Occidental, des., Alg. B6 42
Grand Erg Oriental, des., Alg. B7 42

Name — Map Ref — Page

rande rivière de la Baleine, stm., Que., Can. g11 74
rande Ronde, stm., U.S. C8 124
randes, Salinas, pl., Arg. B4 56
randes-Bergeronnes, Que., Can. A8 74
rande-Terre, i., Guad. F17 64
rand Falls (Grand-Sault), N.B., Can. B2 71
rand Falls, wtfl, Me., U.S. C5 96
rand Falls [-Windsor], Newf., Can. D4 72
randfather Mountain, mtn., N.C., U.S. A1 110
randfield, Ok., U.S. C3 113
rand Forks, B.C., Can. E8 69
rand Forks, N.D., U.S. B8 111
rand Forks, co., N.D., U.S. B8 111
rand Forks Air Force Base, mil., N.D., U.S. B8 111
rand-Fougeray, Fr. E5 10
rand Harbour, N.B., Can. E3 71
rand Haven, Mi., U.S. E4 99
rand Island, Ne., U.S. D7 104
rand Island, i., La., U.S. D6 95
rand Island, i., Mi., U.S. B4 99
rand Isle, La., U.S. E6 95
rand Isle, co., Vt., U.S. B2 122
rand Isle, i., La., U.S. E6 95
rand Junction, Co., U.S. B2 83
rand Junction, Ia., U.S. B3 92
rand Lake, l., N.B., Can. D3 71
rand Lake, l., Newf., Can. D3 72
rand Lake, l., La., U.S. E6 95
rand Lake, l., La., U.S. E3 95
rand Lake, l., Mi., U.S. C7 99
rand Lake, l., Oh., U.S. B1 112
Grand Lake Matagamon, l., Me., U.S. B4 96
Grand Lake Seboeis, l., Me., U.S. B4 96
Grand Ledge, Mi., U.S. F6 99
Grand Manan Island, i., N.B., Can. E3 71
Grand Marais, Mn., U.S. k9 100
Grand Meadow, Mn., U.S. G6 100
Grand-Mère, Que., Can. C5 74
Grand Mound, Ia., U.S. C7 92
Grand Portage Indian Reservation, Mn., U.S. k10 100
Grand Portage National Monument, Mn., U.S. h10 100
Grand Prairie, Tx., U.S. n10 120
Grand Rapids, Mi., U.S. F5 99
Grand Rapids, Mn., U.S. C5 100
Grand Rapids, Oh., U.S. f6 112
Grand Rivière de la Baleine, stm., Que., Can. E17 66
Grand-Saint-Bernard, Tunnel du, Eur. G14 10
Grand Saline, Tx., U.S. C5 120
Grand Terre Islands, is., La., U.S. E6 95
Grand Teton, mtn., Wy., U.S. C2 127
Grand Teton National Park, Wy., U.S. C2 127
Grand Tower, Il., U.S. F4 90
Grand Traverse, co., Mi., U.S. D5 99
Grand Traverse Bay, b., Mi., U.S. C5 99
Grand Turk, T./C. Is. D12 64
Grand Valley, Ont., Can. D4 73
Grandview, Man., Can. D1 70
Grandview, In., U.S. I4 91
Grandview, Mo., U.S. C3 102
Grandview, Wa., U.S. C6 124
Grandview Heights, Oh., U.S. m10 112
Grandville, Mi., U.S. F5 99
Grandy, N.C., U.S. A7 110
Granger, In., U.S. A5 91
Granger, Ia., U.S. C4 92
Granger, Tx., U.S. D4 120
Granger, Wa., U.S. C5 124
Grangeville, Id., U.S. D2 89
Granisle, B.C., Can. B4 69
Granite, Ok., U.S. C2 113
Granite, co., Mt., U.S. D3 103
Granite City, Il., U.S. E3 90
Granite Falls, Mn., U.S. F3 100
Granite Falls, N.C., U.S. B1 110
Granite Falls, Wa., U.S. A4 124
Granite Lake, res., Newf., Can. D3 72
Granite Mountain, mtn., Ak., U.S. B7 79
Granite Mountains, mts., Az., U.S. E2 80
Granite Mountains, mts., Wy., U.S. D5 127
Granite Pass, Wy., U.S. B5 127
Granite Peak, mtn., Mt., U.S. E7 103
Granite Peak, mtn., Nv., U.S. C2 105
Granite Peak, mtn., Nv., U.S. B4 105
Granite Peak, mtn., Ut., U.S. C2 121
Granite Peak, mtn., Ut., U.S. E3 121
Granite Peak, mtn., Wy., U.S. D4 127
Granite Quarry, N.C., U.S. B2 110
Granite Range, mts., Nv., U.S. C2 105
Graniteville, S.C., U.S. D4 117
Graniteville, Vt., U.S. C4 122
Granollers, Spain D14 12
Grant, Al., U.S. A3 78
Grant, Mi., U.S. E5 99
Grant, Ne., U.S. D4 104
Grant, co., Ar., U.S. C3 81
Grant, co., In., U.S. D6 91
Grant, co., Ks., U.S. E2 93
Grant, co., Ky., U.S. B5 94
Grant, co., La., U.S. C3 95
Grant, co., Mn., U.S. E2 100
Grant, co., Ne., U.S. C4 104
Grant, co., N.M., U.S. E1 108
Grant, co., N.D., U.S. C4 111
Grant, co., Ok., U.S. A4 113
Grant, co., Or., U.S. C7 114
Grant, co., S.D., U.S. B8 118
Grant, co., Wa., U.S. B6 124
Grant, co., W.V., U.S. B5 125
Grant, co., Wi., U.S. F3 126
Grant, Mount, mtn., Nv., U.S. E3 105
Grant City, Mo., U.S. A3 102
Grantham, Eng., U.K. I12 7
Grant Park, Il., U.S. B6 90
Grant Range, mts., Nv., U.S. E6 105
Grants, N.M., U.S. B2 108
Grantsburg, Wi., U.S. C1 126
Grants Pass, Or., U.S. E3 114
Grantsville, Ut., U.S. C3 121
Grantsville, W.V., U.S. C3 125
Grant Town, W.V., U.S. B4 125
Grantville, Ga., U.S. C2 87
Granville, Fr. D5 10
Granville, Il., U.S. B4 90
Granville, N.Y., U.S. B7 109
Granville, Oh., U.S. B3 112
Granville, W.V., U.S. h11 125
Granville, co., N.C., U.S. A4 110
Granville Lake, l., Man., Can. A1 70
Granvin, Nor. F6 6
Grapeland, Tx., U.S. D5 120
Grapeview, Wa., U.S. B3 124
Grapevine, Tx., U.S. C4 120
Grapevine Lake, res., Tx., U.S. n9 120
Grapevine Peak, mtn., Nv., U.S. G4 105
Gras, Lac de, l., N.W. Ter., Can. D10 66
Grasonville, Md., U.S. C5 97
Grass, stm., Man., Can. B2 70
Grass, stm., N.Y., U.S. f9 109
Grasse, Fr. I13 10
Grass Lake, Il., U.S. h8 90
Grass Lake, Mi., U.S. F6 99
Grass Lake, l., Il., U.S. h8 90
Grass Valley, Ca., U.S. C3 82
Grassy Brook, stm., Vt., U.S. E3 122
Grassy Lake, l., La., U.S. k9 95
Grates Point, c., Newf., Can. D5 72
Gratiot, co., Mi., U.S. E6 99
Gratis, Oh., U.S. C1 112
Grave Creek, stm., W.V., U.S. g8 125
Gravelly Branch, stm., De., U.S. F4 85
Gravelly Range, mts., Mt., U.S. E4 103
Gravenhurst, Ont., Can. C5 73
Grave Peak, mtn., Id., U.S. C4 89
Graves, co., Ky., U.S. f9 94
Gravette, Ar., U.S. A1 81
Gravina in Puglia, Italy I11 14
Gray, Fr. E12 10
Gray, Ga., U.S. C3 87
Gray, Ky., U.S. D5 94
Gray, La., U.S. k10 95
Gray, Me., U.S. g7 96
Gray, co., Ks., U.S. E3 93
Gray, co., Tx., U.S. B2 120
Grayback Mountain, mtn., Or., U.S. E3 114
Gray Court, S.C., U.S. B3 117
Grayland, Wa., U.S. C1 124
Grayling, Mi., U.S. D6 99
Graylyn Crest, De., U.S. A3 85
Grays Harbor, co., Wa., U.S. B2 124
Grays Harbor, b., Wa., U.S. C1 124
Grayslake, Il., U.S. A5 90
Grays Lake, sw., Id., U.S. F7 89
Grayson, Ky., U.S. B7 94
Grayson, co., Ky., U.S. C3 94
Grayson, co., Tx., U.S. C4 120
Grayson, co., Va., U.S. D1 123
Grayson Lake, res., Ky., U.S. B7 94
Grays Peak, mtn., Co., U.S. B5 83
Gray Summit, Mo., U.S. g12 102
Graysville, Al., U.S. f7 78
Graysville, Tn., U.S. D8 119
Grayville, Il., U.S. E5 90
Graz, Aus. H15 8
Gr'azi, Russia I22 18
Great Abaco, i., Bah. A9 64
Great Artesian Basin, Austl. D8 50
Great Australian Bight, Austl. F5 50
Great Averill Pond, l., Vt., U.S. B5 122
Great Barrier Reef, rf., Austl. C9 50
Great Barrington, Ma., U.S. B1 98
Great Basin National Park, Nv., U.S. E7 105
Great Bay, b., N.H., U.S. D5 106
Great Bay, b., N.J., U.S. D4 107
Great Bear Lake, l., N.W. Ter., Can. C9 66
Great Bend, Ks., U.S. D5 93
Great Captain Island, i., Ct., U.S. F1 84
Great Channel, strt., Asia K3 34
Great Dismal Swamp, sw., U.S. D6 123
Great Divide Basin, Wy., U.S. E4 127
Great Dividing Range, mts., Austl. D9 50
Great East Lake, l., U.S. C5 106
Great Egg Harbor, stm., N.J., U.S. D3 107
Greater Antilles, is., N.A. D10 64
Greater Sunda Islands, is., Asia F4 32
Great Exuma, i., Bah. C10 64
Great Falls, Mt., U.S. C5 103
Great Falls, S.C., U.S. B6 117
Great Falls, wtfl, Md., U.S. B3 97
Great Falls Dam, Tn., U.S. D8 119
Great Guana Cay, i., Bah. B9 64
Great Himalaya Range, mts., Asia F10 38
Greathouse Peak, mtn., Mt., U.S. D7 103
Great Inagua, i., Bah. D11 64
Great Indian Desert (Thar Desert), des., Asia G4 38
Great Island, spit, Ma., U.S. C7 98
Great Island, i., N.C., U.S. B6 110
Great Karroo, plat., S. Afr. H4 44
Great Lakes Naval Training Center, mil., Il., U.S. h9 90
Great Miami, stm., U.S. C1 112
Great Misery Island, i., Ma., U.S. f12 98
Great Moose Lake, l., Me., U.S. D3 96
Great Neck, N.Y., U.S. h13 109
Great Nicobar, i., India K2 34
Great Pee Dee, stm., U.S. D9 117
Great Plain of the Koukdjuak, pl., N.W. Ter., Can. C18 66
Great Plains, pl., N.A. E10 61
Great Point, c., Ma., U.S. D7 98
Great Ruaha, stm., Tan. C7 44
Great Sacandaga Lake, l., N.Y., U.S. C6 109
Great Salt Lake, l., Ut., U.S. B3 121
Great Salt Lake Desert, des., Ut., U.S. C2 121
Great Salt Plains Lake, res., Ok., U.S. A3 113
Great Salt Pond, b., R.I., U.S. h7 116
Great Sand Dunes National Monument, Co., U.S. D5 83
Great Sandy Desert, des., Austl. D4 50
Great Slave Lake, l., N.W. Ter., Can. D10 66
Great Smoky Mountains, mts., U.S. B8 119
Great Smoky Mountains National Park, U.S. B8 119
Great Swamp, sw., R.I., U.S. F3 116
Great Victoria Desert, des., Austl. E5 50
Great Village, N.S., Can. D6 71
Great Wass Island, i., Me., U.S. D5 96
Great Yarmouth, Eng., U.K. I14 7
Greece, N.Y., U.S. B3 109
Greece, ctry., Eur. H12 4
Greeley, Co., U.S. A6 83
Greeley, Pa., U.S. D12 115
Greeley, co., Ks., U.S. D2 93
Greeley, co., Ne., U.S. C7 104
Green, Or., U.S. D3 114
Green, co., Ky., U.S. C4 94
Green, co., Wi., U.S. F4 126
Green, stm., U.S. D5 76
Green, stm., U.S. A1 83
Green, stm., U.S. F3 122
Green, stm., Il., U.S. B4 90
Green, stm., Ky., U.S. C2 94
Green, stm., Wa., U.S. B3 124
Green Acres, De., U.S. h8 85
Greenacres, Wa., U.S. B8 124
Greenacres City, Fl., U.S. F6 86
Greenback, Tn., U.S. D9 119
Green Bay, Wi., U.S. D6 126
Green Bay, b., U.S. D3 99
Greenbelt, Md., U.S. C4 97
Greenbriar, Va., U.S. g12 123
Greenbrier, Ar., U.S. B3 81
Green Brier, Tn., U.S. A5 119
Greenbrier, co., W.V., U.S. D4 125
Greenbrier, stm., W.V., U.S. D4 125
Greenbush, Mn., U.S. B2 100
Greencastle, In., U.S. E4 91
Greencastle, Pa., U.S. G6 115
Green City, Mo., U.S. A5 102
Green Cove Springs, Fl., U.S. C5 86
Greendale, In., U.S. F8 91
Greendale, Wi., U.S. F6 126
Greene, Ia., U.S. B5 92
Greene, N.Y., U.S. C5 109
Greene, co., Al., U.S. C1 78
Greene, co., Ar., U.S. A5 81
Greene, co., Ga., U.S. C3 87
Greene, co., Il., U.S. D3 90
Greene, co., In., U.S. F4 91
Greene, co., Ia., U.S. B3 92
Greene, co., Ms., U.S. D5 101
Greene, co., Mo., U.S. D4 102
Greene, co., N.Y., U.S. C6 109
Greene, co., N.C., U.S. B5 110
Greene, co., Oh., U.S. C2 112
Greene, co., Pa., U.S. G1 115
Greene, co., Tn., U.S. C11 119
Greene, co., Va., U.S. B4 123
Greeneville, Tn., U.S. C11 119
Green Fall, stm., U.S. F1 116
Greenfield, Ca., U.S. D3 82
Greenfield, Il., U.S. D3 90
Greenfield, In., U.S. E6 91
Greenfield, Ia., U.S. C3 92
Greenfield, Ma., U.S. A2 98
Greenfield, Mo., U.S. D4 102
Greenfield, N.H., U.S. E3 106
Greenfield, Oh., U.S. C2 112
Greenfield, Tn., U.S. A3 119
Greenfield, Wi., U.S. n12 126
Greenfield Plaza, Ia., U.S. e8 92
Green Forest, Ar., U.S. A2 81
Green Harbor, Ma., U.S. B6 98
Green Hill Pond, l., R.I., U.S. G3 116
Greenhills, Oh., U.S. n12 112
Green Lake, Wi., U.S. E5 126
Green Lake, co., Wi., U.S. E4 126
Green Lake, l., Me., U.S. D4 96
Green Lake, l., Wi., U.S. E5 126
Greenland, Ar., U.S. B1 81
Greenland, N.H., U.S. D5 106
Greenland, dep., N.A. B16 61
Greenland Sea B13 128
Greenlee, co., Az., U.S. D6 80
Green Lookout Mountain, mtn., Wa., U.S. D3 124
Green Mountain, mtn., Wy., U.S. D5 127
Green Mountain Reservoir, res., Co., U.S. B4 83
Green Mountains, mts., Vt., U.S. F2 122
Greenock, Scot., U.K. F8 7
Greenock, Pa., U.S. F2 115
Green Peter Lake, res., Or., U.S. C4 114
Green Pond, Al., U.S. B2 78
Green Pond, l., N.J., U.S. A4 107
Greenport, N.Y., U.S. m16 109
Green River, Ut., U.S. E5 121
Green River, Wy., U.S. E3 127
Green River Lake, res., Ky., U.S. C4 94
Green River Lock and Dam, U.S. I2 91
Green River Reservoir, res., Vt., U.S. B3 122
Green Rock, Il., U.S. B3 90
Greensboro, Al., U.S. C2 78
Greensboro, Ga., U.S. C3 87
Greensboro, Md., U.S. C6 97
Greensboro, N.C., U.S. A3 110
Greensburg, In., U.S. F7 91
Greensburg, Ks., U.S. E4 93
Greensburg, Ky., U.S. C4 94
Greensburg, Pa., U.S. F2 115
Greens Peak, mtn., Az., U.S. C6 80
Green Springs, Oh., U.S. A2 112
Greensville, co., Va., U.S. D5 123
Green Swamp, sw., N.C., U.S. C4 110
Greentown, In., U.S. D6 91
Greenup, Il., U.S. D5 90
Greenup, Ky., U.S. B7 94
Greenup, co., Ky., U.S. B7 94
Green Valley, Az., U.S. F5 80
Greenview, Il., U.S. C4 90
Greenville, Lib. G4 42
Greenville, Al., U.S. D3 78
Greenville, Ca., U.S. B3 82
Greenville, De., U.S. A3 85
Greenville, Ga., U.S. C2 87
Greenville, Il., U.S. E4 90
Greenville, Ky., U.S. C2 94
Greenville, Me., U.S. C3 96
Greenville, Mi., U.S. E5 99
Greenville, Ms., U.S. B2 101
Greenville, N.H., U.S. E3 106
Greenville, N.C., U.S. B5 110
Greenville, Oh., U.S. B1 112
Greenville, Pa., U.S. D1 115
Greenville, R.I., U.S. C3 116
Greenville, S.C., U.S. B3 117
Greenville, Tx., U.S. C4 120
Greenville, co., S.C., U.S. B3 117
Greenville Creek, stm., Oh., U.S. B1 112
Greenville Junction, Me., U.S. C3 96
Greenwich, Ct., U.S. E1 84
Greenwich, N.Y., U.S. B7 109
Greenwich, Oh., U.S. A3 112
Greenwich Bay, b., R.I., U.S. D4 116
Greenwich Point, c., Ct., U.S. E1 84
Greenwood, B.C., Can. E8 69
Greenwood, Ar., U.S. B1 81
Greenwood, De., U.S. E3 85
Greenwood, In., U.S. E5 91
Greenwood, La., U.S. B2 95
Greenwood, Ms., U.S. B3 101
Greenwood, Mo., U.S. k11 102
Greenwood, Pa., U.S. E5 115
Greenwood, S.C., U.S. C3 117
Greenwood, Wi., U.S. D3 126
Greenwood, co., Ks., U.S. E7 93
Greenwood, co., S.C., U.S. C3 117
Greenwood, Lake, res., In., U.S. G4 91
Greenwood, Lake, res., S.C., U.S. C4 117
Greenwood Lake, N.Y., U.S. D6 109
Greenwood Lake, l., U.S. A4 107
Greenwood Lake, l., Mn., U.S. C7 100
Greer, S.C., U.S. B3 117
Greer, co., Ok., U.S. C2 113
Greers Ferry Lake, res., Ar., U.S. B3 81
Greeson, Lake, res., Ar., U.S. C2 81
Gregg, co., Tx., U.S. C5 120
Gregory, S.D., U.S. D6 118
Gregory, co., S.D., U.S. D6 118
Greifswald, Ger. A13 8
Greilickville, Mi., U.S. D5 99
Greiz, Ger. E12 8
Grenada, Ms., U.S. B4 101
Grenada, co., Ms., U.S. B4 101
Grenada, ctry., N.A. H17 64
Grenada Lake, res., Ms., U.S. B4 101
Grenadine Islands, is., N.A. H17 64
Grenchen, Switz. E14 10
Grenoble, Fr. G12 10
Grenville, Que., Can. D3 74
Grenville, Cape, c., Austl. B8 50
Grenville, Point, c., Wa., U.S. B1 124
Gresham, Or., U.S. B4 114
Gresik, Indon. m16 33a
Gretna, Man., Can. E3 70
Gretna, Fl., U.S. B2 86
Gretna, La., U.S. E5 95
Gretna, Ne., U.S. C9 104
Gretna, Va., U.S. D3 123
Greven, Ger. C7 8
Grevená, Grc. I5 16
Grevesmühlen, Ger. B11 8
Grey, stm., Newf., Can. E3 72
Greybull, Wy., U.S. B4 127
Greybull, stm., Wy., U.S. B4 127
Greylock, Mount, mtn., Ma., U.S. A1 98
Greymouth, N.Z. E3 52
Greys, stm., Wy., U.S. C2 127
Gridley, Ca., U.S. C3 82
Gridley, Il., U.S. C5 90
Griffin, Ga., U.S. C2 87
Griffiss Air Force Base, mil., N.Y., U.S. B5 109
Griffith, Austl. F9 50
Griffith, In., U.S. A3 91
Grifton, N.C., U.S. B5 110
Griggs, co., N.D., U.S. B7 111
Griggsville, Il., U.S. D3 90
Grik, Malay. L6 34
Grimes, Ia., U.S. C4 92
Grimes, co., Tx., U.S. D4 120
Grimmen, Ger. A13 8
Grimsby, Ont., Can. D5 73
Grimsby, Eng., U.K. H12 7
Grimselpass, Switz. F15 10
Grimshaw, Alta., Can. A2 68
Grimsley, Tn., U.S. C9 119
Grimstad, Nor. G7 6
Grindall Creek, Va., U.S. n18 123
Grinnell, Ia., U.S. C5 92
Grinnell Peninsula, pen., N.W. Ter., Can. A14 66
Gris-Nez, Cap, c., Fr. B8 10
Grissom Air Force Base, mil., In., U.S. C5 91
Griswold, Ia., U.S. C2 92
Grizzly Mountain, mtn., Id., U.S. B2 89
Grizzly Mountain, mtn., Or., U.S. C6 114
Grizzly Mountain, mtn., Wa., U.S. A7 124
Groais Island, i., Newf., Can. C4 72
Grodno, Bela. H6 18
Groesbeck, Tx., U.S. D4 120
Grombalia, Tun. M5 14
Gronau, Ger. C6 8
Grong, Nor. D9 6
Groningen, Neth. B6 8
Groom Lake, l., Nv., U.S. F6 105
Groom Range, mts., Nv., U.S. F6 105
Groote Eylandt, i., Austl. B7 50
Grootfontein, Nmb. E3 44
Gros Morne National Park, Newf., Can. D3 72
Grosse Isle Naval Air Station, mil., Mi., U.S. p15 99
Grossenhain, Ger. D13 8
Grosse Pointe, Mi., U.S. *p16 99
Grosse Pointe Park, Mi., U.S. p16 99
Grosse Pointe Woods, Mi., U.S. p16 99
Grosseto, Italy G6 14
Grossglockner, mtn., Aus. H12 8
Grossmont, Ca., U.S. o16 82
Gros Ventre, stm., Wy., U.S. C2 127
Gros Ventre Range, mts., Wy., U.S. C2 127
Groswater Bay, b., Newf., Can. F21 66
Groton, Ct., U.S. D7 84
Groton, N.Y., U.S. C4 109
Groton, S.D., U.S. B7 118
Groton Long Point, Ct., U.S. D7 84
Grottaglie, Italy I12 14
Grottaminarda, Italy H10 14
Grottoes, Va., U.S. B4 123
Grouse Creek, stm., Ut., U.S. B2 121
Grouse Creek Mountain, mtn., Id., U.S. E5 89
Grove, Ok., U.S. A7 113
Grove City, Fl., U.S. F4 86
Grove City, Oh., U.S. C2 112
Grove City, Pa., U.S. D1 115
Grove Hill, Al., U.S. D2 78
Groveland, Fl., U.S. D5 86
Groveland, Ma., U.S. A5 98
Grove Point, c., Md., U.S. B5 97
Groveport, Oh., U.S. C3 112
Grover City, Ca., U.S. E3 82
Groves, Tx., U.S. E6 120
Groveton, N.H., U.S. A3 106
Groveton, Tx., U.S. D5 120
Groveton, Va., U.S. g12 123
Groveton Gardens, Va., U.S. *B5 123
Grovetown, Ga., U.S. C4 87
Groveville, N.J., U.S. C3 107
Growler Peak, mtn., Az., U.S. E2 80
Groznyj, Russia I7 22
Grudziądz, Pol. B18 8
Gruetli-Laager, Tn., U.S. D8 119
Grulla, Tx., U.S. F3 120
Grundy, Va., U.S. e9 123
Grundy, co., Il., U.S. B5 90
Grundy, co., Ia., U.S. B5 92
Grundy, co., Mo., U.S. A4 102
Grundy, co., Tn., U.S. D8 119
Grundy Center, Ia., U.S. B5 92
Grunthal, Man., Can. E3 70
Gruver, Tx., U.S. A2 120
Guacanayabo, Golfo de, b., Cuba D9 64
Guachochic, Mex. D6 62
Guadalajara, Mex. G8 62
Guadalajara, Spain E8 12
Guadalcanal, i., Sol.Is. A11 50
Guadalquivir, stm., Spain H6 12
Guadalupe, Mex. E9 62
Guadalupe, Az., U.S. m9 80
Guadalupe, Ca., U.S. E3 82
Guadalupe, co., N.M., U.S. C5 108
Guadalupe, co., Tx., U.S. E4 120
Guadalupe Garzarón, Mex. E9 62
Guadalupe Mountains, mts., U.S. E5 108
Guadalupe Mountains National Park, Tx., U.S. o12 120
Guadalupe Peak, mtn., Tx., U.S. o12 120
Guadeloupe, dep., N.A. F17 64
Guadeloupe Passage, strt., N.A. F17 64
Guadiana, stm., Eur. H4 12
Guadix, Spain H8 12
Guafo, Isla, i., Chile E2 56
Guajará Mirim, Braz. F5 54
Gualeguaychú, Arg. C5 56
Gualicho, Salina, pl., Arg. E3 56
Guam, dep., Oc. F22 2
Guaminí, Arg. D4 56
Guamo, Col. E5 58
Guampí, Sierra de, mts., Ven. B5 54
Guanaja, Isla de, i., Hond. F5 64
Guanajuato, Mex. G9 62
Guanambi, Braz. C7 57
Guanare, Ven. C8 58
Guanarito, Ven. C8 58
Guanay, Cerro, mtn., Ven. E9 58
Guane, Cuba C5 64
Guang'an, China E8 26
Guangdong, prov., China G9 26
Guanghua, China E9 26
Guangxi Zhuang Zizhiqu, prov., China G8 26
Guangyuan, China E8 26
Guangzhou (Canton), China L2 28
Guano Lake, l., Or., U.S. E7 114
Guantánamo, Cuba D10 64
Guanxian, China E7 26
Guápiles, C.R. I6 64
Guaporé (Iténez), stm., S.A. F6 54
Guaqui, Bol. G5 54
Guarabira, Braz. E11 54
Guaranda, Ec. H3 58
Guarapuava, Braz. B6 56
Guaratinguetá, Braz. G6 57
Guarda, Port. E4 12
Guardo, Spain C7 12
Guárico, Embalse del, res., Ven. C9 58
Guarulhos, Braz. G5 57
Guarus, Braz. F8 57
Guasave, Mex. E5 62
Guasdualito, Ven. D7 58
Guatemala, Guat. G2 64
Guatemala, ctry., N.A. G2 64
Guaviare, stm., Col. F8 58
Guaxupé, Braz. F5 57
Guayama, P.R. F14 64
Guayaquil, Ec. I3 58
Guayaquil, Golfo de, b., S.A. I2 58
Guaymallén, Arg. C3 56
Guaymas, Mex. D4 62
Gubbio, Italy F7 14
Guben, Ger. D14 8
Guchengzi, China D7 26
Güdalūr, India G4 37
Gudiyāttam, India F5 37
Güdūr, India E5 37
Guebwiller, Fr. E14 10
Guelma, Alg. A7 42
Guelph, Ont., Can. D4 73
Guérande, Fr. E4 10
Guéret, Fr. F8 10
Guernsey, Wy., U.S. D8 127
Guernsey, co., Oh., U.S. B4 112
Guernsey, dep., Eur. C4 10
Gueydan, La., U.S. D3 95
Guga, Russia G21 24
Guibes, Nmb. G3 44

Name — Map Ref — Page

Güicán, Col. D6 58
Guichen, Fr. E5 10
Guiding, China A9 34
Guijuelo, Spain E6 12
Guilford, Ct., U.S. D5 84
Guilford, Me., U.S. C3 96
Guilford, co., N.C., U.S. A3 110
Guilin (Kweilin), China B11 34
Guillaumes, Fr. H13 10
Guimarães, Port. D3 12
Guin, Al., U.S. B2 78
Guinea, ctry., Afr. F3 42
Guinea, Gulf of, b., Afr. H6 42
Guinea-Bissau, ctry., Afr. F2 42
Güines, Cuba C6 64
Guingamp, Fr. D3 10
Güira de Melena, Cuba C6 64
Guiratinga, Braz. G8 54
Güiria, Ven. B11 58
Guixian, China C10 34
Guiyang (Kweiyang), China A9 34
Guizhou, prov., China F8 26
Gujarat, state, India I4 38
Gūjar Khān, Pak. D5 38
Gujrānwāla, Pak. D6 38
Gujrāt, Pak. D6 38
Gulbarga, India D4 37
Guledagudda, India D3 37
Gulf, co., Fl., U.S. C1 86
Gulf Gate Estates, Fl., U.S. E4 86
Gulf Islands National Seashore, U.S. E5 101
Gulfport, Fl., U.S. E4 86
Gulfport, Ms., U.S. E4 101
Gulf Shores, Al., U.S. E2 78
Gull Island, i., N.C., U.S. B7 110
Gullivan Bay, b., Fl., U.S. G5 86
Gull Lake, l., Alta., Can. C4 68
Gull Lake, l., Mn., U.S. D4 100
Güllük, Tur. L11 16
Gülpınar, Tur. J10 16
Gulu, Ug. H12 42
Gumal (Gowmal), stm., Asia D3 38
Gumboro, De., U.S. G4 85
Gummersbach, Ger. D7 8
Guna, India H7 38
Gunisao, stm., Man., Can. C3 70
Gunnarn, Swe. D11 6
Gunnison, Co., U.S. C4 83
Gunnison, Ms., U.S. B3 101
Gunnison, Ut., U.S. D4 121
Gunnison, co., Co., U.S. C3 83
Gunnison, stm., Co., U.S. C2 83
Gunnison, Mount, mtn., Co., U.S. C3 83
Gunpowder Neck, c., Md., U.S. B5 97
Gunpowder River, b., Md., U.S. B5 97
Guntakal, India E4 37
Gunter Air Force Base, mil., Al., U.S. C3 78
Guntersville, Al., U.S. A3 78
Guntersville Lake, res., Al., U.S. A3 78
Guntown, Ms., U.S. A5 101
Guntūr, India D6 37
Gunungsitoli, Indon. N4 34
Günzburg, Ger. G10 8
Gunzenhausen, Ger. F10 8
Gurdāspur, India D6 38
Gurdon, Ar., U.S. D2 81
Guri, Embalse, res., Ven. D11 58
Gurley, Al., U.S. A3 78
Gurnee, Il., U.S. h9 90
Gurnet Point, c., Ma., U.S. B6 98
Gurupi, Braz. F9 54
Gurupi, stm., Braz. D9 54
Gusau, Nig. F7 42
Gus'-Chrustal'nyj, Russia F23 18
Gusev, Russia G5 18
Gushi, China C4 28
Gushikawa, Japan y27 31b
Gusinoozersk, Russia G15 24
Guspini, Italy J3 14
Gustav Holm, Kap, c., Grnld. C26 66
Gustine, Ca., U.S. D3 82
Güstrow, Ger. B12 8
Gütersloh, Ger. D8 8
Guthrie, Ky., U.S. D2 94
Guthrie, Ok., U.S. B4 113
Guthrie, W.V., U.S. m12 125
Guthrie, co., Ia., U.S. C3 92
Guthrie Center, Ia., U.S. C3 92
Guttenberg, Ia., U.S. B6 92
Guttenberg, N.J., U.S. h8 107
Guyana, ctry., S.A. B7 54
Guyandotte, stm., W.V., U.S. C2 125
Guymon, Ok., U.S. e9 113
Guysborough, N.S., Can. D8 71
Guyton, Ga., U.S. D5 87
Güzelyurt Körfezi, b., N. Cyp. B3 40
Gwādar, Pak. D1 36
Gwai, Zimb. E5 44
Gwalior, India G8 38
Gwanda, Zimb. F5 44
Gweru, Zimb. E5 44
Gwinhurst, De., U.S. h8 85
Gwinn, Mi., U.S. B3 99
Gwinner, N.D., U.S. C8 111
Gwinnett, co., Ga., U.S. C2 87
Gwydyr Bay, b., Ak., U.S. A10 79
Gwynns Falls, stm., Md., U.S. g10 97
Gympie, Austl. E10 50
Gyöngyös, Hung. H19 8
Győr, Hung. H17 8
Gypsum, Co., U.S. B4 83

H

Haakon, co., S.D., U.S. C4 118
Haapajärvi, Fin. E15 6
Haapamäki, Fin. E15 6
Haar, Ger. G11 8
Haarlem, Neth. C4 8
Haast, N.Z. E2 52
Habersham, co., Ga., U.S. B3 87
Habiganj, Bngl. H14 38
Hachijō-jima, i., Japan E14 26
Hachinohe, Japan B14 30
Hachiōji, Japan G12 30
Hackberry, La., U.S. E2 95
Hackensack, N.J., U.S. B4 107
Hackensack, stm., N.J., U.S. h8 107
Hackettstown, N.J., U.S. B3 107
Hackleburg, Al., U.S. A2 78
Hadd, Ra's al-, c., Oman D6 46
Haddam, Ct., U.S. D5 84
Haddock, Ga., U.S. C3 87
Haddonfield, N.J., U.S. D2 107
Haddon Heights, N.J., U.S. D2 107
Hadejia, stm., Nig. F8 42
Hadera, Isr. C4 40
Haderslev, Den. I7 6
Hadīyah, Sau. Ar. C2 46
Hadjeb el Aïoun, Tun. N4 14
Hadley Bay, b., N.W. Ter., Can. B11 66
Hadley Lake, l., Me., U.S. D5 96
Hadlock, Wa., U.S. A3 124
Ha Dong, Viet. D8 34
Hadramawt, reg., Yemen E4 46
Haeju, N. Kor. D12 26
Hāfizābād, Pak. D5 38
Hafun, Ras, c., Som. F5 46
Hagan, Ga., U.S. D5 87
Hagemeister Island, i., Ak., U.S. D7 79
Hagen, Ger. D7 8
Hagerman, Id., U.S. G4 89
Hagerman, N.M., U.S. D5 108
Hagerstown, In., U.S. E7 91
Hagerstown, Md., U.S. A2 97
Hagfors, Swe. F9 6
Haggin, Mount, mtn., Mt., U.S. D3 103
Hagi, Japan H4 30
Ha Giang, Viet. C8 34
Hague, Sask., Can. E2 75
Hague, Cap de la, c., Fr. C5 10
Haguenau, Fr. D14 10
Hagues Peak, mtn., Co., U.S. A5 83
Ha90 Ha90, Baie des, b., Que., Can. C2 72
Hahira, Ga., U.S. F3 87
Hahnville, La., U.S. E5 95
Haian, China C9 28
Haicheng, China C11 26
Hai Duong, Viet. D9 34
Haifa see Hefa, Isr. C4 40
Haikou, China D11 34
Haiku, Hi., U.S. C5 88
Hā'il, Sau. Ar. C3 46
Hailaer, China B10 26
Hailey, Id., U.S. F4 89
Haileybury, Ont., Can. p20 73
Haileyville, Ok., U.S. C6 113
Haimen, China G10 28
Haimen, China L5 28
Hainan, China H8 26
Hainan Dao, i., China E10 34
Haines, Ak., U.S. D12 79
Haines City, Fl., U.S. D5 86
Haines Junction, Yukon, Can. D5 66
Hainfeld, Aus. G15 8
Haining, China E9 28
Hai Phong, Viet. D9 34
Haiti (Haïti), ctry., N.A. E11 64
Haizhou, China A8 28
Hakodate, Japan r18 30a
Hāla, Pak. H3 38
Halab (Aleppo), Syria A5 40
Halā'ib, Sudan D13 42
Halawa, Cape, c., Hi., U.S. B5 88
Halawa Heights, Hi., U.S. g10 88
Halbā, Leb. B5 40
Halberstadt, Ger. D11 8
Halden, Nor. G8 6
Haldensleben, Ger. C11 8
Haldimand, Ont., Can. E5 73
Haldwāni, India F8 38
Hale, co., Al., U.S. C2 78
Hale, co., Tx., U.S. B2 120
Haleakala Crater, crat., Hi., U.S. C5 88
Haleakala National Park, Hi., U.S. C6 88
Hale Center, Tx., U.S. B2 120
Haleiwa, Hi., U.S. B3 88
Hales Corners, Wi., U.S. n11 126
Halethorpe, Md., U.S. B4 97
Haleyville, Al., U.S. A2 78
Half Moon Bay, Ca., U.S. k8 82
Halfway, Md., U.S. A2 97
Haliburton, Ont., Can. B6 73
Halibut Point, c., Ma., U.S. A6 98
Halifax, N.S., Can. E6 71
Halifax, Va., U.S. D4 123
Halifax, co., N.C., U.S. A5 110
Halifax, co., Va., U.S. D4 123
Halifax Bay, b., Austl. C9 50
Halimaile, Hi., U.S. C5 88
Halkirk, Scot., U.K. C9 7
Hall, co., Ga., U.S. B3 87
Hall, co., Ne., U.S. D7 104
Hall, co., Tx., U.S. B2 120
Hallam Peak, mtn., B.C., Can. C8 69
Hallandale, Fl., U.S. G6 86
Halla-san, mtn., S. Kor. E12 26
Halle, Ger. D11 8
Hällefors, Swe. G10 6
Hallein, Aus. H13 8
Hallettsville, Tx., U.S. E4 120
Hallie, Wi., U.S. D2 126
Hall Island, i., Ak., U.S. C5 79
Hall Meadow Brook Reservoir, res., Ct., U.S. B3 84
Hall Mountain, mtn., Wa., U.S. A8 124
Hällnäs, Swe. D12 6
Hallock, Mn., U.S. B2 100
Hallowell, Me., U.S. D3 96
Hall Peninsula, pen., N.W. Ter., Can. D19 66
Halls, Tn., U.S. B2 119
Hallsberg, Swe. G10 6
Halls Creek, Austl. C5 50
Halls Creek, stm., Ut., U.S. F5 121
Halls Crossroads, Tn., U.S. m14 119
Halls Stream, stm., N.H., U.S. f7 106
Hallstavik, Swe. F12 6
Hallstead, Pa., U.S. C10 115
Hallsville, Mo., U.S. B5 102
Hallsville, Tx., U.S. C5 120
Halmahera, i., Indon. E8 32
Halmahera, Laut, Indon. F8 32
Halmstad, Swe. H9 6
Halsey, Or., U.S. C3 114
Hälsingborg see Helsingborg, Swe. H9 6
Halstad, Mn., U.S. C2 100
Halstead, Ks., U.S. E6 93
Haltern, Ger. D7 8
Haltiatunturi, mtn., Eur. B13 6
Halton Hills, Ont., Can. D5 73
Hamada, Japan H5 30
Hamadān, Iran B4 46
Hamāh, Syria B5 40
Hamamatsu, Japan H10 30
Hamar, Nor. F8 6
Hamblen, co., Tn., U.S. C10 119
Hamburg, Ger. B9 8
Hamburg, Ar., U.S. D4 81
Hamburg, Ia., U.S. D2 92
Hamburg, N.Y., U.S. C2 109
Hamburg, Pa., U.S. E10 115
Hamden, Ct., U.S. D4 84
Hamden, Oh., U.S. C3 112
Hämeenlinna, Fin. F15 6
Hamel, Mn., U.S. m11 100
Hameln, Ger. C9 8
Hamersley Range, mts., Austl. D3 50
Hamhŭng, N. Kor. D12 26
Hami, China C5 26
Hamilton, Ber. E14 76
Hamilton, Ont., Can. D5 73
Hamilton, N.Z. B5 52
Hamilton, Scot., U.K. F8 7
Hamilton, Al., U.S. A2 78
Hamilton, Il., U.S. C2 90
Hamilton, In., U.S. A8 91
Hamilton, Mi., U.S. F4 99
Hamilton, Ms., U.S. B5 101
Hamilton, Mo., U.S. B3 102
Hamilton, Mt., U.S. D2 103
Hamilton, N.Y., U.S. C5 109
Hamilton, Oh., U.S. C1 112
Hamilton, Tx., U.S. D3 120
Hamilton, Va., U.S. A5 123
Hamilton, co., Fl., U.S. B3 86
Hamilton, co., Il., U.S. E5 90
Hamilton, co., In., U.S. D5 91
Hamilton, co., Ia., U.S. B4 92
Hamilton, co., Ks., U.S. E2 93
Hamilton, co., Ne., U.S. D7 104
Hamilton, co., N.Y., U.S. B6 109
Hamilton, co., Oh., U.S. C1 112
Hamilton, co., Tn., U.S. D8 119
Hamilton, co., Tx., U.S. D3 120
Hamilton, Lake, res., Ar., U.S. C2 81
Hamilton, Mount, mtn., Ak., U.S. C8 79
Hamilton, Mount, mtn., Ca., U.S. k9 82
Hamilton, Mount, mtn., Nv., U.S. D6 105
Hamilton Inlet, b., Newf., Can. A2 72
Hamilton Reservoir, res., Ma., U.S. B3 98
Hamilton Sound, strt., Newf., Can. D4 72
Hamilton Square, N.J., U.S. C3 107
Hamiota, Man., Can. D1 70
Hamlet, In., U.S. B4 91
Hamlet, N.C., U.S. C3 110
Hamlet, Mount, mtn., Ak., U.S. B6 79
Hamlin, Pa., U.S. D11 115
Hamlin, Tx., U.S. C2 120
Hamlin, W.V., U.S. C2 125
Hamlin, co., S.D., U.S. C8 118
Hamlin Lake, l., Mi., U.S. D4 99
Hamm, Ger. D7 8
Hammamet, Tun. M5 14
Hammam Lif, Tun. M5 14
Hammerdal, Swe. E10 6
Hammon, Ok., U.S. B2 113
Hammonasset, stm., Ct., U.S. D5 84
Hammonasset Point, c., Ct., U.S. E5 84
Hammond, In., U.S. A2 91
Hammond, La., U.S. D5 95
Hammond, Wi., U.S. D1 126
Hammond Bay, b., Mi., U.S. C6 99
Hammonton, N.J., U.S. D3 107
Hampden, Newf., Can. D3 72
Hampden, Me., U.S. D4 96
Hampden, co., Ma., U.S. B2 98
Hampden Highlands, Me., U.S. D4 96
Hampshire, Il., U.S. A5 90
Hampshire, co., Ma., U.S. B2 98
Hampshire, co., W.V., U.S. B6 125
Hampstead, Md., U.S. A4 97
Hampstead, N.C., U.S. C5 110
Hampton, N.B., Can. D4 71
Hampton, Ar., U.S. D3 81
Hampton, Ga., U.S. C2 87
Hampton, Ia., U.S. B4 92
Hampton, N.H., U.S. E5 106
Hampton, S.C., U.S. F5 117
Hampton, Tn., U.S. C11 119
Hampton, Va., U.S. C6 123
Hampton, co., S.C., U.S. F5 117
Hampton Bays, N.Y., U.S. n16 109
Hampton Beach, N.H., U.S. E5 106
Hampton Butte, mtn., Or., U.S. D6 114
Hampton Roads, Va., U.S. k15 123
Hampton Roads Bridge-Tunnel, Va., U.S. k15 123
Hams Fork, stm., Wy., U.S. E2 127
Hamtramck, Mi., U.S. p15 99
Hana, Hi., U.S. C6 88
Hanahan, S.C., U.S. F7 117
Hanalei Bay, b., Hi., U.S. A2 88
Hanamaki, Japan C14 30
Hanamaulu, Hi., U.S. B2 88
Hanapepe, Hi., U.S. B2 88
Hanau, Ger. E8 8
Hanceville, Al., U.S. A3 78
Hancock, Md., U.S. A1 97
Hancock, Mi., U.S. A2 99
Hancock, Mn., U.S. E3 100
Hancock, co., Ga., U.S. C3 87
Hancock, co., Il., U.S. C2 90
Hancock, co., In., U.S. E6 91
Hancock, co., Ia., U.S. A4 92
Hancock, co., Ky., U.S. C3 94
Hancock, co., Me., U.S. D4 96
Hancock, co., Ms., U.S. E4 101
Hancock, co., Oh., U.S. A2 112
Hancock, co., Tn., U.S. C10 119
Hancock, co., W.V., U.S. A4 125
Hand, co., S.D., U.S. C6 118
Handa, Japan H9 30
Handan, China D9 26
Hando, Som. F5 46
HaNegev, reg., Isr. D4 40
Hanford, Ca., U.S. D4 82
Hangchow see Hangzhou, China E9 28
Hangman Creek, stm., Wa., U.S. B8 124
Hangö (Hanko), Fin. G14 6
Hangzhou (Hangchow), China E9 28
Hangzhou Wan, b., China E9 28
Ḥanīsh, Jazā'ir, is., Yemen F3 46
Hanjiang, China J8 28
Hankinson, N.D., U.S. C9 111
Hanna, Alta., Can. D5 68
Hanna, Wy., U.S. E6 127
Hanna City, Il., U.S. C4 90
Hannahville Indian Reservation, Mi., U.S. C3 99
Hannibal, Mo., U.S. B6 102
Hannover, Ger. C9 8
Ha Noi, Viet. D8 34
Hanover, Ont., Can. C3 73
Hanover, Il., U.S. A3 90
Hanover, In., U.S. G7 91
Hanover, Ks., U.S. C7 93
Hanover, Ma., U.S. B6 98
Hanover, Mn., U.S. m11 100
Hanover, N.H., U.S. C2 106
Hanover, Pa., U.S. G8 115
Hanover, co., Va., U.S. C5 123
Hanover Park, Il., U.S. k8 90
Hansen, Id., U.S. G4 89
Hansford, co., Tx., U.S. A2 120
Hanson, Ma., U.S. B6 98
Hanson, co., S.D., U.S. D8 118
Hantsport, N.S., Can. D5 71
Hanzhong, China E8 26
Haparanda, Swe. D15 6
Hapeville, Ga., U.S. C2 87
Happy Valley, N.M., U.S. E5 108
Happy Valley-Goose Bay, Newf., Can. B1 72
Harahan, La., U.S. k11 95
Haralson, co., Ga., U.S. C1 87
Harare, Zimb. E6 44
Ḥarash, Bi'r al-, well, Libya C10 42
Harbeson, De., U.S. F4 85
Harbin, China B12 26
Harbor, Or., U.S. E2 114
Harbor Beach, Mi., U.S. E8 99
Harborcreek, Pa., U.S. B2 115
Harbor Springs, Mi., U.S. C6 99
Harbour Breton, Newf., Can. E4 72
Harbour Grace, Newf., Can. E5 72
Harcuvar Mountains, mts., Az., U.S. D2 80
Harda, India I7 38
Hardangerfjorden, Nor. F5 6
Hardee, co., Fl., U.S. E5 86
Hardeeville, S.C., U.S. G5 117
Hardeman, co., Tn., U.S. B2 119
Hardeman, co., Tx., U.S. B3 120
Hardin, Il., U.S. D3 90
Hardin, Mt., U.S. E9 103
Hardin, co., Il., U.S. F5 90
Hardin, co., Ia., U.S. B4 92
Hardin, co., Ky., U.S. C4 94
Hardin, co., Oh., U.S. B2 112
Hardin, co., Tn., U.S. B3 119
Hardin, co., Tx., U.S. D5 120
Harding, co., N.M., U.S. B5 108
Harding, co., S.D., U.S. B2 118
Harding, Lake, res., U.S. C4 78
Hardinsburg, Ky., U.S. C3 94
Hardisty, Alta., Can. C5 68
Hardwār, India F8 38
Hardwick, Ga., U.S. C3 87
Hardwick, Vt., U.S. B4 122
Hardwood Ridge, mtn., Pa., U.S. D11 115
Hardy, co., W.V., U.S. B6 125
Hardy Lake, res., In., U.S. G6 91
Hare Bay, Newf., Can. D4 72
Hare Bay, b., Newf., Can. C4 72
Harer, Eth. G3 46
Harford, co., Md., U.S. A5 97
Hargeysa, Som. G3 46
Harihar, India E3 37
Harīrūd (Tedžen), stm., Asia J10 22
Harkers Island, N.C., U.S. C6 110
Harlan, In., U.S. B8 91
Harlan, Ia., U.S. C2 92
Harlan, Ky., U.S. D6 94
Harlan, co., Ky., U.S. D6 94
Harlan, co., Ne., U.S. D6 104
Harlan County Lake, res., Ne., U.S. E6 104
Harlem, Fl., U.S. F6 86
Harlem, Ga., U.S. C4 87
Harlem, Mt., U.S. B8 103
Harleyville, S.C., U.S. E7 117
Harlingen, Neth. B5 8
Harlingen, Tx., U.S. F4 120
Harlow, Eng., U.K. J13 7
Harlowton, Mt., U.S. D7 103
Harmon, co., Ok., U.S. C2 113
Harmon Creek, stm., W.V., U.S. f8 125
Harmony, In., U.S. E3 91
Harmony, Mn., U.S. G6 100
Harmony, Pa., U.S. E1 115
Harmony, R.I., U.S. B3 116
Harnett, co., N.C., U.S. B4 110
Harney, co., Or., U.S. D7 114
Harney, Lake, l., Fl., U.S. D5 86
Harney Lake, l., Or., U.S. D7 114
Harney Peak, mtn., S.D., U.S. D2 118
Härnösand, Swe. E11 6
Haro, Spain C9 12
Haro Strait, strt., Wa., U.S. A2 124
Harper, Lib. H4 42
Harper, Ks., U.S. E5 93
Harper, co., Ks., U.S. E5 93
Harper, co., Ok., U.S. A2 113
Harper, Mount, mtn., Ak., U.S. C11 79
Harpers Ferry, W.V., U.S. B7 125
Harpers Ferry National Historical Park, W.V., U.S. B7 125
Harpersville, Al., U.S. B3 78
Harpeth, stm., Tn., U.S. A5 119
Harquahala Mountain, mtn., Az., U.S. D2 80
Harquahala Mountains, mts., Az., U.S. D2 80
Harrah, Ok., U.S. B4 113
Harricana, stm., Can. F17 66
Harriman, Tn., U.S. D9 119
Harriman Reservoir, res., Vt., U.S. F3 122
Harrington, De., U.S. E3 85
Harrington Park, N.J., U.S. h9 107
Harris, Mn., U.S. E6 100
Harris, R.I., U.S. D3 116
Harris, co., Ga., U.S. D2 87
Harris, co., Tx., U.S. E5 120
Harris, Lake, l., Fl., U.S. D5 86
Harrisburg, Ar., U.S. B5 81
Harrisburg, Il., U.S. F5 90
Harrisburg, Or., U.S. C3 114
Harrisburg, Pa., U.S. F8 115
Harrisburg, S.D., U.S. D9 118
Harrison, Ar., U.S. A2 81
Harrison, Mi., U.S. D6 99
Harrison, N.J., U.S. k8 107
Harrison, N.Y., U.S. h13 109
Harrison, Oh., U.S. C1 112
Harrison, Tn., U.S. h11 119
Harrison, co., In., U.S. H5 91
Harrison, co., Ia., U.S. C2 92
Harrison, co., Ky., U.S. B5 94
Harrison, co., Ms., U.S. E4 101
Harrison, co., Mo., U.S. A3 102
Harrison, co., Oh., U.S. B4 112
Harrison, co., Tx., U.S. C5 120
Harrison, co., W.V., U.S. B4 125
Harrison, Cape, c., Newf., Can. g10 72
Harrison Bay, b., Ak., U.S. A9 79
Harrisonburg, Va., U.S. B4 123
Harrison Hot Springs, B.C., Can. f14 69
Harrison Lake, l., B.C., Can. E7 69
Harrisonville, Mo., U.S. C3 102
Harriston, Ont., Can. D4 73
Harristown, Il., U.S. D4 90
Harrisville, R.I., U.S. B2 116
Harrisville, Ut., U.S. B4 121
Harrisville, W.V., U.S. B3 125
Harrodsburg, Ky., U.S. C5 94
Harrogate, Eng., U.K. G11 7
Harrow, Ont., Can. E2 73
Harry S. Truman Reservoir, res., Mo., U.S. C4 102
Harry Strunk Lake, res., Ne., U.S. D5 104
Harstad, Nor. B11 6
Hart, Mi., U.S. E4 99
Hart, Tx., U.S. B1 120
Hart, co., Ga., U.S. B4 87
Hart, co., Ky., U.S. C4 94
Hart, Lake, l., Fl., U.S. D5 86
Hartford, Al., U.S. D4 78
Hartford, Ar., U.S. B1 81
Hartford, Ct., U.S. B5 84
Hartford, Il., U.S. E3 90
Hartford, Ia., U.S. C4 92
Hartford, Ky., U.S. C3 94
Hartford, Mi., U.S. F4 99
Hartford, S.D., U.S. D9 118
Hartford, Vt., U.S. D4 122
Hartford, Wi., U.S. E5 126
Hartford, co., Ct., U.S. B4 84
Hartford City, In., U.S. D7 91
Hartington, Ne., U.S. B8 104
Hart Lake, l., Or., U.S. E7 114
Hartland, N.B., Can. C2 71
Hartland, Me., U.S. D3 96
Hartland, Wi., U.S. E5 126
Hartland Point, c., Eng., U.K. J8 7
Hartlepool, Eng., U.K. G11 7
Hartley, Ia., U.S. A2 92
Hartley, co., Tx., U.S. B1 120
Hartney, Man., Can. E1 70
Hartselle, Al., U.S. A3 78
Hartshorne, Ok., U.S. C6 113
Hartsville, S.C., U.S. C7 117
Hartsville, Tn., U.S. A5 119
Hartville, Oh., U.S. B4 112
Hartwell, Ga., U.S. B4 87
Hartwell Lake, res., U.S. B1 117
Hārūnābād, Pak. F5 38
Hārūt, stm., Afg. C1 36
Harvard, Il., U.S. A5 90
Harvard, Ne., U.S. D7 104
Harvard, Mount, mtn., Co., U.S. C4 83
Harvey, Il., U.S. B6 90
Harvey, La., U.S. E5 95
Harvey, Mi., U.S. B3 99
Harvey, N.D., U.S. B6 111
Harvey, co., Ks., U.S. D6 93
Harvey Lake, res., Pa., U.S. m16 115
Harveys Creek, stm., Pa., U.S. n16 115
Harwich, Eng., U.K. J14 7
Harwich Port, Ma., U.S. C7 98
Harwinton, Ct., U.S. B3 84
Haryana, state, India F7 38
Harz, mts., Ger. D10 8
Hasbrouck Heights, N.J., U.S. h8 107
Haskell, Ar., U.S. C3 81
Haskell, Ok., U.S. B6 113
Haskell, Tx., U.S. C3 120
Haskell, co., Ks., U.S. E3 93
Haskell, co., Ok., U.S. B6 113
Haskell, co., Tx., U.S. C3 120
Haskovo, Bul. H9 16
Hassan, India F4 37
Hassayampa, stm., Az., U.S. D3 80
Hasselt, Bel. E5 8
Hassfurt, Ger. E10 8
Hässleholm, Swe. H9 6
Hastings, Ont., Can. C7 73
Hastings, N.Z. C6 52
Hastings, Eng., U.K. K13 7
Hastings, Mi., U.S. F5 99
Hastings, Mn., U.S. F6 100
Hastings, Ne., U.S. D7 104
Hastings, Pa., U.S. E4 115
Hastings-on-Hudson, N.Y., U.S. h13 109
Hatch, N.M., U.S. E2 108

Name — Map Ref — Page

atchet Lake, N.S., Can. E6 71
'atchie, stm., Tn., U.S. B2 119
'atchineha, Lake, l., Fl., U.S. D5 86
'at Creek, stm., S.D., U.S. E2 118
atfield, In., U.S. I3 91
atfield, Pa., U.S. F11 115
āthras, India G8 38
a Tinh, Viet. E8 34
'at Mountain, mtn., Az., U.S. E3 80
atteras, N.C., U.S. B7 110
'atteras, Cape, c., N.C., U.S. B7 110
'atteras Inlet, b., N.C., U.S. B7 110
attiesburg, Ms., U.S. D4 101
atton, N.D., U.S. B8 111
at Yai, Thai. K6 34
aubstadt, In., U.S. H2 91
augesund, Nor. G5 6
aughton, La., U.S. B2 95
aukivuori, Fin. E16 6
auser, Or., U.S. D2 114
'aut, Isle au, i., Me., U.S. D4 96
'aut Atlas, mts., Mor. B4 42
auula, Hi., U.S. B4 88
avana, Fl., U.S. B2 86
avana, Il., U.S. C3 90
avana see La Habana, Cuba C6 64
avant, Eng., U.K. K12 7
'avasu, Lake, res., U.S. C1 80
'avasupai Indian Reservation, Az., U.S. A3 80
avelberg, Ger. C12 8
avelock, Ont., Can. C7 73
avelock, N.C., U.S. C6 110
aven, Ks., U.S. E6 93
averford [Township], Pa., U.S. o20 115
averhill, Ma., U.S. A5 98
āveri, India E3 37
averstraw, N.Y., U.S. D7 109
aviland, Ks., U.S. E4 93
avířov, Czech. F18 8
avre, Mt., U.S. B7 103
avre de Grace, Md., U.S. A5 97
avre North, Mt., U.S. B7 103
'aw, stm., N.C., U.S. B3 110
'awaii, co., Hi., U.S. D6 88
'awaii, state, U.S. C5 88
'awaii, i., Hi., U.S. D6 88
'awaiian Islands, is., Hi., U.S. m14 88
'awaii Volcanoes National Park, Hi., U.S. D6 88
awarden, Ia., U.S. A1 92
awesville, Ky., U.S. C3 94
awi, Hi., U.S. C6 88
awick, Scot., U.K. F10 7
'awke Bay, b., N.Z. C6 52
awkesbury, Ont., Can. B10 73
'awkesbury Island, i., B.C., Can. C3 69
'awkins, co., Tn., U.S. C11 119
awkinsville, Ga., U.S. D3 87
awley, Mn., U.S. D2 100
awley, Pa., U.S. D11 115
aworth, N.J., U.S. h9 107
aw River, N.C., U.S. A3 110
awthorne, Ca., U.S. n12 82
awthorne, Fl., U.S. C4 86
awthorne, Nv., U.S. E3 105
awthorne, N.J., U.S. B4 107
awthorne, N.Y., U.S. g13 109
axtun, Co., U.S. A8 83
ay, Austl. F8 50
'ay, stm., Austl. D7 50
'ay, stm., Can. E9 66
'ay, Cape, c., N.W. Ter., Can. B10 66
ayange, Fr. C13 10
ayden, Az., U.S. E5 80
ayden, Co., U.S. A3 83
'ayden Lake, l., Id., U.S. B2 89
ayes, La., U.S. D3 95
'ayes, co., Ne., U.S. D4 104
'ayes, stm., Man., Can. B5 70
'ayes, Mount, mtn., Ak., U.S. C10 79
ayfield, Mn., U.S. G6 100
'ayford Peak, mtn., Nv., U.S. G6 105
'aymock Lake, l., Me., U.S. B3 96
aynesville, La., U.S. B2 95
ayneville, Al., U.S. C3 78
ayrabolu, Tur. H11 16
ay River, N.W. Ter., Can. D9 66
ays, Ks., U.S. D4 93
ays, N.C., U.S. A1 110
'ays, co., Tx., U.S. D3 120
'ays Canyon Peak, mtn., Nv., U.S. B2 105
ay Springs, Ne., U.S. B3 104
'aystack Mountain, mtn., Nv., U.S. B6 105
aysville, Ks., U.S. g12 93
ayti, Mo., U.S. E8 102
ayti Heights, Mo., U.S. E8 102
ayward, Ca., U.S. h8 82
ayward, Wi., U.S. B2 126
'aywood, co., N.C., U.S. f9 110
'aywood, co., Tn., U.S. B2 119
Hazard, Ky., U.S. C6 94
Hazardville, Ct., U.S. B5 84
Hazāribāgh, India I11 38
Hazel Crest, Il., U.S. k9 90
Hazel Dell, Wa., U.S. D3 124
Hazel Green, Al., U.S. A3 78
Hazel Green, Wi., U.S. F3 126
Hazel Park, Mi., U.S. p15 99
Hazelton Pyramid, mtn., Wy., U.S. B5 127
Hazelwood, N.C., U.S. f10 110
Hazen, Ar., U.S. C4 81
Hazen, N.D., U.S. B4 111
Hazen Bay, b., Ak., U.S. C6 79
Hazlehurst, Ga., U.S. E4 87
Hazlehurst, Ms., U.S. D3 101
Hazlet, N.J., U.S. C4 107
Hazleton, Ia., U.S. B6 92
Hazleton, Pa., U.S. E10 115
Head Harbor Island, i., Me., U.S. D5 96
Headland, Al., U.S. D4 78
Headley, Mount, mtn., Mt., U.S. C1 103
Healdsburg, Ca., U.S. C2 82
Healdton, Ok., U.S. C4 113
Healy, Ak., U.S. C10 79
Heard, co., Ga., U.S. C1 87
Hearne, Tx., U.S. D4 120
Hearst, Ont., Can. o19 73
Heart, stm., N.D., U.S. C3 111
Heart Butte Dam, N.D., U.S. C4 111
Heart Lake, l., Wy., U.S. B2 127
Heart's Content, Newf., Can. E5 72
Heath, Oh., U.S. B3 112
Heath Springs, S.C., U.S. B6 117
Heavener, Ok., U.S. C7 113
Hebbronville, Tx., U.S. F3 120
Hebei, prov., China D10 26
Heber, Az., U.S. C5 80
Heber City, Ut., U.S. C4 121
Heber Springs, Ar., U.S. B3 81
Hébertville, Que., Can. A6 74
Hebgen Lake, res., Mt., U.S. F5 103
Hebrides, is., Scot., U.K. D6 4
Hebron, N.S., Can. F3 71
Hebron, Il., U.S. A5 90
Hebron, In., U.S. B3 91
Hebron, Ky., U.S. h13 94
Hebron, Md., U.S. D6 97
Hebron, Ne., U.S. D8 104
Hebron, N.D., U.S. C3 111
Hebron, Oh., U.S. C3 112
Hebron see Al-Khalīl, Jord. D4 40
Hecate Strait, strt., B.C., Can. C2 69
Heceta Island, i., Ak., U.S. n23 79
Hechi, China B9 34
Hechingen, Ger. G8 8
Hechuan, China E8 26
Hecla Island, i., Man., Can. D3 70
Hector, Mn., U.S. F4 100
Hedemora, Swe. F10 6
He Devil, mtn., Id., U.S. D2 89
Hedrick, Ia., U.S. C5 92
Heerenveen, Neth. C5 8
Heerlen, Neth. E5 8
Hefa (Haifa), Isr. C4 40
Hefei, China D6 28
Heflin, Al., U.S. B4 78
Hefner, Lake, res., Ok., U.S. B4 113
Hegang, China B13 26
Hegins, Pa., U.S. E9 115
Heide, Ger. A9 8
Heidelberg, Ger. F8 8
Heidelberg, Ms., U.S. D5 101
Heidenheim, Ger. F10 8
Heidenreichstein, Aus. G15 8
Heidrick, Ky., U.S. D6 94
Heihe (Naquka), China E14 38
Heilbron, S. Afr. G5 44
Heilbronn, Ger. F9 8
Heiligenstadt, Ger. D10 8
Heilongjiang, prov., China B12 26
Heilongjiang (Amur), stm., Asia G19 24
Heinola, Fin. F16 6
Hejaz see Al-Ḥijāz, reg., Sau. Ar. C2 46
Hekla, vol., Ice. C4 4
Hekou, China C7 34
Helena, Al., U.S. B3 78
Helena, Ar., U.S. C5 81
Helena, Ga., U.S. D4 87
Helena, Mt., U.S. D4 103
Helena, Ok., U.S. A3 113
Helensburgh, Scot., U.K. E8 7
Helgoland, i., Ger. A7 8
Helgoländer Bucht, b., Ger. A8 8
Hellam, Pa., U.S. G8 115
Hellertown, Pa., U.S. E11 115
Hellesylt, Nor. E6 6
Hellín, Spain G10 12
Hells Canyon, val., U.S. B10 114
Hells Canyon National Recreation Area, U.S. B10 114
Hell-Ville, Madag. D9 44
Helmand, stm., Asia C2 36
Helmond, Neth. D5 8
Helmsdale, Scot., U.K. C9 7
Helmstedt, Ger. C10 8
Helotes, Tx., U.S. h7 120
Helper, Ut., U.S. D5 121
Helsingborg, Swe. H9 6
Helsingfors see Helsinki, Fin. F15 6
Helsingør (Elsinore), Den. H9 6
Helsinki (Helsingfors), Fin. F15 6
Hematite, Mo., U.S. C7 102
Hemet, Ca., U.S. F5 82
Hemingford, Ne., U.S. B2 104
Hemingway, S.C., U.S. D9 117
Hemlock, Mi., U.S. E6 99
Hemlock Reservoir, res., Ct., U.S. E2 84
Hemmingford, Que., Can. D4 74
Hemphill, Tx., U.S. D6 120
Hemphill, co., Tx., U.S. B2 120
Hempstead, N.Y., U.S. n15 109
Hempstead, Tx., U.S. D4 120
Hempstead, co., Ar., U.S. D2 81
Hemse, Swe. H12 6
Henagar, Al., U.S. A4 78
Henan, prov., China E9 26
Henderson, Ky., U.S. C2 94
Henderson, La., U.S. D4 95
Henderson, Mn., U.S. F5 100
Henderson, Ne., U.S. D8 104
Henderson, Nv., U.S. G7 105
Henderson, N.C., U.S. A4 110
Henderson, Tn., U.S. B3 119
Henderson, Tx., U.S. C5 120
Henderson, co., Il., U.S. C3 90
Henderson, co., Ky., U.S. C2 94
Henderson, co., N.C., U.S. f10 110
Henderson, co., Tn., U.S. B3 119
Henderson, co., Tx., U.S. C5 120
Henderson's Point, Ms., U.S. g7 101
Hendersonville, N.C., U.S. f10 110
Hendersonville, Tn., U.S. A5 119
Hendricks, Mn., U.S. F2 100
Hendricks, co., In., U.S. E4 91
Hendry, co., Fl., U.S. F5 86
Hengelo, Neth. C6 8
Hengshan, China H1 28
Hengyang, China F9 26
Henlawson, W.V., U.S. n12 125
Henlopen, Cape, c., De., U.S. E5 85
Hennef, Ger. E7 8
Hennepin, co., Mn., U.S. E5 100
Hennessey, Ok., U.S. A4 113
Henniker, N.H., U.S. D3 106
Henning, Mn., U.S. D3 100
Henning, Tn., U.S. B2 119
Henrico, co., Va., U.S. C5 123
Henrietta, N.C., U.S. B1 110
Henrietta, Tx., U.S. C3 120
Henrietta Maria, Cape, c., Ont., Can. n19 73
Henry, Il., U.S. B4 90
Henry, co., Al., U.S. D4 78
Henry, co., Ga., U.S. C2 87
Henry, co., Il., U.S. B3 90
Henry, co., In., U.S. E7 91
Henry, co., Ia., U.S. C6 92
Henry, co., Ky., U.S. B4 94
Henry, co., Mo., U.S. C4 102
Henry, co., Oh., U.S. A1 112
Henry, co., Tn., U.S. A3 119
Henry, co., Va., U.S. D3 123
Henry, Mount, mtn., Mt., U.S. B1 103
Henryetta, Ok., U.S. B6 113
Henry Kater, Cape, c., N.W. Ter., Can. C19 66
Henrys Fork, stm., U.S. E2 127
Henryville, Que., Can. D4 74
Henryville, In., U.S. G6 91
Hensall, Ont., Can. D3 73
Henzada, Burma F3 34
Hephzibah, Ga., U.S. C4 87
Heppner, Or., U.S. B7 114
Hepu (Lianzhou), China D10 34
Herāt, Afg. C1 36
Herbes, Isle aux, i., Al., U.S. E1 78
Herbignac, Fr. E4 10
Herculaneum, Mo., U.S. C7 102
Hereford, Eng., U.K. I10 7
Hereford, Md., U.S. A4 97
Hereford, Tx., U.S. B1 120
Hereford Inlet, b., N.J., U.S. E3 107
Herford, Ger. C8 8
Herington, Ks., U.S. D7 93
Herkimer, N.Y., U.S. B6 109
Herkimer, co., N.Y., U.S. B5 109
Hermann, Mo., U.S. C6 102
Hermano Peak, mtn., Co., U.S. D2 83
Hermantown, Mn., U.S. D6 100
Hermanus, S. Afr. H3 44
Herminie, Pa., U.S. F2 115
Hermiston, Or., U.S. B7 114
Hermitage, Newf., Can. E4 72
Hermitage, Ar., U.S. D3 81
Hermitage Bay, b., Newf., Can. E3 72
Hermosillo, Mex. C4 62
Hernando, Fl., U.S. D4 86
Hernando, Ms., U.S. A4 101
Hernando, co., Fl., U.S. D4 86
Herndon, Va., U.S. B5 123
Herning, Den. H7 6
Heron Lake, Mn., U.S. G3 100
Herrera del Duque, Spain F6 12
Herrera de Pisuerga, Spain C7 12
Herrin, Il., U.S. F4 90
Herring Bay, b., Md., U.S. C4 97
Herring Cove, N.S., Can. E6 71
Herrington Lake, res., Ky., U.S. C5 94
Herscher, Il., U.S. B5 90
Hershey, Pa., U.S. F8 115
Hertford, N.C., U.S. A6 110
Hertford, co., N.C., U.S. A5 110
Hervás, Spain E6 12
Hesdin, Fr. B9 10
Hesperia, Ca., U.S. E5 82
Hesperia, Mi., U.S. E4 99
Hesperus Mountain, mtn., Co., U.S. D2 83
Hesston, Ks., U.S. D6 93
Hetian, China B8 38
Hettinger, N.D., U.S. D3 111
Hettinger, co., N.D., U.S. C3 111
Heyburn, Id., U.S. G5 89
Heyworth, Il., U.S. C5 90
Hialeah, Fl., U.S. G6 86
Hiawatha, Ia., U.S. B6 92
Hiawatha, Ks., U.S. C8 93
Hibbing, Mn., U.S. C6 100
Hickam Air Force Base, mil., Hi., U.S. g10 88
Hickman, Ky., U.S. f8 94
Hickman, Ne., U.S. D9 104
Hickman, co., Ky., U.S. f8 94
Hickman, co., Tn., U.S. B4 119
Hickory, N.C., U.S. B1 110
Hickory, co., Mo., U.S. D4 102
Hicksville, N.Y., U.S. E7 109
Hicksville, Oh., U.S. A1 112
Hico, Tx., U.S. D3 120
Hico, W.V., U.S. C3 125
Hidaka-sammyaku, mts., Japan q20 30a
Hidalgo, Mex. E10 62
Hidalgo, Tx., U.S. F3 120
Hidalgo, co., N.M., U.S. F1 108
Hidalgo, co., Tx., U.S. F3 120
Hidalgo del Parral, Mex. D7 62
Hiddenite, N.C., U.S. B1 110
Hieroglyphic Mountains, mts., Az., U.S. k8 80
Hierro, i., Spain C2 42
Higashiōsaka, Japan H8 30
Higbee, Mo., U.S. B5 102
Higganum, Ct., U.S. D5 84
Higgins Lake, l., Mi., U.S. D6 99
Higgins Millpond, res., Md., U.S. C6 97
Higginsville, Mo., U.S. B4 102
High Bridge, N.J., U.S. B3 107
High Falls Reservoir, res., Wi., U.S. C5 126
High Island, i., Mi., U.S. C5 99
Highland, Il., U.S. E4 90
Highland, In., U.S. A3 91
Highland, Ks., U.S. C8 93
Highland, Mi., U.S. o14 99
Highland, N.Y., U.S. D7 109
Highland, Wi., U.S. E3 126
Highland, co., Oh., U.S. C2 112
Highland, co., Va., U.S. B3 123
Highland Lake, l., Me., U.S. g7 96
Highland Lakes, N.J., U.S. A4 107
Highland Park, Il., U.S. A6 90
Highland Park, Mi., U.S. p15 99
Highland Park, Tx., U.S. n10 120
Highland Peak, mtn., Ca., U.S. C4 82
Highland Point, c., Fl., U.S. G5 86
Highlands, N.J., U.S. C5 107
Highlands, N.C., U.S. f9 110
Highlands, Tx., U.S. r14 120
Highlands, co., Fl., U.S. E5 86
Highland Springs, Va., U.S. C5 123
High Level, Alta., Can. F7 68
Highmore, S.D., U.S. C6 118
High Point, N.C., U.S. B2 110
High Prairie, Alta., Can. B2 68
High Ridge, Mo., U.S. g12 102
High River, Alta., Can. D4 68
Highrock Lake, l., Man., Can. B1 70
High Rock Lake, res., N.C., U.S. B2 110
High Spire, Pa., U.S. F8 115
High Springs, Fl., U.S. C4 86
Hightstown, N.J., U.S. C3 107
Highwood, Il., U.S. A6 90
Highwood Baldy, mtn., Mt., U.S. C6 103
Highwood Mountains, mts., Mt., U.S. C6 103
Higuerote, Ven. B9 58
Higüey, Dom. Rep. E13 64
Híjar, Spain D11 12
Hikari, Japan I4 30
Hikone, Japan G9 30
Hiko Range, mts., Nv., U.S. F6 105
Hilbert, Wi., U.S. D5 126
Hildale, Ut., U.S. F3 121
Hilden, N.S., Can. D6 71
Hildesheim, Ger. C9 8
Hill, co., Mt., U.S. B6 103
Hill, co., Tx., U.S. D4 120
Hill City, Ks., U.S. C4 93
Hill City, S.D., U.S. D2 118
Hillcrest, Il., U.S. B4 90
Hillcrest Heights, Md., U.S. C4 97
Hilliard, Fl., U.S. B5 86
Hilliard, Oh., U.S. k10 112
Hill Island Lake, l., N.W. Ter., Can. D11 66
Hill Lake, l., Ar., U.S. h10 81
Hills, Ia., U.S. C6 92
Hills, Mn., U.S. G2 100
Hillsboro, Il., U.S. D4 90
Hillsboro, Ks., U.S. D6 93
Hillsboro, Mo., U.S. C7 102
Hillsboro, N.H., U.S. D3 106
Hillsboro, N.D., U.S. B8 111
Hillsboro, Oh., U.S. C2 112
Hillsboro, Or., U.S. B4 114
Hillsboro, Tx., U.S. C4 120
Hillsboro, Wi., U.S. E3 126
Hillsboro Canal, Fl., U.S. F6 86
Hillsborough, N.B., Can. D5 71
Hillsborough, N.C., U.S. A3 110
Hillsborough, co., Fl., U.S. E4 86
Hillsborough, co., N.H., U.S. E3 106
Hillsborough Bay, b., P.E.I., Can. C6 71
Hillsburgh, Ont., Can. D4 73
Hills Creek Lake, res., Or., U.S. D4 114
Hillsdale, Mi., U.S. G6 99
Hillsdale, N.J., U.S. g8 107
Hillsdale, co., Mi., U.S. G6 99
Hillside, N.J., U.S. k8 107
Hillsville, Pa., U.S. D1 115
Hillsville, Va., U.S. D2 123
Hilo, Hi., U.S. D6 88
Hilo Bay, b., Hi., U.S. D6 88
Hilton, N.Y., U.S. B3 109
Hilton Head Island, S.C., U.S. G6 117
Hilton Head Island, i., S.C., U.S. G6 117
Hilversum, Neth. C5 8
Himachal Pradesh, ter., India E7 38
Himalayas, mts., Asia F10 38
Himeji, Japan H7 30
Himi, Japan F9 30
Ḥimṣ (Homs), Syria B5 40
Hinchinbrook Island, i., Austl. C9 50
Hinchinbrook Island, i., Ak., U.S. g18 79
Hinckley, Il., U.S. B5 90
Hinckley, Mn., U.S. D6 100
Hinckley, Ut., U.S. D3 121
Hinckley Reservoir, res., N.Y., U.S. B5 109
Hindaun, India G7 38
Hindman, Ky., U.S. C7 94
Hinds, co., Ms., U.S. C3 101
Hindu Kush, mts., Asia B4 38
Hindupur, India F4 37
Hines, Or., U.S. D7 114
Hinesville, Ga., U.S. E5 87
Hinganghāt, India B5 37
Hingham, Ma., U.S. B6 98
Hingham Bay, b., Ma., U.S. g12 98
Hingoli, India C4 37
Hinojosa del Duque, Spain G6 12
Hinsdale, Il., U.S. k9 90
Hinsdale, N.H., U.S. E2 106
Hinsdale, co., Co., U.S. D3 83
Hinton, Alta., Can. C2 68
Hinton, Ia., U.S. B1 92
Hinton, Ok., U.S. B3 113
Hinton, W.V., U.S. D4 125
Hirado, Japan I2 30
Hirākud, res., India J10 38
Hiram, Ga., U.S. C2 87
Hiram, Oh., U.S. A4 112
Hirara, Japan G12 26
Hiratsuka, Japan G12 30
Hirosaki, Japan B13 30
Hiroshima, Japan H5 30
Hirson, Fr. C11 10
Hisār, India F6 38
Hispaniola, i., N.A. E12 64
Hita, Japan I3 30
Hitachi, Japan F13 30
Hitchcock, Tx., U.S. r14 120
Hitchcock, co., Ne., U.S. D4 104
Hitchcock Lake, Ct., U.S. C4 84
Hitoyoshi, Japan J3 30
Hitra, i., Nor. E7 6
Hiwassee, stm., Tn., U.S. D9 119
Hiwassee Lake, res., N.C., U.S. f8 110
Hjørring, Den. H7 6
Ho, Ghana G6 42
Hoa Binh, Viet. D8 34
Hoagland, In., U.S. C8 91
Hoback, stm., Wy., U.S. C2 127
Hobart, Austl. H9 50
Hobart, In., U.S. A3 91
Hobart, Ok., U.S. B2 113
Hobbs, N.M., U.S. E6 108
Hobe Sound, Fl., U.S. E6 86
Hobo, Col. F5 58
Hoboken, N.J., U.S. k8 107
Höchstadt an der Aisch, Ger. F10 8
Hockessin, De., U.S. A3 85
Hocking, co., Oh., U.S. C3 112
Hocking, stm., Oh., U.S. C3 112
Hockley, co., Tx., U.S. C1 120
Hodgeman, co., Ks., U.S. D4 93
Hodgenville, Ky., U.S. C4 94
Hodges Village Reservoir, res., Ma., U.S. B4 98
Hódmezővásárhely, Hung. I20 8
Hodna, Chott el, l., Alg. J16 12
Hodonín, Czech. G17 8
Hof, Ger. E11 8
Hoffman Estates, Il., U.S. h8 90
Hofgeismar, Ger. D9 8
Hofheim in Unterfranken, Ger. E10 8
Hofors, Swe. F11 6
Hōfu, Japan H4 30
Hogansville, Ga., U.S. C2 87
Hogback Mountain, mtn., Mt., U.S. F4 103
Hog Island, i., Fl., U.S. C3 86
Hog Island, i., Mi., U.S. C5 99
Hog Island, i., N.C., U.S. B6 110
Hog Island, i., R.I., U.S. D5 116
Hog Island, i., Va., U.S. C7 123
Hoh, stm., Wa., U.S. B1 124
Hohenau an der March, Aus. G16 8
Hohenwald, Tn., U.S. B4 119
Hohe Tauern, mts., Aus. H12 8
Hoh Head, c., Wa., U.S. B1 124
Hohhot, China C9 26
Hohoe, Ghana G5 42
Hōhoku, Japan H3 30
Ho-Ho-Kus, N.J., U.S. h8 107
Hoh Xil Shan, mts., China C13 38
Hoi An, Viet. G10 34
Hoisington, Ks., U.S. D5 93
Hokah, Mn., U.S. G7 100
Hoke, co., N.C., U.S. B3 110
Hokes Bluff, Al., U.S. B4 78
Hokitika, N.Z. E3 52
Hokkaidō, i., Japan p20 30a
Holbrook, Az., U.S. C5 80
Holbrook, Ma., U.S. B5 98
Holcomb, Ks., U.S. E3 93
Holden, Ma., U.S. B4 98
Holden, Mo., U.S. C4 102
Holden, W.V., U.S. D2 125
Holdenville, Ok., U.S. B5 113
Holdrege, Ne., U.S. D6 104
Hole in the Mountain Peak, mtn., Nv., U.S. C6 105
Holgate, Oh., U.S. A1 112
Holguín, Cuba D9 64
Höljes, Swe. F9 6
Hollabrunn, Aus. G16 8
Holladay, Ut., U.S. C4 121
Holland, In., U.S. H3 91
Holland, Mi., U.S. F4 99
Holland, Oh., U.S. A2 112
Holland, Tx., U.S. D4 120
Hollandale, Ms., U.S. B3 101
Holland Island, i., Md., U.S. D5 97
Holland see Netherlands, ctry., Eur. E9 4
Holland Point, c., Md., U.S. C4 97
Holland Straits, strt., Md., U.S. D5 97
Holley, N.Y., U.S. B2 109
Holliday, Tx., U.S. C3 120
Hollidaysburg, Pa., U.S. F5 115
Hollins, Va., U.S. C3 123
Hollis, Ok., U.S. C2 113
Hollister, Ca., U.S. D3 82
Hollister, Mo., U.S. E4 102
Holliston, Ma., U.S. B5 98
Holloman Air Force Base, mil., N.M., U.S. E3 108
Hollow Rock, Tn., U.S. A3 119
Hollowtop Mountain, mtn., Mt., U.S. E4 103
Holly, Co., U.S. C8 83
Holly, Mi., U.S. F7 99
Holly Grove, Ar., U.S. C4 81
Holly Hill, Fl., U.S. C5 86
Holly Hill, S.C., U.S. E7 117
Holly Pond, Al., U.S. A3 78
Holly Ridge, N.C., U.S. C5 110
Holly Shelter Swamp, sw., N.C., U.S. C5 110
Holly Springs, Ga., U.S. B2 87
Holly Springs, Ms., U.S. A4 101
Holly Springs, N.C., U.S. B4 110
Hollywood, Al., U.S. A4 78
Hollywood, Fl., U.S. F6 86
Hollywood, Md., U.S. D4 97
Hollywood, S.C., U.S. k11 117
Hollywood Indian Reservation, Fl., U.S. r3 86
Holman Island, N.W. Ter., Can. B9 66
Holmen, Wi., U.S. E2 126
Holmes, co., Fl., U.S. u16 86
Holmes, co., Ms., U.S. B3 101
Holmes, co., Oh., U.S. B4 112
Holmes, Mount, mtn., Wy., U.S. B2 127
Holmes Reefs, rf., Austl. C9 50
Holstebro, Den. H7 6
Holstein, Ia., U.S. B2 92
Holsteinsborg, Grnld. C22 66
Holston, stm., Tn., U.S. C11 119
Holston, Middle Fork, stm., Va., U.S. f10 123
Holston High Knob, mtn., Tn., U.S. C11 119
Holsworthy, Eng., U.K. K8 7
Holt, Al., U.S. B2 78
Holt, Mi., U.S. F6 99
Holt, co., Mo., U.S. A2 102
Holt, co., Ne., U.S. B7 104

Index

Name — Map Ref — Page

Holt Lake, res., Al., U.S. B2 78
Holton, Ks., U.S. C8 93
Holtville, Ca., U.S. F6 82
Holualoa, Hi., U.S. D6 88
Holy Cross, Mountain of the, mtn., Co., U.S. B4 83
Holyhead, Wales, U.K. H8 7
Holyoke, Co., U.S. A8 83
Holyoke, Ma., U.S. B2 98
Holyoke Range, hills, Ma., U.S. B2 98
Holzminden, Ger. D9 8
Hombori Tondo, mtn., Mali E5 42
Homburg, Ger. F7 8
Home Bay, b., N.W. Ter., Can. C19 66
Homecroft, In., U.S. m10 91
Homedale, Id., U.S. F2 89
Home Hill, Austl. C9 50
Homeland, Ga., U.S. F4 87
Home Place, In., U.S. E5 91
Homer, Ak., U.S. D9 79
Homer, Ga., U.S. B3 87
Homer, Il., U.S. C6 90
Homer, La., U.S. B2 95
Homer, Mi., U.S. F6 99
Homer, N.Y., U.S. C4 109
Homer City, Pa., U.S. E3 115
Homerville, Ga., U.S. E4 87
Homer Youngs Peak, mtn., Mt., U.S. E3 103
Homestead, Fl., U.S. G6 86
Homestead, Pa., U.S. k14 115
Homestead Air Force Base, mil., Fl., U.S. G6 86
Homestead National Monument of America, Ne., U.S. D9 104
Homewood, Al., U.S. g7 78
Homewood, Il., U.S. B6 90
Homewood, Oh., U.S. C1 112
Hominy, Ok., U.S. A5 113
Hominy Creek, stm., Ok., U.S. A5 113
Homme Dam, N.D., U.S. A8 111
Homochitto, stm., Ms., U.S. D2 101
Homosassa, Fl., U.S. D4 86
Homs see Ḥimṣ, Syria B5 40
Honaker, Va., U.S. e10 123
Honaunau, Hi., U.S. D6 88
Honda, Col. E5 58
Hondo, Japan J3 30
Hondo, Tx., U.S. E3 120
Hondo, stm., N.A. H15 62
Hondo, Río, stm., N.M., U.S. D4 108
Honduras, ctry., N.A. G4 64
Honduras, Gulf of, b., N.A. F4 64
Honea Path, S.C., U.S. C3 117
Hønefoss, Nor. F8 6
Honeoye Falls, N.Y., U.S. C3 109
Honesdale, Pa., U.S. C11 115
Honey Brook, Pa., U.S. F10 115
Honey Grove, Tx., U.S. C5 120
Honey Lake, l., Ca., U.S. B3 82
Honeypot Glen, Ct., U.S. C4 84
Honeyville, Ut., U.S. B3 121
Hon Gai, Viet. D9 34
Honga River, b., Md., U.S. D5 97
Hongdong, China D9 26
Honghu, China F2 28
Hong Kong, dep., Asia M3 28
Hongliuyuan, China C6 26
Honguedo, Détroit d', strt., Que., Can. G20 66
Hongze Hu, l., China B7 28
Honiara, Sol.Is. A11 50
Honjō, Japan F12 30
Honningsvåg, Nor. A15 6
Honokaa, Hi., U.S. C6 88
Honolulu, Hi., U.S. B4 88
Honolulu, co., Hi., U.S. B3 88
Honolulu International Airport, Hi., U.S. g10 88
Honomu, Hi., U.S. D6 88
Honouliuli, Hi., U.S. g9 88
Honshū, i., Japan F10 30
Honuapo Bay, b., Hi., U.S. D6 88
Hood, co., Tx., U.S. C4 120
Hood, Mount, mtn., Or., U.S. B5 114
Hood Canal, b., Wa., U.S. B2 124
Hoodoo Peak, mtn., Wa., U.S. A5 124
Hood River, Or., U.S. B5 114
Hood River, co., Or., U.S. B5 114
Hoodsport, Wa., U.S. B2 124
Hoogeveen, Neth. C6 8
Hooker, Ok., U.S. e9 113
Hooker, co., Ne., U.S. C4 104
Hook Head, c., Ire. I6 7
Hooksett, N.H., U.S. D4 106
Hoonah, Ak., U.S. D12 79
Hoopa Valley Indian Reservation, Ca., U.S. B2 82
Hooper, Ne., U.S. C9 104
Hooper Bay, Ak., U.S. C6 79
Hooper Islands, is., Md., U.S. D5 97
Hooper Strait, strt., Md., U.S. D5 97
Hoopes Reservoir, res., De., U.S. A3 85
Hoopeston, Il., U.S. C6 90
Hoorn, Neth. C5 8
Hoosac Range, mts., U.S. A1 98
Hoosic, stm., U.S. C7 109
Hoosick Falls, N.Y., U.S. C7 109
Hoover Dam, U.S. G7 105
Hoover Reservoir, res., Oh., U.S. B3 112
Hooverson Heights, W.V., U.S. f8 125
Hopatcong, N.J., U.S. B3 107
Hopatcong, Lake, l., N.J., U.S. A3 107
Hope, B.C., Can. E7 69
Hope, Ar., U.S. D2 81
Hope, In., U.S. F6 91
Hope, R.I., U.S. D3 116
Hope, Ben, mtn., Scot., U.K. C8 7
Hope, Point, c., Ak., U.S. B6 79
Hopedale, Il., U.S. C4 90
Hopedale, Ma., U.S. B4 98
Hope Island, i., R.I., U.S. E5 116
Hope Mills, N.C., U.S. C4 110
Hopes Advance, Cap, c., Que., Can. f13 74
Hopetown, S. Afr. G4 44
Hope Valley, R.I., U.S. E2 116
Hopewell, Va., U.S. C5 123
Hopewell Junction, N.Y., U.S. D7 109
Hopi Indian Reservation, Az., U.S. A5 80
Hopkins, Mn., U.S. n12 100
Hopkins, S.C., U.S. D6 117
Hopkins, co., Ky., U.S. C2 94
Hopkins, co., Tx., U.S. C5 120
Hopkinsville, Ky., U.S. D2 94
Hopkinton, Ia., U.S. B6 92
Hopkinton, Ma., U.S. B4 98
Hopkinton, R.I., U.S. F1 116
Hopkinton Lake, res., N.H., U.S. D3 106
Hopwood, Pa., U.S. G2 115
Hoquiam, Wa., U.S. C2 124
Horace, N.D., U.S. C9 111
Horace Mountain, mtn., Ak., U.S. B10 79
Horatio, Ar., U.S. D1 81
Horgen, Switz. E15 10
Horicon, Wi., U.S. E5 126
Horine, Mo., U.S. C7 102
Hormuz, Strait of, strt., Asia C6 46
Horn, Aus. G15 8
Horn, Cape see Hornos, Cabo de, c., Chile H3 56
Hornell, N.Y., U.S. C3 109
Hornersville, Mo., U.S. E7 102
Horn Island, i., Ms., U.S. E5 101
Horn Island Pass, strt., Ms., U.S. g8 101
Horn Lake, Ms., U.S. A3 101
Hornos, Cabo de (Cape Horn), c., Chile H3 56
Horn Plateau, plat., N.W. Ter., Can. D9 66
Horqin Youyi Qianqi, China B11 26
Horry, co., S.C., U.S. D10 117
Horse, stm., Ct., U.S. C6 84
Horse Cave, Ky., U.S. C4 94
Horse Creek, stm., U.S. E8 127
Horse Creek Reservoir, res., Co., U.S. C7 83
Horsehead Lake, l., N.D., U.S. B6 111
Horseheads, N.Y., U.S. C4 109
Horse Heaven Hills, hills, Wa., U.S. C6 124
Horsens, Den. I7 6
Horse Peak, mtn., N.M., U.S. D1 108
Horseshoe Bend, Id., U.S. F2 89
Horseshoe Bend National Military Park, Al., U.S. C4 78
Horseshoe Cove, b., Fl., U.S. C3 86
Horseshoe Point, c., Fl., U.S. C3 86
Horseshoe Reservoir, res., Az., U.S. C4 80
Horsham, Austl. G8 50
Horten, Nor. G8 6
Horton, Ks., U.S. C8 93
Hortonia, Lake, l., Vt., U.S. D2 122
Hortonville, Wi., U.S. D5 126
Hoschton, Ga., U.S. B3 87
Hoshangābād, India I7 38
Hoshiārpur, India E6 38
Hospers, Ia., U.S. A2 92
Hospet, India E4 37
Hospitalet, Spain D14 12
Hosta Butte, mtn., N.M., U.S. B1 108
Hoste, Isla, i., Chile H3 56
Hotchkiss, Co., U.S. C3 83
Hot Creek Range, mts., Nv., U.S. E5 105
Hot Creek Valley, val., Nv., U.S. E5 105
Hoting, Swe. D11 6
Hot Spring, co., Ar., U.S. C2 81
Hot Springs, S.D., U.S. D2 118
Hot Springs, co., Wy., U.S. C4 127
Hot Springs National Park, Ar., U.S. C2 81
Hot Springs National Park, Ar., U.S. C2 81
Hot Springs Peak, mtn., Ca., U.S. B3 82
Hot Springs Peak, mtn., Nv., U.S. B4 105
Hottah Lake, l., N.W. Ter., Can. C9 66
Houghton, Mi., U.S. A2 99
Houghton, N.Y., U.S. C2 109
Houghton, co., Mi., U.S. B2 99
Houghton Lake, Mi., U.S. D6 99
Houghton Lake, l., Mi., U.S. D6 99
Houghton Lake Heights, Mi., U.S. D6 99
Houlton, Me., U.S. B5 96
Houma, China D9 26
Houma, La., U.S. E5 95
Housatonic, stm., U.S. D3 84
House Springs, Mo., U.S. g12 102
Houston, De., U.S. E3 85
Houston, Mn., U.S. G7 100
Houston, Ms., U.S. B4 101
Houston, Mo., U.S. D6 102
Houston, Pa., U.S. F1 115
Houston, Tx., U.S. E5 120
Houston, co., Al., U.S. D4 78
Houston, co., Ga., U.S. D3 87
Houston, co., Mn., U.S. G7 100
Houston, co., Tn., U.S. A4 119
Houston, co., Tx., U.S. D5 120
Houston, stm., La., U.S. D2 95
Houston, Lake, res., Tx., U.S. r14 120
Houston Intercontinental Airport, Tx., U.S. r14 120
Houtman Rocks, Austl. E2 50
Houtzdale, Pa., U.S. E5 115
Hovenweep National Monument, Ut., U.S. F6 121
Hovmantorp, Swe. H10 6
Howard, Ks., U.S. E7 93
Howard, S.D., U.S. C8 118
Howard, Wi., U.S. D5 126
Howard, co., Ar., U.S. C2 81
Howard, co., In., U.S. C5 91
Howard, co., Ia., U.S. A5 92
Howard, co., Md., U.S. B4 97
Howard, co., Mo., U.S. B5 102
Howard, co., Ne., U.S. C7 104
Howard, co., Tx., U.S. C2 120
Howard City, Mi., U.S. E5 99
Howard Hanson Reservoir, res., Wa., U.S. B4 124
Howard Lake, Mn., U.S. E4 100
Howard Prairie Lake, res., Or., U.S. E4 114
Howards Grove-Millersville, Wi., U.S. E6 126
Howell, Mi., U.S. F7 99
Howell, co., Mo., U.S. E6 102
Howells, Ne., U.S. C8 104
Howe Sound, strt., B.C., Can. E6 69
Howick, Que., Can. D4 74
Howland, Me., U.S. C4 96
Howrah, India I13 38
Hoxie, Ar., U.S. A5 81
Hoxie, Ks., U.S. C3 93
Höxter, Ger. D9 8
Hoy, i., Scot., U.K. C9 7
Høyanger, Nor. F6 6
Hoyerswerda, Ger. D14 8
Hoyos, Spain E5 12
Hoyt Lakes, Mn., U.S. C6 100
Hradec Králové, Czech. E15 8
Hsilo, Tai. L9 28
Hsinchu, Tai. K9 28
Hsüehchia, Tai. L9 28
Huacho, Peru F3 54
Huachuca City, Az., U.S. F5 80
Hua Hin, Thai. H5 34
Huahua, stm., Nic. G6 64
Huaian, China B8 28
Huainan, China C6 28
Huaiyang, China B3 28
Huaiyin, China B8 28
Huaiyuan, China C6 28
Hualalai, vol., Hi., U.S. D6 88
Hualapai Indian Reservation, Az., U.S. B2 80
Hualapai Mountains, mts., Az., U.S. C2 80
Hualapai Peak, mtn., Az., U.S. B2 80
Hualien, Tai. L10 28
Huallaga, stm., Peru E3 54
Huallanca, Peru E3 54
Huamachuco, Peru E3 54
Huambo, Ang. D3 44
Huancayo, Peru F3 54
Huang (Yellow), stm., China D10 26
Huangchuan, China C4 28
Huangling, China D8 26
Huangshi, China E4 28
Huangyan, China G10 28
Huánuco, Peru E3 54
Huaraz, Peru E3 54
Huascarán, Nevado, mtn., Peru E3 54
Huasco, Chile B2 56
Huatabampo, Mex. D5 62
Huauchinango, Mex. G10 62
Hubbard, Ia., U.S. B4 92
Hubbard, Oh., U.S. A5 112
Hubbard, Or., U.S. B4 114
Hubbard, Tx., U.S. D4 120
Hubbard, co., Mn., U.S. C4 100
Hubbard Creek Lake, res., Tx., U.S. C3 120
Hubbard Lake, l., Mi., U.S. D7 99
Hubbardton, stm., Vt., U.S. D2 122
Hubbell, Mi., U.S. A2 99
Hubei, prov., China E9 26
Hubli, India E3 37
Huckleberry Mountain, mtn., Or., U.S. D4 114
Huddersfield, Eng., U.K. H11 7
Huddinge, Swe. G11 6
Hudiksvall, Swe. F11 6
Hudson, Que., Can. D3 74
Hudson, Co., U.S. A6 83
Hudson, Fl., U.S. D4 86
Hudson, Il., U.S. C5 90
Hudson, Ia., U.S. B5 92
Hudson, Ma., U.S. B4 98
Hudson, Mi., U.S. G6 99
Hudson, N.H., U.S. E4 106
Hudson, N.Y., U.S. C7 109
Hudson, N.C., U.S. B1 110
Hudson, Oh., U.S. A4 112
Hudson, Wi., U.S. D1 126
Hudson, Wy., U.S. D4 127
Hudson, co., N.J., U.S. B4 107
Hudson, stm., U.S. E7 109
Hudson, Lake, res., Ok., U.S. A6 113
Hudson Bay, b., Can. D15 66
Hudson Falls, N.Y., U.S. B7 109
Hudson Hope, B.C., Can. A6 69
Hudson Lake, In., U.S. A4 91
Hudson Strait, strt., Can. D18 66
Hudsonville, Mi., U.S. F5 99
Hudspeth, co., Tx., U.S. o12 120
Hue, Viet. F9 34
Huehuetenango, Guat. G2 64
Huelma, Spain H8 12
Huelva, Spain H5 12
Huércal-Overa, Spain H10 12
Huerfano, co., Co., U.S. D5 83
Huerfano, stm., Co., U.S. D6 83
Huerfano Mountain, mtn., N.M., U.S. A2 108
Huesca, Spain C11 12
Hueytown, Al., U.S. g6 78
Huffakers, Nv., U.S. D2 105
Hugh Butler Lake, res., Ne., U.S. D5 104
Hughenden, Austl. D8 50
Hughes, Ar., U.S. C5 81
Hughes, co., Ok., U.S. B5 113
Hughes, co., S.D., U.S. C5 118
Hughes, North Fork, stm., W.V., U.S. B3 125
Hughes, South Fork, stm., W.V., U.S. B3 125
Hughesville, Md., U.S. C4 97
Hughesville, Pa., U.S. D8 115
Hugo, Co., U.S. B7 83
Hugo, Mn., U.S. m13 100
Hugo, Ok., U.S. C6 113
Hugo Lake, res., Ok., U.S. C6 113
Hugoton, Ks., U.S. E2 93
Huidong, China A7 34
Huila, Nevado del, mtn., Col. F4 58
Huili, China A7 34
Huinan, China C12 26
Huittinen (Lauttakylä), Fin. F14 6
Huitzuco [de los Figueroa], Mex. H10 62
Huixtla, Mex. J13 62
Huiyang (Huizhou), China L3 28
Hulah Lake, res., Ok., U.S. A5 113
Hulan, China B12 26
Hulett, Wy., U.S. B8 127
Hull, Que., Can. D2 74
Hull, Ia., U.S. A1 92
Hull, Ma., U.S. B6 98
Hultsfred, Swe. H10 6
Hulun Nur, l., China B10 26
Humaitá, Braz. E6 54
Humansville, Mo., U.S. D4 102
Humber, stm., Eng., U.K. H12 7
Humble, Tx., U.S. E5 120
Humboldt, Az., U.S. C3 80
Humboldt, Ia., U.S. B3 92
Humboldt, Ks., U.S. E8 93
Humboldt, Ne., U.S. D10 104
Humboldt, Tn., U.S. B3 119
Humboldt, co., Ca., U.S. B2 82
Humboldt, co., Ia., U.S. B3 92
Humboldt, co., Nv., U.S. B3 105
Humboldt, stm., Nv., U.S. C3 105
Humboldt Range, mts., Nv., U.S. C3 105
Hummels Wharf, Pa., U.S. E8 115
Humphrey, Ar., U.S. C4 81
Humphrey, Ne., U.S. C8 104
Humphreys, co., Ms., U.S. B3 101
Humphreys, co., Tn., U.S. A4 119
Humphreys, Mount, mtn., Ca., U.S. D4 82
Humphreys Peak, mtn., Az., U.S. B4 80
Hunan, prov., China F9 26
Hundred Acre Pond, l., R.I., U.S. E3 116
Hunedoara, Rom. D6 16
Hünfeld, Ger. E9 8
Hungary, ctry., Eur. F11 4
Hungf'ou Hsü, i., Tai. M10 28
Hŭngnam, N. Kor. D12 26
Hungry Horse, Mt., U.S. B2 103
Hungry Horse Reservoir, res., Mt., U.S. B3 103
Hunsrück, mts., Ger. F6 8
Hunt, co., Tx., U.S. C4 120
Hunt, stm., R.I., U.S. D4 116
Hunterdon, co., N.J., U.S. B3 107
Hunter Island, i., Austl. H8 50
Hunter Island, i., B.C., Can. D3 69
Huntertown, In., U.S. B7 91
Huntingburg, In., U.S. H4 91
Huntingdon, Que., Can. D3 74
Huntingdon, Pa., U.S. F6 115
Huntingdon, Tn., U.S. A3 119
Huntingdon, co., Pa., U.S. F5 115
Hunting Island, i., S.C., U.S. G7 117
Huntington, Ar., U.S. B1 81
Huntington, In., U.S. C7 91
Huntington, N.Y., U.S. E7 109
Huntington, Tx., U.S. D5 120
Huntington, Ut., U.S. D5 121
Huntington, W.V., U.S. C2 125
Huntington, co., In., U.S. C6 91
Huntington Beach, Ca., U.S. F4 82
Huntington Lake, res., In., U.S. C7 91
Huntington Woods, Mi., U.S. p15 99
Huntingtown, Md., U.S. C4 97
Huntland, Tn., U.S. B5 119
Huntley, Il., U.S. A5 90
Hunt Mountain, mtn., Wy., U.S. B5 127
Huntsville, Ont., Can. B5 73
Huntsville, Al., U.S. A3 78
Huntsville, Ar., U.S. A2 81
Huntsville, Mo., U.S. B5 102
Huntsville, Tn., U.S. C9 119
Huntsville, Tx., U.S. D5 120
Huon Gulf, b., Pap. N. Gui. m16 50a
Hurao, China B13 26
Hurd, Cape, c., Ont., Can. B3 73
Hurley, Ms., U.S. E5 101
Hurley, N.M., U.S. E1 108
Hurley, N.Y., U.S. D6 109
Hurley, Wi., U.S. B3 126
Hurlock, Md., U.S. C6 97
Huron, Oh., U.S. A3 112
Huron, S.D., U.S. C7 118
Huron, co., Mi., U.S. E7 99
Huron, co., Oh., U.S. A3 112
Huron, stm., Mi., U.S. p14 99
Huron, Lake, l., N.A. C10 76
Huron Mountains, hills, Mi., U.S. B3 99
Hurricane, Ut., U.S. F2 121
Hurricane, W.V., U.S. C2 125
Hurst, Il., U.S. F4 90
Hurt, Va., U.S. C3 123
Hurtsboro, Al., U.S. C4 78
Húsavík, Ice. B4 4
Huskvarna, Swe. H10 6
Hustisford, Wi., U.S. E5 126
Husum, Ger. A9 8
Hutchins, Tx., U.S. n10 120
Hutchinson, Ks., U.S. D6 93
Hutchinson, Mn., U.S. F4 100
Hutchinson, co., S.D., U.S. D8 118
Hutchinson, co., Tx., U.S. B2 120
Hutchinson Island, i., Fl., U.S. E6 86
Hutchinson Island, i., S.C., U.S. k11 117
Hutch Mountain, mtn., Az., U.S. C4 80
Hüttental, Ger. E8 8
Huttig, Ar., U.S. D3 81
Huwei, Tai. L9 28
Huxley, Ia., U.S. C4 92
Huy, Bel. E5 8
Huzhou, China E9 28
Hvannadalshnúkur, mtn., Ice. C4 4
Hvar, Cro. F11 14
Hwange, Zimb. E5 44
Hwang Ho see Huang, stm., China D10 26
Hyannis, Ma., U.S. C7 98
Hyannis Port, Ma., U.S. C7 98
Hyattsville, Md., U.S. C4 97
Hybla Valley, Va., U.S. g12 123
Hyco, stm., Va., U.S. D3 123
Hyco Lake, res., N.C., U.S. A3 110
Hydaburg, Ak., U.S. D13 79
Hyde, Pa., U.S. D5 115
Hyde, co., N.C., U.S. B6 110
Hyde, co., S.D., U.S. C6 118
Hyde Park, Guy. D13 58
Hyde Park, N.Y., U.S. D7 109
Hyde Park, Ut., U.S. B4 121
Hyder, Ak., U.S. D13 79
Hyderābād, India D5 37
Hyderābād, Pak. H3 38
Hydeville, Vt., U.S. D2 122
Hydro, Ok., U.S. B3 113
Hyères, Fr. I13 10
Hyesan, N. Kor. C12 26
Hymera, In., U.S. F3 91
Hyndman, Pa., U.S. G4 115
Hyndman Peak, mtn., Id., U.S. F4 89
Hyrum, Ut., U.S. B4 121
Hythe, Alta., Can. B1 68
Hyūga, Japan J4 30
Hyūga-nada, Japan J4 30
Hyvinkää, Fin. F15 6

I

Iamonia, Lake, l., Fl., U.S. B2 86
Iaşi, Rom. B11 16
Iatt, Lake, res., La., U.S. C3 95
Ibadan, Nig. G6 42
Ibagué, Col. E5 58
Ibapah Peak, mtn., Ut., U.S. D2 121
Ibarra, Ec. G3 58
Ibb, Yemen F3 46
Iberia, Mo., U.S. C5 102
Iberia, co., La., U.S. E4 95
Iberville, Que., Can. D4 74
Iberville, co., La., U.S. D4 95
Iberville, Mont d' (Mount Caubvick), mtn., Can. g14 74
Ibiá, Braz. E5 57
Ibicaraí, Braz. C9 57
Ibiza, Spain G13 12
Ibiza, i., Spain G13 12
Ibo, Moz. D8 44
Ica, Peru F3 54
Içá (Putumayo), stm., S.A. I8 58
Içana, Braz. C5 54
Içana, stm., S.A. C5 54
Ice Harbor Dam, Wa., U.S. C7 124
İçel, Tur. H14 4
Iceland, ctry., Eur. B4 4
Ichalkaranji, India D3 37
Ich Bogd Uul, mts., Mong. C7 26
Ichinomiya, Japan G9 30
Ichinoseki, Japan D14 30
Icicle Creek, stm., Wa., U.S. B5 124
Icó, Braz. E11 54
Icy Cape, c., Ak., U.S. A7 79
Icy Strait, strt., Ak., U.S. k22 79
Ida, Mi., U.S. G7 99
Ida, co., Ia., U.S. B2 92
Ida, Lake, l., Mn., U.S. D3 100
Idabel, Ok., U.S. D7 113
Ida Grove, Ia., U.S. B2 92
Idaho, co., Id., U.S. D3 89
Idaho, state, U.S. E3 89
Idaho Falls, Id., U.S. F6 89
Idaho Springs, Co., U.S. B5 83
Idalou, Tx., U.S. C2 120
Idamay, W.V., U.S. k10 125
Idanha-a-Nova, Port. F4 12
Idāppādi, India G4 37
Idar-Oberstein, Ger. F7 8
Idaville, In., U.S. C4 91
Ider, Al., U.S. A4 78
Idfū, Egypt D12 42
Idlib, Syria B5 40
Ídolo, Isla del, i., Mex. G11 62
Ieper, Bel. E2 8
Ierápetra, Grc. N9 16
Iesi, Italy F8 14
Ife, Nig. G6 42
Iferouâne, Niger E7 42
Iforas, Adrar des, mts., Afr. C5 42
Iglesias, Italy J3 14
Igloolik, N.W. Ter., Can. C16 66
Ignacio, Co., U.S. D3 83
Iguaçu, Saltos do (Iguassu Falls), wtfl, S.A. B6 56
Iguala, Mex. H10 62
Igualada, Spain D13 12
Iguape, Braz. A7 56
Iguatu, Braz. E11 54
Iguéla, Gabon B1 44
Iguidi, Erg, dunes, Afr. C4 42
Ihosy, Madag. F9 44
Iida, Japan G10 30
Iisalmi, Fin. E16 6
Iizuka, Japan I3 30
IJmuiden, Neth. C4 8
IJsselmeer (Zuiderzee), Neth. C5 8
Ika, Russia F15 24
Ikela, Zaire B4 44
Ikerre, Nig. G7 42
Ila, Nig. G6 42
Ilagan, Phil. B7 32
Ilan, Tai. K10 28
Ilbenge, Russia E18 24
Île-à-la-Crosse, Lac, l., Sask., Can. B2 75
Ilebo, Zaire B4 44
Île-de-France, hist. reg., Fr. C9 10
Île-Perrot, Que., Can. q19 74
Ilhéus, Braz. C9 57
Ili, stm., Asia I13 22
Iliamna Lake, l., Ak., U.S. D8 79
Iliamna Volcano, vol., Ak., U.S. C9 79
Ilion, N.Y., U.S. B5 109
Ilio Point, c., Hi., U.S. B4 88
Ilirska Bistrica, Slo. D9 14
Il'jinskij, Russia H22 24
Ilkal, India E4 37
Illampu, Nevado, mtn., Bol. G5 54
Illapel, Chile C2 56
Illescas, Mex. F8 62
Illiers, Fr. D8 10
Illimani, Nevado, mtn., Bol. G5 54
Illinois, state, U.S. C4 90
Illinois, stm., U.S. A7 113
Illinois, stm., Il., U.S. B5 90
Illinois, stm., Or., U.S. E3 114
Illinois Peak, mtn., Id., U.S. B3 89
Illiopolis, Il., U.S. D4 90
Illizi, Alg. C7 42

Name Map Ref Page
lmo, Mo., U.S. D8 102
'men', Ozero, l., Russia C14 18
o, Peru G4 54
oilo, Phil. C7 32
omantsi, Fin. E18 6
orin, Nig. G6 42
'pyrskij, Russia F26 24
waco, Wa., U.S. C1 124
nabari, Japan H6 30
nan, Russia H20 24
nari, Japan I2 30
natra, Fin. F17 6
nboden, Ar., U.S. A4 81
nlay, Nv., U.S. C3 105
nlay City, Mi., U.S. E7 99
nmenstadt, Ger. H10 8
nmokalee, Fl., U.S. F5 86
nnaha, stm., Or., U.S. B10 114
nola, Italy E6 14
nperatriz, Braz. E9 54
nperia, Italy F3 14
nperial, Ca., U.S. F6 82
nperial, Mo., U.S. C7 102
nperial, Ne., U.S. D4 104
nperial, Pa., U.S. k13 115
nperial, co., Ca., U.S. F6 82
nperial Beach, Ca., U.S. o15 82
nperial Dam, U.S. E1 80
nperial Reservoir, res., U.S. E1 80
nperial Valley, val., Ca., U.S. F6 82
npfondo, Congo A3 44
nphāl, India H15 38
nst, Aus. H10 8
nuris, Mex. B4 62
na, Japan G10 30
nari, Fin. B16 6
nca, Spain F14 12
ncekum Burnu, c., Tur. A3 40
nch'ŏn, S. Kor. D12 26
ncline Village, Nv., U.S. D2 105
ndependence, Ia., U.S. B6 92
ndependence, Ks., U.S. E8 93
ndependence, Ky., U.S. B5 94
ndependence, La., U.S. D5 95
ndependence, Mo., U.S. B3 102
ndependence, Or., U.S. C3 114
ndependence, Va., U.S. D1 123
ndependence, Wi., U.S. D2 126
ndependence, co., Ar., U.S. B4 81
ndependence, stm., N.Y., U.S. B5 109
ndependence Mountains, mts., Nv., U.S. C5 105
ndependence National Historical Park, Pa., U.S. p21 115
ndependence Rock, mtn., Wy., U.S. D5 127
ndia, ctry., Asia E4 36
ndian, stm., Ont., Can. B7 73
ndian, stm., De., U.S. F4 85
ndian, stm., Mi., U.S. B4 99
ndian, stm., N.Y., U.S. A5 109
ndiana, Pa., U.S. E3 115
ndiana, co., Pa., U.S. E3 115
ndiana, state, U.S. E5 91
ndiana Dunes National Lakeshore, In., U.S. A3 91
ndianapolis, In., U.S. E5 91
ndian Bay, b., Fl., U.S. D4 86
ndian Cedar Swamp, sw., R.I., U.S. F2 116
ndian Creek, stm., Oh., U.S. C1 112
ndian Creek, stm., S.D., U.S. B2 118
ndian Creek, stm., Tn., U.S. B3 119
ndian Creek, stm., W.V., U.S. k9 125
ndian Creek, stm., W.V., U.S. D4 125
ndian Head, Md., U.S. C3 97
ndian Island, i., N.C., U.S. B6 110
ndian Lake, l., Mi., U.S. C4 99
ndian Lake, l., N.Y., U.S. B6 109
ndian Lake, l., Oh., U.S. B2 112
ndian Lake, l., R.I., U.S. F4 116
ndian Neck, Ct., U.S. D4 84
ndian Ocean G17 2
ndianola, Ia., U.S. C4 92
ndianola, Ms., U.S. B3 101
ndianola, Ne., U.S. D5 104
ndian Peak, mtn., Ut., U.S. E2 121
ndian Peak, mtn., Wy., U.S. B3 127
ndian Prairie Canal, Fl., U.S. E5 86
ndian River, co., Fl., U.S. E6 86
ndian River, b., Fl., U.S. D6 86
ndian River Bay, b., De., U.S. F5 85
ndian Rock, mtn., Wa., U.S. D5 124
ndian Rocks Beach, Fl., U.S. p10 86
ndian Springs, Nv., U.S. G6 105
ndian Stream, stm., N.H., U.S. f7 106
ndiantown, Fl., U.S. E6 86
ndian Trail, N.C., U.S. B2 110
ndigirka, stm., Russia C23 24
ndio, Ca., U.S. F5 82
ndispensable Reefs, rf., Sol.Is. B12 50
ndonesia, ctry., Asia F6 32
ndore, India I6 38
ndoukâl-n-Taghès, mtn., Niger E7 42
ndramayu, Indon. m14 33a
ndrāvati, stm., India C6 37
ndus, stm., Asia H2 38
negöl, Tur. I13 16
nfiernillo, Presa del, res., Mex. H9 62
-n-Gall, Niger E7 42
ngalls, In., U.S. E6 91
ngalls Park, Il., U.S. B5 90
ngersoll, Ont., Can. D4 73
ngham, Austl. C9 50
ngham, co., Mi., U.S. F6 99
ngleside, Tx., U.S. F4 120
nglewood, Ca., U.S. n12 82
ngolstadt, Ger. G11 8
ngraham, Lake, l., Fl., U.S. G5 86
ngram, Pa., U.S. k13 115
n Guezzam, Alg. E7 42
nhambane, Moz. F7 44
nhambupe, Braz. F11 54
nhaminga, Moz. E6 44
nharrime, Moz. F7 44
nírida, stm., Col. F8 58
Inkerman, N.B., Can. B5 71
Inkom, Id., U.S. G6 89
Inkster, Mi., U.S. p15 99
Inland Sea see Seto-naikai, Japan H6 30
Inle Lake, l., Burma D4 34
Inman, Ks., U.S. D6 93
Inman, S.C., U.S. A3 117
Inn (En), stm., Eur. G13 8
Innamincka, Austl. E8 50
Inner Hebrides, is., Scot., U.K. E6 7
Innisfail, Alta., Can. C4 68
Innsbruck, Aus. H11 8
Inola, Ok., U.S. A6 113
Inongo, Zaire B3 44
Inowrocław, Pol. C18 8
In Salah, Alg. C6 42
Inscription House Ruin, hist., Az., U.S. A5 80
Insein, Burma F4 34
Institute, W.V., U.S. m12 125
Interlachen, Fl., U.S. C5 86
Interlaken, Switz. F14 10
International Falls, Mn., U.S. B5 100
Inthanon, Doi, mtn., Thai. E5 34
Intiyaco, Arg. B4 56
Intracoastal Waterway, U.S. E4 95
Inukjuak, Que., Can. g11 74
Inveraray, Scot., U.K. E7 7
Invercargill, N.Z. G2 52
Inverell, Austl. E10 50
Inver Grove Heights, Mn., U.S. n12 100
Invermere, B.C., Can. D9 69
Inverness, Scot., U.K. D8 7
Inverness, Ca., U.S. C2 82
Inverness, Fl., U.S. D4 86
Inverness, Ms., U.S. B3 101
Inverurie, Scot., U.K. D10 7
Investigator Group, is., Austl. F6 50
Investigator Strait, strt., Austl. G7 50
Invisible Mountain, mtn., Id., U.S. F5 89
Inwood, Ia., U.S. A1 92
Inwood, N.Y., U.S. k13 109
Inwood, W.V., U.S. B6 125
Inyangani, mtn., Zimb. E6 44
Inyan Kara Creek, stm., Wy., U.S. B8 127
Inyan Kara Mountain, mtn., Wy., U.S. B8 127
Inyo, co., Ca., U.S. D5 82
Inyo, Mount, mtn., Ca., U.S. D5 82
Inyo Mountains, mts., Ca., U.S. D4 82
Ioánnina, Grc. J4 16
Iola, Ks., U.S. E8 93
Iola, Wi., U.S. D4 126
Iona, Id., U.S. F7 89
Ione, Ca., U.S. C3 82
Ionia, Mi., U.S. F5 99
Ionia, co., Mi., U.S. F5 99
Ionian Islands see Iónioi Nísoi, is., Grc. K4 16
Ionian Sea, Eur. H11 4
Iónioi Nísoi, is., Grc. K4 16
Iosco, co., Mi., U.S. D7 99
Iota, La., U.S. D3 95
Iowa, La., U.S. D2 95
Iowa, co., Ia., U.S. C5 92
Iowa, co., Wi., U.S. E3 126
Iowa, state, U.S. C4 92
Iowa, stm., Ia., U.S. C6 92
Iowa, West Branch, stm., Ia., U.S. B4 92
Iowa City, Ia., U.S. C6 92
Iowa Falls, Ia., U.S. B4 92
Iowa Indian Reservation, U.S. C8 93
Iowa Lake, l., U.S. A3 92
Iowa Park, Tx., U.S. C3 120
Ipameri, Braz. D4 57
Iphigenia Bay, b., Ak., U.S. n22 79
Ipiales, Col. G4 58
Ipiaú, Braz. C9 57
Ipoh, Malay. L6 34
Ipswich, Austl. E10 50
Ipswich, Eng., U.K. I14 7
Ipswich, Ma., U.S. A6 98
Ipswich, S.D., U.S. B6 118
Ipswich, stm., Ma., U.S. A5 98
Ipu, Braz. D10 54
Iqaluit, N.W. Ter., Can. D19 66
Iquique, Chile H4 54
Iquitos, Peru D4 54
Iraan, Tx., U.S. D2 120
Iráklion, Grc. N9 16
Iran, ctry., Asia B5 46
Iran Mountains, mts., Asia E5 32
Īrānshahr, Iran C7 46
Irapa, Ven. B11 58
Irapuato, Mex. G9 62
Iraq, ctry., Asia B3 46
Irazú, Volcán, vol., C.R. J6 64
Irbid, Jord. C4 40
Irbīl, Iraq A3 46
Iredell, co., N.C., U.S. B2 110
Ireland, ctry., Eur. E6 4
Iriga, Phil. r20 32
Iringa, Tan. C7 44
Irion, co., Tx., U.S. D2 120
Iriri, stm., Braz. D8 54
Irish, Mount, mtn., Nv., U.S. F6 105
Irish Sea, Eur. H8 7
Irkutsk, Russia G14 24
Irmo, S.C., U.S. C5 117
Iron, co., Mi., U.S. B2 99
Iron, co., Mo., U.S. D7 102
Iron, co., Ut., U.S. F2 121
Iron, co., Wi., U.S. B3 126
Irondale, Al., U.S. f7 78
Irondequoit, N.Y., U.S. B3 109
Iron Gate, val., Eur. E6 16
Iron Gate Reservoir, res., Eur. E5 16
Iron Gate Reservoir, res., Ca., U.S. B2 82
Iron Mountain, Mi., U.S. C2 99
Iron Mountain, mtn., Az., U.S. D4 80
Iron Mountains, mts., U.S. D1 123
Iron Ridge, Wi., U.S. E5 126
Iron River, Mi., U.S. B2 99
Iron River, Wi., U.S. B2 126
Ironton, Mo., U.S. D7 102
Ironton, Oh., U.S. D3 112
Ironwood, Mi., U.S. n11 99
Iroquois, Ont., Can. C9 73
Iroquois, co., Il., U.S. C6 90
Iroquois, stm., U.S. C6 90
Iroquois, Lake, l., Vt., U.S. B2 122
Iroquois Falls, Ont., Can. o19 73
Irrawaddy see Ayeyarwady, stm., Burma G3 34
Irricana, Alta., Can. D4 68
Irrigon, Or., U.S. B7 114
Irtyš (Ertix), stm., Asia F11 22
Irumu, Zaire A5 44
Irún, Spain B10 12
Irurzun, Spain C10 12
Irú Tepuy, mtn., Ven. E12 58
Irvine, Scot., U.K. F8 7
Irvine, Ca., U.S. n13 82
Irvine, Ky., U.S. C6 94
Irving, Tx., U.S. n10 120
Irvington, Al., U.S. E1 78
Irvington, Il., U.S. E4 90
Irvington, Ky., U.S. C3 94
Irvington, N.J., U.S. k8 107
Irvington, N.Y., U.S. g13 109
Irwin, Pa., U.S. F2 115
Irwin, co., Ga., U.S. E3 87
Irwinton, Ga., U.S. D3 87
Isabel, Mount, mtn., Wy., U.S. D2 127
Isabella, co., Mi., U.S. E6 99
Isabella, Cordillera, mts., Nic. G5 64
Isabella Indian Reservation, Mi., U.S. E6 99
Isabella Lake, l., Mn., U.S. C7 100
Ísafjördur, Ice. B3 4
Isahaya, Japan J3 30
Isanti, Mn., U.S. E5 100
Isanti, co., Mn., U.S. E5 100
Isar, stm., Eur. G11 8
Ischia, Italy I8 14
Ise, Japan H9 30
Isernia, Italy H9 14
Isesaki, Japan F12 30
Ise-wan, b., Japan H9 30
Isherton, Guy. F13 58
Ishikari-wan, b., Japan p18 30a
Ishinomaki, Japan D14 30
Ishpeming, Mi., U.S. B3 99
Isinglass, stm., N.H., U.S. D4 106
Isiolo, Kenya A7 44
Isiro, Zaire H11 42
İskele, N. Cyp. B3 40
İskenderun, Tur. H15 4
İskenderun Körfezi, b., Tur. A4 40
Iskitim, Russia G10 24
İslâhiye, Tur. A5 40
Islāmābād, Pak. D5 38
Islamorada, Fl., U.S. H6 86
Isla Mujeres, Mex. G16 62
Island, co., Wa., U.S. A3 124
Island Beach, N.J., U.S. D4 107
Island City, Or., U.S. B8 114
Island Falls, Me., U.S. B4 96
Island Lake, l., Man., Can. C4 70
Island Park, R.I., U.S. E6 116
Island Park Reservoir, res., Id., U.S. E7 89
Island Pond, Vt., U.S. B5 122
Island Pond, l., N.H., U.S. E4 106
Islands, Bay of, b., Newf., Can. D2 72
Isla Vista, Ca., U.S. E4 82
Islay, i., Scot., U.K. F6 7
Isle-aux-Morts, Newf., Can. E2 72
Isle of Man, dep., Eur. E7 4
Isle of Palms, S.C., U.S. k12 117
Isle of Wight, co., Va., U.S. D6 123
Isle of Wight Bay, b., Md., U.S. D7 97
Isle Royale National Park, Mi., U.S. h9 99
Islesboro Island, i., Me., U.S. D4 96
Isleta, N.M., U.S. C3 108
Isleta Indian Reservation, N.M., U.S. C3 108
Islington, Ma., U.S. h11 98
Isola, Ms., U.S. B3 101
Isola della Scala, Italy D5 14
Ispica, Italy M9 14
Israel (Yisra'el), ctry., Asia D4 40
Israel, stm., N.H., U.S. B3 106
Issano, Guy. E13 58
Issaquah, Wa., U.S. B3 124
Issaquena, co., Ms., U.S. C2 101
Issoire, Fr. G10 10
Issoudun, Fr. F8 10
Is-sur-Tille, Fr. E12 10
Issyk-Kul', Kyrg. I13 22
İstanbul, Tur. G13 4
İstanbul Boğazı (Bosporus), strt., Tur. H13 16
Isto, Mount, mtn., Ak., U.S. B11 79
Istokpoga, Lake, l., Fl., U.S. E5 86
Itabaiana, Braz. F11 54
Itaberaí, Braz. G9 54
Itabira, Braz. E7 57
Itabuna, Braz. C9 57
Itacoatiara, Braz. D7 54
Itaguí, Col. D5 58
Itaituba, Braz. D7 54
Itajaí, Braz. B7 56
Itajubá, Braz. G6 57
Italy, Tx., U.S. C4 120
Italy, ctry., Eur. G10 4
Itaperuna, Braz. F8 57
Itapetinga, Braz. C8 57
Itapetininga, Braz. G4 57
Itapeva, Braz. G4 57
Itapicuru, stm., Braz. D10 54
Itapira, Braz. G5 57
Itaquari, Braz. F8 57
Itararé, Braz. H4 57
Itārsi, India I7 38
Itasca, Il., U.S. k8 90
Itasca, Tx., U.S. C4 120
Itasca, co., Mn., U.S. C5 100
Itasca, Lake, l., Mn., U.S. C3 100
Itawamba, co., Ms., U.S. A5 101
Ithaca, Mi., U.S. E6 99
Ithaca, N.Y., U.S. C4 109
Itō, Japan H12 30
Itta Bena, Ms., U.S. B3 101
Ittiri, Italy I3 14
Ituberá, Braz. B9 57
Ituiutaba, Braz. E4 57
Itumbiara, Braz. E4 57
Ituni, Guy. E13 58
Ituri, stm., Zaire A5 44
Iturup, Ostrov (Etorofu-tō), i., Russia I23 24
Ituverava, Braz. F5 57
Ituxi, stm., Braz. E5 54
Itzehoe, Ger. B9 8
Iuka, Ms., U.S. A5 101
Iva, S.C., U.S. C2 117
Ivalo, Fin. B16 6
Ivanhoe, Mn., U.S. F2 100
Ivanić Grad, Cro. D11 14
Ivano-Frankovsk, Ukr. H2 22
Ivanovo, Russia D23 18
Ivigtut, Grnld. D23 66
Ivinheima, stm., Braz. G2 57
Ivins, Ut., U.S. F2 121
Ivory Coast, ctry., Afr. G4 42
Ivoryton, Ct., U.S. D6 84
Ivrea, Italy D2 14
Iwaki (Taira), Japan E13 30
Iwakuni, Japan H5 30
Iwanai, Japan q18 30a
Iwanuma, Japan D13 30
Iwo, Nig. G6 42
Ixtacihuatl, vol., Mex. H10 62
Iyo-nada, Japan I5 30
Izabal, Lago de, l., Guat. G3 64
Izard, co., Ar., U.S. A4 81
Izegem, Bel. E3 8
Iževsk, Russia F8 22
İzmir, Tur. H13 4
İzmit, Tur. G13 4
Iznalloz, Spain H8 12
İznik Gölü, l., Tur. I13 16
Izozog, Bañados de, sw., Bol. G6 54
Izúcar de Matamoros, Mex. H10 62
Izuhara, Japan H2 30
Izumo, Japan G5 30
Izu-shotō, is., Japan H12 30
Izvestij CIK, Ostrova, is., Russia B10 24

J

Jabalpur, India I8 38
Jabbūl, Sabkhat al-, l., Syria A5 40
Jablah, Syria B4 40
Jablonec nad Nisou, Czech. E15 8
Jaboatão, Braz. E11 54
Jabrīn, well, Sau. Ar. D4 46
Jaca, Spain C11 12
Jacarèzinho, Braz. G4 57
Jáchal, Arg. C3 56
Jacinto City, Tx., U.S. r14 120
Jack, co., Tx., U.S. C3 120
Jackfish Lake, l., Sask., Can. D1 75
Jackman, Me., U.S. C2 96
Jackman Station, Me., U.S. C2 96
Jack Mountain, mtn., Mt., U.S. D4 103
Jack Mountain, mtn., Wa., U.S. A5 124
Jackpot, Nv., U.S. B7 105
Jacksboro, Tn., U.S. C9 119
Jacksboro, Tx., U.S. C3 120
Jacks Mountain, mtn., Pa., U.S. E6 115
Jackson, Al., U.S. D2 78
Jackson, Ca., U.S. C3 82
Jackson, Ga., U.S. C3 87
Jackson, Ky., U.S. C6 94
Jackson, La., U.S. D4 95
Jackson, Mi., U.S. F6 99
Jackson, Mn., U.S. G4 100
Jackson, Ms., U.S. C3 101
Jackson, Mo., U.S. D8 102
Jackson, Oh., U.S. C3 112
Jackson, S.C., U.S. E4 117
Jackson, Tn., U.S. B3 119
Jackson, Wi., U.S. E5 126
Jackson, Wy., U.S. C2 127
Jackson, co., Al., U.S. A3 78
Jackson, co., Ar., U.S. B4 81
Jackson, co., Co., U.S. A4 83
Jackson, co., Fl., U.S. B1 86
Jackson, co., Ga., U.S. B3 87
Jackson, co., Il., U.S. F4 90
Jackson, co., In., U.S. G5 91
Jackson, co., Ia., U.S. B7 92
Jackson, co., Ks., U.S. C8 93
Jackson, co., Ky., U.S. C5 94
Jackson, co., La., U.S. B3 95
Jackson, co., Mi., U.S. F6 99
Jackson, co., Mn., U.S. G3 100
Jackson, co., Ms., U.S. E5 101
Jackson, co., Mo., U.S. B3 102
Jackson, co., N.C., U.S. f9 110
Jackson, co., Oh., U.S. C3 112
Jackson, co., Ok., U.S. C2 113
Jackson, co., Or., U.S. E4 114
Jackson, co., S.D., U.S. D4 118
Jackson, co., Tn., U.S. C8 119
Jackson, co., Tx., U.S. E4 120
Jackson, co., W.V., U.S. C3 125
Jackson, co., Wi., U.S. D3 126
Jackson, stm., Va., U.S. C3 123
Jackson, Lake, l., Fl., U.S. E5 86
Jackson, Lake, l., Fl., U.S. B2 86
Jackson, Mount, mtn., N.H., U.S. B4 106
Jackson Center, Oh., U.S. B1 112
Jackson Lake, res., Wy., U.S. C2 127
Jackson Mountains, mts., Nv., U.S. B3 105
Jackson's Arm, Newf., Can. D3 72
Jacksons Gap, Al., U.S. C4 78
Jacksonville, Al., U.S. B4 78
Jacksonville, Ar., U.S. C3 81
Jacksonville, Fl., U.S. B5 86
Jacksonville, Il., U.S. D3 90
Jacksonville, N.C., U.S. C5 110
Jacksonville, Or., U.S. E4 114
Jacksonville, Tx., U.S. D5 120
Jacksonville Beach, Fl., U.S. B5 86
Jacksonville Naval Air Station, mil., Fl., U.S. B5 86
Jacks Peak, mtn., Ut., U.S. E3 121
Jacmel, Haiti E11 64
Jacobābād, Pak. F3 38
Jacques-Cartier, stm., Que., Can. B6 74
Jacques-Cartier, Détroit de, strt., Que., Can. h8 72
Jacquet River, N.B., Can. B4 71
Jadraque, Spain E9 12
Jaén, Peru E3 54
Jaén, Spain H8 12
Jaffna, Sri L. H6 37
Jaffrey, N.H., U.S. E2 106
Jafr, Qā' al-, depr., Jord. D5 40
Jagādhri, India E7 38
Jagdalpur, India C7 37
Jagersfontein, S. Afr. G5 44
Jagodnoje, Russia E23 24
Jagtiāl, India C5 37
Jaguarão, Braz. C6 56
Jahrom, Iran C5 46
Jaidak, Afg. E2 38
Jaipur, India G6 38
Jajce, Bos. E12 14
Jakarta, Indon. m13 32
Jakobshavn, Grnld. C22 66
Jakobstad (Pietarsaari), Fin. E14 6
Jakutsk, Russia E19 24
Jal, N.M., U.S. E6 108
Jalālābād, Afg. C4 38
Jalapa, Guat. G3 64
Jalapa Enríquez, Mex. H11 62
Jālgaon, India B3 37
Jālna, India C3 37
Jalostotitlán, Mex. G8 62
Jalpaiguri, India G13 38
Jalta, Ukr. I4 22
Jaltepec, stm., Mex. I12 62
Jamaica, ctry., N.A. E9 64
Jamaica Bay, b., N.Y., U.S. k13 109
Jamaica Channel, strt., N.A. E10 64
Jamālpur, Bngl. H13 38
Jamālpur, India H12 38
Jamame, Som. A8 44
Jambi, Indon. F3 32
Jambol, Bul. G10 16
James, stm., U.S. C7 76
James, stm., Mo., U.S. E4 102
James, stm., Va., U.S. C5 123
James, Lake, l., In., U.S. A7 91
James, Lake, res., N.C., U.S. B1 110
James Bay, b., Can. F16 66
James Branch, stm., De., U.S. F3 85
Jamesburg, N.J., U.S. C4 107
James City, N.C., U.S. B5 110
James City, co., Va., U.S. C6 123
James Island, S.C., U.S. k12 117
James Island, i., Md., U.S. C5 97
James Island, i., S.C., U.S. F8 117
James River Bridge, Va., U.S. k15 123
Jamestown, In., U.S. E4 91
Jamestown, Ky., U.S. D4 94
Jamestown, N.Y., U.S. C1 109
Jamestown, N.C., U.S. B3 110
Jamestown, N.D., U.S. C7 111
Jamestown, Oh., U.S. C2 112
Jamestown, R.I., U.S. F5 116
Jamestown, Tn., U.S. C9 119
James Town, Wy., U.S. E3 127
Jamestown Dam, N.D., U.S. C7 111
Jamestown Reservoir, res., N.D., U.S. C7 111
Jamiltepec, Mex. I11 62
Jamkhandi, India D3 37
Jammu, India D6 38
Jammu and Kashmir, dep., Asia C6 38
Jāmnagar, India I4 38
Jāmpur, Pak. F4 38
Jämsä, Fin. F15 6
Jamshedpur, India I12 38
Jamsk, Russia F24 24
Jamūi, India H12 38
Jamuna, stm., Bngl. H13 38
Jana, stm., Russia C21 24
Janaucu, Ilha, i., Braz. C8 54
Janesville, Ca., U.S. B3 82
Janesville, Ia., U.S. B5 92
Janesville, Mn., U.S. F5 100
Janesville, Wi., U.S. F4 126
Jangipur, India H13 38
Janīn, Jord. C4 40
Janskij, Russia D20 24
Janskij Zaliv, b., Russia C21 24
Januária, Braz. C6 57
Jaora, India I6 38
Japan, ctry., Asia D14 26
Japan, Sea of, Asia D13 26
Japurá (Caquetá), stm., S.A. D5 54
Jaqué, Pan. K8 64
Jarābulus, Syria A6 40
Jaraiz de la Vera, Spain E6 12
Jarash, Jord. C4 40
Jarcevo, Russia F15 18
Jardines de la Reina, is., Cuba D8 64
Jari, stm., Braz. D8 54
Jaridih, India I12 38
Jaroslavl', Russia D22 18
Jarosław, Pol. E22 8
Jarrettsville, Md., U.S. A5 97
Järvenpää, Fin. F15 6
Järvsö, Swe. F11 6
Jask, Iran C6 46
Jasmine Estates, Fl., U.S. D4 86
Jasnyj, Russia G19 24
Jasonville, In., U.S. F3 91
Jasper, Al., U.S. B2 78
Jasper, Fl., U.S. B4 86
Jasper, Ga., U.S. B2 87
Jasper, In., U.S. H4 91
Jasper, Mo., U.S. D3 102
Jasper, Tn., U.S. D8 119
Jasper, Tx., U.S. D6 120
Jasper, co., Ga., U.S. C3 87
Jasper, co., Il., U.S. D5 90
Jasper, co., In., U.S. B3 91
Jasper, co., Ia., U.S. C4 92
Jasper, co., Ms., U.S. C4 101
Jasper, co., Mo., U.S. D3 102
Jasper, co., S.C., U.S. G5 117

Name — Map Ref — Page

Jasper, co., Tx., U.S. D5 120
Jasper National Park, Alta., Can. C1 68
Jataí, Braz. D3 57
Játiva, Spain G11 12
Jatni, India J11 38
Jaú, Braz. G4 57
Jauaperi, stm., Braz. C6 54
Jauja, Peru F3 54
Jaunpur, India H10 38
Java see Jawa, i., Indon. G4 32
Javari (Yavarí), stm., S.A. D4 54
Java Sea see Jawa, Laut, Indon. G4 32
Jävre, Swe. D13 6
Jawa, i., Indon. G4 32
Jawa, Laut (Java Sea), Indon. G4 32
Jaworzno, Pol. E19 8
Jay, Ok., U.S. A7 113
Jay, co., In., U.S. D7 91
Jaya, Puncak, mtn., Indon. F10 32
Jayapura, Indon. F11 32
Jayb, Wādī al-, val., Asia D4 40
J. B. Thomas, Lake, res., Tx., U.S. C2 120
Jean, Nv., U.S. H6 105
Jeanerette, La., U.S. E4 95
Jean Lafitte National Historical Park, La., U.S. k12 95
Jeannette, Pa., U.S. F2 115
Jebba, Nig. G6 42
Jeddore Lake, res., Newf., Can. D3 72
Jeff Davis, co., Ga., U.S. E4 87
Jeff Davis, co., Tx., U.S. o12 120
Jefferson, Ga., U.S. B3 87
Jefferson, Ia., U.S. B3 92
Jefferson, La., U.S. k11 95
Jefferson, N.C., U.S. A1 110
Jefferson, Oh., U.S. A5 112
Jefferson, Or., U.S. C3 114
Jefferson, S.C., U.S. B7 117
Jefferson, Tx., U.S. C5 120
Jefferson, Wi., U.S. E5 126
Jefferson, co., Al., U.S. B3 78
Jefferson, co., Ar., U.S. C3 81
Jefferson, co., Co., U.S. B5 83
Jefferson, co., Fl., U.S. B3 86
Jefferson, co., Ga., U.S. C4 87
Jefferson, co., Id., U.S. F6 89
Jefferson, co., Il., U.S. E5 90
Jefferson, co., In., U.S. G6 91
Jefferson, co., Ia., U.S. C5 92
Jefferson, co., Ks., U.S. C8 93
Jefferson, co., Ky., U.S. B4 94
Jefferson, co., La., U.S. E5 95
Jefferson, co., Ms., U.S. D2 101
Jefferson, co., Mo., U.S. C7 102
Jefferson, co., Mt., U.S. D4 103
Jefferson, co., Ne., U.S. D8 104
Jefferson, co., N.Y., U.S. A5 109
Jefferson, co., Oh., U.S. B5 112
Jefferson, co., Ok., U.S. C4 113
Jefferson, co., Or., U.S. C5 114
Jefferson, co., Pa., U.S. D3 115
Jefferson, co., Tn., U.S. C10 119
Jefferson, co., Tx., U.S. E5 120
Jefferson, co., Wa., U.S. B1 124
Jefferson, co., W.V., U.S. B7 125
Jefferson, co., Wi., U.S. E5 126
Jefferson, stm., Mt., U.S. E5 103
Jefferson, Mount, mtn., Id., U.S. E7 89
Jefferson, Mount, mtn., Nv., U.S. E5 105
Jefferson, Mount, mtn., Or., U.S. C5 114
Jefferson City, Mo., U.S. C5 102
Jefferson City, Tn., U.S. C10 119
Jefferson Davis, co., La., U.S. D3 95
Jefferson Davis, co., Ms., U.S. D4 101
Jefferson Farms, De., U.S. i7 85
Jefferson Proving Ground, mil., In., U.S. G7 91
Jeffersontown, Ky., U.S. B4 94
Jeffersonville, Ga., U.S. D3 87
Jeffersonville, In., U.S. H6 91
Jeffersonville, Ky., U.S. C6 94
Jeffersonville, Oh., U.S. C2 112
Jeffrey, W.V., U.S. D3 125
Jeffrey City, Wy., U.S. D5 127
Jeffries Creek, stm., S.C., U.S. C8 117
Jefremov, Russia H21 18
Jegorjevsk, Russia F22 18
Jehossee Island, i., S.C., U.S. k11 117
Jejsk, Russia H5 22
Jekaterinburg, Russia F10 22
Jekyll Island, i., Ga., U.S. E5 87
Jelec, Russia I21 18
Jelenia Góra (Hirschberg), Pol. E15 8
Jelgava, Lat. E6 18
Jellico, Tn., U.S. C9 119
Jelm Mountain, mtn., Wy., U.S. E7 127
Jeloguj, stm., Russia E11 24
Jember, Indon. n16 32
Jemez, stm., N.M., U.S. k7 108
Jemez Canyon Dam, N.M., U.S. k7 108
Jemez Indian Reservation, N.M., U.S. h7 108
Jemez Pueblo, N.M., U.S. B3 108
Jemison, Al., U.S. C3 78
Jena, Ger. E11 8
Jena, La., U.S. C3 95
Jenašimskij Polkan, Gora, mtn., Russia F12 24
Jendouba (Souk el Arba), Tun. M3 14
Jenisej, stm., Russia D11 24
Jenisejsk, Russia F12 24
Jenisejskij Zaliv, b., Russia C10 24
Jenkins, Ky., U.S. C7 94
Jenkins, co., Ga., U.S. D5 87
Jenkintown, Pa., U.S. o21 115
Jenks, Ok., U.S. A6 113
Jennings, La., U.S. D3 95
Jennings, Mo., U.S. f13 102
Jennings, co., In., U.S. G6 91
Jensen Beach, Fl., U.S. E6 86
Jepara, Indon. m15 33a
Jequié, Braz. B8 57
Jequitinhonha, stm., Braz. D9 57
Jerada, Mor. B5 42
Jerauld, co., S.D., U.S. C7 118
Jérémie, Haiti E10 64
Jeremoabo, Braz. F11 54
Jerevan, Arm. I6 22
Jerez de García Salinas, Mex. F8 62
Jerez de la Frontera, Spain I5 12
Jerez de los Caballeros, Spain G5 12
Jericho, Vt., U.S. B3 122
Jericho see Arīḥā, Jord. D4 40
Jerimoth Hill, hill, R.I., U.S. C1 116
Jermyn, Pa., U.S. C10 115
Jerofej Pavlovič, Russia G18 24
Jerome, Id., U.S. G4 89
Jerome, Pa., U.S. F4 115
Jerome, co., Id., U.S. G4 89
Jeropol, Russia D27 24
Jersey, co., Il., U.S. D3 90
Jersey, dep., Eur. C4 10
Jersey City, N.J., U.S. B4 107
Jersey Mountain, mtn., Id., U.S. E3 89
Jersey Shore, Pa., U.S. D7 115
Jerseyville, Il., U.S. D3 90
Jerusalem see Yerushalayim, Isr. D4 40
Jervis Inlet, b., B.C., Can. D6 69
Jesenice, Slo. C9 14
Jessamine, co., Ky., U.S. C5 94
Jessore, Bngl. I13 38
Jessup, Md., U.S. B4 97
Jessup, Pa., U.S. m18 115
Jesup, Ga., U.S. E5 87
Jesup, Ia., U.S. B5 92
Jesup, Lake, l., Fl., U.S. D5 86
Jésus, Île, i., Que., Can. p19 74
Jesús Carranza, Mex. I12 62
Jetmore, Ks., U.S. D4 93
Jeumont, Fr. B11 10
Jever, Ger. B7 8
Jevpatorija, Ukr. H4 22
Jewel Cave National Monument, S.D., U.S. D2 118
Jewell, Ia., U.S. B4 92
Jewell, co., Ks., U.S. C5 93
Jewett City, Ct., U.S. C8 84
Jeypore, India C7 37
Jhang Maghiāna, Pak. E5 38
Jhānsi, India H8 38
Jharia, India I12 38
Jhelum, Pak. D5 38
Jhelum, stm., Asia E5 38
Jiading, China D10 28
Jiaganj, India H13 38
Jiamusi, China B13 26
Jian, China H3 28
Jianchuan, China A5 34
Jiangmen, China M2 28
Jiangsu, prov., China E10 26
Jiangxi, prov., China F10 26
Jiangyin, China D9 28
Jiangzi, China F13 38
Jianou, China H7 28
Jianshui, China C7 34
Jiaoxian, China D10 26
Jiaozuo, China D9 26
Jiashan, China C6 28
Jiawang, China A6 28
Jiaxian, China A2 28
Jiaxing, China E9 28
Jiazi, China M5 28
Jicarilla Apache Indian Reservation, N.M., U.S. A2 108
Jiddah, Sau. Ar. D2 46
Jieshou, China B4 28
Jieyang, China L5 28
Jihlava, Czech. F15 8
Jijiga, Eth. G3 46
Jijona, Spain G11 12
Jilemutu, China A11 26
Jilin, China C12 26
Jilin, prov., China C12 26
Jill, Kediet ej, mtn., Maur. D3 42
Jima, Eth. G2 46
Jimena de la Frontera, Spain I6 12
Jim Hogg, co., Tx., U.S. F3 120
Jim Lake, res., N.D., U.S. B7 111
Jim Thorpe, Pa., U.S. E10 115
Jim Wells, co., Tx., U.S. F3 120
Jinan (Tsinan), China D10 26
Jīnd, India F7 38
Jingdezhen (Kingtechen), China F6 28
Jingjiang, China C9 28
Jingxi, China C9 34
Jinhua, China F8 28
Jining, China C9 26
Jining, China D10 26
Jinja, Ug. A6 44
Jinning (Jiukunyang), China B7 34
Jinotega, Nic. H4 64
Jinshi, China F9 26
Jinxian, China D11 26
Jinzhou, China C11 26
Jiparaná, stm., Braz. E6 54
Jipijapa, Ec. H2 58
Jirjā, Egypt C12 42
Jisr ash-Shughūr, Syria B5 40
Jiujiang, China F4 28
Jiuling Shan, mts., China G3 28
Jiumangya, China B14 38
Jiuquan, China D6 26
Jixi, China B13 26
Joaçaba, Braz. B6 56
Joanna, S.C., U.S. C4 117
João Pessoa, Braz. E12 54
Joaquín V. González, Arg. B4 56
Job Peak, mtn., Nv., U.S. D3 105
Jobson (Vera), Arg. B4 56
Jocassee, Lake, res., U.S. B1 117
Jódar, Spain H8 12
Jo Daviess, co., Il., U.S. A3 90
Jodhpur, India G5 38
Joe Batt's Arm [-Barr'd Islands-Shoal Bay], Newf., Can. D4 72
Joensuu, Fin. E17 6
Joes Brook, stm., Vt., U.S. C4 122
Joes Creek, stm., W.V., U.S. m12 125
Joffre, Mount, mtn., Can. D3 68
Jogjakarta see Yogyakarta, Indon. G5 32
Johannesburg, S. Afr. G5 44
Johar, Som. H4 46
John, Cape, c., N.S., Can. D6 71
John Day, Or., U.S. C8 114
John Day, stm., Or., U.S. B6 114
John Day Dam, U.S. D5 124
John Day Fossil Beds National Monument, Or., U.S. C6 114
John F. Kennedy Space Center, sci., Fl., U.S. D6 86
John H. Kerr Dam, Va., U.S. D4 123
John H. Kerr Reservoir, res., U.S. D4 123
John Martin Reservoir, res., Co., U.S. C7 83
John Muir National Historical Site, hist., Ca., U.S. h8 82
John o' Groats, Scot., U.K. C9 7
John Redmond Reservoir, res., Ks., U.S. D8 93
John Sevier, Tn., U.S. m14 119
Johns Island, i., S.C., U.S. F7 117
Johnson, Ks., U.S. E2 93
Johnson, Vt., U.S. B3 122
Johnson, co., Ar., U.S. B2 81
Johnson, co., Ga., U.S. D4 87
Johnson, co., Il., U.S. F5 90
Johnson, co., In., U.S. F5 91
Johnson, co., Ia., U.S. C6 92
Johnson, co., Ks., U.S. D9 93
Johnson, co., Ky., U.S. C7 94
Johnson, co., Mo., U.S. C4 102
Johnson, co., Ne., U.S. D9 104
Johnson, co., Tn., U.S. C12 119
Johnson, co., Tx., U.S. C4 120
Johnson, co., Wy., U.S. B6 127
Johnsonburg, Pa., U.S. D4 115
Johnson City, N.Y., U.S. C5 109
Johnson City, Tn., U.S. C11 119
Johnson City, Tx., U.S. D3 120
Johnson Creek, Wi., U.S. E5 126
Johnsonville, S.C., U.S. D9 117
Johns Pass, strt., Fl., U.S. p10 86
Johnston, Ia., U.S. e8 92
Johnston, R.I., U.S. C4 116
Johnston, S.C., U.S. D4 117
Johnston, co., N.C., U.S. B4 110
Johnston, co., Ok., U.S. C5 113
Johnston City, Il., U.S. F5 90
Johnston Key, i., Fl., U.S. H5 86
Johnstown, Co., U.S. A6 83
Johnstown, N.Y., U.S. B6 109
Johnstown, Oh., U.S. B3 112
Johnstown, Pa., U.S. F4 115
John W. Flannagan Reservoir, res., Va., U.S. e9 123
Johor Baharu, Malay. N7 34
Joigny, Fr. E10 10
Joiner, Ar., U.S. B5 81
Joinvile, Braz. B7 56
Joinville, Fr. D12 10
Jokkmokk, Swe. C12 6
Joliet, Il., U.S. B5 90
Joliette, Que., Can. C4 74
Jolo Island, i., Phil. D7 32
Jombang, Indon. m16 33a
Jones, Ok., U.S. B4 113
Jones, co., Ga., U.S. C3 87
Jones, co., Ia., U.S. B6 92
Jones, co., Ms., U.S. D4 101
Jones, co., N.C., U.S. B5 110
Jones, co., S.D., U.S. D5 118
Jones, co., Tx., U.S. C3 120
Jonesboro, Ar., U.S. B5 81
Jonesboro, Ga., U.S. C2 87
Jonesboro, Il., U.S. F4 90
Jonesboro, In., U.S. D6 91
Jonesboro, La., U.S. B3 95
Jonesborough, Tn., U.S. C11 119
Jonesburg, Mo., U.S. C6 102
Jones Creek, Tx., U.S. s14 120
Jones Mill, Ar., U.S. C3 81
Jonesport, Me., U.S. D5 96
Jones Sound, strt., N.W. Ter., Can. A15 66
Jonestown, Ms., U.S. A3 101
Jonesville, La., U.S. C4 95
Jonesville, Mi., U.S. G6 99
Jonesville, N.C., U.S. A2 110
Jonesville, S.C., U.S. B4 117
Jonesville, Va., U.S. f8 123
Jongkha, China F11 38
Jönköping, Swe. H10 6
Jonquière, Que., Can. A6 74
Jonzac, Fr. G6 10
Joplin, Mo., U.S. D3 102
Joppatowne, Md., U.S. B5 97
Jordan, Mn., U.S. F5 100
Jordan, ctry., Asia D5 40
Jordan, stm., Asia C4 40
Jordan, stm., Ut., U.S. C4 121
Jordan Creek, stm., U.S. E9 114
Jordan Lake, res., Al., U.S. C3 78
Jorhāt, India G16 38
Jörn, Swe. D13 6
Jornado del Muerto, des., N.M., U.S. D3 108
Jos, Nig. G7 42
José Battle y Ordóñez, Ur. C5 56
Joseph, Or., U.S. B9 114
Joseph, Lac, l., Newf., Can. h8 72
Joseph Bonaparte Gulf, b., Austl. B5 50
Joseph City, Az., U.S. C5 80
Josephine, co., Or., U.S. E3 114
Joshua, Tx., U.S. n9 120
Joshua Tree, Ca., U.S. E5 82
Joshua Tree National Monument, Ca., U.S. F6 82
Joškar-Ola, Russia F7 22
Jourdanton, Tx., U.S. E3 120
Joutsijärvi, Fin. C16 6
Jovellanos, Cuba C7 64
J. Percy Priest Lake, res., Tn., U.S. A5 119
Juab, co., Ut., U.S. D2 121
Juan Aldama, Mex. E8 62
Juan de Fuca, Strait of, strt., N.A. G8 66
Juan de Nova, Île, i., Reu. E8 44
Juárez, Arg. D5 56
Juàzeiro, Braz. E10 54
Juàzeiro do Norte, Braz. E11 54
Jūbā, Sudan H12 42
Juba (Genale), stm., Afr. H3 46
Juchitán [de Zaragoza], Mex. I12 62
Judenburg, Aus. H14 8
Judith, stm., Mt., U.S. C7 103
Judith, Point, c., R.I., U.S. G4 85
Judith Basin, co., Mt., U.S. C6 103
Judith Island, i., N.C., U.S. B6 110
Judith Mountains, mts., Mt., U.S. C7 103
Judith Peak, mtn., Mt., U.S. C7 103
Judoma, stm., Russia F21 24
Judsonia, Ar., U.S. B4 81
Juigalpa, Nic. H5 64
Juiz de Fora, Braz. F7 57
Jukagirskoje Ploskogorje, plat., Russia D24 24
Jukte, Russia E15 24
Julesburg, Co., U.S. A8 83
Juliaca, Peru G4 54
Julian, Ca., U.S. F5 82
Julian, W.V., U.S. C3 125
Julian Alps, mts., Eur. C8 14
Juliana Top, mtn., Sur. C7 54
Julianehåb, Grnld. D23 66
Jülich, Ger. E6 8
Jullundur, India E6 38
Jumbo Peak, mtn., Nv., U.S. G7 105
Jumentos Cays, is., Bah. C10 64
Jumet, Bel. E4 8
Jumilla, Spain G10 12
Jump, stm., Wi., U.S. C3 126
Junāgadh, India J4 38
Junction, Tx., U.S. D3 120
Junction City, Ar., U.S. D3 81
Junction City, Ks., U.S. C7 93
Junction City, Ky., U.S. C5 94
Junction City, La., U.S. A3 95
Junction City, Or., U.S. C3 114
Jundiaí, Braz. G5 57
Juneau, Ak., U.S. D13 79
Juneau, Wi., U.S. E5 126
Juneau, co., Wi., U.S. E3 126
June in Winter, Lake, l., Fl., U.S. E5 86
Jungfrau, mtn., Switz. F14 10
Junggar Pendi, China B4 26
Juniata, Ne., U.S. D7 104
Juniata, co., Pa., U.S. F7 115
Juniata, stm., Pa., U.S. F7 115
Junín, Arg. C4 56
Junín, Lago de, l., Peru F3 54
Junín de los Andes, Arg. D2 56
Junior Lake, l., Me., U.S. C4 96
Juniper Mountains, mts., Az., U.S. B2 80
Junipero Serra Peak, mtn., Ca., U.S. D3 82
Junsele, Swe. E11 6
Jupiter, Fl., U.S. F6 86
Jupiter Inlet, b., Fl., U.S. F6 86
Jupiter Island, i., Fl., U.S. E6 86
Jura, mts., Eur. F13 10
Jura, i., Scot., U.K. F7 7
Jurga, Russia F10 24
Jūrmala, Lat. E6 18
Juruá, stm., S.A. D5 54
Juruena, stm., Braz. E7 54
Justin, Tx., U.S. C4 120
Justo Daract, Arg. C3 56
Jutaí, stm., Braz. D5 54
Jüterbog, Ger. D13 8
Jutiapa, Guat. G3 64
Juticalpa, Hond. G4 64
Jutland see Jylland, pen., Den. H7 6
Juventud, Isla de la (Isle of Pines), i., Cuba D6 64
Juwara, Oman E6 46
Juža, Russia E25 18
Južno-Sachalinsk, Russia H22 24
Južnyj, Mys, c., Russia F25 24
Južnyj Bug, stm., Ukr. H3 22
Jwayyā, Leb. C4 40
Jylland, pen., Den. H7 6
Jyväskylä, Fin. E15 6

K

K2 (Qogir Feng), mtn., Asia C7 38
Kaaawa, Hi., U.S. f10 88
Kaala, mtn., Hi., U.S. f9 88
Kaala Djerda, Tun. N3 14
Kaalualu Bay, b., Hi., U.S. E6 88
Kaaumakua, Puu, mtn., Hi., U.S. f10 88
Kabale, Ug. B5 44
Kabalo, Zaire C5 44
Kabambare, Zaire B5 44
Kåbdalis, Swe. C12 6
Kabetogama Lake, l., Mn., U.S. B5 100
Kabīr Kūh, mts., Iran B4 46
Kābol, Afg. C3 38
Kabompo, stm., Zam. D4 44
Kabongo, Zaire C5 44
Kābul, stm., Asia C4 38
Kabwe (Broken Hill), Zam. D5 44
Kachess Lake, res., Wa., U.S. B4 124
K'achta, Russia G15 24
Kačug, Russia G15 24
Kadan Kyun, i., Burma H5 34
Kadiri, India E5 37
Kadoka, S.D., U.S. D4 118
Kaduna, Nig. F7 42
Kāduqlī, Sudan F11 42
Kadykčan, Russia E23 24
Kaédi, Maur. E3 42
Kaena Point, c., Hi., U.S. B3 88
Kaesŏng, N. Kor. D12 26
Kafia Kingi, Sudan G10 42
Kafue, stm., Zam. D5 44
Kaga, Japan F9 30
Kagamigahara, Japan G9 30
Kagaznagar, India C5 37
Kagoshima, Japan K3 30
Kahaluu, Hi., U.S. D6 88
Kahaluu, Hi., U.S. g10 88
Kahana Bay, b., Hi., U.S. f10 88
Kahemba, Zaire C3 44
Kahoka, Mo., U.S. A6 102
Kahoolawe, i., Hi., U.S. C5 88
Kahramanmaraş, Tur. H15 4
Kahuku, Hi., U.S. B4 88
Kahuku Point, c., Hi., U.S. B4 88
Kahului, Hi., U.S. C5 88
Kahului Bay, b., Hi., U.S. C5 88
Kai, Kepulauan, is., Indon. G9 32
Kaibab Indian Reservation, Az., U.S. A3 80
Kaieteur Fall, wtfl, Guy. E13 58
Kaifeng, China E9 26
Kaikoura, N.Z. E4 52
Kaili, China A10 34
Kailua, Hi., U.S. B4 88
Kailua Bay, b., Hi., U.S. g11 88
Kailua Kona, Hi., U.S. D6 88
Kaimana, Indon. F9 32
Kaimanawa Mountains, mts., N.Z. C5 52
Kainan, Japan H8 30
Kaiserslautern, Ger. F7 8
Kaitangata, N.Z. G2 52
Kaiwi Channel, strt., Hi., U.S. B4 88
Kajaani, Fin. D16 6
Kajakī, Band-e, res., Afg. D1 38
Kajan, stm., Indon. E6 32
Kajang, Malay. M6 34
Kakamas, S. Afr. G4 44
Kaka Point, c., Hi., U.S. C5 88
Kake, Ak., U.S. D13 79
Kakegawa, Japan H11 30
Kakie, Bots. F4 44
Kākināda, India D7 37
Kakogawa, Japan H7 30
Kaladan, stm., Asia D2 34
Ka Lae, c., Hi., U.S. E6 88
Kalahari Desert, des., Afr. F4 44
Kālahasti, India F5 37
Kalaheo, Hi., U.S. B2 88
Kalajoki, Fin. D14 6
Kalakan, Russia F17 24
Kalām, Pak. C5 38
Kalama, Wa., U.S. C3 124
Kalámai, Grc. L6 16
Kalamazoo, Mi., U.S. F5 99
Kalamazoo, co., Mi., U.S. F5 99
Kalamazoo, stm., Mi., U.S. F5 99
Kalasin, Thai. F7 34
Kalāt, Pak. F2 38
Kalaupapa Peninsula, pen., Hi., U.S. B5 88
Kalawao, co., Hi., U.S. B5 88
Kalb, Ra's al-, c., Yemen F4 46
Kale, Tur. L12 16
Kaleden, B.C., Can. E8 69
Kalemie (Albertville), Zaire C5 44
Kalena, Puu, mtn., Hi., U.S. g9 88
Kalgin Island, i., Ak., U.S. g16 79
Kalgoorlie, Austl. F4 50
Kalima, Zaire B5 44
Kálimnos, Grc. M10 16
Kaliningrad (Königsberg), Russia G3 18
Kalinkoviči, Bela. I12 18
Kalispel Indian Reservation, Wa., U.S. A8 124
Kalispell, Mt., U.S. B2 103
Kalisz, Pol. D18 8
Kalkaska, Mi., U.S. D5 99
Kalkaska, co., Mi., U.S. D5 99
Kalmar, Swe. H11 6
Kalohi Channel, strt., Hi., U.S. C4 88
Kālol, India I5 38
Kaloli Point, c., Hi., U.S. D7 88
Kalona, Ia., U.S. C6 92
Kalone Peak, mtn., B.C., Can. C4 69
Kaluga, Russia G19 18
Kalutara, Sri L. I5 37
Kamaishi, Japan C14 30
Kamakou, mtn., Hi., U.S. B5 88
Kamakura, Japan G12 30
Kamālia, Pak. E5 38
Kamarān, i., Yemen E3 46
Kamas, Ut., U.S. C4 121
Kamba, China F13 38
Kambam, India H4 37
Kambar, Pak. G2 38
Kamčatka, stm., Russia F25 24
Kamčatka, Poluostrov, pen., Russia F25 24
Kamčatskij Zaliv, b., Russia F26 24
Kamen', Gora, mtn., Russia D12 24
Kamen'-na-Obi, Russia G10 24
Kamenz, Ger. D14 8
Kamiah, Id., U.S. C2 89
Kamiak Butte, mtn., Wa., U.S. C8 124
Kamienna Góra, Pol. E16 8
Kamilukuak Lake, l., N.W. Ter., Can. D12 66
Kamina, Zaire C5 44
Kaminak Lake, l., N.W. Ter., Can. D13 66
Kaminuriak Lake, l., N.W. Ter., Can. D13 66
Kamitsushima, Japan H2 30
Kamloops, B.C., Can. D7 69
Kamo, Japan E12 30
Kāmoke, Pak. E6 38
Kampala, Ug. A6 44
Kampar, Malay. L6 34
Kampen, Neth. C5 8
Kampeska, Lake, l., S.D., U.S. C8 118
Kâmpóng Cham, Camb. H8 34
Kâmpóng Chhnăng, Camb. H8 34
Kâmpóng Saôm, Camb. I7 34
Kâmpóng Saôm, Chhâk, b., Camb. I7 34
Kâmpóng Thum, Camb. H8 34
Kâmpôt, Camb. I8 34
Kāmthi, India B5 37
Kamuela (Waimea), Hi., U.S. C6 88
Kamui-misaki, c., Japan p18 30a
Kan, stm., Asia H9 34

Name Map Ref Page
nab, Ut., U.S. F3 121
nab Creek, stm., U.S. A3 80
nabec, co., Mn., U.S. E5 100
naga Island, i., Ak., U.S. E4 79
nairiktok, stm., Newf., Can. g9 72
nanga (Luluabourg), Zaire C4 44
napou Bay, b., Hi., U.S. C5 88
nata, Ont., Can. B9 73
nawha, Ia., U.S. B4 92
nawha, co., W.V., U.S. C3 125
nawha, stm., W.V., U.S. C3 125
nazawa, Japan F9 30
nchanaburi, Thai. G5 34
nchenjunga, mtn., Asia G13 38
nchipuram, India F5 37
ndhkot, Pak. F3 38
ndi, India I13 38
ndiyohi, co., Mn., U.S. E3 100
ndy, Sri L. I6 37
ne, Pa., U.S. C4 115
ne, co., Il., U.S. B5 90
ne, co., Ut., U.S. F3 121
neohe, Hi., U.S. B4 88
neohe Bay, b., Hi., U.S. g10 88
neohe Bay Marine Corps Air Station, mil., Hi., U.S. g10 88
ngar, Malay. K6 34
ngaroo Island, i., Austl. G7 50
ngean, Kepulauan, is., Indon. G6 32
ngnŭng, S. Kor. D12 26
ngo, Gabon A2 44
ngto, mtn., Asia G15 38
niama, Zaire C4 44
nkakee, Il., U.S. B6 90
nkakee, co., Il., U.S. B6 90
nkakee, stm., U.S. B5 90
nkan, Gui. F4 42
nmaw Kyun, i., Burma I5 34
nnapolis, N.C., U.S. B2 110
nnauj, India G8 38
nnonkoski, Fin. E15 6
nnus, Fin. E14 6
no, Nig. F7 42
nonji, Japan H6 30
nopolis, Ks., U.S. D5 93
nopolis Lake, res., Ks., U.S. D5 93
noya, Japan K3 30
npur, India G9 38
nsas, Il., U.S. D6 90
nsas, state, U.S. D5 93
nsas, stm., Ks., U.S. C7 93
nsas City, Ks., U.S. C9 93
nsas City, Mo., U.S. B3 102
nsk, Russia F13 24
ntō-sammyaku, mts., Japan F11 30
numa, Japan F12 30
nye, Bots. F5 44
ohsiung, Tai. M9 28
ohsiunghsien, Tai. M9 28
okoveld, plat., Nmb. E2 44
olack, Sen. F2 42
paa, Hi., U.S. A2 88
paau, Hi., U.S. C6 88
padvanj, India I5 38
panga, Zaire C4 44
papa Island, i., Hi., U.S. g10 88
pfenberg, Aus. H15 8
plan, La., U.S. D3 95
posvár, Hung. I17 8
ptai, Bngl. I15 38
puas, stm., Indon. F4 32
pūrthala, India E6 38
puskasing, Ont., Can. o19 73
rabük, Tur. G14 4
racabey, Tur. I12 16
racaköy, Tur. H12 16
rāchi, Pak. H2 38
rād, India D3 37
raganda, Kaz. H8 24
raginskij, Ostrov, i., Russia F26 24
raginskij Zaliv, b., Russia F26 24
ragoš, Gora, mtn., Russia G11 24
raikkudi, India G5 37
rakelong, Pulau, i., Indon. E8 32
rakoram Range, mts., Asia C7 38
rakumskij kanal, Turk. J10 22
raman, Tur. H14 4
raman, Tur. L13 16
ramay, China B3 26
ramürsel, Tur. I13 16
ranja, India B4 37
rasburg, Nmb. G3 44
rasjok, Nor. B15 6
ratsu, Japan I2 30
raul, Russia C10 24
rauli, India G7 38
rawang, Indon. m13 33a
rawanken, mts., Eur. C9 14
rbalā', Iraq B3 46
rböle, Swe. F10 6
rcag, Hung. H20 8
rdeljevo, Cro. F12 14
rdhitsa, Grc. J5 16
rdžali, Bul. H9 16
rgasok, Russia F10 24
rhula, Fin. F16 6
riba, Zimb. E5 44
riba, Lake, res., Afr. E5 44
ribib, Nmb. F3 44
rigasniemi, Fin. B15 6
rimata, Kepulauan, is., Indon. F4 32
rimata, Selat (Karimata Strait), strt., Indon. F4 32
rīmganj, India H15 38
rīmnagar, India C5 37
rin, Som. F4 46
ris (Karjaa), Fin. F14 6
riya, Japan H9 30
rkabet, Erit. E2 46
rlovac, Cro. D10 14
rlovo, Bul. G8 16
rlovy Vary, Czech. E12 8
rlshamn, Swe. H10 6
Karlskoga, Swe. G10 6
Karlskrona, Swe. H10 6
Karlsruhe, Ger. F8 8
Karlstad, Swe. G9 6
Karlstad, Mn., U.S. B2 100
Karnāl, India F7 38
Karnaphuli Reservoir, res., Bngl. I15 38
Karnataka, state, India E3 37
Karnes, co., Tx., U.S. E4 120
Karnes City, Tx., U.S. E4 120
Karns, Tn., U.S. n13 119
Karonga, Mwi. C6 44
Kárpathos, i., Grc. N11 16
Karpenísion, Grc. K5 16
Kars, Tur. G16 4
Kärsämäki, Fin. E15 6
Karši, Uzb. J11 22
Kartal, Tur. I13 16
Karufa, Indon. F9 32
Karungi, Swe. C14 6
Karūr, India G5 37
Karviná, Czech. F18 8
Kārwār, India E3 37
Kasai (Cassai), stm., Afr. B3 44
Kasaji, Zaire D4 44
Kasama, Zam. D6 44
Kasanga, Tan. C6 44
Kasaoka, Japan H6 30
Kāsaragod, India F3 37
Kasba Lake, l., N.W. Ter., Can. D12 66
Kaseda, Japan K3 30
Kasempa, Zam. D5 44
Kasenga, Zaire D5 44
Kasese, Zaire B5 44
Kāsganj, India G8 38
Kāshān, Iran B5 46
Kashi, China D2 26
Kashima-nada, Japan F13 30
Kashīpur, India F8 38
Kashiwa, Japan G12 30
Kashiwazaki, Japan E11 30
Kashmir see Jammu and Kashmir, dep., Asia C6 38
Kasimov, Russia G24 18
Kašin, Russia D20 18
Kašira, Russia G21 18
Kaskaskia, stm., Il., U.S. D5 90
Kaskö (Kaskinen), Fin. E13 6
Kaslo, B.C., Can. E9 69
Kasongo, Zaire B5 44
Kasota, Mn., U.S. F5 100
Kasr, Ra's, c., Sudan E13 42
Kassalā, Sudan E13 42
Kassel, Ger. D9 8
Kasson, Mn., U.S. F6 100
Kastoría, Grc. I5 16
Kasugai, Japan G9 30
Kasūr, Pak. E6 38
Katahdin, Mount, mtn., Me., U.S. C4 96
Katanga Plateau, plat., Zaire D5 44
Katchall Island, i., India K2 34
Kateríni, Grc. I6 16
Kates Needle, mtn., Ak., U.S. m24 79
Katherine, Austl. B6 50
Kāthiāwār, pen., India I4 38
Kathleen, Fl., U.S. D4 86
Kāṭhmāṇḍau, Nepal G11 38
Katihār, India H12 38
Katiola, I.C. G4 42
Katmai, Mount, mtn., Ak., U.S. D9 79
Katmai National Park, Ak., U.S. D9 79
Katmandu see Kāṭhmāṇḍau, Nepal G11 38
Katowice, Pol. E19 8
Kātrīnā, Jabal, mtn., Egypt C12 42
Katrineholm, Swe. G11 6
Katsina, Nig. F7 42
Katsuta, Japan F13 30
Kattegat, strt., Eur. H8 6
Katy, Tx., U.S. r14 120
Kauai, co., Hi., U.S. B1 88
Kauai, i., Hi., U.S. A2 88
Kauai Channel, strt., Hi., U.S. B3 88
Kau Desert, des., Hi., U.S. D6 88
Kaufbeuren, Ger. H10 8
Kaufman, Tx., U.S. C4 120
Kaufman, co., Tx., U.S. C4 120
Kauiki Head, c., Hi., U.S. C6 88
Kaukauna, Wi., U.S. D5 126
Kaukauveld, mts., Afr. F3 44
Kaula Island, i., Hi., U.S. m15 88
Kaulakahi Channel, strt., Hi., U.S. A2 88
Kaumakani, Hi., U.S. B2 88
Kaunakakai, Hi., U.S. B4 88
Kauna Point, c., Hi., U.S. D6 88
Kaunas, Lith. G6 18
Kaura Namoda, Nig. F7 42
Kaustinen, Fin. E14 6
Kavača, Russia E27 24
Kavacık, Tur. J12 16
Kavalerovo, Russia I21 24
Kavála, Grc. I8 16
Kavaratti, India G2 37
Kavieng, Pap. N. Gui. k17 50a
Kawagoe, Japan G12 30
Kawaguchi, Japan G12 30
Kawaihoa Point, c., Hi., U.S. B1 88
Kawaikini, mtn., Hi., U.S. A2 88
Kawambwa, Zam. C5 44
Kawanoe, Japan H6 30
Kawasaki, Japan G12 30
Kawich Peak, mtn., Nv., U.S. F5 105
Kawich Range, mts., Nv., U.S. F5 105
Kaw Lake, res., Ok., U.S. A5 113
Kawm Umbū, Egypt D12 42
Kay, co., Ok., U.S. A4 113
Kayankulam, India H4 37
Kaycee, Wy., U.S. C6 127
Kayenta, Az., U.S. A5 80
Kayes, Mali F3 42
Kayseri, Tur. H15 4
Kaysville, Ut., U.S. B4 121
Kažačinskoje, Russia F12 24
Kazačje, Russia C21 24
Kazakhstan, ctry., Asia H11 22
Kazan', Russia F7 22
Kazanlâk, Bul. G9 16
Kāzerūn, Iran C5 46
Keaau, Hi., U.S. D6 88
Keahiakahoe, Puu, mtn., Hi., U.S. g10 88
Keahole Point, c., Hi., U.S. D5 88
Kealaikahiki Channel, strt., Hi., U.S. C5 88
Kealaikahiki Point, c., Hi., U.S. C5 88
Kealakekua, Hi., U.S. D6 88
Kealia, Hi., U.S. A2 88
Keams Canyon, Az., U.S. B5 80
Keanapapa Point, c., Hi., U.S. C4 88
Keansburg, N.J., U.S. C4 107
Kearney, Mo., U.S. B3 102
Kearney, Ne., U.S. D6 104
Kearney, co., Ne., U.S. D7 104
Kearns, Ut., U.S. C4 121
Kearny, Az., U.S. D5 80
Kearny, N.J., U.S. h8 107
Kearny, co., Ks., U.S. D2 93
Kebri Dehar, Eth. G3 46
Kechika, stm., B.C., Can. E7 66
Kecskemét, Hung. I19 8
Kedges Straits, strt., Md., U.S. D5 97
Kedgwick, N.B., Can. B2 71
Kediri, Indon. m16 32
Kedon, Russia E25 24
Kédougou, Sen. F3 42
Kędzierzyn, Pol. E18 8
Keego Harbor, Mi., U.S. o15 99
Keele Peak, mtn., Yukon, Can. D6 66
Keelung see Chilung, Tai. J10 28
Keene, N.H., U.S. E2 106
Keene, Tx., U.S. n9 120
Keeper Hill, hill, Ire. I4 7
Keeseville, N.Y., U.S. f11 109
Keesler Air Force Base, mil., Ms., U.S. E5 101
Keetmanshoop, Nmb. G3 44
Keet Seel Ruin, hist., Az., U.S. A5 80
Keewatin, Ont., Can. E4 70
Keewatin, Mn., U.S. C5 100
Kefallinía, i., Grc. K4 16
Keffi, Nig. G7 42
Keflavík, Ice. C3 4
Ke Ga, Mui, c., Viet. H10 34
Kegonsa, Lake, l., Wi., U.S. F4 126
Keiser, Ar., U.S. B5 81
Keith, Scot., U.K. D10 7
Keith, co., Ne., U.S. C4 104
Keizer, Or., U.S. C3 114
Kejimkujik National Park, N.S., Can. E4 71
Kekaha, Hi., U.S. B2 88
Kelafo, Eth. G3 46
Kelang, Malay. M6 34
Kelheim, Ger. G11 8
Kelibia, Tun. M6 14
Keller, Tx., U.S. n9 120
Kellett, Cape, c., N.W. Ter., Can. B7 66
Kelleys Island, i., Oh., U.S. A3 112
Kellogg, Id., U.S. B2 89
Kellogg, Ia., U.S. C5 92
Kelloselkä, Fin. C17 6
Kelly Air Force Base, mil., Tx., U.S. k7 120
Kelly Island, i., De., U.S. D4 85
Kellyville, Ok., U.S. B5 113
Kélo, Chad G9 42
Kelottijärvi, Fin. B14 6
Kelowna, B.C., Can. E8 69
Kelso, Wa., U.S. C3 124
Keluang, Malay. M7 34
Kemerovo, Russia F11 24
Kemi, Fin. D15 6
Kemijärvi, Fin. C16 6
Kemijoki, stm., Fin. C15 6
Kemmerer, Wy., U.S. E2 127
Kemp, Tx., U.S. C4 120
Kemp, Lake, res., Tx., U.S. C3 120
Kemper, co., Ms., U.S. C5 101
Kemps Bay, Bah. B9 64
Kempt, Lac, l., Que., Can. G18 66
Kempten [Allgäu], Ger. H10 8
Kemptville, Ont., Can. B9 73
Kemul, Kong, mtn., Indon. E6 32
Kenai, Ak., U.S. C9 79
Kenai Fjords National Park, Ak., U.S. D10 79
Kenai Mountains, mts., Ak., U.S. h16 79
Kenai Peninsula, pen., Ak., U.S. h16 79
Kenansville, N.C., U.S. C5 110
Kenbridge, Va., U.S. D4 123
Kendall, Fl., U.S. s13 86
Kendall, co., Il., U.S. B5 90
Kendall, co., Tx., U.S. E3 120
Kendall, Cape, c., N.W. Ter., Can. D15 66
Kendall Park, N.J., U.S. C3 107
Kendallville, In., U.S. B7 91
Kendari, Indon. F7 32
Kenedy, Tx., U.S. E4 120
Kenedy, co., Tx., U.S. F4 120
Kenema, S.L. G3 42
Kenesaw, Ne., U.S. D7 104
Kēng Tung, Burma D5 34
Kenhardt, S. Afr. G4 44
Kenilworth, Il., U.S. h9 90
Kenitra, Mor. B4 42
Kenly, N.C., U.S. B4 110
Kenmare, N.D., U.S. A3 111
Kenmore, N.Y., U.S. C2 109
Kennaday Peak, mtn., Wy., U.S. E6 127
Kennebago Lake, l., Me., U.S. C2 96
Kennebec, co., Me., U.S. D3 96
Kennebec, stm., Me., U.S. D3 96
Kennebunk, Me., U.S. E2 96
Kennebunkport, Me., U.S. E2 96
Kennedy Entrance, strt., Ak., U.S. D9 79
Kennedy Peak, mtn., Burma C2 34
Kenner, La., U.S. E5 95
Kennesaw, Ga., U.S. B2 87
Kennesaw Mountain, mtn., Ga., U.S. C2 87
Kennett, Mo., U.S. E7 102
Kennett Square, Pa., U.S. G10 115
Kennewick, Wa., U.S. C6 124
Kenn Reefs, rf., Austl. D11 50
Kennydale, Wa., U.S. e11 124
Keno, Or., U.S. E5 114
Kénogami, Lac, l., Que., Can. A6 74
Kenora, Ont., Can. o16 73
Kenosha, Wi., U.S. F6 126
Kenosha, co., Wi., U.S. F5 126
Kenova, W.V., U.S. C2 125
Kensett, Ar., U.S. B4 81
Kensico Reservoir, res., N.Y., U.S. g13 109
Kensington, P.E.I., Can. C6 71
Kensington, Ct., U.S. C4 84
Kensington, Md., U.S. B3 97
Kent, Oh., U.S. A4 112
Kent, Wa., U.S. B3 124
Kent, co., De., U.S. D3 85
Kent, co., Md., U.S. B5 97
Kent, co., Mi., U.S. E5 99
Kent, co., R.I., U.S. D2 116
Kent, co., Tx., U.S. C2 120
Kent City, Mi., U.S. E5 99
Kent Island, i., De., U.S. D4 85
Kent Island, i., Md., U.S. C5 97
Kentland, In., U.S. C3 91
Kenton, De., U.S. D3 85
Kenton, Oh., U.S. B2 112
Kenton, Tn., U.S. A2 119
Kenton, co., Ky., U.S. B5 94
Kent Peninsula, pen., N.W. Ter., Can. C11 66
Kent Point, c., Md., U.S. C5 97
Kentucky, state, U.S. C4 94
Kentucky, stm., Ky., U.S. B5 94
Kentwood, La., U.S. D5 95
Kentwood, Mi., U.S. F5 99
Kenvil, N.J., U.S. B3 107
Kenvir, Ky., U.S. D6 94
Kenya, ctry., Afr. B7 44
Kenya, Mount see Kirinyaga, mtn., Kenya B7 44
Kenyon, Mn., U.S. F6 100
Kenyon, R.I., U.S. F2 116
Keokea, Hi., U.S. C5 88
Keokuk, Ia., U.S. D6 92
Keokuk, co., Ia., U.S. C5 92
Keokuk Lock and Dam, U.S. D6 92
Keosauqua, Ia., U.S. D6 92
Keota, Ia., U.S. C6 92
Keota, Ok., U.S. B7 113
Keowee, Lake, res., S.C., U.S. B2 117
Kepi, Indon. G10 32
Kerala, state, India G4 37
Kerč', Ukr. H5 22
Keremeos, B.C., Can. E8 69
Keren, Erit. E2 46
Kerens, Tx., U.S. C4 120
Kerguélen, Îles, is., F.S.A.T. J17 2
Kerhonkson, N.Y., U.S. D6 109
Kericho, Kenya B7 44
Kerinci, Gunung, mtn., Indon. F3 32
Kerkhoven, Mn., U.S. E3 100
Kérkira (Corfu), Grc. J3 16
Kérkira, i., Grc. J3 16
Kermān, Iran B6 46
Kerme Körfezi, b., Tur. M11 16
Kermit, Tx., U.S. D1 120
Kermode, Mount, mtn., B.C., Can. C2 69
Kern, co., Ca., U.S. E4 82
Kern, stm., Ca., U.S. E4 82
Kernersville, N.C., U.S. A2 110
Kernville, Ca., U.S. E4 82
Kerr, co., Tx., U.S. D3 120
Kerr, Lake, l., Fl., U.S. C5 86
Kerrville, Tx., U.S. D3 120
Kerry Head, c., Ire. I3 7
Kersey, Co., U.S. A6 83
Kershaw, S.C., U.S. B6 117
Kershaw, co., S.C., U.S. C6 117
Kerulen (Cherlen), stm., Asia B9 26
Kesagami Lake, l., Ont., Can. F16 66
Keşan, Tur. I10 16
Kesennuma, Japan D14 30
Keshena, Wi., U.S. D5 126
Ket', stm., Russia F11 24
Keta, Ozero, l., Russia D11 24
Ketchikan, Ak., U.S. D13 79
Ketchum, Id., U.S. F4 89
Kettering, Eng., U.K. I12 7
Kettering, Oh., U.S. C1 112
Kettle, stm., Mn., U.S. D6 100
Kettle Creek, stm., Pa., U.S. D6 115
Kettle Creek Lake, res., Pa., U.S. D6 115
Kettle Falls, Wa., U.S. A7 124
Keuka Lake, l., N.Y., U.S. C3 109
Kew, T./C. Is. D11 64
Kewanee, Il., U.S. B4 90
Kewaskum, Wi., U.S. E5 126
Kewaunee, Wi., U.S. D6 126
Kewaunee, co., Wi., U.S. D6 126
Keweenaw, co., Mi., U.S. A2 99
Keweenaw Bay, b., Mi., U.S. B2 99
Keweenaw Peninsula, pen., Mi., U.S. A3 99
Keweenaw Point, c., Mi., U.S. A3 99
Keya Paha, co., Ne., U.S. B6 104
Keya Paha, stm., U.S. A5 104
Keyhole Reservoir, res., Wy., U.S. B8 127
Key Largo, Fl., U.S. G6 86
Keyport, N.J., U.S. C4 107
Keyser, W.V., U.S. B6 125
Keystone, W.V., U.S. D3 125
Keystone Heights, Fl., U.S. C4 86
Keystone Lake, res., Ok., U.S. A5 113
Keystone Peak, mtn., Az., U.S. F4 80
Keysville, Va., U.S. C4 123
Key West, Fl., U.S. H5 86
Key West Naval Air Station, mil., Fl., U.S. H5 86
Kezar Falls, Me., U.S. E2 96
Kezar Lake, l., Me., U.S. D2 96
Kežma, Russia F14 24
Khadki (Kirkee), India C2 37
Khairpur, Pak. G3 38
Khalkís, Grc. K7 16
Khambhāliya, India I3 38
Khambhāt, Gulf of, b., India B2 37
Khāmgaon, India B4 37
Khammam, India D6 37
Khānābād, Afg. B3 38
Khānaqīn, Iraq B4 46
Khandwa, India B4 37
Khānewāl, Pak. E4 38
Khaniá, Grc. N8 16
Khanna, India E7 38
Khānpur, Pak. F4 38
Khān Yūnus, Isr. Occ. D4 40
Kharagpur, India I12 38
Khargon, India J6 38
Kharkov see Char'kov, Ukr. G5 22
Khartoum see Al-Kharṭūm, Sudan E12 42
Kherson see Cherson, Ukr. H4 22
Khíos, Grc. K10 16
Kholm, Afg. B2 38
Khong, Laos G8 34
Khong Sédone, Laos G8 34
Khon Kaen, Thai. F7 34
Khóra Sfakíon, Grc. N8 16
Khorramābād, Iran B4 46
Khorramshahr, Iran B4 46
Khouribga, Mor. B4 42
Khowst, Afg. D3 38
Khulna, Bngl. I13 38
Khunjerab Pass, Asia B6 38
Khurja, India F7 38
Khūryān Mūryān (Kuria Muria Isla, is., Oman E6 46
Khushāb, Pak. D5 38
Khvājeh Moḥammad, Kūh-e, mts., Afg. B4 38
Khvoy, Iran J6 22
Khyber Pass, Asia C4 38
Kiamichi, stm., Ok., U.S. C6 113
Kiamika, stm., Que., Can. C2 74
Kiana, Ak., U.S. B7 79
Kiawah Island, i., S.C., U.S. F7 117
Kibangou, Congo B2 44
Kibombo, Zaire B5 44
Kibre Mengist, Eth. G2 46
Kičevo, Mac. H4 16
Kichčik, Russia G25 24
Kickamuit, stm., R.I., U.S. D5 116
Kickapoo, stm., Wi., U.S. E3 126
Kickapoo, Lake, res., Tx., U.S. C3 120
Kickapoo Indian Reservation, Ks., U.S. C8 93
Kicking Horse Pass, Can. D2 68
Kidal, Mali E6 42
Kidder, co., N.D., U.S. C6 111
Kidira, Sen. F3 42
Kiefer, Ok., U.S. B5 113
Kiel, Ger. A10 8
Kiel, Wi., U.S. E5 126
Kielce, Pol. E20 8
Kieler Bucht, b., Ger. A10 8
Kiester, Mn., U.S. G5 100
Kiev see Kijev, Ukr. G4 22
Kiffa, Maur. E3 42
Kigali, Rw. B6 44
Kigoma, Tan. B5 44
Kihei, Hi., U.S. C5 88
Kihniö, Fin. E14 6
Kiholo Bay, b., Hi., U.S. D5 88
Kii-suidō, strt., Japan I7 30
Kijev (Kiev), Ukr. G4 22
Kikinda, Yugo. D4 16
Kikládhes, is., Grc. L8 16
Kikwit, Zaire C3 44
Kilauea, Hi., U.S. A2 88
Kilauea Crater, crat., Hi., U.S. D6 88
Kilauea Point, c., Hi., U.S. A2 88
Kilgore, Tx., U.S. C5 120
Kilimanjaro, mtn., Tan. B7 44
Kilis, Tur. A5 40
Kilkee, Ire. I3 7
Kilkenny, Ire. I5 7
Kilkís, Grc. H6 16
Killala, Ire. G3 7
Killaloe Station, Ont., Can. B7 73
Killam, Alta., Can. C5 68
Killarney, Man., Can. E2 70
Killarney, Ire. I3 7
Killarney Provincial Park, Ont., Can. A3 73
Killdeer, N.D., U.S. B3 111
Killeen, Tx., U.S. D4 120
Killen, Al., U.S. A2 78
Killian, La., U.S. h10 95
Killik, stm., Ak., U.S. B9 79
Killona, La., U.S. h11 95
Killorglin, Ire. I3 7
Kilmarnock, Scot., U.K. F8 7
Kilmarnock, Va., U.S. C6 123
Kilmichael, Ms., U.S. B4 101
Kiln, Ms., U.S. E4 101
Kilombero, stm., Tan. C7 44
Kilosa, Tan. C7 44
Kilpisjärvi, Fin. B13 6
Kilwa, Zaire C5 44
Kilwa Kivinje, Tan. C7 44
Kimball, Mn., U.S. E4 100
Kimball, Ne., U.S. C2 104
Kimball, S.D., U.S. D7 118
Kimball, co., Ne., U.S. C2 104
Kimball, Mount, mtn., Ak., U.S. C11 79
Kimberley, B.C., Can. E9 69
Kimberley, S. Afr. G4 44
Kimberley Plateau, plat., Austl. C5 50
Kimberlin Heights, Tn., U.S. n14 119
Kimberly, Al., U.S. B3 78
Kimberly, Id., U.S. G4 89
Kimberly, W.V., U.S. m13 125
Kimberly, Wi., U.S. h9 126
Kimble, co., Tx., U.S. D3 120
Kimch'aek, N. Kor. C12 26
Kimovsk, Russia H21 18
Kimry, Russia E20 18
Kinabalu, Gunong, mtn., Malay. D6 32
Kinbasket Lake, res., B.C., Can. D8 69
Kincaid, Il., U.S. D4 90
Kincaid, W.V., U.S. m13 125
Kincaid, Lake, res., Il., U.S. D4 90
Kincardine, Ont., Can. C3 73

Name — Map Ref — Page

Kincheloe Air Force Base, mil., Mi., U.S. B6 99
Kinder, La., U.S. D3 95
Kindia, Gui. F3 42
Kindu, Zaire B5 44
Kinešma, Russia D25 18
King, N.C., U.S. A2 110
King, Wi., U.S. D4 126
King, co., Tx., U.S. C2 120
King, co., Wa., U.S. B3 124
King and Queen, co., Va., U.S. C6 123
Kingaroy, Austl. E10 50
King City, Ca., U.S. D3 82
King City, Mo., U.S. A3 102
King Cove, Ak., U.S. E7 79
Kingfield, Me., U.S. D2 96
Kingfisher, Ok., U.S. B4 113
Kingfisher, co., Ok., U.S. B3 113
King George, co., Va., U.S. B5 123
King Island, i., Austl. G8 50
King Island, i., B.C., Can. C4 69
King Lear Peak, mtn., Nv., U.S. B3 105
King Leopold Ranges, mts., Austl. C5 50
Kingman, Az., U.S. B1 80
Kingman, Ks., U.S. E5 93
Kingman, co., Ks., U.S. E5 93
King Mountain, mtn., Or., U.S. E3 114
King Mountain, mtn., Or., U.S. D8 114
King Peak, mtn., Ca., U.S. B1 82
Kings, Ms., U.S. C3 101
Kings, co., Ca., U.S. D4 82
Kings, co., N.Y., U.S. E7 109
Kings, stm., Ar., U.S. A2 81
Kings, stm., Ca., U.S. D4 82
Kings, stm., Nv., U.S. B3 105
King Salmon, Ak., U.S. D8 79
Kingsburg, Ca., U.S. D4 82
Kingsbury, co., S.D., U.S. C8 118
Kings Canyon National Park, Ca., U.S. D4 82
Kingsey-Falls, Que., Can. D5 74
Kingsford, Mi., U.S. C2 99
Kingsland, Ga., U.S. F5 87
Kingsland, Tx., U.S. D3 120
Kingsley, Ia., U.S. B2 92
Kingsley, Mi., U.S. D5 99
King's Lynn, Eng., U.K. I13 7
Kings Mountain, N.C., U.S. B1 110
King Sound, strt., Austl. C4 50
Kings Park West, Va., U.S. *B5 123
Kings Peak, mtn., Ut., U.S. C5 121
King's Point, Newf., Can. D3 72
Kingsport, Tn., U.S. C11 119
Kingston, Ont., Can. C8 73
Kingston, Jam. E9 64
Kingston, Ga., U.S. B2 87
Kingston, Id., U.S. B2 89
Kingston, Ma., U.S. C6 98
Kingston, N.H., U.S. E4 106
Kingston, N.Y., U.S. D6 109
Kingston, Oh., U.S. C3 112
Kingston, Ok., U.S. D5 113
Kingston, Pa., U.S. D10 115
Kingston, R.I., U.S. F3 116
Kingston, Tn., U.S. D9 119
Kingston Springs, Tn., U.S. A4 119
Kingston upon Hull, Eng., U.K. H12 7
Kingstown, St. Vin. H17 64
Kingstown, Md., U.S. B5 97
Kingstree, S.C., U.S. D8 117
Kingsville, Ont., Can. E2 73
Kingsville, Md., U.S. B5 97
Kingsville (North Kingsville), Oh., U.S. A5 112
Kingsville, Tx., U.S. F4 120
Kingsville Naval Air Station, mil., Tx., U.S. F4 120
King William, co., Va., U.S. C5 123
King William Island, i., N.W. Ter., Can. C13 66
King William's Town, S. Afr. H5 44
Kingwood, W.V., U.S. B5 125
Kinistino, Sask., Can. E3 75
Kinkaid Lake, res., Il., U.S. F4 90
Kinloch, Mo., U.S. f13 102
Kinmundy, Il., U.S. E5 90
Kinna, Swe. H9 6
Kinnairds Head, c., Scot., U.K. D10 7
Kinnelon, N.J., U.S. B4 107
Kinneret, Yam, l., Isr. C4 40
Kinney, co., Tx., U.S. E2 120
Kinross, Scot., U.K. E9 7
Kinsale, Ire. J4 7
Kinsarvik, Nor. F6 6
Kinsey, Al., U.S. D4 78
Kinshasa (Léopoldville), Zaire B3 44
Kinsley, Ks., U.S. E4 93
Kinston, N.C., U.S. B5 110
Kintyre, pen., Scot., U.K. F7 7
Kintyre, Mull of, c., Scot., U.K. F7 7
Kinyeti, mtn., Sudan H12 42
Kiowa, Ks., U.S. E5 93
Kiowa, Ok., U.S. C6 113
Kiowa, co., Co., U.S. C8 83
Kiowa, co., Ks., U.S. E4 93
Kiowa, co., Ok., U.S. C2 113
Kiowa Creek, stm., Ok., U.S. A1 113
Kipembawe, Tan. C6 44
Kipili, Tan. C6 44
Kipnuk, Ak., U.S. C7 79
Kipushi, Zaire D5 44
Kirbyville, Tx., U.S. D6 120
Kirchdorf an der Krems, Aus. H14 8
Kirenga, stm., Russia F15 24
Kirensk, Russia F15 24
Kirghizia see Kyrgyzstan, state, Asia I12 22
Kiribati, ctry., Oc. G24 2
Kırıkhan, Tur. A5 40
Kırıkkale, Tur. H14 4
Kirin see Jilin, China C12 26
Kirinyaga (Mount Kenya), mtn., Kenya B7 44
Kırkağaç, Tur. J11 16
Kirkcaldy, Scot., U.K. E9 7
Kirkcudbright, Scot., U.K. G8 7
Kirkenes, Nor. B18 6
Kirkland, Il., U.S. A5 90
Kirkland, Wa., U.S. B3 124
Kirkland Lake, Ont., Can. o19 73
Kırklareli, Tur. H11 16
Kirklin, In., U.S. D5 91
Kirksville, Mo., U.S. A5 102
Kirkūk, Iraq A3 46
Kirkwall, Scot., U.K. C10 7
Kirkwood, De., U.S. B3 85
Kirkwood, Il., U.S. C3 90
Kirkwood, Mo., U.S. f13 102
Kirov, Russia G17 18
Kirov, Russia F7 22
Kirovograd, Ukr. H4 22
Kirovskij, Russia G25 24
Kırşehir, Tur. H14 4
Kīrthar Range, mts., Pak. G2 38
Kirtland, N.M., U.S. A1 108
Kirtland Air Force Base, mil., N.M., U.S. k7 108
Kiruna, Swe. C13 6
Kirwin Reservoir, res., Ks., U.S. C4 93
Kiryū, Japan F12 30
Kisa, Swe. H10 6
Kisangani (Stanleyville), Zaire A5 44
Kisarazu, Japan G12 30
K.I. Sawyer Air Force Base, mil., Mi., U.S. B3 99
Kisel'ovsk, Russia G11 24
Kishanganj, India G12 38
Kishangarh, India G6 38
Kishinev see Kišin'ov, Mol. H3 22
Kishiwada, Japan H8 30
Kishorganj, Bngl. H14 38
Kishwaukee, stm., Il., U.S. A5 90
Kišin'ov, Mol. H3 22
Kiska Island, i., Ak., U.S. E3 79
Kiskunfélegyháza, Hung. I19 8
Kiskunhalas, Hung. I19 8
Kislovodsk, Russia I6 22
Kismayu, Som. B8 44
Kissidougou, Gui. G3 42
Kissimmee, Fl., U.S. D5 86
Kissimmee, stm., Fl., U.S. E5 86
Kissimmee, Lake, l., Fl., U.S. E5 86
Kississing Lake, l., Man., Can. B1 70
Kistanje, Cro. F10 14
Kistler, W.V., U.S. D3 125
Kisumu, Kenya B6 44
Kitaibaraki, Japan F13 30
Kitakami, stm., Japan C14 30
Kitakami-sanchi, mts., Japan C14 30
Kitakyūshū, Japan I3 30
Kitale, Kenya A6 44
Kitami, Japan p21 30a
Kitami-sanchi, mts., Japan o20 30a
Kit Carson, co., Co., U.S. B8 83
Kitchener, Ont., Can. D4 73
Kíthira, i., Grc. M6 16
Kitimat, B.C., Can. B3 69
Kitsap, co., Wa., U.S. B3 124
Kitscoty, Alta., Can. C5 68
Kittanning, Pa., U.S. E2 115
Kittatinny Mountain, mtn., U.S. B2 107
Kittery, Me., U.S. E2 96
Kittery Point, Me., U.S. E2 96
Kittilä, Fin. C15 6
Kittitas, Wa., U.S. C5 124
Kittitas, co., Wa., U.S. B4 124
Kitts, Ky., U.S. D6 94
Kittson, co., Mn., U.S. B2 100
Kitty Hawk, N.C., U.S. A7 110
Kitty Hawk Bay, b., N.C., U.S. A7 110
Kitwe, Zam. D5 44
Kitzbühel, Aus. H12 8
Kitzingen, Ger. F10 8
Kivu, Lac, l., Afr. B5 44
Kızıl, stm., Tur. G14 4
Kjustendil, Bul. G6 16
Kladno, Czech. E14 8
Klagenfurt, Aus. I14 8
Klaipėda (Memel), Lith. F4 18
Klamath, co., Or., U.S. E5 114
Klamath, stm., U.S. B2 82
Klamath Falls, Or., U.S. E5 114
Klamath Mountains, mts., U.S. E2 114
Klangenan, Indon. m14 33a
Klarälven, stm., Eur. F9 6
Klawock, Ak., U.S. D13 79
Kleberg, co., Tx., U.S. F4 120
Klerksdorp, S. Afr. G5 44
Kleve, Ger. D6 8
Klickitat, Wa., U.S. D4 124
Klickitat, co., Wa., U.S. D4 124
Klickitat, stm., Wa., U.S. C4 124
Klimovsk, Russia F20 18
Klin, Russia E19 18
Klincy, Russia I15 18
Kłodzko, Pol. E16 8
Klondike, hist. reg., Yukon, Can. D5 66
Klondike Gold Rush National Historical Park, Ak., U.S. k22 79
Klosterneuburg, Aus. G16 8
Kluane Lake, l., Yukon, Can. D5 66
Klutina Lake, l., Ak., U.S. g19 79
Knapp Creek, stm., W.V., U.S. C5 125
Knee Lake, l., Man., Can. B4 70
Kneža, Bul. F8 16
Knife, stm., N.D., U.S. B3 111
Knightdale, N.C., U.S. B4 110
Knight Inlet, b., B.C., Can. D5 69
Knight Island, i., Ak., U.S. g18 79
Knightstown, In., U.S. E6 91
Knightsville, In., U.S. E3 91
Knightville Reservoir, res., Ma., U.S. B2 98
Knin, Cro. E11 14
Knittelfeld, Aus. H14 8
Knob Noster, Mo., U.S. C4 102
Knokke, Bel. D3 8
Knollwood, W.V., U.S. m12 125
Knott, co., Ky., U.S. C6 94
Knox, In., U.S. B4 91
Knox, Pa., U.S. D2 115
Knox, co., Il., U.S. B3 90
Knox, co., In., U.S. G3 91
Knox, co., Ky., U.S. D6 94
Knox, co., Me., U.S. D4 96
Knox, co., Mo., U.S. A5 102
Knox, co., Ne., U.S. B8 104
Knox, co., Oh., U.S. B3 112
Knox, co., Tn., U.S. C10 119
Knox, co., Tx., U.S. C3 120
Knox, Cape, c., B.C., Can. B1 69
Knox City, Tx., U.S. C3 120
Knoxville, Il., U.S. C3 90
Knoxville, Ia., U.S. C4 92
Knoxville, Tn., U.S. D10 119
Knysna, S. Afr. H4 44
Kōbe, Japan H8 30
København (Copenhagen), Den. I9 6
Koblenz, Ger. E7 8
Kobrin, Bela. I7 18
Kobuk, stm., Ak., U.S. B8 79
Kobuk Valley National Park, Ak., U.S. B8 79
Kočani, Mac. H6 16
Kočevje, Slo. D9 14
Kōchi, Japan I6 30
Koch Peak, mtn., Mt., U.S. E5 103
Kodiak, Ak., U.S. D9 79
Kodiak Island, i., Ak., U.S. D9 79
Koes, Nmb. G3 44
Kofa Mountains, mts., Az., U.S. D2 80
Köflach, Aus. H15 8
Kōfu, Japan G11 30
Koga, Japan F12 30
Kogaluc, Baie, b., Que., Can. E17 66
Kogaluk, stm., Newf., Can. g9 72
Køge Bugt, b., Grnld. D24 66
Kohala Mountains, mts., Hi., U.S. C6 88
Kohāt, Pak. D4 38
Kohīma, India H16 38
Kohler, Wi., U.S. E6 126
Kohtla-Järve, Est. B10 18
Kokand, Uzb. I12 22
Kokanee Glacier Provincial Park, B.C., Can. E9 69
Kokemäki, Fin. F14 6
Kokkola (Gamlakarleby), Fin. E14 6
Koko Head, c., Hi., U.S. B4 88
Kokolik, stm., Ak., U.S. B7 79
Kokomo, In., U.S. D5 91
Kokonau, Indon. F10 32
Kokopo, Pap. N. Gui. k17 50a
Kokosing, stm., Oh., U.S. B3 112
Koksoak, stm., Que., Can. E19 66
Kokstad, S. Afr. H5 44
Kolaka, Indon. F7 32
Kola Peninsula see Kol'skij poluostrov, pen., Russia D5 22
Kolār, India F5 37
Kolār Gold Fields, India F5 37
Kol'čugino, Russia E22 18
Kolda, Sen. F3 42
Kolding, Den. I7 6
Kolhāpur, India D3 37
Kolín, Czech. E15 8
Kollegāl, India F4 37
Köln (Cologne), Ger. E6 8
Koloa, Hi., U.S. B2 88
Kołobrzeg, Pol. A15 8
Kolomna, Russia F21 18
Kolpaševo, Russia F10 24
Kolpino, Russia B13 18
Kol'skij poluostrov (Kola Peninsula), pen., Russia D5 22
Kolwezi, Zaire D5 44
Kolyma, stm., Russia D25 24
Kolymskaja Nizmennost', pl., Russia D24 24
Komárno, Slov. H18 8
Komatsu, Japan F9 30
Komló, Hung. I18 8
Kommunizma, pik, mtn., Taj. J12 22
Komoé, stm., Afr. G5 42
Komotiní, Grc. H9 16
Komsomolec, Ostrov, i., Russia A12 24
Komsomol'sk-na-Amure, Russia G21 24
Komsomol'skoj Pravdy, Ostrova, is., Russia B15 24
Konahuanui, Puu, mtn., Hi., U.S. g10 88
Konakovo, Russia E19 18
Konawa, Ok., U.S. C5 113
Konch, India H8 38
Kondrovo, Russia G18 18
Kŏng, Kaôh, i., Camb. I7 34
Kongolo, Zaire C5 44
Kongsberg, Nor. G7 6
Kongsvinger, Nor. F8 6
Kongsvoll, Nor. E7 6
Kongur Shan, mtn., China A6 38
Königs Wusterhausen, Ger. C13 8
Konin, Pol. C18 8
Konjic, Bos. F12 14
Konomoc, Lake, res., Ct., U.S. D7 84
Konqi, stm., China C4 26
Konstanz, Ger. H9 8
Kontagora, Nig. F7 42
Kontiomäki, Fin. D17 6
Kon Tum, Viet. G10 34
Konya, Tur. H14 4
Konza, Kenya B7 44
Koochiching, co., Mn., U.S. B4 100
Koolau Range, mts., Hi., U.S. f10 88
Koontz Lake, In., U.S. B5 91
Kooskia, Id., U.S. C3 89
Kootenai, co., Id., U.S. B2 89
Kootenay Lake, l., B.C., Can. E9 69
Kootenay National Park, B.C., Can. D9 69
Kopargaon, India C3 37
Koper, Slo. D8 14
Kopetdag, chrebet, mts., Asia J9 22
Köping, Swe. G10 6
Koppal, India E4 37
Koppang, Nor. F8 6
Koppel, Pa., U.S. E1 115
Koprivnica, Cro. C11 14
Kor'akskoje Nagorje, mts., Russia E27 24
Korba, India I10 38
Korbach, Ger. D8 8
Korçë, Alb. I4 16
Korčula, Cro. G12 14
Korea, North, ctry., Asia C12 26
Korea, South, ctry., Asia D12 26
Korea Bay, b., Asia D11 26
Korea Strait, strt., Asia E12 26
Korf, Russia E27 24
Korhogo, I.C. G4 42
Korinthiakós Kólpos, b., Grc. K6 16
Kórinthos (Corinth), Grc. L6 16
Kōriyama, Japan E13 30
Korliki, Russia E10 24
Korogwe, Tan. C7 44
Koronis, Lake, l., Mn., U.S. E4 100
Koro Toro, Chad E9 42
Korovin Volcano, vol., Ak., U.S. E5 79
Korsakov, Russia H22 24
Korsnäs, Fin. E13 6
Korso, Fin. F15 6
Kortrijk (Courtrai), Bel. E3 8
Koruçam Burnu, c., N. Cyp. B3 40
Koš-Agač, Russia G11 24
Kosciusko, Ms., U.S. B4 101
Kosciusko, co., In., U.S. B6 91
Kosciusko, Mount, mtn., Austl. G9 50
Koshkonong, Lake, l., Wi., U.S. F5 126
Košice, Slov. G21 8
Kosovska Mitrovica, Yugo. G4 16
Kossuth, co., Ia., U.S. A3 92
Kostroma, Russia D23 18
Koszalin (Köslin), Pol. A16 8
Kota, India H6 38
Kota Baharu, Malay. K7 34
Kotabumi, Indon. F3 32
Kot Addu, Pak. E4 38
Kota Kinabalu (Jesselton), Malay. D6 32
Kotel'nyj, Ostrov, i., Russia B21 24
Köthen, Ger. D11 8
Kotka, Fin. F16 6
Kot Kapūra, India E6 38
Kotlas, Russia E7 22
Kotlik, Ak., U.S. C7 79
Kotor Varoš, Bos. E12 14
Kotovsk, Russia I24 18
Kotri, Pak. H3 38
Kötschach [-Mauthen], Aus. I12 8
Kottagūdem, India D6 37
Kottayam, India H4 37
Kotte, Sri L. I5 37
Kotto, stm., Cen. Afr. Rep. G10 42
Kotuj, stm., Russia C14 24
Kotzebue, Ak., U.S. B7 79
Kotzebue Sound, strt., Ak., U.S. B7 79
Kouchibouguac National Park, N.B., Can. C5 71
Koudougou, Burkina F5 42
Koula-Moutou, Gabon B2 44
Koumra, Chad G9 42
Kountze, Tx., U.S. D5 120
Koussi, Emi, mtn., Chad E9 42
Koutiala, Mali F4 42
Kouts, In., U.S. B3 91
Kouvola, Fin. F16 6
Kovrov, Russia E24 18
Kowkcheh, stm., Afg. B4 38
Kowloon (Jiulong), H.K. M3 28
Kowt-e 'Ashrow, Afg. C3 38
Koyukuk, stm., Ak., U.S. B8 79
Koza, Japan y27 31b
Kozáni, Grc. I5 16
Kra, Isthmus of, Asia I5 34
Krâchéh, Camb. H9 34
Kragerø, Nor. G7 6
Kragujevac, Yugo. E4 16
Kraków, Pol. E19 8
Kraljevica, Cro. D9 14
Kraljevo, Yugo. F4 16
Kramfors, Swe. E11 6
Krångede, Swe. E11 6
Kranj, Slo. C9 14
Krasneno, Russia E28 24
Krasnodar, Russia H5 22
Krasnogorsk, Russia F20 18
Krasnojarsk, Russia F12 24
Krasnoje, Ozero, l., Russia E28 24
Krasnosel'kup, Russia D10 24
Krasnozavodsk, Russia E21 18
Krebs, Ok., U.S. C6 113
Kremenčug, Ukr. H4 22
Kremmling, Co., U.S. A4 83
Krems an der Donau, Aus. G15 8
Kresta, Zaliv, b., Russia D30 24
Kribi, Cam. H7 42
Kričov, Bela. H14 18
Krishna, stm., India D5 37
Krishnanagar, India I13 38
Kristiansand, Nor. G7 6
Kristianstad, Swe. H10 6
Kristiansund, Nor. E6 6
Kristinehamn, Swe. G10 6
Kríti, i., Grc. N8 16
Kritikón Pélagos, Grc. N8 16
Krivoj Rog, Ukr. H4 22
Krivoy Rog see Krivoj Rog, Ukr. H4 22
Krnov, Czech. E17 8
Kroken, Nor. D10 6
Kroměříž, Czech. F17 8
Kronach, Ger. E11 8
Krŏng Khémôreáh Phumint, Camb. I7 34
Kronockij Zaliv, b., Russia G26 24
Kronoki, Russia G26 24
Kronštadt, Russia B12 18
Kroonstad, S. Afr. G5 44
Kropotkin, Russia F17 24
Krosno, Pol. F21 8
Krotz Springs, La., U.S. D4 95
Krško, Slo. D10 14
Kr'ukovo, Russia D25 24
Krung Thep (Bangkok), Thai. H6 34
Kruševac, Yugo. F5 16
Krušné hory (Erzgebirge), mts., Eur. E12 8
Kruzenšterna, Proliv, strt., Russia H24 24
Kruzof Island, i., Ak., U.S. m21 79
Krymskij poluostrov (Crimea), pen., Ukr. H4 22
Ksar-es-Souk, Mor. B5 42
Ksenjevka, Russia G17 24
Ksour Essaf, Tun. N5 14
Kuala Kangsar, Malay. L6 34
Kualakapuas, Indon. F5 32
Kuala Krai, Malay. L7 34
Kuala Kubu Baharu, Malay. M6 34
Kuala Lumpur, Malay. M6 34
Kuala Nerang, Malay. K6 34
Kuala Pilah, Malay. M7 34
Kuala Terengganu, Malay. L7 34
Kuantan, Malay. M7 34
Kubokawa, Japan I6 30
Kuche, China C3 26
Kuching, Malay. E5 32
Kudat, Malay. D6 32
Kudus, Indon. m15 32
Kuee Ruins, hist., Hi., U.S. D6 88
Kufstein, Aus. H12 8
Kuhmo, Fin. D17 6
Kuito, Ang. D3 44
Kuiu Island, i., Ak., U.S. m23 79
Kuivaniemi, Fin. D15 6
Kukawa, Nig. F8 42
Kula, Tur. K12 16
Kula, Hi., U.S. C5 88
Kul'ab, Taj. B3 38
Kula Kangri, mtn., Bhu. F14 38
Kulebaki, Russia F25 18
Kulen Vakuf, Bos. E11 14
Kulim, Malay. L6 34
Kulmbach, Ger. E11 8
Kulpmont, Pa., U.S. E9 115
Kulunqi, China C11 26
Kumagaya, Japan F12 30
Kumajri, Arm. I6 22
Kumamoto, Japan J3 30
Kumano, Japan I9 30
Kumano-nada, Japan I9 30
Kumanovo, Mac. G5 16
Kumasi, Ghana G5 42
Kumbakonam, India G5 37
Kume-shima, i., Japan y26 31
Kumo, Nig. F8 42
Kumon Range, mts., Burma B4 34
Kumukahi, Cape, c., Hi., U.S. D7 88
Kuna, Id., U.S. F2 89
Kunašir, Ostrov (Kunashiri-tō), i., Russia I23 24
Kundiān, Pak. D4 38
Kundla, India J4 38
Kunes, Nor. A16 6
Kunghit Island, i., B.C., Can. C2 69
Kuningan, Indon. m14 33
Kunlun Shan, mts., China B12 38
Kunming, China B7 34
Kunsan, S. Kor. D12 26
Kunshan, China D9 28
Kuopio, Fin. E16 6
Kupang, Indon. H7 32
Kupreanof Island, i., Ak., U.S. m23 79
Kupres, Bos. E12 14
Kura, stm., Asia I7 22
Kurashiki, Japan H6 30
Kurayoshi, Japan G6 30
Kure, Japan H5 30
Kure Island, i., Hi., U.S. k12 88
Kurejka, stm., Russia D11 24
Kurenalus, Fin. D16 6
Kurgan-T'ube, Taj. B3 38
Kurikka, Fin. E14 6
Kuril'sk, Russia H23 24
Kuril'skije Ostrova (Kuril Islands), is., Russia H23 24
Kurmuk, Sudan F12 42
Kurnool, India E5 37
Kurow, N.Z. F3 52
Kursk, Russia G5 22
Kurtistown, Hi., U.S. D6 88
Kuruman, S. Afr. G4 44
Kurume, Japan I3 30
Kurumkan, Russia G16 24
Kurunegala, Sri L. I6 37
Kuşadası Körfezi, b., Tur. L11 16
Kuş Gölü, l., Tur. I11 16
Kushima, Japan K4 30
Kushiro, Japan q22 30
Kushtia, Bngl. I13 38
Kushui, China C5 26
Kuskokwim, stm., Ak., U.S. C8 79
Kuskokwim Bay, b., Ak., U.S. D7 79
Kuskokwim Mountains, mts., Ak., U.S. C8 79
Kūstī, Sudan F12 42
K'us'ur, Russia C19 24
Kut, Ko, i., Thai. I7 34
Kutaisi, Geor. I6 22
Kūt al-Imāra, Iraq B4 46
Kutch, Gulf of, b., India I3 38
Kutina, Cro. D11 14
Kutno, Pol. C19 8
Kutu, Zaire B3 44
Kutztown, Pa., U.S. E10 115
Kuujjuaq, Que., Can. g13 74
Kuusamo, Fin. D17 6
Kuusankoski, Fin. F16 6
Kuvango, Ang. D3 44
Kuwait, ctry., Asia C4 46
Kuwait see Al-Kuwayt, Kuw. C4 46
Kuwana, Japan G9 30
Kuybyshev see Samara, Russia G8 22
Kuzneck, Russia G7 22
Kvikkjokk, Swe. C11 6
Kwando (Cuando), stm., Afr. E4 44
Kwangchow see Guangzhou, China L2 28
Kwangju, S. Kor. D12 26
Kwango (Cuango), stm., Afr. B3 44
Kwekwe, Zimb. E5 44
Kwethluk, Ak., U.S. C7 79

Name	Map Ref	Page
vidzyn, Pol.	B18	8
vigillingok, Ak., U.S.	D7	79
vilu (Cuilo), stm., Afr.	B3	44
aiklat, Burma	F3	34
aikto, Burma	F4	34
le, Tx., U.S.	E4	120
le of Lochalsh, Scot., U.K.	D7	7
oga, Lake, l., Ug.	A6	44
ōto, Japan	G8	30
rgyzstan, ctry., Asia	I12	22
uquot Sound, strt., B.C., Can.	E4	69
ūshū, i., Japan	I3	30
ūshū-sanchi, mts., Japan	J4	30
yjärvi, Fin.	E15	6
zyl, Russia	G12	24
yl-Orda, Kaz.	I11	22
a an der Thaya, Aus.	G16	8
Almunia de Doña Godina, Spain	D10	12
Asunción, Ven.	B11	58
au Point, c., Hi., U.S.	B4	88
Abacou, Pointe, c., Haiti	E11	64
badieville, La., U.S.	E5	95
Bañeza, Spain	C6	12
Barca, Mex.	G8	62
Barge, Wy., U.S.	D2	127
Barge Creek, stm., Wy., U.S.	D2	127
Baule, Fr.	E4	10
bé, Gui.	F3	42
be (Elbe), stm., Eur.	E14	8
Belle, Fl., U.S.	F5	86
Belle, Mo., U.S.	A6	102
bette, co., Ks., U.S.	E8	93
bin, Cro.	D9	14
Bisbal, Spain	D15	12
bouheyre, Fr.	H6	10
brador, reg., Newf., Can.	g9	72
brador City, Newf., Can.	h8	72
brador Sea, N.A.	E22	66
brea, Braz.	E6	54
butta, Burma	F3	34
Canada Flintridge, Ca., U.S.	m12	82
canau, Fr.	H5	10
Cañiza, Spain	C3	12
Canourgue, Fr.	H10	10
Carolina, Spain	G8	12
caune, Fr.	I9	10
c-Bouchette, Que., Can.	A5	74
c-Brome, Que., Can.	D5	74
ccadive Sea, Asia	H3	37
c-Carré, Que., Can.	C3	74
c Courte Oreilles Indian Reservation, Wi., U.S.	C2	126
c du Bonnet, Man., Can.	D3	70
c du Flambeau, Wi., U.S.	B4	126
c du Flambeau Indian Reservation, Wi., U.S.	C3	126
Ceiba, Hond.	G4	64
Ceiba, Ven.	C7	58
Center, Ky., U.S.	e9	94
c-Etchemin, Que., Can.	C7	74
cey, Wa., U.S.	B3	124
Charité [-sur-Loire], Fr.	E10	10
Châtre, Fr.	F8	10
Chaux-de-Fonds, Switz.	E13	10
chine, Que., Can.	D4	74
Chorrera, Col.	H6	58
Chorrera, Pan.	J8	64
chute, Que., Can.	D3	74
Ciotat, Fr.	I12	10
ckawanna, N.Y., U.S.	C2	109
ckawanna, co., Pa., U.S.	D10	115
ckland Air Force Base, mil., Tx., U.S.	k7	120
c La Biche, Alta., Can.	B5	68
c la Hache, B.C., Can.	D7	69
clede, co., Mo., U.S.	D5	102
c-Mégantic, Que., Can.	D7	74
colle, Que., Can.	D4	74
combe, Alta., Can.	C4	68
combe, La., U.S.	D6	95
con, Il., U.S.	B4	90
conia, N.H., U.S.	C4	106
Conner, Wa., U.S.	A3	124
coochee, Fl., U.S.	D4	86
Coruña, Spain	B3	12
c qui Parle, co., Mn., U.S.	F2	100
c qui Parle, stm., Mn., U.S.	F2	100
Creek Lake, l., S.D., U.S.	D4	118
Crescent, Mn., U.S.	G7	100
Crete, Alta., Can.	f7	68
Crosse, In., U.S.	B4	91
Crosse, Ks., U.S.	D4	93
Crosse, Wi., U.S.	E2	126
Crosse, co., Wi., U.S.	E2	126
Crosse, stm., Wi., U.S.	E3	126
Cruz, Nic.	H5	64
Cygne, Ks., U.S.	D9	93
dd, Il., U.S.	B4	90
dies Island, i., S.C., U.S.	G6	117
diz, Iran	C7	46
dnun, India	G6	38
doga, In., U.S.	E4	91
doga, Lake see Ladožskoje Ozero, l., Russia	F18	6
Dorada, Col.	E5	58
dožskoje Ozero (Lake Ladoga), l., Russia	F18	6
dson, S.C., U.S.	F7	117
dy Lake, Fl., U.S.	D5	86
dy Laurier, Mount, mtn., B.C., Can.	A6	69
dysmith, B.C., Can.	E6	69
dysmith, S. Afr.	G5	44
dysmith, Wi., U.S.	C2	126
e, Pap. N. Gui.	m16	50a
Encantada, Cerro de, mtn., Mex.	B2	62
Esmeralda, Ven.	F10	58
La Esperanza, Hond.	G3	64
La Estrada, Spain	C3	12
La Farge, Wi., U.S.	E3	126
Lafayette, Al., U.S.	C4	78
Lafayette, Co., U.S.	B5	83
Lafayette, Ga., U.S.	B1	87
Lafayette, In., U.S.	D4	91
Lafayette, La., U.S.	D3	95
Lafayette, N.C., U.S.	B3	110
Lafayette, Or., U.S.	B3	114
La Fayette, R.I., U.S.	E4	116
Lafayette, Tn., U.S.	A5	119
Lafayette, co., Ar., U.S.	D2	81
Lafayette, co., Fl., U.S.	C3	86
Lafayette, co., La., U.S.	D3	95
Lafayette, co., Ms., U.S.	A4	101
Lafayette, co., Mo., U.S.	B4	102
Lafayette, co., Wi., U.S.	F3	126
Lafayette, Mount, mtn., N.H., U.S.	B3	106
La Feria, Tx., U.S.	F4	120
La Ferté-Bernard, Fr.	D7	10
La Ferté-Macé, Fr.	D6	10
La Ferté-Saint-Aubin, Fr.	E8	10
Lafia, Nig.	G7	42
Lafitte, La., U.S.	k11	95
La Flèche, Fr.	E6	10
La Follette, Tn., U.S.	C9	119
La Fontaine, In., U.S.	C6	91
La Fortuna, C.R.	I5	64
Lafourche, La., U.S.	E5	95
Lafourche, co., La., U.S.	E5	95
La France, S.C., U.S.	B2	117
La Fregeneda, Spain	E5	12
La Fría, Ven.	C6	58
La Fuente de San Esteban, Spain	E5	12
Lågen, stm., Nor.	F8	6
Laghouat, Alg.	B6	42
Lago, Mount, mtn., Wa., U.S.	A5	124
Lagonegro, Italy	I10	14
Lagos, Nig.	G6	42
Lagos de Moreno, Mex.	G9	62
La Goulette, Tun.	M5	14
La Grand'Combe, Fr.	H11	10
La Grande, Or., U.S.	B8	114
La Grande, stm., Que., Can.	h11	74
La Grande Deux, Réservoir, res., Que., Can.	h11	74
La Grange, Austl.	C4	50
La Grange, Ga., U.S.	C1	87
La Grange, Il., U.S.	B6	90
Lagrange, In., U.S.	A7	91
La Grange, Ky., U.S.	B4	94
La Grange, Mo., U.S.	A6	102
La Grange, N.C., U.S.	B5	110
Lagrange, Oh., U.S.	A3	112
La Grange, Tx., U.S.	E4	120
Lagrange, co., In., U.S.	A7	91
La Grange Park, Il., U.S.	k9	90
La Gran Sabana, pl., Ven.	E12	58
La Grita, Ven.	C7	58
La Guadeloupe (Saint-Evariste), Que., Can.	D7	74
La Guaira, Ven.	B9	58
La Guajira, Península de, pen., S.A.	A7	58
Laguardia, Spain	C9	12
La Guardia, Spain	D3	12
La Guerche-de-Britagne, Fr.	E5	10
La Guerche-sur-l'aubois, Fr.	F9	10
Laguiole, Fr.	H9	10
Laguna, N.M., U.S.	B2	108
Laguna Beach, Ca., U.S.	F5	82
Laguna Dam, U.S.	E1	80
Laguna Indian Reservation, N.M., U.S.	C2	108
Lagunillas, Bol.	G6	54
La Habana (Havana), Cuba	C6	64
La Habra, Ca., U.S.	n13	82
Lahaina, Hi., U.S.	C5	88
La Harpe, Il., U.S.	C3	90
La Harpe, Ks., U.S.	E8	93
Lahat, Indon.	F3	32
La Have, stm., N.S., Can.	E5	71
La Haye-du-Puits, Fr.	C5	10
Lahij, Yemen	F3	46
Laholm, Swe.	H9	6
Lahoma, Ok., U.S.	A3	113
Lahontan Reservoir, res., Nv., U.S.	D2	105
Lahore, Pak.	E6	38
Lahr, Ger.	G7	8
Lahti, Fin.	F15	6
Laie, Hi., U.S.	B4	88
L'Aigle, Fr.	D7	10
Laignes, Fr.	E11	10
Laihia, Fin.	E14	6
Laingsburg, S. Afr.	H4	44
Laingsburg, Mi., U.S.	F6	99
Lairg, Scot., U.K.	C8	7
Laissac, Fr.	H9	10
Laiyang, China	D11	26
La Jara, Co., U.S.	D5	83
Lajes, Braz.	E11	54
La Jolla, Point, c., Ca., U.S.	o15	82
La Joya, Mex.	A2	62
La Junta, Mex.	C6	62
La Junta, Co., U.S.	D7	83
Lake, co., Ca., U.S.	C2	82
Lake, co., Co., U.S.	B4	83
Lake, co., Fl., U.S.	D5	86
Lake, co., Il., U.S.	A6	90
Lake, co., In., U.S.	B3	91
Lake, co., Mi., U.S.	E5	99
Lake, co., Mn., U.S.	C7	100
Lake, co., Mt., U.S.	C2	103
Lake, co., Oh., U.S.	A4	112
Lake, co., Or., U.S.	E6	114
Lake, co., S.D., U.S.	C8	118
Lake, co., Tn., U.S.	A2	119
Lake Alfred, Fl., U.S.	D5	86
Lake Andes, S.D., U.S.	D7	118
Lake Ariel, Pa., U.S.	D11	115
Lake Arrowhead, Ca., U.S.	E5	82
Lake Arthur, La., U.S.	D3	95
Lake Barcroft, Va., U.S.	*B5	123
Lake Benton, Mn., U.S.	F2	100
Lake Bluff, Il., U.S.	A6	90
Lake Butler, Fl., U.S.	B4	86
Lake Charles, La., U.S.	D2	95
Lake Chelan National Recreation Area, Wa., U.S.	A5	124
Lake City, Ar., U.S.	B5	81
Lake City, Fl., U.S.	B4	86
Lake City, Ia., U.S.	B3	92
Lake City, Mi., U.S.	D5	99
Lake City, Mn., U.S.	F6	100
Lake City, Pa., U.S.	B1	115
Lake City, S.C., U.S.	D8	117
Lake City, Tn., U.S.	C9	119
Lake Clark National Park, Ak., U.S.	C9	79
Lake Cowichan, B.C., Can.	g11	69
Lake Creek, stm., Wa., U.S.	B7	124
Lake Crystal, Mn., U.S.	F4	100
Lake Delta, N.Y., U.S.	B5	109
Lake Delton, Wi., U.S.	E4	126
Lake District National Park, Eng., U.K.	G9	7
Lake Elsinore, Ca., U.S.	F5	82
Lake Erie Beach, N.Y., U.S.	C1	109
Lakefield, Ont., Can.	C6	73
Lakefield, Mn., U.S.	G3	100
Lake Forest, Il., U.S.	A6	90
Lake Fork, stm., Ut., U.S.	C5	121
Lake Geneva, Wi., U.S.	F5	126
Lake Hamilton, Ar., U.S.	g7	81
Lake Harbour, N.W. Ter., Can.	D19	66
Lake Havasu City, Az., U.S.	C1	80
Lake Helen, Fl., U.S.	D5	86
Lakehurst, N.J., U.S.	C4	107
Lakehurst Naval Air Station, mil., N.J., U.S.	C4	107
Lake in the Hills, Il., U.S.	h8	90
Lake Jackson, Tx., U.S.	r14	120
Lake Katrine, N.Y., U.S.	D7	109
Lakeland, Fl., U.S.	D5	86
Lakeland, Ga., U.S.	E3	87
Lake Linden, Mi., U.S.	A2	99
Lake Louise, Alta., Can.	D2	68
Lake Magdalene, Fl., U.S.	o11	86
Lake Mary, Fl., U.S.	D5	86
Lake Mead National Recreation Area, U.S.	H7	105
Lake Meredith National Recreation Area, Tx., U.S.	B2	120
Lake Mills, Ia., U.S.	A4	92
Lake Mills, Wi., U.S.	E5	126
Lakemore, Oh., U.S.	A4	112
Lake Mountain, mtn., Wy., U.S.	E6	127
Lake Nebagamon, Wi., U.S.	B2	126
Lake Odessa, Mi., U.S.	F5	99
Lake of the Woods, co., Mn., U.S.	B4	100
Lake Orion, Mi., U.S.	F7	99
Lake Oswego, Or., U.S.	B4	114
Lake Ozark, Mo., U.S.	C5	102
Lake Park, Fl., U.S.	F6	86
Lake Park, Ia., U.S.	A2	92
Lake Park, Mn., U.S.	D2	100
Lake Placid, Fl., U.S.	E5	86
Lake Placid, N.Y., U.S.	A7	109
Lake Pontchartrain Causeway, La., U.S.	h11	95
Lakeport, Ca., U.S.	C2	82
Lake Preston, S.D., U.S.	C8	118
Lake Providence, La., U.S.	B4	95
Lake Range, mts., Nv., U.S.	C2	105
Lake Ridge, Va., U.S.	*B5	123
Lake Shore, Md., U.S.	B5	97
Lakeshore, Ms., U.S.	E4	101
Lakeside, Az., U.S.	C6	80
Lakeside, Ca., U.S.	F5	82
Lakeside, Ct., U.S.	D3	84
Lakeside, Mt., U.S.	B2	103
Lakeside, Oh., U.S.	A3	112
Lakeside, Or., U.S.	D2	114
Lakeside Park, Ky., U.S.	h13	94
Lake Station, In., U.S.	A3	91
Lake Station, Ok., U.S.	A5	113
Lake Stevens, Wa., U.S.	A3	124
Lake Superior Provincial Park, Ont., Can.	p18	73
Lake Swamp, stm., S.C., U.S.	D8	117
Lake Tansi Village, Tn., U.S.	D8	119
Lake Valley, val., Nv., U.S.	E7	105
Lake View, Ia., U.S.	B2	92
Lakeview, Mi., U.S.	E5	99
Lakeview, Oh., U.S.	B2	112
Lakeview, Or., U.S.	E6	114
Lake View, S.C., U.S.	C9	117
Lake Villa, Il., U.S.	h8	90
Lake Village, Ar., U.S.	D4	81
Lake Village, In., U.S.	B3	91
Lakeville, Ct., U.S.	B2	84
Lakeville, In., U.S.	A5	91
Lakeville, Ma., U.S.	C6	98
Lakeville, Mn., U.S.	F5	100
Lake Waccamaw, N.C., U.S.	C4	110
Lake Wales, Fl., U.S.	E5	86
Lakewood, Ca., U.S.	n12	82
Lakewood, Co., U.S.	B5	83
Lakewood, Il., U.S.	D5	90
Lakewood, Ia., U.S.	f8	92
Lakewood, N.J., U.S.	C4	107
Lakewood, N.Y., U.S.	C1	109
Lakewood, Oh., U.S.	A4	112
Lakewood Center, Wa., U.S.	B3	124
Lake Worth, Fl., U.S.	F6	86
Lake Worth Inlet, b., Fl., U.S.	F7	86
Lake Zurich, Il., U.S.	h8	90
Lakhīmpur, India	G9	38
Lakin, Ks., U.S.	E2	93
Lakota, N.D., U.S.	A7	111
Lakselv, Nor.	A15	6
Lakshadweep, state, India	H3	37
Lakshadweep, is., India	H2	37
Lalbenque, Fr.	H8	10
La Libertad, Guat.	F2	64
La Libertad, Mex.	C3	62
Lalinde, Fr.	H7	10
La Línea, Spain	I6	12
Lalitpur, India	H8	38
Lalitpur, Nepal	G11	38
La Loupe, Fr.	D8	10
La Luz, N.M., U.S.	E4	108
Lama, Ozero, l., Russia	D12	24
La Maddalena, Italy	H4	14
La Madrid, Arg.	B3	56
La Malbaie, Que., Can.	B7	74
La Mancha, Mex.	E8	62
La Mancha, reg., Spain	G8	12
Lamar, Ar., U.S.	B2	81
Lamar, Co., U.S.	C8	83
Lamar, Mo., U.S.	D3	102
Lamar, Pa., U.S.	D7	115
Lamar, S.C., U.S.	C7	117
Lamar, co., Al., U.S.	B1	78
Lamar, co., Ga., U.S.	C2	87
Lamar, co., Ms., U.S.	D4	101
Lamar, co., Tx., U.S.	C5	120
Lamar, stm., Wy., U.S.	B2	127
Lamarche, Fr.	D12	10
La Mauricie, Parc National de, Que., Can.	C5	74
Lamb, co., Tx., U.S.	B1	120
Lamballe, Fr.	D4	10
Lambaréné, Gabon	B2	44
Lambert, Ms., U.S.	A3	101
Lambert Glacier, Ant.	B19	47
Lamberton, Mn., U.S.	F3	100
Lambert's Bay, S. Afr.	H3	44
Lambertville, Mi., U.S.	G7	99
Lambertville, N.J., U.S.	C3	107
Lambton, Cape, c., N.W. Ter., Can.	B8	66
Lame Deer, Mt., U.S.	E10	103
Lamego, Port.	D4	12
Lamèque, N.B., Can.	B5	71
Lamèque, Île, i., N.B., Can.	B5	71
La Mesa, Ca., U.S.	F5	82
La Mesa, N.M., U.S.	E3	108
Lamesa, Tx., U.S.	C2	120
Lamía, Grc.	K6	16
Lamoille, Nv., U.S.	C6	105
Lamoille, co., Vt., U.S.	B3	122
Lamoille, stm., Vt., U.S.	B3	122
La Moine, stm., Il., U.S.	C3	90
Lamoni, Ia., U.S.	D4	92
Lamont, Alta., Can.	C4	68
Lamont, Ca., U.S.	E4	82
La Monte, Mo., U.S.	C4	102
La Motte, Isle, i., Vt., U.S.	B2	122
Lamotte-Beuvron, Fr.	E9	10
La Moure, N.D., U.S.	C7	111
La Moure, co., N.D., U.S.	C7	111
Lampang, Thai.	E5	34
Lampasas, Tx., U.S.	D3	120
Lampasas, co., Tx., U.S.	D3	120
Lampedusa, Isola di, i., Italy	N7	14
Lampertheim, Ger.	F8	8
Lampman, Sask., Can.	H4	75
Lamprey, stm., N.H., U.S.	D4	106
Lamu, Kenya	B8	44
La Mure, Fr.	H12	10
Lanai, i., Hi., U.S.	C4	88
Lanai City, Hi., U.S.	C5	88
Lanaihale, mtn., Hi., U.S.	C5	88
Lanark, Ont., Can.	C8	73
Lanark, Il., U.S.	A4	90
Lanark, W.V., U.S.	D3	125
Lanbi Kyun, i., Burma	I5	34
Lancaster, Ont., Can.	B10	73
Lancaster, Eng., U.K.	G10	7
Lancaster, Ca., U.S.	E4	82
Lancaster, Ky., U.S.	C5	94
Lancaster, Mo., U.S.	A5	102
Lancaster, N.H., U.S.	B3	106
Lancaster, N.Y., U.S.	C2	109
Lancaster, Oh., U.S.	C3	112
Lancaster, Pa., U.S.	F9	115
Lancaster, S.C., U.S.	B6	117
Lancaster, Tx., U.S.	n10	120
Lancaster, Wi., U.S.	F3	126
Lancaster, co., Ne., U.S.	D9	104
Lancaster, co., Pa., U.S.	G9	115
Lancaster, co., S.C., U.S.	B6	117
Lancaster, co., Va., U.S.	C6	123
Lancaster Sound, strt., N.W. Ter., Can.	B16	66
Lance Creek, stm., Wy., U.S.	C8	127
Lanciano, Italy	G9	14
Landau, Ger.	F8	8
Landau an der Isar, Ger.	G12	8
Land Between the Lakes, U.S.	f9	94
Lander, Wy., U.S.	D4	127
Lander, co., Nv., U.S.	C4	105
Landerneau, Fr.	D2	10
Landess, In., U.S.	C6	91
Landete, Spain	F10	12
Landis, N.C., U.S.	B2	110
Lando, S.C., U.S.	B5	117
Landquart, Switz.	F16	10
Landrum, S.C., U.S.	A3	117
Land's End, c., Eng., U.K.	K7	7
Lands End, c., R.I., U.S.	F5	116
Landshut, Ger.	G12	8
Landskrona, Swe.	I9	6
Lane, co., Ks., U.S.	D3	93
Lane, co., Or., U.S.	C4	114
Lanesboro, Mn., U.S.	G7	100
Lanett, Al., U.S.	C4	78
Langar, Afg.	B5	38
Långban, Swe.	G10	6
Langdon, N.D., U.S.	A7	111
Langeac, Fr.	G10	10
Langeais, Fr.	E7	10
Langeloth, Pa., U.S.	F1	115
Langenhagen, Ger.	C9	8
Langenthal, Switz.	E14	10
Langholm, Scot., U.K.	F9	7
Langhorne, Pa., U.S.	F12	115
Langlade, co., Wi., U.S.	C4	126
Langley, B.C., Can.	f13	69
Langley, S.C., U.S.	E4	117
Langley, Wa., U.S.	A3	124
Langley Air Force Base, mil., Va., U.S.	h15	123
Langley Park, Md., U.S.	f9	97
Langnau, Switz.	F14	10
Langogne, Fr.	H10	10
Langon, Fr.	H6	10
Langres, Fr.	E1	10
Langsa, Indon.	E2	32
Lang Son, Viet.	D9	34
Langston, Ok., U.S.	B4	113
Languedoc, hist. reg., Fr.	I9	10
L'Anguille, stm., Ar., U.S.	B5	81
Langzhong, China	E8	26
Lanham, Md., U.S.	C4	97
Lanier, co., Ga., U.S.	E3	87
Lannemezan, Fr.	I7	10
Lannilis, Fr.	D2	10
Lannion, Fr.	D3	10
Lannon, Wi., U.S.	m11	126
L'Annonciation, Que., Can.	C3	74
Lansdale, Pa., U.S.	F11	115
Lansdowne, Md., U.S.	B4	97
L'Anse, Mi., U.S.	B2	99
L'Anse-au-Loup, Newf., Can.	C3	72
L'Anse Indian Reservation, Mi., U.S.	B2	99
Lansford, Pa., U.S.	E10	115
Lansing, Il., U.S.	B6	90
Lansing, Ia., U.S.	A6	92
Lansing, Ks., U.S.	C9	93
Lansing, Mi., U.S.	F6	99
Lantana, Fl., U.S.	F6	86
Lantau Island, i., H.K.	M2	28
Lanusei, Italy	J4	14
Lanxi, China	F8	28
Lanzarote, i., Spain	p27	13b
Lanzhou, China	D7	26
Laoag, Phil.	B7	32
Lao Cai, Viet.	C7	34
Laon, Fr.	C10	10
La Oroya, Peru	F3	54
Laos, ctry., Asia	B3	32
Lapalisse, Fr.	F10	10
La Palma, Col.	E5	58
La Palma, Pan.	J8	64
La Palma, i., Spain	p23	13b
La Paragua, Ven.	D11	58
La Paz, Arg.	C5	56
La Paz, Arg.	C3	56
La Paz, Bol.	G5	54
La Paz, Mex.	E4	62
La Paz, co., Az., U.S.	D2	80
La Paz, Bahía de, b., Mex.	E4	62
Lapeer, Mi., U.S.	E7	99
Lapeer, co., Mi., U.S.	E7	99
Lapel, In., U.S.	D6	91
La Perouse Strait, strt., Asia	B15	26
La Piedad [Cavadas], Mex.	G8	62
La Pine, Or., U.S.	D5	114
Lapinlahti, Fin.	E16	6
La Place, La., U.S.	h11	95
Lapland, reg., Eur.	C14	6
La Plata, Arg.	C5	56
La Plata, Md., U.S.	C4	97
La Plata, Mo., U.S.	A5	102
La Plata, co., Co., U.S.	D3	83
La Plata Mountains, mts., Co., U.S.	D3	83
La Plata Peak, mtn., Co., U.S.	B4	83
La Platte, stm., Vt., U.S.	C2	122
La Pocatière, Que., Can.	B7	74
Laporte, Co., U.S.	A5	83
La Porte, In., U.S.	A4	91
La Porte, Tx., U.S.	r14	120
La Porte, co., In., U.S.	A4	91
La Porte City, Ia., U.S.	B5	92
Lappeenranta, Fin.	F17	6
La Prairie, Que., Can.	D4	74
La Pryor, Tx., U.S.	E3	120
Laptevych, More (Laptev Sea), Russia	B19	24
Lapua, Fin.	E14	6
La Puebla, Spain	F15	12
La Puebla de Montalbán, Spain	F7	12
La Push, Wa., U.S.	B1	124
Lapwai, Id., U.S.	C2	89
La Quiaca, Arg.	A3	56
L'Aquila, Italy	G8	14
Lār, Iran	C5	46
Larache, Mor.	A4	42
Laramie, Wy., U.S.	E7	127
Laramie, co., Wy., U.S.	E8	127
Laramie, stm., U.S.	E7	127
Laramie Mountains, mts., Wy., U.S.	D7	127
Laramie Peak, mtn., Wy., U.S.	D7	127
Larantuka, Indon.	G7	32
L'Arbresle, Fr.	G11	10
Lärbro, Swe.	H12	6
Larche, Col de, Eur.	H13	10
Larchmont, N.Y., U.S.	h13	109
Larchwood, Ia., U.S.	A1	92
Laredo, Tx., U.S.	F3	120
La Réole, Fr.	H6	10
Largeau, Chad	E9	42
L'argentière-la-Bessée, Fr.	H13	10
Lar Gerd, Afg.	C2	38
Largo, Fl., U.S.	E4	86
Largo, Cañon, val., N.M., U.S.	A2	108
Largo, Key, i., Fl., U.S.	G6	86
Largs, Scot., U.K.	F8	7
Larimer, co., Co., U.S.	A5	83
Larimore, N.D., U.S.	B8	111
La Rioja, Arg.	B3	56
Lárisa, Grc.	J6	16
Larjak, Russia	E10	24
Lārkāna, Pak.	G3	38
Lark Harbour, Newf., Can.	D2	72
Larkspur, Ca., U.S.	h7	82
Larksville, Pa., U.S.	n17	115
Lárnax (Larnaca), Cyp.	B3	40
Larne, N. Ire., U.K.	G7	7
Larned, Ks., U.S.	D4	93
La Robla, Spain	C6	12
La Roca de la Sierra, Spain	F5	12
La Rochefoucauld, Fr.	G7	10
La Rochelle, Fr.	F5	10
La Roche-sur-Yon, Fr.	F5	10
La Roda, Spain	F9	12
La Romana, Dom. Rep.	E13	64

Name — Map Ref — Page

Laroquebrou, Fr. H9 10
Larose, La., U.S. E5 95
La Rubia, Arg. C4 56
Larue, co., Ky., U.S. C4 94
Laruns, Fr. J6 10
Larvik, Nor. G7 6
LaSalle, Que., Can. q19 74
La Salle, Co., U.S. A6 83
La Salle, Il., U.S. B4 90
La Salle, co., Il., U.S. B4 90
La Salle, co., La., U.S. C3 95
La Salle, co., Tx., U.S. E3 120
Las Animas, Co., U.S. C7 83
Las Animas, co., Co., U.S. D6 83
Las Anod, Som. G4 46
La Sarre, Que., Can. k11 74
Las Casitas, Cerro, mtn., Mex. F5 62
Las Choapas, Mex. I12 62
La Scie, Newf., Can. D4 72
Las Colimas, Mex. E10 62
Las Cruces, N.M., U.S. E3 108
Las Delicias, Mex. J14 62
La Selle, Pic, mtn., Haiti E11 64
La Serena, Chile B2 56
Las Escobas, Mex. B2 62
La Seyne, Fr. I12 10
Las Flores, Arg. D5 56
Lashio, Burma C4 34
Laško, Slo. C10 14
Las Lomitas, Arg. A4 56
Las Minas, Cerro, mtn., Hond. G3 64
La Solana, Spain G8 12
Las Palmas de Gran Canaria, Spain p25 13b
La Spezia, Italy E4 14
Las Piedras, Ur. C5 56
Las Plumas, Arg. E3 56
Lassen, co., Ca., U.S. B3 82
Lassen Peak, vol., Ca., U.S. B3 82
Lassen Volcanic National Park, Ca., U.S. B3 82
L'Assomption, Que., Can. D4 74
Las Termas, Arg. B4 56
Last Mountain Lake, l., Sask., Can. F3 75
Las Tórtolas, Cerro, mtn., S.A. B3 56
Las Varas, Mex. C5 62
Las Vegas, Nv., U.S. G6 105
Las Vegas, N.M., U.S. B4 108
Latacunga, Ec. H3 58
Latah, co., Id., U.S. C2 89
Latakia see Al-Lādhiqīyah, Syria B4 40
La Teste-de-Buch, Fr. H5 10
Lathrop, Mo., U.S. B3 102
Lathrop Wells, Nv., U.S. G5 105
Latimer, co., Ok., U.S. C6 113
Latina, Italy H7 14
Laton, Ca., U.S. D4 82
La Tortuga, Isla, i., Ven. B10 58
Latour Peak, mtn., Id., U.S. B2 89
Latrobe, Pa., U.S. F3 115
Latta, S.C., U.S. C9 117
La Tuque, Que., Can. B5 74
Lātūr, India C4 37
Latvia, ctry., Eur. E7 18
Lauchhammer, Ger. D13 8
Lauderdale, Ms., U.S. C5 101
Lauderdale, co., Al., U.S. A2 78
Lauderdale, co., Ms., U.S. C5 101
Lauderdale, co., Tn., U.S. B2 119
Lauderdale Lakes, Fl., U.S. r13 86
Lauenburg, Ger. B10 8
Laughlin, Nv., U.S. H7 105
Laughlin Air Force Base, mil., Tx., U.S. E2 120
Laughlin Peak, mtn., N.M., U.S. A5 108
Laughlintown, Pa., U.S. F3 115
Launceston, Austl. H9 50
Launceston, Eng., U.K. K8 7
Launching Point, c., P.E.I., Can. C7 71
La Union, El Sal. H4 64
La Unión, Spain H11 12
La Unión, Ven. C9 58
La Urbana, Ven. D9 58
Laurel, De., U.S. F3 85
Laurel, Fl., U.S. E4 86
Laurel, Md., U.S. B4 97
Laurel, Ms., U.S. D4 101
Laurel, Mt., U.S. E8 103
Laurel, Ne., U.S. B8 104
Laurel, Va., U.S. C5 123
Laurel, co., Ky., U.S. C5 94
Laurel, stm., Ky., U.S. D5 94
Laurel Bay, S.C., U.S. G6 117
Laurel Creek, stm., W.V., U.S. n14 125
Laurel Creek, stm., W.V., U.S. m12 125
Laureldale, Pa., U.S. F10 115
Laurel Fork, stm., W.V., U.S. C5 125
Laurel Hill, N.C., U.S. C3 110
Laurel River Lake, res., Ky., U.S. D5 94
Laurence G. Hanscom Air Force Base, mil., Ma., U.S. g10 98
Laurence Harbor, N.J., U.S. C4 107
Laurens, Ia., U.S. B3 92
Laurens, S.C., U.S. C3 117
Laurens, co., Ga., U.S. D4 87
Laurens, co., S.C., U.S. C4 117
Laurentides, Que., Can. D4 74
Laurentides, Parc Provincial des, Que., Can. B6 74
Laurier, Que., Can. C6 74
Laurière, Fr. F8 10
Laurierville, Que., Can. C6 74
Laurinburg, N.C., U.S. C3 110
Laurium, Mi., U.S. A2 99
Lausanne, Switz. F13 10
Laut, Pulau, i., Indon. F6 32
Laut, Pulau, i., Indon. L9 34
Lautaro, Chile D2 56
Lauterbach, Ger. E9 8
Laut Kecil, Kepulauan, is., Indon. F6 32
Lauzon (part of Lévis-Lauzon), Que., Can. C6 74
Lava Beds National Monument, Ca., U.S. B3 82
Lavaca, Ar., U.S. B1 81
Lavaca, co., Tx., U.S. E4 120
Lavagh More, mtn., Ire. G4 7
Laval, Que., Can. D4 74
Laval, Fr. D6 10
La Vale, Md., U.S. k13 97
Lavaltrie, Que., Can. D4 74
Lavapié, Punta, c., Chile D2 56
Laveen, Az., U.S. m8 80
La Vega, Dom. Rep. E12 64
La Vela, Cabo de, c., Col. A6 58
Lavello, Italy H10 14
L'Avenir, Que., Can. D5 74
La Vergne, Tn., U.S. A5 119
La Verkin, Ut., U.S. F2 121
La Verne, Ca., U.S. m13 82
Laverne, Ok., U.S. A2 113
La Veta, Co., U.S. D5 83
Lavia, Fin. F14 6
La Vista, Ga., U.S. *h8 87
La Vista, Ne., U.S. g12 104
Lavonia, Ga., U.S. B3 87
Lavon Lake, res., Tx., U.S. m10 120
La Voulte-sur-Rhône, Fr. H11 10
Lavras, Braz. F6 57
Lawai, Hi., U.S. B2 88
Lawang, Indon. m16 33a
Lawers, Ben, mtn., Scot., U.K. E8 7
Lawn, Newf., Can. E4 72
Lawrence, In., U.S. E5 91
Lawrence, Ks., U.S. D8 93
Lawrence, Ma., U.S. A5 98
Lawrence, Mi., U.S. F4 99
Lawrence, N.Y., U.S. k13 109
Lawrence, co., Al., U.S. A2 78
Lawrence, co., Ar., U.S. A4 81
Lawrence, co., Il., U.S. E6 90
Lawrence, co., In., U.S. G4 91
Lawrence, co., Ky., U.S. B7 94
Lawrence, co., Ms., U.S. D3 101
Lawrence, co., Mo., U.S. D4 102
Lawrence, co., Oh., U.S. D3 112
Lawrence, co., Pa., U.S. E1 115
Lawrence, co., Tn., U.S. B4 119
Lawrenceburg, In., U.S. F8 91
Lawrenceburg, Ky., U.S. B5 94
Lawrenceburg, Tn., U.S. B4 119
Lawrence Park, Pa., U.S. B1 115
Lawrenceville, Ga., U.S. C3 87
Lawrenceville, Il., U.S. E6 90
Lawrenceville, Va., U.S. D5 123
Lawson, Mo., U.S. B3 102
Lawsonia, Md., U.S. E6 97
Lawtell, La., U.S. D3 95
Lawton, Mi., U.S. F5 99
Lawton, Ok., U.S. C3 113
Lawz, Jabal al-, mtn., Sau. Ar. C2 46
Lay Lake, res., Al., U.S. B3 78
Laysan Island, i., Hi., U.S. k13 88
Layton, Ut., U.S. B4 121
La Zarca, Mex. E7 62
Lazarev, Russia G22 24
Lazi, China F12 38
Lea, co., N.M., U.S. D6 108
Leachville, Ar., U.S. B5 81
Lead, S.D., U.S. C2 118
Leadbetter Point, c., Wa., U.S. C1 124
Leadville, Co., U.S. B4 83
Leadwood, Mo., U.S. D7 102
Leaf, stm., Ms., U.S. D5 101
Leaf Rapids, Man., Can. A1 70
Leake, co., Ms., U.S. C4 101
Leakesville, Ms., U.S. D5 101
Lealman, Fl., U.S. p10 86
Leamington, Ont., Can. E2 73
Leary, Ga., U.S. E2 87
Leatherman Peak, mtn., Id., U.S. E5 89
Leavenworth, Ks., U.S. C9 93
Leavenworth, Wa., U.S. B5 124
Leavenworth, co., Ks., U.S. C8 93
Leavittsburg, Oh., U.S. A5 112
Leawood, Ks., U.S. D9 93
Lebanon, De., U.S. D4 85
Lebanon, Il., U.S. E4 90
Lebanon, In., U.S. D5 91
Lebanon, Ky., U.S. C4 94
Lebanon, Mo., U.S. D5 102
Lebanon, N.H., U.S. C2 106
Lebanon, Oh., U.S. C1 112
Lebanon, Or., U.S. C4 114
Lebanon, Pa., U.S. F9 115
Lebanon, Tn., U.S. A5 119
Lebanon, Va., U.S. f9 123
Lebanon, co., Pa., U.S. F8 115
Lebanon, ctry., Asia C4 40
Lebanon Junction, Ky., U.S. C4 94
Le Blanc, Fr. F8 10
Lebo, Ks., U.S. D8 93
Lębork, Pol. A17 8
Lebrija, Spain I5 12
Lecce, Italy I13 14
Lecco, Italy D4 14
Le Center, Mn., U.S. F5 100
Le Cheylard, Fr. H11 10
Le Claire, Ia., U.S. C7 92
Lecompte, La., U.S. C3 95
Lecompton, Ks., U.S. C8 93
Le Creusot, Fr. F11 10
Le Dorat, Fr. F8 10
Leduc, Alta., Can. C4 68
Lee, Ma., U.S. B1 98
Lee, co., Al., U.S. C4 78
Lee, co., Ar., U.S. C5 81
Lee, co., Fl., U.S. F5 86
Lee, co., Ga., U.S. E2 87
Lee, co., Il., U.S. B4 90
Lee, co., Ia., U.S. D6 92
Lee, co., Ky., U.S. C6 94
Lee, co., Ms., U.S. A5 101
Lee, co., N.C., U.S. B3 110
Lee, co., S.C., U.S. C7 117
Lee, co., Tx., U.S. D4 120
Lee, co., Va., U.S. f8 123
Lee, Lake, l., Ms., U.S. B3 101
Leechburg, Pa., U.S. E2 115
Leech Lake, l., Mn., U.S. C4 100
Leech Lake Indian Reservation, Mn., U.S. C4 100
Lee Creek, stm., U.S. B1 81
Leeds, Eng., U.K. H11 7
Leeds, Al., U.S. B3 78
Leelanau, co., Mi., U.S. D5 99
Leelanau, Lake, l., Mi., U.S. C5 99
Lee Park, Pa., U.S. n17 115
Leer, Ger. B7 8
Leesburg, Fl., U.S. D5 86
Leesburg, Ga., U.S. E2 87
Leesburg, Oh., U.S. C2 112
Leesburg, Va., U.S. A5 123
Lees Summit, Mo., U.S. C3 102
Leesville, La., U.S. C2 95
Leesville, S.C., U.S. D4 117
Leesville Lake, res., Va., U.S. C3 123
Leeton, Mo., U.S. C4 102
Leetonia, Oh., U.S. B5 112
Leetsdale, Pa., U.S. h13 115
Leeuwarden, Neth. B5 8
Leeuwin, Cape, c., Austl. F3 50
Leeward Islands, is., N.A. F17 64
Leflore, co., Ms., U.S. B3 101
Le Flore, co., Ok., U.S. C7 113
Legal, Alta., Can. C4 68
Legazpi, Phil. r20 33b
Leghorn see Livorno, Italy F5 14
Legnago, Italy D6 14
Legnano, Italy D3 14
Legnica (Liegnitz), Pol. D16 8
Le Grand, Ca., U.S. D3 82
Le Grand, Ia., U.S. B5 92
Le Havre, Fr. C7 10
Lehi, Ut., U.S. C4 121
Lehigh, co., Pa., U.S. E10 115
Lehigh, stm., Pa., U.S. E10 115
Lehigh Acres, Fl., U.S. F5 86
Lehighton, Pa., U.S. E10 115
Lehua Island, i., Hi., U.S. A1 88
Lehututu, Bots. F4 44
Leiah, Pak. E4 38
Leibnitz, Aus. I15 8
Leicester, Eng., U.K. I11 7
Leicester, Ma., U.S. B4 98
Leichhardt, stm., Austl. C7 50
Leiden, Neth. C4 8
Leighton, Al., U.S. A2 78
Leikanger, Nor. F6 6
Leinster, hist. reg., Ire. H5 7
Leinster, Mount, mtn., Ire. I6 7
Leipsic, De., U.S. D3 85
Leipsic, Oh., U.S. A2 112
Leipsic, stm., De., U.S. C3 85
Leipzig, Ger. D12 8
Leiria, Port. F3 12
Leisler, Mount, mtn., Austl. D5 50
Leisure City, Fl., U.S. s13 86
Leitchfield, Ky., U.S. C3 94
Leitrim, Ire. G4 7
Leiyang, China I1 28
Leizhou Bandao, pen., China D11 34
Leland, Il., U.S. B5 90
Leland, Ms., U.S. B3 101
Leleiwi Point, c., Hi., U.S. D7 88
Leleque, Arg. E2 56
Le Lion-d'Angers, Fr. E6 10
Leli Shan, mtn., China D9 38
Le Locle, Switz. E13 10
Le Lude, Fr. E7 10
Le Maire, Estrecho de, strt., Arg. G4 56
Le Mans, Fr. D7 10
Le Mars, Ia., U.S. B1 92
Leme, Braz. G5 57
Lemesós (Limassol), Cyp. B3 40
Lemgo, Ger. C8 8
Lemhi, co., Id., U.S. E4 89
Lemhi, stm., Id., U.S. E5 89
Lemhi Pass, Id., U.S. E5 89
Lemhi Range, mts., Id., U.S. E5 89
Lemmon, S.D., U.S. B3 118
Lemmon, Mount, mtn., Az., U.S. E5 80
Lemmon Valley, Nv., U.S. D2 105
Lemon, Lake, l., In., U.S. F5 91
Lemon Fair, stm., Vt., U.S. C2 122
Lemon Grove, Ca., U.S. o15 82
Lemon Island, i., S.C., U.S. G6 117
Lemont, Il., U.S. B5 90
Lemont, Pa., U.S. E6 115
Lemonweir, stm., Wi., U.S. D3 126
Lemoore, Ca., U.S. D4 82
Lemoore Naval Air Station, mil., Ca., U.S. D4 82
Lempa, stm., N.A. H3 64
Lem Peak, mtn., Id., U.S. E5 89
Lena, Il., U.S. A4 90
Lena, stm., Russia C19 24
Lenawee, co., Mi., U.S. G6 99
Lencloître, Fr. F7 10
Lenexa, Ks., U.S. D9 93
Lenghu, China D5 26
Leninabad, Taj. I11 22
Leningrad see Sankt-Peterburg, Russia B13 18
Leninogorsk, Kaz. G10 24
Leninsk-Kuzneckij, Russia G11 24
Leninskoje, Russia H20 24
Lennox, S.D., U.S. D9 118
Lennoxville, Que., Can. D6 74
Lenoir, N.C., U.S. B1 110
Lenoir, co., N.C., U.S. B5 110
Lenoir City, Tn., U.S. D9 119
Lenore Lake, l., Sask., Can. E3 75
Lenore Lake, l., Wa., U.S. B6 124
Lenox, Ga., U.S. E3 87
Lenox, Ia., U.S. D3 92
Lenox, Ma., U.S. B1 98
Lens, Fr. B9 10
Lensk, Russia E16 24
Lentini, Italy L10 14
Leo, In., U.S. B7 91
Leoben, Aus. H15 8
Leominster, Eng., U.K. I10 7
Leominster, Ma., U.S. A4 98
León, Nic. H4 64
León, Spain C6 12
Leon, Ia., U.S. D4 92
Leon, Ks., U.S. E7 93
Leon, co., Fl., U.S. B2 86
Leon, co., Tx., U.S. D4 120
Leonard, Tx., U.S. C4 120
Leonardo, N.J., U.S. C4 107
Leonardtown, Md., U.S. D4 97
Leonberg, Ger. G9 8
León [de los Aldamas], Mex. G9 62
Leonia, N.J., U.S. h9 107
Leonora, Austl. E4 50
Leonville, La., U.S. D4 95
Léopold II, Lac see Mai-Ndombe, Lac, l., Zaire B3 44
Leopoldina, Braz. F7 57
Léopoldville see Kinshasa, Zaire B3 44
Leoti, Ks., U.S. D2 93
Le Palais, Fr. E3 10
Lepanto, Ar., U.S. B5 81
Lepe, Spain H4 12
Leping, China G6 28
L'Épiphanie, Que., Can. D4 74
Lepontine, Alpi, mts., Eur. F15 10
Le Puy, Fr. G10 10
Lercara Friddi, Italy L8 14
Lerici, Italy E4 14
Lérida, Col. G7 58
Lérida, Spain D12 12
Lerma, Spain C8 12
Le Roy, Il., U.S. C5 90
Le Roy, Mn., U.S. G6 100
Le Roy, N.Y., U.S. C3 109
Lerwick, Scot., U.K. A11 7
Léry, Que., Can. q19 74
Lery, Lake, l., La., U.S. k12 95
Les Andelys, Fr. C8 10
Lesbos see Lésvos, i., Grc. J10 16
Les Cayes, Haiti E11 64
Les Échelles, Fr. G12 10
Les Herbiers, Fr. F5 10
Leskovac, Yugo. G5 16
Leslie, Mi., U.S. F6 99
Leslie, S.C., U.S. B6 117
Leslie, co., Ky., U.S. C6 94
Lesotho, ctry., Afr. G5 44
Lesozavodsk, Russia H20 24
Les Sables-d'Olonne, Fr. F5 10
Lesser Antilles, is. G17 64
Lesser Slave Lake, l., Alta., Can. B3 68
Lesser Sunda Islands, is., Indon. G6 32
Lester Prairie, Mn., U.S. F4 100
Le Sueur, Mn., U.S. F5 100
Le Sueur, co., Mn., U.S. F5 100
Lésvos (Lesbos), i., Grc. J10 16
Leszno, Pol. D16 8
Letcher, co., Ky., U.S. C7 94
Lethbridge, Alta., Can. E4 68
Lethbridge, Newf., Can. D5 72
Lethem, Guy. F13 58
Le Thillot, Fr. E13 10
Leti, Kepulauan, is., Indon. G8 32
Leticia, Col. J8 58
Le Tréport, Fr. B8 10
Letsôk-Aw Kyun, i., Burma I5 34
Letterkenny, Ire. G5 7
Leutkirch, Ger. H10 8
Leuven, Bel. E4 8
Levádhia, Grc. K6 16
Levante, Riviera di, Italy E4 14
Levelland, Tx., U.S. C1 120
Leveque, Cape, c., Austl. C4 50
Leverkusen, Ger. D6 8
Le Vigan, Fr. I10 10
Levisa Fork, stm., U.S. C7 94
Lévis [-Lauzon], Que., Can. C6 74
Levittown, N.Y., U.S. E7 109
Levittown, Pa., U.S. F12 115
Levy, co., Fl., U.S. C4 86
Levy Lake, l., Fl., U.S. C4 86
Lewes, Eng., U.K. K13 7
Lewes, De., U.S. E5 85
Lewes and Rehoboth Canal, De., U.S. F5 85
Lewis, co., Id., U.S. C2 89
Lewis, co., Ky., U.S. B6 94
Lewis, co., Mo., U.S. A6 102
Lewis, co., N.Y., U.S. B5 109
Lewis, co., Tn., U.S. B4 119
Lewis, co., Wa., U.S. C3 124
Lewis, co., W.V., U.S. C4 125
Lewis, stm., Wa., U.S. C4 124
Lewis, stm., Wy., U.S. B2 127
Lewis, Isle of, i., Scot., U.K. C6 7
Lewis, Mount, mtn., Nv., U.S. C5 105
Lewis and Clark, co., Mt., U.S. C4 103
Lewis and Clark Cavern, Mt., U.S. D5 103
Lewis and Clark Lake, res., U.S. E8 118
Lewisburg, Ky., U.S. D3 94
Lewisburg, Oh., U.S. C1 112
Lewisburg, Pa., U.S. E8 115
Lewisburg, Tn., U.S. B5 119
Lewisburg, W.V., U.S. D4 125
Lewis Creek, stm., Vt., U.S. C2 122
Lewis Lake, l., Wy., U.S. B2 127
Lewisport, Ky., U.S. C3 94
Lewisporte, Newf., Can. D4 72
Lewis Smith Lake, res., Al., U.S. B2 78
Lewiston, Id., U.S. C1 89
Lewiston, Me., U.S. D2 96
Lewiston, Mn., U.S. G7 100
Lewiston, N.Y., U.S. B1 109
Lewiston, Ut., U.S. B4 121
Lewiston Peak, mtn., Ut., U.S. C3 121
Lewiston Woodville, N.C., U.S. A5 110
Lewistown, Il., U.S. C3 90
Lewistown, Mt., U.S. C7 103
Lewistown, Pa., U.S. E6 115
Lewisville, Ar., U.S. D2 81
Lewisville, Tx., U.S. C4 120
Lewisville Lake, res., Tx., U.S. C4 120
Lexington, Al., U.S. A2 78
Lexington, Il., U.S. C5 90
Lexington, Ky., U.S. B5 94
Lexington, Ma., U.S. B5 98
Lexington, Mi., U.S. E8 99
Lexington, Ms., U.S. B3 101
Lexington, Mo., U.S. B4 102
Lexington, Ne., U.S. D6 104
Lexington, N.C., U.S. B2 110
Lexington, Oh., U.S. B3 112
Lexington, Ok., U.S. B4 113
Lexington, S.C., U.S. D5 117
Lexington, Tn., U.S. B3 119
Lexington, Va., U.S. C3 123
Lexington, co., S.C., U.S. D5 117
Lexington Park, Md., U.S. D5 97
Leyte, i., Phil. C7 32
Leyte Gulf, b., Phil. C8 32
Lhasa, China F14 38
Lhokseumawe, Indon. D2 32
Lianhua Shan, mts., China L4 28
Lianxian, China G9 26
Lianyungang, China E10 26
Liao, stm., China C11 26
Liaocheng, China D10 26
Liaodong Wan, b., China C11 26
Liaoning, prov., China C11 26
Liaotung, Gulf of see Liaodong Wan, b., China C11 26
Liaoyang, China C11 26
Liaoyuan, China C12 26
Liard, stm., Can. E8 66
Libby, Mt., U.S. B1 103
Libenge, Zaire H9 42
Liberal, Ks., U.S. E3 93
Liberal, Mo., U.S. D3 102
Liberec, Czech. E15 8
Liberia, C.R. I5 64
Liberia, ctry., Afr. G4 42
Libertad, Ven. C8 58
Liberty, In., U.S. E8 91
Liberty, Ky., U.S. C5 94
Liberty, Ms., U.S. D3 101
Liberty, Mo., U.S. B3 102
Liberty, N.Y., U.S. D6 109
Liberty, N.C., U.S. B3 110
Liberty, S.C., U.S. B2 117
Liberty, Tx., U.S. D5 120
Liberty, co., Fl., U.S. B2 86
Liberty, co., Ga., U.S. E5 87
Liberty, co., Mt., U.S. B5 103
Liberty, co., Tx., U.S. D5 120
Liberty Center, Oh., U.S. A1 112
Liberty Lake, Wa., U.S. g14 124
Liberty Lake, res., Md., U.S. B4 97
Libertyville, Il., U.S. A6 90
Lībīyah, Aṣ-Ṣaḥrā' al- (Libyan Desert), des., Afr. D11 42
Libourne, Fr. H6 10
Libreville, Gabon A1 44
Libuse, La., U.S. C3 95
Libya, ctry., Afr. C9 42
Libyan Desert see Lībīyah, Aṣ-Ṣaḥrā' al-, des., Afr. D11 42
Licata, Italy L8 14
Lichinga, Moz. D7 44
Lichtenfels, Ger. E11 8
Lick Creek, stm., Tn., U.S. C11 119
Licking, Mo., U.S. D6 102
Licking, co., Oh., U.S. B3 112
Licking, stm., Ky., U.S. B6 94
Lida, Bela. H8 18
Lida, Lake, l., Mn., U.S. D3 100
Lidgerwood, N.D., U.S. C8 111
Lidköping, Swe. G9 6
Lido di Ostia, Italy H7 14
Liechtenstein, ctry., Eur. F9 4
Liège, Bel. E5 8
Lieksa, Fin. E18 6
Lienz, Aus. I12 8
Liepāja, Lat. E4 18
Lier, Bel. D4 8
Liestal, Switz. E14 10
Liévin, Fr. B9 10
Lièvre, Rivière du, stm., Que., Can. D2 74
Liezen, Aus. H14 8
Lifford, Ire. G5 7
Ligao, Phil. r20 33
Lighthouse Inlet, b., S.C., U.S. k12 117
Lighthouse Point, c., Fl., U.S. C2 86
Lighthouse Point, c., La., U.S. E3 95
Lighthouse Point, c., Mi., U.S. C5 99
Lightning Creek, stm., Wy., U.S. C8 127
Ligny-en-Barrois, Fr. D12 10
Ligonier, In., U.S. B6 91
Ligonier, Pa., U.S. F3 115
Ligurian Sea, Eur. F3 14
Lihou Reefs, rf., Austl. C10 50
Lihue, Hi., U.S. B2 88
Lijiang, China F7 26
Likasi (Jadotville), Zaire D5 44
Likino-Dulevo, Russia F22 18
Liknes, Nor. G6 6
Likouala, stm., Congo B3 44
Lilbourn, Mo., U.S. E8 102
Lilburn, Ga., U.S. h8 87
Liling, China H2 28
Lille, Fr. B10 10
Lillehammer, Nor. F8 6
Lillestrøm, Nor. G8 6
Lillian, Al., U.S. E2 78
Lillington, N.C., U.S. B4 110
Lillinonah, Lake, l., Ct., U.S. C2 84
Lillo, Spain F8 12
Lillooet, B.C., Can. D7 69
Lillooet, stm., B.C., Can. D6 69
Lilly, Pa., U.S. F4 115
Lilly Fork, stm., W.V., U.S. m13 125
Lilly Grove, W.V., U.S. D3 125
Lilongwe, Mwi. D6 44
Lily, Ky., U.S. C5 94
Lima, Peru F3 54
Lima, N.Y., U.S. C3 109
Lima, Oh., U.S. B1 112
Lima Reservoir, res., Mt., U.S. F4 103
Limassol see Lemesós, Cyp. B3 40
Limbdi, India I4 38
Limburg an der Lahn, Ger. E8 8
Limeira, Braz. G5 57

Name Map Ref Page
merick, Ire. I4 7
mestone, Me., U.S. B5 96
mestone, co., Al., U.S. A2 78
mestone, co., Tx., U.S. D4 120
mestone Point, pen., Man., Can. C2 70
minka, Fin. D15 6
mmen Bight, Austl. B7 50
mnos, i., Grc. J9 16
moges, Ont., Can. B9 73
moges, Fr. G8 10
món, C.R. I6 64
món, Hond. G5 64
mon, Co., U.S. B7 83
mousins, Plateau du, plat., Fr. G8 10
moux, Fr. I9 10
mpopo, stm., Afr. F6 44
nares, Chile D2 56
nares, Col. G4 58
nares, Mex. E10 62
nares, Spain G8 12
ncoln, Arg. C4 56
ncoln, Ont., Can. D5 73
ncoln, Eng., U.K. H12 7
ncoln, Al., U.S. B3 78
ncoln, Ar., U.S. B1 81
ncoln, Ca., U.S. C3 82
ncoln, De., U.S. E4 85
ncoln, Id., U.S. F6 89
ncoln, Il., U.S. C4 90
ncoln, Ks., U.S. C5 93
ncoln, Me., U.S. C4 96
ncoln, Ma., U.S. g10 98
ncoln, Mo., U.S. C4 102
ncoln, Ne., U.S. D9 104
ncoln, N.H., U.S. B3 106
ncoln, co., Ar., U.S. D4 81
ncoln, co., Co., U.S. C7 83
ncoln, co., Ga., U.S. C4 87
ncoln, co., Id., U.S. G4 89
ncoln, co., Ks., U.S. C5 93
ncoln, co., Ky., U.S. C5 94
ncoln, co., La., U.S. B3 95
ncoln, co., Me., U.S. D3 96
ncoln, co., Mn., U.S. F2 100
ncoln, co., Ms., U.S. D3 101
ncoln, co., Mo., U.S. B7 102
ncoln, co., Mt., U.S. B1 103
ncoln, co., Ne., U.S. D5 104
ncoln, co., Nv., U.S. F6 105
ncoln, co., N.M., U.S. D4 108
ncoln, co., N.C., U.S. B1 110
ncoln, co., Ok., U.S. B5 113
ncoln, co., Or., U.S. C3 114
ncoln, co., S.D., U.S. D9 118
ncoln, co., Tn., U.S. B5 119
ncoln, co., Wa., U.S. B7 124
ncoln, co., W.V., U.S. C2 125
ncoln, co., Wi., U.S. C4 126
ncoln, co., Wy., U.S. D2 127
ncoln, Mount, mtn., Co., U.S. B4 83
ncoln Acres, Ca., U.S. o15 82
ncoln City, Or., U.S. C3 114
ncoln Heights, Oh., U.S. o13 112
ncoln Park, Co., U.S. C5 83
ncoln Park, Ga., U.S. D2 87
ncoln Park, Mi., U.S. p15 99
ncoln Park, N.J., U.S. B4 107
ncolnshire, Il., U.S. h9 90
ncoln Tomb State Memorial, hist., Il., U.S. D4 90
ncolnton, Ga., U.S. C4 87
ncolnton, N.C., U.S. B1 110
ncolnville, S.C., U.S. h11 117
ncolnwood, Il., U.S. h9 90
ncroft, N.J., U.S. C4 107
ndale, Ga., U.S. B1 87
ndale, Tx., U.S. C5 120
ndau, Ger. H9 8
nden, Al., U.S. C2 78
nden, In., U.S. D4 91
nden, Mi., U.S. F7 99
nden, N.J., U.S. k8 107
nden, Tn., U.S. B4 119
nden, Tx., U.S. C5 120
ndenhurst, Il., U.S. h8 90
ndenhurst, N.Y., U.S. n15 109
ndenwold, N.J., U.S. D3 107
ndesnes, c., Nor. G6 6
di, Tan. C7 44
don, Ut., U.S. C4 121
dsay, Ont., Can. C6 73
dsay, Ca., U.S. D4 82
dsay, Ok., U.S. C4 113
dsborg, Ks., U.S. D6 93
dstrom, Mn., U.S. E6 100
esville, Pa., U.S. C1 115
eville, Al., U.S. B4 78
gao, China D10 34
gayen, Phil. B7 32
gen, Ger. C7 8
gga, Kepulauan, is., Indon. F3 32
gle, Wy., U.S. D8 127
glestown, Pa., U.S. F8 115
gling, China A11 34
, Ngoc, mtn., Viet. G9 34
hai, China G10 28
ière, Que., Can. C7 74
jiang, China C12 26
köping, Swe. G10 6
kou, China B13 26
, Mo., U.S. C6 102
n, co., Ia., U.S. C6 92
n, co., Ks., U.S. D9 93
n, co., Mo., U.S. B4 102
n, co., Or., U.S. C4 114
o Lakes, Mn., U.S. m12 100
qing, China D10 26
ru, China A1 28
s, Braz. F4 57
tao, China D7 26
thicum Heights, Md., U.S. B4 97
ton, In., U.S. F3 91
ton, N.D., U.S. C5 111
Linwood, N.J., U.S. E3 107
Linxi, China C10 26
Linxia, China D7 26
Linyi, China D10 26
Linz, Aus. G14 8
Lion, Golfe du, b., Fr. I11 10
Lipa, Phil. r19 33b
Lipeck, Russia I22 18
Lippstadt, Ger. D8 8
Lipscomb, Al., U.S. B3 78
Lipscomb, co., Tx., U.S. A2 120
Lira, Ug. H12 42
Liria, Spain F11 12
Lisala, Zaire A4 44
Lisboa (Lisbon), Port. G2 12
Lisbon, Ia., U.S. C6 92
Lisbon, Me., U.S. D2 96
Lisbon, Md., U.S. B3 97
Lisbon, N.H., U.S. B3 106
Lisbon, N.D., U.S. C8 111
Lisbon, Oh., U.S. B5 112
Lisbon Center, Me., U.S. f7 96
Lisbon Falls, Me., U.S. E2 96
Lisbon see Lisboa, Port. G2 12
Lisburne, Cape, c., Ak., U.S. B6 79
Lishui, China G8 28
Lisianski Island, i., Hi., U.S. k13 88
Lisičansk, Ukr. H5 22
Lisieux, Fr. C7 10
Lisle, Il., U.S. k8 90
L'Isle Jourdain, Fr. F7 10
L'Isle-Jourdain, Fr. I8 10
L'Islet-sur-Mer, Que., Can. B7 74
L'Isle-Verte, Que., Can. A8 74
Lismore, Austl. E10 50
Listowel, Ont., Can. D4 73
Listowel, Ire. I3 7
Lit, Swe. E10 6
Litang, China G8 26
Litchfield, Ct., U.S. C3 84
Litchfield, Il., U.S. D4 90
Litchfield, Mi., U.S. F6 99
Litchfield, Mn., U.S. E4 100
Litchfield, co., Ct., U.S. B2 84
Litchfield Park, Az., U.S. m8 80
Lithia Springs, Ga., U.S. h7 87
Lithonia, Ga., U.S. C2 87
Lithuania, ctry., Eur. F6 18
Litija, Slo. C9 14
Lititz, Pa., U.S. F9 115
Litovko, Russia H21 24
Little, stm., U.S. B5 81
Little, stm., U.S. D7 113
Little, stm., Ct., U.S. C7 84
Little, stm., Ky., U.S. D2 94
Little, stm., La., U.S. C3 95
Little, stm., N.C., U.S. B3 110
Little, stm., Ok., U.S. B5 113
Little, stm., S.C., U.S. C2 117
Little, stm., Tn., U.S. n14 119
Little, stm., Vt., U.S. C3 122
Little, stm., Va., U.S. D2 123
Little Abaco Island, i., Bah. A9 64
Little Acres, Az., U.S. D5 80
Little Andaman, i., India I2 34
Little Arkansas, stm., Ks., U.S. D6 93
Little Belt Mountains, mts., Mt., U.S. D6 103
Little Bighorn, stm., U.S. E9 103
Little Black, stm., Me., U.S. A3 96
Little Blue, stm., U.S. C6 93
Little Blue, stm., In., U.S. H5 91
Little Bow, stm., Alta., Can. D4 68
Little Cacapon, stm., W.V., U.S. B6 125
Little Catalina, Newf., Can. D5 72
Little Cayman, i., Cay. Is. E7 64
Little Cedar, stm., Ia., U.S. A5 92
Little Churchill, stm., Man., Can. A4 70
Little Chute, Wi., U.S. D5 126
Little Coal, stm., W.V., U.S. C3 125
Little Colorado, stm., Az., U.S. B4 80
Little Compton, R.I., U.S. E6 116
Little Creek, De., U.S. D4 85
Little Creek Naval Amphibious Base, mil., Va., U.S. k15 123
Little Creek Peak, mtn., Ut., U.S. F3 121
Little Current, Ont., Can. B3 73
Little Diomede Island, i., Ak., U.S. B6 79
Little Egg Harbor, b., N.J., U.S. D4 107
Little Egg Inlet, b., N.J., U.S. E4 107
Little Falls, Mn., U.S. E4 100
Little Falls, N.J., U.S. B4 107
Little Falls, N.Y., U.S. B6 109
Little Ferry, N.J., U.S. h8 107
Littlefield, Tx., U.S. C1 120
Little Fishing Creek, stm., W.V., U.S. h9 125
Littlefork, Mn., U.S. B5 100
Little Fork, stm., Mn., U.S. B5 100
Little Goose Creek, stm., Wy., U.S. B6 127
Little Gunpowder Falls, stm., Md., U.S. A4 97
Little Humboldt, stm., Nv., U.S. B4 105
Little Inagua, i., Bah. D11 64
Little Kanawha, stm., W.V., U.S. C4 125
Little Lake, Mi., U.S. B3 99
Little Lake, l., La., U.S. E5 95
Little Lynches, stm., S.C., U.S. C7 117
Little Manatee, stm., Fl., U.S. p11 86
Little Mecatina, stm., Can. h9 72
Little Miami, stm., Oh., U.S. C1 112
Little Minch, strt., Scot., U.K. D6 7
Little Missouri, stm., U.S. B6 76
Little Missouri, stm., Ar., U.S. D2 81
Little Muddy, stm., Il., U.S. E4 90
Little Muddy, stm., N.D., U.S. A2 111
Little Nicobar, i., India K2 34
Little Osage, stm., U.S. E9 93
Little Otter Creek, stm., Vt., U.S. C2 122
Little Owyhee, stm., U.S. B5 105
Little Pee Dee, stm., S.C., U.S. C9 117
Little Powder, stm., U.S. F11 103
Little Red, stm., Ar., U.S. B4 81
Little River, co., Ar., U.S. D1 81
Little River Inlet, b., S.C., U.S. D10 117
Little Rock, Ar., U.S. C3 81
Little Rock, stm., U.S. A1 92
Little Rock Air Force Base, mil., Ar., U.S. C3 81
Little Sable Point, c., Mi., U.S. E4 99
Little Salt Lake, l., Ut., U.S. F3 121
Little Sandy, stm., Ky., U.S. B6 94
Little Sandy Creek, stm., Wy., U.S. D3 127
Little Sebago Lake, l., Me., U.S. g7 96
Little Silver, N.J., U.S. C4 107
Little Sioux, stm., U.S. B2 92
Little Sioux, West Fork, stm., Ia., U.S. B2 92
Little Smoky, stm., Alta., Can. B2 68
Little Snake, stm., U.S. A2 83
Little Spokane, stm., Wa., U.S. B8 124
Littlestown, Pa., U.S. G7 115
Little Tallapoosa, stm., U.S. B4 78
Little Tenmile Creek, stm., W.V., U.S. k10 125
Little Tennessee, stm., U.S. D9 119
Littleton, Co., U.S. B6 83
Littleton, Me., U.S. B5 96
Littleton, Ma., U.S. f10 98
Littleton, N.H., U.S. B3 106
Littleton, N.C., U.S. A5 110
Littleville, Al., U.S. A2 78
Little Wabash, stm., Il., U.S. E5 90
Little Walnut, stm., Ks., U.S. g13 93
Little White, stm., S.D., U.S. D5 118
Little Wolf, stm., Wi., U.S. D4 126
Little Wood, stm., Id., U.S. F4 89
Liuan, China D5 28
Liuhe, China C7 28
Liuzhou, China B10 34
Live Oak, Ca., U.S. C3 82
Live Oak, Fl., U.S. B4 86
Live Oak, co., Tx., U.S. E3 120
Livermore, Ca., U.S. h9 82
Livermore, Ky., U.S. C2 94
Livermore, Mount, mtn., Tx., U.S. o12 120
Livermore Falls, Me., U.S. D2 96
Liverpool, Eng., U.K. H10 7
Liverpool, Cape, c., N.W. Ter., Can. B17 66
Livingston, Al., U.S. C1 78
Livingston, Ca., U.S. D3 82
Livingston, Il., U.S. E4 90
Livingston, La., U.S. D5 95
Livingston, Mt., U.S. E6 103
Livingston, N.J., U.S. B4 107
Livingston, Tn., U.S. C8 119
Livingston, Tx., U.S. D5 120
Livingston, co., Il., U.S. C5 90
Livingston, co., Ky., U.S. e9 94
Livingston, co., La., U.S. D5 95
Livingston, co., Mi., U.S. F7 99
Livingston, co., Mo., U.S. B4 102
Livingston, co., N.Y., U.S. C3 109
Livingston, Lake, res., Tx., U.S. D5 120
Livingstone, Zam. E5 44
Livingstonia, Mwi. D6 44
Livno, Bos. F12 14
Livny, Russia I20 18
Livonia, La., U.S. D4 95
Livonia, Mi., U.S. F7 99
Livorno (Leghorn), Italy F5 14
Liyang, China D8 28
Lizard Head Pass, Co., U.S. D3 83
Lizard Head Peak, mtn., Wy., U.S. D3 127
Lizard Point, c., Eng., U.K. L7 7
Lizella, Ga., U.S. D3 87
Ljubljana, Slo. C9 14
Ljungby, Swe. H9 6
Ljusdal, Swe. F11 6
Llandudno, Wales, U.K. H9 7
Llanelli, Wales, U.K. J8 7
Llanes, Spain B7 12
Llanidloes, Wales, U.K. I9 7
Llano, Tx., U.S. D3 120
Llano, co., Tx., U.S. D3 120
Llano, stm., Tx., U.S. D3 120
Llanos, pl., S.A. E7 58
Llanwrtyd Wells, Wales, U.K. I9 7
Llera, Mex. F10 62
Llerena, Spain G5 12
Lloyd, Ky., U.S. B7 94
Lloydminster, Alta., Can. C5 68
Lloyds, stm., Newf., Can. D3 72
Lluchmayor, Spain F14 12
Llullaillaco, Volcán, vol., S.A. A3 56
Lo, stm., Viet. C8 34
Loami, Il., U.S. D4 90
Loange, stm., Afr. C3 44
Löbau, Ger. D14 8
Lobaye, stm., Cen. Afr. Rep. G9 42
Lobelville, Tn., U.S. B4 119
Lobito, Ang. D2 44
Lobos de Afuera, Islas, is., Peru E2 54
Lobos de Tierra, Isla, i., Peru E2 54
Lobster Lake, l., Me., U.S. C3 96
Locarno, Switz. F15 10
Lochaline, Scot., U.K. E7 7
Lochboisdale, Scot., U.K. D5 7
Loches, Fr. E7 10
Lochgilphead, Scot., U.K. E7 7
Loch Lomond, Va., U.S. *B5 123
Loch Raven Reservoir, res., Md., U.S. B4 97
Lochsa, stm., Id., U.S. C3 89
Lockeport, N.S., Can. F4 71
Lockesburg, Ar., U.S. D1 81
Lockhart, Tx., U.S. E4 120
Lock Haven, Pa., U.S. D7 115
Lockland, Oh., U.S. o13 112
Lockney, Tx., U.S. B2 120
Lockport, Il., U.S. B5 90
Lockport, La., U.S. E5 95
Lockport, N.Y., U.S. B2 109
Lockwood, Mo., U.S. D4 102
Lockwood, Mt., U.S. E8 103
Loc Ninh, Viet. I9 34
Locust, N.C., U.S. B2 110
Locust Fork, stm., Al., U.S. B3 78
Locust Grove, Ga., U.S. C2 87
Locust Grove, Ok., U.S. A6 113
Lod, Isr. D4 40
Lodejnoje Pole, Russia A16 18
Lodève, Fr. I10 10
Lodgepole Creek, stm., U.S. C3 104
Lodi, Italy D4 14
Lodi, Ca., U.S. C3 82
Lodi, N.J., U.S. h8 107
Lodi, Oh., U.S. A3 112
Lodi, Wi., U.S. E4 126
Lodja, Zaire B4 44
Lodore, Canyon of, val., Co., U.S. A2 83
Lodwar, Kenya H2 46
Łódź, Pol. D19 8
Loffa, stm., Afr. G3 42
Logan, Ia., U.S. C2 92
Logan, Ks., U.S. C4 93
Logan, N.M., U.S. B6 108
Logan, Oh., U.S. C3 112
Logan, Ut., U.S. B4 121
Logan, W.V., U.S. D3 125
Logan, co., Ar., U.S. B2 81
Logan, co., Co., U.S. A7 83
Logan, co., Il., U.S. C4 90
Logan, co., Ks., U.S. D2 93
Logan, co., Ky., U.S. D3 94
Logan, co., Ne., U.S. C5 104
Logan, co., N.D., U.S. C6 111
Logan, co., Oh., U.S. B2 112
Logan, co., Ok., U.S. B4 113
Logan, co., W.V., U.S. D3 125
Logan, Mount, mtn., Yukon, Can. D4 66
Logan, Mount, mtn., Wa., U.S. A5 124
Logandale, Nv., U.S. G7 105
Logan Lake, B.C., Can. D7 69
Logan Martin Lake, res., Al., U.S. B3 78
Logan Pass, Mt., U.S. B2 103
Logansport, In., U.S. C5 91
Logansport, La., U.S. C2 95
Loganville, Ga., U.S. C3 87
Loganville, Pa., U.S. G8 115
Loggieville, N.B., Can. B4 71
Log Lane Village, Co., U.S. A7 83
Logone, stm., Afr. F9 42
Logroño, Spain C9 12
Logrosán, Spain F6 12
Lohr, Ger. E9 8
Loi-Kaw, Burma E4 34
Loimaa, Fin. F14 6
Loire, stm., Fr. E5 10
Loja, Ec. J3 58
Loja, Spain H7 12
Lokolama, Zaire B3 44
Lol, stm., Sudan G11 42
Lola, Mount, mtn., Ca., U.S. C3 82
Lolo, Mt., U.S. D2 103
Lolo Pass, U.S. C4 89
Lomami, stm., Zaire B4 44
Lombard, Il., U.S. k8 90
Lombien, Pulau, i., Indon. G7 32
Lombok, i., Indon. G6 32
Lomé, Togo G6 42
Lomela, Zaire B4 44
Lomela, stm., Zaire B4 44
Lomira, Wi., U.S. E5 126
Lomond, Loch, l., Scot., U.K. E8 7
Lomonosov, Russia B12 18
Lompoc, Ca., U.S. E3 82
Łomża, Pol. B22 8
Lonaconing, Md., U.S. k13 97
Lonāvale, India C2 37
Loncoche, Chile D2 56
London, Ont., Can. E3 73
London, Eng., U.K. J12 7
London, Ar., U.S. B2 81
London, Ky., U.S. C5 94
London, Oh., U.S. C2 112
Londonderry, N. Ire., U.K. G5 7
Londonderry, N.H., U.S. E4 106
Londonderry, Cape, c., Austl. B5 50
Londonderry, Isla, i., Chile H2 56
Londontown, Md., U.S. C4 97
Londrina, Braz. G3 57
Lone Grove, Ok., U.S. C4 113
Lone Mountain, mtn., Nv., U.S. E4 105
Lone Pine, Ca., U.S. D4 82
Lone Tree, Ia., U.S. C6 92
Long, co., Ga., U.S. E5 87
Longa, Proliv, strt., Russia C29 24
Longarone, Italy C7 14
Long Bar Harbor, Md., U.S. B5 97
Long Beach, Ca., U.S. F4 82
Long Beach, In., U.S. A4 91
Long Beach, Md., U.S. D5 97
Long Beach, Ms., U.S. g7 101
Long Beach, N.Y., U.S. E7 109
Long Beach, Wa., U.S. C1 124
Long Beach Naval Shipyard, mil., Ca., U.S. n12 82
Longboat Key, Fl., U.S. q10 86
Longboat Key, i., Fl., U.S. E4 86
Longboat Pass, strt., Fl., U.S. q10 86
Long Branch, N.J., U.S. C5 107
Longbranch, Wa., U.S. B3 124
Long Creek Mountain, mtn., Wy., U.S. D5 127
Longeau, Fr. E12 10
Long Grove, Ia., U.S. C7 92
Long Harbour [-Mount Arlington Heights], Newf., Can. E5 72
Long Island, i., Bah. C10 64
Long Island, i., N.S., Can. E3 71
Long Island, i., Me., U.S. g7 96
Long Island, i., Ma., U.S. g12 98
Long Island, i., N.Y., U.S. E7 109
Long Island Sound, strt., U.S. E7 109
Longjiang, China B11 26
Long Key, i., Fl., U.S. H6 86
Long Lake, Il., U.S. h8 90
Long Lake, l., Me., U.S. A4 96
Long Lake, l., Me., U.S. D2 96
Long Lake, l., Mi., U.S. D5 99
Long Lake, l., Mi., U.S. C7 99
Long Lake, l., Mn., U.S. D4 100
Long Lake, l., N.Y., U.S. B6 109
Long Lake, l., N.D., U.S. C6 111
Long Lake, l., Wa., U.S. f10 124
Long Lake, l., Wi., U.S. C2 126
Longli, China A9 34
Longmeadow, Ma., U.S. B2 98
Longmont, Co., U.S. A5 83
Long Point, c., Man., Can. C2 70
Long Point, pen., Ont., Can. E4 73
Long Pond, res., Fl., U.S. C4 86
Long Prairie, Mn., U.S. E4 100
Long Range Mountains, mts., Newf., Can. D3 72
Longreach, Austl. D8 50
Longsheng, China B11 34
Longs Peak, mtn., Co., U.S. A5 83
Longué, Fr. E6 10
Longueuil, Que., Can. D4 74
Longuyon, Fr. C12 10
Long View, N.C., U.S. B1 110
Longview, Tx., U.S. C5 120
Longview, Wa., U.S. C3 124
Longwy, Fr. C12 10
Long Xuyen, Viet. I8 34
Lonigo, Italy D6 14
Löningen, Ger. C7 8
Lonoke, Ar., U.S. C4 81
Lonoke, co., Ar., U.S. C4 81
Lønsdal, Nor. C10 6
Lonsdale, Mn., U.S. F5 100
Lonsdale, R.I., U.S. B4 116
Lons-le-Saunier, Fr. F12 10
Loogootee, In., U.S. G4 91
Lookout, Ky., U.S. C7 94
Lookout, Cape, c., N.C., U.S. C6 110
Lookout, Point, c., Mi., U.S. d7 99
Lookout Mountain, Tn., U.S. h11 119
Lookout Mountain, mtn., U.S. D8 119
Lookout Mountain, mtn., Or., U.S. C6 114
Lookout Pass, U.S. B3 89
Lookout Point Lake, res., Or., U.S. D4 114
Loon Lake, Wa., U.S. A8 124
Loon Lake, l., Me., U.S. B3 96
Loop Creek, stm., W.V., U.S. m13 125
Loop Head, c., Ire. I3 7
Loosahatchie, stm., Tn., U.S. B2 119
Lopatina, Gora, mtn., Russia G22 24
Lopatka, Mys, c., Russia G25 24
Lop Buri, Thai. G6 34
Lopez, Cap, c., Gabon B1 44
López Collada, Mex. B3 62
Lopez Island, i., Wa., U.S. A3 124
Lop Nur, l., China C5 26
Lora del Río, Spain H6 12
Lorain, Oh., U.S. A3 112
Lorain, co., Oh., U.S. A3 112
Loramie, Lake, res., Oh., U.S. B1 112
Lorca, Spain H10 12
Lord Howe Island, i., Austl. F11 50
Lordsburg, N.M., U.S. E1 108
Loreauville, La., U.S. D4 95
Lorena, Braz. G6 57
Lorenzo, Tx., U.S. C2 120
Loreto, Braz. E9 54
Loreto, Col. I7 58
Loreto, Mex. F9 62
Lorette, Man., Can. E3 70
Loretteville, Que., Can. C6 74
Loretto, Ky., U.S. C4 94
Loretto, Pa., U.S. F4 115
Loretto, Tn., U.S. B4 119
Lorica, Col. C5 58
Lorient, Fr. E3 10
L'Orignal, Ont., Can. B10 73
Loring Air Force Base, mil., Me., U.S. B5 96
Loriol [-du-Comtat], Fr. H11 10
Loris, S.C., U.S. C10 117
Lorne, N.B., Can. B3 71
Lörrach, Ger. H7 8
Lorraine, hist. reg., Fr. D13 10
Los Alamos, N.M., U.S. B3 108
Los Alamos, co., N.M., U.S. B3 108
Los Aldamas, Mex. D10 62
Los Altos, Ca., U.S. k8 82
Los Ángeles, Chile D2 56
Los Angeles, Ca., U.S. E4 82
Los Angeles, co., Ca., U.S. E4 82
Los Angeles Aqueduct, Ca., U.S. E4 82
Los Banos, Ca., U.S. D3 82
Los Blancos, Arg. A4 56
Los Fresnos, Tx., U.S. F4 120
Los Gatos, Ca., U.S. D2 82
Los Lagos, Chile D2 56
Los Lunas, N.M., U.S. C3 108
Los Mochis, Mex. E5 62
Los Palacios y Villafranca, Spain H6 12
Los Pinos, stm., Co., U.S. D3 83
Los Ranchos de Albuquerque, N.M., U.S. B3 108
Los Roques, Islas, is., Ven. B9 58
Lost, stm., In., U.S. G4 91
Lost, stm., Wa., U.S. A5 124
Lost, stm., W.V., U.S. B6 125
Lost Creek, stm., Wy., U.S. D4 127
Los Teques, Ven. B9 58
Los Testigos, Islas, is., Ven. B11 58
Lost Peak, mtn., Ut., U.S. F2 121
Lost Ranger Peak, mtn., Co., U.S. A4 83
Lost River Glacial Caverns, N.H., U.S. B3 106
Lost River Range, mts., Id., U.S. E5 89
Lost Trail Pass, U.S. D5 89
Los Vilos, Chile C2 56
Los Yébenes, Spain F8 12
Lota, Chile D2 56
Lotawana, Lake, res., Mo., U.S. k11 102
Lotbinière, Que., Can. C6 74
Louang Namtha, Laos D6 34
Louangphrabang, Laos E7 34
Loudéac, Fr. D4 10
Loudon, Tn., U.S. D9 119
Loudon, co., Tn., U.S. D9 119
Loudonville, Oh., U.S. B3 112
Loudoun, co., Va., U.S. A5 123
Loudun, Fr. E7 10
Louga, Sen. E2 42

Name	Map Ref	Page
Loughrea, Ire.	H4	7
Louhans, Fr.	F12	10
Louisa, Ky., U.S.	B7	94
Louisa, Va., U.S.	B4	123
Louisa, co., Ia., U.S.	C6	92
Louisa, co., Va., U.S.	C5	123
Louisa, Lake, l., Fl., U.S.	D5	86
Louisbourg, N.S., Can.	D10	71
Louisburg, Ks., U.S.	D9	93
Louisburg, N.C., U.S.	A4	110
Louisdale, N.S., Can.	D8	71
Louise, Lake, l., Ak., U.S.	f18	79
Louise Island, i., B.C., Can.	C2	69
Louiseville, Que., Can.	C5	74
Louisiade Archipelago, is., Pap. N. Gui.	B10	50
Louisiana, Mo., U.S.	B6	102
Louisiana, state, U.S.	C3	95
Louisiana Point, c., La., U.S.	E2	95
Louis Trichardt, S. Afr.	F5	44
Louisville, Al., U.S.	D4	78
Louisville, Co., U.S.	B5	83
Louisville, Ga., U.S.	C4	87
Louisville, Il., U.S.	E5	90
Louisville, Ky., U.S.	B4	94
Louisville, Ms., U.S.	B4	101
Louisville, Ne., U.S.	D9	104
Louisville, Oh., U.S.	B4	112
Louis-XIV, Pointe, c., Que., Can.	h11	74
Loulé, Port.	H3	12
Loup, co., Ne., U.S.	C6	104
Loup, stm., Ne., U.S.	C8	104
Loup City, Ne., U.S.	C7	104
Lourdes, Newf., Can.	D2	72
Lourdes, Fr.	I6	10
Lourenço Marques see Maputo, Moz.	G6	44
Louth, Eng., U.K.	H12	7
Louviers, Fr.	C8	10
Louviers, Co., U.S.	B6	83
Love, co., Ok., U.S.	D4	113
Loveč, Bul.	F8	16
Loveland, Co., U.S.	A5	83
Loveland, Oh., U.S.	n13	112
Loveland Park, Oh., U.S.	C1	112
Loveland Pass, Co., U.S.	B5	83
Lovell, Wy., U.S.	B4	127
Lovelock, Nv., U.S.	C3	105
Lovely, Ky., U.S.	C7	94
Lovenia, Mount, mtn., Ut., U.S.	C5	121
Love Point, c., Md., U.S.	B5	97
Lovere, Italy	D5	14
Loves Park, Il., U.S.	A4	90
Lovettsville, Va., U.S.	A5	123
Loving, N.M., U.S.	E5	108
Loving, co., Tx., U.S.	D1	120
Lovington, Il., U.S.	D5	90
Lovington, Ia., U.S.	e8	92
Lovington, N.M., U.S.	E6	108
Lövstabruk, Swe.	F11	6
Low, Cape, c., N.W. Ter., Can.	D15	66
Lowden, Ia., U.S.	C7	92
Lowell, Ar., U.S.	A1	81
Lowell, In., U.S.	B3	91
Lowell, Ma., U.S.	A5	98
Lowell, Mi., U.S.	F5	99
Lowell, N.C., U.S.	B1	110
Lowell, Or., U.S.	D4	114
Lowell, Lake, res., Id., U.S.	F2	89
Lowellville, Oh., U.S.	A5	112
Lower Arrow Lake, res., B.C., Can.	E8	69
Lower Brule Indian Reservation, S.D., U.S.	C6	118
Lower California see Baja California, pen., Mex.	D3	62
Lower Hutt, N.Z.	D5	52
Lower Klamath Lake, l., Ca., U.S.	B3	82
Lower Matecumbe Key, i., Fl., U.S.	H6	86
Lower Monumental Lake, res., Wa., U.S.	C7	124
Lower New York Bay, b., N.J., U.S.	B4	107
Lower Otay Lake, res., Ca., U.S.	o16	82
Lower Paia, Hi., U.S.	C5	88
Lower Red Lake, l., Mn., U.S.	C3	100
Lower Rice Lake, l., Mn., U.S.	C3	100
Lower Salmon Dam, Id., U.S.	G4	89
Lower West Pubnico, N.S., Can.	F4	71
Lowestoft, Eng., U.K.	I14	7
Lowndes, co., Al., U.S.	C3	78
Lowndes, co., Ga., U.S.	F3	87
Lowndes, co., Ms., U.S.	B5	101
Lowry Air Force Base, mil., Co., U.S.	B6	83
Lowry City, Mo., U.S.	C4	102
Lowville, N.Y., U.S.	B5	109
Loxley, Al., U.S.	E2	78
Loyal, Wi., U.S.	D3	126
Loyall, Ky., U.S.	D6	94
Loyalsock Creek, stm., Pa., U.S.	D8	115
Loznica, Yugo.	E3	16
Lozoyuela, Spain	E8	12
Lua, stm., Zaire	H9	42
Lualaba, stm., Zaire	B5	44
Lua Makika, crat., Hi., U.S.	C5	88
Luanda, Ang.	C2	44
Luang Praban Range, mts., Asia	E6	34
Luanguinga, stm., Afr.	D4	44
Luangwa, stm., Afr.	D6	44
Luanshya, Zam.	D5	44
Luarca, Spain	B5	12
Luau, Ang.	D4	44
Lubang Island, i., Phil.	C7	32
Lubango, Ang.	D2	44
Lübben, Ger.	D13	8
Lübbenau, Ger.	D13	8
Lubbock, Tx., U.S.	C2	120
Lubbock, co., Tx., U.S.	C2	120
Lubec, Me., U.S.	D6	96
Lübeck, Ger.	B10	8
Lübecker Bucht, b., Ger.	A11	8
L'ubercy, Russia	F20	18
Lubilash, stm., Zaire	C4	44
Lubin, Pol.	D16	8
Lublin, Pol.	D22	8
Lubudi, Zaire	C4	44
Lubuksikaping, Indon.	N6	34
Lubumbashi (Élisabethville), Zaire	D5	44
Lubutu, Zaire	B5	44
Lucama, N.C., U.S.	B4	110
Lucan, Ont., Can.	D3	73
Lucania, Mount, mtn., Yukon, Can.	D4	66
Lucas, co., Ia., U.S.	C4	92
Lucas, co., Oh., U.S.	A2	112
Lucasville, Oh., U.S.	D3	112
Lucca, Italy	F5	14
Luce, co., Mi., U.S.	B5	99
Luce Bay, b., Scot., U.K.	G8	7
Lucedale, Ms., U.S.	E5	101
Lucena, Phil.	r19	33b
Lucena, Spain	H7	12
Lucena del Cid, Spain	E11	12
Luc-en-Diois, Fr.	H12	10
Lucera, Italy	H10	14
Lucerne, Ca., U.S.	C2	82
Lucerne see Luzern, Switz.	E15	10
Lucernemines, Pa., U.S.	E3	115
Lucerne Valley, Ca., U.S.	E5	82
Luceville, Que., Can.	A9	74
Luchiang, Tai.	K9	28
Lüchow, Ger.	C11	8
Lucira, Ang.	D2	44
Luck, Ukr.	G3	22
Luck, Wi., U.S.	C1	126
Luckeesarai, India	H12	38
Luckenwalde, Ger.	C13	8
Lucknow, Ont., Can.	D3	73
Lucknow, India	G9	38
Lucky Peak Lake, res., Id., U.S.	F3	89
Luçon, Fr.	F5	10
Lüderitz, Nmb.	G3	44
Ludhiāna, India	E6	38
Ludington, Mi., U.S.	E4	99
L'udinovo, Russia	H17	18
Ludlow, Ky., U.S.	h13	94
Ludlow, Ma., U.S.	B3	98
Ludlow, Vt., U.S.	E3	122
Ludowici, Ga., U.S.	E5	87
Ludvika, Swe.	F10	6
Ludwigsburg, Ger.	G9	8
Ludwigsfelde, Ger.	C13	8
Ludwigshafen, Ger.	F8	8
Luena, stm., Ang.	D4	44
Luene, Ang.	D3	44
Lufeng, China	M4	28
Lufkin, Tx., U.S.	D5	120
Luga, Russia	C12	18
Lugano, Switz.	F15	10
Lugansk, Ukr.	H5	22
Lugenda, stm., Moz.	D7	44
Lugh Ganane, Som.	H3	46
Lugnaquillia Mountain, mtn., Ire.	I6	7
Lugo, Italy	E6	14
Lugo, Spain	B4	12
Lugoff, S.C., U.S.	C6	117
Lugoj, Rom.	D5	16
Luhit, stm., Asia	G16	38
Luilaka, stm., Zaire	B4	44
Luino, Italy	C3	14
Lukachukai, Az., U.S.	A6	80
Luke Air Force Base, mil., Az., U.S.	D3	80
Lukulu, Zam.	D4	44
Lula, Ga., U.S.	B3	87
Luleå, Swe.	D14	6
Lüleburgaz, Tur.	H11	16
Luling, La., U.S.	k11	95
Luling, Tx., U.S.	E4	120
Lulonga, stm., Zaire	A3	44
Lumajang, Indon.	n16	33a
Lumber, stm., U.S.	C9	117
Lumber City, Ga., U.S.	E4	87
Lumberport, W.V., U.S.	B4	125
Lumberton, Ms., U.S.	D4	101
Lumberton, N.C., U.S.	C3	110
Lumbrales, Spain	E5	12
Lumby, B.C., Can.	D8	69
Lumding, India	H15	38
Lummi Indian Reservation, Wa., U.S.	A3	124
Lumpkin, Ga., U.S.	D2	87
Lumpkin, co., Ga., U.S.	B2	87
Lumsden, Newf., Can.	D5	72
Luna, co., N.M., U.S.	E2	108
Luna Pier, Mi., U.S.	G7	99
Lund, Swe.	I9	6
Lund, Nv., U.S.	E6	105
Lundar, Man., Can.	D2	70
Lundazi, Zam.	D6	44
Lüneburg, Ger.	B10	8
Lüneburger Heide, reg., Ger.	B10	8
Lunel, Fr.	I11	10
Lunenburg, Ma., U.S.	A4	98
Lunenburg, co., Va., U.S.	D4	123
Lunéville, Fr.	D13	10
Lunga, stm., Zam.	D5	44
Luohe, China	B3	28
Luolong, China	E17	38
Luopu, China	B9	38
Luoyang, China	E9	26
Lūrah, stm., Afg.	D2	38
Luray, Va., U.S.	B4	123
Lure, Fr.	E13	10
Lure, Lake, res., N.C., U.S.	f10	110
Lurgan, N. Ire., U.K.	G6	7
Lúrio, stm., Moz.	D7	44
Lusaka, Zam.	E5	44
Lusambo, Zaire	B4	44
Lusby, Md., U.S.	D5	97
Luseland, Sask., Can.	E1	75
Lushan, China	B1	28
Lushnje, Alb.	I3	16
Lushoto, Tan.	B7	44
Lüshun (Port Arthur), China	D11	26
Lusk, Wy., U.S.	D8	127
Lussac-les-Châteaux, Fr.	F7	10
Lūt, Dasht-e, des., Iran	B6	46
Lutcher, La., U.S.	D5	95
Luther, Ok., U.S.	B4	113
Luthersville, Ga., U.S.	C2	87
Lutherville-Timonium, Md., U.S.	B4	97
Luton, Eng., U.K.	J12	7
Lutsk see Luck, Ukr.	G3	22
Luttrell, Tn., U.S.	C10	119
Lutz, Fl., U.S.	D4	86
Luverne, Al., U.S.	D3	78
Luverne, Mn., U.S.	G2	100
Luwegu, stm., Tan.	C7	44
Luxapallila Creek, stm., U.S.	B5	101
Luxembourg, Lux.	F6	8
Luxembourg, ctry., Eur.	F9	4
Luxemburg, Wi., U.S.	D6	126
Luxomni, Ga., U.S.	h8	87
Luxora, Ar., U.S.	B6	81
Luzern, Switz.	E15	10
Luzerne, Pa., U.S.	n17	115
Luzerne, co., Pa., U.S.	D9	115
Luzhou, China	F8	26
Luzon, i., Phil.	B7	32
Luzon Strait, strt., Asia	G11	26
Luzy, Fr.	F10	10
L'vov, Ukr.	H2	22
Lycksele, Swe.	D12	6
Lycoming, co., Pa., U.S.	D7	115
Lycoming Creek, stm., Pa., U.S.	D7	115
Lydenburg, S. Afr.	G6	44
Lyell, Mount, mtn., Can.	D2	68
Lyford, Tx., U.S.	F4	120
Lykens, Pa., U.S.	E8	115
Lyle, Wa., U.S.	D4	124
Lyman, S.C., U.S.	B3	117
Lyman, Wy., U.S.	E2	127
Lyman, co., S.D., U.S.	D6	118
Lyman Lake, res., Az., U.S.	C6	80
Lynch, Ky., U.S.	D7	94
Lynchburg, Oh., U.S.	C2	112
Lynchburg, Tn., U.S.	B5	119
Lynchburg, Va., U.S.	C3	123
Lynches, stm., S.C., U.S.	D8	117
Lynden, Wa., U.S.	A3	124
Lynde Point, c., Ct., U.S.	D6	84
Lyndhurst, N.J., U.S.	h8	107
Lyndhurst, Oh., U.S.	g9	112
Lyndon, Ks., U.S.	D8	93
Lyndon, Ky., U.S.	g11	94
Lyndon B. Johnson National Historical Site, hist., Tx., U.S.	D3	120
Lyndon B. Johnson Space Center, sci., Tx., U.S.	r14	120
Lyndonville, Vt., U.S.	B4	122
Lyndora, Pa., U.S.	E2	115
Lynher Reef, rf., Austl.	C4	50
Lynn, Al., U.S.	A2	78
Lynn, In., U.S.	D8	91
Lynn, Ma., U.S.	B6	98
Lynn, co., Tx., U.S.	C2	120
Lynn, Lake, res., W.V., U.S.	B5	125
Lynn Canal, b., Ak., U.S.	k22	79
Lynne Acres, Md., U.S.	*B4	97
Lynnfield, Ma., U.S.	f11	98
Lynn Garden, Tn., U.S.	C11	119
Lynn Garden, Tn., U.S.	A9	119
Lynn Haven, Fl., U.S.	u16	86
Lynnhaven Roads, b., Va., U.S.	k15	123
Lynnville, In., U.S.	H3	91
Lynnwood, Wa., U.S.	B3	124
Lynton, Eng., U.K.	J9	7
Lynwood, Ca., U.S.	n12	82
Lyon, Fr.	G11	10
Lyon, co., Ia., U.S.	A1	92
Lyon, co., Ks., U.S.	D7	93
Lyon, co., Ky., U.S.	C1	94
Lyon, co., Mn., U.S.	F3	100
Lyon, co., Nv., U.S.	D2	105
Lyons, Co., U.S.	A5	83
Lyons, Ga., U.S.	D4	87
Lyons, Il., U.S.	k9	90
Lyons, In., U.S.	G3	91
Lyons, Ks., U.S.	D5	93
Lyons, Mi., U.S.	F6	99
Lyons, Ne., U.S.	C9	104
Lyons, N.Y., U.S.	B3	109
Lyons, Or., U.S.	C4	114
Lyster Station, Que., Can.	C6	74
Lytle, Tx., U.S.	E3	120
M		
Ma, stm., Asia	D8	34
Maalaea Bay, b., Hi., U.S.	C5	88
Ma'ān, Jord.	D4	40
Maanshan, China	D7	28
Ma'arrat an-Nu'mān, Syria	B5	40
Maas (Meuse), stm., Eur.	D5	8
Maastricht, Neth.	E5	8
Mabank, Tx., U.S.	C4	120
Mabaruma, Guy.	C13	58
Mabel, Mn., U.S.	G7	100
Maben, Ms., U.S.	B4	101
Mableton, Ga., U.S.	h7	87
Mabscott, W.V., U.S.	D3	125
Mabton, Wa., U.S.	C5	124
Mača, Russia	F17	24
Macaé, Braz.	G8	57
Macão, Port.	F3	12
Macao see Macau, dep., Asia	M2	28
Macapá, Braz.	C8	54
Macará, Ec.	J3	58
Macarani, Braz.	C8	57
Macas, Ec.	I3	58
Macau, Braz.	E11	54
Macau (Aomen), Macao	M2	28
Macau (Aomen), dep., Asia	M2	28
MacClenny, Fl., U.S.	B4	86
MacDill Air Force Base, mil., Fl., U.S.	E4	86
Macdonnell Ranges, mts., Austl.	D6	50
MacDowell Reservoir, res., N.H., U.S.	E2	106
Macduff, Scot., U.K.	D10	7
Macdui, Ben, mtn., Scot., U.K.	D9	7
Macedo de Cavaleiros, Port.	D5	12
Macedonia, Oh., U.S.	A4	112
Macedonia, hist. reg., Eur.	H6	16
Macedonia, ctry., Eur.	H5	16
Maceió, Braz.	E11	54
Macerata, Italy	F8	14
Maces Bay, b., N.B., Can.	D3	71
MacGregor, Man., Can.	E2	70
Machačkala, Russia	I7	22
Machagai, Arg.	B4	56
Machala, Ec.	I3	58
Machecoul, Fr.	E5	10
Machias, Me., U.S.	D5	96
Machias, stm., Me., U.S.	B4	96
Machias, stm., Me., U.S.	D5	96
Machias Bay, b., Me., U.S.	D5	96
Machias Lakes, l., Me., U.S.	C5	96
Machilīpatnam (Bandar), India	D6	37
Machiques, Ven.	B6	58
Macho, Arroyo del, val., N.M., U.S.	C4	108
Machupicchu, Peru	F4	54
Macina, reg., Mali	F4	42
Mackay, Austl.	D9	50
Mackay, Lake, l., Austl.	D5	50
MacKenzie, B.C., Can.	B6	69
Mackenzie, stm., N.W. Ter., Can.	C6	66
Mackenzie Bay, b., Can.	C5	66
Mackenzie Mountains, mts., Can.	D7	66
Mackinac, co., Mi., U.S.	B5	99
Mackinac, Straits of, strt., Mi., U.S.	C6	99
Mackinac Bridge, Mi., U.S.	C6	99
Mackinac Island, i., Mi., U.S.	C6	99
Mackinaw, Il., U.S.	C4	90
Mackinaw, stm., Il., U.S.	C4	90
Mackinaw City, Mi., U.S.	C6	99
Maclear, S. Afr.	H5	44
Macmillan, stm., Yukon, Can.	D6	66
Macomb, Il., U.S.	C3	90
Macomb, co., Mi., U.S.	F8	99
Macomer, Italy	I3	14
Mâcon, Fr.	F11	10
Macon, Ga., U.S.	D3	87
Macon, Il., U.S.	D5	90
Macon, Ms., U.S.	B5	101
Macon, Mo., U.S.	B5	102
Macon, co., Al., U.S.	C4	78
Macon, co., Ga., U.S.	D2	87
Macon, co., Il., U.S.	D4	90
Macon, co., Mo., U.S.	B5	102
Macon, co., N.C., U.S.	f9	110
Macon, co., Tn., U.S.	A5	119
Macon, Bayou, stm., U.S.	B4	95
Macoupin, co., Il., U.S.	D4	90
MacTier, Ont., Can.	B5	73
Macungie, Pa., U.S.	E10	115
Mad, stm., Ca., U.S.	B2	82
Mad, stm., Ct., U.S.	B3	84
Mad, stm., N.H., U.S.	C3	106
Mad, stm., Oh., U.S.	C2	112
Mad, stm., Vt., U.S.	C3	122
Ma'dabā, Jord.	D4	40
Madagascar, ctry., Afr.	E9	44
Madame, Isle, i., N.S., Can.	D9	71
Madanapalle, India	F5	37
Madang, Pap. N. Gui.	m16	50a
Mādārīpur, Bngl.	I14	38
Madawaska, Me., U.S.	A4	96
Madawaska, stm., Can.	B9	74
Madawaska, stm., Ont., Can.	B7	73
Madawaska Lake, l., Me., U.S.	A4	96
Maddaloni, Italy	H9	14
Madeira, Oh., U.S.	o13	112
Madeira, i., Port.	B2	42
Madeira, stm., S.A.	E6	54
Madeira, Arquipélago da (Madeira Islands), is., Port.	m20	13a
Mädelegabel, mtn., Eur.	E17	10
Madeleine, Îles de la, is., Que., Can.	B8	71
Madelia, Mn., U.S.	F4	100
Madeline Island, i., Wi., U.S.	B3	126
Madera, Ca., U.S.	D3	82
Madera, co., Ca., U.S.	D4	82
Madhubani, India	G12	38
Madhya Pradesh, state, India	I8	38
Madill, Ok., U.S.	C5	113
Madīnat ash-Sha'b, Yemen	F3	46
Madingou, Congo	B2	44
Madison, Al., U.S.	A3	78
Madison, Ar., U.S.	B5	81
Madison, Ct., U.S.	D5	84
Madison, Fl., U.S.	B3	86
Madison, Ga., U.S.	C3	87
Madison, Il., U.S.	E3	90
Madison, In., U.S.	G7	91
Madison, Ks., U.S.	D7	93
Madison, Me., U.S.	D3	96
Madison, Mn., U.S.	E2	100
Madison, Ms., U.S.	C3	101
Madison, Ne., U.S.	C8	104
Madison, N.J., U.S.	B4	107
Madison, N.C., U.S.	A3	110
Madison, Oh., U.S.	A4	112
Madison, S.D., U.S.	D8	118
Madison, W.V., U.S.	C3	125
Madison, Wi., U.S.	E4	126
Madison, co., Al., U.S.	A3	78
Madison, co., Ar., U.S.	B2	81
Madison, co., Fl., U.S.	B3	86
Madison, co., Ga., U.S.	B3	87
Madison, co., Id., U.S.	F7	89
Madison, co., Il., U.S.	E4	90
Madison, co., In., U.S.	D6	91
Madison, co., Ia., U.S.	C3	92
Madison, co., Ky., U.S.	C5	94
Madison, co., La., U.S.	B4	95
Madison, co., Ms., U.S.	C4	101
Madison, co., Mo., U.S.	D7	102
Madison, co., Mt., U.S.	E5	103
Madison, co., Ne., U.S.	C8	104
Madison, co., N.Y., U.S.	C5	109
Madison, co., N.C., U.S.	f10	110
Madison, co., Oh., U.S.	C2	112
Madison, co., Tn., U.S.	B3	119
Madison, co., Tx., U.S.	D5	120
Madison, co., Va., U.S.	B4	123
Madison, stm., Mt., U.S.	E5	103
Madison Heights, Mi., U.S.	o15	99
Madison Heights, Va., U.S.	C3	123
Madison Lake, Mn., U.S.	F5	100
Madison Range, mts., Mt., U.S.	E5	103
Madisonville, Ky., U.S.	C2	94
Madisonville, La., U.S.	D5	95
Madisonville, Tn., U.S.	D9	119
Madisonville, Tx., U.S.	D5	120
Madiun, Indon.	m15	32
Madoc, Ont., Can.	C7	73
Mado Gashi, Kenya	B7	44
Madras, India	F6	37
Madras, Or., U.S.	C5	114
Madre, Laguna, b., Mex.	E11	62
Madre, Laguna, b., Tx., U.S.	F4	120
Madre, Sierra, mts., N.A.	J14	62
Madre, Sierra, mts., Phil.	B7	32
Madre de Dios, stm., S.A.	F5	54
Madre de Dios, Isla, i., Chile	G1	56
Madre del Sur, Sierra, mts., Mex.	I10	62
Madre Occidental, Sierra, mts., Mex.	E6	62
Madre Oriental, Sierra, mts., Mex.	F9	62
Madrid, Spain	E8	12
Madrid, Ia., U.S.	C4	92
Madridejos, Spain	F8	12
Maduo, China	E6	26
Madura, i., Indon.	G5	32
Madurai, India	H5	37
Maebashi, Japan	F12	30
Mae Hong Son, Thai.	E4	34
Maeser, Ut., U.S.	C6	121
Mae Sot, Thai.	F5	34
Maestra, Sierra, mts., Cuba	D9	64
Maevatanana, Madag.	E9	44
Mafia Island, i., Tan.	C7	44
Mafikeng, S. Afr.	G5	44
Mafra, Braz.	B7	56
Magadan, Russia	F24	24
Magadi, Kenya	B7	44
Magallanes, Estrecho de (Strait of Magellan), strt., S.A.	G2	56
Magangué, Col.	C5	58
Magazine, Ar., U.S.	B2	81
Magazine Mountain, mtn., Ar., U.S.	B2	81
Magdagači, Russia	G19	24
Magdalena, Bol.	F6	54
Magdalena, Mex.	B4	62
Magdalena, N.M., U.S.	C2	108
Magdalena, stm., Col.	B5	58
Magdalena, Bahía, b., Mex.	E3	62
Magdalena, Isla, i., Chile	E2	56
Magdalena Mountains, mts., N.M., U.S.	D2	108
Magdeburg, Ger.	C11	8
Magee, Ms., U.S.	D4	101
Magelang, Indon.	m15	33
Magellan, Strait of see Magallanes, Estrecho de, strt., S.A.	G2	56
Magenta, Italy	D3	14
Maggie Creek, stm., Nv., U.S.	C5	105
Maggiore, Lago, l., Eur.	C3	14
Magic Reservoir, res., Id., U.S.	F4	89
Magione, Italy	F7	14
Magna, Ut., U.S.	C3	121
Magnetawan, stm., Ont., Can.	B4	73
Magnitogorsk, Russia	G9	22
Magnolia, Ar., U.S.	D2	81
Magnolia, Ky., U.S.	C4	94
Magnolia, Ms., U.S.	D3	101
Magnolia, N.C., U.S.	C4	110
Magnolia, Oh., U.S.	B4	112
Magoffin, co., Ky., U.S.	C6	94
Magog, Que., Can.	D5	74
Magothy River, b., Md., U.S.	B4	97
Magpie, Lac, l., Que., Can.	F20	66
Magrath, Alta., Can.	E4	68
Magruder Mountain, mtn., Nv., U.S.	F4	105
Maguarinho, Cabo, c., Braz.	D9	54
Magway, Burma	D3	34
Mahābād, Iran	J7	22
Mahābhārat Range, mts., Nepal	F10	38
Mahaicony Village, Guy.	D14	58
Mahajamba, Baie de la, b., Madag.	E9	44
Mahajanga, Madag.	E9	44
Mahakam, stm., Indon.	E6	32
Mahānadi, stm., India	J11	38
Mahanoro, Madag.	E9	44
Mahanoy City, Pa., U.S.	E9	115
Mahārāshtra, state, India	C3	37
Maha Sarakham, Thai.	F7	34
Mahaska, co., Ia., U.S.	C5	92
Mahaṭṭat al-Qaṭrānah, Jord.	D5	40
Mahaṭṭat Ḥaraḍ, Sau. Ar.	D4	46
Mahbūbnagar, India	D4	37
Mahé Island, i., Sey.	B11	44
Mahenge, Tan.	C7	44
Mahi, stm., India	I5	38
Mahmūd-e 'Erāqī, Afg.	C3	38
Mahnomen, Mn., U.S.	C3	100
Mahnomen, co., Mn., U.S.	C3	100
Mahoba, India	H8	38
Mahogany Mountain, mtn., Or., U.S.	D9	114
Mahomet, Il., U.S.	C5	90
Mahón, Spain	F16	12
Mahone Bay, N.S., Can.	E5	71
Mahoning, co., Oh., U.S.	B5	112
Mahoning, stm., U.S.	A5	112
Mahopac, N.Y., U.S.	D7	109
Mahuva, India	J4	38
Mahwah, N.J., U.S.	A4	107
Maiden, N.C., U.S.	B1	110
Maidstone, Eng., U.K.	J13	7
Maidstone Lake, l., Vt., U.S.	B5	122
Maiduguri, Nig.	F8	42
Maili, Hi., U.S.	g9	88
Maili Point, c., Hi., U.S.	g9	88
Maillezais, Fr.	F6	10

Name | Map Ref | Page
ain, stm., Ger. F9 8
ainburg, Ger. G11 8
ain Channel, strt., Ont., Can. B3 73
ai-Ndombe, Lac, l., Zaire B3 44
aine, state, U.S. C3 96
ainland, i., Scot., U.K. B9 7
ainland, i., Scot., U.K. A11 7
ain Pass, strt., La., U.S. E6 95
ainz, Ger. E8 8
aipo, Volcán, vol., S.A. C3 56
aipú, Arg. D5 56
aiquetía, Ven. B9 58
aisonnette, N.B., Can. B4 71
aitland, Austl. F10 50
aitland, Ont., Can. C9 73
aize, Ks., U.S. g12 93
aizuru, Japan G8 30
aja, stm., Russia F20 24
ajene, Indon. F6 32
aji, Eth. G2 46
ajkop, Russia I6 22
ajno-Pyl'gino, Russia E29 24
ajor, co., Ok., U.S. A3 113
ajorca see Mallorca, i., Spain F15 12
akaha, Hi., U.S. g9 88
akaha Point, c., Hi., U.S. A2 88
akah Indian Reservation, Wa., U.S. A1 124
akahuena Point, c., Hi., U.S. B2 88
akakilo City, Hi., U.S. g9 88
akale, Indon. F6 32
akapuu Head, c., Hi., U.S. B4 88
akarska, Cro. F12 14
akasar, Selat (Makassar Strait), strt., Indon. F6 32
akasar see Ujungpandang, Indon. G6 32
akawao, Hi., U.S. C5 88
akaweli, Hi., U.S. B2 88
akeni, S.L. G3 42
akgadikgadi Pans, pl., Bots. F5 44
akhachkala see Machačkala, Russia I7 22
akindu, Kenya B7 44
akit, Russia E24 24
akkah (Mecca), Sau. Ar. D2 46
aklakovo, Russia F12 24
akó, Hung. I20 8
akokou, Gabon A2 44
akthar, Tun. N4 14
akumbi, Zaire C4 44
akurazaki, Japan K3 30
akurdi, Nig. G7 42
akushin Volcano, vol., Ak., U.S. E6 79
alabar, Fl., U.S. D6 86
alabar Coast, India G4 37
alabo, Eq. Gui. H7 42
alacca, Strait of, strt., Asia M6 34
alad City, Id., U.S. G6 89
alaga, Col. D6 58
alaga, Spain I7 12
alagón, Spain F8 12
alaimbandy, Madag. F9 44
alaja Kuril'skaja Gr'ada (Habomai-shotō), is., Russia p24 30a
alakāl, Sudan G12 42
alakoff, Tx., U.S. C4 120
alang, Indon. m16 32
alanje, Ang. C3 44
alanville, Benin F6 42
alaren, l., Swe. G11 6
alargüe, Arg. D3 56
alartic, Que., Can. k11 74
alaspina Glacier, Ak., U.S. D11 79
alatya, Tur. H15 4
alawi, ctry., Afr. D6 44
alaya, reg., Malay. M7 34
alay Peninsula, pen., Asia K6 34
alaysia, ctry., Asia E3 32
albaie, stm., Que., Can. B7 74
albork, Pol. A19 8
alcolm, Austl. E4 50
alden, Ma., U.S. B5 98
alden, Mo., U.S. E8 102
alden, W.V., U.S. m12 125
aldives, ctry., Asia I2 37
aldonado, Ur. C6 56
alegaon, India B3 37
alek Dīn, Afg. D3 38
alha Wells, Sudan E11 42
alheur, co., Or., U.S. D9 114
alheur, stm., Or., U.S. D9 114
alheur Lake, l., Or., U.S. D8 114
ali, ctry., Afr. E5 42
alibu, Ca., U.S. m11 82
alik, Wādī al-, val., Sudan E11 42
alin, Or., U.S. E5 114
alindi, Kenya B8 44
alino, Bukit, mtn., Indon. E7 32
alka, Russia G25 24
alkāpur, India B4 37
alkara, Tur. I10 16
allaig, Scot., U.K. D7 7
allawī, Egypt C12 42
alletts Bay, b., Vt., U.S. B2 122
allnitz, Aus. I13 8
allorca, i., Spain F14 12
allow, Ire. I4 7
almberget, Swe. C13 6
almédy, Bel. E6 8
almesbury, S. Afr. H3 44
almö, Swe. I9 6
almstrom Air Force Base, mil., Mt., U.S. C5 103
alolos, Phil. q19 33b
alone, N.Y., U.S. f10 109
aloney Reservoir, res., Ne., U.S. C5 104
aløy, Nor. F5 6
alpaso, Presa de, res., Mex. I13 62
alpelo, Isla de, i., Col. C2 54
alpeque Bay, b., P.E.I., Can. C6 71
alta, Il., U.S. B5 90
alta, Mt., U.S. B9 103
Malta, ctry., Eur. H10 4
Malta Channel, strt., Eur. M9 14
Maltahöhe, Nmb. F3 44
Maluku (Moluccas), is., Indon. F8 32
Maluku, Laut (Molucca Sea), Indon. F7 32
Malung, Swe. F9 6
Malvern, Ar., U.S. C3 81
Malvern, Ia., U.S. D2 92
Malvern, Oh., U.S. B4 112
Malvern, Pa., U.S. o19 115
Malverne, N.Y., U.S. k13 109
Malyj An'uj, stm., Russia D26 24
Malyj Tajmyr, Ostrov, i., Russia B15 24
Mama, Russia F16 24
Mamala Bay, b., Hi., U.S. g10 88
Mamaroneck, N.Y., U.S. h13 109
Mamberamo, stm., Indon. F10 32
Mamers, Fr. D7 10
Mamfe, Cam. G7 42
Mammoth, Az., U.S. E5 80
Mammoth Cave National Park, Ky., U.S. C4 94
Mammoth Lakes, Ca., U.S. D4 82
Mammoth Spring, Ar., U.S. A4 81
Mamoré, stm., S.A. F5 54
Mamou, Gui. F3 42
Mamou, La., U.S. D3 95
Man, I.C. G4 42
Man, W.V., U.S. D3 125
Manacapuru, Braz. D6 54
Manacor, Spain F15 12
Manado, Indon. E7 32
Managua, Nic. H4 64
Managua, Lago de, l., Nic. H4 64
Manakara, Madag. F9 44
Manama see Al-Manāmah, Bahr. C5 46
Manana Island, i., Hi., U.S. g11 88
Mananara, Madag. E9 44
Mananjary, Madag. F9 44
Manantico Creek, stm., N.J., U.S. E3 107
Mana Point, c., Hi., U.S. A2 88
Manas, China C4 26
Manasquan, N.J., U.S. C4 107
Manasquan, stm., N.J., U.S. C4 107
Manassa, Co., U.S. D5 83
Manassas, Va., U.S. B5 123
Manassas National Battlefield Park, Va., U.S. g11 123
Manassas Park, Va., U.S. B5 123
Manatee, co., Fl., U.S. E4 86
Manatee, stm., Fl., U.S. E4 86
Manaus, Braz. D6 54
Manawa, Wi., U.S. D5 126
Manbij, Syria A5 40
Mancelona, Mi., U.S. D5 99
Mancha Real, Spain H8 12
Manchester, Eng., U.K. H10 7
Manchester, Ct., U.S. B5 84
Manchester, Ga., U.S. D2 87
Manchester, Ia., U.S. B6 92
Manchester, Ky., U.S. C6 94
Manchester, Me., U.S. D3 96
Manchester, Md., U.S. A4 97
Manchester, Ma., U.S. A6 98
Manchester, Mi., U.S. F6 99
Manchester, Mo., U.S. f12 102
Manchester, N.H., U.S. E4 106
Manchester, N.Y., U.S. C3 109
Manchester, Oh., U.S. D2 112
Manchester, Pa., U.S. F8 115
Manchester, Tn., U.S. B5 119
Manchester, Vt., U.S. E2 122
Manchester Center, Vt., U.S. E2 122
Manchuria, reg., China B12 26
Manciano, Italy G6 14
Mancos, Co., U.S. D2 83
Mancos, stm., U.S. D2 83
Mand, stm., Iran C5 46
Manda, Tan. D6 44
Mandal, Nor. G6 6
Mandalay, Burma C4 34
Mandalgov', Mong. B8 26
Mandan, N.D., U.S. C5 111
Mandas, Italy J4 14
Mandasor, India H6 38
Mandeb, Bāb el-, strt. F3 46
Mandeville, Ar., U.S. D2 81
Mandeville, La., U.S. D5 95
Mandi Bahāuddīn, Pak. D5 38
Mandimba, Moz. D7 44
Mandla, India I9 38
Manduria, Italy I12 14
Māndvi, India I3 38
Mandya, India F4 37
Manerbio, Italy D5 14
Manfredonia, Italy H10 14
Mangabeiras, Chapada das, hills, Braz. F9 54
Mangalore, India F3 37
Mangkalihat, Tanjung, c., Indon. E6 32
Manglares, Cabo, c., Col. G3 58
Mangoche, Mwi. D7 44
Mangoky, stm., Madag. F8 44
Mangole, Pulau, i., Indon. F8 32
Māngrol, India J4 38
Mangrove Cay, i., Bah. B9 64
Mangualde, Port. E4 12
Mangum, Ok., U.S. C2 113
Mangya, China D5 26
Manhattan, Ks., U.S. C7 93
Manhattan, Mt., U.S. E5 103
Manhattan Beach, Ca., U.S. n12 82
Manhattan Island, i., N.Y., U.S. h13 109
Manheim, Pa., U.S. F9 115
Manhuaçu, Braz. F7 57
Manicoré, Braz. E6 54
Manicouagan, stm., Que., Can. F19 66
Manicouagan, Réservoir, res., Que., Can. h13 74
Manila, Phil. q19 32
Manila, Ar., U.S. B5 81
Manila Bay, b., Phil. C7 32
Manilla, Ia., U.S. C2 92
Manipur, ter., India H15 38
Manisa, Tur. K11 16
Manistee, Mi., U.S. D4 99
Manistee, co., Mi., U.S. D4 99
Manistee, stm., Mi., U.S. D5 99
Manistique, Mi., U.S. C4 99
Manistique, stm., Mi., U.S. B4 99
Manistique Lake, l., Mi., U.S. B5 99
Manito, Il., U.S. C4 90
Manitoba, prov., Can. C3 70
Manitoba, Lake, l., Man., Can. D2 70
Manitou, Man., Can. E2 70
Manitou, Lake, l., Ont., Can. B3 73
Manitou Island, i., Mi., U.S. A3 99
Manitou Lake, l., Sask., Can. E1 75
Manitoulin Island, i., Ont., Can. B2 73
Manitou Springs, Co., U.S. C6 83
Manitowoc, Wi., U.S. D6 126
Manitowoc, co., Wi., U.S. D6 126
Manitowoc, stm., Wi., U.S. h10 126
Maniwaki, Que., Can. C2 74
Manizales, Col. E5 58
Manjacaze, Moz. F6 44
Mānjra, stm., India C4 37
Mankato, Ks., U.S. C5 93
Mankato, Mn., U.S. F5 100
Mankoya, Zam. D4 44
Manlius, N.Y., U.S. C5 109
Manlléu, Spain C14 12
Manly, Ia., U.S. A4 92
Manmād, India B3 37
Mannar, Gulf of, b., Asia H5 37
Mannārgudi, India G5 37
Mannar Island, i., Sri L. H5 37
Mannford, Ok., U.S. A5 113
Mannheim, Ger. F8 8
Manning, Alta., Can. A2 68
Manning, Ia., U.S. C2 92
Manning, S.C., U.S. D7 117
Mannington, W.V., U.S. B4 125
Manns Creek, stm., W.V., U.S. n14 125
Mannville, Alta., Can. C5 68
Manokin, stm., Md., U.S. D6 97
Manokotak, Ak., U.S. D8 79
Manokwari, Indon. F9 32
Manomet, Ma., U.S. C6 98
Manomet Point, c., Ma., U.S. C6 98
Manono, Zaire C5 44
Manor, Tx., U.S. D4 120
Manosque, Fr. I12 10
Manouane, Lac, l., Que., Can. h12 74
Manresa, Spain D13 12
Mānsa, India F6 38
Mansa, Zam. D5 44
Manseau, Que., Can. C5 74
Mansel Island, i., N.W. Ter., Can. D17 66
Mansfield, Eng., U.K. H11 7
Mansfield, Ar., U.S. B1 81
Mansfield, Il., U.S. C5 90
Mansfield, La., U.S. B2 95
Mansfield, Ma., U.S. B5 98
Mansfield, Mo., U.S. D5 102
Mansfield, Oh., U.S. B3 112
Mansfield, Pa., U.S. C7 115
Mansfield, Tx., U.S. n9 120
Mansfield, Mount, mtn., Vt., U.S. B3 122
Mansfield Center, Ct., U.S. B7 84
Mansfield Hollow Lake, res., Ct., U.S. B7 84
Manson, Ia., U.S. B3 92
Manson, Wa., U.S. B5 124
Mansonville, Que., Can. D5 74
Mansura, La., U.S. C3 95
Manta, Ec. H2 58
Mantachie, Ms., U.S. A5 101
Manteca, Ca., U.S. D3 82
Manteno, Il., U.S. B6 90
Manteo, N.C., U.S. B7 110
Mantes-la-Jolie, Fr. D8 10
Manti, Ut., U.S. D4 121
Mantiqueira, Serra da, mts., Braz. F6 57
Manton, Mi., U.S. D5 99
Mantorville, Mn., U.S. F6 100
Mantova, Italy D5 14
Mantua, Oh., U.S. A4 112
Mantua, Ut., U.S. B4 121
Manturovo, Russia C27 18
Manukau Harbour, b., N.Z. B5 52
Manumuskin, stm., N.J., U.S. E3 107
Manus Island, i., Pap. N. Gui. k16 50a
Manvel, Tx., U.S. r14 120
Manville, N.J., U.S. B3 107
Manville, R.I., U.S. B4 116
Many, La., U.S. C2 95
Many Farms, Az., U.S. A6 80
Manzanares, Spain F8 12
Manzanillo, Cuba D9 64
Manzanillo, Mex. H7 62
Manzano Mountains, mts., N.M., U.S. C3 108
Manzano Peak, mtn., N.M., U.S. C3 108
Manzhouli, China B10 26
Mao, Chad F9 42
Maoke, Pegunungan, mts., Indon. F10 32
Mapastepec, Mex. J13 62
Mapi, Indon. G10 32
Mapia, Kepulauan, is., Indon. E9 32
Mapimí, Mex. E8 62
Mapimí, Bolsón de, des., Mex. D8 62
Mapire, Ven. D10 58
Maple, stm., U.S. A7 118
Maple, stm., Ia., U.S. B2 92
Maple, stm., N.D., U.S. C8 111
Maple Bluff, Wi., U.S. E4 126
Maple Grove, Mn., U.S. m12 100
Maple Heights, Oh., U.S. h9 112
Maple Lake, Mn., U.S. E5 100
Maple Plain, Mn., U.S. m11 100
Maple Shade, N.J., U.S. D2 107
Maplesville, Al., U.S. C3 78
Mapleton, Ia., U.S. B2 92
Mapleton, Mn., U.S. G5 100
Mapleton, N.D., U.S. C8 111
Mapleton, Or., U.S. C3 114
Mapleton, Ut., U.S. C4 121
Maple Valley, Wa., U.S. f11 124
Mapleville, R.I., U.S. B2 116
Maplewood, Mn., U.S. n12 100
Maplewood, Mo., U.S. f13 102
Maplewood, N.J., U.S. B4 107
Mapuera, stm., Braz. D7 54
Maputo (Lourenço Marques), Moz. G6 44
Maqueda, Spain E7 12
Maquela do Zombo, Ang. C3 44
Maquinchao, Arg. E3 56
Maquoketa, Ia., U.S. B7 92
Maquoketa, stm., Ia., U.S. B6 92
Maquoketa, North Fork, stm., Ia., U.S. B7 92
Mar, Serra do, clf, Braz. A7 56
Marabá, Braz. E9 54
Maracá, Ilha de, i., Braz. C8 54
Maracaibo, Ven. B7 58
Maracaibo, Lago de, l., Ven. C7 58
Maracay, Ven. B9 58
Marādah, Libya C9 42
Maradi, Niger F7 42
Marāgheh, Iran J7 22
Maragogipe, Braz. B9 57
Marahuaca, Cerro, mtn., Ven. F10 58
Marais des Cygnes, stm., U.S. D8 93
Marajó, Baía de, b., Braz. D9 54
Marajó, Ilha de, i., Braz. D9 54
Maralal, Kenya A7 44
Marambaia, Ilha da, i., Braz. G7 57
Marana, Az., U.S. E4 80
Marang, Malay. L7 34
Marañón, stm., Peru D3 54
Marans, Fr. F5 10
Marapanim, Braz. D9 54
Marathon, Fl., U.S. H5 86
Marathon, Wi., U.S. D4 126
Marathon, co., Wi., U.S. D4 126
Marawī, Sudan E1 46
Marble, Mn., U.S. C5 100
Marble, N.C., U.S. f9 110
Marble Bar, Austl. D3 50
Marble Canyon, val., Az., U.S. A4 80
Marble Falls, Tx., U.S. D3 120
Marblehead, Ma., U.S. B6 98
Marble Hill, Mo., U.S. D8 102
Marbleton, Wy., U.S. D2 127
Marburg an der Lahn, Ger. E8 8
Marbury, Md., U.S. C3 97
Marcaria, Italy D5 14
Marceline, Mo., U.S. B5 102
Marcellus, Mi., U.S. F5 99
March (Morava), stm., Eur. G16 8
Marcha, Russia E18 24
March Air Force Base, mil., Ca., U.S. F5 82
Marche-en-Famenne, Bel. E5 8
Marchena, Spain H6 12
Mar Chiquita, Laguna, l., Arg. C4 56
Marco, Fl., U.S. G5 86
Marcus, Ia., U.S. B2 92
Marcus Baker, Mount, mtn., Ak., U.S. g18 79
Marcus Hook, Pa., U.S. G11 115
Marcy, Mount, mtn., N.Y., U.S. A7 109
Mardān, Pak. C5 38
Mar del Plata, Arg. D5 56
Mardin, Tur. H16 4
Mareeba, Austl. C9 50
Mareg, Som. H4 46
Marengo, Il., U.S. A5 90
Marengo, In., U.S. H5 91
Marengo, Ia., U.S. C5 92
Marengo, co., Al., U.S. C2 78
Marennes, Fr. G5 10
Marfa, Tx., U.S. o12 120
Margaret, Al., U.S. B3 78
Margarita, Isla de, i., Ven. B10 58
Margate, Fl., U.S. F6 86
Margate City, N.J., U.S. E3 107
Margherita Peak, mtn., Afr. A5 44
Marghī, Afg. C2 38
Margrethe, Lake, l., Mi., U.S. D6 99
María Cleofas, Isla, i., Mex. G6 62
María Madre, Isla, i., Mex. G6 62
María Magdalena, Isla, i., Mex. G6 62
Marian, Lake, l., Fl., U.S. E5 86
Marianao, Cuba C6 64
Marianna, Ar., U.S. C5 81
Marianna, Fl., U.S. B1 86
Marias, stm., Mt., U.S. B4 103
Marias, Islas, is., Mex. G6 62
Marias Pass, Mt., U.S. B3 103
Mariato, Punta, c., Pan. K7 64
Mariazell, Aus. H15 8
Maribor, Slo. C10 14
Marica (Évros) (Meriç), stm., Eur. G9 16
Maricopa, Az., U.S. E3 80
Maricopa, Ca., U.S. E4 82
Maricopa, co., Az., U.S. D3 80
Maricopa Mountains, mts., Az., U.S. m7 80
Marie-Galante, i., Guad. G17 64
Mariehamn, Fin. F12 6
Mariemont, Oh., U.S. o13 112
Mariental, Nmb. F3 44
Marienville, Pa., U.S. D3 115
Maries, co., Mo., U.S. C6 102
Mariestad, Swe. G9 6
Marietta, Ga., U.S. C2 87
Marietta, Oh., U.S. C4 112
Marietta, Ok., U.S. D4 113
Marietta, S.C., U.S. A2 117
Marieville, Que., Can. D4 74
Marília, Braz. G4 57
Marimba, Ang. C3 44
Marín, Spain C3 12
Marin, co., Ca., U.S. C2 82
Marinduque Island, i., Phil. C7 32
Marine, Il., U.S. E4 90
Marine City, Mi., U.S. F8 99
Marine On St. Croix, Mn., U.S. E6 100
Marinette, Wi., U.S. C6 126
Marinette, co., Wi., U.S. C5 126
Maringá, Braz. G3 57
Maringouin, La., U.S. D4 95
Marinha Grande, Port. F3 12
Marion, Al., U.S. C2 78
Marion, Ar., U.S. B5 81
Marion, Il., U.S. F5 90
Marion, In., U.S. C6 91
Marion, Ia., U.S. B6 92
Marion, Ks., U.S. D6 93
Marion, Ky., U.S. e9 94
Marion, La., U.S. B3 95
Marion, Mi., U.S. D5 99
Marion, Ms., U.S. C5 101
Marion, N.C., U.S. B1 110
Marion, Oh., U.S. B2 112
Marion, Pa., U.S. G6 115
Marion, S.C., U.S. C9 117
Marion, S.D., U.S. D8 118
Marion, Va., U.S. f10 123
Marion, Wi., U.S. D5 126
Marion, co., Al., U.S. A2 78
Marion, co., Ar., U.S. A3 81
Marion, co., Fl., U.S. C4 86
Marion, co., Ga., U.S. D2 87
Marion, co., Il., U.S. E4 90
Marion, co., In., U.S. E5 91
Marion, co., Ia., U.S. C4 92
Marion, co., Ks., U.S. D6 93
Marion, co., Ky., U.S. C4 94
Marion, co., Ms., U.S. D4 101
Marion, co., Mo., U.S. B6 102
Marion, co., Oh., U.S. B2 112
Marion, co., Or., U.S. C4 114
Marion, co., S.C., U.S. C9 117
Marion, co., Tn., U.S. D8 119
Marion, co., Tx., U.S. C5 120
Marion, co., W.V., U.S. B4 125
Marion, Lake, res., S.C., U.S. E7 117
Marion Station, Md., U.S. D6 97
Marionville, Mo., U.S. D4 102
Maripa, Ven. D10 58
Mariposa, co., Ca., U.S. D3 82
Mariscal Estigarribia, Para. A4 56
Marissa, Il., U.S. E4 90
Maritime Alps, mts., Eur. H14 10
Mariupol' (Ždanov), Ukr. H5 22
Marka, Som. H3 46
Markaryd, Swe. H9 6
Markdale, Ont., Can. C4 73
Marked Tree, Ar., U.S. B5 81
Markesan, Wi., U.S. E5 126
Markham, Ont., Can. D5 73
Markham, Il., U.S. k9 90
Markham, Tx., U.S. E4 120
Markham, Mount, mtn., Ant. A29 47
Markland Lock and Dam, U.S. B5 94
Markle, In., U.S. C7 91
Markovo, Russia E28 24
Marks, Ms., U.S. A3 101
Marksville, La., U.S. C3 95
Marktredwitz, Ger. E12 8
Mark Twain Lake, res., Mo., U.S. B6 102
Marlboro, N.Y., U.S. D6 109
Marlboro, Va., U.S. n17 123
Marlboro, co., S.C., U.S. B8 117
Marlborough, Ct., U.S. C6 84
Marlborough, Ma., U.S. B4 98
Marlborough, N.H., U.S. E2 106
Marle, Fr. C10 10
Marlette, Mi., U.S. E7 99
Marley, Md., U.S. B4 97
Marlin, Tx., U.S. D4 120
Marlinton, W.V., U.S. C4 125
Marlow, Ok., U.S. C4 113
Marlowe, W.V., U.S. B7 125
Marlton, N.J., U.S. D3 107
Marmaduke, Ar., U.S. A5 81
Marmande, Fr. H7 10
Marmara Adası, i., Tur. I11 16
Marmara Denizi (Sea of Marmara), Tur. I12 16
Marmaris, Tur. M12 16
Marmet, W.V., U.S. C3 125
Marmora, Ont., Can. C7 73
Marne, stm., Fr. C10 10
Maroa, Il., U.S. C5 90
Maroa, Ven. F9 58
Maroantsetra, Madag. E9 44
Maromokotro, mtn., Madag. D9 44
Marondera, Zimb. E6 44
Maros (Mureș), stm., Eur. C4 16
Maroua, Cam. F8 42
Marovoay, Madag. E9 44
Marquesas Keys, is., Fl., U.S. H4 86
Marquette, Mi., U.S. B3 99
Marquette, co., Mi., U.S. B3 99
Marquette, co., Wi., U.S. E4 126
Marquette Heights, Il., U.S. C4 90
Marquise, Fr. B8 10
Marrah, Jabal, mtn., Sudan F10 42
Marrakech, Mor. B4 42
Marrero, La., U.S. E5 95
Mars, Pa., U.S. E1 115
Marsabit, Kenya H2 46
Marsala, Italy L7 14
Marsā Matrūh, Egypt B11 42
Marseille, Fr. J12 10
Marseille-en-Beauvaisis, Fr. C8 10
Marseilles, Il., U.S. B5 90
Marshall, Sask., Can. D1 75
Marshall, Ar., U.S. B3 81
Marshall, Il., U.S. D6 90
Marshall, Mi., U.S. F6 99
Marshall, Mn., U.S. F3 100
Marshall, Mo., U.S. B4 102
Marshall, N.C., U.S. f10 110
Marshall, Tx., U.S. C5 120
Marshall, Va., U.S. B5 123
Marshall, Wi., U.S. E4 126
Marshall, co., Al., U.S. A3 78
Marshall, co., Il., U.S. B4 90
Marshall, co., In., U.S. B5 91
Marshall, co., Ia., U.S. C4 92
Marshall, co., Ks., U.S. C7 93
Marshall, co., Ky., U.S. f9 94
Marshall, co., Mn., U.S. B2 100
Marshall, co., Ms., U.S. A4 101
Marshall, co., Ok., U.S. C5 113
Marshall, co., S.D., U.S. B8 118
Marshall, co., Tn., U.S. B5 119

Name	Map Ref	Page
Marshall, co., W.V., U.S.	B4	125
Marshallton, De., U.S.	B3	85
Marshalltown, Ia., U.S.	B5	92
Marshallville, Ga., U.S.	D3	87
Marshes Siding, Ky., U.S.	D5	94
Marshfield, Ma., U.S.	B6	98
Marshfield, Mo., U.S.	D5	102
Marshfield, Wi., U.S.	D3	126
Marshfield Hills, Ma., U.S.	B6	98
Marsh Fork, stm., W.V., U.S.	n13	125
Marsh Harbour, Bah.	A9	64
Mars Hill, Me., U.S.	B5	96
Mars Hill, N.C., U.S.	f10	110
Marsh Island, i., La., U.S.	E4	95
Marsh Lake, res., Mn., U.S.	E2	100
Marsh Peak, mtn., Ut., U.S.	C6	121
Marshville, N.C., U.S.	C2	110
Marsing, Id., U.S.	F2	89
Märsta, Swe.	G11	6
Marston, Mo., U.S.	E8	102
Mart, Tx., U.S.	D4	120
Martaban, Gulf of, b., Burma	F4	34
Marthasville, Mo., U.S.	C6	102
Martha's Vineyard, i., Ma., U.S.	D6	98
Martigny, Switz.	F14	10
Martigues, Fr.	I12	10
Martin, Slov.	F18	8
Martin, Ky., U.S.	C7	94
Martin, S.D., U.S.	D4	118
Martin, Tn., U.S.	A3	119
Martin, co., Fl., U.S.	E6	86
Martin, co., In., U.S.	G4	91
Martin, co., Ky., U.S.	C7	94
Martin, co., Mn., U.S.	G4	100
Martin, co., N.C., U.S.	B5	110
Martin, co., Tx., U.S.	C2	120
Martina Franca, Italy	I12	14
Martinez, Ca., U.S.	C2	82
Martinez, Ga., U.S.	C4	87
Martínez de la Torre, Mex.	G11	62
Martinique, dep., N.A.	G17	64
Martin Lake, res., Al., U.S.	C4	78
Martin Point, c., Ak., U.S.	A11	79
Martinsberg, Aus.	G15	8
Martinsburg, Pa., U.S.	F5	115
Martinsburg, W.V., U.S.	B7	125
Martins Ferry, Oh., U.S.	B5	112
Martinsville, Il., U.S.	D6	90
Martinsville, In., U.S.	F5	91
Martinsville, Va., U.S.	D3	123
Martos, Spain	H8	12
Martre, Lac la, l., N.W. Ter., Can.	D9	66
Martti, Fin.	C17	6
Marugame, Japan	H6	30
Ma'rūt, Afg.	E2	38
Marvejols, Fr.	H10	10
Marvell, Ar., U.S.	C5	81
Marvine, Mount, mtn., Ut., U.S.	E4	121
Mary, Turk.	J10	22
Mary, Lake, l., Mn., U.S.	E3	100
Mary, Lake, l., Ms., U.S.	D2	101
Maryborough, Austl.	E10	50
Maryland, state, U.S.	B4	97
Maryland City, Md., U.S.	B4	97
Maryland Heights, Mo., U.S.	f13	102
Maryland Point, c., Md., U.S.	D3	97
Maryport, Eng., U.K.	G9	7
Marys, stm., Nv., U.S.	B6	105
Marys Peak, mtn., Or., U.S.	C3	114
Marystown, Newf., Can.	E4	72
Marysville, Ca., U.S.	C3	82
Marysville, Ks., U.S.	C7	93
Marysville, Mi., U.S.	F8	99
Marysville, Oh., U.S.	B2	112
Marysville, Pa., U.S.	F8	115
Marysville, Wa., U.S.	A3	124
Maryville, Mo., U.S.	A3	102
Maryville, Tn., U.S.	D10	119
Marzūq, Libya	C8	42
Marzūq, Idehan, reg., Libya	C8	42
Masai Steppe, plat., Tan.	B7	44
Masaka, Ug.	B6	44
Masan, S. Kor.	D12	26
Masasi, Tan.	D7	44
Masaya, Nic.	I4	64
Masbate Island, i., Phil.	C7	32
Mascarene Islands, is., Afr.	F11	44
Mascoma, stm., N.H., U.S.	C2	106
Mascoma Lake, l., N.H., U.S.	C2	106
Mascot, Tn., U.S.	C10	119
Mascota, Mex.	G7	62
Mascouche, Que., Can.	D4	74
Mascoutah, Il., U.S.	E4	90
Maseru, Leso.	G5	44
Mashābih, i., Sau. Ar.	C2	46
Mashapaug Pond, l., Ct., U.S.	A7	84
Masherbrum, mtn., Pak.	C7	38
Mashhad, Iran	J9	22
Masi Manimba, Zaire	B3	44
Masindi, Ug.	H12	42
Masjed Soleymān, Iran	B4	46
Mask, Lough, l., Ire.	H3	7
Maskanah, Syria	A6	40
Maskinongé, Que., Can.	C4	74
Mason, Mi., U.S.	F6	99
Mason, Nv., U.S.	E2	105
Mason, Oh., U.S.	C1	112
Mason, Tx., U.S.	D3	120
Mason, W.V., U.S.	B2	125
Mason, co., Il., U.S.	C4	90
Mason, co., Ky., U.S.	B6	94
Mason, co., Mi., U.S.	D4	99
Mason, co., Tx., U.S.	D3	120
Mason, co., Wa., U.S.	B2	124
Mason, co., W.V., U.S.	C3	125
Mason City, Il., U.S.	C4	90
Mason City, Ia., U.S.	A4	92
Masontown, Pa., U.S.	G2	115
Masontown, W.V., U.S.	B5	125
Masqaṭ (Muscat), Oman	D6	46
Massa, Italy	E5	14
Massabesic Lake, l., N.H., U.S.	E4	106
Massac, co., Il., U.S.	F5	90
Massachusetts, state, U.S.	B4	98
Massachusetts Bay, b., Ma., U.S.	B6	98
Massacre Lake, l., Nv., U.S.	B2	105
Massafra, Italy	I12	14
Massa Marittima, Italy	F5	14
Massangena, Moz.	F6	44
Massapoag Lake, l., Ma., U.S.	h11	98
Massarosa, Italy	F5	14
Massasecum, Lake, l., N.H., U.S.	D3	106
Massena, N.Y., U.S.	f10	109
Massenya, Chad	F9	42
Masset, B.C., Can.	C1	69
Massey, Ont., Can.	A2	73
Massif Central see Central, Massif, mts., Fr.	G10	10
Massillon, Oh., U.S.	B4	112
Massive, Mount, mtn., Co., U.S.	B4	83
Masterton, N.Z.	D5	52
Mastic Beach, N.Y., U.S.	n16	109
Mastung, Pak.	F2	38
Masuda, Japan	H4	30
Masury, Oh., U.S.	A5	112
Matadi, Zaire	C2	44
Matagalpa, Nic.	H5	64
Matagorda, co., Tx., U.S.	E5	120
Matagorda Bay, b., Tx., U.S.	E4	120
Matagorda Island, i., Tx., U.S.	E4	120
Matagorda Peninsula, pen., Tx., U.S.	E5	120
Matale, Sri L.	I6	37
Matamoras, Pa., U.S.	D12	115
Matamoros, Mex.	E11	62
Matamoros de la Laguna, Mex.	E8	62
Matandu, stm., Tan.	C7	44
Matane, Que., Can.	k13	74
Matanuska, stm., Ak., U.S.	g18	79
Matanzas, Cuba	C7	64
Matanzas Inlet, b., Fl., U.S.	C5	86
Matara, Sri L.	J6	37
Mataró, Spain	D14	12
Matatiele, S. Afr.	H5	44
Matawan, N.J., U.S.	C4	107
Matehuala, Mex.	F9	62
Mateira, Braz.	E3	57
Matelica, Italy	F7	14
Matera, Italy	I11	14
Mateur, Tun.	L4	14
Matewan, W.V., U.S.	D2	125
Mather, Pa., U.S.	G1	115
Mather Air Force Base, mil., Ca., U.S.	C3	82
Mather Peaks, mts., Wy., U.S.	B5	127
Mathews, La., U.S.	E5	95
Mathews, Va., U.S.	C6	123
Mathews, co., Va., U.S.	C6	123
Mathews, Lake, l., Ca., U.S.	n14	82
Mathis, Tx., U.S.	E4	120
Mathiston, Ms., U.S.	B4	101
Mathura, India	G7	38
Matías Romero, Mex.	I12	62
Matinicus Island, i., Me., U.S.	E3	96
Mātli, Pak.	H3	38
Mato, Cerro, mtn., Ven.	D10	58
Matoaca, Va., U.S.	n18	123
Mato Grosso, Braz.	F7	54
Mato Grosso, Planalto do, plat., Braz.	G7	54
Matosinhos, Port.	D3	12
Matou, Tai.	L9	28
Maṭraḥ, Oman	D6	46
Matsqui, B.C., Can.	f13	69
Matsudo, Japan	G12	30
Matsue, Japan	G6	30
Matsumae, Japan	r18	30a
Matsumoto, Japan	F10	30
Matsusaka, Japan	H9	30
Matsu Tao, i., Tai.	I8	28
Matsuyama, Japan	I5	30
Mattagami, stm., Ont., Can.	F16	66
Mattamiscontis Lake, l., Me., U.S.	C4	96
Mattamuskeet, Lake, l., N.C., U.S.	B6	110
Mattāncheri, India	H4	37
Mattapoisett, Ma., U.S.	C6	98
Mattaponi, stm., Va., U.S.	C5	123
Mattawa, Ont., Can.	A6	73
Mattawamkeag, Me., U.S.	C4	96
Mattawamkeag, stm., Me., U.S.	C4	96
Mattawamkeag Lake, l., Me., U.S.	C4	96
Matterhorn, mtn., Eur.	G14	10
Matterhorn, mtn., Nv., U.S.	B6	105
Matteson, Il., U.S.	k9	90
Matthews, Mo., U.S.	E8	102
Matthews, N.C., U.S.	B2	110
Matthews Ridge, Guy.	D12	58
Matthew Town, Bah.	D11	64
Mattighofen, Aus.	G13	8
Mattituck, N.Y., U.S.	n16	109
Mattoon, Il., U.S.	D5	90
Mattoon, Lake, res., Il., U.S.	D5	90
Mattydale, N.Y., U.S.	B4	109
Matunuck, R.I., U.S.	G3	116
Maturín, Ven.	C11	58
Maúa, Moz.	D7	44
Maubeuge, Fr.	B10	10
Maud, Ok., U.S.	B5	113
Maugansville, Md., U.S.	A2	97
Maui, co., Hi., U.S.	B5	88
Maui, i., Hi., U.S.	C6	88
Mauldin, S.C., U.S.	B3	117
Mauléon-Licharre, Fr.	I6	10
Maulvi Bāzār, Bngl.	H14	38
Maumee, Oh., U.S.	A2	112
Maumee, stm., U.S.	A2	112
Maumee Bay, b., U.S.	G7	99
Maumelle, Lake, res., Ar., U.S.	C3	81
Maun, Bots.	E4	44
Mauna Kea, vol., Hi., U.S.	D6	88
Maunaloa, Hi., U.S.	B4	88
Mauna Loa, vol., Hi., U.S.	D6	88
Maunalua Bay, b., Hi., U.S.	g10	88
Maunath Bhanjan, India	H10	38
Maunawili, Hi., U.S.	g10	88
Mau Rānīpur, India	H8	38
Maurepas, Lake, l., La., U.S.	D5	95
Mauriac, Fr.	G9	10
Maurice, Ia., U.S.	B1	92
Maurice, stm., N.J., U.S.	E2	107
Mauritania, ctry., Afr.	D3	42
Mauritius, ctry., Afr.	F11	44
Maurs, Fr.	H9	10
Maury, co., Tn., U.S.	B4	119
Maury City, Tn., U.S.	B2	119
Maury Island, i., Wa., U.S.	f11	124
Mauston, Wi., U.S.	E3	126
Mauterndorf, Aus.	H13	8
Mauthausen, Aus.	G14	8
Maverick, co., Tx., U.S.	E2	120
Maw-Daung Pass, Asia	I5	34
Mawlaik, Burma	C3	34
Mawlamyine (Moulmein), Burma	F4	34
Maw Taung, mtn., Asia	I5	34
Maxinkuckee, Lake, l., In., U.S.	B5	91
Max Meadows, Va., U.S.	D2	123
Maxton, N.C., U.S.	C3	110
Maxville, Ont., Can.	B10	73
Maxwell, Ia., U.S.	C4	92
Maxwell Acres, W.V., U.S.	g8	125
Maxwell Air Force Base, mil., Al., U.S.	C3	78
Mayaguana, i., Bah.	C11	64
Mayaguana Passage, strt., Bah.	C11	64
Mayagüez, P.R.	E14	64
Maya Mountains, mts., N.A.	F3	64
Maybole, Scot., U.K.	F8	7
Mayen, Ger.	E7	8
Mayenne, Fr.	D6	10
Mayer, Az., U.S.	C3	80
Mayerthorpe, Alta., Can.	C3	68
Mayes, co., Ok., U.S.	A6	113
Mayesville, S.C., U.S.	D7	117
Mayfield, Ky., U.S.	f9	94
Mayfield, Pa., U.S.	C10	115
Mayfield Heights, Oh., U.S.	A4	112
Mayfield Lake, res., Wa., U.S.	C3	124
Mayflower, Ar., U.S.	C3	81
Mayking, Ky., U.S.	C7	94
Maykop see Majkop, Russia	I6	22
Maymyo, Burma	C4	34
Maynard, Ma., U.S.	B5	98
Maynardville, Tn., U.S.	C10	119
Mayne, B.C., Can.	g12	69
Mayo, Yukon, Can.	D5	66
Mayo, Md., U.S.	C4	97
Mayo, S.C., U.S.	A4	117
Mayodan, N.C., U.S.	A3	110
Mayotte, ter., Afr.	D9	44
Mayotte, i., May.	D9	44
May Park, Or., U.S.	B8	114
Mayport Naval Station, mil., Fl., U.S.	B5	86
Maysville, Ga., U.S.	B3	87
Maysville, Ky., U.S.	B6	94
Maysville, Mo., U.S.	B3	102
Maysville, N.C., U.S.	C5	110
Maysville, Ok., U.S.	C4	113
Mayumba, Gabon	B2	44
Māyūram, India	G5	37
Mayville, Mi., U.S.	E7	99
Mayville, N.Y., U.S.	C1	109
Mayville, N.D., U.S.	B8	111
Mayville, Wi., U.S.	E5	126
Maywood, Il., U.S.	k9	90
Maywood, N.J., U.S.	h8	107
Maywood Park, Or., U.S.	*B4	114
Mazabuka, Zam.	E5	44
Mazamet, Fr.	I9	10
Mazara del Vallo, Italy	L7	14
Mazār-e Sharīf, Afg.	B2	38
Mazaruni, stm., Guy.	E13	58
Mazatenango, Guat.	G2	64
Mazatlán, Mex.	F6	62
Mazatzal Mountains, mts., Az., U.S.	C4	80
Mazatzal Peak, mtn., Az., U.S.	C4	80
Mazeppa, Mn., U.S.	F6	100
Mazoe, stm., Afr.	E6	44
Mazomanie, Wi., U.S.	E4	126
Mazon, Il., U.S.	B5	90
Mbabane, Swaz.	G6	44
Mbaïki, Cen. Afr. Rep.	H9	42
Mbala, Zam.	C6	44
Mbale, Ug.	A6	44
Mbandaka (Coquilhatville), Zaire	A3	44
Mbanza-Ngungu, Zaire	C2	44
M'banz Congo, Ang.	C2	44
Mbeya, Tan.	C6	44
Mbomou (Bomu), stm., Afr.	H10	42
Mbout, Maur.	E3	42
Mbuji-Mayi (Bakwanga), Zaire	C4	44
McAdam, N.B., Can.	D2	71
McAdoo, Pa., U.S.	E9	115
McAfee Peak, mtn., Nv., U.S.	B6	105
McAlester, Ok., U.S.	C6	113
McAlester, Lake, res., Ok., U.S.	B6	113
McAllen, Tx., U.S.	F3	120
McAlmont, Ar., U.S.	h10	81
McAlpine, Md., U.S.	B4	97
McAlpine Lock and Dam, U.S.	H6	91
McArthur, Oh., U.S.	C3	112
McBee, S.C., U.S.	C7	117
McCall, Id., U.S.	E2	89
McCalla, Al., U.S.	g6	78
McCamey, Tx., U.S.	D1	120
McCammon, Id., U.S.	G6	89
McCandless, Pa., U.S.	h13	115
McCartney Mountain, mtn., Mt., U.S.	E4	103
McCaysville, Ga., U.S.	B2	87
McChord Air Force Base, mil., Wa., U.S.	f11	124
McClain, co., Ok., U.S.	C4	113
McCleary, Wa., U.S.	B2	124
McClellan Air Force Base, mil., Ca., U.S.	C3	82
McClintock, Mount, mtn., Ant.	A28	47
McCloud, Ca., U.S.	B2	82
McClure, Pa., U.S.	E7	115
McColl, S.C., U.S.	B8	117
McComas, W.V., U.S.	D3	125
McComb, Ms., U.S.	D3	101
McComb, Oh., U.S.	A2	112
McCone, co., Mt., U.S.	C11	103
McConnell Air Force Base, mil., Ks., U.S.	g12	93
McConnellsburg, Pa., U.S.	G6	115
McConnelsville, Oh., U.S.	C4	112
McCook, Ne., U.S.	D5	104
McCook, co., S.D., U.S.	D8	118
McCordsville, In., U.S.	E6	91
McCormick, S.C., U.S.	D3	117
McCormick, co., S.C., U.S.	D3	117
McCracken, co., Ky., U.S.	e9	94
McCreary, Man., Can.	D2	70
McCreary, co., Ky., U.S.	D5	94
McCrory, Ar., U.S.	B4	81
McCulloch, co., Tx., U.S.	D3	120
McCullough Mountain, mtn., Nv., U.S.	H6	105
McCurtain, co., Ok., U.S.	C7	113
McDermitt, Nv., U.S.	B4	105
McDonald, co., Mo., U.S.	E3	102
McDonough, Ga., U.S.	C2	87
McDonough, co., Il., U.S.	C3	90
McDougall, Mount, mtn., Wy., U.S.	D2	127
McDowell, Ky., U.S.	C7	94
McDowell, co., N.C., U.S.	f10	110
McDowell, co., W.V., U.S.	D3	125
McDowell Mountains, mts., Az., U.S.	k9	80
McDowell Peak, mtn., Az., U.S.	k9	80
McDuffie, co., Ga., U.S.	C4	87
McElroy Creek, stm., W.V., U.S.	k9	125
Mcensk, Russia	H19	18
McEwen, Tn., U.S.	A4	119
McFarland, Ca., U.S.	E4	82
McFarland, Wi., U.S.	E4	126
McGehee, Ar., U.S.	D4	81
McGill, Nv., U.S.	D7	105
McGrath, Ak., U.S.	C8	79
McGregor, Ia., U.S.	A6	92
McGregor, Tx., U.S.	D4	120
McGregor, stm., B.C., Can.	B7	69
McGregor Lake, l., Alta., Can.	D4	68
McGuire, Mount, mtn., Id., U.S.	D4	89
McGuire Air Force Base, mil., N.J., U.S.	C3	107
McHenry, Il., U.S.	A5	90
McHenry, Md., U.S.	k12	97
McHenry, co., Il., U.S.	A5	90
McHenry, co., N.D., U.S.	A5	111
McIntosh, Mn., U.S.	C3	100
McIntosh, co., Ga., U.S.	E5	87
McIntosh, co., N.D., U.S.	C6	111
McIntosh, co., Ok., U.S.	B6	113
McKean, co., Pa., U.S.	C4	115
McKee, Ky., U.S.	C6	94
McKeesport, Pa., U.S.	F2	115
McKees Rocks, Pa., U.S.	F1	115
McKenzie, Tn., U.S.	A3	119
McKenzie, co., N.D., U.S.	B2	111
McKenzie, stm., Or., U.S.	C4	114
McKinley, co., N.M., U.S.	B1	108
McKinley, Mount, mtn., Ak., U.S.	C9	79
McKinleyville, Ca., U.S.	B1	82
McKinney, Tx., U.S.	C4	120
McKinney, Lake, l., Ks., U.S.	E2	93
McKittrick Summit, mtn., Ca., U.S.	E4	82
McLaughlin, S.D., U.S.	B5	118
McLean, Il., U.S.	C4	90
McLean, Va., U.S.	g12	123
McLean, co., Il., U.S.	C4	90
McLean, co., Ky., U.S.	C2	94
McLean, co., N.D., U.S.	B4	111
McLeansboro, Il., U.S.	E5	90
McLennan, Alta., Can.	B2	68
McLennan, co., Tx., U.S.	D4	120
McLeod, co., Mn., U.S.	F4	100
McLeod, Lake, l., Austl.	D2	50
M'Clintock Channel, strt., N.W. Ter., Can.	B12	66
McLoud, Ok., U.S.	B4	113
McLoughlin, Mount, mtn., Or., U.S.	D4	114
McLouth, Ks., U.S.	C8	93
McMechen, W.V., U.S.	B4	125
McMillan, Lake, res., N.M., U.S.	E5	108
McMinn, co., Tn., U.S.	D9	119
McMinnville, Or., U.S.	B3	114
McMinnville, Tn., U.S.	D8	119
McMullen, co., Tx., U.S.	E3	120
McNairy, co., Tn., U.S.	B3	119
McNary, Az., U.S.	C6	80
McNary Dam, U.S.	B7	114
McNeil, Ar., U.S.	D2	81
McNeil, Mount, mtn., B.C., Can.	B2	69
McNeil Island, i., Wa., U.S.	f10	124
McNeill, Ms., U.S.	E4	101
McPherson, Ks., U.S.	D6	93
McPherson, co., Ks., U.S.	D6	93
McPherson, co., Ne., U.S.	C4	104
McPherson, co., S.D., U.S.	B6	118
McQueeney, Tx., U.S.	h7	120
McRae, Ar., U.S.	B4	81
McRae, Ga., U.S.	D4	87
McRoberts, Ky., U.S.	C7	94
McSherrystown, Pa., U.S.	G7	115
Mead, Wa., U.S.	B8	124
Mead, Lake, res., U.S.	A1	80
Meade, Ks., U.S.	E3	93
Meade, co., Ks., U.S.	E3	93
Meade, co., Ky., U.S.	C3	94
Meade, co., S.D., U.S.	C3	118
Meade, stm., Ak., U.S.	B8	79
Meaden Peak, mtn., Co., U.S.	A3	83
Meade Peak, mtn., Id., U.S.	G7	89
Meadow, stm., W.V., U.S.	C4	125
Meadow Creek, stm., W.V., U.S.	n14	125
Meadow Lands, Pa., U.S.	F1	115
Meadow Valley Wash, val., Nv., U.S.	F7	105
Meadowview, Va., U.S.	f10	123
Meadville, Pa., U.S.	C1	115
Meaford, Ont., Can.	C4	73
Meagher, co., Mt., U.S.	D6	103
Mealhada, Port.	E3	12
Meander Creek Reservoir, res., Oh., U.S.	A5	112
Meath, hist. reg., Ire.	H5	7
Meaux, Fr.	D9	10
Mebane, N.C., U.S.	A3	110
Mecca, Ca., U.S.	F5	82
Mecca see Makkah, Sau. Ar.	D2	46
Mechanic Falls, Me., U.S.	D2	96
Mechanicsburg, Oh., U.S.	B2	112
Mechanicsburg, Pa., U.S.	F7	115
Mechanicsville, Ia., U.S.	C6	92
Mechanicsville, Md., U.S.	D4	97
Mechanicsville, Va., U.S.	C5	123
Mechanicville, N.Y., U.S.	C7	109
Mechant, Lake, l., La., U.S.	E4	95
Mechelen, Bel.	D4	8
Mecklenburg, co., N.C., U.S.	B2	110
Mecklenburg, co., Va., U.S.	D4	123
Mecklenburg, hist. reg., Ger.	B12	8
Mecklenburger Bucht, b., Ger.	A11	8
Mecosta, co., Mi., U.S.	E5	99
Medan, Indon.	E2	32
Medanosa, Punta, c., Arg.	F3	56
Medaryville, In., U.S.	B4	91
Meddybumps Lake, l., Me., U.S.	C5	96
Medeiros Neto, Braz.	D8	57
Medellín, Col.	D5	58
Médenine, Tun.	B8	42
Medfield, Ma., U.S.	h10	98
Medford, Ma., U.S.	B5	98
Medford, Mn., U.S.	F5	100
Medford, Ok., U.S.	A4	113
Medford, Or., U.S.	E4	114
Medford, Wi., U.S.	C3	126
Medford Lakes, N.J., U.S.	D3	107
Medgidia, Rom.	E12	16
Media, Pa., U.S.	G11	115
Mediapolis, Ia., U.S.	C6	92
Mediaș, Rom.	C8	16
Medical Lake, Wa., U.S.	B8	124
Medicine Bow, Wy., U.S.	E6	127
Medicine Bow, stm., Wy., U.S.	E6	127
Medicine Bow Mountains, mts., U.S.	E6	127
Medicine Bow Peak, mtn., Wy., U.S.	E6	127
Medicine Hat, Alta., Can.	D5	68
Medicine Lodge, Ks., U.S.	E5	93
Medicine Lodge, stm., U.S.	E4	93
Medina, N.Y., U.S.	B2	109
Medina, Oh., U.S.	A4	112
Medina, Tn., U.S.	B3	119
Medina, Wa., U.S.	e11	124
Medina, co., Oh., U.S.	A4	112
Medina, co., Tx., U.S.	E3	120
Medina, stm., Tx., U.S.	k7	120
Medina see Al-Madīnah, Sau. Ar.	D2	46
Medinaceli, Spain	D9	12
Medina del Campo, Spain	D7	12
Medina de Ríoseco, Spain	D6	12
Mediterranean Sea	D14	2
Medjez el Bab, Tun.	M4	14
Médoc, reg., Fr.	G5	10
Medora, In., U.S.	G5	91
Médouneu, Gabon	A2	44
Medway, Me., U.S.	C4	96
Medway, Ma., U.S.	B5	98
Medway, stm., N.S., Can.	E5	71
Meekatharra, Austl.	E3	50
Meeker, Co., U.S.	A3	83
Meeker, Ok., U.S.	B5	113
Meeker, co., Mn., U.S.	E4	100
Meelpaeg Lake, res., Newf., Can.	D3	72
Meerut, India	F7	38
Meeteetse, Wy., U.S.	B4	127
Mega, Eth.	H2	46
Mégantic, Lac, l., Que., Can.	D7	74
Mégantic, Mont, mtn., Que., Can.	D6	74
Mégara, Grc.	K7	16
Meggett, S.C., U.S.	F7	117
Meghalaya, state, India	H14	38
Meherrin, stm., U.S.	A4	110
Mehlville, Mo., U.S.	f13	102
Mehsāna, India	I5	38
Mehtar Lām, Afg.	C4	38
Mehun-sur-Yèvre, Fr.	E9	10
Meigs, Ga., U.S.	E2	87
Meigs, co., Oh., U.S.	C3	112
Meigs, co., Tn., U.S.	D9	119
Meiktila, Burma	D3	34
Meiningen, Ger.	E10	8
Meissen, Ger.	D13	8
Meixian, China	K5	28
Mekambo, Gabon	A2	44
Mekele, Eth.	F2	4[illegible]
Meknès, Mor.	B4	42
Mekong, stm., Asia	H8	34
Melaka, Malay.	M7	34
Melanesia, is., Oc.	G23	[illegible]
Melbourne, Austl.	G8	5[illegible]
Melbourne, Ar., U.S.	A4	8[illegible]
Melbourne, Fl., U.S.	D6	8[illegible]
Melbourne, Ia., U.S.	C4	9[illegible]
Melbourne, Ky., U.S.	h14	9[illegible]
Melbourne Beach, Fl., U.S.	D6	8[illegible]
Melcher, Ia., U.S.	C4	9[illegible]
Meldorf, Ger.	A9	[illegible]
Mélèzes, Rivière aux, stm., Que., Can.	g12	74
Melfi, Chad	F9	42
Melfi, Italy	I10	14
Melgaço, Port.	C3	12
Melhus, Nor.	E8	[illegible]
Melilla, Sp. N. Afr.	A5	42
Melita, Man., Can.	E1	7[illegible]
Melito di Porto Salvo, Italy	L10	1[illegible]
Melitopol', Ukr.	H5	22
Melk, Aus.	G15	[illegible]
Mellansel, Swe.	E12	[illegible]
Melle, Fr.	F6	1[illegible]
Mellen, Wi., U.S.	B3	12[illegible]
Mellerud, Swe.	G9	[illegible]
Mellette, co., S.D., U.S.	D5	11[illegible]
Mellish Reef, atoll, Austl.	C11	5[illegible]
Melo, Ur.	C6	5[illegible]
Melocheville, Que., Can.	q19	7[illegible]
Melrhir, Chott, l., Alg.	B7	4[illegible]
Melrose, Fl., U.S.	C4	8[illegible]

Name — Map Ref — Page

elrose, Ma., U.S. B5 98
elrose, Mn., U.S. E4 100
elrose, N.M., U.S. C6 108
eltaus, Fin. C15 6
elton Hill Lake, res., Tn., U.S. D9 119
elton Mowbray, Eng., U.K. I12 7
elun, Fr. D9 10
elvern Lake, res., Ks., U.S. D8 93
elville, La., U.S. D4 95
elville, Lake, l., Newf., Can. B2 72
elville Hills, hills, N.W. Ter., Can. C8 66
elville Island, i., Austl. B6 50
elville Island, i., N.W. Ter., Can. A10 66
elville Peninsula, pen., N.W. Ter., Can. C16 66
elvin, Ky., U.S. C7 94
emmingen, Ger. H10 8
emphis, Fl., U.S. p10 86
emphis, Mi., U.S. F8 99
emphis, Mo., U.S. A5 102
emphis, Tn., U.S. B1 119
emphis, Tx., U.S. B2 120
emphis Naval Air Station, mil., Tn., U.S. B2 119
ena, Ar., U.S. C1 81
enahga, Mn., U.S. D3 100
énaka, Mali E6 42
enan, Id., U.S. F7 89
enands, N.Y., U.S. C7 109
enard, Tx., U.S. D3 120
enard, co., Il., U.S. C4 90
enard, co., Tx., U.S. D3 120
enasha, Wi., U.S. D5 126
endawai, stm., Indon. F5 32
ende, Fr. H10 10
endenhall, Ms., U.S. D4 101
éndez, Ec. I3 58
endham, N.J., U.S. B3 107
endi, Eth. G2 46
endip Hills, hills, Eng., U.K. J10 7
endocino, co., Ca., U.S. C2 82
endon, Il., U.S. C2 90
endon, Mi., U.S. F5 99
endon, Ut., U.S. B4 121
endota, Ca., U.S. D3 82
endota, Il., U.S. B4 90
endota, Lake, l., Wi., U.S. E4 126
endoza, Arg. C3 56
ene de Mauroa, Ven. B7 58
ene Grande, Ven. C7 58
enemen, Tur. K11 16
enfi, Italy L7 14
engzhi, China C7 34
engzi, China B5 34
enifee, co., Ky., U.S. C6 94
enlo Park, Ca., U.S. k8 82
enno, S.D., U.S. D8 118
enominee, Mi., U.S. C3 99
enominee, co., Mi., U.S. C3 99
enominee, co., Wi., U.S. C5 126
enominee, stm., U.S. C6 126
enominee Indian Reservation, Wi., U.S. C5 126
enomonee, stm., Wi., U.S. m11 126
enomonee Falls, Wi., U.S. E5 126
enomonie, Wi., U.S. D2 126
enongue, Ang. D3 44
enorca, i., Spain F16 12
entawai, Kepulauan, is., Indon. F2 32
enton, Fr. I14 10
entone, In., U.S. B5 91
entor, Oh., U.S. A4 112
entor-on-the-Lake, Oh., U.S. A4 112
enzel Bourguiba, Tun. L4 14
eoqui, Mex. C7 62
eppel, Neth. C6 8
eppen, Ger. C7 8
equon, Wi., U.S. E6 126
er, Fr. E8 10
eramec, stm., Mo., U.S. C7 102
erano (Meran), Italy C6 14
erasheen Island, i., Newf., Can. E4 72
erauke, Indon. G11 32
eraux, La., U.S. k12 95
ercaderes, Col. G4 58
erced, Ca., U.S. D3 82
erced, co., Ca., U.S. D3 82
erced, stm., Ca., U.S. D3 82
ercedes, Arg. B5 56
ercedes, Arg. C3 56
ercedes, Tx., U.S. F4 120
ercedes, Ur. C5 56
ercer, Pa., U.S. D1 115
ercer, Wi., U.S. B3 126
ercer, co., Il., U.S. B3 90
ercer, co., Ky., U.S. C5 94
ercer, co., Mo., U.S. A4 102
ercer, co., N.J., U.S. C3 107
ercer, co., N.D., U.S. B4 111
ercer, co., Oh., U.S. B1 112
ercer, co., Pa., U.S. D1 115
ercer, co., W.V., U.S. D3 125
ercer Island, Wa., U.S. B3 124
ercer Island, i., Wa., U.S. e11 124
ercersburg, Pa., U.S. G6 115
ercerville, N.J., U.S. C3 107
ercier, Que., Can. D4 74
eredith, N.H., U.S. C3 106
eredith, Lake, l., Co., U.S. C7 83
eredith, Lake, res., Tx., U.S. B2 120
eredosia, Il., U.S. D3 90
eredosia Lake, l., Il., U.S. D3 90
ergui (Myeik), Burma H5 34
ergui Archipelago, is., Burma H4 34
eriç (Marica) (évros), stm., Eur. H10 16
érida, Mex. G15 62
érida, Spain G5 12
érida, Ven. C7 58
eriden, Ct., U.S. C4 84
eriden, Ks., U.S. C8 93
eridian, Id., U.S. F2 89
eridian, Ms., U.S. C5 101
eridian, Pa., U.S. E2 115

Meridian, Tx., U.S. D4 120
Meridian Hills, In., U.S. k10 91
Meridian Naval Air Station, mil., Ms., U.S. C5 101
Meridianville, Al., U.S. A3 78
Mérignac, Fr. H6 10
Merikarvia, Fin. F13 6
Meriwether, co., Ga., U.S. C2 87
Merkel, Tx., U.S. C2 120
Merlin, Ont., Can. E2 73
Mermentau, La., U.S. D3 95
Mermentau, stm., La., U.S. E3 95
Meron, Hare, mtn., Isr. C4 40
Merriam, Ks., U.S. k16 93
Merrick, co., Ne., U.S. C7 104
Merrickville, Ont., Can. C9 73
Merrill, Ia., U.S. B1 92
Merrill, Mi., U.S. E6 99
Merrill, Or., U.S. E5 114
Merrill, Wi., U.S. C4 126
Merrillville, In., U.S. B3 91
Merrimac, Ma., U.S. A5 98
Merrimack, N.H., U.S. E4 106
Merrimack, co., N.H., U.S. D3 106
Merrimack, stm., U.S. A5 98
Merritt, B.C., Can. D7 69
Merritt Island, Fl., U.S. D6 86
Merritt Reservoir, res., Ne., U.S. B5 104
Merrymeeting Lake, l., N.H., U.S. D4 106
Merryville, La., U.S. D2 95
Merseburg, Ger. D11 8
Merthyr Tydfil, Wales, U.K. J9 7
Mértola, Port. H4 12
Merton, Wi., U.S. m11 126
Méru, Fr. C9 10
Merwin Lake, res., Wa., U.S. C3 124
Merzig, Ger. F6 8
Mesa, Az., U.S. D4 80
Mesa, co., Co., U.S. C2 83
Mesabi Range, hills, Mn., U.S. C6 100
Mesagne, Italy I12 14
Mesa Mountain, mtn., Co., U.S. D4 83
Mesa Verde National Park, Co., U.S. D2 83
Mescalero, N.M., U.S. D4 108
Mescalero Indian Reservation, N.M., U.S. D4 108
Mesilla, N.M., U.S. E3 108
Mesolóngion, Grc. K5 16
Mesopotamia, reg., Asia B3 46
Mesquite, Nv., U.S. G7 105
Mesquite, N.M., U.S. E3 108
Mesquite, Tx., U.S. n10 120
Messalo, stm., Moz. D7 44
Messalonskee Lake, l., Me., U.S. D3 96
Messina, Italy K10 14
Messina, S. Afr. F5 44
Messina, Stretto di, strt., Italy K10 14
Mesta (Néstos), stm., Eur. H7 16
Mestre, Italy D7 14
Meta, stm., S.A. D9 58
Métabetchouan, Que., Can. A6 74
Métabetchouane, stm., Que., Can. A5 74
Metairie, La., U.S. k11 95
Metamora, Il., U.S. C4 90
Metán, Arg. B3 56
Metcalfe, Ont., Can. B9 73
Metcalfe, Ms., U.S. B2 101
Metcalfe, co., Ky., U.S. C4 94
Metedeconk, North Branch, stm., N.J., U.S. C4 107
Metedeconk, South Branch, stm., N.J., U.S. C3 107
Meteghan, N.S., Can. E3 71
Meteghan River, N.S., Can. E3 71
Meteor Crater, crat., Az., U.S. C4 80
Methow, stm., Wa., U.S. A5 124
Methuen, Ma., U.S. A5 98
Metković, Cro. F12 14
Metlakatla, Ak., U.S. D13 79
Metlatonoc, Mex. I10 62
Metlika, Slo. D10 14
Metonga, Lake, l., Wi., U.S. C5 126
Metro, Indon. k12 33a
Metropolis, Il., U.S. F5 90
Mettawee, stm., U.S. E2 122
Metter, Ga., U.S. D4 87
Mettūr, India G4 37
Metuchen, N.J., U.S. B4 107
Metz, Fr. C13 10
Metzger, Or., U.S. h12 114
Meuse (Maas), stm., Eur. E5 8
Mexia, Tx., U.S. D4 120
Mexia, Lake, res., Tx., U.S. D4 120
Mexiana, Ilha, i., Braz. D9 54
Mexicali, Mex. A2 62
Mexico, In., U.S. C5 91
Mexico, Me., U.S. D2 96
Mexico, Mo., U.S. B6 102
Mexico (México), ctry., N.A. F8 62
Mexico, Gulf of, b., N.A. F9 76
Mexico City see Ciudad de México, Mex. H10 62
Meximieux, Fr. G12 10
Meycauayan, Phil. q19 33b
Meyersdale, Pa., U.S. G3 115
Meymaneh, Afg. C1 38
Meyrueis, Fr. H10 10
Meždurečensk, Russia G11 24
Mèze, Fr. I10 10
Mezőtúr, Hung. H20 8
Mezquital, Mex. F7 62
Mezzolombardo, Italy C6 14
Mhow, India I6 38
Miami, Az., U.S. D5 80
Miami, Fl., U.S. G6 86
Miami, Ok., U.S. A7 113
Miami, co., In., U.S. C5 91
Miami, co., Ks., U.S. D9 93
Miami, co., Oh., U.S. B1 112
Miami Beach, Fl., U.S. G6 86
Miami Canal, Fl., U.S. F6 86
Miami International Airport, Fl., U.S. G6 86
Miamisburg, Oh., U.S. C1 112
Miami Shores, Fl., U.S. G6 86

Miami Springs, Fl., U.S. G6 86
Miandrivazo, Madag. E9 44
Mīāneh, Iran J7 22
Mianus Reservoir, res., U.S. E1 84
Miānwāli, Pak. D4 38
Mica Mountain, mtn., Az., U.S. E5 80
Micco, Fl., U.S. E6 86
Miccosukee, Lake, res., Fl., U.S. B2 86
Michelson, Mount, mtn., Ak., U.S. B11 79
Michie, Tn., U.S. B3 119
Michigamme, Lake, l., Mi., U.S. B2 99
Michigamme Reservoir, res., Mi., U.S. B2 99
Michigan, state, U.S. E6 99
Michigan, stm., Co., U.S. A4 83
Michigan, Lake, l., U.S. C9 76
Michigan Center, Mi., U.S. F6 99
Michigan City, In., U.S. A4 91
Michigan Island, i., Wi., U.S. B3 126
Michikamau Lake, l., Newf., Can. F20 66
Michipicoten Island, i., Ont., Can. G15 66
Micronesia, is., Oc. F23 2
Mičurinsk, Russia I23 18
Middelburg, Neth. D3 8
Middelburg, S. Afr. H4 44
Middelharnis, Neth. D4 8
Middle, stm., Ia., U.S. C3 92
Middle, stm., Mn., U.S. B2 100
Middle Andaman, i., India H2 34
Middleboro (Middleborough Center), Ma., U.S. C6 98
Middlebourne, W.V., U.S. B4 125
Middleburg, Fl., U.S. B5 86
Middleburg, Pa., U.S. E7 115
Middleburg Heights, Oh., U.S. h9 112
Middlebury, Ct., U.S. C3 84
Middlebury, In., U.S. A6 91
Middlebury, Vt., U.S. C2 122
Middlefield, Ct., U.S. C5 84
Middlefield, Oh., U.S. A4 112
Middle Island Creek, stm., W.V., U.S. B3 125
Middle Nodaway, stm., Ia., U.S. C3 92
Middle Park, val., Co., U.S. A4 83
Middle Patuxent, stm., Md., U.S. B4 97
Middleport, N.Y., U.S. B2 109
Middleport, Oh., U.S. C3 112
Middle Raccoon, stm., Ia., U.S. C3 92
Middle River, Md., U.S. B5 97
Middlesboro, Ky., U.S. D6 94
Middlesex, N.J., U.S. B4 107
Middlesex, N.C., U.S. B4 110
Middlesex, co., Ct., U.S. D5 84
Middlesex, co., Ma., U.S. A5 98
Middlesex, co., N.J., U.S. C4 107
Middlesex, co., Va., U.S. C6 123
Middlesex Fells Reservation, Ma., U.S. g11 98
Middleton, N.S., Can. E4 71
Middleton, Id., U.S. F2 89
Middleton, Ma., U.S. A5 98
Middleton, Wi., U.S. E4 126
Middleton Reef, atoll, Austl. E11 50
Middletown, Ca., U.S. C2 82
Middletown, Ct., U.S. C5 84
Middletown, De., U.S. C3 85
Middletown, In., U.S. D6 91
Middletown, Ky., U.S. g11 94
Middletown, Md., U.S. B2 97
Middletown, N.J., U.S. C4 107
Middletown, N.Y., U.S. D6 109
Middletown, Oh., U.S. C1 112
Middletown, Pa., U.S. F8 115
Middletown, R.I., U.S. E5 116
Middletown, Va., U.S. A4 123
Middleville, Mi., U.S. F5 99
Midfield, Al., U.S. g7 78
Midland, Ont., Can. C5 73
Midland, Mi., U.S. E6 99
Midland, N.C., U.S. B2 110
Midland, Pa., U.S. E1 115
Midland, Tx., U.S. D1 120
Midland, co., Mi., U.S. E6 99
Midland, co., Tx., U.S. D1 120
Midland City, Al., U.S. D4 78
Midland Park, Ks., U.S. g12 93
Midland Park, N.J., U.S. B4 107
Midland Park, S.C., U.S. k11 117
Midleton, Ire. J4 7
Midlothian, Il., U.S. k9 90
Midlothian, Tx., U.S. C4 120
Midnapore, India I12 38
Midongy Sud, Madag. F9 44
Midvale, Ut., U.S. C4 121
Midville, Ga., U.S. D4 87
Midway, B.C., Can. E8 69
Midway, De., U.S. F5 85
Midway, Ky., U.S. B5 94
Midway, Pa., U.S. G7 115
Midway, Ut., U.S. C4 121
Midway Islands, dep., Oc. E1 2
Midwest, Wy., U.S. C6 127
Midwest City, Ok., U.S. B4 113
Mielec, Pol. E21 8
Mieres, Spain B6 12
Miesbach, Ger. H11 8
Mifflin, co., Pa., U.S. E6 115
Mifflinburg, Pa., U.S. E7 115
Mifflinville, Pa., U.S. D9 115
Miguel Alemán, Presa, res., Mex. H11 62
Miguel Auza, Mex. E8 62
Mihajlovgrad, Bul. F7 16
Mihara, Japan H6 30
Mikasa, Japan p19 30a
Mikkeli, Fin. F16 6
Mikumi, Tan. C7 44
Milaca, Mn., U.S. E5 100
Milagro, Arg. C3 56
Milagro, Ec. I3 58
Milam, co., Tx., U.S. D4 120
Milan, Ga., U.S. D3 87
Milan, Il., U.S. B3 90
Milan, In., U.S. F7 91
Milan, Mi., U.S. F7 99
Milan, Mo., U.S. A4 102
Milan, N.M., U.S. B2 108

Milan, Oh., U.S. A3 112
Milan, Tn., U.S. B3 119
Milan see Milano, Italy D4 14
Milano (Milan), Italy D4 14
Milâs, Tur. L11 16
Milazzo, Italy K10 14
Milbank, S.D., U.S. B9 118
Mildmay, Ont., Can. C3 73
Mildura, Austl. F8 50
Milesburg, Pa., U.S. E6 115
Miles City, Mt., U.S. D11 103
Milestone, Sask., Can. G3 75
Milford, Ct., U.S. E3 84
Milford, De., U.S. E4 85
Milford, Il., U.S. C6 90
Milford, In., U.S. B6 91
Milford, Ia., U.S. A2 92
Milford, Me., U.S. D4 96
Milford, Ma., U.S. B4 98
Milford, Mi., U.S. F7 99
Milford, Ne., U.S. D8 104
Milford, N.H., U.S. E3 106
Milford, Oh., U.S. C1 112
Milford, Pa., U.S. D12 115
Milford, Ut., U.S. E2 121
Milford Haven, Wales, U.K. J7 7
Milford Lake, res., Ks., U.S. C6 93
Milford Station, N.S., Can. D6 71
Mililani Town, Hi., U.S. g9 88
Mil'kovo, Russia G25 24
Milk River, Alta., Can. E4 68
Mill, stm., Ma., U.S. h9 98
Millard, co., Ut., U.S. D2 121
Millau, Fr. H10 10
Millbrae, Ca., U.S. h8 82
Millbrook, Ont., Can. C6 73
Millbrook, Al., U.S. C3 78
Mill Brook, stm., Vt., U.S. B5 122
Millburn, N.J., U.S. B4 107
Millbury, Ma., U.S. B4 98
Millbury, Oh., U.S. e7 112
Mill City, Or., U.S. C4 114
Millcreek, Ut., U.S. C4 121
Mill Creek, W.V., U.S. C5 125
Mill Creek, stm., N.J., U.S. D4 107
Mill Creek, stm., Oh., U.S. B2 112
Mill Creek, stm., Tn., U.S. g10 119
Mill Creek, stm., W.V., U.S. m13 125
Mill Creek, stm., W.V., U.S. C3 125
Millcreek Township, Pa., U.S. B1 115
Milledgeville, Ga., U.S. C3 87
Milledgeville, Il., U.S. B4 90
Mille Îles, Rivière des, stm., Que., Can. p19 74
Mille Lacs, co., Mn., U.S. E5 100
Mille Lacs, Lac des, l., Ont., Can. G14 66
Mille Lacs Indian Reservation, Mn., U.S. D5 100
Mille Lacs Lake, l., Mn., U.S. D5 100
Millen, Ga., U.S. D5 87
Miller, S.D., U.S. C7 118
Miller, co., Ar., U.S. D2 81
Miller, co., Ga., U.S. E2 87
Miller, co., Mo., U.S. C5 102
Miller, Mount, mtn., Ak., U.S. C11 79
Miller Peak, mtn., Az., U.S. F5 80
Miller Run, stm., Vt., U.S. B4 122
Millers, stm., Ma., U.S. A3 98
Millersburg, In., U.S. A6 91
Millersburg, Ky., U.S. B5 94
Millersburg, Oh., U.S. B4 112
Millersburg, Pa., U.S. E8 115
Millersport, Oh., U.S. C3 112
Millersville, Pa., U.S. F9 115
Millet, Alta., Can. C4 68
Mill Hall, Pa., U.S. D7 115
Milliken, Co., U.S. A6 83
Millington, Mi., U.S. E7 99
Millington, Tn., U.S. B2 119
Millinocket, Me., U.S. C4 96
Millinocket Lake, l., Me., U.S. C4 96
Millinocket Lake, l., Me., U.S. B4 96
Millis, Ma., U.S. B5 98
Millport, Al., U.S. B1 78
Millry, Al., U.S. D1 78
Mills, Wy., U.S. D6 127
Mills, co., Ia., U.S. C2 92
Mills, co., Tx., U.S. D3 120
Millsboro, De., U.S. F4 85
Millsboro, Pa., U.S. G1 115
Millstadt, Il., U.S. E3 90
Millstone, stm., N.J., U.S. C4 107
Milltown, In., U.S. H5 91
Milltown, N.J., U.S. C4 107
Milltown, Wi., U.S. C1 126
Milltown [-Head of Bay d'Espoir], Newf., Can. E4 72
Milltown Malbay, Ire. I3 7
Millvale, Pa., U.S. k14 115
Mill Valley, Ca., U.S. D2 82
Millville, Ma., U.S. B4 98
Millville, N.J., U.S. E2 107
Millville, Pa., U.S. D9 115
Millville, Ut., U.S. B4 121
Millville Lake, N.H., U.S. E4 106
Millwood, Wa., U.S. g14 124
Millwood Lake, res., Ar., U.S. D1 81
Milner Dam, Id., U.S. G5 89
Milnor, N.D., U.S. C8 111
Milo, Ia., U.S. C4 92
Milo, Me., U.S. C4 96
Milparinka, Austl. E8 50
Milroy, In., U.S. F7 91
Milroy, Pa., U.S. E6 115
Milstead, Ga., U.S. C3 87
Milton, Ont., Can. D5 73
Milton, De., U.S. E4 85
Milton, Fl., U.S. u14 86
Milton, In., U.S. E7 91
Milton, Ma., U.S. B5 98
Milton, N.H., U.S. D5 106
Milton, Pa., U.S. D8 115
Milton, Vt., U.S. B2 122
Milton, Wa., U.S. f11 124
Milton, W.V., U.S. C2 125
Milton, Wi., U.S. F5 126

Milton, Lake, l., Oh., U.S. A4 112
Miltona, Lake, l., Mn., U.S. D3 100
Milton-Freewater, Or., U.S. B8 114
Milton Reservoir, res., Co., U.S. A6 83
Milverton, Ont., Can. D4 73
Milwaukee, Wi., U.S. E6 126
Milwaukee, co., Wi., U.S. E6 126
Milwaukee, stm., Wi., U.S. m12 126
Milwaukie, Or., U.S. B4 114
Mimizan, Fr. H5 10
Mims, Fl., U.S. D6 86
Min, stm., China I7 28
Mina, Nv., U.S. E3 105
Minahasa, pen., Indon. E7 32
Minamata, Japan J3 30
Minas, Ur. C5 56
Minas, Sierra de las, mts., Guat. G3 64
Minas Basin, b., N.S., Can. D5 71
Minas Channel, strt., N.S., Can. D5 71
Minas de Barroterán, Mex. D9 62
Minas Novas, Braz. D7 57
Minatare, Ne., U.S. C2 104
Minatitlán, Mex. I12 62
Minco, Ok., U.S. B4 113
Mindanao, i., Phil. D7 32
Mindanao, stm., Phil. D7 32
Mindanao Sea, Phil. D7 32
Mindelheim, Ger. G10 8
Minden, Ger. C8 8
Minden, La., U.S. B2 95
Minden, Ne., U.S. D7 104
Minden, Nv., U.S. E2 105
Minden, W.V., U.S. D3 125
Mindoro, i., Phil. C7 32
Mindoro Strait, strt., Phil. C7 32
Mine Hill, N.J., U.S. B3 107
Mineiros, Braz. D2 57
Mineola, N.Y., U.S. E7 109
Mineola, Tx., U.S. C5 120
Miner, Mo., U.S. E8 102
Miner, co., S.D., U.S. D8 118
Mineral, co., Co., U.S. D4 83
Mineral, co., Mt., U.S. C1 103
Mineral, co., Nv., U.S. E3 105
Mineral, co., W.V., U.S. B6 125
Mineral Point, Wi., U.S. F3 126
Mineral Springs, Ar., U.S. D2 81
Mineral Wells, Tx., U.S. C3 120
Minersville, Pa., U.S. E9 115
Minersville, Ut., U.S. E3 121
Minerva, Oh., U.S. B4 112
Minervino Murge, Italy H11 14
Minetto, N.Y., U.S. B4 109
Mingo, co., W.V., U.S. D2 125
Mingo Junction, Oh., U.S. B5 112
Minho (Miño), stm., Eur. D3 12
Minidoka, co., Id., U.S. G5 89
Minidoka Dam, Id., U.S. G5 89
Minier, Il., U.S. C4 90
Minisink Island, i., N.J., U.S. A3 107
Minitonas, Man., Can. C1 70
Minna, Nig. G7 42
Minneapolis, Ks., U.S. C6 93
Minneapolis, Mn., U.S. F5 100
Minnedosa, Man., Can. D2 70
Minnedosa, stm., Man., Can. D1 70
Minnehaha, co., S.D., U.S. D9 118
Minneola, Ks., U.S. E3 93
Minneota, Mn., U.S. F3 100
Minnesota, state, U.S. E4 100
Minnesota, stm., Mn., U.S. F2 100
Minnesota Lake, Mn., U.S. G5 100
Minnetonka, Mn., U.S. n12 100
Minnetonka, Lake, l., Mn., U.S. n11 100
Minnewaska, Lake, l., Mn., U.S. E3 100
Miño (Minho), stm., Eur. D3 12
Minocqua, Wi., U.S. C4 126
Minonk, Il., U.S. C4 90
Minooka, Il., U.S. B5 90
Minot, N.D., U.S. A4 111
Minot Air Force Base, mil., N.D., U.S. A4 111
Minquadale, De., U.S. i7 85
Minsk, Bela. H10 18
Mińsk Mazowiecki, Pol. C21 8
Minster, Oh., U.S. B1 112
Mint Hill, N.C., U.S. B2 110
Minto, N.B., Can. C3 71
Minto Inlet, b., N.W. Ter., Can. B9 66
Minturn, Co., U.S. B4 83
Minturno, Italy H8 14
Minusinsk, Russia G12 24
Minute Man National Historical Park, Ma., U.S. g10 98
Minxian, China E7 26
Mio, Mi., U.S. D6 99
Mira, Italy D7 14
Mirabel, Que., Can. D3 74
Miraflores, Col. E6 58
Miraflores, Col. G6 58
Miraj, India D3 37
Miramar, Fl., U.S. s13 86
Miramar Naval Air Station, mil., Ca., U.S. F5 82
Miramas, Fr. I11 10
Mirambeau, Fr. G6 10
Miramichi Bay, b., N.B., Can. B5 71
Miranda de Ebro, Spain C9 12
Miranda do Douro, Port. D5 12
Mirande, Fr. I7 10
Mirandela, Port. D4 12
Mirandola, Italy E6 14
Mirbāt, Oman E5 46
Mirebeau-sur-Bèze, Fr. E12 10
Miri, Malay. E5 32
Mirnyj, Russia E16 24
Mīrpur Khās, Pak. H3 38
Mirror Lake, l., N.H., U.S. C4 106
Mirzāpur, India H10 38
Misawa, Japan B14 30
Miscouche, P.E.I., Can. C6 71
Miscou Island, i., N.B., Can. B5 71
Miscou Point, c., N.B., Can. A5 71
Misenheimer, N.C., U.S. B2 110
Mishawaka, In., U.S. A5 91

Name	Map Ref	Page
Misheguk Mountain, mtn., Ak., U.S.	B7	79
Mishicot, Wi., U.S.	D6	126
Mishmi Hills, hills, Asia	F16	38
Misima Island, i., Pap. N. Gui.	B10	50
Miskitos, Cayos, is., Nic.	G6	64
Miskolc, Hung.	G20	8
Misool, Pulau, i., Indon.	F9	32
Mispillion, stm., De., U.S.	E4	85
Misrātah, Libya	B9	42
Missaukee, co., Mi., U.S.	D5	99
Missaukee, Lake, l., Mi., U.S.	D5	99
Mission, Ks., U.S.	m16	93
Mission, S.D., U.S.	D5	118
Mission, Tx., U.S.	F3	120
Mission Range, mts., Mt., U.S.	C3	103
Mission Viejo, Ca., U.S.	n13	82
Missisquoi, stm., Vt., U.S.	B3	122
Missisquoi Bay, b., Vt., U.S.	A2	122
Mississauga, Ont., Can.	D5	73
Mississinewa, stm., U.S.	D7	91
Mississinewa Lake, res., In., U.S.	C6	91
Mississippi, co., Ar., U.S.	B5	81
Mississippi, co., Mo., U.S.	E8	102
Mississippi, state, U.S.	C4	101
Mississippi, stm., U.S.	E8	76
Mississippi Delta, La., U.S.	E6	95
Mississippi Sound, strt., U.S.	E5	101
Mississippi State, Ms., U.S.	B5	101
Missoula, Mt., U.S.	D2	103
Missoula, co., Mt., U.S.	D2	103
Missouri, state, U.S.	C5	102
Missouri, stm., U.S.	C7	76
Missouri City, Tx., U.S.	r14	120
Missouri Valley, Ia., U.S.	C2	92
Mistassini, Que., Can.	h12	74
Mistassini, Lac, l., Que., Can.	h12	74
Misti, Volcán, vol., Peru	G4	54
Mistretta, Italy	L9	14
Mita, Punta de, c., Mex.	G7	62
Mitchell, Austl.	E9	50
Mitchell, Ont., Can.	D3	73
Mitchell, Il., U.S.	E3	90
Mitchell, In., U.S.	G5	91
Mitchell, Ne., U.S.	C2	104
Mitchell, S.D., U.S.	D7	118
Mitchell, co., Ga., U.S.	E2	87
Mitchell, co., Ia., U.S.	A5	92
Mitchell, co., Ks., U.S.	C5	93
Mitchell, co., N.C., U.S.	e10	110
Mitchell, co., Tx., U.S.	C2	120
Mitchell, stm., Austl.	C8	50
Mitchell, Lake, l., Mi., U.S.	D5	99
Mitchell, Lake, res., Al., U.S.	C3	78
Mitchell, Mount, mtn., N.C., U.S.	f10	110
Mitchell Island, i., La., U.S.	E6	95
Mitchellville, Ia., U.S.	C4	92
Mitilíni, Grc.	J10	16
Mitkof Island, i., Ak., U.S.	m23	79
Mito, Japan	F13	30
Mitsiwa, Erit.	E2	46
Mitsuke, Japan	E11	30
Mittenwald, Ger.	H11	8
Mittweida, Ger.	E12	8
Mitú, Col.	G7	58
Mitumba, Monts, mts., Zaire	C5	44
Mitwaba, Zaire	C5	44
Mitzic, Gabon	A2	44
Miura, Japan	G12	30
Mixian, China	A2	28
Miyako, Japan	C14	30
Miyako-jima, i., Japan	G12	26
Miyakonojō, Japan	K4	30
Miyazaki, Japan	K4	30
Miyoshi, Japan	H5	30
Miyun, China	C10	26
Mizdah, Libya	B8	42
Mizen Head, c., Ire.	J3	7
Mizoram, ter., India	I15	38
Mizpe Ramon, Isr.	D4	40
Mizque, Bol.	G5	54
Mjölby, Swe.	G10	6
Mjøsa, l., Nor.	F8	6
Mkalama, Tan.	B6	44
Mladá Boleslav, Czech.	E14	8
Mława, Pol.	B20	8
Mo, Nor.	C10	6
Moab, Ut., U.S.	E6	121
Moanda, Gabon	B2	44
Moapa River Indian Reservation, Nv., U.S.	G7	105
Moate, Ire.	H5	7
Mobara, Japan	G13	30
Mobaye, Cen. Afr. Rep.	H10	42
Moberly, Mo., U.S.	B5	102
Mobile, Al., U.S.	E1	78
Mobile, co., Al., U.S.	E1	78
Mobile, stm., Al., U.S.	E1	78
Mobile Bay, b., Al., U.S.	E1	83
Mobridge, S.D., U.S.	B5	118
Moçambique, Moz.	E8	44
Mocanaqua, Pa., U.S.	D9	115
Mocha, Isla, i., Chile	D2	56
Mochudi, Bots.	F5	44
Mocksville, N.C., U.S.	B2	110
Moclips, Wa., U.S.	B1	124
Môco, Serra do, mtn., Ang.	D3	44
Mocoa, Col.	G4	58
Mococa, Braz.	F5	57
Moctezuma, Mex.	C5	62
Mocuba, Moz.	E7	44
Modane, Fr.	G13	10
Model Reservoir, res., Co., U.S.	D6	83
Modena, Italy	E5	14
Modesto, Ca., U.S.	D3	82
Modica, Italy	M9	14
Mödling, Aus.	G16	8
Modoc, co., Ca., U.S.	B3	82
Modowi, Indon.	F9	32
Moengo, Sur.	B8	54
Moenkopi, Az., U.S.	A4	80
Moffat, Scot., U.K.	F9	7
Moffat, co., Co., U.S.	A2	83
Moffat Tunnel, Co., U.S.	B5	83
Moffett Field Naval Air Station, mil., Ca., U.S.	k8	82
Moga, India	E6	38
Mogadisho see Muqdisho, Som.	H4	46
Mogadore, Oh., U.S.	A4	112
Mogadouro, Port.	D5	12
Mogaung, Burma	B4	34
Mogi das Cruzes, Braz.	G5	57
Mogil'ov, Bela.	H13	18
Mogi-Mirim, Braz.	G5	57
Mogincual, Moz.	E8	44
Mogoča, Russia	G17	24
Mogočin, Russia	F10	24
Mogok, Burma	C4	34
Mogollon Mountains, mts., N.M., U.S.	D1	108
Mogollon Rim, clf, Az., U.S.	C5	80
Mogotón, Pico, mtn., N.A.	H4	64
Mohall, N.D., U.S.	A4	111
Mohave, co., Az., U.S.	B1	80
Mohave, Lake, res., U.S.	H7	105
Mohave Mountains, mts., Az., U.S.	C1	80
Mohave Valley, Az., U.S.	C1	80
Mohawk, N.Y., U.S.	C5	109
Mohawk, stm., N.H., U.S.	g7	106
Mohawk, stm., N.Y., U.S.	C6	109
Mohawk Lake, l., N.J., U.S.	A3	107
Mohawk Mountains, mts., Az., U.S.	E2	80
Moheli, i., Com.	D8	44
Mohican, stm., Oh., U.S.	B3	112
Mohinora, Cerro, mtn., Mex.	D6	62
Mohnton, Pa., U.S.	F10	115
Moi, Nor.	G6	6
Moisie, Que., Can.	h8	72
Moisie, stm., Que., Can.	F19	66
Moissac, Fr.	H8	10
Mojave, Ca., U.S.	E4	82
Mojave, stm., Ca., U.S.	E5	82
Mojave Desert, des., Ca., U.S.	E5	82
Mojjero, stm., Russia	D14	24
Mojo, Eth.	G2	46
Mokapu Peninsula, pen., Hi., U.S.	g10	88
Mokapu Point, c., Hi., U.S.	g11	88
Mokelumne, stm., Ca., U.S.	C3	82
Mokena, Il., U.S.	k9	90
Mokp'o, S. Kor.	E12	26
Moku Manu, i., Hi., U.S.	g11	88
Mol, Bel.	D5	8
Molalla, Or., U.S.	B4	114
Moldau see Vltava, stm., Czech.	F14	8
Moldavia see Moldova, ctry., Eur.	H3	22
Molde, Nor.	E6	6
Moldova, ctry., Eur.	H3	22
Molepolole, Bots.	F5	44
Molfetta, Italy	H11	14
Molina de Aragón, Spain	E10	12
Molina de Segura, Spain	G10	12
Moline, Il., U.S.	B3	90
Moline, Mi., U.S.	F5	99
Molino, Fl., U.S.	u14	86
Molins de Rey, Spain	D14	12
Mollendo, Peru	G4	54
Mölln, Ger.	B10	8
Mölndal, Swe.	H9	6
Molodečno, Bela.	G9	18
Molokai, i., Hi., U.S.	B5	88
Molokini, i., Hi., U.S.	C5	88
Molson Lake, l., Man., Can.	B3	70
Molucca Sea see Maluku, Laut, Indon.	F7	32
Moluccas see Maluku, is., Indon.	F8	32
Moma, Moz.	E7	44
Moma, stm., Russia	D22	24
Mombasa, Kenya	B7	44
Mombetsu, Japan	o21	30a
Momence, Il., U.S.	B6	90
Momotombo, Volcán, vol., Nic.	H4	64
Mon, stm., Burma	D3	34
Mona, Canal de la, strt., N.A.	E14	64
Mona, Isla, i., P.R.	E14	64
Monaca, Pa., U.S.	E1	115
Monaco, ctry., Eur.	G9	4
Monadhliath Mountains, mts., Scot., U.K.	D8	7
Monadnock, Mount, mtn., N.H., U.S.	E2	106
Monadnock Mountain, mtn., Vt., U.S.	B5	122
Monahans, Tx., U.S.	D1	120
Monarch Mills, S.C., U.S.	B4	117
Monarch Pass, Co., U.S.	C4	83
Monashee Mountains, mts., B.C., Can.	D8	69
Monastir, Tun.	N5	14
Moncalieri, Italy	D2	14
Monção, Braz.	D9	54
Mönchengladbach, Ger.	D6	8
Monchique, Port.	H3	12
Moncks Corner, S.C., U.S.	E7	117
Monclova, Mex.	D9	62
Moncton, N.B., Can.	C5	71
Mondoñedo, Spain	B4	12
Mondovì, Italy	E2	14
Mondovi, Wi., U.S.	D2	126
Mondragone, Italy	H8	14
Monee, Il., U.S.	B6	90
Monessen, Pa., U.S.	F2	115
Monett, Mo., U.S.	E4	102
Monette, Ar., U.S.	B5	81
Monfalcone, Italy	D8	14
Monforte de Lemos, Spain	C4	12
Monfort Heights, Oh., U.S.	*o12	112
Mong Cai, Viet.	D9	34
Möng Hsat, Burma	D5	34
Monghyr, India	H12	38
Mongo, Chad	F9	42
Mongol Altajn Nuruu, mts., Asia	B5	26
Mongolia, ctry., Asia	B7	26
Mongu, Zam.	E4	44
Monhegan Island, i., Me., U.S.	E3	96
Monida Pass, U.S.	E6	89
Moniteau, co., Mo., U.S.	C5	102
Monitor Range, mts., Nv., U.S.	E5	105
Monitor Valley, val., Nv., U.S.	D5	105
Monmouth, Il., U.S.	C3	90
Monmouth, Or., U.S.	C3	114
Monmouth, co., N.J., U.S.	C4	107
Monmouth Beach, N.J., U.S.	C5	107
Monmouth Mountain, mtn., B.C., Can.	D6	69
Mono, co., Ca., U.S.	D4	82
Monocacy, stm., Md., U.S.	B3	97
Mono Lake, l., Ca., U.S.	D4	82
Monomonac, Lake, l., U.S.	E3	106
Monomoy Island, i., Ma., U.S.	C7	98
Monomoy Point, c., Ma., U.S.	C7	98
Monon, In., U.S.	C4	91
Monona, Ia., U.S.	A6	92
Monona, Wi., U.S.	E4	126
Monona, co., Ia., U.S.	B1	92
Monona, Lake, l., Wi., U.S.	E4	126
Monongah, W.V., U.S.	B4	125
Monongahela, Pa., U.S.	F2	115
Monongahela, stm., U.S.	G2	115
Monongalia, co., W.V., U.S.	B4	125
Monopoli, Italy	I12	14
Monóvar, Spain	G11	12
Monreal del Campo, Spain	E10	12
Monroe, Ga., U.S.	C3	87
Monroe, In., U.S.	C8	91
Monroe, Ia., U.S.	C4	92
Monroe, La., U.S.	B3	95
Monroe, Mi., U.S.	G7	99
Monroe, N.Y., U.S.	D6	109
Monroe, N.C., U.S.	C2	110
Monroe, Oh., U.S.	C1	112
Monroe, Ut., U.S.	E3	121
Monroe, Wa., U.S.	B4	124
Monroe, Wi., U.S.	F4	126
Monroe, co., Al., U.S.	D2	78
Monroe, co., Ar., U.S.	C4	81
Monroe, co., Fl., U.S.	G5	86
Monroe, co., Ga., U.S.	D3	87
Monroe, co., Il., U.S.	E3	90
Monroe, co., In., U.S.	F4	91
Monroe, co., Ia., U.S.	D5	92
Monroe, co., Ky., U.S.	D4	94
Monroe, co., Mi., U.S.	G7	99
Monroe, co., Ms., U.S.	B5	101
Monroe, co., Mo., U.S.	B5	102
Monroe, co., N.Y., U.S.	B3	109
Monroe, co., Oh., U.S.	C4	112
Monroe, co., Pa., U.S.	D11	115
Monroe, co., Tn., U.S.	D9	119
Monroe, co., W.V., U.S.	D4	125
Monroe, co., Wi., U.S.	E3	126
Monroe Center, Ct., U.S.	D3	84
Monroe City, Mo., U.S.	B6	102
Monroe Lake, res., In., U.S.	F5	91
Monroe Park, De., U.S.	h7	85
Monroeville, Al., U.S.	D2	78
Monroeville, In., U.S.	C8	91
Monroeville, Oh., U.S.	A3	112
Monroeville, Pa., U.S.	k14	115
Monrovia, Lib.	G3	42
Monrovia, Ca., U.S.	m13	82
Monrovia, In., U.S.	E5	91
Mons, Bel.	E3	8
Monson, Ma., U.S.	B3	98
Montague, P.E.I., Can.	C7	71
Montague, Ca., U.S.	B2	82
Montague, Mi., U.S.	E4	99
Montague, co., Tx., U.S.	C4	120
Montague, Isla, i., Mex.	B2	62
Montague Island, i., Ak., U.S.	D10	79
Montague Peak, mtn., Ak., U.S.	g18	79
Montague Strait, strt., Ak., U.S.	h18	79
Montaigu, Fr.	F5	10
Montalbán, Spain	E11	12
Montalcino, Italy	F6	14
Montalegre, Port.	D4	12
Mont Alto, Pa., U.S.	G6	115
Montana, state, U.S.	D7	103
Montánchez, Spain	F5	12
Montargis, Fr.	D9	10
Montauban, Fr.	H8	10
Montauk, N.Y., U.S.	m17	109
Montbard, Fr.	E11	10
Montbéliard, Fr.	E13	10
Mont Belvieu, Tx., U.S.	E5	120
Montblanch, Spain	D13	12
Montbrison, Fr.	G11	10
Montcalm, co., Mi., U.S.	E5	99
Montchanin, De., U.S.	h7	85
Montclair, Ca., U.S.	m13	82
Montclair, N.J., U.S.	B4	107
Mont Clare, Pa., U.S.	o19	115
Mont-de-Marsan, Fr.	I6	10
Montdidier, Fr.	C9	10
Monteagle, Tn., U.S.	D8	119
Monteagudo, Bol.	G6	54
Monte Azul, Braz.	C7	57
Montebello, Que., Can.	D3	74
Montebello, Ca., U.S.	m12	82
Monte Caseros, Arg.	C5	56
Montecatini Terme, Italy	F5	14
Monte Comán, Arg.	C3	56
Montecristi, Dom. Rep.	E12	64
Montecristi, Ec.	H2	58
Montefiascone, Italy	G7	14
Montego Bay, Jam.	E9	64
Montegut, La., U.S.	E5	95
Montélimar, Fr.	H11	10
Montello, Nv., U.S.	B7	105
Montello, Wi., U.S.	E4	126
Montemorelos, Mex.	E10	62
Montemor-o-Novo, Port.	G3	12
Montendre, Fr.	G6	10
Montenero di Bisaccia, Italy	H9	14
Montepuez, Moz.	D8	44
Montepulciano, Italy	F6	14
Monte Quemado, Arg.	B4	56
Montereau-faut-Yonne, Fr.	D9	10
Monterey, Ca., U.S.	D3	82
Monterey, Tn., U.S.	C8	119
Monterey, co., Ca., U.S.	D3	82
Monterey Bay, b., Ca., U.S.	D2	82
Monterey Park, Ca., U.S.	m12	82
Montería, Col.	C5	58
Monterotondo, Italy	G7	14
Monterrey, Mex.	E9	62
Montesano, Wa., U.S.	C2	124
Monte Sant'Angelo, Italy	H10	14
Montes Claros, Braz.	D7	57
Montevallo, Al., U.S.	B3	78
Montevarchi, Italy	F6	14
Montevideo, Mn., U.S.	F3	100
Montevideo, Ur.	C5	56
Monte Vista, Co., U.S.	D4	83
Montezuma, Ga., U.S.	D2	87
Montezuma, In., U.S.	E3	91
Montezuma, Ia., U.S.	C5	92
Montezuma, Ks., U.S.	E3	93
Montezuma, co., Co., U.S.	D2	83
Montezuma Castle National Monument, Az., U.S.	C4	80
Montezuma Peak, mtn., Az., U.S.	D3	80
Montgomery, Al., U.S.	C3	78
Montgomery, Il., U.S.	B5	90
Montgomery, La., U.S.	C3	95
Montgomery, Mn., U.S.	F5	100
Montgomery, N.Y., U.S.	D6	109
Montgomery, Oh., U.S.	o13	112
Montgomery, Pa., U.S.	D8	115
Montgomery, W.V., U.S.	C3	125
Montgomery, co., Al., U.S.	C3	78
Montgomery, co., Ar., U.S.	C2	81
Montgomery, co., Ga., U.S.	D4	87
Montgomery, co., Il., U.S.	D4	90
Montgomery, co., In., U.S.	D4	91
Montgomery, co., Ia., U.S.	C2	92
Montgomery, co., Ks., U.S.	E8	93
Montgomery, co., Ky., U.S.	B6	94
Montgomery, co., Md., U.S.	B3	97
Montgomery, co., Ms., U.S.	B4	101
Montgomery, co., Mo., U.S.	C6	102
Montgomery, co., N.Y., U.S.	C6	109
Montgomery, co., N.C., U.S.	B3	110
Montgomery, co., Oh., U.S.	C1	112
Montgomery, co., Pa., U.S.	F11	115
Montgomery, co., Tn., U.S.	A4	119
Montgomery, co., Tx., U.S.	D5	120
Montgomery, co., Va., U.S.	C2	123
Montgomery City, Mo., U.S.	C6	102
Monthey, Switz.	F13	10
Monticello, Ar., U.S.	D4	81
Monticello, Fl., U.S.	B3	86
Monticello, Ga., U.S.	C3	87
Monticello, Il., U.S.	C5	90
Monticello, In., U.S.	C4	91
Monticello, Ia., U.S.	B6	92
Monticello, Ky., U.S.	D5	94
Monticello, Mn., U.S.	E5	100
Monticello, Ms., U.S.	D3	101
Monticello, N.Y., U.S.	D6	109
Monticello, Ut., U.S.	F6	121
Monticello, Wi., U.S.	F4	126
Montichiari, Italy	D5	14
Montignac, Fr.	G8	10
Montijo, Port.	G3	12
Montijo, Spain	G5	12
Montilla, Spain	H7	12
Montivilliers, Fr.	C7	10
Mont-Joli, Que., Can.	A9	74
Mont-Laurier, Que., Can.	C2	74
Mont-Louis, Fr.	J9	10
Montluçon, Fr.	F9	10
Montmagny, Que., Can.	C7	74
Montmorenci, S.C., U.S.	D4	117
Montmorency, co., Mi., U.S.	C6	99
Montmorillon, Fr.	F7	10
Montmort, Fr.	D10	10
Montoro, Spain	G7	12
Montour, co., Pa., U.S.	D8	115
Montour Falls, N.Y., U.S.	C4	109
Montoursville, Pa., U.S.	D8	115
Montpelier, Id., U.S.	G7	89
Montpelier, In., U.S.	C7	91
Montpelier, Oh., U.S.	A1	112
Montpelier, Vt., U.S.	C3	122
Montpellier, Fr.	I10	10
Montréal, Que., Can.	D4	74
Montreal, Wi., U.S.	B3	126
Montréal, Île de, i., Que., Can.	q19	74
Montreal Lake, l., Sask., Can.	C3	75
Montréal-Nord, Que., Can.	p19	74
Montreat, N.C., U.S.	f10	110
Montreuil-Bellay, Fr.	E6	10
Montreux, Switz.	F13	10
Mont-Rolland, Que., Can.	D3	74
Montrose, B.C., Can.	E9	69
Montrose, Scot., U.K.	E10	7
Montrose, Al., U.S.	E2	78
Montrose, Co., U.S.	C3	83
Montrose, Ia., U.S.	D6	92
Montrose, Mi., U.S.	E7	99
Montrose, Pa., U.S.	C10	115
Montrose, Va., U.S.	m18	123
Montrose, co., Co., U.S.	C2	83
Mont-Royal, Que., Can.	p19	74
Montserrat, dep., N.A.	F16	64
Mont-Tremblant, Parc Provincial du, Que., Can.	C3	74
Montvale, N.J., U.S.	A4	107
Montville, Ct., U.S.	D7	84
Monument, Co., U.S.	B6	83
Monument Beach, Ma., U.S.	C6	98
Monument Peak, mtn., Co., U.S.	B3	83
Monument Peak, mtn., Id., U.S.	G4	89
Monument Valley, val., Az., U.S.	A5	80
Monywa, Burma	C3	34
Monza, Italy	D4	14
Monzón, Spain	D12	12
Moodus, Ct., U.S.	D6	84
Moodus Reservoir, res., Ct., U.S.	C6	84
Moody, Tx., U.S.	D4	120
Moody, co., S.D., U.S.	C9	118
Moon Lake, l., Ms., U.S.	A3	101
Moora, Austl.	F3	50
Moorcroft, Wy., U.S.	B8	127
Moore, Ok., U.S.	B4	113
Moore, co., N.C., U.S.	B3	110
Moore, co., Tn., U.S.	B5	119
Moore, co., Tx., U.S.	B2	120
Moore Dam, U.S.	B3	106
Moorefield, W.V., U.S.	B6	125
Moore Haven, Fl., U.S.	F5	86
Mooreland, Ok., U.S.	A2	113
Moore Reservoir, res., U.S.	B3	106
Moores Creek National Military Park, N.C., U.S.	C4	110
Moores Hill, In., U.S.	F7	91
Moorestown, N.J., U.S.	D3	107
Mooresville, In., U.S.	E5	91
Mooresville, N.C., U.S.	B2	110
Moorhead, Mn., U.S.	D2	100
Moorhead, Ms., U.S.	B3	101
Mooringsport, La., U.S.	B2	95
Moose, stm., N.H., U.S.	B4	106
Moose, stm., N.Y., U.S.	B5	109
Moose, stm., Vt., U.S.	B5	122
Moosehead Lake, l., Me., U.S.	C3	96
Moose Jaw, stm., Sask., Can.	G3	75
Moose Lake, Man., Can.	C1	70
Moose Lake, Mn., U.S.	D6	100
Moose Lake, l., Wi., U.S.	B2	126
Mooseleuk Stream, stm., Me., U.S.	B4	96
Mooselookmeguntic Lake, l., Me., U.S.	D2	96
Moose Mountain Creek, stm., Sask., Can.	H4	75
Moose Mountain Provincial Park, Sask., Can.	H4	75
Moosic, Pa., U.S.	m18	115
Moosup, Ct., U.S.	C8	84
Moosup, stm., U.S.	C1	116
Mopang Lake, l., Me., U.S.	D5	96
Mopti, Mali	F5	42
Moquegua, Peru	G4	54
Mora, Port.	G3	12
Mora, Spain	F8	12
Mora, Swe.	F10	6
Mora, Mn., U.S.	E5	100
Mora, N.M., U.S.	B4	108
Mora, co., N.M., U.S.	A5	108
Mora, stm., N.M., U.S.	B5	108
Morādābād, India	F8	38
Morada Nova de Minas, Braz.	E6	57
Morafenobe, Madag.	E8	44
Moraleda, Canal, strt., Chile	E2	56
Morant Cays, is., Jam.	F9	64
Mor'arovskij Zaton, Russia	F10	24
Moratuwa, Sri L.	I5	37
Morava, hist. reg., Czech.	F17	8
Morava (March), stm., Eur.	G16	8
Moravia, Ia., U.S.	D5	92
Moravia see Morava, hist. reg., Czech.	F17	8
Morawhanna, Guy.	C13	58
Moray Firth, est., Scot., U.K.	D9	7
Morden, Man., Can.	E2	70
More, Ben, mtn., Scot., U.K.	E8	7
More Assynt, Ben, mtn., Scot., U.K.	C8	7
Moreau, stm., S.D., U.S.	B3	118
Moreauville, La., U.S.	C4	95
Morecambe, Eng., U.K.	G10	7
Moree, Austl.	E9	50
Morehead, Ky., U.S.	B6	94
Morehead City, N.C., U.S.	C6	110
Morehouse, Mo., U.S.	E8	102
Morehouse, co., La., U.S.	B4	95
Morelia, Mex.	H9	62
Morella, Spain	E11	12
Morena, India	G8	38
Morenci, Az., U.S.	D6	80
Morenci, Mi., U.S.	G6	99
Moresby Island, i., B.C., Can.	C2	69
Moreuil, Fr.	C9	10
Morey, Lake, l., Vt., U.S.	D4	122
Morey Peak, mtn., Nv., U.S.	E5	105
Morgan, Mn., U.S.	F4	100
Morgan, Ut., U.S.	B4	121
Morgan, co., Al., U.S.	A3	78
Morgan, co., Co., U.S.	A7	83
Morgan, co., Ga., U.S.	C3	87
Morgan, co., Il., U.S.	D3	90
Morgan, co., In., U.S.	F5	91
Morgan, co., Ky., U.S.	C6	94
Morgan, co., Mo., U.S.	C5	102
Morgan, co., Oh., U.S.	C4	112
Morgan, co., Tn., U.S.	C9	119
Morgan, co., Ut., U.S.	B4	121
Morgan, co., W.V., U.S.	B6	125
Morgan City, La., U.S.	E4	95
Morganfield, Ky., U.S.	C2	94
Morgan Hill, Ca., U.S.	D3	82
Morgan Island, i., S.C., U.S.	G6	117
Morgan Point, c., Ct., U.S.	E4	84
Morganton, N.C., U.S.	B1	110
Morgantown, In., U.S.	F5	91
Morgantown, Ky., U.S.	C3	94
Morgantown, Ms., U.S.	D2	101
Morgantown, Tn., U.S.	D8	119
Morgantown, W.V., U.S.	B5	125
Morganza, La., U.S.	D4	95
Mori, Japan	q18	30
Moriah, Mount, mtn., Nv., U.S.	D7	105
Moriarty, N.M., U.S.	C3	108
Morinville, Alta., Can.	C4	68
Morioka, Japan	C14	30
Morkoka, stm., Russia	D16	24
Morlaix, Fr.	D3	10
Morley, Mo., U.S.	D8	102
Mormon Peak, mtn., Nv., U.S.	G7	105
Morning Sun, Ia., U.S.	C6	92
Mornington Island, i., Austl.	C7	50
Morobe, Pap. N. Gui.	m16	50
Morocco, In., U.S.	C3	91
Morocco, ctry., Afr.	B4	42
Morogoro, Tan.	C7	44
Moro Gulf, b., Phil.	D7	32
Morombe, Madag.	F8	44
Morón, Cuba	C8	64
Morondava, Madag.	F8	44
Morón de la Frontera, Spain	H6	12
Moroni, Com.	D8	44
Moroni, Ut., U.S.	D4	121
Morošečnoje, Russia	F25	24
Morotai, i., Indon.	E8	32

Name Map Ref Page
Morrill, Ne., U.S. C2 104
Morrill, co., Ne., U.S. C2 104
Morrilton, Ar., U.S. B3 81
Morrinhos, Braz. D4 57
Morris, Man., Can. E3 70
Morris, Al., U.S. B3 78
Morris, Il., U.S. B5 90
Morris, Mn., U.S. E3 100
Morris, Ok., U.S. B6 113
Morris, co., Ks., U.S. D7 93
Morris, co., N.J., U.S. B3 107
Morris, co., Tx., U.S. C5 120
Morrisburg, Ont., Can. C9 73
Morris Island, i., S.C., U.S. F8 117
Morrison, Il., U.S. B4 90
Morrison, Ok., U.S. A4 113
Morrison, co., Mn., U.S. D4 100
Morrison City, Tn., U.S. C11 119
Morrisonville, Il., U.S. D4 90
Morrisonville, N.Y., U.S. f11 109
Morris Plains, N.J., U.S. B4 107
Morristown, In., U.S. E6 91
Morristown, Mn., U.S. F5 100
Morristown, N.J., U.S. B4 107
Morristown, Tn., U.S. C10 119
Morristown National Historical Park, N.J., U.S. B3 107
Morrisville, N.Y., U.S. C5 109
Morrisville, Pa., U.S. F12 115
Morrisville, Vt., U.S. B3 122
Morro, Ec. I2 58
Morro, Punta, c., Chile B2 56
Morro Bay, Ca., U.S. E3 82
Morro do Chapéu, Braz. F10 54
Morrow, Ga., U.S. C2 87
Morrow, Oh., U.S. C1 112
Morrow, co., Oh., U.S. B3 112
Morrow, co., Or., U.S. B7 114
Moršansk, Russia H24 18
Morse, La., U.S. D3 95
Morse Reservoir, res., In., U.S. D5 91
Morses Creek, stm., N.J., U.S. k8 107
Mortagne, Fr. D7 10
Mortagne-sur-Sèvre, Fr. E6 10
Mortara, Italy D3 14
Mortes, Rio das, stm., Braz. G8 54
Morton, Il., U.S. C4 90
Morton, Ms., U.S. C4 101
Morton, Tx., U.S. C1 120
Morton, Wa., U.S. C3 124
Morton, co., Ks., U.S. E2 93
Morton, co., N.D., U.S. C4 111
Morton Grove, Il., U.S. h9 90
Morton Pass, Wy., U.S. E7 127
Mortons Gap, Ky., U.S. C2 94
Morven, mtn., Scot., U.K. C9 7
Morvi, India I4 38
Morwell, Austl. G9 50
Mosbach, Ger. F9 8
Moscos Islands, is., Burma G4 34
Moscow, Id., U.S. C2 89
Moscow, Pa., U.S. m18 115
Moscow Mills, Mo., U.S. C7 102
Moscow see Moskva, Russia F20 18
Mosel (Moselle), stm., Eur. F6 8
Moselle, Ms., U.S. D4 101
Moselle (Mosel), stm., Eur. F6 8
Moses Coulee, val., Wa., U.S. B6 124
Moses Lake, Wa., U.S. B6 124
Moses Lake, l., Wa., U.S. B6 124
Mosheim, Tn., U.S. C11 119
Moshi, Tan. B7 44
Mosinee, Wi., U.S. D4 126
Mosjøen, Nor. D9 6
Moskva (Moscow), Russia F20 18
Mosquera, Col. F3 58
Mosquito Creek Lake, res., Oh., U.S. A5 112
Mosquito Lagoon, b., Fl., U.S. D6 86
Mosquitos, Golfo de los, b., Pan. J7 64
Moss, Nor. G8 6
Mossaka, Congo B3 44
Moss Bluff, La., U.S. D2 95
Mosselbaai, S. Afr. H4 44
Mossendjo, Congo B2 44
Mossoró, Braz. E11 54
Moss Point, Ms., U.S. E5 101
Most, Czech. E13 8
Mostaganem, Alg. A6 42
Mostar, Bos. F12 14
Mostardas, Braz. C6 56
Møsting, Kap, c., Grnld. D24 66
Moswansicut Pond, l., R.I., U.S. C3 116
Mota del Marqués, Spain D6 12
Motala, Swe. G10 6
Motherwell, Scot., U.K. F8 7
Motīhāri, India G11 38
Motilla del Palancar, Spain F10 12
Motley, co., Tx., U.S. B2 120
Motril, Spain I8 12
Mott, N.D., U.S. C3 111
Motueka, N.Z. D4 52
Motul de Felipe Carrillo Puerto, Mex. G15 62
Motygino, Russia F12 24
Mouchoir Passage, strt., N.A. D12 64
Moudjéria, Maur. E3 42
Mouila, Gabon B2 44
Moulamein Creek, stm., Austl. G8 50
Moulins, Fr. F10 10
Moulmeingyun, Burma F3 34
Moulouya, Oued, stm., Mor. B5 42
Moulton, Al., U.S. A2 78
Moulton, Ia., U.S. D5 92
Moultrie, Ga., U.S. E3 87
Moultrie, co., Il., U.S. D5 90
Moultrie, Lake, res., S.C., U.S. E7 117
Mound, Mn., U.S. n11 100
Mound Bayou, Ms., U.S. B3 101
Mound City, Il., U.S. F4 90
Mound City, Ks., U.S. D9 93
Mound City, Mo., U.S. A2 102
Mound City Group National Monument, Oh., U.S. C2 112
Moundou, Chad G9 42
Moundridge, Ks., U.S. D6 93
Mounds, Il., U.S. F4 90
Mounds, Ok., U.S. B5 113
Mounds View, Mn., U.S. m12 100
Moundsville, W.V., U.S. B4 125
Moundville, Al., U.S. C2 78
Mountainair, N.M., U.S. C3 108
Mountainaire, Az., U.S. B4 80
Mountain Brook, Al., U.S. g7 78
Mountain City, Ga., U.S. B3 87
Mountain City, Nv., U.S. B6 105
Mountain City, Tn., U.S. C12 119
Mountain Fork, stm., U.S. C7 113
Mountain Grove, Mo., U.S. D5 102
Mountain Home, Ar., U.S. A3 81
Mountain Home, Id., U.S. F3 89
Mountain Home Air Force Base, mil., Id., U.S. F3 89
Mountain Iron, Mn., U.S. C6 100
Mountain Lake, Mn., U.S. G4 100
Mountain Lake Park, Md., U.S. m12 97
Mountain Nile (Baḥr al-Jabal), stm., Sudan G12 42
Mountain Pine, Ar., U.S. C2 81
Mountainside, N.J., U.S. B4 107
Mountain View, Ar., U.S. B3 81
Mountain View, Ca., U.S. k8 82
Mountain View, Mo., U.S. D6 102
Mountain View, N.M., U.S. C3 108
Mountain View, Ok., U.S. B3 113
Mountain View, Wy., U.S. E2 127
Mountain Village, Ak., U.S. C7 79
Mount Airy, Md., U.S. B3 97
Mount Airy, N.C., U.S. A2 110
Mount Albert, Ont., Can. C5 73
Mount Angel, Or., U.S. B4 114
Mount Arlington, N.J., U.S. B3 107
Mount Ayr, Ia., U.S. D3 92
Mount Carmel, Il., U.S. E6 90
Mount Carmel, Oh., U.S. o13 112
Mount Carmel, Pa., U.S. E9 115
Mount Carmel [-Mitchell's Brook-Saint Catherine's], Newf., Can. E5 72
Mount Carroll, Il., U.S. A4 90
Mount Clare, W.V., U.S. B4 125
Mount Clemens, Mi., U.S. F8 99
Mount Desert Island, i., Me., U.S. D4 96
Mount Dora, Fl., U.S. D5 86
Mount Forest, Ont., Can. D4 73
Mount Gambier, Austl. G8 50
Mount Gay, W.V., U.S. D2 125
Mount Gilead, N.C., U.S. B3 110
Mount Gilead, Oh., U.S. B3 112
Mount Healthy, Oh., U.S. o12 112
Mount Holly, N.J., U.S. D3 107
Mount Holly, N.C., U.S. B1 110
Mount Holly Springs, Pa., U.S. F7 115
Mount Hope, Austl. F7 50
Mount Hope, Ks., U.S. E6 93
Mount Hope, W.V., U.S. D3 125
Mount Hope, stm., Ct., U.S. B7 84
Mount Hope Bay, b., U.S. D6 116
Mount Horeb, Wi., U.S. E4 126
Mount Ida, Ar., U.S. C2 81
Mount Isa, Austl. D7 50
Mount Jackson, Va., U.S. B4 123
Mount Jewett, Pa., U.S. C4 115
Mount Joy, Pa., U.S. F9 115
Mount Juliet, Tn., U.S. A5 119
Mount Kisco, N.Y., U.S. D7 109
Mount Lebanon, Pa., U.S. F1 115
Mount Magnet, Austl. E3 50
Mount Morris, Il., U.S. A4 90
Mount Morris, Mi., U.S. E7 99
Mount Morris, N.Y., U.S. C3 109
Mount Olive, Al., U.S. B3 78
Mount Olive, Il., U.S. D4 90
Mount Olive, Ms., U.S. D4 101
Mount Olive, N.C., U.S. B4 110
Mount Olive, Tn., U.S. n14 119
Mount Orab, Oh., U.S. C2 112
Mount Pearl, Newf., Can. E5 72
Mount Penn, Pa., U.S. F10 115
Mount Pleasant, Ia., U.S. D6 92
Mount Pleasant, Mi., U.S. E6 99
Mount Pleasant, N.C., U.S. B2 110
Mount Pleasant, Pa., U.S. F2 115
Mount Pleasant, S.C., U.S. F8 117
Mount Pleasant, Tn., U.S. B4 119
Mount Pleasant, Tx., U.S. C5 120
Mount Pleasant, Ut., U.S. D4 121
Mount Pocono, Pa., U.S. D11 115
Mount Prospect, Il., U.S. A6 90
Mount Pulaski, Il., U.S. C4 90
Mountrail, co., N.D., U.S. A3 111
Mount Rainier, Md., U.S. f9 97
Mount Rainier National Park, Wa., U.S. C4 124
Mount Revelstoke National Park, B.C., Can. D8 69
Mount Rogers National Recreation Area, Va., U.S. D1 123
Mount Rushmore National Memorial, hist., S.D., U.S. D2 118
Mount Savage, Md., U.S. k13 97
Mount Shasta, Ca., U.S. B2 82
Mount Sterling, Il., U.S. D3 90
Mount Sterling, Ky., U.S. B6 94
Mount Sterling, Oh., U.S. C2 112
Mount Uniacke, N.S., Can. E6 71
Mount Union, Pa., U.S. F6 115
Mount Vernon, Al., U.S. D1 78
Mount Vernon, Ga., U.S. D4 87
Mount Vernon, Il., U.S. E5 90
Mount Vernon, In., U.S. I2 91
Mount Vernon, Ia., U.S. C6 92
Mount Vernon, Ky., U.S. C5 94
Mount Vernon, Mo., U.S. D4 102
Mount Vernon, N.Y., U.S. h13 109
Mount Vernon, Oh., U.S. B3 112
Mount Vernon, Tx., U.S. C5 120
Mount Vernon, Wa., U.S. A3 124
Mount View, R.I., U.S. D4 116
Mount Washington, Ky., U.S. B4 94
Mount Wolf, Pa., U.S. F8 115
Mount Zion, Il., U.S. D5 90
Moura, Braz. D6 54
Moura, Port. G4 12
Mourne Mountains, mts., N. Ire., U.K. G6 7
Moussoro, Chad F9 42
Moutong, Indon. E7 32
Moville, Ia., U.S. B1 92
Moweaqua, Il., U.S. D4 90
Mower, co., Mn., U.S. G6 100
Moxee City, Wa., U.S. C5 124
Moxos, Llanos de, pl., Bol. G6 54
Moyahua, Mex. G8 62
Moyale, Kenya H2 46
Moyen Atlas, mts., Mor. B5 42
Moyeuvre-Grande, Fr. C13 10
Moyock, N.C., U.S. A6 110
Moyu, China B8 38
Možajsk, Russia F19 18
Mozambique, ctry., Afr. E6 44
Mozambique Channel, strt., Afr. E8 44
Mozyr', Bela. G3 22
Mpanda, Tan. C6 44
Mpika, Zam. D6 44
Mrkonjić Grad, Bos. E12 14
Msaken, Tun. N5 14
Mtwara, Tan. D8 44
Muang Khammouan, Laos F8 34
Muang Pakxan, Laos E7 34
Muar, Malay. M7 34
Muaratewe, Indon. F5 32
Muāri, Rās, c., Pak. H2 38
Mücheln, Ger. D11 8
Muchinga Mountains, mts., Zam. D6 44
Muckleshoot Indian Reservation, Wa., U.S. f11 124
Mud, stm., Ky., U.S. C3 94
Mud, stm., Mn., U.S. B3 100
Mud, stm., W.V., U.S. C2 125
Mudanjiang, China C12 26
Mud Creek, stm., Ok., U.S. C4 113
Muddy Boggy Creek, stm., Ok., U.S. C6 113
Muddy Creek, stm., Ut., U.S. E4 121
Muddy Creek, stm., Wy., U.S. E2 127
Muddy Creek, stm., Wy., U.S. E5 127
Muddy Creek, stm., Wy., U.S. D6 127
Muddy Creek, stm., Wy., U.S. C4 127
Muddy Mountains, mts., Nv., U.S. G7 105
Muddy Peak, mtn., Nv., U.S. G7 105
Mud Lake, l., Me., U.S. A4 96
Mud Lake, l., Nv., U.S. F4 105
Mudon, Burma F4 34
Muenster, Tx., U.S. C4 120
Mufulira, Zam. D5 44
Mu Gia, Deo (Mu Gia Pass), Asia F8 34
Muğla, Tur. H13 4
Mühldorf, Ger. G12 8
Muhlenberg, co., Ky., U.S. C2 94
Mühlhausen, Ger. D10 8
Mühlviertel, reg., Aus. G14 8
Muhola, Fin. E15 6
Muirkirk, Md., U.S. B4 97
Muiron Islands, is., Austl. D2 50
Muir Woods National Monument, Ca., U.S. h7 82
Mukden see Shenyang, China C11 26
Mukilteo, Wa., U.S. B3 124
Mukwonago, Wi., U.S. F5 126
Mula, Spain G10 12
Mulanje, Mwi. E7 44
Mulberry, Ar., U.S. B1 81
Mulberry, Fl., U.S. E4 86
Mulberry, In., U.S. D4 91
Mulberry, N.C., U.S. A1 110
Mulberry, stm., Ar., U.S. B1 81
Mulberry Fork, stm., Al., U.S. B3 78
Muldraugh, Ky., U.S. C4 94
Muldrow, Ok., U.S. B7 113
Muleshoe, Tx., U.S. B1 120
Mulgrave, N.S., Can. D8 71
Mulhacén, mtn., Spain H8 12
Mulhouse, Fr. E14 10
Mull, Island of, i., Scot., U.K. E6 7
Mullan, Id., U.S. B3 89
Mullan Pass, Mt., U.S. D4 103
Mullens, W.V., U.S. D3 125
Muller, Pegunungan, mts., Indon. E5 32
Mullet Key, i., Fl., U.S. p10 86
Mullett Lake, l., Mi., U.S. C6 99
Mullewa, Austl. E3 50
Mullica, stm., N.J., U.S. D3 107
Mullins, S.C., U.S. C9 117
Multān, Pak. E4 38
Multnomah, co., Or., U.S. B4 114
Mulvane, Ks., U.S. E6 93
Mumbwa, Zam. D5 44
Mummy Range, mts., Co., U.S. A5 83
Muna, Pulau, i., Indon. F7 32
Muncar, Indon. n17 33a
München (Munich), Ger. G11 8
Muncie, In., U.S. D7 91
Muncy, Pa., U.S. D8 115
Munday, Tx., U.S. C3 120
Mundelein, Il., U.S. A5 90
Münden, Ger. D9 8
Munford, Al., U.S. B4 78
Munford, Tn., U.S. B2 119
Munfordville, Ky., U.S. C4 94
Mungbere, Zaire H11 42
Munhall, Pa., U.S. k14 115
Munhango, Ang. D3 44
Munich see München, Ger. G11 8
Munising, Mi., U.S. B4 99
Münster, Ger. C10 8
Münster, Ger. D7 8
Munster, In., U.S. A2 91
Munster, hist. reg., Ire. I4 7
Munsungan Lake, l., Me., U.S. B3 96
Munuscong Lake, l., Mi., U.S. B6 99
Muong Sing, Laos D6 34
Muqayshit, i., U.A.E. D5 46
Muqdisho, Som. H4 46
Mur (Mura), stm., Eur. I15 8
Mura (Mur), stm., Eur. I16 8
Murat, Fr. G9 10
Murat, stm., Tur. H16 4
Murau, Aus. H14 8
Muravera, Italy J4 14
Murča, Port. D4 12
Murchison, stm., Austl. E3 50
Murcia, Spain H10 12
Murderkill, stm., De., U.S. D4 85
Murdo, S.D., U.S. D5 118
Mureș (Maros), stm., Eur. C5 16
Muret, Fr. I8 10
Murfreesboro, Ar., U.S. C2 81
Murfreesboro, N.C., U.S. A5 110
Murfreesboro, Tn., U.S. B5 119
Mūrīān, Hāmūn-e, l., Iran C6 46
Murmansk, Russia D4 22
Murom, Russia F25 18
Muroran, Japan q18 30a
Muros, Spain C2 12
Muroto, Japan I7 30
Muroto-zaki, c., Japan I7 30
Murphy, Mo., U.S. g13 102
Murphy, N.C., U.S. f8 110
Murphy Island, i., S.C., U.S. E9 117
Murphysboro, Il., U.S. F4 90
Murray, Ia., U.S. C4 92
Murray, Ky., U.S. f9 94
Murray, Ut., U.S. C4 121
Murray, co., Ga., U.S. B2 87
Murray, co., Mn., U.S. F3 100
Murray, co., Ok., U.S. C4 113
Murray, stm., Austl. F7 50
Murray, Lake, res., Ok., U.S. C4 113
Murray, Lake, res., S.C., U.S. C5 117
Murray Head, c., P.E.I., Can. C7 71
Murraysburg, S. Afr. H4 44
Murrayville, Ga., U.S. B3 87
Murrells Inlet, S.C., U.S. D9 117
Murrells Inlet, b., S.C., U.S. D10 117
Murten, Switz. F14 10
Murukta, Russia D14 24
Murwāra, India I9 38
Murwillumbah, Austl. E10 50
Mürzzuschlag, Aus. H15 8
Muş, Tur. H16 4
Musay'īd, Qatar D5 46
Muscat and Oman see Oman, ctry., Asia D6 46
Muscatatuck, stm., In., U.S. G5 91
Muscatine, Ia., U.S. C6 92
Muscatine, co., Ia., U.S. C6 92
Muscat see Masqaṭ, Oman D6 46
Mus-Chaja, Gora, mtn., Russia E22 24
Muscle Shoals, Al., U.S. A2 78
Musclow, Mount, mtn., B.C., Can. C4 69
Muscoda, Wi., U.S. E3 126
Muscogee, co., Ga., U.S. D2 87
Musconetcong, stm., N.J., U.S. B4 107
Muscooten Bay, l., Il., U.S. C3 90
Muse, Pa., U.S. F1 115
Musgrave, Austl. B8 50
Musgrave Harbour, Newf., Can. D5 72
Musgrave Ranges, mts., Austl. E6 50
Musgravetown, Newf., Can. D5 72
Mushin, Nig. G6 42
Muskeg Bay, b., Mn., U.S. B3 100
Muskeget Island, i., Ma., U.S. D7 98
Muskego, Wi., U.S. F5 126
Muskego Lake, l., Wi., U.S. n11 126
Muskegon, Mi., U.S. E4 99
Muskegon, co., Mi., U.S. E4 99
Muskegon, stm., Mi., U.S. E4 99
Muskegon Heights, Mi., U.S. E4 99
Muskegon Lake, l., Mi., U.S. E4 99
Muskingum, co., Oh., U.S. B4 112
Muskingum, stm., Oh., U.S. C4 112
Muskogee, Ok., U.S. B6 113
Muskogee, co., Ok., U.S. B6 113
Musoma, Tan. B6 44
Musquacook Lakes, l., Me., U.S. B3 96
Musquodoboit Harbour, N.S., Can. E6 71
Musselshell, co., Mt., U.S. D8 103
Musselshell, stm., Mt., U.S. D9 103
Mussidan, Fr. G7 10
Mussuma, Ang. D4 44
Mustafakemalpaşa, Tur. I12 16
Mustang, Ok., U.S. B4 113
Mustinka, stm., Mn., U.S. E2 100
Mut, Tur. A3 40
Mutare, Zimb. E6 44
Mutoraj, Russia E14 24
Mutsu, Japan A14 30
Mutsu-wan, b., Japan A13 30
Mutton Mountains, mts., Or., U.S. C5 114
Muzaffarābād, Pak. C5 38
Muzaffarnagar, India F7 38
Muzaffarpur, India G11 38
Muzon, Cape, c., Ak., U.S. n23 79
Muztag, mtn., China B9 38
Muztag, mtn., China B12 38
Mvuma, Zimb. E6 44
Mwanza, Tan. B6 44
Mweelrea, mtn., Ire. H3 7
Mweka, Zaire B4 44
Mwenezi, Zimb. F6 44
Mweru, Lake, l., Afr. C5 44
Mwinilunga, Zam. D4 44
Myakka, stm., Fl., U.S. E4 86
Myanaung, Burma E3 34
Myaungmya, Burma F3 34
Myerstown, Pa., U.S. F9 115
Myingyan, Burma D3 34
Myitkyinā, Burma B4 34
Myllymäki, Fin. E15 6
Mymensingh, Bngl. H14 38
Mynämäki, Fin. F13 6
Myrskylä (Mörskom), Fin. F15 6
Myrtle Beach, S.C., U.S. D10 117
Myrtle Beach Air Force Base, mil., S.C., U.S. D10 117
Myrtle Grove, Fl., U.S. u14 86
Myrtle Point, Or., U.S. D2 114
Mysen, Nor. G8 6
Mysore, India F4 37
Mys Šmidta, Russia D30 24
Mystic, Ct., U.S. D8 84
Mystic Lakes, l., Ma., U.S. g11 98
My Tho, Viet. I9 34
Mytišči, Russia F20 18
Mzimba, Mwi. D6 44
Mzuzu, Mwi. D6 44

N

Naalehu, Hi., U.S. D6 88
Naas, Ire. H6 7
Nabadwīp, India I13 38
Naberežnyje Čelny, Russia F8 22
Nabeul, Tun. M5 14
Nabī Shu'ayb, Jabal an-, mtn., Yemen E3 46
Nabnasset, Ma., U.S. A5 98
Nābulus, Isr. Occ. C4 40
Nacala-Velha, Moz. D8 44
Naches, stm., Wa., U.S. C5 124
Nachingwea, Tan. D7 44
Nachodka, Russia I20 24
Nacimiento, Lake, res., Ca., U.S. E3 82
Naco, Mex. B5 62
Naco, Az., U.S. F6 80
Nacogdoches, Tx., U.S. D5 120
Nacogdoches, co., Tx., U.S. D5 120
Nadiād, India I5 38
Nadym, stm., Russia E8 24
Næstved, Den. I8 6
Naga, Phil. r20 32
Nagahama, Japan G9 30
Nagaland, state, India H16 38
Nagano, Japan F11 30
Nagaoka, Japan E11 30
Nāgappattinam, India G5 37
Nagasaki, Japan J2 30
Nāgaur, India G5 38
Nāgda, India I6 38
Nāgercoil, India H4 37
Nago, Japan y27 31b
Nagornyj, Russia F18 24
Nagoya, Japan G9 30
Nāgpur, India B5 37
Nags Head, N.C., U.S. B7 110
Nagykanizsa, Hung. I16 8
Nagykőrös, Hung. H19 8
Naha, Japan y27 31b
Nahant, Ma., U.S. g12 98
Nahariya, Isr. C4 40
Nahmakanta Lake, l., Me., U.S. C3 96
Nahunta, Ga., U.S. E5 87
Naidong, China F14 38
Nain, Newf., Can. g9 72
Nā'īn, Iran B5 46
Nairn, Scot., U.K. D9 7
Nairobi, Kenya B7 44
Najafābād, Iran B5 46
Nájera, Spain C9 12
Najin, N. Kor. C13 26
Nakaminato, Japan F13 30
Nakatsu, Japan I4 30
Nakatsugawa, Japan G10 30
Nakhon Pathom, Thai. H6 34
Nakhon Phanom, Thai. F8 34
Nakhon Ratchasima, Thai. G7 34
Nakhon Sawan, Thai. G6 34
Nakhon Si Thammarat, Thai. J5 34
Nakina, Ont., Can. o18 73
Naknek, Ak., U.S. D8 79
Naknek Lake, l., Ak., U.S. D8 79
Nakskov, Den. I8 6
Nakuru, Kenya B7 44
Nakusp, B.C., Can. D9 69
Nalchik see Nal'čik, Russia I6 22
Nal'čik, Russia I6 22
Nalgonda, India D5 37
Nālūt, Libya B8 42
Namak, Daryācheh-ye, l., Iran K8 22
Namangan, Uzb. I12 22
Namanock Island, i., N.J., U.S. A3 107
Namapa, Moz. D7 44
Namatanai, Pap. N. Gui. k17 50a
Nambour, Austl. E10 50
Namcha Barwa see Namjagbarwa Feng, mtn., China F16 38
Nam Co, l., China E14 38
Nam Dinh, Viet. D9 34
Namekagon, stm., Wi., U.S. B2 126
Namekagon Lake, l., Wi., U.S. B2 126
Namhkam, Burma C4 34
Namib Desert, des., Nmb. F2 44
Namibe, Ang. E2 44
Namibia, ctry., Afr. F3 44
Namjagbarwa Feng, mtn., China F16 38
Namlea, Indon. F8 32
Nampa, Id., U.S. F2 89
Namp'o, N. Kor. D12 26
Nampula, Moz. E7 44
Namsos, Nor. D8 6
Namur, Bel. E4 8
Nanaimo, B.C., Can. E5 69
Nanakuli, Hi., U.S. B3 88
Nanao, Japan E9 30
Nance, co., Ne., U.S. C7 104
Nanchang, China G4 28
Nanchong, China E8 26
Nancy, Fr. D13 10
Nanda Devi, mtn., India E8 38
Nānded, India C4 37
Nandurbār, India B3 37
Nandyāl, India E5 37
Nānga Parbat, mtn., Pak. C6 38
Nangqian (Xiangda), China D17 38
Nanjing (Nanking), China C7 28
Nanking see Nanjing, China C7 28
Nankoku, Japan I6 30
Nankou, China C10 26
Nan Ling, mts., China F9 26
Nanning, China C10 34
Nanping, China I7 28
Nansei-shotō (Ryukyu Islands), is., Japan F12 26
Nansemond, stm., Va., U.S. k14 123

Name	Map Ref	Page
Nantes, Fr.	E5	10
Nanticoke, Ont., Can.	E4	73
Nanticoke, Pa., U.S.	D10	115
Nanticoke, stm., U.S.	D6	97
Nanton, Alta., Can.	D4	68
Nantong, China	C9	28
Nant'ou, Tai.	L9	28
Nantua, Fr.	F12	10
Nantucket, Ma., U.S.	D7	98
Nantucket, co., Ma., U.S.	D7	98
Nantucket Island, i., Ma., U.S.	D7	98
Nantucket Sound, strt., Ma., U.S.	C7	98
Nantuxent Point, c., N.J., U.S.	E2	107
Nanty Glo, Pa., U.S.	F4	115
Nanuet, N.Y., U.S.	g12	109
Nanuque, Braz.	D8	57
Nanxiang, China	D10	28
Nanxiong, China	J3	28
Nanyang, China	B1	28
Naoetsu, Japan	E11	30
Naoma, W.V., U.S.	n13	125
Naomi Peak, mtn., Ut., U.S.	B4	121
Náousa, Grc.	I6	16
Napa, Ca., U.S.	C2	82
Napa, co., Ca., U.S.	C2	82
Napanee, Ont., Can.	C8	73
Napatree Point, c., R.I., U.S.	G1	116
Napavine, Wa., U.S.	C3	124
Naperville, Il., U.S.	B5	90
Napier, N.Z.	C6	52
Napierville, Que., Can.	D4	74
Naples, Fl., U.S.	F5	86
Naples, Tx., U.S.	C5	120
Naples, Ut., U.S.	C6	121
Naples see Napoli, Italy	I9	14
Napo, stm., S.A.	I6	58
Napoleon, N.D., U.S.	C6	111
Napoleon, Oh., U.S.	A1	112
Napoleonville, La., U.S.	E4	95
Napoli (Naples), Italy	I9	14
Nappanee, In., U.S.	B5	91
Nara, Japan	H8	30
Nara, Mali	E4	42
Naracoorte, Austl.	G8	50
Naramata, B.C., Can.	E8	69
Naranja, Fl., U.S.	G6	86
Narasapur, India	D6	37
Narasaraopet, India	D6	37
Narathiwat, Thai.	K6	34
Nārāyanganj, Bngl.	I14	38
Narberth, Pa., U.S.	p20	115
Narbonne, Fr.	I9	10
Nardò, Italy	I13	14
Narew, stm., Eur.	C21	8
Nārīn Ghar, Afg.	B3	38
Narita, Japan	G13	30
Narmada, stm., India	J5	38
Nārnaul, India	F7	38
Narni, Italy	G7	14
Naro-Fominsk, Russia	F19	18
Narragansett, R.I., U.S.	F4	116
Narragansett Bay, b., R.I., U.S.	E5	116
Narraguagus, stm., Me., U.S.	D5	96
Narrows, Va., U.S.	C2	123
Narsimhapur, India	I8	38
Narssag, Grnld.	D23	66
Naruto, Japan	H7	30
Narva, Est.	B11	18
Narvik, Nor.	B11	6
Naselle, Wa., U.S.	C2	124
Nash, Tx., U.S.	C5	120
Nash, co., N.C., U.S.	A4	110
Nashawena Island, i., Ma., U.S.	D6	98
Nash Stream, stm., N.H., U.S.	A4	106
Nashua, Ia., U.S.	B5	92
Nashua, N.H., U.S.	E4	106
Nashua, stm., U.S.	E3	106
Nashville, Ar., U.S.	D2	81
Nashville, Ga., U.S.	E3	87
Nashville, Il., U.S.	E4	90
Nashville, In., U.S.	F5	91
Nashville, Mi., U.S.	F5	99
Nashville, N.C., U.S.	B5	110
Nashville, Tn., U.S.	A5	119
Nashwauk, Mn., U.S.	C5	100
Nāsik, India	C2	37
Nāsir, Sudan	G12	42
Naskaupi, stm., Newf., Can.	g9	72
Nassau, Bah.	B9	64
Nassau, co., Fl., U.S.	B5	86
Nassau, co., N.Y., U.S.	E7	109
Nassau, stm., Fl., U.S.	k8	86
Nassau Sound, b., Fl., U.S.	B5	86
Nasser, Lake, res., Afr.	D12	42
Nässjö, Swe.	H10	6
Nasukoin Mountain, mtn., Mt., U.S.	B2	103
Natal, Braz.	E11	54
Natalbany, La., U.S.	D5	95
Natalia, Tx., U.S.	E3	120
Natashquan, stm., Can.	h9	72
Natchaug, stm., Ct., U.S.	B7	84
Natchez, Ms., U.S.	D2	101
Natchitoches, La., U.S.	C2	95
Natchitoches, co., La., U.S.	C2	95
Nāthdwāra, India	H5	38
Natick, Ma., U.S.	B5	98
National City, Ca., U.S.	F5	82
Natron, Lake, l., Afr.	B7	44
Natrona, co., Wy., U.S.	D5	127
Natrona Heights, Pa., U.S.	E2	115
Nattaung, mtn., Burma	E4	34
Natuna Besar, i., Indon.	M10	34
Natuna Besar, Kepulauan, is., Indon.	M10	34
Natuna Selatan, Kepulauan, is., Indon.	M10	34
Natural Bridge, Ut., U.S.	F3	121
Natural Bridge, Va., U.S.	C3	123
Natural Bridges National Monument, Ut., U.S.	F6	121
Naturaliste, Cape, c., Austl.	F3	50
Nauen, Ger.	C12	8
Naugatuck, Ct., U.S.	D3	84
Naugatuck, stm., Ct., U.S.	D3	84
Naumburg, Ger.	D11	8
Naushon Island, i., Ma., U.S.	D6	98
Nautilus Park, Ct., U.S.	D7	84
Nauvoo, Il., U.S.	C2	90
Nava del Rey, Spain	D6	12
Navahermosa, Spain	F7	12
Navajo, co., Az., U.S.	B5	80
Navajo Dam, N.M., U.S.	A2	108
Navajo Indian Reservation, U.S.	A4	80
Navajo Mountain, mtn., Ut., U.S.	F5	121
Navajo National Monument, Az., U.S.	A5	80
Navajo Reservoir, res., U.S.	A2	108
Navalcarnero, Spain	E7	12
Navalmoral de la Mata, Spain	F6	12
Navalvillar de Pela, Spain	F6	12
Navan, Ont., Can.	B9	73
Navan, Ire.	H6	7
Navarin, Mys, c., Russia	E29	24
Navarino, Isla, i., Chile	H3	56
Navarre, Oh., U.S.	B4	112
Navarro, co., Tx., U.S.	D4	120
Navasota, Tx., U.S.	D4	120
Navassa Island, i., N.A.	E10	64
Navoi, Uzb.	I11	22
Navojoa, Mex.	D5	62
Navolato, Mex.	E6	62
Navsāri, India	B2	37
Nawābganj, Bngl.	H13	38
Nawābganj, India	G9	38
Nawābshāh, Pak.	G3	38
Nāwah, Afg.	D2	38
Nawalgarh, India	G6	38
Nawiliwili Bay, b., Hi., U.S.	B2	88
Náxos, i., Grc.	L9	16
Nayak, Afg.	C2	38
Naylor, Mo., U.S.	E7	102
Nayoro, Japan	o20	30a
Nazaré, Braz.	B9	57
Nazaré, Port.	F2	12
Nazareth, Pa., U.S.	E11	115
Nazca, Peru	F4	54
Naze, Japan	w29	31b
Nazilli, Tur.	L12	16
Nazko, stm., B.C., Can.	C6	69
Ndélé, Cen. Afr. Rep.	G10	42
N'Djamena (Fort-Lamy), Chad	F9	42
Ndola, Zam.	D5	44
Neagh, Lough, l., N. Ire., U.K.	G6	7
Neah Bay, Wa., U.S.	A1	124
Néa Páfos (Paphos), Cyp.	B3	40
Neápolis, Grc.	M7	16
Near Islands, is., Ak., U.S.	E2	79
Nebo, Mount, mtn., Ut., U.S.	D4	121
Nebraska, state, U.S.	C6	104
Nebraska City, Ne., U.S.	D10	104
Nechako, stm., B.C., Can.	C5	69
Neches, stm., Tx., U.S.	D5	120
Nechí, Col.	C5	58
Neckar, stm., Ger.	F9	8
Necker Island, i., Hi., U.S.	m15	88
Necochea, Arg.	D5	56
Nederland, Co., U.S.	B5	83
Nederland, Tx., U.S.	E6	120
Nedrow, N.Y., U.S.	C4	109
Needham, Ma., U.S.	g11	98
Needle Mountain, mtn., Wy., U.S.	B3	127
Needles, Ca., U.S.	E6	82
Needville, Tx., U.S.	r14	120
Neenah, Wi., U.S.	D5	126
Neepawa, Man., Can.	D2	70
Neffs, Oh., U.S.	B5	112
Neffsville, Pa., U.S.	F9	115
Negage, Ang.	C3	44
Negaunee, Mi., U.S.	B3	99
Negele, Eth.	G2	46
Negev Desert see Hanegev, reg., Isr.	D4	40
Negley, Oh., U.S.	B5	112
Negombo, Sri L.	I5	37
Negra, Punta, c., Peru	E2	54
Negro, stm., Arg.	E4	56
Negro, stm., S.A.	H12	58
Negros, i., Phil.	C7	32
Neguac, N.B., Can.	B4	71
Nehalem, stm., Or., U.S.	A3	114
Nehbandān, Iran	B7	46
Neheim-Hüsten, Ger.	D7	8
Neiba, Bahía de, b., Dom. Rep.	E12	64
Neijiang, China	F8	26
Neill Point, c., Wa., U.S.	f11	124
Neillsville, Wi., U.S.	D3	126
Nei Monggol Zizhiqu (Inner Mongolia), prov., China	C10	26
Neisse (Nysa Łużycka), stm., Eur.	D14	8
Neiva, Col.	F5	58
Neja, Russia	C26	18
Nekemte, Eth.	G2	46
Nekoosa, Wi., U.S.	D4	126
Nelidovo, Russia	E15	18
Neligh, Ne., U.S.	B7	104
Nel'kan, Russia	F21	24
Nellikuppam, India	G5	37
Nellis Air Force Base, mil., Nv., U.S.	G6	105
Nellore, India	E5	37
Nelson, B.C., Can.	E9	69
Nelson, N.Z.	D4	52
Nelson, Ne., U.S.	D7	104
Nelson, co., Ky., U.S.	C4	94
Nelson, co., N.D., U.S.	B7	111
Nelson, co., Va., U.S.	C4	123
Nelson, stm., Man., Can.	A4	70
Nelsonville, Oh., U.S.	C3	112
Néma, Maur.	E4	42
Nemacolin, Pa., U.S.	G2	115
Nemadji, stm., U.S.	B1	126
Nemaha, co., Ks., U.S.	C7	93
Nemaha, co., Ne., U.S.	D10	104
Nemours, Fr.	D9	10
Nemuro, Japan	p23	30a
Nemuro Strait, strt., Asia	o23	30a
Nenagh, Ire.	I4	7
Nenana, Ak., U.S.	C10	79
Neodesha, Ks., U.S.	E8	93
Neoga, Il., U.S.	D5	90
Neola, Ia., U.S.	C2	92
Neola, Ut., U.S.	C5	121
Neopit, Wi., U.S.	D5	126
Neosho, Mo., U.S.	E3	102
Neosho, co., Ks., U.S.	E8	93
Neosho, stm., Ok., U.S.	A6	113
Nepal (Nepāl), ctry., Asia	D5	36
Nepālganj, Nepal	F9	38
Nepaug Reservoir, res., Ct., U.S.	B3	84
Nepean, Ont., Can.	h12	73
Nepewassi Lake, l., Ont., Can.	A4	73
Nephi, Ut., U.S.	D4	121
Nepisiguit, stm., N.B., Can.	B3	71
Nepisiguit Bay, b., N.B., Can.	B4	71
Neponset, stm., Ma., U.S.	h11	98
Neptune, N.J., U.S.	C4	107
Neptune Beach, Fl., U.S.	B5	86
Neptune City, N.J., U.S.	C4	107
Nérac, Fr.	H7	10
Nerastro, Sarīr, des., Libya	D10	42
Nerčinskij Zavod, Russia	G17	24
Nerechta, Russia	D23	18
Neriquinha, Ang.	E4	44
Nerva, Spain	H5	12
Nesbyen, Nor.	F7	6
Nescopeck, Pa., U.S.	D9	115
Neshanic, stm., N.J., U.S.	C3	107
Neshoba, co., Ms., U.S.	C4	101
Neskaupstaður, Ice.	B5	4
Nesna, Nor.	C9	6
Nesowadnehunk, l., Me., U.S.	B3	96
Nesquehoning, Pa., U.S.	E10	115
Ness, co., Ks., U.S.	D4	93
Ness, Loch, l., Scot., U.K.	D8	7
Ness City, Ks., U.S.	D4	93
Néstos (Mesta), stm., Eur.	H8	16
Netanya, Isr.	C4	40
Netcong, N.J., U.S.	B3	107
Netherlands, ctry., Eur.	E9	4
Netherlands Antilles (Nederlandse Antillen), dep., N.A.	H13	64
Netrakona, Bngl.	H14	38
Nettie, W.V., U.S.	C4	125
Nettilling Lake, l., N.W. Ter., Can.	C18	66
Nett Lake, l., Mn., U.S.	B5	100
Nett Lake Indian Reservation, Mn., U.S.	B6	100
Nettleton, Ms., U.S.	A5	101
Nettuno, Italy	H7	14
Neubrandenburg, Ger.	B13	8
Neuburg an der Donau, Ger.	G11	8
Neuchâtel, Switz.	F13	10
Neuchâtel, Lac de, l., Switz.	F13	10
Neufchâteau, Bel.	F5	8
Neufchâteau, Fr.	D12	10
Neufchâtel-en-Bray, Fr.	C8	10
Neuillé-Pont-Pierre, Fr.	E7	10
Neumarkt in der Oberpfalz, Ger.	F11	8
Neumünster, Ger.	A9	8
Neunkirchen, Aus.	H16	8
Neunkirchen/Saar, Ger.	F7	8
Neuquén, Arg.	D3	56
Neuruppin, Ger.	C12	8
Neuse, stm., N.C., U.S.	B6	110
Neusiedler See, l., Eur.	H16	8
Neuss, Ger.	D6	8
Neustadt Jan der Aisch—, Ger.	F10	8
Neustadt an der Weinstrasse, Ger.	F8	8
Neustadt in Holstein, Ger.	A10	8
Neustrelitz, Ger.	B13	8
Neu-Ulm, Ger.	G10	8
Neuville, Que., Can.	C6	74
Neuville-de-Poitou, Fr.	F7	10
Neuwied, Ger.	E7	8
Nevada, Ia., U.S.	B4	92
Nevada, Mo., U.S.	D3	102
Nevada, co., Ar., U.S.	D2	81
Nevada, co., Ca., U.S.	C3	82
Nevada, state, U.S.	D5	105
Nevada, Sierra, mts., Spain	H8	12
Nevada, Sierra, mts., Ca., U.S.	D4	82
Nevada City, Ca., U.S.	C3	82
Nevado, Cerro, mtn., Arg.	D3	56
Nevado, Cerro, mtn., Col.	F5	58
Never, Russia	G18	24
Nevers, Fr.	E10	10
Neversink, stm., N.Y., U.S.	D6	109
Nevis, i., St. K./N.	F16	64
Nevis, Ben, mtn., Scot., U.K.	E7	7
New, stm., U.S.	C3	125
New, stm., Az., U.S.	k8	80
New, stm., N.C., U.S.	C5	110
New Albany, In., U.S.	H6	91
New Albany, Ms., U.S.	A4	101
New Albany, Oh., U.S.	k11	112
New Amsterdam, Guy.	D14	58
Newark, Ar., U.S.	B4	81
Newark, Ca., U.S.	h8	82
Newark, De., U.S.	B3	85
Newark, Il., U.S.	B5	90
Newark, N.J., U.S.	B4	107
Newark, N.Y., U.S.	B3	109
Newark, Oh., U.S.	B3	112
Newark Bay, b., N.J., U.S.	k8	107
Newark Lake, l., Nv., U.S.	D6	105
New Athens, Il., U.S.	E4	90
New Augusta, Ms., U.S.	D4	101
Newaygo, Mi., U.S.	E5	99
Newaygo, co., Mi., U.S.	E5	99
New Baden, Il., U.S.	E4	90
New Baltimore, Mi., U.S.	F8	99
New Bedford, Ma., U.S.	C6	98
New Bedford, Pa., U.S.	D1	115
Newberg, Or., U.S.	B4	114
New Berlin, Il., U.S.	D4	90
New Berlin, Wi., U.S.	n11	126
New Bern, N.C., U.S.	B5	110
Newbern, Tn., U.S.	A2	119
Newberry, Fl., U.S.	C4	86
Newberry, Mi., U.S.	B5	99
Newberry, S.C., U.S.	C4	117
Newberry, co., S.C., U.S.	C4	117
New Bethlehem, Pa., U.S.	D3	115
New Bloomfield, Pa., U.S.	F7	115
New Boston, Mi., U.S.	p15	99
New Boston, Oh., U.S.	D3	112
New Boston, Tx., U.S.	C5	120
New Braunfels, Tx., U.S.	E3	120
New Bremen, Oh., U.S.	B1	112
New Brighton, Mn., U.S.	m12	100
New Brighton, Pa., U.S.	E1	115
New Britain, Ct., U.S.	C4	84
New Britain, i., Pap. N. Gui.	m16	50a
New Brockton, Al., U.S.	D4	78
New Brunswick, N.J., U.S.	C4	107
New Brunswick, prov., Can.	C3	71
New Buffalo, Mi., U.S.	G4	99
Newburg, Wi., U.S.	E5	126
Newburgh, Ont., Can.	C8	73
Newburgh, In., U.S.	I3	91
Newburgh, N.Y., U.S.	D6	109
Newburgh Heights, Oh., U.S.	h9	112
Newburyport, Ma., U.S.	A6	98
New Caledonia, dep., Oc.	H24	2
New Canaan, Ct., U.S.	E2	84
New Carlisle, In., U.S.	A4	91
New Carlisle, Oh., U.S.	C1	112
Newcastle, Austl.	F10	50
Newcastle, N.B., Can.	C4	71
Newcastle, Ont., Can.	D6	73
Newcastle, S. Afr.	G5	44
Newcastle, N. Ire., U.K.	G7	7
New Castle, Al., U.S.	B3	78
New Castle, Co., U.S.	B3	83
New Castle, De., U.S.	B3	85
New Castle, In., U.S.	E7	91
New Castle, Ky., U.S.	B4	94
Newcastle, Ok., U.S.	B4	113
New Castle, Pa., U.S.	D1	115
Newcastle, Wy., U.S.	C8	127
New Castle, co., De., U.S.	B3	85
Newcastle upon Tyne, Eng., U.K.	G11	7
Newcastle Waters, Austl.	C6	50
New City, N.Y., U.S.	D6	109
Newcomerstown, Oh., U.S.	B4	112
New Concord, Oh., U.S.	C4	112
New Cumberland, Pa., U.S.	F8	115
New Cumberland, W.V., U.S.	A4	125
Newdegate, Austl.	F3	50
New Delhi, India	F7	38
Newell, Ia., U.S.	B2	92
Newell, S.D., U.S.	C2	118
Newell, W.V., U.S.	A4	125
New Ellenton, S.C., U.S.	E4	117
Newellton, La., U.S.	B4	95
New England, N.D., U.S.	C3	111
Newenham, Cape, c., Ak., U.S.	D7	79
New Fairfield, Ct., U.S.	D2	84
Newfane, N.Y., U.S.	B2	109
Newfields, N.H., U.S.	D5	106
New Florence, Mo., U.S.	C6	102
Newfound Gap, U.S.	f9	110
Newfound Lake, l., N.H., U.S.	C3	106
Newfoundland, prov., Can.	D4	72
Newfoundland, i., Newf., Can.	D3	72
New Franklin, Mo., U.S.	B5	102
New Freedom, Pa., U.S.	G8	115
New Georgia, i., Sol.Is.	A11	50
New Germany, N.S., Can.	E5	71
New Glarus, Wi., U.S.	F4	126
New Guinea, i.	m14	50a
Newhall, Ia., U.S.	C6	92
New Hampshire, state, U.S.	C3	106
New Hampton, Ia., U.S.	A5	92
New Hanover, co., N.C., U.S.	C5	110
New Hanover, i., Pap. N. Gui.	k17	50a
New Harbour, Newf., Can.	E5	72
New Harmony, In., U.S.	H2	91
New Hartford, Ct., U.S.	B4	84
New Hartford, Ia., U.S.	B5	92
New Haven, Ct., U.S.	D4	84
New Haven, In., U.S.	B7	91
New Haven, Ky., U.S.	C4	94
New Haven, Mi., U.S.	F8	99
New Haven, Mo., U.S.	C6	102
New Haven, W.V., U.S.	C3	125
New Haven, co., Ct., U.S.	D4	84
New Haven, stm., Vt., U.S.	C2	122
New Haven Harbor, b., Ct., U.S.	E4	84
New Hazelton, B.C., Can.	B4	69
New Hebrides see Vanuatu, ctry., Oc.	H24	2
New Holland, Ga., U.S.	B3	87
New Holland, Pa., U.S.	F9	115
New Holstein, Wi., U.S.	E5	126
New Hope, Al., U.S.	A3	78
New Hope, Ky., U.S.	C4	94
New Hope, Mn., U.S.	m12	100
New Hope, Pa., U.S.	F12	115
New Hudson, Mi., U.S.	o14	99
New Iberia, La., U.S.	D4	95
Newington, Ct., U.S.	C5	84
New Inlet, b., N.C., U.S.	D5	110
New Ireland, i., Pap. N. Gui.	k17	50a
New Jersey, state, U.S.	C4	107
New Johnsonville, Tn., U.S.	A4	119
New Kensington, Pa., U.S.	E2	115
New Kent, co., Va., U.S.	C5	123
Newkirk, Ok., U.S.	A4	113
New Laguna, N.M., U.S.	B2	108
New Lake, l., N.C., U.S.	B6	110
New Lenox, Il., U.S.	B6	90
New Lexington, Oh., U.S.	C3	112
New Lisbon, Wi., U.S.	E3	126
New Liskeard, Ont., Can.	p20	73
Newllano, La., U.S.	C2	95
New London, Ct., U.S.	D7	84
New London, Ia., U.S.	D6	92
New London, Mn., U.S.	E4	100
New London, Mo., U.S.	B6	102
New London, N.H., U.S.	D3	106
New London, Oh., U.S.	A3	112
New London, Wi., U.S.	D5	126
New London, co., Ct., U.S.	C7	84
New London Submarine Base, mil., Ct., U.S.	D7	84
New Madison, Oh., U.S.	C1	112
New Madrid, Mo., U.S.	E8	102
New Madrid, co., Mo., U.S.	E8	102
Newman, Ca., U.S.	D3	82
Newman, Il., U.S.	D6	90
New Manchester, W.V., U.S.	e8	125
Newman Grove, Ne., U.S.	C8	104
Newman Lake, l., Wa., U.S.	B8	124
Newmanstown, Pa., U.S.	F9	115
Newmarket, Ont., Can.	C5	73
New Market, Al., U.S.	A3	78
New Market, In., U.S.	E4	91
Newmarket, N.H., U.S.	D5	106
New Market, Tn., U.S.	C10	119
New Market, Va., U.S.	B4	123
New Martinsville, W.V., U.S.	B4	125
New Matamoras, Oh., U.S.	C4	112
New Mexico, state, U.S.	C3	108
New Miami, Oh., U.S.	C1	112
New Milford, Ct., U.S.	C2	84
New Milford, N.J., U.S.	h8	107
New Milford, Pa., U.S.	C10	115
Newnan, Ga., U.S.	C2	87
Newnans Lake, l., Fl., U.S.	C4	86
New Norfolk, Austl.	H9	50
New Orleans, La., U.S.	E5	95
New Orleans Naval Air Station, mil., La., U.S.	k11	95
New Oxford, Pa., U.S.	G7	115
New Palestine, In., U.S.	E6	91
New Paltz, N.Y., U.S.	D6	109
New Paris, In., U.S.	B6	91
New Paris, Oh., U.S.	C1	112
New Philadelphia, Oh., U.S.	B4	112
New Philadelphia, Pa., U.S.	E9	115
New Plymouth, N.Z.	C5	52
New Plymouth, Id., U.S.	F2	89
New Point Comfort, c., Va., U.S.	C6	123
Newport, Eng., U.K.	K11	7
Newport, Wales, U.K.	J9	7
Newport, Ar., U.S.	B4	81
Newport, De., U.S.	B3	85
Newport, In., U.S.	E3	91
Newport, Ky., U.S.	A5	94
Newport, Me., U.S.	D3	96
Newport, Mi., U.S.	G7	99
Newport, Mn., U.S.	n13	100
Newport, N.H., U.S.	D2	106
Newport, N.C., U.S.	C6	110
Newport, Oh., U.S.	C4	112
Newport, Or., U.S.	C2	114
Newport, Pa., U.S.	F7	115
Newport, R.I., U.S.	F5	116
Newport, Tn., U.S.	D10	119
Newport, Vt., U.S.	B4	122
Newport, Wa., U.S.	A8	124
Newport, co., R.I., U.S.	E5	116
Newport Beach, Ca., U.S.	n13	82
Newport News, Va., U.S.	D6	123
New Port Richey, Fl., U.S.	D4	86
New Prague, Mn., U.S.	F5	100
New Preston, Ct., U.S.	C2	84
New Providence, N.J., U.S.	B4	107
New Providence, i., Bah.	B9	64
Newquay, Eng., U.K.	K7	7
New Richland, Mn., U.S.	G5	100
New Richmond, Que., Can.	A4	71
New Richmond, Oh., U.S.	D1	112
New Richmond, Wi., U.S.	C1	126
New River Inlet, b., N.C., U.S.	C5	110
New Roads, La., U.S.	D4	95
New Rochelle, N.Y., U.S.	E7	109
New Rockford, N.D., U.S.	B6	111
New Ross, Ire.	I6	7
Newry, N. Ire., U.K.	G6	7
New Salem, N.D., U.S.	C4	111
New Sarpy, La., U.S.	k11	95
New Sharon, Ia., U.S.	C5	92
New Site, Al., U.S.	B4	78
New Smyrna Beach, Fl., U.S.	C6	86
New South Wales, state, Austl.	F9	50
New Straitsville, Oh., U.S.	C3	112
New Tazewell, Tn., U.S.	C10	119
Newton, Al., U.S.	D4	78
Newton, Ga., U.S.	E2	87
Newton, Il., U.S.	E5	90
Newton, Ia., U.S.	C4	92
Newton, Ks., U.S.	D6	93
Newton, Ma., U.S.	B5	98
Newton, Ms., U.S.	C4	101
Newton, N.J., U.S.	A3	107
Newton, N.C., U.S.	B1	110
Newton, Tx., U.S.	D6	120
Newton, Ut., U.S.	B4	121
Newton, co., Ar., U.S.	B2	81
Newton, co., Ga., U.S.	C3	87
Newton, co., In., U.S.	B3	91
Newton, co., Ms., U.S.	C4	101
Newton, co., Mo., U.S.	E3	102
Newton, co., Tx., U.S.	D6	120
Newton Falls, Oh., U.S.	A5	112
Newton Lake, res., Il., U.S.	E5	90
Newton Stewart, Scot., U.K.	G8	7
Newtown, Ct., U.S.	D2	84
New Town, N.D., U.S.	B3	111
Newtown, Oh., U.S.	C1	112
Newtownabbey, N. Ire., U.K.	G7	7
Newtownards, N. Ire., U.K.	G7	7
Newtown Square, Pa., U.S.	p20	115
New Ulm, Mn., U.S.	F4	100
New Vienna, Oh., U.S.	C2	112
Newville, Pa., U.S.	F7	115
New Washington, In., U.S.	G6	91
New Washington, Oh., U.S.	B3	112
New Waterford, Oh., U.S.	B5	112
New Westminster, B.C., Can.	E6	69
New Whiteland, In., U.S.	E5	91
New Wilmington, Pa., U.S.	D1	115
New Windsor, Il., U.S.	B3	90
New Windsor, Md., U.S.	A3	97
New Windsor, N.Y., U.S.	D6	109
New World Island, i., Newf., Can.	D4	72
New York, N.Y., U.S.	E7	109
New York, co., N.Y., U.S.	k13	109
New York, state, U.S.	C6	109
New York Mills, Mn., U.S.	D3	100
New Zealand, ctry., Oc.	D4	52
Nežin, Ukr.	G4	22
Nez Perce, co., Id., U.S.	C2	89

Name | Map Ref | Page

Nez Perce Indian Reservation, Id., U.S. C2 89
Ngami, Lake, l., Bots. F4 44
Nganglong Kangri, mts., China D10 38
Nganjuk, Indon. m15 33a
Ngaoundéré, Cam. G8 42
Nguigmi, Niger F8 42
Nguru, Nig. F8 42
Nha Trang, Viet. H10 34
Niafounké, Mali E5 42
Niagara, Wi., U.S. C6 126
Niagara, co., N.Y., U.S. B2 109
Niagara Falls, Ont., Can. D5 73
Niagara Falls, N.Y., U.S. B1 109
Niagara-on-the-Lake, Ont., Can. D5 73
Niamey, Niger F6 42
Niangara, Zaire H11 42
Niangua, stm., Mo., U.S. D5 102
Niantic, Ct., U.S. D7 84
Nias, Pulau, i., Indon. N4 34
Nibley, Ut., U.S. B4 121
Nicaragua, ctry., N.A. H5 64
Nicaragua, Lago de, l., Nic. I5 64
Nicastro (Lamezia Terme), Italy K11 14
Nicatous Lake, l., Me., U.S. C4 96
Nice, Fr. I14 10
Niceville, Fl., U.S. u15 86
Nichinan, Japan K4 30
Nicholas, co., Ky., U.S. B6 94
Nicholas, co., W.V., U.S. C4 125
Nicholas Channel, strt., N.A. C7 64
Nicholasville, Ky., U.S. C5 94
Nicholls, Ga., U.S. E4 87
Nichols Hills, Ok., U.S. B4 113
Nicholson, Ms., U.S. E4 101
Nickajack Lake, res., Tn., U.S. D8 119
Nickel Centre, Ont., Can. p19 73
Nickerson, Ks., U.S. D5 93
Nicobar Islands, is., India J2 34
Nicolet, Que., Can. C5 74
Nicolet, stm., Que., Can. C5 74
Nicolet, Lake, l., Mi., U.S. B6 99
Nicollet, Mn., U.S. F4 100
Nicollet, co., Mn., U.S. F4 100
Nicolls Town, Bah. B8 64
Nicoma Park, Ok., U.S. B4 113
Nicosia, Cyp. B3 40
Nicosia, N. Cyp. B3 40
Nicosia, Italy L9 14
Nicoya, Golfo de, b., C.R. J5 64
Nicoya, Península de, pen., C.R. I5 64
Niebüll, Ger. A8 8
Nienburg, Ger. C9 8
Nieuw Nickerie, Sur. B7 54
Nieves, Mex. E8 62
Nigadoo, N.B., Can. B4 71
Niger, ctry., Afr. E7 42
Niger, stm., Afr. G7 42
Nigeria, ctry., Afr. G7 42
Nigríta, Grc. I7 16
Nihoa, i., Hi., U.S. m15 88
Niigata, Japan E12 30
Niihama, Japan I6 30
Niihau, i., Hi., U.S. B1 88
Niinisalo, Fin. F14 6
Niitsu, Japan E12 30
Níjar, Spain I9 12
Nijmegen, Neth. D5 8
Nikishka, Ak., U.S. g16 79
Nikkō, Japan F12 30
Nikolajev, Ukr. H4 22
Nikolajevsk-na-Amure, Russia G22 24
Nikolajev see Nikolajev, Ukr. H4 22
Nikšić, Yugo. G2 16
Niland, Ca., U.S. F6 82
Nile (Nahr an-Nīl), stm., Afr. C12 42
Niles, Il., U.S. h9 90
Niles, Mi., U.S. G4 99
Niles, Oh., U.S. A5 112
Nileshwar, India F3 37
Nīmach, India H6 38
Nimba, Mont, mtn., Afr. G4 42
Nîmes, Fr. I11 10
Nimrod Lake, res., Ar., U.S. C2 81
Nine Degree Channel, strt., India H2 37
Nine Mile Creek, stm., Ut., U.S. D5 121
Ninemile Point, c., Mi., U.S. C6 99
Ninety Six, S.C., U.S. C3 117
Ningbo, China F10 28
Ningming, China C9 34
Ningxia Huizu Zizhiqu, prov., China D8 26
Ninh Binh, Viet. D8 34
Ninigret Pond, l., R.I., U.S. G2 116
Ninilchik, Ak., U.S. C9 79
Ninnescah, stm., Ks., U.S. E6 93
Niobrara, co., Wy., U.S. C8 127
Niobrara, stm., U.S. B7 104
Niono, Mali F4 42
Nioro du Sahel, Mali E4 42
Niort, Fr. F6 10
Niota, Tn., U.S. D9 119
Nipāni, India D3 37
Nipigon, Lake, l., Ont., Can. o17 73
Nipissing, Lake, l., Ont., Can. A5 73
Nipomo, Ca., U.S. E3 82
Nipple Mountain, mtn., Co., U.S. D2 83
Nirmal, India C5 37
Niš, Yugo. F5 16
Nisa, Port. F4 12
Nishinoomote, Japan u30 31b
Nishiwaki, Japan H7 30
Niskayuna, N.Y., U.S. C7 109
Nisqually, stm., Wa., U.S. C3 124
Nisswa, Mn., U.S. D4 100
Niterói, Braz. G7 57
Nitra, Slov. G18 8
Nitro, W.V., U.S. C3 125
Niue, dep., Oc. H1 2
Nivelles, Bel. E4 8
Niverville, Man., Can. E3 70
Niwot, Co., U.S. A5 83
Nixa, Mo., U.S. D4 102
Nixon, Nv., U.S. D2 105
Nixon, Tx., U.S. E4 120
Nizāmābād, India C5 37
Nizip, Tur. A5 40
Nižn'aja Pojma, Russia F13 24
Nižn'aja Tunguska, stm., Russia E12 24
Nižneangarsk, Russia F15 24
Nižneilimsk, Russia F14 24
Nižneudinsk, Russia G13 24
Nižnij Novgorod (Gorki), Russia E27 18
Nizza Monferrato, Italy E3 14
Njombe, Tan. C6 44
Nkhota Kota, Mwi. D6 44
Nkongsamba, Cam. H7 42
Noākhāli, Bngl. I14 38
Noank, Ct., U.S. D8 84
Noatak, Ak., U.S. B7 79
Noatak, stm., Ak., U.S. B7 79
Nobel, Ont., Can. B4 73
Nobeoka, Japan J4 30
Noble, Ok., U.S. B4 113
Noble, co., In., U.S. B7 91
Noble, co., Oh., U.S. C4 112
Noble, co., Ok., U.S. A4 113
Nobles, co., Mn., U.S. G3 100
Noblesville, In., U.S. D6 91
Noboribetsu, Japan q19 30a
Nocatee, Fl., U.S. E5 86
Nocera [Inferiore], Italy I9 14
Nochixtlán, Mex. I11 62
Nocona, Tx., U.S. C4 120
Nodaway, co., Mo., U.S. A3 102
Nodaway, stm., U.S. A2 102
Noel, Mo., U.S. E3 102
Nogales, Mex. B4 62
Nogales, Az., U.S. F5 80
Nōgata, Japan I3 30
Nogent-le-Rotrou, Fr. D7 10
Noginsk, Russia F21 18
Nogoyá, Arg. C5 56
Noirmoutier, Fr. E4 10
Nojima-zaki, c., Japan H12 30
Nokia, Fin. F14 6
Nokomis, Fl., U.S. E4 86
Nokomis, Il., U.S. D4 90
Nokomis, Lake, res., Wi., U.S. C4 126
Nolan, co., Tx., U.S. C2 120
Nolichucky, stm., Tn., U.S. C10 119
Nolin, stm., Ky., U.S. C3 94
Nolin Lake, res., Ky., U.S. C3 94
Nomans Land, i., Ma., U.S. D6 98
Nombre de Dios, Mex. F7 62
Nome, Ak., U.S. C6 79
Nominingue, Que., Can. C2 74
Nonacho Lake, l., N.W. Ter., Can. D11 66
Nonesuch, stm., Me., U.S. g7 96
Nong'an, China C12 26
Nong Khai, Thai. F7 34
Nonquit Pond, l., R.I., U.S. E6 116
Nontron, Fr. G7 10
Nooksack, North Fork, stm., Wa., U.S. A4 124
Nooksack, South Fork, stm., Wa., U.S. A3 124
Noordoost Polder, reg., Neth. C5 8
Noorvik, Ak., U.S. B7 79
Nootka Island, i., B.C., Can. G7 66
Nootka Sound, strt., B.C., Can. E4 69
No Point, Point, c., Md., U.S. D5 97
Noquebay, Lake, l., Wi., U.S. C6 126
Noranda (part of Rouyn [-Noranda]), Que., Can. k11 74
Nora Springs, Ia., U.S. A5 92
Norborne, Mo., U.S. B4 102
Norco, La., U.S. E5 95
Norcross, Ga., U.S. C2 87
Norden, Ger. B7 8
Nordenham, Ger. B8 8
Nordenšel'da, Archipelag, is., Russia B13 24
Norderney, i., Ger. B7 8
Nordfjordeid, Nor. F5 6
Nordfold, Nor. C10 6
Nordhausen, Ger. D10 8
Nordhorn, Ger. C7 8
Nordkapp, c., Nor. A15 6
Nordkjosbotn, Nor. B12 6
Nördlingen, Ger. G10 8
Nordmaling, Swe. E12 6
Nordreisa, Nor. B13 6
Nordre Strømfjord, Grnld. C22 66
Nordvik, Russia C16 24
Norfolk, Ct., U.S. B3 84
Norfolk, Ne., U.S. B8 104
Norfolk, N.Y., U.S. f9 109
Norfolk, Va., U.S. D6 123
Norfolk, co., Ma., U.S. B5 98
Norfolk Naval Base, mil., Va., U.S. k15 123
Norfolk Naval Shipyard, mil., Va., U.S. k15 123
Norfork Dam, Ar., U.S. A3 81
Norfork Lake, res., U.S. A3 81
Noril'sk, Russia D11 24
Norland, Fl., U.S. s13 86
Norlina, N.C., U.S. A4 110
Normal, Il., U.S. C5 90
Norman, Ok., U.S. B4 113
Norman, co., Mn., U.S. C2 100
Norman, Lake, res., N.C., U.S. B2 110
Normandie, hist. reg., Fr. D6 10
Normandy, Mo., U.S. f13 102
Normandy see Normandie, hist. reg., Fr. D6 10
Norman Park, Ga., U.S. E3 87
Normanton, Austl. C8 50
Norman Wells, N.W. Ter., Can. C7 66
Norphlet, Ar., U.S. D3 81
Ñorquincó, Arg. E2 56
Norridge, Il., U.S. k9 90
Norridgewock, Me., U.S. D3 96
Norris, S.C., U.S. B2 117
Norris, Tn., U.S. C9 119
Norris Arm, Newf., Can. D4 72
Norris City, Il., U.S. F5 90
Norris Dam, Tn., U.S. C9 119
Norris Lake, res., Tn., U.S. C10 119
Norris Point, Newf., Can. D3 72
Norristown, Pa., U.S. F11 115
Norrköping, Swe. G11 6
Norrtälje, Swe. G12 6
Norseman, Austl. F4 50
Norsk, Russia G19 24
Norte, Serra do, plat., Braz. F7 54
North, S.C., U.S. D5 117
North, stm., Al., U.S. B2 78
North, stm., Ia., U.S. f8 92
North, stm., Ma., U.S. h12 98
North, stm., W.V., U.S. B6 125
North, Cape, c., N.S., Can. B9 71
North Adams, Ma., U.S. A1 98
North Albany, Or., U.S. k11 114
Northam, Austl. F3 50
North America E10 61
North Amherst, Ma., U.S. B2 98
Northampton, Eng., U.K. I12 7
Northampton, Ma., U.S. B2 98
Northampton, Pa., U.S. E11 115
Northampton, co., N.C., U.S. A5 110
Northampton, co., Pa., U.S. E11 115
Northampton, co., Va., U.S. C7 123
North Andaman, i., India H2 34
North Andover, Ma., U.S. A5 98
North Andrews Gardens, Fl., U.S. *r13 86
North Anna, stm., Va., U.S. B5 123
North Anson, Me., U.S. D3 96
North Apollo, Pa., U.S. E2 115
North Arapaho Peak, mtn., Co., U.S. A5 83
North Arlington, N.J., U.S. h8 107
North Atlanta, Ga., U.S. h8 87
North Attleboro, Ma., U.S. C5 98
North Augusta, S.C., U.S. D4 117
North Aurora, Il., U.S. k8 90
North Baltimore, Oh., U.S. A2 112
North Bay, Ont., Can. A5 73
North Beach, Md., U.S. C4 97
North Belmont, N.C., U.S. B1 110
North Bend, Ne., U.S. C9 104
North Bend, Or., U.S. D2 114
North Bend, Wa., U.S. B4 124
North Bennington, Vt., U.S. F2 122
North Bergen, N.J., U.S. h8 107
North Berwick, Me., U.S. E2 96
North Billerica, Ma., U.S. A5 98
Northborough, Ma., U.S. B4 98
North Branch, Mi., U.S. E7 99
North Branch, Mn., U.S. E6 100
North Branch, N.H., U.S. D3 106
North Branch, N.J., U.S. B3 107
North Branford, Ct., U.S. D4 84
Northbridge, Ma., U.S. B4 98
Northbrook, Il., U.S. h9 90
North Brookfield, Ma., U.S. B3 98
North Brunswick, N.J., U.S. C4 107
North Caldwell, N.J., U.S. B4 107
North Canadian, stm., Ok., U.S. A5 113
North Canton, Ga., U.S. B2 87
North Canton, Oh., U.S. B4 112
North Cape, c., P.E.I., Can. B6 71
North Cape May, N.J., U.S. F3 107
North Cape see Nordkapp, c., Nor. A15 6
North Caribou Lake, l., Ont., Can. F14 66
North Carolina, state, U.S. B3 110
North Cascades National Park, Wa., U.S. A4 124
North Channel, strt., Ont., Can. A2 73
North Channel, strt., U.K. F7 7
North Charleston, S.C., U.S. F8 117
North Chicago, Il., U.S. A6 90
North Clarendon, Vt., U.S. D3 122
North College Hill, Oh., U.S. o12 112
North Conway, N.H., U.S. B4 106
North Corbin, Ky., U.S. D5 94
North Crossett, Ar., U.S. D4 81
North Cyprus, ctry., Asia B3 40
North Dakota, state, U.S. B5 111
North Dartmouth, Ma., U.S. C6 98
North Druid Hills, Ga., U.S. *h8 87
North Eagle Butte, S.D., U.S. B4 118
North East, Md., U.S. A6 97
North East, Pa., U.S. B2 115
Northeast, stm., Md., U.S. A6 97
Northeast Cape, c., Ak., U.S. C6 79
Northeast Cape Fear, stm., N.C., U.S. C5 110
Northeast Harbor, Me., U.S. D4 96
Northeast Henrietta, N.Y., U.S. *B3 109
North Easton, Ma., U.S. B5 98
Northeast Pond, l., N.H., U.S. D5 106
Northeast Providence Channel, strt., Bah. B9 64
North Edisto, stm., S.C., U.S. k11 117
Northeim, Ger. D9 8
North English, Ia., U.S. C5 92
North English, stm., Ia., U.S. C5 92
North Enid, Ok., U.S. A4 113
Northern Cheyenne Indian Reservation, Mt., U.S. E10 103
Northern Indian Lake, l., Man., Can. A3 70
Northern Ireland, ter., U.K. G6 7
Northern Territory, ter., Austl. C6 50
North Falmouth, Ma., U.S. C6 98
Northfield, Mn., U.S. F5 100
Northfield, N.H., U.S. D3 106
Northfield, N.J., U.S. E3 107
Northfield, Oh., U.S. h9 112
Northfield, Vt., U.S. C3 122
Northfield Falls, Vt., U.S. C3 122
North Flinders Ranges, mts., Austl. F7 50
North Fond du Lac, Wi., U.S. E5 126
Northford, Ct., U.S. D4 84
North Fork Reservoir, res., Or., U.S. B4 114
North Fort Myers, Fl., U.S. F5 86
North Fox Island, i., Mi., U.S. C5 99
North Frisian Islands, is., Eur. A8 8
Northglenn, Co., U.S. B6 83
North Gower, Ont., Can. B9 73
North Grafton, Ma., U.S. B4 98
North Grosvenordale, Ct., U.S. B8 84
North Gulfport, Ms., U.S. E4 101
North Haledon, N.J., U.S. B4 107
North Hampton, N.H., U.S. E5 106
North Hartland Reservoir, res., Vt., U.S. D4 122
North Hatley, Que., Can. D6 74
North Haven, Ct., U.S. D4 84
North Head, N.B., Can. E3 71
North Hero Island, i., Vt., U.S. B2 122
North Horn Lake, l., Tn., U.S. e8 119
North Industry, Oh., U.S. B4 112
North Inlet, b., S.C., U.S. E9 117
North Island, i., N.Z. C5 52
North Island, i., S.C., U.S. E9 117
North Island Naval Air Station, mil., Ca., U.S. o15 82
North Islands, is., La., U.S. E7 95
North Judson, In., U.S. B4 91
North Kansas City, Mo., U.S. h10 102
North Kingstown, R.I., U.S. E4 116
North Kingsville, Oh., U.S. A5 112
North La Junta, Co., U.S. C7 83
Northlake, Il., U.S. k9 90
North Laramie, stm., Wy., U.S. D7 127
North Las Vegas, Nv., U.S. G6 105
North La Veta Pass, Co., U.S. D5 83
North Lewisburg, Oh., U.S. B2 112
North Liberty, In., U.S. A5 91
North Liberty, Ia., U.S. C6 92
North Lima, Oh., U.S. B5 112
North Little Rock, Ar., U.S. C3 81
North Logan, Ut., U.S. B4 121
North Loon Mountain, mtn., Id., U.S. D3 89
North Magnetic Pole B22 128
North Mamm Peak, mtn., Co., U.S. B3 83
North Manchester, In., U.S. C6 91
North Manitou Island, i., Mi., U.S. C4 99
North Mankato, Mn., U.S. F4 100
North Merrydale, La., U.S. *D4 95
North Miami, Fl., U.S. G6 86
North Miami Beach, Fl., U.S. s13 86
North Middletown, Ky., U.S. B5 94
North Moose Lake, l., Man., Can. B1 70
North Mountain, mtn., Pa., U.S. D9 115
North Muskegon, Mi., U.S. E4 99
North Myrtle Beach, S.C., U.S. D10 117
North Naples, Fl., U.S. F5 86
North New River Canal, Fl., U.S. F6 86
North Ogden, Ut., U.S. B4 121
North Olmsted, Oh., U.S. h9 112
North Palisade, mtn., Ca., U.S. D4 82
North Park, Il., U.S. A4 90
North Park, val., Co., U.S. A4 83
North Pass, strt., La., U.S. E7 95
North Pembroke, Ma., U.S. B6 98
North Plainfield, N.J., U.S. B4 107
North Plains, Or., U.S. B4 114
North Plains, pl., N.M., U.S. C1 108
North Platte, Ne., U.S. C5 104
North Platte, stm., U.S. C6 76
North Point, c., Md., U.S. B5 97
North Point, c., Mi., U.S. C7 99
North Pole A12 128
Northport, Al., U.S. B2 78
North Prairie, Wi., U.S. F5 126
North Providence, R.I., U.S. C4 116
North Raccoon, stm., Ia., U.S. C3 92
North Reading, Ma., U.S. f11 98
North Richland Hills, Tx., U.S. n9 120
Northridge, Oh., U.S. C2 112
North Ridgeville, Oh., U.S. A3 112
North Royalton, Oh., U.S. h9 112
North Rustico, P.E.I., Can. C6 71
North Salem, N.H., U.S. E4 106
North Salt Lake, Ut., U.S. C4 121
North Santee, stm., S.C., U.S. E9 117
North Saskatchewan, stm., Can. F10 66
North Schell Peak, mtn., Nv., U.S. D7 105
North Scituate, Ma., U.S. h12 98
North Sea, Eur. D8 4
North Shoshone Peak, mtn., Nv., U.S. D4 105
North Sioux City, S.D., U.S. E9 118
North Skunk, stm., Ia., U.S. C5 92
North Springfield, Vt., U.S. E3 122
North Springfield Reservoir, res., Vt., U.S. E4 122
North Star, De., U.S. A3 85
North St. Paul, Mn., U.S. m13 100
North Stratford, N.H., U.S. A3 106
North Sudbury, Ma., U.S. g10 98
North Swanzey, N.H., U.S. E2 106
North Syracuse, N.Y., U.S. B4 109
North Tarrytown, N.Y., U.S. D7 109
North Terre Haute, In., U.S. E3 91
North Thompson, stm., B.C., Can. D8 69
North Tonawanda, N.Y., U.S. B2 109
North Troy, Vt., U.S. B4 122
North Tunica, Ms., U.S. A3 101
North Twin Lake, l., Wi., U.S. B4 126
Northumberland, Pa., U.S. E8 115
Northumberland, co., Pa., U.S. D8 115
Northumberland, co., Va., U.S. C6 123
Northumberland National Park, Eng., U.K. F10 7
Northumberland Strait, strt., Can. C6 71
North Umpqua, stm., Or., U.S. D3 114
North Uxbridge, Ma., U.S. B4 98
Northvale, N.J., U.S. g9 107
North Vancouver, B.C., Can. E6 69
North Vassalboro, Me., U.S. D3 96
North Vernon, In., U.S. F6 91
Northville, Mi., U.S. p15 99
North Wales, Pa., U.S. F11 115
North Walpole, N.H., U.S. D2 106
North Warren, Pa., U.S. C3 115
North Webster, In., U.S. B6 91
North West Cape, c., Austl. D2 50
Northwest Miramichi, stm., N.B., Can. B3 71
Northwest Providence Channel, strt., Bah. A8 64
Northwest Territories, prov., Can. C13 66
North Wildwood, N.J., U.S. E3 107
North Wilkesboro, N.C., U.S. A1 110
North Windham, Ct., U.S. C7 84
North Windham, Me., U.S. E2 96
Northwood, Ia., U.S. A4 92
Northwood, N.D., U.S. B8 111
North Woodstock, N.H., U.S. B3 106
North York, Ont., Can. D5 73
North York, Pa., U.S. G8 115
North York Moors National Park, Eng., U.K. G12 7
Norton, N.B., Can. D4 71
Norton, Ks., U.S. C4 93
Norton, Ma., U.S. C5 98
Norton, Oh., U.S. A4 112
Norton, Va., U.S. f9 123
Norton, co., Ks., U.S. C4 93
Norton Air Force Base, mil., Ca., U.S. E5 82
Norton Bay, b., Ak., U.S. C7 79
Norton Pond, l., Vt., U.S. B5 122
Norton Reservoir, res., Ks., U.S. C3 93
Norton Shores, Mi., U.S. E4 99
Norton Sound, strt., Ak., U.S. C6 79
Nortonville, Ks., U.S. C8 93
Nortonville, Ky., U.S. C2 94
Norwalk, Ca., U.S. n12 82
Norwalk, Ct., U.S. E2 84
Norwalk, Ia., U.S. C4 92
Norwalk, Oh., U.S. A3 112
Norwalk, stm., Ct., U.S. E2 84
Norwalk Islands, is., Ct., U.S. E2 84
Norway, Me., U.S. D2 96
Norway, Mi., U.S. C3 99
Norway, ctry., Eur. C9 4
Norway Bay, b., N.W. Ter., Can. B12 66
Norway House, Man., Can. C3 70
Norway Lake, l., Mn., U.S. E3 100
Norwegian Sea, Eur. C12 128
Norwich, Eng., U.K. I14 7
Norwich, Ct., U.S. C7 84
Norwich, N.Y., U.S. C5 109
Norwich, Vt., U.S. D4 122
Norwood, Ont., Can. C7 73
Norwood, Ma., U.S. B5 98
Norwood, Mn., U.S. F5 100
Norwood, N.J., U.S. h9 107
Norwood, N.Y., U.S. f10 109
Norwood, N.C., U.S. B2 110
Norwood, Oh., U.S. o13 112
Norwood, Pa., U.S. p20 115
Norwoodville, Ia., U.S. e8 92
Noshiro, Japan B13 30
Notasulga, Al., U.S. C4 78
Notch Peak, mtn., Ut., U.S. D2 121
Noto, Italy M10 14
Notodden, Nor. G7 6
Notre Dame, Monts, mts., Que., Can. k13 74
Notre Dame Bay, b., Newf., Can. D4 72
Notre Dame de Lourdes, Man., Can. E2 70
Notre-Dame-du-Lac, Que., Can. B9 74
Nottawasaga Bay, b., Ont., Can. C4 73
Nottaway, stm., Que., Can. h11 74
Nottingham, Eng., U.K. I11 7
Nottingham Island, i., N.W. Ter., Can. D17 66
Nottoway, co., Va., U.S. C4 123
Nottoway, stm., Va., U.S. D5 123
Nouadhibou, Maur. D2 42
Nouakchott, Maur. E2 42
Nouamrhar, Maur. E2 42
Noupoort, S. Afr. H4 44
Nouveau-Québec, Cratère du, crat., Que., Can. D18 66
Nova América, Braz. C4 57
Nova Cruz, Braz. E11 54
Nova Freixo, Moz. D7 44
Nova Friburgo, Braz. G7 57
Nova Gaia, Ang. D3 44
Nova Gradiška, Cro. D12 14
Nova Iguaçu, Braz. G7 57
Novaja Sibir', Ostrov, i., Russia B23 24
Novaja Zeml'a, is., Russia C5 24
Nova Lima, Braz. E7 57
Nova Lisboa see Huambo, Ang. D3 44
Nova Mambone, Moz. F7 44
Novara, Italy D3 14
Nova Scotia, prov., Can. D6 71
Nova Sofala, Moz. F6 44
Novato, Ca., U.S. C2 82
Novelda, Spain G11 12
Nové Zámky, Slov. H18 8
Novgorod, Russia C14 18
Novi, Mi., U.S. p15 99
Novi Ligure, Italy E3 14
Novi Pazar, Bul. F11 16
Novi Pazar, Yugo. F4 16
Novi Sad, Yugo. D3 16
Novoaltajsk, Russia G10 24
Novo Aripuanã, Braz. E6 54
Novogrudok, Bela. H8 18
Novokuzneck, Russia G11 24
Novo Mesto, Slo. D10 14
Novo Redondo, Ang. D2 44
Novorossijsk, Russia I5 22
Novorybnoje, Russia C15 24
Novosibirsk, Russia D4 128
Novosibirskije Ostrova, is., Russia B22 24
Novosibirskoje Vodochranilišče, res., Russia G10 24
Novotroick, Russia G9 22
Novozybkov, Russia I14 18
Novska, Cro. D11 14
Nowa Sól (Neusalz), Pol. D15 8
Nowata, Ok., U.S. A6 113
Nowata, co., Ok., U.S. A6 113
Nowgong, India G15 38
Nowood, stm., Wy., U.S. B5 127
Nowshāk, mtn., Asia B4 38
Nowshera, Pak. C4 38
Nowy Sącz, Pol. F20 8
Nowy Targ, Pol. F20 8
Noxon Reservoir, res., Mt., U.S. C1 103
Noxontown Lake, res., De., U.S. C3 85

Index

Name	Map Ref	Page
Noxubee, co., Ms., U.S.	B5	101
Noxubee, stm., U.S.	B5	101
Noyes Island, i., Ak., U.S.	n22	79
Noyon, Fr.	C9	10
Nozay, Fr.	E5	10
Nsanje, Mwi.	E7	44
Nsawam, Ghana	G5	42
Nubanusit Lake, l., N.H., U.S.	E2	106
Nubian Desert, des., Sudan	D12	42
Nuckolls, co., Ne., U.S.	D7	104
Nucla, Co., U.S.	C2	83
Nueces, co., Tx., U.S.	F4	120
Nueces, stm., Tx., U.S.	E3	120
Nueltin Lake, l., Can.	E13	66
Nueva Casas Grandes, Mex.	B6	62
Nueva Rosita, Mex.	D9	62
Nueva San Salvador, El Sal.	H3	64
Nueve de Julio, Arg.	D4	56
Nuevitas, Cuba	D9	64
Nuevo, Golfo, b., Arg.	E4	56
Nuevo Laredo, Mex.	D10	62
Nuevo Rocafuerte, Ec.	H5	58
Nuits-Saint-Georges, Fr.	E11	10
Nukus, Uzb.	I9	22
Nulato, Ak., U.S.	C8	79
Nulhegan, stm., Vt., U.S.	B5	122
Nullagine, Austl.	D4	50
Nullarbor Plain, pl., Austl.	F5	50
Numata, Japan	F12	30
Numazu, Japan	G11	30
Numfoor, Pulau, i., Indon.	F9	32
Nun, stm., China	A12	26
Nunivak Island, i., Ak., U.S.	D6	79
Nunjiang, China	B12	26
Nuoro, Italy	I4	14
N'urba, Russia	E17	24
Nuremberg, Pa., U.S.	E9	115
Nuremberg see Nürnberg, Ger.	F11	8
Nürnberg, Ger.	F11	8
Nurri, Italy	J4	14
Nutley, N.J., U.S.	B4	107
Nutter Fort, W.V., U.S.	k10	125
Nutting Lake, Ma., U.S.	f10	98
Nuuanu Pali, Hi., U.S.	g10	88
Nyack, N.Y., U.S.	D7	109
Nyainqêntanglha Shan, mts., China	E13	38
Nyala, Sudan	F10	42
Nyanda, Zimb.	F6	44
Nyasa, Lake, l., Afr.	D6	44
Nyaunglebin, Burma	F4	34
Nybro, Swe.	H10	6
Nye, co., Nv., U.S.	E5	105
Nyenyam, China	F11	38
Nyeri, Kenya	B7	44
Nyíregyháza, Hung.	H21	8
Nykøbing, Den.	I8	6
Nyköping, Swe.	G11	6
Nylstroom, S. Afr.	F5	44
Nynäshamn, Swe.	G11	6
Nyngan, Austl.	F9	50
Nyon, Switz.	F13	10
Nyons, Fr.	H12	10
Nysa, Pol.	E17	8
Nysa Łużycka (Neisse) (Nisa), stm., Eur.	D14	8
Nyssa, Or., U.S.	D9	114
Nzérékoré, Gui.	G4	42
N'zeto, Ang.	C2	44
O		
Oahe, Lake, res., U.S.	B6	76
Oahe Dam, S.D., U.S.	C5	118
Oahu, i., Hi., U.S.	B4	88
Oak Bay, B.C., Can.	h12	69
Oak Bluffs, Ma., U.S.	D6	98
Oak Creek, Co., U.S.	A4	83
Oak Creek, Wi., U.S.	n12	126
Oakdale, Ca., U.S.	D3	82
Oakdale, Ga., U.S.	h8	87
Oakdale, La., U.S.	D3	95
Oakdale, Pa., U.S.	k13	115
Oakes, N.D., U.S.	C7	111
Oakfield, N.Y., U.S.	B2	109
Oakfield, Wi., U.S.	E5	126
Oak Forest, Il., U.S.	k9	90
Oak Grove, Ky., U.S.	D2	94
Oak Grove, La., U.S.	B4	95
Oak Grove, Or., U.S.	B4	114
Oak Harbor, Oh., U.S.	A2	112
Oak Harbor, Wa., U.S.	A3	124
Oak Hill, Mi., U.S.	D4	99
Oak Hill, Oh., U.S.	D3	112
Oak Hill, W.V., U.S.	D3	125
Oak Hill, mtn., Ma., U.S.	f9	98
Oakhurst, Ok., U.S.	A5	113
Oak Island, i., Wi., U.S.	B3	126
Oak Lake, l., Man., Can.	E1	70
Oakland, Ca., U.S.	D2	82
Oakland, Il., U.S.	D5	90
Oakland, Ia., U.S.	C2	92
Oakland, Me., U.S.	D3	96
Oakland, Md., U.S.	m12	97
Oakland, Ne., U.S.	C9	104
Oakland, N.J., U.S.	A4	107
Oakland, Ok., U.S.	C5	113
Oakland, Or., U.S.	D3	114
Oakland, R.I., U.S.	B2	116
Oakland, co., Mi., U.S.	F7	99
Oakland City, In., U.S.	H3	91
Oakland Park, Fl., U.S.	r13	86
Oak Lawn, Il., U.S.	B6	90
Oaklawn, Ks., U.S.	g12	93
Oakley, Id., U.S.	G5	89
Oakley, Ks., U.S.	C3	93
Oakman, Al., U.S.	B2	78
Oakmont, Pa., U.S.	E2	115
Oak Mountain, mtn., Ga., U.S.	D2	87
Oak Orchard, De., U.S.	F5	85
Oak Park, Il., U.S.	B6	90
Oak Park, Mi., U.S.	p15	99
Oak Ridge, N.C., U.S.	A3	110
Oakridge, Or., U.S.	D4	114
Oak Ridge, Tn., U.S.	C9	119
Oak Ridge Reservoir, res., N.J., U.S.	A3	107
Oakton, Va., U.S.	g12	123
Oaktown, In., U.S.	G3	91
Oak Valley, N.J., U.S.	D2	107
Oakville, Ont., Can.	D5	73
Oakville, Ct., U.S.	C3	84
Oakville, Mo., U.S.	g13	102
Oakwood, Ga., U.S.	B3	87
Oakwood, Il., U.S.	C6	90
Oakwood, Oh., U.S.	C1	112
Oamaru, N.Z.	F3	52
Oaxaca [de Juárez], Mex.	I11	62
Ob', stm., Russia	D7	24
Oban, Scot., U.K.	E7	7
Obbia, Som.	G4	46
Obed, stm., Tn., U.S.	C9	119
Oberlin, Ks., U.S.	C3	93
Oberlin, La., U.S.	D3	95
Oberlin, Oh., U.S.	A3	112
Oberwart, Aus.	H16	8
Obetz, Oh., U.S.	C3	112
Obi, Kepulauan, is., Indon.	F8	32
Obi, Pulau, i., Indon.	F8	32
Óbidos, Braz.	D7	54
Obihiro, Japan	q21	30a
Obion, Tn., U.S.	A2	119
Obion, co., Tn., U.S.	A2	119
Obion, stm., Tn., U.S.	A2	119
Oblong, Il., U.S.	D6	90
Oblučje, Russia	H20	24
Obninsk, Russia	F19	18
Obock, Dji.	F3	46
O'Brien, co., Ia., U.S.	A2	92
Obrovac, Cro.	E10	14
Observation Peak, mtn., Ca., U.S.	B3	82
Observatoire, Caye de l', i., N. Cal.	D11	50
Obuasi, Ghana	G5	42
Ocala, Fl., U.S.	C4	86
Ocaña, Col.	C6	58
Ocaña, Spain	F8	12
Occidental, Cordillera, mts., Col.	E4	58
Occidental, Cordillera, mts., Peru	F4	54
Ocean, co., N.J., U.S.	D4	107
Oceana, W.V., U.S.	D3	125
Oceana, co., Mi., U.S.	E4	99
Oceana Naval Air Station, mil., Va., U.S.	k15	123
Ocean Bluff, Ma., U.S.	B6	98
Ocean City, Fl., U.S.	u15	86
Ocean City, Md., U.S.	D7	97
Ocean City, N.J., U.S.	E3	107
Ocean Grove, Ma., U.S.	C5	98
Ocean Park, Wa., U.S.	C1	124
Oceanport, N.J., U.S.	C4	107
Oceanside, Ca., U.S.	F5	82
Ocean Springs, Ms., U.S.	E5	101
Ocean [Township], N.J., U.S.	C4	107
Ocean View, De., U.S.	F5	85
Ocha, Russia	G22	24
Ocheda Lake, l., Mn., U.S.	G3	100
Ocheyedan, stm., Ia., U.S.	A2	92
Ochiltree, co., Tx., U.S.	A2	120
Ochlockonee, stm., Fl., U.S.	B2	86
Ochoco Lake, res., Or., U.S.	C6	114
Ocho Rios, Jam.	E9	64
Ochota, stm., Russia	F22	24
Ochotsk, Russia	F22	24
Ochsenfurt, Ger.	F10	8
Ocilla, Ga., U.S.	E3	87
Ockelbo, Swe.	F11	6
Ocmulgee, stm., Ga., U.S.	D3	87
Ocoee, Fl., U.S.	D5	86
Ocoee, Lake, res., Tn., U.S.	D9	119
Oconee, co., Ga., U.S.	C3	87
Oconee, co., S.C., U.S.	B1	117
Oconee, stm., Ga., U.S.	C3	87
Oconee, Lake, res., Ga., U.S.	C3	87
Oconomowoc, Wi., U.S.	E5	126
Oconto, Wi., U.S.	D6	126
Oconto, co., Wi., U.S.	D5	126
Oconto, stm., Wi., U.S.	D5	126
Oconto Falls, Wi., U.S.	D5	126
Ocotal, Nic.	H4	64
Ocotlán, Mex.	G8	62
Ocracoke Inlet, b., N.C., U.S.	B6	110
Ocracoke Island, i., N.C., U.S.	B7	110
Octoraro Creek, stm., U.S.	A5	97
Ocumare del Tuy, Ven.	B9	58
Ocussi, Indon.	G7	32
Oda, Ghana	G5	42
Oda, Jabal, mtn., Sudan	D13	42
Ōdate, Japan	B13	30
Odawara, Japan	G12	30
Odda, Nor.	F6	6
Odebolt, Ia., U.S.	B2	92
Odell, Il., U.S.	B5	90
Odell, Or., U.S.	B5	114
Odell Lake, l., Or., U.S.	E5	114
Odem, Tx., U.S.	F4	120
Odemira, Port.	H3	12
Ödemiş, Tur.	K11	16
Odense, Den.	I8	6
Odenton, Md., U.S.	B4	97
Odenville, Al., U.S.	B3	78
Oder (Odra), stm., Eur.	C14	8
Oderberg, Ger.	C14	8
Odessa, Ont., Can.	C8	73
Odessa, Ukr.	H4	22
Odessa, De., U.S.	C3	85
Odessa, Mo., U.S.	C4	102
Odessa, Tx., U.S.	D1	120
Odessa, Wa., U.S.	B7	124
Odienné, I.C.	G4	42
Odin, Il., U.S.	E4	90
Odincovo, Russia	F20	18
Odon, In., U.S.	G4	91
O'Donnell, Tx., U.S.	C2	120
Odra (Oder), stm., Eur.	C14	8
Oelsnitz, Ger.	E12	8
Oelwein, Ia., U.S.	B6	92
O'Fallon, Il., U.S.	E4	90
O'Fallon, Mo., U.S.	f12	102
Offenbach, Ger.	E8	8
Offenburg, Ger.	G7	8
Offutt Air Force Base, mil., Ne., U.S.	g3	104
Ōfunato, Japan	C14	30
Ōgaki, Japan	G9	30
Ogallala, Ne., U.S.	C4	104
Ogbomosho, Nig.	G6	42
Ogden, Ia., U.S.	B3	92
Ogden, Ks., U.S.	C7	93
Ogden, Ut., U.S.	B4	121
Ogden, Mount, mtn., N.A.	k23	79
Ogdensburg, N.J., U.S.	A3	107
Ogdensburg, N.Y., U.S.	f9	109
Ogeechee, stm., Ga., U.S.	D5	87
Ogemaw, co., Mi., U.S.	D6	99
Ogilvie Mountains, mts., Yukon, Can.	D5	66
Ogle, co., Il., U.S.	A4	90
Oglesby, Il., U.S.	B4	90
Oglethorpe, Ga., U.S.	D2	87
Oglethorpe, co., Ga., U.S.	C3	87
Oglethorpe, Mount, mtn., Ga., U.S.	B2	87
Ogooué, stm., Afr.	B2	44
Ogulin, Cro.	D10	14
Ogunquit, Me., U.S.	E2	96
Oğuzeli, Tur.	A5	40
Ohanet, Alg.	C7	42
Ōhata, Japan	A14	30
Ohatchee, Al., U.S.	B3	78
O'Higgins, Lago (Lago San Martín), l., S.A.	F2	56
Ohio, co., In., U.S.	G7	91
Ohio, co., Ky., U.S.	C3	94
Ohio, co., W.V., U.S.	A4	125
Ohio, state, U.S.	B3	112
Ohio, stm., U.S.	D9	76
Ohio Brush Creek, stm., Oh., U.S.	D2	112
Ohio City, Oh., U.S.	B1	112
Ohio Peak, mtn., Co., U.S.	C3	83
Ohioville, Pa., U.S.	E1	115
Ohoopee, stm., Ga., U.S.	D4	87
Ohrid, Lake, l., Eur.	H4	16
Öhringen, Ger.	F9	8
Oiapoque, Braz.	C8	54
Oil City, La., U.S.	B2	95
Oil City, Pa., U.S.	D2	115
Oil Creek, stm., Pa., U.S.	C2	115
Oildale, Ca., U.S.	E4	82
Oil Springs, Ont., Can.	E2	73
Oilton, Ok., U.S.	A5	113
Ōita, Japan	I4	30
Ojai, Ca., U.S.	E4	82
Ojinaga, Mex.	C7	62
Ojm'akon, Russia	E22	24
Ojo de Liebre, Laguna, b., Mex.	D2	62
Ojos del Salado, Cerro, mtn., S.A.	B3	56
Oka, stm., Russia	F25	18
Oka, stm., Russia	G14	24
Okaba, Indon.	G10	32
Okahandja, Nmb.	F3	44
Okaloosa, co., Fl., U.S.	u15	86
Okamanpeedan Lake, l., U.S.	A3	92
Okanagan Falls, B.C., Can.	E8	69
Okanagan Lake, l., B.C., Can.	D8	69
Okanagan Landing, B.C., Can.	D8	69
Okanogan, Wa., U.S.	A6	124
Okanogan, co., Wa., U.S.	A5	124
Okāra, Pak.	E5	38
Okarche, Ok., U.S.	B4	113
Okatibbee Reservoir, res., Ms., U.S.	C5	101
Okauchee Lake, Wi., U.S.	*E5	126
Okavango (Cubango), stm., Afr.	E3	44
Okavango Swamp, sw., Bots.	E4	44
Ōkawa, Japan	I3	30
Okawville, Il., U.S.	E4	90
Okaya, Japan	F11	30
Okayama, Japan	H6	30
Okazaki, Japan	H10	30
Okeechobee, Fl., U.S.	E6	86
Okeechobee, co., Fl., U.S.	E6	86
Okeechobee, Lake, l., Fl., U.S.	F6	86
Okeene, Ok., U.S.	A3	113
Okefenokee Swamp, sw., U.S.	F4	87
Okemah, Ok., U.S.	B5	113
Okfuskee, co., Ok., U.S.	B5	113
Okhotsk, Sea of (Ochotskoje More), Asia	G23	24
Oki-guntō, is., Japan	F6	30
Okinawa-jima, i., Japan	y27	31b
Okinoerabu-shima, i., Japan	x28	31b
Okino-Tori-shima, i., Japan	G14	26
Oklahoma, co., Ok., U.S.	B4	113
Oklahoma, state, U.S.	B4	113
Oklahoma City, Ok., U.S.	B4	113
Oklawaha, Fl., U.S.	C5	86
Oklawaha, stm., Fl., U.S.	C5	86
Oklawaha, Lake, res., Fl., U.S.	C5	86
Okmulgee, Ok., U.S.	B6	113
Okmulgee, co., Ok., U.S.	B5	113
Okoboji, Ia., U.S.	A2	92
Okobojo Creek, stm., S.D., U.S.	C5	118
Okolona, Ky., U.S.	g11	94
Okolona, Ms., U.S.	B5	101
Okotoks, Alta., Can.	D4	68
Okt'abr'skoj Revol'ucii, Ostrov, i., Russia	B13	24
Oktibbeha, co., Ms., U.S.	B5	101
Ola, Ar., U.S.	B2	81
Olancha Peak, mtn., Ca., U.S.	D4	82
Olanchito, Hond.	G4	64
Öland, i., Swe.	H11	6
Olanta, S.C., U.S.	D8	117
Olathe, Co., U.S.	C3	83
Olathe, Ks., U.S.	D9	93
Olavarría, Arg.	D4	56
Olbia, Italy	I4	14
Ol'chon, Ostrov, i., Russia	G15	24
Olcott, N.Y., U.S.	B2	109
Old Bahama Channel, strt., N.A.	C8	64
Old Bridge, N.J., U.S.	C4	107
Oldenburg, Ger.	B8	8
Oldenburg, In., U.S.	F7	91
Oldenburg [in Holstein], Ger.	A10	8
Old Faithful Geyser, Wy., U.S.	B2	127
Old Forge, Pa., U.S.	D10	115
Old Fort, N.C., U.S.	f10	110
Oldham, co., Ky., U.S.	B4	94
Oldham, co., Tx., U.S.	B1	120
Old Harbor, Ak., U.S.	D9	79
Old Head of Kinsale, c., Ire.	J4	7
Old Hickory Lake, res., Tn., U.S.	A5	119
Oldman, stm., Alta., Can.	E4	68
Old Man of the Mountain, N.H., U.S.	B3	106
Oldmans Creek, stm., N.J., U.S.	D2	107
Old Orchard Beach, Me., U.S.	E2	96
Old Perlican, Newf., Can.	D5	72
Old Point Comfort, c., Va., U.S.	h15	123
Old Rhodes Key, i., Fl., U.S.	G6	86
Old River Lake, l., Ar., U.S.	k10	81
Olds, Alta., Can.	D3	68
Old Saybrook, Ct., U.S.	D6	84
Oldsmar, Fl., U.S.	o10	86
Old Tampa Bay, b., Fl., U.S.	p10	86
Old Tappan, N.J., U.S.	g9	107
Old Topsail Inlet, b., N.C., U.S.	C5	110
Old Town, Me., U.S.	D4	96
Old Wives Lake, l., Sask., Can.	G2	75
Olean, N.Y., U.S.	C2	109
O'Leary, P.E.I., Can.	C5	71
Ølen, Nor.	G5	6
Olenij, Ostrov, i., Russia	C9	24
Olen'ok, Russia	D16	24
Olen'ok, stm., Russia	C18	24
Olen'okskij Zaliv, b., Russia	C18	24
Olentangy, stm., Oh., U.S.	B3	112
Oleśnica, Pol.	D17	8
Ol'ga, Russia	I21	24
Olga, Mount, mtn., Austl.	E6	50
Olhão, Port.	H3	12
Ólimbos, mtn., Cyp.	B3	40
Ólimbos, Óros, mtn., Grc.	I6	16
Olímpia, Braz.	F4	57
Olin, Ia., U.S.	B6	92
Olinda, Braz.	E12	54
Olite, Spain	C10	12
Oliva, Arg.	C4	56
Oliva, Spain	G11	12
Oliva de la Frontera, Spain	G5	12
Olive Branch, Ms., U.S.	A4	101
Olive Hill, Ky., U.S.	B6	94
Olivehurst, Ca., U.S.	C3	82
Oliveira, Braz.	F6	57
Olivenza, Spain	G4	12
Oliver, B.C., Can.	E8	69
Oliver, Pa., U.S.	G2	115
Oliver, co., N.D., U.S.	B4	111
Oliver Dam, U.S.	C5	78
Oliver Springs, Tn., U.S.	C9	119
Olivet, Mi., U.S.	F6	99
Olivia, Mn., U.S.	F4	100
Olla, La., U.S.	C3	95
Ollagüe, Chile	A3	56
Olmedo, Spain	D7	12
Olmito, Tx., U.S.	F4	120
Olmos, Peru	E3	54
Olmos Park, Tx., U.S.	k7	120
Olmsted, co., Mn., U.S.	G6	100
Olmsted Falls, Oh., U.S.	h9	112
Olney, Il., U.S.	E5	90
Olney, Md., U.S.	B3	97
Olney, Tx., U.S.	C3	120
Oloj, stm., Russia	D26	24
Ol'okma, stm., Russia	F18	24
Ol'okminsk, Russia	E18	24
Olomouc, Czech.	F17	8
Olongapo, Phil.	q19	33b
Oloron-Sainte-Marie, Fr.	I6	10
Olot, Spain	C14	12
Olov'annaja, Russia	G17	24
Olsztyn (Allenstein), Pol.	B20	8
Olten, Switz.	E14	10
Olton, Tx., U.S.	B1	120
Oluan Pi, c., Tai.	N9	28
Olustee, Ok., U.S.	C2	113
Ol'utorskij, Mys, c., Russia	F28	24
Olympia, Wa., U.S.	B3	124
Olympic Mountains, mts., Wa., U.S.	B2	124
Olympic National Park, Wa., U.S.	B2	124
Olympus, Mount, mtn., Wa., U.S.	B2	124
Olympus, Mount see Ólimbos, Óros, mtn., Grc.	I6	16
Olyphant, Pa., U.S.	D10	115
Omae-zaki, c., Japan	H11	30
Omagh, N. Ire., U.K.	G5	7
Omaha, Ne., U.S.	C10	104
Omaha Indian Reservation, Ne., U.S.	B9	104
Omak, Wa., U.S.	A6	124
Omak Lake, l., Wa., U.S.	A6	124
Oman, ctry., Asia	D6	46
Oman, Gulf of, b., Asia	D6	46
Omar, W.V., U.S.	D3	125
Ōma-zaki, c., Japan	A13	30
Omčak, Russia	E23	24
Omega, Ga., U.S.	E3	87
Omegna, Italy	D3	14
Omemee, Ont., Can.	C6	73
Omerville, Que., Can.	D5	74
Ometepe, Isla de, i., Nic.	I5	64
Ometepec, Mex.	I10	62
Omineca, stm., B.C., Can.	B5	69
Omineca Mountains, mts., B.C., Can.	A4	69
Ōmiya, Japan	G12	30
Ommaney, Cape, c., Ak., U.S.	D12	79
Ommanney Bay, b., N.W. Ter., Can.	B12	66
Ommen, Neth.	C6	8
Omo, stm., Eth.	G2	46
Omolon, stm., Russia	D25	24
Ompompanoosuc, stm., Vt., U.S.	D4	122
Omro, Wi., U.S.	D5	126
Omsk, Russia	F8	24
Omsukčan, Russia	E25	24
Ōmura, Japan	J2	30
Ōmuta, Japan	I3	30
Onaga, Ks., U.S.	C7	93
Onalaska, Wa., U.S.	C3	124
Onalaska, Wi., U.S.	E2	126
Onamia, Mn., U.S.	D5	100
Onancock, Va., U.S.	C7	123
Onarga, Il., U.S.	C6	90
Onawa, Ia., U.S.	B1	92
Onawa, Lake, l., Me., U.S.	C3	96
Onaway, Mi., U.S.	C6	99
Onda, Spain	F11	12
Ondangua, Nmb.	E3	44
Ondjiva, Ang.	E3	44
Öndörchaan, Mong.	B9	26
Oneco, Fl., U.S.	E4	86
Onega, Lake see Onežskoje ozero, l., Russia	E5	22
One Hundred Fifty Mile House, B.C., Can.	C7	69
One Hundred Mile House, B.C., Can.	D7	69
Oneida, Ky., U.S.	C6	94
Oneida, N.Y., U.S.	B5	109
Oneida, Oh., U.S.	C1	112
Oneida, Tn., U.S.	C9	119
Oneida, co., Id., U.S.	G6	89
Oneida, co., N.Y., U.S.	B5	109
Oneida, co., Wi., U.S.	C4	126
Oneida Lake, l., N.Y., U.S.	B5	109
O'Neill, Ne., U.S.	B7	104
Onekotan, Ostrov, i., Russia	H24	24
Oneonta, Al., U.S.	B3	78
Oneonta, N.Y., U.S.	C5	109
Onești, Rom.	C10	16
Onežskoje ozero, l., Russia	E5	22
Ongole, India	E6	37
Onida, S.D., U.S.	C5	118
Onitsha, Nig.	G7	42
Onoda, Japan	I4	30
Onomichi, Japan	H6	30
Onondaga, co., N.Y., U.S.	C4	109
Onondaga Indian Reservation, N.Y., U.S.	C4	109
Onota Lake, l., Ma., U.S.	B1	98
Onoway, Alta., Can.	C3	68
Onset, Ma., U.S.	C6	98
Onslow, Austl.	D3	50
Onslow, co., N.C., U.S.	C5	110
Onslow Bay, b., N.C., U.S.	C5	110
Onsted, Mi., U.S.	F6	99
Ontario, Ca., U.S.	E5	82
Ontario, Oh., U.S.	B3	112
Ontario, Or., U.S.	C10	114
Ontario, co., N.Y., U.S.	C3	109
Ontario, prov., Can.	C6	73
Ontario, Lake, l., N.A.	C11	76
Onteniente, Spain	G11	12
Ontonagon, Mi., U.S.	m12	99
Ontonagon, co., Mi., U.S.	m12	99
Ontonagon Indian Reservation, Mi., U.S.	B1	99
Onverwacht, Sur.	B7	54
Oodnadatta, Austl.	E7	50
Ooldea, Austl.	F6	50
Oolitic, In., U.S.	G4	91
Oologah, Ok., U.S.	A6	113
Oologah Lake, res., Ok., U.S.	A6	113
Ooltewah, Tn., U.S.	D8	119
Oostburg, Wi., U.S.	E6	126
Oostende (Ostende), Bel.	D2	8
Oosterhout, Neth.	D4	8
Ootacamund, India	G4	37
Ootsa Lake, l., B.C., Can.	C4	69
Opala, Zaire	B4	44
Opa-Locka, Fl., U.S.	s13	86
Opatija, Cro.	D9	14
Opava, Czech.	F17	8
Opelika, Al., U.S.	C4	78
Opelousas, La., U.S.	D3	95
Opequon Creek, stm., W.V., U.S.	B6	125
Opiscotéo, Lac, l., Que., Can.	F19	66
Opole (Oppeln), Pol.	E17	8
Opotiki, N.Z.	C6	52
Opp, Al., U.S.	D3	78
Oppdal, Nor.	E7	6
Oppelo, Ar., U.S.	B3	81
Opportunity, Wa., U.S.	B8	124
Optima Reservoir, res., Ok., U.S.	e9	113
Oquawka, Il., U.S.	C3	90
Ora, Italy	C6	14
Oracle, Az., U.S.	E5	80
Oradea, Rom.	B5	16
Oradell, N.J., U.S.	h8	107
Oradell Reservoir, res., N.J., U.S.	h9	107
Orai, India	H8	38
Oraibi, Az., U.S.	B5	80
Oran (Wahran), Alg.	A5	42
Oran, Mo., U.S.	D8	102
Orange, Austl.	F9	50
Orange, Fr.	H11	10
Orange, Ca., U.S.	n13	82
Orange, Ct., U.S.	D3	84
Orange, Ma., U.S.	A3	98
Orange, N.J., U.S.	B4	107
Orange, Tx., U.S.	D6	120
Orange, Va., U.S.	B4	123
Orange, co., Ca., U.S.	F5	82
Orange, co., Fl., U.S.	D5	86
Orange, co., In., U.S.	G4	91
Orange, co., N.Y., U.S.	D6	109
Orange, co., N.C., U.S.	A3	110
Orange, co., Tx., U.S.	D6	120
Orange, co., Vt., U.S.	D3	122
Orange, co., Va., U.S.	B4	123
Orange (Oranje), stm., Afr.	G3	44
Orange, Cabo, c., Braz.	C8	54
Orange Beach, Al., U.S.	E2	78
Orangeburg, S.C., U.S.	E6	117
Orangeburg, co., S.C., U.S.	E6	117
Orange City, Fl., U.S.	D5	86
Orange City, Ia., U.S.	B1	92
Orange Grove, Ms., U.S.	E5	101
Orange Grove, Tx., U.S.	F4	120
Orange Lake, l., Fl., U.S.	C4	86
Orange Park, Fl., U.S.	B5	86
Orangeville, Ont., Can.	D4	73
Orangeville, Ut., U.S.	D4	121

Name — Map Ref — Page

Orange Walk, Belize E3 64
Orani, Phil. q19 33b
Oranienburg, Ger. C13 8
Oranjestad, Aruba H12 64
Orbetello, Italy G6 14
Orbost, Austl. G9 50
Orbyhus, Swe. F11 6
Orcas Island, i., Wa., U.S. A3 124
Orcera, Spain G9 12
Orchard City, Co., U.S. C3 83
Orchard Homes, Mt., U.S. D2 103
Orchard Park, N.Y., U.S. C2 109
Orchards, Wa., U.S. D3 124
Orchard Valley, Wy., U.S. E8 127
Orchila, Isla, i., Ven. B9 58
Orchon, stm., Mong. B7 26
Orcutt, Ca., U.S. E3 82
Ord, Ne., U.S. C7 104
Ord, Mount, mtn., Austl. C5 50
Ordenes, Spain B3 12
Ordway, Co., U.S. C7 83
Ordzhonikidze see Vladikavkaz, Russia I6 22
Oreana, Il., U.S. D5 90
Örebro, Swe. G10 6
Orechovo-Zujevo, Russia F21 18
Oregon, Il., U.S. A4 90
Oregon, Mo., U.S. B2 102
Oregon, Oh., U.S. A2 112
Oregon, Wi., U.S. F4 126
Oregon, co., Mo., U.S. E6 102
Oregon, state, U.S. C6 114
Oregon Caves National Monument, Or., U.S. E2 114
Oregon City, Or., U.S. B4 114
Oregon Inlet, b., N.C., U.S. B7 110
Orel, Russia I19 18
Orem, Ut., U.S. C4 121
Orenburg, Russia G9 22
Orense, Spain C4 12
Orestiás, Grc. H10 16
Orfordville, Wi., U.S. F4 126
Organ Mountains, mts., N.M., U.S. E3 108
Organ Pipe Cactus National Monument, Az., U.S. E3 80
Orgūn, Afg. D3 38
Oriental, N.C., U.S. B6 110
Oriental, Cordillera, mts., Col. E6 58
Oriental, Cordillera, mts., Peru F4 54
Orihuela, Spain G11 12
Orillia, Ont., Can. C5 73
Orinoco, stm., S.A. C11 58
Orinoco, Delta del, Ven. C12 58
Orion, Il., U.S. B3 90
Oripää, Fin. F14 6
Orissa, state, India J11 38
Oristano, Italy I3 14
Orivesi, Fin. F15 6
Orizaba, Mex. H11 62
Orizaba, Pico de (Volcán Citlaltépetl), vol., Mex. H11 62
Orkney Islands, is., Scot., U.K. B9 7
Orland, Ca., U.S. C2 82
Orlando, Fl., U.S. D5 86
Orland Park, Il., U.S. k9 90
Orléans, Fr. E8 10
Orleans, Ma., U.S. C7 98
Orleans, Vt., U.S. B4 122
Orleans, co., La., U.S. E6 95
Orleans, co., N.Y., U.S. B2 109
Orleans, co., Vt., U.S. B4 122
Orléans, Île d', i., Que., Can. C6 74
Orman Dam, S.D., U.S. C2 118
Ormond Beach, Fl., U.S. C5 86
Ormož, Slo. C11 14
Ormstown, Que., Can. D3 74
Ornans, Fr. E13 10
Örnsköldsvik, Swe. E12 6
Orocué, Col. E7 58
Orofino, Id., U.S. C2 89
Oromocto, N.B., Can. D3 71
Oromocto Lake, l., N.B., Can. D2 71
Orono, Me., U.S. D4 96
Oronoco, Mn., U.S. F6 100
Oroville, Ca., U.S. C3 82
Oroville, Wa., U.S. A6 124
Oroville, Lake, res., Ca., U.S. C3 82
Orrick, Mo., U.S. B3 102
Orrville, Oh., U.S. B4 112
Orsk, Russia G9 22
Orta Nova, Italy H10 14
Ortegal, Cabo, c., Spain B4 12
Orting, Wa., U.S. B3 124
Ortiz, Ven. C9 58
Ortona, Italy G9 14
Ortonville, Mi., U.S. F7 99
Ortonville, Mn., U.S. E2 100
Orūmīyeh (Reżā'īyeh), Iran J7 22
Orūmīyeh, Daryācheh-ye, l., Iran J7 22
Oruro, Bol. G5 54
Orūzgān (Qala-I-Hazār Qadam), Afg. D2 38
Orvieto, Italy G7 14
Orwell, Oh., U.S. A5 112
Orwigsburg, Pa., U.S. E9 115
Oš, Kyrg. I12 22
Osa, Península de, pen., C.R. J6 64
Osage, Ia., U.S. A5 92
Osage, Wy., U.S. C8 127
Osage, co., Ks., U.S. D8 93
Osage, co., Mo., U.S. C6 102
Osage, co., Ok., U.S. A5 113
Osage, stm., Mo., U.S. C3 102
Osage Beach, Mo., U.S. C5 102
Osage City, Ks., U.S. D8 93
Ōsaka, Japan H8 30
Ōsaka-wan, b., Japan H8 30
Osakis, Mn., U.S. E3 100
Osakis, Lake, l., Mn., U.S. E3 100
Osawatomie, Ks., U.S. D9 93
Osborne, Ks., U.S. C5 93
Osborne, co., Ks., U.S. C5 93
Osburn, Id., U.S. B3 89
Osceola, Ar., U.S. B6 81
Osceola, In., U.S. A5 91
Osceola, Ia., U.S. C4 92
Osceola, Mo., U.S. C4 102
Osceola, Ne., U.S. C8 104
Osceola, Wi., U.S. C1 126
Osceola, co., Fl., U.S. E5 86
Osceola, co., Ia., U.S. A2 92
Osceola, co., Mi., U.S. E5 99
Osceola Mills, Pa., U.S. E5 115
Oschersleben, Ger. C11 8
Oscoda, Mi., U.S. D7 99
Oscoda, co., Mi., U.S. D6 99
Oscura Mountains, mts., N.M., U.S. D3 108
Osen, Nor. D8 6
Osgood, In., U.S. F7 91
Oshawa, Ont., Can. D6 73
Oshima-hantō, pen., Japan q18 30a
Oshkosh, Ne., U.S. C3 104
Oshkosh, Wi., U.S. D5 126
Oshogbo, Nig. G6 42
Osh see Oš, Kyrg. I12 22
Oshwe, Zaire B3 44
Osijek, Cro. D2 16
Osimo, Italy F8 14
Osinniki, Russia G11 24
Osipoviči, Bela. H11 18
Oskaloosa, Ia., U.S. C5 92
Oskaloosa, Ks., U.S. C8 93
Oskarshamn, Swe. H11 6
Oslo, Nor. G8 6
Osmānābād, India G4 37
Osmaniye, Tur. A5 40
Osmond, Ne., U.S. B8 104
Osnabrück, Ger. C8 8
Osorno, Chile E2 56
Osorno, Spain C7 12
Osoyoos, B.C., Can. E8 69
Osoyoos Lake, l., Wa., U.S. A6 124
Ospino, Ven. C8 58
Osprey, Fl., U.S. E4 86
Osprey Reef, rf., Austl. B9 50
Ossa, Mount, mtn., Austl. H9 50
Ossabaw Island, i., Ga., U.S. E5 87
Osseo, Mn., U.S. m12 100
Osseo, Wi., U.S. D2 126
Ossian, In., U.S. C7 91
Ossian, Ia., U.S. A6 92
Ossining, N.Y., U.S. D7 109
Ossipee, stm., U.S. C5 106
Ossipee Lake, l., N.H., U.S. C4 106
Ostaškov, Russia D16 18
Osterholz-Scharmbeck, Ger. B8 8
Osterode, Ger. D10 8
Östersund, Swe. E10 6
Osterville, Ma., U.S. C7 98
Ostrava, Czech. F18 8
Ostrołęka, Pol. B21 8
Ostrov, Russia D11 18
Ostrowiec Świętokrzyski, Pol. E21 8
Ostrów Wielkopolski, Pol. D17 8
Ostuni, Italy I12 14
Ōsumi-kaikyō, strt., Japan L3 30
Ōsumi-shotō, is., Japan u30 31b
Osuna, Spain H6 12
Osvaldo Cruz, Braz. F3 57
Oswegatchie, stm., N.Y., U.S. f9 109
Oswego, Il., U.S. B5 90
Oswego, Ks., U.S. E8 93
Oswego, N.Y., U.S. B4 109
Oswego, co., N.Y., U.S. B4 109
Oswego, stm., N.J., U.S. D4 107
Oswego, stm., N.Y., U.S. B4 109
Oswestry, Eng., U.K. I9 7
Oświęcim, Pol. E19 8
Ōta, Japan F12 30
Otaki, N.Z. D5 52
Otaru, Japan p18 30a
Otavi, Nmb. E3 44
Oteen, N.C., U.S. f10 110
Otero, co., Co., U.S. D7 83
Otero, co., N.M., U.S. E3 108
Othello, Wa., U.S. C6 124
Oti, stm., Afr. G6 42
Otish, Monts, mts., Que., Can. F18 66
Otis Orchards, Wa., U.S. g14 124
Otis Reservoir, res., Ma., U.S. B1 98
Otisville, Mi., U.S. E7 99
Otjiwarongo, Nmb. F3 44
Otočac, Cro. E10 14
Otoe, co., Ne., U.S. D9 104
Otranto, Italy I13 14
Otranto, Strait of, mth., Eur. I2 16
Otsego, Mi., U.S. F5 99
Otsego, co., Mi., U.S. C6 99
Otsego, co., N.Y., U.S. C5 109
Otsego Lake, l., N.Y., U.S. C6 109
Ōtsu, Japan G8 30
Otta, Nor. F7 6
Ottauquechee, stm., Vt., U.S. D4 122
Ottawa, Ont., Can. B9 73
Ottawa, Il., U.S. B5 90
Ottawa, Ks., U.S. D8 93
Ottawa, Oh., U.S. A1 112
Ottawa, co., Ks., U.S. C6 93
Ottawa, co., Mi., U.S. F4 99
Ottawa, co., Oh., U.S. A2 112
Ottawa, co., Ok., U.S. A7 113
Ottawa, stm., Can. G17 66
Ottawa, stm., Oh., U.S. e6 112
Ottawa Hills, Oh., U.S. e6 112
Ottawa Islands, is., N.W. Ter., Can. E16 66
Ottenby, Swe. H11 6
Otterbein, In., U.S. D3 91
Otter Brook, stm., N.H., U.S. E2 106
Otter Brook Lake, res., N.H., U.S. E2 106
Otter Creek, stm., Ut., U.S. E4 121
Otter Creek, stm., Vt., U.S. C2 122
Otter Creek Reservoir, res., Ut., U.S. E4 121
Otter Islands, is., S.C., U.S. m11 117
Otter Tail, co., Mn., U.S. D3 100
Otter Tail, stm., Mn., U.S. D2 100
Otter Tail Lake, l., Mn., U.S. D3 100
Otterville, Ont., Can. E4 73
Ottumwa, Ia., U.S. C5 92
Otwock, Pol. C21 8
Ötztaler Alpen, mts., Eur. C5 14
Ouachita, co., Ar., U.S. D3 81
Ouachita, co., La., U.S. B3 95
Ouachita, Lake, res., Ar., U.S. C2 81
Ouachita Mountains, mts., U.S. E8 76
Ouadda, Cen. Afr. Rep. G10 42
Ouagadougou, Burkina F5 42
Ouahigouya, Burkina F5 42
Oualâta, Maur. E4 42
Ouallene, Alg. D6 42
Ouanda Djallé, Cen. Afr. Rep. G10 42
Ouarane, reg., Maur. D3 42
Ouargla, Alg. B7 42
Ouarzazate, Mor. B4 42
Oubangui, stm., Afr. A3 44
Oudtshoorn, S. Afr. H4 44
Oued Meliz, Tun. M3 14
Oued Zarga, Tun. M4 14
Ouémé, stm., Benin G6 42
Ouesso, Congo A3 44
Ouezzane, Mor. B4 42
Oujda, Mor. B5 42
Oulu, Fin. D15 6
Oulujärvi, l., Fin. D16 6
Oum Chalouba, Chad E10 42
Ounianga Kébir, Chad E10 42
Ouray, Co., U.S. C3 83
Ouray, co., Co., U.S. C3 83
Ouray, Mount, mtn., Co., U.S. C4 83
Ourinhos, Braz. G4 57
Ourique, Port. H3 12
Ouro Prêto, Braz. F7 57
Ōu-sammyaku, mts., Japan D13 30
Outagamie, co., Wi., U.S. D5 126
Outardes Quatre, Réservoir, res., Que., Can. h13 74
Outer Hebrides, is., Scot., U.K. D5 7
Outer Island, i., Wi., U.S. A3 126
Outer Santa Barbara Passage, strt., Ca., U.S. F4 82
Outpost Mountain, mtn., Ak., U.S. B9 79
Outremont, Que., Can. p19 74
Ovalle, Chile C2 56
Ovamboland, hist. reg., Nmb. E3 44
Ovana, Cerro, mtn., Ven. E9 58
Ovar, Port. E3 12
Overbrook, Ks., U.S. D8 93
Overgaard, Az., U.S. C5 80
Overland, Mo., U.S. f13 102
Overland Park, Ks., U.S. m16 93
Overlea, Md., U.S. B4 97
Overton, Nv., U.S. G7 105
Overton, Tx., U.S. C5 120
Overton, co., Tn., U.S. C8 119
Övertorneå, Swe. C14 6
Ovett, Ms., U.S. D4 101
Ovid, Mi., U.S. E6 99
Oviedo, Spain B6 12
Owando, Congo B3 44
Owasco Lake, l., N.Y., U.S. C4 109
Owase, Japan H9 30
Owasso, Ok., U.S. A6 113
Owatonna, Mn., U.S. F5 100
Owego, N.Y., U.S. C4 109
Owen, Wi., U.S. D3 126
Owen, co., In., U.S. F4 91
Owen, co., Ky., U.S. B5 94
Owen, Lake, l., Wi., U.S. B2 126
Owen, Mount, mtn., Co., U.S. C3 83
Owens, stm., Ca., U.S. D4 82
Owensboro, Ky., U.S. C2 94
Owens Cross Roads, Al., U.S. A3 78
Owens Lake, l., Ca., U.S. D5 82
Owen Sound, Ont., Can. C4 73
Owen Sound, b., Ont., Can. C4 73
Owen Stanley Range, mts., Pap. N. Gui. m16 50a
Owensville, In., U.S. H2 91
Owensville, Mo., U.S. C6 102
Owensville, Oh., U.S. C1 112
Owenton, Ky., U.S. B5 94
Owings Mills, Md., U.S. B4 97
Owingsville, Ky., U.S. B6 94
Owl Creek, stm., Wy., U.S. C4 127
Owl Creek Mountains, mts., Wy., U.S. C4 127
Owo, Nig. G7 42
Owosso, Mi., U.S. E6 99
Owsley, co., Ky., U.S. C6 94
Owyhee, Nv., U.S. B5 105
Owyhee, co., Id., U.S. G2 89
Owyhee, stm., U.S. E9 114
Owyhee, Lake, res., Or., U.S. D9 114
Owyhee Dam, Or., U.S. D9 114
Owyhee Mountains, mts., U.S. G2 89
Oxbow Dam, U.S. E2 89
Oxelösund, Swe. G11 6
Oxford, N.S., Can. D6 71
Oxford, N.Z. E4 52
Oxford, Eng., U.K. J11 7
Oxford, Al., U.S. B4 78
Oxford, Ct., U.S. D3 84
Oxford, Ga., U.S. C3 87
Oxford, In., U.S. C3 91
Oxford, Ia., U.S. C6 92
Oxford, Ks., U.S. E6 93
Oxford, Me., U.S. D2 96
Oxford, Md., U.S. C5 97
Oxford, Ma., U.S. B4 98
Oxford, Mi., U.S. F7 99
Oxford, Ms., U.S. A4 101
Oxford, Ne., U.S. D6 104
Oxford, N.Y., U.S. C5 109
Oxford, N.C., U.S. A4 110
Oxford, Oh., U.S. C1 112
Oxford, Pa., U.S. G10 115
Oxford, co., Me., U.S. D2 96
Oxford Lake, l., Man., Can. B4 70
Oxford Peak, mtn., Id., U.S. G6 89
Oxnard, Ca., U.S. E4 82
Oxon Hill, Md., U.S. f9 97
Oxus see Amu Darya, stm., Asia I10 22
Oyama, B.C., Can. D8 69
Oyama, Japan F12 30
Oyem, Gabon A2 44
Oyen, Alta., Can. D5 68
Oyonnax, Fr. F12 10
Oyster Bay, N.Y., U.S. E7 109
Oyster Keys, is., Fl., U.S. G6 86
Ozamiz, Phil. D7 32
Ozark, Al., U.S. D4 78
Ozark, Ar., U.S. B2 81
Ozark, Mo., U.S. D4 102
Ozark, co., Mo., U.S. E5 102
Ozark Plateau, plat., U.S. D8 76
Ozark Reservoir, res., Ar., U.S. B1 81
Ozarks, Lake of the, res., Mo., U.S. C5 102
Ozaukee, co., Wi., U.S. E6 126
Ózd, Hung. G20 8
Ozernovskij, Russia G25 24
Ozette Lake, l., Wa., U.S. A1 124
Ozieri, Italy I3 14
Ožogino, Ozero, l., Russia D23 24
Ozona, Fl., U.S. o10 86
Ozona, Tx., U.S. D2 120
Ōzu, Japan I5 30

P

Paarl, S. Afr. H3 44
Paauilo, Hi., U.S. C6 88
Pabianice, Pol. D19 8
Pābna, Bngl. H13 38
Pacasmayo, Peru E3 54
Pace, Fl., U.S. u14 86
Pachaug Pond, l., Ct., U.S. C8 84
Pachino, Italy M10 14
Pachuca [de Soto], Mex. G10 62
Pacific, Mo., U.S. C7 102
Pacific, Wa., U.S. f11 124
Pacific, co., Wa., U.S. C2 124
Pacifica, Ca., U.S. h8 82
Pacific Beach, Wa., U.S. B1 124
Pacific City, Or., U.S. B3 114
Pacific Creek, stm., Wy., U.S. D3 127
Pacific Grove, Ca., U.S. D3 82
Pacific Ocean F2 2
Pacific Palisades, Hi., U.S. g10 88
Pacific Ranges, mts., B.C., Can. D4 69
Pacific Rim National Park, B.C., Can. E5 69
Pack Monadnock Mountain, mtn., N.H., U.S. E3 106
Packwood, Wa., U.S. C4 124
Pacolet, S.C., U.S. B4 117
Pacolet, stm., S.C., U.S. A4 117
Pacolet Mills, S.C., U.S. B4 117
Pactola Reservoir, res., S.D., U.S. C2 118
Padang, Indon. F3 32
Padangpanjang, Indon. O6 34
Padangsidempuan, Indon. N5 34
Paddock Lake, Wi., U.S. n11 126
Paden City, W.V., U.S. B4 125
Paderborn, Ger. D8 8
Padova, Italy D6 14
Padre Island, i., Tx., U.S. F4 120
Padre Island National Seashore, Tx., U.S. F4 120
Padrón, Spain C3 12
Padstow, Eng., U.K. K8 7
Padua see Padova, Italy D6 14
Paducah, Ky., U.S. e9 94
Paducah, Tx., U.S. B2 120
Paektu-san, mtn., Asia C12 26
Pafúri, Moz. F6 44
Pag, Cro. E10 14
Pagai Selatan, Pulau, i., Indon. F3 32
Pagai Utara, Pulau, i., Indon. F3 32
Page, Az., U.S. A4 80
Page, W.V., U.S. C3 125
Page, co., Ia., U.S. D2 92
Page, co., Va., U.S. B4 123
Pageland, S.C., U.S. B7 117
Pagoda Peak, mtn., Co., U.S. A3 83
Pagoda Point, c., Burma G3 34
Pagosa Springs, Co., U.S. D3 83
Paguate, N.M., U.S. B2 108
Pahala, Hi., U.S. D6 88
Pahang, stm., Malay. M7 34
Pahoa, Hi., U.S. D7 88
Pahokee, Fl., U.S. F6 86
Pahrump, Nv., U.S. G6 105
Pahute Mesa, mtn., Nv., U.S. F5 105
Paia, Hi., U.S. C5 88
Päijänne, l., Fin. F15 6
Pailolo Channel, strt., Hi., U.S. B5 88
Paimpol, Fr. D3 10
Paincourtville, La., U.S. k9 95
Painesville, Oh., U.S. A4 112
Paint, stm., Mi., U.S. B2 99
Paint Creek, stm., Oh., U.S. C2 112
Paint Creek, stm., W.V., U.S. m13 125
Paint Creek, North Fork, stm., Oh., U.S. C2 112
Paint Creek Lake, res., Oh., U.S. C2 112
Painted Desert, des., Az., U.S. B4 80
Painted Post, N.Y., U.S. C3 109
Painted Rock Reservoir, res., Az., U.S. D3 80
Paintsville, Ky., U.S. C7 94
Paisley, Ont., Can. C3 73
Paisley, Scot., U.K. F8 7
Paita, Peru E2 54
Pajala, Swe. C14 6
Paján, Ec. H2 58
Pakanbaru, Indon. E3 32
Pakaraima Mountains, mts., S.A. E12 58
Pakistan (Pākistān), ctry., Asia D2 36
Pakistan, East see Bangladesh, ctry., Asia E6 36
Pakokku, Burma D3 34
Pakowki Lake, l., Alta., Can. E5 68
P'akupur, stm., Russia E9 24
Pakxé, Laos G8 34
Pala, Chad G8 42
Palacios, Tx., U.S. E4 120
Palamós, Spain D15 12
Palana, Russia F25 24
Pālanpur, India H5 38
Palaoa Point, c., Hi., U.S. C4 88
Palapye, Bots. F5 44
Palatine, Il., U.S. A5 90
Palatka, Russia E24 24
Palatka, Fl., U.S. C5 86
Palawan, i., Phil. D6 32
Pālayankottai, India H4 37
Palembang, Indon. F3 32
Palencia, Spain C7 12
Palermo, Italy K8 14
Palestine, Ar., U.S. C5 81
Palestine, Il., U.S. D6 90
Palestine, Tx., U.S. D5 120
Palestine, ctry., Asia C4 40
Palestine, Lake, res., Tx., U.S. C5 120
Paletwa, Burma D2 34
Pālghāt, India G4 37
Pāli, India H5 38
Palikea, mtn., Hi., U.S. g9 88
Palisade, Co., U.S. B2 83
Palisades Park, N.J., U.S. h8 107
Palisades Reservoir, res., U.S. F7 89
Pālitāna, India J4 38
Palk Strait, strt., Asia H5 37
Pallastunturi, mtn., Fin. B14 6
Palma, Moz. D8 44
Palma del Río, Spain H6 12
Palma [de Mallorca], Spain F14 12
Palma di Montechiaro, Italy L8 14
Palmanova, Italy D8 14
Palmarito, Ven. D7 58
Palmas, Cape, c., Lib. H4 42
Palma Soriano, Cuba D9 64
Palm Bay, Fl., U.S. D6 86
Palm Beach, Fl., U.S. F6 86
Palm Beach, co., Fl., U.S. F6 86
Palm Beach Gardens, Fl., U.S. *F6 86
Palmdale, Ca., U.S. E4 82
Palmelo, Braz. D4 57
Palmer, Ak., U.S. C10 79
Palmer, Ma., U.S. B3 98
Palmer, Mi., U.S. B3 99
Palmer, Ms., U.S. D4 101
Palmer, Ne., U.S. C7 104
Palmer, Tn., U.S. D8 119
Palmer, Tx., U.S. n10 120
Palmer Lake, Co., U.S. B6 83
Palmerston, Ont., Can. D4 73
Palmerston, Cape, c., Austl. D9 50
Palmerston North, N.Z. D5 52
Palmerton, Pa., U.S. E10 115
Palmetto, Fl., U.S. E4 86
Palmetto, Ga., U.S. C2 87
Palm Harbor, Fl., U.S. o10 86
Palmi, Italy K10 14
Palmira, Col. F4 58
Palmira, Ec. I3 58
Palms, Isle of, i., S.C., U.S. F8 117
Palm Springs, Ca., U.S. F5 82
Palm Springs, Fl., U.S. *F6 86
Palmyra, In., U.S. H5 91
Palmyra, Mo., U.S. B6 102
Palmyra, N.J., U.S. C2 107
Palmyra, N.Y., U.S. B3 109
Palmyra, Pa., U.S. F8 115
Palmyra, Wi., U.S. F5 126
Palni, India G4 37
Palo Alto, Ca., U.S. D2 82
Palo Alto, co., Ia., U.S. A3 92
Paloich, Sudan F12 42
Palomar Mountain, mtn., Ca., U.S. F5 82
Palomas Mountains, mts., Az., U.S. D2 80
Palo Pinto, co., Tx., U.S. C3 120
Palos Park, Il., U.S. k9 90
Palos Verdes Estates, Ca., U.S. n12 82
Palourde, Lake, l., La., U.S. k9 95
Palouse, Wa., U.S. C8 124
Palouse, stm., Wa., U.S. C7 124
Palu, Indon. F6 32
Palwal, India F7 38
Pamekasan, Indon. m16 33a
Pamiers, Fr. I8 10
Pamir, mts., Asia B3 36
Pamlico, co., N.C., U.S. B6 110
Pamlico, stm., N.C., U.S. B6 110
Pamlico Sound, strt., N.C., U.S. B6 110
Pampa, Tx., U.S. B2 120
Pampas, reg., Arg. C4 56
Pamplico, S.C., U.S. D8 117
Pamplona, Col. D6 58
Pamplona, Spain C10 12
Pamunkey, stm., Va., U.S. C5 123
Pana, Il., U.S. D4 90
Panaca, Nv., U.S. F7 105
Panache, Lake, l., Ont., Can. A3 73
Panaji (Panjim), India E2 37
Panamá, Pan. J8 64
Panama, Ok., U.S. B7 113
Panama, ctry., N.A. J7 64
Panama, Gulf of, b., Pan. J8 64
Panama, Isthmus of, Pan. J8 64
Panama Canal, Pan. J8 64
Panama City, Fl., U.S. u16 86
Panama City Beach, Fl., U.S. u16 86
Panamint Range, mts., Ca., U.S. D5 82
Panay, i., Phil. C7 32
Pancake Range, mts., Nv., U.S. E6 105
Pandharpur, India D3 37
Pandora, Oh., U.S. B2 112
P'andž (Panj), stm., Asia A4 38
Panevėžys, Lith. F7 18
Pangala, Congo B2 44
Pangburn, Ar., U.S. B4 81
Pangkalanbuun, Indon. F5 32
Pangkalpinang, Indon. F4 32
Pangnirtung, N.W. Ter., Can. C19 66
Panguitch, Ut., U.S. F3 121
Pangutaran Group, is., Phil. D7 32
Panhandle, Tx., U.S. B2 120
Paniau, mtn., Hi., U.S. B1 88
Pānīpat, India F7 38
Panj (P'andž), stm., Asia B4 38

Name	Map Ref	Page
Panjāb, Afg.	C2	38
Panjgūr, Pak.	D1	36
Panola, co., Ms., U.S.	A3	101
Panola, co., Tx., U.S.	C5	120
Panora, Ia., U.S.	C3	92
Pantelleria, Italy	M6	14
Panvel, India	C2	37
Panxian, China	B8	34
Panyam, Nig.	G7	42
Panyu, China	M2	28
Paola, Italy	J11	14
Paola, Ks., U.S.	D9	93
Paoli, In., U.S.	G5	91
Paoli, Pa., U.S.	o20	115
Paonia, Co., U.S.	C3	83
Pápa, Hung.	H17	8
Papago Indian Reservation, Az., U.S.	E3	80
Papaikou, Hi., U.S.	D6	88
Papantla [de Olarte], Mex.	G11	62
Papawai Point, c., Hi., U.S.	C5	88
Papenburg, Ger.	B7	8
Papillion, Ne., U.S.	C9	104
Papineauville, Que., Can.	D2	74
Papua, Gulf of, b., Pap. N. Gui.	m15	50a
Papua New Guinea, ctry., Oc.	m15	50a
Pará, stm., Braz.	D9	54
Paracatu, Braz.	D5	57
Paracatu, stm., Braz.	D6	57
Paracel Islands, is., Asia	B5	32
Parachute, Co., U.S.	B2	83
Paradis, La., U.S.	k11	95
Paradise, Ca., U.S.	C3	82
Paradise, Nv., U.S.	G6	105
Paradise, stm., Newf., Can.	B3	72
Paradise Hills, N.M., U.S.	B3	108
Paradise Valley, Az., U.S.	k9	80
Paradise Valley, Nv., U.S.	B4	105
Paragould, Ar., U.S.	A5	81
Paraguaçu Paulista, Braz.	G3	57
Paraguaipoa, Ven.	B7	58
Paraguaná, Península de, pen., Ven.	B7	58
Paraguarí, Para.	B5	56
Paraguay, ctry., S.A.	A5	56
Paraguay, stm., S.A.	B5	56
Paraíba do Sul, stm., Braz.	F7	57
Parakou, Benin	G6	42
Paramagudi, India	H5	37
Paramaribo, Sur.	B7	54
Paramirim, Braz.	B7	57
Paramount, Md., U.S.	A2	97
Paramus, N.J., U.S.	h8	107
Paramušir, Ostrov, i., Russia	G25	24
Paraná, Arg.	C4	56
Paranã, Braz.	B5	57
Paranã, stm., Braz.	B5	57
Paraná, stm., S.A.	C5	56
Paranaguá, Braz.	B7	56
Paranaíba, Braz.	E3	57
Paranaíba, stm., Braz.	E3	57
Paranapanema, stm., Braz.	G3	57
Paranavaí, Braz.	G2	57
Parangaba, Braz.	D11	54
Paratinga, Braz.	B7	57
Paraúna, Braz.	D3	57
Paray-le-Monial, Fr.	F11	10
Pārbati, stm., India	H7	38
Parbhani, India	C4	37
Parchim, Ger.	B11	8
Parchment, Mi., U.S.	F5	99
Pardeeville, Wi., U.S.	E4	126
Pardo, stm., Braz.	F5	57
Pardubice, Czech.	E15	8
Parece Vela see Okino-Tori-shima, i., Japan	G14	26
Parecis, Serra dos, mts., Braz.	F7	54
Paredes de Nava, Spain	C7	12
Paren', Russia	E26	24
Parepare, Indon.	F6	32
Pargas (Parainen), Fin.	F14	6
Paria, stm., U.S.	A4	80
Paria, Gulf of, b.	I16	64
Pariaguán, Ven.	C10	58
Pariaman, Indon.	O6	34
Parícutin, vol., Mex.	H8	62
Parikkala, Fin.	F17	6
Parima, Sierra, mts., S.A.	F10	58
Pariñas, Punta, c., Peru	D2	54
Parintins, Braz.	D7	54
Paris, Ont., Can.	D4	73
Paris, Fr.	D9	10
Paris, Ar., U.S.	B2	81
Paris, Il., U.S.	D6	90
Paris, Ky., U.S.	B5	94
Paris, Mo., U.S.	B5	102
Paris, Tn., U.S.	A3	119
Paris, Tx., U.S.	C5	120
Paris Peak, mtn., Id., U.S.	G7	89
Parit Buntar, Malay.	L6	34
Park, co., Co., U.S.	B5	83
Park, co., Mt., U.S.	E6	103
Park, co., Wy., U.S.	B3	127
Park, stm., N.D., U.S.	A8	111
Parkano, Fin.	E14	6
Park City, Ks., U.S.	g12	93
Park City, Ut., U.S.	C4	121
Parkdale, P.E.I., Can.	C6	71
Parke, co., In., U.S.	E3	91
Parker, Az., U.S.	C1	80
Parker, Co., U.S.	B6	83
Parker, Fl., U.S.	u16	86
Parker, S.D., U.S.	D8	118
Parker, co., Tx., U.S.	C4	120
Parker, Cape, c., N.W. Ter., Can.	A17	66
Parker City, In., U.S.	D7	91
Parker Dam, U.S.	C1	80
Parkersburg, Ia., U.S.	B5	92
Parkersburg, W.V., U.S.	B3	125
Parkers Prairie, Mn., U.S.	D3	100
Parkesburg, Pa., U.S.	G10	115
Park Falls, Wi., U.S.	C3	126
Park Forest, Il., U.S.	B6	90
Park Hall, Md., U.S.	D5	97
Parkhill, Ont., Can.	D3	73
Park Hills, Ky., U.S.	h13	94
Parkin, Ar., U.S.	B5	81
Parkland, Wa., U.S.	f11	124
Park Layne, Oh., U.S.	C1	112
Park Range, mts., Co., U.S.	A4	83
Park Rapids, Mn., U.S.	D3	100
Park Ridge, Il., U.S.	B6	90
Park Ridge, N.J., U.S.	g8	107
Park River, N.D., U.S.	A8	111
Parkrose, Or., U.S.	B4	114
Parksley, Va., U.S.	C7	123
Parkston, S.D., U.S.	D8	118
Parksville, B.C., Can.	E5	69
Parkville, Md., U.S.	B4	97
Parkville, Mo., U.S.	B3	102
Parkwater, Wa., U.S.	g14	124
Parkwood, N.C., U.S.	B4	110
Parlākimidi, India	C8	37
Parle, Lac qui, l., Mn., U.S.	E3	100
Parlier, Ca., U.S.	D4	82
Parma, Italy	E5	14
Parma, Id., U.S.	F2	89
Parma, Mi., U.S.	F6	99
Parma, Mo., U.S.	E8	102
Parma, Oh., U.S.	A4	112
Parmachenee Lake, l., Me., U.S.	C2	96
Parma Heights, Oh., U.S.	h9	112
Parmer, co., Tx., U.S.	B1	120
Parnaíba, Braz.	D10	54
Parnaíba, stm., Braz.	D10	54
Pärnu, Est.	C7	18
Paro, Bhu.	G13	38
Parowan, Ut., U.S.	F3	121
Par Pond, res., S.C., U.S.	D5	117
Parral, Chile	D2	56
Parramore Island, i., Va., U.S.	C7	123
Parras de la Fuente, Mex.	E8	62
Parrish, Al., U.S.	B2	78
Parrsboro, N.S., Can.	D5	71
Parry, Cape, c., N.W. Ter., Can.	B8	66
Parry, Mount, mtn., B.C., Can.	C3	69
Parry Bay, b., N.W. Ter., Can.	C16	66
Parry Sound, Ont., Can.	B4	73
Parshall, N.D., U.S.	B3	111
Parsons, Ks., U.S.	E8	93
Parsons, Tn., U.S.	B3	119
Parsons, W.V., U.S.	B5	125
Parsonsburg, Md., U.S.	D7	97
Parthenay, Fr.	F6	10
Partinico, Italy	K8	14
Partridge Point, c., Newf., Can.	C3	72
Paru, stm., Braz.	D8	54
Pārvatīpuram, India	C7	37
Parys, S. Afr.	G5	44
Pasadena, Newf., Can.	D3	72
Pasadena, Ca., U.S.	E4	82
Pasadena, Md., U.S.	B4	97
Pasadena, Tx., U.S.	r14	120
Pascagoula, Ms., U.S.	E5	101
Pascagoula, stm., Ms., U.S.	E5	101
Pascagoula Bay, b., Ms., U.S.	f8	101
Pasco, Wa., U.S.	C6	124
Pasco, co., Fl., U.S.	D4	86
Pascoag, R.I., U.S.	B2	116
Pascoag Reservoir, res., R.I., U.S.	B2	116
Pascua, Isla de (Easter Island), i., Chile	H5	2
Pasewalk, Ger.	B13	8
Pasig, Phil.	q19	33b
P'asina, stm., Russia	C11	24
P'asino, Ozero, l., Russia	D11	24
P'asinskij Zaliv, b., Russia	C10	24
Pasirpengarajan, Indon.	N6	34
Pasir Puteh, Malay.	L7	34
Pasni, Pak.	D1	36
Paso de Indios, Arg.	E3	56
Paso de los Libres, Arg.	B5	56
Paso Robles, Ca., U.S.	E3	82
Pasque Island, i., Ma., U.S.	D6	98
Pasquotank, co., N.C., U.S.	A6	110
Passagem, Braz.	B7	57
Passaic, N.J., U.S.	B4	107
Passaic, co., N.J., U.S.	A4	107
Passaic, stm., N.J., U.S.	h8	107
Passamaquoddy Bay, b., Me., U.S.	C6	96
Passau, Ger.	G13	8
Pass Christian, Ms., U.S.	E4	101
Passo Fundo, Braz.	B6	56
Passos, Braz.	F5	57
Passumpsic, stm., Vt., U.S.	C4	122
Pasto, Col.	G4	58
Pastora Peak, mtn., Az., U.S.	A6	80
Pastrana, Spain	E9	12
Pasuruan, Indon.	m16	33a
Patagonia, Az., U.S.	F5	80
Patagonia, reg., Arg.	E3	56
Pātan, India	I5	38
Patapsco, stm., Md., U.S.	B4	97
Pataskala, Oh., U.S.	C3	112
Patchet Brook Reservoir, res., R.I., U.S.	E6	116
Patchogue, N.Y., U.S.	n15	109
Pate Island, i., Kenya	B8	44
Paternò, Italy	L9	14
Paterson, N.J., U.S.	B4	107
Pathānkot, India	D6	38
Pathein, Burma	F3	34
Pathfinder Reservoir, res., Wy., U.S.	D6	127
Pati, Indon.	m15	33a
Patiāla, India	E7	38
Patience Island, i., R.I., U.S.	D5	116
P'atigorsk, Russia	I6	22
Pātkai Range, mts., Asia	G16	38
Patman, Lake, res., Tx., U.S.	C5	120
Patna, India	H11	38
Patoka, In., U.S.	H2	91
Patoka, stm., In., U.S.	H2	91
Patoka Lake, res., In., U.S.	H4	91
Patos, Braz.	E11	54
Patos, Lagoa dos, b., Braz.	C6	56
Patos de Minas, Braz.	E5	57
Patquía, Arg.	C3	56
Pátrai, Grc.	K5	16
Patricio Lynch, Isla, i., Chile	F1	56
Patrick, co., Va., U.S.	D2	123
Patrick Air Force Base, mil., Fl., U.S.	D6	86
Patrocínio, Braz.	E5	57
Pattani, Thai.	K6	34
Patten, Me., U.S.	C4	96
Patterson, Ga., U.S.	E4	87
Patterson, La., U.S.	E4	95
Patterson Creek, stm., W.V., U.S.	B5	125
Pattoki, Pak.	E5	38
Patton, Pa., U.S.	E4	115
Patuākhāli, Bngl.	I14	38
Patuca, stm., Hond.	G5	64
Patuxent, stm., Md., U.S.	D4	97
Patuxent Naval Air Test Center, mil., Md., U.S.	D5	97
Pátzcuaro, Mex.	H9	62
Pau, Fr.	I6	10
Paul, Id., U.S.	G5	89
Paulding, Oh., U.S.	A1	112
Paulding, co., Ga., U.S.	C2	87
Paulding, co., Oh., U.S.	A1	112
Paulina, La., U.S.	h10	95
Paulina Mountains, mts., Or., U.S.	D5	114
Paulina Peak, mtn., Or., U.S.	E5	114
Paulins Kill, stm., N.J., U.S.	A3	107
Paulistana, Braz.	E10	54
Paulistas, Braz.	E7	57
Paullina, Ia., U.S.	B2	92
Paulo Afonso, Braz.	E11	54
Paulsboro, N.J., U.S.	D2	107
Paul Stream, stm., Vt., U.S.	B5	122
Pauls Valley, Ok., U.S.	C4	113
Paungde, Burma	E3	34
Pavia, Italy	D4	14
Pavilion Key, i., Fl., U.S.	G5	86
Pavlodar, Kaz.	G9	24
Pavlof Volcano, vol., Ak., U.S.	D7	79
Pavlovo, Russia	F26	18
Pavlovsk, Russia	G7	24
Pavlovskij Posad, Russia	F21	18
Pavo, Ga., U.S.	F3	87
Pavón, Col.	F6	58
Pavullo nel Frignano, Italy	E5	14
Pawcatuck, Ct., U.S.	D8	84
Pawcatuck, stm., R.I., U.S.	G1	116
Paw Creek, N.C., U.S.	B2	110
Pawhuska, Ok., U.S.	A5	113
Pawling, N.Y., U.S.	D7	109
Pawnee, Il., U.S.	D4	90
Pawnee, Ok., U.S.	A5	113
Pawnee, co., Ks., U.S.	D4	93
Pawnee, co., Ne., U.S.	D9	104
Pawnee, co., Ok., U.S.	A5	113
Pawnee, stm., Ks., U.S.	D3	93
Pawnee City, Ne., U.S.	D9	104
Pawpaw, Il., U.S.	B5	90
Paw Paw, Mi., U.S.	F5	99
Paw Paw, stm., Mi., U.S.	F4	99
Pawpaw Creek, stm., W.V., U.S.	h10	125
Pawtuckaway Pond, l., N.H., U.S.	D4	106
Pawtucket, R.I., U.S.	C4	116
Pawtuxet, stm., R.I., U.S.	C4	116
Paxton, Il., U.S.	C5	90
Paxton, Ma., U.S.	B4	98
Payakumbuh, Indon.	O6	34
Payette, Id., U.S.	E2	89
Payette, co., Id., U.S.	E2	89
Payette, North Fork, stm., Id., U.S.	E2	89
Payette, South Fork, stm., Id., U.S.	E3	89
Payette Lake, res., Id., U.S.	E3	89
Payne, Oh., U.S.	A1	112
Payne, co., Ok., U.S.	A4	113
Paynesville, Mn., U.S.	E4	100
Paysandú, Ur.	C5	56
Payson, Az., U.S.	C4	80
Payson, Il., U.S.	D2	90
Payson, Ut., U.S.	C4	121
Pazardžik, Bul.	G8	16
Pazarköy, Tur.	J11	16
Paz de Río, Col.	E6	58
Pazin, Cro.	D8	14
Pea, stm., Al., U.S.	D3	78
Peabody, Ks., U.S.	D6	93
Peabody, Ma., U.S.	A6	98
Peabody, stm., N.H., U.S.	B4	106
Peace, stm., Can.	E9	66
Peace, stm., Fl., U.S.	E5	86
Peace Dale, R.I., U.S.	F3	116
Peace River, Alta., Can.	A2	68
Peach, co., Ga., U.S.	D3	87
Peacham Pond, res., Vt., U.S.	C4	122
Peach Point, c., Ma., U.S.	f12	98
Peach Springs, Az., U.S.	B2	80
Peak District National Park, Eng., U.K.	H11	7
Peaks Island, i., Me., U.S.	g7	96
Peale, Mount, mtn., Ut., U.S.	E6	121
Pea Patch Island, i., De., U.S.	B3	85
Pea Ridge, Ar., U.S.	A1	81
Pea Ridge National Military Park, Ar., U.S.	A1	81
Pearisburg, Va., U.S.	C2	123
Pearl, Ms., U.S.	C3	101
Pearl, stm., U.S.	D3	101
Pearland, Tx., U.S.	r14	120
Pearl and Hermes Reef, rf., Hi., U.S.	k12	88
Pearl City, Hi., U.S.	B4	88
Pearl Harbor, b., Hi., U.S.	B3	88
Pearl Harbor Naval Station, mil., Hi., U.S.	g10	88
Pearlington, Ms., U.S.	E4	101
Pearl River, La., U.S.	D6	95
Pearl River, N.Y., U.S.	g12	109
Pearl River, co., Ms., U.S.	E4	101
Pearsall, Tx., U.S.	E3	120
Pearsoll Peak, mtn., Or., U.S.	E3	114
Pearson, Ga., U.S.	E4	87
Peary Land, reg., Grnld.	A16	128
Pease, stm., Tx., U.S.	B3	120
Pease Air Force Base, mil., N.H., U.S.	D5	106
Pebane, Moz.	E7	44
Peć, Yugo.	G4	16
Pecatonica, Il., U.S.	A4	90
Pecatonica, stm., U.S.	A4	90
Pecatonica, East Branch, stm., Wi., U.S.	F4	126
Peckerwood Lake, res., Ar., U.S.	C4	81
Pečora, stm., Russia	D5	24
Pecos, N.M., U.S.	B4	108
Pecos, Tx., U.S.	D1	120
Pecos, co., Tx., U.S.	D1	120
Pecos, stm., U.S.	E6	76
Pecos National Monument, N.M., U.S.	B4	108
Pécs, Hung.	I18	8
Peculiar, Mo., U.S.	C3	102
Peddocks Island, i., Ma., U.S.	g12	98
Pedernales, Ven.	C11	58
Pedregal, Ven.	B7	58
Pedro, Point, c., Sri L.	H6	37
Pedro de Valdivia, Chile	A3	56
Pedro Juan Caballero, Para.	G1	57
Peebles, Oh., U.S.	D2	112
Peekskill, N.Y., U.S.	D7	109
Peel, I. of Man	G8	7
Peel, stm., Can.	C5	66
Peel Point, c., N.W. Ter., Can.	B10	66
Peel Sound, strt., N.W. Ter., Can.	B13	66
Pegram, Tn., U.S.	A4	119
Pehuajó, Arg.	D4	56
Peikang, Tai.	L9	28
Peine, Ger.	C10	8
Pekalongan, Indon.	m14	32
Pekin, Il., U.S.	C4	90
Pekin, In., U.S.	G5	91
Peking see Beijing, China	D10	26
Pelagie, Isole, is., Italy	N7	14
Pelahatchie, Ms., U.S.	C4	101
Pelée, Montagne, mtn., Mart.	G17	64
Pelee Island, i., Ont., Can.	F2	73
Peleng, Pulau, i., Indon.	F7	32
Pelham, Ont., Can.	D5	73
Pelham, Al., U.S.	B3	78
Pelham, Ga., U.S.	E2	87
Pelham, N.H., U.S.	E4	106
Pelham Manor, N.Y., U.S.	h13	109
Pelican Bay, b., Man., Can.	C1	70
Pelican Lake, l., Man., Can.	C1	70
Pelican Lake, l., Mn., U.S.	D4	100
Pelican Lake, l., Mn., U.S.	D3	100
Pelican Lake, l., Mn., U.S.	B6	100
Pelican Lake, l., Mn., U.S.	E5	100
Pelican Lake, l., Wi., U.S.	C4	126
Pelican Mountain, mtn., Alta., Can.	B4	68
Pelican Rapids, Mn., U.S.	D2	100
Pella, Ia., U.S.	C5	92
Pell City, Al., U.S.	B3	78
Pell Lake, Wi., U.S.	n11	126
Pello, Fin.	C14	6
Pelly Mountains, mts., Yukon, Can.	D6	66
Pelopónnisos, reg., Grc.	L5	16
Pelotas, Braz.	C6	56
Pelton, Lake, l., La., U.S.	E5	95
Pemadumcook Lake, l., Me., U.S.	C3	96
Pemalang, Indon.	m14	33a
Pematangsiantar, Indon.	E2	32
Pemba, Moz.	D8	44
Pemba Island, i., Tan.	C7	44
Pemberton, Austl.	F3	50
Pemberville, Oh., U.S.	A2	112
Pembina, N.D., U.S.	A8	111
Pembina, co., N.D., U.S.	A8	111
Pembina, stm., Alta., Can.	C3	68
Pembroke, Ont., Can.	B7	73
Pembroke, Wales, U.K.	J8	7
Pembroke, Ga., U.S.	D5	87
Pembroke, Ky., U.S.	D2	94
Pembroke, Ma., U.S.	B6	98
Pembroke, N.C., U.S.	C3	110
Pembroke, Va., U.S.	C2	123
Pembroke Pines, Fl., U.S.	r13	86
Pemigewasset, stm., N.H., U.S.	C3	106
Pemiscot, co., Mo., U.S.	E8	102
Peñafiel, Spain	D7	12
Penápolis, Braz.	F3	57
Peñaranda de Bracamonte, Spain	E6	12
Pen Argyl, Pa., U.S.	E11	115
Peñarroya-Pueblonuevo, Spain	G6	12
Penas, Golfo de, b., Chile	F1	56
Penasco, N.M., U.S.	A4	108
Peñasco, Rio, stm., N.M., U.S.	E4	108
Penbrook, Pa., U.S.	F8	115
Pender, Ne., U.S.	B9	104
Pender, co., N.C., U.S.	C4	110
Pendleton, In., U.S.	E6	91
Pendleton, Or., U.S.	B8	114
Pendleton, S.C., U.S.	B2	117
Pendleton, co., Ky., U.S.	B5	94
Pendleton, co., W.V., U.S.	C5	125
Pendley Hills, Ga., U.S.	*h8	87
Pend Oreille, co., Wa., U.S.	A8	124
Pend Oreille, Lake, l., Id., U.S.	A2	89
Pend Oreille, Mount, mtn., Id., U.S.	A2	89
Penetanguishene, Ont., Can.	C5	73
P'enghu Liehtao, is., Tai.	L8	28
Penglai, China	D11	26
Penhold, Alta., Can.	C4	68
Peniche, Port.	F2	12
Penjamo, Mex.	G9	62
Pennant Point, c., N.S., Can.	E6	71
Pennask Mountain, mtn., B.C., Can.	E7	69
Penne, Italy	G8	14
Pennell, Mount, mtn., Ut., U.S.	F5	121
Penner, stm., India	E5	37
Penn Hills, Pa., U.S.	k14	115
Pennines, mts., Eng., U.K.	G10	7
Pennines, Alpes, mts., Eur.	F14	10
Pennington, co., Mn., U.S.	B2	100
Pennington, co., S.D., U.S.	D2	118
Pennington Gap, Va., U.S.	f8	123
Pennsauken, N.J., U.S.	D2	107
Pennsboro, W.V., U.S.	B4	125
Pennsburg, Pa., U.S.	F11	115
Penns Grove, N.J., U.S.	D2	107
Pennsville, N.J., U.S.	D1	107
Pennsylvania, state, U.S.	E7	115
Pennville, In., U.S.	D7	91
Penn Yan, N.Y., U.S.	C3	109
Penobscot, co., Me., U.S.	C4	96
Penobscot, stm., Me., U.S.	C4	96
Penobscot Bay, b., Me., U.S.	D3	96
Penobscot Lake, l., Me., U.S.	C2	96
Penonomé, Pan.	J7	64
Penrith, Eng., U.K.	G10	7
Pensacola, Fl., U.S.	u14	86
Pensacola Bay, b., Fl., U.S.	u14	86
Pensacola Dam, Ok., U.S.	A6	113
Pensacola Naval Air Station, mil., Fl., U.S.	u14	86
Pentagon Mountain, mtn., Mt., U.S.	C3	103
Penticton, B.C., Can.	E8	69
Pentland Firth, strt., Scot., U.K.	C9	7
Pentwater, Mi., U.S.	E4	99
Penyu, Kepulauan, is., Indon.	G8	32
Penza, Russia	G7	22
Penzance, Eng., U.K.	K7	7
Penžina, stm., Russia	E27	24
Penžinskaja Guba, b., Russia	E26	24
Penžinskij Chrebet, mts., Russia	E27	24
Peonan Point, c., Man., Can.	D2	70
Peoria, Az., U.S.	D3	80
Peoria, Il., U.S.	C4	90
Peoria, co., Il., U.S.	C4	90
Peoria Heights, Il., U.S.	C4	90
Peotone, Il., U.S.	B6	90
Pepacton Reservoir, res., N.Y., U.S.	C6	109
Pepeekeo, Hi., U.S.	D6	88
Pepin, Wi., U.S.	D1	126
Pepin, co., Wi., U.S.	D2	126
Pepin, Lake, U.S.	D1	126
Pepperell, Ma., U.S.	A4	98
Pequannock, N.J., U.S.	B4	107
Pequest, stm., N.J., U.S.	B2	107
Pequop Mountains, mts., Nv., U.S.	C7	105
Pequot Lakes, Mn., U.S.	D4	100
Perabumulih, Indon.	F3	32
Percy, Il., U.S.	E4	90
Perdido, Al., U.S.	D2	78
Perdido, stm., U.S.	E2	78
Perdido Bay, b., Al., U.S.	E2	78
Pereira, Col.	E5	58
Pere Marquette, stm., Mi., U.S.	E4	99
Pereslavl'-Zalesskij, Russia	E21	18
Pergamino, Arg.	C4	56
Pergine Valsugana, Italy	C6	14
Perham, Mn., U.S.	D3	100
Péribonca, stm., Que., Can.	G18	66
Peridot, Az., U.S.	D5	80
Périgueux, Fr.	G7	10
Perijá, Sierra de, mts., S.A.	B6	58
Perkasie, Pa., U.S.	F11	115
Perkins, Ok., U.S.	B4	113
Perkins, co., Ne., U.S.	D4	104
Perkins, co., S.D., U.S.	B3	118
Perkinston, Ms., U.S.	E4	101
Perlas, Archipiélago de las, is., Pan.	J8	64
Perlas, Laguna de, b., Nic.	H6	64
Perleberg, Ger.	B11	8
Perm', Russia	F9	22
Pernik, Bul.	G7	16
Péronne, Fr.	C9	10
Perpignan, Fr.	J9	10
Perquimans, co., N.C., U.S.	A6	110
Perrine, Fl., U.S.	G6	86
Perris, Ca., U.S.	F5	82
Perro, Laguna del, l., N.M., U.S.	C4	108
Perros-Guirec, Fr.	D3	10
Perrot, Île, i., Que., Can.	q19	74
Perry, Fl., U.S.	B3	86
Perry, Ga., U.S.	D3	87
Perry, Ia., U.S.	C3	92
Perry, Ks., U.S.	C8	93
Perry, Mi., U.S.	F6	99
Perry, Mo., U.S.	B6	102
Perry, N.Y., U.S.	C2	109
Perry, Oh., U.S.	A4	112
Perry, Ok., U.S.	A4	113
Perry, Ut., U.S.	B3	121
Perry, co., Al., U.S.	C2	78
Perry, co., Ar., U.S.	C3	81
Perry, co., Il., U.S.	E4	90
Perry, co., In., U.S.	H4	91
Perry, co., Ky., U.S.	C6	94
Perry, co., Ms., U.S.	D4	101
Perry, co., Mo., U.S.	D8	102
Perry, co., Oh., U.S.	C3	112
Perry, co., Pa., U.S.	F7	115
Perry, co., Tn., U.S.	B4	119
Perry Hall, Md., U.S.	B5	97
Perry Lake, res., Ks., U.S.	C8	93
Perryman, Md., U.S.	B5	97
Perrysburg, Oh., U.S.	A2	112
Perry Stream, stm., N.H., U.S.	f7	106
Perry's Victory and International Peace Memorial, hist., Oh., U.S.	A2	112
Perryton, Tx., U.S.	A2	120
Perryville, Ar., U.S.	B3	81
Perryville, Ky., U.S.	C5	94
Perryville, Md., U.S.	A5	97
Perryville, Mo., U.S.	D8	102
Pershing, co., Nv., U.S.	C3	105
Persia see Iran, ctry., Asia	B5	46
Persian Gulf, b., Asia	C5	46
Person, co., N.C., U.S.	A3	110
Perth, Austl.	F3	50
Perth, Ont., Can.	C8	73
Perth, Scot., U.K.	E9	7
Perth Amboy, N.J., U.S.	B4	107
Perth-Andover, N.B., Can.	D10	71
Pertuis, Fr.	I12	10
Peru, Il., U.S.	B4	90
Peru, In., U.S.	C5	91

Name — Map Ref — Page
eru, Ne., U.S. D10 104
eru, N.Y., U.S. f11 109
eru (Perú), ctry., S.A. E3 54
erugia, Italy F7 14
erušić, Cro. E10 14
esaro, Italy F7 14
escadores see P'enghu Liehtao, is., Tai. L8 28
escara, Italy G9 14
escia, Italy F5 14
eshastin, Wa., U.S. B5 124
eshāwar, Pak. C4 38
eshtigo, Wi., U.S. C6 126
eshtigo, stm., Wi., U.S. C5 126
esqueira, Braz. E11 54
essac, Fr. H6 10
etah Tiqwa, Isr. C4 40
etal, Ms., U.S. D4 101
etaluma, Ca., U.S. C2 82
etatlán, Mex. I9 62
etawawa, Ont., Can. B7 73
etawawa, stm., Ont., Can. A6 73
etenwell Lake, res., Wi., U.S. D4 126
eterborough, Austl. F7 50
eterborough, Ont., Can. C6 73
eterborough, Eng., U.K. I12 7
eterborough, N.H., U.S. E3 106
eterhead, Scot., U.K. D11 7
eter Pond Lake, l., Sask., Can. m7 75
etersburg, Ak., U.S. D13 79
etersburg, Il., U.S. C4 90
etersburg, In., U.S. H3 91
etersburg, Mi., U.S. G7 99
etersburg, Oh., U.S. B5 112
etersburg, Tx., U.S. C2 120
etersburg, Va., U.S. C5 123
etersburg, W.V., U.S. B5 125
eters Creek, stm., W.V., U.S. m14 125
eterson, Al., U.S. B2 78
eterson Field, mil., Co., U.S. C6 83
etersville, Al., U.S. A2 78
etit Bois Island, i., Ms., U.S. E5 101
etitcodiac, N.B., Can. D4 71
etitcodiac, stm., N.B., Can. C5 71
etite Amite, stm., La., U.S. h10 95
etit Jean, stm., Ar., U.S. B2 81
etit Lac Des Allemands, l., La., U.S. k11 95
etit Lake, l., La., U.S. k12 95
etitot, stm., Can. E8 66
etit-Rocher, N.B., Can. B4 71
etitsikapau Lake, l., Newf., Can. g8 72
etlād, India I5 38
etone, N.Z. D5 52
etoskey, Mi., U.S. C6 99
etrified Forest National Park, Az., U.S. B6 80
etrila, Rom. D7 16
etrinja, Cro. D11 14
etroleum, co., Mt., U.S. C8 103
etrolia, Ont., Can. E2 73
etrolina, Braz. E10 54
etropavlovsk-Kamčatskij, Russia G25 24
etrópolis, Braz. G7 57
etros, Tn., U.S. C9 119
etroşani, Rom. D7 16
etrovsk-Zabajkal'skij, Russia G15 24
etrozavodsk, Russia E4 22
ettaquamscutt Lake Shores, R.I., U.S. F4 116
ettingell Peak, mtn., Co., U.S. B5 83
ettis, co., Mo., U.S. C4 102
evek, Russia D28 24
evely, Mo., U.S. g13 102
ewaukee, Wi., U.S. E5 126
ewaukee Lake, l., Wi., U.S. m11 126
ewee Valley, Ky., U.S. B4 94
ezenas, Fr. I10 10
forzheim, Ger. G8 8
ungstadt, Ger. F8 8
a-an, Burma F4 34
agwāra, India E6 38
alsbourg, Fr. D14 10
altan, India D3 37
angan, Ko, i., Thai. J6 34
angnga, Thai. J5 34
anom Dongrak, Thiu Khao, mts., Asia G7 34
an Rang, Viet. I10 34
an Si Pan, mtn., Viet. C7 34
an Thiet, Viet. I10 34
arr, Tx., U.S. F3 120
atthalung, Thai. K6 34
ayao, Thai. E5 34
elps, Ky., U.S. C7 94
elps, N.Y., U.S. C3 109
elps, Wi., U.S. B4 126
elps, co., Mo., U.S. D6 102
elps, co., Ne., U.S. D6 104
elps Lake, l., N.C., U.S. B6 110
enix City, Al., U.S. C4 70
etchaburi, Thai. H5 34
iladelphia, Ms., U.S. C4 101
iladelphia, Pa., U.S. G11 115
iladelphia, co., Pa., U.S. G12 115
iladelphia Naval Shipyard, mil., Pa., U.S. P21 115
il Campbell, Al., U.S. A2 78
ilip, S.D., U.S. C4 118
ilippeville, Bel. E4 8
ilippi, W.V., U.S. B4 125
ilippines, ctry., Asia C7 32
ilippine Sea E21 2
ilipsburg, Mt., U.S. D3 103
ilipsburg, Pa., U.S. E5 115
illeo Lake, l., Wa., U.S. h14 124
illips, Me., U.S. D2 96
illips, Tx., U.S. B2 120
illips, Wi., U.S. C3 126
illips, co., Ar., U.S. C5 81
illips, co., Co., U.S. A8 83
illips, co., Ks., U.S. C4 93
illips, co., Mt., U.S. B8 103
Phillips Brook, stm., N.H., U.S. A4 106
Phillipsburg, Ks., U.S. C4 93
Phillipsburg, N.J., U.S. B2 107
Philmont, N.Y., U.S. C7 109
Philo, Il., U.S. C5 90
Philomath, Or., U.S. C3 114
Philpots Island, i., N.W. Ter., Can. B17 66
Philpott Reservoir, res., Va., U.S. D2 123
Phitsanulok, Thai. F6 34
Phnom Penh see Phnum Pénh, Camb. I8 34
Phnum Pénh (Phnom Penh), Camb. I8 34
Phoenix, Az., U.S. D3 80
Phoenix, Il., U.S. k9 90
Phoenix, N.Y., U.S. B4 109
Phoenix, Or., U.S. E4 114
Phoenixville, Pa., U.S. F10 115
Phôngsali, Laos D7 34
Phrae, Thai. E6 34
Phra Nakhon Si Ayutthaya, Thai. G6 34
Phuket, Thai. K5 34
Phuket, Ko, i., Thai. K5 34
Phu Ly, Viet. D8 34
Phumĭ Béng, Camb. H8 34
Phumĭ Kâmpóng Trâbêk, Camb. H8 34
Phu Quoc, Dao, i., Viet. I7 34
Phu Tho, Viet. D8 34
Piacenza, Italy D4 14
Piatra-Neamţ, Rom. C10 16
Piatt, co., Il., U.S. D5 90
Piazza Armerina, Italy L9 14
Pibor Post, Sudan G12 42
Picacho, Az., U.S. E4 80
Picardie, hist. reg., Fr. C9 10
Picayune, Ms., U.S. E4 101
Piccadilly, Newf., Can. D2 72
Pichanal, Arg. A4 56
Picher, Ok., U.S. A7 113
Pickaway, co., Oh., U.S. C2 112
Pickens, Ms., U.S. C4 101
Pickens, S.C., U.S. B2 117
Pickens, co., Al., U.S. B1 78
Pickens, co., Ga., U.S. B2 87
Pickens, co., S.C., U.S. B2 117
Pickerel Lake, l., Wi., U.S. C5 126
Pickering, Ont., Can. D5 73
Pickerington, Oh., U.S. C3 112
Pickett, co., Tn., U.S. C8 119
Pickwick Lake, res., U.S. A6 101
Pickworth Point, c., Ma., U.S. f12 98
Pico Rivera, Ca., U.S. n12 82
Picos, Braz. E10 54
Picquigny, Fr. C9 10
Picton, Ont., Can. D7 73
Pictou Island, i., N.S., Can. D7 71
Picture Butte, Alta., Can. E4 68
Pictured Rocks National Lakeshore, Mi., U.S. B4 99
Pidálion, Akrotírion, c., Cyp. B4 40
Pidurutalagala, mtn., Sri L. I6 37
Piedmont, Al., U.S. B4 78
Piedmont, Ca., U.S. h8 82
Piedmont, Mo., U.S. D7 102
Piedmont, Ok., U.S. B4 113
Piedmont, S.C., U.S. B3 117
Piedmont, W.V., U.S. B5 125
Piedmont Lake, res., Oh., U.S. B4 112
Piedra, stm., Co., U.S. D3 83
Piedrabuena, Spain F7 12
Piedrahita, Spain E6 12
Piedras Blancas, Point, c., Ca., U.S. E3 82
Piedras Negras, Guat. F2 64
Piedras Negras, Mex. C9 62
Pieksämäki, Fin. E16 6
Pierce, Co., U.S. A6 83
Pierce, Id., U.S. C3 89
Pierce, Ne., U.S. B8 104
Pierce, co., Ga., U.S. E4 87
Pierce, co., Ne., U.S. B8 104
Pierce, co., N.D., U.S. A5 111
Pierce, co., Wa., U.S. C3 124
Pierce, co., Wi., U.S. D1 126
Pierce, Lake, l., Fl., U.S. E5 86
Pierce City, Mo., U.S. E3 102
Pierceton, In., U.S. B6 91
Pierre, S.D., U.S. C5 118
Pierre-Buffière, Fr. G8 10
Pierrefonds, Que., Can. q19 74
Pierre Part, La., U.S. k9 95
Pierreville, Que., Can. C5 74
Pierson, Fl., U.S. C5 86
Pierz, Mn., U.S. E4 100
Pietermaritzburg, S. Afr. G6 44
Pietersburg, S. Afr. F5 44
Pietrasanta, Italy F5 14
Piet Retief, S. Afr. G6 44
Pigeon, Mi., U.S. E7 99
Pigeon, stm., U.S. f9 110
Pigeon, stm., In., U.S. A6 91
Pigeon, stm., Mn., U.S. h10 100
Pigeon, stm., Wi., U.S. k10 126
Pigeon Cove, Ma., U.S. A6 98
Pigeon Forge, Tn., U.S. D10 119
Pigeon Point, c., Mn., U.S. h10 100
Pigg, stm., Va., U.S. D3 123
Piggott, Ar., U.S. A5 81
Pihlajavesi, l., Fin. F17 6
Pihtipudas, Fin. E15 6
Pijijiapan, Mex. J13 62
Pikal'ovo, Russia B17 18
Pike, co., Al., U.S. D4 78
Pike, co., Ar., U.S. C2 81
Pike, co., Ga., U.S. C2 87
Pike, co., Il., U.S. D2 90
Pike, co., In., U.S. H3 91
Pike, co., Ky., U.S. C7 94
Pike, co., Ms., U.S. D3 101
Pike, co., Mo., U.S. B6 102
Pike, co., Oh., U.S. C2 112
Pike, co., Pa., U.S. D11 115
Pike, stm., Wi., U.S. C6 126
Pike Island Dam, U.S. f8 125
Pike Lake, Mn., U.S. D6 100
Pikes Peak, mtn., Co., U.S. C5 83
Pikesville, Md., U.S. B4 97
Piketberg, S. Afr. H3 44
Piketon, Oh., U.S. C2 112
Pikeville, Ky., U.S. C7 94
Pikeville, Tn., U.S. D8 119
Piła (Schneidemühl), Pol. B16 8
Pilar do Sul, Braz. G5 57
Pilcomayo, stm., S.A. A4 56
Pīlībhīt, India F8 38
Pillar Point, c., Ca., U.S. k7 82
Pilot Grove, Mo., U.S. C5 102
Pilot Knob, Mo., U.S. D7 102
Pilot Knob, mtn., Id., U.S. D3 89
Pilot Mound, Man., Can. E2 70
Pilot Mountain, N.C., U.S. A2 110
Pilot Peak, mtn., Nv., U.S. B7 105
Pilot Peak, mtn., Nv., U.S. E4 105
Pilot Peak, mtn., Wy., U.S. B3 127
Pilot Point, Tx., U.S. C4 120
Pilot Range, mts., Nv., U.S. B7 105
Pilot Rock, Or., U.S. B8 114
Pilot Station, Ak., U.S. C7 79
Pima, Az., U.S. E6 80
Pima, co., Az., U.S. E3 80
Pimentel, Peru E3 54
Pimmit Hills, Va., U.S. g12 123
Pina, Spain D11 12
Pinal, co., Az., U.S. E4 80
Pinaleno Mountains, mts., Az., U.S. E5 80
Pinal Mountains, mts., Az., U.S. D5 80
Pinang see George Town, Malay. L6 34
Pinar del Río, Cuba C6 64
Pinardville, N.H., U.S. E3 106
Pincher Creek, Alta., Can. E4 68
Pinckard, Al., U.S. D4 78
Pinckney, Mi., U.S. F7 99
Pinckney Island, i., S.C., U.S. G6 117
Pinckneyville, Il., U.S. E4 90
Pinconning, Mi., U.S. E7 99
Píndhos Óros, mts., Grc. J5 16
Pindi Gheb, Pak. D5 38
Pindus Mountains see Píndhos Óros, mts., Grc. J5 16
Pine, Az., U.S. C4 80
Pine, co., Mn., U.S. D6 100
Pine, stm., Mi., U.S. D7 99
Pine, stm., Mi., U.S. D5 99
Pine, stm., N.H., U.S. C4 106
Pine, stm., Wi., U.S. D4 126
Pine, stm., Wi., U.S. C5 126
Pine Barrens, reg., N.J., U.S. D3 107
Pine Bluff, Ar., U.S. C3 81
Pinebluff, N.C., U.S. B3 110
Pine Bluffs, Wy., U.S. E8 127
Pine Bridge, Ct., U.S. D3 84
Pine Castle, Fl., U.S. D5 86
Pine City, Mn., U.S. E6 100
Pine Creek, stm., Nv., U.S. C5 105
Pine Creek, stm., Pa., U.S. C6 115
Pine Creek, stm., Wa., U.S. B8 124
Pine Creek Lake, res., Ok., U.S. C6 113
Pinedale, Wy., U.S. D3 127
Pine Falls, Man., Can. D3 70
Pine Forest Range, mts., Nv., U.S. B3 105
Pine Grove, Pa., U.S. E9 115
Pine Grove Mills, Pa., U.S. E6 115
Pine Hill, N.J., U.S. D3 107
Pine Hills, Fl., U.S. D5 86
Pinehouse Lake, Sask., Can. B2 75
Pinehouse Lake, l., Sask., Can. B2 75
Pinehurst, Ma., U.S. f11 98
Pinehurst, N.C., U.S. B3 110
Pine Island, Mn., U.S. F6 100
Pine Island, i., Fl., U.S. F4 86
Pine Island Sound, strt., Fl., U.S. F4 86
Pine Key, i., Fl., U.S. p10 86
Pine Knot, Ky., U.S. D5 94
Pine Lake, Ga., U.S. h8 87
Pine Lake, l., In., U.S. A4 91
Pine Lake, l., Wi., U.S. C5 126
Pine Lawn, Mo., U.S. f13 102
Pine Level, N.C., U.S. B4 110
Pinellas, co., Fl., U.S. D4 86
Pinellas, Point, c., Fl., U.S. p10 86
Pinellas Park, Fl., U.S. E4 86
Pine Mountain, Ga., U.S. D2 87
Pine Mountain, mtn., Or., U.S. D6 114
Pine Mountain, mtn., Wy., U.S. E3 127
Pine Point, N.W. Ter., Can. D10 66
Pine Point, Me., U.S. E2 96
Pine Prairie, La., U.S. D3 95
Pine Ridge, S.D., U.S. D3 118
Pine Ridge Indian Reservation, S.D., U.S. D3 118
Pine River, Mn., U.S. D4 100
Pinerolo, Italy E2 14
Pines, Lake O' the, res., Tx., U.S. C5 120
Pinesdale, Mt., U.S. D2 103
Pinetops, N.C., U.S. B5 110
Pine Valley, val., Ut., U.S. E2 121
Pineville, Ky., U.S. D6 94
Pineville, La., U.S. C3 95
Pineville, N.C., U.S. B2 110
Pineville, W.V., U.S. D3 125
Pinewood, S.C., U.S. D7 117
Piney Creek, stm., W.V., U.S. n13 125
Piney Fork, stm., W.V., U.S. h9 125
Piney Point, Md., U.S. D4 97
Piney View, W.V., U.S. n13 125
Ping, stm., Thai. F5 34
Pingdingshan, China E9 26
Pinghu, China E10 28
Pingliang, China D8 26
Pingtan Dao, i., China J8 28
P'ingtung, Tai. M9 28
Pingxiang, China H2 28
Pingyao, China D9 26
Pinhel, Port. E4 12
Pinnacles National Monument, Ca., U.S. D3 82
Pinneberg, Ger. B9 8
Pinole, Ca., U.S. h8 82
Pinopolis Dam, S.C., U.S. E8 117
Pinos, Mount, mtn., Ca., U.S. E4 82
Pins, Pointe aux, c., Ont., Can. E3 73
Pinsk, Bela. I9 18
Pinson, Al., U.S. f7 78
Pinta, Sierra, mts., Az., U.S. E2 80
Pintwater Range, mts., Nv., U.S. G6 105
Pioche, Nv., U.S. F7 105
Piombino, Italy G5 14
Pioneer, Oh., U.S. A1 112
Pioneer Mountains, mts., Id., U.S. F5 89
Pioneer Mountains, mts., Mt., U.S. E3 103
Pioner, Ostrov, i., Russia B12 24
Piotrków Trybunalski, Pol. D19 8
Pipe Spring National Monument, Az., U.S. A3 80
Pipestem Creek, stm., N.D., U.S. B6 111
Pipestone, Mn., U.S. G2 100
Pipestone, co., Mn., U.S. F2 100
Pipestone, stm., Ont., Can. F14 66
Pipestone National Monument, Mn., U.S. G2 100
Pipestone Pass, Mt., U.S. E4 103
Pipmuacan, Réservoir, res., Que., Can. k12 74
Piqua, Oh., U.S. B1 112
Piracicaba, Braz. G5 57
Piraeus see Piraiévs, Grc. L7 16
Piraí do Sul, Braz. A7 56
Piraiévs (Piraeus), Grc. L7 16
Piraju, Braz. G4 57
Piran, Slo. D8 14
Pirané, Arg. B5 56
Pirapora, Braz. D6 57
Pires do Rio, Braz. D4 57
Pírgos, Grc. L5 16
Pirmasens, Ger. F7 8
Pirna, Ger. E13 8
Pirtleville, Az., U.S. F6 80
Piru, Indon. F8 32
Pisa, Italy F5 14
Pisagua, Chile G4 54
Piscataqua, stm., N.H., U.S. D5 106
Piscataquis, co., Me., U.S. C3 96
Piscataquis, stm., Me., U.S. C3 96
Piscataquog, stm., N.H., U.S. D3 106
Piscataway, N.J., U.S. B4 107
Pisco, Peru F3 54
Piseco Lake, l., N.Y., U.S. B6 109
Písek, Czech. F14 8
Pisgah, Al., U.S. A4 78
Pisgah, Oh., U.S. n13 112
Pisgah, Mount, mtn., Wy., U.S. B8 127
Pisgah Forest, N.C., U.S. f10 110
Pishan, China B8 38
Pismo Beach, Ca., U.S. E3 82
Pisticci, Italy I11 14
Pistoia, Italy F5 14
Pistolet Bay, b., Newf., Can. C4 72
Pit, stm., Ca., U.S. B3 82
Pitalito, Col. G4 58
Pitcairn, Pa., U.S. k14 115
Pitcairn, dep., Oc. H4 2
Piteå, Swe. D13 6
Piteşti, Rom. E8 16
Pithāpuram, India D7 37
Pithiviers, Fr. D9 10
Pitiquito, Mex. B3 62
Pitkin, co., Co., U.S. B4 83
Pitlochry, Scot., U.K. E9 7
Pitman, N.J., U.S. D2 107
Pitt, co., N.C., U.S. B5 110
Pitt Island, i., B.C., Can. C3 69
Pittsboro, In., U.S. E5 91
Pittsboro, N.C., U.S. B3 110
Pittsburg, Ca., U.S. g9 82
Pittsburg, Ks., U.S. E9 93
Pittsburg, Ky., U.S. C5 94
Pittsburg, Tx., U.S. C5 120
Pittsburg, co., Ok., U.S. C6 113
Pittsburgh, Pa., U.S. F1 115
Pittsfield, Il., U.S. D3 90
Pittsfield, Me., U.S. D3 96
Pittsfield, Ma., U.S. B1 98
Pittsfield, N.H., U.S. D4 106
Pittsford, Vt., U.S. D2 122
Pittston, Pa., U.S. D10 115
Pittsville, Md., U.S. D7 97
Pittsville, Wi., U.S. D3 126
Pittsylvania, co., Va., U.S. D3 123
Piu, Cerro, mtn., Nic. H5 64
Piura, Peru E2 54
Piute, co., Ut., U.S. E3 121
Piute Peak, mtn., Ca., U.S. E4 82
Piute Reservoir, res., Ut., U.S. E3 121
Pixley, Ca., U.S. E4 82
Pizzo, Italy K11 14
Placentia, Newf., Can. E5 72
Placentia Bay, b., Newf., Can. E4 72
Placer, co., Ca., U.S. C3 82
PLacer Mountain, mtn., N.M., U.S. k8 108
Placerville, Ca., U.S. C3 82
Placetas, Cuba C8 64
Placid, Lake, l., Fl., U.S. E5 86
Placid, Lake, l., N.Y., U.S. f11 109
Placitas, N.M., U.S. B3 108
Plain City, Oh., U.S. B2 112
Plain City, Ut., U.S. B3 121
Plain Dealing, La., U.S. B2 95
Plainfield, Ct., U.S. C8 84
Plainfield, Il., U.S. B5 90
Plainfield, In., U.S. E5 91
Plainfield, N.J., U.S. B4 107
Plainfield, Vt., U.S. C4 122
Plainfield, Wi., U.S. D4 126
Plainfield Heights, Mi., U.S. *E5 99
Plains, Ga., U.S. D2 87
Plains, Ks., U.S. E3 93
Plains, Mt., U.S. C2 103
Plains, Pa., U.S. n17 115
Plains, Tx., U.S. C1 120
Plainview, Ar., U.S. C2 81
Plainview, Mn., U.S. F6 100
Plainview, Ne., U.S. B8 104
Plainview, Tx., U.S. B2 120
Plainville, Ct., U.S. C4 84
Plainville, Ks., U.S. C4 93
Plainville, Ma., U.S. B5 98
Plainwell, Mi., U.S. F5 99
Plaistow, N.H., U.S. E4 106
Plankinton, S.D., U.S. D7 118
Plano, Il., U.S. B5 90
Plano, Tx., U.S. C4 120
Plantagenet, Ont., Can. B9 73
Plantation, Fl., U.S. r13 86
Plant City, Fl., U.S. D4 86
Plantersville, Al., U.S. C3 78
Plantersville, Ms., U.S. A5 101
Plantsite, Az., U.S. D6 80
Plantsville, Ct., U.S. C4 84
Plaquemine, La., U.S. D4 95
Plaquemines, co., La., U.S. E6 95
Plasencia, Spain E5 12
Plaški, Cro. D10 14
Plaster Rock, N.B., Can. C2 71
Plata, Río de la, est., S.A. D5 56
Platte, S.D., U.S. D7 118
Platte, co., Mo., U.S. B3 102
Platte, co., Ne., U.S. C8 104
Platte, co., Wy., U.S. D7 127
Platte, stm., U.S. B3 102
Platte, stm., Mn., U.S. E4 100
Platte, stm., Ne., U.S. D6 104
Platte City, Mo., U.S. B3 102
Platte Island, i., Sey. C11 44
Platteville, Co., U.S. A6 83
Platteville, Wi., U.S. F3 126
Plattling, Ger. G12 8
Plattsburg, Mo., U.S. B3 102
Plattsburgh, N.Y., U.S. f11 109
Plattsburgh Air Force Base, mil., N.Y., U.S. f11 109
Plattsmouth, Ne., U.S. D10 104
Plau, Ger. B12 8
Plauen, Ger. E12 8
Playas Lake, l., N.M., U.S. F2 108
Play Cu, Viet. H9 34
Playgreen Lake, l., Man., Can. B2 70
Pleasant, stm., Me., U.S. C3 96
Pleasant, Lake, res., Az., U.S. D3 80
Pleasant Gap, Pa., U.S. E6 115
Pleasant Garden, N.C., U.S. B3 110
Pleasant Grove, Al., U.S. g7 78
Pleasant Grove, Ut., U.S. C4 121
Pleasant Hill, Ca., U.S. h8 82
Pleasant Hill, Il., U.S. D3 90
Pleasant Hill, Ia., U.S. e8 92
Pleasant Hill, La., U.S. C2 95
Pleasant Hill, Mo., U.S. C3 102
Pleasant Hill, Oh., U.S. B1 112
Pleasant Lake, In., U.S. A7 91
Pleasant Lake, l., Me., U.S. C5 96
Pleasant Lake, l., N.H., U.S. D4 106
Pleasanton, Ca., U.S. h9 82
Pleasanton, Ks., U.S. D9 93
Pleasanton, Tx., U.S. E3 120
Pleasant Prairie, Wi., U.S. n12 126
Pleasants, co., W.V., U.S. B3 125
Pleasant Valley, Ia., U.S. g11 92
Pleasant Valley, Mo., U.S. h11 102
Pleasant View, Ut., U.S. B3 121
Pleasantville, Ia., U.S. C4 92
Pleasantville, N.J., U.S. E3 107
Pleasantville, N.Y., U.S. D7 109
Pleasantville, Oh., U.S. C3 112
Pleasure Beach, Ct., U.S. D7 84
Pleasure Ridge Park, Ky., U.S. g11 94
Pleasureville, Ky., U.S. B4 94
Pleiku see Play Cu, Viet. H9 34
Pléneuf, Fr. D4 10
Plenty, Bay of, b., N.Z. B6 52
Plentywood, Mt., U.S. B12 103
Plessisville, Que., Can. C6 74
Pleternica, Cro. D12 14
Plétipi, Lac, l., Que., Can. F18 66
Pleven, Bul. F8 16
Pljevlja, Yugo. F3 16
Płock, Pol. C19 8
Ploërmel, Fr. E4 10
Ploieşti, Rom. E10 16
Plomosa Mountains, mts., Az., U.S. D1 80
Plonge, Lac la, l., Sask., Can. B2 75
Plouguenast, Fr. D4 10
Plovdiv, Bul. G8 16
Plover, Wi., U.S. D4 126
Plover, stm., Wi., U.S. D4 126
Plum, Pa., U.S. k14 115
Plumas, co., Ca., U.S. B3 82
Plum Coulee, Man., Can. E3 70
Plumerville, Ar., U.S. B3 81
Plum Island, i., Ma., U.S. A6 98
Plummer, Id., U.S. B2 89
Plumsteadville, Pa., U.S. F11 115
Plumtree, Zimb. F5 44
Plymouth, Monts. F16 64
Plymouth, Eng., U.K. K8 7
Plymouth, Ct., U.S. C3 84
Plymouth, Fl., U.S. D5 86
Plymouth, In., U.S. B5 91
Plymouth, Ma., U.S. C6 98
Plymouth, Mi., U.S. p15 99
Plymouth, Mn., U.S. m12 100
Plymouth, N.H., U.S. C3 106
Plymouth, N.C., U.S. B6 110
Plymouth, Oh., U.S. A3 112
Plymouth, Pa., U.S. D10 115
Plymouth, Wi., U.S. E6 126
Plymouth, co., Ia., U.S. B1 92
Plymouth, co., Ma., U.S. C6 98
Plymouth Bay, b., Ma., U.S. C6 98
Plzeň, Czech. F13 8
Po, stm., Italy E7 14
Po, stm., Va., U.S. B5 123
Pobeda, Gora, mtn., Russia D23 24
Pocahontas, Ar., U.S. A5 81
Pocahontas, Il., U.S. E4 90
Pocahontas, Ia., U.S. B3 92
Pocahontas, co., Ia., U.S. B3 92
Pocahontas, co., W.V., U.S. C4 125
Pocasset, Ma., U.S. C6 98
Pocatalico, W.V., U.S. C3 125
Pocatalico, stm., W.V., U.S. C3 125

Name	Map Ref	Page
Pocatello, Id., U.S.	G6	89
Počep, Russia	I16	18
Pochutla, Mex.	J11	62
Poções, Braz.	C8	57
Pocola, Ok., U.S.	B7	113
Pocomoke, stm., Md., U.S.	D7	97
Pocomoke City, Md., U.S.	D6	97
Pocomoke Sound, strt., Md., U.S.	E6	97
Pocono Mountains, hills, Pa., U.S.	E11	115
Pocono Pines, Pa., U.S.	D11	115
Poços de Caldas, Braz.	F5	57
Pocotopaug Lake, res., Ct., U.S.	C6	84
Podensac, Fr.	H6	10
Podgorica, Yugo.	G3	16
Podkamennaja Tunguska, Russia	E12	24
Podkamennaja Tunguska, stm., Russia	E13	24
Podol'sk, Russia	F20	18
Podor, Sen.	E3	42
Podravska Slatina, Cro.	D12	14
Pofadder, S. Afr.	G3	44
Poge, Cape, c., Ma., U.S.	D7	98
Poggibonsi, Italy	F6	14
P'ohang, S. Kor.	D12	26
Pohénégamook, Que., Can.	B8	74
Pohue Bay, b., Hi., U.S.	E6	88
Poinsett, co., Ar., U.S.	B5	81
Poinsett, Lake, l., Fl., U.S.	D6	86
Poinsett, Lake, l., S.D., U.S.	C8	118
Point Clear, Al., U.S.	E2	78
Pointe a la Hache, La., U.S.	E6	95
Pointe-à-Pitre, Guad.	F17	64
Pointe-au-Pic, Que., Can.	B7	74
Pointe-Calumet, Que., Can.	p19	74
Pointe-Claire, Que., Can.	D4	74
Pointe Coupee, co., La., U.S.	D4	95
Pointe-des-Cascades, Que., Can.	q19	74
Point Edward, Ont., Can.	D2	73
Pointe-Noire, Congo	B2	44
Pointe-Verte, N.B., Can.	B4	71
Point Fortin, Trin.	I17	64
Point Hope, Ak., U.S.	B6	79
Point Imperial, mtn., Az., U.S.	A4	80
Point Judith Pond, l., R.I., U.S.	F4	116
Point Lake, l., N.W. Ter., Can.	C10	66
Point Leamington, Newf., Can.	D4	72
Point Marion, Pa., U.S.	G2	115
Point Mugu Naval Air Station, mil., Ca., U.S.	E4	82
Point of Rocks, Md., U.S.	B2	97
Point Pelee National Park, Ont., Can.	F2	73
Point Pleasant, N.J., U.S.	C4	107
Point Pleasant, W.V., U.S.	C2	125
Point Pleasant Beach, N.J., U.S.	C4	107
Point Reyes National Seashore, Ca., U.S.	C2	82
Point Roberts, Wa., U.S.	A2	124
Poipu, Hi., U.S.	B2	88
Poison Creek, stm., Wy., U.S.	C5	127
Poisson Blanc, Lac du, res., Que., Can.	C2	74
Poitiers, Fr.	F7	10
Poitou, reg., Fr.	F6	10
Poix, Fr.	C8	10
Pokegama Lake, l., Mn., U.S.	C5	100
Pokegama Lake, l., Wi., U.S.	C2	126
Polacca, Az., U.S.	B5	80
Poland, ctry., Eur.	E11	4
Polar Bear Provincial Park, Ont., Can.	n18	73
Polecat Creek, stm., Ok., U.S.	B5	113
Pol-e Khomrī, Afg.	C3	38
Polesje, reg., Eur.	I10	18
Pólis, Cyp.	B3	40
Polistena, Italy	K11	14
Polk, Pa., U.S.	D2	115
Polk, co., Ar., U.S.	C1	81
Polk, co., Fl., U.S.	E5	86
Polk, co., Ga., U.S.	C1	87
Polk, co., Ia., U.S.	C4	92
Polk, co., Mn., U.S.	C2	100
Polk, co., Mo., U.S.	D4	102
Polk, co., Ne., U.S.	C8	104
Polk, co., N.C., U.S.	f10	110
Polk, co., Or., U.S.	C3	114
Polk, co., Tn., U.S.	D9	119
Polk, co., Tx., U.S.	D5	120
Polk, co., Wi., U.S.	C1	126
Polk City, Fl., U.S.	D5	86
Polk City, Ia., U.S.	C4	92
Pol'kino, Russia	C13	24
Pollāchi, India	G4	37
Polo, Il., U.S.	B4	90
Polock, Bela.	F11	18
Polson, Mt., U.S.	C2	103
Poltava, Ukr.	H4	22
Polynesia, is., Oc.	G2	2
Pomabamba, Peru	E3	54
Pomaro, Mex.	H8	62
Pombal, Port.	F3	12
Pomerania, hist. reg., Pol.	A16	8
Pomeranian Bay, b., Eur.	A14	8
Pomeroy, Ia., U.S.	B3	92
Pomeroy, Oh., U.S.	C3	112
Pomeroy, Wa., U.S.	C8	124
Pomme de Terre, stm., Mn., U.S.	E3	100
Pomme de Terre, stm., Mo., U.S.	D4	102
Pomme de Terre Lake, res., Mo., U.S.	D4	102
Pomona, Ca., U.S.	E5	82
Pomona, Ks., U.S.	D8	93
Pomona Lake, res., Ks., U.S.	D7	93
Pompano Beach, Fl., U.S.	F6	86
Pompton Lakes, N.J., U.S.	A4	107
Ponaganset, stm., R.I., U.S.	C2	116
Ponaganset Reservoir, res., R.I., U.S.	B2	116
Ponca, Ne., U.S.	B9	104
Ponca City, Ok., U.S.	A4	113
Ponca Creek, stm., U.S.	A6	104
Ponca Indian Reservation, Ne., U.S.	B7	104
Ponce, P.R.	E14	64
Ponce de Leon Bay, b., Fl., U.S.	G5	86
Ponce de Leon Inlet, b., Fl., U.S.	C6	86
Poncha Pass, Co., U.S.	C4	83
Ponchatoula, La., U.S.	D5	95
Pond, stm., Ky., U.S.	C2	94
Pond Creek, Ok., U.S.	A3	113
Pondera, co., Mt., U.S.	B4	103
Pond Fork, stm., W.V., U.S.	D3	125
Pondicherry, India	G5	37
Pondicherry, ter., India	G5	37
Pond Inlet, N.W. Ter., Can.	B17	66
Pone Island, i., Md., U.S.	D5	97
Ponferrada, Spain	C5	12
Ponoka, Alta., Can.	C4	68
Ponorogo, Indon.	m15	33a
Pons, Fr.	G6	10
Ponta Grossa, Braz.	B6	56
Pont-à-Mousson, Fr.	D13	10
Ponta Porã, Braz.	G1	57
Pontarlier, Fr.	F13	10
Pontassieve, Italy	F6	14
Pont-Audemer, Fr.	C7	10
Pontchartrain, Lake, l., La., U.S.	D5	95
Pontchâteau, Fr.	E4	10
Pont de Suert, Spain	C12	12
Ponte Branca, Braz.	D2	57
Ponte da Barca, Port.	D3	12
Pontedera, Italy	F5	14
Ponte de Sor, Port.	F3	12
Ponteix, Sask., Can.	H2	75
Ponte Nova, Braz.	F7	57
Pontevedra, Spain	C3	12
Ponte Vedra Beach, Fl., U.S.	B5	86
Pontgibaud, Fr.	F9	10
Pontiac, Il., U.S.	C5	90
Pontiac, Mi., U.S.	F7	99
Pontianak, Indon.	F4	32
Pontivy, Fr.	D4	10
Pont-l'Abbé, Fr.	E2	10
Pontoise, Fr.	C9	10
Pontoosuc Lake, l., Ma., U.S.	B1	98
Pontorson, Fr.	D5	10
Pontotoc, Ms., U.S.	A4	101
Pontotoc, co., Ms., U.S.	A4	101
Pontotoc, co., Ok., U.S.	C5	113
Pont-Rouge, Que., Can.	C6	74
Pontypool, Ont., Can.	C6	73
Pontypool, Wales, U.K.	J9	7
Poole, Eng., U.K.	K11	7
Pooler, Ga., U.S.	D5	87
Pooles Island, i., Md., U.S.	B5	97
Poolesville, Md., U.S.	B3	97
Poopó, Lago de, l., Bol.	G5	54
Popayán, Col.	F4	58
Pope, co., Ar., U.S.	B2	81
Pope, co., Il., U.S.	F5	90
Pope, co., Mn., U.S.	E3	100
Pope Air Force Base, mil., N.C., U.S.	B3	110
Poplar, Mt., U.S.	B11	103
Poplar, stm., Can.	C3	70
Poplar, stm., Mn., U.S.	C2	100
Poplar Bluff, Mo., U.S.	E7	102
Poplar Island, i., Md., U.S.	C5	97
Poplarville, Ms., U.S.	E4	101
Popocatépetl, Volcán, vol., Mex.	H10	62
Popokabaka, Zaire	C3	44
Popomanasiu, Mount, mtn., Sol.Is.	A11	50
Popondetta, Pap. N. Gui.	m16	50a
Popple, stm., Wi., U.S.	C5	126
Poquonock, Ct., U.S.	B5	84
Poquonock Bridge, Ct., U.S.	D7	84
Poquoson, Va., U.S.	C6	123
Porangatu, Braz.	F9	54
Porbandar, India	J3	38
Porcher Island, i., B.C., Can.	C2	69
Porcupine Mountains, mts., Mi., U.S.	m12	99
Pordenone, Italy	D7	14
Poreč, Cro.	D8	14
Pori, Fin.	F13	6
Porkkala, Fin.	G15	6
Porlamar, Ven.	B11	58
Poronajsk, Russia	H22	24
Porsgrunn, Nor.	G7	6
Portadown, N. Ire., U.K.	G6	7
Portage, In., U.S.	A3	91
Portage, Mi., U.S.	F5	99
Portage, Pa., U.S.	F4	115
Portage, Wi., U.S.	E4	126
Portage, co., Oh., U.S.	A4	112
Portage, co., Wi., U.S.	D4	126
Portage, stm., Oh., U.S.	B2	112
Portage Bay, b., Man., Can.	D2	70
Portage Head, c., Wa., U.S.	A1	124
Portage Lake, l., Me., U.S.	B4	96
Portage Lakes, Oh., U.S.	B4	112
Portage la Prairie, Man., Can.	E2	70
Portageville, Mo., U.S.	E8	102
Port Alberni, B.C., Can.	E5	69
Portalegre, Port.	F4	12
Portales, N.M., U.S.	C6	108
Port Alice, B.C., Can.	D4	69
Port Allegany, Pa., U.S.	C5	115
Port Allen, La., U.S.	D4	95
Port Angeles, Wa., U.S.	A2	124
Port Antonio, Jam.	E9	64
Port Aransas, Tx., U.S.	F4	120
Port Arthur, Tx., U.S.	E6	120
Port Arthur see Lüshun, China	D11	26
Port Augusta, Austl.	F7	50
Port au Port Bay, b., Newf., Can.	D2	72
Port au Port [West-Aguathuna-Felix Cove], Newf., Can.	D2	72
Port-au-Prince, Haiti	E11	64
Port au Prince Peninsula, pen., Newf., Can.	D2	72
Port Austin, Mi., U.S.	D7	99
Port Barre, La., U.S.	D4	95
Port-Bergé, Madag.	E9	44
Port Blair, India	I2	34
Port Blandford, Newf., Can.	D4	72
Port Bolivar, Tx., U.S.	E5	120
Port Burwell, Ont., Can.	E4	73
Port Byron, Il., U.S.	B3	90
Port Carbon, Pa., U.S.	E9	115
Port Carling, Ont., Can.	B5	73
Port-Cartier-Ouest, Que., Can.	k13	74
Port Chalmers, N.Z.	F3	52
Port Charlotte, Fl., U.S.	F4	86
Port Chester, N.Y., U.S.	E7	109
Port Clinton, Oh., U.S.	A3	112
Port Colborne, Ont., Can.	E5	73
Port Coquitlam, B.C., Can.	E6	69
Port Deposit, Md., U.S.	A5	97
Port Dickinson, N.Y., U.S.	C5	109
Port Dickson, Malay.	M6	34
Port Edward, B.C., Can.	B2	69
Port Edwards, Wi., U.S.	D4	126
Portel, Braz.	D8	54
Portel, Port.	G4	12
Port Elgin, Ont., Can.	C3	73
Port Elizabeth, S. Afr.	H5	44
Port Ellen, Scot., U.K.	F6	7
Porter, In., U.S.	A3	91
Porter, Tx., U.S.	D5	120
Porter, co., In., U.S.	B3	91
Porter Creek, stm., W.V., U.S.	m13	125
Porterdale, Ga., U.S.	C3	87
Porterville, Ca., U.S.	D4	82
Port Ewen, N.Y., U.S.	D7	109
Port Gamble Indian Reservation, Wa., U.S.	B3	124
Port-Gentil, Gabon	B1	44
Port Gibson, Ms., U.S.	D3	101
Port Harcourt, Nig.	H7	42
Port Hedland, Austl.	D3	50
Port Hood, N.S., Can.	C8	71
Port Hope, Ont., Can.	D6	73
Port Hope Simpson, Newf., Can.	B3	72
Port Hueneme, Ca., U.S.	E4	82
Port Huron, Mi., U.S.	F8	99
Portimão, Port.	H3	12
Port Isabel, Tx., U.S.	F4	120
Port Jefferson, N.Y., U.S.	n15	109
Port Jervis, N.Y., U.S.	D6	109
Portland, Austl.	G8	50
Portland, Ct., U.S.	C5	84
Portland, In., U.S.	D8	91
Portland, Me., U.S.	E2	96
Portland, Mi., U.S.	F6	99
Portland, N.D., U.S.	B8	111
Portland, Or., U.S.	B4	114
Portland, Tn., U.S.	A5	119
Portland, Tx., U.S.	F4	120
Portland, Bill of, c., Eng., U.K.	K10	7
Portland Inlet, b., B.C., Can.	B2	69
Portland Point, c., Jam.	F9	64
Port Lavaca, Tx., U.S.	E4	120
Port Lincoln, Austl.	F7	50
Port Loko, S.L.	G3	42
Port Louis, Mrts.	F11	44
Port Ludlow, Wa., U.S.	B3	124
Port-Lyautey see Kenitra, Mor.	B4	42
Port Macquarie, Austl.	F10	50
Port Madison Indian Reservation, Wa., U.S.	B3	124
Port McNeil, B.C., Can.	D4	69
Port McNicoll, Ont., Can.	C5	73
Port Monmouth, N.J., U.S.	C4	107
Port Moresby, Pap. N. Gui.	m16	50a
Port Morien, N.S., Can.	C10	71
Port Neches, Tx., U.S.	E6	120
Portneuf, Que., Can.	C6	74
Port Nolloth, S. Afr.	G3	44
Porto, Port.	D3	12
Porto Alegre, Braz.	C6	56
Porto Amboim, Ang.	D2	44
Portobelo, Pan.	J8	64
Porto de Moz, Braz.	D8	54
Porto Esperança, Braz.	G7	54
Porto Esperidião, Braz.	G7	54
Pôrto Feliz, Braz.	G5	57
Portoferraio, Italy	G5	14
Pôrto Ferreira, Braz.	F5	57
Port of Spain, Trin.	I17	64
Portogruaro, Italy	D7	14
Portola, Ca., U.S.	C3	82
Porto Murtinho, Braz.	H7	54
Porto Nacional, Braz.	F9	54
Porto-Novo, Benin	G6	42
Port Orange, Fl., U.S.	C6	86
Port Orchard, Wa., U.S.	B3	124
Port Orford, Or., U.S.	E2	114
Porto San Giorgio, Italy	F8	14
Porto Santo Stefano, Italy	G6	14
Pôrto São José, Braz.	G2	57
Pôrto Seguro, Braz.	D9	57
Porto Torres, Italy	I3	14
Porto União, Braz.	B6	56
Porto Velho, Braz.	E6	54
Portoviejo, Ec.	H2	58
Port Penn, De., U.S.	B3	85
Port Pirie, Austl.	F7	50
Port Richey, Fl., U.S.	D4	86
Port Rowan, Ont., Can.	E4	73
Port Royal, S.C., U.S.	G6	117
Port Royal Island, i., S.C., U.S.	G6	117
Port Royal Sound, strt., S.C., U.S.	G6	117
Port Said see Būr Sa'īd, Egypt	B12	42
Port-Sainte-Marie, Fr.	H7	10
Port Saint Joe, Fl., U.S.	C1	86
Port Saint Johns, S. Afr.	H5	44
Port Saint Lucie, Fl., U.S.	E6	86
Port Salerno, Fl., U.S.	E6	86
Port Saunders, Newf., Can.	C3	72
Port Shepstone, S. Afr.	H6	44
Portsmouth, Eng., U.K.	K11	7
Portsmouth, N.H., U.S.	D5	106
Portsmouth, Oh., U.S.	D3	112
Portsmouth, R.I., U.S.	E6	116
Portsmouth, Va., U.S.	D6	123
Portsmouth Naval Shipyard, mil., Me., U.S.	D5	106
Port Stanley, Ont., Can.	E3	73
Port Sulphur, La., U.S.	E6	95
Port Talbot, Wales, U.K.	J9	7
Port Townsend, Wa., U.S.	A3	124
Portugal, ctry., Eur.	H6	4
Portugalete, Spain	B8	12
Portuguese Guinea see Guinea-Bissau, ctry., Afr.	F2	42
Portumna, Ire.	H4	7
Port Union, Newf., Can.	D5	72
Port-Vendres, Fr.	J10	10
Port Washington, N.Y., U.S.	h13	109
Port Washington, Wi., U.S.	E6	126
Port Wentworth, Ga., U.S.	D5	87
Porum, Ok., U.S.	B6	113
Porz, Ger.	E7	8
Porzuna, Spain	F7	12
Posadas, Arg.	B5	56
Poschiavo, Switz.	F17	10
Posen, Il., U.S.	k9	90
Posey, co., In., U.S.	H2	91
Poseyville, In., U.S.	H2	91
Poso, Indon.	F7	32
Posse, Braz.	C5	57
Pössneck, Ger.	E11	8
Post, Tx., U.S.	C2	120
Post Falls, Id., U.S.	B2	89
Post Maurice Cortier (Bidon Cinq), Alg.	D6	42
Postojna, Slo.	D9	14
P'ostraja Dresva, Russia	E25	24
Postville, Ia., U.S.	A6	92
Potawatomi Indian Reservation, Ks., U.S.	C8	93
Potchefstroom, S. Afr.	G5	44
Poté, Braz.	D8	57
Poteau, Ok., U.S.	B7	113
Poteau, stm., U.S.	B7	113
Poteet, Tx., U.S.	E3	120
Potenza, Italy	I10	14
Potes, Spain	B7	12
Potgietersrus, S. Afr.	F5	44
Poth, Tx., U.S.	E3	120
Potholes Reservoir, res., Wa., U.S.	B6	124
Potiraguá, Braz.	C9	57
Potiskum, Nig.	F8	42
Potlatch, Id., U.S.	C2	89
Potomac, Md., U.S.	B3	97
Potomac, stm., U.S.	D4	97
Potomac Heights, Md., U.S.	C3	97
Potomac Park, Md., U.S.	k13	97
Potosí, Bol.	G5	54
Potosi, Mo., U.S.	D7	102
Potosí, Cerro, mtn., Mex.	E9	62
Potsdam, Ger.	C13	8
Potsdam, N.Y., U.S.	f10	109
Pottawatomie, co., Ks., U.S.	C7	93
Pottawatomie, co., Ok., U.S.	B4	113
Pottawattamie, co., Ia., U.S.	C2	92
Potter, co., Pa., U.S.	C6	115
Potter, co., S.D., U.S.	B6	118
Potter, co., Tx., U.S.	B2	120
Potter Valley, Ca., U.S.	C2	82
Potts Creek, stm., U.S.	C2	123
Pottstown, Pa., U.S.	F10	115
Pottsville, Ar., U.S.	B2	81
Pottsville, Pa., U.S.	E9	115
P'otzu, Tai.	L9	28
Pouce Coupe, B.C., Can.	B7	69
Pouch Cove, Newf., Can.	E5	72
Poughkeepsie, N.Y., U.S.	D7	109
Poulan, Ga., U.S.	E3	87
Poulsbo, Wa., U.S.	B3	124
Poultney, Vt., U.S.	D2	122
Poultney, stm., Vt., U.S.	D2	122
Pound, Va., U.S.	e9	123
Pound Gap, U.S.	C7	94
Pouso Alegre, Braz.	G6	57
Poŭthĭsăt, Camb.	H7	34
Pouzauges, Fr.	F6	10
Póvoa de Varzim, Port.	D3	12
Povungnituk, Que., Can.	f11	74
Powassan, Ont., Can.	A5	73
Poway, Ca., U.S.	F5	82
Powder, stm., U.S.	B5	76
Powder, stm., Or., U.S.	C9	114
Powder, Middle Fork, stm., Wy., U.S.	C6	127
Powder, North Fork, stm., Wy., U.S.	C6	127
Powder, South Fork, stm., Wy., U.S.	C6	127
Powder River, co., Mt., U.S.	E11	103
Powder River Pass, Wy., U.S.	B5	127
Powder Springs, Ga., U.S.	h8	87
Powell, Oh., U.S.	B2	112
Powell, Tn., U.S.	m13	119
Powell, Wy., U.S.	B4	127
Powell, co., Ky., U.S.	C6	94
Powell, co., Mt., U.S.	D4	103
Powell, stm., U.S.	C10	119
Powell, Lake, res., U.S.	F5	121
Powell, Mount, mtn., Co., U.S.	B4	83
Powell, Mount, mtn., N.M., U.S.	B1	108
Powell Butte, Or., U.S.	C5	114
Powell Park, reg., Co., U.S.	A2	83
Powell River, B.C., Can.	E5	69
Powellton, W.V., U.S.	C3	125
Power, co., Id., U.S.	G5	89
Powers, Or., U.S.	E2	114
Powerview, Man., Can.	D3	70
Poweshiek, co., Ia., U.S.	C5	92
Powhatan, Va., U.S.	C5	123
Powhatan, co., Va., U.S.	C5	123
Powhatan Point, Oh., U.S.	C5	112
Poxoreu, Braz.	C1	57
Poyang, China	G5	28
Poyang Hu, l., China	F5	28
Poygan, Lake, l., Wi., U.S.	D5	126
Poynette, Wi., U.S.	E4	126
Poza Rica de Hidalgo, Mex.	G11	62
Poznań, Pol.	C16	8
Pozo Alcón, Spain	H9	12
Pozoblanco, Spain	G7	12
Pozo Redondo Mountains, mts., Az., U.S.	E3	80
Pozuelo de Alarcón, Spain	E8	12
Pozzuoli, Italy	I9	14
Prachin Buri, Thai.	G6	34
Prachuap Khiri Khan, Thai.	I5	34
Prague, Ok., U.S.	B5	113
Prague see Praha, Czech.	E14	8
Praha (Prague), Czech.	E14	8
Prainha, Braz.	E6	54
Prairie, co., Ar., U.S.	C4	81
Prairie, co., Mt., U.S.	D11	103
Prairie, stm., Mn., U.S.	C5	100
Prairie, stm., Wi., U.S.	C4	126
Prairie City, Ia., U.S.	C4	92
Prairie City, Or., U.S.	C8	114
Prairie Creek Reservoir, res., In., U.S.	D7	91
Prairie Dog Creek, stm., U.S.	C3	93
Prairie du Chien, Wi., U.S.	E2	126
Prairie du Sac, Wi., U.S.	E4	126
Prairie Grove, Ar., U.S.	B1	81
Prairies, Rivière des, stm., Que., Can.	p19	74
Prairie View, Tx., U.S.	D5	120
Prairie Village, Ks., U.S.	m16	93
Praslin Island, i., Sey.	B11	44
Pratas Islands see Tungsha Tao, is., Tai.	G10	26
Prat de Llobregat, Spain	D14	12
Prater Mountain, mtn., Wy., U.S.	C2	127
Prato, Italy	F6	14
Pratt, Ks., U.S.	E5	93
Pratt, co., Ks., U.S.	E5	93
Prattville, Al., U.S.	C3	78
Pravia, Spain	B5	12
Preble, co., Oh., U.S.	C1	112
Predazzo, Italy	C6	14
Predlitz [-Turrach], Aus.	H13	8
Pré-en-Pail, Fr.	D6	10
Preetz, Ger.	A10	8
Premont, Tx., U.S.	F3	120
Prentiss, Ms., U.S.	D4	101
Prentiss, co., Ms., U.S.	A5	101
Prenzlau, Ger.	B13	8
Preparis Island, i., Burma	G2	34
Preparis North Channel, strt., Burma	G2	34
Preparis South Channel, strt., Burma	G2	34
Přerov, Czech.	F17	8
Prescott, Ont., Can.	C9	73
Prescott, Az., U.S.	C3	80
Prescott, Ar., U.S.	D2	81
Prescott, Wi., U.S.	D1	126
Presho, S.D., U.S.	D5	118
Presidencia Roca, Arg.	B5	56
Presidente Epitácio, Braz.	F2	57
Presidente Prudente, Braz.	G3	57
Presidential Range, mts., N.H., U.S.	B4	106
Presidio, Tx., U.S.	p12	120
Presidio, co., Tx., U.S.	o12	120
Presidio of San Francisco, mil., Ca., U.S.	h8	82
Prešov, Slov.	F21	8
Prespa, Lake, l., Eur.	I4	16
Presque Isle, Me., U.S.	B5	96
Presque Isle, co., Mi., U.S.	C6	99
Preston, Eng., U.K.	H10	7
Preston, Id., U.S.	G7	89
Preston, Ia., U.S.	B7	92
Preston, Mn., U.S.	G6	100
Preston, co., W.V., U.S.	B5	125
Preston Peak, mtn., Ca., U.S.	B2	82
Prestonsburg, Ky., U.S.	C7	94
Presumpscot, stm., Me., U.S.	g7	96
Pretoria, S. Afr.	G5	44
Prettyboy Reservoir, res., Md., U.S.	A4	97
Pretty Prairie, Ks., U.S.	E5	93
Préveza, Grc.	K4	16
Prewitt Reservoir, res., Co., U.S.	A7	83
Prey Vêng, Camb.	I8	34
Pribilof Islands, is., Ak., U.S.	D5	79
Příbram, Czech.	F14	8
Price, Ut., U.S.	D5	121
Price, co., Wi., U.S.	C3	126
Price, stm., Ut., U.S.	D5	121
Price Inlet, b., S.C., U.S.	k12	117
Prichard, Al., U.S.	E1	78
Priego, Spain	E9	12
Priego de Córdoba, Spain	H7	12
Prien, Ger.	H12	8
Prieska, S. Afr.	G4	44
Priest Lake, l., Id., U.S.	A2	89
Priest Rapids Dam, Wa., U.S.	C6	124
Priest Rapids Lake, res., Wa., U.S.	C6	124
Priest River, Id., U.S.	A2	89
Prievidza, Slov.	G18	8
Prijedor, Bos.	E11	14
Prilep, Mac.	H5	16
Prim, Point, c., P.E.I., Can.	C6	71
Primghar, Ia., U.S.	A2	92
Primrose, R.I., U.S.	B3	116
Primrose Lake, l., Can.	F11	66
Prince, Lake, res., Va., U.S.	k14	123
Prince Albert National Park, Sask., Can.	C2	75
Prince Albert Sound, strt., N.W. Ter., Can.	B9	66
Prince Charles Island, i., N.W. Ter., Can.	C17	66
Prince-de-Galles, Cap du, c., Que., Can.	D18	66
Prince Edward, co., Va., U.S.	C4	123
Prince Edward Island, prov., Can.	C6	71
Prince Edward Island National Park, P.E.I., Can.	C6	71
Prince Frederick, Md., U.S.	C4	97
Prince George, B.C., Can.	C6	69
Prince George, co., Va., U.S.	C5	123
Prince Georges, co., Md., U.S.	C4	97
Prince of Wales, Cape, c., Ak., U.S.	B6	79
Prince of Wales Island, i., Austl.	B8	50
Prince of Wales Island, i., N.W. Ter., Can.	B13	66
Prince of Wales Island, i., Ak., U.S.	n23	79
Prince of Wales Strait, strt., N.W. Ter., Can.	B9	66

Name / Map Ref / Page

rince Regent Inlet, b., N.W. Ter., Can. B14 66
ince Rupert, B.C., Can. B2 69
inces Lakes, In., U.S. F5 91
incess Anne, Md., U.S. D6 97
incess Royal Channel, strt., B.C., Can. C3 69
incess Royal Island, i., B.C., Can. C3 69
inceton, B.C., Can. E7 69
inceton, Fl., U.S. G6 86
inceton, Il., U.S. B4 90
inceton, In., U.S. H2 91
inceton, Ia., U.S. C7 92
inceton, Ky., U.S. C2 94
inceton, Me., U.S. C5 96
inceton, Mn., U.S. E5 100
inceton, Mo., U.S. A4 102
inceton, N.J., U.S. C3 107
inceton, N.C., U.S. B4 110
inceton, W.V., U.S. D3 125
inceton, Wi., U.S. E4 126
inceton, Mount, mtn., Co., U.S. C4 83
inceville, Que., Can. C6 74
inceville, Il., U.S. C4 90
inceville, N.C., U.S. B5 110
ince William, co., Va., U.S. B5 123
ince William Sound, strt., Ak., U.S. g18 79
incipe, i., S. Tom./P. A1 44
incipe Channel, strt., B.C., Can. C3 69
incipe da Beira, Braz. F6 54
ineville, Or., U.S. C6 114
ineville Reservoir, res., Or., U.S. C6 114
ingsewu, Indon. k12 33a
inzapolca, Nic. H6 64
ior Lake, Mn., U.S. F5 100
iština, Yugo. G5 16
itchards Island, i., S.C., U.S. G6 117
itzwalk, Ger. B12 8
ivas, Fr. H11 10
ivolžsk, Russia D24 18
obolinggo, Indon. m16 33a
octor, Mn., U.S. D6 100
octor, Vt., U.S. D2 122
octor Lake, res., Tx., U.S. C3 120
octorsville, Vt., U.S. E3 122
oddatūr, India E5 37
ofessor Dr. Ir. W.J. van Blommestein Meer, res., Sur. C7 54
ogreso, Mex. G15 62
okopjevsk, Russia G11 24
okuplje, Yugo. F5 16
omontory Mountains, mts., Ut., U.S. B3 121
ophetstown, Il., U.S. B4 90
opriá, Braz. F11 54
ospect, Ct., U.S. C4 84
ospect, Ky., U.S. g11 94
ospect, Oh., U.S. B2 112
ospect, Or., U.S. E4 114
ospect, Pa., U.S. E1 115
ospect Hill, mtn., Or., U.S. k11 114
ospect Park, N.J., U.S. B4 107
ospect Park, Pa., U.S. p20 115
osperity, S.C., U.S. C4 117
osperity, W.V., U.S. n13 125
osser, Wa., U.S. C6 124
ostějov, Czech. F17 8
otection, Ks., U.S. E4 93
otville, Tun. M5 14
ovence, hist. reg., Fr. I13 10
ovidence, Ky., U.S. C2 94
ovidence, R.I., U.S. C4 116
ovidence, Ut., U.S. B4 121
ovidence, co., R.I., U.S. C2 116
ovidence, stm., R.I., U.S. C5 116
ovidence Island, i., Sey. C10 44
ovidence Point, c., R.I., U.S. D5 116
ovidencia, Isla de, i., Col. H7 64
ovidenija, Russia E31 24
ovince Lake, l., N.H., U.S. C5 106
ovincetown, Ma., U.S. B7 98
ovins, Fr. D10 10
ovo, Ut., U.S. C4 121
ovo, stm., Ut., U.S. C4 121
ovost, Alta., Can. C5 68
owers, co., Co., U.S. D8 83
ozor, Bos. F12 14
udence Island, i., R.I., U.S. E5 116
udenville, Mi., U.S. D6 99
udhoe Bay, Ak., U.S. A10 79
udhoe Bay, b., Ak., U.S. A10 79
üm, Ger. E6 8
uszków, Pol. C20 8
ut, stm., Eur. D12 16
yor, Mt., U.S. E8 103
yor, Ok., U.S. A6 113
yor Mountains, mts., Mt., U.S. E8 103
zemyśl, Pol. F22 8
kov, Russia D11 18
olemais, Grc. I5 16
uj, Slo. C10 14
callpa, Peru E4 54
cheng, China H7 28
ckaway Lake, l., Wi., U.S. E4 126
dukkottai, India G5 37
ebla de Sanabria, Spain C5 12
ebla de Trives, Spain C4 12
ebla [de Zaragoza], Mex. H10 62
eblo, Co., U.S. C6 83
eblo, co., Co., U.S. C6 83
eblo Hundido, Chile B2 56
eblo Mountain, mtn., Or., U.S. E8 114
eblo Mountains, mts., Or., U.S. E8 114
eblo Reservoir, res., Co., U.S. C6 83
entedeume, Spain B3 12
ente-Genil, Spain H7 12
eo Point, c., Hi., U.S. B1 88
erco, stm., U.S. C6 80
erco, Rio, stm., N.M., U.S. B2 108
erto Aisén, Chile F2 56
erto Alfonso, Col. I7 58
Puerto Ángel, Mex. J11 62
Puerto Armuelles, Pan. J6 64
Puerto Asís, Col. G4 58
Puerto Ayacucho, Ven. E9 58
Puerto Barrios, Guat. G3 64
Puerto Berrío, Col. D5 58
Puerto Boyacá, Col. E5 58
Puerto Cabello, Ven. B8 58
Puerto Cabezas, Nic. G6 64
Puerto Carreño, Col. D9 58
Puerto Casado, Para. A5 56
Puerto Chicama, Peru E3 54
Puerto Cortés, C.R. J6 64
Puerto Cortés, Hond. G4 64
Puerto Cumarebo, Ven. B8 58
Puerto de Pollensa, Spain F15 12
Puerto de San José, Guat. H2 64
Puerto Deseado, Arg. F3 56
Puerto Escondido, Mex. J11 62
Puerto Francisco de Orellana, Ec. H4 58
Puerto Inírida, Col. F9 58
Puerto Juárez, Mex. G16 62
Puerto la Cruz, Ven. B10 58
Puerto Leguízamo, Col. H5 58
Puerto Limón, Col. F6 58
Puertollano, Spain G7 12
Puerto Lobos, Arg. E3 56
Puerto Madryn, Arg. E3 56
Puerto Maldonado, Peru F5 54
Puerto Montt, Chile E2 56
Puerto Morelos, Mex. G16 62
Puerto Nariño, Col. E9 58
Puerto Natales, Chile G2 56
Puerto Padre, Cuba D9 64
Puerto Peñasco, Mex. B3 62
Puerto Plata, Dom. Rep. E12 64
Puerto Princesa, Phil. D6 32
Puerto Real, Spain I5 12
Puerto Rico, dep., N.A. E14 64
Puerto Rondón, Col. D7 58
Puerto Suárez, Bol. G7 54
Puerto Tejada, Col. F4 58
Puerto Vallarta, Mex. G7 62
Puerto Wilches, Col. D6 58
Puget Sound, strt., Wa., U.S. B3 124
Puget Sound Naval Shipyard, mil., Wa., U.S. e10 124
Pugwash, N.S., Can. D6 71
Puhi, Hi., U.S. B2 88
Puigcerdá, Spain C13 12
Pukalani, Hi., U.S. C5 88
Pukaskwa National Park, Ont., Can. o18 73
Pukch'ŏng, N. Kor. C12 26
Pukë, Alb. G3 16
Pukeashun Mountain, mtn., B.C., Can. D8 69
Pukekohe, N.Z. B5 52
Pukou, China C7 28
Pula, Cro. E8 14
Pulacayo, Bol. H5 54
Pulaski, N.Y., U.S. B4 109
Pulaski, Tn., U.S. B4 119
Pulaski, Va., U.S. C2 123
Pulaski, Wi., U.S. D5 126
Pulaski, co., Ar., U.S. C3 81
Pulaski, co., Ga., U.S. D3 87
Pulaski, co., Il., U.S. F4 90
Pulaski, co., In., U.S. B4 91
Pulaski, co., Ky., U.S. C5 94
Pulaski, co., Mo., U.S. D5 102
Pulaski, co., Va., U.S. C2 123
Puli, Tai. L9 28
Puliyangudi, India H4 37
Pulkkila, Fin. D15 6
Pullman, Wa., U.S. C8 124
Pulog, Mount, mtn., Phil. B7 32
Pumphrey, Md., U.S. h11 97
Puná, Isla, i., Ec. I2 58
Punakha, Bhu. G13 38
Pūnch, India D6 38
Pune (Poona), India C2 37
Pungo Lake, l., N.C., U.S. B6 110
Punjab, state, India E6 38
Puno, Peru G4 54
Punta, Cerro de, mtn., P.R. E14 64
Punta Alta, Arg. D4 56
Punta Arenas, Chile G2 56
Punta Delgada, Arg. E4 56
Punta de Mata, Ven. C11 58
Punta Gorda, Belize F3 64
Punta Gorda, Nic. I6 64
Punta Gorda, Fl., U.S. F4 86
Puntarenas, C.R. J5 64
Punto Fijo, Ven. B7 58
Punxsutawney, Pa., U.S. E4 115
Puolanka, Fin. D16 6
Purcell, Ok., U.S. B4 113
Purcellville, Va., U.S. A5 123
Purdy, Mo., U.S. E4 102
Purgatoire, stm., Co., U.S. D7 83
Purgatoire Peak, mtn., Co., U.S. D5 83
Puri, India K11 38
Purli, India C4 37
Purnea, India H12 38
Purūlia, India I12 38
Purus (Purús), stm., S.A. D6 54
Purvis, Ms., U.S. D4 101
Purwakarta, Indon. m13 33a
Purwokerto, Indon. m14 32
Purworejo, Indon. m15 33a
Pusan, S. Kor. D12 26
Pushaw Lake, l., Me., U.S. D4 96
Pushmataha, co., Ok., U.S. C6 113
Puškin, Russia B13 18
Puškino, Russia E20 18
Putao, Burma F6 26
Putian, China J8 28
Puting, Tanjung, c., Indon. F5 32
Putnam, Ct., U.S. B8 84
Putnam, co., Fl., U.S. C5 86
Putnam, co., Ga., U.S. C3 87
Putnam, co., Il., U.S. B4 90
Putnam, co., In., U.S. E4 91
Putnam, co., Mo., U.S. A4 102
Putnam, co., N.Y., U.S. D7 109
Putnam, co., Oh., U.S. B1 112
Putnam, co., Tn., U.S. C8 119
Putnam, co., W.V., U.S. C3 125
Putney, Ga., U.S. E2 87
Putney, Vt., U.S. F3 122
Putorana, Plato, plat., Russia D12 24
Puttalam, Sri L. H5 37
Puttgarden, Ger. A11 8
Putumayo (Içá), stm., S.A. I7 58
Putuo, China F11 28
Puukohola Heiau National Historic Site, hist., Hi., U.S. D6 88
Puxico, Mo., U.S. E7 102
Puyallup, Wa., U.S. B3 124
Puyallup, stm., Wa., U.S. C3 124
Puy de Dôme, mtn., Fr. G9 10
Puy de Sancy, mtn., Fr. G9 10
Puylaurens, Fr. I9 10
Puyo, Ec. H4 58
Pweto, Zaire C5 44
Pwllheli, Wales, U.K. I8 7
Pyapon, Burma F3 34
Pyatigorsk see P'atigorsk, Russia I6 22
Pyè (Prome), Burma E3 34
Pyhäjoki, Fin. D15 6
Pyhäselkä, Fin. E17 6
Pyinmana, Burma E4 34
Pyles Fork, stm., W.V., U.S. h10 125
Pymatuning Reservoir, res., U.S. C1 115
P'yŏngyang, N. Kor. D12 26
Pyramid Lake, l., Nv., U.S. C2 105
Pyramid Lake Indian Reservation, Nv., U.S. D2 105
Pyramid Mountains, mts., N.M., U.S. E1 108
Pyramid Peak, mtn., N.M., U.S. E1 108
Pyramid Peak, mtn., Wy., U.S. C2 127
Pyrenees, mts., Eur. C12 12
Pyskowice, Pol. E18 8
Pyu, Burma E4 34

Q

Qaidam Pendi, China B16 38
Qalāt, Afg. D2 38
Qal'at Bīshah, Sau. Ar. E3 46
Qal'eh-ye Kānsī, Afg. C2 36
Qal'eh-ye Sarkārī, Afg. C2 38
Qallābāt, Sudan F13 42
Qamar, Ghubbat al-, b., Yemen E5 46
Qamdo, China E6 26
Qandahār, Afg. E1 38
Qandala, Som. F4 46
Qarqan, stm., China B11 38
Qarqīn, Afg. B2 38
Qaṣr al-Burayqah, Libya B9 42
Qaṣr al-Farāfirah, Egypt C11 42
Qaṭanā, Syria C5 40
Qatar, ctry., Asia C5 46
Qazvīn, Iran J8 22
Qeshm, i., Iran C6 46
Qeyṣār, Afg. C1 38
Qeẓi'ot, Isr. D4 40
Qiemo, China A11 38
Qijiang, China F8 26
Qinā, Egypt C12 42
Qingdao (Tsingtao), China D11 26
Qinghai, prov., China D6 26
Qinghai Hu, l., China D7 26
Qingjiang, China G4 28
Qinglong, China B8 34
Qingyang, China D8 26
Qingyuan, China G8 26
Qingyuan, China L2 28
Qinhuangdao, China D10 26
Qin Ling, mts., China E8 26
Qinzhou, China D10 34
Qiongzhou Haixia, strt., China D11 34
Qiqihar, China B11 26
Qiryat Shemona, Isr. C4 40
Qitai, China C4 26
Qīzān, Sau. Ar. E3 46
Qom, Iran B5 46
Qomsheh, Iran B5 46
Qondūz, Afg. B3 38
Qondūz, stm., Afg. C3 38
Quabbin Reservoir, res., Ma., U.S. B3 98
Quaddick Reservoir, res., Ct., U.S. B8 84
Quail Oaks, Va., U.S. n18 123
Quaker Hill, Ct., U.S. D7 84
Quakertown, Pa., U.S. F11 115
Qualicum Beach, B.C., Can. E5 69
Quanah, Tx., U.S. B3 120
Quang Ngai, Viet. G10 34
Quannapowitt, Lake, l., Ma., U.S. f11 98
Quantico, Va., U.S. B5 123
Quantico Marine Corps Air Station, mil., Va., U.S. B5 123
Quanzhou, China K7 28
Quapaw, Ok., U.S. A7 113
Qu'Appelle, Sask., Can. G4 75
Qu'Appelle, stm., Can. G4 75
Quarryville, Pa., U.S. G9 115
Quartu Sant'Elena, Italy J4 14
Quartz Lake, l., N.W. Ter., Can. B16 66
Quartz Mountain, mtn., Or., U.S. D4 114
Quartzsite, Az., U.S. D1 80
Quassapaug, Lake, l., Ct., U.S. C3 84
Quatsino Sound, strt., B.C., Can. D3 69
Quay, co., N.M., U.S. C6 108
Qūchān, Iran J9 22
Québec, Que., Can. C6 74
Quebec, prov., Can. C5 74
Quechee, Vt., U.S. D4 122
Quedlinburg, Ger. D11 8
Queen, stm., R.I., U.S. E3 116
Queen Annes, co., Md., U.S. B5 97
Queen Bess, Mount, mtn., B.C., Can. D5 69
Queen Charlotte, B.C., Can. C1 69
Queen Charlotte Islands, is., B.C., Can. C1 69
Queen Charlotte Mountains, mts., B.C., Can. C1 69
Queen Charlotte Sound, strt., B.C., Can. n17 69
Queen Charlotte Strait, strt., B.C., Can. D4 69
Queen City, Mo., U.S. A5 102
Queen City, Tx., U.S. C5 120
Queen Creek, Az., U.S. m9 80
Queen Maud Gulf, b., N.W. Ter., Can. C12 66
Queen Maud Land, reg., Ant. B14 47
Queens, co., N.Y., U.S. E7 109
Queens Channel, strt., N.W. Ter., Can. A13 66
Queensland, state, Austl. D8 50
Queenstown, N.Z. F2 52
Queenstown, S. Afr. H5 44
Quelimane, Moz. E7 44
Quemoy see Chinmen Tao, i., Tai. K7 28
Querétaro, Mex. G9 62
Querobabi, Mex. B4 62
Quesnel, B.C., Can. C6 69
Quesnel, stm., B.C., Can. C6 69
Quesnel Lake, l., B.C., Can. C7 69
Questa, N.M., U.S. A4 108
Questembert, Fr. E4 10
Quetico Provincial Park, Ont., Can. o17 73
Quetta, Pak. E2 38
Quevedo, Ec. H3 58
Quevedo, stm., Ec. H3 58
Quezaltenango, Guat. G2 64
Quezon City, Phil. q19 32
Qufu, China D10 26
Quibdó, Col. E4 58
Quiberon, Fr. E3 10
Quicksand Pond, l., R.I., U.S. E6 116
Quidnessett, R.I., U.S. E4 116
Quidnick, R.I., U.S. D3 116
Quidnick Reservoir, res., R.I., U.S. D2 116
Quilá, Mex. E6 62
Quilcene, Wa., U.S. B3 124
Quileute Indian Reservation, Wa., U.S. B1 124
Quillan, Fr. J9 10
Quilon, India H4 37
Quilpie, Austl. E8 50
Quimilí, Arg. B4 56
Quimper, Fr. D2 10
Quimperlé, Fr. E3 10
Quinault, stm., Wa., U.S. B1 124
Quinault, Lake, l., Wa., U.S. B2 124
Quinault Indian Reservation, Wa., U.S. B1 124
Quincemil, Peru F4 54
Quincy, Ca., U.S. C3 82
Quincy, Fl., U.S. B2 86
Quincy, Il., U.S. D2 90
Quincy, Ma., U.S. B5 98
Quincy, Mi., U.S. G6 99
Quincy, Wa., U.S. B6 124
Quincy Bay, b., Ma., U.S. g12 98
Quinebaug, Ct., U.S. A8 84
Quinebaug, stm., Ct., U.S. C8 84
Quinhagak, Ak., U.S. D7 79
Qui Nhon, Viet. H10 34
Quinlan, Tx., U.S. C4 120
Quinn, stm., Nv., U.S. B3 105
Quinn Canyon Range, mts., Nv., U.S. F6 105
Quinnesec, Mi., U.S. C3 99
Quinnipiac, stm., Ct., U.S. D4 84
Quintanar de la Orden, Spain F8 12
Quinter, Ks., U.S. C3 93
Quinton, Ok., U.S. B6 113
Quiroga, Spain C4 12
Quitman, Ar., U.S. B3 81
Quitman, Ga., U.S. F3 87
Quitman, Ms., U.S. C5 101
Quitman, Tx., U.S. C5 120
Quitman, co., Ga., U.S. E1 87
Quitman, co., Ms., U.S. A3 101
Quito, Ec. H3 58
Quixadá, Braz. D11 54
Qujing, China B7 34
Qumalai (Sewugou), China C16 38
Quoich, stm., N.W. Ter., Can. D14 66
Quonnipaug Lake, l., Ct., U.S. D5 84
Quonochontaug, R.I., U.S. G2 116
Quonochontaug Pond, l., R.I., U.S. G2 116
Quonset Point, c., R.I., U.S. E4 116
Qutdligssat, Grnld. B22 66
Quthing, Leso. H5 44
Quxian, China G7 28

R

Raalte, Neth. C6 8
Rab, Cro. E9 14
Raba, Indon. G6 32
Rába (Raab), stm., Eur. H17 8
Rábade, Spain B4 12
Rabat (Victoria), Malta M9 14
Rabat, Mor. B4 42
Rabaul, Pap. N. Gui. k17 50a
Rabbit Creek, stm., S.D., U.S. B3 118
Rabbit Ears Pass, Co., U.S. A4 83
Rābigh, Sau. Ar. D2 46
Rabun, co., Ga., U.S. B3 87
Rabun Bald, mtn., Ga., U.S. B3 87
Raccoon Creek, stm., Oh., U.S. D3 112
Raccourci Island, i., La., U.S. D4 95
Race, Cape, c., Newf., Can. E5 72
Raceland, Ky., U.S. B7 94
Raceland, La., U.S. E5 95
Race Point, c., Ma., U.S. B7 98
Rach Gia, Viet. I8 34
Racibórz (Ratibor), Pol. E18 8
Racine, W.V., U.S. C3 125
Racine, Wi., U.S. F6 126
Racine, co., Wi., U.S. F5 126
Racine Dam, U.S. C3 125
Radcliff, Ky., U.S. C4 94
Radeberg, Ger. D13 8
Radebeul, Ger. D13 8
Radeče, Slo. C10 14
Radford, Va., U.S. C2 123
Radolfzell, Ger. H8 8
Radom, Pol. D21 8
Radomsko, Pol. D19 8
Rae, N.W. Ter., Can. D9 66
Rāe Bareli, India G9 38
Raeford, N.C., U.S. C3 110
Rae Isthmus, N.W. Ter., Can. C15 66
Rae Strait, strt., N.W. Ter., Can. C13 66
Raetihi, N.Z. C5 52
Rafaela, Arg. C4 56
Rafaḥ, Isr. Occ. D4 40
Rafḥā', Sau. Ar. C3 46
Rafsanjān, Iran K9 22
Rafsanjān, Iran B6 46
Raft, stm., Id., U.S. G5 89
Raft River Mountains, mts., Ut., U.S. B2 121
Raga, Sudan G11 42
Ragged Island, i., Me., U.S. E4 96
Ragged Lake, l., Me., U.S. C3 96
Ragged Top Mountain, mtn., Wy., U.S. E7 127
Ragland, Al., U.S. B3 78
Ragusa, Italy M9 14
Ragusa see Dubrovnik, Cro. G13 14
Raḥīmyār Khān, Pak. F4 38
Rahway, N.J., U.S. B4 107
Rahway, stm., N.J., U.S. k7 107
Rāichūr, India D4 37
Raigarh, India B7 37
Railroad Valley, val., Nv., U.S. E6 105
Rainbow Bridge National Monument, Ut., U.S. F5 121
Rainbow Falls, wtfl, Tn., U.S. D10 119
Rainbow Flowage, res., Wi., U.S. C4 126
Rainbow Lake, l., Me., U.S. C3 96
Rainelle, W.V., U.S. D4 125
Rainier, Or., U.S. A4 114
Rainier, Wa., U.S. C3 124
Rainier, Mount, mtn., Wa., U.S. C4 124
Rains, co., Tx., U.S. C5 120
Rainsville, Al., U.S. A4 78
Rainy Lake, l., N.A. G14 66
Rainy Lake, l., Mn., U.S. B5 100
Rainy River, Ont., Can. o16 73
Raipur, India B6 37
Rājahmundry, India D6 37
Raja-Jooseppi, Fin. B17 6
Rājapālaiyam, India H4 37
Rājasthān, prov., India G5 38
Rājasthān Canal, India F5 38
Rajčichinsk, Russia H19 24
Rājkot, India I4 38
Rāj-Nāndgaon, India B6 37
Rājpīpla, India J5 38
Rājshāhi, Bngl. H13 38
Rakaposhi, mtn., Pak. B6 38
Rakata, Pulau, i., Indon. m12 33a
Råkvåg, Nor. E8 6
Raleigh, Ms., U.S. C4 101
Raleigh, N.C., U.S. B4 110
Raleigh, W.V., U.S. n13 125
Raleigh, co., W.V., U.S. D3 125
Raleigh Bay, b., N.C., U.S. C6 110
Ralls, Tx., U.S. C2 120
Ralls, co., Mo., U.S. B6 102
Ralston, Ne., U.S. g12 104
Ralston Valley, val., Nv., U.S. E4 105
Rama, Nic. H5 64
Ramah, N.M., U.S. B1 108
Ramah Indian Reservation, N.M., U.S. C1 108
Rām Allāh, Jord. D4 40
Ramapo, stm., N.J., U.S. A4 107
Ramblewood, N.J., U.S. D3 107
Rambouillet, Fr. D8 10
Ramea, Newf., Can. E3 72
Ramenskoje, Russia F21 18
Rāmeswaram, India H5 37
Rāmgarh, Bngl. I14 38
Ramla, Isr. D4 40
Ramlo, mtn., Erit. F3 46
Ramona, Ca., U.S. F5 82
Rampart Range, mts., Co., U.S. B5 83
Rāmpur, India F8 38
Ramree Island, i., Burma E2 34
Ramsay, Mi., U.S. n12 99
Ramseur, N.C., U.S. B3 110
Ramsey, I. of Man G8 7
Ramsey, Il., U.S. D4 90
Ramsey, Mn., U.S. *E5 100
Ramsey, N.J., U.S. A4 107
Ramsey, co., Mn., U.S. E5 100
Ramsey, co., N.D., U.S. A7 111
Ramsgate, Eng., U.K. J14 7
Ramshorn Peak, mtn., Mt., U.S. E5 103
Ramshorn Peak, mtn., Wy., U.S. C3 127
Rāmu, Bngl. J15 38
Ramu, stm., Pap. N. Gui. m16 50a
Rancagua, Chile C2 56
Rancharia, Braz. G3 57
Rancheria Rock, mtn., Or., U.S. C6 114
Ranchester, Wy., U.S. B5 127
Rānchī, India I11 38
Rancho Palos Verdes, Ca., U.S. *n12 82
Ranchos de Taos, N.M., U.S. A4 108
Rancocas Creek, stm., N.J., U.S. C3 107
Rand, W.V., U.S. C3 125
Randall, co., Tx., U.S. B2 120
Randallstown, Md., U.S. B4 97
Randazzo, Italy L9 14
Randers, Den. H8 6
Randle, Wa., U.S. C4 124
Randleman, N.C., U.S. B3 110
Randolph, Me., U.S. D3 96
Randolph, Ma., U.S. B5 98
Randolph, Ne., U.S. B8 104
Randolph, Vt., U.S. D3 122
Randolph, Wi., U.S. E5 126
Randolph, co., Al., U.S. B4 78
Randolph, co., Ar., U.S. A4 81
Randolph, co., Ga., U.S. E2 87
Randolph, co., Il., U.S. E4 90
Randolph, co., In., U.S. D7 91

Name	Map Ref	Page
Randolph, co., Mo., U.S.	B5	102
Randolph, co., N.C., U.S.	B3	110
Randolph, co., W.V., U.S.	C5	125
Randolph Air Force Base, mil., Tx., U.S.	h7	120
Randolph Hills, Md., U.S.	B3	97
Random Island, i., Newf., Can.	D5	72
Random Lake, Wi., U.S.	E6	126
Rangeley, Me., U.S.	D2	96
Rangeley Lake, l., Me., U.S.	D2	96
Rangely, Co., U.S.	A2	83
Ranger, Tx., U.S.	C3	120
Ranger Lake, l., N.M., U.S.	D6	108
Rangoon see Yangon, Burma	B2	32
Rangpur, Bngl.	H13	38
Rankin, Pa., U.S.	k14	115
Rankin, co., Ms., U.S.	C4	101
Rankin Inlet, N.W. Ter., Can.	D14	66
Rann of Kutch, pl., Asia	H3	38
Ransom, co., N.D., U.S.	C8	111
Ranson, W.V., U.S.	B7	125
Rantauprapat, Indon.	E2	32
Rantekombola, Bulu, mtn., Indon.	F7	32
Rantoul, Il., U.S.	C5	90
Raoping, China	L6	28
Raoul, Ga., U.S.	B3	87
Rapallo, Italy	E4	14
Rapid, stm., Mn., U.S.	B4	100
Rapid City, S.D., U.S.	C2	118
Rapides, co., La., U.S.	C3	95
Rapid River, Mi., U.S.	C4	99
Rapids City, Il., U.S.	B3	90
Rappahannock, co., Va., U.S.	B4	123
Rappahannock, stm., Va., U.S.	B5	123
Raquette, stm., N.Y., U.S.	f10	109
Raquette Lake, l., N.Y., U.S.	B6	109
Raritan, N.J., U.S.	B3	107
Raritan, stm., N.J., U.S.	C4	107
Raritan Bay, b., N.J., U.S.	C4	107
Ra's al-'Ayn, Syria	A7	40
Ra's an-Naqb, Jord.	D4	40
Ras Dashen, mtn., Eth.	F2	46
Ras Djebel, Tun.	L5	14
Rasht, Iran	J7	22
Rāsipuram, India	G5	37
Rasskazovo, Russia	I24	18
Rastatt, Ger.	G8	8
Ratangarh, India	F6	38
Rätansbyn, Swe.	E10	6
Rathbun Lake, res., Ia., U.S.	D5	92
Rathdrum, Id., U.S.	B2	89
Rathenow, Ger.	C12	8
Rathkeale, Ire.	I4	7
Rathlin Island, i., N. Ire., U.K.	F6	7
Rat Islands, is., Ak., U.S.	E3	79
Ratlām, India	I6	38
Ratnāgiri, India	D2	37
Ratnapura, Sri L.	I6	37
Raton, N.M., U.S.	A5	108
Raton Pass, N.M., U.S.	A5	108
Rattlesnake Creek, stm., Oh., U.S.	C2	112
Rattlesnake Creek, stm., Wa., U.S.	C6	124
Rättvik, Swe.	F10	6
Ratz, Mount, mtn., B.C., Can.	E6	66
Ratzeburg, Ger.	B10	8
Raub, Malay.	M6	34
Rauch, Arg.	D5	56
Rauma, Fin.	F13	6
Raurkela, India	I11	38
Ravalli, co., Mt., U.S.	D2	103
Raven, Va., U.S.	e10	123
Ravena, N.Y., U.S.	C7	109
Ravenel, S.C., U.S.	k11	117
Ravenna, Italy	E7	14
Ravenna, Ky., U.S.	C6	94
Ravenna, Mi., U.S.	E5	99
Ravenna, Ne., U.S.	C7	104
Ravenna, Oh., U.S.	A4	112
Raven Park, reg., Co., U.S.	A2	83
Ravensburg, Ger.	H9	8
Ravenshoe, Austl.	C9	50
Ravensthorpe, Austl.	F3	50
Ravenswood, W.V., U.S.	C3	125
Rāwalpindi, Pak.	D5	38
Rawdon, Que., Can.	C4	74
Rawhide Creek, stm., Wy., U.S.	D8	127
Rawlings, Md., U.S.	k13	97
Rawlinna, Austl.	F5	50
Rawlins, Wy., U.S.	E5	127
Rawlins, co., Ks., U.S.	C2	93
Rawson, Arg.	E3	56
Ray, N.D., U.S.	A2	111
Ray, co., Mo., U.S.	B3	102
Ray, Cape, c., Newf., Can.	E2	72
Raya, Bukit, mtn., Indon.	F5	32
Rāyadrug, India	E4	37
Ray City, Ga., U.S.	E3	87
Raymond, Alta., Can.	E4	68
Raymond, Il., U.S.	D4	90
Raymond, Mn., U.S.	E3	100
Raymond, Ms., U.S.	C3	101
Raymond, N.H., U.S.	D4	106
Raymond, Wa., U.S.	C2	124
Raymondville, Tx., U.S.	F4	120
Raymore, Sask., Can.	F3	75
Raymore, Mo., U.S.	C3	102
Rayne, La., U.S.	D3	95
Raynham, Ma., U.S.	C5	98
Raynham Center, Ma., U.S.	C5	98
Raytown, Mo., U.S.	h11	102
Rayville, La., U.S.	B4	95
R'azan', Russia	G22	18
Razgrad, Bul.	F10	16
R'ažsk, Russia	H23	18
Reader, W.V., U.S.	B4	125
Reading, Eng., U.K.	J12	7
Reading, Ma., U.S.	A5	98
Reading, Mi., U.S.	G6	99
Reading, Oh., U.S.	C1	112
Reading, Pa., U.S.	F10	115
Readlyn, Ia., U.S.	B5	92
Reagan, co., Tx., U.S.	D2	120
Real, co., Tx., U.S.	E3	120
Realicó, Arg.	D4	56
Réalmont, Fr.	I9	10
Reamstown, Pa., U.S.	F9	115
Recanati, Italy	F8	14
Recherche, Archipelago of the, is., Austl.	F4	50
Rečica, Bela.	I13	18
Recife, Braz.	E12	54
Recklinghausen, Ger.	D7	8
Recreo, Arg.	B3	56
Rector, Ar., U.S.	A5	81
Red (Hong) (Yuan), stm., Asia	C8	34
Red, stm., N.A.	B7	76
Red, stm., U.S.	E8	76
Red, stm., Ky., U.S.	C6	94
Red, stm., Tn., U.S.	A4	119
Red Bank, N.J., U.S.	C4	107
Red Bank, Tn., U.S.	D8	119
Red Bay, Al., U.S.	A1	78
Redberry Lake, l., Sask., Can.	E2	75
Redbird, Oh., U.S.	A4	112
Red Bird, stm., Ky., U.S.	C6	94
Red Bluff, Ca., U.S.	B2	82
Red Bluff Lake, res., U.S.	o12	120
Red Boiling Springs, Tn., U.S.	C8	119
Red Bud, Il., U.S.	E4	90
Red Butte, mtn., Ut., U.S.	B2	121
Red Cedar, stm., Wi., U.S.	C2	126
Red Cedar Lake, l., Wi., U.S.	C2	126
Redcliff, Alta., Can.	D5	68
Redcliffe, Mount, mtn., Austl.	E4	50
Red Cliff Indian Reservation, Wi., U.S.	B2	126
Red Cloud, Ne., U.S.	D7	104
Redcloud Peak, mtn., Co., U.S.	D3	83
Red Deer, Alta., Can.	C4	68
Red Deer, stm., Can.	D4	68
Red Deer, stm., Can.	E4	75
Redding, Ca., U.S.	B2	82
Redding, Ct., U.S.	D2	84
Redeye, stm., Mn., U.S.	D3	100
Redfield, Ar., U.S.	C3	81
Redfield, Ia., U.S.	C3	92
Redfield, S.D., U.S.	C7	118
Redford, Mi., U.S.	F7	99
Redgranite, Wi., U.S.	D4	126
Red Hook, N.Y., U.S.	C7	109
Red Indian Lake, l., Newf., Can.	D3	72
Red Jacket, W.V., U.S.	D2	125
Redkey, In., U.S.	D7	91
Redlake, Mn., U.S.	C3	100
Red Lake, co., Mn., U.S.	C2	100
Red Lake, l., Az., U.S.	B1	80
Red Lake, stm., Mn., U.S.	C2	100
Red Lake Falls, Mn., U.S.	C2	100
Red Lake Indian Reservation, Mn., U.S.	B3	100
Redlands, Ca., U.S.	E5	82
Red Lion, Pa., U.S.	G8	115
Red Lodge, Mt., U.S.	E7	103
Red Mill Pond, l., De., U.S.	E5	85
Redmond, Or., U.S.	C5	114
Redmond, Ut., U.S.	E4	121
Redmond, Wa., U.S.	e11	124
Red Mountain, mtn., Ca., U.S.	B2	82
Red Mountain, mtn., Mt., U.S.	C4	103
Red Mountain Pass, Co., U.S.	D3	83
Red Oak, Ga., U.S.	h7	87
Red Oak, Ia., U.S.	D2	92
Red Oak, Ok., U.S.	C6	113
Red Oak, Tx., U.S.	n10	120
Red Oaks, La., U.S.	h9	95
Redon, Fr.	E4	10
Redondela, Spain	C3	12
Redondo, Port.	G4	12
Redondo, Wa., U.S.	f11	124
Redondo Beach, Ca., U.S.	n12	82
Redoubt Volcano, vol., Ak., U.S.	g15	79
Red Peak, mtn., Co., U.S.	B4	83
Red River, co., La., U.S.	B2	95
Red River, co., Tx., U.S.	C5	120
Red Rock, stm., Mt., U.S.	F4	103
Red Rock, Lake, res., Ia., U.S.	C4	92
Red Sea	D2	46
Red Springs, N.C., U.S.	C3	110
Red Table Mountain, mts., Co., U.S.	B4	83
Redwater, Alta., Can.	C4	68
Redwater, stm., Mt., U.S.	C11	103
Red Willow, co., Ne., U.S.	D5	104
Redwillow, stm., Can.	B7	69
Red Wing, Mn., U.S.	F6	100
Redwood, co., Mn., U.S.	F3	100
Redwood, stm., Mn., U.S.	F3	100
Redwood City, Ca., U.S.	D2	82
Redwood Falls, Mn., U.S.	F3	100
Redwood National Park, Ca., U.S.	B2	82
Redwood Valley, Ca., U.S.	C2	82
Ree, Lough, l., Ire.	H4	7
Reed City, Mi., U.S.	E5	99
Reedley, Ca., U.S.	D4	82
Reedsburg, Wi., U.S.	E3	126
Reeds Peak, mtn., N.M., U.S.	D2	108
Reedsport, Or., U.S.	D2	114
Reedsville, Pa., U.S.	E6	115
Reedsville, Wi., U.S.	D6	126
Reedy, stm., S.C., U.S.	C3	117
Reedy Lake, l., Fl., U.S.	E5	86
Reelfoot Lake, l., Tn., U.S.	A2	119
Reese, Mi., U.S.	E7	99
Reese, stm., Nv., U.S.	C4	105
Reese Air Force Base, mil., Tx., U.S.	C1	120
Reeves, co., Tx., U.S.	o13	120
Reform, Al., U.S.	B1	78
Refugio, Tx., U.S.	E4	120
Refugio, co., Tx., U.S.	E4	120
Regen, Ger.	G13	8
Regencia, Braz.	E9	57
Regensburg, Ger.	F12	8
Reggane, Alg.	C6	42
Reggio di Calabria, Italy	K10	14
Reggio nell'Emilia, Italy	E5	14
Regina, Sask., Can.	G3	75
Regina Beach, Sask., Can.	G3	75
Rehoboth, Nmb.	E3	44
Rehoboth Bay, b., De., U.S.	F5	85
Rehoboth Beach, De., U.S.	F5	85
Reḥovot, Isr.	D4	40
Reichenbach, Ger.	E12	8
Reid, Mount, mtn., Ak., U.S.	n24	79
Reidland, Ky., U.S.	e9	94
Reidsville, Ga., U.S.	D4	87
Reidsville, N.C., U.S.	A3	110
Reims, Fr.	C11	10
Reina Adelaida, Archipiélago, is., Chile	G2	56
Reinbeck, Ia., U.S.	B5	92
Reindeer Island, i., Man., Can.	C3	70
Reindeer Lake, l., Can.	m8	75
Reinosa, Spain	B7	12
Reisterstown, Md., U.S.	B4	97
Reliance, Wy., U.S.	E3	127
Remada, Tun.	B8	42
Remanso, Braz.	E10	54
Rembang, Indon.	m15	33a
Remington, In., U.S.	C3	91
Remiremont, Fr.	D13	10
Remmel Dam, Ar., U.S.	g8	81
Remscheid, Ger.	D7	8
Remsen, Ia., U.S.	B2	92
Rend Lake, res., Il., U.S.	E5	90
Rendova, i., Sol.Is.	A11	50
Rendsburg, Ger.	A9	8
Renforth, N.B., Can.	D4	71
Renfrew, Ont., Can.	B8	73
Rengat, Indon.	O7	34
Rennell Island, i., Sol.Is.	B12	50
Rennes, Fr.	D5	10
Reno, Nv., U.S.	D2	105
Reno, co., Ks., U.S.	E5	93
Reno, Lake, l., Mn., U.S.	E3	100
Reno Hill, mtn., Wy., U.S.	D6	127
Renovo, Pa., U.S.	D6	115
Rensselaer, In., U.S.	C3	91
Rensselaer, N.Y., U.S.	C7	109
Rensselaer, co., N.Y., U.S.	C7	109
Renton, Wa., U.S.	B3	124
Renville, Mn., U.S.	F3	100
Renville, co., Mn., U.S.	F4	100
Renville, co., N.D., U.S.	A4	111
Reo, Indon.	G7	32
Repentigny, Que., Can.	D4	74
Republic, Mi., U.S.	B3	99
Republic, Mo., U.S.	D4	102
Republic, Pa., U.S.	G2	115
Republic, Wa., U.S.	A7	124
Republic, co., Ks., U.S.	C6	93
Republican, stm., U.S.	C6	93
Repulse Bay, N.W. Ter., Can.	C15	66
Repvåg, Nor.	A15	6
Réquista, Fr.	H9	10
Reschenpass, Eur.	C5	14
Reserve, La., U.S.	h10	95
Resistencia, Arg.	B5	56
Reşiţa, Rom.	D5	16
Resolute, N.W. Ter., Can.	B14	66
Resolution Island, i., N.W. Ter., Can.	D20	66
Reston, Man., Can.	E1	70
Reston, Va., U.S.	B5	123
Resülhınzır, c., Tur.	A4	40
Retalhuleu, Guat.	G2	64
Rethel, Fr.	C11	10
Réthimnon, Grc.	N8	16
Reunion (Réunion), dep., Afr.	F11	44
Reus, Spain	D13	12
Reutlingen, Ger.	G9	8
Revelo, Ky., U.S.	D5	94
Revelstoke, B.C., Can.	D8	69
Revelstoke, Lake, res., B.C., Can.	D8	69
Revere, Ma., U.S.	g11	98
Revillagigedo, Islas de, is., Mex.	H4	62
Revillagigedo Island, i., Ak., U.S.	n24	79
Revin, Fr.	C11	10
Rewa, India	H9	38
Rewāri, India	F7	38
Rex, Ga., U.S.	h8	87
Rexburg, Id., U.S.	F7	89
Rexton, N.B., Can.	C5	71
Rey, Iran	J8	22
Rey, Isla del, i., Pan.	J8	64
Reyes, Bol.	F5	54
Reyes, Point, c., Ca., U.S.	C2	82
Reyhanlı, Tur.	A5	40
Reykjavík, Ice.	C3	4
Reynolds, Ga., U.S.	D2	87
Reynolds, co., Mo., U.S.	D6	102
Reynoldsburg, Oh., U.S.	C3	112
Reynoldsville, Pa., U.S.	D4	115
Reynosa, Mex.	D10	62
Rēzekne, Lat.	E10	18
Rhaetian Alps, mts., Eur.	F16	10
Rhea, co., Tn., U.S.	D9	119
Rheine, Ger.	C7	8
Rheydt, Ger.	D6	8
Rhine (Rhein) (Rhin), stm., Eur.	D6	8
Rhinebeck, N.Y., U.S.	D7	109
Rhinelander, Wi., U.S.	C4	126
Rho, Italy	D4	14
Rhode Island, state, U.S.	D3	116
Rhode Island, i., R.I., U.S.	E5	116
Rhode Island Sound, strt., U.S.	F5	116
Rhodesia see Zimbabwe, ctry., Afr.	E5	44
Rhodes Peak, mtn., Id., U.S.	C4	89
Rhodes see Ródhos, Grc.	M12	16
Rhodope Mountains, mts., Eur.	H8	16
Rhondda, Wales, U.K.	J9	7
Rhône, stm., Eur.	H11	10
Rialto, Ca., U.S.	m14	82
Riau, Kepulauan, is., Indon.	N8	34
Riaza, Spain	D8	12
Ribadeo, Spain	B4	12
Ribadesella, Spain	B6	12
Ribeirão Prêto, Braz.	F5	57
Ribera, Italy	L8	14
Riberalta, Bol.	F5	54
Rib Lake, Wi., U.S.	C3	126
Ribnitz-Damgarten, Ger.	A12	8
Riccione, Italy	F7	14
Rice, Mn., U.S.	E4	100
Rice, co., Ks., U.S.	D5	93
Rice, co., Mn., U.S.	F5	100
Riceboro, Ga., U.S.	E5	87
Rice Lake, Wi., U.S.	C2	126
Rice Lake, l., Ont., Can.	C6	73
Rice Lake, l., Mn., U.S.	D5	100
Riceville, Ia., U.S.	A5	92
Rich, co., Ut., U.S.	B4	121
Rich, Cape, c., Ont., Can.	C4	73
Richards-Gebaur Air Force Base, mil., Mo., U.S.	C3	102
Richards Island, i., N.W. Ter., Can.	C6	66
Richardson, Tx., U.S.	n10	120
Richardson, co., Ne., U.S.	D10	104
Richardson Lakes, l., Me., U.S.	D2	96
Richardson Mountains, mts., Can.	C5	66
Richardton, N.D., U.S.	C3	111
Rich Creek, Va., U.S.	C2	123
Riche, Pointe, c., Newf., Can.	C3	72
Richfield, Mn., U.S.	F5	100
Richfield, Ut., U.S.	E3	121
Richford, Vt., U.S.	B3	122
Rich Hill, Mo., U.S.	C3	102
Richibucto, N.B., Can.	C5	71
Richland, Ga., U.S.	D2	87
Richland, Mo., U.S.	D5	102
Richland, Wa., U.S.	C6	124
Richland, co., Il., U.S.	E5	90
Richland, co., La., U.S.	B4	95
Richland, co., Mt., U.S.	C12	103
Richland, co., N.D., U.S.	C8	111
Richland, co., Oh., U.S.	B3	112
Richland, co., S.C., U.S.	D6	117
Richland, co., Wi., U.S.	E3	126
Richland Balsam, mtn., N.C., U.S.	f10	110
Richland Center, Wi., U.S.	E3	126
Richland Creek, stm., Tn., U.S.	B5	119
Richlands, N.C., U.S.	C5	110
Richlands, Va., U.S.	e10	123
Richlandtown, Pa., U.S.	F11	115
Richmond, Austl.	D8	50
Richmond, B.C., Can.	E6	69
Richmond, Que., Can.	D5	74
Richmond, Ca., U.S.	D2	82
Richmond, Il., U.S.	A5	90
Richmond, In., U.S.	E8	91
Richmond, Ky., U.S.	C5	94
Richmond, Me., U.S.	D3	96
Richmond, Mi., U.S.	F8	99
Richmond, Mn., U.S.	E4	100
Richmond, Mo., U.S.	B4	102
Richmond, Tx., U.S.	E5	120
Richmond, Ut., U.S.	B4	121
Richmond, Vt., U.S.	C3	122
Richmond, Va., U.S.	C5	123
Richmond, co., Ga., U.S.	C4	87
Richmond, co., N.Y., U.S.	E6	109
Richmond, co., N.C., U.S.	B3	110
Richmond, co., Va., U.S.	C6	123
Richmond Beach, Wa., U.S.	B3	124
Richmond Heights, Fl., U.S.	s13	86
Richmond Heights, Mo., U.S.	f13	102
Richmond Highlands, Wa., U.S.	B3	124
Richmond Hill, Ont., Can.	D5	73
Richmond Hill, Ga., U.S.	E5	87
Richmond National Battlefield Park, Va., U.S.	n18	123
Rich Square, N.C., U.S.	A5	110
Richthofen, Mount, mtn., Co., U.S.	A5	83
Richton, Ms., U.S.	D5	101
Richwood, Oh., U.S.	B2	112
Richwood, W.V., U.S.	C4	125
Rickenbacker Air Force Base, mil., Oh., U.S.	m11	112
Rickman, Tn., U.S.	C8	119
Riddle, Or., U.S.	E3	114
Riddle Mountain, mtn., Or., U.S.	D8	114
Rideau, stm., Ont., Can.	B9	73
Ridgecrest, Ca., U.S.	E5	82
Ridge Farm, Il., U.S.	D6	90
Ridgefield, Ct., U.S.	D2	84
Ridgefield, N.J., U.S.	h8	107
Ridgefield, Wa., U.S.	D3	124
Ridgefield Park, N.J., U.S.	B4	107
Ridgeland, Ms., U.S.	C3	101
Ridgeland, S.C., U.S.	G6	117
Ridgeley, W.V., U.S.	B6	125
Ridgely, Md., U.S.	C6	97
Ridgely, Tn., U.S.	A2	119
Ridge Spring, S.C., U.S.	D4	117
Ridgetop, Tn., U.S.	A5	119
Ridgetown, Ont., Can.	E3	73
Ridgeview, W.V., U.S.	C3	125
Ridgeville, In., U.S.	D7	91
Ridgeville, S.C., U.S.	E7	117
Ridgeway, Va., U.S.	D3	123
Ridgewood, N.J., U.S.	B4	107
Ridgway, Il., U.S.	F5	90
Ridgway, Pa., U.S.	D4	115
Riding Mountain National Park, Man., Can.	D1	70
Ridley Park, Pa., U.S.	p20	115
Ried im Innkreis, Aus.	G13	8
Riesa, Ger.	D13	8
Riesi, Italy	L9	14
Rieti, Italy	G7	14
Rif, mts., Mor.	A5	42
Riffe Lake, res., Wa., U.S.	C3	124
Rifle, Co., U.S.	B3	83
Rifle, stm., Mi., U.S.	D6	99
Rift Valley, val., Afr.	B5	44
Rīga, Lat.	E7	18
Riga, Gulf of, b., Eur.	D6	18
Rigaud, Que., Can.	D3	74
Rigby, Id., U.S.	F7	89
Rīgestān, reg., Afg.	C1	36
Riihimäki, Fin.	F15	6
Rijeka, Cro.	D9	14
Riley, Ks., U.S.	C7	93
Riley, co., Ks., U.S.	C7	93
Riley, Mount, mtn., N.M., U.S.	F2	108
Rimbey, Alta., Can.	C3	68
Rimersburg, Pa., U.S.	D3	115
Rimini, Italy	E7	14
Rimouski, Que., Can.	A9	74
Rimouski, stm., Que., Can.	A9	74
Rimouski-Est, Que., Can.	A9	74
Rimrock Lake, res., Wa., U.S.	C4	124
Rincon, Ga., U.S.	D5	87
Rincon Mountains, mts., Az., U.S.	E5	80
Rindal, Nor.	E7	6
Ringebu, Nor.	F8	6
Ringgold, Ga., U.S.	B1	87
Ringgold, La., U.S.	B2	95
Ringgold, co., Ia., U.S.	D3	92
Ringling, Ok., U.S.	C4	113
Ringwood, N.J., U.S.	A4	107
Rio, Fl., U.S.	E6	86
Rio, Wi., U.S.	E4	126
Rio Arriba, co., N.M., U.S.	A2	108
Riobamba, Ec.	H3	58
Río Benito, Eq. Gui.	H7	42
Rio Blanco, co., Co., U.S.	B2	83
Rio Branco, Braz.	E5	54
Rio Claro, Braz.	G5	57
Río Colorado, Arg.	D4	56
Río Cuarto, Arg.	C4	56
Rio de Janeiro, Braz.	G7	57
Rio Dell, Ca., U.S.	B1	82
Rio do Sul, Braz.	B7	56
Río Gallegos, Arg.	G3	56
Río Grande, Arg.	G3	56
Rio Grande, Braz.	C6	56
Río Grande, Mex.	F8	62
Río Grande, Nic.	H6	64
Rio Grande, Oh., U.S.	D3	112
Rio Grande, co., Co., U.S.	D4	83
Rio Grande City, Tx., U.S.	F3	120
Rio Grande Reservoir, res., Co., U.S.	D3	83
Ríohacha, Col.	B6	58
Rio Hondo, Tx., U.S.	F4	120
Rioja, Peru	E3	54
Riom, Fr.	G10	10
Río Mayo, Arg.	F2	56
Río Negro, Embalse del, res., Ur.	C5	56
Rio Negro, Pantanal do, sw., Braz.	G7	54
Rionero in Vulture, Italy	I10	14
Rio Pardo, Braz.	B6	56
Rio Pardo de Minas, Braz.	G10	54
Rio Rancho, N.M., U.S.	B3	108
Río Sucio, Col.	E5	58
Rio Verde, Braz.	D3	57
Ríoverde, Mex.	G10	62
Rio Vista, Ca., U.S.	C3	82
Rioz, Fr.	E13	10
Ripley, Ms., U.S.	A5	101
Ripley, Oh., U.S.	D2	112
Ripley, Tn., U.S.	B2	119
Ripley, W.V., U.S.	C3	125
Ripley, co., In., U.S.	F7	91
Ripley, co., Mo., U.S.	E7	102
Ripoll, Spain	C14	12
Ripon, Eng., U.K.	G11	7
Ripon, Wi., U.S.	E5	126
Rippowam, stm., Ct., U.S.	E1	84
Ririe Lake, res., Id., U.S.	F7	89
Rishon leẔiyyon, Isr.	D4	40
Rising Sun, De., U.S.	D3	85
Rising Sun, In., U.S.	G8	91
Rising Sun, Md., U.S.	A5	97
Rison, Ar., U.S.	D3	81
Ritchie, co., W.V., U.S.	B3	125
Ritter, Mount, mtn., Ca., U.S.	D4	82
Rittman, Oh., U.S.	B4	112
Ritzville, Wa., U.S.	B7	124
Riva, Italy	D5	14
Rivanna, stm., Va., U.S.	C4	123
Rivas, Nic.	I5	64
Rivera, Ur.	C5	56
Riverbank, Ca., U.S.	D3	82
River Bourgeois, N.S., Can.	D9	71
Riverdale, Ca., U.S.	D4	82
Riverdale, Il., U.S.	k9	90
Riverdale, Md., U.S.	C4	97
River Edge, N.J., U.S.	h8	107
River Falls, Al., U.S.	D3	78
River Falls, Wi., U.S.	D1	126
River Forest, Il., U.S.	k9	90
River Grove, Il., U.S.	k9	90
Riverhead, N.Y., U.S.	n16	109
River Hebert, N.S., Can.	D5	71
River Heights, Ut., U.S.	B4	121
River Hills, Wi., U.S.	m12	126
River Pines, Ma., U.S.	f10	98
River Ridge, La., U.S.	k11	95
River Road, Or., U.S.	C3	114
River Rouge, Mi., U.S.	p15	99
Rivers, Man., Can.	D1	70
Riverside, Al., U.S.	B3	78
Riverside, Ca., U.S.	F5	82
Riverside, Il., U.S.	k9	90
Riverside, Ia., U.S.	C6	92
Riverside, N.J., U.S.	C3	107
Riverside, Pa., U.S.	E8	115
Riverside, co., Ca., U.S.	F5	82
Riverside Reservoir, res., Co., U.S.	A6	83
Riverton, Man., Can.	D3	70
Riverton, Il., U.S.	D4	90
Riverton, Ks., U.S.	E9	93
Riverton, N.J., U.S.	C3	107
Riverton, Ut., U.S.	C4	121
Riverton, Vt., U.S.	C3	122
Riverton, Wy., U.S.	C4	127
Riverton Heights, Wa., U.S.	f11	124
River Vale, N.J., U.S.	h8	107
Riverview, Fl., U.S.	p11	86
Riverview, Mi., U.S.	p15	99
Rivesaltes, Fr.	J9	10
Rivesville, W.V., U.S.	B4	125
Riviera Beach, Fl., U.S.	F6	86
Riviera Beach, Md., U.S.	B4	97
Rivière-du-Loup, Que., Can.	B8	74
Rivière-Verte, N.B., Can.	B1	71
Rivoli, Italy	D2	14
Riyadh see Ar-Riyāḍ, Sau. Ar.	D4	46

Name | Map Ref | Page

ze, Tur. G16 4
oa, Spain D8 12
oachdale, In., U.S. E4 91
oane, co., Tn., U.S. D9 119
oane, co., W.V., U.S. C3 125
oan Mountain, Tn., U.S. C11 119
oanne, Fr. F11 10
oanoke, Al., U.S. B4 78
oanoke, Il., U.S. C4 90
oanoke, In., U.S. C7 91
oanoke, La., U.S. D3 95
oanoke, Tx., U.S. m9 120
oanoke, Va., U.S. C3 123
oanoke, co., Va., U.S. C2 123
oanoke, stm., U.S. A5 110
oanoke Island, i., N.C., U.S. B7 110
oanoke Rapids, N.C., U.S. A5 110
oanoke Rapids Lake, res., U.S. A5 110
oaring Fork, stm., Co., U.S. C4 83
oaring Spring, Pa., U.S. F5 115
oatán, Isla de, i., Hond. F4 64
obbins, Il., U.S. k9 90
obbins, N.C., U.S. B3 110
obbinsdale, Mn., U.S. m12 100
obbinsville, N.C., U.S. f9 110
obel, Ger. B12 8
obersonville, N.C., U.S. B5 110
oberta, Ga., U.S. D2 87
obert Lee, Tx., U.S. D2 120
oberts, Wi., U.S. C1 126
oberts, co., S.D., U.S. B8 118
oberts, co., Tx., U.S. B2 120
oberts, Point, c., Wa., U.S. A2 124
obert's Arm, Newf., Can. D4 72
oberts Creek Mountain, mtn., Nv., U.S. D5 105
obertsdale, Al., U.S. E2 78
obertsfors, Swe. D13 6
obert S. Kerr Reservoir, res., Ok., U.S. B6 113
oberts Mountain, mtn., Ak., U.S. C6 79
oberts Mountain, mtn., Wy., U.S. D3 127
obertson, co., Ky., U.S. B5 94
obertson, co., Tn., U.S. A5 119
obertson, co., Tx., U.S. D4 120
obertsonville, Que., Can. C6 74
oberts Peak, mtn., B.C., Can. F8 66
obertsport, Lib. G3 42
obertville, N.B., Can. B4 71
oberval, Que., Can. A5 74
obeson, co., N.C., U.S. C3 110
obins, Ia., U.S. B6 92
obinson, Il., U.S. D6 90
obinson Fork, stm., W.V., U.S. m14 125
obinson Fork, stm., W.V., U.S. k9 125
oblin, Man., Can. D1 70
oboré, Bol. G7 54
obson, Mount, mtn., B.C., Can. C8 69
obstown, Tx., U.S. F4 120
oca Partida, Isla, i., Mex. H3 62
oca Partida, Punta, c., Mex. H12 62
ocas, Atol das, atoll, Braz. D12 54
occastrada, Italy F6 14
ocha, Ur. C6 56
ochefort, Fr. G6 10
ochelle, Ga., U.S. E3 87
ochelle, Il., U.S. B4 90
ochelle Park, N.J., U.S. h8 107
ochester, Il., U.S. D4 90
ochester, In., U.S. B5 91
ochester, Mi., U.S. F7 99
ochester, Mn., U.S. F6 100
ochester, N.H., U.S. D5 106
ochester, N.Y., U.S. B3 109
ochester, Pa., U.S. E1 115
ochester, Vt., U.S. D3 122
ochester, Wa., U.S. C2 124
ochester, Wi., U.S. n11 126
ock, co., Mn., U.S. G2 100
ock, co., Ne., U.S. B6 104
ock, co., Wi., U.S. F4 126
ock, stm., U.S. B3 90
ock, stm., U.S. A1 92
ockall, i., Scot., U.K. D5 4
ockaway, N.J., U.S. B3 107
ockaway, Or., U.S. B3 114
ockbridge, co., Va., U.S. C3 123
ockcastle, co., Ky., U.S. C5 94
ockcastle, stm., Ky., U.S. C5 94
ockcliffe Park, Ont., Can. h12 73
ock Creek, Mn., U.S. E6 100
ock Creek, stm., U.S. B3 97
ock Creek, stm., U.S. h14 124
ock Creek, stm., Nv., U.S. C5 105
ock Creek, stm., Or., U.S. B6 114
ock Creek, stm., Wa., U.S. D5 124
ock Creek, stm., Wa., U.S. B8 124
ock Creek, stm., Wy., U.S. E6 127
ock Creek Butte, mtn., Or., U.S. C8 114
ockdale, Il., U.S. B5 90
ockdale, Md., U.S. B4 97
ockdale, Tx., U.S. D4 120
ockdale, co., Ga., U.S. C3 87
ockfall, Ct., U.S. C5 84
ock Falls, Il., U.S. B4 90
ockford, Il., U.S. A4 90
ockford, Ia., U.S. A5 92
ockford, Mi., U.S. E5 99
ockford, Mn., U.S. E5 100
ockford, Oh., U.S. B1 112
ockford, Tn., U.S. D10 119
ock Hall, Md., U.S. B5 97
ockhampton, Austl. D10 50
ock Hill, S.C., U.S. B5 117
ockingham, N.C., U.S. C3 110
ockingham, co., N.H., U.S. D4 106
ockingham, co., N.C., U.S. A3 110
ockingham, co., Va., U.S. B4 123
ock Island, Que., Can. D5 74
ock Island, Il., U.S. B3 90
ock Island, co., Il., U.S. B3 90
ock Island, i., Fl., U.S. C3 86

Rock Island, i., Wi., U.S. C7 126
Rock Lake, I., Wa., U.S. B8 124
Rockland, Ont., Can. B9 73
Rockland, Me., U.S. D3 96
Rockland, Ma., U.S. B6 98
Rockland, co., N.Y., U.S. D6 109
Rockledge, Fl., U.S. D6 86
Rockledge, Pa., U.S. o20 115
Rocklin, Ca., U.S. C3 82
Rockmart, Ga., U.S. B1 87
Rock Mountain, mtn., Co., U.S. D3 83
Rockport, In., U.S. I3 91
Rockport, Me., U.S. D3 96
Rockport, Ma., U.S. A6 98
Rock Port, Mo., U.S. A2 102
Rockport, Tx., U.S. F4 120
Rock Rapids, Ia., U.S. A1 92
Rock River, Wy., U.S. E7 127
Rock Sound, Bah. B9 64
Rocksprings, Tx., U.S. D2 120
Rock Springs, Wy., U.S. E3 127
Rockstone, Guy. E13 58
Rockton, Il., U.S. A4 90
Rock Valley, Ia., U.S. A1 92
Rockville, In., U.S. E3 91
Rockville, Md., U.S. B3 97
Rockville Centre, N.Y., U.S. n15 109
Rockwall, Tx., U.S. C4 120
Rockwall, co., Tx., U.S. C4 120
Rockwell, Ia., U.S. B4 92
Rockwell, N.C., U.S. B2 110
Rockwell City, Ia., U.S. B3 92
Rockwell Park, N.C., U.S. B2 110
Rockwood, Mi., U.S. F7 99
Rockwood, Pa., U.S. G3 115
Rockwood, Tn., U.S. D9 119
Rocky, stm., N.C., U.S. B2 110
Rocky, stm., S.C., U.S. C2 117
Rocky, East Branch, stm., Oh., U.S. h9 112
Rocky, West Branch, stm., Oh., U.S. h9 112
Rocky Boys Indian Reservation, Mt., U.S. B7 103
Rocky Ford, Co., U.S. C7 83
Rocky Fork Lake, I., Oh., U.S. C2 112
Rocky Harbour, Newf., Can. D3 72
Rocky Hill, Ct., U.S. C5 84
Rocky Lake, I., Me., U.S. D5 96
Rocky Mount, N.C., U.S. B5 110
Rocky Mount, Va., U.S. D3 123
Rocky Mountain, mtn., Mt., U.S. C4 103
Rocky Mountain House, Alta., Can. C3 68
Rocky Mountain National Park, Co., U.S. A5 83
Rocky Mountains, mts., N.A. E9 61
Rocky Ripple, In., U.S. k10 91
Rocky River, Oh., U.S. A4 112
Rocky Top, mtn., Or., U.S. C4 114
Roddickton, Newf., Can. C3 72
Roderfield, W.V., U.S. D3 125
Rodez, Fr. H9 10
Ródhos (Rhodes), Grc. M12 16
Ródhos, i., Grc. M11 16
Rodney, Ont., Can. E3 73
Rodney, Cape, c., Ak., U.S. C6 79
Rodney Village, De., U.S. D3 85
Rodniki, Russia D24 18
Roebourne, Austl. D3 50
Roebuck, S.C., U.S. B4 117
Roeland Park, Ks., U.S. k16 93
Roeselare, Bel. E3 8
Roes Welcome Sound, strt., N.W. Ter., Can. D15 66
Roff, Ok., U.S. C5 113
Rogagua, Lago, I., Bol. F5 54
Roger Mills, co., Ok., U.S. B2 113
Rogers, Ar., U.S. A1 81
Rogers, Mn., U.S. E5 100
Rogers, Tx., U.S. D4 120
Rogers, co., Ok., U.S. A6 113
Rogers, Mount, mtn., Va., U.S. f10 123
Rogers City, Mi., U.S. C7 99
Rogers Lake, res., Ct., U.S. D6 84
Rogers Pass, Mt., U.S. C4 103
Rogersville, N.B., Can. C4 71
Rogersville, Al., U.S. A2 78
Rogersville, Mo., U.S. D4 102
Rogersville, Tn., U.S. C10 119
Roggiano Gravina, Italy J11 14
Rogue, stm., Or., U.S. E2 114
Rogue River, Or., U.S. E3 114
Rohtak, India F7 38
Roi Et, Thai. F7 34
Rojo, Cabo, c., Mex. G11 62
Roland, Ia., U.S. B4 92
Roland, Ok., U.S. B7 113
Roland, Lake, res., Md., U.S. g11 97
Rolândia, Braz. G3 57
Røldal, Nor. G6 6
Rolette, N.D., U.S. A6 111
Rolette, co., N.D., U.S. A6 111
Rolfe, Ia., U.S. B3 92
Rolla, Mo., U.S. D6 102
Rolla, N.D., U.S. A6 111
Rollingbay, Wa., U.S. e10 124
Rolling Fork, Ms., U.S. C3 101
Rolling Fork, stm., Ar., U.S. C1 81
Rolling Fork, stm., Ky., U.S. C4 94
Rolling Meadows, Il., U.S. h8 90
Rollingstone, Mn., U.S. F7 100
Rollinsford, N.H., U.S. D5 106
Roma (Rome), Italy H7 14
Roma, Tx., U.S. F3 120
Romain, Cape, c., S.C., U.S. F9 117
Roman, Rom. C10 16
Romania, ctry., Eur. F13 4
Roman Nose Mountain, mtn., Or., U.S. D3 114
Romano, Cape, c., Fl., U.S. G5 86
Romano, Cayo, i., Cuba C8 64
Romans [-sur-Isère], Fr. G12 10
Romanzof, Cape, c., Ak., U.S. C6 79
Romanzof Mountains, mts., Ak., U.S. B11 79

Rome, Ga., U.S. B1 87
Rome, Il., U.S. C4 90
Rome, N.Y., U.S. B5 109
Rome City, In., U.S. B7 91
Romeo, Mi., U.S. F7 99
Romeoville, Il., U.S. k8 90
Rome see Roma, Italy H7 14
Romilly-sur-Seine, Fr. D10 10
Romney, W.V., U.S. B6 125
Romorantin-Lanthenay, Fr. E8 10
Romulus, Mi., U.S. p15 99
Ron, Mui, c., Viet. E9 34
Ronan, Mt., U.S. C2 103
Roncador, Serra do, plat., Braz. F8 54
Roncesvalles, Spain B10 12
Ronceverte, W.V., U.S. D4 125
Ronda, Spain I6 12
Rondônia, Braz. F6 54
Rondonópolis, Braz. D1 57
Ronge, Lac la, I., Sask., Can. B3 75
Rønne, Den. I10 6
Ronneby, Swe. H10 6
Ronne Ice Shelf, Ant. B6 47
Ronse, Bel. E3 8
Roodhouse, Il., U.S. D3 90
Rooks, co., Ks., U.S. C4 93
Roorkee, India F7 38
Roosendaal, Neth. D4 8
Roosevelt, Ut., U.S. C5 121
Roosevelt, co., Mt., U.S. B11 103
Roosevelt, co., N.M., U.S. C6 108
Roosevelt, stm., Braz. E6 54
Roosevelt Park, Mi., U.S. E4 99
Root, stm., Mn., U.S. G7 100
Root, stm., Wi., U.S. n12 126
Roper, N.C., U.S. B6 110
Roquefort, Fr. H6 10
Roraima, Mount, mtn., S.A. E12 58
Røros, Nor. E8 6
Rorschach, Switz. E16 10
Rørvik, Nor. D8 6
Rošal', Russia F22 18
Rosamond, Ca., U.S. E4 82
Rosamorada, Mex. F7 62
Rosario, Arg. C4 56
Rosário, Braz. D10 54
Rosario, Mex. F7 62
Rosario, Mex. B2 62
Rosario, Ven. B6 58
Rosário Oeste, Braz. F7 54
Rosarno, Italy K10 14
Rosas, Golfo de, b., Spain C15 12
Roscoe, Il., U.S. A5 90
Roscoe, Tx., U.S. C2 120
Roscommon, Ire. H4 7
Roscommon, Mi., U.S. D6 99
Roscommon, co., Mi., U.S. D6 99
Roscrea, Ire. I5 7
Rose, Mount, mtn., Nv., U.S. D2 105
Roseau, Dom. G17 64
Roseau, Mn., U.S. B3 100
Roseau, co., Mn., U.S. B3 100
Roseau, South Fork, stm., Mn., U.S. B3 100
Rose-Blanche [-Harbour le Cou], Newf., Can. E2 72
Roseboro, N.C., U.S. C4 110
Rosebud, S.D., U.S. D5 118
Rosebud, Tx., U.S. D4 120
Rosebud, co., Mt., U.S. D10 103
Rosebud Indian Reservation, S.D., U.S. D5 118
Roseburg, Or., U.S. D3 114
Rosedale, In., U.S. E3 91
Rosedale, Md., U.S. g11 97
Rosedale, Ms., U.S. B2 101
Rose Hill, Ks., U.S. E6 93
Rose Hill, N.C., U.S. C4 110
Rose Hill, Va., U.S. f8 123
Roseland, Fl., U.S. E6 86
Roseland, In., U.S. A5 91
Roseland, La., U.S. D5 95
Roseland, Oh., U.S. B3 112
Roselle, Il., U.S. k8 90
Roselle, N.J., U.S. k7 107
Roselle Park, N.J., U.S. k7 107
Rosemère, Que., Can. p19 74
Rosemount, Mn., U.S. F5 100
Rosenberg, Tx., U.S. E5 120
Rosendale, Wi., U.S. E5 126
Rosenheim, Ger. H12 8
Rose Peak, mtn., Az., U.S. D6 80
Rosepine, La., U.S. D2 95
Rose Point, c., B.C., Can. B2 69
Roseto, Pa., U.S. E11 115
Roseville, Ca., U.S. C3 82
Roseville, Il., U.S. C3 90
Roseville, Mi., U.S. o16 99
Roseville, Mn., U.S. m12 100
Roseville, Oh., U.S. C3 112
Rosewood Heights, Il., U.S. E3 90
Rosiclare, Il., U.S. F5 90
Rosignano Marittimo, Italy F5 14
Roskilde, Den. I9 6
Roslags-Näsby, Swe. G12 6
Roslavl', Russia H15 18
Roslyn, Wa., U.S. B4 124
Roslyn Heights, N.Y., U.S. h13 109
Ross, Oh., U.S. C1 112
Ross, co., Oh., U.S. C2 112
Rossano, Italy J11 14
Rossan Point, c., Ire. G4 7
Ross Barnett Reservoir, res., Ms., U.S. C3 101
Rossburn, Man., Can. D1 70
Ross Dam, Wa., U.S. A4 124
Rossel Island, i., Pap. N. Gui. B10 50
Rossford, Oh., U.S. A2 112
Ross Ice Shelf, Ant. A31 47
Rossignol, Lake, I., N.S., Can. E4 71
Ross Island, i., Man., Can. B3 70
Ross Lake National Recreation Area, Wa., U.S. A5 124
Rossland, B.C., Can. E9 69
Rosslare, Ire. I6 7
Rosso, Maur. E2 42

Ross River, Yukon, Can. D6 66
Ross Sea, Ant. B31 47
Rossville, Ga., U.S. B1 87
Rossville, Il., U.S. C6 90
Rossville, In., U.S. D4 91
Rossville, Ks., U.S. C8 93
Rostock, Ger. A12 8
Rostov, Russia D22 18
Rostov-na-Donu, Russia H5 22
Roswell, Ga., U.S. B2 87
Roswell, N.M., U.S. D5 108
Rotan, Tx., U.S. C2 120
Rotenburg, Ger. B9 8
Rothaargebirge, mts., Ger. D8 8
Rothenburg ob der Tauber, Ger. F10 8
Rothesay, N.B., Can. D4 71
Rothschild, Wi., U.S. D4 126
Rothsville, Pa., U.S. F9 115
Roti, Pulau, i., Indon. H7 32
Rotondella, Italy I11 14
Rotorua, N.Z. C6 52
Rotterdam, Neth. D4 8
Rotterdam, N.Y., U.S. C6 109
Rottweil, Ger. G8 8
Roubaix, Fr. B10 10
Rouen, Fr. C8 10
Rouge, stm., Que., Can. D3 74
Rough, stm., Ky., U.S. C3 94
Rough River Lake, res., Ky., U.S. C3 94
Roulette, Pa., U.S. C5 115
Round Island, i., Ms., U.S. g8 101
Round Lake, Il., U.S. h8 90
Round Lake Beach, Il., U.S. h8 90
Round Mountain, Nv., U.S. E4 105
Round Rock, Tx., U.S. D4 120
Roundup, Mt., U.S. D8 103
Round Valley Indian Reservation, Ca., U.S. C2 82
Round Valley Reservoir, res., N.J., U.S. B3 107
Rouses Point, N.Y., U.S. f11 109
Roussillon, hist. reg., Fr. J9 10
Routt, co., Co., U.S. A3 83
Rouyn [-Noranda], Que., Can. k11 74
Rouzerville, Pa., U.S. G6 115
Rovaniemi, Fin. C15 6
Rovato, Italy D4 14
Rovereto, Italy D6 14
Rovigo, Italy D6 14
Rovinj, Cro. D8 14
Rovno, Ukr. G3 22
Rowan, co., Ky., U.S. B6 94
Rowan, co., N.C., U.S. B2 110
Rowland, N.C., U.S. C3 110
Rowlesburg, W.V., U.S. B5 125
Rowley Island, i., N.W. Ter., Can. C17 66
Rowley Shoals, rf., Austl. C3 50
Roxboro, N.C., U.S. A4 110
Roxton Falls, Que., Can. D5 74
Roxton Pond, Que., Can. D5 74
Roy, Ut., U.S. B3 121
Royal, stm., Me., U.S. g7 96
Royal Canal, Ire. H5 7
Royal Center, In., U.S. C4 91
Royale, Isle, i., Mi., U.S. h9 99
Royal Gorge, val., Co., U.S. C5 83
Royal Oak, Mi., U.S. F7 99
Royal Pines, N.C., U.S. f10 110
Royalton, Il., U.S. F4 90
Royalton, Mn., U.S. E4 100
Royan, Fr. G5 10
Royersford, Pa., U.S. F10 115
Royerton, In., U.S. D7 91
Royse City, Tx., U.S. C4 120
Royston, B.C., Can. E5 69
Royston, Ga., U.S. B3 87
Rubbestadneset, Nor. G5 6
Rubcovsk, Russia G10 24
Rubidoux, Ca., U.S. n14 82
Rubio, Ven. D6 58
Ruby Dome, mtn., Nv., U.S. C6 105
Ruby Lake, I., Nv., U.S. C6 105
Ruby Mountains, mts., Nv., U.S. C6 105
Ruby Range, mts., Co., U.S. C3 83
Ruby Range, mts., Mt., U.S. E4 103
Rudolf, Lake, I., Afr. H2 46
Rudolstadt, Ger. E11 8
Rudyard, Mi., U.S. B6 99
Rue, Fr. B8 10
Rufā'ah, Sudan F12 42
Ruffec, Fr. F7 10
Rufino, Arg. C4 56
Rufus Woods Lake, res., Wa., U.S. A6 124
Rugao, China C9 28
Rugby, Eng., U.K. I11 7
Rugby, N.D., U.S. A6 111
Ruian, China H9 28
Ruidoso, N.M., U.S. D4 108
Ruidoso Downs, N.M., U.S. D4 108
Ruijin, China F10 26
Ruijin, China J4 28
Rukwa, Lake, I., Tan. C6 44
Ruleville, Ms., U.S. B3 101
Rum, stm., Mn., U.S. D5 100
Ruma, Yugo. D3 16
Rumbek, Sudan G11 42
Rum Cay, i., Bah. C10 64
Rum Creek, stm., W.V., U.S. n12 125
Rumford, Me., U.S. D2 96
Rumia, Pol. A18 8
Rum Jungle, Austl. B6 50
Rumoi, Japan p19 30a
Rumson, N.J., U.S. C4 107
Rumstick Point, c., R.I., U.S. D5 116
Ru'nan, China B3 28
Runanga, N.Z. E3 52
Runge, Tx., U.S. E4 120
Rungwa, Tan. C6 44
Runnels, co., Tx., U.S. D3 120
Runnemede, N.J., U.S. D2 107
Ruoqiang, China D4 26
Rupert, Id., U.S. G5 89
Rupert, W.V., U.S. D4 125
Rupert, Rivière de, stm., Que., Can. h11 74

Rural Hall, N.C., U.S. A2 110
Rural Retreat, Va., U.S. D1 123
Rusagonis, N.B., Can. D3 71
Ruse, Bul. F9 16
Rush, co., In., U.S. E6 91
Rush, co., Ks., U.S. D4 93
Rush, stm., Mn., U.S. F4 100
Rush, stm., Wi., U.S. D1 126
Rush City, Mn., U.S. E6 100
Rush Creek, stm., Oh., U.S. B2 112
Rush Creek, stm., Ok., U.S. C4 113
Rushford, Mn., U.S. G7 100
Rush Lake, I., Mn., U.S. E5 100
Rush Lake, I., Mn., U.S. D3 100
Rush Lake, I., Wi., U.S. E5 126
Rushmere, Va., U.S. h14 123
Rush Springs, Ok., U.S. C4 113
Rushville, Il., U.S. C3 90
Rushville, In., U.S. E7 91
Rushville, Ne., U.S. B3 104
Rusk, Tx., U.S. D5 120
Rusk, co., Tx., U.S. C5 120
Rusk, co., Wi., U.S. C2 126
Ruskin, Fl., U.S. E4 86
Russas, Braz. D11 54
Russell, Man., Can. D1 70
Russell, Ont., Can. B9 73
Russell, Ks., U.S. D5 93
Russell, Ky., U.S. B7 94
Russell, Pa., U.S. C3 115
Russell, co., Al., U.S. C4 78
Russell, co., Ks., U.S. D5 93
Russell, co., Ky., U.S. D4 94
Russell, co., Va., U.S. f9 123
Russell, Mount, mtn., Ak., U.S. f16 79
Russell Cave National Monument, Al., U.S. A4 78
Russell Fork, stm., U.S. C7 94
Russell Island, i., N.W. Ter., Can. B13 66
Russell Springs, Ky., U.S. C4 94
Russellville, Al., U.S. A2 78
Russellville, Ar., U.S. B2 81
Russellville, Ky., U.S. D3 94
Russellville, Mo., U.S. C5 102
Russellville, Tn., U.S. C10 119
Rüsselsheim, Ger. E8 8
Russia, ctry., Eur. E15 22
Russian, stm., Ca., U.S. C2 82
Russiaville, In., U.S. D5 91
Rustavi, Geor. I7 22
Rustburg, Va., U.S. C3 123
Rustenburg, S. Afr. G5 44
Ruston, La., U.S. B3 95
Ruston, Wa., U.S. B3 124
Ruth, Nv., U.S. D6 105
Rutherford, N.J., U.S. B4 107
Rutherford, Tn., U.S. A3 119
Rutherford, co., N.C., U.S. B1 110
Rutherford, co., Tn., U.S. B5 119
Rutherfordton, N.C., U.S. B1 110
Ruthven, Ia., U.S. A3 92
Rutland, Ma., U.S. B4 98
Rutland, Vt., U.S. D3 122
Rutland, co., Vt., U.S. D2 122
Rutledge, Ga., U.S. C3 87
Rutledge, Tn., U.S. C10 119
Ruukki, Fin. D15 6
Ruvuma (Rovuma), stm., Afr. D7 44
Ružomberok, Slov. F19 8
Rwanda, ctry., Afr. B5 44
Ryan, Ok., U.S. C4 113
Ryan Peak, mtn., Id., U.S. F4 89
Rybinsk, Russia C21 18
Rybinskoje Vodochranilišče, res., Russia C21 18
Rybnik, Pol. E18 8
Rycroft, Alta., Can. B1 68
Ryde, Eng., U.K. K11 7
Rye, N.H., U.S. D5 106
Rye, N.Y., U.S. h13 109
Rye Beach, N.H., U.S. E5 106
Rye Patch Dam, Nv., U.S. C3 105
Rye Patch Reservoir, res., Nv., U.S. C3 105
Ryfoss, Nor. F7 6
Ryōtsu, Japan D11 30
Rysy, mtn., Eur. F20 8
Ryukyu Islands see Nansei-shotō, is., Japan F12 26
Rzeszów, Pol. E21 8
Ržev, Russia E17 18

S

Saalfeld, Ger. E11 8
Saarbrücken, Ger. F6 8
Saaremaa, i., Est. C5 18
Saarijärvi, Fin. E15 6
Saarlouis, Ger. F6 8
Sab, Tônlé, I., Camb. H7 34
Saba, i., Neth. Ant. F16 64
Sabadell, Spain D14 12
Sabae, Japan G9 30
Sabana, Archipiélago de, is., Cuba C8 64
Sabanagrande, Hond. H4 64
Sabanalarga, Col. B5 58
Sabang, Indon. E6 32
Sabanilla, Mex. E9 62
Sabará, Braz. E7 57
Sabattus, Me., U.S. D2 96
Sabetha, Ks., U.S. C8 93
Sabhah, Libya C8 42
Sabi (Save), stm., Afr. F6 44
Sabillasville, Md., U.S. A3 97
Sabina, Oh., U.S. C2 112
Sabinal, Tx., U.S. E3 120
Sabiñánigo, Spain C11 12
Sabinas, Mex. D9 62
Sabinas Hidalgo, Mex. D9 62
Sabine, co., La., U.S. C2 95
Sabine, co., Tx., U.S. D6 120
Sabine, stm., U.S. D6 120
Sabine Lake, I., U.S. E2 95
Sabine Pass, strt., U.S. E2 95
Sable, Cape, c., N.S., Can. H19 66

Name	Map Ref	Page
Sable, Cape, c., Fl., U.S.	G5	86
Sable, Îles de, i., N. Cal.	C11	50
Sable Island, i., N.S., Can.	F10	71
Sabula, Ia., U.S.	B7	92
Sabzevār, Iran	J9	22
Sac, co., Ia., U.S.	B2	92
Sac, stm., Mo., U.S.	D4	102
Sacajawea, Lake, res., Wa., U.S.	C7	124
Sacajawea Peak, mtn., Or., U.S.	B9	114
Sacandaga Lake, l., N.Y., U.S.	B6	109
Sac and Fox Indian Reservation, Ia., U.S.	C5	92
Sacaton, Az., U.S.	D4	80
Sac City, Ia., U.S.	B2	92
Sacedón, Spain	E9	12
Sachalin, Ostrov (Sakhalin), i., Russia	G22	24
Sachalinskij Zaliv, b., Russia	G22	24
Sachigo, stm., Ont., Can.	F14	66
Sachse, Tx., U.S.	n10	120
Şachs Harbour, N.W. Ter., Can.	B8	66
Šachty, Russia	H6	22
Sachuest Point, c., R.I., U.S.	F6	116
Sackville, N.B., Can.	D5	71
Saco, Me., U.S.	E2	96
Saco, stm., U.S.	E2	96
Saco, East Branch, stm., N.H., U.S.	B4	106
Sacramento, Ca., U.S.	C3	82
Sacramento, co., Ca., U.S.	C3	82
Sacramento, stm., Ca., U.S.	C3	82
Sacramento, stm., N.M., U.S.	E4	108
Sacramento Mountains, mts., N.M., U.S.	E4	108
Sacramento Valley, val., Ca., U.S.	C2	82
Sacré-Coeur-Saguenay, Que., Can.	A8	74
Sacred Heart, Mn., U.S.	F3	100
Sádaba, Spain	C10	12
Şa'dah, Yemen	E3	46
Saddle, stm., N.J., U.S.	h8	107
Saddleback Mountain, mtn., Az., U.S.	k8	80
Saddle Brook, N.J., U.S.	h8	107
Saddlebunch Keys, is., Fl., U.S.	H5	86
Saddle Mountain, mtn., Or., U.S.	B3	114
Saddle Mountains, mts., Wa., U.S.	C5	124
Saddle River, N.J., U.S.	A4	107
Sa Dec, Viet.	I8	34
Sādiqābad, Pak.	F4	38
Sado, i., Japan	D11	30
Sado-kaikyō, strt., Japan	E11	30
Saegertown, Pa., U.S.	C1	115
Safety Harbor, Fl., U.S.	E4	86
Säffle, Swe.	G9	6
Safford, Az., U.S.	E6	80
Safi, Mor.	B4	42
Safīd, stm., Afg.	B1	38
Sāfīd Kūh, Selseleh-ye, mts., Afg.	C1	36
Safonovo, Russia	F16	18
Saga, Japan	I3	30
Sagadahoc, co., Me., U.S.	E3	96
Sagaing, Burma	D3	34
Sagamihara, Japan	G12	30
Sagami-nada, b., Japan	G12	30
Sagamore Hills, Oh., U.S.	h9	112
Saganaga Lake, l., Mn., U.S.	B7	100
Sāgar, India	E3	37
Sāgar, India	I8	38
Sag Harbor, N.Y., U.S.	m16	109
Saginaw, Mi., U.S.	E7	99
Saginaw, Tx., U.S.	n9	120
Saginaw, co., Mi., U.S.	E6	99
Saginaw Bay, b., Mi., U.S.	E7	99
Saglek Bay, b., Newf., Can.	f9	72
Sagres, Port.	H3	12
Saguache, co., Co., U.S.	C4	83
Sagua de Tánamo, Cuba	D10	64
Sagua la Grande, Cuba	C7	64
Saguaro Lake, res., Az., U.S.	k10	80
Saguaro National Monument, Az., U.S.	E5	80
Saguaro National Monument (Tucson Mountain Section), Az., U.S.	E4	80
Saguenay, stm., Que., Can.	A7	74
Sagunto, Spain	F11	12
Sahagún, Col.	C5	58
Sahagún, Spain	C6	12
Sahara, des., Afr.	D6	42
Sahāranpur, India	F7	38
Sāhiwāl (Montgomery), Pak.	E5	38
Sahuaripa, Mex.	C5	62
Sahuarita, Az., U.S.	F5	80
Sahuayo, Mex.	G8	62
Saibai, i., Austl.	A8	50
Saïda, Alg.	B6	42
Saidpur, Bngl.	H13	38
Saidu, Pak.	C5	38
Saigō, Japan	F6	30
Saigon see Thanh Pho Ho Chi Minh, Viet.	I9	34
Saijō, Japan	I6	30
Saimaa, l., Fin.	F16	6
Saint Abb's Head, c., Scot., U.K.	F10	7
Saint Adolphe, Man., Can.	E3	70
Saint-Affrique, Fr.	I9	10
Sainte-Agathe, Que., Can.	C6	74
Sainte-Agathe-des-Monts, Que., Can.	C3	74
Saint-Aimé (Massueville), Que., Can.	D5	74
Saint-Alban, Que., Can.	C5	74
Saint Alban's, Newf., Can.	E4	72
Saint Albans, Eng., U.K.	J12	7
Saint Albans, Vt., U.S.	B2	122
Saint Albans, W.V., U.S.	C3	125
Saint Albans Bay, b., Vt., U.S.	B2	122
Saint Albert, Alta., Can.	C4	68
Saint-Amand-Mont-Rond, Fr.	F9	10
Saint-Ambroise, Que., Can.	A6	74
Saint-Ambroix, Fr.	H11	10
Saint-André, Cap, c., Madag.	E8	44
Saint-André-Avellin, Que., Can.	D2	74
Saint-André-Est, Que., Can.	D3	74
Saint-André-les-Alpes, Fr.	I13	10
Saint Andrew Bay, b., Fl., U.S.	u16	86
Saint Andrews, N.B., Can.	D2	71
Saint Andrews, Scot., U.K.	E10	7
Saint Andrews, S.C., U.S.	F7	117
Saint Andrews, S.C., U.S.	C5	117
Saint Anne, Il., U.S.	B6	90
Sainte-Anne-de-Beaupré, Que., Can.	B7	74
Sainte-Anne [-de-Bellevue], Que., Can.	q19	74
Sainte Anne-de-Madawaska, N.B., Can.	B1	71
Sainte Anne-des-Chênes, Man., Can.	E3	70
Saint-Anselme, Que., Can.	C7	74
Saint Ansgar, Ia., U.S.	A5	92
Saint Anthony, Newf., Can.	C4	72
Saint Anthony, Id., U.S.	F7	89
Saint Antoine, N.B., Can.	C5	71
Saint-Apollinaire, Que., Can.	C6	74
Saint Arthur, N.B., Can.	B3	71
Saint-Astier, Fr.	G7	10
Saint-Aubert, Que., Can.	B7	74
Saint Augustin, stm., Can.	C2	72
Saint Augustine, Fl., U.S.	C5	86
Saint Austell, Eng., U.K.	K8	7
Saint-Avold, Fr.	C13	10
Saint-Barthélemy, i., Guad.	F16	64
Saint Basile, N.B., Can.	B1	71
Saint-Basile [-Sud], Que., Can.	C6	74
Saint-Benoît-du-Sault, Fr.	F8	10
Saint-Bernard, Que., Can.	C6	74
Saint Bernard, Al., U.S.	A3	78
Saint Bernard, La., U.S.	E6	95
Saint Bernard, Oh., U.S.	o13	112
Saint Bernard, co., La., U.S.	E6	95
Saint Bernice, In., U.S.	E2	91
Saint Bride, Mount, mtn., Alta., Can.	D3	68
Saint Bride's, Newf., Can.	E4	72
Saint-Brieuc, Fr.	D4	10
Saint-Bruno, Que., Can.	A6	74
Saint-Calais, Fr.	E7	10
Saint-Casimir, Que., Can.	C5	74
Saint Catharines, Ont., Can.	D5	73
Saint Catherine, Lake, l., Vt., U.S.	E2	122
Saint Catherines Island, i., Ga., U.S.	E5	87
Saint-Célestin (Annaville), Que., Can.	C5	74
Saint-Céré, Fr.	H8	10
Saint-Césaire, Que., Can.	D4	74
Saint-Chamond, Fr.	G11	10
Saint-Charles, Que., Can.	C7	74
Saint Charles, Il., U.S.	B5	90
Saint Charles, Mi., U.S.	E6	99
Saint Charles, Mn., U.S.	G6	100
Saint Charles, Mo., U.S.	C7	102
Saint Charles, co., La., U.S.	E5	95
Saint Charles, co., Mo., U.S.	C7	102
Saint-Chély-d'Apcher, Fr.	H10	10
Saint Christopher (Saint Kitts), i., St. K./N.	F16	64
Saint Christopher-Nevis see Saint Kitts and Nevis, ctry., N.A.	F16	64
Saint-Chrysostome, Que., Can.	D4	74
Saint Clair, Mi., U.S.	F8	99
Saint Clair, Mn., U.S.	F5	100
Saint Clair, Mo., U.S.	C6	102
Saint Clair, Pa., U.S.	E9	115
Saint Clair, co., Al., U.S.	B3	78
Saint Clair, co., Il., U.S.	E3	90
Saint Clair, co., Mi., U.S.	F8	99
Saint Clair, co., Mo., U.S.	C4	102
Saint Clair Shores, Mi., U.S.	p16	99
Saint Clairsville, Oh., U.S.	B5	112
Saint Claude, Man., Can.	E2	70
Saint-Claude, Fr.	F12	10
Saint Cloud, Fl., U.S.	D5	86
Saint Cloud, Mn., U.S.	E4	100
Saint-Coeur-de-Marie, Que., Can.	A6	74
Saint-Constant, Que., Can.	q19	74
Sainte-Croix, Que., Can.	C6	74
Saint Croix, co., Wi., U.S.	C1	126
Saint Croix, i., V.I.U.S.	F15	64
Saint Croix, stm., U.S.	C1	126
Saint Croix, Lake, l., U.S.	D1	126
Saint Croix Falls, Wi., U.S.	C1	126
Saint Croix Stream, stm., Me., U.S.	B4	96
Saint-Damase, Que., Can.	D4	74
Saint David, Az., U.S.	F5	80
Saint-David-de-l'Auberivière, Que., Can.	n17	74
Saint David's, Wales, U.K.	J7	7
Saint-Denis, Que., Can.	D4	74
Saint-Denis, Fr.	D9	10
Saint-Denis, Reu.	F11	44
Saint-Dié, Fr.	D13	10
Saint-Dizier, Fr.	D11	10
Saint-Dominique, Que., Can.	D5	74
Saint Edward, Ne., U.S.	C8	104
Saint Eleanor's, P.E.I., Can.	C6	71
Saint Elias, Cape, c., Ak., U.S.	D11	79
Saint Elmo, Al., U.S.	E1	78
Saint Elmo, Il., U.S.	D5	90
Saint-Éphrem [-de-Tring], Que., Can.	C7	74
Saint Étienne, Fr.	G11	10
Saint-Eustache, Que., Can.	D4	74
Saint-Félicien, Que., Can.	A5	74
Saint-Félix-de-Valois, Que., Can.	C4	74
Saint-Ferdinand (Bernierville), Que., Can.	C6	74
Saint-Ferréol [-les-Neiges], Que., Can.	B7	74
Saint-Flavien, Que., Can.	C6	74
Saint-Florentin, Fr.	D10	10
Saint-Florent-sur-Cher, Fr.	F9	10
Saint-Flour, Fr.	G10	10
Sainte-Foy, Que., Can.	n17	74
Sainte-Foy-la-Grande, Fr.	H7	10
Saint Francis, Ks., U.S.	C2	93
Saint Francis, Mn., U.S.	E5	100
Saint Francis, S.D., U.S.	D5	118
Saint Francis, Wi., U.S.	n12	126
Saint Francis, co., Ar., U.S.	B5	81
Saint Francis, stm., U.S.	A5	81
Saint Francis, Cape, c., Newf., Can.	E5	72
Saint Francisville, Il., U.S.	E6	90
Saint Francisville, La., U.S.	D4	95
Saint Francois, co., Mo., U.S.	D7	102
Saint-François, stm., Que., Can.	D5	74
Saint-François, Lac, l., Que., Can.	D6	74
Saint Francois Mountains, hills, Mo., U.S.	D7	102
Saint Froid Lake, l., Me., U.S.	B4	96
Saint-Fulgence, Que., Can.	A7	74
Saint-Gabriel, Que., Can.	C4	74
Saint-Gaudens, Fr.	I7	10
Saint-Gédéon, Que., Can.	D7	74
Sainte Genevieve, Mo., U.S.	D7	102
Sainte Genevieve, co., Mo., U.S.	D7	102
Saint George, Austl.	E9	50
Saint George, N.B., Can.	D3	71
Saint George, Ont., Can.	D4	73
Saint George, S.C., U.S.	E6	117
Saint George, Ut., U.S.	F2	121
Saint George, Cape, c., Newf., Can.	D2	72
Saint George, Cape, c., Fl., U.S.	C1	86
Saint George Island, i., Ak., U.S.	D6	79
Saint George Island, i., Fl., U.S.	C2	86
Saint George's, Newf., Can.	D2	72
Saint-Georges, Que., Can.	C5	74
Saint-Georges, Fr. Gu.	C8	54
Saint George's, Gren.	H17	64
Saint Georges, De., U.S.	B3	85
Saint George's Bay, b., Newf., Can.	D2	72
Saint Georges Bay, b., N.S., Can.	D8	71
Saint George's Channel, strt., Eur.	J6	7
Saint-Georges-Ouest (part of Ville-Saint-Georges), Que., Can.	C7	74
Saint-Germain, Fr.	D9	10
Saint-Gervais, Que., Can.	C7	74
Saint-Gilles, Que., Can.	C6	74
Saint-Gilles-Croix-de-Vie, Fr.	F5	10
Saint-Girons, Fr.	J8	10
Saint-Grégoire (Larochelle), Que., Can.	C5	74
Saint-Guénolé, Fr.	E2	10
Saint-Guillaume-d'Upton, Que., Can.	D5	74
Saint Helen, Lake, l., Mi., U.S.	D6	99
Saint Helena, Ca., U.S.	C2	82
Saint Helena, co., La., U.S.	D5	95
Saint Helena Bay, b., S. Afr.	H3	44
Saint Helena Island, i., S.C., U.S.	G6	117
Saint Helena Sound, strt., S.C., U.S.	G7	117
Saint Helens, Or., U.S.	B4	114
Saint Helens, Mount, vol., Wa., U.S.	C3	124
Saint Helier, Jersey	C4	10
Saint Henry, Oh., U.S.	B1	112
Saint-Hippolyte, Fr.	E13	10
Saint-Honoré, Que., Can.	D7	74
Saint-Hubert, Que., Can.	q20	74
Saint-Hubert-de-Témiscouata, Que., Can.	B8	74
Saint-Hyacinthe, Que., Can.	D5	74
Saint Ignace, Mi., U.S.	C6	99
Saint Ignace Island, i., Ont., Can.	G15	66
Saint Ignatius, Mt., U.S.	C2	103
Saint Isidore de Prescott, Ont., Can.	B10	73
Saint Jacobs, Ont., Can.	D4	73
Saint Jacques, N.B., Can.	B1	71
Saint-Jacques, Que., Can.	D4	74
Saint James, Mn., U.S.	G4	100
Saint James, Mo., U.S.	D6	102
Saint James, co., La., U.S.	D5	95
Saint James, Cape, c., B.C., Can.	D2	69
Saint James City, Fl., U.S.	F4	86
Saint-Jean, stm., Que., Can.	A7	74
Saint-Jean, Lac, l., Que., Can.	A5	74
Saint Jean Baptiste, Man., Can.	E3	70
Saint-Jean-Chrysostome, Que., Can.	o17	74
Saint-Jean-d'Angély, Fr.	G6	10
Saint-Jean-de-Luz, Fr.	I5	10
Saint-Jean-de-Maurienne, Fr.	G13	10
Saint-Jean-de-Monts, Fr.	F4	10
Saint-Jean-Pied-de-Port, Fr.	I5	10
Saint-Jean-sur-Richelieu, Que., Can.	D4	74
Saint-Jérôme, Que., Can.	D3	74
Saint Jo, Tx., U.S.	C4	120
Saint-Joachim, Que., Can.	B7	74
Saint Joe, stm., Id., U.S.	B3	89
Saint John, N.B., Can.	D3	71
Saint John, In., U.S.	B3	91
Saint John, Ks., U.S.	E5	93
Saint John, i., V.I.U.S.	E15	64
Saint John, stm., N.A.	G19	66
Saint John, Cape, c., Newf., Can.	D4	72
Saint John Bay, b., Newf., Can.	C3	72
Saint Johns, Antig.	F17	64
Saint John's, Newf., Can.	E5	72
Saint Johns, Az., U.S.	C6	80
Saint Johns, Mi., U.S.	F6	99
Saint Johns, co., Fl., U.S.	C5	86
Saint Johns, stm., Fl., U.S.	B5	86
Saint Johnsbury, Vt., U.S.	C4	122
Saint Johnsville, N.Y., U.S.	B6	109
Saint John the Baptist, co., La., U.S.	D5	95
Saint Jones, stm., De., U.S.	D4	85
Saint Joseph, N.B., Can.	D5	71
Saint Joseph, Il., U.S.	C5	90
Saint Joseph, La., U.S.	C4	95
Saint Joseph, Mi., U.S.	F4	99
Saint Joseph, Mn., U.S.	E4	100
Saint Joseph, Mo., U.S.	B3	102
Saint Joseph, Tn., U.S.	B4	119
Saint Joseph, co., In., U.S.	A5	91
Saint Joseph, co., Mi., U.S.	G5	99
Saint Joseph, stm., U.S.	F5	99
Saint-Joseph, Lac, l., Que., Can.	n16	74
Saint Joseph, Lake, l., Ont., Can.	o17	73
Saint Joseph Bay, b., Fl., U.S.	C1	86
Saint-Joseph-de-Beauce, Que., Can.	C7	74
Saint Joseph Point, c., Fl., U.S.	v16	86
Saint Joseph Sound, strt., Fl., U.S.	o10	86
Saint-Jovite, Que., Can.	C3	74
Saint-Julien-en-Born, Fr.	H5	10
Saint-Junien, Fr.	G7	10
Saint-Just-en-Chaussée, Fr.	C9	10
Saint Kilda, i., Scot., U.K.	D4	7
Saint Kitts-Nevis, ctry., N.A.	F16	64
Saint-Lambert, Que., Can.	p19	74
Saint Landry, co., La., U.S.	D3	95
Saint-Laurent, Que., Can.	p19	74
Saint Lawrence, Newf., Can.	E4	72
Saint Lawrence, co., N.Y., U.S.	A5	109
Saint Lawrence, stm., N.A.	G19	66
Saint Lawrence, Cape, c., N.S., Can.	B9	71
Saint Lawrence, Gulf of, b., Can.	G20	66
Saint Lawrence Island, i., Ak., U.S.	C5	79
Saint Lawrence Islands National Park, Ont., Can.	C9	73
Saint Léonard, N.B., Can.	B2	71
Saint-Léonard [-d'Aston], Que., Can.	C5	74
Saint-Liboire, Que., Can.	D5	74
Saint-Lô, Fr.	C5	10
Saint-Louis, Sen.	E2	42
Saint Louis, Mi., U.S.	E6	99
Saint Louis, Mo., U.S.	C7	102
Saint Louis, co., Mn., U.S.	C6	100
Saint Louis, co., Mo., U.S.	C7	102
Saint Louis, stm., U.S.	D6	100
Saint-Louis, Lac, l., Que., Can.	q19	74
Saint Louis Bay, b., Ms., U.S.	f7	101
Saint-Louis-de-Gonzague, Que., Can.	D3	74
Saint Louis-de-Kent, N.B., Can.	C5	71
Saint-Louis-du-Ha! Ha!, Que., Can.	B8	74
Saint Louis Park, Mn., U.S.	n12	100
Saint-Luc, Que., Can.	D4	74
Saint Lucia, ctry., N.A.	H17	64
Saint Lucia Channel, strt., N.A.	G17	64
Saint Lucie, co., Fl., U.S.	E6	86
Saint Lucie Canal, Fl., U.S.	F6	86
Saint Lucie Inlet, b., Fl., U.S.	E6	86
Sainte-Madeleine, Que., Can.	D4	74
Saint Malo, Man., Can.	E3	70
Saint-Malo, Fr.	D4	10
Saint-Malo, Golfe de, b., Fr.	D4	10
Saint-Marc, Haiti	E11	64
Saint-Marc [-des-Carrières], Que., Can.	C5	74
Saint-Marcellin, Fr.	G12	10
Saint Margaret Bay, b., Newf., Can.	C3	72
Sainte-Marguerite, stm., Que., Can.	A7	74
Sainte-Marie, Que., Can.	C6	74
Sainte-Marie, Cap, c., Madag.	G9	44
Saint Maries, Id., U.S.	B2	89
Sainte-Marthe, Que., Can.	D3	74
Saint Martin, co., La., U.S.	D4	95
Saint-Martin (Sint Maarten), i., N.A.	E16	64
Saint Martin, Lake, l., Man., Can.	D2	70
Saint Martin Island, i., Mi., U.S.	C4	99
Saint Martinville, La., U.S.	D4	95
Saint Mary, co., La., U.S.	E4	95
Saint Mary-of-the-Woods, In., U.S.	E3	91
Saint Mary Peak, mtn., Austl.	F7	50
Saint Marys, Austl.	H9	50
Saint Mary's, Newf., Can.	E5	72
Saint Mary's, Ont., Can.	D3	73
Saint Marys, Ak., U.S.	C7	79
Saint Marys, Ga., U.S.	F5	87
Saint Marys, In., U.S.	A5	91
Saint Marys, Ks., U.S.	C7	93
Saint Marys, Oh., U.S.	B1	112
Saint Marys, Pa., U.S.	D4	115
Saint Marys, W.V., U.S.	B3	125
Saint Marys, co., Md., U.S.	D4	97
Saint Marys, stm., N.S., Can.	D8	71
Saint Marys, stm., U.S.	F5	87
Saint Marys, stm., U.S.	C8	91
Saint Marys, stm., Md., U.S.	D5	97
Saint Mary's, Cape, c., Newf., Can.	E4	72
Saint Mary's Bay, b., Newf., Can.	E5	72
Saint Marys Bay, b., N.S., Can.	E3	71
Saint Marys City, Md., U.S.	D5	97
Saint-Mathieu, Pointe de, c., Fr.	D2	10
Saint Matthew Island, i., Ak., U.S.	C5	79
Saint Matthews, Ky., U.S.	B4	94
Saint Matthews, S.C., U.S.	D6	117
Sainte-Maure-du-Touraine, Fr.	E7	10
Saint-Maurice, stm., Que., Can.	C5	74
Sainte-Maxime, Fr.	I13	10
Saint-Méen-le-Grand, Fr.	D4	10
Sainte-Menehould, Fr.	C11	10
Sainte-Mère-Église, Fr.	C5	10
Saint Michael, Mn., U.S.	E5	100
Saint Michaels, Md., U.S.	C5	97
Saint-Michel [-de-Bellechasse], Que., Can.	C7	74
Saint-Mihiel, Fr.	D12	10
Saint-Moritz see Sankt Moritz, Switz.	F16	10
Saint-Nazaire, Fr.	E4	10
Saint-Nicolas, Que., Can.	o17	74
Saint-Odilon, Que., Can.	C7	74
Saint-Omer, Fr.	B9	10
Saint-Ours, Que., Can.	D4	74
Saint-Pacôme, Que., Can.	B8	74
Saint-Pamphile, Que., Can.	C8	74
Saint Paris, Oh., U.S.	B2	112
Saint-Pascal, Que., Can.	B8	74
Saint Paul, Alta., Can.	B5	68
Saint Paul, Ak., U.S.	D5	79
Saint Paul, In., U.S.	F6	91
Saint Paul, Ks., U.S.	E8	93
Saint Paul, Mn., U.S.	F5	100
Saint Paul, Mo., U.S.	f12	102
Saint Paul, Ne., U.S.	C7	104
Saint Paul, Va., U.S.	f9	123
Saint Paul Island, i., Ak., U.S.	D5	79
Saint Paul Park, Mn., U.S.	n12	100
Saint Pauls, N.C., U.S.	C4	110
Sainte-Perpétue-de-L'Islet, Que., Can.	B8	74
Saint Peter, Mn., U.S.	F5	100
Saint Peter Port, Guernsey	C4	10
Saint Peters, N.S., Can.	D9	71
Saint Peters, Mo., U.S.	C7	102
Saint Petersburg, Fl., U.S.	E4	86
Saint Petersburg Beach, Fl., U.S.	p10	86
Saint Petersburg see Sankt-Peterburg, Russia	B13	18
Saint Phillips Island, i., S.C., U.S.	G6	117
Saint-Pie, Que., Can.	D5	74
Saint-Pierre, Reu.	F11	44
Saint-Pierre, St. P./M.	E3	72
Saint-Pierre, Lac, l., Que., Can.	C5	74
Saint Pierre and Miquelon, dep., N.A.	G21	66
Saint Pierre Island, i., Sey.	C10	44
Saint Pierre-Jolys, Man., Can.	E3	70
Saint-Pierre-le-Moûtier, Fr.	F10	10
Saint-Pol-de-Léon, Fr.	D3	10
Saint-Pons, Fr.	I9	10
Saint-Pourçain-sur-Sioule, Fr.	F10	10
Saint-Prime, Que., Can.	A5	74
Saint Quentin, N.B., Can.	B2	71
Saint-Quentin, Fr.	C10	10
Saint-Raphaël, Que., Can.	C7	74
Saint-Raphaël, Fr.	I13	10
Saint-Raymond, Que., Can.	C6	74
Saint-Rédempteur, Que., Can.	o17	74
Saint Regis, Mt., U.S.	C1	103
Saint Regis, West Branch, stm., N.Y., U.S.	f10	109
Saint-Rémi, Que., Can.	D4	74
Saint-Romuald, Que., Can.	C6	74
Saint Rose, La., U.S.	k11	95
Sainte Rose du Lac, Man., Can.	D2	70
Saintes, Fr.	G6	10
Saint Sauveur, N.B., Can.	B4	71
Saint-Sauveur-des-Monts, Que., Can.	D3	74
Saint-Sébastien, Cap, c., Madag.	D9	44
Saint-Siméon, Que., Can.	B8	74
Saint Simons Island, Ga., U.S.	E5	87
Saint Simons Island, i., Ga., U.S.	E5	87
Saint Stephen, N.B., Can.	D2	71
Saint Stephen, S.C., U.S.	E8	117
Saint Tammany, co., La., U.S.	D5	95
Sainte-Thècle, Que., Can.	C5	74
Sainte-Thérèse, Que., Can.	D4	74
Saint Thomas, Ont., Can.	E3	73
Saint Thomas, i., V.I.U.S.	E15	64
Saint Timothée, Que., Can.	q18	74
Saint-Tite, Que., Can.	C5	74
Saint-Tropez, Fr.	I13	10
Saint-Valéry-en-Caux, Fr.	C7	10
Saint-Varent, Fr.	F6	10
Sainte-Véronique, Que., Can.	C3	74
Saint-Victor, Que., Can.	C7	74
Saint-Vincent, Cap, c., Madag.	F8	44
Saint Vincent, Gulf, b., Austl.	F7	50
Saint Vincent and the Grenadines, ctry., N.A.	H17	64
Saint Vincent Island, i., Fl., U.S.	C1	86
Saint Vincent Passage, strt., N.A.	H17	64
Saint Vincent's [-Saint Stephens-Peter's River], Newf., Can.	E5	72
Saint-Vith, Bel.	E6	8
Saint Walburg, Sask., Can.	D1	75
Saint-Zacharie, Que., Can.	C7	74
Sairecábur, Cerro, mtn., S.A.	A3	56
Saito, Japan	J4	30
Saitula, China	B8	38
Sajama, Nevado, mtn., Bol.	G5	54
Sajia, China	F13	38
Sajnšand, Mong.	C9	26
Sakai, Japan	H8	30
Sakaide, Japan	H6	30
Sakai-minato, Japan	G6	30
Sakakawea, Lake, res., N.D., U.S.	B3	11
Sakami, Lac, l., Que., Can.	F17	66
Sakata, Japan	D12	30
Sakhalin see Sachalin, Ostrov, i., Russia	G22	24
Sākhar, Afg.	D1	38
Sakishima-shotō, is., Japan	G11	26
Sakon Nakhon, Thai.	F8	34
Sakonnet, stm., R.I., U.S.	E6	116
Sakonnet Point, c., R.I., U.S.	F6	116
Saku, Japan	F11	3
Sakurai, Japan	H8	3
Sal, Point, c., Ca., U.S.	E3	8
Sala, Swe.	G11	
Salaberry-de-Valleyfield, Que., Can.	D3	7
Sala Consilina, Italy	I10	1
Salado, stm., Arg.	C4	5
Salado, Rio, stm., N.M., U.S.	C2	10
Şalālah, Oman	E5	4
Salamanca, Mex.	G9	6
Salamanca, Spain	E6	1
Salamanca, N.Y., U.S.	C2	10
Salamina, Col.	E5	5
Salamonie, stm., In., U.S.	C6	9
Salamonie Lake, res., In., U.S.	C6	9
Salatiga, Indon.	m15	3
Salavat, Russia	G9	2
Salawati, i., Indon.	F9	3
Saldanha, S. Afr.	H3	4
Sale, Austl.	G9	5
Sale Creek, Tn., U.S.	D8	11
Salem, India	G5	3
Salem, Ar., U.S.	A4	8
Salem, Il., U.S.	E5	9
Salem, In., U.S.	G5	9
Salem, Ky., U.S.	e9	9

Name Map Ref Page
lem, Ma., U.S. A6 98
lem, Mo., U.S. D6 102
lem, N.H., U.S. E4 106
lem, N.J., U.S. D2 107
lem, Oh., U.S. B5 112
lem, Or., U.S. C4 114
lem, S.D., U.S. D8 118
lem, Ut., U.S. C4 121
lem, Va., U.S. C2 123
lem, W.V., U.S. B4 125
lem, Wi., U.S. n11 126
lem, co., N.J., U.S. D2 107
lem, stm., N.J., U.S. D2 107
lem, Lake, l., Vt., U.S. B4 122
lemi, Italy L7 14
len, Swe. F9 6
lerno, Italy I9 14
lford, Eng., U.K. H10 7
lgótarján, Hung. G19 8
li, Cro. F10 14
lida, Co., U.S. C5 83
lies-de-Béarn, Fr. I6 10
lihli, Tur. K12 16
lina, Ks., U.S. D6 93
lina, Ok., U.S. A6 113
lina, Ut., U.S. E4 121
lina Cruz, Mex. I12 62
linas, Braz. D7 57
linas, Ca., U.S. D3 82
linas, stm., Ca., U.S. D3 82
linas de Hidalgo, Mex. F9 62
linas Peak, mtn., N.M., U.S. D3 108
linas Pueblo Missions National Monument, N.M., U.S. C3 108
line, Mi., U.S. F7 99
line, co., Ar., U.S. C3 81
line, co., Il., U.S. F5 90
line, co., Ks., U.S. D6 93
line, co., Mo., U.S. B4 102
line, co., Ne., U.S. D8 104
line, stm., Ar., U.S. C1 81
line, stm., Ar., U.S. D4 81
line, stm., Ks., U.S. C3 93
line, North Fork, stm., Il., U.S. F5 90
line Lake, res., La., U.S. C3 95
lineville, Oh., U.S. B5 112
lisbury, N.B., Can. C4 71
lisbury, Eng., U.K. J11 7
lisbury, Ct., U.S. B2 84
lisbury, Md., U.S. D6 97
lisbury, Ma., U.S. A6 98
lisbury, Mo., U.S. B5 102
lisbury, N.C., U.S. B2 110
lisbury see Harare, Zimb. E6 44
lisbury Island, i., N.W. Ter., Can. D17 66
lisbury Plain, pl., Eng., U.K. J11 7
lish Mountains, mts., Mt., U.S. B2 103
lkehatchie, stm., S.C., U.S. E5 117
lkhad, Syria C5 40
les-Curan, Fr. H9 10
llisaw, Ok., U.S. B7 113
luit, Que., Can. f11 74
mo, B.C., Can. E9 69
mon, Id., U.S. D5 89
lmon, stm., N.B., Can. C4 71
lmon, stm., Id., U.S. D3 89
mon Creek, Wa., U.S. D3 124
mon Creek Reservoir, res., Id., U.S. G4 89
lmon Falls, stm., U.S. D5 106
lmon Falls Creek, stm., U.S. G4 89
mon Mountains, mts., Ca., U.S. B2 82
mon Point, c., Ont., Can. D7 73
mon River Mountains, mts., Id., U.S. E3 89
lmon River Reservoir, res., N.Y., U.S. B5 109
o, Fin. F14 6
ome, Az., U.S. D2 80
on-De-Provence, Fr. I12 10
onika see Thessaloníki, Grc. I6 16
somaggiore Terme, Italy E4 14
t, stm., Az., U.S. D4 80
t, stm., Ky., U.S. C4 94
t, stm., Mo., U.S. B6 102
ta, Arg. A3 56
t Creek, stm., N.M., U.S. D5 108
t Creek, stm., Oh., U.S. C3 112
t Creek, stm., Wy., U.S. C6 127
ter Path, N.C., U.S. C6 110
t Fork Lake, res., Oh., U.S. B4 112
tillo, Mex. E9 62
tillo, Ms., U.S. A5 101
t Lake, co., Ut., U.S. C3 121
t Lake, l., Hi., U.S. g10 88
t Lake, l., N.M., U.S. E6 108
t Lake City, Ut., U.S. C4 121
to, Ur. C5 56
ton Sea, l., Ca., U.S. F5 82
tonstall, Lake, l., Ct., U.S. D4 84
t Point, c., Ca., U.S. C2 82
t River Indian Reservation, Az., U.S. k9 80
t River Range, mts., Wy., U.S. D2 127
tsburg, Pa., U.S. F3 115
t Springs, Fl., U.S. C5 86
tville, Va., U.S. f10 123
t Wells Creek, stm., Wy., U.S. E4 127
uda, S.C., U.S. C4 117
uda, co., S.C., U.S. C4 117
uda, stm., S.C., U.S. C4 117
uda Dam, S.C., U.S. C5 117
ūr, India C7 37
uzzo, Italy E2 14
vador, Braz. B9 57
vador, Lake, l., La., U.S. E5 95
vatierra, Mex. G9 62
ween (Nu) (Thanlwin), stm., Asia D5 34
yersville, Ky., U.S. C6 94
zburg, Aus. H13 8

Salzgitter, Ger. C10 8
Salzwedel, Ger. C11 8
Sama [de Langreo], Spain B6 12
Samaná, Bahía de, b., Dom. Rep. E13 64
Samana Cay, i., Bah. C11 64
Samandağı, Tur. A4 40
Samar, i., Phil. C8 32
Samara, Russia G8 22
Samarai, Pap. N. Gui. n17 50a
Samariapo, Ven. E9 58
Samarinda, Indon. F6 32
Samarkand, Uzb. J11 22
Sāmarrā', Iraq B3 46
Samāstipur, India H11 38
Sambalpur, India J10 38
Sambas, Indon. E4 32
Sambava, Madag. D10 44
Sambhal, India F8 38
Sāmbhar, India G6 38
Samborondón, Ec. H3 58
Sammamish Lake, l., Wa., U.S. e11 124
Samneua, Laos D8 34
Samobor, Cro. D10 14
Sámos, i., Grc. L10 16
Samoset, Fl., U.S. q10 86
Sampit, Indon. F5 32
Sampit, stm., S.C., U.S. E9 117
Sampson, co., N.C., U.S. B4 110
Sam Rayburn Reservoir, res., Tx., U.S. D5 120
Samson, Al., U.S. D3 78
Samsun, Tur. G15 4
Samuels, Id., U.S. A2 89
Samui, Ko, i., Thai. J6 34
Samut Prakan, Thai. H6 34
Samut Sakhon, Thai. H6 34
San, Mali F5 42
San, stm., Eur. E22 8
Şan'ā', Yemen E3 46
Sanaga, stm., Cam. H7 42
San Agustín, Col. G4 58
San Agustin, Cape, c., Phil. D8 32
San Agustin, Plains of, pl., N.M., U.S. C2 108
Sanak Islands, is., Ak., U.S. E7 79
Sanana, Pulau, i., Indon. F8 32
Sanandaj, Iran A4 46
San Andreas, Ca., U.S. C3 82
San Andrés, Isla de, i., Col. H7 64
San Andres Mountains, mts., N.M., U.S. E3 108
San Andres Peak, mtn., N.M., U.S. E3 108
San Andrés Tuxtla, Mex. H12 62
San Angelo, Tx., U.S. D2 120
San Anselmo, Ca., U.S. h7 82
San Antonio, Tx., U.S. E3 120
San Antonio, Cabo, c., Arg. D5 56
San Antonio, Cabo, c., Cuba D5 64
San Antonio Abad, Spain G13 12
San Antonio Bay, b., Tx., U.S. E4 120
San Antonio de Bravo, Mex. B7 62
San Antonio de los Cobres, Arg. A3 56
San Antonio del Táchira, Ven. D6 58
San Antonio Mountain, mtn., N.M., U.S. A3 108
San Antonio Oeste, Arg. E4 56
San Augustine, Tx., U.S. D5 120
San Augustine, co., Tx., U.S. D5 120
San Benedetto del Tronto, Italy G8 14
San Benedicto, Isla, i., Mex. H4 62
San Benito, Guat. F3 64
San Benito, Tx., U.S. F4 120
San Benito, co., Ca., U.S. D3 82
San Benito Mountain, mtn., Ca., U.S. D3 82
San Bernardino, Ca., U.S. E5 82
San Bernardino, co., Ca., U.S. E5 82
San Bernardo, Chile C2 56
San Blas, Mex. G7 62
San Blas, Mex. D5 62
San Blas, Cape, c., Fl., U.S. v16 86
San Borja, Bol. F5 54
Sanborn, Ia., U.S. A2 92
Sanborn, co., S.D., U.S. D7 118
Sanbornville, N.H., U.S. C4 106
San Bruno, Ca., U.S. D2 82
San Carlos, Nic. I5 64
San Carlos, Az., U.S. D5 80
San Carlos, Ca., U.S. k8 82
San Carlos, Ven. C8 58
San Carlos de Bariloche, Arg. E2 56
San Carlos de Guaroa, Col. F6 58
San Carlos de la Rápita, Spain E12 12
San Carlos del Zulia, Ven. C7 58
San Carlos de Río Negro, Ven. G9 58
San Carlos Indian Reservation, Az., U.S. D5 80
San Carlos Lake, res., Az., U.S. D5 80
San Cataldo, Italy L9 14
Sancerre, Fr. E9 10
Sánchez, Mex. D10 62
San Clemente, Ca., U.S. F5 82
San Clemente Island, i., Ca., U.S. F4 82
Sancoins, Fr. F9 10
San Cristóbal, Arg. C4 56
San Cristóbal, Ven. D6 58
San Cristóbal, Volcán, vol., Nic. H4 64
San Cristóbal las Casas, Mex. I13 62
Sancti-Spíritus, Cuba D8 64
Sand, Nor. G6 6
Sandakan, Malay. D6 32
Sanday, i., Scot., U.K. B10 7
Sand Creek, stm., Wy., U.S. C7 127
Sanders, Az., U.S. B6 80
Sanders, co., Mt., U.S. C1 103
Sanderson, Tx., U.S. D1 120
Sandersville, Ga., U.S. D4 87
Sandersville, Ms., U.S. D4 101
Sand Hill, Ma., U.S. h13 98
Sand Hill, stm., Mn., U.S. C2 100
Sandia, Peru F5 54
Sandia Crest, mtn., N.M., U.S. k8 108
Sandia Indian Reservation, N.M., U.S. k7 108
Sandia Mountains, mts., N.M., U.S. k8 108
San Diego, Ca., U.S. F5 82
San Diego, Tx., U.S. F3 120
San Diego, co., Ca., U.S. F5 82
San Diego, stm., Ca., U.S. o15 82
San Diego Naval Station, mil., Ca., U.S. o15 82
San Diego Naval Training Center, mil., Ca., U.S. o15 82
Sand Island, i., Hi., U.S. g10 88
Sand Island, i., Wi., U.S. B3 126
Sand Key, i., Fl., U.S. E4 86
Sandlick Creek, stm., W.V., U.S. n13 125
Sandnes, Nor. G5 6
Sandoa, Zaire C4 44
San Donà di Piave, Italy D7 14
Sandoval, Il., U.S. E4 90
Sandoval, co., N.M., U.S. B2 108
Sandoway, Burma E3 34
Sand Point, Ak., U.S. D7 79
Sandpoint, Id., U.S. A2 89
Sands Key, i., Fl., U.S. s3 86
Sand Springs, Ok., U.S. A5 113
Sandston, Va., U.S. m18 123
Sandstone, Austl. E3 50
Sandstone, Mn., U.S. D6 100
Sandusky, Mi., U.S. E8 99
Sandusky, Oh., U.S. A3 112
Sandusky, co., Oh., U.S. A2 112
Sandusky, stm., Oh., U.S. B2 112
Sandviken, Swe. F11 6
Sandwich, Il., U.S. B5 90
Sandwich, Ma., U.S. C7 98
Sandwich Bay, b., Newf., Can. B3 72
Sandy, Or., U.S. B4 114
Sandy, Ut., U.S. C4 121
Sandy, stm., Me., U.S. D2 96
Sandy Creek, stm., Oh., U.S. B4 112
Sandy Creek, stm., Ok., U.S. C2 113
Sandy Hook, Ct., U.S. D2 84
Sandy Hook, spit, N.J., U.S. C5 107
Sandy Island, i., S.C., U.S. D9 117
Sandy Lake, l., Newf., Can. D3 72
Sandy Lake, l., Ont., Can. n16 73
Sandy Neck, pen., Ma., U.S. C7 98
Sandy Point, c., R.I., U.S. h7 116
Sandy Springs, Ga., U.S. h8 87
Sandy Springs, S.C., U.S. B2 117
Sandyville, Md., U.S. A4 97
San Felipe, Ven. B8 58
San Felipe Indian Reservation, N.M., U.S. k8 108
San Felipe Pueblo, N.M., U.S. B3 108
San Feliu de Guixols, Spain D15 12
San Fernando, Chile C2 56
San Fernando, Mex. E10 62
San Fernando, Phil. B7 32
San Fernando, Phil. q19 32
San Fernando, Spain I5 12
San Fernando, Trin. I17 64
San Fernando, Ca., U.S. m12 82
San Fernando de Apure, Ven. D9 58
San Fernando de Atabapo, Ven. E9 58
Sanford, Co., U.S. D5 83
Sanford, Fl., U.S. D5 86
Sanford, Me., U.S. E2 96
Sanford, Mi., U.S. E6 99
Sanford, N.C., U.S. B3 110
Sanford, Mount, mtn., Ak., U.S. C11 79
San Francisco, Arg. C4 56
San Francisco, Ca., U.S. D2 82
San Francisco, co., Ca., U.S. D2 82
San Francisco, stm., U.S. D6 80
San Francisco Bay, b., Ca., U.S. h8 82
San Francisco de Borja, Mex. D6 62
San Francisco del Oro, Mex. D7 62
San Francisco del Rincón, Mex. G9 62
San Francisco de Macorís, Dom. Rep. E12 64
San Fratello, Italy K9 14
San Gabriel, Ec. G4 58
San Gabriel, Ca., U.S. *m12 82
San Gabriel Mountains, mts., Ca., U.S. m12 82
Sangamner, India C3 37
Sangamon, co., Il., U.S. D4 90
Sangamon, stm., Il., U.S. C3 90
San Gavino Monreale, Italy J3 14
Sangay, Volcán, vol., Ec. H3 58
Sang-e Māsheh, Afg. D2 38
Sanger, Ca., U.S. D4 82
Sanger, Tx., U.S. C4 120
Sangerhausen, Ger. D11 8
Sangha, stm., Afr. B3 44
Sanghar, Pak. G3 38
Sangihe, Kepulauan, is., Indon. E8 32
Sangihe, Pulau, i., Indon. E8 32
San Gil, Col. D6 58
San Giovanni in Fiore, Italy J11 14
San Giovanni in Persiceto, Italy E6 14
San Giovanni Valdarno, Italy F6 14
Sāngli, India D3 37
Sangolquí, Ec. H3 58
San Gorgonio Mountain, mtn., Ca., U.S. E5 82
San Gregorio, Ur. C5 56
Sangrūr, India E6 38
Sangüesa, Spain C10 12
Sanibel, Fl., U.S. F4 86
Sanibel Island, i., Fl., U.S. F4 86
San Ignacio, Arg. B5 56
San Ignacio, Hond. G4 64
Sanilac, co., Mi., U.S. E8 99
San Isidro, Arg. C5 56
San Isidro, C.R. J6 64
San Jacinto, Col. C5 58
San Jacinto, Ca., U.S. F5 82
San Jacinto, co., Tx., U.S. D5 120
San Jacinto, stm., Tx., U.S. r14 120
Sanjō, Japan E11 30
San Joaquin, co., Ca., U.S. D3 82
San Joaquin, stm., Ca., U.S. D3 82
San Joaquin Valley, val., Ca., U.S. D3 82
San Jorge, Golfo, b., Arg. F3 56
San Jorge, Golfo de, b., Spain E12 12
San José, C.R. J5 64
San Jose, Ca., U.S. D3 82
San José, Isla, i., Mex. E4 62
San José de Chiquitos, Bol. G6 54
San José de Guanipa, Ven. C10 58
San José del Cabo, Mex. F5 62
San José del Guaviare, Col. F6 58
San José de Mayo, Ur. C5 56
San José de Ocuné, Col. E7 58
San José de Raíces, Mex. E9 62
San Jose Island, i., Tx., U.S. E4 120
San Juan, Arg. C3 56
San Juan, Mex. D8 62
San Juan, P.R. E14 64
San Juan, Tx., U.S. F3 120
San Juan, co., Co., U.S. D3 83
San Juan, co., N.M., U.S. A1 108
San Juan, co., Ut., U.S. F5 121
San Juan, co., Wa., U.S. A2 124
San Juan, stm., N.A. I6 64
San Juan Capistrano, Ca., U.S. F5 82
San Juan de Colón, Ven. C6 58
San Juan [de la Maguana], Dom. Rep. E12 64
San Juan del Norte, Nic. I6 64
San Juan de los Cayos, Ven. B8 58
San Juan de los Morros, Ven. C9 58
San Juan del Río, Mex. G9 62
San Juan del Sur, Nic. I5 64
San Juan Island, i., Wa., U.S. A2 124
San Juan Mountains, mts., Co., U.S. D3 83
San Julián, Arg. F3 56
San Justo, Arg. C4 56
Sankt Gallen, Aus. H14 8
Sankt Gallen, Switz. E16 10
Sankt Johann im Pongau, Aus. H13 8
Sankt Moritz, Switz. F16 10
Sankt Peter, Ger. A8 8
Sankt-Peterburg (Saint Petersburg), Russia B13 18
Sankt Pölten, Aus. G15 8
Sankt Veit an der Glan, Aus. I14 8
Sankt Wendel, Ger. F7 8
Sankuru, stm., Zaire B4 44
San Lázaro, Cabo, c., Mex. E3 62
San Leandro, Ca., U.S. h8 82
Şanliurfa, Tur. H15 4
San Lope, Col. D7 58
San Lorenzo, Arg. C4 56
San Lorenzo, Ec. G3 58
San Lorenzo, Isla, i., Peru F3 54
San Lorenzo de El Escorial, Spain E7 12
San Lorenzo de la Parrilla, Spain F9 12
Sanlúcar de Barrameda, Spain I5 12
San Lucas, Ec. I3 58
San Lucas, Cabo, c., Mex. F5 62
San Luis, Arg. C3 56
San Luis, Cuba D10 64
San Luis, Guat. F3 64
San Luis, Az., U.S. E1 80
San Luis, Co., U.S. D5 83
San Luis, Ven. B8 58
San Luis, Lago de, l., Bol. F6 54
San Luis, Point, c., Ca., U.S. E3 82
San Luis de la Paz, Mex. G9 62
San Luis Obispo, Ca., U.S. E3 82
San Luis Obispo, co., Ca., U.S. E3 82
San Luis Pass, strt., Tx., U.S. r14 120
San Luis Peak, mtn., Co., U.S. D4 83
San Luis Potosí, Mex. F9 62
San Luis Río Colorado, Mex. A2 62
San Luis Valley, val., Co., U.S. D4 83
San Manuel, Az., U.S. E5 80
San Marcos, Col. C5 58
San Marcos, Mex. D8 62
San Marcos, Mex. I10 62
San Marcos, Tx., U.S. E4 120
San Marcos, stm., Tx., U.S. h8 120
San Marino, Ca., U.S. m12 82
San Marino, ctry., Eur. G10 4
San Martín de Valdeiglesias, Spain E7 12
San Mateo, Spain E12 12
San Mateo, Ca., U.S. D2 82
San Mateo, co., Ca., U.S. D2 82
San Mateo Mountains, mts., N.M., U.S. B2 108
San Mateo Mountains, mts., N.M., U.S. D2 108
San Matías, Golfo, b., Arg. E4 56
San Miguel, El Sal. H3 64
San Miguel, co., Co., U.S. D2 83
San Miguel, co., N.M., U.S. B5 108
San Miguel, stm., Bol. F6 54
San Miguel, stm., Co., U.S. C2 83
San Miguel de Allende, Mex. G9 62
San Miguel del Monte, Arg. D5 56
San Miguel de Tucumán, Arg. B3 56
San Miguel el Alto, Mex. G8 62
San Miguel Island, i., Ca., U.S. E3 82
San Miguel Mountains, mts., Co., U.S. D2 83
Sannār, Sudan F12 42
Sannicandro Garganico, Italy H10 14
San Nicolas, Phil. o19 33b
San Nicolás de los Arroyos, Arg. C4 56
San Nicolas Island, i., Ca., U.S. F4 82
Sannikova, Proliv, strt., Russia C21 24
Sanniquellie, Lib. G4 42
Sano, Japan F12 30
Sanok, Pol. F22 8
San Onofre, Col. C5 58
San Pablo, Col. G4 58
San Pablo, Phil. q19 32
San Pablo Balleza, Mex. D6 62
San Pablo Bay, b., Ca., U.S. g8 82
San Patricio, co., Tx., U.S. E4 120
San Pedro, stm., Az., U.S. E5 80
San Pedro, Punta, c., Chile B2 56
San Pedro, Volcán, vol., Chile A3 56
San Pedro Bay, b., Ca., U.S. n12 82
San Pedro Carchá, Guat. G2 64
San Pedro de las Colonias, Mex. E8 62
San Pedro de Macorís, Dom. Rep. E13 64
San Pedro Mártir, Sierra, mts., Mex. B2 62
San Pedro Peaks, mts., N.M., U.S. A3 108
San Pedro Sula, Hond. G4 64
Sanpete, co., Ut., U.S. D4 121
Sanpoil, stm., Wa., U.S. A7 124
San Quintín, Cabo, c., Mex. B1 62
San Rafael, Arg. C3 56
San Rafael, Mex. E9 62
San Rafael, Ca., U.S. D2 82
San Rafael, N.M., U.S. B2 108
San Rafael, stm., Ut., U.S. D5 121
San Rafael Knob, mtn., Ut., U.S. E5 121
San Rafael Mountains, mts., Ca., U.S. E4 82
San Ramón, Nic. G5 64
San Ramon, Ca., U.S. h9 82
San Remo, Italy F2 14
San Saba, Tx., U.S. D3 120
San Saba, co., Tx., U.S. D3 120
San Salvador, El Sal. H3 64
San Salvador (Watling Island), i., Bah. B10 64
San Salvador de Jujuy, Arg. A3 56
Sansanné-Mango, Togo F6 42
San Sebastián, Spain B10 12
Sansepolcro, Italy F7 14
San Severo, Italy H10 14
San Simon, stm., Az., U.S. E6 80
Sanski Most, Bos. E11 14
Santa Ana, Bol. G5 54
Santa Ana, Bol. F5 54
Santa Ana, El Sal. H3 64
Santa Ana, Mex. E9 62
Santa Ana, Mex. B4 62
Santa Ana, Ca., U.S. F5 82
Santa Ana, stm., Ca., U.S. n13 82
Santa Ana Indian Reservation, N.M., U.S. h7 108
Santa Ana Mountains, mts., Ca., U.S. n13 82
Santa Anna, Tx., U.S. D3 120
Santa Bárbara, Mex. D7 62
Santa Barbara, Ca., U.S. E4 82
Santa Barbara, co., Ca., U.S. E3 82
Santa Barbara Channel, strt., Ca., U.S. E3 82
Santa Barbara Island, i., Ca., U.S. F4 82
Santa Catalina, Gulf of, b., Ca., U.S. F5 82
Santa Catalina Island, i., Ca., U.S. F4 82
Santa Catalina Mountains, mts., Az., U.S. E5 80
Santa Catarina, Ilha de, i., Braz. B7 56
Santa Clara, Cuba C8 64
Santa Clara, Ca., U.S. D2 82
Santa Clara, Ut., U.S. F2 121
Santa Clara, co., Ca., U.S. D3 82
Santa Clara, stm., Ca., U.S. E4 82
Santa Claus, In., U.S. H4 91
Santa Coloma de Farnés, Spain D14 12
Santa Comba Dão, Port. E3 12
Santa Cruz, Arg. F3 56
Santa Cruz, Bol. G6 54
Santa Cruz, C.R. I5 64
Santa Cruz, Phil. q19 33b
Santa Cruz, Ca., U.S. D2 82
Santa Cruz, N.M., U.S. B3 108
Santa Cruz, co., Az., U.S. F5 80
Santa Cruz, co., Ca., U.S. D2 82
Santa Cruz, stm., Az., U.S. E4 80
Santa Cruz del Quiché, Guat. G2 64
Santa Cruz de Tenerife, Spain p24 13b
Santa Cruz do Rio Pardo, Braz. G4 57
Santa Cruz Island, i., Ca., U.S. F4 82
Santa Elena, Ec. I2 58
Santa Elena, Punta, c., Ec. I2 58
Santa Eugenia, Spain C2 12
Santa Eulalia, Spain E10 12
Santa Eulalia del Río, Spain G13 12
Santa Fe, Arg. C4 56
Santa Fé, Braz. C3 57
Santa Fé, Cuba D6 64
Santa Fe, Spain H8 12
Santa Fe, N.M., U.S. B4 108
Santa Fe, Tx., U.S. r14 120
Santa Fe, co., N.M., U.S. B3 108
Santa Fe, stm., N.M., U.S. h8 108
Santa Fe Baldy, mtn., N.M., U.S. B4 108
Santa Fe de Bogotá, Col. E5 58
Santa Inés, Isla, i., Chile G2 56
Santa Isabel, Ec. I3 58
Santa Isabel, i., Sol.Is. A11 50
Santa Isabel see Malabo, Eq. Gui. H7 42
Santa Lucia Range, mts., Ca., U.S. E3 82
Santa Magdalena, Isla, i., Mex. E3 62
Santa Margarita, Ca., U.S. E3 82
Santa Margarita, Isla de, i., Mex. E4 62
Santa Maria, Braz. B6 56
Santa Maria, Ca., U.S. E3 82
Santa Maria, stm., Az., U.S. C2 80
Santa Maria, Cabo de, c., Ang. D2 44
Santa Maria do Suaçuí, Braz. E7 57
Santa Maria Mountains, mts., Az., U.S. C3 80
Santa Marta, Col. B5 58
Santa Monica, Ca., U.S. m12 82
Santana do Livramento, Braz. C5 56
Santander, Col. F4 58
Santander, Spain B8 12
Sant' Antioco, Italy J3 14
Santa Paula, Ca., U.S. E4 82
Santaquin, Ut., U.S. D4 121
Sant'Arcangelo, Italy I11 14
Santarém, Braz. D8 54
Santarém, Port. F3 12
Santa Rita, Col. G6 58
Santa Rita, Hond. G4 64
Santa Rosa, Arg. D4 56
Santa Rosa, Arg. C3 56
Santa Rosa, Ec. I3 58
Santa Rosa, Ca., U.S. C2 82
Santa Rosa, N.M., U.S. C5 108
Santa Rosa, co., Fl., U.S. u14 86

Name — Map Ref — Page

Santa Rosa de Cabal, Col. E5 58
Santa Rosa [de Copán], Hond. G3 64
Santa Rosa Island, i., Ca., U.S. F3 82
Santa Rosa Island, i., Fl., U.S. u14 86
Santa Rosa Range, mts., Nv., U.S. B4 105
Šantarskije Ostrova, is., Russia F21 24
Santa Teresa Gallura, Italy H4 14
Santa Vitória do Palmar, Braz. C6 56
Santa Ynez, Ca., U.S. E3 82
Santee, Ca., U.S. o16 82
Santee, stm., S.C., U.S. E8 117
Santee Dam, S.C., U.S. E7 117
Santee Indian Reservation, Ne., U.S. B8 104
Santhià, Italy D3 14
Santiago, Chile C2 56
Santiago, Dom. Rep. E12 64
Santiago, Pan. J7 64
Santiago de Compostela, Spain C3 12
Santiago de Cuba, Cuba D10 64
Santiago del Estero, Arg. B4 56
Santiago do Cacém, Port. G3 12
Santiago Ixcuintla, Mex. G7 62
Santiago Papasquiaro, Mex. E7 62
Santiago Peak, mtn., Ca., U.S. n13 82
Santiago Reservoir, res., Ca., U.S. n13 82
Santiaguillo, Laguna de, l., Mex. E7 62
Santiam Pass, Or., U.S. C4 114
Sāntipur, India I13 38
Santisteban del Puerto, Spain G8 12
Santo Amaro, Braz. B9 57
Santo Anastácio, Braz. F3 57
Santo André, Braz. G5 57
Santo Ângelo, Braz. B6 56
Santo Antônio de Jesus, Braz. B9 57
Santo Antônio do Içá, Braz. D5 54
Santo Domingo, Dom. Rep. E13 64
Santo Domingo, Nic. H5 64
Santo Domingo de la Calzada, Spain C9 12
Santo Domingo de los Colorados, Ec. H3 58
Santo Domingo Indian Reservation, N.M., U.S. h8 108
Santo Domingo Pueblo, N.M., U.S. B3 108
Santoña, Spain B8 12
Santos, Braz. G5 57
Santos Dumont, Braz. F7 57
Santo Tomás, Mex. B1 62
Santo Tomé, Arg. B5 56
San Valentín, Monte, mtn., Chile F2 56
San Vicente, El Sal. H3 64
San Vicente, Mex. B1 62
San Vicente de Baracaldo, Spain B9 12
San Vicente de la Barquera, Spain B7 12
San Vicente del Caguán, Col. F5 58
San Vicente Reservoir, res., Ca., U.S. o16 82
San Xavier Indian Reservation, Az., U.S. E4 80
Sanzao Dao, i., China M2 28
Sanza Pombo, Ang. C3 44
São Bento, Braz. D10 54
São Borja, Braz. B5 56
São Caetano do Sul, Braz. G5 57
São Carlos, Braz. G5 57
São Domingos, Braz. B5 57
São Francisco, stm., Braz. E11 54
São Francisco do Sul, Braz. B7 56
São Gabriel, Braz. C6 56
São João da Boa Vista, Braz. F5 57
São João da Madeira, Port. E3 12
São João del Rei, Braz. F6 57
São Joaquim da Barra, Braz. F5 57
São José do Rio Prêto, Braz. F4 57
São José dos Campos, Braz. G6 57
São Leopoldo, Braz. B6 56
São Lourenço, Braz. G6 57
São Lourenço, Pantanal de, sw., Braz. G7 54
São Luís, Braz. D10 54
São Manuel, Braz. G4 57
São Mateus, Braz. E9 57
Saona, Isla, i., Dom. Rep. E13 64
Saône, stm., Fr. F11 10
São Paulo, Braz. G5 57
São Pedro do Ivaí, Braz. G3 57
São Pedro do Sul, Port. E3 12
São Romão, Braz. D6 57
São Roque, Cabo de, c., Braz. E11 54
São Sebastião, Ponta, c., Moz. F7 44
São Sebastião do Paraíso, Braz. F5 57
São Tomé, S. Tom./P. A1 44
São Tomé, i., S. Tom./P. A1 44
São Tomé, Cabo de, c., Braz. F8 57
Sao Tome and Principe, ctry., Afr. A1 44
São Vicente, Braz. G5 57
São Vicente, Cabo de, c., Port. H2 12
Sapé, Braz. E11 54
Sapele, Nig. G7 42
Sapelo Island, i., Ga., U.S. E5 87
Sapitwa, mtn., Mwi. E7 44
Sappa Creek, stm., U.S. E5 104
Sapphire Mountains, mts., Mt., U.S. D3 103
Sappington, Mo., U.S. f13 102
Sapporo, Japan p19 30a
Sapri, Italy I10 14
Sapulpa, Ok., U.S. B5 113
Sara Buri, Thai. G6 34
Sarajevo, Bos. F2 16
Saraland, Al., U.S. E1 78
Saranac, Mi., U.S. F5 99
Saranac, stm., N.Y., U.S. F11 109
Saranac Lake, N.Y., U.S. f10 109
Saranac Lakes, l., N.Y., U.S. f10 109
Sarangani Islands, is., Phil. D8 32
Saransk, Russia G7 22
Sarapul, Russia F8 22
Sarasota, Fl., U.S. E4 86
Sarasota, co., Fl., U.S. E4 86
Sarasota Bay, b., Fl., U.S. E4 86
Saratoga, Ca., U.S. k8 82
Saratoga, Tx., U.S. D5 120
Saratoga, Wy., U.S. E6 127
Saratoga, co., N.Y., U.S. B7 109
Saratoga Lake, l., N.Y., U.S. C7 109
Saratoga National Historical Park, N.Y., U.S. B7 109
Saratoga Springs, N.Y., U.S. B7 109
Saratov, Russia G7 22
Saravane, Laos G9 34
Sarcoxie, Mo., U.S. D3 102
Sardalas, Libya C8 42
Sardārshahr, India F6 38
Sardegna, i., Italy I3 14
Sardinia see Sardegna, i., Italy I3 14
Sardis, Ga., U.S. D5 87
Sardis, Ms., U.S. A4 101
Sardis Lake, res., Ms., U.S. A4 101
Sar-e Pol, Afg. B1 38
Sarepta, La., U.S. B2 95
Sarera, Teluk, b., Indon. F10 32
Sargent, Ga., U.S. C2 87
Sargent, Ne., U.S. C6 104
Sargent, co., N.D., U.S. C8 111
Sargodha, Pak. D5 38
Sarh, Chad G9 42
Sariñena, Spain D11 12
Şarköy, Tur. I11 16
Sarlat-la-Canéda, Fr. H8 10
Sarmi, Indon. F10 32
Sarmiento, Arg. F3 56
Särna, Swe. F9 6
Sarnia, Ont., Can. E2 73
Sarpy, co., Ne., U.S. C9 104
Sarralbe, Fr. C14 10
Sarrebourg, Fr. D14 10
Sarreguemines, Fr. C14 10
Sarria, Spain C4 12
Sartang, stm., Russia D20 24
Sartell, Mn., U.S. E4 100
Sarthe, stm., Fr. E6 10
Sarufutsu, Japan n20 30a
Sarzeau, Fr. E4 10
Sasarām, India H11 38
Sasebo, Japan I2 30
Saskatchewan, prov., Can. E3 75
Saskatchewan, stm., Can. F12 66
Saskylach, Russia C16 24
Sasovo, Russia G24 18
Sassafras, stm., Md., U.S. B5 97
Sassafras Mountain, mtn., U.S. A2 117
Sassandra, I.C. H4 42
Sassandra, stm., I.C. G4 42
Sassari, Italy I3 14
Sassnitz, Ger. A13 8
Sassuolo, Italy E5 14
Sastown, Lib. H4 42
Satah Mountain, mtn., B.C., Can. C5 69
Sata-misaki, c., Japan L3 30
Satanta, Ks., U.S. E3 93
Sātāra, India D2 37
Satilla, stm., Ga., U.S. E5 87
Satkānia, Bngl. I15 38
Satna, India H9 38
Sātpura Range, mts., India B4 37
Satsuma, Al., U.S. E1 78
Satsunan-shotō, is., Japan v29 31b
Şatu Mare, Rom. B6 16
Šatura, Russia F22 18
Satus Creek, stm., Wa., U.S. C5 124
Sauceda Mountains, mts., Az., U.S. E3 80
Sauda, Nor. G6 6
Saudi Arabia, ctry., Asia D4 46
Saufley Field Naval Air Station, mil., Fl., U.S. u14 86
Saugatuck, Mi., U.S. F4 99
Saugatuck, stm., Ct., U.S. D2 84
Saugatucket, stm., R.I., U.S. F4 116
Saugatuck Reservoir, res., Ct., U.S. D2 84
Saugerties, N.Y., U.S. C7 109
Saugus, Ma., U.S. B5 98
Saugus, stm., Ma., U.S. g11 98
Sauk, co., Wi., U.S. E4 126
Sauk, stm., Mn., U.S. E4 100
Sauk, stm., Wa., U.S. A4 124
Sauk Centre, Mn., U.S. E4 100
Sauk City, Wi., U.S. E4 126
Sauk Rapids, Mn., U.S. E4 100
Saukville, Wi., U.S. E6 126
Saulgau, Ger. G9 8
Saulnierville, N.S., Can. E3 71
Sault-au-Mouton, Que., Can. A8 74
Sault Sainte Marie, Ont., Can. p18 73
Sault Sainte Marie, Mi., U.S. B6 99
Saumarez Reef, rf., Austl. D10 50
Saumur, Fr. E6 10
Saunders, co., Ne., U.S. C9 104
Saunderstown, R.I., U.S. E4 116
Saurimo, Ang. C4 44
Sausalito, Ca., U.S. D2 82
Sava, Italy I12 14
Sava, stm., Eur. E3 16
Savage, Md., U.S. B4 97
Savage, stm., Md., U.S. k12 97
Savage River Reservoir, res., Md., U.S. k12 97
Savanna, Il., U.S. A3 90
Savanna, Ok., U.S. C6 113
Savannah, Ga., U.S. D5 87
Savannah, Mo., U.S. B3 102
Savannah, Tn., U.S. B3 119
Savannah, stm., U.S. F5 117
Savannah River Plant, sci., S.C., U.S. E4 117
Savannakhet, Laos F8 34
Savanna Lake, l., Md., U.S. D6 97
Savanna-la-Mar, Jam. E8 64
Savaştepe, Tur. J11 16
Save (Sabi), stm., Afr. F6 44
Savenay, Fr. E5 10
Saverdun, Fr. I8 10
Saverne, Fr. D14 10
Savigliano, Italy E2 14
Saville Dam, Ct., U.S. B4 84
Savona, Italy E3 14
Savonlinna, Fin. F17 6
Savonranta, Fin. E17 6
Savoonga, Ak., U.S. C5 79
Savoy, Il., U.S. C5 90
Savu Sea see Sawu, Laut, Indon. G7 32
Sawai Mādhopur, India G7 38
Sawākin, Sudan E13 42
Sawang, Indon. N7 34
Sawatch Range, mts., Co., U.S. B4 83
Sawdā', Qurnat as-, mtn., Leb. B5 40
Sawel Mountain, mtn., N. Ire., U.K. G5 7
Sawhāj, Egypt C12 42
Sawknah, Libya C9 42
Sawnee Mountain, mtn., Ga., U.S. B2 87
Sawtooth Mountains, mts., Id., U.S. F4 89
Sawtooth National Recreation Area, Id., U.S. E3 89
Sawu, Laut (Savu Sea), Indon. G7 32
Sawu, Pulau, i., Indon. H7 32
Şawwān, Arḍ aş-, pl., Jord. D5 40
Sawyer, co., Wi., U.S. C2 126
Sawyerville, Que., Can. D6 74
Saxmundham, Eng., U.K. I14 7
Saxonburg, Pa., U.S. E2 115
Saxtons, stm., Vt., U.S. E3 122
Saxtons River, Vt., U.S. E3 122
Sayaboury, Laos E6 34
Sayan Mountains (Sajany), mts., Asia G12 24
Sayaxché, Guat. F2 64
Saybrook, Il., U.S. C5 90
Saybrook Manor, Ct., U.S. D6 84
Şaydā (Sidon), Leb. C4 40
Saydel, Ia., U.S. e8 92
Sayhūt, Yemen E5 46
Saylesville, R.I., U.S. B4 116
Saylorsburg, Pa., U.S. E11 115
Saylorville, Ia., U.S. e8 92
Saylorville Lake, res., Ia., U.S. C4 92
Sayre, Al., U.S. B3 78
Sayre, Ok., U.S. B2 113
Sayre, Pa., U.S. C8 115
Sayreville, N.J., U.S. C4 107
Sayula, Mex. H8 62
Say'ūn, Yemen E4 46
Sayville, N.Y., U.S. n15 109
Scafell Pikes, mtn., Eng., U.K. G9 7
Scalp Level, Pa., U.S. F4 115
Scanlon, Mn., U.S. D6 100
Scapegoat Mountain, mtn., Mt., U.S. C3 103
Ščapino, Russia F25 24
Scappoose, Or., U.S. B4 114
Scarborough, Ont., Can. m15 73
Scarborough, Trin. I17 64
Scarborough, Me., U.S. E2 96
Scarbro, W.V., U.S. n13 125
Scarsdale, N.Y., U.S. h13 109
Ščelkovo, Russia F21 18
Ščerbakovo, Russia D26 24
Schaefferstown, Pa., U.S. F9 115
Schaffhausen, Switz. E15 10
Schaller, Ia., U.S. B2 92
Schaumburg, Il., U.S. h8 90
Schell Creek Range, mts., Nv., U.S. D7 105
Schenectady, N.Y., U.S. C7 109
Schenectady, co., N.Y., U.S. C6 109
Schererville, In., U.S. B3 91
Schertz, Tx., U.S. h7 120
Schiller Park, Il., U.S. k9 90
Schio, Italy D6 14
Schladming, Aus. H13 8
Schleicher, co., Tx., U.S. D2 120
Schleiden, Ger. E6 8
Schleswig, Ger. A9 8
Schleswig, Ia., U.S. B2 92
Schley, co., Ga., U.S. D2 87
Schneverdingen, Ger. B9 8
Schofield, Wi., U.S. D4 126
Schofield Barracks, mil., Hi., U.S. g9 88
Schoharie, co., N.Y., U.S. C6 109
Schoharie Creek, stm., N.Y., U.S. C6 109
Schönebeck, Ger. B13 8
Schongau, Ger. H10 8
Schoodic Lake, l., Me., U.S. C4 96
Schoolcraft, Mi., U.S. F5 99
Schoolcraft, co., Mi., U.S. B4 99
Schramberg, Ger. G8 8
Schrobenhausen, Ger. G11 8
Schroon Lake, l., N.Y., U.S. B7 109
Schulenburg, Tx., U.S. E4 120
Schulter, Ok., U.S. B6 113
Schurz, Nv., U.S. E3 105
Schuyler, Ne., U.S. C8 104
Schuyler, co., Il., U.S. C3 90
Schuyler, co., Mo., U.S. A5 102
Schuyler, co., N.Y., U.S. C4 109
Schuylkill, co., Pa., U.S. E9 115
Schuylkill, stm., Pa., U.S. F10 115
Schuylkill Haven, Pa., U.S. E9 115
Schwabach, Ger. F11 8
Schwaben, hist. reg., Ger. G10 8
Schwäbische Alb, mts., Ger. G9 8
Schwäbisch Gmünd, Ger. G9 8
Schwäbisch Hall, Ger. F9 8
Schwandorf in Bayern, Ger. F12 8
Schwaner, Pegunungan, mts., Indon. F5 32
Schwarzwald, mts., Ger. G8 8
Schwaz, Aus. H11 8
Schwechat, Aus. G16 8
Schwedt, Ger. B14 8
Schweinfurt, Ger. E10 8
Schwerin, Ger. B11 8
Schwyz, Switz. E15 10
Sciacca, Italy L8 14
Scicli, Italy M9 14
Science Hill, Ky., U.S. C5 94
Scilly, Isles of, is., Eng., U.K. L6 7
Scio, Or., U.S. C4 114
Scioto, co., Oh., U.S. D3 112
Scioto, stm., Oh., U.S. B2 112
Scituate, Ma., U.S. B6 98
Scituate Reservoir, res., R.I., U.S. C3 116
Scobey, Mt., U.S. B11 103
Scofield Reservoir, res., Ut., U.S. D4 121
Ščokino, Russia G20 18
Scotch Plains, N.J., U.S. B4 107
Scotia, Ca., U.S. B1 82
Scotia, N.Y., U.S. C7 109
Scotland, Ont., Can. D4 73
Scotland, S.D., U.S. D8 118
Scotland, co., Mo., U.S. A5 102
Scotland, co., N.C., U.S. C3 110
Scotland, ter., U.K. D8 7
Scotland Neck, N.C., U.S. A5 110
Scotlandville, La., U.S. D4 95
Scotrun, Pa., U.S. D11 115
Scottstown, Que., Can. D6 74
Scott, La., U.S. D3 95
Scott, co., Ar., U.S. C1 81
Scott, co., Il., U.S. D3 90
Scott, co., In., U.S. G6 91
Scott, co., Ia., U.S. C7 92
Scott, co., Ks., U.S. D3 93
Scott, co., Ky., U.S. B5 94
Scott, co., Mn., U.S. F5 100
Scott, co., Ms., U.S. C4 101
Scott, co., Mo., U.S. D8 102
Scott, co., Tn., U.S. C9 119
Scott, co., Va., U.S. f9 123
Scott, Cape, c., B.C., Can. D3 69
Scott, Mount, mtn., Or., U.S. E4 114
Scott Air Force Base, mil., Il., U.S. E4 90
Scott City, Ks., U.S. D3 93
Scott City, Mo., U.S. D8 102
Scottdale, Ga., U.S. h8 87
Scottdale, Pa., U.S. F2 115
Scott Islands, is., B.C., Can. F7 66
Scott Mountain, mtn., Id., U.S. E3 89
Scott Peak, mtn., Id., U.S. E6 89
Scott Reef, rf., Austl. B4 50
Scott Reservoir, res., N.C., U.S. A1 110
Scottsbluff, Ne., U.S. C2 104
Scotts Bluff, co., Ne., U.S. C2 104
Scotts Bluff National Monument, Ne., U.S. C2 104
Scottsboro, Al., U.S. A3 78
Scottsburg, In., U.S. G6 91
Scottsdale, Austl. H9 50
Scottsdale, Az., U.S. D4 80
Scottsville, Ky., U.S. D3 94
Scottsville, N.Y., U.S. B3 109
Scottville, Mi., U.S. E4 99
Scourie, Scot., U.K. C7 7
Scraggly Lake, l., Me., U.S. B4 96
Scranton, Ks., U.S. D8 93
Scranton, Pa., U.S. D10 115
Scranton, S.C., U.S. D8 117
Screven, Ga., U.S. E4 87
Screven, co., Ga., U.S. D5 87
Scribner, Ne., U.S. C9 104
Scugog, Lake, l., Ont., Can. C6 73
Scurry, co., Tx., U.S. C2 120
Scutari, Lake, l., Eur. G3 16
Seaboard, N.C., U.S. A5 110
Seabreeze, De., U.S. F5 85
Seabrook, N.H., U.S. E5 106
Seabrook, Tx., U.S. r14 120
Seabrook Island, i., S.C., U.S. F7 117
Seadrift, Tx., U.S. E4 120
Seaford, De., U.S. F3 85
Seaford, Va., U.S. h15 123
Seaforth, Ont., Can. D3 73
Seagoville, Tx., U.S. n10 120
Seagraves, Tx., U.S. C1 120
Seaham, Eng., U.K. G11 7
Sea Isle City, N.J., U.S. E3 107
Seal, stm., Man., Can. E13 66
Seal Cove, Newf., Can. D3 72
Seal Point, c., P.E.I., Can. C5 71
Seal Rock, Or., U.S. C2 114
Sealy, Tx., U.S. E4 120
Seaman, Oh., U.S. D2 112
Seaman Range, mts., Nv., U.S. F6 105
Searchlight, Nv., U.S. H7 105
Searcy, Ar., U.S. B4 81
Searcy, co., Ar., U.S. B3 81
Searles Lake, l., Ca., U.S. E5 82
Searsport, Me., U.S. D4 96
Seaside, Or., U.S. B3 114
Seat Pleasant, Md., U.S. C4 97
Seattle, Wa., U.S. B3 124
Seattle-Tacoma International Airport, Wa., U.S. f11 124
Seaview, Wa., U.S. C1 124
Sebago Lake, Me., U.S. E2 96
Šebalino, Russia G11 24
Sebastian, Fl., U.S. E6 86
Sebastian, co., Ar., U.S. B1 81
Sebastian, Cape, c., Or., U.S. E2 114
Sebastian Inlet, b., Fl., U.S. E6 86
Sebastián Vizcaíno, Bahía, b., Mex. C2 62
Sebasticook Lake, l., Me., U.S. D3 96
Sebec Lake, l., Me., U.S. C3 96
Sebeka, Mn., U.S. D3 100
Sebewaing, Mi., U.S. E7 99
Seboeis, stm., Me., U.S. B4 96
Seboeis Lake, l., Me., U.S. C4 96
Seboomook Lake, l., Me., U.S. C3 96
Sebree, Ky., U.S. C2 94
Sebring, Fl., U.S. E5 86
Sebring, Oh., U.S. B4 112
Secaucus, N.J., U.S. h8 107
Sechelt, B.C., Can. E6 69
Second Lake, l., N.H., U.S. f7 106
Second Mesa, Az., U.S. B5 80
Secret Lake, l., R.I., U.S. E4 116
Section, Al., U.S. A4 78
Security, Co., U.S. C6 83
Sedalia, Mo., U.S. C4 102
Sedan, Fr. C11 10
Sedan, Ks., U.S. E7 93
Sedano, Spain C8 12
Sedgewick, Alta., Can. C5 68
Sedgewick, Mount, mtn., N.M., U.S. B1 108
Sedgwick, Ks., U.S. E6 93
Sedgwick, co., Co., U.S. A8 83
Sedgwick, co., Ks., U.S. E6 93
Sedley, Va., U.S. D6 123
Sedona, Az., U.S. C4 80
Sedro Woolley, Wa., U.S. A3 124
Seeheim, Nmb. G3 44
Seekonk, Ma., U.S. C5 98
Seekonk, stm., R.I., U.S. C4 116
Seeley, Ca., U.S. F6 82
Seeley Lake, Mt., U.S. C3 103
Seelyville, In., U.S. F3 91
Sées, Fr. D7 10
Segamat, Malay. M7 34
Ségou, Mali F4 42
Segovia, Col. D5 58
Segovia, Spain E7 12
Segré, Fr. E6 10
Seguam Island, i., Ak., U.S. E5 79
Seguam Pass, strt., Ak., U.S. E5 79
Séguédine, Niger D8 42
Seguin, Tx., U.S. E4 120
Sehore, India I7 38
Seia, Port. E4 12
Seiling, Ok., U.S. A3 113
Seinäjoki, Fin. E14 6
Seine, stm., Fr. C7 10
Seki, Tur. M13 16
Sekiu, Wa., U.S. A1 124
Şekondi-Takoradi, Ghana H5 42
Šelagskij, Mys, c., Russia C28 24
Selah, Wa., U.S. C5 124
Selaru, Pulau, i., Indon. G9 32
Selatan, Tanjung, c., Indon. F5 32
Selawik, Ak., U.S. B7 79
Selawik Lake, l., Ak., U.S. B7 79
Selayar, Pulau, i., Indon. G7 32
Selb, Ger. E12 8
Selby, S.D., U.S. B5 118
Selbyville, De., U.S. G5 85
Selçuk, Tur. L11 16
Seldovia, Ak., U.S. D9 79
Selemdža, stm., Russia G20 24
Selenn'ach, stm., Russia D21 24
Sélestat, Fr. D14 10
Şélibaby, Maur. E3 42
Šelichova, Zaliv, b., Russia E25 24
Seligman, Az., U.S. B3 80
Selinsgrove, Pa., U.S. E8 115
Selkirk, Man., Can. D3 70
Selkirk, Scot., U.K. F10 7
Selkirk Mountains, mts., N.A. F9 66
Sellersburg, In., U.S. H6 91
Sellersville, Pa., U.S. F11 115
Selles-sur-Cher, Fr. E8 10
Sells, Az., U.S. F4 80
Selma, Al., U.S. C2 78
Selma, Ca., U.S. D4 82
Selma, In., U.S. D7 91
Selma, N.C., U.S. B4 110
Selmer, Tn., U.S. B3 119
Selva, Arg. B4 56
Selvas, for., Braz. E6 54
Selway, stm., Id., U.S. C3 89
Selwyn Mountains, mts., Can. D6 66
Semara, W. Sah. C3 42
Semarang, Indon. m15 32
Semeru, Gunung, vol., Indon. n16 33
Seminoe Mountains, mts., Wy., U.S. D6 127
Seminoe Reservoir, res., Wy., U.S. D6 127
Seminole, Ok., U.S. B5 113
Seminole, Tx., U.S. C1 120
Seminole, co., Fl., U.S. D5 86
Seminole, co., Ga., U.S. F2 87
Seminole, co., Ok., U.S. B5 113
Seminole, Lake, res., U.S. F2 87
Semipalatinsk, Kaz. G10 24
Semisopochnoi Island, i., Ak., U.S. E3 79
Şemmes, Al., U.S. E1 78
Šemonaicha, Kaz. G10 24
Semur-en-Auxois, Fr. E11 1
Sên, stm., Camb. H8 34
Sena, Moz. E6 4
Senachwine Lake, l., Il., U.S. B4 9
Senador Pompeu, Braz. E11 5
Sena Madureira, Braz. E5 5
Senanga, Zam. E4 4
Senath, Mo., U.S. E7 10
Senatobia, Ms., U.S. A4 10
Sendai, Japan K3 3
Sendai, Japan D13 3
Seneca, Il., U.S. B5 9
Seneca, Ks., U.S. C7 9
Seneca, Mo., U.S. E3 10
Seneca, Pa., U.S. D2 11
Seneca, S.C., U.S. B2 11
Seneca, co., N.Y., U.S. C4 10
Seneca, co., Oh., U.S. A2 11
Seneca Falls, N.Y., U.S. C4 10
Seneca Lake, l., N.Y., U.S. C4 10
Senecaville Lake, res., Oh., U.S. C4 11
Senegal (Sénégal), ctry., Afr. F3 4
Sénégal, stm., Afr. E3 4
Senekal, S. Afr. G5 4
Senftenberg, Ger. D13
Senigallia, Italy F8 1
Senise, Italy I11 1
Senmonorom, Camb. H9 3
Senneterre, Que., Can. k11 7
Sennori, Italy I3 1
Senoia, Ga., U.S. C2 8
Sens, Fr. D10 1
Senta, Yugo. D4 1
Sentinel, Ok., U.S. B2 11
Seo de Urgel, Spain C13 1
Seoni, India I8 3
Seoul see Sŏul, S. Kor. D12 2
Sept-Îles (Seven Islands), Que., Can. h13 7
Sepulga, stm., Al., U.S. D3 7
Sepúlveda, Spain D8 1
Sequatchie, co., Tn., U.S. D8 11

Name	Map Ref	Page
equatchie, stm., Tn., U.S.	D8	119
equim, Wa., U.S.	A2	124
equoia National Park, Ca., U.S.	D4	82
equoyah, co., Ok., U.S.	B7	113
eraing, Bel.	E5	8
eram, i., Indon.	F8	32
eram, Laut (Ceram Sea), Indon.	F8	32
erang, Indon.	m13	33a
eremban, Malay.	M6	34
erengeti Plain, pl., Tan.	B6	44
erenje, Zam.	D6	44
ergeant Bluff, Ia., U.S.	B1	92
ergeja Kirova, Ostrova, is., Russia	B11	24
ergijev Podad, Russia	E21	18
erowe, Bots.	F5	44
erpa, Port.	H4	12
erpuchov, Russia	G20	18
érrai, Grc.	H7	16
erra San Bruno, Italy	K11	14
erra Talhada, Braz.	E11	54
erres, Fr.	H12	10
errezuela, Arg.	C3	56
erri, Italy	J4	14
errinha, Braz.	F11	54
ertã, Port.	F3	12
esfontein, Nmb.	E2	44
esheke, Zam.	E4	44
essa Aurunca, Italy	H8	14
esser, Il., U.S.	E4	90
estri Levante, Italy	E4	14
ète, Fr.	I10	10
ete Lagoas, Braz.	E6	57
eth, W.V., U.S.	C3	125
étif, Alg.	A7	42
eto, Japan	G10	30
eto-naikai, Japan	H6	30
etúbal, Port.	G3	12
eul, Lac, l., Ont., Can.	o16	73
eul Choix Point, c., Mi., U.S.	C5	99
evan, ozero, l., Arm.	I7	22
evastopol', Ukr.	I4	22
even Devils Lake, res., Ar., U.S.	D4	81
even Devils Mountains, mts., Id., U.S.	D2	89
even Hills, Oh., U.S.	h9	112
even Mile Beach, N.J., U.S.	E3	107
évérac-le-Château, Fr.	H10	10
evern, Md., U.S.	B4	97
evern, stm., Ont., Can.	n17	73
evern, stm., Eng., U.K.	J10	7
evernaja Dvina, stm., Russia	E6	22
evernaja Zemľa, is., Russia	B13	24
everna Park, Md., U.S.	B4	97
evern River, b., Md., U.S.	B4	97
everodvinsk, Russia	E5	22
evero-Kuril'sk, Russia	G25	24
evero-Sibirskaja Nizmennosť, pl., Russia	C13	24
evero-Zadonsk, Russia	G21	18
evettijärvi, Fin.	B17	6
evier, co., Ar., U.S.	D1	81
evier, co., Tn., U.S.	D10	119
evier, co., Ut., U.S.	E4	121
evier, stm., Ut., U.S.	D3	121
evier Bridge Reservoir, res., Ut., U.S.	D4	121
evier Lake, l., Ut., U.S.	E2	121
evierville, Tn., U.S.	D10	119
evilla, Col.	E5	58
evilla, Spain	H6	12
eville, Oh., U.S.	A4	112
eville see Sevilla, Spain	H6	12
ewanee, Tn., U.S.	D8	119
eward, Ak., U.S.	C10	79
eward, Ne., U.S.	D8	104
eward, co., Ks., U.S.	E3	93
eward, co., Ne., U.S.	D8	104
eward Peninsula, pen., Ak., U.S.	B7	79
ewickley, Pa., U.S.	E1	115
exsmith, Alta., Can.	B1	68
eychelles, ctry., Afr.	B11	44
eydisfjördur, Ice.	B5	4
eymour, Ct., U.S.	D3	84
eymour, In., U.S.	G6	91
eymour, Ia., U.S.	D4	92
eymour, Mo., U.S.	D5	102
eymour, Tx., U.S.	C3	120
eymour, Wi., U.S.	D5	126
eymour Inlet, b., B.C., Can.	D4	69
eymour Johnson Air Force Base, mil., N.C., U.S.	B5	110
eymour Lake, l., Vt., U.S.	B4	122
eymourville, La., U.S.	h9	95
eyne, Fr.	H13	10
eyssel, Fr.	G12	10
ézanne, Fr.	D10	10
ezze, Italy	H8	14
fax, Tun.	B8	42
s-Gravenhage (The Hague), Neth.	C4	8
habbona, Il., U.S.	B5	90
hache, China	A7	38
hackelford, co., Tx., U.S.	C3	120
hackleton Ice Shelf, Ant.	C22	47
haddādī, Syria	A7	40
hadehill Dam, S.D., U.S.	B3	118
hadehill Reservoir, res., S.D., U.S.	B3	118
hadow Mountain National Recreation Area, Co., U.S.	A4	83
hady Cove, Or., U.S.	E4	114
hady Side, Md., U.S.	C4	97
hadyside, Oh., U.S.	C5	112
hady Spring, W.V., U.S.	D3	125
hafer, Lake, l., In., U.S.	C4	91
hafer Butte, mtn., Id., U.S.	F2	89
hafter, Ca., U.S.	E4	82
haftsbury, Vt., U.S.	E2	122
hāhdādkot, Pak.	G2	38
hahdol, India	I9	38
hāhjahānpur, India	G8	38
hāh Jūy, Afg.	D2	38
hahrak, Afg.	C1	38
Shājāpur, India	I7	38
Shakawe, Bots.	E4	44
Shaker Heights, Oh., U.S.	A4	112
Shakhty see Šachty, Russia	H6	22
Shaki, Nig.	G6	42
Shakopee, Mn., U.S.	F5	100
Shaler Mountains, mts., N.W. Ter., Can.	B10	66
Shallotte, N.C., U.S.	D4	110
Shallotte Inlet, b., N.C., U.S.	D4	110
Shallowater, Tx., U.S.	C2	120
Shām, Bādiyat ash-, des., Asia	C6	40
Shām, Jabal ash-, mtn., Oman	D6	46
Shamokin, Pa., U.S.	E8	115
Shamokin Dam, Pa., U.S.	E8	115
Shamrock, Tx., U.S.	B2	120
Shandī, Sudan	E12	42
Shandong, prov., China	D10	26
Shandong Bandao, pen., China	D11	26
Shanghai, China	D10	28
Shanghai Shih, China	E11	28
Shangqiu, China	A4	28
Shangrao, China	G6	28
Shangshui, China	B3	28
Shangzhi, China	B12	26
Shannock, R.I., U.S.	F2	116
Shannon, Ga., U.S.	B1	87
Shannon, Il., U.S.	A4	90
Shannon, Ms., U.S.	A5	101
Shannon, co., Mo., U.S.	D6	102
Shannon, co., S.D., U.S.	D3	118
Shannon, stm., Ire.	I3	7
Shannon, Lake, l., Wa., U.S.	A4	124
Shannontown, S.C., U.S.	D7	117
Shantou (Swatow), China	L5	28
Shantung Peninsula see Shandong Bandao, pen., China	D11	26
Shănxī, prov., China	D8	26
Shănxī, prov., China	D9	26
Shanyin, China	D9	26
Shaoguan, China	K2	28
Shaowu, China	H6	28
Shaoxing, China	E9	28
Shaoyang, China	F9	26
Shark Bay, b., Austl.	E2	50
Sharkey, co., Ms., U.S.	C3	101
Shark Point, c., Fl., U.S.	H5	86
Sharktooth Mountain, mtn., B.C., Can.	E7	66
Sharon, Ct., U.S.	B2	84
Sharon, Ma., U.S.	B5	98
Sharon, Pa., U.S.	D1	115
Sharon, Tn., U.S.	A3	119
Sharon, Wi., U.S.	F5	126
Sharon Hill, Pa., U.S.	p20	115
Sharon Park, Oh., U.S.	n12	112
Sharon Springs, Ks., U.S.	D2	93
Sharonville, Oh., U.S.	n13	112
Sharp, co., Ar., U.S.	A4	81
Sharpe, Lake, res., S.D., U.S.	C6	118
Sharpes, Fl., U.S.	D6	86
Sharpley, De., U.S.	h7	85
Sharpsburg, Md., U.S.	B2	97
Sharpsburg, N.C., U.S.	B5	110
Sharpsburg, Pa., U.S.	k14	115
Sharpsville, In., U.S.	D5	91
Sharpsville, Pa., U.S.	D1	115
Sharptown, Md., U.S.	C6	97
Sharqīyah, Aş-Şahrā' ash- (Arabian Desert), des., Egypt	C12	42
Shashi, China	E9	26
Shashi, stm., Afr.	F5	44
Shasta, co., Ca., U.S.	B3	82
Shasta, Mount, vol., Ca., U.S.	B2	82
Shasta Lake, res., Ca., U.S.	B2	82
Shattuck, Ok., U.S.	A2	113
Shaw, Ms., U.S.	B3	101
Shaw Air Force Base, mil., S.C., U.S.	D7	117
Shawano, Wi., U.S.	D5	126
Shawano, co., Wi., U.S.	D5	126
Shawano Lake, l., Wi., U.S.	D5	126
Shawinigan, Que., Can.	C5	74
Shawinigan-Sud, Que., Can.	C5	74
Shawnee, Ks., U.S.	k16	93
Shawnee, Ok., U.S.	B5	113
Shawnee, co., Ks., U.S.	D8	93
Shawneetown, Il., U.S.	F5	90
Shawsheen, stm., Ma., U.S.	f11	98
Shaybārā, i., Sau. Ar.	C2	46
Shaykh, Jabal ash-, mtn., Asia	C4	40
Shebele (Shebelle), stm., Afr.	G3	46
Sheberghān, Afg.	B1	38
Sheboygan, Wi., U.S.	E6	126
Sheboygan, co., Wi., U.S.	E6	126
Sheboygan, stm., Wi., U.S.	k10	126
Sheboygan Falls, Wi., U.S.	E6	126
Shediac, N.B., Can.	C5	71
Sheenjek, stm., Ak., U.S.	B11	79
Sheep Mountain, mtn., Az., U.S.	E1	80
Sheep Mountain, mtn., Wy., U.S.	B5	127
Sheep Mountain, mtn., Wy., U.S.	C2	127
Sheep Peak, mtn., Nv., U.S.	G6	105
Sheep Range, mts., Nv., U.S.	G6	105
Sheet Harbour, N.S., Can.	E7	71
Sheffield, Eng., U.K.	H11	7
Sheffield, Al., U.S.	A2	78
Sheffield, Il., U.S.	B4	90
Sheffield, Ia., U.S.	B4	92
Sheffield, Pa., U.S.	C3	115
Sheffield Lake, Oh., U.S.	A3	112
Sheila, N.B., Can.	B5	71
Shēkhābād, Afg.	C3	38
Shekhūpura, Pak.	E5	38
Shelagyote Peak, mtn., B.C., Can.	B4	69
Shelbiana, Ky., U.S.	C7	94
Shelbina, Mo., U.S.	B5	102
Shelburn, In., U.S.	F3	91
Shelburne, Ont., Can.	C4	73
Shelburne Falls, Ma., U.S.	A2	98
Shelburne Pond, l., Vt., U.S.	C2	122
Shelby, Al., U.S.	B3	78
Shelby, In., U.S.	B3	91
Shelby, Ia., U.S.	C2	92
Shelby, Mi., U.S.	E4	99
Shelby, Ms., U.S.	B3	101
Shelby, Mt., U.S.	B5	103
Shelby, Ne., U.S.	C8	104
Shelby, N.C., U.S.	B1	110
Shelby, Oh., U.S.	B3	112
Shelby, co., Al., U.S.	B3	78
Shelby, co., Il., U.S.	D5	90
Shelby, co., In., U.S.	E6	91
Shelby, co., Ia., U.S.	C2	92
Shelby, co., Ky., U.S.	B4	94
Shelby, co., Mo., U.S.	B5	102
Shelby, co., Oh., U.S.	B1	112
Shelby, co., Tn., U.S.	B2	119
Shelby, co., Tx., U.S.	D5	120
Shelbyville, Il., U.S.	D5	90
Shelbyville, In., U.S.	F6	91
Shelbyville, Ky., U.S.	B4	94
Shelbyville, Tn., U.S.	B5	119
Shelbyville, Lake, res., Il., U.S.	D5	90
Sheldon, Il., U.S.	C6	90
Sheldon, Ia., U.S.	A2	92
Sheldon, Tx., U.S.	r14	120
Shelikof Strait, strt., Ak., U.S.	D9	79
Shell Creek, stm., U.S.	A2	83
Shell Creek, stm., Wy., U.S.	B5	127
Shelley, Id., U.S.	F6	89
Shell Lake, Wi., U.S.	C2	126
Shell Lake, l., Mn., U.S.	D3	100
Shell Lake, l., Wi., U.S.	C2	126
Shellman, Ga., U.S.	E2	87
Shell Rock, Ia., U.S.	B5	92
Shell Rock, stm., Ia., U.S.	B5	92
Shellsburg, Ia., U.S.	B6	92
Shelly Mountain, mtn., Id., U.S.	F5	89
Shelter Island, N.Y., U.S.	m16	109
Shelton, Ct., U.S.	D3	84
Shelton, Ne., U.S.	D7	104
Shelton, Wa., U.S.	B2	124
Shemya Air Force Base, mil., Ak., U.S.	E2	79
Shenandoah, Ia., U.S.	D2	92
Shenandoah, Pa., U.S.	E9	115
Shenandoah, Va., U.S.	B4	123
Shenandoah, co., Va., U.S.	B4	123
Shenandoah, stm., U.S.	A5	123
Shenandoah, North Fork, stm., Va., U.S.	B4	123
Shenandoah, South Fork, stm., Va., U.S.	B4	123
Shenandoah Mountain, mtn., U.S.	B3	123
Shenandoah National Park, Va., U.S.	B4	123
Shenango River Lake, res., U.S.	D1	115
Shengfang, China	D10	26
Shengze, China	E9	28
Shenipsit Lake, l., Ct., U.S.	B6	84
Shenyang (Mukden), China	C11	26
Shenzha, China	E13	38
Shepaug, stm., Ct., U.S.	C2	84
Shepaug Dam, Ct., U.S.	D2	84
Shepaug Reservoir, res., Ct., U.S.	C2	84
Shepherd, Mi., U.S.	E6	99
Shepherd, Tx., U.S.	D5	120
Shepherdstown, W.V., U.S.	B7	125
Shepherdsville, Ky., U.S.	C4	94
Sheppard Air Force Base, mil., Tx., U.S.	C3	120
Shepparton, Austl.	G9	50
Sherborn, Ma., U.S.	h10	98
Sherbro Island, i., S.L.	G3	42
Sherbrooke, Que., Can.	D6	74
Sherburn, Mn., U.S.	G4	100
Sherburne, co., Mn., U.S.	E5	100
Sheridan, Ar., U.S.	C3	81
Sheridan, Il., U.S.	B5	90
Sheridan, In., U.S.	D5	91
Sheridan, Mi., U.S.	E5	99
Sheridan, Mt., U.S.	E4	103
Sheridan, Or., U.S.	B3	114
Sheridan, Wy., U.S.	B6	127
Sheridan, co., Ks., U.S.	C3	93
Sheridan, co., Mt., U.S.	B12	103
Sheridan, co., Ne., U.S.	B3	104
Sheridan, co., N.D., U.S.	B5	111
Sheridan, co., Wy., U.S.	B5	127
Sheridan, Mount, mtn., Wy., U.S.	B2	127
Sheringham Cromer, Eng., U.K.	I14	7
Sherman, Tx., U.S.	C4	120
Sherman, co., Ks., U.S.	C2	93
Sherman, co., Ne., U.S.	C6	104
Sherman, co., Or., U.S.	B6	114
Sherman, co., Tx., U.S.	A2	120
Sherman Reservoir, res., Ne., U.S.	C7	104
Sherrelwood, Co., U.S.	*B6	83
Sherrill, N.Y., U.S.	B5	109
's-Hertogenbosch, Neth.	D5	8
Sherwood, P.E.I., Can.	C6	71
Sherwood, Ar., U.S.	C3	81
Sherwood, Or., U.S.	h12	114
Sherwood, Wi., U.S.	h9	126
Sherwood Manor, Ct., U.S.	A5	84
Sherwood Park, De., U.S.	i7	85
Shetek, Lake, l., Mn., U.S.	G3	100
Shetland Islands, is., Scot., U.K.	A11	7
Shetucket, stm., Ct., U.S.	C7	84
Sheyenne, stm., N.D., U.S.	C8	111
Sheyenne Lake, res., N.D., U.S.	B5	111
Shiawassee, co., Mi., U.S.	F6	99
Shibata, Japan	E12	30
Shibetsu, Japan	p23	30a
Shibukawa, Japan	F11	30
Shickshinny, Pa., U.S.	D9	115
Shijiazhuang, China	D9	26
Shijushan, China	D8	26
Shikārpur, Pak.	G3	38
Shikohābād, India	G8	38
Shikoku, i., Japan	I6	30
Shikoku-sanchi, mts., Japan	I6	30
Shikotsu-ko, l., Japan	q19	30a
Shillington, Pa., U.S.	F10	115
Shillong, India	H14	38
Shiloh National Military Park, Tn., U.S.	B3	119
Shilong, China	L2	28
Shimabara, Japan	J3	30
Shimada, Japan	H11	30
Shimbiris, mtn., Som.	F4	46
Shimizu, Japan	G11	30
Shimminato, Japan	F10	30
Shimodate, Japan	F12	30
Shimoga, India	F3	37
Shimonoseki, Japan	I3	30
Shinano, stm., Japan	E11	30
Shīndand, Afg.	C1	36
Shiner, Tx., U.S.	E4	120
Shinglehouse, Pa., U.S.	C5	115
Shingū, Japan	I8	30
Shinjō, Japan	D13	30
Shinnston, W.V., U.S.	B4	125
Shinshār, Syria	B5	40
Shinyanga, Tan.	B6	44
Shiocton, Wi., U.S.	D5	126
Shiogama, Japan	D14	30
Shiojiri, Japan	F10	30
Shiping, China	C7	34
Ship Island, i., Ms., U.S.	E5	101
Ship Island Pass, strt., Ms., U.S.	g7	101
Shippegan, N.B., Can.	B5	71
Shippensburg, Pa., U.S.	F6	115
Shiprock, N.M., U.S.	A1	108
Ship Rock, mtn., N.M., U.S.	A1	108
Shirakawa, Japan	E13	30
Shīrāz, Iran	C5	46
Shire, stm., Afr.	E6	44
Shiretoko-misaki, c., Japan	o23	30a
Shirley, In., U.S.	E6	91
Shirley, Ma., U.S.	A4	98
Shirley Mountains, mts., Wy., U.S.	D6	127
Shirpur, India	B3	37
Shishaldin Volcano, vol., Ak., U.S.	E7	79
Shishmaref, Ak., U.S.	B6	79
Shively, Ky., U.S.	B4	94
Shivpuri, India	H7	38
Shizuoka, Japan	H11	30
Shkodër, Alb.	G3	16
Shoal Creek, stm., U.S.	B4	119
Shoal Harbour, Newf., Can.	D4	72
Shoal Lake, Man., Can.	D1	70
Shoals, In., U.S.	G4	91
Shoals, Isles of, is., Me., U.S.	E2	96
Shoalwater, Cape, c., Wa., U.S.	C1	124
Shōdo-shima, i., Japan	H7	30
Shoemakersville, Pa., U.S.	F10	115
Sholāpur, India	D3	37
Shongopovi, Az., U.S.	B5	80
Shonto, Az., U.S.	A5	80
Shoreham, Mi., U.S.	F4	99
Shores Acres, R.I., U.S.	E4	116
Shoreview, Mn., U.S.	m12	100
Shorewood, Il., U.S.	k8	90
Shorewood, Mn., U.S.	n11	100
Shorewood, Wi., U.S.	E6	126
Short Beach, Ct., U.S.	D4	84
Shoshone, Id., U.S.	G4	89
Shoshone, co., Id., U.S.	B2	89
Shoshone, stm., Wy., U.S.	B4	127
Shoshone Falls, wtfl, Id., U.S.	G4	89
Shoshone Lake, l., Wy., U.S.	B2	127
Shoshone Mountains, mts., Nv., U.S.	E4	105
Shoshone Peak, mtn., Nv., U.S.	G5	105
Shoshone Range, mts., Nv., U.S.	C5	105
Shoshong, Bots.	F5	44
Shoshoni, Wy., U.S.	C4	127
Shoup, Id., U.S.	D4	89
Shouxian, China	C5	28
Show Low, Az., U.S.	C5	80
Shreve, Oh., U.S.	B3	112
Shreveport, La., U.S.	B2	95
Shrewsbury, Eng., U.K.	I10	7
Shrewsbury, Ma., U.S.	B4	98
Shrewsbury, N.J., U.S.	C4	107
Shrewsbury, Pa., U.S.	G8	115
Shuajingsi, China	E7	26
Shuangcheng, China	B12	26
Shuangyashan, China	B13	26
Shubenacadie, N.S., Can.	D6	71
Shuksan, Mount, mtn., Wa., U.S.	A4	124
Shullsburg, Wi., U.S.	F3	126
Shumagin Islands, is., Ak., U.S.	E7	79
Shunde, China	M2	28
Shungnak, Ak., U.S.	B8	79
Shuqrā', Yemen	F4	46
Shūshtar, Iran	B4	46
Shuswap Lake, l., B.C., Can.	D8	69
Shwebo, Burma	C3	34
Siaksriinderapura, Indon.	N7	34
Siālkot, Pak.	D6	38
Siam, Gulf of see Thailand, Gulf of, b., Asia	J6	34
Sian see Xi'an, China	E8	26
Siargao Island, i., Phil.	D8	32
Šiaškotan, Ostrov, i., Russia	H24	24
Šiauliai, Lith.	F6	18
Šibenik, Cro.	F10	14
Siberia see Sibir', reg., Russia	D16	24
Siberut, Pulau, i., Indon.	F2	32
Sibi, Pak.	F2	38
Sibir' (Siberia), reg., Russia	D16	24
Sibir'akova, Ostrov, i., Russia	C9	24
Sibiti, Congo	B2	44
Sibiu, Rom.	D8	16
Sibley, Ia., U.S.	A2	92
Sibley, La., U.S.	B2	95
Sibley, co., Mn., U.S.	F4	100
Sibolga, Indon.	E2	32
Sibsāgar, India	G16	38
Sibu, Malay.	E5	32
Sibutu Island, i., Phil.	E6	32
Sibuyan Island, i., Phil.	C7	32
Sibuyan Sea, Phil.	C7	32
Sicamous, B.C., Can.	D8	69
Sichote-Alin', mts., Russia	H21	24
Sichuan, prov., China	E7	26
Sicié, Cap, c., Fr.	I12	10
Sicilia, i., Italy	L9	14
Sicily, Strait of, strt.	L7	14
Sicily see Sicilia, i., Italy	L9	14
Sico, stm., Hond.	G5	64
Sicuani, Peru	F4	54
Siddipet, India	C5	37
Siderno, Italy	K11	14
Sidhpur, India	I5	38
Sidi bel Abbès, Alg.	A5	42
Sidi Ifni, Mor.	C3	42
Sidmouth, Eng., U.K.	K9	7
Sidney, B.C., Can.	E6	69
Sidney, Il., U.S.	C5	90
Sidney, Ia., U.S.	D2	92
Sidney, Mt., U.S.	C12	103
Sidney, Ne., U.S.	C3	104
Sidney, N.Y., U.S.	C5	109
Sidney, Oh., U.S.	B1	112
Sidney Lanier, Lake, res., Ga., U.S.	B2	87
Sidon see Şaydā, Leb.	C4	40
Sidra, Gulf of see Surt, Khalīj, b., Libya	B9	42
Siedlce, Pol.	C22	8
Siegburg, Ger.	E7	8
Siegen, Ger.	E8	8
Siĕmréab, Camb.	H7	34
Siena, Italy	F6	14
Sierra, co., Ca., U.S.	C3	82
Sierra, co., N.M., U.S.	D2	108
Sierra Blanca Peak, mtn., N.M., U.S.	D4	108
Sierra Colorada, Arg.	E3	56
Sierra Estrella, mts., Az., U.S.	m8	80
Sierra Leone, ctry., Afr.	G3	42
Sierra Madre, Ca., U.S.	m12	82
Sierra Vista, Az., U.S.	F5	80
Sierre, Switz.	F14	10
Siesta Key, i., Fl., U.S.	E4	86
Sighetul Marmaţiei, Rom.	B7	16
Sighişoara, Rom.	C8	16
Siglufjördur, Ice.	B4	4
Signal Mountain, Tn., U.S.	D8	119
Signal Peak, mtn., Az., U.S.	D1	80
Signal Peak, mtn., Ut., U.S.	F2	121
Signy-l'Abbaye, Fr.	C11	10
Sigourney, Ia., U.S.	C5	92
Sigüenza, Spain	D9	12
Sigües, Spain	C10	12
Siguiri, Gui.	F4	42
Siilinjärvi, Fin.	E16	6
Si-Kacha, Thai.	H6	34
Sīkar, India	G6	38
Sikasso, Mali	F4	42
Sikeston, Mo., U.S.	E8	102
Sikiá, Grc.	I7	16
Síkinos, Grc.	M9	16
Sikkim, state, India	G13	38
Šikotan, Ostrov (Shikotan-tō), i., Russia	I23	24
Sikt'ach, Russia	D19	24
Silandro, Italy	C5	14
Silao, Mex.	G9	62
Silay, Phil.	C7	32
Silba, Cro.	E9	14
Silchar, India	H15	38
Siler City, N.C., U.S.	B3	110
Silesia, hist. reg., Pol.	E16	8
Siletz, Or., U.S.	C3	114
Silifke, Tur.	A3	40
Silīguri, India	G13	38
Siling Co, l., China	E13	38
Silistra, Bul.	E11	16
Šilka, Russia	G18	24
Šilka, stm., Russia	G17	24
Silkeborg, Den.	H7	6
Sillamäe, Est.	B10	18
Sillé-le-Guillaume, Fr.	D6	10
Sillery, Que., Can.	n17	74
Sillon de Talbert, pen., Fr.	D3	10
Siloam Springs, Ar., U.S.	A1	81
Silsbee, Tx., U.S.	D5	120
Silt, Co., U.S.	B3	83
Silvânia, Braz.	G9	54
Silvassa, India	B2	37
Silver Bay, Mn., U.S.	C7	100
Silver Bow, co., Mt., U.S.	E4	103
Silver City, Nv., U.S.	D2	105
Silver City, N.M., U.S.	E1	108
Silver Creek, Ne., U.S.	C8	104
Silver Creek, N.Y., U.S.	C1	109
Silver Creek, stm., Or., U.S.	D7	114
Silverdale, Wa., U.S.	B3	124
Silver Grove, Ky., U.S.	h14	94
Silver Hill, Md., U.S.	f9	97
Silver Lake, Ks., U.S.	C8	93
Silver Lake, Ma., U.S.	f11	98
Silver Lake, Mn., U.S.	F4	100
Silver Lake, Wi., U.S.	F5	126
Silver Lake, l., De., U.S.	D3	85
Silver Lake, l., Ia., U.S.	A3	92
Silver Lake, l., Me., U.S.	C3	96
Silver Lake, l., N.H., U.S.	E2	106
Silver Lake, l., N.H., U.S.	C4	106
Silver Lake, l., Or., U.S.	D7	114
Silver Lake, l., Wa., U.S.	g13	124
Silverpeak, Nv., U.S.	F4	105
Silver Peak Range, mts., Nv., U.S.	F4	105
Silver Spring, Md., U.S.	C3	97
Silver Springs, Nv., U.S.	D2	105
Silver Star Mountain, mtn., Wa., U.S.	A5	124
Silverthrone Mountain, mtn., B.C., Can.	D4	69
Silvertip Mountain, mtn., Mt., U.S.	C3	103
Silverton, Co., U.S.	D3	83
Silverton, Id., U.S.	B3	89
Silverton, N.J., U.S.	C4	107
Silverton, Oh., U.S.	o13	112
Silverton, Or., U.S.	C4	114
Silvi, Italy	G9	14
Silvies, stm., Or., U.S.	D7	114
Silview, De., U.S.	B3	85
Silvis, Il., U.S.	B3	90
Simanggang, Malay.	E5	32
Simanovsk, Russia	G19	24
Simav, Tur.	J12	16
Simcoe, Ont., Can.	E4	73
Simcoe, Lake, l., Ont., Can.	C5	73
Simeulue, Pulau, i., Indon.	M3	34
Simferopol', Ukr.	I4	22
Simi Valley, Ca., U.S.	E4	82
Simla, India	E7	38

Name	Map Ref	Page
Simmesport, La., U.S.	D4	95
Simms Stream, stm., N.H., U.S.	g7	106
Simojovel [de Allende], Mex.	I13	62
Simonette, stm., Alta., Can.	B1	68
Simplon Pass, Switz.	F15	10
Simpson, Pa., U.S.	C11	115
Simpson, co., Ky., U.S.	D3	94
Simpson, co., Ms., U.S.	D4	101
Simpson Creek, stm., W.V., U.S.	k10	125
Simpson Desert, des., Austl.	D7	50
Simpson Peninsula, pen., N.W. Ter., Can.	C15	66
Simpsonville, Ky., U.S.	B4	94
Simpsonville, S.C., U.S.	B3	117
Simsboro, La., U.S.	B3	95
Simsbury, Ct., U.S.	B4	84
Simušir, Ostrov, i., Russia	H24	24
Sīnā', Shibh Jazīrat (Sinai Peninsula), pen., Egypt	C12	42
Sinabang, Indon.	M4	34
Sinai Peninsula see Sīnā', Shibh Jazīrat, pen., Egypt	C12	42
Sin'aja, stm., Russia	E18	24
Sinaloa, stm., Mex.	E5	62
Sināwan, Libya	B8	42
Sincé, Col.	C5	58
Sincé, Col.	J10	64
Sincelejo, Col.	C5	58
Sinclair, Wy., U.S.	E5	127
Sindri, India	I12	38
Sines, Port.	H3	12
Sinfães, Port.	D3	12
Singānallūr, India	G4	37
Singapore, Sing.	N7	34
Singapore, ctry., Asia	E3	32
Singapore Strait, strt., Asia	N7	34
Singen [Hohentwiel], Ger.	H8	8
Singida, Tan.	B6	44
Singkang, Indon.	F7	32
Singkawang, Indon.	E4	32
Siniscola, Italy	I4	14
Sinj, Cro.	F11	14
Sinjah, Sudan	F12	42
Sinkāt, Sudan	E13	42
Sinnamary, Fr. Gu.	B8	54
Sinnemahoning Creek, stm., Pa., U.S.	D5	115
Sinop, Tur.	G15	4
Sinskoje, Russia	E19	24
Sintang, Indon.	E5	32
Sint Eustatius, i., Neth. Ant.	F16	64
Sint Marten (Saint-Martin), i., N.A.	E16	64
Sint-Niklaas, Bel.	D4	8
Sinton, Tx., U.S.	E4	120
Sintra, Port.	G2	12
Sinŭiju, N. Kor.	C11	26
Sion, Switz.	F14	10
Sioux, co., Ia., U.S.	A1	92
Sioux, co., Ne., U.S.	B2	104
Sioux, co., N.D., U.S.	C4	111
Sioux Center, Ia., U.S.	A1	92
Sioux City, Ia., U.S.	B1	92
Sioux Falls, S.D., U.S.	D9	118
Sioux Lookout, Ont., Can.	o17	73
Sioux Rapids, Ia., U.S.	B2	92
Siping, China	C11	26
Sipiwesk Lake, l., Man., Can.	B3	70
Sipsey, stm., Al., U.S.	B2	78
Sipsey Fork, stm., Al., U.S.	A2	78
Siracusa, Italy	L10	14
Sirājganj, Bngl.	H13	38
Sir Douglas, Mount, mtn., Can.	D3	68
Sir Edward Pellew Group, is., Austl.	C7	50
Siren, Wi., U.S.	C1	126
Siret, stm., Eur.	C11	16
Sirevåg, Nor.	G5	6
Sir James MacBrien, Mount, mtn., N.W. Ter., Can.	D7	66
Sirohi, India	H5	38
Sirsa, India	F6	38
Sir Sandford, Mount, mtn., B.C., Can.	D9	69
Sirsi, India	E3	37
Sir Wilfrid Laurier, Mount, mtn., B.C., Can.	C8	69
Sisak, Cro.	D11	14
Siskiyou, co., Ca., U.S.	B2	82
Siskiyou Mountains, mts., U.S.	F3	114
Siskiyou Pass, Or., U.S.	E4	114
Sisseton, S.D., U.S.	B8	118
Sisseton Indian Reservation, U.S.	B8	118
Sissiboo, stm., N.S., Can.	E4	71
Sisson Branch Reservoir, res., N.B., Can.	B2	71
Sissonville, W.V., U.S.	C3	125
Sisteron, Fr.	H12	10
Sisters, Or., U.S.	C5	114
Sistersville, W.V., U.S.	B4	125
Sītāpur, India	G9	38
Sitka, Ak., U.S.	D12	79
Sitka National Historical Park, Ak., U.S.	m22	79
Sitka Sound, strt., Ak., U.S.	m22	79
Sittard, Neth.	D5	8
Sittoung, stm., Burma	E4	34
Sittwe (Akyab), Burma	D2	34
Situbondo, Indon.	m16	33a
Sivas, Tur.	H15	4
Sīwah, Egypt	C11	42
Siwān, India	G11	38
Sjælland, i., Den.	I8	6
Skagen, Den.	H8	6
Skagerrak, strt., Eur.	H7	6
Skagit, co., Wa., U.S.	A4	124
Skagway, Ak., U.S.	D12	79
Skaidi, Nor.	A15	6
Skamania, co., Wa., U.S.	D3	124
Skaneateles, N.Y., U.S.	C4	109
Skaneateles Lake, l., N.Y., U.S.	C4	109
Skārdu, Pak.	C6	38
Skarżysko-Kamienna, Pol.	D20	8
Skeena Mountains, mts., B.C., Can.	E7	66
Skegness, Eng., U.K.	H13	7
Skeleton Lake, l., Ont., Can.	B5	73
Skellefteå, Swe.	D13	6
Skelleftehamn, Swe.	D13	6
Skiatook, Ok., U.S.	A5	113
Skiatook Reservoir, res., Ok., U.S.	A5	113
Skibotn, Nor.	B13	6
Skiddaw, mtn., Eng., U.K.	G9	7
Skien, Nor.	G7	6
Skierniewice, Pol.	D20	8
Skihist Mountain, mtn., B.C., Can.	D7	69
Skikda, Alg.	A7	42
Skillet Fork, stm., Il., U.S.	E5	90
Skillingaryd, Swe.	H10	6
Šklad, Russia	C18	24
Škofja Loka, Slo.	C9	14
Skokie, Il., U.S.	A6	90
Skokomish Indian Reservation, Wa., U.S.	B2	124
Skopje, Mac.	H5	16
Skövde, Swe.	G9	6
Skovorodino, Russia	G18	24
Skowhegan, Me., U.S.	D3	96
Skull Valley, val., Ut., U.S.	C3	121
Skull Valley Indian Reservation, Ut., U.S.	C3	121
Skuna, stm., Ms., U.S.	B4	101
Skunk, stm., Ia., U.S.	D6	92
Skwentna, stm., Ak., U.S.	g15	79
Skye, Island of, i., Scot., U.K.	D6	7
Skykomish, stm., Wa., U.S.	B4	124
Skyland, Nv., U.S.	D2	105
Skyland, N.C., U.S.	f10	110
Skyline, Al., U.S.	A3	78
Slagnäs, Swe.	D12	6
Slamet, Gunung, vol., Indon.	m14	33a
Slancy, Russia	B11	18
Slano, Cro.	G12	14
Slater, Ia., U.S.	C4	92
Slater, Mo., U.S.	B4	102
Slater, S.C., U.S.	A3	117
Slatersville, R.I., U.S.	A3	116
Slatersville Reservoir, res., R.I., U.S.	B3	116
Slatington, Pa., U.S.	E10	115
Slaton, Tx., U.S.	C2	120
Slaughter, La., U.S.	D4	95
Slave, stm., Can.	D10	66
Slave Lake, Alta., Can.	B3	68
Slavonia see Slavonija, reg., Cro.	D12	14
Slavonija, reg., Cro.	D12	14
Slavonska Požega, Cro.	D12	14
Slavonski Brod, Cro.	D2	16
Slayton, Mn., U.S.	G3	100
Sleeping Bear Dunes National Lakeshore, Mi., U.S.	D4	99
Sleeping Bear Point, c., Mi., U.S.	D4	99
Sleepy Eye, Mn., U.S.	F4	100
Slickville, Pa., U.S.	F2	115
Slidell, La., U.S.	D6	95
Sliderock Mountain, mtn., Mt., U.S.	D3	103
Sligo, Ire.	G4	7
Slinger, Wi., U.S.	E5	126
Slippery Rock, Pa., U.S.	D1	115
Sliven, Bul.	G10	16
Sloan, Ia., U.S.	B1	92
Sloan, N.Y., U.S.	C2	109
Slocomb, Al., U.S.	D4	78
Slonim, Bela.	H8	18
Slope, co., N.D., U.S.	C2	111
Slovakia, ctry., Eur.	G19	8
Slovenia, ctry., Eur.	C9	14
Slovenjgradec, Slo.	C10	14
Slovenska Bistrica, Slo.	C10	14
Sluck, Bela.	H10	18
Sl'ud'anka, Russia	G14	24
Słupsk (Stolp), Pol.	A17	8
Smackover, Ar., U.S.	D3	81
Small Point, c., Me., U.S.	g8	96
Smallwood Reservoir, res., Newf., Can.	g8	72
Smederevo, Yugo.	E4	16
Smethport, Pa., U.S.	C5	115
Smidovič, Russia	H20	24
Šmidta, Ostrov, i., Russia	A12	24
Smith, co., Ks., U.S.	C5	93
Smith, co., Ms., U.S.	C4	101
Smith, co., Tn., U.S.	A5	119
Smith, co., Tx., U.S.	C5	120
Smith, stm., U.S.	D3	123
Smith, stm., Mt., U.S.	D5	103
Smith and Sayles Reservoir, res., R.I., U.S.	B2	116
Smith Bay, b., Ak., U.S.	A9	79
Smith Canyon, val., Co., U.S.	D7	83
Smith Center, Ks., U.S.	C5	93
Smithers, B.C., Can.	B4	69
Smithers, W.V., U.S.	C3	125
Smithfield, N.C., U.S.	B4	110
Smithfield, Pa., U.S.	G2	115
Smithfield, Ut., U.S.	B4	121
Smithfield, Va., U.S.	D6	123
Smith Island, i., U.S.	D5	97
Smith Island, i., Va., U.S.	C7	123
Smith Mountain Lake, res., Va., U.S.	C3	123
Smith Peak, mtn., Id., U.S.	A2	89
Smith Point, c., Ma., U.S.	D7	98
Smith Point, c., Va., U.S.	C6	123
Smiths, Al., U.S.	C4	78
Smithsburg, Md., U.S.	A2	97
Smiths Falls, Ont., Can.	C8	73
Smiths Grove, Ky., U.S.	C3	94
Smithton, Austl.	H9	50
Smithton, Il., U.S.	E4	90
Smithtown, N.Y., U.S.	n15	109
Smithville, Ga., U.S.	E2	87
Smithville, Ms., U.S.	A5	101
Smithville, Mo., U.S.	B3	102
Smithville, Oh., U.S.	B4	112
Smithville, Tn., U.S.	D8	119
Smithville, Tx., U.S.	D4	120
Smithville Lake, res., Mo., U.S.	B3	102
Smoke Creek Desert, des., Nv., U.S.	C2	105
Smokey, Cape, c., N.S., Can.	C9	71
Smokey Dome, mtn., Id., U.S.	F4	89
Smoky, stm., Alta., Can.	B1	68
Smoky Hill, stm., U.S.	D5	93
Smoky Lake, Alta., Can.	B4	68
Smoky Mountains, mts., Id., U.S.	F4	89
Smolensk, Russia	G15	18
Smooth Rock Falls, Ont., Can.	o19	73
Smoothstone Lake, l., Sask., Can.	C2	75
Smyrna, De., U.S.	C3	85
Smyrna, Ga., U.S.	C2	87
Smyrna, Tn., U.S.	B5	119
Smyrna, stm., De., U.S.	C3	85
Smyth, co., Va., U.S.	f10	123
Smythe, Mount, mtn., B.C., Can.	E8	66
Snake, stm., U.S.	D5	100
Snake, stm., Mn., U.S.	B1	100
Snake, stm., Ne., U.S.	B4	104
Snake Range, mts., Nv., U.S.	E7	105
Snake River Plain, pl., Id., U.S.	F2	89
Snake River Range, mts., U.S.	C2	127
Sneads, Fl., U.S.	B2	86
Sneedville, Tn., U.S.	C10	119
Sneek, Neth.	B5	8
Snipe Keys, is., Fl., U.S.	H5	86
Snohomish, Wa., U.S.	B3	124
Snohomish, co., Wa., U.S.	A4	124
Snoqualmie, Wa., U.S.	B4	124
Snoqualmie, stm., Wa., U.S.	B4	124
Snoqualmie Pass, Wa., U.S.	B4	124
Snowbank Lake, l., Mn., U.S.	B7	100
Snowdon, mtn., Wales, U.K.	H8	7
Snowdonia National Park, Wales, U.K.	I9	7
Snowdrift, N.W. Ter., Can.	D10	66
Snowflake, Az., U.S.	C5	80
Snow Hill, Md., U.S.	D7	97
Snow Hill, N.C., U.S.	B5	110
Snowking Mountain, mtn., Wa., U.S.	A4	124
Snow Lake, Man., Can.	B1	70
Snowmass Mountain, mtn., Co., U.S.	B3	83
Snow Peak, mtn., Wa., U.S.	A7	124
Snowshoe Lake, l., Me., U.S.	B4	96
Snowshoe Peak, mtn., Mt., U.S.	B1	103
Snow Water Lake, l., Nv., U.S.	C7	105
Snowyside Peak, mtn., Id., U.S.	F4	89
Snyder, Ok., U.S.	C3	113
Snyder, Tx., U.S.	C2	120
Snyder, co., Pa., U.S.	E7	115
Soacha, Col.	E5	58
Soalala, Madag.	E9	44
Soap Lake, Wa., U.S.	B6	124
Sobat, stm., Sudan	G12	42
Sobinka, Russia	F23	18
Sobral, Braz.	D10	54
Socastee, S.C., U.S.	D9	117
Sochi see Soči, Russia	I5	22
Soči, Russia	I5	22
Social Circle, Ga., U.S.	C3	87
Society Hill, S.C., U.S.	B8	117
Socorro, Col.	D6	58
Socorro, N.M., U.S.	C3	108
Socorro, co., N.M., U.S.	D2	108
Socorro, Isla, i., Mex.	H4	62
Socotra see Suquṭrā, i., Yemen	F5	46
Soc Trang, Viet.	J8	34
Socuéllamos, Spain	F9	12
Sodankylä, Fin.	C16	6
Soda Springs, Id., U.S.	G7	89
Soddy-Daisy, Tn., U.S.	D8	119
Söderhamn, Swe.	F11	6
Södertälje, Swe.	G11	6
Sodo, Eth.	G2	46
Sodus, N.Y., U.S.	B3	109
Soest, Ger.	D8	8
Sofia, stm., Madag.	E9	44
Sofia see Sofija, Bul.	G7	16
Sofija (Sofia), Bul.	G7	16
Sogamoso, Col.	E6	58
Sognafjorden, Nor.	F5	6
Søgne, Nor.	G6	6
Soignies, Bel.	E4	8
Sointula, B.C., Can.	D4	69
Soissons, Fr.	C10	10
Sokal'skogo, Proliv, strt., Russia	B14	24
Söke, Tur.	L11	16
Sokodé, Togo	G6	42
Sokol, Russia	B23	18
Sokol, Russia	C19	24
Sokoto, Nig.	F7	42
Sol, Costa del, Spain	I7	12
Solana, Fl., U.S.	F5	86
Solano, Phil.	p19	33b
Solano, co., Ca., U.S.	C3	82
Solbad Hall in Tirol, Aus.	H11	8
Soldier, stm., Ia., U.S.	C2	92
Soldier Key, i., Fl., U.S.	s3	86
Soldotna, Ak., U.S.	g16	79
Soledad, Col.	B5	58
Soledad, Ca., U.S.	D3	82
Soledad, Ven.	C11	58
Soleduck, stm., Wa., U.S.	B1	124
Solingen, Ger.	D7	8
Sollefteå, Swe.	E11	6
Sollentuna, Swe.	G11	6
Sóller, Spain	F14	12
Solnečnogorsk, Russia	E19	18
Sologoncy, Russia	D16	24
Solok, Indon.	O6	34
Solomon, Ks., U.S.	D6	93
Solomon, stm., Ks., U.S.	C6	93
Solomon Islands, ctry., Oc.	G23	2
Solomons, Md., U.S.	D5	97
Solomon Sea, Oc.	A10	50
Solon, Ia., U.S.	C6	92
Solon, Oh., U.S.	A4	112
Solothurn, Switz.	E14	10
Solsona, Spain	D13	12
Soltau, Ger.	C9	8
Solvay, N.Y., U.S.	B4	109
Solwezi, Zam.	D5	44
Soma, Tur.	J11	16
Somalia, ctry., Afr.	G4	46
Sombor, Yugo.	D3	16
Sombrerete, Mex.	F8	62
Somerdale, N.J., U.S.	D2	107
Somers, Ct., U.S.	B6	84
Somers, Mt., U.S.	B2	103
Somerset, Man., Can.	E2	70
Somerset, Ky., U.S.	C5	94
Somerset, Ma., U.S.	C5	98
Somerset, N.J., U.S.	B3	107
Somerset, Oh., U.S.	C3	112
Somerset, Pa., U.S.	F3	115
Somerset, Tx., U.S.	k7	120
Somerset, Wi., U.S.	C1	126
Somerset, co., Me., U.S.	C2	96
Somerset, co., Md., U.S.	D6	97
Somerset, co., N.J., U.S.	B3	107
Somerset, co., Pa., U.S.	G3	115
Somerset Island, i., N.W. Ter., Can.	B14	66
Somerset Reservoir, res., Vt., U.S.	E3	122
Somers Point, N.J., U.S.	E3	107
Somersville, Ct., U.S.	B6	84
Somersworth, N.H., U.S.	D5	106
Somerton, Az., U.S.	E1	80
Somervell, co., Tx., U.S.	C4	120
Somerville, Ma., U.S.	B5	98
Somerville, N.J., U.S.	B3	107
Somerville, Tn., U.S.	B2	119
Somerville, Tx., U.S.	D4	120
Somerville Lake, res., Tx., U.S.	D4	120
Someș (Szamos), stm., Eur.	B6	16
Sömmerda, Ger.	D11	8
Somonauk, Il., U.S.	B5	90
Somoto, Nic.	H4	64
Son, stm., India	H10	38
Sønderborg, Den.	I7	6
Sondershausen, Ger.	D10	8
Søndre Strømfjord, Grnld.	C22	66
Sondrio, Italy	C4	14
Song Cau, Viet.	H10	34
Songea, Tan.	D7	44
Songhua, stm., China	B12	26
Songjiang, China	D10	28
Songkhla, Thai.	K6	34
Songnim, N. Kor.	D12	26
Sonīpat, India	F7	38
Son La, Viet.	D7	34
Sonmiāni Bay, b., Pak.	H2	38
Sonneberg, Ger.	E11	8
Sonoita, Mex.	B3	62
Sonoma, Ca., U.S.	C2	82
Sonoma, co., Ca., U.S.	C2	82
Sonoma Peak, mtn., Nv., U.S.	C4	105
Sonoma Range, mts., Nv., U.S.	C4	105
Sonora, Ca., U.S.	D3	82
Sonora, Tx., U.S.	D2	120
Sonora, stm., Mex.	C4	62
Sonseca, Spain	F8	12
Sonsón, Col.	E5	58
Sonsonate, El Sal.	H3	64
Sonsorol Islands, is., Palau	D9	32
Son Tay, Viet.	D8	34
Sonthofen, Ger.	H10	8
Soochow see Suzhou, China	D9	28
Soperton, Ga., U.S.	D4	87
Sophia, W.V., U.S.	D3	125
Sopot, Pol.	A18	8
Sopron, Hung.	H16	8
Sopur, India	C6	38
Sora, Italy	H8	14
Sore, Fr.	H6	10
Sorel, Que., Can.	C4	74
Sorgono, Italy	I4	14
Sorgues, Fr.	H11	10
Soria, Spain	D9	12
Sorocaba, Braz.	G5	57
Sorong, Indon.	F9	32
Soroti, Ug.	H12	42
Sorrento, Italy	I9	14
Sorrento, La., U.S.	D5	95
Sorsele, Swe.	D11	6
Sorsogon, Phil.	C7	32
Sort, Spain	C13	12
Sorūbī, Afg.	C3	38
Sos del Rey Católico, Spain	C10	12
Sosnovo-Oz'orskoje, Russia	G16	24
Sosnowiec, Pol.	E19	8
Šoštanj, Slo.	C10	14
Sotkamo, Fin.	D17	6
Soto la Marina, Mex.	F10	62
Sotteville, Fr.	C8	10
Soucook, stm., N.H., U.S.	D4	106
Soudan, Mn., U.S.	C6	100
Souderton, Pa., U.S.	F11	115
Souhegan, stm., N.H., U.S.	E3	106
Souillac, Fr.	H8	10
Soŭl (Seoul), S. Kor.	D12	26
Soulac-sur-Mer, Fr.	G5	10
Souris, Man., Can.	E1	70
Souris, P.E.I., Can.	C7	71
Sousa, Braz.	E11	54
Sousse, Tun.	N5	14
South, stm., Ia., U.S.	C4	92
South, stm., N.C., U.S.	C4	110
South Acton, Ma., U.S.	g10	98
South Africa, ctry., Afr.	G5	44
South Amboy, N.J., U.S.	C4	107
South America	E4	53
South Amherst, Ma., U.S.	B2	98
South Amherst, Oh., U.S.	A3	112
Southampton, Ont., Can.	C3	73
Southampton, Eng., U.K.	K11	7
Southampton, N.Y., U.S.	n16	109
Southampton, co., Va., U.S.	D5	123
Southampton Island, i., N.W. Ter., Can.	D16	66
South Andaman, i., India	I2	34
South Anna, stm., Va., U.S.	C5	123
South Aulatsivik Island, i., Newf., Can.	E20	66
South Australia, state, Austl.	F7	50
Southaven, Ms., U.S.	A3	101
South Bald Mountain, mtn., Co., U.S.	A5	83
South Baldy, mtn., N.M., U.S.	D2	108
South Barre, Vt., U.S.	C3	122
South Bay, Fl., U.S.	F6	86
South Beloit, Il., U.S.	A4	90
South Bend, In., U.S.	A5	91
South Bend, Wa., U.S.	C2	124
South Berwick, Me., U.S.	E2	96
South Bloomfield, Oh., U.S.	C3	112
South Boston, Va., U.S.	D4	123
South Bound Brook, N.J., U.S.	B3	107
South Branch Lake, l., Me., U.S.	C4	96
Southbridge, Ma., U.S.	B3	98
South Bristol, Me., U.S.	E3	96
South Britain, Ct., U.S.	D3	84
South Broadway, Wa., U.S.	C5	124
South Bruny, i., Austl.	H9	50
South Burlington, Vt., U.S.	C2	122
Southbury, Ct., U.S.	D3	84
South Carolina, state, U.S.	D6	117
South Charleston, Oh., U.S.	C2	112
South Charleston, W.V., U.S.	C3	125
South Chicago Heights, Il., U.S.	m9	90
South China Sea, Asia	C5	32
South Coffeyville, Ok., U.S.	A6	113
South Congaree, S.C., U.S.	D5	117
South Connellsville, Pa., U.S.	G2	115
South Dakota, state, U.S.	C5	118
South Dartmouth, Ma., U.S.	C6	98
South Daytona, Fl., U.S.	C5	86
South Deerfield, Ma., U.S.	B2	98
South Dennis, Ma., U.S.	C7	98
South Duxbury, Ma., U.S.	B6	98
South East Cape, c., Austl.	H9	50
Southeast Cape, c., Ak., U.S.	C6	79
South Easton, Ma., U.S.	B5	98
Southeast Pass, strt., La., U.S.	E7	95
Southeast Point, c., R.I., U.S.	h7	116
South Elgin, Il., U.S.	B5	90
Southend-on-Sea, Eng., U.K.	J13	7
Southern Alps, mts., N.Z.	E3	52
Southern Cross, Austl.	F3	50
Southern Indian Lake, l., Man., Can.	f8	70
Southern Pines, N.C., U.S.	B3	110
Southern Ute Indian Reservation, Co., U.S.	D2	83
South Euclid, Oh., U.S.	g9	112
Southey, Sask., Can.	G3	75
South Fabius, stm., Mo., U.S.	A5	102
South Fallsburg, N.Y., U.S.	D6	109
Southfield, Mi., U.S.	o15	99
South Fork, Pa., U.S.	F4	115
South Fox Island, i., Mi., U.S.	C5	99
South Fulton, Tn., U.S.	A3	119
South Gastonia, N.C., U.S.	B1	110
South Gate, Ca., U.S.	n12	82
Southgate, Ky., U.S.	h14	94
Southgate, Mi., U.S.	p15	99
South Georgia, i., Falk. Is.	G9	56
South Glastonbury, Ct., U.S.	C5	84
South Glens Falls, N.Y., U.S.	B7	109
South Grafton, Ma., U.S.	B4	98
South Grand, stm., Mo., U.S.	C3	102
South Hadley, Ma., U.S.	B2	98
South Hadley Falls, Ma., U.S.	B2	98
South Hamilton, Ma., U.S.	A6	98
South Haven, In., U.S.	A3	91
South Haven, Mi., U.S.	F4	99
South Henik Lake, l., N.W. Ter., Can.	D13	66
South Hero Island, i., Vt., U.S.	B2	122
South Hill, Va., U.S.	D4	123
South Hingham, Ma., U.S.	h12	98
South Holland, Il., U.S.	k9	90
South Holston Lake, res., U.S.	A9	119
South Hooksett, N.H., U.S.	D4	106
South Hopkinton, R.I., U.S.	F1	116
South Houston, Tx., U.S.	r14	120
South Hutchinson, Ks., U.S.	f11	93
South Indian Lake, Man., Can.	A2	70
Southington, Ct., U.S.	C4	84
South International Falls, Mn., U.S.	B5	100
South Island, i., N.Z.	E3	52
South Island, i., S.C., U.S.	E9	117
South Jacksonville, Il., U.S.	D3	90
South Jordan, Ut., U.S.	C3	121
South Kenosha, Wi., U.S.	F6	126
South Lake Tahoe, Ca., U.S.	C4	82
South Lancaster, Ma., U.S.	B4	98
South Laurel, Md., U.S.	*B4	97
South Lebanon, Oh., U.S.	C1	112
South Lyon, Mi., U.S.	F7	99
South Magnetic Pole	C26	47
South Manitou Island, i., Mi., U.S.	C4	99
South Marsh Island, i., Md., U.S.	D5	97
South Miami, Fl., U.S.	G6	86
South Miami Heights, Fl., U.S.	s13	86
South Mills, N.C., U.S.	A6	110
South Milwaukee, Wi., U.S.	F6	126
Southmont, N.C., U.S.	B2	110
South Moose Lake, l., Man., Can.	C1	70
South Mountain, mtn., Id., U.S.	G2	89
South Mountain, mtn., N.M., U.S.	k8	108
South Mountains, mts., Az., U.S.	m8	80
South Mountains, mts., N.C., U.S.	B1	110
South Nahanni, stm., N.W. Ter., Can.	D7	66
South New River Canal, Fl., U.S.	r3	86
South Ogden, Ut., U.S.	B4	121
Southold, N.Y., U.S.	m16	109
South Orange, N.J., U.S.	B4	107
South Orkney Islands, is., B.A.T.	C8	47
South Paris, Me., U.S.	D2	96
South Park, val., Co., U.S.	B5	83
South Pass, Wy., U.S.	D4	127
South Pass, strt., La., U.S.	F6	95
South Patrick Shores, Fl., U.S.	D6	86
South Pekin, Il., U.S.	C4	90
South Pittsburg, Tn., U.S.	D8	119
South Plainfield, N.J., U.S.	B4	107
South Platte, stm., U.S.	C6	83
South Point, c., Mi., U.S.	D7	99
South Pole, Ant.	A12	47

Name | Map Ref | Page

outhport, Eng., U.K. H9 7
outhport, Fl., U.S. u16 86
outhport, In., U.S. E5 91
outhport, N.Y., U.S. C4 109
outhport, N.C., U.S. D4 110
outh Portland, Me., U.S. E2 96
outh Portsmouth, Ky., U.S. B6 94
outh Range, Mi., U.S. A2 99
outh River, Ont., Can. B5 73
outh River, N.J., U.S. C4 107
outh River, b., Md., U.S. C4 97
outh Ronaldsay, i., Scot., U.K. C10 7
outh Royalton, Vt., U.S. D3 122
outh Saint Paul, Mn., U.S. n12 100
outh Sandwich Islands, is., Falk. Is. D10 47
outh San Francisco, Ca., U.S. h8 82
outh Saskatchewan, stm., Can. F11 66
outh Shetland Islands, is., B.A.T. C7 47
outh Shields, Eng., U.K. F11 7
outhside, Al., U.S. B3 78
outhside Place, Tx., U.S. r14 120
outh Sioux City, Ne., U.S. B9 104
outh Skunk, stm., Ia., U.S. C4 92
outh Stony Brook, N.Y., U.S. *n15 109
outh Streator, Il., U.S. B5 90
outh Toms River, N.J., U.S. D4 107
outh Torrington, Wy., U.S. D8 127
outh Tucson, Az., U.S. E5 80
outh Valley Stream, N.Y., U.S. *n15 109
outh Venice, Fl., U.S. E4 86
outh Ventana Cone, vol., Ca., U.S. D3 82
outh Waverly, Pa., U.S. C8 115
outh Wellfleet, Ma., U.S. C8 98
outh Wellington, B.C., Can. f12 69
outh West Africa see Namibia, ctry., Afr. F3 44
outh Westbury, N.Y., U.S. *n15 109
outh West Cape, c., Austl. H9 50
outhwest Channel, strt., Fl., U.S. E4 86
outhwest City, Mo., U.S. E3 102
outhwest Harbor, Me., U.S. D4 96
outhwest Head, c., N.B., Can. E3 71
outhwest Miramichi, stm., N.B., Can. C3 71
outhwest Pass, strt., La., U.S. E3 95
outhwest Pass, strt., La., U.S. E6 95
outhwest Point, c., R.I., U.S. h7 116
outh Weymouth Naval Air Station, mil., Ma., U.S. h12 98
outh Whitley, In., U.S. B6 91
outh Williamson, Ky., U.S. C7 94
outh Williamsport, Pa., U.S. D7 115
outh Windham, Ct., U.S. C7 84
outh Windham, Me., U.S. E2 96
outh Windsor, Ct., U.S. B5 84
outhwood, Co., U.S. *B6 83
outhwood Acres, Ct., U.S. A5 84
outh Woodstock, Ct., U.S. B8 84
outh Yarmouth, Ma., U.S. C7 98
outh Zanesville, Oh., U.S. C3 112
ovetsk (Tilsit), Russia F4 18
ovetskaja Gavan', Russia H22 24
pa, Bel. E5 8
pain, ctry., Eur. G7 4
palding, co., Ga., U.S. C2 87
panaway, Wa., U.S. B3 124
pangler, Pa., U.S. E4 115
paniard's Bay, Newf., Can. E5 72
panish Fork, Ut., U.S. C4 121
panish Fort, Al., U.S. E2 78
panish Lake, Mo., U.S. f13 102
panish North Africa, dep., Afr. A4 42
panish Peak, mtn., Or., U.S. C7 114
panish Sahara see Western Sahara, dep., Afr. D3 42
panish Town, Jam. E9 64
parks, Ga., U.S. E3 87
parks, Nv., U.S. D2 105
parta, Ga., U.S. C4 87
parta, Il., U.S. E4 90
parta, Mi., U.S. E5 99
parta, Mo., U.S. D4 102
parta (Lake Mohawk), N.J., U.S. A3 107
parta, N.C., U.S. A1 110
parta, Tn., U.S. D8 119
parta, Wi., U.S. E3 126
partanburg, S.C., U.S. B4 117
partanburg, co., S.C., U.S. B3 117
parta see Spárti, Grc. L6 16
partel, Cap, c., Mor. J6 12
párti (Sparta), Grc. L6 16
partivento, Capo, c., Italy K3 14
parwood, B.C., Can. E10 69
passk-Dal'nij, Russia I20 24
pavinaw Creek, stm., Ok., U.S. A7 113
pear, Cape, c., Newf., Can. E5 72
pearfish, S.D., U.S. C2 118
pearman, Tx., U.S. A2 120
pearville, Ks., U.S. E4 93
peed, In., U.S. H6 91
peedway, In., U.S. E5 91
pence Bay, N.W. Ter., Can. C14 66
pencer, In., U.S. F4 91
pencer, Ia., U.S. A2 92
pencer, Ma., U.S. B4 98
pencer, N.C., U.S. B2 110
pencer, Tn., U.S. D8 119
pencer, W.V., U.S. C3 125
pencer, Wi., U.S. D3 126
pencer, co., In., U.S. H4 91
pencer, co., Ky., U.S. B4 94
pencer, Cape, c., Ak., U.S. k21 79
pencer Gulf, b., Austl. F7 50
pencer Lake, l., Me., U.S. C2 96
pencerport, N.Y., U.S. B3 109
pencerville, Md., U.S. B4 97
pencerville, Oh., U.S. B1 112
perry, Ok., U.S. A6 113
pesutie Island, i., Md., U.S. B5 97
pey, stm., Scot., U.K. D9 7
peyer, Ger. F8 8

Spiceland, In., U.S. E7 91
Spicer, Mn., U.S. E4 100
Spider Lake, l., Wi., U.S. B2 126
Spindale, N.C., U.S. B1 110
Spink, co., S.D., U.S. C7 118
Spirit Lake, Id., U.S. B2 89
Spirit Lake, Ia., U.S. A2 92
Spirit Lake, l., Ia., U.S. A2 92
Spirit Lake, l., Wa., U.S. C3 124
Spirit River, Alta., Can. B1 68
Spirit River Flowage, res., Wi., U.S. C4 126
Spiro, Ok., U.S. B7 113
Spittal an der Drau, Aus. I13 8
Spitz, Aus. G15 8
Split, Cro. F11 14
Split, Cape, c., N.S., Can. D5 71
Split Lake, l., Man., Can. A4 70
Split Rock Creek, stm., U.S. G2 100
Splügen, Switz. F16 10
Spofford Lake, l., N.H., U.S. E2 106
Spokane, Wa., U.S. B8 124
Spokane, co., Wa., U.S. B8 124
Spokane, stm., U.S. B8 124
Spokane, Mount, mtn., Wa., U.S. B8 124
Spokane Indian Reservation, Wa., U.S. B8 124
Spoleto, Italy G7 14
Spoon, stm., Il., U.S. C3 90
Spooner, Wi., U.S. C2 126
Spooner Lake, l., Wi., U.S. C2 126
Spornoje, Russia E24 24
Spotswood, N.J., U.S. C4 107
Spotsylvania, co., Va., U.S. B5 123
Sprague, W.V., U.S. n13 125
Sprague, stm., Or., U.S. E5 114
Sprague Lake, l., Wa., U.S. B7 124
Spratly Island, i., Asia D5 32
Spremberg, Ger. D14 8
Spring, stm., Ar., U.S. A4 81
Spring Arbor, Mi., U.S. F6 99
Spring Bay, b., Ut., U.S. B3 121
Springbok, S. Afr. G3 44
Springboro, Oh., U.S. C1 112
Spring Brook, stm., Pa., U.S. n18 115
Spring City, Pa., U.S. F10 115
Spring City, Tn., U.S. D9 119
Spring City, Ut., U.S. D4 121
Spring Creek, stm., U.S. D4 104
Spring Creek, stm., Nv., U.S. C4 105
Spring Creek, stm., N.D., U.S. B3 111
Springdale, Newf., Can. D3 72
Springdale, Ar., U.S. A1 81
Springdale, Oh., U.S. n13 112
Springdale, Pa., U.S. E2 115
Springdale, S.C., U.S. D5 117
Springer, N.M., U.S. A5 108
Springerville, Az., U.S. C6 80
Springfield, Co., U.S. D8 83
Springfield, Fl., U.S. u16 86
Springfield, Ga., U.S. D5 87
Springfield, Il., U.S. D4 90
Springfield, Ky., U.S. C4 94
Springfield, Ma., U.S. B2 98
Springfield, Mn., U.S. F4 100
Springfield, Mo., U.S. D4 102
Springfield, Ne., U.S. C9 104
Springfield, N.J., U.S. B4 107
Springfield, Oh., U.S. C2 112
Springfield, Or., U.S. C4 114
Springfield, Pa., U.S. p20 115
Springfield, S.D., U.S. E8 118
Springfield, Tn., U.S. A5 119
Springfield, Vt., U.S. E4 122
Springfield, Va., U.S. g12 123
Springfield, Lake, res., Il., U.S. D4 90
Springfontein, S. Afr. H5 44
Spring Garden, Guy. D13 58
Spring Glen, Ut., U.S. D5 121
Spring Green, Wi., U.S. E3 126
Spring Grove, Il., U.S. h8 90
Spring Grove, Mn., U.S. G7 100
Spring Grove, Pa., U.S. G8 115
Spring Hill, Fl., U.S. D4 86
Spring Hill, Ks., U.S. D9 93
Springhill, La., U.S. A2 95
Spring Hill, Tn., U.S. B5 119
Spring Hope, N.C., U.S. B4 110
Spring Island, i., S.C., U.S. G6 117
Spring Lake, Mi., U.S. E4 99
Spring Lake, N.J., U.S. C4 107
Spring Lake, N.C., U.S. B4 110
Spring Lake, l., Me., U.S. C2 96
Spring Lake, res., U.S. B3 90
Spring Lake Heights, N.J., U.S. C4 107
Spring Mountains, mts., Nv., U.S. G6 105
Springport, Mi., U.S. F6 99
Springs, S. Afr. G5 44
Springside, Sask., Can. F4 75
Springvale, Me., U.S. E2 96
Spring Valley, Ca., U.S. o16 82
Spring Valley, Il., U.S. B4 90
Spring Valley, Mn., U.S. G6 100
Spring Valley, N.Y., U.S. g12 109
Spring Valley, Wi., U.S. D1 126
Springville, Al., U.S. B3 78
Springville, Ia., U.S. B6 92
Springville, N.Y., U.S. C2 109
Springville, Ut., U.S. C4 121
Spruce Fork, stm., W.V., U.S. m12 125
Spruce Grove, Alta., Can. C4 68
Spruce Knob, mtn., W.V., U.S. C6 125
Spruce Knob-Seneca Rocks National Recreation Area, W.V., U.S. C5 125
Spruce Mountain, mtn., Az., U.S. C3 80
Spruce Mountain, mtn., Nv., U.S. C7 105
Spruce Pine, N.C., U.S. f10 110
Spruce Run Reservoir, res., N.J., U.S. B3 107
Spur, Tx., U.S. C2 120
Spurr, Mount, mtn., Ak., U.S. g15 79
Squam Lake, l., N.H., U.S. C4 106
Squapan Lake, l., Me., U.S. B4 96
Square Lake, l., Me., U.S. A4 96
Squatec, Que., Can. B9 74

Squaw Cap Mountain, mtn., N.B., Can. B3 71
Squaw Hill, mtn., Wy., U.S. E7 127
Squaw Peak, mtn., Mt., U.S. C2 103
Squibnocket Point, c., Ma., U.S. D6 98
Squinzano, Italy I13 14
Squire, W.V., U.S. D3 125
Sragen, Indon. m15 33a
Sredinnyj Chrebet, mts., Russia F26 24
Srednekolymsk, Russia D24 24
Sredneresskaja Vozvyšennost', plat., Russia H20 18
Srednesibirskoje Ploskogorje, plat., Russia D14 24
Sremska Mitrovica, Yugo. E3 16
Sri Gangānagar, India F5 38
Srīkākulam, India C7 37
Sri Lanka, ctry., Asia H5 36
Srīnagar, India C6 38
Srīrampur, India C3 37
Stack Reservoir, res., R.I., U.S. C3 116
Stade, Ger. B9 8
Stadthagen, Ger. C9 8
Stafford, Eng., U.K. I10 7
Stafford, Ks., U.S. E5 93
Stafford, Va., U.S. B5 123
Stafford, co., Ks., U.S. D5 93
Stafford, co., Va., U.S. B5 123
Stafford Pond, l., R.I., U.S. D6 116
Stafford Springs, Ct., U.S. B6 84
Staked Plain see Estacado, Llano, pl., U.S. E6 76
Stalheim, Nor. F6 6
Stalingrad see Volgograd, Russia H6 22
Stalowa Wola, Pol. E22 8
Stambaugh, Mi., U.S. B2 99
Stamford, Ct., U.S. E1 84
Stamford, Tx., U.S. C3 120
Stamford, Vt., U.S. F2 122
Stamford, Lake, res., Tx., U.S. C3 120
Stamping Ground, Ky., U.S. B5 94
Stamps, Ar., U.S. D2 81
Stanaford, W.V., U.S. D3 125
Stanberry, Mo., U.S. A3 102
Standerton, S. Afr. G5 44
Standing Rock Indian Reservation, U.S. B4 118
Standish, Mi., U.S. E7 99
Stanfield, Az., U.S. E3 80
Stanfield, Or., U.S. B7 114
Stanford, Ky., U.S. C5 94
Stanhope, N.J., U.S. B3 107
Stanislaus, co., Ca., U.S. D3 82
Stanke Dimitrov, Bul. G7 16
Stanley, Falk. Is. G5 56
Stanley, N.C., U.S. B1 110
Stanley, N.D., U.S. A3 111
Stanley, Va., U.S. B4 123
Stanley, Wi., U.S. D3 126
Stanley, co., S.D., U.S. C5 118
Stanley Falls, wtfl, Zaire A5 44
Stanleytown, Va., U.S. D3 123
Stanleyville, N.C., U.S. A2 110
Stanleyville see Kisangani, Zaire A5 44
Stanly, co., N.C., U.S. B2 110
Stann Creek, Belize F3 64
Stanovoj Chrebet, mts., Russia F19 24
Stanovoje Nagorje (Stanovoy Mountains), mts., Russia F16 24
Stanstead, Que., Can. D5 74
Stanton, Ia., U.S. D2 92
Stanton, Ky., U.S. C6 94
Stanton, Mi., U.S. E5 99
Stanton, Ne., U.S. C8 104
Stanton, Tx., U.S. C2 120
Stanton, co., Ks., U.S. E2 93
Stanton, co., Ne., U.S. C8 104
Stantonsburg, N.C., U.S. B5 110
Stanwood, Ia., U.S. C6 92
Stanwood, Wa., U.S. A3 124
Staples, Mn., U.S. D4 100
Stapleton, Al., U.S. E2 78
Star, Id., U.S. F2 89
Star, N.C., U.S. B3 110
Starachowice, Pol. D21 8
Staraja Russa, Russia C14 18
Stara Planina (Balkan Mountains), mts., Eur. G8 16
Stara Zagora, Bul. G9 16
Starbuck, Mn., U.S. E3 100
Star City, Ar., U.S. D4 81
Star City, W.V., U.S. B5 125
Stargard Szczeciński (Stargard in Pommern), Pol. B15 8
Stargo, Az., U.S. D6 80
Stark, co., Il., U.S. B4 90
Stark, co., N.D., U.S. C3 111
Stark, co., Oh., U.S. B4 112
Starke, Fl., U.S. C4 86
Starke, co., In., U.S. B4 91
Starks, La., U.S. D2 95
Starkville, Ms., U.S. B5 101
Star Lake, l., Mn., U.S. D3 100
Starnberg, Ger. G11 8
Starogard Gdański, Pol. B18 8
Star Peak, mtn., Nv., U.S. C3 105
Starr, co., Tx., U.S. F3 120
Startex, S.C., U.S. B3 117
Start Point, c., Eng., U.K. K9 7
Startup, Wa., U.S. B4 124
State Center, Ia., U.S. B4 92
State College, Pa., U.S. E6 115
Stateline, Nv., U.S. E2 105
State Line, Pa., U.S. G6 115
Staten Island, i., N.Y., U.S. k12 109
Statenville, Ga., U.S. F4 87
Statesboro, Ga., U.S. D5 87
Statesville, N.C., U.S. B2 110
Statham, Ga., U.S. C3 87
Statue of Liberty National Monument, N.J., U.S. k8 107
Staunton, Il., U.S. D4 90
Staunton, Va., U.S. B3 123
Stavanger, Nor. G5 6
Stavropol', Russia H6 22
Stayner, Ont., Can. C4 73

Stayton, Or., U.S. C4 114
Steamboat, Nv., U.S. D2 105
Steamboat Mountain, mtn., Mt., U.S. C4 103
Steamboat Mountain, mtn., Wy., U.S. E4 127
Steamboat Springs, Co., U.S. A4 83
Stearns, Ky., U.S. D5 94
Stearns, co., Mn., U.S. E4 100
Stearns Brook, stm., N.H., U.S. A4 106
Stebbins, Ak., U.S. C7 79
Steele, Al., U.S. B3 78
Steele, Mo., U.S. E8 102
Steele, N.D., U.S. C6 111
Steele, co., Mn., U.S. F5 100
Steele, co., N.D., U.S. B8 111
Steele, Mount, mtn., Wy., U.S. E6 127
Steeleville, Il., U.S. E4 90
Steelton, Pa., U.S. F8 115
Steelville, Mo., U.S. D6 102
Steenkool, Indon. F9 32
Steens Mountain, mts., Or., U.S. E8 114
Stefansson Island, i., N.W. Ter., Can. B11 66
Steger, Il., U.S. B6 90
Steilacoom, Wa., U.S. f10 124
Steinbach, Man., Can. E3 70
Steinhatchee, stm., Fl., U.S. C3 86
Steinkjer, Nor. D8 6
Stellenbosch, S. Afr. H3 44
Stenay, Fr. C12 10
Stendal, Ger. C11 8
Stephen, Mn., U.S. B2 100
Stephens, Ar., U.S. D2 81
Stephens, co., Ga., U.S. B3 87
Stephens, co., Ok., U.S. C4 113
Stephens, co., Tx., U.S. C3 120
Stephens City, Va., U.S. A4 123
Stephens Lake, res., Man., Can. A4 70
Stephenson, Mi., U.S. C3 99
Stephenson, co., Il., U.S. A4 90
Stephens Passage, strt., Ak., U.S. m23 79
Stephenville, Newf., Can. D2 72
Stephenville, Tx., U.S. C3 120
Stephenville Crossing, Newf., Can. D2 72
Sterling, Ak., U.S. g16 79
Sterling, Co., U.S. A7 83
Sterling, Il., U.S. B4 90
Sterling, Ks., U.S. D5 93
Sterling, Ok., U.S. C3 113
Sterling, Va., U.S. A5 123
Sterling, co., Tx., U.S. D2 120
Sterling City, Tx., U.S. D2 120
Sterling Heights, Mi., U.S. o15 99
Sterling Reservoir, res., Co., U.S. A7 83
Sterlington, La., U.S. B3 95
Sterlitamak, Russia G9 22
Stettin see Szczecin, Pol. B14 8
Stettler, Alta., Can. C4 68
Steuben, co., In., U.S. A7 91
Steuben, co., N.Y., U.S. C3 109
Steubenville, Oh., U.S. B5 112
Stevenage, Eng., U.K. J12 7
Stevens, co., Ks., U.S. E2 93
Stevens, co., Mn., U.S. E3 100
Stevens, co., Wa., U.S. A7 124
Stevens Creek Dam, U.S. C4 87
Stevenson, Al., U.S. A4 78
Stevenson, Ct., U.S. D3 84
Stevenson, Wa., U.S. D4 124
Stevenson Lake, l., Man., Can. C4 70
Stevens Pass, Wa., U.S. B4 124
Stevens Peak, mtn., Id., U.S. B3 89
Stevens Point, Wi., U.S. D4 126
Stevensville, Md., U.S. C5 97
Stevensville, Mi., U.S. F4 99
Stevensville, Mt., U.S. D2 103
Stewart, co., Ga., U.S. D2 87
Stewart, co., Tn., U.S. A4 119
Stewart Island, i., N.Z. G1 52
Stewart Mountain, mtn., Az., U.S. k9 80
Stewartstown, Pa., U.S. G8 115
Stewartsville, Mo., U.S. B3 102
Stewartville, Mn., U.S. G6 100
Stewiacke, N.S., Can. D6 71
Steyr, Aus. G14 8
Stigler, Ok., U.S. B6 113
Stigliano, Italy I11 14
Stikine, stm., B.C., Can. E7 66
Stikine, stm., Ak., U.S. D13 79
Stikine Ranges, mts., B.C., Can. E6 66
Still, stm., Ct., U.S. B3 84
Stillaguamish, North Fork, stm., Wa., U.S. A4 124
Stillaguamish, South Fork, stm., Wa., U.S. A4 124
Stillhouse Hollow Lake, res., Tx., U.S. D4 120
Stillman Valley, Il., U.S. A4 90
Stillmore, Ga., U.S. D4 87
Stillwater, Mn., U.S. E6 100
Stillwater, Ok., U.S. A4 113
Stillwater, co., Mt., U.S. E7 103
Stillwater Range, mts., Nv., U.S. D3 105
Stillwater Reservoir, res., N.Y., U.S. B5 109
Stillwater Reservoir, res., R.I., U.S. B3 116
Stilwell, Ok., U.S. B7 113
Stimson, Mount, mtn., Mt., U.S. B3 103
Stine Mountain, mtn., Mt., U.S. E3 103
Stinking Lake, l., N.M., U.S. A3 108
Stinnett, Tx., U.S. B2 120
Štip, Mac. H6 16
Stirling, Alta., Can. E4 68
Stirling, Ont., Can. C7 73
Stirling, Scot., U.K. E9 7
Stjørdalshalsen, Nor. E8 6
Stockbridge, Ga., U.S. C2 87
Stockbridge, Mi., U.S. F6 99
Stockbridge-Munsee Indian Reservation, Wi., U.S. D5 126
Stockdale, Tx., U.S. E4 120
Stockerau, Aus. G16 8
Stockholm, Swe. G12 6

Stockton, Ca., U.S. D3 82
Stockton, Il., U.S. A3 90
Stockton, Ks., U.S. C4 93
Stockton, Md., U.S. D7 97
Stockton, Mo., U.S. D4 102
Stockton Island, i., Wi., U.S. B3 126
Stockton Lake, res., Mo., U.S. D4 102
Stoddard, Wi., U.S. E2 126
Stoddard, co., Mo., U.S. E8 102
Stoke-on-Trent, Eng., U.K. H10 7
Stokes, co., N.C., U.S. A2 110
Stokesdale, N.C., U.S. A3 110
Stolbovoj, Ostrov, i., Russia C21 24
Stollings, W.V., U.S. n12 125
Ston, Cro. G12 14
Stone, co., Ar., U.S. B3 81
Stone, co., Ms., U.S. E4 101
Stone, co., Mo., U.S. E4 102
Stoneboro, Pa., U.S. D1 115
Stone Corral Lake, l., Or., U.S. E7 114
Stoneham, Ma., U.S. g11 98
Stonehaven, Scot., U.K. E10 7
Stone Mountain, Ga., U.S. C2 87
Stone Mountain, mtn., Ga., U.S. C2 87
Stones River National Battlefield, hist., Tn., U.S. B4 119
Stoneville, N.C., U.S. A3 110
Stonewall, Man., Can. D3 70
Stonewall, La., U.S. B2 95
Stonewall, Ms., U.S. C5 101
Stonewall, co., Tx., U.S. C2 120
Stonewood, W.V., U.S. k10 125
Stoney Creek, Ont., Can. D5 73
Stonington, Ct., U.S. D8 84
Stonington, Il., U.S. D4 90
Stonington, Me., U.S. D4 96
Stono, stm., S.C., U.S. k11 117
Stono Inlet, b., S.C., U.S. F8 117
Stony Brook, N.Y., U.S. n15 109
Stony Brook, stm., N.J., U.S. C3 107
Stony Creek, stm., Va., U.S. C5 123
Stony Island, i., N.Y., U.S. B4 109
Stony Plain, Alta., Can. C3 68
Stony Point, N.C., U.S. B1 110
Storby, Fin. F12 6
Støren, Nor. E8 6
Storey, co., Nv., U.S. D2 105
Storfors, Swe. G10 6
Storkerson Peninsula, pen., N.W. Ter., Can. B11 66
Storlien, Swe. E9 6
Storm Lake, Ia., U.S. B2 92
Storm Lake, l., Ia., U.S. B2 92
Storm Mountain, mtn., Ak., U.S. h16 79
Stornoway, Scot., U.K. C6 7
Storrs, Ct., U.S. B7 84
Storuman, Swe. D11 6
Storvreta, Swe. G11 6
Story, Wy., U.S. B6 127
Story, co., Ia., U.S. B4 92
Story City, Ia., U.S. B4 92
Stoughton, Sask., Can. H4 75
Stoughton, Ma., U.S. B5 98
Stoughton, Wi., U.S. F4 126
Stover, Mo., U.S. C5 102
Stow, Oh., U.S. A4 112
Stow Creek, stm., N.J., U.S. E2 107
Stowe, Pa., U.S. F10 115
Stowe, Vt., U.S. C3 122
Stoyoma Mountain, mtn., B.C., Can. E7 69
Strabane, Pa., U.S. F1 115
Strafford, Mo., U.S. D4 102
Strafford, co., N.H., U.S. D4 106
Straffordville, Ont., Can. E4 73
Strahan, Austl. H9 50
Strakonice, Czech. F13 8
Stralsund, Ger. A13 8
Stranraer, Scot., U.K. G7 7
Strasbourg, Fr. D14 10
Strasburg, Co., U.S. B6 83
Strasburg, Oh., U.S. B4 112
Strasburg, Pa., U.S. G9 115
Strasburg, Va., U.S. B4 123
Stratford, Ont., Can. D3 73
Stratford, Ct., U.S. E3 84
Stratford, Ia., U.S. B4 92
Stratford, N.J., U.S. D2 107
Stratford, Ok., U.S. C5 113
Stratford, Tx., U.S. A1 120
Stratford, Wi., U.S. D3 126
Stratford Point, c., Ct., U.S. E3 84
Stratford-upon-Avon, Eng., U.K. I11 7
Stratham, N.H., U.S. D5 106
Strathmore, Alta., Can. D4 68
Strathmore, Ca., U.S. D4 82
Strathroy, Ont., Can. E3 73
Stratton, Co., U.S. B8 83
Straubing, Ger. G12 8
Strausberg, Ger. C13 8
Strawberry, stm., Ar., U.S. A4 81
Strawberry, stm., Ut., U.S. C5 121
Strawberry Mountain, mtn., Or., U.S. C8 114
Strawberry Point, Ia., U.S. B6 92
Strawberry Point, c., Ma., U.S. B6 98
Strawberry Range, mts., Or., U.S. C8 114
Strawberry Reservoir, res., Ut., U.S. C4 121
Streator, Il., U.S. B5 90
Stretensk, Russia G17 24
Strickland, stm., Pap. N. Gui. m15 50a
Strimón (Struma), stm., Eur. I7 16
Stromness, Scot., U.K. C9 7
Stromsburg, Ne., U.S. C8 104
Strömstad, Swe. G8 6
Strömsund, Swe. E10 6
Strong, Ar., U.S. D3 81
Strong, Me., U.S. D2 96
Strong, stm., Ms., U.S. C4 101
Strong City, Ks., U.S. D7 93
Stronghurst, Il., U.S. C3 90
Strongsville, Oh., U.S. A4 112
Stronsay, i., Scot., U.K. B10 7
Stroud, Ok., U.S. B5 113
Stroudsburg, Pa., U.S. E11 115

Name Map Ref Page
Stroudwater, stm., Me., U.S. g7 96
Strum, Wi., U.S. D2 126
Struma (Strimón), stm., Eur. H7 16
Strumble Head, c., Wales, U.K. I7 7
Strumica, Mac. H6 16
Strunino, Russia E21 18
Struthers, Oh., U.S. A5 112
Stryker, Oh., U.S. A1 112
Stuart, Fl., U.S. E6 86
Stuart, Ia., U.S. C3 92
Stuart, Ne., U.S. B6 104
Stuart, Va., U.S. D2 123
Stuart, Mount, mtn., Wa., U.S. B5 124
Stuart Lake, l., B.C., Can. B5 69
Stuarts Draft, Va., U.S. B3 123
Stull, stm., Can. B5 70
Stump Lake, l., N.D., U.S. B7 111
Stump Pond, res., R.I., U.S. D2 116
Stung Treng, Camb. H8 34
Stupino, Russia G21 18
Sturbridge, Ma., U.S. B3 98
Sturgeon, Mo., U.S. B5 102
Sturgeon, stm., Mi., U.S. B4 99
Sturgeon Bay, Wi., U.S. D6 126
Sturgeon Bay, b., Man., Can. C3 70
Sturgeon Falls, Ont., Can. A5 73
Sturgeon Lake, l., Ont., Can. C6 73
Sturgis, Sask., Can. F4 75
Sturgis, Ky., U.S. e10 94
Sturgis, Mi., U.S. G5 99
Sturgis, S.D., U.S. C2 118
Sturtevant, Wi., U.S. F6 126
Stutsman, co., N.D., U.S. B6 111
Stuttgart, Ger. G9 8
Stuttgart, Ar., U.S. C4 81
Suaita, Col. D6 58
Subang, Indon. m13 33a
Subansiri, stm., Asia G16 38
Subiaco, Italy H8 14
Sublette, Ks., U.S. E3 93
Sublette, co., Wy., U.S. D2 127
Sublett Range, mts., Id., U.S. G6 89
Sublimity, Or., U.S. C4 114
Subotica, Yugo. C3 16
Sučan, Russia I20 24
Sucarnoochee, stm., Al., U.S. C1 78
Succasunna, N.J., U.S. B3 107
Suceava, Rom. B10 16
Sūchbaatar, Mong. A8 26
Suchumi, Geor. I6 22
Sucre, Bol. G5 54
Sucuaro, Col. E8 58
Sudan, ctry., Afr. F12 42
Sudan, reg., Afr. F7 42
Sudbury, Ont., Can. A4 73
Sudbury, Ma., U.S. B5 98
Sudbury, stm., Ma., U.S. B5 98
Sudbury Center, Ma., U.S. g10 98
Sudbury Reservoir, res., Ma., U.S. g10 98
Sudeten see Sudety, mts., Eur. E15 8
Sudety, mts., Eur. E15 8
Sue, stm., Sudan G11 42
Sueca, Spain F11 12
Suez see As-Suways, Egypt C12 42
Suez Canal see Suways, Qanāt as-, Egypt D3 40
Suffern, N.Y., U.S. D6 109
Suffield, Ct., U.S. B5 84
Suffolk, Va., U.S. D6 123
Suffolk, co., Ma., U.S. B5 98
Suffolk, co., N.Y., U.S. n15 109
Sugar, stm., U.S. F4 126
Sugar, stm., N.H., U.S. D2 106
Sugar City, Id., U.S. F7 89
Sugar Creek, Mo., U.S. h11 102
Sugarcreek, Pa., U.S. D2 115
Sugar Creek, stm., Oh., U.S. C2 112
Sugar Creek, stm., Pa., U.S. C8 115
Sugar Grove, Va., U.S. D1 123
Sugar Hill, Ga., U.S. B2 87
Sugar Island, i., Mi., U.S. B6 99
Sugar Land, Tx., U.S. E5 120
Sugarland Run, Va., U.S. *A5 123
Sugar Loaf, Va., U.S. C3 123
Sugarloaf Mountain, mtn., Mt., U.S. C4 103
Sugar Notch, Pa., U.S. n17 115
Suggi Lake, l., Sask., Can. C4 75
Sugoj, stm., Russia E25 24
Şuḥār, Oman D6 46
Suhl, Ger. E10 8
Suiattle, stm., Wa., U.S. A4 124
Suide, China D9 26
Suihua, China B12 26
Suining, China E8 26
Suiping, China B2 28
Suitland, Md., U.S. C4 97
Şuizhong, China C11 26
Šuja, Russia E24 18
Sukabumi, Indon. m13 32
Sukagawa, Japan E13 30
Sukhumi see Suchumi, Geor. I6 22
Sukkertoppen, Grnld. C22 66
Sukkur, Pak. G3 38
Sukumo, Japan J5 30
Sula, Kepulauan, is., Indon. F8 32
Sulaimān Range, mts., Pak. F3 38
Sulawesi (Celebes), i., Indon. F7 32
Sullana, Peru D2 54
Sulligent, Al., U.S. B1 78
Sullivan, Il., U.S. D5 90
Sullivan, In., U.S. F3 91
Sullivan, Mo., U.S. C6 102
Sullivan, co., In., U.S. F3 91
Sullivan, co., Mo., U.S. A4 102
Sullivan, co., N.H., U.S. D2 106
Sullivan, co., N.Y., U.S. D6 109
Sullivan, co., Pa., U.S. D9 115
Sullivan, co., Tn., U.S. C11 119
Sullivan Lake, l., Alta., Can. D5 68
Sullivans Island, S.C., U.S. k12 117
Sully, Fr. E9 10
Sully, Ia., U.S. C5 92
Sully, co., S.D., U.S. C5 118
Sulmona, Italy G8 14
Sulphur, La., U.S. D2 95
Sulphur, Ok., U.S. C5 113
Sulphur, stm., U.S. D2 81
Sulphur Spring Range, mts., Nv., U.S. C5 105
Sulphur Springs, Tx., U.S. C5 120
Sultan, Wa., U.S. B4 124
Sultānpur, India G10 38
Sulu Archipelago, is., Phil. D7 32
Sulu Sea, Asia D6 32
Sulzbach-Rosenberg, Ger. F11 8
Sumas, Wa., U.S. A3 124
Sumatera (Sumatra), i., Indon. F3 32
Sumatra see Sumatera, i., Indon. F3 32
Sumba, i., Indon. G7 32
Sumbawa, i., Indon. G6 32
Sumbawanga, Tan. C6 44
Sumedang, Indon. m13 33a
Šumen, Bul. F10 16
Sumenep, Indon. m16 33a
Sumgait, Azer. I7 22
Sumiton, Al., U.S. B2 78
Summerfield, N.C., U.S. A3 110
Summerford, Newf., Can. D4 72
Summer Island, i., Mi., U.S. C4 99
Summer Lake, l., Or., U.S. E6 114
Summerland, B.C., Can. E8 69
Summers, co., W.V., U.S. D4 125
Summerside, P.E.I., Can. C6 71
Summersville, W.V., U.S. C4 125
Summersville Lake, res., W.V., U.S. C4 125
Summerton, S.C., U.S. D7 117
Summertown, Tn., U.S. B4 119
Summerville, Ga., U.S. B1 87
Summerville, S.C., U.S. E7 117
Summit, Il., U.S. k9 90
Summit, Ms., U.S. D3 101
Summit, N.J., U.S. B4 107
Summit, Tn., U.S. h11 119
Summit, co., Co., U.S. B4 83
Summit, co., Oh., U.S. A4 112
Summit, co., Ut., U.S. C5 121
Summit Hill, Pa., U.S. E10 115
Summit Lake, l., Ia., U.S. C3 92
Summit Lake Indian Reservation, Nv., U.S. B2 105
Summit Mountain, mtn., Nv., U.S. D5 105
Summit Peak, mtn., Co., U.S. D4 83
Summitville, In., U.S. D6 91
Sumner, Il., U.S. E6 90
Sumner, Ia., U.S. B5 92
Sumner, Wa., U.S. B3 124
Sumner, co., Ks., U.S. E6 93
Sumner, co., Tn., U.S. A5 119
Sumner, Lake, res., N.M., U.S. C5 108
Sumner Dam, N.M., U.S. C5 108
Sumner Strait, strt., Ak., U.S. m23 79
Sumoto, Japan H7 30
Šumperk, Czech. F16 8
Sumrall, Ms., U.S. D4 101
Šumšu, Ostrov, i., Russia G25 24
Sumter, S.C., U.S. D7 117
Sumter, co., Al., U.S. C1 78
Sumter, co., Fl., U.S. D4 86
Sumter, co., Ga., U.S. D2 87
Sumter, co., S.C., U.S. D7 117
Sumy, Ukr. G4 22
Sun, stm., Mt., U.S. C4 103
Sunagawa, Japan p19 30a
Sunapee, N.H., U.S. D2 106
Sunapee Lake, l., N.H., U.S. D2 106
Sunbright, Tn., U.S. C9 119
Sunbury, Oh., U.S. B3 112
Sunbury, Pa., U.S. E8 115
Sunchales, Arg. C4 56
Sun City, Az., U.S. k8 80
Suncook, N.H., U.S. D4 106
Suncook, stm., N.H., U.S. D4 106
Suncook Lakes, l., N.H., U.S. D4 106
Sunda, Selat, strt., Indon. G4 32
Sundance, Wy., U.S. B8 127
Sundance Mountain, mtn., Wy., U.S. B8 127
Sundarbans, reg., Asia J13 38
Sunderland, Ont., Can. C5 73
Sunderland, Eng., U.K. G11 7
Sundown, Tx., U.S. C1 120
Sundre, Alta., Can. D3 68
Sundridge, Ont., Can. B5 73
Sundsvall, Swe. E11 6
Sunflower, Ms., U.S. B3 101
Sunflower, co., Ms., U.S. B3 101
Sunflower, Mount, mtn., Ks., U.S. C2 93
Sungaidareh, Indon. O6 34
Sungei Patani, Malay. L6 34
Suniteyouqi, China C9 26
Sunland Park, N.M., U.S. F3 108
Sunlight Creek, stm., Wy., U.S. B3 127
Sunman, In., U.S. F7 91
Sunndalsøra, Nor. E7 6
Sunnyside, Newf., Can. E5 72
Sunnyside, Wa., U.S. C5 124
Sunnyvale, Ca., U.S. k8 82
Sun Prairie, Wi., U.S. E4 126
Sunray, Tx., U.S. A2 120
Sunrise Manor, Nv., U.S. *G6 105
Sunset, La., U.S. D3 95
Sunset, Ut., U.S. B4 121
Sunset Beach, Hi., U.S. f9 88
Sunset Crater National Monument, Az., U.S. B4 80
Sunset Lake, l., Vt., U.S. D2 122
Suntar, Russia E17 24
Suntar-Chajata, Chrebet, mts., Russia E22 24
Suntaug Lake, l., Ma., U.S. f11 98
Sun Valley, Id., U.S. F4 89
Sun Valley, Nv., U.S. D2 105
Sunyani, Ghana G5 42
Suō-nada, Japan I4 30
Suonenjoki, Fin. E16 6
Suordach, Russia D20 24
Superior, Az., U.S. D4 80
Superior, Mt., U.S. C2 103
Superior, Ne., U.S. D7 104
Superior, Wi., U.S. B1 126
Superior, Wy., U.S. E4 127
Superior, Lake, l., N.A. B9 76
Superstition Mountains, mts., Az., U.S. m10 80
Supetar, Cro. F11 14
Suphan Buri, Thai. G6 34
Suqian, China B7 28
Suquamish, Wa., U.S. B3 124
Suquṭrā (Socotra), i., Yemen F5 46
Şūr (Tyre), Leb. C4 40
Şūr, Oman D6 46
Sur, Point, c., Ca., U.S. D3 82
Surabaya, Indon. m16 32
Surakarta, Indon. m15 32
Şūrān, Syria B5 40
Surat, India B2 37
Surat Thani (Ban Don), Thai. J5 34
Surendranagar, India I4 38
Surfside, Fl., U.S. s13 86
Surfside Beach, S.C., U.S. D10 117
Surgoinsville, Tn., U.S. C11 119
Sūri, India I12 38
Surigao, Phil. D8 32
Surin, Thai. G7 34
Suriname, ctry., S.A. C7 54
Sūrmaq, Iran B5 46
Surprise, Az., U.S. k8 80
Surrey, N.D., U.S. A4 111
Surry, co., N.C., U.S. A2 110
Surry, co., Va., U.S. C6 123
Surry Mountain Lake, res., N.H., U.S. D2 106
Surt, Libya B9 42
Surt, Khalīj, b., Libya B9 42
Sürüç, Tur. A6 40
Suruga-wan, b., Japan H11 30
Susa, Italy D2 14
Susanville, Ca., U.S. B3 82
Susitna, stm., Ak., U.S. C10 79
Susquehanna, Pa., U.S. C10 115
Susquehanna, co., Pa., U.S. C10 115
Susquehanna, stm., U.S. A5 97
Susquehanna, West Branch, stm., Pa., U.S. D5 115
Sussex, N.B., Can. D4 71
Sussex, N.J., U.S. A3 107
Sussex, Wi., U.S. m11 126
Sussex, co., De., U.S. F4 85
Sussex, co., N.J., U.S. A3 107
Sussex, co., Va., U.S. D5 123
Susurluk, Tur. J12 16
Sutherland, S. Afr. H4 44
Sutherland, Ia., U.S. B2 92
Sutherland, Ne., U.S. C4 104
Sutherlin, Or., U.S. D3 114
Sutlej (Satluj) (Langqên), stm., Asia F4 38
Sutter, co., Ca., U.S. C3 82
Sutter Creek, Ca., U.S. C3 82
Sutton, Que., Can. D5 74
Sutton, Ne., U.S. D8 104
Sutton, W.V., U.S. C4 125
Sutton, co., Tx., U.S. D2 120
Sutton Lake, res., W.V., U.S. C4 125
Sutwik Island, i., Ak., U.S. D8 79
Suur Munamägi, hill, Est. D10 18
Suwa, Japan F11 30
Suwałki, Pol. A22 8
Suwanee, Ga., U.S. B2 87
Suwannee, co., Fl., U.S. B3 86
Suwannee, stm., U.S. C4 86
Suwannee Sound, strt., Fl., U.S. C3 86
Suways, Qanāt as- (Suez Canal), Egypt D3 40
Suwŏn, S. Kor. D12 26
Suxian, China B5 28
Suzaka, Japan F11 30
Suzhou (Soochow), China D9 28
Suzuka, Japan H9 30
Suzu-misaki, c., Japan E10 30
Suzzara, Italy D5 14
Svappavaara, Swe. C13 6
Svartenhuk, pen., Grnld. B22 66
Sv'atoj Nos, Mys, c., Russia C22 24
Sveg, Swe. E10 6
Svenljunga, Swe. H9 6
Svensen, Or., U.S. A3 114
Sverdlovsk see Jekaterinburg, Russia F10 22
Svetlaja, Russia H21 24
Svetlyj, Russia F17 24
Svištov, Bul. F9 16
Svobodnyj, Russia G19 24
Svolvær, Nor. B10 6
Swain, co., N.C., U.S. f9 110
Swainsboro, Ga., U.S. D4 87
Swakopmund, Nmb. F2 44
Swampscott, Ma., U.S. B6 98
Swan, stm., Can. C1 70
Swan Creek, stm., Oh., U.S. e6 112
Swan Falls, wtfl, Id., U.S. F2 89
Swan Hill, Austl. G8 50
Swan Hills, Alta., Can. B3 68
Swan Islands, is., Hond. F6 64
Swan Lake, l., Man., Can. C1 70
Swan Lake, l., Me., U.S. D4 96
Swan Lake, l., Ne., U.S. C3 104
Swannanoa, N.C., U.S. f10 110
Swan Peak, mtn., Mt., U.S. C3 103
Swan Range, mts., Mt., U.S. C3 103
Swan River, Man., Can. C1 70
Swansboro, N.C., U.S. C5 110
Swansea, Wales, U.K. J9 7
Swansea, Il., U.S. E4 90
Swanson Lake, res., Ne., U.S. D4 104
Swanton, Oh., U.S. A2 112
Swanton, Vt., U.S. B2 122
Swanzey Center, N.H., U.S. E2 106
Swarthmore, Pa., U.S. p20 115
Swartswood Lake, l., N.J., U.S. A3 107
Swartz Creek, Mi., U.S. F7 99
Swayzee, In., U.S. C6 91
Swaziland, ctry., Afr. G6 44
Swea City, Ia., U.S. A3 92
Sweden, ctry., Eur. C10 4
Sweeny, Tx., U.S. r14 120
Sweet Grass, co., Mt., U.S. E7 103
Sweet Home, Or., U.S. C4 114
Sweetser, In., U.S. C6 91
Sweet Springs, Mo., U.S. C4 102
Sweetwater, Tn., U.S. D9 119
Sweetwater, Tx., U.S. C2 120
Sweetwater, co., Wy., U.S. E3 127
Sweetwater, stm., Wy., U.S. D4 127
Sweetwater Creek, Fl., U.S. p10 86
Sweetwater Creek, stm., Ok., U.S. B1 113
Swellendam, S. Afr. H4 44
Swepsonville, N.C., U.S. A3 110
Świdnica (Schweidnitz), Pol. E16 8
Swift, co., Mn., U.S. E3 100
Swift, stm., N.H., U.S. B4 106
Swift Creek, stm., N.C., U.S. B5 110
Swift Creek, stm., Va., U.S. n17 123
Swift Creek Reservoir, res., Wa., U.S. C3 124
Swift Diamond, stm., N.H., U.S. g7 106
Swifton, Ar., U.S. B4 81
Swinburne, Cape, c., N.W. Ter., Can. B13 66
Swindon, Eng., U.K. J11 7
Swinford, Ire. H4 7
Swinomish Indian Reservation, Wa., U.S. A3 124
Świnoujście (Swinemünde), Pol. B14 8
Swisher, Ia., U.S. C6 92
Swisher, co., Tx., U.S. B2 120
Swissvale, Pa., U.S. k14 115
Switzer, W.V., U.S. D3 125
Switzerland, Fl., U.S. m8 86
Switzerland, co., In., U.S. G7 91
Switzerland, ctry., Eur. F9 4
Swoyerville, Pa., U.S. D10 115
Syalach, Russia D18 24
Sycamore, Al., U.S. B3 78
Sycamore, Il., U.S. B5 90
Sycamore, Oh., U.S. B2 112
Sycamore Creek, stm., W.V., U.S. m13 125
Sydenham, Ont., Can. C8 73
Sydney, Austl. F10 50
Syke, Ger. C8 8
Sykesville, Md., U.S. B4 97
Sykesville, Pa., U.S. D4 115
Sykkylven, Nor. E6 6
Syktyvkar, Russia E8 22
Sylacauga, Al., U.S. B3 78
Sylhet, Bngl. H14 38
Sylva, N.C., U.S. f9 110
Sylvania, Al., U.S. A4 78
Sylvania, Ga., U.S. D5 87
Sylvania, Oh., U.S. A2 112
Sylvan Lake, Alta., Can. C3 68
Sylvan Lake, Mi., U.S. o15 99
Sylvan Lake, l., In., U.S. B7 91
Sylvan Pass, Wy., U.S. B2 127
Sylvester, Ga., U.S. E3 87
Sym, Russia E11 24
Symmes Creek, stm., Oh., U.S. D3 112
Symsonia, Ky., U.S. f9 94
Syracuse, In., U.S. B6 91
Syracuse, Ks., U.S. E2 93
Syracuse, Ne., U.S. D9 104
Syracuse, N.Y., U.S. B4 109
Syracuse, Ut., U.S. B3 121
Syrdarja (Syr Darya), stm., Asia I11 22
Syria, ctry., Asia B5 40
Syriam, Burma F4 34
Syrian Desert see Shām, Bādiyat ash-, des., Asia C6 40
Sysladobsis Lake, l., Me., U.S. C4 96
Syzran', Russia G7 22
Szamos (Someş), stm., Eur. B6 16
Szczecin (Stettin), Pol. B14 8
Szczecinek (Neustettin), Pol. B16 8
Szeged, Hung. I20 8
Székesfehérvár, Hung. H18 8
Szentes, Hung. I20 8
Szolnok, Hung. H20 8
Szombathely, Hung. H16 8

T

Taal, Lake, l., Phil. r19 33b
Tabaco, Phil. r20 33b
Tabarka, Tun. M3 14
Tabatinga, Serra da, hills, Braz. F10 54
Tabbys Peak, mtn., Ut., U.S. C3 121
Tabelbala, Alg. C5 42
Taber, Alta., Can. E4 68
Tabernes de Valldigna, Spain F11 12
Tablas Island, i., Phil. C7 32
Table Head, c., Newf., Can. B4 72
Table Mountain, mtn., Az., U.S. E5 80
Table Rock Lake, res., U.S. E4 102
Table Top, mtn., Az., U.S. E3 80
Tabor, Russia C24 24
Tabor, Ia., U.S. D2 92
Tabora, Tan. C6 44
Tabor City, N.C., U.S. C4 110
Tobou, I.C. H4 42
Tabrīz, Iran J7 22
Tabūk, Sau. Ar. C2 46
Tacámbaro de Codallos, Mex. H9 62
Tachikawa, Japan G12 30
Tacna, Peru G4 54
Tacoma, Wa., U.S. B3 124
Taconic Range, mts., U.S. A1 98
Tacuarembó, Ur. C5 56
Tacubaya, Mex. C7 62
Tadjerouine, Tun. N3 14
Tadoule Lake, l., Man., Can. E13 66
Tadoussac, Que., Can. A8 74
Tādpatri, India E5 37
Taegu, S. Kor. D12 26
Taejŏn, S. Kor. D12 26
Tafalla, Spain C10 12
Taft, Ca., U.S. E4 82
Taft, Tx., U.S. F4 120
Tagajō, Japan D13 30
Taganrog, Russia H5 22
Taglio di Po, Italy D7 14
Taguatinga, Braz. B5 57
Taguke, China D11 38
Tagula Island, i., Pap. N. Gui. B10 50
Tagus (Tejo) (Tajo), stm., Eur. F3 12
Tahan, Gunong, mtn., Malay. L7 34
Tahat, mtn., Alg. D7 42
Tahlequah, Ok., U.S. B7 113
Tahoe, Lake, l., U.S. E1 105
Tahoe City, Ca., U.S. C3 82
Tahoka, Tx., U.S. C2 120
Taholah, Wa., U.S. B1 124
Tahoua, Niger F7 42
Tahquamenon, stm., Mi., U.S. B5 99
Tahsis, B.C., Can. E4 69
Tahtsa Peak, mtn., B.C., Can. C4 69
T'aichung, Tai. K9 28
T'aichunghsien, Tai. K9 28
Taihape, N.Z. C5 52
Tai Hu, l., China D9 28
Tailai, China B11 26
Tain, Scot., U.K. D8 7
T'ainan, Tai. L9 28
T'aipei, Tai. J10 28
T'aipeihsien, Tai. J10 28
Taiping, Malay. L6 34
Taishun, China H8 28
Taitao, Península de, pen., Chile F2 56
T'aitung, Tai. M10 28
Taivalkoski, Fin. D17 6
Taiwan (T'aiwan), ctry., Asia G11 26
Taiwan Strait, strt., Asia K8 28
Taixian, China C9 28
Taixing, China C9 28
Taiyuan, China D9 26
Taizhou, China C8 28
Ta'izz, Yemen F3 46
Tajikistan, ctry., Asia J12 22
Tajitos, Mex. B3 62
Tajmyr, Ozero, l., Russia C14 24
Tajmyr, Poluostrov, pen., Russia B14 24
Tajšet, Russia F13 24
Tajumulco, Volcań, vol., Guat. G2 64
Tak, Thai. F5 34
Takada, Japan E11 30
Takalar, Indon. G6 32
Takamatsu, Japan H7 30
Takaoka, Japan F10 30
Takapuna, N.Z. B5 52
Takasaki, Japan F12 30
Takatsuki, Japan H8 30
Takawa, Japan I3 30
Takayama, Japan F10 30
Takefu, Japan G9 30
Takêv, Camb. I8 34
Takijuq Lake, l., N.W. Ter., Can. C10 66
Takikawa, Japan p19 30a
Takla Lake, l., B.C., Can. B5 69
Taklimakan Shamo, des., China D3 26
Takoma Park, Md., U.S. f8 97
Taku Glacier, Ak., U.S. k22 79
Tala, Mex. G8 62
Talagang, Pak. D5 38
Talaimannar, Sri L. H5 37
Talara, Peru D2 54
Talarrubias, Spain F6 12
Talasea, Pap. N. Gui. m17 50a
Talaud, Kepulauan, is., Indon. E8 32
Talavera de la Reina, Spain F7 12
Talawdī, Sudan F12 42
Talbot, co., Ga., U.S. D2 87
Talbot, co., Md., U.S. C5 97
Talbot Island, i., Fl., U.S. B5 86
Talbot Lake, l., Man., Can. B2 70
Talbotton, Ga., U.S. D2 87
Talca, Chile D2 56
Talcahuano, Chile D2 56
Talent, Or., U.S. E4 114
Taliabu, Pulau, i., Indon. F7 32
Taliaferro, co., Ga., U.S. C4 87
Talihina, Ok., U.S. C6 113
Talkeetna, Ak., U.S. C10 79
Talkeetna Mountains, mts., Ak., U.S. f17 79
Talladega, Al., U.S. B3 78
Talladega, co., Al., U.S. B3 78
Tallahassee, Fl., U.S. B2 86
Tallahatchie, co., Ms., U.S. B3 101
Tallahatchie, stm., Ms., U.S. B3 101
Tallapoosa, Ga., U.S. C1 87
Tallapoosa, co., Al., U.S. C4 78
Tallapoosa, stm., Al., U.S. C3 78
Tallassee, Al., U.S. C4 78
Talleyville, De., U.S. A3 85
Tallinn, Est. B7 18
Tall Kalakh, Syria B5 40
Tallmadge, Oh., U.S. A4 112
Tall Tamir, Syria A7 40
Tallulah, La., U.S. B4 95
Tal'menka, Russia G10 24
Talo, mtn., Eth. F2 46
Tāloqān, Afg. B3 38
Talquin, Lake, res., Fl., U.S. B2 86
Talu, Indon. N5 34
Taluk, Indon. O6 34
Tama, Ia., U.S. C5 92
Tama, co., Ia., U.S. B5 92
Tamale, Ghana G5 42
Tamalpais, Mount, mtn., Ca., U.S. h7 82
Tamana, Japan J3 30
Tamanrasset, Alg. D7 42
Tamaqua, Pa., U.S. E10 115
Tamaroa, Il., U.S. E4 90
Tamazula de Gordiano, Mex. H8 62
Tamazunchale, Mex. G10 62
Tambacounda, Sen. F3 42
Tambohorano, Madag. E8 44
Tambov, Russia I24 18
Tambura, Sudan G11 42
Tamchaket, Maur. E3 42
Tamel Aike, Arg. F2 56
Tamiahua, Laguna de, b., Mex. G11 62
Tamiami Canal, Fl., U.S. G6 86
Tamil Nadu, state, India G5 37

Name — Map Ref — Page

Tam Ky, Viet. G10 34
Tampa, Fl., U.S. E4 86
Tampa Bay, b., Fl., U.S. E4 86
Tampere, Fin. F14 6
Tampico, Mex. F11 62
Tampico, Il., U.S. B4 90
Tamrida, Yemen F5 46
Tamsagbulag, Mong. B10 26
Tamworth, Austl. F10 50
Tana, Nor. A17 6
Tana, stm., Eur. A16 6
Tana, stm., Kenya B7 44
Tana, Lake, l., Eth. F2 46
Tanabe, Japan I8 30
Tanaga Island, i., Ak., U.S. E4 79
Tanahjampea, Pulau, i., Indon. G7 32
Tanami Desert, des., Austl. C5 50
Tanana, Ak., U.S. B9 79
Tanana, stm., Ak., U.S. C10 79
Tananarive see Antananarivo, Madag. E9 44
Tanda, India G10 38
Tandil, Arg. D5 56
Tando Ādam, Pak. H3 38
Tando Muhammad Khān, Pak. H3 38
Tanega-shima, i., Japan u30 31b
Taney, co., Mo., U.S. E4 102
Taneycomo, Lake, res., Mo., U.S. E4 102
Taneytown, Md., U.S. A3 97
Tanezrouft, des., Afr. D5 42
Tanga, Tan. C7 44
Tangail, Bngl. H13 38
Tanganyika, Lake, l., Afr. C5 44
Tanger (Tangier), Mor. A4 42
Tangerang, Indon. m13 33a
Tangermünde, Ger. C11 8
Tanggula Shan, mts., China D13 38
Tangier, Va., U.S. C7 123
Tangier Island, i., Va., U.S. C6 123
Tangier Sound, strt., Md., U.S. D6 97
Tangier see Tanger, Mor. A4 42
Tangipahoa, co., La., U.S. D5 95
Tangipahoa, stm., La., U.S. D5 95
Tangra Yumco, l., China E12 38
Tangshan, China D10 26
Tanimbar, Kepulauan, is., Indon. G9 32
Tanjungbalai, Indon. M5 34
Tanjungkarang-Telukbetung, Indon. k12 32
Tanjungpinang, Indon. N8 34
Tanjungselor, Indon. E6 32
Tānk, Pak. D4 38
Tännäs, Swe. E9 6
Tanner, Al., U.S. A3 78
Tânout, Niger F7 42
Tanshui, Tai. J10 28
Tanṭā, Egypt B12 42
Tanuku, India D6 37
Tanzania, ctry., Afr. C6 44
Taos, Mo., U.S. C5 102
Taos, N.M., U.S. A4 108
Taos, co., N.M., U.S. A4 108
Taos Pueblo, N.M., U.S. A4 108
Taoudenni, Mali D5 42
Tapachula, Mex. J13 62
Tapah, Malay. L6 34
Tapajós, stm., Braz. E7 54
Taphan Hin, Thai. F6 34
Tāpi, stm., India B2 37
Tappahannock, Va., U.S. C6 123
Tappan, N.Y., U.S. g13 109
Tappan, Lake, res., N.J., U.S. g9 107
Tappan Lake, res., Oh., U.S. B4 112
Taqātu' Hayyā, Sudan E13 42
Taquaritinga, Braz. F4 57
Tar, stm., N.C., U.S. B5 110
Tara, Ont., Can. C3 73
Tarābulus (Tripoli), Leb. B4 40
Tarābulus (Tripoli), Libya B8 42
Tarābulus (Tripolitania), reg., Libya B8 42
Tarakan, Indon. E6 32
Tarancón, Spain E8 12
Taranto, Italy I12 14
Taranto, Golfo di, b., Italy I12 14
Tarapacá, Col. I8 58
Tarare, Fr. G11 10
Tarascon, Fr. J8 10
Tarata, Bol. G5 54
Tarazona, Spain D10 12
Tarazona de la Mancha, Spain F10 12
Tarbert, Scot., U.K. F7 7
Tarbert, Scot., U.K. D6 7
Tarbes, Fr. I7 10
Tarboro, N.C., U.S. B5 110
Tarcento, Italy C8 14
Taree, Austl. F10 50
Tareja, Russia C12 24
Tarentum, Pa., U.S. E2 115
Tarfaya, Mor. C3 42
Targhee Pass, U.S. E7 89
Tarifa, Punta de, c., Spain I6 12
Tariffville, Ct., U.S. B4 84
Tarija, Bol. H6 54
Tarim, stm., China C3 26
Tarīn Kowt, Afg. D1 38
Tarkio, Mo., U.S. A2 102
Tarkwa, Ghana G5 42
Tarlac, Phil. q19 32
Tarn, stm., Fr. I8 10
Tärnaby, Swe. D10 6
Tarnak, stm., Afg. D2 38
Tarnów, Pol. E20 8
Tarnowskie Góry, Pol. E18 8
Tarpey, Ca., U.S. D4 82
Tarpon, Lake, l., Fl., U.S. o10 86
Tarpon Springs, Fl., U.S. D4 86
Tarquinia, Italy G6 14
Tarragona, Spain D13 12
Tarrant, Al., U.S. B3 78
Tarrant, co., Tx., U.S. C4 120
Tarrasa, Spain D14 12
Tarryall Mountains, mts., Co., U.S. B5 83
Tarrytown, N.Y., U.S. D7 109
Tarsus, Tur. A4 40
Tartagal, Arg. A4 56
Tartas, Fr. I6 10
Tartu, Est. C9 18
Ṭarṭūs, Syria B4 40
Tarutung, Indon. M5 34
Tašauz, Turk. I9 22
Tasejeva, stm., Russia F12 24
Tasejevo, Russia F12 24
Taseko Mountain, mtn., B.C., Can. D6 69
Tashi Gang Dzong, Bhu. G14 38
Tashkent see Taškent, Uzb. I11 22
Tasikmalaya, Indon. m14 32
Taškent, Uzb. I11 22
Tasmania, state, Austl. H9 50
Tasman Sea, Oc. G11 50
Tasso, Tn., U.S. D9 119
Taštagol, Russia G11 24
Tatabánya, Hung. H18 8
Tatarskij Proliv, strt., Russia H22 24
Tate, Ga., U.S. B2 87
Tate, co., Ms., U.S. A4 101
Tateville, Ky., U.S. D5 94
Tateyama, Japan H12 30
Tathlina Lake, l., N.W. Ter., Can. D9 66
Tatnam, Cape, c., Man., Can. f9 70
Tatta, Pak. H2 38
Tattnall, co., Ga., U.S. D4 87
Tatum, N.M., U.S. D6 108
Tatvan, Tur. H16 4
Tau, Nor. G5 6
Taubaté, Braz. G6 57
Tauberbischofsheim, Ger. F9 8
Taujskaja Guba, b., Russia F24 24
Taumarunui, N.Z. C5 52
Taum Sauk Mountain, mtn., Mo., U.S. D6 102
Taungdwingyi, Burma D3 34
Taunggyi, Burma D4 34
Taungup Pass, Burma E3 34
Taunton, Eng., U.K. J9 7
Taunton, Ma., U.S. C5 98
Taunton, stm., Ma., U.S. C5 98
Taupo, Lake, l., N.Z. C5 52
Tauranga, N.Z. B6 52
Taureau, Réservoir, res., Que., Can. C4 74
Taurus Mountains see Toros Dağları, mts., Tur. H14 4
Tauste, Spain D10 12
Tavares, Fl., U.S. D5 86
Tavernier, Fl., U.S. G6 86
Tavira, Port. H4 12
Tavoy Point, c., Burma H5 34
Tavşanlı, Tur. J13 16
Tawakoni, Lake, res., Tx., U.S. C4 120
Tawas City, Mi., U.S. D7 99
Tawas Lake, l., Mi., U.S. D7 99
Tawau, Malay. E6 32
Tawitawi Island, i., Phil. D6 32
Ṭawkar, Sudan E13 42
Taxco de Alarcón, Mex. H10 62
Tay, Loch, l., Scot., U.K. E8 7
Taylor, B.C., Can. A7 69
Taylor, Az., U.S. C5 80
Taylor, Ar., U.S. D2 81
Taylor, Mi., U.S. p15 99
Taylor, Pa., U.S. D10 115
Taylor, Tx., U.S. D4 120
Taylor, co., Fl., U.S. B3 86
Taylor, co., Ga., U.S. D2 87
Taylor, co., Ia., U.S. D3 92
Taylor, co., Ky., U.S. C4 94
Taylor, co., Tx., U.S. C3 120
Taylor, co., W.V., U.S. B4 125
Taylor, co., Wi., U.S. C3 126
Taylor, stm., Co., U.S. C4 83
Taylor, Mount, mtn., N.M., U.S. B2 108
Taylor Mill, Ky., U.S. k14 94
Taylor Mountain, mtn., Id., U.S. E4 89
Taylor Park Reservoir, res., Co., U.S. C4 83
Taylors, S.C., U.S. B3 117
Taylors Falls, Mn., U.S. E6 100
Taylors Island, i., Md., U.S. D5 97
Taylorsville, In., U.S. F6 91
Taylorsville, Ky., U.S. B4 94
Taylorsville, Ms., U.S. D4 101
Taylorsville, N.C., U.S. B1 110
Taylorville, Il., U.S. D4 90
Taymā', Sau. Ar. C2 46
Tay Ninh, Viet. I9 34
Tayoltita, Mex. E7 62
Taytay, Phil. C6 32
Taz, stm., Russia D10 24
Taza, Mor. B5 42
Tazewell, Tn., U.S. C10 119
Tazewell, Va., U.S. e10 123
Tazewell, co., Il., U.S. C4 90
Tazewell, co., Va., U.S. e10 123
Tazin Lake, l., Sask., Can. E11 66
Tbessa, Alg. A7 42
Tbilisi, Geor. I6 22
Tbong, Camb. H8 34
Tchefuncta, stm., La., U.S. D5 95
Tchibanga, Gabon B2 44
Tchien, Lib. G4 42
Tchula, Ms., U.S. B3 101
Tczew, Pol. A18 8
Tea, S.D., U.S. D9 118
Teacapán, Mex. F7 62
Teague, Tx., U.S. D4 120
Teakean Butte, mtn., Id., U.S. C2 89
Te Anau, Lake, l., N.Z. F1 52
Teaneck, N.J., U.S. h8 107
Teano, Italy H9 14
Teaticket, Ma., U.S. C6 98
Tebingtinggi, Indon. M5 34
Téboursouk, Tun. M4 14
Tecate, Mex. A1 62
Tecolotlan, Mex. G7 62
Tecomán, Mex. H8 62
Tecpan de Galeana, Mex. I9 62
Tecuala, Mex. F7 62
Tecuci, Rom. D11 16
Tecumseh, Ont., Can. E2 73
Tecumseh, Ks., U.S. k14 93
Tecumseh, Mi., U.S. G7 99
Tecumseh, Ne., U.S. D9 104
Tecumseh, Ok., U.S. B5 113
Tedžen (Harīrūd), stm., Asia J10 22
Teeswater, Ont., Can. C3 73
Tefé, Braz. D6 54
Tegal, Indon. m14 32
Tegucigalpa, Hond. G4 64
Tehachapi, Ca., U.S. E4 82
Tehachapi Mountains, mts., Ca., U.S. E4 82
Tehama, co., Ca., U.S. B2 82
Tehrān, Iran J8 22
Tehuacán, Mex. H11 62
Tehuantepec, Mex. I12 62
Tehuantepec, Golfo de, b., Mex. J12 62
Tehuantepec, Istmo de, Mex. I12 62
Teide, Pico de, mtn., Spain p24 13b
Tejamén, Mex. E7 62
Tejkovo, Russia E23 18
Tejupan, Punta, c., Mex. H8 62
Tekamah, Ne., U.S. C9 104
Tekirdağ, Tur. I11 16
Tekoa, Wa., U.S. B8 124
Tekonsha, Mi., U.S. F5 99
Tela, Hond. G4 64
Telavåg, Nor. F5 6
Tel Aviv-Yafo, Isr. C4 40
Teleckoje, Ozero, l., Russia G11 24
Telén, Arg. D3 56
Telescope Peak, mtn., Ca., U.S. D5 82
Teles Pires, stm., Braz. E7 54
Telfair, co., Ga., U.S. E4 87
Telford, Pa., U.S. F11 115
Telfs, Aus. H11 8
Teli, Russia G12 24
Telkwa, B.C., Can. B4 69
Tell City, In., U.S. I4 91
Teller, co., Co., U.S. C5 83
Tellicherry, India G3 37
Tellico Plains, Tn., U.S. D9 119
Telluride, Co., U.S. D3 83
Telok Anson, Malay. L6 34
Telos Lake, l., Me., U.S. B3 96
Temagami, Lake, l., Ont., Can. G16 66
Tembeling, stm., Malay. L7 34
Tembenči, stm., Russia D13 24
Temecula, Ca., U.S. F5 82
Temerloh, Malay. M7 34
Teminabuan, Indon. F9 32
Témiscouata, Lac, l., Que., Can. B9 74
Te-Moak Indian Reservation, Nv., U.S. C6 105
Temósachic, Mex. C6 62
Tempe, Az., U.S. D4 80
Temperance, Mi., U.S. G7 99
Temperance, stm., Mn., U.S. C8 100
Tempio Pausania, Italy I4 14
Temple, Ga., U.S. C1 87
Temple, Ok., U.S. C3 113
Temple, Pa., U.S. F10 115
Temple, Tx., U.S. D4 120
Temple Terrace, Fl., U.S. o11 86
Templin, Ger. B13 8
Temuco, Chile D2 56
Tena, Ec. H4 58
Tenafly, N.J., U.S. B5 107
Tenaha, Tx., U.S. D5 120
Tenāli, India D6 37
Tendaho, Eth. F3 46
Tende, Col de, Eur. H14 10
Ten Degree Channel, strt., India J2 34
Ténéré, des., Niger E8 42
Tenerife, i., Spain p24 13b
Tengchong, China B5 34
Tenino, Wa., U.S. C3 124
Tenkāsi, India H4 37
Tenkiller Ferry Lake, res., Ok., U.S. B6 113
Tenkodogo, Burkina F5 42
Tenmile, stm., U.S. B5 116
Tenmile Creek, stm., W.V., U.S. k10 125
Tenmile Lake, l., Mn., U.S. D4 100
Tennant Creek, Austl. C6 50
Tennessee, state, U.S. B5 119
Tennessee, stm., U.S. D9 76
Tennessee Pass, Co., U.S. B4 83
Tennessee Ridge, Tn., U.S. A4 119
Tennille, Ga., U.S. D4 87
Tenom, Malay. D6 32
Tenryū, stm., Japan G10 30
Tensas, co., La., U.S. B4 95
Tensas, stm., La., U.S. B4 95
Tensaw, stm., Al., U.S. E2 78
Ten Sleep, Wy., U.S. B5 127
Tenterfield, Austl. E10 50
Ten Thousand Islands, is., Fl., U.S. G5 86
Teocaltiche, Mex. G8 62
Teófilo Otoni, Braz. D8 57
Tepa, Indon. G8 32
Tepatitlán [de Morelos], Mex. G8 62
Tepic, Mex. G7 62
Teplice, Czech. E13 8
Teramo, Italy G8 14
Teresina, Braz. E10 54
Teresópolis, Braz. G7 57
Termez, Uzb. B2 38
Termini Imerese, Italy L8 14
Términos, Laguna de, b., Mex. H14 62
Termoli, Italy G9 14
Ternej, Russia H21 24
Terni, Italy G7 14
Ternopol', Ukr. H3 22
Terpenija, Mys, c., Russia H22 24
Terpenija, Zaliv, b., Russia H22 24
Terra Alta, W.V., U.S. B5 125
Terrace, B.C., Can. B3 69
Terracina, Italy H8 14
Terralba, Italy J3 14
Terra Nova National Park, Newf., Can. D4 72
Terrebonne, Que., Can. D4 74
Terrebonne, Or., U.S. C5 114
Terrebonne, co., La., U.S. E5 95
Terrebonne Bay, b., La., U.S. E5 95
Terre Haute, In., U.S. F3 91
Terre Hill, Pa., U.S. F9 115
Terrell, Tx., U.S. C4 120
Terrell, co., Ga., U.S. E2 87
Terrell, co., Tx., U.S. D1 120
Terrell Hills, Tx., U.S. k7 120
Terrenceville, Newf., Can. E4 72
Terry, Ms., U.S. C3 101
Terry, Mt., U.S. D11 103
Terry, co., Tx., U.S. C1 120
Terrytown, Ne., U.S. C2 104
Terryville, Ct., U.S. C3 84
Teruel, Spain E10 12
Tervola, Fin. C15 6
Teseney, Erit. E2 46
Teshekpuk Lake, l., Ak., U.S. A9 79
Teshio, Japan o19 30a
Teslin, Yukon, Can. D6 66
Teslin, stm., Can. D6 66
Tesouro, Braz. D2 57
Tessalit, Mali D6 42
Tesuque, N.M., U.S. B4 108
Tete, Moz. E6 44
Teterow, Ger. B12 8
Teton, co., Id., U.S. F7 89
Teton, co., Mt., U.S. C4 103
Teton, co., Wy., U.S. C2 127
Teton, stm., Mt., U.S. C5 103
Teton Pass, Wy., U.S. C2 127
Teton Range, mts., Wy., U.S. C2 127
Teton Village, Wy., U.S. C2 127
Tétouan, Mor. A4 42
Tetovo, Mac. G4 16
Tet'uche, Russia I21 24
Teulada, Italy K3 14
Teulon, Man., Can. D3 70
Teutopolis, Il., U.S. D5 90
Teuva, Fin. E13 6
Tevere (Tiber), stm., Italy G7 14
Teverya, Isr. C4 40
Tewksbury, Ma., U.S. A5 98
Texada Island, i., B.C., Can. E5 69
Texarkana, Ar., U.S. D1 81
Texarkana, Tx., U.S. C5 120
Texas, co., Mo., U.S. D5 102
Texas, co., Ok., U.S. e9 113
Texas, state, U.S. D3 120
Texas City, Tx., U.S. E5 120
Texhoma, Ok., U.S. e9 113
Texico, N.M., U.S. C6 108
Texoma, Lake, res., U.S. D5 113
Teyvareh, Afg. D1 38
Teziutlán, Mex. H11 62
Tezpur, India G15 38
Thabazimbi, S. Afr. F5 44
Thai Binh, Viet. D9 34
Thailand, ctry., Asia B3 32
Thailand, Gulf of, b., Asia J6 34
Thai Nguyen, Viet. D8 34
Thal, Pak. D4 38
Thames, stm., Ont., Can. E3 73
Thames, stm., Eng., U.K. J14 7
Thames, stm., Ct., U.S. D7 84
Thamesville, Ont., Can. E3 73
Thāna, India C2 37
Thanh Hoa, Viet. E8 34
Thanh Pho Ho Chi Minh (Saigon), Viet. I9 34
Thanjāvūr, India G5 37
Thar Desert (Great Indian Desert), des., Asia G3 38
Thargomindah, Austl. E8 50
Thatcher, Az., U.S. E6 80
Thaton, Burma F4 34
Thayer, Mo., U.S. E6 102
Thayer, co., Ne., U.S. D8 104
Thayetmyo, Burma E3 34
Thayne, Wy., U.S. D1 127
Thealka, Ky., U.S. C7 94
The Barrens, plat., Tn., U.S. B5 119
The Bight, Bah. B10 64
The Cheviot, mtn., Eng., U.K. F10 7
The Colony, Tx., U.S. *C4 120
The Dalles, Or., U.S. B5 114
The Dells, val., Wi., U.S. E4 126
Thedford, Ont., Can. D3 73
The English Company's Islands, is., Austl. B7 50
The Everglades, sw., Fl., U.S. G6 86
The Fens, sw., Eng., U.K. I12 7
The Flat Tops, mts., Co., U.S. B3 83
The Flume, wtfl, N.H., U.S. B3 106
The Graves, is., Ma., U.S. g12 98
The Hague see 's-Gravenhage, Neth. C4 8
The Heads, c., Or., U.S. E2 114
Thelon, stm., N.W. Ter., Can. D12 66
The Narrows, strt., Wa., U.S. f10 124
Theodore, Austl. D10 50
Theodore, Al., U.S. E1 78
Theodore Roosevelt Lake, res., Az., U.S. D4 80
Theodore Roosevelt National Park (South Unit), N.D., U.S. C2 111
Theodore Roosevelt National Park (North Unit), N.D., U.S. B2 111
The Pas, Man., Can. C1 70
The Plains, Oh., U.S. C3 112
Theresa, Wi., U.S. E5 126
Thermopolis, Wy., U.S. C4 127
The Rockies, mts., Wa., U.S. C3 124
Thessalon, Ont., Can. p19 73
Thessaloníki (Salonika), Grc. I6 16
Thetford Mines, Que., Can. C6 74
The Thimbles, is., Ct., U.S. E5 84
The Village, Ok., U.S. B4 113
The Warburton, stm., Austl. E7 50
The Wash, b., Eng., U.K. I13 7
The Weald, reg., Eng., U.K. J13 7
Thibodaux, La., U.S. E5 95
Thief, stm., Mn., U.S. B3 100
Thief Lake, l., Mn., U.S. B3 100
Thief River Falls, Mn., U.S. B2 100
Thielsen, Mount, mtn., Or., U.S. D4 114
Thiene, Italy D6 14
Thiensville, Wi., U.S. E6 126
Thiers, Fr. G10 10
Thiès, Sen. F2 42
Thika, Kenya B7 44
Thimphu, Bhu. G13 38
Thingangyun, Burma F4 34
Thionville, Fr. C13 10
Thíra, i., Grc. M9 16
Third Lake, l., N.H., U.S. f7 106
Thirsk, Eng., U.K. G11 7
Thisted, Den. H7 6
Thívai (Thebes), Grc. K7 16
Thiviers, Fr. G7 10
Thomas, Ok., U.S. B3 113
Thomas, co., Ga., U.S. F3 87
Thomas, co., Ks., U.S. C2 93
Thomas, co., Ne., U.S. C5 104
Thomasboro, Il., U.S. C5 90
Thomaston, Ct., U.S. C3 84
Thomaston, Ga., U.S. D2 87
Thomaston, Me., U.S. D3 96
Thomaston Reservoir, res., Ct., U.S. C3 84
Thomastown, Ire. I5 7
Thomasville, Al., U.S. D2 78
Thomasville, Ga., U.S. F3 87
Thomasville, N.C., U.S. B2 110
Thompson, Man., Can. B3 70
Thompson, Ct., U.S. B8 84
Thompson, N.D., U.S. B8 111
Thompson, stm., U.S. A4 102
Thompson Falls, Mt., U.S. C1 103
Thompson Island, i., Ma., U.S. g11 98
Thompson Lake, l., U.S. D2 96
Thompson Peak, mtn., Ca., U.S. B2 82
Thompson Peak, mtn., N.M., U.S. h9 108
Thompson Reservoir, res., Or., U.S. E5 114
Thomsen, stm., N.W. Ter., Can. B9 66
Thomson, Ga., U.S. C4 87
Thon Buri, Thai. H6 34
Thongwa, Burma F4 34
Thonon-les-Bains, Fr. F13 10
Thonotosassa, Fl., U.S. D4 86
Thonze, Burma F3 34
Thorburn, N.S., Can. D7 71
Thoreau, N.M., U.S. B1 108
Thornbury, Ont., Can. C4 73
Thorndale, Tx., U.S. D4 120
Thornton, Ont., Can. C5 73
Thorntown, In., U.S. D4 91
Thorold, Ont., Can. D5 73
Thorp, Wi., U.S. D3 126
Thorsby, Al., U.S. C3 78
Thouars, Fr. F6 10
Thousand Islands, is., N.Y., U.S. A4 109
Thousand Lake Mountain, mtn., Ut., U.S. E4 121
Thousand Springs Creek, stm., U.S. B7 105
Thrace, hist. reg., Eur. G13 4
Thrakikón Pélagos, Grc. I8 16
Three Fingered Jack, mtn., Or., U.S. C5 114
Three Forks, Mt., U.S. E5 103
Three Hills, Alta., Can. D4 68
Three Lakes, Wi., U.S. C4 126
Three Mile Plains, N.S., Can. E5 71
Three Oaks, Mi., U.S. G4 99
Three Pagodas Pass, Asia G5 34
Three Points, Cape, c., Ghana H5 42
Three Rivers, Ma., U.S. B3 98
Three Rivers, Mi., U.S. G5 99
Three Rivers, Tx., U.S. E3 120
Three Sisters, mtn., Or., U.S. C5 114
Three Springs, Austl. E3 50
Throckmorton, co., Tx., U.S. C3 120
Throop, Pa., U.S. m18 115
Throssell Range, mts., Austl. D4 50
Thu Dao Mot, Viet. I9 34
Thule, Grnld. B19 128
Thun, Switz. F14 10
Thunder Bay, Ont., Can. o17 73
Thunder Bay, b., Mi., U.S. D7 99
Thunder Bay, stm., Mi., U.S. D6 99
Thunderbird, Lake, res., Ok., U.S. B4 113
Thunderbolt, Ga., U.S. D5 87
Thunder Butte Creek, stm., S.D., U.S. B3 118
Thunersee, l., Switz. F14 10
Thüringen, hist. reg., Ger. D11 8
Thurles, Ire. I5 7
Thurmont, Md., U.S. A3 97
Thurso, Que., Can. D2 74
Thurso, Scot., U.K. C9 7
Thurston, co., Ne., U.S. B9 104
Thurston, co., Wa., U.S. C2 124
Tiancang, China C7 26
Tiandong, China C9 34
Tianjin (Tientsin), China D10 26
Tianjun, China D6 26
Tianmen, China E2 28
Tianshui, China E8 26
Tiaret, Alg. A6 42
Tibagi, Braz. A6 56
Tibasti, Sarīr, des., Libya D9 42
Tiber see Tevere, stm., Italy G7 14
Tibesti, mts., Chad D9 42
Tibet, hist. reg., China E12 38
Tiburón, Isla, i., Mex. C3 62
Tice, Fl., U.S. F5 86
Tīchīt, Maur. E4 42
Tichvin, Russia B16 18
Tickfaw, stm., La., U.S. C5 95
Ticonderoga, N.Y., U.S. B7 109
Ticul, Mex. G15 62
Tide Head, N.B., Can. B3 71
Tidjikdja, Maur. E3 42
Tieling, China C11 26
Tienen, Bel. E4 8
Tien Shan, mts., Asia C2 26
Tientsin see Tianjin, China D10 26
Tierra Amarilla, N.M., U.S. A3 108
Tierra Blanca, Mex. H11 62

Name	Map Ref	Page

Tierra del Fuego, Isla Grande de, i., S.A. G3 56
Tierralta, Col. C4 58
Tietê, stm., Braz. F3 57
Tieton, Wa., U.S. C5 124
Tieton, stm., Wa., U.S. C4 124
Tieton Dam, Wa., U.S. C4 124
Tiffany Mountain, mtn., Wa., U.S. A6 124
Tiffin, Oh., U.S. A2 112
Tiffin, stm., Oh., U.S. A1 112
Tift, co., Ga., U.S. E3 87
Tifton, Ga., U.S. E3 87
Tigard, Or., U.S. h12 114
Tigerton, Wi., U.S. D4 126
Tigil', Russia F25 24
Tignall, Ga., U.S. C4 87
Tignish, P.E.I., Can. C5 71
Tigre, stm., Peru D3 54
Tigris (Dijlah), stm., Asia A3 46
Tiguentourine, Alg. C7 42
Tijesno, Cro. F10 14
Tijuana, Mex. A1 62
Tikamgarh, India H8 38
Tikrīt, Iraq B3 46
Tilburg, Neth. D5 8
Tilbury, Ont., Can. E2 73
Tilden, Il., U.S. E4 90
Tilden, Ne., U.S. B8 104
Tilghman, Md., U.S. C5 97
Tilghman Island, i., Md., U.S. C5 97
Tilhar, India G8 38
Tillabéry, Niger F6 42
Tillamook, Or., U.S. B3 114
Tillamook, co., Or., U.S. B3 114
Tillanchong Island, i., India J2 34
Tillery, Lake, res., N.C., U.S. B2 110
Tillman, co., Ok., U.S. C2 113
Tillmans Corner, Al., U.S. E1 78
Tillsonburg, Ont., Can. E4 73
Tilton, Il., U.S. C6 90
Tilton, N.H., U.S. D3 106
Tiltonsville, Oh., U.S. B5 112
Timaru, N.Z. F3 52
Timbalier Island, i., La., U.S. E5 95
Timberlake, Va., U.S. C3 123
Timberville, Va., U.S. B4 123
Timbuktu see Tombouctou, Mali E5 42
Timimoun, Alg. C6 42
Timiris, Cap, c., Maur. E2 42
Timișoara, Rom. D5 16
Timmins, Ont., Can. o19 73
Timmonsville, S.C., U.S. C8 117
Timms Hill, hill, Wi., U.S. C3 126
Timor, i., Indon. G8 32
Timor Sea B5 50
Timotes, Ven. C7 58
Timpanogos Cave National Monument, Ut., U.S. C4 121
Timpton, stm., Russia F19 24
Tims Ford Lake, res., Tn., U.S. B5 119
Tinaquillo, Ven. C8 58
Tindivanam, India F5 37
Tindouf, Alg. C4 42
Tingmerkpuk Mountain, mtn., Ak., U.S. B7 79
Tingo María, Peru E3 54
Tingvoll, Nor. E7 6
Tinharé, Ilha de, i., Braz. F11 54
Tinker Air Force Base, mil., Ok., U.S. B4 113
Tinley Park, Il., U.S. k9 90
Tinniswood, Mount, mtn., B.C., Can. D6 69
Tinogasta, Arg. B3 56
Tinsukia, India G16 38
Tinton Falls, N.J., U.S. C4 107
Tioga, La., U.S. C3 95
Tioga, N.D., U.S. A3 111
Tioga, co., N.Y., U.S. C4 109
Tioga, co., Pa., U.S. C7 115
Tioga, stm., Pa., U.S. B7 115
Tiogue Lake, res., R.I., U.S. D3 116
Tioman, Pulau, i., Malay. M8 34
Tionesta Creek, stm., Pa., U.S. C3 115
Tionesta Lake, res., Pa., U.S. D3 115
Tioughnioga, stm., N.Y., U.S. C4 109
Tippah, co., Ms., U.S. A5 101
Tippah, stm., Ms., U.S. A4 101
Tipp City, Oh., U.S. C1 112
Tippecanoe, co., In., U.S. D4 91
Tippecanoe, stm., In., U.S. C4 91
Tipperary, Ire. I4 7
Tipton, Ca., U.S. D4 82
Tipton, In., U.S. D5 91
Tipton, Ia., U.S. C6 92
Tipton, Mo., U.S. C5 102
Tipton, Ok., U.S. C2 113
Tipton, co., In., U.S. D5 91
Tipton, co., Tn., U.S. B2 119
Tipton, Mount, mtn., Az., U.S. B1 80
Tiptonville, Tn., U.S. A2 119
Tiquisate, Guat. G2 64
Tiracambu, Serra do, plat., Braz. D9 54
Tīrān, Maḍīq, strt. F4 40
Tiran, Strait of see Tīrān, Maḍīq, strt. F4 40
Tiranë, Alb. H3 16
Tirano, Italy C5 14
Tiraspol', Mol. H3 22
Tirat Karmel, Isr. C4 40
Tire, Tur. K11 16
Tiree, i., Scot., U.K. E6 7
Tîrgoviște, Rom. E9 16
Tîrgu-Jiu, Rom. D7 16
Tîrgu Mureș, Rom. C8 16
Tîrgu-Ocna, Rom. C10 16
Tírnavos, Grc. J6 16
Tirschenreuth, Ger. F12 8
Tiruchchirāppalli, India G5 37
Tirunelveli, India H4 37
Tirupati, India F5 37
Tiruppattūr, India F5 37
Tiruppur, India G4 37
Tiruvannāmalai, India F5 37
Tishomingo, Ok., U.S. C5 113
Tishomingo, co., Ms., U.S. A5 101
Tiskilwa, Il., U.S. B4 90
Tisza (Tisa), stm., Eur. C4 16
Tit-Ary, Russia C19 24
Titicaca, Lago, l., S.A. G5 54
Titonka, Ia., U.S. A3 92
Titov Veles, Mac. H5 16
Titule, Zaire H11 42
Titus, co., Tx., U.S. C5 120
Titusville, Fl., U.S. D6 86
Titusville, Pa., U.S. C2 115
Tiverton, Ont., Can. C3 73
Tiverton, Eng., U.K. K9 7
Tiverton, R.I., U.S. D6 116
Tivoli, Italy H7 14
Tizimín, Mex. G15 62
Tizi-Ouzou, Alg. A6 42
Tlahualilo de Zaragoza, Mex. D8 62
Tlaltenango de Sánchez Román, Mex. G8 62
Tlaxiaco, Mex. I11 62
Tlemcen, Alg. B5 42
Tlētē Ouāte Gharbī, Jabal, mtn., Syria B6 40
Toamasina, Madag. E9 44
Toano, Va., U.S. C6 123
Toano Range, mts., Nv., U.S. C7 105
Toast, N.C., U.S. A2 110
Toba, Japan H9 30
Toba, Danau, l., Indon. M5 34
Tobacco Root Mountains, mts., Mt., U.S. E5 103
Tobago, i., Trin. I17 64
Toba Inlet, b., B.C., Can. D5 69
Toba Kākar Range, mts., Pak. E2 38
Tobarra, Spain G10 12
Tobermory, Scot., U.K. E6 7
Tobin, Mount, mtn., Nv., U.S. C4 105
Tobin Lake, l., Sask., Can. D4 75
Tobin Range, mts., Nv., U.S. C4 105
Tobique, stm., N.B., Can. B2 71
Tobruk see Ţubruq, Libya B10 42
Tobyhanna, Pa., U.S. D11 115
Tocantínia, Braz. E9 54
Tocantinópolis, Braz. E9 54
Tocantins, stm., Braz. D9 54
Toccoa, Ga., U.S. B3 87
Toccoa, stm., Ga., U.S. B2 87
Toccoa Falls, Ga., U.S. B3 87
Tochigi, Japan F12 30
Töcksfors, Swe. G8 6
Toco, Chile A3 56
Tocopilla, Chile A2 56
Todd, co., Ky., U.S. D2 94
Todd, co., Mn., U.S. D4 100
Todd, co., S.D., U.S. D5 118
Todi, Italy G7 14
Todos Santos, Mex. F4 62
Todtnau, Ger. H7 8
Tofield, Alta., Can. C4 68
Tofino, B.C., Can. E5 69
Togiak, Ak., U.S. D7 79
Togian, Kepulauan, is., Indon. F7 32
Togo, ctry., Afr. G6 42
Togwotee Pass, Wy., U.S. C2 127
Tohakum Peak, mtn., Nv., U.S. C2 105
Tohatchi, N.M., U.S. B1 108
Tohopekaliga, Lake, l., Fl., U.S. D5 86
Toiyabe Range, mts., Nv., U.S. D4 105
Tok, Ak., U.S. C11 79
Tōkamachi, Japan E11 30
Tokara-kaikyō, strt., Japan u30 31b
Tokara-rettō, is., Japan v29 31b
Tokat, Tur. G15 4
Tokelau Islands, dep., Oc. G1 2
Toki, Japan G10 30
Tokuno-shima, i., Japan x28 31b
Tokushima, Japan H7 30
Tokuyama, Japan H4 30
Tōkyō, Japan G12 30
Tokzār, Afg. C2 38
Toleak Point, c., Wa., U.S. B1 124
Toledo, Spain F7 12
Toledo, Il., U.S. D5 90
Toledo, Ia., U.S. B5 92
Toledo, Oh., U.S. A2 112
Toledo, Or., U.S. C3 114
Toledo Bend Reservoir, res., U.S. C2 95
Tolentino, Italy F8 14
Toler, Ky., U.S. C7 94
Toliara, Madag. F8 44
Toljatti, Russia G7 22
Tol'ka, Russia E10 24
Tolland, Ct., U.S. B6 84
Tolland, co., Ct., U.S. B6 84
Tollesboro, Ky., U.S. B6 94
Tolleson, Az., U.S. m8 80
Tolmezzo, Italy C8 14
Tolmin, Slo. C8 14
Tolo, Teluk, b., Indon. F7 32
Tolono, Il., U.S. D5 90
Tolosa, Spain B9 12
Tolstoj, Mys, c., Russia F25 24
Tolt Reservoir, res., Wa., U.S. B4 124
Toluca, Il., U.S. C4 90
Toluca, Nevado de, vol., Mex. H10 62
Toluca [de Lerdo], Mex. H10 62
Tom', stm., Russia F11 24
Tomah, Wi., U.S. E3 126
Tomahawk, Wi., U.S. C4 126
Tomahawk Lake, l., Wi., U.S. C4 126
Tomakomai, Japan q19 30a
Tomar, Port. F3 12
Tomaszów Mazowiecki, Pol. D20 8
Tomatlán, Mex. H7 62
Tombador, Serra do, plat., Braz. F7 54
Tomball, Tx., U.S. D5 120
Tombigbee, stm., U.S. D1 78
Tombouctou (Timbuktu), Mali E5 42
Tombstone, Az., U.S. F5 80
Tombua, Ang. E2 44
Tomelloso, Spain F9 12
Tom Green, co., Tx., U.S. D2 120
Tomini, Teluk, b., Indon. F7 32
Tommot, Russia F19 24
Tom Nevers Head, c., Ma., U.S. D8 98
Tomo, stm., Col. E8 58
Tompkins, co., N.Y., U.S. C4 109
Tompkinsville, Ky., U.S. D4 94
Tomptokan, Russia F20 24
Tomra, Nor. E6 6
Toms, stm., N.J., U.S. C4 107
Tomsk, Russia F10 24
Toms River, N.J., U.S. D4 107
Tonalá, Mex. I13 62
Tonasket, Wa., U.S. A6 124
Tonawanda Indian Reservation, N.Y., U.S. B2 109
Tondabayashi, Japan H8 30
Tone, stm., Japan F12 30
Tonga, ctry., Oc. H1 2
Tonganoxie, Ks., U.S. C8 93
Tongbai, China C2 28
Tongchuan, China D8 26
Tongeren, Bel. E5 8
Tongguan, China E9 26
Tonghai, China B7 34
Tonghua, China C12 26
Tongliao, China C11 26
Tongling, China E6 28
Tongsa Dzong, Bhu. G14 38
Tongtianheyan, China D15 38
Tongue, Scot., U.K. C8 7
Tongue, stm., Mt., U.S. E10 103
Tongue, stm., Tx., U.S. p13 120
Tongzi, China F8 26
Tonk, India G6 38
Tonkawa, Ok., U.S. A4 113
Tonkin, Gulf of, b., Asia E9 34
Tonle Sap see Sab, Tônlé, l., Camb. H7 34
Tonneins, Fr. H7 10
Tonnerre, Fr. E10 10
Tonopah, Nv., U.S. E4 105
Tønsberg, Nor. G8 6
Tonstad, Nor. G6 6
Tonto National Monument, Az., U.S. D4 80
Tonto Natural Bridge, Az., U.S. C4 80
Tooele, Ut., U.S. C3 121
Tooele, co., Ut., U.S. C2 121
Toole, co., Mt., U.S. B5 103
Toombs, co., Ga., U.S. D4 87
Toomsboro, Ga., U.S. D3 87
Toowoomba, Austl. E10 50
Topeka, In., U.S. A6 91
Topeka, Ks., U.S. C8 93
Topia, Mex. E6 62
Topock, Az., U.S. C1 80
Toppenish, Wa., U.S. C5 124
Topsfield, Ma., U.S. A6 98
Topsham, Me., U.S. E3 96
Topton, Pa., U.S. F10 115
Toquima Range, mts., Nv., U.S. E5 105
Torbay, Newf., Can. E5 72
Torbert, Mount, mtn., Ak., U.S. g15 79
Torch Lake, l., Mi., U.S. D5 99
Tordesillas, Spain D6 12
Töre, Swe. D14 6
Torgau, Ger. D12 8
Torhout, Bel. D3 8
Torino (Turin), Italy D2 14
Torit, Sudan H12 42
Torkestān, Band-e, mts., Afg. C2 38
Torneälven, stm., Eur. B12 4
Torngat Mountains, mts., Can. f8 72
Toro, Spain D6 12
Toronto, Ont., Can. D5 73
Toronto, Oh., U.S. B5 112
Toronto Lake, res., Ks., U.S. E7 93
Toro Peak, mtn., Ca., U.S. F5 82
Tororo, Ug. A6 44
Toros Dağları, mts., Tur. H14 4
Torquay (Torbay), Eng., U.K. K9 7
Torquemada, Spain C7 12
Torrance, Ca., U.S. n12 82
Torrance, co., N.M., U.S. C3 108
Torrão, Port. G3 12
Torre Annunziata, Italy I9 14
Torre Baja, Spain E10 12
Torreblanca, Spain E12 12
Torrecilla en Cameros, Spain C9 12
Torre de Moncorvo, Port. D4 12
Torredonjimeno, Spain H8 12
Torrelaguna, Spain E8 12
Torrelavega, Spain B7 12
Torremaggiore, Italy H10 14
Torremolinos, Spain I7 12
Torrens, Lake, l., Austl. F7 50
Torrente, Spain F11 12
Torreón, Mex. E8 62
Torres Novas, Port. F3 12
Torres Strait, strt., Oc. B8 50
Torres Vedras, Port. F2 12
Torrevieja, Spain H11 12
Torridon, Scot., U.K. D7 7
Torriglia, Italy E4 14
Torrijos, Spain F7 12
Torrington, Ct., U.S. B3 84
Torrington, Wy., U.S. D8 127
Torrox, Spain I8 12
Torsby, Swe. F9 6
Tórshavn, Faer. Is. C6 4
Tortola, i., Br. Vir. Is. E15 64
Tortoli, Italy J4 14
Tortona, Italy E3 14
Tortosa, Spain E12 12
Tortue, Île de la, i., Haiti D11 64
Toruń, Pol. B18 8
Toržok, Russia D17 18
Tosa-shimizu, Japan J5 30
Tosa-wan, b., Japan I6 30
Tostado, Arg. B4 56
Totagatic, stm., Wi., U.S. B2 126
Totana, Spain H10 12
Toteng, Bots. F4 44
Tôtes, Fr. C8 10
Tot'ma, Russia B25 18
Totowa, N.J., U.S. B4 107
Totson Mountain, mtn., Ak., U.S. C8 79
Tottenham (part of Alliston Beeton Tecumseth and Tottenham), Ont., Can. C5 73
Tottori, Japan G7 30
Toubkal, Jbel, mtn., Mor. B4 42
Touchet, stm., Wa., U.S. C7 124
Touggourt, Alg. B7 42
Touisset, Ma., U.S. C5 98
Toul, Fr. D12 10
Toulon, Fr. I12 10
Toulon, Il., U.S. B4 90
Toulouse, Fr. I8 10
Tounan, Tai. L9 28
Toungoo, Burma E4 34
Tourcoing, Fr. B10 10
Tournai, Bel. E3 8
Tournon, Fr. G11 10
Tournus, Fr. F11 10
Tours, Fr. E7 10
Touside, Pic, mtn., Chad D9 42
Toussaint Creek, stm., Oh., U.S. f7 112
Toutle, North Fork, stm., Wa., U.S. C3 124
Tovar, Ven. C7 58
Towanda, Il., U.S. C5 90
Towanda, Ks., U.S. E7 93
Towanda, Pa., U.S. C9 115
Towanda Creek, stm., Pa., U.S. C8 115
Tower City, Pa., U.S. E8 115
Town Creek, Al., U.S. A2 78
Towner, N.D., U.S. A5 111
Towner, co., N.D., U.S. A6 111
Towns, co., Ga., U.S. B3 87
Townsend, De., U.S. C3 85
Townsend, Mt., U.S. D5 103
Townshend Reservoir, res., Vt., U.S. E3 122
Townsville, Austl. C9 50
Towson, Md., U.S. B4 97
Toyama, Japan F10 30
Toyohashi, Japan H10 30
Toyokawa, Japan H10 30
Toyonaka, Japan H8 30
Toyooka, Japan G7 30
Toyota, Japan G10 30
Tozeur, Tun. B7 42
Trabzon, Tur. G15 4
Tracadie, N.B., Can. B5 71
Tracy, N.B., Can. D3 71
Tracy, Que., Can. C4 74
Tracy, Ca., U.S. D3 82
Tracy, Mn., U.S. F3 100
Tracy City, Tn., U.S. D8 119
Tracyton, Wa., U.S. e10 124
Tradewater, stm., Ky., U.S. C2 94
Traer, Ia., U.S. B5 92
Trafford, Pa., U.S. k14 115
Trafford, Lake, l., Fl., U.S. F5 86
Trail, B.C., Can. E9 69
Trail Creek, In., U.S. A4 91
Traill, co., N.D., U.S. B8 111
Trail Ridge, mtn., U.S. F4 87
Tralee, Ire. I3 7
Tranås, Swe. G10 6
Trancas, Arg. B3 56
Trang, Thai. K5 34
Trangan, Pulau, i., Indon. G9 32
Trani, Italy H11 14
Transylvania, co., N.C., U.S. f10 110
Transylvania, hist. reg., Rom. C7 16
Transylvanian Alps see Carpații Meridionali, mts., Rom. D8 16
Trapani, Italy K7 14
Trappe, Md., U.S. C5 97
Trapper Peak, mtn., Mt., U.S. E2 103
Traun, Aus. G14 8
Traunstein, Ger. H12 8
Travelers Rest, S.C., U.S. B3 117
Traverse, co., Mn., U.S. E2 100
Traverse, Lake, l., U.S. B9 118
Traverse City, Mi., U.S. D5 99
Tra Vinh, Viet. J9 34
Travis, co., Tx., U.S. D4 120
Travis Air Force Base, mil., Ca., U.S. C2 82
Travnik, Bos. E12 14
Tray Mountain, mtn., Ga., U.S. B3 87
Treasure, co., Mt., U.S. D9 103
Treasure Island Naval Station, mil., Ca., U.S. h8 82
Trecate, Italy D3 14
Trego, co., Ks., U.S. D4 93
Tregosse Islets, is., Austl. C10 50
Tréguier, Fr. D3 10
Treherne, Man., Can. E2 70
Treinta y Tres, Ur. C6 56
Trélazé, Fr. E6 10
Trelew, Arg. E3 56
Trelleborg, Swe. I9 6
Tremblant, Mont, mtn., Que., Can. C3 74
Tremont, Il., U.S. C4 90
Tremont, Pa., U.S. E9 115
Tremonton, Ut., U.S. B3 121
Tremp, Spain C12 12
Trempealeau, Wi., U.S. D2 126
Trempealeau, co., Wi., U.S. D2 126
Trempealeau, stm., Wi., U.S. D2 126
Trenche, stm., Que., Can. B5 74
Trenčín, Slov. G18 8
Trenque Lauquen, Arg. D4 56
Trent, stm., N.C., U.S. B5 110
Trente et un Milles, Lac des, l., Que., Can. C2 74
Trento, Italy C6 14
Trenton, Ont., Can. C7 73
Trenton, Fl., U.S. C4 86
Trenton, Ga., U.S. B1 87
Trenton, Il., U.S. E4 90
Trenton, Mi., U.S. F7 99
Trenton, Mo., U.S. A4 102
Trenton, Ne., U.S. D4 104
Trenton, N.J., U.S. C3 107
Trenton, Oh., U.S. C1 112
Trenton, Tn., U.S. B3 119
Trepassey, Newf., Can. E5 72
Trepassey Bay, b., Newf., Can. E5 72
Tres Arroyos, Arg. D4 56
Tresckow, Pa., U.S. E10 115
Três Corações, Braz. F6 57
Tres Esquinas, Col. G5 58
Três Lagoas, Braz. F3 57
Três Marias, Represa, res., Braz. E6 57
Tres Picos, Cerro, mtn., Arg. D4 56
Três Pontas, Braz. F6 57
Tres Puntas, Cabo, c., Arg. F3 56
Três Rios, Braz. G7 57
Treutlen, co., Ga., U.S. D4 87
Treviglio, Italy D4 14
Treviso, Italy D7 14
Trevor, Wi., U.S. n11 126
Trevorton, Pa., U.S. E8 115
Treynor, Ia., U.S. C2 92
Trezevant, Tn., U.S. A3 119
Triadelphia, W.V., U.S. A4 125
Triadelphia Reservoir, res., Md., U.S. B3 97
Triangle, Va., U.S. B5 123
Tribune, Ks., U.S. D2 93
Trichūr, India G4 37
Tri City, Or., U.S. E3 114
Trident Peak, mtn., Nv., U.S. B3 105
Trieben, Aus. H14 8
Trier, Ger. F6 8
Trieste, Italy D8 14
Trigg, co., Ky., U.S. D2 94
Triglav, mtn., Slo. C8 14
Trigo Mountains, mts., Az., U.S. D1 80
Tríkala, Grc. J5 16
Trikora, Puncak, mtn., Indon. F10 32
Tri Lakes, In., U.S. B7 91
Trim, Ire. H6 7
Trimble, Tn., U.S. A2 119
Trimble, co., Ky., U.S. B4 94
Trimont, Mn., U.S. G4 100
Trincheras, Mex. B4 62
Trincomalee, Sri L. H6 37
Třinec, Czech. F18 8
Tring Jonction, Que., Can. C6 74
Trinidad, Bol. F6 54
Trinidad, Col. E7 58
Trinidad, Cuba D8 64
Trinidad, Co., U.S. D6 83
Trinidad, Tx., U.S. C4 120
Trinidad, i., Trin. I17 64
Trinidad and Tobago, ctry., N.A. I17 64
Trinidad Head, c., Ca., U.S. B1 82
Trinity, Al., U.S. A2 78
Trinity, Tx., U.S. D5 120
Trinity, co., Ca., U.S. B2 82
Trinity, co., Tx., U.S. D5 120
Trinity, stm., Ca., U.S. B2 82
Trinity, stm., Tx., U.S. D5 120
Trinity Bay, b., Newf., Can. D5 72
Trinity Islands, is., Ak., U.S. D9 79
Trinity Mountain, mtn., Id., U.S. F3 89
Trinity Mountains, mts., Ca., U.S. B2 82
Trinity Peak, mtn., Nv., U.S. C3 105
Trinity Range, mts., Nv., U.S. C3 105
Trion, Ga., U.S. B1 87
Tripoli, Ia., U.S. B5 92
Tripolis, Grc. L6 16
Tripoli see Ţarābulus, Leb. B4 40
Tripoli see Ţarābulus, Libya B8 42
Tripp, S.D., U.S. D8 118
Tripp, co., S.D., U.S. D6 118
Triumph, La., U.S. E6 95
Trivandrum, India H4 37
Trnava, Slov. G17 8
Troarn, Fr. C6 10
Trobriand Islands, is., Pap. N. Gui. A10 50
Trochu, Alta., Can. D4 68
Trogir, Cro. F11 14
Trois-Pistoles, Que., Can. A8 74
Trois-Rivières, Que., Can. C5 74
Trois-Rivières-Ouest, Que., Can. C5 74
Trojan, Bul. G8 16
Trollhättan, Swe. G9 6
Trombetas, stm., Braz. C7 54
Tromelin, i., Afr. E10 44
Tromsø, Nor. B12 6
Trona, Ca., U.S. E5 82
Tronador, Monte, mtn., S.A. E2 56
Trondheim, Nor. E8 6
Trondheimsfjorden, Nor. E8 6
Tropea, Italy K10 14
Trophy Mountain, mtn., B.C., Can. D8 69
Trotwood, Oh., U.S. C1 112
Troup, co., Ga., U.S. C1 87
Trousdale, co., Tn., U.S. A5 119
Trout, stm., Fl., U.S. m8 86
Trout, stm., Vt., U.S. B3 122
Trout Creek, Ont., Can. B5 73
Trout Creek Pass, Co., U.S. C5 83
Trout Lake, Wa., U.S. D4 124
Trout Lake, l., N.W. Ter., Can. D8 66
Trout Lake, l., Ont., Can. o16 73
Trout Lake, l., Mn., U.S. B6 100
Trout Lake, l., Wi., U.S. B4 126
Troutman, N.C., U.S. B2 110
Trout Peak, mtn., Wy., U.S. B3 127
Trout River, Newf., Can. D2 72
Trouville [-sur-Mer], Fr. C7 10
Troy, Al., U.S. D4 78
Troy, Id., U.S. C2 89
Troy, Il., U.S. E4 90
Troy, Ks., U.S. C8 93
Troy, Mi., U.S. o15 99
Troy, Mo., U.S. C7 102
Troy, Mt., U.S. B1 103
Troy, N.H., U.S. E2 106
Troy, N.Y., U.S. C7 109
Troy, N.C., U.S. B3 110
Troy, Oh., U.S. B1 112
Troy, Pa., U.S. C8 115
Troy, Tn., U.S. A2 119
Troyes, Fr. D11 10
Troy Peak, mtn., Nv., U.S. E6 105
Truchas Peak, mtn., N.M., U.S. B4 108
Trucial States see United Arab Emirates, ctry., Asia D5 46
Truckee, Ca., U.S. C3 82
Truckee, stm., U.S. D2 105

Name Map Ref Page
Trujillo, Hond. G4 64
Trujillo, Peru E3 54
Trujillo, Spain F6 12
Trujillo, Ven. C7 58
Truman, Mn., U.S. G4 100
Trumann, Ar., U.S. B5 81
Trumansburg, N.Y., U.S. C4 109
Trumbull, Ct., U.S. E3 84
Trumbull, co., Oh., U.S. A5 112
Trumbull, Mount, mtn., Az., U.S. A2 80
Truro, Eng., U.K. K7 7
Trussville, Al., U.S. B3 78
Trustom Pond, l., R.I., U.S. G3 116
Truth or Consequences (Hot Springs), N.M., U.S. D2 108
Trutnov, Czech. E15 8
Tryon, N.C., U.S. f10 110
Tržič, Slo. C9 14
Tsala Apopka Lake, l., Fl., U.S. D4 86
Tsaratanana, Madag. E9 44
Tsaratanana, Massif du, mts., Madag. D9 44
Tschida, Lake, res., N.D., U.S. C4 111
Tshabong, Bots. G4 44
Tshangalele, Lac, l., Zaire D5 44
Tshikapa, Zaire C4 44
Tshofa, Zaire C5 44
Tshuapa, stm., Zaire B4 44
Tsoying, Tai. M9 28
Tsu, Japan H9 30
Tsubame, Japan E11 30
Tsuchiura, Japan F13 30
Tsugaru-kaikyō, strt., Japan A13 30
Tsukumi, Japan I4 30
Tsukushi-sanchi, mts., Japan I3 30
Tsumeb, Nmb. E3 44
Tsuruga, Japan G9 30
Tsuruoka, Japan D12 30
Tsushima, is., Japan H2 30
Tsushima-kaikyō, strt., Japan I2 30
Tsuyama, Japan G7 30
Tual, Indon. G9 32
Tualatin, stm., Or., U.S. h11 114
Tuba City, Az., U.S. A4 80
Tuban, Indon. m16 33a
Tubarão, Braz. B7 56
Tubruq, Libya B10 42
Tucannon, stm., Wa., U.S. C8 124
Tucano, Braz. F11 54
Tuckahoe, N.Y., U.S. h13 109
Tuckahoe, stm., N.J., U.S. E3 107
Tucker, Ga., U.S. h8 87
Tucker, co., W.V., U.S. B5 125
Tucker Island, i., N.J., U.S. E4 107
Tuckerman, Ar., U.S. B4 81
Tuckernuck Island, i., Ma., U.S. D7 98
Tuckerton, N.J., U.S. D4 107
Tucson, Az., U.S. E5 80
Tucumcari, N.M., U.S. B6 108
Tucumcari Mountain, mtn., N.M., U.S. B6 108
Tucupita, Ven. C11 58
Tucuruí, Braz. D9 54
Tudela, Spain C10 12
Tudmur (Palmyra), Syria B6 40
Tugaloo Lake, res., U.S. B1 117
Tug Fork, stm., U.S. C2 125
Tuguegarao, Phil. p19 32
Tugur, Russia G21 24
Tukangbesi, Kepulauan, is., Indon. G7 32
Tuktoyaktuk, N.W. Ter., Can. C6 66
Tukwila, Wa., U.S. f11 124
Tula, Mex. F10 62
Tula, Russia G20 18
Tulalip Indian Reservation, Wa., U.S. A3 124
Tulancingo, Mex. G10 62
Tulare, Ca., U.S. D4 82
Tulare, co., Ca., U.S. D4 82
Tulare Lake, l., Ca., U.S. D4 82
Tularosa, N.M., U.S. D3 108
Tularosa Mountains, mts., N.M., U.S. D1 108
Tularosa Valley, val., N.M., U.S. E3 108
Tulcán, Ec. G4 58
Tulcea, Rom. D12 16
Tule Lake, sw., Ca., U.S. B3 82
Tule River Indian Reservation, Ca., U.S. E4 82
Tule Valley, val., Ut., U.S. D2 121
Tulia, Tx., U.S. B2 120
Tūlkarm, Jord. C4 40
Tullahoma, Tn., U.S. B5 119
Tullamore, Ire. H5 7
Tulle, Fr. G8 10
Tullins, Fr. G12 10
Tulsa, Ok., U.S. A6 113
Tulsa, co., Ok., U.S. B6 113
Tuluá, Col. E4 58
Tulum, Mex. G16 62
Tulun, Russia G14 24
Tulungagung, Indon. n15 33a
Tuma, stm., Nic. H5 64
Tumacacori National Monument, Az., U.S. F4 80
Tumaco, Col. G3 58
Tuman-gang, stm., Asia C12 26
Tumany, Russia E25 24
Tumatumari, Guy. E13 58
Tumba, Lac, l., Zaire B3 44
Tumbes, Peru D2 54
Tumble Mountain, mtn., Mt., U.S. E7 103
Tumbler Ridge, B.C., Can. B7 69
Tumen, China C12 26
Tumiritinga, Braz. E8 57
Tumkūr, India F4 37
Tummo, Libya D8 42
Tumsar, India B5 37
Tumuc-Humac Mountains, mts., S.A. C8 54
Tumwater, Wa., U.S. B3 124
Tunbridge Wells, Eng., U.K. J13 7
Tunduru, Tan. D7 44
Tundža, stm., Eur. G10 16
T'ung, stm., Russia D17 24
Tungabhadra, stm., India E4 37
Tungabhadra Reservoir, res., India E4 37
Tungchiang, Tai. M9 28
Tungsha Tao (Pratas Islands), is., Tai. G10 26
Tungshih, Tai. K9 28
Tunica, Ms., U.S. A3 101
Tunica, co., Ms., U.S. A3 101
Tunis, Tun. M5 14
Tunisia, ctry., Afr. B7 42
Tunja, Col. E6 58
Tunkhannock, Pa., U.S. C10 115
Tunk Lake, l., Me., U.S. D4 96
Tunnel Hill, Ga., U.S. B1 87
Tunp Range, mts., Wy., U.S. D2 127
Tununak, Ak., U.S. C6 79
Tunxi, China F7 28
Tuobuja, Russia E18 24
Tuolumne, Ca., U.S. D3 82
Tuolumne, co., Ca., U.S. C4 82
Tuolumne, stm., Ca., U.S. D3 82
Tupã, Braz. F3 57
Tupaciguara, Braz. E4 57
Tupanciretã, Braz. B6 56
Tupelo, Ms., U.S. A5 101
Tupiza, Bol. H5 54
Tupper Lake, N.Y., U.S. A6 109
Tupper Lake, l., N.Y., U.S. A6 109
Túquerres, Col. G4 58
Tura, India H14 38
Tura, Russia E14 24
Turan, Russia G12 24
Turbat, Pak. D1 36
Turbeville, S.C., U.S. D7 117
Turbo, Col. C4 58
Turda, Rom. C7 16
Turgutlu, Tur. K11 16
Turimiquire, Cerro, mtn., Ven. B11 58
Turin see Torino, Italy D2 14
Turkey, ctry., Asia H14 4
Turkey, stm., Ia., U.S. B6 92
Turkey Creek, stm., Ok., U.S. A3 113
Turkey Point, c., Md., U.S. B5 97
Turkmenistan, ctry., Asia I9 22
Turks and Caicos Islands, dep., N.A. D12 64
Turks Islands, is., T./C. Is. D12 64
Turku (Åbo), Fin. F14 6
Turley, Ok., U.S. A6 113
Turlock, Ca., U.S. D3 82
Turnbull, Mount, mtn., Az., U.S. D5 80
Turneffe Islands, is., Belize F4 64
Turner, Or., U.S. C4 114
Turner, co., Ga., U.S. E3 87
Turner, co., S.D., U.S. D8 118
Turners Falls, Ma., U.S. A2 98
Turner Valley, Alta., Can. D3 68
Turnhout, Bel. D4 8
Turnor Lake, l., Sask., Can. m7 75
Turnu-Măgurele, Rom. F8 16
Turpan, China C4 26
Turquino, Pico, mtn., Cuba E9 64
Turrell, Ar., U.S. B5 81
Turret Peak, mtn., Az., U.S. C4 80
Turtle Creek, Pa., U.S. k14 115
Turtle Flambeau Flowage, res., Wi., U.S. B3 126
Turtle Lake, N.D., U.S. B5 111
Turtle Lake, Wi., U.S. C1 126
Turtle Lake, l., Sask., Can. D1 75
Turtle Mountain Indian Reservation, N.D., U.S. A6 111
Turu, stm., Russia D14 24
Turuchan, stm., Russia D11 24
Turuchansk, Russia D11 24
Tuscaloosa, Al., U.S. B2 78
Tuscaloosa, co., Al., U.S. B2 78
Tuscarawas, co., Oh., U.S. B4 112
Tuscarawas, stm., Oh., U.S. B4 112
Tuscarora Indian Reservation, N.Y., U.S. B2 109
Tuscarora Mountain, mtn., Pa., U.S. F6 115
Tuscarora Mountains, mts., Nv., U.S. B5 105
Tuscola, Il., U.S. D5 90
Tuscola, co., Mi., U.S. E7 99
Tuscumbia, Al., U.S. A2 78
Tuskegee, Al., U.S. C4 78
Tusket, stm., N.S., Can. E4 71
Tustumena Lake, l., Ak., U.S. g16 79
Tuticorin, India H5 37
Tutóia, Braz. D10 54
Tuttle, Ok., U.S. B4 113
Tuttle Creek Lake, res., Ks., U.S. C7 93
Tututalak Mountain, mtn., Ak., U.S. B7 79
Tutwiler, Ms., U.S. A3 101
Tuvalu, ctry., Oc. G24 2
Ṭuwayq, Jabal, mts., Sau. Ar. D4 46
Tuxedo, N.C., U.S. f10 110
Tuxedo Park, De., U.S. i7 85
Tuxpan, Mex. G7 62
Tuxpan de Rodríguez Cano, Mex. G11 62
Tuxtla Gutiérrez, Mex. I13 62
Túy, Spain C3 12
Tuy Hoa, Viet. H10 34
Tuz Gölü, l., Tur. H14 4
Tuzigoot National Monument, Az., U.S. C4 80
Tuzla, Bos. E2 16
Tveitsund, Nor. G7 6
Tver', Russia E18 18
Tweed, Ont., Can. C7 73
Tweedsmuir Provincial Park, B.C., Can. C4 69
Tweedy Mountain, mtn., Mt., U.S. E4 103
Twelvepole Creek, stm., W.V., U.S. C2 125
Twentymile Creek, stm., W.V., U.S. C3 125
Twentynine Palms, Ca., U.S. E5 82
Twentynine Palms Marine Corps Base, mil., Ca., U.S. E5 82
Twiggs, co., Ga., U.S. D3 87
Twillingate, Newf., Can. D4 72
Twin Buttes, mtn., Or., U.S. C4 114
Twin Buttes Reservoir, res., Tx., U.S. D2 120
Twin City, Ga., U.S. D4 87
Twin Creek, stm., Oh., U.S. C1 112
Twin Falls, Id., U.S. G4 89
Twin Falls, co., Id., U.S. G4 89
Twin Knolls, Az., U.S. m9 80
Twin Lakes, Ga., U.S. F3 87
Twin Lakes, Wi., U.S. F5 126
Twin Lakes, l., Ct., U.S. A2 84
Twin Lakes, l., Ia., U.S. B3 92
Twin Lakes, l., Me., U.S. C4 96
Twin Mountains, mtn., Wy., U.S. E7 127
Twin Peaks, mts., Id., U.S. E4 89
Twin Rivers, N.J., U.S. C4 107
Twinsburg, Oh., U.S. A4 112
Twin Valley, Mn., U.S. C2 100
Twisp, Wa., U.S. A5 124
Two Harbors, Mn., U.S. C7 100
Two Hills, Alta., Can. C5 68
Two Mile Beach, N.J., U.S. F3 107
Two Rivers, Wi., U.S. D6 126
Two Rivers, North Branch, stm., Mn., U.S. B2 100
Two Rivers, South Branch, stm., Mn., U.S. B2 100
Tybee Island, Ga., U.S. D6 87
Tychy, Pol. E18 8
Tygart Lake, res., W.V., U.S. B5 125
Tygart River, Falls of the, wtfl, W.V., U.S. k10 125
Tygart Valley, stm., W.V., U.S. B4 125
Tyger, stm., S.C., U.S. B4 117
Tyler, Mn., U.S. F2 100
Tyler, Tx., U.S. C5 120
Tyler, co., Tx., U.S. D5 120
Tyler, co., W.V., U.S. B4 125
Tyler, Lake, res., Tx., U.S. C5 120
Tyler Branch, stm., Vt., U.S. B3 122
Tyler Heights, W.V., U.S. C3 125
Tylertown, Ms., U.S. D3 101
Tymochtee Creek, stm., Oh., U.S. B2 112
Tyndall, S.D., U.S. E8 118
Tyndall Air Force Base, mil., Fl., U.S. u16 86
Tyonek, Ak., U.S. C9 79
Tyre see Ṣūr, Leb. C4 40
Tyrma, Russia G20 24
Tyrone, N.M., U.S. E1 108
Tyrone, Ok., U.S. e9 113
Tyrone, Pa., U.S. E5 115
Tyronza, Ar., U.S. B5 81
Tyrrell, co., N.C., U.S. B6 110
Tyrrhenian Sea (Mare Tirreno), Eur. I6 14
Tysse, Nor. F5 6
Tzaneen, S. Afr. F6 44

U

Uatumã, stm., Braz. D7 54
Uaupés, Braz. D5 54
Ubá, Braz. F7 57
Ubangi (Oubangui), stm., Afr. H9 42
Ube, Japan I4 30
Úbeda, Spain G8 12
Uberaba, Braz. E5 57
Uberlândia, Braz. E4 57
Ubly, Mi., U.S. E8 99
Ubon Ratchathani, Thai. G8 34
Ubundi, Zaire B5 44
Učami, Russia E13 24
Ucayali, stm., Peru E4 54
Uchiura-wan, b., Japan q18 30a
Ucluelet, B.C., Can. E5 69
Ucon, Id., U.S. F7 89
Uda, stm., Russia G13 24
Uda, stm., Russia G20 24
Udaipur, India H5 38
Udall, Ks., U.S. E6 93
Uddevalla, Swe. G8 6
Udgīr, India C4 37
Udine, Italy C8 14
Udipi, India F3 37
Udon Thani, Thai. F7 34
Udskaja Guba, b., Russia G21 24
Udža, Russia C17 24
Ueckermünde, Ger. B14 8
Ueda, Japan F11 30
Uele, stm., Zaire H10 42
Uelen, Russia D31 24
Uelzen, Ger. C10 8
Ueno, Japan H9 30
Uere, stm., Zaire H11 42
Ufa, Russia G9 22
Uganda, ctry., Afr. A6 44
Ugashik Lakes, l., Ak., U.S. D8 79
Ugine, Fr. G13 10
Uglegorsk, Russia H22 24
Uglič, Russia D21 18
Uhrichsville, Oh., U.S. B4 112
Uíge, Ang. C3 44
Uinta, co., Wy., U.S. E2 127
Uinta, stm., Ut., U.S. C5 121
Uintah, co., Ut., U.S. D6 121
Uintah and Ouray Indian Reservation, Ut., U.S. C5 121
Uinta Mountains, mts., Ut., U.S. C5 121
Uitenhage, S. Afr. H5 44
Uivak, Cape, c., Newf., Can. f9 72
Ujandina, stm., Russia D22 24
Uji, Japan H8 30
Ujiji, Tan. B5 44
Ujjain, India I6 38
Ujungpandang, Indon. G6 32
Uka, Russia F26 24
Ukiah, Ca., U.S. C2 82
Ukraine, ctry., Eur. H4 22
Ulaanbaatar (Ulan Bator), Mong. B8 26
Ulaangom, Mong. B5 26
Ulak Island, i., Ak., U.S. E4 79
Ulan Bator see Ulaanbaatar, Mong. B8 26
Ulan-Ude, Russia G15 24
Ulhāsnagar, India C2 37
Uliastaj, Mong. B6 26
Ulindi, stm., Zaire B5 44
Ulja, Russia F22 24
Uljanovsk, Russia G7 22
Ullapool, Scot., U.K. D7 7
Ullŭng-do, i., S. Kor. D13 26
Ulm, Ger. G10 8
Ulsan, S. Kor. D12 26
Ulster, co., N.Y., U.S. D6 109
Ulster, hist. reg., Eur. G5 7
Ulu, Russia E19 24
Ulubat Gölü, l., Tur. I12 16
Ulungur Hu, l., China B4 26
Ulysses, Ks., U.S. E2 93
Umag, Cro. D8 14
Uman', Ukr. H4 22
Umanak, Grnld. B22 66
Umanak Fjord, Grnld. B22 66
Umatilla, Fl., U.S. D5 86
Umatilla, Or., U.S. B7 114
Umatilla, co., Or., U.S. B8 114
Umatilla, stm., Or., U.S. B7 114
Umatilla Indian Reservation, Or., U.S. B8 114
Umbagog Lake, l., U.S. A4 106
Umcolcus Lake, l., Me., U.S. B4 96
Umeå, Swe. E13 6
Umm Durmān (Omdurman), Sudan E12 42
Umnak Island, i., Ak., U.S. E6 79
Umnäs, Swe. D11 6
Umpqua, stm., Or., U.S. D3 114
Umsaskis Lake, l., Me., U.S. B3 96
Umtata, S. Afr. H5 44
Umzinto, S. Afr. H6 44
Unadilla, Ga., U.S. D3 87
Unadilla, stm., N.Y., U.S. C5 109
Unalakleet, Ak., U.S. C7 79
Unalaska Island, i., Ak., U.S. E6 79
'Unayzah, Sau. Ar. C3 46
Uncasville, Ct., U.S. D7 84
Uncompahgre, stm., Co., U.S. C3 83
Uncompahgre Mountains, mts., Co., U.S. C3 83
Uncompahgre Peak, mtn., Co., U.S. C3 83
Underwood, Al., U.S. B3 78
Underwood, N.D., U.S. B4 111
Ungava, Péninsule d', pen., Que., Can. g12 74
Ungava Bay, b., Can. E19 66
União dos Palmares, Braz. E11 54
Unicoi, Tn., U.S. C11 119
Unicoi, co., Tn., U.S. C11 119
Unicoi Mountains, mts., U.S. D9 119
Unimak Island, i., Ak., U.S. D7 79
Unimak Pass, strt., Ak., U.S. E6 79
Union, Ky., U.S. k13 94
Union, Ms., U.S. C4 101
Union, Mo., U.S. C6 102
Union, Or., U.S. B9 114
Union, S.C., U.S. B4 117
Union, Wa., U.S. B2 124
Union, co., Ar., U.S. D3 81
Union, co., Fl., U.S. B4 86
Union, co., Ga., U.S. B2 87
Union, co., Il., U.S. F4 90
Union, co., In., U.S. E8 91
Union, co., Ia., U.S. C3 92
Union, co., Ky., U.S. C2 94
Union, co., La., U.S. B3 95
Union, co., Ms., U.S. A4 101
Union, co., N.J., U.S. B4 107
Union, co., N.M., U.S. A6 108
Union, co., N.C., U.S. B2 110
Union, co., Oh., U.S. B2 112
Union, co., Or., U.S. B8 114
Union, co., Pa., U.S. E7 115
Union, co., S.C., U.S. B4 117
Union, co., S.D., U.S. E9 118
Union, co., Tn., U.S. C10 119
Union, West Branch, stm., Me., U.S. D4 96
Union Beach, N.J., U.S. C4 107
Union Bridge, Md., U.S. A3 97
Union City, Ca., U.S. h8 82
Union City, Ga., U.S. C2 87
Union City, In., U.S. D8 91
Union City, Mi., U.S. F5 99
Union City, N.J., U.S. h8 107
Union City, Oh., U.S. B1 112
Union City, Ok., U.S. B4 113
Union City, Pa., U.S. C2 115
Union City, Tn., U.S. A2 119
Union Flat Creek, stm., Wa., U.S. C8 124
Union Gap, Wa., U.S. C5 124
Union Grove, Wi., U.S. F5 126
Union Lake, l., N.J., U.S. E2 107
Union Pier, Mi., U.S. G4 99
Union Point, Ga., U.S. C3 87
Union Springs, Al., U.S. C4 78
Uniontown, Al., U.S. C2 78
Uniontown, Ky., U.S. C2 94
Uniontown, Oh., U.S. B4 112
Uniontown, Pa., U.S. G2 115
Union Village, R.I., U.S. B3 116
Union Village Reservoir, res., Vt., U.S. D4 122
Unionville, Ct., U.S. B4 84
Unionville, Mo., U.S. A4 102
United Arab Emirates, ctry., Asia D5 46
United Kingdom, ctry., Eur. E7 4
United Nations Headquarters, N.Y., U.S. h12 109
United States, ctry., N.A. D7 76
United States Air Force Academy, mil., Co., U.S. B6 83
United States Military Academy, mil., N.Y., U.S. C6 109
United States Naval Academy, mil., Md., U.S. C4 97
Unity Reservoir, res., Or., U.S. C8 114
University City, Mo., U.S. C7 102
University Heights, Ia., U.S. C6 92
University Heights, Oh., U.S. h9 112
University Park, Ia., U.S. C5 92
University Park, N.M., U.S. E3 108
University Park, Tx., U.S. n10 120
University Place, Wa., U.S. f10 124
Unnão, India G9 38
Uozu, Japan F10 30
Upata, Ven. C11 58
Upemba, Lac, l., Zaire C5 44
Upernavik, Grnld. B21 66
Upington, S. Afr. G4 44
Upland, Ca., U.S. E5 82
Upland, In., U.S. D7 91
Upleta, India J4 38
Upolu Point, c., Hi., U.S. C6 88
Upper Ammonoosuc, stm., N.H., U.S. A4 106
Upper Arlington, Oh., U.S. B2 112
Upper Arrow Lake, l., B.C., Can. F9 66
Upper Arrow Lake, res., B.C., Can. D9 69
Upperco, Md., U.S. A4 97
Upper Darby, Pa., U.S. G11 115
Upper Greenwood Lake, N.J., U.S. A4 107
Upper Humber, stm., Newf., Can. D3 72
Upper Iowa, stm., Ia., U.S. A5 92
Upper Island Cove, Newf., Can. E5 72
Upper Kapuas Mountains, mts., Asia E5 32
Upper Klamath Lake, l., Or., U.S. E4 114
Upper Marlboro, Md., U.S. C4 97
Upper New York Bay, b., U.S. k8 107
Upper Red Lake, l., Mn., U.S. B4 100
Upper Saddle River, N.J., U.S. A4 107
Upper Sandusky, Oh., U.S. B2 112
Upper Sheila [Haut Sheila], N.B., Can. B5 71
Upper Volta see Burkina Faso, ctry., Afr. F5 42
Uppsala, Swe. G11 6
Upright, Cape, c., Ak., U.S. C5 79
Upshur, co., Tx., U.S. C5 120
Upshur, co., W.V., U.S. C4 125
Upson, co., Ga., U.S. D2 87
Upton, Que., Can. D5 74
Upton, Ky., U.S. C4 94
Upton, Ma., U.S. B4 98
Upton, Wy., U.S. B8 127
Upton, co., Tx., U.S. D2 120
Uquía, Cerro, mtn., Ven. E11 58
Urabá, Golfo de, b., Col. C4 58
Ural, stm., Asia H8 22
Ural Mountains see Ural'skije gory, mts., Russia F9 22
Ural'sk, Kaz. G8 22
Ural'skije gory (Ural Mountains), mts., Russia F9 22
Urania, La., U.S. C3 95
Urbana, Il., U.S. C5 90
Urbana, Oh., U.S. B2 112
Urbancrest, Oh., U.S. m10 112
Urbandale, Ia., U.S. C4 92
Urbino, Italy F7 14
Urgenč, Uzb. I10 22
Uribe, Col. F5 58
Uribia, Col. B6 58
Urla, Tur. K10 16
Uruaçu, Braz. C4 57
Uruapan [del Progreso], Mex. H8 62
Urubamba, stm., Peru F4 54
Urucuia, stm., Braz. D6 57
Uruguaiana, Braz. B5 56
Uruguay, ctry., S.A. C5 56
Uruguay (Uruguai), stm., S.A. C5 56
Ürümqi, China C4 26
Ur'ung-Chaja, Russia C16 24
Urun-Islāmpur, India D3 37
Urup, Ostrov, i., Russia H23 24
Usa, Japan I4 30
Uşak, Tur. K13 16
Usedom, i., Eur. B14 8
Ushibuka, Japan J3 30
Ushuaia, Arg. G3 56
Usolje-Sibirskoje, Russia G14 24
Usquepaug, R.I., U.S. F3 116
Ussel, Fr. G9 10
Ussuri (Wusuli), stm., Asia B14 26
Ussurijsk, Russia I20 24
Ust'-Barguzin, Russia G15 24
Ust'-Belaja, Russia D28 24
Ust'Čaun, Russia D28 24
Ústí nad Labem, Czech. E14 8
Ust'-Kamčatsk, Russia F26 24
Ust'-Kamenogorsk, Kaz. H10 24
Ust'-Kut, Russia F15 24
Ust'-Maja, Russia E20 24
Ust'-Nera, Russia E22 24
Usu, China C3 26
Usuki, Japan I4 30
Usulután, El Sal. H3 64
Usumacinta, stm., N.A. I14 62
Utah, co., Ut., U.S. C4 121
Utah, state, U.S. D4 121
Utah Lake, l., Ut., U.S. C4 121
Utashinai, Japan p20 30a
Ute Creek, stm., N.M., U.S. A6 108
Ute Mountain Indian Reservation, U.S. D2 83
Ute Reservoir, res., N.M., U.S. B6 108
Utete, Tan. C7 44
Uthai Thani, Thai. G6 34
Utiariti, Braz. F7 54
Utica, Il., U.S. B5 90
Utica, Mi., U.S. F7 99
Utica, Ms., U.S. C3 101
Utica, Ne., U.S. D8 104
Utica, N.Y., U.S. B5 109
Utica, Oh., U.S. B3 112
Utiel, Spain F10 12
Utikuma Lake, l., Alta., Can. B3 68
Utrecht, Neth. C5 8
Utrera, Spain H6 12
Utsunomiya, Japan F12 30
Uttar Pradesh, state, India G8 38

Name — Map Ref — Page

Uusikaupunki (Nystad), Fin. F13 6
Uvá, stm., Col. F8 58
Uvalde, Tx., U.S. E3 120
Uvalde, co., Tx., U.S. E3 120
Uvdal, Nor. F7 6
Uvinza, Tan. C6 44
Uvs Nuur, l., Asia A5 26
Uwajima, Japan I5 30
'Uwaynāt, Jabal al-, mtn., Afr. D10 42
Uwharrie, stm., N.C., U.S. B3 110
Uxbridge, Ma., U.S. B4 98
Uyuni, Bol. H5 54
Uyuni, Salar de, pl., Bol. H5 54
Uzbekistan, state, Asia I10 22
Uzerche, Fr. G8 10
Uzès, Fr. H11 10
Užice, Yugo. F3 16
Uzlovaja, Russia H21 18
Uzunköprü, Tur. H10 16
Užur, Russia F11 24

V

Vaala, Fin. D16 6
Vaasa (Vasa), Fin. E13 6
Vác, Hung. H19 8
Vaca Key, i., Fl., U.S. H5 86
Vacaville, Ca., U.S. C3 82
Vaccarès, Étang de, b., Fr. I11 10
Vach, stm., Russia E9 24
Vacherie, La., U.S. h10 95
Vadsø, Nor. A17 6
Vaduz, Liech. H9 8
Váh, stm., Slov. G18 8
Vaiden, Ms., U.S. B4 101
Vail, Co., U.S. B4 83
Vākhān, stm., Afg. B5 38
Vākhān, reg., Afg. B5 38
Vålådalen, Swe. E9 6
Val-Bélair, Que., Can. n17 74
Valcheta, Arg. E3 56
Valcourt, Que., Can. D5 74
Valdagno, Italy D6 14
Val-David, Que., Can. C3 74
Valdecañas, Embalse de, res., Spain F6 12
Valdemarsvik, Swe. G11 6
Valdepeñas, Spain G8 12
Valderrobres, Spain E12 12
Valders, Wi., U.S. D6 126
Valdés, Península, pen., Arg. E4 56
Valdese, N.C., U.S. B1 110
Valdez, Ak., U.S. C10 79
Val-d'Isère, Fr. G13 10
Valdivia, Chile D2 56
Valdivia, Col. D5 58
Val-d'Or, Que., Can. k11 74
Valdosta, Ga., U.S. F3 87
Vale, Or., U.S. D9 114
Valemount, B.C., Can. C8 69
Valença, Braz. B9 57
Valença, Port. C3 12
Valençay, Fr. E8 10
Valence, Fr. H11 10
Valencia, Spain F11 12
Valencia, Az., U.S. m7 80
Valencia, Ven. C8 58
Valencia, co., N.M., U.S. C3 108
Valencia, Golfo de, b., Spain F12 12
Valencia de Alcántata, Spain F4 12
Valencia de Don Juan, Spain C6 12
Valencia Heights, S.C., U.S. D6 117
Valenciennes, Fr. B10 10
Valentine, Ne., U.S. B5 104
Valenza, Italy D3 14
Valera, Ven. C7 58
Valga, Est. D9 18
Valhalla, N.Y., U.S. D7 109
Valhermoso Springs, Al., U.S. A3 78
Valjevo, Yugo. E3 16
Valkeakoski, Fin. F15 6
Valkenswaard, Neth. D5 8
Valladolid, Mex. G15 62
Valladolid, Spain D7 12
Vall de Uxó, Spain F11 12
Vallecito Reservoir, res., Co., U.S. D3 83
Valle de Guanape, Ven. C10 58
Valle de la Pascua, Ven. C9 58
Valle de Santiago, Mex. G9 62
Valle de Zaragoza, Mex. D7 62
Valledupar, Col. B6 58
Vallée-Jonction, Que., Can. C7 74
Valle Hermoso, Mex. E11 62
Vallejo, Ca., U.S. C2 82
Vallelunga Pratameno, Italy L8 14
Vallenar, Chile B2 56
Valletta, Malta N9 14
Valley, Ne., U.S. C9 104
Valley, co., Id., U.S. E3 89
Valley, co., Mt., U.S. B10 103
Valley, co., Ne., U.S. C6 104
Valley, stm., Man., Can. D1 70
Valley Center, Ks., U.S. E6 93
Valley City, N.D., U.S. C8 111
Valley Cottage, N.Y., U.S. g13 109
Valley East, Ont., Can. p19 73
Valley Falls, Ks., U.S. C8 93
Valley Falls, R.I., U.S. B4 116
Valley Forge, Pa., U.S. o20 115
Valley Mills, Tx., U.S. D4 120
Valley Park, Mo., U.S. f12 102
Valley Springs, S.D., U.S. D9 118
Valley Station, Ky., U.S. g11 94
Valley Stream, N.Y., U.S. n15 109
Valleyview, Alta., Can. B2 68
Valley View, Pa., U.S. E8 115
Valliant, Ok., U.S. D6 113
Vallo della Lucania, Italy I10 14
Valls, Spain D13 12
Vallscreek, W.V., U.S. D3 125
Valmeyer, Il., U.S. E3 90
Valognes, Fr. C5 10
Valparai, India G4 37
Valparaíso, Chile C2 56
Valparaíso, Mex. F8 62
Valparaiso, Fl., U.S. u15 86
Valparaiso, In., U.S. B3 91
Valréas, Fr. H11 10
Vals, Tanjung, c., Indon. G10 32
Valtimo, Fin. E17 6
Val Verda, Ut., U.S. C4 121
Valverde, Dom. Rep. E12 64
Val Verde, co., Tx., U.S. E2 120
Valverde del Camino, Spain H5 12
Van, Tur. H16 4
Van, Tx., U.S. C5 120
Van, W.V., U.S. n12 125
Van Alstyne, Tx., U.S. C4 120
Vanavara, Russia E14 24
Van Buren, Ar., U.S. B1 81
Van Buren, In., U.S. C6 91
Van Buren, Me., U.S. A5 96
Van Buren, Mo., U.S. E6 102
Van Buren, co., Ar., U.S. B3 81
Van Buren, co., Ia., U.S. D6 92
Van Buren, co., Mi., U.S. F4 99
Van Buren, co., Tn., U.S. D8 119
Vance, co., N.C., U.S. A4 110
Vance Air Force Base, mil., Ok., U.S. A3 113
Vanceboro, N.C., U.S. B5 110
Vanceburg, Ky., U.S. B6 94
Vancleave, Ms., U.S. E5 101
Vancouver, B.C., Can. E6 69
Vancouver, Wa., U.S. D3 124
Vancouver, Cape, c., Austl. G3 50
Vancouver Island, i., B.C., Can. E4 69
Vancouver Island Ranges, mts., B.C., Can. D4 69
Vandalia, Il., U.S. E4 90
Vandalia, Mo., U.S. B6 102
Vandenberg Air Force Base, mil., Ca., U.S. E3 82
Vander, N.C., U.S. B4 110
Vanderbilt Peak, mtn., N.M., U.S. E1 108
Vanderburgh, co., In., U.S. H2 91
Vandergrift, Pa., U.S. E2 115
Vanderhoof, B.C., Can. C5 69
Van Diemen Gulf, b., Austl. B6 50
Vänern, l., Swe. G9 6
Vänersborg, Swe. G9 6
Vangaindrano, Madag. F9 44
Van Gölü, l., Tur. H16 4
Vangunu, i., Sol.Is. A11 50
Van Horn, Tx., U.S. o12 120
Van Horne, Ia., U.S. B5 92
Vanier, Ont., Can. h12 73
Vāniyambādi, India F5 37
Vankarem, Russia D30 24
Vankleek Hill, Ont., Can. B10 73
Van Kull, Kill, stm., N.J., U.S. k8 107
Van Lear, Ky., U.S. C7 94
Van Meter, Ia., U.S. C4 92
Vännäs, Swe. E12 6
Vannes, Fr. E4 10
Van Rees, Pegunungan, mts., Indon. F10 32
Vanrhynsdorp, S. Afr. H3 44
Vansant, Va., U.S. e9 123
Vansbro, Swe. F10 6
Vansittart Island, i., N.W. Ter., Can. C16 66
Vanuatu, ctry., Oc. H24 2
Van Vleck, Tx., U.S. r14 120
Van Wert, Oh., U.S. B1 112
Van Wert, co., Oh., U.S. B1 112
Van Zandt, co., Tx., U.S. C5 120
Varades, Fr. E5 10
Vārānasi (Benares), India H10 38
Varaždin, Cro. C11 14
Varazze, Italy E3 14
Varberg, Swe. H9 6
Vardaman, Ms., U.S. B4 101
Vardar (Axiós), stm., Eur. H6 16
Vardø, Nor. A18 6
Varennes, Que., Can. D4 74
Varennes-sur-Allier, Fr. F10 10
Varese, Italy D3 14
Varginha, Braz. F6 57
Varina, Va., U.S. C5 123
Varkaus, Fin. E16 6
Varkhān, stm., Afg. D1 38
Varna, Bul. F11 16
Värnamo, Swe. H10 6
Varnville, S.C., U.S. F5 117
Varzy, Fr. E10 10
Vasai (Bassein), India C2 37
Vashon, Point, c., Wa., U.S. e11 124
Vashon Island, i., Wa., U.S. f11 124
Vass, N.C., U.S. B3 110
Vassar, Mi., U.S. E7 99
Västerås, Swe. G11 6
Västervik, Swe. H11 6
Vasto, Italy G9 14
Vas'ugan, stm., Russia F9 24
Vatican City (Città del Vaticano), ctry., Eur. H7 14
Vatnajökull, Ice. C4 4
Vättern, l., Swe. G10 6
Vaucouleurs, Fr. D12 10
Vaudreuil, Que., Can. D3 74
Vaughan, Ont., Can. D5 73
Vaughn, Mt., U.S. C5 103
Vaughn, N.M., U.S. C4 108
Vaupés (Uaupés), stm., S.A. G7 58
Vauxhall, Alta., Can. D4 68
Växjö, Swe. H10 6
Vazante, Braz. D5 57
V'azemskij, Russia H20 24
V'az'ma, Russia F17 18
V'azniki, Russia E25 18
Veazie, Me., U.S. D4 96
Vechta, Ger. C8 8
Veedersburg, In., U.S. D3 91
Veendam, Neth. B6 8
Vegreville, Alta., Can. C4 68
Vejer de la Frontera, Spain I6 12
Vejle, Den. I7 6
Vela Luka, Cro. G11 14
Velda Rose Estates, Az., U.S. *D4 80
Velenje, Slo. C10 14
Vélez-Málaga, Spain I7 12
Vélez Rubio, Spain H9 12
Velhas, Rio das, stm., Braz. D6 57
Velike Lašče, Slo. D9 14
Velikije Luki, Russia E13 18
Veliko Târnovo, Bul. F9 16
Vella Lavella, i., Sol.Is. A11 50
Velletri, Italy H7 14
Vellore, India F5 37
Velma, Ok., U.S. C4 113
Velva, N.D., U.S. A5 111
Venado Tuerto, Arg. C4 56
Venango, co., Pa., U.S. D2 115
Venda Nova, Braz. E7 57
Vendeuvre-sur-Barse, Fr. D11 10
Vendôme, Fr. E8 10
Veneta, Or., U.S. C3 114
Venezia (Venice), Italy D7 14
Venezuela, ctry., S.A. B5 54
Venezuela, Golfo de, b., S.A. B7 58
Veniaminof, Mount, mtn., Ak., U.S. D8 79
Venice, Fl., U.S. E4 86
Venice, Il., U.S. E3 90
Venice, Gulf of, b., Eur. D7 14
Venice see Venezia, Italy D7 14
Vénissieux, Fr. G11 10
Venlo, Neth. D6 8
Venosa, Italy I10 14
Ventanas, Ec. H3 58
Ventnor City, N.J., U.S. E4 107
Ventspils, Lat. D4 18
Ventuari, stm., Ven. E9 58
Ventura (San Buenaventura), Ca., U.S. E4 82
Ventura, co., Ca., U.S. E4 82
Venustiano Carranza, Mex. I13 62
Vera, Spain H10 12
Veracruz [Llave], Mex. H11 62
Verāval, India J4 38
Verbania, Italy D3 14
Vercelli, Italy D3 14
Verchères, Que., Can. D4 74
Verchn'aja Amga, Russia F19 24
Verchneimbatskoje, Russia E11 24
Verchojansk, Russia D20 24
Verchojanskij Chrebet, mts., Russia D19 24
Verda, Ky., U.S. D6 94
Verde, stm., Az., U.S. C4 80
Verden, Ger. C9 8
Verdi, Nv., U.S. D2 105
Verdigre, Ne., U.S. B7 104
Verdigris, Ok., U.S. A6 113
Verdigris, stm., U.S. A6 113
Verdi Peak, mtn., Nv., U.S. C6 105
Verdun, Que., Can. q19 74
Verdun, Fr. C12 10
Vereeniging, S. Afr. G5 44
Vergara, Spain B9 12
Vergennes, Vt., U.S. C2 122
Veríssimo, Braz. E4 57
Vermilion, Alta., Can. C5 68
Vermilion, Oh., U.S. A3 112
Vermilion, co., Il., U.S. C6 90
Vermilion, co., La., U.S. E3 95
Vermilion, stm., Alta., Can. C5 68
Vermilion, stm., Il., U.S. C5 90
Vermilion, stm., La., U.S. E3 95
Vermilion, stm., Mn., U.S. B6 100
Vermilion, stm., Oh., U.S. A3 112
Vermilion Bay, b., La., U.S. E3 95
Vermilion Lake, l., Mn., U.S. C6 100
Vermilion Pass, Can. D2 68
Vermillion, S.D., U.S. E9 118
Vermillion, co., In., U.S. E2 91
Vermillion, East Fork, stm., S.D., U.S. D8 118
Vermillon, stm., Que., Can. B4 74
Vermont, Il., U.S. C3 90
Vermont, state, U.S. D3 122
Vermontville, Mi., U.S. F5 99
Vernal, Ut., U.S. C6 121
Verneuil-sur-Avre, Fr. D7 10
Vernon, B.C., Can. D8 69
Vernon, Fr. C8 10
Vernon, Al., U.S. B1 78
Vernon, Tx., U.S. B3 120
Vernon, co., La., U.S. C2 95
Vernon, co., Mo., U.S. D3 102
Vernon, co., Wi., U.S. E3 126
Vernon Hills, Il., U.S. h9 90
Vernonia, Or., U.S. B3 114
Vero Beach, Fl., U.S. E6 86
Véroia, Grc. I6 16
Verona, Ont., Can. C8 73
Verona, Italy D6 14
Verona, Ms., U.S. A5 101
Verona, N.J., U.S. B4 107
Verona, Pa., U.S. k14 115
Verona, Wi., U.S. E4 126
Verret, Lake, l., La., U.S. E4 95
Versailles, Fr. D9 10
Versailles, In., U.S. F7 91
Versailles, Ky., U.S. B5 94
Versailles, Mo., U.S. C5 102
Versailles, Oh., U.S. B1 112
Vert, Cap, c., Sen. F2 42
Vertientes, Cuba D8 64
Vertou, Fr. E5 10
Verviers, Bel. E5 8
Vesoul, Fr. E13 10
Vestal, N.Y., U.S. C4 109
Vestavia Hills, Al., U.S. g7 78
Vestmannaeyjar, Ice. C3 4
Vesuvio, vol., Italy I9 14
Vesuvius see Vesuvio, vol., Italy I9 14
Veszprém, Hung. H17 8
Vetlanda, Swe. H10 6
Vevay, In., U.S. G7 91
Vevey, Switz. F13 10
Veynes, Fr. H12 10
Viadana, Italy E5 14
Vian, Ok., U.S. B7 113
Viana del Bollo, Spain C4 12
Viana do Alentejo, Port. G3 12
Viana do Castelo, Port. D3 12
Viangchan, Laos F7 34
Viareggio, Italy F5 14
Viborg, Den. H7 6
Viborg, S.D., U.S. D8 118
Vibo Valentia, Italy K11 14
Viburnum, Mo., U.S. D6 102
Vic-en-Bigorre, Fr. I7 10
Vicente, Point, c., Ca., U.S. n12 82
Vicenza, Italy D6 14
Vich, Spain D14 12
Vichada, stm., Col. E8 58
Vichy, Fr. F10 10
Vici, Ok., U.S. A2 113
Vicksburg, Mi., U.S. F5 99
Vicksburg, Ms., U.S. C3 101
Vicksburg National Military Park, Ms., U.S. C3 101
Viçosa, Braz. F7 57
Victor, Ia., U.S. C5 92
Victor, N.Y., U.S. C3 109
Victoria, B.C., Can. E6 69
Victoria, Newf., Can. E5 72
Victoria (Xianggang), H.K. M3 28
Victoria, Sey. B11 44
Victoria, Ks., U.S. D4 93
Victoria, Tx., U.S. E4 120
Victoria, Va., U.S. *C4 123
Victoria, state, Austl. G9 50
Victoria, co., Tx., U.S. E4 120
Victoria, Lake, l., Afr. B6 44
Victoria, Mount, mtn., Burma D2 34
Victoria de las Tunas, Cuba D9 64
Victoria Falls, wtfl, Afr. E5 44
Victoria Harbour, Ont., Can. C5 73
Victoria Island, i., N.W. Ter., Can. B10 66
Victoria Lake, res., Newf., Can. D3 72
Victoria Land, reg., Ant. B28 47
Victoria Nile, stm., Ug. H12 42
Victoria Peak, mtn., Belize F3 64
Victoria Strait, strt., N.W. Ter., Can. C12 66
Victoriaville, Que., Can. C6 74
Victoria West, S. Afr. H4 44
Victorville, Ca., U.S. E5 82
Vičuga, Russia D24 18
Vidalia, Ga., U.S. D4 87
Vidalia, La., U.S. C4 95
Vidisha, India I7 38
Vidor, Tx., U.S. D5 120
Viechtach, Ger. F12 8
Viedma, Arg. E4 56
Viedma, Lago, l., Arg. F2 56
Viella, Spain C12 12
Vienna, Ga., U.S. D3 87
Vienna, Il., U.S. F5 90
Vienna, Mo., U.S. C6 102
Vienna, Va., U.S. B5 123
Vienna, W.V., U.S. B3 125
Vienna see Wien, Aus. G16 8
Vienne, Fr. G11 10
Vientiane see Viangchan, Laos F7 34
Vieques, Isla de, i., P.R. E15 64
Vieremä, Fin. E16 6
Vierwaldstätter See, l., Switz. F15 10
Vierzon, Fr. E9 10
Vieste, Italy H11 14
Vietnam, ctry., Asia B4 32
Vieux Desert, Lac, l., Wi., U.S. B4 126
Vigan, Phil. p19 33b
Vigevano, Italy D3 14
Vignola, Italy E5 14
Vigo, Spain C3 12
Vigo, co., In., U.S. F3 91
Vihti, Fin. F15 6
Vijayawāda, India D6 37
Vijosë (Aóös), stm., Eur. I3 16
Vikajärvi, Fin. C16 6
Viking, Alta., Can. C5 68
Vila Coutinho, Moz. D6 44
Vila do Conde, Port. D3 12
Vila Fontes, Moz. E7 44
Vilafranca del Panadés, Spain D13 12
Vila Franca de Xira, Port. G3 12
Vilanculos, Moz. F7 44
Vila Nova de Famalicão, Port. D3 12
Vila Nova de Foz Côa, Port. D4 12
Vila Nova de Gaia, Port. D3 12
Vila Pery, Moz. E6 44
Vila Real, Port. D4 12
Vilas, co., Wi., U.S. B4 126
Vila Velha, Braz. F8 57
Vila Velha de Ródão, Port. F4 12
Vilhelmina, Swe. D11 6
Vilhena, Braz. F6 54
Vil'kickogo, Proliv, strt., Russia B14 24
Villa Ahumada, Mex. B6 62
Villa Bella, Bol. F5 54
Villablino, Spain C5 12
Villa Bruzual, Ven. C8 58
Villacañas, Spain F8 12
Villacarriedo, Spain B8 12
Villacarrillo, Spain G8 12
Villach, Aus. I13 8
Villacidro, Italy J3 14
Villa Colón (Caucete), Arg. C3 56
Villa del Rosario, Ven. I11 64
Villa de Méndez, Mex. E10 62
Villadiego, Spain C7 12
Villafranca del Bierzo, Spain C5 12
Villafranca de los Barros, Spain G5 12
Villafranca di Verona, Italy D5 14
Villa Frontera, Mex. D9 62
Villagaracía, Spain C3 12
Villa Grove, Il., U.S. D5 90
Villaguay, Arg. C5 56
Villa Hayes, Para. B5 56
Villahermosa, Mex. I13 62
Villajoyosa, Spain G11 12
Villalón de Campos, Spain C6 12
Villalonga, Arg. D4 56
Villalpando, Spain D6 12
Villa María, Arg. C4 56
Villamartín, Spain I6 12
Villa Montes, Bol. H6 54
Villanova Monteleone, Italy I3 14
Villanueva, Col. B6 58
Villanueva de Córdoba, Spain G7 12
Villanueva de la Serana, Spain G6 12
Villanueva de los Infantes, Spain G9 12
Villanueva del Río y Minas, Spain H6 12
Villanueva y Geltrú, Spain D13 12
Villa Park, Il., U.S. k8 90
Villa Pedro Montoya, Mex. G10 62
Villarcayo, Spain C8 12
Villa Rica, Ga., U.S. C2 87
Villarreal, Spain F11 12
Villarrica, Chile D2 56
Villarrobledo, Spain F9 12
Villas, N.J., U.S. E3 107
Villa San Giovanni, Italy K10 14
Villasayas, Spain D9 12
Villa Unión, Arg. B4 56
Villavicencio, Col. E6 58
Villaviciosa de Córdoba, Spain G6 12
Villedieu, Fr. D5 10
Villefort, Fr. H10 10
Villefranche, Fr. G11 10
Villefranche-de-Rouergue, Fr. H9 10
Villena, Spain G11 12
Villeneuve-de-Berg, Fr. H11 10
Villeneuve-Saint-Georges, Fr. D9 10
Villeneuve-sur-Lot, Fr. H7 10
Ville Platte, La., U.S. D3 95
Villers-Bocage, Fr. C6 10
Villers-Cotterêts, Fr. C10 10
Ville Saint-Georges, Que., Can. C7 74
Villeurbanne, Fr. G11 10
Villingen-Schwenningen, Ger. G8 8
Villisca, Ia., U.S. D3 92
Villupuram, India G5 37
Vilnius, Lith. G8 18
Vilonia, Ar., U.S. B3 81
Vilsbiburg, Ger. G12 8
Vil'uj, stm., Russia E18 24
Vil'ujsk, Russia E18 24
Vimianzo, Spain B2 12
Vimoutiers, Fr. D7 10
Vina, stm., Cam. G8 42
Viña del Mar, Chile C2 56
Vinalhaven, Me., U.S. D4 96
Vinalhaven Island, i., Me., U.S. D4 96
Vinaroz, Spain E12 12
Vincennes, In., U.S. G2 91
Vincent, Al., U.S. B3 78
Vinces, Ec. H3 58
Vindeln, Swe. D12 6
Vindhya Range, mts., India I7 38
Vine Brook, stm., Ma., U.S. g11 98
Vinegar Hill, mtn., Or., U.S. C8 114
Vine Grove, Ky., U.S. C4 94
Vineland, N.J., U.S. E2 107
Vineyard Haven, Ma., U.S. D6 98
Vineyard Sound, strt., Ma., U.S. D6 98
Vinh, Viet. E8 34
Vinhais, Port. D4 12
Vinh Long, Viet. I8 34
Vinita, Ok., U.S. A6 113
Vinkovci, Cro. D2 16
Vinnica, Ukr. H3 22
Vinnitsa see Vinnica, Ukr. H3 22
Vinson Massif, mtn., Ant. B4 47
Vinton, Ia., U.S. B5 92
Vinton, La., U.S. D2 95
Vinton, Va., U.S. C3 123
Vinton, co., Oh., U.S. C3 112
Viola, Il., U.S. B3 90
Violet, La., U.S. k12 95
Vipava, Slo. D8 14
Vipiteno, Italy C6 14
Virac, Phil. C7 32
Viramgām, India I5 38
Viranşehir, Tur. A6 40
Virden, Man., Can. E1 70
Virden, Il., U.S. D4 90
Vire, Fr. D6 10
Virgin, stm., U.S. G8 105
Virginia, S. Afr. G5 44
Virginia, Al., U.S. g6 78
Virginia, Il., U.S. D3 90
Virginia, Mn., U.S. C6 100
Virginia, state, U.S. C4 123
Virginia Beach, Va., U.S. D7 123
Virginia City, Nv., U.S. D2 105
Virginia Peak, mtn., Nv., U.S. D2 105
Virgin Islands, dep., N.A. E15 64
Virje, Cro. C11 14
Virkie, Scot., U.K. B11 7
Viroqua, Wi., U.S. E3 126
Virovitica, Cro. D12 14
Virtaniemi, Fin. B17 6
Virudunagar, India H4 37
Vis, Cro. F11 14
Visalia, Ca., U.S. D4 82
Visby, Swe. H12 6
Viscount Melville Sound, strt., N.W. Ter., Can. B10 66
Viseu, Port. E4 12
Vishākhapatnam, India D7 37
Vislinskij Zaliv, b., Eur. A19 8
Visnagar, India I5 38
Vista, Ca., U.S. F5 82
Vistula see Wisła, stm., Pol. A18 8
Vitarte, Peru F3 54
Vitebsk, Bela. F13 18
Viterbo, Italy G7 14
Vitigudino, Spain D5 12
Vitim, Russia F16 24
Vitim, stm., Russia F16 24
Vitória, Braz. F8 57
Vitoria, Spain C9 12
Vitória da Conquista, Braz. C8 57
Vitré, Fr. D5 10
Vitry-le-François, Fr. D11 10
Vitteaux, Fr. E11 10
Vittel, Fr. D12 10
Vittoria, Italy M9 14
Vittorio Veneto, Italy D7 14
Viver, Spain F11 12

Name Map Ref Page
ivero, Spain B4 12
ivian, La., U.S. B2 95
iviers, Fr. H11 10
ivonne, Fr. F7 10
'izcachas, Meseta de las, plat., Arg. G2 56
'izcaíno, Desierto de, des., Mex. D3 62
izianagaram, India C7 37
izille, Fr. G12 10
laardingen, Neth. D4 8
ladikavkaz, Russia I6 22
ladimir, Russia E23 18
ladivostok, Russia E35 128
lissingen (Flushing), Neth. D3 8
lorë, Alb. I3 16
'ltava, stm., Czech. F14 8
öcklabruck, Aus. G13 8
odnjan, Cro. E8 14
'ogelsberg, mts., Ger. E9 8
oghera, Italy E4 14
ohenstrauss, Ger. F12 8
ohibinany, Madag. E9 44
ohimarina, Madag. D10 44
oi, Kenya B7 44
oinjama, Lib. G4 42
oiron, Fr. G12 10
oitsberg, Aus. H15 8
olcano, Hi., U.S. D6 88
olchov, Russia B15 18
olda, Nor. E6 6
olga, S.D., U.S. C9 118
'olga, stm., Russia H7 22
olgograd (Stalingrad), Russia H6 22
olkovysk, Bela. H7 18
oločanka, Russia C12 24
ologda, Russia B22 18
olokolamsk, Russia E18 18
ólos, Grc. J6 16
'olta, Lake, res., Ghana G5 42
'olta Blanche (White Volta), stm., Afr. F5 42
'olta Noire (Black Volta), stm., Afr. F6 42
olta Redonda, Braz. G6 57
olterra, Italy F5 14
'olusia, co., Fl., U.S. C5 86
olžskij, Russia H6 22
'on Frank Mountain, mtn., Ak., U.S. C9 79
onore, Tn., U.S. D9 119
'oríai Sporádhes, is., Grc. J7 16
oronež, Russia G5 22
oronezh see Voronež, Russia G5 22
'osges, mts., Fr. D14 10
oskresensk, Russia F21 18
oss, Nor. F6 6
ostočno-Sibirskoje More (East Siberian Sea), Russia C25 24
'ostočnyj Sajan, mts., Russia G13 24
otkinsk, Russia F8 22
otuporanga, Braz. F4 57
ouziers, Fr. C11 10
'oyageurs National Park, Mn., U.S. B5 100
raca, Bul. F7 16
'rangel'a, Ostrov, i., Russia C29 24
ranje, Yugo. G5 16
rhnika, Slo. D9 14
ryburg, S. Afr. G4 44
ryheid, S. Afr. G6 44
'sevidof, Mount, mtn., Ak., U.S. E6 79
sevoložsk, Russia A13 18
ukovar, Cro. D2 16
ulcan, Alta., Can. D4 68
ung Tau (Cap-St.-Jacques), Viet. I9 34
'uoggatjålme, Swe. C11 6
uoksenniska, Fin. F17 6
'yborg, Russia A11 18
yška, Russia D18 18
yšnij Voloček, Russia D17 18
ysokogornyj, Russia G21 24

W

/a, Ghana F5 42
/aawaa, Puu, mtn., Hi., U.S. D6 88
/abana (Bell Island), Newf., Can. E5 72
/abasca, Alta., Can. B4 68
/abasca, stm., Alta., Can. f1 68
/abash, In., U.S. C6 91
/abash, co., Il., U.S. E6 90
/abash, co., In., U.S. C6 91
/abash, stm., U.S. H2 91
/abasha, Mn., U.S. F6 100
/abasha, co., Mn., U.S. F6 100
/abasso, Fl., U.S. E6 86
/abasso, Mn., U.S. F3 100
/abaunsee, co., Ks., U.S. D7 93
/abeno, Wi., U.S. C5 126
/abowden, Man., Can. B2 70
/abush, Newf., Can. h8 72
/accamaw, stm., U.S. D9 117
/accamaw, Lake, l., N.C., U.S. C4 110
/accasassa Bay, b., Fl., U.S. C4 86
/achusett Mountain, mtn., Ma., U.S. B4 98
/achusett Reservoir, res., Ma., U.S. B4 98
/aco, Tx., U.S. D4 120
/aco Lake, res., Tx., U.S. D4 120
/aconda Lake, res., Ks., U.S. C5 93
/aconia, Mn., U.S. F5 100
/addeneilanden, is., Neth. B5 8
/addenzee, Neth. B5 8
/addi, Chappal, mtn., Nig. G8 42
/addington, Mount, mtn., B.C., Can. D5 69
'adena, Mn., U.S. D3 100
'adena, co., Mn., U.S. D4 100
'ädenswil, Switz. E15 10
'adesboro, N.C., U.S. C2 110
'ādī Halfā', Sudan D12 42
Wading, stm., N.J., U.S. D3 107
Wadley, Ga., U.S. D4 87
Wad Madanī, Sudan F12 42
Wadmalaw Island, i., S.C., U.S. F7 117
Wadsworth, Il., U.S. h9 90
Wadsworth, Nv., U.S. D2 105
Wadsworth, Oh., U.S. A4 112
Wagener, S.C., U.S. D5 117
Wageningen, Neth. D5 8
Wager Bay, b., N.W. Ter., Can. C15 66
Wagga Wagga, Austl. G9 50
Wagin, Austl. F3 50
Wagner, S.D., U.S. D7 118
Wagoner, Ok., U.S. B6 113
Wagoner, co., Ok., U.S. B6 113
Wagontire Mountain, mtn., Or., U.S. D7 114
Wągrowiec, Pol. C17 8
Wah, Pak. D5 38
Waha, Libya C9 42
Wahiawa, Hi., U.S. B3 88
Wahiawa Reservoir, res., Hi., U.S. g9 88
Wahkiakum, co., Wa., U.S. C2 124
Wahoo, Ne., U.S. C9 104
Wahpeton, N.D., U.S. C9 111
Wahweap Creek, stm., Ut., U.S. F4 121
Waialua, Hi., U.S. B3 88
Waialua Bay, b., Hi., U.S. B3 88
Waianae, Hi., U.S. B3 88
Waianae Range, mts., Hi., U.S. f9 88
Waidhofen an der Ybbs, Aus. H14 8
Waigeo, Pulau, i., Indon. F9 32
Waihi, N.Z. B5 52
Waikapu, Hi., U.S. C5 88
Waikiki Beach, Hi., U.S. g10 88
Wailua, Hi., U.S. A2 88
Wailuku, Hi., U.S. C5 88
Waimanalo, Hi., U.S. B4 88
Waimanalo Bay, b., Hi., U.S. g11 88
Waimea, Hi., U.S. f9 88
Waimea, Hi., U.S. B2 88
Wainwright, Alta., Can. C5 68
Wainwright, Ak., U.S. A8 79
Waipahu, Hi., U.S. B3 88
Waipio Acres, Hi., U.S. g9 88
Waipio Peninsula, pen., Hi., U.S. g10 88
Waipukurau, N.Z. D6 52
Waite Park, Mn., U.S. E4 100
Waits, stm., Vt., U.S. C4 122
Waitsburg, Wa., U.S. C7 124
Wajir, Kenya H3 46
Wakarusa, In., U.S. A5 91
Wakarusa, stm., Ks., U.S. D8 93
Wakasa-wan, b., Japan G8 30
Wakatomika Creek, stm., Oh., U.S. B3 112
Wakayama, Japan H8 30
Wake, co., N.C., U.S. B4 110
WaKeeney, Ks., U.S. C4 93
Wakefield, Que., Can. D2 74
Wakefield, Ks., U.S. C6 93
Wakefield, Ma., U.S. B5 98
Wakefield, Mi., U.S. n12 99
Wakefield, Ne., U.S. B9 104
Wakefield, R.I., U.S. F3 116
Wakefield, Va., U.S. D6 123
Wake Forest, N.C., U.S. B4 110
Wake Island, dep., Oc. E24 2
Wakema, Burma F3 34
Wakeman, Oh., U.S. A3 112
Wakkanai, Japan n19 30a
Wakulla, co., Fl., U.S. B2 86
Walbridge, Oh., U.S. e6 112
Wałbrzych (Waldenburg), Pol. E16 8
Walcott, Ia., U.S. C7 92
Walcott Lake, res., Id., U.S. G5 89
Walden, Ont., Can. A3 73
Walden, Co., U.S. A4 83
Walden, N.Y., U.S. D6 109
Walden Ridge, mtn., Tn., U.S. D8 119
Waldheim, Sask., Can. E2 75
Waldo, Ar., U.S. D2 81
Waldo, co., Me., U.S. D3 96
Waldoboro, Me., U.S. D3 96
Waldo Lake, l., Ma., U.S. h11 98
Waldo Lake, l., Or., U.S. D4 114
Waldport, Or., U.S. C2 114
Waldron, Ar., U.S. C1 81
Waldron, In., U.S. F6 91
Waldshut, Ger. H8 8
Waldwick, N.J., U.S. A4 107
Wales, ter., U.K. I9 7
Wales Island, i., N.W. Ter., Can. C15 66
Waleska, Ga., U.S. B2 87
Walgett, Austl. E9 50
Walhalla, N.D., U.S. A8 111
Walhalla, S.C., U.S. B1 117
Walhonding, stm., Oh., U.S. B3 112
Walker, Ia., U.S. B6 92
Walker, La., U.S. g10 95
Walker, Mi., U.S. E5 99
Walker, Mn., U.S. C4 100
Walker, co., Al., U.S. B2 78
Walker, co., Ga., U.S. B1 87
Walker, co., Tx., U.S. D5 120
Walker, stm., Nv., U.S. D3 105
Walker Lake, l., Nv., U.S. E3 105
Walker River Indian Reservation, Nv., U.S. D3 105
Walkersville, Md., U.S. B3 97
Walkerton, Ont., Can. C3 73
Walkerton, In., U.S. B5 91
Walkertown, N.C., U.S. A2 110
Walkerville, Mt., U.S. D4 103
Wall, S.D., U.S. D3 118
Wallace, Id., U.S. B3 89
Wallace, N.C., U.S. B4 110
Wallace, co., Ks., U.S. D2 93
Wallaceburg, Ont., Can. E2 73
Wallace Lake, res., La., U.S. B2 95
Walla Walla, Wa., U.S. C7 124
Walla Walla, co., Wa., U.S. C7 124
Walla Walla, stm., U.S. C7 124
Walled Lake, Mi., U.S. o15 99
Wallen, In., U.S. B7 91
Wallenpaupack, Lake, l., Pa., U.S. D11 115
Waller, Tx., U.S. q14 120
Waller, co., Tx., U.S. E4 120
Wallingford, Ct., U.S. D4 84
Wallingford, Vt., U.S. E3 122
Wallington, N.J., U.S. h8 107
Wallis and Futuna, dep., Oc. G1 2
Wallkill, N.Y., U.S. D6 109
Wallkill, stm., N.Y., U.S. D6 109
Wall Lake, Ia., U.S. B2 92
Wall Lake, l., Ia., U.S. B4 92
Walloomsac, stm., U.S. F2 122
Walloon Lake, l., Mi., U.S. C6 99
Wallowa, Or., U.S. B9 114
Wallowa, co., Or., U.S. B9 114
Wallowa Mountains, mts., Or., U.S. B9 114
Wallula, Lake, res., U.S. C7 124
Wallum Lake, l., U.S. A1 116
Walnut, Il., U.S. B4 90
Walnut, Ia., U.S. C2 92
Walnut, stm., Ks., U.S. E6 93
Walnut Canyon National Monument, Az., U.S. B4 80
Walnut Cove, N.C., U.S. A2 110
Walnut Creek, Ca., U.S. h8 82
Walnut Creek, stm., Ks., U.S. D4 93
Walnut Grove, Al., U.S. A3 78
Walnut Grove, Mn., U.S. F3 100
Walnutport, Pa., U.S. E10 115
Walnut Ridge, Ar., U.S. A5 81
Walpole, Ma., U.S. B5 98
Walpole, N.H., U.S. D2 106
Walsall, Eng., U.K. I11 7
Walsenburg, Co., U.S. D6 83
Walsh, Co., U.S. D8 83
Walsh, co., N.D., U.S. A8 111
Walsrode, Ger. C9 8
Walterboro, S.C., U.S. F6 117
Walter F. George Dam, U.S. D4 78
Walter F. George Lake, res., U.S. D4 78
Walters, Ok., U.S. C3 113
Walthall, co., Ms., U.S. D3 101
Waltham, Ma., U.S. B5 98
Walthill, Ne., U.S. B9 104
Walthourville, Ga., U.S. E5 87
Walton, In., U.S. C5 91
Walton, Ky., U.S. B5 94
Walton, N.Y., U.S. C5 109
Walton, co., Fl., U.S. u15 86
Walton, co., Ga., U.S. C3 87
Walvisbaai (Walvis Bay), S. Afr. F2 44
Walworth, Wi., U.S. F5 126
Walworth, co., S.D., U.S. B5 118
Walworth, co., Wi., U.S. F5 126
Wamac, Il., U.S. E4 90
Wamba, stm., Afr. C3 44
Wamego, Ks., U.S. C7 93
Wamesit, Ma., U.S. A5 98
Wamsutter, Wy., U.S. E5 127
Wanaka, N.Z. F2 52
Wanamingo, Mn., U.S. F6 100
Wanapum Dam, Wa., U.S. C6 124
Wanapum Lake, res., Wa., U.S. B6 124
Wanaque, N.J., U.S. A4 107
Wanaque Reservoir, res., N.J., U.S. A4 107
Wanatah, In., U.S. B4 91
Wanchese, N.C., U.S. B7 110
Wando, stm., S.C., U.S. F8 117
Wando Woods, S.C., U.S. k11 117
Wanganui, N.Z. C5 52
Wanganui, stm., N.Z. C5 52
Wangaratta, Austl. G9 50
Wangen [im Allgäu], Ger. H9 8
Wangpan Yang, b., China E10 28
Wānkāner, India I4 38
Wanxian, China E8 26
Wapakoneta, Oh., U.S. B1 112
Wapato, Wa., U.S. C5 124
Wapawekka Lake, l., Sask., Can. C3 75
Wapello, Ia., U.S. C6 92
Wapello, co., Ia., U.S. C5 92
Wapiti, stm., Can. B1 68
Wappapello, Lake, res., Mo., U.S. D7 102
Wappingers Falls, N.Y., U.S. D7 109
Wapsipinicon, stm., Ia., U.S. B6 92
War, W.V., U.S. D3 125
Waramaug, Lake, l., Ct., U.S. C2 84
Warangal, India C5 37
Ward, Ar., U.S. B4 81
Ward, co., N.D., U.S. A4 111
Ward, co., Tx., U.S. D1 120
Warden, Wa., U.S. C6 124
Wardha, India B5 37
Ward Mountain, mtn., Mt., U.S. D2 103
Ware, Ma., U.S. B3 98
Ware, co., Ga., U.S. E4 87
Ware, stm., Ma., U.S. B3 98
War Eagle Mountain, mtn., Id., U.S. G2 89
Wareham, Ma., U.S. C6 98
Warehouse Point, Ct., U.S. B5 84
Waren, Ger. B12 8
Warendorf, Ger. D7 8
Ware Shoals, S.C., U.S. C3 117
Warfield, B.C., Can. E9 69
Warminster, Eng., U.K. J10 7
Warminster, Pa., U.S. F11 115
Warm Springs Indian Reservation, Or., U.S. C5 114
Warm Springs Reservoir, res., Or., U.S. D8 114
Warnemünde, Ger. A12 8
Warner, N.H., U.S. D3 106
Warner, Ok., U.S. B6 113
Warner, stm., N.H., U.S. D3 106
Warner Mountains, mts., Ca., U.S. B3 82
Warner Peak, mtn., Or., U.S. E7 114
Warner Robins, Ga., U.S. D3 87
Warr Acres, Ok., U.S. B4 113
Warren, Ar., U.S. D3 81
Warren, Il., U.S. A4 90
Warren, In., U.S. C7 91
Warren, Ma., U.S. B3 98
Warren, Mi., U.S. F7 99
Warren, Mn., U.S. B2 100
Warren, Oh., U.S. A5 112
Warren, Or., U.S. B4 114
Warren, Pa., U.S. C3 115
Warren, R.I., U.S. D5 116
Warren, Vt., U.S. C3 122
Warren, co., Ga., U.S. C4 87
Warren, co., Il., U.S. C3 90
Warren, co., In., U.S. D3 91
Warren, co., Ia., U.S. C4 92
Warren, co., Ky., U.S. C3 94
Warren, co., Ms., U.S. C3 101
Warren, co., Mo., U.S. C6 102
Warren, co., N.J., U.S. B3 107
Warren, co., N.Y., U.S. B7 109
Warren, co., N.C., U.S. A4 110
Warren, co., Oh., U.S. C1 112
Warren, co., Pa., U.S. C3 115
Warren, co., Tn., U.S. D8 119
Warren, co., Va., U.S. B4 123
Warren, stm., U.S. D5 116
Warren Park, In., U.S. k10 91
Warren Peaks, mts., Wy., U.S. B8 127
Warrensburg, Il., U.S. D4 90
Warrensburg, Mo., U.S. C4 102
Warrensburg, N.Y., U.S. B7 109
Warrensville Heights, Oh., U.S. h9 112
Warrenton, S. Afr. G4 44
Warrenton, Ga., U.S. C4 87
Warrenton, Mo., U.S. C6 102
Warrenton, N.C., U.S. A4 110
Warrenton, Or., U.S. A3 114
Warrenton, Va., U.S. B5 123
Warrenville, Il., U.S. k8 90
Warrenville, S.C., U.S. D4 117
Warri, Nig. G7 42
Warrick, co., In., U.S. H3 91
Warrina, Austl. E7 50
Warrington, Eng., U.K. H10 7
Warrington, Fl., U.S. u14 86
Warrior, Al., U.S. B3 78
Warrior Lake, res., Al., U.S. C2 78
Warrnambool, Austl. G8 50
Warroad, Mn., U.S. B3 100
Warsaw, Il., U.S. C2 90
Warsaw, In., U.S. B6 91
Warsaw, Ky., U.S. B5 94
Warsaw, Mo., U.S. C4 102
Warsaw, N.Y., U.S. C2 109
Warsaw, N.C., U.S. B4 110
Warsaw, Va., U.S. C6 123
Warsaw see Warszawa, Pol. C21 8
Warszawa (Warsaw), Pol. C21 8
Warta, stm., Pol. C15 8
Wartburg, Tn., U.S. C9 119
Warthe see Warta, stm., Pol. C15 8
Warwick, Austl. E10 50
Warwick, Que., Can. D6 74
Warwick, Eng., U.K. I11 7
Warwick, Md., U.S. B6 97
Warwick, N.Y., U.S. D6 109
Warwick, R.I., U.S. D4 116
Wasaga Beach, Ont., Can. C4 73
Wasatch, co., Ut., U.S. C4 121
Wasco, Ca., U.S. E4 82
Wasco, co., Or., U.S. B5 114
Waseca, Mn., U.S. F5 100
Waseca, co., Mn., U.S. F5 100
Washakie, co., Wy., U.S. C5 127
Washakie Needles, mts., Wy., U.S. C3 127
Washburn, Il., U.S. C4 90
Washburn, Ia., U.S. B5 92
Washburn, Me., U.S. B4 96
Washburn, N.D., U.S. B5 111
Washburn, Wi., U.S. B3 126
Washburn, co., Wi., U.S. C2 126
Washburn, Mount, mtn., Wy., U.S. B2 127
Washington, D.C., U.S. C3 97
Washington, Ga., U.S. C4 87
Washington, Il., U.S. C4 90
Washington, In., U.S. G3 91
Washington, Ia., U.S. C6 92
Washington, Ks., U.S. C6 93
Washington, Ky., U.S. B6 94
Washington, La., U.S. D3 95
Washington, Ms., U.S. D2 101
Washington, Mo., U.S. C6 102
Washington, N.J., U.S. B3 107
Washington, N.C., U.S. B5 110
Washington, Pa., U.S. F1 115
Washington, Ut., U.S. F2 121
Washington, co., Al., U.S. D1 78
Washington, co., Ar., U.S. A1 81
Washington, co., Co., U.S. B7 83
Washington, co., Fl., U.S. u16 86
Washington, co., Ga., U.S. C4 87
Washington, co., Id., U.S. E2 89
Washington, co., Il., U.S. E4 90
Washington, co., In., U.S. G5 91
Washington, co., Ia., U.S. C6 92
Washington, co., Ks., U.S. C6 93
Washington, co., Ky., U.S. C4 94
Washington, co., La., U.S. D5 95
Washington, co., Me., U.S. D5 96
Washington, co., Md., U.S. A2 97
Washington, co., Mn., U.S. E6 100
Washington, co., Ms., U.S. B3 101
Washington, co., Mo., U.S. D7 102
Washington, co., Ne., U.S. C9 104
Washington, co., N.Y., U.S. B7 109
Washington, co., N.C., U.S. B6 110
Washington, co., Oh., U.S. C4 112
Washington, co., Ok., U.S. A6 113
Washington, co., Or., U.S. B3 114
Washington, co., Pa., U.S. F1 115
Washington, co., R.I., U.S. E2 116
Washington, co., Tn., U.S. C11 119
Washington, co., Tx., U.S. D4 120
Washington, co., Ut., U.S. F2 121
Washington, co., Vt., U.S. C3 122
Washington, co., Va., U.S. f9 123
Washington, co., Wi., U.S. E5 126
Washington, state, U.S. B5 124
Washington, Lake, l., Fl., U.S. D6 86
Washington, Lake, l., Mn., U.S. E4 100
Washington, Lake, l., Ms., U.S. B3 101
Washington, Lake, l., Wa., U.S. e11 124
Washington, Mount, mtn., N.H., U.S. B4 106
Washington Court House, Oh., U.S. C2 112
Washington Island, i., Wi., U.S. C7 126
Washington Park, Il., U.S. E3 90
Washington Terrace, Ut., U.S. B4 121
Washita, co., Ok., U.S. B2 113
Washita, stm., Ok., U.S. C4 113
Washoe, co., Nv., U.S. C2 105
Washoe City, Nv., U.S. D2 105
Washougal, Wa., U.S. D3 124
Washow Bay, b., Man., Can. D3 70
Washtenaw, co., Mi., U.S. F7 99
Wasilla, Ak., U.S. C10 79
Wasior, Indon. F9 32
Waskom, Tx., U.S. C5 120
Waspán, Nic. G5 64
Wasque Point, c., Ma., U.S. D7 98
Wassen, Switz. F15 10
Wassookeag, Lake, l., Me., U.S. C3 96
Wassuk Range, mts., Nv., U.S. E3 105
Wataga, Il., U.S. B3 90
Watauga, co., N.C., U.S. A1 110
Watauga, stm., Tn., U.S. C12 119
Watauga Lake, res., Tn., U.S. C12 119
Watchaug Pond, l., R.I., U.S. F2 116
Watch Hill Point, c., R.I., U.S. G1 116
Watchung, N.J., U.S. B4 107
Waterbury, Ct., U.S. C3 84
Waterbury, Vt., U.S. C3 122
Waterbury Center, Vt., U.S. C3 122
Waterbury Reservoir, res., Vt., U.S. C3 122
Wateree, stm., S.C., U.S. D6 117
Wateree Lake, res., S.C., U.S. C6 117
Waterford, Ire. I5 7
Waterford, Ct., U.S. D7 84
Waterford, N.Y., U.S. C7 109
Waterford, Pa., U.S. C2 115
Waterford, Wi., U.S. F5 126
Waterhen Lake, l., Man., Can. C2 70
Waterloo, Bel. E4 8
Waterloo, Ont., Can. D4 73
Waterloo, Que., Can. D5 74
Waterloo, Il., U.S. E3 90
Waterloo, In., U.S. B7 91
Waterloo, Ia., U.S. B5 92
Waterloo, N.Y., U.S. C4 109
Waterloo, Wi., U.S. E5 126
Waterman, Il., U.S. B5 90
Waterman Reservoir, res., R.I., U.S. B3 116
Waterproof, La., U.S. C4 95
Watersmeet, Mi., U.S. n12 99
Waterton Lakes National Park, Alta., Can. E3 68
Watertown, Ct., U.S. C3 84
Watertown, Ma., U.S. g11 98
Watertown, N.Y., U.S. B5 109
Watertown, S.D., U.S. C8 118
Watertown, Tn., U.S. A5 119
Watertown, Wi., U.S. E5 126
Water Valley, Ms., U.S. A4 101
Waterville, Ks., U.S. C7 93
Waterville, Me., U.S. D3 96
Waterville, Mn., U.S. F5 100
Waterville, N.Y., U.S. C5 109
Waterville, Oh., U.S. A2 112
Waterville, Wa., U.S. B5 124
Watervliet, Mi., U.S. F4 99
Watervliet, N.Y., U.S. C7 109
Watford, Ont., Can. E3 73
Watford City, N.D., U.S. B2 111
Wathena, Ks., U.S. C9 93
Watkins, Mn., U.S. E4 100
Watkins Glen, N.Y., U.S. C4 109
Watkinsville, Ga., U.S. C3 87
Watonga, Ok., U.S. B3 113
Watonwan, co., Mn., U.S. F4 100
Watonwan, stm., Mn., U.S. G4 100
Watseka, Il., U.S. C6 90
Watson Lake, Yukon, Can. D7 66
Watsontown, Pa., U.S. D8 115
Watsonville, Ca., U.S. D3 82
Watts Bar Dam, Tn., U.S. D9 119
Watts Bar Lake, res., Tn., U.S. D9 119
Wattsville, S.C., U.S. B4 117
Wattwil, Switz. E16 10
Watubela, Kepulauan, is., Indon. F9 32
Waubaushene, Ont., Can. C5 73
Waubay, S.D., U.S. B8 118
Waubay Lake, l., S.D., U.S. B8 118
Wauchula, Fl., U.S. E5 86
Wauconda, Il., U.S. h8 90
Waugh Mountain, mtn., Id., U.S. D4 89
Waukee, Ia., U.S. C4 92
Waukegan, Il., U.S. A6 90
Waukesha, Wi., U.S. F5 126
Waukesha, co., Wi., U.S. E5 126
Waukewan, Lake, l., N.H., U.S. C3 106
Waukomis, Ok., U.S. A4 113
Waukon, Ia., U.S. A6 92
Waunakee, Wi., U.S. E4 126
Wauneta, Ne., U.S. D4 104
Waungumbaug Lake, l., Ct., U.S. B6 84
Waupaca, Wi., U.S. D4 126
Waupaca, co., Wi., U.S. D5 126
Waupun, Wi., U.S. E5 126
Wauregan, Ct., U.S. C8 84
Waurika, Ok., U.S. C4 113
Waurika Lake, res., Ok., U.S. C3 113
Wausau, Wi., U.S. D4 126
Wausau, Lake, res., Wi., U.S. D4 126
Wauseon, Oh., U.S. A1 112
Waushara, co., Wi., U.S. D4 126
Wautoma, Wi., U.S. D4 126
Wauwatosa, Wi., U.S. m12 126
Wave Hill, Austl. C6 50
Waveland, Ms., U.S. E4 101
Waverley, N.S., Can. E6 71
Waverly, Il., U.S. D4 90
Waverly, Ia., U.S. B5 92
Waverly, Ks., U.S. D8 93
Waverly, Mn., U.S. E5 100

Name	Map Ref	Page
Waverly, Mo., U.S.	B4	102
Waverly, Ne., U.S.	D9	104
Waverly, N.Y., U.S.	C4	109
Waverly, Oh., U.S.	C3	112
Waverly, Tn., U.S.	A4	119
Waverly, Va., U.S.	C5	123
Waverly, W.V., U.S.	B3	125
Waverly Hall, Ga., U.S.	D2	87
Wāw, Sudan	G11	42
Wawanesa, Man., Can.	E2	70
Wawasee, Lake, l., In., U.S.	B6	91
Wawayanda Lake, l., N.J., U.S.	A4	107
Wawota, Sask., Can.	H4	75
Waxahachie, Tx., U.S.	C4	120
Waxhaw, N.C., U.S.	C2	110
Waycross, Ga., U.S.	E4	87
Wayland, Ia., U.S.	C6	92
Wayland, Ma., U.S.	g10	98
Wayland, Mi., U.S.	F5	99
Wayland, N.Y., U.S.	C3	109
Waylyn, S.C., U.S.	k12	117
Waymart, Pa., U.S.	C11	115
Wayne, Mi., U.S.	p15	99
Wayne, Ne., U.S.	B8	104
Wayne, N.J., U.S.	B4	107
Wayne, W.V., U.S.	C2	125
Wayne, co., Ga., U.S.	E5	87
Wayne, co., Il., U.S.	E5	90
Wayne, co., In., U.S.	E7	91
Wayne, co., Ia., U.S.	D4	92
Wayne, co., Ky., U.S.	D5	94
Wayne, co., Mi., U.S.	F7	99
Wayne, co., Ms., U.S.	D5	101
Wayne, co., Mo., U.S.	D7	102
Wayne, co., Ne., U.S.	B8	104
Wayne, co., N.Y., U.S.	B3	109
Wayne, co., N.C., U.S.	B4	110
Wayne, co., Oh., U.S.	B4	112
Wayne, co., Pa., U.S.	C11	115
Wayne, co., Tn., U.S.	B4	119
Wayne, co., Ut., U.S.	E4	121
Wayne, co., W.V., U.S.	C2	125
Wayne City, Il., U.S.	E5	90
Waynesboro, Ga., U.S.	C4	87
Waynesboro, Ms., U.S.	D5	101
Waynesboro, Pa., U.S.	G6	115
Waynesboro, Tn., U.S.	B4	119
Waynesboro, Va., U.S.	B4	123
Waynesburg, Oh., U.S.	B4	112
Waynesburg, Pa., U.S.	G1	115
Waynesville, Mo., U.S.	D5	102
Waynesville, N.C., U.S.	f10	110
Waynesville, Oh., U.S.	C1	112
Waynetown, In., U.S.	D3	91
Waynewood, Va., U.S.	g12	123
Waynoka, Ok., U.S.	A3	113
Wayzata, Mn., U.S.	n11	100
Wazīrābād, Pak.	D6	38
Weakley, co., Tn., U.S.	A3	119
Weatherford, Ok., U.S.	B3	113
Weatherford, Tx., U.S.	C4	120
Weatherly, Pa., U.S.	E10	115
Weatogue, Ct., U.S.	B4	84
Weaver, Al., U.S.	B4	78
Weaver Mountains, mts., Az., U.S.	C3	80
Weaverville, Ca., U.S.	B2	82
Weaverville, N.C., U.S.	f10	110
Webb, Al., U.S.	D4	78
Webb, Ms., U.S.	B3	101
Webb, co., Tx., U.S.	F3	120
Webb City, Mo., U.S.	D3	102
Webbers Falls, Ok., U.S.	B6	113
Webberville, Mi., U.S.	F6	99
Webb Lake, l., Me., U.S.	D2	96
Weber, co., Ut., U.S.	B4	121
Weber City, Va., U.S.	f9	123
Webster, Ma., U.S.	B4	98
Webster, N.Y., U.S.	B3	109
Webster, Pa., U.S.	F2	115
Webster, S.D., U.S.	B8	118
Webster, co., Ga., U.S.	D2	87
Webster, co., Ia., U.S.	B3	92
Webster, co., Ky., U.S.	C2	94
Webster, co., La., U.S.	B2	95
Webster, co., Ms., U.S.	B4	101
Webster, co., Mo., U.S.	D5	102
Webster, co., Ne., U.S.	D7	104
Webster, co., W.V., U.S.	C4	125
Webster City, Ia., U.S.	B4	92
Webster Groves, Mo., U.S.	f13	102
Webster Reservoir, res., Ks., U.S.	C4	93
Webster Springs, W.V., U.S.	C4	125
Websterville, Vt., U.S.	C4	122
Weddell Sea, Ant.	B8	47
Wedgeport, N.S., Can.	F4	71
Wedgewood, Mo., U.S.	f13	102
Wedowee, Al., U.S.	B4	78
Weed, Ca., U.S.	B2	82
Weed Heights, Nv., U.S.	E2	105
Weedon, Que., Can.	D6	74
Weedsport, N.Y., U.S.	B4	109
Weedville, Pa., U.S.	D5	115
Weehawken, N.J., U.S.	h8	107
Weeksbury, Ky., U.S.	C7	94
Weeping Water, Ne., U.S.	D9	104
Wegscheid, Ger.	G13	8
Weiden in der Oberpfalz, Ger.	F12	8
Weifang, China	D10	26
Weihai, China	D11	26
Weilburg, Ger.	E8	8
Weilheim, Ger.	H11	8
Weimar, Ger.	E11	8
Weimar, Tx., U.S.	E4	120
Weiner, Ar., U.S.	B5	81
Weinheim, Ger.	F8	8
Weipa, Austl.	B8	50
Weippe, Id., U.S.	C3	89
Weir, Ks., U.S.	E9	93
Weir, Lake, l., Fl., U.S.	C5	86
Weirsdale, Fl., U.S.	D5	86
Weirton, W.V., U.S.	A4	125
Weiser, Id., U.S.	E2	89
Weiser, stm., Id., U.S.	E2	89
Weishi, China	A3	28
Weissenburg in Bayern, Ger.	F10	8
Weissenfels, Ger.	D11	8
Weiss Lake, res., U.S.	A4	78
Weisswasser, Ger.	D14	8
Weiz, Aus.	H15	8
Wejherowo, Pol.	A18	8
Welch, W.V., U.S.	D3	125
Welcome, Mn., U.S.	G4	100
Welcome, S.C., U.S.	B3	117
Weld, co., Co., U.S.	A6	83
Weldon, N.C., U.S.	A5	110
Weldon Spring, Mo., U.S.	f12	102
Weleetka, Ok., U.S.	B5	113
Welkom, S. Afr.	G5	44
Welland, Ont., Can.	E5	73
Wellesley, Ont., Can.	D4	73
Wellesley, Ma., U.S.	B5	98
Wellesley Islands, is., Austl.	C7	50
Wellford, S.C., U.S.	B3	117
Wellington, Ont., Can.	D7	73
Wellington, N.Z.	D5	52
Wellington, Co., U.S.	A5	83
Wellington, Ks., U.S.	E6	93
Wellington, Mo., U.S.	B4	102
Wellington, Nv., U.S.	E2	105
Wellington, Oh., U.S.	A3	112
Wellington, Tx., U.S.	B2	120
Wellington, Ut., U.S.	D5	121
Wellington, Isla, i., Chile	F2	56
Wellington Channel, strt., N.W. Ter., Can.	A14	66
Wellman, Ia., U.S.	C6	92
Wells, Me., U.S.	E2	96
Wells, Mi., U.S.	C3	99
Wells, Mn., U.S.	G5	100
Wells, Nv., U.S.	B7	105
Wells, co., In., U.S.	C7	91
Wells, co., N.D., U.S.	B6	111
Wells, stm., Vt., U.S.	C4	122
Wellsboro, Pa., U.S.	C7	115
Wellsburg, Ia., U.S.	B5	92
Wellsburg, W.V., U.S.	A4	125
Wellston, Oh., U.S.	C3	112
Wellston, Ok., U.S.	B4	113
Wellsville, Ks., U.S.	D8	93
Wellsville, Mo., U.S.	B6	102
Wellsville, N.Y., U.S.	C3	109
Wellsville, Oh., U.S.	B5	112
Wellsville, Ut., U.S.	B4	121
Wellton, Az., U.S.	E1	80
Wels, Aus.	G14	8
Welsh, La., U.S.	D3	95
Welshpool, Wales, U.K.	I9	7
Wembley, Alta., Can.	B1	68
Wenatchee, Wa., U.S.	B5	124
Wenatchee, stm., Wa., U.S.	B5	124
Wenatchee Lake, l., Wa., U.S.	B5	124
Wenatchee Mountains, mts., Wa., U.S.	B5	124
Wendell, Id., U.S.	G4	89
Wendell, N.C., U.S.	B4	110
Wendover, Ut., U.S.	C1	121
Wenham, Ma., U.S.	A6	98
Wenham Lake, l., Ma., U.S.	f12	98
Wenona, Il., U.S.	B4	90
Wenshan, China	C8	34
Wentworth, Lake, l., N.H., U.S.	C4	106
Wentzville, Mo., U.S.	C7	102
Wenzhou, China	G9	28
Weohyakapka, Lake, l., Fl., U.S.	E5	86
Wernigerode, Ger.	D10	8
Wertheim, Ger.	F9	8
Wesel, Ger.	D6	8
Weser, stm., Ger.	B8	8
Weslaco, Tx., U.S.	F4	120
Wesleyville, Newf., Can.	D5	72
Wesleyville, Pa., U.S.	B2	115
Wessel Islands, is., Austl.	B7	50
Wesserunsett Lake, l., Me., U.S.	D3	96
Wessington Springs, S.D., U.S.	C7	118
Wesson, Ms., U.S.	D3	101
West, Tx., U.S.	D4	120
West, stm., Ct., U.S.	D5	84
West, stm., Ma., U.S.	h9	98
West, stm., Vt., U.S.	E3	122
West Acton, Ma., U.S.	g10	98
West Alexandria, Oh., U.S.	C1	112
West Allis, Wi., U.S.	m11	126
West Alton, Mo., U.S.	f13	102
West Andover, Ma., U.S.	A5	98
West Baden Springs, In., U.S.	G4	91
West Baton Rouge, co., La., U.S.	D4	95
West Bay, b., Fl., U.S.	u16	86
West Bay, b., N.C., U.S.	B6	110
West Bay, b., Tx., U.S.	r15	120
West Bend, Ia., U.S.	B3	92
West Bend, Wi., U.S.	E5	126
West Bengal, state, India	I12	38
West Berlin, N.J., U.S.	D3	107
West Billerica, Ma., U.S.	f10	98
West Blocton, Al., U.S.	B2	78
Westborough, Ma., U.S.	B4	98
West Bountiful, Ut., U.S.	C4	121
West Boylston, Ma., U.S.	B4	98
West Branch, Ia., U.S.	C6	92
West Branch, Mi., U.S.	D6	99
West Branch Reservoir, res., Ct., U.S.	B3	84
West Bridgewater, Ma., U.S.	B5	98
Westbrook, Ct., U.S.	D6	84
Westbrook, Me., U.S.	E2	96
Westbrook, Mn., U.S.	F3	100
West Burlington, Ia., U.S.	D6	92
West Butte, mtn., Mt., U.S.	B5	103
Westby, Wi., U.S.	E3	126
West Cache Creek, stm., Ok., U.S.	C3	113
West Caldwell, N.J., U.S.	B4	107
West Canada Creek, stm., N.Y., U.S.	B6	109
West Carroll, co., La., U.S.	B4	95
West Carrollton, Oh., U.S.	C1	112
West Carthage, N.Y., U.S.	B5	109
Westchester, Il., U.S.	k9	90
West Chester, Pa., U.S.	G10	115
Westchester, co., N.Y., U.S.	D7	109
West Chicago, Il., U.S.	k8	90
West Chop, c., Ma., U.S.	D6	98
West College Corner, In., U.S.	E8	91
West Columbia, S.C., U.S.	D5	117
West Columbia, Tx., U.S.	E5	120
West Concord, Ma., U.S.	B5	98
West Concord, Mn., U.S.	F6	100
West Concord, N.C., U.S.	B2	110
Westconnaug Reservoir, res., R.I., U.S.	C2	116
West Cote Blanche Bay, b., La., U.S.	E4	95
West Covina, Ca., U.S.	m13	82
West Crossett, Ar., U.S.	D4	81
West Cumberland, Me., U.S.	E2	96
West Dennis, Ma., U.S.	C7	98
West Des Moines, Ia., U.S.	C4	92
West Elk Mountains, mts., Co., U.S.	C3	83
West Elk Peak, mtn., Co., U.S.	C3	83
Westerly, R.I., U.S.	F1	116
Western Australia, state, Austl.	D4	50
Western Desert see Gharbīyah, Aṣ-Ṣaḥrā' al-, des., Egypt	C11	42
Western Ghāts, mts., India	E3	37
Westernport, Md., U.S.	m12	97
Western Sahara, dep., Afr.	D3	42
Western Samoa, ctry., Oc.	G1	2
Western Springs, Il., U.S.	k9	90
Westerstede, Ger.	B7	8
Westerville, Oh., U.S.	B3	112
West Falkland, i., Falk. Is.	G4	56
West Falmouth, Ma., U.S.	C6	98
West Fargo, N.D., U.S.	C9	111
West Feliciana, co., La., U.S.	D4	95
Westfield, N.B., Can.	D3	71
Westfield, In., U.S.	D5	91
Westfield, Ma., U.S.	B2	98
Westfield, N.J., U.S.	B4	107
Westfield, N.Y., U.S.	C1	109
Westfield, Pa., U.S.	C6	115
Westfield, Wi., U.S.	E4	126
Westfield, stm., Ma., U.S.	B2	98
West Fork, Ar., U.S.	B1	81
West Fork, stm., W.V., U.S.	B4	125
West Frankfort, Il., U.S.	F5	90
West Freehold, N.J., U.S.	C4	107
West Friendship, Md., U.S.	B4	97
Westgate, Fl., U.S.	F6	86
West Grand Lake, l., Me., U.S.	C5	96
West Grove, Pa., U.S.	G10	115
West Hanover, Ma., U.S.	h12	98
West Hartford, Ct., U.S.	B4	84
West Haven, Ct., U.S.	D4	84
West Hazleton, Pa., U.S.	E9	115
West Helena, Ar., U.S.	C5	81
West Hill Reservoir, res., Ma., U.S.	B4	98
Westhope, N.D., U.S.	A4	111
West Indies, is.	E12	64
West Island, i., Ma., U.S.	C6	98
West Jefferson, N.C., U.S.	A1	110
West Jefferson, Oh., U.S.	C2	112
West Jordan, Ut., U.S.	C3	121
West Kingston, R.I., U.S.	F3	116
West Lafayette, In., U.S.	D4	91
West Lafayette, Oh., U.S.	B4	112
Westlake, La., U.S.	D2	95
Westlake, Oh., U.S.	h9	112
West Lake, l., Me., U.S.	C4	96
Westland, Mi., U.S.	F7	99
West Laramie, Wy., U.S.	E7	127
West Lawn, Pa., U.S.	F10	115
West Lebanon, In., U.S.	D3	91
West Liberty, Ia., U.S.	C6	92
West Liberty, Ky., U.S.	C6	94
West Liberty, Oh., U.S.	B2	112
West Liberty, W.V., U.S.	f8	125
West Linn, Or., U.S.	B4	114
Westlock, Alta., Can.	B4	68
West Long Branch, N.J., U.S.	C4	107
West Lorne, Ont., Can.	E3	73
West Marion, N.C., U.S.	f10	110
West Medway, Ma., U.S.	B5	98
West Memphis, Ar., U.S.	B5	81
West Miami, Fl., U.S.	s13	86
West Middlesex, Pa., U.S.	D1	115
West Mifflin, Pa., U.S.	F2	115
West Milton, Oh., U.S.	C1	112
West Milwaukee, Wi., U.S.	m12	126
Westminster, Ca., U.S.	n12	82
Westminster, Co., U.S.	B5	83
Westminster, Md., U.S.	A4	97
Westminster, S.C., U.S.	B1	117
West Monroe, La., U.S.	B3	95
Westmont, Ca., U.S.	*n12	82
Westmont, Il., U.S.	k9	90
Westmont, N.J., U.S.	D2	107
Westmont, Pa., U.S.	F4	115
Westmoreland, Tn., U.S.	A5	119
Westmoreland, co., Pa., U.S.	F2	115
Westmoreland, co., Va., U.S.	B6	123
Westmorland, Ca., U.S.	F6	82
West Musquash Lake, l., Me., U.S.	C5	96
West Mystic, Ct., U.S.	D8	84
West Newton, Pa., U.S.	F2	115
West New York, N.J., U.S.	h8	107
West Nishnabotna, stm., Ia., U.S.	C2	92
West Norriton, Pa., U.S.	o20	115
Weston, Ct., U.S.	E2	84
Weston, Ma., U.S.	g10	98
Weston, Mo., U.S.	B3	102
Weston, Oh., U.S.	A2	112
Weston, Or., U.S.	B8	114
Weston, W.V., U.S.	B4	125
Weston, Wi., U.S.	*D4	126
Weston, co., Wy., U.S.	C8	127
Weston-super-Mare, Eng., U.K.	J10	7
West Orange, N.J., U.S.	B4	107
Westover, Md., U.S.	D6	97
Westover, W.V., U.S.	B5	125
Westover Air Force Base, mil., Ma., U.S.	B2	98
West Palm Beach, Fl., U.S.	F6	86
West Pawlet, Vt., U.S.	E2	122
West Pearl, stm., La., U.S.	D6	95
West Pelzer, S.C., U.S.	B3	117
West Pensacola, Fl., U.S.	u14	86
West Peoria, Il., U.S.	C4	90
Westphalia, Mi., U.S.	F6	99
West Pittsburg, Pa., U.S.	E1	115
West Pittston, Pa., U.S.	m17	115
West Plains, Mo., U.S.	E6	102
West Point, Ca., U.S.	C3	82
West Point, Ga., U.S.	D1	87
West Point, Ia., U.S.	D6	92
West Point, Ky., U.S.	C4	94
West Point, Ms., U.S.	B5	101
West Point, Ne., U.S.	C9	104
West Point, N.Y., U.S.	D7	109
West Point, Va., U.S.	C6	123
West Point, mtn., Ak., U.S.	C11	79
West Point Lake, res., U.S.	C1	87
Westport, Ont., Can.	C8	73
Westport, N.Z.	D3	52
Westport, Ct., U.S.	E2	84
Westport, In., U.S.	F6	91
Westport, Wa., U.S.	C1	124
West Portsmouth, Oh., U.S.	D2	112
West Quoddy Head, c., Me., U.S.	D6	96
Westray, i., Scot., U.K.	B10	7
Westray Firth, strt., Scot., U.K.	B9	7
West Reading, Pa., U.S.	F10	115
West Rutland, Vt., U.S.	D2	122
West Saint Paul, Mn., U.S.	n12	100
West Salem, Il., U.S.	E5	90
West Salem, Oh., U.S.	B3	112
West Salem, Wi., U.S.	E2	126
West Scarborough, Me., U.S.	E2	96
West Seneca, N.Y., U.S.	C2	109
West Simsbury, Ct., U.S.	B4	84
West Slope, Or., U.S.	g12	114
West Spanish Peak, mtn., Co., U.S.	D6	83
West Springfield, Ma., U.S.	B2	98
West Springfield, Va., U.S.	g12	123
West Swanzey, N.H., U.S.	E2	106
West Terre Haute, In., U.S.	F3	91
West Thompson Lake, res., Ct., U.S.	B8	84
West Union, Ia., U.S.	B6	92
West Union, Oh., U.S.	D2	112
West Union, W.V., U.S.	B4	125
West Unity, Oh., U.S.	A1	112
West University Place, Tx., U.S.	r14	120
West Valley City, Ut., U.S.	C4	121
West Vancouver, B.C., Can.	f12	69
West Van Lear, Ky., U.S.	C7	94
West View, Pa., U.S.	h13	115
Westville, Il., U.S.	C6	90
Westville, In., U.S.	A4	91
Westville, N.H., U.S.	E4	106
Westville, N.J., U.S.	D2	107
Westville, Ok., U.S.	A7	113
Westville Lake, res., Ma., U.S.	B3	98
West Virginia, state, U.S.	C4	125
West Walker, stm., U.S.	E2	105
West Wareham, Ma., U.S.	C6	98
West Warwick, R.I., U.S.	D3	116
Westwego, La., U.S.	k11	95
Westwood, Ca., U.S.	B3	82
Westwood, Ks., U.S.	k16	93
Westwood, Ky., U.S.	B7	94
Westwood, Ma., U.S.	B5	98
Westwood, N.J., U.S.	B4	107
Westwood Lakes, Fl., U.S.	s13	86
West Wyoming, Pa., U.S.	n17	115
West Yarmouth, Ma., U.S.	C7	98
West Yellowstone, Mt., U.S.	F5	103
West York, Pa., U.S.	G8	115
Wetar, Pulau, i., Indon.	G8	32
Wetaskiwin, Alta., Can.	C4	68
Wethersfield, Ct., U.S.	C5	84
Wet Mountains, mts., Co., U.S.	C5	83
Wetumka, Ok., U.S.	B5	113
Wetumpka, Al., U.S.	C3	78
Wetzel, co., W.V., U.S.	B4	125
Wetzlar, Ger.	E8	8
Wewahitchka, Fl., U.S.	B1	86
Wewak, Pap. N. Gui.	k15	50a
Wewoka, Ok., U.S.	B5	113
Wexford, Ire.	I6	7
Wexford, co., Mi., U.S.	D5	99
Weyauwega, Wi., U.S.	D5	126
Weymouth, Eng., U.K.	K10	7
Weymouth, Ma., U.S.	B6	98
Whaleysville, Md., U.S.	D7	97
Whalsay, i., Scot., U.K.	A12	7
Whangarei, N.Z.	A5	52
Wharton, N.J., U.S.	B3	107
Wharton, Tx., U.S.	E4	120
Wharton, co., Tx., U.S.	E4	120
What Cheer, Ia., U.S.	C5	92
Whatcom, co., Wa., U.S.	A4	124
Whatcom, Lake, l., Wa., U.S.	A3	124
Wheatfield, In., U.S.	B3	91
Wheatland, Ca., U.S.	C3	82
Wheatland, Ia., U.S.	C7	92
Wheatland, Wy., U.S.	D8	127
Wheatland, co., Mt., U.S.	D7	103
Wheatland Reservoir, res., Wy., U.S.	E7	127
Wheatley, Ont., Can.	E2	73
Wheaton, Il., U.S.	B5	90
Wheaton, Md., U.S.	B3	97
Wheaton, Mn., U.S.	E2	100
Wheaton, Mo., U.S.	E3	102
Wheat Ridge, Co., U.S.	B5	83
Wheelbarrow Peak, mtn., Nv., U.S.	F5	105
Wheeler, Ms., U.S.	A5	101
Wheeler, Tx., U.S.	B2	120
Wheeler, co., Ga., U.S.	D4	87
Wheeler, co., Ne., U.S.	C7	104
Wheeler, co., Or., U.S.	C6	114
Wheeler, co., Tx., U.S.	B2	120
Wheeler Air Force Base, mil., Hi., U.S.	g9	88
Wheeler Lake, res., Al., U.S.	A2	78
Wheeler Peak, mtn., Ca., U.S.	C4	82
Wheeler Peak, mtn., Nv., U.S.	E7	105
Wheeler Peak, mtn., N.M., U.S.	A4	108
Wheelersburg, Oh., U.S.	D3	112
Wheeling, Il., U.S.	h9	90
Wheeling, W.V., U.S.	A4	125
Wheeling Creek, stm., W.V., U.S.	f8	125
Wheelwright, Ky., U.S.	C7	94
Whetstone, stm., U.S.	E2	100
Whidbey Island, i., Wa., U.S.	A3	124
Whidbey Island Naval Air Station, mil., Wa., U.S.	A3	124
Whigham, Ga., U.S.	F2	87
Whiskey Peak, mtn., Wy., U.S.	D5	127
Whiskeytown-Shasta-Trinity National Recreation Area, Ca., U.S.	B2	82
Whistler, B.C., Can.	D6	69
Whitacres, Ct., U.S.	A5	84
Whitakers, N.C., U.S.	A5	110
Whitbourne, Newf., Can.	E5	72
Whitby, Ont., Can.	D6	73
Whitchurch-Stouffville, Ont., Can.	D5	73
White, co., Ar., U.S.	B4	81
White, co., Ga., U.S.	B3	87
White, co., Il., U.S.	E5	90
White, co., In., U.S.	C4	91
White, co., Tn., U.S.	D8	119
White, stm., N.A.	D4	66
White, stm., U.S.	C4	81
White, stm., U.S.	D5	118
White, stm., U.S.	C7	121
White, stm., Az., U.S.	D5	80
White, stm., In., U.S.	H2	91
White, stm., Mi., U.S.	E4	99
White, stm., Nv., U.S.	E6	105
White, stm., Tx., U.S.	C2	120
White, stm., Vt., U.S.	D4	122
White, stm., Wa., U.S.	B4	124
White, stm., Wa., U.S.	B5	124
White, Lake, l., Austl.	D5	50
White Bay, b., Newf., Can.	D3	72
White Bear, stm., Newf., Can.	E3	72
White Bear Lake, Mn., U.S.	E5	100
White Bluff, Tn., U.S.	A4	119
White Butte, mtn., N.D., U.S.	C2	111
White Castle, La., U.S.	D4	95
White Center, Wa., U.S.	e11	124
White City, Or., U.S.	E4	114
White Clay Creek, stm., U.S.	A3	104
White Cloud, Mi., U.S.	E5	99
Whitecourt, Alta., Can.	B3	68
White Creek, stm., U.S.	E2	122
Whiteday, stm., W.V., U.S.	h10	125
White Deer, Tx., U.S.	B2	120
White Earth Indian Reservation, Mn., U.S.	C3	100
White Earth Lake, l., Mn., U.S.	C3	100
Whiteface, stm., Mn., U.S.	C6	100
Whiteface Mountain, mtn., N.Y., U.S.	f11	109
Whitefield, N.H., U.S.	B3	106
Whitefish, Mt., U.S.	B2	103
Whitefish Bay, Wi., U.S.	m12	126
Whitefish Bay, b., Mi., U.S.	B6	99
Whitefish Lake, l., Mn., U.S.	D4	100
Whitefish Range, mts., Mt., U.S.	B2	103
Whiteford, Md., U.S.	A5	97
White Hall, Al., U.S.	C3	78
White Hall, Ar., U.S.	C3	81
White Hall, Il., U.S.	D3	90
Whitehall, Mi., U.S.	E4	99
Whitehall, Mt., U.S.	E4	103
Whitehall, N.Y., U.S.	B7	109
Whitehall, Oh., U.S.	m11	112
Whitehall, Wi., U.S.	D2	126
Whitehall Reservoir, res., Ma., U.S.	h9	98
Whitehaven, Eng., U.K.	G9	7
White Haven, Pa., U.S.	D10	115
Whitehorn, Point, c., Wa., U.S.	A3	124
Whitehorse, Yukon, Can.	D5	66
White Horse, N.J., U.S.	C3	107
Whitehouse, Oh., U.S.	A2	112
White House, Tn., U.S.	A5	119
White Island Shores, Ma., U.S.	C6	98
White Knob Mountains, mts., Id., U.S.	F5	89
White Lake, l., La., U.S.	E3	95
Whiteman Air Force Base, mil., Mo., U.S.	C4	102
White Meadow Lake, N.J., U.S.	*B3	107
White Mesa Natural Bridge, Az., U.S.	A4	80
White Mountain Peak, mtn., Ca., U.S.	D4	82
White Mountains, mts., U.S.	D4	82
White Mountains, mts., N.H., U.S.	B3	106
Whitemouth, stm., Man., Can.	E4	70
Whitemouth Lake, l., Man., Can.	E4	70
White Nile (Al-Baḩr al-Abyaḑ), stm., Sudan	F12	42
White Oak, Oh., U.S.	o12	112
White Oak Creek, stm., Oh., U.S.	D2	112
Whiteoak Creek, stm., Tn., U.S.	A4	119
White Oak Lake, res., Ar., U.S.	D2	81
White Pigeon, Mi., U.S.	G5	99
White Pine, Mi., U.S.	m12	99
White Pine, Tn., U.S.	C10	119
White Pine, co., Nv., U.S.	D6	105
White Plains, Md., U.S.	C4	97
White Plains, N.Y., U.S.	D7	109
Whiteriver, Az., U.S.	D6	80
White River Junction, Vt., U.S.	D4	122
White Rock, B.C., Can.	E6	69
White Russia see Belarus, ctry., Eur.	G3	18
White Salmon, Wa., U.S.	D4	124
White Salmon, stm., Wa., U.S.	D4	124
White Sands Missile Range, mil., N.M., U.S.	E3	108
White Sands National Monument, N.M., U.S.	E3	108
Whitesboro, N.Y., U.S.	B5	109
Whitesboro, Tx., U.S.	C4	120
Whitesburg, Ga., U.S.	C2	87